The Mayfield Anthology of
Western Philosophy

The Mayfield Anthology of
Western Philosophy

DANIEL KOLAK

The William Paterson University of New Jersey

MAYFIELD PUBLISHING COMPANY

Mountain View, California

London • Toronto

Library of Congress Cataloging-in-Publication Data

Kolak, Daniel.
    The Mayfield anthology of Western philosophy / Daniel Kolak.
      p.   cm.
    Includes index.
    ISBN 1-55934-972-7
    1. Philosophy.   I. Mayfield Publishing Company.   II. Title.
    B21.K65   1997
    190—dc21   97-27184
                                           CIP

Manufactured in the United States of America
10 9 8 7 6 5 4 3 2 1

Mayfield Publishing Company
1280 Villa Street
Mountain View, California 94041

Sponsoring editor, Ken King; production editor, Carla White; manuscript editor, Margaret Moore; design and art manager, Jean Mailander; text and cover designer, Donna Davis; cover art, © Jim Brandenburg/Fall Reflections/Minden Pictures; manufacturing manager, Randy Hurst. The text was set in 10/12 Garamond by G & S Typesetters, Inc. and printed on 30# Nyalite by R. R. Donnelley & Sons Company, Harrisonburg.

For Ken

CONTENTS

FOREWORD

I find myself in awesome company, rounding out a full deck of fifty-two philosophers drawn from two and a half millennia of Western philosophy. My inclusion in this illustrious company is more flattering in view of the selflessness of the selecting; for none of us fifty-two had a hand in it. Of this I am confident, since all but me have been dead for fifteen years or more.

Whatever its omissions, this giant sampler is a convenient addition to a private philosophical library. It is a handy first resort for ready consultation before seeking elsewhere, and it is richly suited to edifying bouts of idle browsing.

W. V. QUINE

PREFACE

This book presents in their entirety or in representational selections the great works of fifty-two major Western philosophers arranged chronologically. Each philosopher is introduced with an essay that provides biographical and historical background as well as information about the philosophical context of the work. In making accessible between two covers the whole range of Western philosophy, I have tried to provide a functional gallery of all leading figures and representatives of every major school.

This text is appropriate for a variety of introductory philosophy courses and can be used in several different ways. You can ask students to read the philosophers chronologically, or you can pick any one of a variety of possible thematic paths through the book—epistemology, metaphysics, philosophy of religion, philosophy of mind, ethics, social and political thought, or anything else—and follow that path with students chronologically. A third way to use this text is to take a particular issue or issues and compare and contrast the various views of the philosophy by reading the appropriate selections, but as organized by movements: for example, skepticism, idealism, empiricism, rationalism, materialism, irrationalism, and so on. There are, of course, many other ways to use this text; it is certainly large enough, and no doubt once you are familiar with it still other approaches will present themselves.

I should make a few points of detail regarding translations, the content of the selections, and the choice of the selections themselves. In dealing with the variety of translations, I have been guided by several factors. First, when I have included selections from different works by the same author, I have sought to achieve, as far as possible, a standardization of usage. Nothing is more distracting and misleading than reading one philosopher's views on the nature of *spirit,* another's on the nature of *mind,* and another's on the nature of *soul,* only to find at some later point that these philosophers had the same concept in mind, or, as in many cases, that each used *the same term* for a different concept; this sometimes happens even in the course of reading various translations of a series of works by the same author. Second, nothing is more frustrating to students than encountering such words in translation as "nominatum" when "reference" will just as easily do. I have tried, therefore, whenever possible, either to use different works under the same translator or, if not possible, to amend the works of the different translators to achieve, as far as possible, a uniform terminology. This I believe to be the worst solution with the exception of all the others. I have, however, always had the originals at hand against which I have checked the various translations. I have also consulted not just with translators and scholars but also with native speakers. I should also point out that in many cases I have tried out on my own students a variety of translations to see which works best for them. I have often been surprised. Accuracy is always the most important issue, of course, but just what accuracy in translation even *means* is deeply controversial. I am of the school that a great translation has as far as possible the same effect on readers in the new language as the original work had on readers of the original language. Therefore, I have amended the translations in this spirit wherever I saw fit.

Likewise, there are probably as many approaches to introducing philosophers and their writings as there are philosophers. In writing the introductory essays I have again been guided by several factors. First, when it comes to those figures about whose meaning and intention scholars most vehemently disagree, I have taken great pains to be as neutral as possible without compromising the intent of this text. As a result, although my fifty-two introductory essays contain basically the same type of biographical information, historical background, and philosophical explanation, the balance is quite varied. In some cases I have found it prudent to include a fuller discussion of a view, provide a philosophical synopsis, or include a more detailed exposition of certain technicalities; whereas, in other cases a greater emphasis was needed on the historical context, the prior and later influences, and so on. For instance, to be told that William James is a pragmatist or a radical empiricist, and to read some selections without explanation of the three very different stages of James's development makes it difficult, if not impossible, to make coherent sense, for instance, of his study of religious experience and his claim that "consciousness does not exist." Similarly, Averroes and Maimonedes seem to come out of nowhere unless the proper bridges have first been pointed out and a historical explanation given as to the reasons they were important in the development of Western thought. And it is easy to completely misunderstand not just Locke but all the so-called British Empiricists unless one clearly explains Locke's theory of perception as a type of *representation*. Likewise, Kant's "solution" to Hume's fork, his division of the world into the phenomenal and the noumenal, and his notion of the "thing-in-itself," requires a rather elaborate philosophical topography along with the reading to make it comprehensible enough so that it can later be further discussed or explored in the works of other philosophers.

I have thus, in various ways, sought to fill in more detail for the philosophers who needed it so that all readers can more easily connect them as part of the synthetic collection that I have here assembled. The philosopher and student will both, I believe, find these minor variations in my introductory essays quite natural and so will the general reader. Also, if I have described certain historical developments in one essay, I have generally not redescribed them in another (except perhaps to make the minimal necessary reference).

I have omitted most footnotes to the original works, except where the footnotes are very brief but essential (such as one- or two-word phrases). These I have placed in brackets and inserted into the main text; foreign phrases in the original have been translated wherever I saw it appropriate to do so. Finally, I have omitted paragraph numbers unless a good reason existed to leave them in; Wittgenstein's notation, for instance (because the numbered propositions refer to each other), is one of several exceptions.

As to the selection of philosophers and their works presented in this text, I must say in conclusion that the choices have in only a few cases been difficult, both in terms of what to include and what to exclude as well as what to say about a philosopher and his work. This entire exhibit of Western philosophy has been guided by one overarching goal: to willfully and consciously display the best selections of the best philosophers in the best light possible, and thus to open wide the doors and make accessible to all visitors the whole conceptual world called philosophy—an endless labyrinth of thought with room enough for everything, a view of all views.

ACKNOWLEDGMENTS

I thank all the many colleagues and friends who in one way or another have contributed to making this work possible, especially: Willard Quine, Jaakko Hintikka, Raymond Martin, Garrett Thompson, Burton Drebin, John White, Horst Ungerer, Bill Boos, Victor Velarde, John O'Connor, Arthur Hyman, Salvatore Andreani, Ghiyath Mohammed, Robert Nanteuil, Lucius Afrani, Lucila Mistral, and Eilert Ekwall. Thomas Nenon, University of Memphis and Richard Cole, University of Kansas reviewed the manuscript and offered helpful advice. I am profoundly indebted to my editor Ken King and all the wonderful people at Mayfield for their tremendous dedication, energy, and skill in the art of making beautiful books.

THALES

624–546 B.C.E.

Thales was born in the early part of the sixth century B.C.E.,[1] several generations before the birth of Socrates and Plato, more than 2,600 years ago, in Miletus, an ancient seaport on the west coast of Ionia in Asia Minor (present-day Turkey). Subsequent centuries have called it the Age of the Seven Wise Men; there have been some variations as to who they were,[2] but Thales makes every list. It is not hard to see why. Ancient Greece was not just a land, the Greece of Europe, but also a sea, the Grecian sea, with all its coasts from Asia Minor to Sicily and from Cyrene to Thrace. This sea, with all its islands and coasts peopled since the earliest recorded time, linked the three great continents from the Black Sea to the Pillars of Hercules. It was Thales' nautical star guide that made it possible for Grecian seafarers to sail at night; he taught pilots how to navigate using the stars and how to estimate the distance of a ship at sea by triangulating from two points on land.

Thales' understanding of mathematics and the laws of nature was so astounding that many regard him as the first scientist. He showed how to calculate the height of a pyramid by measuring its shadow at the time of day when a man's shadow is equal to his height and even predicted the solar eclipse of May 28, 585 B.C.E. During the Persian War he showed the army how to cross a wide river by building a dam and diverting its flow into two narrower rivers across which bridges could then be built. According to legend, at one point Thales gained control over the entire economy of Miletus—just to make a point! Plato describes in his *Theaetetus* how this happened: a young woman laughed at Thales when he "was looking up to study the stars and tumbled down a well. She scoffed at him for being so eager to know what was happening in the sky that he could not see what lay at his feet." And here is how Aristotle tells the story in his *Politics:*

> There is . . . the story which is told of Thales of Miletus. It is a story about a scheme for making money, which is fathered on Thales owing to his reputation for wisdom. . . . He was reproached for his poverty, which was supposed to show the uselessness of philosophy. According to the story,

---

1. Before the Common Era, which coincides with and replaces the locution "B.C."

2. Four names appear on all of the lists, including Plato's (*Protagoras,* 343a): Bias of Priene, who saved the Ionians during the Persian invasion with a migration to Sardinia; Pittacus, the tyrant of Mitylene; Solon, a Gnomic poet who became the "lawgiver" of Athens; and Thales.

observing from his knowledge of meteorology while it was yet winter that there would be a great harvest of olives in the coming year, he gave deposits for all the olive-presses in Miletus and Chios, which he hired at a low price because no one bid against him. When the harvest time came, and there was a sudden and simultaneous demand for the olive presses, he let out the stock he had collected at any rate he chose to fix; and making a considerable fortune, he succeeded in proving that it is easy for philosophers to become rich if they like, but that their ambition lies elsewhere.[3]

According to Aristotle, Thales originated the idea that some underlying *material* substance forms the basis of the existence of all things:

ARISTOTLE, "ON THALES"

Now, most of the earliest philosophers regarded principles of a *material* kind as the only principles of all things. That of which all things consist, from which they are originally generated, and into which they are finally dissolved, is substance persisting though its attributes change; this, they affirm, is an element and first principle of Being. Hence, too, they hold that nothing is ever generated or annihilated, since this primary entity always persists. Similarly, we do not say of Socrates that he comes into being, in an absolute sense, when he becomes handsome or cultivated, nor that he is annihilated when he loses these qualifications, because their *substrate,* viz., Socrates himself, persists. In the same way, they held, nothing else absolutely comes into being or perishes. For there must be one or more entities which persist, and out of which all other things are generated. They do not, however, all agree as to the number and character of these principles. Thales, the founder of this type of philosophy, says it is *water.* Hence, he also put forward the view that the earth floats on the water. Perhaps he was led to this conviction by observing that the nutriment of all things is moist, and that even heat is generated from moisture, and lives upon it. (Now, that from which anything is generated is in every case a first principle of it.) He based his conviction, then, on this, and on the fact that the germs of all things are of a moist nature, while water is the first principle of the nature of moist things. There are also some who think that even the men of remote antiquity who first speculated about the gods, long before our own era, held this same view about the primary entity. For they represented Oceanus and Tethys as the progenitors of creation, and the oath of the gods as being by water, or, as they [the poets] call it, Styx. Now, the most ancient of things is most venerable, while the most venerable thing is taken to swear by. Whether this opinion about the primary entity is really so original and ancient is very possibly uncertain; in any case, Thales is said to have put forward this doctrine about the first cause.[4]

Certainly *it does not seem to be the case that everything is made of water.* So why would Thales say this? We have seen a good deal of evidence to suggest that Thales was neither an idiot nor crazy, but was one of the smartest people of the time. So what could he mean?

Well, if we take his statement at its word, the first thing it tells us—if, indeed, everything *is* made of water—is that *appearances are deceiving.* More than that: in what way are they deceiving? Looking around, you see many different sorts of things: tables, chairs, rocks, stars, people, air, fire, and so on. Plato, whom you will meet in Chapter 10, will refer to this multitudinous aspect of existence as "the many." In speaking of "the many," the ancient philosophers referred to all the multiplicity you see around you. They also referred to "the appearances." In speaking of "the appearances," they are referring, simply and directly, to the way everything *appears.* And the way things appear is not always the way they actually

3. From A. E. Taylor, *Aristotle on His Predecessors* (La Salle, Ill.: Open Court, 1962; first printed in 1907).
4. From A. E. Taylor, *Aristotle on His Predecessors.*

are. More than that: not only are appearances deceiving, the *least obvious and most deceptive way in which the appearances are deceiving is that they do not appear to be appearances!*[5] They appear to be *reality*. But reality is something beyond mere appearance. The first and main aspect of the appearances that Thales draws attention to is that they appear as a *many*. In suggesting that everything is made of water, he is saying that what appears to be a many is, in reality, a one. The appearances are but different aspects of one and the same underlying reality. But why water?

Water has no shape, no "form" of its own. If you pour water into a round glass, the water becomes round. If you pour water into a square cup, it becomes square. Thales is suggesting that behind the appearances, which are a many, reality is to be understood as some sort of underlying unity. That is, ultimately, everything is made of one single substance.

Thales calls this universal substance "water." If you think this idea is scientifically naive, then consider this: during the subsequent twenty-five centuries, science has altered Thales' statement by only one word! Consider tables, chairs, books, rocks, people, cars . . . what are these things? From the perspective of our looking at them (how they appear to us) these seem to be very different things. But what are all these things made of? Tables are made of atoms. Chairs are made of atoms. Books are made of atoms. People and cars are made of atoms. Everything is made of atoms! And what about the atoms themselves? They're made of the ultimate subatomic particles: *quarks!* Indeed, in the twentieth century, post-Einsteinian physics has come to understand all matter in terms of one universal substance, *mass-energy*. Some quantum physicists have even come up with theories equating mass-energy with space, one universal medium, a single reality underlying all things.[6]

There is but one other statement made by Thales that we can be sure was his: "Everything is full of gods."

---

5. Of course, as always in philosophy, language is especially tricky here in that the word *appearance* is ambiguous; for there is the sense in which my hand (i.e., the image of my hand) appears to get smaller as I move it farther from my eyes and there is the sense in which my hand does *not* "appear" to change in size at all: that is, only by paying special attention do I notice relative size differences. Under ordinary circumstances there is what is called "object constancy," the mind's ability to interpret varying image relations in such a way as to make the visual appearances appear more constant than that given by their actual visual geometries.

6. See my "Quantum Cosmology, the Anthropic Principle, and Why Is There Something Rather Than Nothing?" in *The Experience of Philosophy,* 3d ed. (Belmont, Calif.: Wadsworth, 1995), pp. 427–59.

2

ANAXIMANDER

d. 546 B.C.E.

Our historical information about Anaximander comes from one of Aristotle's students, Theophrastus (370–287 B.C.E.), who wrote many volumes of ancient history of which only a few fragments remain. Fortunately, in one of the remaining fragments Theophrastus quotes directly from Anaximander's lost book:

ON THE INFINITE

Anaximander of Miletos, son of Praxiades, a fellow-citizen and associate of Thales, said that the material cause and first element of things was the Infinite, he being the first to introduce this name of the material cause. He says it is neither water nor any other of the so-called elements, but a substance different from them which is infinite, from which arise all the heavens and the worlds within them.

He says that this is "eternal and ageless," and that it "encompasses all the worlds."

And into that from which things take their rise they pass away once more, "as is meet: for they make reparation and satisfaction to one another for their injustice according to the ordering of time," as he says in these somewhat poetical terms.

And besides this, there was an external motion, in which was brought about the origin of the worlds.

He did not ascribe the origin of things to any alteration in matter, but said that the oppositions in the substratum, which was a boundless body, were separated out.[1]

Notice that Anaximander agrees with his teacher, Thales, that the many individual things derive their existence from some eternal, indestructible universal *one* thing into which the many things ultimately return when they cease to exist as individuals. Anaximander claims that this one underlying existence underlying everything is *not* water, however, but something *like* water, having the sorts of properties that water has, such as shapelessness, infinite elasticity, and so on. He calls this the *infinite boundless.* Anaximander's reasoning is preserved for us by Aristotle:

Further, there cannot be a single, simple body which is infinite, either, as some hold, one distinct from the elements, which they then derive from it, or without this qualification. For there are

---

1. From John Burnet, *Early Greek Philosophy,* 2d ed. (London: A & C Black, 1902).

some who make this (*i.e.* a body distinct from the elements) the infinite, and not air or water, in order that the other things may not be destroyed by their infinity. *They are in opposition one to another*—air is cold, water moist, and fire hot—and therefore, *if any one of them were infinite, the rest would have ceased to be by this time.* Accordingly they say that what is infinite is something other than the elements, and from it the elements arise.[2]

The most important disagreement between Anaximander and Thales can be summarized in the following question, about which philosophers have continued to argue to this day: To what degree can truth be expressed using ordinary language?

Experience consists of appearances. If, as Thales and his students all readily assert, appearances are deceiving (because there is, according to them, an underlying reality beyond appearance that is radically different from things as they appear to us through our senses), then isn't language, too, deceiving? That is, since language evolved to describe what we see, how can we use it to understand what is beyond appearance? This is the question that Anaximander asked, and then answered in the negative.

According to Anaximander, philosophy can solve this problem by creating new terms to stand for new concepts. These new, "technical" terms will not simply be an attempt to refer to immediate appearances. He thus takes what he thinks to be the essential aspects of water and abstracts from them their underlying concept to create a new, "nonvisualizable," abstract concept. In thus trying to capture the abstract "form" of water, he comes up with the abstract concept: the "infinite boundless." This is the key formal aspect of the type of thing water is, which makes water such a good metaphor for the underlying substance, the "stuff of reality." But water is just a metaphor, and the infinite boundless is, paradoxically, the more *literal* truth. In other words, the concrete empirical concept is, for Anaximander, not the literal truth but the truth expressed *metaphorically*. Individual things have a specific, finite shape; water has none. Individual things have an intrinsic, built-in boundary; water has none. The basic idea is that the world exists as an undifferentiated, infinite substance, a cosmic, frothing ocean in which individual things arise through its various, internal motions, among which are the appearances as reflected in the mind's eye, the human soul.

---

2. From John Burnet, *Early Greek Philosophy*, 2d ed.

3

ANAXIMENES
585–528 B.C.E.

Just as Anaximander made his mark by disagreeing with and rethinking his teacher's philosophy, so his own young student, Anaximenes, found Anaximander's notion of an "infinite boundless" utterly unsatisfactory. Anaximenes argues that Anaximander's teacher, Thales, had originally been on the right track. According to Anaximenes, we ought to stick to known terms as they arise in common language and not invent new, abstract ones. Moving away from ordinary language into abstract terms should be avoided at all costs because, ultimately, such terms are meaningless. Only words arising in reference to specific things referred to in our immediate experience are meaningful. Anaximenes' philosophy mirrors this idea; he writes using simple, ordinary language in an unpretentious, lean style much opposed to Anaximander's lyrical, poetic prose. Although his book has since been lost, it was celebrated for centuries to come not just for its wisdom but for the lucidity of its prose as well. Fortunately, Theophrastus devotes a long passage to Anaximenes' book, giving us a brief glimpse into his ideas and his style:

LOGOS: THE BREATH OF THE WORLD

Anaximenes of Miletos, son of Eurystratos, who had been an associate of Anaximander, said, like him, that the underlying substance was one and infinite. He did not, however, say it was indeterminate, like Anaximander, but determinate; for he said it was Air.

From it, he said, the things that are, and have been, and shall be, the gods and things divine, took their rise, while other things come from its offspring.

"Just as," he said, "our soul, being air, holds us together, so do breath and air encompass the whole world."

And the form of the air is as follows. Where it is most even, it is invisible to our sight; but cold and heat, moisture and motion, make it visible. It is always in motion; for, if it were not, it would not change so much as it does.

It differs in different substances in virtue of its rarefaction and condensation.

When it is dilated so as to be rarer, it becomes fire; while winds, on the other hand, are condensed Air. Cloud is formed from Air by felting; and this, still further condensed, becomes water. Water, condensed still more, turns to earth; and when condensed as much as it can be, to stones.[1]

According to Anaximenes, the primary, infinite substance underlying everything is not water, nor is it the infinite boundless. Rather, it is *air*. This in his view is a great improvement over the work of both his predecessors, while preserving the best wisdom of both. Air has properties that evoke the abstract idea of a substance that is an "infinite boundless" even better than water because air, unlike water, is invisible. The fact is that no one can see air, and yet we can all infer its existence through its effects. For instance, without air you cannot breathe and quickly die. You can feel the wind. And so on. Further, and most important, air is an ordinary word.

To explain differentiation within the single primary substance underlying all things, Anaximander had to rely on the problematic concept of motion (see Chapter 7, Zeno of Elea). Anaximenes avoids motion and instead uses "rarefaction" and "condensation" to explain, for instance, how "air that is condensed forms winds . . . if this process goes further, it gives water, still further earth, and the greatest condensation of all is found in stones."

---

1. From John Burnet, *Early Greek Philosophy,* 2d ed. (London: A & C Black, 1902).

PYTHAGORAS

c. 572–497 B.C.E.

Bertrand Russell (Chapter 49) called Pythagoras "intellectually one of the most important men that ever lived . . . one of the most interesting and puzzling men in history." Pythagoras was born on Samos, a small island in the Aegean Sea. Located between Miletus and Athens, Samos was the main commercial rival of Miletus. Expelled by Polycrates, the tyrant of Samos, Pythagoras migrated to Crotona, a Dorian colony in southern Italy. Here he could develop his philosophy freely, and he founded his own school in which he and his students practiced ancient Orphic rites, similar to the Hindu religious tradition, designed to purify the soul so as to free it from the "wheel of birth." But whereas the religious traditions of the time involved mystical rituals, Pythagoras's method relied on mathematics and music to achieve philosophical enlightenment.

It was Pythagoras who invented the mathematical system of deduction based on demonstrative argument, the foundation of mathematical thinking up to the present day. At the same time, his philosophy gave rise to a brand of mathematical and philosophical mysticism that became the basis for a new religion. Pythagoras also invented the Western musical scale. By measuring the appropriate lengths of string on a monochord, Pythagoras showed how musical intervals correspond to simple numerical ratios between the first four integers: the lengths in the ratio 2:3:4 emit a tonic, its fifth, and its octave, respectively, and the major triad has relative frequencies expressible in the ratio 4:5:6. Pythagoras even invented new string instruments, one of which became the basis for the guitar. And he showed how the ratios for vibrating strings hold as well as for resonating air columns, thereby laying the foundation for the subsequent construction of pipe organs. His students, sworn to secrecy about his musical, mathematical, and philosophical discoveries, swore oaths on the tetractys, a series of ten dots summarizing the musical harmonies:

octave (2:1)   •

                    •   •   fifth (3:2)

fourth (4:3)   •   •   •

          •   •   •   •

So impressed where the Pythagoreans by the tetractys that they saw in it the secret insight that all of nature can be understood through mathematics—an idea that not only influenced later thinkers for centuries to come but one that is still today accepted by most scientists.

Pythagoras thought that by using the concept of number and the methods of mathematics he could decipher the inner workings of the mind. Further, he believed that by using mathematical philosophy he could perfect the mind's intellectual and perceptual abilities by "purifying" its many deceptions and errors. Thus, according to Pythagoras, it is not religion but philosophy, mathematics, and science that are the true path to enlightenment.

His famous theorem, which still today bears his name, revealed for the first time the important relationship between arithmetic and geometry—between number and magnitude. It lay the conceptual foundation for subsequent philosophers and scientists to create systems of thought based on the view that the structure and order of the universe can be completely understood by the human mind—provided that its logical and reasoning abilities are perfected along with its powers of mystical insight. Unlike today, when these two tendencies of the human mind are viewed in sharp contrast, the Pythagoreans tried to create a complete understanding of themselves and the world through combining mathematics, philosophy, and mysticism into an integrated system of thought. The most important and fundamental aspect of their thought, with intriguing implications for us today, is that the point of contact between the rational and the mystical, in their view, was mathematics. This is because the universe itself, and everything in it, according to the Pythagoreans, revealed itself as consisting of numbers.

Just as Thales said that "everything is made of water," Pythagoras argued that "everything is made of numbers." There is both a striking difference between the two statements and a striking similarity. Obviously, Pythagoras's proposition is a variation of the same formula, according to which all separately existing individual things in the universe—"the many"—ultimately consist of the same sort of thing. Though of course it must be kept in mind that numbers are not "things." Similarly, it certainly doesn't *seem* as if everything is made of numbers. Thus, once again, the fundamental idea is that appearances are deceiving. But notice that according to Pythagoras the underlying oneness is not some sort of *stuff* or *matter,* as Thales, Anaximander, and Anaximenes (the Milesian philosophers) thought; indeed, reality is not a *thing* at all. This is one of the most important philosophical insights of all time: the recognition that there is a distinction between tangible *things* and intangible *ideas.* Think about it: if numbers are not things and everything is made of numbers, then everything must ultimately be made not of *things* but of *ideas.* The profound importance of this move can best be understood in contrast to the Milesians' view that the world is an undifferentiated, unified, single substance—"water," "the indeterminate boundless," "air," and so on. For whereas Thales, Anaximander, and Anaximenes could only allude to what accounted for the differentiation observed among all things using complex and obscure notions, Pythagoras could explain the observed differences among things with the all-important concept of *ideal form,* based on his concepts of *limit* and *proportion,* both of which can be understood in purely numerical terms. The concept of ideal forms will turn out to be the key notion in the philosophy of Plato. Further, it is the numbers themselves that represent the application of a specific *limit,* or *form,* to the *unlimited* stuff of the world (matter or substance). This line of Pythagoras's thought paved the way for the philosophy of Plato, one of the greatest philosophers of all time.

Philosophy students often wonder what makes the Pythagorean theorem so special. The theorem states: Let a triangle in the plane have sides of length *a, b,* and *c.* Then this triangle is a right triangle whose hypotenuse has length c if and only if $a^2 + b^2 = c^2$. This formula says that the sum of the squares of the lengths of the legs equals the square of the length of the hypotenuse:

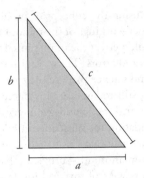

Now, why is this theorem so important? It is of course nice as a tool to calculate distances. But Thales was already able to do this, and Pythagoras is merely formalizing his predecessor's methods. What is so *philosophically* astounding about that? Well, you may have noticed that the proposition "The sum of the squares of adjoining perpendicular lines having length a and b respectively is the square of the line connecting their endpoints, length c," is not obviously true. In other words, you can't tell just by looking at the two sides of a right triangle that the ratio of the length of the hypotenuse to the sum of the two sides is as Pythagoras proves it must be. Indeed, one can *see* no reason for why it must be so. And yet it must be so. So it isn't just that the ratio is as Pythagoras says it is, but that it can be proven by *showing what cannot be seen*. If you think about our discussion about the appearances, you will see the significance at once: we are discovering, through mathematics, truths that cannot be seen. We are seeing beyond the appearances.

A theorem, like Pythagoras's, is a type of proposition. Propositions are statements that are either true or false. Some propositions, like "Two points determine a line," can be seen to be true without proof. These are sometimes called "self-evident." When the authors of the U.S. Constitution wrote, "We take these truths to be self-evident," they were evoking this ancient notion. In mathematics, such fundamental propositions are called *axioms*. Once the axioms are stated, then further propositions can be proven to be true by using the *axiomatic method;* the propositions proved in this manner, as in the case of Pythagoras, are called *theorems.*

The axiomatic method begins with axioms and moves step by step, using other axioms, to derive some new proposition, called the *conclusion.* This is in part what Pythagoras gave to mathematics and philosophy. The whole procedure is called an *argument.* The type of argument Pythagoras gave to the world, which has been the foundation of mathematical thought and much of philosophy for the past twenty-five centuries, is the *demonstrative deductive argument.* You may have noticed, for instance, that in Pythagoras's proof each proposition leading up to the conclusion is intuitively obvious, while the conclusion is not at all intuitively obvious. This is how the deductive method of reasoning works. Yet this is also what gave impetus to Pythagoras's mysticism. The idea is that you can take one intuitively obvious step after another until you end up with an intuitively unobvious conclusion which is itself known to be true with perfect certainty. This method will have a profound influence on all subsequent Western thought, especially on the work of Plato.

ARISTOTLE, "ON THE PYTHAGOREANS"

At the same time, and even earlier, the so-called Pythagoreans attached themselves to the mathematics and were the first to advance that science by their education, in which they were led to suppose that the principles of mathematics are the principles of all things. So as *numbers* are logically first among these principles, and as they fancied they could perceive in numbers many analogues of what is and what comes into being, much more readily than in fire and earth and water (such and such a property of number being *justice,* such and such another *soul* or *mind,* another *opportunity,* and so on, speaking generally, with all the other individual cases), and since they further observed that the properties and determining ratios of *harmonies* depend on numbers—since, in fact, everything else manifestly appeared to be modeled in its entire character on numbers, and numbers to be the ultimate things in the whole Universe, they became convinced that the elements of numbers are the elements of everything, and that the whole "Heaven" is harmony and number. So, all the admitted analogies they could show between numbers and harmonies and the properties or parts of the "Heaven" and the whole order of the universe, they collected and accommodated to the facts; if any gaps were left in the analogy, they eagerly caught at some additional notion, so as to introduce connection into their system as a whole. I mean, e.g., that since the number 10 is thought to be perfect, and to embrace the whole essential nature of the numerical system, they declare also that the number of revolving heavenly bodies is ten, and as there are only nine visible, they invent the Antichthon as a tenth. But I have discussed this subject more in detail elsewhere. I only enter on it here for the purpose of discovering from these philosophers as well as from the others what principles they assume, and how those principles fit into our previous classification of causes. Well, they, too, manifestly regard number as a principle, both in the sense that it is the *material* of things, and in the sense that it constitutes their *properties* and *states.* The elements of number are, they think, the Even and the Odd, the former being unlimited, the latter limited. Unity is composed of both factors, for, they say, it is both even and odd. Number is derived from unity, and numbers, as I have said, constitute the whole "Heaven."

Other members of the same school say that the principles are ten, which they arrange in a series of corresponding pairs:

Limit—the Unlimited.	Rest—Motion.
Odd—Even.	Straight—Curved.
Unity—Multitude.	Light—Darkness.
Right—Left.	Good—Evil.
Male—Female.	Square—Oblong.

From A. E. Taylor, *Aristotle on His Predecessors* (La Salle, Ill.: Open Court, 1962; first printed in 1907).

HERACLITUS

540–480 B.C.E.

Anaximenes, the youngest of the three great Milesian philosophers, was already an old man by the time Heraclitus was born in Ephesus, a town between Miletus and Colophon, on the west coast of Ionia (today's Turkey). Unlike his predecessors, Heraclitus was of noble descent from the earlier kings of Ephesus. He was a rich nobleman, but he renounced any pretense to the throne and gave up all family privileges to his younger brother so that he could pursue philosophy. Unlike Thales, Anaximander, and Anaximenes, who were respectful of their society and their positions as figures of authority, Heraclitus was the first of a long tradition of philosophers who openly criticized their society and fellow citizens, including other philosophers. For instance, when his fellow Ephesians—in a foreshadowing of the similar fate awaiting the future philosophical rebel, Socrates—put one of Heraclitus's teachers, Hermodorus, on trial for corrupting the youth and raising questions about the accepted gods, Heraclitus declares: "The Ephesians would do well to hang themselves, every adult man, and bequeath their City-State to adolescents." The idea is that the leaders, being full of ignorance and pretense, should give way to the youth because the youth have not yet been corrupted. We shall see this same theme again in the trial and death of Socrates.

When the ancient Greek philosophers referred to the world as a whole, they called it *kosmos,* meaning, literally, "ordered whole." In Heraclitus's philosophy, the human mind must ignore the world of deceptive appearances so as to be guided by the invisible logic of its own operations, in order to apprehend through the dark light of reason the hidden, underlying logic of existence. In this way the mind becomes a mirror of the universal, cosmic law, the *logos.* This is possible because the mind can perceive regularities from out of the flux of ever-changing and ephemeral sensations so as to think and speak about them. And this, in turn, is possible because the mind and the cosmos are inextricably linked by the same principle, the *logos.* The human mind and the cosmos are ultimately guided by the same laws and principles, according to which all the many individual, separately existing things in the world are united by the same underlying principles of reason, the *logos.* The appearances show the individual things of the world to be many and in constant flux, but reason reveals a hidden cosmic unity beneath the apparent diversity. This mystical insight cannot be seen directly, however; it must be intuited. It transcends the subjective opinions of those barely conscious souls who sleepwalk through life:

> To those who are awake the world-order is one, common to all; but the sleeping turn aside each into a world of his own. We ought not to act and speak like men asleep. We ought to follow what is common to all; but though the *logos* is common to all, the many live as though their thought were private to themselves.

The word *logos* is derived from a verb meaning "to speak," but it had several different meanings in ancient Greek. Most important, it referred both to the words used by a speaker and to the thought, or meaning, thereby expressed, which exists independently of the words. *Logos* thus signified reason or order both in words (which makes language and thought possible) and in things (which makes existence and the world possible).

Logos both guides the world and makes it intelligible to the mind. It is at once the source of all natural processes and of human reason. The Stoics will use this very notion in their view of the world as a living, breathing unity, supremely perfect in its conjoinment between individuals to the whole. The *logos* according to the Stoics gives rise to the concept of divine Providence as well as to the idea of Nature conceived as an ordered course of events. Subsequent thinkers interpret *logos* as an immaterial instrument, the personal agency through which God guides the course of events in the world. Thus in Christian philosophy, the *logos* became the second person of the Trinity, Jesus Christ. The fourth Gospel of the New Testament begins with the cryptic statement "In the beginning was the Word," where "Word" is a translation of "Logos." And "the word became flesh."

Heraclitus's idea that the inner workings of the human mind and the inner workings of the world are structured by the same underlying reality will find its fullest expression in the work of Immanuel Kant (Chapter 32). Unfortunately, according to Heraclitus, the majority of people ignore the *logos,* even after it has been explained to them. This is because the human mind, not enlightened to its own presence in the world, tends to constantly divide its understanding into oversimplified, black-and-white thinking, disagreeing with itself. The mind's own naive concepts suggest that things must be one way or another, never both. The problem, in other words, is that we think in simplistic, rigid terms using words that are limited and incapable of expressing the whole truth except through reasoning. Our concepts are divisive of the whole and therefore cannot render the world as it really is. Thus, according to Heraclitus, we must learn to make room for what to the unenlightened mind will seem like utterly perplexing contradictions.

Is the cosmos *one* or *many?* Heraclitus says it is *both.* How is that possible? Because the answer depends on your perspective. From the point of view of our perceptions—the appearances, the images the mind makes in response to its senses—what we see is a *many.* This is because our perceptions consist of opposites: small and large, infinite and finite, hot and cold, dead and living, wet and dry, and so on—all of which constantly undergo change, going from one to the other. But why, then, does everything not vanish? The fact that it doesn't, says Heraclitus, suggests that there must be something behind everything, keeping it all going, always present but nowhere to be seen: the *logos.* It is reason that corrects our ever-flickering view of the world due to our constantly changing perceptions, revealing that despite all the changes something must nevertheless remain the same.

Heraclitus published his main philosophical work around 500 B.C.E. Only about a hundred fragments remain, as quoted by subsequent writers. But these aphorisms reveal a vivid, cryptic, and prophetic style that earned him the nickname "the Obscure."

FRAGMENTS

1. It is wise to hearken, not to me, but to my Logos, and to confess that all things are one.

2. Though this, Logos is true evermore, yet men are as unable to understand it when they hear it for the first time as before they have heard it at all. For, though all things come to pass in accordance with this Logos, men seem as if they had no experience of them, when they make trial of words and deeds such as I set forth, dividing each thing according to its kind and showing how it truly is. But other men know not what they are doing when awake, even as they forget what they do in sleep.

3. Fools when they do hear are like the deaf: of them does the saying bear witness that they are absent when present.

4. Eyes and ears are bad witnesses to men if they have souls that understand not their language.

5. The many do not take heed of such things as those they meet with, nor do they mark them when they are taught, though they think they do.

6. Knowing not how to listen nor how to speak.

7. If you do not expect the unexpected, you will not find it; for it is hard to be sought out and difficult.

8. Those who seek for gold dig up much earth and find a little.

10. Nature loves to hide.

11. The lord whose is the oracle at Delphi neither utters nor hides his meaning, but shows it by a sign.

12. And the Sibyl, with raving lips uttering things mirthless, unbedizened, and unperfumed, reaches over a thousand years with her voice, thanks to the god in her.

13. The things that can be seen, heard, and learned are what I prize the most.

14. . . . bringing untrustworthy witnesses in support of disputed points.

15. The eyes are more exact witnesses than the ears.

From John Burnet, *Early Greek Philosophy* (London: World, 1910).

16. The learning of many things teacheth not understanding, else would it have taught Hesiod and Pythagoras, and again Xenophanes and Hekataios.

17. Pythagoras, son of Mnesarchos, practised scientific inquiry beyond all other men, and making a selection of these writings, claimed for his own wisdom what was but a knowledge of many things and an imposture.

18. Of all those discourses I have heard, there is not one who attains to understanding that wisdom is apart from all.

19. Wisdom is one thing. It is to know the thought by which all things are steered through all things.

20. This world, which is the same for all, no one of gods or men has made; but it was ever, is now, and ever shall be an ever-living Fire, with measures of it kindling, and measures going out.

21. The transformations of Fire are, first of all, sea; and half of the sea is earth, half whirlwind. . . .

22. All things are an exchange for Fire, and Fire for all things, even as wares for gold and gold for wares.

23. It becomes liquid sea, and is measured by the same tale as before it became earth.

24. Fire is want and surfeit.

25. Fire lives the death of air, and air lives the death of fire; water lives the death of earth, earth that of water.

26. Fire in its advance will judge and convict all things.

27. How can one hide from that which never sets?

28. It is the thunderbolt that steers the course of all things.

29. The sun will not overstep his measures; if he does, the Erinyes, the handmaids of Justice, will find him out.

30. The limit of dawn and evening is the Bear; and opposite the Bear is the boundary of bright Zeus.

31. If there were no sun it would be night, for all the other stars could do.

32. The sun is new every day.

33. Thales foretold an eclipse.

34. . . . the seasons that bring all things.

35. Hesiod is most men's teacher. Men are sure he knew very many things, a man who did not know day or night! They are one.

36. God is day and night, winter and summer, war and peace, surfeit and hunger; but he takes various shapes, just as fire, when it is mingled with spices, is named according to the savour of each.

37. If all things were turned to smoke, the nostrils would distinguish them.

38. Souls smell in Hades.

39. Cold things become warm, and what is warm cools; what is wet dries, and the parched is moistened.

40. It scatters and it gathers; it advances and retires.

41. You cannot step twice into the same rivers; for fresh waters are ever flowing in upon you.

43. Homer was wrong in saying: "Would that strife might perish from among gods and men!" He did not see that he was praying for the destruction of the universe; for, if his prayer were heard, all things would pass away. . . .

44. War is the father of all and the king of all; and some he has made gods and some men, some bond and some free.

45. Men do not know how what is at variance agrees with itself. It is an attunement of opposite tensions, like that of the bow and the lyre.

46. It is the opposite which is good for us.

47. The hidden attunement is better than the open.

48. Let us not conjecture at random about the greatest things.

49. Men that love wisdom must be acquainted with very many things indeed.

50. The straight and the crooked path of the fuller's comb is one and the same.

51. Asses would rather have straw than gold.

51a. Oxen are happy when they find bitter vetches to eat.

52. The sea is the purest and the impurest water. Fish can drink it, and it is good for them; to men it is undrinkable and destructive.

53. Swine wash in the mire, and barnyard fowls in dust.

54. . . . to delight in the mire.

55. Every beast is driven to pasture with blows.

56. (Same as 45.)

57. Good and ill are one.

58. Physicians who cut, burn, stab, and rack the sick, demand a fee for it which they do not deserve to get.

59. Couples are things whole and things not whole, what is drawn together and what is drawn asunder, the harmonious and the discordant. The one is made up of all things, and all things issue from the one.

60. Men would not have known the name of justice if these things were not.

61. To God all things are fair and good and right, but men hold some things wrong and some right.

62. We must know that war is common to all and strife is justice, and that all things come into being and pass away through strife.

64. All the things we see when awake are death, even as all we see in slumber are sleep.

65. The wise is one only. It is unwilling and willing to be called by the name of Zeus.

66. The bow (βιός) is called life (βίος), but its work is death.

67. Mortals are immortals and immortals are mortals, the one living the others' death and dying the others' life.

68. For it is death to souls to become water, and death to water to become earth. But water comes from earth; and from water, soul.

69. The way up and the way down is one and the same.

70. In the circumference of a circle the beginning and end are common.

71. You will not find the boundaries of soul by travelling in any direction, so deep is the measure of it.

72. It is pleasure to souls to become moist.

73. A man, when he gets drunk, is led by a beardless lad, tripping, knowing not where he steps, having his soul moist.

74–76. The dry soul is the wisest and best.

77. Man kindles a light for himself in the night-time, when he has died but is alive. The sleeper, whose vision has been put out, lights up from the dead; he that is awake lights up from the sleeping.

78. And it is the same thing in us that is quick and dead, awake and asleep, young and old; the former are shifted and become the latter, and the latter in turn are shifted and become the former.

79. Time is a child playing draughts, the kingly power is a child's.

80. I have sought myself.

81. We step and do not step into the same rivers; we are and are not.

82. It is a weariness to labour for the same masters and be ruled by them.

83. It rests by changing.

84. Even the posset separates if it is not stirred.

85. Corpses are more fit to be cast out than dung.

86. When they are born, they wish to live and to meet with their dooms—or rather to rest—and they leave children behind them to meet with their dooms in turn.

87–89. A man may be a grandfather in thirty years.

90. Those who are asleep are fellow-workers (in what goes on in the world).

91*a*. Thought is common to all.

91*b*. Those who speak with understanding must hold fast to what is common to all as a city holds fast to its law, and even more strongly. For all human laws are fed by the one divine law. It prevails as much as it will, and suffices for all things with something to spare.

92. So we must follow the common, yet though my Logos is common, the many live as if they had a wisdom of their own.

93. They are estranged from that with which they have most constant intercourse.

94. It is not meet to act and speak like men asleep.

95. The waking have one common world, but the sleeping turn aside each into a world of his own.

96. The way of man has no wisdom, but that of God has.

97. Man is called a baby by God, even as a child by a man.

98, 99. The wisest man is an ape compared to God, just as the most beautiful ape is ugly compared to man.

100. The people must fight for its law as for its walls.

101. Greater deaths win greater portions.

102. Gods and men honour those who are slain in battle.

103. Wantonness needs putting out, even more than a house on fire.

104. It is not good for men to get all they wish to get. It is sickness that makes health pleasant; evil, good; hunger, plenty; weariness, rest.

105–107. It is hard to fight with one's heart's desire. Whatever it wishes to get, it purchases at the cost of soul.

108, 109. It is best to hide folly; but it is hard in times of relaxation, over our cups.

110. And it is law, too, to obey the counsel of one.

111. For what thought or wisdom have they? They follow the poets and take the crowd as their teacher, knowing not that there are many bad and few good. For even the best of them choose one thing above all others, immortal glory among mortals, while most of them are glutted like beasts.

112. In Priene lived Bias, son of Teutamas, who is of more account than the rest. (He said, "Most men are bad.")

113. One is ten thousand to me, if he be the best.

114. The Ephesians would do well to hang themselves, every grown man of them, and leave the city to beardless lads; for they have cast out Hermodoros, the best man among them, saying, "We will have none who is best among us; if there be any such, let him be so elsewhere and among others."

115. Dogs bark at every one they do not know.

116. . . . (The wise man) is not known because of men's want of belief.

117. The fool is flattered at every word.

118. The most esteemed of them knows but fancies, and holds fast to them, yet of a truth justice shall overtake the artificers of lies and the false witnesses.

119. Homer should be turned out of the lists and whipped, and Archilochos likewise.

120. One day is like any other.

121. Man's character is his fate.

122. There awaits men when they die such things as they look not for nor dream of.

123. . . . that they rise up and become the wakeful guardians of the quick and dead.

124. Night-walkers, Magians, Bakchoi, Lenai, and the initiated . . .

125. The mysteries practised among men are unholy mysteries.

126. And they pray to these images, as if one were to talk with a man's house, knowing not what gods or heroes are.

127. For if it were not to Dionysos that they made a procession and sang the shameful phallic hymn, they would be acting most shamelessly. But Hades is the same as Dionysos in whose honour they go mad and rave.

129, 130. They vainly purify themselves by defiling themselves with blood, just as if one who had stepped into the mud were to wash his feet in mud. Any man who marked him doing thus, would deem him mad.

PARMENIDES

515–445 B.C.E.

Parmenides was a student of Anaximander's who joined Pythagoras's religious and philosophical brotherhood in Crotona. But he was born in Elea, a Greek city in southern Italy (today called Velia) that lay at the other end of the known world from where Heraclitus and other Ionians lived. Of his writings, all that remains are 160 lines of *Nature,* a poem he wrote in honor of his most illustrious student, Zeno. Parmenides' style is a mix of Pythagorean mysticism combined with myths and allegories. He may have written the work to confound and mislead the uninitiated while passing on to his initiates the secret teachings of the wise and enlightened masters.

The poem describes a journey from darkness into light and beyond, where Parmenides finds the Goddess of Wisdom who then instructs him about the nature of the ultimate truth. She urges him not just to learn the absolute truth, about which there can be no disagreement, but also to acquaint himself with all the misleading opinions among which there can be no truth, so that he will himself not be deceived. There are three ways one might try to discover truth. The first is to speak of what does not exist: "*It is not,* and there must be non-being." But this is impossible. What does not exist cannot even be thought of (since thinking is itself something). The second way is to speak of "what is" and to say both that "it is and is not" or that "it is both the same and not the same." This is the Heraclitan way. The third and only correct path to truth is to start from the fundamental proposition "*It is,* and non-being is impossible."

Clearly, although it seems we can think either about what is or about what is not, in truth we cannot think about what is not. We can think only about what is since whatever we think about is, itself, an object of thought. This is what Parmenides means in identifying *thought* and *being* as one and the same. Thoughts themselves—even the thought "Goblins exist"—exist and have being regardless of whether the things described by the thoughts themselves exist. When we think that goblins exist, for instance, we are merely thinking something false about what exists, namely, that the existence contains goblins. But we are not thereby thinking about non-being, which is impossible. Non-being is not a possible object of thought for it is not an object, it is just nothing. And since nothing is not, we must reject the first of the three possible ways of inquiry into truth.

By similar reasoning we should reject the second possible way of inquiry, as advocated by Heraclitus. To say of "what is" that it both is "the same and not the same," as Heraclitus does, is according to Parmenides a grave mistake. Such a false way of thinking comes about because the mind is seduced by its own appearances. We must therefore rise above the senses and rely solely on reason in determining what the truth is. If we do this, he claims, we will find that the world as a whole exists in and of itself and is uncreated. Ultimate reality is permanent and unchangeable; it is whole, indivisible, and everywhere continuous. According to Heraclitus, however, reality is identical with the thought that recognizes it. In this way, all the things that our ordinary, commonsense conception predicates of reality—generation and destruction, being and non-being, change of position, change in qualities—are nothing more than illusions.

PROLOGUE TO "NATURE"

The car that bears me carried me as far as ever my heart desired, when it had brought me and set me on the renowned way of the goddess, which leads the man who knows through all the towns. On that way was I borne along; for on it did the wise steeds carry me, drawing my car, and maidens showed the way. And the axle, glowing in the socket—for it was urged round by the whirling wheels at each end—gave forth a sound as of a pipe, when the daughters of the Sun, hasting to convey me into the light, threw back their veils from off their faces and left the abode of Night.

There are the gates of the ways of Night and Day, fitted above with a lintel and below with a threshold of stone. They themselves, high in the air, are closed by mighty doors, and Avenging Justice keeps the keys that fit them. Her did the maidens entreat with gentle words and cunningly persuade to unfasten without demur the bolted bars from the gates. Then, when the doors were thrown back, they disclosed a wide opening, when their brazen posts fitted with rivets and nails swung back one after the other. Straight through them, on the broad way, did the maidens guide the horses and the car, and the goddess greeted me kindly, and took my right hand in hers, and spake to me these words:

Welcome, O youth, that comest to my abode on the car that bears thee tended by immortal charioteers! It is no ill chance, but right and justice that has sent thee forth to travel on this way. Far, indeed, does it lie from the beaten track of men! Meet it is that thou shouldst learn all things, as well the unshaken heart of well-rounded truth, as the opinions of mortals in which is no true belief at all. Yet none the less shalt thou learn these things also,—how passing right through all things one should judge the things that seem to be.

But do thou restrain thy thought from this way of inquiry, nor let habit by its much experience force thee to cast upon this way a wandering eye or sounding ear or tongue; but judge by argument the much disputed proof uttered by me. There is only one way left that can be spoken of. . . .

THE WAY OF TRUTH

Look steadfastly with thy mind at things though afar as if they were at hand. Thou canst not cut off what is from holding fast to what is, neither scattering itself abroad in order nor coming together.

It is all one to me where I begin; for I shall come back again there.

Come now, I will tell thee—and do thou hearken to my saying and carry it away—the only two ways of search that can be thought of. The first, namely, that *It is,* and that it is impossible for it not to be, is the way of belief, for truth is its companion. The other, namely, that *It is not,* and that it must needs not be,—that, I tell thee, is a path that none can learn of at all. For thou canst not know what is *not*—that is impossible—nor utter it; for it is the same thing that can be thought and that can be.

It needs must be that what can be spoken and thought *is;* for it is possible for it to be, and it is not possible for what is nothing to be. This is what I bid thee ponder. I hold thee back from this first way of inquiry, and from this other also, upon which mortals knowing naught wander two-faced; for helplessness guides the wandering thought in their breasts, so that they are borne along stupefied like men deaf and blind. Undiscerning crowds, who hold that it is and is not the same and not the same, and all things travel in opposite directions!

For this shall never be proved, that the things that are not are; and do thou restrain thy thought from this way of inquiry.

One path only is left for us to speak of, namely, that *It is.* In this path are very many tokens that what is is uncreated and indestructible; for it is complete, immovable, and without end. Nor was it ever, nor will it be; for now *it is,* all at once, a continuous one. For what kind of origin for it wilt thou look for? In what way and from what source could it have drawn its increase? . . . I shall not let thee say nor think that it came from what is not; for it can neither be thought nor uttered that anything is not. And, if it came from nothing, what need could have made it arise later rather than sooner? Therefore must it either be altogether or be not at all. Nor will the force of truth suffer aught to arise besides itself from that which is not. Wherefore, Justice doth not loose her fetters and let anything come into being or pass away, but holds it fast. Our judgment thereon depends on this: "*Is it* or *is it not?*" Surely it is adjudged, as it needs must be, that we are to set aside the one way as unthinkable and nameless (for it is no true way), and that the other path is real and true. How, then, can what *is* be going to be in the future? Or how could it come into being? If it came into being, it is not; nor is it if it is going to be in the future. Thus is becoming extinguished and passing away not to be heard of.

Nor is it divisible, since it is all alike, and there is no more of it in one place than in another, to hinder it from holding together, nor less of it, but everything is full of what is. Wherefore it is wholly continuous; for what is, is in contact with what is.

Moreover, it is immovable in the bonds of mighty chains, without beginning and without end, since coming into being and passing away have been driven afar, and true belief has cast them away. It is the same, and it rests in the self-same place, abiding in itself. And thus it remaineth constant in its place; for hard necessity keeps it in the bonds of the limit that holds it fast on every side. Wherefore it is not permitted to what is to be infinite; for it is in need of nothing; while, if it were infinite, it would stand in need of everything.

The thing that can be thought and that for the sake of which the thought exists is the same; for you cannot find thought without something that is, as to which it is uttered. And there is not, and never shall be, anything besides what is, since fate has chained it so as to be whole and immovable. Wherefore all these things are but names which mortals have given, believing them to be true—coming into being and passing away, being and not being, change of place and alteration of bright colour.

Since, then, it has a furthest limit, it is complete on every side, like the mass of a rounded sphere, equally poised from the centre in every direction; for it cannot be greater or smaller in one place than in another. For there is no nothing that could keep it from reaching out equally, nor can aught that is be more here and less there than what is, since it is all inviolable. For the point from which it is equal in every direction tends equally to the limits.

THE WAY OF BELIEF

Here shall I close my trustworthy speech and thought about the truth. Henceforward learn the beliefs of mortals, giving ear to the deceptive ordering of my words.

Mortals have made up their minds to name two forms, one of which they should not name, and that is where they go astray from the truth. They have distinguished them as opposite in form, and have assigned to them marks distinct from one another. To the one they allot the fire of heaven, gentle, very light, in every direction the same as itself, but not the same as the other. The other is just the opposite to it, dark night, a compact and heavy body. Of these I tell thee the whole arrangement as it seems likely; for so no thought of mortals will ever outstrip thee.

Now that all things have been named light and night, and the names which belong to the power of each have been assigned to these things and to those, everything is full at once of light and dark night, both equal, since neither has aught to do with the other.

And thou shalt know the substance of the sky, and all the signs in the sky, and the resplendent works of the glowing sun's pure torch, and whence they arose. And thou shalt learn likewise of the wandering deeds of the round-faced moon, and of her substance. Thou shalt know, too, the heavens that surround us, whence they arose, and how Necessity took them and bound them to keep the limits of the stars . . . how the earth, and the sun, and the moon, and the sky that is common to all, and the Milky Way, and the outermost Olympos, and the burning might of the stars arose.

The narrower bands were filled with unmixed fire, and those next them with night, and in the midst of these rushes their portion of fire. In the midst of these is the divinity that directs the course of all things; for she is the beginner of all painful birth and all begetting, driving the female to the embrace of the male, and the male to that of the female.

First of all the gods she contrived Eros.

Shining by night with borrowed light, wandering round the earth.

Always looking to the beams of the sun.

For just as thought stands at any time to the mixture of its erring organs, so does it come to men; for that which thinks is the same, namely, the substance of the limbs, in each and every man; for their thought is that of which there is more in them.

On the right boys; on the left girls.

Thus, according to men's opinions, did things come into being, and thus they are now. In time they will grow up and pass away. To each of these things men have assigned a fixed name.

ZENO OF ELEA

490–430 B.C.E.

The ancient Greeks' discovery that appearances are not the direct apprehension of reality as it exists independently of the mind leads naturally to the metaphysical question of what that reality, behind or beyond the appearances, *is* like. It may be nothing like the appearances, or it may to some degree be like the appearances. It may even be exactly similar to the appearances, in which case the appearances are an accurate representation of reality. In either of these cases, it is natural to ask the epistemological question: How can we know to what degree the appearances correspond to reality?

According to Parmenides, as we just saw, reality is nothing like the appearances. Appearances are a many; reality is a one: you and I and everything in the world are in reality one. Beyond the appearances is the unity and indivisibility of Being. Now, to the ordinary person whose life consists in living among and dealing with the appearances, such a view of reality seems obviously false. The reason is obvious: it seems that one can tell, just by looking, that there are lots of different things separated by space and other things, that there is change, and so on. The senses seem to paint a picture in which Parmenides' view looks literally like *nonsense*. Parmenides and the Eleatic philosophers can offer arguments to the contrary, but will such arguments make one doubt the reality of what one sees? Perhaps in an intellectual sense, but not in the *actual* sense *of altering the appearances*. It seems, in other words, that there is an inescapable primacy in the appearances themselves that no amount of argument can dispel: the philosophers can declare and perhaps even prove that the appearances are an illusion, but this in no way dispels the illusion.

It is to this problem that Parmenides' greatest student, and one of the most powerful and enigmatic of the ancient philosophers, Zeno of Elea, turned his sights. His method is as powerful as it is subtle: show that the commonsense view of reality based on the appearances *is itself nonsensical*. More than that: the commonsense view is *more* nonsensical than is Parmenides' view!

Zeno does this not with poetry or mystical proclamations, but with the same sort of carefully reasoned *proof* as offered by Pythagoras's famous theorem, relying on a careful analysis of the appearances and the concepts involved in our interpreting them, buttressed by the incontrovertible logic of mathematics. We do know that Zeno, like Parmenides, had been initiated into both the Pythagorean mysteries and their mathematical methods. But

Zeno put his arguments not in terms of any abstract metaphysics, nor in allegories or myths; rather, he used mathematically precise rigor to come up with a completely new form of argument known as *dialectic,* whose invention in the *Sophist* Aristotle attributes to Zeno. And in Plato we find the following description of Zeno's book:

> In reality, this writing is a sort of reinforcement for the argument of Parmenides against those who try to turn it into ridicule on the ground that, if reality is one, the argument becomes involved in many absurdities and contradictions. This writing argues against those who uphold a Many, and gives them back as good and better than they gave; its aim is to show that their assumption of multiplicity will be involved in still more absurdities than the assumption of unity, if it is sufficiently worked out.

Only fragments remain of Zeno's books, but they contain some of the most puzzling paradoxes of all time, ones which confound philosophers and mathematicians to the present day. The most famous of these focuses on the concept of motion. In asserting that Being is ultimately not a collection of many individual things but continuous and unified, Parmenides had asserted that the cosmos is one undifferentiated, unchanging, eternal whole. This implies that all change, even the simplest change such as one thing moving from one place to another, is but an illusion. If, on the other hand, Being is *not* a one but a many, what then separates one thing from another? Such a separation between one thing and another would have itself to be not something but nothing (for if it is something, then the "two" things are but one continuous thing). But if the separation is a nothing, the separation does not exist, which would be an absurdity: if there exist two things between which there exists nothing, then these are not two things but one thing.

Zeno now tries in a clever and subtle way to *prove* Parmenides right by proving that the reasons we may have for thinking he is wrong are bad reasons, and that the absurdity which we may think is involved in Parmenides' view applies to our own commonsense view. In other words, instead of directly supporting Parmenides' view of reality, Zeno offers proofs that go against our own beliefs about what we take to be the commonsense reality. He does it by presenting *paradoxes,* which means, literally, "beyond" or "above" (*para*) "belief" (*doxa*). He invented about forty paradoxes designed to show that our ordinary, commonsense view of reality is, literally, nonsensical, that it is more absurd to believe what the appearances tell us is real than what philosophers such as Parmenides say is real. The first three given here, fragments from Zeno's book, are his paradoxes of magnitude. The four that follow are his paradoxes of motion, as preserved by Aristotle.

THE PARADOXES

PARADOXES OF MAGNITUDE

1. If what is had no magnitude, it would not even be. . . . But, if it is, each one must have a certain magnitude and a certain thickness, and must be at a certain distance from

another, and the same may be said of what is in front of it; for it, too, will have magnitude, and something will be in front of it. It is all the same to say this once and to say it always; for no such part of it will be the last, nor will one thing not be as compared with another. So, if things are a many, they must be both small and great, so small as not to have any magnitude at all, and so great as to be infinite.

2. For if it were added to any other thing it would not make it any larger; for nothing can gain in magnitude by the addition of what has no magnitude, and thus it follows at once that what was added was nothing. But if, when this is taken away from another thing, that thing is no less; and again, if, when it is added to another thing, that does not increase, it is plain that what was added was nothing, and what was taken away was nothing.

3. If things are a many, they must be just as many as they are, and neither more nor less. Now, if they are as many as they are, they will be finite in number.

If things are a many, they will be infinite in number; for there will always be other things between them, and others again between these. And so things are infinite in number.

PARADOXES OF MOTION

1. You cannot cross a race-course. You cannot traverse an infinite number of points in a finite time. You must traverse the half of any given distance before you traverse the whole, and the half of that again before you can traverse it. This goes on *ad infinitum,* so that there are an infinite number of points in any given space, and you cannot touch an infinite number one by one in a finite time.

2. Achilles will never overtake the tortoise. He must first reach the place from which the tortoise started. By that time the tortoise will have got some way ahead. Achilles must then make up that, and again the tortoise will be ahead. He is always coming nearer, but he never makes up to it.

3. The arrow in flight is at rest. For, if everything is at rest when it occupies a space equal to itself, and what is in flight at any given moment always occupies a space equal to itself, it cannot move.

4. Half the time may be equal to double the time. Let us suppose three rows of bodies, one of which (A) is at rest while the other two (B, C) are moving with equal velocity in opposite directions (Fig. 1). By the time they are all in the same part of the course, B will have passed twice as many of the bodies in C as in A (Fig. 2).

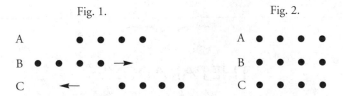

Therefore the time which it takes to pass C is twice as long as the time it takes to pass A. But the time which B and C take to reach the position of A is the same. Therefore double the time is equal to the half.

CHAPTER

8

PROTAGORAS

480–410 B.C.E.

Protagoras was born in Abdera, a coastal town in a region of Greece called Thrace. Along with Anaxagoras and Zeno of Elea, he enjoyed the patronage of Pericles (495–429), the enlightened political leader and military general most responsible for the development of the Athenian democracy and the rise of the Greek Empire. Protagoras spent most of his life traveling about the world, teaching anyone who could afford his modest fees. His travels brought him in contact with many different societies, each steeped in different religious customs and laws, which showed him the vastly different ideas the human mind could accept as true.

Recognized as one of the wisest sages of the time, Protagoras became a teacher of Pericles, who pioneered democracy in Athens against the plutocracies of neighboring Corinth and the warrior nobilities of Sparta. It was Protagoras who impressed upon Pericles the extent to which religious and moral codes are based not upon human nature, nor are they God-given truths—else why would there be so many different types of societies? Rather, ways of life are but socially constructed conventions. Therefore, according to Protagoras, rhetoric—the art of persuasive speech—should be used to influence people's opinions and change them in ways that only great enlightened leaders like Pericles could openly debate, so as to find what would be in the best interests of their societies. This of course would require that the leaders themselves be sophists, which anticipates Plato's notion of the philosopher-king as being the best type of ruler.

The word *sophist* appears in the word *philosophy,* which consists of the Greek *philein* ("to love") and *sophia* ("wisdom"). The word *philosophy* means, literally, "love of wisdom," and *philosopher* means "lover of wisdom." Thus the early "sophists" were, literally, "wise men." They appeared in the Greek city-states during the fifth century B.C.E. as traveling teachers for hire, who taught the youth of the aristocracy who aspired to power. With the advent of democracy in that century, a new and profound power shift had occurred among the ruling class, one that had a definite and positive effect on the birth of philosophy. Before the power shift, to attain power you had merely to have inherited a political position, wealth, or land; now to attain positions of political authority you had to demonstrate your intellectual skills and earn the right to power. This required skills of argumentation and rhetoric; you had to win your case in open debate.

Sophists like Protagoras came from all over the known world, often from nondemocratic localities where their brand of disputation had gotten them in trouble with the authorities, to take advantage of these new freedoms by seeking employment for their knowledge and abilities. Thus the word *sophist* did not originally have the pejorative connotation it has today, that of someone who uses a superficial grasp of knowledge and truth to confuse, confound, and manipulate. The sophists came to Athens at a time when no education as such existed and no provisions were made on the part of the state for the education of youth. It was not until Plato's Academy—built in part as an alternative to the public teaching of the sophists—that the first university was born, one which is still the model of most institutions of higher learning today. Up to the time of Plato, education in ancient Greece was for the privileged and the few; the sophists, however, had already begun to tip the balance by teaching anyone—noble or commoner—who could afford their rates. Since success in Athenian society depended on oratory skills and appealing to the masses, the sophists—much like the lawyers of today—became highly sought by everyone who sought a position of power.

Plato's own teacher, Socrates, was educated by the sophists and originally made his living as one, distinguishing himself at a young age as the most skilled of all the sophists. The one sophist for whom Plato seemed to have great respect, however—probably because of his theory of perception which in many ways was very similar to Plato's—was Protagoras, to whom Plato devoted an entire dialogue. Like his most famous student, Socrates, Protagoras raised doubts in the minds of the youth about the gods they had come by tradition to accept, saying, "About the gods, I am not able to know whether they exist or do not exist, nor what they are like in form; for the factors preventing knowledge are many: the obscurity of the subject, and the shortness of human life."

Protagoras summed up his philosophy in his famous proposition: "Man is the measure of all things." This idea was expressed and developed in his book *On Truth,* of which only the first sentence remains: "Of all things the measure is man; of existing things, that they exist; of nonexistent things, that they do not exist."

In Plato's dialogue *Cratylus,* Socrates ponders Protagoras's cryptic meaning. The dialogue is named after another of Socrates' enigmatic sophist teachers, Cratylus, who was such a nihilist (believing that nothing can be known about anything) that not only did he refuse to write anything down, just as Socrates did, he went further: Cratylus refused even to speak. He merely wagged his finger occasionally to acknowledge that sensations seemed to be occurring.

> *Socrates:* So what is true of existing things, according to Protagoras, is this: what each thing itself is depends on the individual perceiving it. This is what Protagoras means when he says "Man is the measure of all things." The way things appear to me is the way they are for me; the way things appear to you is the way they are for you.

Protagoras's philosophy had important *pragmatic* repercussions for his theory of education, which is remarkably similar to nineteenth-century American pragmatists William James and John Dewey (Chapters 42 and 48) and their German avatar F. C. S. Schiller. This pragmatist philosophy comes out in Plato's dialogue *Protagoras,* in which Protagoras responds to Socrates's criticism that if truth and knowledge are relative in the way Protagoras is claiming, then no one is wiser than anyone else. Protagoras denies this statement by arguing that the wise man has a special responsibility due to the freedom conferred upon him through the realization that truth does not exist independently of the mind, but is itself a product of human thought.

PLATO, "PROTAGORAS"

Each of us is the measure of what is and of what is not, but people differ from one another in this: that different things appear and are to different people. . . .

Don't quibble with my use of language, but try to understand what I mean. Remember what was said earlier: to the man who is sick his food seems bitter and is bitter; to the man who is well it is and seems just the opposite. Now neither of these men is to be made wiser, for that is impossible; nor should it be claimed that the sick man is ignorant because he believes what he does, or the well man wise because he believes otherwise. But a change must be brought about from the one condition to the other, because the other is better. So it is with education: a change must be brought about from a worse condition to a better; but whereas the physician produces this change by drugs, the sophist does it by words. No one has ever yet made anyone who previously had false beliefs have true ones; for it is impossible to believe what is not, nor anything but what one experiences, and this is always true. But I believe that one can make a man who is in a depraved condition of soul and has beliefs of a like nature good, so that he has different beliefs. These appearances some, through inexperience, call "true"; but I say that some are "better" than others, but not "truer." And the wise, friend Socrates, I am very far from calling frogs, but when they have to do with the body I call them physicians, and when they have to do with plants, farmers. For I maintain that the latter induce in sickly plants good and healthy and true sensations instead of bad, and that wise and good orators make good things instead of wicked things appear just to their cities. For I believe that whatever *seems* right or wrong to each city *is* right or wrong for it, so long as it continues to think so. But the wise man causes the good things instead of the bad to appear and to be for them in each case.[1]

Although Protagoras, like his fellow sophists, is deeply critical about the possibility of truth and knowledge in some absolute sense, he relies on careful methods of demonstration and argument. He even came up with a clever experiment to show the relativity of truth as he saw it. He assembled an audience in front of a stage and took three volunteers to a secluded area behind the stage. The first put his hand in a bucket of cold water, the second put his hand in a bucket of hot water, and the third put his hand in a bucket of lukewarm water. After a few minutes, Protagoras brought them back on stage where they all put their hands in the same bucket of water at air temperature. Much to the audience's surprise, they claimed the same bucket of water was cold, hot, and lukewarm!

It would be easy to try to dismiss Protagoras's demonstration by saying that the only reason the same water felt different was because the three people had gotten used to three different temperatures. But Protagoras's argument goes much deeper. After all, he himself openly revealed what accounted for the differences, because his point isn't that he is "manipulating" what each person feels. Rather, the words *hot, cold,* and *lukewarm* refer to actual sensations experienced by each mind involved in the experiment. These sensations are something the mind conjures up among its perceptions in response to some stimulus. Protagoras's deep and subtle point is that the stimulus itself is neither hot nor cold nor lukewarm. This is an incredibly advanced insight about the nature of the appearances— perception—in its relation to the world beyond the appearances.

Indeed, today science tells us that temperature is a measure of the relative motion of atomic particles. Now, think about it: *the motion of particles,* by itself—is this the *feeling* of warmth or coldness? One can try to reduce, via a scientific theory, the sensation of warmth

---

1. From *The Dialogues of Plato,* trans. B. Jowett (London: Clarendon Press, 1892).

to the motion of particles, but warmth as an experience certainly does not seem to be the same thing as motion. And that the same motions, or vibrations, can give rise to different sensations is precisely the sort of relativistic truth that Protagoras is after. Insofar as the appearances themselves consist not of physical things as they exist independently of the mind but rather of mental phenomena, they are not a direct apprehension of objective reality but constructions by the mind relative to the observer. It is to Protagoras's credit that he could make such a sophisticated type of argument using something as simple as three buckets of water.

DEMOCRITUS

460–360 B.C.E.

Democritus, like Protagoras, was born in the coastal town of Abdera. Twenty years younger than Protagoras, ten years younger than Socrates, he overlapped with the young Plato, but the latter makes no mention of him nor of his atomic theory of physical reality. However, Plato's star pupil and philosophical successor, Aristotle, wrote knowingly about his fellow northern Ionian. Democritus himself complained that unlike Protagoras, who received a great welcome in Athens, "I went to Athens, and no one knew me." The ancient biographer Diogenes Laertius, from whom we get most of our biographical information on the pre-Socratic philosophers, claims that Plato despised Democritus so much that he wanted all of his books burned. Protagoras was almost as prolific a writer as Plato, with more than fifty books to his credit, and all his writings were indeed destroyed, but not until the fourth century C.E. (Common Era).

Democritus studied with Leucippus at his highly influential School of Abdera, at the same time as Protagoras. Leucippus based his theory of reality on Parmenides's theory but with an original twist: he took the primary aspects of being that Parmenides had ascribed to the whole of reality and applied them not to the whole but to the ultimate parts, which he called *atoms.* He taught his students both the Ionian philosophers (Thales, Anaxagoras, Anaximenes, Pythagoras, Heraclitus) and the Eleatic philosophers (Parmenides, Zeno), hoping thereby to create a new synthesis of apparently irreconcilable philosophical positions. This is the ideal to which Democritus devoted his entire, long life (he lived to be one hundred).

Democritus took the atomic physical theory of Leucippus and combined it with Protagoras's representational theory of the mind. In Leucippus's view the Parmenidean properties of being apply not to the whole of existence but only to its ultimate, indivisible, eternal, units, or *atoms* (literally, *a*["non"]*tom*["divisible"]). To the question of what separated atoms, he gave a brilliant answer: not a nothingness but an emptiness. Thus the concept of *nothing,* or non-being, gave rise to the concept of *space.* But whereas Parmenides had claimed that reality is a single, undifferentiated, and indivisible unit—the One—which is completely full, Democritus claims that there is an *infinite* number of separate, individual things—atoms—each one which is completely full and contains no void (no empty space). Because the atoms are so small, they are invisible. Being themselves eternal, the atoms are neither created nor destroyed. In other words, reality consists not of one type of being but of two very different types of beings: existent things and existent non-things. Atoms are existent things, but space, which is a non-thing, also exists. Space is a vacuum having only the property of extension. In this way the atoms can freely move about such that their motions give rise to the various physical objects that we perceive as representations.

In this way, Democritus was the first to try to use atomic theory to circumvent Zeno's paradoxes. Motion, according to Democritus, is possible because everything consists of atoms that combine and recombine in empty space into the various shapes and forms we see. In the same way that Pythagoras relied on ideal objects and numbers, represented as dots, to explain the formation of various shapes, Democritus used the minimal physical dots of existence: atoms. He thus combines Leucippus's atomic theory not just with mathematics but also with Protagoras's theory of perception.

According to Democritus, the various arrangements that atoms can make account for the qualitative differences among perceived objects. These perceived qualities do not belong to the atoms themselves but only appear at the level of perception; they are the result of the subjective manner in which the mind of the perceiving object (the observer) constructs the representation. But the behavior of these atoms is purely mechanical, the result of laws of motion that are always and everywhere the same. Democritus's philosophy is thus the first multiperspectival philosophy, in that there is according to him *both* an absolute reality (beyond the perceptions) and a relative reality which we perceive; the two are related by cause: the physical causes the mental.

Democritus was convinced that an atomic theory of matter and the void could answer Zeno's objections to the possibility of motion. At the same time, it raises and then tries to solve the Parmenidean problem of how to reconcile appearances with ultimate reality so that we could have true knowledge of the world. Democritus's brilliant solution takes both the Heraclitan (Ionian) and Parmenidean (Eleatic) philosophies—as his colleague Protagoras would similarly claim—to be true. But both philosophies are true not simply in the subjective way that Protagoras and other sophists had claimed. Rather, according to Democritus, the Parmenidean and Heraclitan views are both *objectively* true of the world. The fact is that the objective world contains *both* material reality ("the physical world") and ideal reality ("the ideal world").

Such a dualistic and multiperspectival view of reality persists to this day. Most people today believe that there exists an objective, external, physical reality consisting of atoms in motion through empty space, as well as a subjective, internal, mental world of perceptions, ideas, and thoughts. Which is the more fundamental reality? According to Democritus, the mental world is itself to be explained in terms of the mind-independent reality of the physical world. In that regard, he was the first thoroughgoing materialist: the mind and all of its phenomena are ultimately of derivative reality, to be explained the same way the physical phenomena of nature are explained: by the movement of atoms. The materialist world view, overshadowed for centuries by the emerging philosophies of Plato and Aristotle, came into its own again in the works of Epicurus, Epictetus, and the stoics. During the Middle Ages it disappeared but then resurfaced in the seventeenth century, when it became the foundation for the newly developing physical sciences, especially in Newton's work. In the passage that follows, Aristotle relates the historical development of the materialist world view.

ARISTOTLE, "FRAGMENTS"

Leukippos and Democritus have decided about all things practically by the same method and on the same theory, taking as their starting-point what naturally comes first. Some of the ancients had held that the real must necessarily be one and immovable; for, said they, empty space is not real, and motion would be impossible without empty space separated from matter; nor, further, could reality be a many, if there were nothing to separate things. And it makes no difference if any one holds that the All is not continuous, but discrete, with its parts in contact (*the Pythagorean view*), instead of holding that reality is many, not one, and that there is empty space. For, if it is divisible at every point there is no one, and therefore no many, and the Whole is empty (*Zeno*); while, if we say it is divisible in one place and not in another, this looks like an arbitrary fiction; for up to what point and for what reason will part of the Whole be in this state and be full, while the rest is discrete? And, on the same grounds, they further say that there can be no motion. In consequence of these reasonings, then, going beyond perception and overlooking it in the belief that we ought to follow the argument, they say that the All is one and immovable (*Parmenides*), and some of them that it is infinite (*Melissos*), for any limit would be bounded by empty space. This, then, is the opinion they expressed about the truth, and these are the reasons which led them to do so. Now, so far as arguments go, this conclusion does seem to follow; but, if we appeal to facts, to hold such a view looks like madness. No one who is mad is so far out of his senses that fire and ice appear to him to be one; it is only things that are right, and things that appear right from habit, in which madness makes some people see no difference.

Leukippos, however, thought he had a theory which was in harmony with sense, and did not do away with coming into being and passing away, nor motion, nor the multiplicity of things. He conceded this to experience, while he conceded, on the other hand, to those who invented the One that motion was impossible without the void, that the void was not real, and that nothing of what was real was not real. "For," said he, "that which is strictly speaking real is an absolute *plenum;* but the *plenum* is not one. On the contrary, there are an infinite number of them, and they are invisible owing to the smallness of their bulk. They move in the void (for there is a void); and by their coming together they effect coming into being; by their separation, passing away."

From John Burnet, *Early Greek Philosophy* (London: World, 1910).

IO

PLATO

428–348 B.C.E.

Plato was born in Athens to a prominent aristocratic family. The Peloponnesian War, between Athens and Sparta, had been raging for many years and continued for the next several decades. In 404 B.C.E., when Plato was only twenty-four, Athens surrendered to Sparta. Disillusioned by politics and warfare, Plato gave up the political life in favor of philosophy. He became a disciple of none other than Socrates and went on in his own right to become one of the greatest and most influential philosophers. He founded the Academy, the first university, which lasted nearly a thousand years.

Socrates, who claimed that philosophy ought not to be written down, wrote nothing. Plato, on the other hand, produced dozens of works on nearly every topic. He wrote so much and covered so much ground that the twentieth-century philosopher Alfred North Whitehead has called the entire history of Western philosophy "a series of footnotes to Plato." No one knows why Plato disregarded his teacher's prohibition against writing. Indeed, Socrates not only shunned the written word, he claimed that writing down philosophy was unphilosophical. Even more surprising, Plato himself preserves Socrates' arguments against writing in his own written works, such as *The Republic.* Indeed, Plato gives explicit and detailed arguments against the very types of books Plato wrote!

As far as we know, Plato began writing his dialogues after Socrates was executed by his fellow Athenians for "corrupting" the youth and raising doubts in their minds about accepted gods. No doubt, the trial and death of his beloved mentor had a profound effect on young Plato and may well have changed his mind about the role of writing. We do know that Plato left Athens shortly thereafter. For nearly ten years he traveled in southern Italy and Sicily, where he began writing his first dialogues in which Socrates appears as a philosophical gadfly seeking human excellence not by offering solutions to philosophical problems. Rather, Socrates goads his adversaries into offering a definition of some term, such as justice, courage, intelligence, piety, and so on, and then draws inferences from his opponents' responses so as to elicit explicit contradictions. In this way, Socrates shows the profound ignorance in which most people live. By unmasking their pretense, Socrates frustrates his adversaries not into some better view of reality but into his own befuddled state of puzzlement and unknowing. This was probably the method used by the actual Socrates, but of course we have no way of knowing since we are getting this not from Socrates himself but from Plato.

One of the best examples of the Socratic method is in our first selection, the *Euthyphro.* This dialogue takes place shortly before Socrates' infamous trial and subsequent execution in 399 B.C.E. It contains one of the most devastating assaults ever mounted against a religion-based ethics, in the form of a simple, piercing question: Is an action pious because it pleases the gods, or does it please the gods because it is pious?

In other words, *is some action, X, right because God says so or does God say so because X is right?* This question cuts so deeply to the heart of the issue that contemporary philosopher Anthony Flew has remarked that "one good test of a person's aptitude for philosophy is to discover whether he can grasp its force and point." Socrates' famous question thus forces Euthyphro into a dilemma (literally, "two-forked path"), each fork of which leads to a contradiction from within Euthyphro's own point of view.

In our second selection, the *Apology,* Plato tells the famous story of how Socrates became a philosopher. Like other sophists, he traveled about seeking wisdom by asking questions of everyone who would talk to him, questions about anything and everything. One day, a friend of his went to the official priestess through whom the gods supposedly spoke, called an *oracle.* This friend asked whether anyone in Athens was wiser than Socrates and "the Delphic prophetess answered that there was no one wiser." According to Socrates' testimony in the *Apology,* he himself did not believe the oracle; indeed, he set out to prove the gods wrong. The method was simple. He would go to those who were far wiser than himself and question them until he could demonstrate their superiority. But then a surprising thing happened: all the people he talked to invariably pretended to know more than they actually knew. Socrates then proclaims that, if he is wise, it is only because he does not pretend to know more than he knows. Further, he is not deceived by pretense to knowledge: that is, he is not just ignorant, he knows the unknown.

Socrates' trial and subsequent imprisonment are described in the *Apology* and *Crito.* Already in his seventies, Socrates was by then famous throughout the Hellenic world. Plays had been written about him, the most famous of which, *The Clouds* by Aristophanes, satirized Socrates and his students, making them the objects of public ridicule. The *Apology* (the Greek word means "defense," not "request for forgiveness") begins, as was traditional at the time, with a defense by the accused. But instead of offering a real defense, Socrates repeats the charges against him and then goes on to insult his audience and ridicule his accusers. In the end, he suggests what his punishment should be: a lifelong pension! He is then found guilty by a vote of 281 to 220—more voting against him than before his apology.

In the *Crito,* sentenced to die in prison by drinking the infamous hemlock, Socrates is awaiting execution. Here we find that the citizens of Athens apparently expected Socrates would not take the poison but would flee to another country. But Socrates, always the gadfly, does not flee. He stays, and the *Crito* ends with Socrates choosing death instead of exile. The fourth selection, *Phaedo,* written during Plato's so-called middle period, is a detailed version of Socrates' final conversations with his students. These first four dialogues complete the initial formulations of Plato's philosophy.

The fifth selection is from the *Meno.* Here Plato argues not only that knowledge is possible, but also that it is possible before one has complete knowledge of everything: knowledge attained in life is but remembrance. All human knowledge is nothing more than *recollection.* He illustrates this concept by showing how a slave, completely ignorant of mathematics, has already within him a storehouse of knowledge that he has forgotten. Once awakened, this inner knowledge allows him to learn what otherwise would be impossible.

In the *Phaedrus,* written in the middle of his life, Plato presents his theory of immortality using the examples of love and beauty. He argues that the formal ideas are the ultimate constituents of reality that make possible the evolution and enlightenment of the soul. From here on, the dialogues of Plato's so-called middle and late periods carry on this positive theme. Written at the Academy, they focus on many of the same questions as the earlier dialogues. Instead of the dialectical cross-examination by Socrates leaving his interlocutors without any viable solutions, Socrates in the middle and late dialogues is much less adversarial and offers positive answers to even the most difficult philosophical questions. In this way, by relying on the Parmenidean distinction between reality and appearance and using the method of Pythagorean mathematics, Plato moves beyond the Socratic state of unknowing to the direct knowledge of the formal ideas as revealed "through a glass darkly," the "mind's eye."

According to Plato, the objects of our knowledge do not exist among the appearances. Indeed, the objects that appear to us only obscure the true nature of the real objects that are themselves nowhere to be seen. Real objects exist beyond appearances, in the world of Ideas. Plato explains this relationship between appearance and reality allegorically. He suggests that the objects we perceive are at best but shadows of real things using his allegory of the cave, the simile of the sun, and the divided line. They are found in *The Republic,* from which the next selection is taken, a major work that Plato kept revising the rest of his life. It takes place during a pause in the Peloponnesian War, ten or so years before Socrates' trial. Athens was then still a democracy. The "I" of the narrator is Socrates; Glaucon is one of Plato's older brothers.

In the *Parmenides,* written in the third and final period of his life, Plato comes to question his own Theory of Ideas. The dialogue describes a meeting that took place before Plato's birth. Socrates, then a young man, meets Parmenides and his most famous pupil, Zeno of Elea. Parmenides, as we saw, claimed that being is not many but one, an undifferentiated, unchanging, eternal whole. All change is an illusion. Zeno used his famous paradoxes to show that those who claimed Parmenides' view was absurd were starting from an even *more* absurd view. The narrator, Cephalus, describes the conversation as told to him by Plato's older half-brother, Antiphon, in which Socrates tries to solve one of Zeno's paradoxes using Plato's theory of Ideas. As is often the case with the dialogues from Plato's later period, there is a detailed examination of philosophical logic directed toward a critical and often unflattering scrutiny of Plato's own theory of Ideas. Parmenides criticizes Socrates' solution as a devastating reductio ad absurdum of Plato's entire theory. Plato's lack of an adequate response to Parmenides' criticism has been interpreted by some scholars as a move away from his former dualism, that is, an abandonment of the separation between the world of Ideas and the sensible world of appearances. In any case, this is exactly the move that will later be made by Aristotle, the most famous of Plato's formidable students at the Academy.

The *Philebus,* our ninth selection, is a more rigorous version of the Socratic dialectical method, applied to specific topics such as the relationship between the one and the many. The final selection is from the *Timaeus,* in which Plato presents his theory of cosmology, physics, and biology, as well as his theory of time, through the character of Timaeus. He does this by combining Pythagorean mathematics and astronomy with the biology of Empedocles. He presents two different models of the origin of the world. The first is based on the principles of reason, the second on the principle of individuality.

EUTHYPHRO

EUTHYPHRO: Why have you left the Lyceum, Socrates? and what are you doing in the Porch of the King Archon? Surely you cannot be concerned in a suit before the King, like myself?

SOCRATES: Not in a suit, Euthyphro: impeachment is the word which the Athenians use.

EUTH.: What! I suppose that some one has been prosecuting you, for I cannot believe that you are the prosecutor of another.

SOC.: Certainly not.

EUTH.: Then some one else has been prosecuting you?

SOC.: Yes.

EUTH.: And who is he?

SOC.: A young man who is little known, Euthyphro: and I hardly know him: his name is Meletus, and he is of the deme of Pitthis. Perhaps you may remember his appearance: he has a beak, and long straight hair, and a beard which is ill grown.

EUTH.: No, I do not remember him, Socrates. But what is the charge which he brings against you?

SOC.: What is the charge? Well, a very serious charge, which shows a good deal of character in the young man, and for which he is certainly not to be despised. He says he knows how the youth are corrupted and who are their corruptors. I fancy that he must be a wise man, and seeing that I am the reverse of a wise man, he has found me out, and is going to accuse me of corrupting his young friends. And of this our mother the state is to be the judge. Of all our political men he is the only one who seems to me to begin in the right way, with the cultivation of virtue in youth; like a good husbandman, he makes the young shoots his first care, and clears away us who are the destroyers of them. This is only the first step; he will afterwards attend to the elder branches; and if he goes on as he has begun, he will be a very great public benefactor.

EUTH.: I hope that he may; but I rather fear, Socrates, that the opposite will turn out to be the truth. My opinion is that in attacking you he is simply aiming a blow at the foundation of the state. But in what way does he say that you corrupt the young?

SOC.: He brings a wonderful accusation against me, which at first hearing excites surprise: he says that I am a poet or maker of gods, and that I invent

From "Euthyphro," in *The Dialogues of Plato,* trans. B. Jowett (London: Oxford University Press, 1920).

new gods and deny the existence of old ones; this is the ground of his indictment.

EUTH.: I understand, Socrates; he means to attack you about the familiar sign which occasionally, as you say, comes to you. He thinks that you are a neologian, and he is going to have you up before the court for this. He knows that such a charge is readily received by the world, as I myself know too well; for when I speak in the assembly about divine things, and foretell the future to them, they laugh at me and think me a madman. Yet every word that I say is true. But they are jealous of us all; and we must be brave and go at them.

SOC.: Their laughter, friend Euthyphro, is not a matter of much consequence. For a man may be thought wise; but the Athenians, I suspect, do not much trouble themselves about him until he begins to impart his wisdom to others; and then for some reason or other, perhaps, as you say, from jealousy, they are angry.

EUTH.: I am never likely to try their temper in this way.

SOC.: I dare say not, for you are reserved in your behaviour, and seldom impart your wisdom. But I have a benevolent habit of pouring out myself to everybody, and would even pay for a listener, and I am afraid that the Athenians may think me too talkative. Now if, as I was saying, they would only laugh at me, as you say that they laugh at you, the time might pass gaily enough in the court; but perhaps they may be in earnest, and then what the end will be you soothsayers only can predict.

EUTH.: I dare say that the affair will end in nothing, Socrates, and that you will win your cause; and I think that I shall win my own.

SOC.: And what is your suit, Euthyphro? are you the pursuer or the defendant?

EUTH.: I am the pursuer.

SOC.: Of whom?

EUTH.: You will think me mad when I tell you.

SOC.: Why, has the fugitive wings?

EUTH.: Nay, he is not very volatile at his time of life.

SOC.: Who is he?

EUTH.: My father.

SOC.: Your father! my good man?

EUTH.: Yes.

SOC.: And of what is he accused?

EUTH.: Of murder, Socrates.

SOC.: By the powers, Euthyphro! how little does the common herd know of the nature of right and truth. A man must be an extraordinary man, and have made great strides in wisdom, before he could have seen his way to bring such an action.

EUTH.: Indeed, Socrates, he must.

SOC.: I suppose that the man whom your father murdered was one of your rela-tives—clearly he was; for if he had been a stranger you would never have thought of prosecuting him.

EUTH.: I am amused, Socrates, at your making a distinction between one who is a relation and one who is not a relation; for surely the pollution is the same in either case, if you knowingly associate with the murderer when you ought to clear yourself and him by proceeding against him. The real ques-tion is whether the murdered man has been justly slain. If justly, then your duty is to let the matter alone; but if unjustly, then even if the murderer lives under the same roof with you and eats at the same table, proceed against him. Now the man who is dead was a poor dependant of mine who worked for us as a field labourer on our farm in Naxos, and one day in a fit of drunken passion he got into a quarrel with one of our domestic servants and slew him. My father bound him hand and foot and threw him into a ditch, and then sent to Athens to ask of a diviner what he should do with him. Meanwhile he never attended to him and took no care about him, for he regarded him as a murderer; and thought that no great harm would be done even if he did die. Now this was just what happened. For such was the effect of cold and hunger and chains upon him, that before the mes-senger returned from the diviner, he was dead. And my father and family are angry with me for taking the part of the murderer and prosecuting my father. They say that he did not kill him, and that if he did, the dead man was but a murderer, and I ought not to take any notice, for that a son is impious who prosecutes a father. Which shows, Socrates, how little they know what the gods think about piety and impiety.

SOC.: Good heavens, Euthyphro! and is your knowledge of religion and of things pious and impious so very exact, that, supposing the circumstances to be as you state them, you are not afraid lest you too may be doing an impious thing in bringing an action against your father?

EUTH.: The best of Euthyphro, and that which distinguishes him, Socrates, from other men, is his exact knowledge of all such matters. What should I be good for without it?

SOC.: Rare friend! I think that I cannot do better than be your disciple. Then before the trial with Meletus comes on I shall challenge him, and say that I have always had a great interest in religious questions, and now, as he charges me with rash imaginations and innovations in religion, I have be-come your disciple. You, Meletus, as I shall say to him, acknowledge Eu-thyphro to be a great theologian, and sound in his opinions; and if you approve of him you ought to approve of me, and not have me into court; but if you disapprove, you should begin by indicting him who is my teacher, and who will be the ruin, not of the young, but of the old; that is to say, of myself whom he instructs, and of his old father whom he admon-ishes and chastises. And if Meletus refuses to listen to me, but will go on, and will not shift the indictment from me to you, I cannot do better than repeat this challenge in the court.

EUTH.:   Yes, indeed, Socrates; and if he attempts to indict me I am mistaken if I do not find a flaw in him; the court shall have a great deal more to say to him than to me.

SOC.:   And I, my dear friend, knowing this, am desirous of becoming your disciple. For I observe that no one appears to notice you—not even this Meletus; but his sharp eyes have found me out at once, and he has indicted me for impiety. And therefore, I adjure you to tell me the nature of piety and impiety, which you said that you knew so well, and of murder, and of other offences against the gods. What are they? Is not piety in every action always the same? and impiety, again—is it not always the opposite of piety, and also the same with itself, having, as impiety, one notion which includes whatever is impious?

EUTH.:   To be sure, Socrates.

SOC.:   And what is piety, and what is impiety?

EUTH.:   Piety is doing as I am doing; that is to say, prosecuting any one who is guilty of murder, sacrilege, or of any similar crime—whether he be your father or mother, or whoever he may be—that makes no difference; and not to prosecute them is impiety. And please to consider, Socrates, what a notable proof I will give you of the truth of my words, a proof which I have already given to others:—of the principle, I mean, that the impious, whoever he may be, ought not to go unpunished. For do not men regard Zeus as the best and most righteous of the gods?—and yet they admit that he bound his father (Cronos) because he wickedly devoured his sons, and that he too had punished his own father (Uranus) for a similar reason, in a nameless manner. And yet when I proceed against my father, they are angry with me. So inconsistent are they in their way of talking when the gods are concerned, and when I am concerned.

SOC.:   May not this be the reason, Euthyphro, why I am charged with impiety—that I cannot away with these stories about the gods? and therefore I suppose that people think me wrong. But, as you who are well informed about them approve of them, I cannot do better than assent to your superior wisdom. What else can I say, confessing as I do, that I know nothing about them? Tell me, for the love of Zeus, whether you really believe that they are true.

EUTH.:   Yes, Socrates; and things more wonderful still, of which the world is in ignorance.

SOC.:   And do you really believe that the gods fought with one another, and had dire quarrels, battles, and the like, as the poets say, and as you may see represented in the works of great artists? The temples are full of them; and notably the robe of Athene, which is carried up to the Acropolis at the great Panathenaea, is embroidered with them. Are all these tales of the gods true, Euthyphro?

EUTH.:   Yes, Socrates; and, as I was saying, I can tell you, if you would like to hear them, many other things about the gods which would quite amaze you.

SOC.:   I dare say; and you shall tell me them at some other time when I have leisure. But just at present I would rather hear from you a more precise answer, which you have not as yet given, my friend, to the question, What is 'piety'? When asked, you only replied, Doing as you do, charging your father with murder.

EUTH.: And what I said was true, Socrates.

SOC.: No doubt, Euthyphro; but you would admit that there are many other pious acts?

EUTH.: There are.

SOC.: Remember that I did not ask you to give me two or three examples of piety, but to explain the general idea which makes all pious things to be pious. Do you not recollect that there was one idea which made the impious impious, and the pious pious?

EUTH.: I remember.

SOC.: Tell me what is the nature of this idea, and then I shall have a standard to which I may look, and by which I may measure actions, whether yours or those of any one else, and then I shall be able to say that such and such an action is pious, such another impious.

EUTH.: I will tell you, if you like.

SOC.: I should very much like.

EUTH.: Piety, then, is that which is dear to the gods, and impiety is that which is not dear to them.

SOC.: Very good, Euthyphro; you have now given me the sort of answer which I wanted. But whether what you say is true or not I cannot as yet tell, although I make no doubt that you will prove the truth of your words.

EUTH.: Of course.

SOC.: Come, then, and let us examine what we are saying. That thing or person which is dear to the gods is pious, and that thing or person which is hateful to the gods is impious, these two being the extreme opposites of one another. Was not that said?

EUTH.: It was.

SOC.: And well said?

EUTH.: Yes, Socrates, I thought so; it was certainly said.

SOC.: And further, Euthyphro, the gods were admitted to have enmities and hatreds and differences?

EUTH.: Yes, that was also said.

SOC.: And what sort of difference creates enmity and anger? Suppose for example that you and I, my good friend, differ about a number; do differences of this sort make us enemies and set us at variance with one another? Do we not go at once to arithmetic, and put an end to them by a sum?

EUTH.: True.

SOC.: Or suppose that we differ about magnitudes, do we not quickly end the differences by measuring?

EUTH.: Very true.

SOC.: And we end a controversy about heavy and light by resorting to a weighing machine?

EUTH.: To be sure.

SOC.: But what differences are there which cannot be thus decided, and which therefore make us angry and set us at enmity with one another? I dare say the answer does not occur to you at the moment, and therefore I will suggest that these enmities arise when the matters of difference are the just and unjust, good and evil, honourable and dishonourable. Are not these the points about which men differ, and about which when we are unable satisfactorily to decide our differences, you and I and all of us quarrel, when we do quarrel?

EUTH.: Yes, Socrates, the nature of the differences about which we quarrel is such as you describe.

SOC.: And the quarrels of the gods, noble Euthyphro, when they occur, are of a like nature?

EUTH.: Certainly they are.

SOC.: They have differences of opinion, as you say, about good and evil, just and unjust, honourable and dishonourable: there would have been no quarrels among them, if there had been no such differences—would there now?

EUTH.: You are quite right.

SOC.: Does not every man love that which he deems noble and just and good, and hate the opposite of them?

EUTH.: Very true.

SOC.: But, as you say, people regard the same things, some as just and others as unjust,—about these they dispute; and so there arise wars and fightings among them.

EUTH.: Very true.

SOC.: Then the same things are hated by the gods and loved by the gods, and are both hateful and dear to them?

EUTH.: True.

SOC.: And upon this view the same things, Euthyphro, will be pious and also impious?

EUTH.: So I should suppose.

SOC.: Then, my friend, I remark with surprise that you have not answered the question which I asked. For I certainly did not ask you to tell me what action is both pious and impious: but now it would seem that what is loved by the gods is also hated by them. And therefore, Euthyphro, in thus chastising your father you may very likely be doing what is agreeable to Zeus but disagreeable to Cronos or Uranus, and what is acceptable to Hephaestus but unacceptable to Herè, and there may be other gods who have similar differences of opinion.

EUTH.: But I believe, Socrates, that all the gods would be agreed as to the propriety of punishing a murderer: there would be no difference of opinion about that.

SOC.: Well, but speaking of men, Euthyphro, did you ever hear any one arguing that a murderer or any sort of evil-doer ought to be let off?

EUTH.: I should rather say that these are the questions which they are always arguing, especially in courts of law: they commit all sorts of crimes, and there is nothing which they will not do or say in their own defence.

SOC.: But do they admit their guilt, Euthyphro, and yet say that they ought not to be punished?

EUTH.: No; they do not.

SOC.: Then there are some things which they do not venture to say and do: for they do not venture to argue that the guilty are to be unpunished, but they deny their guilt, do they not?

EUTH.: Yes.

SOC.: Then they do not argue that the evil-doer should not be punished, but they argue about the fact of who the evil-doer is, and what he did and when?

EUTH.: True.

SOC.: And the gods are in the same case, if as you assert they quarrel about just and unjust, and some of them say while others deny that injustice is done among them. For surely neither God nor man will ever venture to say that the doer of injustice is not to be punished?

EUTH.: That is true, Socrates, in the main.

SOC.: But they join issue about the particulars—gods and men alike; and, if they dispute at all, they dispute about some act which is called in question, and which by some is affirmed to be just, by others to be unjust. Is not that true?

EUTH.: Quite true.

SOC.: Well then, my dear friend Euthyphro, do tell me, for my better instruction and information, what proof have you that in the opinion of all the gods a servant who is guilty of murder, and is put in chains by the master of the dead man, and dies because he is put in chains before he who bound him can learn from the interpreters of the gods what he ought to do with him, dies unjustly; and that on behalf of such an one a son ought to proceed against his father and accuse him of murder. How would you show that all the gods absolutely agree in approving of his act? Prove to me that they do, and I will applaud your wisdom as long as I live.

EUTH.: It will be a difficult task; but I could make the matter very clear indeed to you.

SOC.: I understand; you mean to say that I am not so quick of apprehension as the judges: for to them you will be sure to prove that the act is unjust, and hateful to the gods.

EUTH.: Yes indeed, Socrates; at least if they will listen to me.

SOC.: But they will be sure to listen if they find that you are a good speaker. There was a notion that came into my mind while you were speaking; I said to myself: "Well, and what if Euthyphro does prove to me that all the gods regarded the death of the serf as unjust, how do I know anything more of the nature of piety and impiety? for granting that this action may be hateful to the gods, still piety and impiety are not adequately defined by these distinctions, for that which is hateful to the gods has been shown to be also pleasing and dear to them." And therefore, Euthyphro, I do not ask you to prove this; I will suppose, if you like, that all the gods condemn and abominate such an action. But I will amend the definition so far as to say that what all the gods hate is impious, and what they love pious or holy; and what some of them love and others hate is both or neither. Shall this be our definition of piety and impiety?

EUTH.: Why not, Socrates?

SOC.: Why not! certainly, as far as I am concerned, Euthyphro, there is no reason why not. But whether this admission will greatly assist you in the task of instructing me as you promised, is a matter for you to consider.

EUTH.: Yes, I should say that what all the gods love is pious and holy, and the opposite which they all hate, impious.

SOC.: Ought we to enquire into the truth of this, Euthyphro, or simply to accept the mere statement on our own authority and that of others? What do you say?

EUTH.: We should enquire; and I believe that the statement will stand the test of enquiry.

SOC.: We shall know better, my good friend, in a little while. The point which I should first wish to understand is whether the pious or holy is beloved by the gods because it is holy, or holy because it is beloved of the gods.

EUTH.: I do not understand your meaning, Socrates.

SOC.: I will endeavour to explain: we speak of carrying and we speak of being carried, of leading and being led, seeing and being seen. You know that in all such cases there is a difference, and you know also in what the difference lies?

EUTH.: I think that I understand.

SOC.: And is not that which is beloved distinct from that which loves?

EUTH.: Certainly.

SOC.: Well; and now tell me, is that which is carried in this state of carrying because it is carried, or for some other reason?

EUTH.: No; that is the reason.

SOC.: And the same is true of what is led and of what is seen?

EUTH.: True.

SOC.: And a thing is not seen because it is visible, but conversely, visible because it is seen; nor is a thing led because it is in the state of being led, or carried because it is in the state of being carried, but the converse of this. And now

I think, Euthyphro, that my meaning will be intelligible; and my meaning is, that any state of action or passion implies previous action or passion. It does not become because it is becoming, but it is in a state of becoming because it becomes; neither does it suffer because it is in a state of suffering, but it is in a state of suffering because it suffers. Do you not agree?

EUTH.: Yes.

SOC.: Is not that which is loved in some state either of becoming or suffering?

EUTH.: Yes.

SOC.: And the same holds as in the previous instances; the state of being loved follows the act of being loved, and not the act the state.

EUTH.: Certainly.

SOC.: And what do you say of piety, Euthyphro: is not piety, according to your definition, loved by all the gods?

EUTH.: Yes.

SOC.: Because it is pious or holy, or for some other reason?

EUTH.: No, that is the reason.

SOC.: It is loved because it is holy, not holy because it is loved?

EUTH.: Yes.

SOC.: And that which is dear to the gods is loved by them, and is in a state to be loved of them because it is loved of them?

EUTH.: Certainly.

SOC.: Then that which is dear to the gods, Euthyphro, is not holy, nor is that which is holy loved of God, as you affirm; but they are two different things.

EUTH.: How do you mean, Socrates?

SOC.: I mean to say that the holy has been acknowledged by us to be loved of God because it is holy, not to be holy because it is loved.

EUTH.: Yes.

SOC.: But that which is dear to the gods is dear to them because it is loved by them, not loved by them because it is dear to them.

EUTH.: True.

SOC.: But, friend Euthyphro, if that which is holy is the same with that which is dear to God, and is loved because it is holy, then that which is dear to God would have been loved as being dear to God; but if that which is dear to God is dear to him because loved by him, then that which is holy would have been holy because loved by him. But now you see that the reverse is the case, and that they are quite different from one another. For one ($\theta\epsilon o\phi\iota\lambda\grave{\epsilon}\cdot$) is of a kind to be loved because it is loved, and the other ($\H{o}\sigma\iota o\nu$) is loved because it is of a kind to be loved. Thus you appear to me, Euthyphro, when I ask you what is the essence of holiness, to offer an attribute only, and not the essence—the attribute of being loved by all the gods. But you still refuse to explain to me the nature of holiness. And therefore, if you please, I will ask you not to hide your treasure, but to tell me once more what holiness or piety really is, whether dear to the gods or not (for that is a matter about which we will not quarrel); and what is impiety?

EUTH.: I really do not know, Socrates, how to express what I mean. For somehow or other our arguments, on whatever ground we rest them, seem to turn round and walk away from us.

SOC.: Your words, Euthyphro, are like the handiwork of my ancestor Daedalus; and if I were the sayer or propounder of them, you might say that my arguments walk away and will not remain fixed where they are placed because I am a descendant of his. But now, since these notions are your own, you must find some other gibe, for they certainly, as you yourself allow, show an inclination to be on the move.

EUTH.: Nay, Socrates, I shall still say that you are the Daedalus who sets arguments in motion; not I, certainly, but you make them move or go round, for they would never have stirred, as far as I am concerned.

SOC.: Then I must be a greater than Daedalus: for whereas he only made his own inventions to move, I move those of other people as well. And the beauty of it is, that I would rather not. For I would give the wisdom of Daedalus, and the wealth of Tantalus, to be able to detain them and keep them fixed. But enough of this. As I perceive that you are lazy, I will myself endeavour to show you how you might instruct me in the nature of piety; and I hope that you will not grudge your labour. Tell me, then,—Is not that which is pious necessarily just?

EUTH.: Yes.

SOC.: And is, then, all which is just pious? or, is that which is pious all just, but that which is just, only in part and not all, pious?

EUTH.: I do not understand you, Socrates.

SOC.: And yet I know that you are as much wiser than I am, as you are younger. But, as I was saying, revered friend, the abundance of your wisdom makes you lazy. Please to exert yourself, for there is no real difficulty in understanding me. What I mean I may explain by an illustration of what I do not mean. The poet (Stasinus) sings—

> "Of Zeus, the author and creator of all these things,
> You will not tell: for where there is fear there is also reverence."

Now I disagree with this poet. Shall I tell you in what respect?

EUTH.: By all means.

SOC.: I should not say that where there is fear there is also reverence; for I am sure that many persons fear poverty and disease, and the like evils, but I do not perceive that they reverence the objects of their fear.

EUTH.: Very true.

SOC.: But where reverence is, there is fear; for he who has a feeling of reverence and shame about the commission of any action, fears and is afraid of an ill reputation.

EUTH.: No doubt.

SOC.: Then we are wrong in saying that where there is fear there is also reverence; and we should say, where there is reverence there is also fear. But there is not always reverence where there is fear; for fear is a more extended notion, and reverence is a part of fear, just as the odd is a part of number, and number is a more extended notion than the odd. I suppose that you follow me now?

EUTH.: Quite well.

SOC.: That was the sort of question which I meant to raise when I asked whether the just is always the pious, or the pious always the just; and whether there may not be justice where there is not piety; for justice is the more extended notion of which piety is only a part. Do you dissent?

EUTH.: No, I think that you are quite right.

SOC.: Then, if piety is a part of justice, I suppose that we should enquire what part? If you had pursued the enquiry in the previous cases; for instance, if you had asked me what is an even number, and what part of number the even is, I should have had no difficulty in replying, a number which represents a figure having two equal sides. Do you not agree?

EUTH.: Yes, I quite agree.

SOC.: In like manner, I want you to tell me what part of justice is piety or holiness, that I may be able to tell Meletus not to do me injustice, or indict me for impiety, as I am now adequately instructed by you in the nature of piety or holiness, and their opposites.

EUTH.: Piety or holiness, Socrates, appears to me to be that part of justice which attends to the gods, as there is the other part of justice which attends to men.

SOC.: That is good, Euthyphro; yet still there is a little point about which I should like to have further information. What is the meaning of "attention"? For attention can hardly be used in the same sense when applied to the gods as when applied to other things. For instance, horses are said to require attention, and not every person is able to attend to them, but only a person skilled in horsemanship. Is it not so?

EUTH.: Certainly.

SOC.: I should suppose that the art of horsemanship is the art of attending to horses?

EUTH.: Yes.

SOC.: Nor is every one qualified to attend to dogs, but only the huntsman?

EUTH.: True.

SOC.: And I should also conceive that the art of the huntsman is the art of attending to dogs?

EUTH.: Yes.

SOC.: As the art of the oxherd is the art of attending to oxen?

EUTH.: Very true.

SOC.:   In like manner holiness or piety is the art of attending to the gods?—that would be your meaning, Euthyphro?

EUTH.:   Yes.

SOC.:   And is not attention always designed for the good or benefit of that to which the attention is given? As in the case of horses, you may observe that when attended to by the horseman's art they are benefited and improved, are they not?

EUTH.:   True.

SOC.:   As the dogs are benefited by the huntsman's art, and the oxen by the art of the oxherd, and all other things are tended or attended for their good and not for their hurt?

EUTH.:   Certainly, not for their hurt.

SOC.:   But for their good?

EUTH.:   Of course.

SOC.:   And does piety or holiness, which has been defined to be the art of attending to the gods, benefit or improve them? Would you say that when you do a holy act you make any of the gods better?

EUTH.:   No, no; that was certainly not what I meant.

SOC.:   And I, Euthyphro, never supposed that you did. I asked you the question about the nature of the attention, because I thought that you did not.

EUTH.:   You do me justice, Socrates; that is not the sort of attention which I mean.

SOC.:   Good; but I must still ask what is this attention to the gods which is called piety?

EUTH.:   It is such, Socrates, as servants show to their masters.

SOC.:   I understand—a sort of ministration to the gods.

EUTH.:   Exactly.

SOC.:   Medicine is also a sort of ministration or service, having in view the attainment of some object—would you not say of health?

EUTH.:   I should.

SOC.:   Again, there is an art which ministers to the ship-builder with a view to the attainment of some result?

EUTH.:   Yes, Socrates, with a view to the building of a ship.

SOC.:   As there is an art which ministers to the housebuilder with a view to the building of a house?

EUTH.:   Yes.

SOC.:   And now tell me, my good friend, about the art which ministers to the gods: what work does that help to accomplish? For you must surely know if, as you say, you are of all men living the one who is best instructed in religion.

EUTH.:   And I speak the truth, Socrates.

SOC.:   Tell me then, oh tell me—what is that fair work which the gods do by the help of our ministrations?

EUTH.: Many and fair, Socrates, are the works which they do.

SOC.: Why, my friend, and so are those of a general. But the chief of them is easily told. Would you not say that victory in war is the chief of them?

EUTH.: Certainly.

SOC.: Many and fair, too, are the works of the husbandman, if I am not mistaken; but his chief work is the production of food from the earth?

EUTH.: Exactly.

SOC.: And of the many and fair things done by the gods, which is the chief or principal one?

EUTH.: I have told you already, Socrates, that to learn all these things accurately will be very tiresome. Let me simply say that piety or holiness is learning how to please the gods in word and deed, by prayers and sacrifices. Such piety is the salvation of families and states, just as the impious, which is unpleasing to the gods, is their ruin and destruction.

SOC.: I think that you could have answered in much fewer words the chief question which I asked, Euthyphro, if you had chosen. But I see plainly that you are not disposed to instruct me—clearly not: else why, when we reached the point, did you turn aside? Had you only answered me I should have truly learned of you by this time the nature of piety. Now, as the asker of a question is necessarily dependent on the answerer, whither he leads I must follow; and can only ask again, what is the pious, and what is piety? Do you mean that they are a sort of science of praying and sacrificing?

EUTH.: Yes, I do.

SOC.: And sacrificing is giving to the gods, and prayer is asking of the gods?

EUTH.: Yes, Socrates.

SOC.: Upon this view, then, piety is a science of asking and giving?

EUTH.: You understand me capitally, Socrates.

SOC.: Yes, my friend; the reason is that I am a votary of your science, and give my mind to it, and therefore nothing which you say will be thrown away upon me. Please then to tell me, what is the nature of this service to the gods? Do you mean that we prefer requests and give gifts to them?

EUTH.: Yes, I do.

SOC.: Is not the right way of asking to ask of them what we want?

EUTH.: Certainly.

SOC.: And the right way of giving is to give to them in return what they want of us. There would be no meaning in an art which gives to any one that which he does not want.

EUTH.: Very true, Socrates.

SOC.: Then piety, Euthyphro, is an art which gods and men have of doing business with one another?

EUTH.: That is an expression which you may use, if you like.

SOC.: But I have no particular liking for anything but the truth. I wish, however, that you would tell me what benefit accrues to the gods from our gifts. There is no doubt about what they give to us; for there is no good thing which they do not give; but how we can give any good thing to them in return is far from being equally clear. If they give everything and we give nothing, that must be an affair of business in which we have very greatly the advantage of them.

EUTH.: And do you imagine, Socrates, that any benefit accrues to the gods from our gifts?

SOC.: But if not, Euthyphro, what is the meaning of gifts which are conferred by us upon the gods?

EUTH.: What else, but tributes of honour; and, as I was just now saying, what pleases them?

SOC.: Piety, then, is pleasing to the gods, but not beneficial or dear to them?

EUTH.: I should say that nothing could be dearer.

SOC.: Then once more the assertion is repeated that piety is dear to the gods?

EUTH.: Certainly.

SOC.: And when you say this, can you wonder at your words not standing firm, but walking away? Will you accuse me of being the Daedalus who makes them walk away, not perceiving that there is another and far greater artist than Daedalus who makes them go round in a circle, and he is yourself; for the argument, as you will perceive, comes round to the same point. Were we not saying that the holy or pious was not the same with that which is loved of the gods? Have you forgotten?

EUTH.: I quite remember.

SOC.: And are you not saying that what is loved of the gods is holy; and is not this the same as what is dear to them—do you see?

EUTH.: True.

SOC.: Then either we were wrong in our former assertion; or, if we were right then, we are wrong now.

EUTH.: One of the two must be true.

SOC.: Then we must begin again and ask, What is piety? That is an enquiry which I shall never be weary of pursuing as far as in me lies; and I entreat you not to scorn me, but to apply your mind to the utmost, and tell me the truth. For, if any man knows, you are he; and therefore I must detain you, like Proteus, until you tell. If you had not certainly known the nature of piety and impiety, I am confident that you would never, on behalf of a serf, have charged your aged father with murder. You would not have run such a risk of doing wrong in the sight of the gods, and you would have had too much respect for the opinions of men. I am sure, therefore, that you know the nature of piety and impiety. Speak out then, my dear Euthyphro, and do not hide your knowledge.

EUTH.: Another time, Socrates; for I am in a hurry, and must go now.

SOC.: Alas! my companion, and will you leave me in despair? I was hoping that you would instruct me in the nature of piety and impiety; and then I might have cleared myself of Meletus and his indictment. I would have told him that I had been enlightened by Euthyphro, and had given up rash innovations and speculations, in which I indulged only through ignorance, and that now I am about to lead a better life.

APOLOGY

How you have felt, O men of Athens, at hearing the speeches of my accusers, I cannot tell; but I know that their persuasive words almost made me forget who I was, such was the effect of them; and yet they have hardly spoken a word of truth. But many as their falsehoods were, there was one of them which quite amazed me: I mean when they told you to be upon your guard, and not to let yourself be deceived by the force of my eloquence. They ought to have been ashamed of saying this, because they were sure to be detected as soon as I opened my lips and displayed my deficiency; they certainly did appear to be most shameless in saying this, unless by the force of eloquence they mean the force of truth: for then I do indeed admit that I am eloquent. But in how different a way from theirs! . . .

Well, then, I will make my defence, and I will endeavor in the short time which is allowed to do away with this evil opinion of me which you have held for such a long time; and I hope I may succeed, if this be well for you and me, and that my words may find favor with you. But I know that to accomplish this is not easy—I quite see the nature of the task. Let the event be as God wills: in obedience to the law I make my defence.

I will begin at the beginning, and ask what the accusation is which has given rise to this slander of me, and which has encouraged Meletus to proceed against me. What do the slanderers say? They shall be my prosecutors, and I will sum up their words in an affidavit: "Socrates is an evil-doer, and a curious person, who searches into things under the earth and in heaven, and he makes the worse appear the better cause; and he teaches the aforesaid doctrines to others." That is the nature of the accusation. . . . But the simple truth is, O Athenians, that I have nothing to do with these studies. Very many of those here present are witnesses to the truth of this, and to them I appeal. . . . As little foundation is there for the report that I am a teacher, and take money; that is no more true than the other. . . .

I dare say that someone will ask the question, "Why is this, Socrates, and what is the origin of these accusations of you: for there must have been something strange which you have been doing? All this great fame and talk about you would never have arisen if you had been like other men: tell us, then, why this is, as we should be sorry to judge hastily of you." Now I regard this as a fair challenge, and I will endeavor to explain to you the origin of this name of "wise," and of this evil fame. Please to attend them. And although some of you may think I am joking, I declare that I will tell you the entire truth. Men of Athens, this reputation of mine has come of a certain sort of wisdom which I possess. If you ask me what kind of wisdom, I reply, such wisdom as is attainable by man, for to that extent I am

From "Apology," in *The Dialogues of Plato,* trans. B. Jowett (Oxford: Clarendon Press, 1892).

inclined to believe that I am wise; whereas the persons of whom I was speaking have a superhuman wisdom, which I may fail to describe, because I have it not myself; and he who says that I have, speaks falsely, and is taking away my character. And here, O men of Athens, I must beg you not to interrupt me, even if I seem to say something extravagant. For the word which I will speak is not mine. I will refer you to a witness who is worthy of credit, and will tell you about my wisdom—whether I have any, and of what sort—and that witness shall be the god of Delphi. . . . [A] friend of mine . . . went to Delphi and boldly asked the oracle to tell him whether—as I was saying, I must beg you not to interrupt—he asked the oracle to tell him whether there was anyone wiser than I was, and the Pythian prophetess answered that there was no man wiser. . . .

Why do I mention this? Because I am going to explain to you why I have such an evil name. When I heard the answer, I said to myself, What can the god mean? and what is the interpretation of this riddle? for I know that I have no wisdom, small or great. What can he mean when he says that I am the wisest of men? And yet he is a god and cannot lie; that would be against his nature. After a long consideration, I at last thought of a method of trying the question. I reflected that if I could only find a man wiser than myself, then I might go to the god with a refutation in my hand. I should say to him, "Here is a man who is wiser than I am; but you said that I was the wisest." Accordingly I went to one who had the reputation of wisdom, and observed to him—his name I need not mention; he was a politician whom I selected for examination—and the result was as follows: When I began to talk with him, I could not help thinking that he was not really wise, although he was thought wise by many, and wiser still by himself; and I went and tried to explain to him that he thought himself wise, but was not really wise; and the consequence was that he hated me, and his enmity was shared by several who were present and heard me. So I left him, saying to myself, as I went away: Well, although I do not suppose that either of us knows anything really beautiful and good, I am better off than he is—for he knows nothing, and thinks that he knows. I neither know nor think that I know. In this latter particular, then, I seem to have slightly the advantage of him. Then I went to another, who had still higher philosophical pretensions, and my conclusion was exactly the same. I made another enemy of him, and of many others besides him.

After this I went to one man after another, being not unconscious of the enmity which I provoked, and I lamented and feared this: but necessity was laid upon me—the word of God, I thought, ought to be considered first. And I said to myself, Go I must to all who appear to know, and find out the meaning of the oracle. And I swear to you, Athenians, by the dog I swear!—for I must tell you the truth—the result of my mission was just this: I found that the men most in repute were all but the most foolish; and that some inferior men were really wiser and better. I will tell you the tale of my wanderings and of the "Herculean" labors, as I may call them, which I endured only to find at last the oracle irrefutable. When I left the politicians, I went to the poets; tragic, dithyrambic, and all sorts. And there, I said to myself, you will be detected; now you will find out that you are more ignorant than they are. Accordingly, I took them some of the most elaborate passages in their own writings, and asked what was the meaning of them—thinking that they would teach me something. Will you believe me? I am almost ashamed to speak of this, but still I must say that there is hardly a person present who would not have talked better about their poetry than they did themselves. That showed me in an instant that not by wisdom do poets write poetry, but by a sort of genius and inspiration; they are like diviners or sooth-sayers who also say many fine things, but do not understand the meaning of them. And the poets appeared to me to be much in the same case; and I further observed that upon the strength of their poetry they believed themselves to be the wisest of men in other things in which they were not wise. So I departed, conceiving myself to be superior to them for the same reason that I was superior to the politicians.

At last I went to the artisans, for I was conscious that I knew nothing at all, as I may say, and I was sure that they knew many fine things; and in this I was not mistaken, for they did know many things of which I was ignorant, and in this they certainly were wiser than I was. But I observed that even the good artisans fell into the same error as the poets; because they were good workmen they thought that they also knew all sorts of high matters, and this defect in them overshadowed their wisdom—therefore I asked myself on behalf of the oracle, whether I would like to be as I was, neither having their knowledge nor their ignorance, or like them in both; and I made answer to myself and the oracle that I was better off as I was.

This investigation has led to my having many enemies of the worst and most dangerous kind, and has given occasion also to many calumnies, and I am called wise, for my hearers always imagine that I myself possess the wisdom which I find wanting in others; but the truth is, O men of Athens, that God only is wise; and in this oracle he means to say that the wisdom of men is little or nothing; he is not speaking of Socrates, he is only using my name as an illustration, as if he said, He, O men, is the wisest, who, like Socrates, knows that his wisdom is in truth worth nothing. And so I go my way, obedient to the god, and make inquisition into the wisdom of anyone, whether citizen or stranger, who appears to be wise; and if he is not wise, then in vindication of the oracle I show him that he is not wise; and this occupation quite absorbs me, and I have no time to give either to any public matter of interest or to any concern of my own, but I am in utter poverty by reason of my devotion to the god.

There is another thing:—young men of the richer classes, who have not much to do, come about me of their own accord; they like to hear the pretenders examined, and they often imitate me, and examine others themselves; there are plenty of persons, as they soon enough discover, who think that they know something, but really know little or nothing: and then those who are examined by them instead of being angry with themselves are angry with me: This confounded Socrates, they say; this villainous misleader of youth!—and then if somebody asks them, Why, what evil does he practise or teach? they do not know, and cannot tell; but in order that they may not appear to be at a loss, they repeat the ready-made charges which are used against all philosophers about teaching things up in the clouds and under the earth, and having no gods, and making the worse appear the better cause; for they do not like to confess that their pretence of knowledge has been detected—which is the truth: and as they are numerous and ambitious and energetic, and are all in battle array and have persuasive tongues, they have filled your ears with their loud and inveterate calumnies. And this is the reason why my three accusers, Meletus and Anytus and Lycon, have set upon me; Meletus, who has a quarrel with me on behalf of the poets; Anytus, on behalf of the craftsmen; Lycon, on behalf of the rhetoricians; and as I said at the beginning, I cannot expect to get rid of this mass of calumny all in a moment. And this, O men of Athens, is the truth and the whole truth; I have concealed nothing, I have dissembled nothing. And yet I know that this plainness of speech makes them hate me, and what is their hatred but a proof that I am speaking the truth?—this is the occasion and reason of their slander of me, as you will find out either in this or in any future inquiry.

I have said enough in my defence against the first class of my accusers; I turn to the second class, who are headed by Meletus, that good and patriotic man, as he calls himself. And now I will try to defend myself against them: these new accusers must also have their affidavit read. What do they say? Something of this sort: That Socrates is a doer of evil, and corrupter of the youth, and he does not believe in the gods of the State, and has other new divinities of his own. That is the sort of charge; and now let us examine the particular counts. He says that I am a doer of evil, who corrupt the youth; but I say, O men of Athens, that Meletus is a doer of evil, and the evil is that he makes a joke of a serious matter, and is too ready at bringing other men to trial from a pretended zeal and interest about matters in which he really never had the smallest interest. And the truth of this I will endeavor to prove.

Come hither, Meletus, and let me ask a question of you. You think a great deal about the improvement of youth?

Yes, I do.

Tell the judges, then, who is their improver; for you must know, as you have taken the pains to discover their corrupter, and are citing and accusing me before them. Speak, then, and tell the judges who their improver is. Observe, Meletus, that you are silent, and have nothing to say. But is not this rather disgraceful, and a very considerable proof of what I was saying, that you have no interest in the matter? Speak up, friend, and tell us who their improver is.

The laws.

But that, my good sir, is not my meaning. I want to know who the person is, who, in the first place, knows the laws.

The judges, Socrates, who are present in court.

What do you mean to say, Meletus, that they are able to instruct and improve youth?

Certainly they are.

What, all of them, or some only and not others?

All of them.

By the goddess Here, that is good news! There are plenty of improvers, then. And what do you say of the audience—do they improve them?

Yes, they do.

And the Senators?

Yes, the Senators improve them.

But perhaps the ecclesiasts corrupt them?—or do they too improve them?

They improve them.

Then every Athenian improves and elevates them; all with the exception of myself; and I alone am their corrupter? Is that what you affirm?

That is what I stoutly affirm.

I am very unfortunate if that is true. But suppose I ask you a question: Would you say that this also holds true in the case of horses? Does one man do them harm and all the world good? Is not the exact opposite of this true? One man is able to do them good, or at least not many; the trainer of horses, that is to say, does them good, and others who have to do with them rather injure them? Is not that true, Meletus, of horses, or any other animals? Yes, certainly. Whether you and Anytus say yes or no, that is no matter. Happy indeed would be the condition of youth if they had one corrupter only, and all the rest of the world were their improvers. And you, Meletus, have sufficiently shown that you never had a thought about the young: your carelessness is seen in your not caring about matters spoken of in this very indictment.

And now, Meletus, I must ask you another question: Which is better, to live among bad citizens, or among good ones? Answer, friend, I say; for that is a question which may be easily answered. Do not the good do their neighbors good, and the bad do them evil?

Certainly.

And is there anyone who would rather be injured than benefited by those who live with him? Answer, my good friend; the law requires you to answer—does anyone like to be injured?

Certainly not.

And when you accuse me of corrupting and deteriorating the youth, do you allege that I corrupt them intentionally or unintentionally?

Intentionally, I say.

But you have just admitted that the good do their neighbors good, and the evil do them evil. Now is that a truth which your superior wisdom has recognized thus early in life, and am I, at my age, in such darkness and ignorance as not to know that if a man with whom I have to live is corrupted by me, I am very likely to be harmed by him, and yet I corrupt him, and intentionally, too? that is what you are saying, and of that you will never persuade me or any other human being. But either I do not corrupt them, or I corrupt them unintentionally, so that on either view of the case you lie. If my offence is unintentional, the law has no cognizance of unintentional offences: you ought to have taken me privately, and warned and admonished me; for if I had been better advised, I should have left off doing what I only did unintentionally—no doubt I should; whereas you hated to converse with me or teach me, but you indicted me in this court, which is a place not of instruction, but of punishment.

I have shown, Athenians, as I was saying, that Meletus has no care at all, great or small, about the matter. But still I should like to know, Meletus, in what I am affirmed to corrupt the young. I suppose you mean, as I infer from your indictment, that I teach them not to acknowledge the gods which the State acknowledges, but some other new divinities or spiritual agencies in their stead. These are the lessons which corrupt the youth, as you say.

Yes, that I say emphatically.

Then, by the gods, Meletus, of whom we are speaking, tell me and the court, in somewhat plainer terms, what you mean! for I do not as yet understand whether you affirm that I teach others to acknowledge some gods, and therefore do believe in gods and am not an entire atheist—this you do not lay to my charge; but only that they are not the same gods which the city recognizes—the charge is that they are different gods. Or, do you mean to say that I am an atheist simply, and a teacher of atheism?

I mean the latter—that you are a complete atheist.

That is an extraordinary statement, Meletus. Why do you say that? Do you mean that I do not believe in the god-head of the sun or moon, which is the common creed of all men?

I assure you, judges, that he does not believe in them; for he says that the sun is stone, and the moon earth.

Friend Meletus, you think that you are accusing Anaxagoras; and you have but a bad opinion of the judges, if you fancy them ignorant to such a degree as not to know that those doctrines are found in the books of Anaxagoras the Clazomenian, who is full of them. And these are the doctrines which the youth are said to learn of Socrates, when there are not unfrequently exhibitions of them at the theatre (price of admission one drachma at the most); and they might cheaply purchase them, and laugh at Socrates if he pretends to father such eccentricities. And so, Meletus, you really think that I do not believe in any god?

I swear by Zeus that you believe absolutely in none at all.

You are a liar, Meletus, not believed even by yourself. For I cannot help thinking, O men of Athens, that Meletus is reckless and impudent, and that he has written this indictment in a spirit of mere wantonness and youthful bravado. Has he not compounded a riddle, thinking to try me? He said to himself: I shall see whether this wise Socrates will discover my ingenious contradiction, or whether I shall be able to deceive him and the rest of them. For he certainly does appear to me to contradict himself in the indictment as much as if he said that Socrates is guilty of not believing in the gods, and yet of believing in them—but this surely is a piece of fun.

I should like you, O men of Athens, to join me in examining what I conceive to be his inconsistency; and do you, Meletus, answer. And I must remind you that you are not to interrupt me if I speak in my accustomed manner.

Did ever man, Meletus, believe in the existence of human things, and not of human beings? . . . I wish, men of Athens, that he would answer, and not be always trying to get up an interruption. Did ever any man believe in horsemanship, and not in horses? or in flute-playing and not in flute-players? No, my friend; I will answer to you and to the court, as you refuse to answer for yourself. There is no man who ever did. But now please to answer the next question: Can a man believe in spiritual and divine agencies, and not in spirits or demigods?

He cannot.

I am glad that I have extracted that answer, by the assistance of the court; nevertheless you swear in the indictment that I teach and believe in divine or spiritual agencies (new or old, no matter for that); at any rate, I believe in spiritual agencies, as you say and swear in the affidavit; but if I believe in divine beings, I must believe in spirits or demigods; is not that true? Yes, that is true, for I may assume that your silence gives assent to that. Now what are spirits or demigods? are they not either gods or the sons of gods? Is that true?

Yes, that is true.

But this is just the ingenious riddle of which I was speaking: the demigods or spirits are gods, and you say first that I don't believe in gods, and then again that I do believe in gods; that is, if I believe in demigods. For if the demigods are the illegitimate sons of gods, whether by the Nymphs or by any other mothers, as is thought, that, as all men will allow, necessarily implies the existence of their parents. You might as well affirm the existence of mules, and deny that of horses and asses. Such nonsense, Meletus, could only have been intended by you as a trial of me. You have put this into the indictment because you had nothing real of which to accuse me. But no one who has a particle of understanding will ever be convinced by you that the same man can believe in divine and superhuman things, and yet not believe that there are gods and demigods and heroes.

I have said enough in answer to the charge of Meletus: any elaborate defence is unnecessary; but as I was saying before, I certainly have many enemies, and this is what will be my destruction if I am destroyed; of that I am certain; not Meletus, nor yet Anytus, but the envy and detraction of the world, which has been the death of many good men, and will probably be the death of many more; there is no danger of my being the last of them.

Someone will say: And are you not ashamed, Socrates, of a course of life which is likely to bring you to an untimely end? To him I may fairly answer: There you are mistaken: a man who is good for anything ought not to calculate the chance of living or dying; he ought only to consider whether in doing anything he is doing right or wrong—acting the part of a good man or of a bad. . . .

Strange, indeed, would be my conduct, O men of Athens, if I who, when I was ordered by the generals whom you chose to command me at Potidaea and Amphipolis and Delium, remained where they placed me, like any other man, facing death—if, I say, now, when, as I conceive and imagine, God orders me to fulfil the philosopher's mission of searching into myself and other men, I were to desert my post through fear of death, or any other fear;

that would indeed be strange, and I might justly be arraigned in court for denying the existence of the gods, if I disobeyed the oracle because I was afraid of death: then I should be fancying that I was wise when I was not wise. For this fear of death is indeed the pretence of wisdom, and not real wisdom, being the appearance of knowing the unknown; since no one knows whether death, which they in their fear apprehend to be the greatest evil, may not be the greatest good. Is there not here conceit of knowledge, which is a disgraceful sort of ignorance? And this is the point in which, as I think, I am superior to men in general, and in which I might perhaps fancy myself wiser than other men—that whereas I know but little of the world below, I do not suppose that I know: but I do know that injustice and disobedience to a better, whether God or man, is evil and dishonorable, and I will never fear or avoid a possible good rather than a certain evil. And therefore if you let me go now, and reject the counsels of Anytus, who said that if I were not put to death I ought not to have been prosecuted, and that if I escape now, your sons will all be utterly ruined by listening to my words—if you say to me, Socrates, this time we will not mind Anytus, and will let you off, but upon one condition, that you are not to inquire and speculate in this way any more, and that if you are caught doing this again you shall die—if this was the condition on which you let me go, I should reply: Men of Athens, I honor and love you; but I shall obey God rather than you, and while I have life and strength I shall never cease from the practice and teaching of philosophy, exhorting anyone whom I meet after my manner, and convincing him, saying: O my friend, why do you who are a citizen of the great and mighty and wise city of Athens, care so much about laying up the greatest amount of money and honor and reputation, and so little about wisdom and truth and the greatest improvement of the soul, which you never regard or heed at all? Are you not ashamed of this? And if the person with whom I am arguing says: Yes, but I do care; I do not depart or let him go at once; I interrogate and examine and cross-examine him, and if I think that he has no virtue, but only says that he has, I reproach him with undervaluing the greater, and overvaluing the less. And this I should say to everyone whom I meet, young and old, citizen and alien, but especially to the citizens, inasmuch as they are my brethren. For this is the command of God, as I would have you know; and I believe that to this day no greater good has ever happened in the State than my service to the God. For I do nothing but go about persuading you all, old and young alike, not to take thought for your persons and your properties, but first and chiefly to care about the greatest improvement of the soul. I tell you that virtue is not given by money, but that from virtue come money and every other good of man, public as well as private. This is my teaching, and if this is the doctrine which corrupts the youth, my influence is ruinous indeed. But if anyone says that this is not my teaching, he is speaking an untruth. Wherefore, O men of Athens, I say to you, do as Anytus bids or not as Anytus bids, and either acquit me or not; but whatever you do, know that I shall never alter my ways, not even if I have to die many times.

Men of Athens, do not interrupt, but hear me; there was an agreement between us that you should hear me out. And I think that what I am going to say will do you good: for I have something more to say, at which you may be inclined to cry out; but I beg that you will not do this. I would have you know that, if you kill such a one as I am, you will injure yourselves more than you will injure me. Meletus and Anytus will not injure me: they cannot; for it is not in the nature of things that a bad man should injure a better than himself. I do not deny that he may, perhaps, kill him, or drive him into exile, or deprive him of civil rights; and he may imagine, and others may imagine, that he is doing him a great injury: but in that I do not agree with him; for the evil of doing as Anytus is doing— of unjustly taking away another man's life—is greater far. And now, Athenians, I am not going to argue for my own sake, as you may think, but for yours, that you may not sin against the God, or lightly reject his boon by condemning me. For if you kill me you will not easily find another like me, who, if I may use such a ludicrous figure of speech, am a sort of gadfly, given to the State by the God; and the State is like a great and noble steed who is tardy in his motions owing to his very size, and requires to be stirred into life. I am that gadfly which God has given the State and all day long and in all places am always fastening upon you, arousing and persuading and reproaching you. And as you will not easily find another like me, I would advise you to spare me. I dare say that you may feel irritated at being suddenly awakened when you are caught napping; and you may think that if you were to strike me dead, as Anytus advises, which you easily might, then you would sleep on for the remainder of your lives, unless God in his care of you gives you another gadfly. And that I am given to you by God is proved by this: that if I had been like other men, I should not have neglected all my own concerns, or patiently seen the neglect of them during all these years, and have been doing yours, coming to you individually, like a father or elder brother, exhorting you to regard virtue; this, I say, would not be like human nature. And had I gained anything, or if my exhortations had been paid, there would have been some sense in that: but now, as you will perceive, not even the impudence of my accusers dares to say that I have ever exacted or sought pay of anyone; they have no witness of that. And I have a witness of the truth of what I say; my poverty is a sufficient witness.

Someone may wonder why I go about in private, giving advice and busying myself with the concerns of others, but do not venture to come forward in public and advise the State. I will tell you the reason of this. You have often heard me speak of an oracle or sign which comes to me, and is the divinity which Meletus ridicules in the indictment. This sign I have had ever since I was a child. The sign is a voice which comes to me and always forbids me to do something which I am going to do, but never commands me to do anything, and this is what stands in the way of my being a politician. And rightly, as I think. For I am certain, O men of Athens, that if I had engaged in politics, I should have perished long ago and done no good either to you or to myself. And don't be offended at my telling you the truth: for the truth is that no man who goes to war with you or any other multitude, honestly struggling against the commission of unrighteousness and wrong in the State, will save his life; he who will really fight for the right, if he would live even for a little while, must have a private station and not a public one.

I can give you as proofs of this, not words only, but deeds, which you value more than words. Let me tell you a passage of my own life, which will prove to you that I should never have yielded to injustice from any fear of death, and that if I had not yielded I should have died at once. I will tell you a story—tasteless, perhaps, and commonplace, but nevertheless true. The only office of State which I ever held, O men of Athens, was that of Senator; the tribe Antiochis, which is my tribe, had the presidency at the trial of the generals who had not taken up the bodies of the slain after the battle of Arginusae; and you proposed to try them all together, which was illegal, as you all thought afterwards; but at the time I was the only one of the Prytanes who was opposed to the illegality, and I gave my vote against you; and when the orators threatened to impeach and arrest me, and have me taken away, and you called and shouted, I made up my mind that I would run the risk, having law and justice with me, rather than take part in your injustice because I feared imprisonment and death. This happened in the days of the democracy. But when the oligarchy of the Thirty was in power, they sent for me and four others into the rotunda, and bade us bring Leon the Salaminian from Salamis, as they wanted to execute him. This was a specimen of the sort of commands which they were always giving with the view of implicating as many as possible in their crimes; and then I showed, not in words only, but in deed, that, if I may be allowed to use such an expression, I cared not a straw for death, and that my only fear was the fear of doing an unrighteous or unholy thing. For the strong arm of that oppressive power did not frighten me into doing wrong; and when we came out of the rotunda the other four went to Salamis and fetched Leon, but I went quietly home. For which I might have lost my life, had not the power of the Thirty shortly afterwards come to an end. And to this many will witness.

Now do you really imagine that I could have survived all these years, if I had led a public life, supposing that like a good man I had always supported the right and had made justice, as I ought, the first thing? No, indeed, men of Athens, neither I nor any other. But I have been always the same in all my actions, public as well as private, and never have I yielded any base compliance to those who are slanderously termed my disciples or to any other. For the truth is that I have no regular disciples: but if anyone likes to come and hear me while I am pursuing my mission, whether he be young or old, he may freely come. Nor do I converse with those who pay only, and not with those who do not pay; but any one, whether he be rich or poor, may ask and answer me and listen to my words; and whether he turns out to be a bad man or a good one; that cannot be justly laid to my charge, as I never taught him anything. And if anyone says that he has ever learned or heard anything from me in private which all the world has not heard, I should like you to know that he is speaking an untruth.

But I shall be asked, Why do people delight in continually conversing with you? I have told you already, Athenians, the whole truth about this: they like to hear the cross examination of the pretenders to wisdom; there is amusement in this. And this is a duty which the God has imposed upon me, as I am assured by oracles, visions, and in every sort of way in which the will of divine power was ever signified to anyone. This is true, O Athenians; or, if not true, would be soon refuted. For if I am really corrupting the youth, and have corrupted some of them already, those of them who have grown up and have become sensible that I gave them bad advice in the days of their youth should come forward as accusers and take their revenge; and if they do not like to come themselves, some of their relatives, fathers, brothers, or other kinsmen, should say what evil their families suffered at my hands. . . . [A]ny of whom Meletus should have produced as witnesses in the course of his speech; and let him still produce them, if he has forgotten; I will make way for him. And let him say, if he has any testimony of the sort which he can produce. Nay, Athenians, the very opposite is the truth. For all these are ready to witness on behalf of the corrupter, of the destroyer of their kindred, as Meletus and Anytus call me; not the corrupted youth only—there might have been a motive for that—but their uncorrupted elder relatives. Why should they too support me with their testimony? Why, indeed, except for the sake of truth and justice, and because they know that I am speaking the truth and that Meletus is lying.

Well, Athenians, this and the like of this is nearly all the defence which I have to offer. Yet a word more. Perhaps there may be someone who is offended at me, when he calls to mind how he himself, on a similar or even a less serious occasion, had recourse to prayers and supplications with many tears, and how he produced his children in court, which was a moving spectacle, together with a posse of his relations and friends; whereas I, who am probably in danger of my life, will do none of these things. Perhaps this may come into his mind, and he may be set against me, and vote in anger because he is displeased at this. Now if there be such a person among you, which I am far from affirming, I may fairly reply to him: My friend, I am a man, and like other men, a creature of flesh and blood, and not of wood or stone, as Homer says; and I have a family, yes, and sons, O Athenians, three in number, one of whom is growing up, and the two others are still young; and yet I will not bring any of them hither in order to petition you for an acquittal. And why not? Not from any self-will or disregard of you. Whether I am or am not afraid of death is another question, of which I will not now speak. But my reason simply is that I feel such conduct to be discreditable to myself, and you, and the whole State. One who has reached my years, and who has a name for wisdom, whether deserved or not, ought not to debase himself. At any rate, the world has decided that Socrates is in some way superior to other men. And if those among you who are said to be superior in wisdom and courage, and any other virtue, demean themselves in this way, how shameful is their conduct! I have seen men of reputation, when they have been condemned, behaving in the strangest manner: they seemed to fancy that they were going to suffer something dreadful if they died, and that they could be immortal if you only allowed them to live; and I think that they were a dishonor to the State, and that any stranger coming in would say of them that the most eminent men of Athens, to whom the Athenians themselves give honor and command, are no better than women. And I say that these things ought not to be done by those of us who are of reputation; and if they are done, you ought not to permit them; you ought rather to show that you are more inclined to condemn, not the man who is quiet, but the man who gets up a doleful scene, and makes the city ridiculous.

But, setting aside the question of dishonor, there seems to be something wrong in petitioning a judge, and thus procuring an acquittal instead of informing and convincing him. For his duty is, not to make a present of justice, but to give judgment; and he has sworn that he will judge according to the laws, and not according to his own good pleasure; and neither he nor we should get into the habit of perjuring ourselves—there can be no piety in that. Do not then require me to do what I consider dishonorable and impious and wrong, especially now, when I am being tried for impiety on the indictment of Meletus. For if, O men of Athens, by force of persuasion and entreaty, I could overpower your oaths, then I should be teaching you to believe that there are no gods, and convict myself, in my own defence, of not believing in them. But that is not the case; for I do believe that there are gods, and in a far higher sense than that in which any of my accusers believe in them. And to you and to God I commit my cause, to be determined by you as is best for you and me. [He is found guilty by a vote of 281 to 220.]

There are many reasons why I am not grieved, O men of Athens, at the vote of condemnation. I expected this, and am only surprised that the votes are so nearly equal; for I had thought that the majority against me would have been far larger; but now, had thirty votes gone over to the other side, I should have been acquitted. And I may say that I have escaped Meletus. And I may say more; for without the assistance of Anytus and Lycon, he would not have had a fifth part of the votes, as the law requires, in which case he would have incurred a fine of a thousand drachmæ, as is evident.

And so he proposes death as the penalty. And what shall I propose on my part, O men of Athens? Clearly that which is my due. And what is that which I ought to pay or to receive? What shall be done to the man who has never had the wit to be idle during his whole life; but has been careless of what the many care about—wealth and family interests, and military offices, and speaking in the assembly, and magistracies, and plots, and parties. Reflecting that I was really too honest a man to follow in this way and live, I did not go where I could do no good to you or to myself; but where I could do the greatest good privately to every one of you, thither I went, and sought to persuade every man among you that he must look to himself, and seek virtue and wisdom before he looks to his private interests, and look to the State before he looks to the interests of the State; and that this should be the order which he observes in all his actions. What shall be done to such a one? Doubtless some good thing, O men of Athens, if he has his reward; and the good should be of a kind suitable to him. What would be a reward suitable to a poor man who is your benefactor, who desires leisure that he may instruct you? There can be no more fitting reward than maintenance in the Prytaneum, O men of Athens, a reward which he deserves far more than the citizen who has won the prize at Olympia in the horse or chariot race, whether the chariots were drawn by two horses or by many. For I am in want, and he has enough; and he only gives you the appearance of happiness, and I give you the reality. And if I am to estimate the penalty justly, I say that maintenance in the Prytaneum is the just return.

Perhaps you may think that I am braving you in saying this, as in what I said before about the tears and prayers. But that is not the case. I speak rather because I am convinced that I never intentionally wronged anyone, although I cannot convince you of that—for we have had a short conversation only; but if there were a law at Athens, such as there is in other cities, that a capital cause should not be decided in one day, then I believe that I should have convinced you; but now the time is too short. I cannot in a moment refute great slanders; and, as I am convinced that I never wronged another, I will assuredly not wrong myself. I will not say of myself that I deserve any evil, or propose any penalty. Why should I? Because I am afraid of the penalty of death which Meletus proposes? When I do not know whether death is a good or an evil, why should I propose a penalty which would certainly be an evil? Shall I say imprisonment? And why should I live in prison, and be the slave of the magistrates of the year—of the Eleven? Or shall the penalty be a fine, and imprisonment until the fine is paid? There is the same objection. I should have to lie in prison, for money I have none, and I cannot pay. And if I say exile (and this may possibly be the penalty which you will affix), I must indeed be blinded by the love of life if I were to consider that when you, who are my own citizens, cannot endure my discourses and words, and have found them so grievous and odious that you would fain have done with them, others are likely to endure me. No, indeed, men of Athens, that is not very likely. And what a life should I lead, at my age, wandering from city to city, living in ever-changing exile, and always being driven out! For I am quite sure that into whatever place I go, as here so also there, the young men will come to me; and if I drive them away, their elders will drive me out at their desire: and if I let them come, their fathers and friends will drive me out for their sakes.

Someone will say: Yes, Socrates, but cannot you hold your tongue, and then you may go into a foreign city, and no one will interfere with you? Now I have great difficulty in making you understand my answer to this. For if I tell you that this would be a disobedience to a divine command, and therefore that I cannot hold my tongue, you will not believe that I am serious; and if I say again that the greatest good of man is daily to converse about virtue, and all that concerning which you hear me examining myself and others, and that the life which is unexamined is not worth living—that you are still less likely to believe. And yet what I say is true, although a thing of which it is hard for me to persuade you. Moreover, I am not accustomed to think that I deserve any punishment. Had I money I might have proposed to give you what I had, and have been none the worse. But you see that I have none, and can only ask you to proportion the fine to my means. However, I think that I could afford a mina, and therefore, I propose that penalty: Plato, Crito, Critobulus, and

Apollodorus, my friends here, bid me say thirty minae, and they will be the sureties. Well then, say thirty minae, let that be the penalty; for that they will be ample security to you. [He is condemned to death.]

Not much time will be gained, O Athenians, in return for the evil name which you will get from the detractors of the city, who will say that you killed Socrates, a wise man; for they will call me wise even although I am not wise when they want to reproach you. If you had waited a little while, your desire would have been fulfilled in the course of nature. For I am far advanced in years, as you may perceive and not far from death. I am speaking now only to those of you who have condemned me to death. And I have another thing to say to them: you think that I was convicted through deficiency of words—I mean, that if I had thought fit to leave nothing undone, nothing unsaid, I might have gained an acquittal. Not so; the deficiency which led to my conviction was not of words—certainly not. But I had not the boldness or impudence or inclination to address you as you would have liked me to address you, weeping and wailing and lamenting, and saying and doing many things which you have been accustomed to hear from others, and which, as I say, are unworthy of me. But I thought that I ought not to do anything common or mean in the hour of danger: nor do I now repent of the manner of my defence, and I would rather die having spoken after my manner, than speak in your manner and live. For neither in war nor yet at law ought any man to use every way of escaping death. For often in battle there is no doubt that if a man will throw away his arms, and fall on his knees before his pursuers, he may escape death; and in other dangers there are other ways of escaping death, if a man is willing to say and do anything. The difficulty, my friends, is not in avoiding death, but in avoiding un-righteousness; for that runs faster than death. I am old and move slowly, and the slower runner has overtaken me, and my accusers are keen and quick, and the faster runner, who is unrighteousness, has overtaken them. And now I depart hence condemned by you to suffer the penalty of death, and they, too, go their ways condemned by the truth to suffer the penalty of villainy and wrong; and I must abide by my award—let them abide by theirs. I suppose that these things may be regarded as fated—and I think that they are well.

And now, O men who have condemned me, I would fain prophesy to you; for I am about to die, and that is the hour in which men are gifted with prophetic power. And I prophesy to you who are my murderers, that immediately after my death punishment far heavier than you have inflicted on me will surely await you. Me you have killed because you wanted to escape the accuser, and not to give an account of your lives. But that will not be as you suppose: far otherwise. For I say that there will be more accusers of you than there are now; accusers whom hitherto I have restrained: and as they are younger they will be more severe with you, and you will be more offended at them. For if you think that by killing men you can avoid the accuser censuring your lives, you are mistaken; that is not a way of escape which is either possible or honorable; the easiest and noblest way is not to be crushing others, but to be improving yourselves. This is the prophecy which I utter before my departure, to the judges who have condemned me.

Friends, who would have acquitted me, I would like also to talk with you about this thing which has happened, while the magistrates are busy, and before I go to the place at which I must die. Stay then awhile, for we may as well talk with one another while there is time. You are my friends, and I should like to show you the meaning of this event which has happened to me. O my judges—for you I may truly call judges—I should like to tell you of a wonderful circumstance. Hitherto the familiar oracle within me has constantly been in the habit of opposing me even about trifles, if I was going to make a slip or error about anything; and now as you see there has come upon me that which may be thought, and is generally believed to be, the last and worst evil. But the oracle made no sign of opposition, either as I was leaving my house and going out in the morning, or when I was going up into this court, or while I was speaking, at anything which I was going to say; and yet I have often been stopped in the middle of a speech; but now in nothing I either said or did touching this matter has the oracle opposed me. What do I take to be the explanation of this? I will tell you. I regard this as a proof that what has happened to me is a good, and that those of us who think that death is an evil are in error. This is a great proof to me of what I am saying, for the customary sign would surely have opposed me had I been going to evil and not to good.

Let us reflect in another way, and we shall see that there is great reason to hope that death is a good, for one of two things: either death is a state of nothingness and utter unconsciousness, or, as men say, there is a change and migration of the soul from this world to another. Now if you suppose that there is no consciousness, but a sleep like the sleep of him who is undisturbed even by the sight of dreams, death will be an unspeakable gain. For if a person were to select the night in which his sleep was undisturbed even by dreams, and were to compare with this the other days and nights of his life, and then were to tell us how many days and nights he had passed in the course of his life better and more pleasantly than this one, I think that any man, I will not say a private man, but even the great king, will not find many such days or nights, when compared with the others. Now if death is like this, I say that to die, is gain; for eternity is then only a single night. But if death is the journey to another place, and there, as men say, all the dead are, what good, O my friends and judges, can be greater than this? If indeed when the pilgrim arrives in the world below, he is delivered from the professors of justice in this world, and finds the true judges who are said to give judgment there, Minos and Rhadamanthus and Aeacus and Triptolemus, and other sons of God who were righteous in their own life, that pilgrimage will be worth making. What would not a man give if he might converse with Orpheus and Musaeus and Hesiod and Homer? Nay, if this be true, let me die again and again. I, too, shall have a wonderful interest in a place where I can converse with Palamedes, and Ajax the son of Telamon, and other heroes of old, who have suffered death through an unjust judgment; and there will be no small pleasure, as I think, in comparing my own sufferings with theirs. Above all, I shall be able to continue my search into true and false knowledge; as in this world, so also in that; I shall find out who is wise, and who pretends to be wise, and is not. What should not a man give, O judges, to be able to examine the leader of the great Trojan expedition; or Odysseus or Sisyphus, or numberless others, men and women too! What infinite delight would there be in conversing with them and asking them questions! For in that world they do not put a man to death for this; certainly not. For besides being happier in that world than in this, they will be immortal, if what is said is true.

Wherefore, O judges, be of good cheer about death, and know this of a truth—that no evil can happen to a good man, either in life or after death. He and his are not neglected by the gods; nor has my own approaching end happened by mere chance. But I see clearly that to die and be released was better for me; and therefore the oracle gave no sign. For which reason also, I am not angry with my accusers, or my condemners; they have done me no harm, although neither of them meant to do me any good; and for this I may gently blame them.

Still I have a favor to ask of them. When my sons are grown up, I would ask you, O my friends, to punish them; and I would have you trouble them, as I have troubled you, if they seem to care about riches, or anything, more than about virtue; or if they pretend to be something when they are really nothing—then reprove them, as I have reproved you, for not caring about that for which they ought to care, and thinking that they are something when they are really nothing. And if you do this, I and my sons will have received justice at your hands.

The hour of departure has arrived, and we go our ways—I to die, and you to live. Which is better, God only knows.

CRITO

SOCRATES: Why have you come at this hour, Crito? it must be quite early.

CRITO: Yes, certainly.

SOC.: What is the exact time?

CR.: The dawn is breaking.

SOC.: I wonder why the keeper of the prison would let you in.

CR.: He knows me because I often come, Socrates; moreover, I have done him a kindness.

SOC.: And are you only just come?

CR.: No, I came some time ago.

SOC.: Then why did you sit and say nothing, instead of awakening me at once?

CR.: Why, indeed, Socrates, I myself would rather not have all this sleeplessness and sorrow. But I have been wondering at your peaceful slumbers, and that was the reason why I did not awaken you, because I wanted you to be out of pain. I have always thought you happy in the calmness of your temperament; but never did I see the like of the easy, cheerful way in which you bear this calamity.

SOC.: Why, Crito, when a man has reached my age he ought not to be repining at the prospect of death.

CR.: And yet other old men find themselves in similar misfortunes, and age does not prevent them from repining.

SOC.: That may be. But you have not told me why you come at this early hour.

CR.: I come to bring you a message which is sad and painful; not, as I believe, to yourself, but to all of us who are your friends, and saddest of all to me.

SOC.: What! I suppose that the ship has come from Delos, on the arrival of which I am to die?

CR.: No, the ship has not actually arrived, but she will probably be here to-day, as

From "Crito," in *The Dialogues of Plato,* trans. B. Jowett (London: Clarendon Press, 1892).

persons who have come from Sunium tell me that they have left her there; and therefore to-morrow, Socrates, will be the last day of your life.

SOC.: Very well, Crito; if such is the will of God, I am willing; but my belief is that there will be a delay of a day.

CR.: Why do you say this?

SOC.: I will tell you. I am to die on the day after the arrival of the ship?

CR.: Yes; that is what the authorities say.

SOC.: But I do not think that the ship will be here until to-morrow; this I gather from a vision which I had last night, or rather only just now, when you fortunately allowed me to sleep.

CR.: And what was the nature of the vision?

SOC.: There came to me the likeness of a woman, fair and comely, clothed in white raiment, who called to me and said: O Socrates—

The third day hence, to Phthia shalt thou go.

CR.: What a singular dream, Socrates!

SOC.: There can be no doubt about the meaning, Crito, I think.

CR.: Yes: the meaning is only too clear. But, O! my beloved Socrates, let me entreat you once more to take my advice and escape. For if you die I shall not only lose a friend who can never be replaced, but there is another evil: people who do not know you and me will believe that I might have saved you if I had been willing to give money, but that I did not care. Now, can there be a worse disgrace than this—that I should be thought to value money more than the life of a friend? For the many will not be persuaded that I wanted you to escape, and that you refused.

SOC.: But why, my dear Crito, should we care about the opinion of the many? Good men, and they are the only persons who are worth considering, will think of these things truly as they happened.

CR.: But do you see, Socrates, that the opinion of the many must be regarded, as is evident in your own case, because they can do the very greatest evil to anyone who has lost their good opinion?

SOC.: I only wish, Crito, that they could; for then they could also do the greatest good, and that would be well. But the truth is, that they can do neither good nor evil; they cannot make a man wise or make him foolish; and whatever they do is the result of chance.

CR.: Well, I will not dispute about that; but please to tell me, Socrates, whether you are not acting out of regard to me and your other friends: are you not afraid that if you escape hence we may get into trouble with the informers for having stolen you away, and lose either the whole or a great part of our property; or that even a worse evil may happen to us? Now, if this is your fear, be at ease; for in order to save you, we ought surely to run this or even a greater risk; be persuaded, then, and do as I say.

SOC.: Yes, Crito, that is one fear which you mention, but by no means the only one.

CR.:   Fear not. There are persons who at no great cost are willing to save you and bring you out of prison; and as for the informers, you may observe that they are far from being exorbitant in their demands; a little money will satisfy them. My means, which, as I am sure, are ample, are at your service, and if you have a scruple about spending all mine, here are strangers who will give you the use of theirs; and one of them, Simmias the Theban, has brought a sum of money for this very purpose; and Cebes and many others are willing to spend their money too. I say, therefore, do not on that account hesitate about making your escape, and do not say, as you did in the court, that you will have a difficulty in knowing what to do with yourself if you escape. For men will love you in other places to which you may go, and not in Athens only; there are friends of mine in Thessaly, if you like to go to them, who will value and protect you, and no Thessalian will give you any trouble. Nor can I think that you are justified, Socrates, in betraying your own life when you might be saved; this is playing into the hands of your enemies and destroyers; and moreover I should say that you were betraying your children; for you might bring them up and educate them; instead of which you go away and leave them, and they will have to take their chance; and if they do not meet with the usual fate of orphans, there will be small thanks to you. No man should bring children into the world who is unwilling to persevere to the end in their nurture and education. But you are choosing the easier part, as I think, not the better and manlier, which would rather have become one who professes virtue in all his actions, like yourself. And, indeed, I am ashamed not only of you, but of us who are your friends, when I reflect that this entire business of yours will be attributed to our want of courage. The trial need never have come on, or might have been brought to another issue; and the end of all, which is the crowning absurdity, will seem to have been permitted by us, through cowardice and baseness, who might have saved you, as you might have saved yourself, if we had been good for anything (for there was no difficulty in escaping); and we did not see how disgraceful, Socrates, and also miserable all this will be to us as well as to you. Make your mind up then, or rather have your mind already made up, for the time of deliberation is over, and there is only one thing to be done, which must be done, if at all, this very night, and which any delay will render all but impossible; I beseech you therefore, Socrates, to be persuaded by me, and to do as I say.

SOC.:   Dear Crito, your zeal is invaluable, if a right one; but if wrong, the greater the zeal the greater the evil; and therefore we ought to consider whether these things shall be done or not. For I am and always have been one of those natures who must be guided by reason, whatever the reason may be which upon reflection appears to me to be the best; and now that this fortune has come upon me, I cannot put away the reasons which I have before given: the principles which I have hitherto honored and revered I still honor, and unless we can find other and better principles on the instant, I am certain not to agree with you; no, not even if the power of the multitude could inflict many more imprisonments, confiscations, deaths, frightening us like children with hobgoblin terrors. But what will be the fairest way of considering the question? Shall I return to your old argument about the opinions of men, some of which are to be regarded, and others, as we were saying, are not to be regarded? Now were we right in maintaining this before I was condemned? And has the argument which was once good now proved to be talk for the sake of talking; in fact an amusement only, and altogether vanity? That is what I want to consider with your help, Crito: whether, under my present circumstances, the argument appears to be in any way different or not; and is to be allowed by me or disallowed. That argument, which, as I believe, is maintained by many who assume to be authorities, was to the effect, as I was saying, that the opinions of some men are to be regarded, and of other men not to be regarded. Now you, Crito, are a disinterested person who are not going to die to-morrow—at least, there is no human probability of this, and you are therefore not liable to be deceived by the circumstances in which you are placed. Tell me, then, whether I am right in saying that some opinions, and the opinions of some men only, are to be valued, and other opinions, and the opinions of other men, are not to be valued. I ask you whether I was right in maintaining this?

CR.: Certainly.

SOC.: The good are to be regarded, and not the bad?

CR.: Yes.

SOC.: And the opinions of the wise are good, and the opinions of the unwise are evil?

CR.: Certainly.

SOC.: And what was said about another matter? Was the disciple in gymnastics supposed to attend to the praise and blame and opinion of every man, or of one man only—his physician or trainer, whoever that was?

CR.: Of one man only.

SOC.: And he ought to fear the censure and welcome the praise of that one only, and not of the many?

CR.: That is clear.

SOC.: And he ought to live and train, and eat and drink in the way which seems good to his single master who has understanding, rather than according to the opinion of all other men put together?

CR.: True.

SOC.: And if he disobeys and disregards the opinion and approval of the one, and regards the opinion of the many who have no understanding, will he not suffer evil?

CR.: Certainly he will.

SOC.: And what will the evil be, whither tending and what affecting, in the disobedient person?

CR.: Clearly, affecting the body; that is what is destroyed by the evil.

SOC.: Very good; and is not this true, Crito, of other things which we need not separately enumerate? In the matter of just and unjust, fair and foul, good and evil, which are the subjects of our present consultation, ought we to follow the opinion of the many and to fear them; or the opinion of the one man who has understanding, and whom we ought to fear and reverence more than all the rest of the world: and whom deserting we shall destroy and injure that principle in us which may be assumed to be improved by justice and deteriorated by injustice; is there not such a principle?

CR.: Certainly there is, Socrates.

SOC.: Take a parallel instance; if, acting under the advice of men who have no understanding, we destroy that which is improvable by health and deteriorated by disease—when that has been destroyed, I say, would life be worth having? And that is—the body?.

CR.: Yes.

SOC.: Could we live, having an evil and corrupted body?

CR.: Certainly not.

SOC.: And will life be worth having, if that higher part of man be depraved, which is improved by justice and deteriorated by injustice? Do we suppose that principle, whatever it may be in man, which has to do with justice and injustice, to be inferior to the body?

CR.: Certainly not.

SOC.: More honored, then?

CR.: Far more honored.

SOC.: Then, my friend, we must not regard what the many say of us: but what he, the one man who has understanding of just and unjust, will say, and what the truth will say. And therefore you begin in error when you suggest that we should regard the opinion of the many about just and unjust, good and evil, honorable and dishonorable. Well, someone will say, "But the many can kill us."

CR.: Yes, Socrates; that will clearly be the answer.

SOC.: That is true; but still I find with surprise that the old argument is, as I conceive, unshaken as ever. And I should like to know whether I may say the same of another proposition—that not life, but a good life, is to be chiefly valued?

CR.: Yes, that also remains.

SOC.: And a good life is equivalent to a just and honorable one—that holds also?

CR.: Yes, that holds.

SOC.: From these premises I proceed to argue the question whether I ought or ought not to try to escape without the consent of the Athenians: and if I am clearly right in escaping, then I will make the attempt; but if not, I will abstain. The other considerations which you mention, of money and loss of character, and the duty of educating children, are as I hear, only the doctrines of the multitude, who would be as ready to call people to life, if they were able, as they are to put them to death—and with as little reason. But now, since the argument has thus far prevailed, the only question which remains to be considered is, whether we shall do rightly either in escaping or in suffering others to aid in our escape and paying them in money and thanks, or whether we shall not do rightly; and if the latter, then death or any other calamity which may ensue on my remaining here must not be allowed to enter into the calculation.

CR.: I think that you are right, Socrates; how then shall we proceed?

SOC.: Let us consider the matter together, and do you either refute me if you can, and I will be convinced; or else cease, my dear friend, from repeating to me that I ought to escape against the wishes of the Athenians: for I am extremely desirous to be persuaded by you, but not against my own better judgment. And now please to consider my first position, and do your best to answer me.

CR.: I will do my best.

SOC.: Are we to say that we are never intentionally to do wrong, or that in one way we ought and in another way we ought not to do wrong, or is doing wrong always evil and dishonorable, as I was just now saying, and as has been already acknowledged by us? Are all our former admissions which were made within a few days to be thrown away? And have we, at our age, been earnestly discoursing with one another all our life long only to discover that we are no better than children? Or are we to rest assured, in spite of the opinion of the many, and in spite of consequences whether better or worse, of the truth of what was then said, that injustice is always an evil and dishonor to him who acts unjustly? Shall we affirm that?

CR.: Yes.

SOC.: Then we must do no wrong?

CR.: Certainly not.

SOC.: Nor when injured injure in return, as the many imagine; for we must injure no one at all?

CR.: Clearly not.

SOC.: Again, Crito, may we do evil?

CR.: Surely not, Socrates.

SOC.: And what of doing evil in return for evil, which is the morality of the many—is that just or not?

CR.: Not just.

SOC.: For doing evil to another is the same as injuring him?

CR.: Very true.

SOC.: Then we ought not to retaliate or render evil for evil to anyone, whatever evil we may have suffered from him. But I would have you consider, Crito, whether you really mean what you are saying. For this opinion has never been held, and never will be held, by any considerable number of persons; and those who are agreed and those who are not agreed upon this point have no common ground, and can only despise one another, when they see how widely they differ. Tell me, then, whether you agree with and assent to my first principle, that neither injury nor retaliation nor warding off evil by evil is ever right. And shall that be the premise of our argument? Or do you decline and dissent from this? For this has been of old and is still my opinion; but, if you are of another opinion, let me hear what you have to say. If, however, you remain of the same mind as formerly, I will proceed to the next step.

CR.: You may proceed, for I have not changed my mind.

SOC.: Then I will proceed to the next step, which may be put in the form of a question: Ought a man to do what he admits to be right, or ought he to betray the right?

CR.: He ought to do what he thinks right.

SOC.: But if this is true, what is the application? In leaving the prison against the will of the Athenians, do I wrong any? or rather do I not wrong those whom I ought least to wrong? Do I not desert the principles which were acknowledged by us to be just? What do you say?

CR.: I cannot tell, Socrates, for I do not know.

SOC.: Then consider the matter in this way: Imagine that I am about to play truant (you may call the proceeding by any name which you like), and the laws and the government come and interrogate me: "Tell us, Socrates," they say; "what are you about? are you going by an act of yours to overturn us—the laws and the whole State, as far as in you lies? Do you imagine that a State can subsist and not be overthrown, in which the decisions of law have no power, but are set aside and overthrown by individuals?" What will be our answer, Crito, to these and the like words? Anyone, and especially a clever rhetorician, will have a good deal to urge about the evil of setting aside the law which requires a sentence to be carried out; and we might reply, "Yes; but the State has injured us and given an unjust sentence." Suppose I say that?

CR.: Very good, Socrates.

SOC.: "And was that our agreement with you?" the law would say; "or were you to abide by the sentence of the State?" And if I were to express astonishment at their saying this, the law would probably add: "Answer, Socrates, instead of opening your eyes; you are in the habit of asking and answering questions. Tell us what complaint you have to make against us which justifies you in attempting to destroy us and the State? In the first place did we not bring you into existence? Your father married your mother by our aid and begat you. Say whether you have any objection to urge against those of us who regulate marriage?" None, I should reply. "Or against those of us who regulate the system of nurture and education of children in which you were trained? Were not the laws, who have the charge of this, right in commanding your father to train you in music and gymnastic?" Right, I should reply. "Well, then, since you were brought into the world and nurtured and educated by us, can you deny in the first place that you are our child and slave, as your fathers were before you? And if this is true you are not on equal terms with us; nor can you think that you have a right to do to us what we are doing to you. Would you have any right to strike or revile or do any other evil to a father or to your master, if you had one, when you have been struck or reviled by him, or received some other evil at his hands?—you would not say this? And because we think right to destroy you, do you think that you have any right to destroy us in return, and your country as far as in you lies? And will you, O professor of true virtue, say that you are justified in this? Has a philosopher like you failed to discover that our country is more to be valued and higher and holier far than mother or father or any ancestor, and more to be regarded in the eyes of the gods and of men of understanding? also to be soothed, and gently and reverently entreated when angry, even more than a father, and if not persuaded, obeyed? And when we are punished by her, whether with imprisonment or stripes, the punishment is to be endured in silence; and if she leads us to wounds or death in battle, thither we follow as is right; neither may anyone yield or retreat or leave his rank, but whether in battle or in a court of law, or in any other place, he must do what his city and his country order him; or he must change their view of what is just; and if he may do no violence to his father or mother, much less may he do violence to his country." What answer shall we make to this, Crito? Do the laws speak truly, or do they not?

CR.: I think that they do.

SOC.: Then the laws will say: "Consider, Socrates, if this is true, that in your present attempt you are going to do us wrong. For, after having brought you into the world, and nurtured and educated you, and given you and every other citizen a share in every good that we had to give, we further proclaim and give the right to every Athenian, that if he does not like us when he has come of age and has seen the ways of the city, and made our acquaintance, he may go where he pleases and take his goods with him; and none of our laws will forbid him or interfere with him. Any of you who does not like us and the city, and who wants to go to a colony or to any other city, may go where he likes, and take his goods with him. But he who has experience of the manner in which we order justice and administer the State, and still remains, has entered into an implied contract that he will do as we command him. And he who disobeys us is, as we maintain, thrice wrong: first, because in disobeying us he is disobeying his parents; secondly, because we are the authors of his education; thirdly, because he has made an agreement with us that he will duly obey our commands; and he neither obeys them nor convinces us that our commands are wrong; and we do not rudely impose them, but give him the alternative of obeying or convincing us; that is what we offer, and he does neither. These are the sort of accusations to which, as we were saying, you, Socrates, will be exposed if you accomplish your intentions; you, above all other Athenians." Suppose I ask, why is this? they will justly retort upon me that I above all other men have acknowledged the agreement. "There is clear proof," they will say, "Socrates, that we and the city were not displeasing to you. Of all Athenians you have been the most constant resident in the city, which, as you never leave, you may be supposed to love. For you never went out of the city either to see the games, except once when you went to the Isthmus, or to any other place unless you were on military service; nor did you travel as other men do. Nor had you any curiosity to know other States or their laws: your affections did not go beyond us and our State; we were your especial favorites, and you acquiesced in our government of you; and this is the State in which you begat your children, which is a proof of your satisfaction. Moreover, you might, if you had liked, have fixed the penalty at banishment in the course of the trial—the State which refuses to let you go now would have let you go then. But you pretended that you preferred death to exile, and that you were not grieved at death. And now you have forgotten these fine sentiments, and pay no respect to us, the laws, of whom you are the destroyer; and are doing what only a miserable slave would do, running away and turning your back upon the compacts and agreements which you made as a citizen. And first of all answer this very question: Are we right in saying that you agreed to be governed according to us in deed, and not in word only? Is that true or not?" How shall we answer that, Crito? Must we not agree?

CR.: There is no help, Socrates.

SOC.: Then will they not say: "You, Socrates, are breaking the covenants and agreements which you made with us at your leisure, not in any haste or under any compulsion or deception, but having had seventy years to think of them, during which time you were at liberty to leave the city, if we were not to your mind, or if our covenants appeared to you to be unfair. You had your choice, and might have gone either to Lacedaemon or Crete, which you often praise for their good government, or to some other Hellenic or foreign State. Whereas you, above all other Athenians, seemed to be so fond of the State, or, in other words, of us her laws (for who would like a State that has no laws?), that you never stirred out of her: the halt, the blind, the maimed, were not more stationary in her than you were. And now you run away and forsake your agreements. Not so, Socrates, if you will take our advice; do not make yourself ridiculous by escaping out of the city.

"For just consider, if you transgress and err in this sort of way, what good will you do, either to yourself or to your friends? That your friends will be driven into exile and deprived of citizenship, or will lose their property, is tolerably certain; and you yourself, if you fly to one of the neighboring cities, as, for example, Thebes or Megara, both of which are well-governed cities, will come to them as an enemy, Socrates, and their government will be against you, and all patriotic citizens will cast an evil eye upon you as a subverter of the laws, and you will confirm in the minds of the judges the justice of their own condemnation of you. For he who is a corrupter of the laws is more than likely to be corrupter of the young and foolish portion of mankind. Will you then flee from well-ordered cities and virtuous men? and is existence worth having on these terms? Or will you go to them without shame, and talk to them, Socrates? And what will you say to them? What you say here about virtue and justice and institutions and laws being the best things among men? Would that be decent of you? Surely not. But if you go away from well-governed States to Crito's friends in Thessaly, where there is great disorder and license, they will be charmed to have the tale of your escape from prison, set off with ludicrous particulars of the manner in which you were wrapped in a goatskin or some other disguise, and metamorphosed as the fashion of runaways is—that is very likely; but will there be no one to remind you that in your old age you violated the most sacred laws from a miserable desire of a little more life? Perhaps not, if you keep them in a good temper; but if they are out of temper you will hear many degrading things; you will live, but how?—as the flatterer of all men, and the servant of all men; and doing what?—eating and drinking in Thessaly, having gone abroad in order that you may get a dinner. And where will be your fine sentiments about justice and virtue then? Say that you wish to live for the sake of your children, that you may bring them up and educate them—will you take them into Thessaly and deprive them of Athenian citizenship? Is that the benefit which you would confer upon them? Or are you under the impression that they will be better cared for and educated here if you are still alive, although absent from them; for that your friends will take care of them? Do you fancy that if you are an inhabitant of Thessaly they will take care of them, and if you are an inhabitant of the other world they will not take care of them? Nay; but if they who call themselves friends are truly friends, they surely will.

"Listen, then, Socrates, to us who have brought you up. Think not of life and children first, and of justice afterwards, but of justice first, that you may be justified before the princes of the world below. For neither will you nor any that belong to you be happier or holier or juster in this life, or happier in another, if you do as Crito bids. Now you depart in innocence, a sufferer and not a doer of evil; a victim, not of the laws, but of men. But if you go forth, returning evil for evil, and injury for injury, breaking the covenants and agreements which you have made with us, and wronging those whom you ought least to wrong, that is to say, yourself, your friends, your country, and us, we shall be angry with you while you live, and our brethren, the laws in the world below, will receive you as an enemy; for they will know that you have done your best to destroy us. Listen, then, to us and not to Crito."

This is the voice which I seem to hear murmuring in my ears, like the sound of the flute in the ears of the mystic; that voice, I say, is humming in my ears, and prevents me from hearing any other. And I know that anything more which you will say will be in vain. Yet speak, if you have anything to say.

CR.: I have nothing to say, Socrates.

SOC.: Then let me follow the intimations of the will of God.

PHAEDO

ECHECRATES: Were you yourself, Phaedo, in the prison with Socrates on the day when he drank the poison?

PHAEDO: Yes, Echecrates, I was.

ECH.: I wish that you would tell me about his death. What did he say in his last

From "Phaedo," in *The Dialogues of Plato*, trans. B. Jowett (London: Clarendon Press, 1892).

hours? We were informed that he died by taking poison, but no one knew anything more; for no Phliasian ever goes to Athens now, and a long time has elapsed since any Athenian found his way to Phlius, and therefore we had no clear account. . . .

PHAED.:   I will begin at the beginning, and endeavour to repeat the entire conversation. You must understand that we had been previously in the habit of assembling early in the morning at the court in which the trial was held, and which is not far from the prison. There we remained talking with one another until the opening of the prison doors (for they were not opened very early), and then went in and generally passed the day with Socrates. . . .

But do you mean to take away your thoughts with you, Socrates? said Simmias. Will you not communicate them to us? . . .

I will do my best, replied Socrates. But you must first let me hear what Crito wants; he was going to say something to me.

Only this, Socrates, replied Crito: the attendant who is to give you the poison has been telling me that you are not to talk much, and he wants me to let you know this; for that by talking heat is increased, and this interferes with the action of the poison; those who excite themselves are sometimes obliged to drink the poison two or three times.

Then, said Socrates, let him mind his business and be prepared to give the poison two or three times, if necessary; that is all.

I was almost certain that you would say that, replied Crito; but I was obliged to satisfy him.

Never mind him, he said.

And now I will make answer to you, O my judges, and show that he who has lived as a true philosopher has reason to be of good cheer when he is about to die, and that after death he may hope to receive the greatest good in the other world. And how this may be, Simmias and Cebes, I will endeavour to explain. For I deem that the true disciple of philosophy is likely to be misunderstood by other men; they do not perceive that he is ever pursuing death and dying; and if this is true, why, having had the desire of death all his life long, should he repine at the arrival of that which he has been always pursuing and desiring?

Simmias laughed and said: Though not in a laughing humor I swear that I cannot help laughing when I think what the wicked world will say when they hear this. They will say that this is very true, and our people at home will agree with them in saying that the life which philosophers desire is truly death, and that they have found them out to be deserving of the death which they desire.

And they are right, Simmias, in saying this, with the exception of the words "They have found them out"; for they have not found out what is the nature of this death which the true philosopher desires, or how he deserves or desires death. But let us leave them and have a word with ourselves: Do we believe that there is such a thing as death?

To be sure, replied Simmias.

And is this anything but the separation of soul and body? And being dead is the attainment of this separation when the soul exists in herself, and is parted from the body and the body is parted from the soul—that is death?

Just so, he replied.

Whereas, Simmias, the rest of the world are of opinion that a life which has no bodily pleasures and no part in them is not worth having; but that he who thinks nothing of bodily pleasures is almost as though he were dead.

That is quite true.

What again shall we say of the actual requirement of knowledge?—is the body, if invited to share in the inquiry, a hinderer or a helper? I mean to say, have sight and hearing any truth in them? Are they not, as the poets are always telling us, inaccurate witnesses? and yet, if even they are inaccurate and indistinct, what is to be said of the other senses?—for you will allow that they are the best of them?

Certainly, he replied.

Then when does the soul attain truth?—for in attempting to consider anything in company with the body she is obviously deceived.

Yes, that is true.

Then must not existence be revealed to her in thought, if at all?

Yes.

And thought is best when the mind is gathered into herself and none of these things trouble her—neither sounds nor sights nor pain nor any pleasure—when she has as little as possible to do with the body, and has no bodily sense of feeling, but is aspiring after being?

That is true.

And in this the philosopher dishonors the body; his soul runs away from the body and desires to be alone and by herself?

That is true.

Well, but there is another thing, Simmias: Is there or is there not an absolute justice?

Assuredly there is.

And an absolute beauty and absolute good?

Of course.

But did you ever behold any of them with your eyes?

Certainly not.

Or did you ever reach them with any other bodily sense? (and I speak not of these alone, but of absolute greatness, and health and strength, and of the essence or true nature of everything). Has the reality of them ever been perceived by you through the bodily organs? or rather, is not the nearest approach to the knowledge of their several natures made by him who so orders his intellectual vision as to have the most exact conception of the essence of that which he considers?

Certainly.

And he attains to the knowledge of them in their highest purity who goes to each of them with the mind alone, not allowing when in the act of thought the intrusion or introduction of sight or any other sense in the company of reason, but with the very light of the mind in her clearness penetrates into the very light of truth in each; he has got rid, as far as he can, of eyes and ears and of the whole body, which he conceives of only as a disturbing element, hindering the soul from the acquisition of knowledge when in company with her—is not this the sort of man who, if ever man did, is likely to attain the knowledge of existence?

There is admirable truth in that, Socrates, replied Simmias.

And when they consider all this, must not true philosophers make a reflection, of which they will speak to one another in such words as these: We have found, they will say, a path of speculation which seems to bring us and the argument to the conclusion that while we are in the body, and while the soul is mingled with this mass of evil, our desire will not be satisfied, and our desire is of the truth. For the body is a source of endless trouble to us by reason of the mere requirement of food; and also is liable to diseases which overtake and impede us in the search after truth: and by filling us so full of loves, and lusts, and fears, and fancies, and idols, and every sort of folly, prevents our ever having, as people say, so much as a thought. For whence come wars, and fightings, and factions? whence but from the body and the lusts of the body? For wars are occasioned by the love of money, and money has to be acquired for the sake and in the service of the body; and in consequence of all these things the time which ought to be given to philosophy is lost. Moreover, if there is time and an inclination toward philosophy, yet the body introduces a turmoil and confusion and fear into the course of speculation, and hinders us from seeing the truth: and all experience shows that if we would have pure knowledge of anything we must be quit of the body, and the soul in herself must behold all things in themselves: then I suppose that we shall attain that which we desire, and of which we say that we are lovers, and that is wisdom, not while we live, but after death, as the argument shows; for if while in company with the body the soul cannot have pure knowledge, one of two things seems to follow—either knowledge is not to be attained at all, or, if at all, after death. For then, and not till then, the soul will be in herself alone and without the body. In this present life, I reckon that we make the nearest approach to knowledge when we have the least possible concern or interest in the body, and are not saturated with the bodily nature, but remain pure until the hour when God himself is pleased to release us. And when the foolishness of the body will be cleared away and we shall be pure and hold converse with other pure souls, and know of ourselves the clear light everywhere; and this is surely the light of truth. For no impure thing is allowed to approach the pure. These are the sort of words, Simmias, which the true lovers of wisdom cannot help saying to one another, and thinking. You will agree with me in that?

Certainly, Socrates.

But if this is true, O my friend, then there is great hope that, going whither I go, I shall there be satisfied with that which has been the chief concern of you and me in our past lives. And now that the hour of departure is appointed to me, this is the hope with which I depart, and not I only, but every man who believes that he has his mind purified.

Certainly, replied Simmias.

And what is purification but the separation of the soul from the body, as I was saying before; the habit of the soul gathering and collecting herself into herself, out of all the courses of the body; the dwelling in her own place alone, as in another life, so also in this, as far as she can; the release of the soul from the chains of the body?

Very true, he said.

And what is that which is termed death, but this very separation and release of the soul from the body?

To be sure, he said.

And the true philosophers, and they only, study and are eager to release the soul. Is not the separation and release of the soul from the body their especial study?

That is true.

And as I was saying at first, there would be a ridiculous contradiction in men studying to live as nearly as they can in a state of death, and yet repining when death comes.

Certainly.

Then, Simmias, as the true philosophers are ever studying death, to them, of all men, death is the least terrible. . . .

Cebes answered: I agree, Socrates, in the greater part of what you say. But in what relates to the soul, men are apt to be incredulous; they fear that when she leaves the body her place may be nowhere, and that on the very day of death she may be destroyed and perish—immediately on her release from the body, issuing forth like smoke or air and vanishing away into nothingness. For if she could only hold together and be herself after she was released from the evils of the body, there would be good reason to hope, Socrates, that what you say is true. But much persuasion and many arguments are required in order to prove that when the man is dead the soul yet exists, and has any force of intelligence.

True, Cebes, said Socrates; and shall I suggest that we talk a little of the probabilities of these things?

I am sure, said Cebes, that I should greatly like to know your opinion about them.

I reckon, said Socrates, that no one who heard me now, not even if he were one of my old enemies, the comic poets, could accuse me of idle talking about matters in which I have no concern. Let us, then, if you please, proceed with the inquiry.

Whether the souls of men after death are or are not in the world below, is a question which may be argued in this manner. The ancient doctrine of which I have been speaking affirms that they go from this into the other world, and return hither, and are born from the dead. Now if this be true, and the living come from the dead, then our souls must be in the other world, for if not, how could they be born again? And this would be conclusive, if there were any real evidence that the living are only born from the dead; but if there is no evidence of this, then other arguments will have to be adduced.

That is very true, replied Cebes.

Then let us consider this question, not in relation to man only, but in relation to animals generally, and to plants, and to everything of which there is generation, and the proof will be easier. Are not all things which have opposites generated out of their opposites? I mean such things as good and evil, just and unjust—and there are innumerable other opposites which are generated out of opposites. And I want to show that this holds universally of all opposites; I mean to say, for example, that anything which becomes greater must become greater after being less.

True.

And that which becomes less must have been once greater and then become less.

Yes. . . .

Well; but let me tell you something more. There was a time when I thought that I understood the meaning of greater and less pretty well; and when I saw a great man standing by a little one, I fancied that one was taller than the other by a head; or one horse would appear to be greater than another horse; and still more clearly did I seem to perceive that ten is two more than eight, and that two cubits are more than one, because two is the double of one.

And what is now your notion of such matters? said Cebes.

I should be far enough from imagining, he replied, that I knew the cause of any of them, by heaven I should; for I cannot satisfy myself that, when one is added to one, the one to which the addition is made becomes two, or that the two units added together make two by reason of the addition. I cannot understand how, when separated from the other, each of them was one and not two, and now, when they are brought together, the mere juxtaposition or meeting of them should be the cause of their becoming two: neither can I understand how the division of one is the way to make two; for then a different cause would produce the same effect,—as in the former instance the addition and juxtaposition of one to one was the cause of two, in this the separation and subtraction of one from the other would be the cause. Nor am I any longer satisfied that I understand the reason why one or anything else is either generated or destroyed or is at all, but I have in my mind some confused notion of a new method, and can never admit the other.

Then I heard some one reading, as he said, from a book of Anaxagoras, that mind was the disposer and cause of all, and I was delighted at this notion, which appeared quite admirable, and I said to myself: If mind is the disposer, mind will dispose all for the best, and put each particular in the best place; and I argued that if any one desired to find out the cause of the generation or destruction or existence of anything, he must find out what state of being or doing or suffering was best for that thing, and therefore a man had only to consider the best for himself and others, and then he would also know the worse, since the same science comprehended both. And I rejoiced to think that I had found in Anaxagoras a teacher of the causes of existence such as I desired, and I imagined that he would tell me first whether the earth is flat or round; and whichever was true, he would proceed to explain the cause and the necessity of this being so, and then he would teach me the nature of the best and show that this was best; and if he said that the earth was in the centre, he would further explain that this position was the best, and I should be satisfied with the explanation given, and not want any other sort of cause. And I thought that I would then go on and ask him about the sun and moon and stars, and that he would explain to me their comparative swiftness, and their returnings and various states, active and passive, and how all of them were for the best. For I could not imagine that when he spoke of mind as the disposer of them, he would give any other account of their being as they are, except that this was best; and I thought that when he had explained to me in detail the cause of each and the cause of all, he would go on to explain to me what was best for each and what was good for all. These hopes I would not have sold for a large sum of money, and I seized the books and read them as fast as I could in my eagerness to know the better and the worse.

What expectations I had formed, and how grievously was I disappointed! As I proceeded, I found my philosopher altogether forsaking mind or any other principle of order, but having recourse to air, and ether, and water, and other eccentricities. I might compare him to a person who began by maintaining generally that mind is the cause of the actions of Socrates, but who, when he endeavoured to explain the causes of my several actions in detail, went on to show that I sit here because my body is made up of bones and muscles; and the bones, as he would say, are hard and have joints which divide them, and the muscles are elastic, and they cover the bones, which have also a covering or environment of flesh and skin which contains them; and as the bones are lifted at their joints by the contraction or relaxation of the muscles, I am able to bend my limbs, and this is why I am sitting here in a curved posture—that is what he would say; and he would have a similar explanation of my talking to you, which he would attribute to sound, and air, and hearing, and he would assign ten thousand other causes of the same sort, forgetting to mention the true cause, which is, that the Athenians have thought fit to condemn me, and accordingly I have thought it better and more right to remain here and undergo my sentence; for I am inclined to think that these muscles and bones of mine would have gone off long ago to Megara or Boeotia—by the dog, they would, if they had been moved only by their own idea of what was best, and if I had not chosen the better and nobler part, instead of playing truant and running away, of enduring any punishment which the state inflicts. There is surely a strange confusion of causes and conditions in all this. It may be said, indeed, that without bones and muscles and the other parts of the body I cannot execute my purposes. But to say that I do as I do because of them, and that this is the way in which mind acts, and not from the choice of the best, is a very careless and idle mode of speaking. I wonder that they cannot distinguish the cause from the condition, which the many, feeling about in the dark, are always mistaking and misnaming. And thus one man makes a vortex all round and steadies the earth by the heaven; another gives the air as a support to the earth, which is a sort of broad trough. Any power which in arranging them as they are arranges them for the best never enters into their minds; and instead of finding any superior strength in it, they rather expect to discover another Atlas of the world who is stronger and more everlasting and more containing than the good;—of the obligatory and containing power of the good they think nothing; and yet this is the principle which I would fain learn if any one would teach me. But as I have failed either to discover myself, or to learn of any one else, the nature of the best, I will exhibit to you, if you like, what I have found to be the second best mode of enquiring into the cause.

I should very much like to hear, he replied.

Socrates proceeded: I thought that as I had failed in the contemplation of true existence, I ought to be careful that I did not lose the eye of my soul; as people may injure their bodily eye by observing and gazing on the sun during an eclipse, unless they take the precaution of only looking at the image reflected in the water, or in some similar medium. That occurred to me, and I was afraid that my soul might be blinded altogether if I looked at things with my eyes or tried by the help of the senses to apprehend them. And I thought that I had better have recourse to ideas, and seek in them the truth of existence. I dare say that the simile is not perfect—for I am very far from admitting that he who contemplates existence through the medium of ideas, sees them only "through a glass darkly," any more than he who sees in their working and effects. However, this was the method which I adopted: I first assumed some principle which I judged to be the strongest, and then I affirmed as true whatever seemed to agree with this, whether relating to the cause or to anything else; and that which disagreed I regarded as untrue. But I should like to explain my meaning clearly, as I do not think that you understand me.

No, indeed, replied Cebes, not very well.

There is nothing new, he said, in what I am about to tell you; but only what I have been always and everywhere repeating in the previous discussion and on other occasions; I want to show you the nature of that cause which has occupied my thoughts, and I shall have to go back to those familiar words which are in the mouth of every one, and first of all assume that there is an absolute beauty and goodness, and greatness, and the like; grant me this, and I hope to be able to show you the nature of the cause, and to prove the immortality of the soul.

Cebes said: You may proceed at once with the proof, as I readily grant you this.

Well, he said, then I should like to know whether you agree with me in the next step; for I cannot help thinking that if there be anything beautiful other than absolute beauty, that can only be beautiful in as far as it partakes of absolute beauty—and this I should say of everything. Do you agree in this notion of the cause?

Yes, he said, I agree.

He proceeded: I know nothing and can understand nothing of any other of those wise causes which are alleged; and if a person says to me that the bloom of color, or form, or anything else of that sort is a source of beauty, I leave all that, which is only confusing to me, and simply and singly, and perhaps foolishly, hold and am assured in my own mind that nothing makes a thing beautiful but the presence and participation of beauty in whatever way or manner obtained; for as to the manner I am uncertain, but I stoutly contend that by beauty all beautiful things become beautiful. That appears to me to be the only safe answer that I can give, either to myself or to any other, and to that I cling, in the persuasion that I shall never be overthrown, and that I may safely answer to myself or any other that by beauty beautiful things become beautiful. Do you not agree to that?

Yes, I agree.

And that by greatness only great things become great and greater greater, and by smallness the less becomes less.

True.

Then if a person remarks that A is taller by a head than B, and B less by a head than A, you would refuse to admit this, and would stoutly contend that what you mean is only that the greater is greater by, and by reason of, greatness, and the less is less only by, or by reason of, smallness; and thus you would avoid the danger of saying that the greater is greater and the less less by the measure of the head, which is the same in both and would also avoid the monstrous absurdity of supposing that the greater man is greater by reason of the head, which is small. Would you not be afraid of that?

Indeed, I should, said Cebes, laughing.

In like manner you would be afraid to say that ten exceeded eight by, and by reason of, two; but would say by, and by reason of, number; or that two cubits exceed one cubit by a half, but by magnitude—that is what you would say, for there is the same danger in both cases.

Very true, he said.

Again, would you not be cautious of affirming that the addition of one to one, or the division of one, is the cause of two? And you would loudly asseverate that you know of no way in which anything comes into existence except by participation in its own proper essence, and consequently, as far as you know, the only cause of two is the participation in duality; that is, the way to make two, and the participation in one is the way to make one. You would say: I will let alone puzzles of division and addition—wiser heads than mine may answer them; inexperienced as I am, and ready to start, as the proverb says, at my own shadow, I cannot afford to give up the sure ground of a principle. And if any one assails you there, you would not mind him, or answer him until you had seen whether the consequences which follow agree with one another or not, and when you are further required to give an explanation of this principle, you would go on to assume a higher principle, and the best of the higher ones until you found a resting-place; but you would not refuse the principle and the consequences in your reasoning like the Eristics—at least if you wanted to discover real existence. Not that this confusion signifies to them who never care or think about the matter at all, for they have the wit to be well pleased with themselves, however great may be the turmoil of their ideas. But you, if you are a philosopher, will, I believe, do as I say.

What you say is most true, said Simmias and Cebes, both speaking at once.

ECH.:   Yes, Phaedo; and I don't wonder at their assenting. Anyone who has the least sense will acknowledge the wonderful clearness of Socrates's reasoning.

PHAED.:   Certainly, Echecrates; and that was the feeling of the whole company at the time.

ECH.:   Yes, and equally of ourselves, who were not of the company, and are now listening to your recital. But what followed?

PHAED.:   After all this was admitted, and they had agreed about the existence of ideas and the participation in them of the other things which derive their names from them, Socrates, if, I remember rightly, said:—...

Then not only do opposite ideas repel the advance of one another, but also there are other things which repel the approach of opposites.

That is quite true, he said.

Suppose, he said, that we endeavor, if possible, to determine what these are.

By all means.

Are they not, Cebes, such as compel the things of which they have possession, not only to take their own form, but also the form of some opposite?

What do you mean?

I mean, as I was just now saying, and have no need to repeat to you, that those things which are possessed by the number three must not only be three in number, but must also be odd.

Quite true.

And on this oddness, of which the number three has the impress, the opposite idea will never intrude?

No.

And this impress was given by the odd principle?

Yes.

And to the odd is opposed the even?

True.

Then the idea of the even number will never arrive at three?

No.

Then three has no part in the even?

None.

Then the triad or number three is uneven?

Very true.

To return then to my distinction of natures which are not opposites, and yet do not admit opposites: as in this instance, three although not opposed to the even, does not any the more admit of the even, but always brings the opposite into play on the other side; or as two does not receive the odd, or fire the cold—from these examples (and there are many more of them) perhaps you may be able to arrive at the general conclusion that not only opposites will not receive opposites, but also that nothing which brings the opposite will admit the opposite of that which it brings in that to which it is brought. And here let me recapitulate—for there is no harm in repetition. The number five will not admit the nature of the even, any more than ten, which is the double of five, will admit the nature of the odd—the double, though not strictly opposed to the odd, rejects the odd altogether. Nor again will parts of the ratio of 3:2, nor any fraction in which there is a half, nor again in which there is a third, admit the notion of the whole, although they are not opposed to the whole. You will agree to that?

Yes, he said, I entirely agree and go along with you in that.

And now, he said, I think that I may begin again; and to the question which I am about to ask I will beg you to give not the old safe answer, but another, of which I will offer you an example; and I hope that you will find in what has been just said another foundation which is as safe. I mean that if anyone asks you, "What that is, the inherence of which makes the body hot," you will reply not heat (this is what I call the safe and stupid answer), but fire, a far better answer, which we are now in a condition to give. Or if anyone asks you, "Why a body is diseased," you will not say from disease, but from fever; and instead of saying that oddness is the cause of odd numbers, you will say that the monad is the cause of them: and so of things in general, as I dare say that you will understand sufficiently without my adducing any further examples.

Yes, he said, I quite understand you.

Tell me, then, what is that the inherence of which will render the body alive?

The soul, he replied.

And is this always the case?

Yes, he said, of course.

Then whatever the soul possesses, to that she comes bearing life?

Yes, certainly.

And is there any opposite to life?

There is, he said.

And what is that?

Death.

Then the soul, as has been acknowledged, will never receive the opposite of what she brings. And now, he said, what did we call that principle which repels the even?

The odd.

And that principle which repels the musical, or the just?

The unmusical, he said, and the unjust.

And what do we call the principle which does not admit of death?

The immortal, he said.

And does the soul admit of death?

No.

Then the soul is immortal?

Yes, he said.

And may we say that this is proven?

Yes, abundantly proven, Socrates, he replied.

And supposing that the odd were imperishable, must not three be imperishable?

Of course. . . .

And the same may be said of the immortal: if the immortal is also imperishable, then the soul will be imperishable as well as immortal; but if not, some other proof of her imperishableness will have to be given.

No other proof is needed, he said; for if the immortal, being eternal, is liable to perish, then nothing is imperishable.

Yes, replied Socrates, all men will agree that God, and the essential form of life, and the immortal in general will never perish.

Yes, all men, he said—that is true; and what is more, gods, if I am not mistaken, as well as men.

Seeing then that the immortal is indestructible, must not the soul, if she is immortal, be also imperishable?

Most certainly.

Then when death attacks a man, the mortal portion of him may be supposed to die, but the immortal goes out of the way of death and is preserved safe and sound?

True.

Then, Cebes, beyond question the soul is immortal and imperishable, and our souls will truly exist in another world! . . .

But then, O my friends, he said, if the soul is really immortal, what care should be taken of her, not only in respect of the portion of time which is called life, but of eternity! And the danger of neglecting her from this point of view does indeed appear to be awful. If death had only been the end of all, the wicked would have had a good bargain in dying, for they would have been happily quit not only of their body, but of their own evil together with their souls. But now, as the soul plainly appears to be immortal, there is no release or salvation from evil except the attainment of the highest virtue and wisdom. For the soul when on her progress to the world below takes nothing with her but nurture and education; which are indeed said greatly to benefit or greatly to injure the departed, at the very beginning of its pilgrimage in the other world.

For after death, as they say, the genius of each individual, to whom he belonged in life, leads him to a certain place in which the dead are gathered together for judgment, whence they go into the world below, following the guide who is appointed to conduct them from this world to the other: and when they have there received their due and remained their time, another guide brings them back again after many revolutions of ages. Now this journey to the other world is not, as Aeschylus says in the "Telephus," a single and straight path—no guide would be wanted for that, and no one could miss a single path; but there are many partings of the road, and windings, as I must infer from the rites and sacrifices which are offered to the gods below in places where three ways meet on earth. The wise and orderly soul is conscious of her situation and follows in the path; but the soul which desires the body, and which, as I was relating before, has long been fluttering about the lifeless frame and the world of sight, is after many struggles and many sufferings hardly and with violence carried away by her attendant genius, and when she arrives at the place where the other souls are gathered, if she be impure and have done impure deeds, or been concerned in foul murders or other crimes which are the brothers of these, and the works of brothers in crime—from that soul every one flees and turns away; no one will be her companion, no one her guide, but alone she wanders in extremity of evil until certain times are fulfilled, and when they are fulfilled, she is borne irresistibly to her own fitting habitation; as every pure and just soul which has passed through life in the company and under the guidance of the gods has also her own proper home. . . .

Wherefore, Simmias, seeing all these things, what ought not we to do in order to obtain virtue and wisdom in this life? Fair is the prize, and the hope great.

I do not mean to affirm that the description which I have given of the soul and her mansions is exactly true—a man of sense ought hardly to say that. But I do say that, inasmuch as the soul is shown to be immortal, he may venture to think not improperly or unworthily, that something of the kind is true. The venture is a glorious one, and he ought to comfort himself with words like these, which is the reason why I lengthen out the tale. Wherefore, I say, let a man be of good cheer about his soul, who hast cast away the pleasures and ornaments of the body as alien to him, and rather hurtful in their effects, and has followed after the pleasures of knowledge in this life; who has adorned the soul in her own proper jewels, which are temperance, and justice, and courage, and nobility, and truth—in these arrayed she is ready to go on her journey to the world below, when her time comes. You, Simmias and Cebes, and all other men, will depart at some time or other. Me already, as the tragic poet would say, the voice of fate calls. Soon I must drink the poison; and I think that I had better repair to the bath first, in order that the women may not have the trouble of washing my body after I am dead.

When he had done speaking, Crito said: And have you any commands for us, Socrates—anything to say about your children, or any other matter in which we can serve you?

Nothing particular, he said: only, as I have always told you, I would have you to look to yourselves; that is a service which you may always be doing to me and mine as well as to yourselves. And you need not make professions; for if you take no thought for yourselves, and walk not according to the precepts which I have given you, not now for the first time, the warmth of your professions will be of no avail.

We will do our best, said Crito. But in what way would you have us bury you?

In any way that you like; only you must get hold of me, and take care that I do not walk away from you. Then he turned to us, and added with a smile: I cannot make Crito believe that I am the same Socrates who have been talking and conducting the argument; he fancies that I am the other Socrates whom he will soon see, a dead body—and he asks, How shall he bury me? And though I have spoken many words in the endeavour to show that when I have drunk the poison I shall leave you and go to the joys of the blessed—these words of mine, with which I comforted you and myself, have had, I perceive, no effect upon Crito. And therefore I want you to be surety for me now, as he was surety for me at the trial: but let the promise be of another sort; for he was my surety to the judges that I would remain, but you must be my surety to him that I shall not remain, but go away and depart; and then he will suffer less at my death, and not be grieved when he sees my body being burned or buried. I would not have him sorrow at my hard lot, or say at the burial, Thus we lay out Socrates, or, Thus we follow him to the grave or bury him; for false words are not only evil in themselves, but they infect the soul with evil. Be of good cheer, then, my dear Crito, and say that you are burying my body only, and do with that as is usual, and as you think best.

When he had spoken these words, he arose and went into the bath chamber with Crito, who bade us wait; and we waited, talking and thinking of the subject of discourse, and also of the greatness of our sorrow; he was like a father of whom we were being bereaved, and we were about to pass the rest of our lives as orphans. When he had taken the bath his children were brought to him—(he had two young sons and an elder one); and the women of his family also came, and he talked to them and gave them a few directions in the presence of Crito; and he then dismissed them and returned to us.

Now the hour of sunset was near, for a good deal of time had passed while he was within. When he came out, he sat down with us again after his bath, but not much was said. Soon the jailer, who was the servant of the Eleven, entered and stood by him, saying: To you, Socrates, whom I know to be the noblest and gentlest and best of all who ever came to this place, I will not impute the angry feelings of other men, who rage and swear at me when, in obedience to the authorities, I bid them drink the poison—indeed I am sure that you will not be angry with me; for others, as you are aware, and not I, are the guilty cause. And so fare you well, and try to bear lightly what must needs be; you know my errand. Then bursting into tears he turned away and went out.

Socrates looked at him and said: I return your good wishes, and will do as you bid. Then, turning to us, he said, How charming the man is: since I have been in prison he has always been coming to see me, and at times he would talk to me, and was as good as could be to me, and now see how generously he sorrows for me. But we must do as he says, Crito; let the cup be brought, if the poison is prepared: if not, let the attendant prepare some.

Yet, said Crito, the sun is still upon the hilltops, and many a one has taken the draught late, and after the announcement has been made to him, he has eaten and drunk, and indulged in sensual delights; do not hasten, then, there is still time.

Socrates said: Yes, Crito, and they of whom you speak are right in doing thus, for they think that they will gain by the delay; but I am right in not doing thus, for I do not think that I should gain anything by drinking the poison a little later; I should be sparing and saving a life which is already gone: I could only laugh at myself for this. Please then to do as I say, and not refuse me.

Crito, when he heard this, made a sign to the servant, and the servant went in, and remained for some time, and then returned with the jailer carrying a cup of poison. Socrates said: You, my good friend, who are experienced in these matters, shall give me directions how I am to proceed. The man answered: You have only to walk about until your legs are heavy, and then to lie down, and the poison will act. At the same time he handed the cup to Socrates, who in the easiest and gentlest manner, without the least fear or change of color or feature, looking at the man with all his eyes, Echecrates, as his manner was, took the cup and said: What do you say about making a libation out of this cup to any god? May I, or not? The man answered: We only prepare, Socrates, just so much as we deem enough. I understand, he said: yet I may and must pray to the gods to prosper my journey from this to that other world—may this, then, which is my prayer, be granted to me. Then holding the cup to his lips, quite readily and cheerfully he drank off the poison. And hitherto most of us had been able to control our sorrow; but now when we saw him drinking, and saw too that he had finished the draught, we could no longer forbear, and in spite of myself my own tears were flowing fast; so that I covered my face and wept over myself, for certainly I was not weeping over him, but at the thought of my own calamity in having lost such a companion. Nor was I the first, for Crito, when he found himself unable to restrain his tears, had got up and moved away, and I followed; and at that moment, Apollodorus, who had been weeping all the time, broke out in a loud cry which made cowards of us all. Socrates alone retained his calmness: What is this strange outcry? he said. I sent away the women mainly in order that they might not offend in this way, for I have heard that a man should die in peace. Be quiet, then, and have patience.

When we heard that, we were ashamed, and refrained our tears; and he walked about until, as he said, his legs began to fail, and then he lay on his back, according to the directions, and the man who gave him the poison now and then looked at his feet and legs; and after a while he pressed his foot hard and asked him if he could feel; and he said, no; and then his leg, and so upwards and upwards and showed us that he was cold and stiff. And he felt them himself, and said: When the poison reaches the heart, that will be the end. He was beginning to grow cold about the groin, when he uncovered his face, for he had covered himself up, and said (they were his last words)—he said: Crito, I owe a cock to Asclepius; will you remember to pay the debt? The debt shall be paid, said Crito; is there anything else? There was no answer to this question; but in a minute or two a movement was heard, and the attendants uncovered him; his eyes were set, and Crito closed his eyes and mouth.

Such was the end, Echecrates, of our friend, whom I may truly call the wisest, and justest, and best of all the men whom I have ever known.

MENO

MENO: And how will you enquire, Socrates, into that which you do not know? What will you put forth as the subject of enquiry? And if you find what you want, how will you ever know that this is the thing which you did not know?

SOCRATES: I know, Meno, what you mean; but just see what a tiresome dispute you are introducing. You argue that a man cannot enquire either about that which he knows, or about that which he does not know; for if he knows, he has no need to enquire; and if not, he cannot; for he does not know the very subject about which he is to enquire.

MEN.:   Well, Socrates, and is not the argument sound?

SOC.:   I think not.

MEN.:   Why not?

SOC.:   I will tell you why: I have heard from certain wise men and women who spoke of things divine that—

MEN.:   What did they say?

SOC.:   They spoke of a glorious truth, as I conceive.

MEN.:   What was it? and who were they?

SOC.:   Some of them were priests and priestesses, who had studied how they might be able to give a reason of their profession: there have been poets also, who spoke of these things by inspiration, like Pindar, and many others who were inspired. And they say—mark, now, and see whether their words are true— they say that the soul of man is immortal, and at one time has an end, which is termed dying, and at another time is born again, but is never destroyed. And the moral is, that a man ought to live always in perfect holiness. "*For in the ninth year Persephone sends the souls of those from whom she has received the penalty of ancient crime back again from beneath into the light of the sun above, and these are they who become noble kings and mighty men and great in wisdom and are called saintly heroes in after ages.*" The soul, then, as being immortal, and having been born again many times, and having seen all things that exist, whether in this world or in the world below, has knowledge of them all; and it is no wonder that she should be able to call to remembrance all that she ever knew about virtue, and about everything; for as all nature is akin, and the soul has learned all things, there is no difficulty in her eliciting or as men say learning, out of a single recollection all the rest, if a man is strenuous and does not faint; for all enquiry and all learning is but recollection. And therefore we ought not to listen to this sophistical argument about the impossibility of enquiry: for it will make us idle, and is sweet only to the sluggard;

From "Crito," in *The Dialogues of Plato,* trans. B. Jowett (Oxford: Clarendon Press, 1892).

but the other saying will make us active and inquisitive. In that confiding, I will gladly enquire with you into the nature of virtue.

MEN.: Yes, Socrates; but what do you mean by saying that we do not learn, and that what we call learning is only a process of recollection? Can you teach me how this is?

SOC.: I told you, Meno, just now that you were a rogue, and now you ask whether I can teach you, when I am saying that there is no teaching, but only recollection; and thus you imagine that you will involve me in a contradiction.

MEN.: Indeed, Socrates, I protest that I had no such intention. I only asked the question from habit; but if you can prove to me that what you say is true, I wish that you would.

SOC.: It will be no easy matter, but I will try to please you to the utmost of my power. Suppose that you call one of your numerous attendants, that I may demonstrate on him.

MEN.: Certainly. Come hither, boy.

SOC.: He is Greek, and speaks Greek, does he not?

MEN.: Yes, indeed; he was born in the house.

SOC.: Attend now to the questions which I ask him, and observe whether he learns of me or only remembers.

MEN.: I will.

SOC.: Tell me, boy, do you know that a figure like this is a square?

BOY: I do.

SOC.: And you know that a square figure has these four lines equal?

BOY: Certainly.

SOC.: And these lines which I have drawn through the middle of the square are also equal?

BOY: Yes.

SOC.: A square may be of any size?

BOY: Certainly.

SOC.: And if one side of the figure be of two feet, and the other side be of two feet, how much will the whole be? Let me explain: if in one direction the space was of two feet, and in the other direction of one foot, the whole would be of two feet taken once?

BOY: Yes.

SOC.: But since this side is also of two feet, there are twice two feet?

BOY: There are.

SOC.: Then the square is of twice two feet?

BOY: Yes.

SOC.: And how many are twice two feet? Count and tell me.

BOY: Four, Socrates.

SOC.:   And might there not be another square twice as large as this, and having like this the lines equal?

BOY: Yes.

SOC.:   And of how many feet will that be?

BOY: Of eight feet.

SOC.:   And now try and tell me the length of the line which forms the side of that double square: this is two feet—what will that be?

BOY: Clearly, Socrates, it will be double.

SOC.:   Do you observe, Meno, that I am not teaching the boy anything, but only asking him questions; and now he fancies that he knows how long a line is necessary in order to produce a figure of eight square feet; does he not?

MEN.:   Yes.

SOC.:   And does he really know?

MEN.:   Certainly not.

SOC.:   He only guesses that because the square is double, the line is double.

MEN.:   True.

SOC.:   Observe him while he recalls the steps in regular order. (*To the Boy.*) Tell me, boy, do you assert that a double space comes from a double line? Remember that I am not speaking of an oblong, but of a figure equal every way, and twice the size of this—that is to say of eight feet; and I want to know whether you still say that a double square comes from a double line?

BOY: Yes.

SOC.:   But does not this line become doubled if we add another such line here?

BOY: Certainly.

SOC.:   And four such lines will make a space containing eight feet?

BOY: Yes.

SOC.:   Let us describe such a figure: Would you not say that this is the figure of eight feet?

BOY: Yes.

SOC.:   And are there not these four divisions in the figure, each of which is equal to the figure of four feet?

BOY: True.

SOC.:   And is not that four times four?

BOY: Certainly.

SOC.:   And four times is not double?

BOY: No, indeed.

SOC.:   But how much?

BOY: Four times as much.

SOC.:   Therefore the double line, boy, has given a space, not twice, but four times as much.

BOY: True.

SOC.:   Four times four are sixteen—are they not?

BOY: Yes.

SOC.:   What line would give you a space of eight feet, as this gives one of sixteen feet;—do you see?

BOY: Yes.

SOC.:   And the space of four feet is made from this half line?

BOY: Yes.

SOC.:   Good; and is not a space of eight feet twice the size of this, and half the size of the other?

BOY: Certainly.

SOC.:   Such a space, then, will be made out of a line greater than this one, and less than that one?

BOY: Yes; I think so.

SOC.:   Very good; I like to hear you say what you think. And now tell me, is not this a line of two feet and that of four?

BOY: Yes.

SOC.:   Then the line which forms the side of eight feet ought to be more than this line of two feet, and less than the other of four feet?

BOY: It ought.

SOC.:   Try and see if you can tell me how much it will be.

BOY: Three feet.

SOC.:   Then if we add a half to this line of two, that will be the line of three. Here are two and there is one; and on the other side, here are two also and there is one: and that makes the figure of which you speak?

BOY: Yes.

SOC.:   But if there are three feet this way and three feet that way, the whole space will be three times three feet?

BOY: That is evident.

SOC.:   And how much are three times three feet?

BOY: Nine.

SOC.:   And how much is the double of four?

BOY: Eight.

SOC.:   Then the figure of eight is not made out of a line of three?

BOY: No.

SOC.:   But from what line?—tell me exactly; and if you would rather not reckon, try and show me the line.

BOY: Indeed, Socrates, I do not know.

SOC.:   Do you see, Meno, what advances he has made in his power of recollection? He did not know at first, and he does not know now, what is the side of a figure of eight feet: but then he thought that he knew, and answered confidently as if he knew, and had no difficulty; now he has a difficulty, and neither knows nor fancies that he knows.

MEN.:   True.

SOC.:   Is he not better off in knowing his ignorance?

MEN.:   I think that he is.

SOC.:   If we have made him doubt, and given him the "torpedo's shock," have we done him any harm?

MEN.:   I think not.

SOC.:   We have certainly, as would seem, assisted him in some degree to the discovery of the truth; and now he will wish to remedy his ignorance, but then he would have been ready to tell all the world again and again that the double space should have a double side.

MEN.:   True.

SOC.:   But do you suppose that he would ever have enquired into or learned what he fancied that he knew, though he was really ignorant of it, until he had fallen into perplexity under the idea that he did not know, and had desired to know?

MEN.:   I think not, Socrates. . . .

SOC.:   Mark now the farther development. I shall only ask him, and not teach him, and he shall share the enquiry with me: and do you watch and see if you find me telling or explaining anything to him, instead of eliciting his opinion. Tell me, boy, is not this a square of four feet which I have drawn?

BOY: Yes.

SOC.:   And now I add another square equal to the former one?

BOY: Yes.

SOC.:   And a third, which is equal to either of them?

BOY: Yes.

SOC.:   Suppose that we fill up the vacant corner?

BOY: Very good.

SOC.:   Here, then, there are four equal spaces?

BOY: Yes.

SOC.:   And how many times larger is this space than this other?

BOY: Four times.

SOC.:   But it ought to have been twice only, as you will remember.

BOY: True.

SOC.:   And does not this line, reaching from corner to corner, bisect each of these spaces?

BOY: Yes.

SOC.:   And are there not here four equal lines which contain this space?

BOY: There are.

SOC.: Look and see how much this space is.

BOY: I do not understand.

SOC.: Has not each interior line cut off half of the four spaces?

BOY: Yes.

SOC.: And how many such spaces are there in this section?

BOY: Four.

SOC.: And how many in this?

BOY: Two.

SOC.: And four is how many times two?

BOY: Twice.

SOC.: And this space is of how many feet?

BOY: Of eight feet.

SOC.: And from what line do you get this figure?

BOY: From this.

SOC.: That is, from the line which extends from corner to corner of the figure of four feet?

BOY: Yes.

SOC.: And that is the line which the learned call the diagonal. And if this is the proper name, then you, Meno's slave, are prepared to affirm that the double space is the square of the diagonal?

BOY: Certainly, Socrates.

SOC.: What do you say of him, Meno? Were not all these answers given out of his own head?

MEN.: Yes, they were all his own.

SOC.: And yet, as we were just now saying, he did not know?

MEN.: True.

SOC.: But still he had in him those notions of his—had he not?

MEN.: Yes.

SOC.: Then he who does not know may still have true notions of that which he does not know?

MEN.: He has.

SOC.: And at present these notions have just been stirred up in him, as in a dream; but if he were frequently asked the same questions, in different forms, he would know as well as any one at last?

MEN.: I dare say.

SOC.: Without any one teaching him he will recover his knowledge for himself, if he is only asked questions?

MEN.: Yes.

SOC.: And this spontaneous recovery of knowledge in him is recollection?

MEN.:   True.

SOC.:   And this knowledge which he now has must he not either have acquired or always possessed?

MEN.:   Yes.

SOC.:   But if he always possessed this knowledge he would always have known; or if he has acquired the knowledge he could not have acquired it in this life, unless he has been taught geometry; for he may be made to do the same with all geometry and every other branch of knowledge. Now, has any one ever taught him all this? You must know about him, if, as you say, he was born and bred in your house.

MEN.:   And I am certain that no one ever did teach him.

SOC.:   And yet he has the knowledge?

MEN.:   The fact, Socrates, is undeniable.

SOC.:   But if he did not acquire the knowledge in this life, then he must have had and learned it at some other time?

MEN.:   Clearly he must.

SOC.:   Which must have been the time when he was not a man?

MEN.:   Yes.

SOC.:   And if there have been always true thoughts in him, both at the time when he was and was not a man, which only need to be awakened into knowledge by putting questions to him, his soul must have always possessed this knowledge, for he always either was or was not a man?

MEN.:   Obviously.

SOC.:   And if the truth of all things always existed in the soul, then the soul is immortal. Wherefore be of good cheer, and try to recollect what you do not know, or rather what you do not remember.

MEN.:   I feel, somehow, that I like what you are saying.

SOC.:   And I, Meno, like what I am saying. Some things I have said of which I am not altogether confident. But that we shall be better and braver and less helpless if we think that we ought to enquire, than we should have been if we indulged in the idle fancy that there was no knowing and no use in seeking to know what we do not know;—that is a theme upon which I am ready to fight, in word and deed, to the utmost of my power. . . .

PHAEDRUS

To explain what the soul is, would be a long and most assuredly a godlike labour; to say what it resembles, is a shorter and a human task. Let us attempt then the latter; let us say that the soul resembles the combined efficacy of a pair of winged steeds and a charioteer. Now the horses and drivers of the gods are all both good themselves and of good extraction, but the character and breed of all others is mixed. In the first place, with us men the supreme ruler has a pair of horses to manage, and then of these horses he finds one generous and of generous breed, the other of opposite descent and opposite character. And thus it necessarily follows that driving in our case is no easy or agreeable work. We must at this point endeavour to express what we mean respectively by a mortal and an immortal animal. All that is soul presides over all that is without soul, and patrols all heaven, now appearing in one form and now in another. When it is perfect and fully feathered, it roams in upper air, and regulates the entire universe; but the soul that has lost its feathers is carried down till it finds some solid resting-place; and when it has settled there, when it has taken to itself, that is, an earthly body, which seems capable of self-motion, owing to the power of its new inmate, the name of animal is given to the whole; to this compound, I mean, of soul and body, with the addition of the epithet mortal. The immortal, on the other hand, has received its name from the conclusion of no human reasoning; but without either having seen or formed any conception of a god, we picture him to ourselves as an immortal animal, possessed of soul and possessed of body, and of both in intimate conjunction from all eternity. But this matter I leave to be and to be told as Heaven pleases—my task is to discover what is the cause that makes the feathers fall off the soul. It is something, I conceive, of the following kind.

The natural efficacy of a wing is to lift up heavy substances, and bear them aloft to those upper regions which are inhabited by the race of the gods. And of all the parts connected with the body it has perhaps shared most largely (with the soul) in the divine nature. Now of this nature are beauty, wisdom, virtue, and all similar qualities. By these then the plumage of the soul is chiefly fostered and increased; by ugliness, vice, and all such contraries, it is wasted and destroyed. Zeus, the great chieftain in heaven, driving a winged car, travels first, arranging and presiding over all things; and after him comes a host of gods and inferior deities, marshalled in eleven divisions, for Hestia stays at home alone in the mansion of the gods; but all the other ruling powers, that have their place in the number of the twelve, march at the head of a troop in the order to which they have been severally appointed. Now there are, it is true, many ravishing views and opening paths within the bounds of heaven, whereon the family of the blessed gods go to and fro, each in performance of his own proper work; and they are followed by all who from time to time possess both will and power; for envy has no place in the celestial choir. But whenever they go to feast and revel, they forthwith journey by an uphill path to the summit of the heavenly vault. Now the chariots of the gods being of equal poise, and obedient to the rein, move easily, but all others with

From "Phaedrus," in *The Phaedrus, Lysis, and Protagoras of Plato*, trans. J. Wright (London: Macmillan, 1909).

difficulty; for they are burdened by the horse of vicious temper, which sways and sinks them towards the earth, if haply he has received no good training from his charioteer. Whereupon there awaits the soul a crowning pain and agony. For those which we called immortal go outside when they are come to the topmost height, and stand on the outer surface of heaven, and as they stand they are borne round by its evolution, and gaze on the external scene. Now of that region beyond the sky no earthly bard has ever yet sung or ever will sing in worthy strains. But this is the fashion of it; for sure I must venture to speak the truth, especially as truth is my theme. Real existence, colourless, formless, and intangible, visible only to the intelligence which sits at the helm of the soul, and with which the family of true science is concerned, has its abode in this region. The mind then of deity, as it is fed by intelligence and pure science, and the mind of every soul that is destined to receive its due inheritance, is delighted at seeing the essence to which it has been so long a stranger, and by the light of truth is fostered and made to thrive, until, by the revolution of the heaven, it is brought round again to the same point. And during the circuit it sees distinctly absolute justice, and absolute temperance, and absolute science; not such as they appear in creation, nor under the variety of forms to which we nowadays give the name of realities, but the justice, the temperance, the science, which exist in that which is real and essential being. And when in like manner it has seen all the rest of the world of essence, and feasted on the sight, it sinks down again into the interior of heaven, and returns to its own home. And on its arrival, the charioteer takes his horses to the manger, and sets before them ambrosia, and gives them nectar to drink with it. Such is the life of the gods; but of the other souls, that which follows a god most closely and resembles him most nearly, succeeds in raising the head of its charioteer into the outer region, and is carried round with the immortals in their revolution, though sore encumbered by its horses, and barely able to contemplate the real existences; while another rises and sinks by turns, his horses plunging so violently that he can discern no more than a part of these existences. But the common herd follow at a distance, all of them indeed burning with desire for the upper world, but, failing to reach it, they make the revolution in the moisture of the lower element, trampling on one another, and striking against one another, in their efforts to rush one before the other. Hence ensues the extremest turmoil and struggling and sweating; and herein, by the awkwardness of the drivers, many souls are maimed, and many lose many feathers in the crush; and all after painful labour go away without being blessed by admission to the spectacle of truth, and thenceforth live on the food of mere opinion.

And now will I tell you the motives of this great anxiety to behold the fields of truth. The suitable pasturage for the noblest portion of the soul is grown on the meadows there, and it is the nature of the wing, which bears aloft the soul, to be fostered thereby; and moreover, there is an irrevocable decree, that if any soul has followed a god in close companionship and discerned any of the true essences, it shall continue free from harm till the next revolution, and if it be ever thus successful, it shall be ever thus unharmed: but whenever, from inability to follow, it has missed that glorious sight, and, through some mishap it may have encountered, has become charged with forgetfulness and vice, and been thereby so burdened as to shed its feathers and fall to the earth, in that case there is a law that the soul thus fallen be not planted in any bestial nature during the first generation, but that if it has seen more than others of essential verity, it pass into the germ of a man who is to become a lover of wisdom, or a lover of beauty, or some votary of the Muses and Love; if it be of second rank, it is to enter the form of a constitutional ruler, a warrior, or a man fitted for command; the third will belong to a politician, or economist, or merchant; the fourth, to a labourious professor of gymnastics, or some disciple of the healing art; the fifth will be possessed by a soothsayer, or some person connected with mysteries; the sixth will be best suited by the life of a poet or some other imitative artist; the seventh, by the labour of an artisan or a farmer; the eighth, by the trade of a sophist or a demagogue; and the ninth, by the lot of an absolute monarch. And in all these various conditions those who have lived justly receive afterwards a better lot; those who have lived unjustly, a worse. For to that same place from which each soul set out, it does not return for ten thousand years; so long is it before it recovers its plumage, unless it has belonged to a guileless lover of philosophy, or a philosophic lover of boys. But these souls, during their third millennium, if only they have chosen thrice in succession this form of existence, do in this case regain their feathers, and at its conclusion wing their departure. But all the rest are, on the termination of their first life, brought to trial; and, according to their sentence, some go to the prison-houses beneath the earth, to suffer for their sins; while others, by virtue of their trial, are borne lightly upwards to some celestial spot, where they pass their days in a manner worthy of the life they have lived in their mortal form. But in the thousandth year both divisions come back again to share and choose their second life, and they select that which they severally please. And then it is that a human soul passes into the life of a beast, and from a beast who was once a man the soul comes back into a man again. For the soul which has never seen the truth at all can never enter into the human form; it being a necessary condition of a man that he should apprehend according to that which is called a generic form, which, proceeding from a variety of perceptions, is by reflection combined into unity. And this is nothing more nor less than a recollection of those things which in time past our soul beheld when it travelled with a god, and, looking high over what we now call real, lifted up its head into the region of eternal essence. And thus you see it is with justice that the mind of the philosopher alone recovers its plumage, for to the best of its power it is ever fixed in memory on that glorious spectacle, by the contemplation of which the godhead is divine. And it is only by the right use of such memorials as these, and by ever perfecting himself in perfect mysteries, that a man becomes really perfect. But because such an one stands aloof from human interests, and is rapt in contemplation of the divine, he is taken to task by the multitude as a man demented, because the multitude do not see that he is by God inspired.

It will now appear what conclusion the whole course of our argument has reached with regard to the fourth kind of madness, with which a man is inspired whenever, by the sight of beauty in this lower world, the true beauty of the world above is so brought to his remembrance that he begins to recover his plumage, and feeling new wings longs to soar aloft; but the power failing him gazes upward like a bird, and becomes heedless of all lower matters, thereby exposing himself to the imputation of being crazed. And the conclusion is this, that of all kinds of enthusiasm this is the best, as well in character as in origin, for those who possess it, whether fully or in part; and further, that he who loves beautiful objects must partake of this madness before he can deserve the name of lover. For though, as I said before, every man's soul has by the law of his birth been a spectator of eternal truth, or it would never have passed into this our mortal frame, yet still it is no easy matter for all to be reminded of their past by their present existence. It is not easy either for those who, during that struggle I told you of, caught but a brief glimpse of upper glories, nor for those who, after their fall to this world, were so unfortunate as to be turned aside by evil associations into the paths of wickedness, and so made to forget that holy spectacle. Few, few only are there left, with whom the world of memory is duly present. And these few, whenever they see here any resemblance of what they witnessed there, are struck with wonder, and can no longer contain themselves, though what it is that thus affects them they know not, for want of sufficient discernment. Now in the likenesses existing here of justice, and temperance, and all else which souls hold precious, there is no brightness; but through the medium of dull dim instruments it is but seldom and with difficulty that people are enabled on meeting with the copies to recognise the character of the original. But beauty not only shone brightly on our view at the time when in the heavenly choir we, for our part, followed in the band of Zeus, as others in the bands of other gods, and saw that blissful sight and spectacle, and were initiated into that mystery which I fear not to pronounce the most blessed of all mysteries; for we who celebrated it were perfect and untainted by the evil that awaited us in time to come, and perfect too, and simple, and calm, and blissful were the visions which we were solemnly admitted to gaze upon in the purest light, ourselves being no less pure, nor as yet entombed in that which we now drag about with us and call the body, being fettered to it as an oyster to his shell. Excuse my so far indulging memory, which has carried me to a greater length than I intended, in my yearning for a happiness that is past. I return to beauty. Not only, as I said before, did she shine brightly arteries, and prick each at the outlet which is shut against it; so that the soul, being stung all over, is frantic with pain. But then again it calls to mind the beautiful one, and rejoices. And both these feelings being combined, it is sore perplexed by the strangeness of its condition, and not knowing what to do with itself, becomes frenzied, and in its frenzy can neither sleep by night, nor by day remain at rest, but runs to and fro with wistful look wherever it may expect to see the possessor of the beauty. And after it has seen him, and drunk in fresh streams of desire, it succeeds in opening the stoppages which absence had made, and taking breath it enjoys a respite from sting and throe, and now again delights itself for the time being in that most delicious pleasure. And therefore, if it can help, it never quits the side of its beloved, nor holds any one of more account than him, but forgets mother, and brothers, and friends, and though its substance be wasting by neglect, it regards that as nothing, and of all observances and decorums, on which it prided itself once, it now thinks scorn, and is ready to be a slave and lie down as closely as may be allowed to the object of its yearnings; for, besides its reverence for the possessor of beauty, it has found in him the sole physician for its bitterest pains. Now this affection, my beautiful boy—you I mean to whom my speech is addressed—is called by mortals Eros (Love); on hearing its name among the gods, your young wit will naturally laugh. There are put forth, if I mistake not, by certain Homerids, out of their secret poems, two verses on Eros, of which the second is quite outrageous, and not at all particularly metrical. Thus they sing:

> Him mortals indeed call winged Eros,
> But immortals Pteros (Flyer), for his flighty nature.

Now these verses you may believe or not believe, as you think proper; but whatever is thought of them the cause of love, and the condition of lovers, is all the same, just such as has been here stated.

Now, if it be one of the former followers of Zeus who is seized by love, he is able to bear in greater weight than others the burden of the wing-named god. But all who were in the service of Ares, and patrolled the heavens in his company, when they are taken captive by Love, and fancy themselves in aught injured by the object of their love, are thirsty of blood, and ready to immolate both themselves and their favourites. And so it is with the followers of the other gods. Every man spends his life in honouring and imitating to the best of his power that particular god of whose choir he was a member, so long as he is exempt from decay, and living his first generation here; and in keeping with the bent thus acquired, he conducts his intercourse and behaviour towards the beloved object, as well as all the world. Accordingly, each man chooses himself his love out of the ranks of beauty to suit his peculiar turn; and then, as though his choice were his god, he builds him up for himself, and attires him like a holy image, for the purpose of doing him reverence, and worshipping him with ecstatic festival. They then that belong to Zeus seek to have for their beloved one who resembles Zeus in his soul. And so they look for a youth who is by nature a lover of wisdom, and fitted for command; and when they have found one, and become enamoured of him, they strive all they can to make him truly such. And if they have never previously entered upon this task, they now apply themselves to it, both seeking instruction from every possible quarter, and searching in their own souls. And this endeavour to discover the nature of their patron god, by following the track in themselves, is attended with success, by reason of their being ever constrained to gaze upon their god unflinchingly; and when they grasp him with their memory, they are inspired with his inspiration, and take from him their character and habits, so far as it is possible for man to partake of god. And attributing these blessings to their beloved, they love him still more dearly than ever; and whatever streams they may have drawn from Zeus, like the inspired draughts of the Bacchanals, they pour into their darling's soul, thereby making him resemble, as far as possible, the god whom they resemble themselves. Those again who followed in the train of Hera, search out a youth of kingly mould, and when he is found, act towards him in exactly the same manner as the former. And so it is with the adherents of Apollo, and all other gods. Walking themselves in the steps of their own proper god, they look for the youth whom they are to love to be of kindred nature; and when they have gained such an one, both by imitation on their own part, and by urging and attuning the soul of their beloved, they guide him into the particular pursuit and character of that god, so far as they are severally able, not treating him with jealous or illiberal harshness, but using every endeavour to bring him into all possible conformity with themselves and the god whom they adore. So beautiful is the desire of those who truly love; and if they accomplish their desire, so beautiful is the initiation, as I call it, into their holy mystery, and so fraught with blessing at the hand of the friend, whom love has maddened, to the object of the friendship, if he be but won. Now he who is won, is won in the following manner.

As at the commencement of this account I divided every soul into three parts, two of them resembling horses, and the third a charioteer, so let us here still keep to that division. Now of the horses one, if you remember, we said, was good, and the other bad; but wherein consists the goodness of the one, and the badness of the other, is a point which, not distinguished then, must be stated now. That horse of the two which occupies the nobler rank, is in form erect and firmly knit, high-necked, hook-nosed, white-coloured, black-eyed; he loves honour with temperance and modesty, and, a votary of genuine glory, he is driven without stroke of the whip by voice and reason alone. The bad horse, on the other hand, is crooked, bulky, clumsily put together, with thick neck, short throat, flat face, black coat, gray and bloodshot eyes, a friend to all riot and insolence, shaggy about the ears, dull of hearing, scarce yielding to lash and goad united. Whenever therefore the driver sees the sight which inspires love, and his whole soul being thoroughly heated by sense, is surcharged with irritation and the stings of desire, the obedient horse, yielding then as ever to the check of shame, restrains himself from springing on the loved one; but the other pays heed no longer to his driver's goad or lash, but struggles on with unruly bounds, and doing all violence to his yoke-fellow and master, forces them to approach the beautiful youth, and bethink themselves of the joys of dalliance. And though at first they resist him with indignation at the lawless and fearful crime he is urging, yet at last, when there is no end to the evil, they move onward as he leads them, having yielded him submission and agreed to do his bidding. So they come up to the beautiful boy, and see his face all gleaming with beauty. But at the sight the driver's memory is carried back to the essence of beauty, and again he sees her by the side of Continence standing on a holy pedestal. And at the sight he shudders, and with a holy awe falls backward to the ground, and falling cannot help pulling back the reins so violently that he brings both the horses on their haunches, the one indeed willingly, because he is not resisting, but the rebel in spite of struggling. And when they are withdrawn to some distance, the former in his shame and ravishment drenches all the soul with sweat; but the other, when he is recovered from the pain which the bit and the fall inflicted, and has with difficulty regained his breath, breaks out into passionate revilings, vehemently railing at his master and his comrade for their treacherous cowardice in deserting their ranks and agreement. And again he urges them, again refusing, to approach, and barely yields a reluctant consent when they beg to defer the attempt to another time. But soon as the covenanted time is come, though they affect forgetfulness, he reminds them of their engagement, and plunging and neighing and dragging, he again obliges them to approach the beautiful youth to make the same proposals. And when they are near, he stoops his head and gets the bit between his teeth, and drags them on incontinently. But the driver experiences, though still more strongly, the same sensation as at first; backward he falls like racers at the barrier, and with a wrench still more violent than before pulls back the bit from between the teeth of the riotous horse, thereby drenching his jaws and railing tongue with blood: and bruising against the ground his legs and haunches, consigns him to anguish. But as soon as by this treatment oft repeated the evil horse is recovered from his vice, he follows with humbled steps the guidance of his driver, and at sight of the fair one is consumed with terror. So that then, and not till then, does it happen that the soul of the lover follows his beloved with reverence and awe. And the consequence is, that the youth being now worshipped with all the worship of a god by a lover who does not feign the passion, but feels it in his soul, and being himself by nature fondly inclined to his worshipper, even though haply in time past he may have been set against lovers by the remarks of his schoolfellows or others on the scandal of allowing their approaches, and is therefore disposed to reject his present wooer, yet now that the latter is thus changed he is led in course of time, by the instinct of his years, and the law of destiny, to admit him to familiarity. For surely it was never destined for the bad to be friends of the bad, or the good aught but friendly to the good. But when the advances have been accepted and speech and intercourse allowed, the affection of the lover being brought into near connection with the loved one, strikes him with wonder, as it compels him to feel that the friendship shown him by all the rest of his friends and relations put together is as nothing beside the love of his god-inspired friend. And if he continues long thus to indulge him, and allows him the closest contact both in gymnastic schools and other places of meeting, then it is that the stream of that effluence, to which Zeus when enamoured of Ganymedes gave the name of desire, pours upon the lover in a plenteous flood, and partly sinks within him, partly flows off him when he is full; and just as a wind or a noise rebounds from smooth and hard substances and is carried back again to the place from which it came; so the tide of beauty passes back into the beautiful boy through his eyes, the natural channel into his soul; and when it is come there and has fledged it anew, it waters the outlets of the feathers, and forcing them to shoot up afresh fills the soul of the loved one as well as that of his lover with love. He is in love therefore, but with whom he cannot say; nay, what it is that is come over him he knows not, neither can he tell, but like one who has caught a disease in the eye from the diseased gaze of another, he can assign no reason for the affection, but sees himself in his lover, as in a glass, without knowing who it is that he sees. And when they are together, he enjoys the same respite that his lover does from his anguish; but when they are parted, he yearns for him as he himself is yearned for, since he holds in his bosom love's reflected image, love returned. He calls it, however, and believes it to be not love but friendship, albeit, he feels the same desire as the other does, though in a feebler degree, for the sight, the touch, the kiss, the embrace. And consequently, as might be expected, his conduct henceforward is as follows. When they are lying side by side, the lover's unbridled horse has much to say to its driver, and claims as the recompense of many labours a short enjoyment; but the vicious horse of the other has nothing to say, but burning and restless clasps the lover and kisses him as he would kiss a dear friend, and when they are folded in each other's embrace, is just of such a temper as not for his part to refuse indulging the lover in any pleasure he might request to enjoy; but his yoke-fellow, on the other hand, joins the driver in struggling against him with chastity and reason. Should it appear then that the better part of their nature has succeeded in bringing both the lover and loved into a life of order and philosophy, and established its own ascendency, in bliss and harmony they live out their existence here, being masters of themselves and decorous before the world, having enslaved that portion of the soul wherein vice is contained, and liberated that where virtue dwells; and at last when they come to die, being winged and lightened, they have in one of their three truly Olympic combats achieved the prize, than which no greater good can either human prudence or godly madness bestow on man. But if they have given in to a coarser habit of life, and one unfriendly to wisdom, though not to honour, it may well happen that in a moment of drunkenness or like abandonment, those two unruly beasts will surprise the souls off their guard, and bringing them together into one place will choose and consummate that practice which the world deems happy, and once consummated will for the future indulge in it, though sparingly, as doing what is not approved by all their mind. Dear, therefore, to each other, though not so dear as the former two, do these continue both while their love is burning and when it is extinct; for they conceive themselves to have given and received the strongest pledges, which it were impious at any time to violate by becoming alienated. And in the end, without their wings it is true, but not without having started feathers, they go forth from the body, so that they carry off no paltry prize for their impassioned madness; for there is a law that the paths of darkness beneath the earth shall never again be trodden by those who have so much as set their foot on the heavenward road, but that walking hand in hand they shall live a bright and blessed life, and when they recover their wings, recover them together for their love's sake.

So great and so godly, my beautiful boy, are the blessings which the affection of a lover will bestow. But the commerce of one who does not love, being alloyed with mortal prudence, and dispensing only mortal and niggardly gifts, will breed in the soul of the loved one a sordidness which the vulgar laud as virtue, and doom it for nine thousand years to be tossed about the earth and under the earth without reason.

THE REPUBLIC

Book II

. . . Glaucon and the rest entreated me by all means not to let the question drop, but to proceed in the investigation. They wanted to arrive at the truth, first, about the nature of justice and injustice, and secondly, about their relative advantages. I told them, what I really thought, that the enquiry would be of a serious nature, and would require very good eyes. Seeing then, I said, that we are no great wits, I think that we had better adopt a method which I may illustrate thus; suppose that a short-sighted person had been asked by some one to read small letters from a distance; and it occurred to some one else that they might be found in another place which was larger and in which the letters were larger—if they were the same and he could read the larger letters first, and then proceed to the lesser—this would have been thought a rare piece of good fortune.

Very true. said Adeimantus; but how does the illustration apply to our enquiry?

I will tell you, I replied; justice, which is the subject of our enquiry, is, as you know, sometimes spoken of as the virtue of an individual, and sometimes as the virtue of a State.

True, he replied.

And is not a State larger than an individual?

It is.

Then in the larger the quantity of justice is likely to be larger and more easily discernible. I propose therefore that we enquire into the nature of justice and injustice, first as they appear in the State, and secondly in the individual, proceeding from the greater to the lesser and comparing them.

That, he said, is an excellent proposal.

And if we imagine the State in process of creation, we shall see the justice and injustice of the State in process of creation also.

I dare say.

When the State is completed there may be a hope that the object of our search will be more easily discovered.

Yes, far more easily.

But ought we to attempt to construct one? I said; for to do so, as I am inclined to think, will be a very serious task. Reflect therefore.

I have reflected, said Adeimantus, and am anxious that you should proceed.

A State, I said, arises, as I conceive, out of the needs of mankind; no one is self-sufficing, but all of us have many wants. Can any other origin of a State be imagined?

There can be no other.

Then, as we have many wants, and many persons are needed to supply them, one takes a helper for one purpose and another for another; and when these partners and helpers are gathered together in one habitation the body of inhabitants is termed a State.

True, he said.

And they exchange with one another, and one gives, and another receives, under the idea that the exchange will be for their good.

From "The Republic," in *The Dialogues of Plato,* trans. B. Jowett (Oxford: Clarendon Press, 1892).

Very true.

Then, I said, let us begin and create in idea a State; and yet the true creator is necessity, who is the mother of our invention.

Of course, he replied.

Now the first and greatest of necessities is food, which is the condition of life and existence.

Certainly.

The second is a dwelling, and the third clothing and the like.

True.

And now let us see how our city will be able to supply this great demand: We may suppose that one man is a husbandman, another a builder, some one else a weaver—shall we add to them a shoemaker, or perhaps some other purveyor to our bodily wants?

Quite right.

The barest notion of a State must include four or five men.

Clearly.

And how will they proceed? Will each bring the result of his labours into a common stock?—the individual husbandman, for example, producing for four, and labouring four times as long and as much as he need in the provision of food with which he supplies others as well as himself; or will he have nothing to do with others and not be at the trouble of producing for them, but provide for himself alone a fourth of the food in a fourth of the time, and in the remaining three-fourths of his time be employed in making a house or a coat or a pair of shoes, having no partnership with others, but supplying himself all his own wants?

Adeimantus thought that he should aim at producing food only and not at producing everything.

Probably, I replied, that would be the better way; and when I hear you say this, I am myself reminded that we are not all alike; there are diversities of natures among us which are adapted to different occupations.

Very true.

And will you have a work better done when the workman has many occupations, or when he has only one?

When he has only one.

Further, there can be no doubt that a work is spoilt when not done at the right time?

No doubt.

For business is not disposed to wait until the doer of the business is at leisure; but the doer must follow up what he is doing, and make the business his first object.

He must.

And if so, we must infer that all things are produced more plentifully and easily and of a better quality when one man does one thing which is natural to him and does it at the right time, and leaves other things.

Undoubtedly.

Then more than four citizens will be required; for the husbandman will not make his own plough or mattock, or other implements of agriculture, if they are to be good for anything. Neither will the builder make his tools—and he too needs many; and in like manner the weaver and shoemaker.

True.

Then carpenters, and smiths, and many other artisans, will be sharers in our little State, which is already beginning to grow?

True.

Yet even if we add neatherds, shepherds, and other herdsmen, in order that our husbandmen may have oxen to plough with, and builders as well as husbandmen may have draught cattle, and curriers and weavers fleeces and hides—still our State will not be very large.

That is true; yet neither will it be a very small State which contains all these.

Then, again, there is the situation of the city—to find a place where nothing need be imported is well-nigh impossible.

Impossible.

Then there must be another class of citizens who will bring the required supply from another city?

There must.

But if the trader goes empty-handed, having nothing which they require who would supply his need, he will come back empty-handed.

That is certain.

And therefore what they produce at home must be not only enough for themselves, but such both in quantity and quality as to accommodate those from whom their wants are supplied.

Very true.

Then more husbandmen and more artisans will be required?

They will.

Not to mention the importers and exporters, who are called merchants?

Yes.

Then we shall want merchants?

We shall.

And if merchandise is to be carried over the sea, skilful sailors will also be needed, and in considerable numbers?

Yes, in considerable numbers.

Then, again, within the city, how will they exchange their productions? To secure such an exchange was, as you will remember, one of our principal objects when we formed them into a society and constituted a State.

Clearly they will buy and sell.

Then they will need a market-place, and a money-token for purposes of exchange.

Certainly.

Suppose now that a husbandman, or an artisan, brings some production to market, and he comes at a time when there is no one to exchange with him,—is he to leave his calling and sit idle in the market-place?

Not at all; he will find people there who, seeing the want, undertake the office of salesmen. In well-ordered states they are commonly those who are the weakest in bodily strength, and therefore of little use for any other purpose; their duty is to be in the market, and to give money in exchange for goods to those who desire to sell and to take money from those who desire to buy.

This want, then, creates a class of retail-traders in our State. Is not "retailer" the term which is applied to those who sit in the market-place engaged in buying and selling, while those who wander from one city to another are called merchants?

Yes, he said.

And there is another class of servants, who are intellectually hardly on the level of companionship; still they have plenty of bodily strength for labour, which accordingly they sell, and are called, if I do not mistake, hirelings, hire being the name which is given to the price of their labour.

True.

Then hirelings will help to make up our population?

Yes.

And now, Adeimantus, is our State matured and perfected?

I think so.

Where, then, is justice, and where is injustice, and in what part of the State did they spring up?

Probably in the dealings of these citizens with one another. I cannot imagine that they are more likely to be found anywhere else.

I dare say that you are right in your suggestion, I said; we had better think the matter out, and not shrink from the enquiry.

Let us then consider, first of all, what will be their way of life, now that we have thus established them. Will they not produce corn, and wine, and clothes, and shoes, and build houses for themselves? And when they are housed, they will work, in summer, commonly, stripped and barefoot, but in winter substantially clothed and shod. They will feed on barley-meal and flour of wheat, baking and kneading them, making noble cakes and loaves; these they will serve up on a mat of reeds or on clean leaves, themselves reclining the while upon beds strewn with yew or myrtle. And they and their children will feast, drinking of the wine which they have made, wearing garlands on their heads, and hymning the praises of the gods, in happy converse with one another. And they will take care that their families do not exceed their means; having an eye to poverty or war.

But, said Glaucon, interposing, you have not given them a relish to their meal.

True, I replied, I had forgotten; of course they must have a relish—salt, and olives, and cheese, and they will boil roots and herbs such as country people prepare; for a dessert we shall give them figs, and peas, and beans; and they will roast myrtle-berries and acorns at the fire, drinking in moderation. And with such a diet they may be expected to live in peace and health to a good old age, and bequeath a similar life to their children after them.

Yes, Socrates, he said, and if you were providing for a city of pigs, how else would you feed the beasts?

But what would you have, Glaucon? I replied.

Why, he said, you should give them the ordinary conveniences of life. People who are to be comfortable are accustomed to lie on sofas, and dine off tables, and they should have sauces and sweets in the modern style.

Yes, I said, now I understand: the question which you would have me consider is, not only how a State, but how a luxurious State is created; and possibly there is no harm in this, for in such a state we shall be more likely to see how justice and injustice originate. In my opinion the true and healthy constitution of the State is the one which I have described. But if you wish also to see a State at fever heat, I have no objection. For I suspect that many will not be satisfied with the simpler way of life. They will be for adding sofas, and tables, and other furniture; also dainties, and perfumes, and incense, and courtesans, and cakes, all these not of one sort only, but in every variety; we must go beyond the necessaries of which I was at first speaking, such as houses, and clothes, and shoes: the arts of the painter and the embroiderer will have to be set in motion, and gold and ivory and all sorts of materials must be procured.

True, he said.

Then we must enlarge our borders; for the original healthy State is no longer sufficient. Now will the city have to fill and swell with a multitude of callings which are not required by any natural want; such as the whole tribe of hunters and actors, of whom one large class have to do with forms and colours; another will be votaries of music—poets and their attendant train of rhapsodists, players, dancers, contractors; also makers of divers kinds of articles, including women's dresses. And we shall want more servants. Will not tutors be also in request, and nurses wet and dry, tirewomen and barbers, as well as confectioners and cooks; and swineherds, too, who were not needed and therefore had no place in the former edition of our State, but are needed now? They must not be forgotten: and there will be animals of many other kinds, if people eat them.

Certainly.

And living in this way we shall have much greater need of physicians than before?

Much greater.

And the country which was enough to support the original inhabitants will be too small now, and not enough?

Quite true.

Then a slice of our neighbours' land will be wanted by us for pasture and tillage, and they will want a slice of ours, if, like ourselves, they exceed the limit of necessity, and give themselves up to the unlimited accumulation of wealth?

That, Socrates, will be inevitable.

And so we shall go to war, Glaucon. Shall we not?

Most certainly, he replied.

Then, without determining as yet whether war does good or harm, thus much we may affirm, that now we have discovered war to be derived from causes which are also the causes of almost all the evils in States, private as well as public.

Undoubtedly.

And our State must once more enlarge; and this time the enlargement will be nothing short of a whole army, which will have to go out and fight with the invaders for all that we have, as well as for the things and persons whom we were describing above.

Why? he said; are they not capable of defending themselves?

No, I said; not if we were right in the principle which was acknowledged by all of us when we were framing the State: the principle, as you will remember, was that one man cannot practise many arts with success.

Very true, he said.

But is not war an art?

Certainly.

And an art requiring as much attention as shoemaking?

Quite true.

And the shoemaker was not allowed by us to be a husbandman, or a weaver, or a builder—in order that we might have our shoes well made; but to him and to every other worker was assigned one work for which he was by nature fitted, and at that he was to continue working all his life long and at no other; he was not to let opportunities slip, and then he would become a good workman. Now nothing can be more important than that the work of a soldier should be well done. But is war an art so easily acquired that a man may be a warrior who is also a husbandman, or shoemaker, or other artisan; although no one in the world would be a good dice or draught player who merely took up the game as a recreation, and had not from his earliest years devoted himself to this and nothing else? No tools will make a man a skilled workman, or master of defence, nor be of any use to him who has not learned how to handle them, and has never bestowed any attention upon them. How then will he who takes up a shield or other implement of war become a good fighter all in a day, whether with heavy-armed or any other kind of troops?

Yes, he said, the tools which would teach men their own use would be beyond price.

And the higher the duties of the guardian, I said, the more time, and skill, and art, and application will be needed by him?

No doubt, he replied.

Will he not also require natural aptitude for his calling?

Certainly.

Then it will be our duty to select, if we can, natures which are fitted for the task of guarding the city?

It will.

And the selection will be no easy matter, I said; but we must be brave and do our best.

We must.

Is not the noble youth very like a well-bred dog in respect of guarding and watching?

What do you mean?

I mean that both of them ought to be quick to see, and swift to overtake the enemy when they see him; and strong too if, when they have caught him, they have to fight with him.

All these qualities, he replied, will certainly be required by them.

Well, and your guardian must be brave if he is to fight well?

Certainly.

And is he likely to be brave who has no spirit, whether horse or dog or any other animal? Have you never observed how invincible and unconquerable is spirit and how the presence of it makes the soul of any creature to be absolutely fearless and indomitable?

I have.

Then now we have a clear notion of the bodily qualities which are required in the guardian.

True.

And also of the mental ones; his soul is to be full of spirit?

Yes.

But are not these spirited natures apt to be savage with one another, and with everybody else?

A difficulty by no means easy to overcome, he replied.

Whereas, I said, they ought to be dangerous to their enemies, and gentle to their friends; if not, they will destroy themselves without waiting for their enemies to destroy them.

True, he said.

What is to be done then? I said; how shall we find a gentle nature which has also a great spirit, for the one is the contradiction of the other?

True.

He will not be a good guardian who is wanting in either of these two qualities; and yet the combination of them appears to be impossible; and hence we must infer that to be a good guardian is impossible.

I am afraid that what you say is true, he replied.

Here feeling perplexed I began to think over what had preceded.—My friend, I said, no wonder that we are in a perplexity; for we have lost sight of the image which we had before us.

What do you mean? he said.

I mean to say that there do exist natures gifted with those opposite qualities.

And where do you find them?

Many animals, I replied, furnish examples of them; our friend the dog is a very good one: you know that well-bred dogs are perfectly gentle to their familiars and acquaintances, and the reverse to strangers.

Yes, I know.

Then there is nothing impossible or out of the order of nature in our finding a guardian who has a similar combination of qualities?

Certainly not.

Would not he who is fitted to be a guardian, besides the spirited nature, need to have the qualities of a philosopher?

I do not apprehend your meaning.

The trait of which I am speaking, I replied, may be also seen in the dog, and is remarkable in the animal.

What trait?

Why, a dog, whenever he sees a stranger, is angry; when an acquaintance, he welcomes him although the one has never done him any harm, nor the other any good. Did this never strike you as curious?

The matter never struck me before; but I quite recognise the truth of your remark.

And surely this instinct of the dog is very charming;—your dog is a true philosopher.

Why?

Why, because he distinguishes the face of a friend and of an enemy only by the criterion of knowing and not knowing. And must not an animal be a lover of learning who determines what he likes and dislikes by the test of knowledge and ignorance?

Most assuredly.

And is not the love of learning the love of wisdom, which is philosophy?

They are the same, he replied.

And may we not say confidently of man also, that he who is likely to be gentle to his friends and acquaintances, must by nature be a lover of wisdom and knowledge?

That we may safely affirm.

Then he who is to be a really good and noble guardian of the State will require to unite in himself philosophy and spirit and swiftness and strength?

Undoubtedly. . . .

BOOK III

. . . Very good, I said; then what is the next question? Must we not ask who are to be rulers and who subjects?

Certainly.

There can be no doubt that the elder must rule the younger.

Clearly.

And that the best of these must rule.

That is also clear.

Now, are not the best husbandmen those who are most devoted to husbandry?

Yes.

And as we are to have the best of guardians for our city, must they not be those who have most the character of guardians?

Yes.

And to this end they ought to be wise and efficient, and to have a special care of the State?

True.

And a man will be most likely to care about that which he loves?

To be sure.

And he will be most likely to love that which he regards as having the same interests with himself, and that of which the good or evil fortune is supposed by him at any time most to affect his own?

Very true, he replied.

Then there must be a selection. Let us note among the guardians those who in their whole life show the greatest eagerness to do what is for the good of their country, and the greatest repugnance to do what is against her interests.

Those are the right men.

And they will have to be watched at every age, in order that we may see whether they preserve their resolution, and never, under the influence either of force or enchantment, forget or cast off their sense of duty to the State.

How cast off? he said.

I will explain to you, I replied. A resolution may go out of a man's mind either with his will or against his will; with his will when he gets rid of a falsehood and learns better, against his will whenever he is deprived of a truth.

I understand, he said, the willing loss of a resolution; the meaning of the unwilling I have yet to learn.

Why, I said, do you not see that men are unwillingly deprived of good, and willingly of evil? Is not to have lost the truth an evil, and to possess the truth a good? and you would agree that to conceive things as they are is to possess the truth?

Yes, he replied; I agree with you in thinking that mankind are deprived of truth against their will.

And is not this involuntary deprivation caused either by theft, or force, or enchantment?

Still, he replied, I do not understand you.

I fear that I must have been talking darkly, like the tragedians. I only mean that some men are changed by persuasion and that others forget; argument steals away the hearts of one class, and time of the other; and this I call theft. Now you understand me?

Yes.

Those again who are forced are those whom the violence of some pain or grief compels to change their opinion.

I understand, he said, and you are quite right.

And you would also acknowledge that the enchanted are those who change their minds either under the softer influence of pleasure, or the sterner influence of fear?

Yes, he said; everything that deceives may be said to enchant.

Therefore, as I was just now saying, we must enquire who are the best guardians of their own conviction that what they think the interest of the State is to be the rule of their lives. We must watch them from their youth upwards, and make them perform actions in which they are most likely to forget or to be deceived, and he who remembers and is not deceived is to be selected, and he who fails in the trial is to be rejected. That will be the way?

Yes.

And there should also be toils and pains and conflicts prescribed for them, in which they will be made to give further proof of the same qualities.

Very right, he replied.

And then, I said, we must try them with enchantments—that is the third sort of test— and see what will be their behaviour: like those who take colts amid noise and tumult to see if they are of a timid nature, so must we take our youth amid terrors of some kind, and again pass them into pleasures, and prove them more thoroughly than gold is proved in the furnace, that we may discover whether they are armed against all enchantments, and of a noble bearing always, good guardians of themselves and of the music which they have learned, and retaining under all circumstances a rhythmical and harmonious nature, such as will be most serviceable to the individual and to the State. And he who at every age, as boy and youth and in mature life, has come out of the trial victorious and pure, shall be appointed a ruler and guardian of the State; he shall be honoured in life and death, and shall receive sepulture and other memorials of honour, the greatest that we have to give. But him who fails, we must reject. I am inclined to think that this is the sort of way in which our rulers and guardians should be chosen and appointed. I speak generally, and not with any pretension to exactness.

And, speaking generally, I agree with you, he said.

And perhaps the word "guardian" in the fullest sense ought to be applied to this higher class only who preserve us against foreign enemies and maintain peace among our citizens at home, that the one may not have the will, or the others the power, to harm us. The young men who we before called guardians may be more properly designated auxiliaries and sup- porters of the principles of the rulers.

I agree with you, he said.

How then may we devise one of those needful falsehoods of which we lately spoke— just one royal lie which may deceive the rulers, if that be possible, and at any rate the rest of the city?

What sort of lie? he said.

Nothing new, I replied; only an old Phoenician tale of what has often occurred before now in other places, (as the poets say, and have made the world believe,) though not in our time, and I do not know whether such an event could ever happen again, or could now even be made probable, if it did.

How your words seem to hesitate on your lips!

You will not wonder, I replied, at my hesitation when you have heard.

Speak, he said, and fear not.

Well then, I will speak, although I really know not how to look you in the face, or in what words to utter the audacious fiction, which I propose to communicate gradually, first to the rulers, then to the soldiers, and lastly to the people. They are to be told that their youth was a dream, and the education and training which they received from us, an ap- pearance only; in reality during all that time they were being formed and fed in the womb of the earth, where they themselves and their arms and appurtenances were manufactured; when they were completed, the earth, their mother, sent them up; and so, their country being their mother and also their nurse, they are bound to advise for her good, and to defend her against attacks, and her citizens they are to regard as children of the earth and their own brothers.

You had good reason, he said, to be ashamed of the lie which you were going to tell.

True, I replied, but there is more coming; I have only told you half. Citizens, we shall say to them in our tale, you are brothers, yet God has framed you differently. Some of you have the power of command, and in the composition of these he has mingled gold, where- fore also they have the greatest honour; others he has made of silver, to be auxiliaries; others again who are to be husbandmen and craftsmen he has composed of brass and iron; and the species will generally be preserved in the children. But as all are of the same original stock, a golden parent will sometimes have a silver son, or a silver parent a golden son. And God proclaims as a first principle to the rulers, and above all else, that there is nothing which they should so anxiously guard, or of which they are to be such good guardians, as of the purity of the race. They should observe what elements mingle in their offspring; for if the son of a golden or silver parent has an admixture of brass and iron, then nature orders a transposition of ranks, and the eye of the ruler must not be pitiful towards the child because he has to descend in the scale and become a husbandman or artisan, just as there may be sons of artisans who having an admixture of gold or silver in them are raised to honour, and become guardians or auxiliaries. For an oracle says that when a man of brass or iron guards the State, it will be destroyed. Such is the tale; is there any possibility of making our citizens believe in it?

Not in the present generation, he replied; there is no way of accomplishing this; but their sons may be made to believe in the tale, and their sons' sons, and posterity after them.

I see the difficulty, I replied; yet the fostering of such a belief will make them care more for the city and for one another. Enough, however, of the fiction, which may now fly abroad upon the wings of rumour, while we arm our earth-born heroes, and lead them forth under the command of their rulers. Let them look round and select a spot whence they can best suppress insurrection, if any prove refractory within, and also defend themselves against enemies who like wolves may come down on the fold from without; there let them encamp, and when they have encamped, let them sacrifice to the proper Gods and prepare their dwellings.

Just so, he said.

And their dwellings must be such as will shield them against the cold of winter and the heat of summer.

I suppose that you mean houses, he replied.

Yes, I said; but they must be the houses of soldiers, and not of shop-keepers.

What is the difference? he said.

That I will endeavour to explain, I replied. To keep watch-dogs, who, from want of discipline or hunger, or some evil habit or other, would turn upon the sheep and worry them, and behave not like dogs but wolves, would be a foul and monstrous thing in a shepherd?

Truly monstrous, he said.

And therefore every care must be taken that our auxiliaries, being stronger than our citizens, may not grow to be too much for them and become savage tyrants instead of friends and allies?

Yes, great care should be taken.

And would not a really good education furnish the best safeguard?

But they are well-educated already, he replied.

I cannot be so confident, my dear Glaucon, I said; I am much more certain that they ought to be, and that true education, whatever that may be, will have the greatest tendency to civilize and humanize them in their relations to one another, and to those who are under their protection.

Very true, he replied.

And not only their education, but their habitations, and all that belongs to them, should be such as will neither impair their virtue as guardians, nor tempt them to prey upon the other citizens. Any man of sense must acknowledge that.

He must.

Then let us consider what will be their way of life, if they are to realize our idea of them. In the first place, none of them should have any property of his own beyond what is absolutely necessary; neither should they have a private house or store closed against any one who has a mind to enter; their provisions should be only such as are required by trained warriors, who are men of temperance and courage; they should agree to receive from the citizens a fixed rate of pay, enough to meet the expenses of the year and no more; and they will go to mess and live together like soldiers in a camp. Gold and silver we will tell them that they have from God; the diviner metal is within them, and they have therefore no need of the dross which is current among men, and ought not to pollute the divine by any such earthly admixture; for that commoner metal has been the source of many unholy deeds, but their own is undefiled. And they alone of all the citizens may not touch or handle silver or gold, or be under the same roof with them, or wear them, or drink from them. And this will be their salvation, and they will be saviours of the State. But should they ever acquire homes or lands or moneys of their own, they will become housekeepers and husbandmen instead of guardians, enemies and tyrants instead of allies of the other citizens; hating and being hated, plotting and being plotted against, they will pass their whole life in much greater terror of internal than of external enemies, and the hour of ruin, both to themselves and to the rest of the State, will be at hand. For all which reasons may we not say that thus shall our State be ordered, and that these shall be the regulations appointed by us for our guardians concerning their houses and all other matters?

Yes, said Glaucon.

BOOK IV

Here Adeimantus interposed a question: How would you answer, Socrates, said he, if a person were to say that you are making these people miserable, and that they are the cause of their own unhappiness; the city in fact belongs to them, but they are none the better for it; whereas other men acquire lands, and build large and handsome houses, and have everything handsome about them, offering sacrifices to the gods on their own account, and practising hospitality; moreover, as you were saying just now, they have gold and silver, and all that is usual among the favourites of fortune; but our poor citizens are no better than mercenaries who are quartered in the city and are always mounting guard?

Yes, I said; and you may add that they are only fed, and not paid in addition to their food, like other men; and therefore they cannot, if they would, take a journey of pleasure; they have no money to spend on a mistress or any other luxurious fancy, which, as the world goes, is thought to be happiness; and many other accusations of the same nature might be added.

But, said he, let us suppose all this to be included in the charge.

You mean to ask, I said, what will be our answer?

Yes.

If we proceed along the old path, my belief, I said, is that we shall find the answer. And our answer will be that, even as they are, our guardians may very likely be the happiest of men; but that our aim in founding the State was not the disproportionate happiness of any one class, but the greatest happiness of the whole; we thought that in a State which is ordered with a view to the good of the whole we should be most likely to find justice, and in the ill-ordered State injustice: and, having found them, we might then decide which of the two is the happier. At present, I take it, we are fashioning the happy State, not piecemeal, or with a view of making a few happy citizens, but as a whole; and by-and-by we will proceed to view the opposite kind of State. Suppose that we were painting a statue, and some one came up to us and said, Why do you not put the most beautiful colours on the most beautiful parts of the body—the eyes ought to be purple, but you have made them black—to him we might fairly answer, Sir, you would not surely have us beautify the eyes to such a degree that they are no longer eyes; consider rather whether, by giving this and the other features their due proportion, we make the whole beautiful. And so I say to you, do not compel us to assign to the guardians a sort of happiness which will make them anything but guardians; for we too can clothe our husbandmen in royal apparel, and set crowns of gold on their heads, and bid them till the ground as much as they like, and no more. Our potters also might be allowed to repose on couches, and feast by the fireside, passing round the winecup, while their wheel is conveniently at hand, and working at pottery only as much as they like; in this way we might make every class happy—and then, as you imagine, the whole State would be happy. But do not put this idea into our heads; for, if we listen to you, the husbandman will be no longer a hubandman, the potter will cease to be a potter, and no one will have the character of any distinct class in the State. Now this is not of much consequence where the corruption of society, and pretension to be what you are not, is confined to cobblers; but when the guardians of the laws and of the government are only seemingly and not real guardians, then see how they turn the State upside down; and on the other hand they alone have the power of giving order and happiness to the State. We mean our guardians to be true saviours and not the destroyers of the State, whereas our opponent is thinking of peasants at a festival, who are enjoying a life of revelry, not of citizens who are doing their duty to the State. But, if so, we mean different things, and he is speaking of something which is not a State. And therefore we must consider whether in appointing our guardians we would look to their greatest happiness individually, or whether this principle of happiness does not rather reside in the State as a whole. But if the latter be the truth, then the guardians and auxiliaries, and all others equally with them, must be compelled or induced to do their own work in the best way. And thus the whole State will grow up in a noble order, and the several classes will receive the proportion of happiness which nature assigns to them.

I think that you are quite right.

I wonder whether you will agree with another remark which occurs to me.

What may that be?

There seem to be two causes of the deterioration of the arts.

What are they?

Wealth, I said, and poverty.

How do they act?

The process is as follows: When a potter becomes rich, will he, think you, any longer take the same pains with his art?

Certainly not.

He will grow more and more indolent and careless?

Very true.

And the result will be that he becomes a worse potter?

Yes; he greatly deteriorates.

But, on the other hand, if he has no money, and cannot provide himself with tools or instruments, he will not work equally well himself, nor will he teach his sons or apprentices to work equally well.

Certainly not.

Then, under the influence either of poverty or of wealth, workmen and their work are equally liable to degenerate?

That is evident.

Here, then, is a discovery of new evils, I said, against which the guardians will have to watch, or they will creep into the city unobserved.

What evils?

Wealth, I said, and poverty; the one is the parent of luxury and indolence, and the other of meanness and viciousness, and both of discontent.

That is very true, he replied; but still I should like to know, Socrates, how our city will be able to go to war, especially against an enemy who is rich and powerful, if deprived of the sinews of war.

There would certainly be a difficulty, I replied, in going to war with one such enemy; but there is no difficulty where there are two of them.

How so? he asked.

In the first place, I said, if we have to fight, our side will be trained warriors fighting against an army of rich men.

That is true, he said.

And do you not suppose, Adeimantus, that a single boxer who was perfect in his art would easily be a match for two stout and well-to-do gentlemen who were not boxers?

Hardly, if they came upon him at once.

What, not, I said, if he were able to run away and then turn and strike at the one who first came up? And supposing he were to do this several times under the heat of a scorching sun, might he not, being an expert, overturn more than one stout personage?

Certainly, he said, there would be nothing wonderful in that.

And yet rich men probably have a greater superiority in the science and practise of boxing than they have in military qualities.

Likely enough.

Then we may assume that our athletes will be able to fight with two or three times their own number?

I agree with you, for I think you right.

And suppose that, before engaging, our citizens send an embassy to one of the two cities, telling them what is the truth: Silver and gold we neither have nor are permitted to have, but you may; do you therefore come and help us in war, and take the spoils of the other city: Who, on hearing these words, would choose to fight against lean wiry dogs, rather than, with the dogs on their side, against fat and tender sheep?

That is not likely; and yet there might be a danger to the poor State if the wealth of many States were to be gathered into one.

But how simple of you to use the term State at all of any but our own!

Why so?

You ought to speak of other States in the plural number; not one of them is a city, but many cities, as they say in the game. For indeed any city, however small, is in fact divided into two, one the city of the poor, the other of the rich; these are at war with one another; and in either there are many smaller divisions, and you would be altogether beside the mark if you treated them all as a single State. But if you deal with them as many, and give the wealth or power or persons of the one to the others, you will always have a great many friends and not many enemies. And your State, while the wise order which has now been prescribed continues to prevail in her, will be the greatest of States, I do not mean to say in reputation or appearance, but in deed and truth, though she number not more than a thousand defenders. A single State which is her equal you will hardly find, either among Hellenes or barbarians, though many that appear to be as great and many times greater.

That is most true, he said.

And what, I said, will be best limit for our rulers to fix when they are considering the size of the State and the amount of territory which they are to include, and beyond which they will not go?

What limit would you propose?

I would allow the State to increase so far as is consistent with unity; that, I think, is the proper limit.

Very good, he said.

Here then, I said, is another order which will have to be conveyed to our guardians: Let our city be accounted neither large nor small, but one and self-sufficing.

And surely, said he, this is not a very severe order which we impose upon them.

And the other, said I, of which we were speaking before is lighter still,—I mean the duty of degrading the offspring of the guardians when inferior, and of elevating into the rank of guardians the offspring of the lower classes, when naturally superior. The intention was, that, in the case of the citizens generally, each individual should be put to the use for which nature intended him, one to one work, and then every man would do his own business, and be one and not many; and so the whole city would be one and not many.

Yes, he said; that is not so difficult.

The regulations which we are prescribing, my good Adeimantus, are not, as might be supposed, a number of great principles, but trifles all, if care be taken, as the saying is, of the one great thing,—a thing, however, which I would rather call, not great, but sufficient for our purpose.

What may that be? he asked.

Education, I said, and nurture: If our citizens are well educated, and grow into sensible men, they will easily see their way through all these, as well as other matter which I omit; such, for example, as marriage, the possession of women and the procreation of children, which will all follow the general principle that friends have all things in common, as the proverb says.

That will be the best way of settling them.

Also, I said, the State, if once started well, moves with accumulating force like a wheel. For good nurture and education implant good constitutions, and these good constitutions taking root in a good education improve more and more, and this improvement affects the breed in man as in other animals.

Very possibly, he said.

Then to sum up: This is the point to which, above all, the attention of our rulers should be directed,—that music and gymnastic be preserved in their original form, and no innovation made. They must do their utmost to maintain them intact. And when any one says that mankind most regard

"The newest song which the singers have,"

they will be afraid that he may be praising, not new songs, but a new kind of song; and this ought not to be praised, or conceived to be the meaning of the poet; for any musical innovation is full of danger to the whole State, and ought to be prohibited. So Damon tells me, and I can quite believe him;—he says that when modes of music change, the fundamental laws of the State always change with them.

Yes, said Adeimantus; and you may add my suffrage to Damon's and your own.

Then, I said, our guardians must lay the foundations of their fortress in music?

Yes, he said; the lawlessness of which you speak too easily steals in.

Yes, I replied, in the form of amusement; and at first sight it appears harmless.

Why, yes, he said, and there is no harm; were it not that little by little this spirit of licence, finding a home, imperceptibly penetrates into manners and customs; whence, issuing with greater force, it invades contracts between man and man, and from contracts goes on to laws and constitutions, in utter recklessness, ending at last, Socrates, by an over-throw of all rights, private as well as public.

Is that true? I said.

That is my belief, he replied.

Then, as I was saying, our youth should be trained from the first in a stricter system, for if amusements become lawless, and the youths themselves become lawless, they can never grow up into well-conducted and virtuous citizens.

Very true, he said.

And when they have made a good beginning in play, and by the help of music have gained the habit of good order, then this habit of order, in a manner how unlike the lawless play of the others! will accompany them in all their actions and be a principle of growth to them, and if there be any fallen places in the State will raise them up again.

Very true, he said.

Thus educated, they will invent for themselves any lesser rules which their predecessors have altogether neglected.

What do you mean?

I mean such things as these:—when the young are to be silent before their elders; how they are to show respect to them by standing and making them sit; what honour is due to parents; what garments or shoes are to be worn; the mode of dressing the hair; deportment and manners in general. You would agree with me?

Yes.

But there is, I think, small wisdom in legislating about such matters,—I doubt if it is ever done; nor are any precise written enactments about them likely to be lasting.

Impossible.

It would seem, Adeimantus, that the direction in which education starts a man, will determine his future life. Does not like always attract like?

To be sure.

Until some one rare and grand result is reached which may be good, and may be the reverse of good?

That is not to be denied.

And for this reason, I said, I shall not attempt to legislate further about them.

Naturally enough, he replied.

Well, and about the business of the agora, and the ordinary dealings between man and man, or again about agreements with artisans; about insult and injury, or the commence-ment of actions, and the appointment of juries, what would you say? there may also arise questions about any impositions and extractions of market and harbour dues which may be requried, and in general about the regulations of markets, police, harbours, and the like. But, oh heavens! shall we condescend to legislate on any of these particulars?

I think, he said, that there is no need to impose laws about them on good men; what regulations are necessary they will find out soon enough for themselves.

Yes, I said, my friend, if God will only preserve to them the laws which we have given them.

And without divine help, said Adeimantus, they will go on for ever making and mending their laws and their lives in the hope of attaining perfection.

You would compare them, I said, to those invalids who, having no self-restraint, will not leave off their habits of intemperance?

Exactly.

Yes, I said; and what a delightful life they lead! they are always doctoring and increasing and complicating their disorders, and always fancying that they will be cured by any nostrum which anybody advises them to try.

Such cases are very common, he said, with invalids of this sort.

Yes, I replied; and the charming thing is that they deem him their worst enemy who tells them the truth, which is simply that, unless they give up eating and drinking and wenching and idling, neither drug nor cautery nor spell nor amulet nor any other remedy will avail.

Charming! he replied. I see nothing charming in going into a passion with a man who tells you what is right.

These gentlemen, I said, do not seem to be in your good graces.

Assuredly not.

Nor would you praise the behaviour of States which act like the men whom I was just now describing. For are there not ill-ordered States in which the citizens are forbidden under pain of death to alter the constitution; and yet he who most sweetly courts those who live under this régime and indulges them and fawns upon them and is skilful in anticipating and gratifying their humours is held to be a great and good statesman—do not these States resemble the persons whom I was describing?

Yes, he said; the States are as bad as the men; and I am very far from praising them.

But do you not admire, I said, the coolness and dexterity of these ready ministers of political corruption?

Yes, he said, I do; but not of all of them, for there are some whom the applause of the multitude has deluded into the belief that they are really statesmen, and these are not much to be admired.

What do you mean? I said; you should have more feeling for them. When a man cannot measure, and a great many others who cannot measure declare that he is four cubits high, can he help believing what they say?

Nay, he said, certainly not in that case.

Well, then, do not be angry with them; for are they not as good as a play, trying their hand at paltry reforms such as I was describing; they are always fancying that by legislation they will make an end of frauds in contracts, and the other rascalities which I was mentioning, not knowing that they are in reality cutting off the heads of a hydra?

Yes, he said; that is just what they are doing.

I conceive, I said, that the true legislator will not trouble himself with this class of enactments whether concerning laws or the constitution either in an ill-ordered or in a well-ordered State; for in the former they are quite useless, and in the latter there will be no difficulty in devising them; and many of them will naturally flow out of our previous regulations.

What, then, he said, is still remaining to us of the work of legislation?

Nothing to us, I replied; but to Apollo, the God of Delphi, there remains the ordering of the greatest and noblest and chiefest things of all.

Which are they? he said.

The institution of temples and sacrifices, and the entire service of gods, demigods, and heroes; also the ordering of the repositories of the dead, and the rites which have to be observed by him who would propitiate the inhabitants of the world below. These are matters of which we are ignorant ourselves, and as founders of a city we should be unwise in trusting them to any interpreter but our ancestral deity. He is the god who sits in the centre, on the navel of the earth, and he is the interpreter of religion to all mankind.

You are right, and we will do as you propose.

But where, amid all this, is justice? son of Ariston, tell me where. Now that our city has been made habitable, light a candle and search, and get your brother and Polemarchus and the rest of our friends to help, and let us see where in it we can discover justice and where injustice, and in what they differ from one another, and which of them the man who would be happy should have for his portion, whether seen or unseen by gods and men.

Nonsense, said Glaucon: did you not promise to search yourself, saying that for you not to help justice in her need would be an impiety?

I do not deny that I said so, and as you remind me, I will be as good as my word; but you must join.

We will, he replied.

Well, then, I hope to make the discovery in this way: I mean to begin with the assumption that our State, if rightly ordered, is perfect.

That is most certain.

And being perfect, is therefore wise and valiant and temperate and just.

That is likewise clear.

And whichever of these qualities we find in the State, the one which is not found will be the residue?

Very good.

If there were four things, and we were searching for one of them, wherever it might be, the one sought for might be known to us from the first, and there would be no further trouble; or we might know the other three first, and then the fourth would clearly be the one left.

Very true, he said.

And is not a similar method to be pursued about the virtues, which are also four in number?

Clearly.

First among the virtues found in the State, wisdom comes into view, and in this I detect a certain peculiarity.

What is that?

The State which we have been describing is said to be wise as being good in counsel?

Very true.

And good counsel is clearly a kind of knowledge, for not by ignorance, but by knowledge, do men counsel well?

Clearly.

And the kinds of knowledge in a State are many and diverse?

Of course.

There is the knowledge of the carpenter; but is that the sort of knowledge which gives a city the title of wise and good in counsel?

Certainly not; that would only give a city the reputation of skill in carpentering.

Then a city is not to be called wise because possessing a knowledge which counsels for the best about wooden implements?

Certainly not.

Nor by reason of a knowledge which advises about brazen pots, I said, nor as possessing any other similar knowledge?

Not by reason of any of them, he said.

Nor yet by reason of a knowledge which cultivates the earth; that would give the city the name of agricultural?

Yes.

Well, I said, and is there any knowledge in our recently founded State among any of the citizens which advises, not about any particular thing in the State, but about the whole, and considers how a State can best deal with itself and with other States?

There certainly is.

And what is this knowledge, and among whom is it found? I asked.

It is the knowledge of the guardians, he replied, and is found among those whom we were just now describing as perfect guardians.

And what is the name which the city derives from the possession of this sort of knowledge?

The name of good in counsel and truly wise.

And will there be in our city more of these true guardians or more smiths?

The smiths, he replied, will be far more numerous.

Will not the guardians be the smallest of all the classes who receive a name from the profession of some kind of knowledge?

Much the smallest.

And so by reason of the smallest part or class, and of the knowledge which resides in this presiding and ruling part of itself, the whole State, being thus constituted according to nature, will be wise; and this, which has the only knowledge worthy to be called wisdom, has been ordained by nature to be of all classes the least.

Most true.

Thus, then, I said, the nature and place in the State of one of the four virtues has some-how or other been discovered.

And, in my humble opinion, very satisfactorily discovered, he replied.

Again, I said, there is no difficulty in seeing the nature of courage, and in what part that quality resides which gives the name of courageous to the State.

How do you mean?

Why, I said, every one who calls any State courageous or cowardly, will be thinking of the part which fights and goes out to war on the State's behalf.

No one, he replied, would ever think of any other.

Certainly not.

The rest of the citizens may be courageous or may be cowardly but their courage or cowardice will not, as I conceive, have the effect of making the city either the one or the other.

The city will be courageous in virtue of a portion of herself which preserves under all circumstances that opinion about the nature of things to be feared and not to be feared in which our legislator educated them; and this is what you term courage.

I should like to hear what you are saying once more, for I do not think that I perfectly understand you.

I mean that courage is a kind of salvation.

Salvation of what?

Of the opinion respecting things to be feared, what they are and of what nature, which the law implants through education; and I mean by the words "under all circumstances" to intimate that in pleasure or in pain, or under the influence of desire or fear, a man preserves, and does not lose this opinion. Shall I give you an illustration?

If you please.

You know, I said, that dyers, when they want to dye wool for making the true sea-purple, begin by selecting their white colour first; this they prepare and dress with much care and pains, in order that the white ground may take the purple hue in full perfection. The dyeing then proceeds; and whatever is dyed in this manner becomes a fast colour, and no washing either with lyes or without them can take away the bloom. But, when the ground has not been duly prepared, you will have noticed how poor is the look either of purple or of any other colour.

Yes, he said; I know that they have a washed-out and ridiculous appearance.

Then now, I said, you will understand what our object was in selecting our soldiers, and educating them in music and gymnastic; we were contriving influences which would prepare them to take the dye of the laws in perfection, and the colour of their opinion about dangers and of every other opinion was to be indelibly fixed by their nurture and training, not to be washed away by such potent lyes as pleasure—mightier agent far in washing the soul than any soda or lye; or by sorrow, fear, and desire, the mightiest of all other solvents. And this sort of universal saving power of true opinion in conformity with law about real and false dangers I call and maintain to be courage, unless you disagree.

But I agree, he replied; for I suppose that you mean to exclude mere uninstructed courage, such as that of a wild beast or of a slave—this, in your opinion, is not the courage which the law ordains, and ought to have another name.

Most certainly.

Then I may infer courage to be such as you describe?

Why, yes, said I, you may, and if you add the words "of a citizen," you will not be far wrong;— hereafter, if you like, we will carry the examination further, but at present we are seeking not for courage but justice; and for the purpose of our enquiry we have said enough.

You are right, he replied.

Two virtues remain to be discovered in the State—first temperance, and then justice which is the end of our search.

Very true.

Now, can we find justice without troubling ourselves about temperance?

I do not know how that can be accomplished, he said, nor do I desire that justice should be brought to light and temperance lost sight of; and therefore I wish that you would do me the favour of considering temperance first.

Certainly, I replied, I should not be justified in refusing your request.

Then consider, he said.

Yes, I replied; I will; and as far as I can at present see, the virtue of temperance has more of the nature of harmony and symphony than the preceding.

How so? he asked.

Temperance, I replied, is the ordering or controlling of certain pleasures and desires; this is curiously enough implied in the saying of "a man being his own master"; and other traces of the same notion may be found in language.

No doubt, he said.

There is something ridiculous in the expression "master of himself"; for the master is also the servant and the servant the master; and in all these modes of speaking the same person is denoted.

Certainly.

The meaning is, I believe, that in the human soul there is a better and also a worse principle; and when the better has the worse under control, then a man is said to be master of himself; and this is a term of praise: but when, owing to evil education or association, the better principle, which is also the smaller, is overwhelmed by the greater mass of the worse—in this case he is blamed and is called the salve of self and unprincipled.

Yes, there is reason in that.

And now, I said, look at our newly created State, and there you will find one of these two conditions realised; for the State, as you will acknowledge, may be justly called master of itself, if the words "temperance" and "self-mastery" truly express the rule of the better part over the worse.

Yes, he said, I see that what you say is true.

Let me further note that the manifold and complex pleasures and desires and pains are generally found in children and women and servants, and in the freemen so called who are of the lowest and more numerous class.

Certainly, he said.

Whereas the simple and moderate desires which follow reason, and are under the guidance of mind and true opinion, are to be found only in a few, and those the best born and best educated.

Very true.

These two, as you may perceive, have a place in our State; and the meaner desires of the many are held down by the virtuous desires and wisdom of the few.

That I perceive, he said.

Then if there be any city which may be described as master of its own pleasures and desires, and master of itself, ours may claim such a designation?

Certainly, he replied.

It may also be called temperate, and for the same reasons?

Yes.

And if there be any State in which rulers and subjects will be agreed as to the question who are to rule, and again will be our State?

Undoubtedly.

And the citizens being thus agreed among themselves, in which class will temperance be found—in the rulers or in the subjects?

In both, as I should imagine, he replied.

Do you observe that we were not far wrong in our guess that temperance was a sort of harmony?

Why so?

Why, because temperance is unlike courage and wisdom, each of which resides in a part only, the one making the State wise and the other valiant; not so temperance, which extends to the whole, and runs through all the notes of the scale, and produces a harmony of the weaker and the stronger and the middle class, whether you suppose them to be stronger or weaker in wisdom or power or numbers or wealth, or anything else. Most truly then may we deem temperance to be the agreement of the naturally superior and inferior, as to the right to rule of either, both in states and individuals.

I entirely agree with you.

And so, I said, we may consider three out of the four virtues to have been discovered in our State. The last of those qualities which make a state virtuous must be justice, if we only knew what that was.

The inference is obvious.

The time then has arrived, Glaucon, when, like huntsmen, we should surround the cover, and look sharp that justice does not steal away, and pass out of sight and escape us; for beyond a doubt she is somewhere in this country: watch therefore and strive to catch a sight of her, and if you see her first, let me know.

Would that I could! but you should regard me rather as a follower who has just eyes enough to see what you show him—that is about as much as I am good for.

Offer up a prayer with me and follow.

I will, but you must show me the way.

Here is no path, I said, and the wood is dark and perplexing; still we must push on.

Let us push on.

Here I saw something: Halloo! I said, I begin to perceive a track, and I believe that the quarry will not escape.

Good news, he said.

Truly, I said, we are stupid fellows.

Why so?

Why, my good sir, at the beginning of our enquiry, ages ago, there was justice tumbling out at our feet, and we never saw her; nothing could be more ridiculous. Like people who go about looking for what they have in their hands—that was the way with us—we looked not at what we were seeking, but at what was far off in the distance; and therefore, I suppose, we missed her.

What do you mean?

I mean to say that in reality for a long time past we have been talking of justice, and have failed to recognise her.

I grow impatient at the length of your exordium.

Well then, tell me, I said, whether I am right or not: You remember the original principle which we were always laying down at the foundation of the State, that one man should practise one thing only, the thing to which his nature was best adapted;—now justice is this principle of a part of it.

Yes, we often said that one man should do one thing only.

Further, we affirmed that justice was doing one's own business, and not being a busy-body; we said so again and again, and many others have said the same to us.

Yes, we said so.

Then to do one's own business in a certain way may be assumed to be justice. Can you tell me whence I derive this inference?

I cannot, but I should like to be told.

Because I think that this is the only virtue which remains in the State when the other virtues of temperance and courage and wisdom are abstracted; and, that this is the ultimate cause and condition of the existence of all of them, and while remaining in them is also their preservative; and we were saying that if the three were discovered by us, justice would be the fourth or remaining one.

That follows of necessity.

If we are asked to determine which of these four qualities by its presence contributes most to the excellence of the State, whether the agreement of rulers and subjects, or the preservation in the soldiers of the opinion which the law ordains about the true nature of dangers, or wisdom and watchfulness in the rulers, or whether this other which I am mentioning, and which is found in children and women, slave and freeman, artisan, ruler, subject,—the quality, I mean, of every one doing his own work, and not being a busybody, would claim the palm—the question is not so easily answered.

Certainly, he replied, there would be a difficulty in saying which.

Then the power of each individual in the State to do his own work appears to compete with the other political virtues, wisdom, temperance, courage.

Yes, he said.

And the virtue which enters into this competition is justice?

Exactly.

Let us look at the question from another point of view: Are not the rulers in a State those to whom you would entrust the office of determining suits at law?

Certainly.

And are suits decided on any other ground but that a man may neither take what is another's, nor be deprived of what is his own?

Yes; that is their principle.

Which is a just principle?

Yes.

Then on this view also justice will be admitted to be the having and doing what is a man's own, and belongs to him?

Very true.

Think, now, and say whether you agree with me or not. Suppose a carpenter to be doing the business of a cobbler, or a cobbler of a carpenter; and suppose them to exchange their implements or their duties, or the same person to be doing the work of both, or whatever be the change; do you think that any great harm would result to the State?

Not much.

But when the cobbler or any other man whom nature designed to be a trader, having his heart lifted up by wealth or strength or the number of his followers, or any like advantage, attempts to force his way into the class of warriors, or a warrior into that of legislators and guardians, for which he is unfitted, and either to take the implements or the duties of the other; or when one man is trader, legislator, and warrior all in one, then I think you will agree with me in saying that this interchange and this meddling of one with another is the ruin of the State.

Most true.

Seeing then, I said, that there are three distinct classes, any meddling of one with another, or the change of one into another, is the greatest harm to the State, and may be most justly termed evil-doing?

Precisely.

And the greatest degree of evil-doing to one's own city would be termed by you injustice?

Certainly.

This then is injustice; and on the other hand when the trader, the auxiliary, and the guardian each do their own business, that is justice, and will make the city just.

I agree with you.

We will not, I said, be over-positive as yet; but if, on trial, this conception of justice be verified in the individual as well as in the State, there will be no longer any room for doubt; if it be not verified, we must have a fresh enquiry. First let us complete the old investigation, which we began, as you remember, under the impression that, if we could previously examine justice on the larger scale, there would be less difficulty in discerning her in the individual. That larger example appeared to be the State, and accordingly we constructed as good a one as we could, knowing well that in the good State justice would be found. Let the discovery which we made be now applied to the individual—if they agree, we shall be satisfied; or, if there be a difference in the individual, we will come back to the State and have another trial of the theory. The friction of the two when rubbed together may possibly strike a light in which justice will shine forth, and the vision which is then revealed we will fix in our souls.

That will be in regular course; let us do as you say.

I proceeded to ask: When two things, a greater and less, are called by the same name, are they like or unlike in so far as they are called the same?

Like, he replied.

The just man then, if we regard the idea of justice only, will be like the just State?

He will.

And a State was thought by us to be just when the three classes in the State severally did their own business; and also thought to be temperate and valiant and wise by reason of certain other affections and qualities of these same classes?

True, he said.

And so of the individual; we may assume that he has the same three principles in his own soul which are found in the State; and he may be rightly described in the same terms, because he is affected in the same manner?

Certainly, he said.

Once more then, O my friend, we have alighted upon an easy question—whether the soul has these three principles or not?

An easy question! Nay, rather, Socrates, the proverb holds that hard is the good.

Very true, I said; and I do not think that the method which we are employing is at all adequate to the accurate solution of this question; the true method is another and a longer one. Still we may arrive at a solution not below the level of the previous enquiry.

May we not be satisfied with that? he said;—under the circumstances, I am quite content.

I too, I replied, shall be extremely well satisfied.

Then faint not in pursuing the speculation, he said.

Must we not acknowledge, I said, that in each of us there are the same principles and habits which there are in the State; and that from the individual they pass into the State?—how else can they come there? Take the quality of passion or spirit;—it would be ridiculous to imagine that this quality, when found in States, is not derived from the individuals who are supposed to possess it, e.g. the Thracians, Scythians, and in general the northern nations; and the same may be said of the love of knowledge, which is the special characteristic of our part of the world, or of the love of money, which may, with equal truth, be attributed to the Phoenicians and Egyptians.

Exactly so, he said.

There is no difficulty in understanding this.

None whatever.

But the question is not quite so easy when we proceed to ask whether these principles are three or one; whether, that is to say, we learn with one part of our nature, are angry with another, and with a third part desire the satisfaction of our natural appetites; or whether the whole soul comes into play in each sort of action—to determine that is the difficulty.

Yes, he said; there lies the difficulty.

Then let us now try and determine whether they are the same or different.

How can we? he asked.

I replied as follows: The same thing clearly cannot act or be acted upon in the same part or in relation to the same thing at the same time, in contrary ways; and therefore whenever this contradiction occurs in things apparently the same, we know that they are really not the same, but different.

Good.

For example, I said, can the same thing be at rest and in motion at the same time in the same part?

Impossible.

Still, I said, let us have a more precise statement of terms, lest we should hereafter fall out by the way. Imagine the case of a man who is standing and also moving his hands and his head, and suppose a person to say that one and the same person is in motion and at rest at the same moment—to such a mode of speech we should object, and should rather say that one part of him is in motion while another is at rest.

Very true.

And suppose the objector to refine still further, and to draw the nice distinction that not only parts of tops, but whole tops, when they spin round with their pegs fixed on the spot, are at rest and in motion at the same time (and he may say the same of anything which revolves in the same spot), his objection would not be admitted by us, because in such cases things are not at rest and in motion in the same parts of themselves; we should rather say that they have both an axis and a circumference, and that the axis stands still, for there is no deviation from the perpendicular; and that the circumference goes round. But if, while revolving, the axis inclines either to the right or left, forwards or backwards, then in no point of view can they be at rest.

That is the correct mode of describing them, he replied.

Then none of these objections will confuse us, or incline us to believe that the same thing at the same time, in the same part or in relation to the same thing, can act or be acted upon in contrary ways.

Certainly not, according to my way of thinking.

Yet, I said, that we may not be compelled to examine all such objections, and prove at length that they are untrue, let us assume their absurdity, and go forward on the understanding that hereafter, if this assumption turn out to be untrue, all the consequences which follow shall be withdrawn.

Yes, he said, that will be the best way.

Well, I said, would you not allow that assent and dissent, desire and aversion, attraction and repulsion, are all of them opposites, whether they are regarded as active or passive (for that makes no difference in the fact of their opposition)?

Yes, he said, they are opposites.

Well, I said, and hunger and thirst, and the desires in general, and again willing and wishing,—all these you would refer to the classes already mentioned. You would say— would you not?—that the soul of him who desires is seeking after the object of his desires; or that he is drawing to himself the thing which he wishes to possess: or again, when a person wants anything to be given him, his mind, longing for the realisation of his desires, intimates his wish to have it by a nod of assent, as if he had been asked a question?

Very true.

And what would you say of unwillingness and dislike and the absence of desire; should not these be referred to the opposite class of repulsion and rejection?

Certainly.

Admitting this to be true of desire generally, let us suppose a particular class of desires, and out of these we will select hunger and thirst, as they are termed, which are the most obvious of them?

Let us take that class, he said.

The object of one is food, and of the other drink?

Yes.

And here comes the point: is not thirst the desire which the soul has of drink, and of drink only; not of drink qualified by anything else; for example, warm or cold, or much or little, or, in a word, drink of any particular sort: but if the thirst be accompanied by heat, then the desire is of cold drink; or, if accompanied by cold, then of warm drink; or, if the thirst be excessive, then the drink which is desired will be excessive; or, if not great, the quantity of drink will also be small: but thirst pure and simple will desire drink pure and simple, which is the natural satisfaction of thirst, as food is of hunger?

Yes, he said; the simple desire is, as you say, in every case of the simple object, and the qualified desire of the qualified object.

But here a confusion may arise; and I should wish to guard against an opponent starting up and saying that no man desires drink only, but good drink, or food only, but good food; for good is the universal object of desire, and thirst being a desire, will necessarily be thirst after good drink; and the same is true of every other desire.

Yes, he replied, the opponent might have something to say.

Nevertheless I should still maintain, that of relatives some have a quality attached to either term of the relation; others are simple and have their correlatives simple.

I do not know what you mean.

Well, you know of course that the greater is relative to the less?

Certainly.

And the much greater to the much less?

Yes.

And the sometime greater to the sometime less, and the greater that is to be to the less that is to be?

Certainly, he said.

And so of more and less, and of other correlative terms, such as the double and the half, or again, the heavier and the lighter, the swifter and the slower; and of hot and cold, and of any other relatives;—is not this true of all of them?

Yes.

And does not the same principle hold in the sciences? The object of science is knowledge (assuming that to be the true definition), but the object of a particular science is a particular kind of knowledge; I mean, for example, that the science of house-building is a kind of knowledge which is defined and distinguished from other kinds and is therefore termed architecture.

Certainly.

Because it has a particular quality which no other has?

Yes.

And it has this particular quality because it has an object of a particular kind; and this is true of the other arts and sciences?

Yes.

Now, then, if I have made myself clear, you will understand my original meaning in what I said about relatives. My meaning was, that if one term of a relation is taken alone, the other is taken alone; if one term is qualified, the other is also qualified. I do not mean to say that relatives may not be disparate, or that the science of health is healthy, or of disease necessarily diseased, or that the sciences of good and evil are therefore good and evil; but only that, when the term science is no longer used absolutely, but has a qualified object which in this case is the nature of health and disease, it becomes defined, and is hence called not merely science, but the science of medicine.

I quite understand, and I think as you do.

Would you not say that thirst is one of these essentially relative terms, having clearly a relation—

Yes, thirst is relative to drink.

And a certain kind of thirst is relative to a certain kind of drink; but thirst taken alone is neither of much nor little, nor of good nor bad, nor of any particular kind of drink, but of drink only?

Certainly.

Then the soul of the thirsty one, in so far as he is thirsty, desires only drink; for this he yearns and tries to obtain it?

That is plain.

And if you suppose something which pulls a thirsty soul away from drink, that must be different from the thirsty principle which draws him like a beast to drink; for, as we were saying, the same thing cannot at the same time with the same part of itself act in contrary ways about the same.

Impossible.

No more than you can say that the hands of the archer push and pull the bow at the same time, but what you say is that one hand pushes and the other pulls.

Exactly so, he replied.

And might a man be thirsty, and yet unwilling to drink?

Yes, he said, it constantly happens.

And in such a case what is one to say? Would you not say that there was something in the soul bidding a man to drink, and something else forbidding him, which is other and stronger than the principle which bids him?

I should say so.

And the forbidding principle is derived from reason, and that which bids and attracts proceeds from passion and disease?

Clearly.

Then we may fairly assume that they are two, and that they differ from one another; the one with which a man reasons, we may call the rational principle of the soul, the other, with which he loves and hungers and thirsts and feels the flutterings of any other desire, may be termed the irrational or appetitive, the ally of sundry pleasures and satisfactions?

Yes, he said, we may fairly assume them to be different.

Then let us finally determine that there are two principles existing in the soul. And what of passion, or spirit? Is it a third, or akin to one of the preceding?

I should be inclined to say—akin to desire.

Well, I said, there is a story which I remember to have heard, and in which I put faith. The story is, that Leontius, the son of Aglaion, coming up one day from the Piraeus, under the north wall on the outside, observed some dead bodies lying on the ground at the place of execution. He felt a desire to see them, and also a dread and abhorrence of them; for a time he struggled and covered his eyes, but at length the desire got the better of him; and forcing them open, he ran up to the dead bodies, saying, Look, ye wretches, take your fill of the fair sight.

I have heard the story myself, he said.

The moral of the tale is, that anger at times goes to war with desire, as though they were two distinct things.

Yes; that is the meaning, he said.

And are there not many other cases in which we observe that when a man's desires violently prevail over his reason, he reviles himself, and is angry at the violence within him, and that in this struggle, which is like the struggle of factions in a State, his spirit is on the side of his reason;—but for the passionate or spirited element to take part with the desires when reason decides that she should not be opposed, is a sort of thing which I believe that you never observed occurring in yourself, nor, as I should imagine, in any one else?

Certainly not.

Suppose that a man thinks he has done a wrong to another, the nobler he is the less able is he to feel indignant at any suffering, such as hunger, or cold, or any other pain which the injured person may inflict upon him—these he deems to be just, and, as I say, his anger refuses to be excited by them.

True, he said.

But when he thinks that the is the sufferer of the wrong, then he boils and chafes, and is on the side of what he believes to be justice; and because he suffers hunger or cold or other pain he is only the more determined to persevere and conquer. His noble spirit will not be quelled until he either slays or is slain; or until he hears the voice of the shepherd, that is, reason, bidding his dog bark no more.

The illustration is perfect, he replied; and in our State, as we were saying, the auxiliaries were to be dogs, and to hear the voice of the rulers, who are their shepherds.

I perceive, I said, that you quite understand me; there is, however, a further point which I wish you to consider.

What point?

You remember that passion or spirit appeared at first sight to be a kind of desire, but now we should say quite the contrary; for in the conflict of the soul spirit is arrayed on the side of the rational principle.

Most assuredly.

But a further question arises: Is passion different from reason also, or only a kind of reason; in which latter case, instead of three principles in the soul, there will only be two, the rational and the concupiscent; or rather, as the State was composed of three classes, traders, auxiliaries, counsellors, so may there not be in the individual soul a third element which is passion or spirit, and when not corrupted by bad education is the natural auxiliary of reason?

Yes, he said, there must be a third.

Yes, I replied, if passion, which has already been shown to be different from desire, turn out also to be different from reason.

But that is easily proved;—We may observe even in young children that they are full of spirit almost as soon as they are born, whereas some of them never seem to attain to the use of reason, and most of them late enough.

Excellent, I said, and you may see passion equally in brute animals, which is a further proof of the truth of what you are saying. And we may once more appeal to the words of Homer, which have been already quoted by us,

"He smote his breast, and thus rebuked his soul";

for in this verse Homer has clearly supposed the power which reasons about the better and worse to be different from the unreasoning anger which is rebuked by it.

Very true, he said.

And so, after much tossing, we have reached land, and are fairly agreed that the same principles which exist in the State exist also in the individual, and that they are three in number.

Exactly.

Must we not then infer that the individual is wise in the same way, and in virtue of the same quality which makes the State wise?

Certainly.

Also that the same quality which constitutes courage in the State constitutes courage in the individual; and that both the State and the individual bear the same relation to all the other virtues?

Assuredly.

And the individual will be acknowledged by us to be just in the same way in which the State is just?

That follows, of course.

We cannot but remember that the justice of the State consisted in each of the three classes doing the work of its own class?

We are not very likely to have forgotten, he said.

We must recollect that the individual in whom the several qualities of his nature do their own work will be just, and will do his own work?

Yes, he said, we must remember that too.

And ought not the rational principle, which is wise, and has the care of the whole soul, to rule, and the passionate or spirited principle to be the subject and ally?

Certainly.

And, as we were saying, the united influence of music and gymnastic will bring them into accord, nerving and sustaining the reason with noble words and lessons, and moderating and soothing and civilizing the wildness of passion by harmony and rhythm?

Quite true, he said.

And these two, thus nurtured and educated, and having learned truly to know their own functions, will rule over the concupiscent, which in each of us is the largest part of the soul and by nature most insatiable of gain; over this they will keep guard, lest, waxing great and strong with the fulness of bodily pleasures, as they are termed, the concupiscent soul, no longer confined to her own sphere, should attempt to enslave and rule those who are not her natural-born subjects, and overturn the whole life of man?

Very true, he said.

Both together will they not be the best defenders of the whole soul and the whole body against attacks from without; the one counselling, and the other fighting under his leader, and courageously executing his commands and counsels?

True.

And he is to be deemed courageous whose spirit retains in pleasure and in pain the commands of reason about what he ought or ought not to fear?

Right, he replied.

And him we call wise who has in him that little part which rules, and which proclaims these commands; that part too being supposed to have a knowledge of what is for the interest of each of the three parts and of the whole?

Assuredly.

And would you not say that he is temperate who has these same elements in friendly harmony, in whom the one ruling principle of reason, and the two subject ones of spirit and desire are equally agreed that reason ought to rule, and do not rebel?

Certainly, he said, that is the true account of temperance whether in the State or individual.

And surely, I said, we have explained again and again how and by virtue of what quality a man will be just.

That is very certain.

And is justice dimmer in the individual, and is her form different, or is she the same which we found her to be in the State?

There is no difference in my opinion, he said.

Because, if any doubt is still lingering in our minds, a few commonplace instances will satisfy us of the truth of what I am saying.

What sort of instances do you mean?

If the case is put to us, must we not admit that the just State, or the man who is trained in the principles of such a State, will be less likely than the unjust to make away with a deposit of gold or silver? Would any one deny this?

No one, he replied.

Will the just man or citizen ever be guilty of sacrilege or theft, or treachery either to his friends or to his country?

Never.

Neither will he ever break faith where there have been oaths or agreements?

Impossible.

No one will be less likely to commit adultery, or to dishonour his father and mother, or to fail in his religious duties?

No one.

And the reason is that each part of him is doing its own business, whether in ruling or being ruled?

Exactly so.

Are you satisfied then that the quality which makes such men and such states is justice, or do you hope to discover some other?

Not I, indeed.

Then our dream has been realized; and the suspicion which we entertained at the beginning of our work of construction, that some divine power must have conducted us to a primary form of justice, has now been verified?

Yes, certainly.

And the division of labour which required the carpenter and the shoemaker and the rest of the citizens to be doing each his own business, and not another's, was a shadow of justice, and for that reason it was of use?

Clearly.

But in reality justice was such as we were describing, being concerned however, not with the outward man, but with the inward, which is the true self and concernment of man: for the just man does not permit the several elements within him to interfere with one another, or any of them to do the work of others,—he sets in order his own inner life, and is his own master and his own law, and at peace with himself; and when he has bound together the three principles within him, which may be compared to the higher, lower, and middle notes of the scale, and the intermediate intervals—when he has bound all these together, and is no longer many, but has become one entirely temperate and perfectly adjusted nature, then he proceeds to act, if he has to act, whether in a matter of property, or in the treatment of the body, or in some affair of politics or private business; always thinking and calling that which preserves and co-operates with this harmonious condition, just and good action, and the knowledge which presides over it, wisdom, and that which at any time impairs this condition, he will call unjust action, and the opinion which presides over it ignorance.

You have said the exact truth, Socrates.

Very good; and if we were to affirm that we had discovered the just man and the just State, and the nature of justice in each of them, we should not be telling a falsehood?

Most certainly not.

May we say so, then?

Let us say so.

And now, I said, injustice has to be considered.

Clearly.

Must not injustice be a strife which arises among the three principles—a meddlesomeness, and interference, and rising up of a part of the soul against the whole, an assertion of unlawful authority, which is made by a rebellious subject against a true prince, of whom he is the natural vassal,—what is all this confusion and delusion but injustice, and intemperance and cowardice and ignorance, and every form of vice?

Exactly so.

And if the nature of justice and injustice be known, then the meaning of acting unjustly and being unjust, or, again, of acting justly, will also be perfectly clear?

What do you mean? he said.

Why, I said, they are like disease and health; being in the soul just what disease and health are in the body.

How so? he said.

Why, I said, that which is healthy causes health, and that which is unhealthy causes disease.

Yes.

And just actions cause justice, and unjust actions cause injustice?

That is certain.

And the creation of health is the institution of a natural order and government of one by another in the parts of the body; and the creation of disease is the production of a state of things at variance with this natural order?

True.

And is not the creation of justice the institution of a natural order and government of one by another in the parts of the soul, and the creation of injustice the production of a state of things at variance with the natural order?

Exactly so, he said.

Then virtue is the health and beauty and well-being of the soul, and vice the disease and weakness and deformity of the same?

True.

And do not good practices lead to virtue, and evil practices to vice?

Assuredly.

Still our old question of the comparative advantage of justice and injustice has not been answered: Which is the more profitable, to be just and act justly and practise virtue, whether seen or unseen of gods and men, or to be unjust and act unjustly, if only unpunished and unreformed?

In my judgment, Socrates, the question has now become ridiculous. We know that, when the bodily constitution is gone, life is no longer endurable, though pampered with all kinds of meats and drinks, and having all wealth and all power; and shall we be told that when the very essence of the vital principle is undermined and corrupted, life is still worth having to a man, if only he be allowed to do whatever he likes with the single exception that he is not to acquire justice and virtue, or to escape from injustice and vice; assuming them both to be such as we have described?

Yes, I said, the question is, as you say, ridiculous. Still, as we are near the spot at which we may see the truth in the clearest manner with our own eyes, let us not faint by the way.

Certainly not, he replied.

Come up hither, I said, and behold the various forms of vice, those of them, I mean, which are worth looking at.

I am following you, he replied: proceed.

I said, The argument seems to have reached a height from which, as from some tower of speculation, a man may look down and see that virtue is one, but that the forms of vice are innumerable; there being four special ones which are deserving of note.

What do you mean? he said.

I mean, I replied, that there appear to be as many forms of the soul as there are distinct forms of the State.

How many?

There are five of the State, and five of the soul, I said.

What are they?

The first, I said, is that which we have been describing, and which may be said to have two names, monarchy and aristocracy, accordingly as rule is exercised by one distinguished man or by many.

True, he replied.

But I regard the two names as describing one form only; for whether the government is in the hands of one or many, if the governors have been trained in the manner which we have supposed, the fundamental laws of the State will be maintained.

That is true, he replied.

BOOK V

Such is the good and true City or State, and the good and true man is of the same pattern; and if this is right every other is wrong; and the evil is one which affects not only the ordering of the State, but also the regulation of the individual soul, and is exhibited in four forms.

What are they? he said.

I was proceeding to tell the order in which the four evil forms appeared to me to succeed one another, when Polemarchus, who was sitting a little way off, just beyond Adeimantus, began to whisper to him: stretching forth his hand, he took hold of the upper part of his coat by the shoulder, and drew him towards him, leaning forward himself so as to be quite close and saying something in his ear, of which I only caught the words, "Shall we let him off, or what shall we do?"

Certainly not, said Adeimantus, raising his voice.

Who is it, I said, whom you are refusing to let off?

You, he said.

I repeated, Why am I especially not to be let off?

Why, he said, we think that you are lazy, and mean to cheat us out of a whole chapter which is a very important part of the story; and you fancy that we shall not notice your airy way of proceeding; as if it were self-evident to everybody, that in the matter of women and children "friends have all things in common."

And was I not right, Adeimantus?

Yes, he said; but what is right in this particular case, like everything else, requires to be explained; for community may be of many kinds. Please, therefore, to say what sort of community you mean. We have been long expecting that you would tell us something about the family life of your citizens—how they will bring children into the world, and rear them when they have arrived, and, in general, what is the nature of this community of women and children—for we are of opinion that the right or wrong management of such matters will have a great and paramount influence on the State for good or for evil. And now, since the question is still undetermined, and you are taking in hand another State, we have resolved, as you heard, not to let you go until you give an account of all this.

To that resolution, said Glaucon, you may regard me as saying Agreed.

And without more ado, said Thrasymachus, you may consider us all to be equally agreed.

I said, You know not what you are doing in thus assailing me: What an argument are you raising about the State! Just as I thought that I had finished, and was only too glad that I had laid this question to sleep, and was reflecting how fortunate I was in your acceptance of what I then said, you ask me to begin again at the very foundation, ignorant of what a hornet's nest of words you are stirring. Now I foresaw this gathering trouble, and avoided it.

For what purpose do you conceive that we have come here, said Thrasymachus,—to look for gold, or to hear discourse?

Yes, but discourse should have a limit.

Yes, Socrates, said Glaucon, and the whole of life is the only limit which wise men assign to the hearing of such discourses. But never mind about us; take heart yourself and answer the question in your own way: What sort of community of women and children is this which is to prevail among our guardians? and how shall we manage the period between birth and education, which seems to require the greatest care? Tell us how these things will be.

Yes, my simple friend, but the answer is the reverse of easy; many more doubts arise about this than about our previous conclusions. For the practicability of what is said may be doubted; and looked at in another point of view, whether the scheme, if ever so practicable, would be for the best, is also doubtful. Hence I feel a reluctance to approach the subject, lest our aspiration, my dear friend, should turn out to be a dream only.

Fear not, he replied, for your audience will not be hard upon you; they are not skeptical or hostile.

I said: My good friend, I suppose that you mean to encourage me by these words.

Yes, he said.

Then let me tell you that you are doing just the reverse; the encouragement which you offer would have been all very well had I myself believed that I knew what I was talking about: to declare the truth about matters of high interest which a man honours and loves among wise men who love him need occasion no fear or faltering in his mind; but to carry on an argument when you are yourself only a hesitating enquirer, which is my condition, is a dangerous and slippery thing; and the danger is not that I shall be laughed at (of which the fear would be childish), but that I shall miss the truth where I have most need to be sure of my footing, and drag my friends after me in my fall. And I pray Nemesis not to visit upon me the words which I am going to utter. For I do indeed believe that to be an involuntary homicide is a less crime than to be a deceiver about beauty or goodness or justice in the matter of laws. And that is a risk which I would rather run among enemies than among friends, and therefore you do well to encourage me.

Glaucon laughed and said: Well then, Socrates, in case you and your argument do us any serious injury you shall be acquitted beforehand of the homicide, and shall not be held to be a deceiver; take courage then and speak.

Well, I said, the law says that when a man is acquitted he is free from guilt, and what holds at law may hold in argument.

Then why should you mind?

Well, I replied, I suppose that I must retrace my steps and say what I perhaps ought to have said before in the proper place. The part of the men has been played out, and now properly enough comes the turn of the women. Of them I will proceed to speak, and the more readily since I am invited by you.

For men born and educated like our citizens, the only way, in my opinion, of arriving at a right conclusion about the possession and use of women and children is to follow the path on which we originally started, when we said that the men were to be the guardians and watchdogs of the herd.

True.

Let us further suppose the birth and education of our women to be subject to similar or nearly similar regulations; then we shall see whether the result accords with our design.

What do you mean?

What I mean may be put into the form of a question, I said: Are dogs divided into hes and shes, or do they both share equally in hunting and in keeping watch and in the other duties of dogs? or do we entrust to the males the entire and exclusive care of the flocks, while we leave the females at home, under the idea that the bearing and suckling their puppies is labour enough for them?

No, he said, they share alike; the only difference between them is that the males are stronger and the females weaker.

But can you use different animals for the same purpose, unless they are bred and fed in the same way?

You cannot.

Then, if women are to have the same duties as men, they must have the same nurture and education?

Yes.

The education which was assigned to the men was music and gymnastic.

Yes.

Then women must be taught music and gymnastic and also the art of war, which they must practise like the men?

That is the inference, I suppose.

I should rather expect, I said, that several of our proposals, if they are carried out, being unusual, may appear ridiculous.

No doubt of it.

Yes, and the most ridiculous thing of all will be the sight of women naked in the palaestra, exercising with the men, especially when they are no longer young; they certainly will not be a vision of beauty, any more than the enthusiastic old men who in spite of wrinkles and ugliness continue to frequent the gymnasia.

Yes, indeed, he said: according to present notions the proposal would be thought ridiculous.

But then, I said, as we have determined to speak our minds, we must not fear the jests of the wits which will be directed against this sort of innovation; how they will talk of women's attainments both in music and gymnastic, and above all about their wearing armour and riding upon horseback!

Very true, he replied.

Yet having begun we must go forward to the rough places of the law; at the same time begging of these gentlemen for once in their life to be serious. Not long ago, as we shall remind them, the Hellenes were of the opinion, which is still generally received among the barbarians, that the sight of a naked man was ridiculous and improper; and when first the Cretans and then the Lacedaemonians introduced the custom, the wits of that day might equally have ridiculed the innovation.

No doubt.

But when experience showed that to let all things be uncovered was far better than to cover them up, and the ludicrous effect to the outward eye vanished before the better principle which reason asserted, then the man was perceived to be a fool who directs the shafts of his ridicule at any other sight but that of folly and vice, or seriously inclines to weigh the beautiful by any other standard but that of the good.

Very true, he replied.

First, then, whether the question is to be put in jest or in earnest, let us come to an understanding about the nature of woman: Is she capable of sharing either wholly or partially in the actions of men, or not at all? And is the art of war one of those arts in which she can or can not share? That will be the best way of commencing the enquiry, and will probably lead to the fairest conclusion.

That will be much the best way.

Shall we take the other side first and begin by arguing against ourselves; in this manner the adversary's position will not be undefended.

Why not? he said.

Then let us put a speech into the mouths of our opponents. They will say: "Socrates and Glaucon, no adversary need convict you, for you yourselves, at the first foundation of the State, admitted the principle that everybody was to do the one work suited to his own nature." And certainly, if I am not mistaken, such an admission was made by us. "And do not the natures of men and women differ very much indeed?" And we shall reply: Of course they do. Then we shall be asked, "Whether the tasks assigned to men and to women should not be different, and such as are agreeable to their different natures?" Certainly they should. "But if so, have you not fallen into a serious inconsistency in saying that men and women, whose natures are so entirely different, ought to perform the same actions?"—What defence will you make for us, my good Sir, against any one who offers these objections?

That is not an easy question to answer when asked suddenly; and I shall and I do beg of you to draw out the case on our side.

These are the objections, Glaucon, and there are many others of a like kind, which I foresaw long ago; they made me afraid and reluctant to take in hand any law about the possession and nurture of women and children.

By Zeus, he said, the problem to be solved is anything but easy.

Why yes, I said, but the fact is that when a man is out of his depth, whether he has fallen into a little swimming bath or into mid-ocean, he has to swim all the same.

Very true.

And must not we swim and try to reach the shore: we will hope that Arion's dolphin or some other miraculous help may save us?

I suppose so, he said.

Well then, let us see if any way of escape can be found. We acknowledged—did we not? that different natures ought to have different pursuits, and that men's and women's natures are different. And now what are we saying?—that different natures ought to have the same pursuits,— this is the inconsistency which is charged upon us.

Precisely.

Verily, Glaucon, I said, glorious is the power of the art of contradiction!

Why do you say so?

Because I think that many a man falls into the practice against his will. When he thinks that he is reasoning he is really disputing, just because he cannot define and divide, and so know that of which he is speaking; and he will pursue a merely verbal opposition in the spirit of contention and not of fair discussion.

Yes, he replied, such is very often the case; but what has that to do with us and our argument?

A great deal; for there is certainly a danger of our getting unintentionally into a verbal opposition.

In what way?

Why we valiantly and pugnaciously insist upon the verbal truth, that different natures ought to have different pursuits, but we never considered at all what was the meaning of sameness or difference of nature, or why we distinguished them when we assigned different pursuits to different natures and the same to the same natures.

Why, no, he said, that was never considered by us.

I said: Suppose that by way of illustration we were to ask the question whether there is not an opposition in nature between bald men and hairy men; and if this is admitted by us, then, if bald men are cobblers, we should forbid the hairy men to be cobblers, and conversely?

That would be a jest, he said.

Yes, I said, a jest; and why? because we never meant when we constructed the State, that the opposition of natures should extend to every difference, but only to those differences which affected the pursuit in which the individual is engaged; we should have argued, for example, that a physician and one who is in mind a physician may be said to have the same nature.

True.

Whereas the physician and the carpenter have different natures?

Certainly.

And if, I said, the male and female sex appear to differ in their fitness for any art or pursuit, we should say that such pursuit or art ought to be assigned to one or the other of them, but if the difference consists only in women bearing and men begetting children, this does not amount to a proof that a woman differs from a man in respect of the sort of education she should receive; and we shall therefore continue to maintain that our guardians and their wives ought to have the same pursuits.

Very true, he said.

Next, we shall ask our opponent how, in reference to any of the pursuits or arts of civic life, the nature of a woman differs from that of a man?

That will be quite fair.

And perhaps he, like yourself, will reply that to give a sufficient answer on the instant is not easy; but after a little reflection there is no difficulty.

Yes, perhaps.

Suppose then that we invite him to accompany us in the argument, and then we may hope to show him that there is nothing peculiar in the constitution of women which would affect them in the administration of the State.

By all means.

Let us say to him: Come now, and we will ask you a question:—when you spoke of a nature gifted or not gifted in any respect, did you mean to say that one man will acquire a thing easily, another with difficulty; a little learning will lead the one to discover a great deal; whereas the other, after much study and application, no sooner learns than he forgets; or again, did you mean, that the one has a body which is a good servant to his mind, while the body of the other is a hindrance to him?—would not these be the sort of differences which distinguish the man gifted by nature from the one who is ungifted?

No one will deny that.

And can you mention any pursuit of mankind in which the male sex has not all these gifts and qualities in a higher degree than the female? Need I waste time in speaking of the art of weaving, and the management of pancakes and preserves, in which womankind does really appear to be great, and in which for her to be beaten by a man is of all things the most absurd?

You are quite right, he replied, in maintaining the general inferiority of the female sex: although many women are in many things superior to many men, yet on the whole what you say is true.

And if so, my friend, I said, there is no special faculty of administration in a state which a woman has because she is a woman, or which a man has by virtue of his sex, but the gifts of nature are alike diffused in both; all the pursuits of men are the pursuits of women also, but in all of them a woman is inferior to a man.

Very true.

Then are we to impose all our enactments on men and none of them on women?

That will never do.

One woman has a gift of healing, another not; one is a musician, and another has no music in her nature?

Very true.

And one woman has a turn for gymnastic and military exercises, and another is unwar-like and hates gymnastics?

Certainly.

And one woman is a philosopher, and another is an enemy of philosophy; one has spirit, and another is without spirit?

That is also true.

Then one woman will have the temper of a guardian, and another not. Was not the selection of the male guardians determined by differences of this sort?

Yes.

Men and women alike possess the qualities which make a guardian; they differ only in their comparative strength or weakness.

Obviously.

And those women who have such qualities are to be selected as the companions and colleagues of men who have similar qualities and whom they resemble in capacity and in character?

Very true.

And ought not the same natures to have the same pursuits?

They ought.

Then, as we were saying before, there is nothing unnatural in assigning music and gymnastic to the wives of the guardians—to that point we come round again.

Certainly not.

The law which we then enacted was agreeable to nature, and therefore not an impossibility or mere aspiration; and the contrary practice, which prevails at present, is in reality a violation of nature.

That appears to be true.

We had to consider, first, whether our proposals were possible, and secondly whether they were the most beneficial?

Yes.

And the possibility has been acknowledged?

Yes.

The very great benefit has next to be established?

Quite so.

You will admit that the same education which makes a man a good guardian will make a woman a good guardian; for their original nature is the same?

Yes.

I should like to ask you a question.

What is it?

Would you say that all men are equal in excellence, or is one man better than another?

The latter.

And in the commonwealth which we were founding do you conceive the guardians who have been brought up on our model system to be more perfect men, or the cobblers whose education has been cobbling?

What a ridiculous question!

You have answered me, I replied: Well, and may we not further say that our guardians are the best of our citizens?

By far the best.

And will not their wives be the best women?

Yes, by far the best.

And can there be anything better for the interests of the State than that the men and women of a State should be as good as possible?

There can be nothing better.

And this is what the arts of music and gymnastic, when present in such manner as we have described, will accomplish?

Certainly.

Then we have made an enactment not only possible but in the highest degree beneficial to the State?

True.

Then let the wives of our guardians strip, for their virtue will be their robe, and let them share in the toils of war and the defence of their country; only in the distribution of labours the lighter are to be assigned to the women, who are the weaker natures, but in other respects their duties are to be the same. And as for the man who laughs at naked women exercising their bodies from the best of motives, in his laughter he is plucking

"A fruit of unripe wisdom,"

and he himself is ignorant of what he is laughing at, or what he is about;—for that is, and ever will be, the best of sayings, *That the useful is the noble and the hurtful is the base.*

Very true.

Here, then, is one difficulty in our law about women, which we may say that we have now escaped; the wave has not swallowed us up alive for enacting that the guardians of either sex should have all their pursuits in common; to the utility and also to the possibility of this arrangement the consistency of the argument with itself bears witness.

Yes, that was a mighty wave which you have escaped.

Yes, I said, but a greater is coming; you will not think much of this when you see the next.

Go on; let me see.

The law, I said, which is the sequel of this and of all that has preceded, is to the following effect,—"that the wives of our guardians are to be common, and their children are to be common, and no parent is to know his own child, nor any child his parent."

Yes, he said, that is a much greater wave than the other; and the possibility as well as the utility of such a law are far more questionable.

I do not think, I said, that there can be any dispute about the very great utility of having wives and children in common; the possibility is quite another matter, and will be very much disputed.

I think that a good many doubts may be raised about both. . . .

—Is such an order of things possible, and how, if at all? For I am quite ready to acknowledge that the plan which you propose, if only feasible, would do all sorts of good to the State. I will add, what you have omitted, that your citizens will be the bravest of warriors, and will never leave their ranks, for they will all know one another, and each will call the other father, brother, son; and if you suppose the women to join their armies, whether in the same rank or in the rear, either as a terror to the enemy, or as auxiliaries in case of need, I know that they will then be absolutely invincible; and there are many domestic advantages which might also be mentioned and which I also fully acknowledge: but, as I admit all these advantages and as many more as you please, if only this State of yours were to come into existence, we need say no more about them; assuming then the existence of the State, let us now turn to the question of possibility and ways and means—the rest may be left.

If I loiter for a moment, you instantly make a raid upon me, I said, and have no mercy; I have hardly escaped the first and second waves, and you seem not to be aware that you are now bringing upon me the third, which is the greatest and heaviest. When you have seen and heard the third wave, I think you will be more considerate and will acknowledge that some fear and hesitation was natural respecting a proposal so extraordinary as that which I have now to state and investigate.

The more appeals of this sort which you make, he said, the more determined are we that you shall tell us how such a State is possible: speak out and at once.

Let me begin by reminding you that we found our way hither in the search after justice and injustice.

True, he replied; but what of that?

I was only going to ask whether, if we have discovered them, we are to require that the just man should in nothing fail of absolute justice; or may we be satisfied with an approximation, and the attainment in him of a higher degree of justice than is to be found in other men?

The approximation will be enough.

We are enquiring into the nature of absolute justice and into the character of the perfectly just, and into injustice and the perfectly unjust, that we might have an ideal. We were to look at these in order that we might judge of our own happiness and unhappiness according to the standard which they exhibited and the degree in which we resembled them, but not with any view of showing that they could exist in fact.

True, he said.

Would a painter be any the worse because, after having delineated with consummate art an ideal of a perfectly beautiful man, he was unable to show that any such man could ever have existed?

He would be none the worse.

Well, and were we not creating an ideal of a perfect State?

To be sure.

And is our theory a worse theory because we are unable to prove the possibility of a city being ordered in the manner described?

Surely not, he replied.

That is the truth, I said. But if, at your request, I am to try and show how and under what conditions the possibility is highest, I must ask you, having this in view, to repeat your former admissions.

What admissions?

I want to know whether ideals are ever fully realised in language? Does not the word express more than the fact, and must not the actual, whatever a man may think, always, in the nature of things, fall short of the truth? What do you say?

I agree.

Then you must not insist on my proving that the actual State will in every respect coincide with the ideal: if we are only able to discover how a city may be governed nearly as we proposed, you will admit that we have discovered the possibility which you demand; and will be contented. I am sure that I should be contented—will not you?

Yes, I will.

Let me next endeavour to show what is that fault in States which is the cause of their present maladministration, and what is the least change which will enable a State to pass into the truer form; and let the change, if possible, be of one thing only, or if not, of two; at any rate, let the changes be as few and slight as possible.

Certainly, he replied.

I think, I said, that there might be a reform of the State if only one change were made, which is not a slight or easy though still a possible one.

What is it? he said.

Now then, I said, I go to meet that which I liken to the greatest of the waves; yet shall the word be spoken, even though the wave break and drown me in laughter and dishonour; and do you mark my words.

Proceed.

I said: Until philosophers are kings, or the kings and princes of this world have the spirit and power of philosophy, and political greatness and wisdom meet in one, and those commoner natures who pursue either to the exclusion of the other are compelled to stand aside, cities will never have rest from their evils,—no, nor the human race, as I believe,—and then only will this our State have a possibility of life and behold the light of day. Such was the thought, my dear Glaucon, which I would fain have uttered if it had not seemed too extravagant; for to be convinced that in no other State can there be happiness private or public is indeed a hard thing.

Socrates, what do you mean? I would have you consider that the word which you have uttered is one at which numerous persons, and very respectable persons too, in a figure pulling off their coats all in a moment, and seizing any weapon that comes to hand, will run at you might and main, before you know where you are, intending to do heaven knows what; and if you don't prepare an answer, and put yourself in motion, you will be "pared by their fine wits," and no mistake.

You got me into the scrape, I said.

And I was quite right; however, I will do all I can to get you out of it; but I can only give you goodwill and good advice, and, perhaps, I may be able to fit answers to your questions better than another—that is all. And now, having such an auxiliary, you must do your best to show the unbelievers that you are right.

I ought to try, I said, since you offer me such invaluable assistance. And I think that, if there is to be a chance of our escaping, we must explain to them whom we mean when we say that philosophers are to rule in the State; then we shall be able to defend ourselves: There will be discovered to be some natures who ought to study philosophy and to be leaders in the State; and others who are not born to be philosophers, and are meant to be followers rather than leaders.

Then now for a definition, he said.

Follow me, I said, and I hope that I may in some way or other be able to give you a satisfactory explanation.

Proceed.

I dare say that you remember, and therefore I need not remind you, that a lover, if he is worthy of the name, ought to show his love, not to some one part of that which he loves, but to the whole.

I really do not understand, and therefore beg of you to assist my memory.

Another person, I said, might fairly reply as you do; but a man of pleasure like yourself ought to know that all who are in the flower of youth do somehow or other raise a pang or emotion in a lover's breast, and are thought by him to be worthy of his affectionate regards. Is not this a way which you have with the fair: one has a snub nose, and you praise his charming face; the hook-nose of another has, you say, a royal look; while he who is neither snub nor hooked has the grace of regularity: the dark visage is manly, the fair are children of the gods; and as to the sweet "honey pale," as they are called, what is the very name but the invention of a lover who talks in diminutives, and is not adverse to paleness if appearing on the cheek of youth? In a word, there is no excuse which you will not make, and nothing which you will not say, in order not to lose a single flower that blooms in the spring-time of youth.

If you make me an authority in matters of love, for the sake of the argument, I assent.

And what do you say of lovers of wine? Do you not see them doing the same? They are glad of any pretext of drinking any wine.

Very good.

And the same is true of ambitious men; if they cannot command an army, they are willing to command a file; and if they cannot be honoured by really great and important persons, they are glad to be honoured by lesser and meaner people,—but honour of some kind they must have.

Exactly.

Once more let me ask: Does he who desires any class of goods, desire the whole class or a part only?

The whole.

And may we not say of the philosopher that he is a lover, not of a part of wisdom only, but of the whole?

Yes, of the whole.

And he who dislikes learning, especially in youth, when he has no power of judging what is good and what is not, such an one we maintain not to be a philosopher or a lover of knowledge, just as he who refuses his food is not hungry, and may be said to have a bad appetite and not a good one?

Very true, he said.

Whereas he who has a taste for every sort of knowledge and who is curious to learn and is never satisfied, may be justly termed a philosopher? Am I not right?

Glaucon said: If curiosity makes a philosopher, you will find many a strange being will have a title to the name. All the lovers of sights have a delight in learning, and must therefore be included. Musical amateurs, too, are a folk strangely out of place among philosophers, for they are the last persons in the world who would come to anything like a philosophical discussion, if they could help, while they run about at the Dionysiac festivals as if they had let out their ears to hear every chorus; whether the performance is in town or country—that makes no difference—they are there. Now are we to maintain that all these and any who have similar tastes, as well as the professors of quite minor arts, are philosophers?

Certainly not, I replied; they are only an imitation.

He said: Who then are the true philosophers?

Those, I said, who are lovers of the vision of truth.

That is also good, he said; but I should like to know what you mean?

To another, I replied, I might have a difficulty in explaining; but I am sure that you will admit a proposition which I am about to make.

What is the proposition?

That since beauty is the opposite of ugliness, they are two?

Certainly.

And inasmuch as they are two, each of them is one?

True again.

And of just and unjust, good and evil, and of every other class, the same remark holds: taken singly, each of them is one; but from the various combinations of them with actions and things and with one another, they are seen in all sorts of lights and appear many?

Very true.

And this is the distinction which I draw between the sight-loving, art-loving, practical class and those of whom I am speaking, and who are alone worthy of the name of philosophers.

How do you distinguish them? he said.

The lovers of sounds and sights, I replied, are, as I conceive, fond of fine tones and colours and forms and all the artificial products that are made out of them, but their mind is incapable of seeing or loving absolute beauty.

True, he replied.

Few are they who are able to attain to the sight of this.

Very true.

And he who, having a sense of beautiful things has no sense of absolute beauty, or who, if another lead him to a knowledge of that beauty is unable to follow—of such an one I ask, Is he awake or in a dream only? Reflect: is not the dreamer, sleeping or waking, one who likens dissimilar things, who puts the copy in the place of the real object?

I should certainly say that such an one was dreaming.

But take the case of the other, who recognises the existence of absolute beauty and is able to distinguish the idea from the objects which participate in the idea, neither putting the objects in the place of the idea nor the idea in the place of the objects—is he a dreamer, or is he awake?

He is wide awake.

And may we not say that the mind of the one who knows has knowledge, and that the mind of the other, who opines only, has opinion?

Certainly.

But suppose that the latter should quarrel with us and dispute our statement, can we administer any soothing cordial or advice to him, without revealing to him that there is sad disorder in his wits?

We must certainly offer him some good advice, he replied.

Come, then, and let us think of something to say to him. Shall we begin by assuring him that he is welcome to any knowledge which he may have, and that we are rejoiced at his having it? But we should like to ask him a question: Does he who has knowledge know something or nothing? (You must answer for him.)

I answer that he knows something.

Something that is or is not?

Something that is; for how can that which is not ever be known?

And are we assured, after looking at the matter from many points of view, that absolute being is or may be absolutely known, but that the utterly nonexistent is utterly unknown?

Nothing can be more certain.

Good. But if there be anything which is of such a nature as to be and not to be, that will have a place intermediate between pure being and the absolute negation of being?

Yes, between them.

And, as knowledge corresponded to being and ignorance of necessity to not-being, for that intermediate between being and not-being there has to be discovered a corresponding intermediate between ignorance and knowledge, if there be such?

Certainly.

Do we admit the existence of opinion?

Undoubtedly.

As being the same with knowledge, or another faculty?

Another faculty.

Then opinion and knowledge have to do with different kinds of matter corresponding to this difference of faculties?

Yes.

And knowledge is relative to being and knows being. But before I proceed further I will make a division.

What division?

I will begin by placing faculties in a class by themselves: they are powers in us, and in all other things, by which we do as we do. Sight and hearing, for example, I should call faculties. Have I clearly explained the class which I mean?

Yes, I quite understand.

Then let me tell you my view about them. I do not see them, and therefore the distinctions of figure, colour, and the like, which enable me to discern the differences of some things, do not apply to them. In speaking of a faculty I think only of its sphere and its result; and that which has the same sphere and the same result I call the same faculty, but that which has another sphere and another result I call different. Would that be your way of speaking?

Yes.

And will you be so very good as to answer one more question? Would you say that knowledge is a faculty, or in what class would you place it?

Certainly knowledge is a faculty, and the mightiest of all faculties.

And is opinion also a faculty?

Certainly, he said; for opinion is that with which we are able to form an opinion.

And yet you were acknowledging a little while ago that knowledge is not the same as opinion?

Why, yes, he said: how can any reasonable being ever identify that which is infallible with that which errs?

An excellent answer, proving, I said, that we are quite conscious of a distinction between them.

Yes.

Then knowledge and opinion having distinct powers have also distinct spheres or subject-matters?

That is certain.

Being is the sphere or subject-matter of knowledge, and knowledge is to know the nature of being?

Yes.

And opinion is to have an opinion?

Yes.

And do we know what we opine? or is the subject-matter of opinion the same as the subject-matter of knowledge?

Nay, he replied, that has been already disproven; if difference in faculty implies difference in the sphere or subject-matter, and if, as we were saying, opinion and knowledge are distinct faculties, then the sphere of knowledge and of opinion cannot be the same.

Then if being is the subject-matter of knowledge, something else must be the subject-matter of opinion?

Yes, something else.

Well then, is not-being the subject-matter of opinion? or, rather, how can there be an opinion at all about not-being? Reflect: when a man has an opinion, has he not an opinion about something? Can he have an opinion which is an opinion about nothing?

Impossible.

He who has an opinion has an opinion about some one thing?

Yes.

And not-being is not one thing but, properly speaking, nothing?

True.

Of not-being, ignorance was assumed to be the necessary correlative; of being, knowledge?

True, he said.

Then opinion is not concerned either with being or with not-being?

Not with either.

And can therefore neither be ignorance nor knowledge?

That seems to be true.

But is opinion to be sought without and beyond either of them, in a greater clearness than knowledge, or in a greater darkness than ignorance?

In neither.

Then I suppose that opinion appears to you to be darker than knowledge, but lighter than ignorance?

Both; and in no small degree.

And also to be within and between them?

Yes.

Then you would infer that opinion is intermediate?

No question.

But were we not saying before, that if anything appeared to be of a sort which is and is not at the same time, that sort of thing would appear also to lie in the interval between pure being and absolute not-being; and that the corresponding faculty is neither knowledge nor ignorance, but will be found in the interval between them?

True.

And in that interval there has now been discovered something which we call opinion?

There has.

Then what remains to be discovered is the object which partakes equally of the nature of being and not-being, and cannot rightly be termed either, pure and simple; this unknown term, when discovered, we may truly call the subject of opinion, and assign each to its proper faculty,—the extremes to the faculties of the extremes and the mean to the faculty of the mean.

True.

This being premised, I would ask the gentleman who is of opinion that there is no absolute or unchangeable idea of beauty—in whose opinion the beautiful is the manifold— he, I say, your lover of beautiful sights, who cannot bear to be told that the beautiful is one, and the just is one, or that anything is one—to him I would appeal, saying, Will you be so very kind, sir, as to tell us whether, of all these beautiful things, there is one which will not be found ugly; or of the just, which will not be found unjust; or of the holy, which will not also be unholy?

No, he replied; the beautiful will in some point of view be found ugly; and the same is true of the rest.

And may not the many which are doubles be also halves?—doubles, that is, of one thing, and halves of another?

Quite true.

And things great and small, heavy and light, as they are termed, will not be denoted by these any more than by the opposite names?

True; both these and the opposite names will always attach to all of them.

And can any one of those many things which are called by particular names be said to be this rather than not to be this?

He replied: They are like the punning riddles which are asked at feasts or the children's puzzle about the eunuch aiming at the bat, with what he hit him, as they say in the puzzle, and upon what the bat was sitting. The individual objects of which I am speaking are also a riddle, and have a double sense: nor can you fix them in your mind, either as being or not-being, or both, or neither.

Then what will you do with them? I said. Can they have a better place than between being and not-being? For they are clearly not in greater darkness or negation than not-being, or more full of light and existence than being.

That is quite true, he said.

Thus then we seem to have discovered that the many ideas which the multitude entertain about the beautiful and about all other things are tossing about in some region which is half-way between pure being and pure not-being?

We have.

Yes; and we had before agreed that anything of this kind which we might find was to be described as matter of opinion, and not as matter of knowledge; being the intermediate flux which is caught and detained by the intermediate faculty.

Quite true.

Then those who see the many beautiful, and who yet neither see absolute beauty, nor can follow any guide who points the way thither; who see the many just, and not absolute justice, and the like,—such persons may be said to have opinion but not knowledge?

That is certain.

But those who see the absolute and eternal and immutable may be said to know, and not to have opinion only?

Neither can that be denied.

The one loves and embraces the subjects of knowledge, the other those of opinion? The latter are the same, as I dare say you will remember, who listened to sweet sounds and gazed upon fair colours, but would not tolerate the existence of absolute beauty.

Yes, I remember.

Shall we then be guilty of any impropriety in calling them lovers of opinion rather than lovers of wisdom, and will they be very angry with us for thus describing them?

I shall tell them not to be angry; no man should be angry at what is true.

But those who love the truth in each thing are to be called lovers of wisdom and not lovers of opinion.

Assuredly.

BOOK VI

And thus, Glaucon, after the argument has gone a weary way, the true and the false philosophers have at length appeared in view.

I do not think, he said, that the way could have been shortened.

I suppose not, I said; and yet I believe that we might have had a better view of both of them if the discussion could have been confined to this one subject and if there were not many other questions awaiting us, which he who desires to see in what respect the life of the just differs from that of the unjust must consider.

And what is the next question? he asked.

Surely, I said, the one which follows next in order. Inasmuch as philosophers only are able to grasp the eternal and unchangeable, and those who wander in the region of the many and variable are not philosophers, I must ask you which of the two classes should be the rulers of our State?

And how can we rightly answer that question?

Whichever of the two are best able to guard the laws and institutions of our State—let them be our guardians.

Very good.

Neither, I said, can there be any question that the guardian who is to keep anything should have eyes rather than no eyes?

There can be no question of that.

And are not those who are verily and indeed wanting in the knowledge of the true being of each thing, and who have in their souls no clear pattern, and are unable as with a painter's eye to look at the absolute truth and to that original to repair, and having perfect vision of the other world to order the laws about beauty, goodness, justice in this, if not already ordered, and to guard and preserve the order of them—are not such persons, I ask, simply blind?

Truly, he replied, they are much in that condition.

And shall they be our guardians when there are others who, besides being their equals in experience and falling short of them in no particular of virtue, also know the very truth of each thing?

There can be no reason, he said, for rejecting those who have this greatest of all great qualities; they must always have the first place unless they fail in some other respect.

Suppose then, I said, that we determine how far they can unite this and the other excellences.

By all means.

In the first place, as we began by observing, the nature of the philosopher has to be ascertained. We must come to an understanding about him, and, when we have done so, then, if I am not mistaken, we shall also acknowledge that such an union of qualities is possible, and that those in whom they are united, and those only, should be rulers in the State.

What do you mean?

Let us suppose that philosophical minds always love knowledge of a sort which shows them the eternal nature not varying from generation and corruption.

Agreed.

And further, I said, let us agree that they are lovers of all true being; there is no part whether greater or less, or more or less honourable, which they are willing to renounce; as we said before of the lover and the man of ambition.

True.

And if they are to be what we were describing, is there not another quality which they should also possess?

What quality?

Truthfulness: they will never intentionally receive into their mind falsehood, which is their detestation, and they will love the truth.

Yes, that may be safely affirmed of them.

"May be," my friend, I replied, is not the word; say rather "must be affirmed": for he whose nature is amorous of anything cannot help loving all that belongs or is akin to the object of his affections.

Right, he said.

And is there anything more akin to wisdom than truth?

How can there be?

Can the same nature be a lover of wisdom and a lover of falsehood?

Never.

The true lover of learning then must from his earliest youth, as far as in him lies, desire all truth?

Assuredly.

But then again, as we know by experience, he whose desires are strong in one direction will have them weaker in others; they will be like a stream which has been drawn off into another channel.

True.

He whose desires are drawn towards knowledge in every form will be absorbed in the pleasures of the soul, and will hardly feel bodily pleasure—I mean, if he be a true philosopher and not a sham one.

That is most certain.

Such an one is sure to be temperate and the reverse of covetous; for the motives which make another man desirous of having and spending, have no place in his character.

Very true.

Another criterion of the philosophical nature has also to be considered.

What is that?

There should be no secret corner of illiberality; nothing can be more antagonistic than meanness to a soul which is ever longing after the whole of things both divine and human.

Most true, he replied.

Then how can he who has magnificence of mind and is the spectator of all time and all existence, think much of human life?

He cannot.

Or can such an one account death fearful?

No indeed.

Then the cowardly and mean nature has no part in true philosophy?

Certainly not.

Or again: can he who is harmoniously constituted, who is not covetous or mean, or a boaster, or a coward—can he, I say, ever be unjust or hard in his dealings?

Impossible.

Then you will soon observe whether a man is just and gentle, or rude and unsociable; these are the signs which distinguish even in youth the philosophical nature from the unphilosophical.

True.

There is another point which should be remarked.

What point?

Whether he has or has not a pleasure in learning; for no one will love that which gives him pain, and in which after much toil he makes little progress.

Certainly not.

And again, if he is forgetful and retains nothing of what he learns, will he not be an empty vessel?

That is certain.

Labouring in vain, he must end in hating himself and his fruitless occupation?

Yes.

Then a soul which forgets cannot be ranked among genuine philosophic natures; we must insist that the philosopher should have a good memory?

Certainly.

And once more, the inharmonious and unseemly nature can only tend to disproportion?

Undoubtedly.

And do you consider truth to be akin to proportion or to disproportion?

To proportion.

Then, besides other qualities, we must try to find a naturally well-proportioned and gracious mind, which will move spontaneously towards the true being of everything.

Certainly.

Well, and do not all these qualities, which we have been enumerating, go together, and are they not, in a manner, necessary to a soul, which is to have a full and perfect participation of being?

They are absolutely necessary, he replied.

And must not that be a blameless study which he only can pursue who has the gift of a good memory, and is quick to learn,—noble, gracious, the friend of truth, justice, courage, temperance, who are his kindred?

The god of jealousy himself, he said, could find no fault with such a study.

And to men like him, I said, when perfected by years and education, and to these only you will entrust the State.

Here Adeimantus interposed and said: To these statements, Socrates, no one can offer a reply; but when you talk in this way, a strange feeling passes over the minds of your hearers: They fancy that they are led astray a little at each step in the argument, owing to their own want of skill in asking and answering questions; these littles accumulate, and at the end of the discussion they are found to have sustained a mighty overthrow and all their former notions appear to be turned upside down. And as unskilful players of draughts are at last shut up by their more skilful adversaries and have no piece to move, so they too find themselves shut up at last; for they have nothing to say in this new game of which words are the counters; and yet all the time they are in the right. The observation is suggested to me by what is now occurring. For any one of us might say, that although in words he is not able to meet you at each step of the argument, he sees as a fact that the votaries of philosophy, when they carry on the study, not only in youth as a part of education, but as the pursuit of their maturer years, most of them become strange monsters, not to say utter rogues, and that those who may be considered the best of them are made useless to the world by the very study which you extol.

Well, and do you think that those who say so are wrong?

I cannot tell, he replied; but I should like to know what is your opinion.

Hear my answer; I am of opinion that they are quite right.

Then how can you be justified in saying that cities will not cease from evil until philosophers rule in them, when philosophers are acknowledged by us to be of no use to them?

You ask a question, I said, to which a reply can only be given in a parable.

Yes, Socrates; and that is a way of speaking to which you are not at all accustomed, I suppose.

I perceive, I said, that you are vastly amused at having plunged me into such a hopeless discussion; but now hear the parable, and then you will be still more amused at the meagreness of my imagination: for the manner in which the best men are treated in their own States is so grievous that no single thing on earth is comparable to it; and therefore, if I am to plead their cause, I must have recourse to fiction, and put together a figure made up of many things, like the fabulous unions of goats and stags which are found in pictures. Imagine then a fleet or a ship in which there is a captain who is taller and stronger than any of the crew, but he is a little deaf and has a similar infirmity in sight, and his knowledge of navigation is not much better. The sailors are quarrelling with one another about the steering—every one is of opinion that he has a right to steer, though he has never learned the art of navigation and cannot tell who taught him or when he learned, and will further assert that it cannot be taught, and they are ready to cut in pieces any one who says the contrary. They throng about the captain, begging and praying him to commit the helm to them; and if at any time they do not prevail, but others are preferred to them, they kill the others or throw them overboard, and having first chained up the noble captain's senses with drink or some narcotic drug, they mutiny and take possession of the ship and make free with the stores; thus, eating and drinking, they proceed on their voyage in such a manner as might be expected of them. Him who is their partisan and cleverly aids them in their plot for getting the ship out of the captain's hands into their own whether by force or persuasion, they compliment with the name of sailor, pilot, able seaman, and abuse the other sort of man, whom they call a good-for-nothing; but that the true pilot must pay attention to the year and seasons and sky and stars and winds, and whatever else belongs to his art, if he intends to be really qualified for the command of a ship, and that he must and will be the steerer, whether other people like or not—the possibility of this union of authority with the steerer's art has never seriously entered into their thoughts or been made part of their calling. Now in vessels which are in a state of mutiny and by sailors who are mutineers, how will the true pilot be regarded? Will he not be called by them a prater, a star-gazer, a good-for-nothing?

Of course, said Adeimantus.

Then you will hardly need, I said, to hear the interpretation of the figure, which describes the true philosopher in his relation to the State; for you understand already.

Certainly.

Then suppose you now take this parable to the gentleman who is surprised at finding that philosophers have no honour in their cities; explain it to him and try to convince him that their having honour would be far more extraordinary.

I will.

Say to him, that, in deeming the best votaries of philosophy to be useless to the rest of the world, he is right; but also tell him to attribute their uselessness to the fault of those who will not use them, and not to themselves. The pilot should not humbly beg the sailors to be commanded by him—that is not the order of nature; neither are "the wise to go to the doors of the rich"—the ingenious author of this saying told a lie—but the truth is, that, when a man is ill, whether he be rich or poor, to the physician he must go, and he who wants to be governed, to him who is able to govern. The ruler who is good for anything ought not to beg his subjects to be ruled by him; although the present governors of mankind are of a different stamp; they may be justly compared to the mutinous sailors, and the true helmsmen to those who are called by them good-for-nothings and star-gazers.

Precisely so, he said.

For these reasons, and among men like these, philosophy, the noblest pursuit of all, is not likely to be much esteemed by those of the opposite faction; not that the greatest and most lasting injury is done to her by her opponents, but by her own professing followers, the same of whom you suppose the accuser to say, that the greater number of them are arrant rogues, and the best are useless; in which opinion I agreed.

Yes.

And the reason why the good are useless has now been explained?

True.

Then shall we proceed to show that the corruption of the majority is also unavoidable, and that this is not to be laid to the charge of philosophy any more than the other?

By all means.

And let us ask and answer in turn, first going back to the description of the gentle and noble nature. Truth, as you will remember, was his leader, whom he followed always and in all things; failing in this, he was an impostor, and had no part or lot in true philosophy.

Yes, that was said.

Well, and is not this one quality, to mention no others, greatly at variance with present notions of him?

Certainly, he said.

And have we not a right to say in his defence, that the true lover of knowledge is always striving after being—that is his nature; he will not rest in the multiplicity of individuals which is an appearance only, but will go on—the keen edge will not be blunted, nor the force of his desire abate until he have attained the knowledge of the true nature of every essence by a sympathetic and kindred power in the soul, and by that power drawing near and mingling and becoming incorporate with very being, having begotten mind and truth, he will have knowledge and will live and grow truly, and then, and not till then, will he cease from his travail.

Nothing, he said, can be more just than such a description of him.

And will the love of a lie be any part of a philosopher's nature? Will he not utterly hate a lie?

He will.

And when truth is the captain, we cannot suspect any evil of the band which he leads?

Impossible.

Justice and health of mind will be of the company, and temperance will follow after?

True, he replied.

Neither is there any reason why I should again set in array the philosopher's virtues, as you will doubtless remember that courage, magnificence, apprehension, memory, were his natural gifts. And you objected that, although no one could deny what I then said, still, if you leave words and look at facts, the persons who are thus described are some of them manifestly useless, and the greater number utterly depraved; we were then led to enquire into the grounds of these accusations, and have now arrived at the point of asking why are the majority bad, which question of necessity brought us back to the examination and definition of the true philosopher.

Exactly.

And we have next to consider the corruptions of the philosophic nature, why so many are spoiled and so few escape spoiling—I am speaking of those who were said to be useless but not wicked—and, when we have done with them, we will speak of the imitators of philosophy, what manner of men are they who aspire after a profession which is above them and of which they are unworthy, and then, by their manifold inconsistencies, bring upon philosophy, and upon all philosophers, that universal reprobation of which we speak.

What are these corruptions? he said.

I will see if I can explain them to you. Every one will admit that a nature having in perfection all the qualities which we required in a philosopher, is a rare plant which is seldom seen among men.

Rare indeed.

And what numberless and powerful causes tend to destroy these rare natures!

What causes?

In the first place there are their own virtues, their courage, temperance, and the rest of them, every one of which praiseworthy qualities (and this is a most singular circumstance) destroys and distracts from philosophy the soul which is the possessor of them.

That is very singular, he replied.

Then there are all the ordinary goods of life—beauty, wealth, strength, rank, and great connections in the State—you understand the sort of things—these also have a corrupting and distracting effect.

I understand; but I should like to know more precisely what you mean about them.

Grasp the truth as a whole, I said, and in the right way; you will then have no difficulty in apprehending the preceding remarks, and they will no longer appear strange to you.

And how am I to do so? he asked.

Why, I said, we know that all germs or seeds, whether vegetable or animal, when they fail to meet with proper nutriment or climate or soil, in proportion to their vigour, are all the more sensitive to the want of a suitable environment, for evil is a greater enemy to what is good than what is not.

Very true.

There is reason in supposing that the finest natures, when under alien conditions, receive more injury than the inferior, because the contrast is greater.

Certainly.

And may we not say, Adeimantus, that the most gifted minds, when they are ill-educated, become preeminently bad? Do not great crimes and the spirit of pure evil spring out of a fulness of nature ruined by education rather than from any inferiority, whereas weak natures are scarcely capable of any very great good or very great evil?

There I think that you are right.

And our philosopher follows the same analogy—he is like a plant which, having proper nurture, must necessarily grow and mature into all virtue, but, if sown and planted in an alien soil, becomes the most noxious of all weeds, unless he be preserved by some divine power. Do you really think, as people so often say, that our youth are corrupted by Sophists, or that private teachers of the art corrupt them in any degree worth speaking of? Are not the public who say these things the greatest of all Sophists? And do they not educate to perfection young and old, men and women alike, and fashion them after their own hearts?

When is this accomplished? he said.

When they meet together, and the world sits down at an assembly, or in a court of law, or a theatre, or a camp, or in any other popular resort, and there is a great uproar, and they praise some things which are being said or done, and blame other things, equally exaggerating both, shouting and clapping their hands, and the echo of the rocks and the place in which they are assembled redoubles the sound of the praise or blame—at such a time will not a young man's heart, as they say, leap within him? Will any private training enable him to stand firm against the overwhelming flood of popular opinion? or will he be carried away by the stream? Will he not have the notions of good and evil which the public in general have—he will do as they do, and as they are, such will he be?

Yes, Socrates; necessity will compel him.

And yet, I said, there is a still greater necessity, which has not been mentioned.

What is that?

The gentle force of attainder or confiscation or death, which, as you are aware, these new Sophists and educators, who are the public, apply when their words are powerless.

Indeed they do; and in right good earnest.

Now what opinion of any other Sophist, or of any private person, can be expected to overcome in such an unequal contest?

None, he replied.

No, indeed, I said, even to make the attempt is a great piece of folly; there neither is, nor has been, nor is ever likely to be, any different type of character which has had no other training in virtue but that which is supplied by public opinion—I speak, my friend, of human virtue only; what is more than human, as the proverb says, is not included: for I would not have you ignorant that, in the present evil state of governments, whatever is saved and comes to good is saved by the power of God, as we may truly say.

I quite assent, he replied.

Then let me crave your assent also to a further observation.

What are you going to say?

Why, that all those mercenary individuals, whom the many call Sophists and whom they deem to be their adversaries, do, in fact, reach nothing but the opinion of the many, that is to say, the opinions of their assemblies; and this is their wisdom. I might compare them to a man who should study the tempers and desires of a mighty strong beast who is fed by him—he would learn how to approach and handle him, also at what times and from what causes he is dangerous or the reverse, and what is the meaning of his several cries, and by what sounds, when another utters them, he is soothed or infuriated; and you may suppose further, that when, by continually attending upon him, he has become perfect in all this, he calls his knowledge wisdom, and makes of it a system or art, which he proceeds to teach, although he has no real notion of what he means by the principles or passions of which he is speaking, but calls this honourable and that dishonourable, or good or evil, or just or unjust, all in accordance with the tastes and tempers of the great brute. Good he pronounces to be that in which the beast delights and evil to be that which he dislikes; and he can give no other account of them except that the just and noble are the necessary, having never himself seen, and having no power of explaining to others the nature of either, or the difference between them, which is immense. By heaven, would not such an one be a rare educator?

Indeed, he would.

And in what way does he who thinks that wisdom is the discernment of the tempers and tastes of the motley multitude, whether in painting or music, or, finally, in politics, differ from him whom I have been describing? For when a man consorts with the many, and exhibits to them his poem or other work of art or the service which he has done the State, making them his judges when he is not obliged, the so-called necessity of Diomede will oblige him to produce whatever they praise. And yet the reasons are utterly ludicrous which they give in confirmation of their own notions about the honourable and good. Did you ever hear any of them which were not?

No, nor am I likely to hear.

You recognise the truth of what I have been saying? Then let me ask you to consider further whether the world will ever be induced to believe in the existence of absolute beauty rather than of the many beautiful, or of the absolute in each kind rather than of the many in each kind?

Certainly not.

Then the world cannot possibly be a philosopher?

Impossible.

And therefore philosophers must inevitably fall under the censure of the world?

They must.

And of individuals who consort with the mob and seek to please them?

That is evident.

Then, do you see any way in which the philosopher can be preserved in his calling to the end? and remember what we were saying of him, that he was to have quickness and memory and courage and magnificence—these were admitted by us to be the true philosopher's gifts.

Yes.

Will not such an one from his early childhood be in all things first among all, especially if his bodily endowments are like his mental ones?

Certainly, he said.

And his friends and fellow-citizens will want to use him as he gets older for their own purposes?

No question.

Falling at his feet, they will make requests to him and do him honour and flatter him, because they want to get into their hands now, the power which he will one day possess.

That often happens, he said.

And what will a man such as he is be likely to do under such circumstances, especially if he be a citizen of a great city, rich and noble, and a tall proper youth? Will he not be full of boundless aspirations, and fancy himself able to manage the affairs of Hellenes and of barbarians, and having got such notions into his head will he not dilate and elevate himself in the fulness of vain pomp and senseless pride?

To be sure he will.

Now, when he is in this state of mind, if some one gently comes to him and tells him that he is a fool and must get understanding, which can only be got by slaving for it, do you think that, under such adverse circumstances, he will be easily induced to listen?

Far otherwise.

And even if there be some one who through inherent goodness or natural reasonableness has had his eyes opened a little and is humbled and taken captive by philosophy, how will his friends behave when they think that they are likely to lose the advantage which they were hoping to reap from his companionship? Will they not do and say anything to prevent him from yielding to his better nature and to render his teacher powerless, using to this end private intrigues as well as public prosecutions?

There can be no doubt of it.

And how can one who is thus circumstanced ever become a philosopher?

Impossible.

Then were we not right in saying that even the very qualities which make a man a philosopher may, if he be ill-educated, divert him from philosophy, no less than riches and their accompaniments and the other so-called goods of life?

We were quite right.

Thus, my excellent friend, is brought about all that ruin and failure which I have been describing of the natures best adapted to the best of all pursuits; they are natures which we maintain to be rare at any time; this being the class out of which come the men who are the authors of the greatest evil to States and individuals; and also of the greatest good when the tide carries them in that direction; but a small man never was the doer of any great thing either to individuals or to States.

That is most true, he said.

And so philosophy is left desolate, with her marriage rite incomplete: for her own have fallen away and forsaken her, and while they are leading a false and unbecoming life, other unworthy persons, seeing that she has no kinsmen to be her protectors, enter in and dishonour her; and fasten upon her the reproaches which, as you say, her reprovers utter, who affirm of her votaries that some are good for nothing, and that the greater number deserve the severest punishment.

That is certainly what people say.

Yes; and what else would you expect, I said, when you think of the puny creatures who, seeing this land open to them—a land well stocked with fair names and showy titles—like prisoners running out of prison into a sanctuary, take a leap out of their trades into philosophy; those who do so being probably the clevered hands at their own miserable crafts? For, although philosophy be in this evil case, still there remains a dignity about her which is not to be found in the arts. And many are thus attracted by her whose natures are imperfect and whose souls are maimed and disfigured by their meannesses, as their bodies are by their trades and crafts. Is not this unavoidable?

Yes.

Are they not exactly like a bald little tinker who has just got out of durance and come into a fortune; he takes a bath and puts on a new coat, and is decked out as a bridegroom going to marry his master's daughter, who is left poor and desolate?

A most exact parallel.

What will be the issue of such marriages? Will they not be vile and bastard?

There can be no question of it.

And when persons who are unworthy of education approach philosophy and make an alliance with her who is a rank above them what sort of ideas and opinions are likely to be generated? Will they not be sophisms captivating to the ear, having nothing in them genuine, or worthy of or akin to true wisdom?

No doubt, he said.

Then, Adeimantus, I said, the worthy disciples of philosophy will be but a small remnant: perchance some noble and well-educated person, detained by exile in her service, who in the absence of corrupting influences remains devoted to her; or some lofty soul born in a mean city, the politics of which he contemns and neglects; and there may be a gifted few who leave the arts, which they justly despise, and come to her—or peradventure there are some who are restrained by our friend Theages' bridle; for everything in the life of Theages conspired to divert him from philosophy; but ill-health kept him away from politics. My own case of the internal sign is hardly worth mentioning, for rarely, if ever, has such a monitor been given to any other man. Those who belong to this small class have tasted how sweet and blessed a possession philosophy is, and have also seen enough of the madness of the multitude; and they know that no politician is honest, nor is there any champion of justice at whose side they may fight and be saved. Such an one may be compared to a man who has fallen among wild beasts—he will not join in the wickedness of his fellows, but neither is he able singly to resist all their fierce natures, and therefore seeing that he would be of no use to the State or to his friends, and reflecting that he would have to throw away his life without doing any good either to himself or others, he holds his peace, and goes his own way. He is like one who, in the storm of dust and sleet which the driving wind hurries along, retires under the shelter of a wall; and seeing the rest of mankind full of wickedness, he is content, if only he can live his own life and be pure from evil or unrighteousness, and depart in peace and good-will, with bright hopes.

Yes, he said, and he will have done a great work before he departs.

A great work—yes; but not the greatest, unless he find a State suitable to him; for in a State which is suitable to him, he will have a larger growth and be the saviour of his country, as well as of himself.

The causes why philosophy is in such an evil name have now been sufficiently explained: the injustice of the charges against her has been shown—is there anything more which you wish to say?

Nothing more on that subject, he replied; but I should like to know which of the governments now existing is in your opinion the one adapted to her.

Not any of them, I said; and that is precisely the accusation which I bring against them—not one of them is worthy of the philosophic nature, and hence that nature is warped and estranged—as the exotic seed which is sown in a foreign land becomes denaturalized, and is wont to be overpowered and to lose itself in the new soil, even so this growth of philosophy, instead of persisting, degenerates and receives another character. But if philosophy ever finds in the State that perfection which she herself is, then will be seen that she is in truth divine, and that all other things, whether natures of men or institutions, are but human—and now, I know that you are going to ask, what that State is.

No, he said; there you are wrong, for I was going to ask another question—whether it is the State of which we are the founders and inventors, or some other?

Yes, I replied, ours in most respects; but you may remember my saying before, that some living authority would always be required in the State having the same idea of the constitution which guided you when as legislator you were laying down the laws.

That was said, he replied.

Yes, but not in a satisfactory manner; you frightened us by interposing objections, which certainly showed that the discussion would be long and difficult; and what still remains is the reverse of easy.

What is there remaining?

The question how the study of philosophy may be so ordered as not to be the ruin of the State: All great attempts are attended with risk; "hard is the good," as men say.

Still, he said, let the point be cleared up, and the enquiry will then be complete.

I shall not be hindered, I said, by any want of will, but, if at all, by a want of power: my zeal you may see for yourselves; and please to remark in what I am about to say how boldly and unhesitatingly I declare that States should pursue philosophy, not as they do now, but in a different spirit.

In what manner?

At present, I said, the students of philosophy are quite young; beginning when they are hardly past childhood, they devote only the time saved from moneymaking and housekeeping to such pursuits; and even those of them who are reputed to have most of the philosophic spirit, when they come within sight of the great difficulty of the subject, I mean dialectic, take themselves off. In after life when invited by some one else, they may, perhaps, go and hear a lecture, and about this they make much ado, for philosophy is not considered by them to be their proper business: at last, when they grow old, in most cases they are extinguished more truly than Heracleitus' sun, inasmuch as they never light up again.

But what ought to be their course?

Just the opposite. In childhood and youth their study, and what philosophy they learn, should be suited to their tender years: during this period while they are growing up towards manhood, the chief and special care should be given to their bodies that they may have them to use in the service of philosophy; as life advances and the intellect begins to mature, let them increase the gymnastics of the soul; but when the strength of our citizens fails and is past civil and military duties, then let them range at will and engage in no serious labour, as we intend them to live happily here, and to crown this life with a similar happiness in another.

How truly in earnest you are, Socrates! he said; I am sure of that; and yet most of your hearers, if I am not mistaken, are likely to be still more earnest in their opposition to you, and will never be convinced; Thrasymachus least of all.

Do not make a quarrel, I said, between Thrasymachus and me, who have recently become friends, although, indeed, we were never enemies; for I shall go on striving to the utmost until I either convert him and other men, or do something which may profit them against the day when they live again, and hold the like discourse in another state of existence.

You are speaking of a time which is not very near.

Rather, I replied, of a time which is as nothing in comparison with eternity. Nevertheless, I do not wonder that the many refuse to believe; for they have never seen that of which we are now speaking realised; they have seen only a conventional imitation of philosophy, consisting of words artificially brought together, not like these of ours having a natural unity. But a human being who in word and work is perfectly moulded, as far as he can be, into the proportion and likeness of virtue—such a man ruling in a city which bears the same image, they have never yet seen, neither one nor many of them—do you think that they ever did?

No indeed.

No, my friend, and they have seldom, if ever, heard free and noble sentiments; such as men utter when they are earnestly and by every means in their power seeking after truth for the sake of knowledge, while they look coldly on the subtleties of controversy, of which the end is opinion and strife, whether they meet with them in the courts of law or in society.

They are strangers, he said, to the words of which you speak.

And this was what we foresaw, and this was the reason why truth forced us to admit, not without fear and hesitation, that neither cities nor States nor individuals will ever attain perfection until the small class of philosophers whom we termed useless but not corrupt are providentially compelled, whether they will or not, to take care of the State, and until a like necessity be laid on the State to obey them; or until kings, or if not kings, the sons of kings or princes, are divinely inspired with a true love of true philosophy. That either or both of these alternatives are impossible, I see no reason to affirm: if they were so, we might indeed be justly ridiculed as dreamers and visionaries. Am I not right?

Quite right.

If then, in the countless ages of the past, or at the present hour in some foreign clime which is far away and beyond our ken, the perfected philosopher is or has been or hereafter shall be compelled by a superior power to have the charge of the State, we are ready to assert to the death, that this our constitution has been, and is—yea, and will be whenever the Muse of Philosophy is queen. There is no impossibility in all this; that there is a difficulty, we acknowledge ourselves.

My opinion agrees with yours, he said.

But do you mean to say that this is not the opinion of the multitude?

I should imagine not, he replied.

O my friend, I said, do not attack the multitude: they will change their minds, if, not in an aggressive spirit, but gently and with the view of soothing them and removing their dislike of over-education, you show them your philosophers as they really are and describe as you were just now doing their character and profession, and then mankind will see that he of whom you are speaking is not such as they supposed—if they view him in this new light, they will surely change their notion of him, and answer in another strain. Who can be at enmity with one who loves them, who that is himself gentle and free from envy will be jealous of one in whom there is no jealousy? Nay, let me answer for you, that in a few this harsh temper may be found but not in the majority of mankind.

I quite agree with you, he said.

And do you not also think, as I do, that the harsh feeling which the many entertain towards philosophy originates in the pretenders, who rush in uninvited, and are always abusing them, and finding fault with them, who make persons instead of things the theme of their conversation? and nothing can be more unbecoming in philosophers than this.

It is most unbecoming.

For he, Adeimantus, whose mind is fixed upon true being, has surely no time to look down upon the affairs of earth, or to be filled with malice and envy, contending against men; his eye is ever directed towards things fixed and immutable, which he sees neither injuring nor injured by one another, but all in order moving according to reason; these he imitates, and to these he will, as far as he can, conform himself. Can a man help imitating that with which he holds reverential converse?

Impossible.

And the philosopher holding converse with the divine order, becomes orderly and divine, as far as the nature of man allows; but like every one else, he will suffer from detraction.

Of course.

And if a necessity be laid upon him of fashioning, not only himself, but human nature generally, whether in States or individuals, into that which he beholds elsewhere, will he, think you, be an unskilful artificer of justice, temperance, and every civil virtue?

Anything but unskilful.

And if the world perceives that what we are saying about him is the truth, will they be angry with philosophy? Will they disbelieve us, when we tell them that no State can be happy which is not designed by artists who imitate the heavenly pattern?

They will not be angry if they understand, he said. But how will they draw out the plan of which you are speaking?

They will begin by taking the State and the manners of men, from which, as from a tablet, they will rub out the picture, and leave a clean surface. This is no easy task. But whether easy or not, herein will lie the difference between them and every other legislator,—they will have nothing to do either with individual or State, and will inscribe no laws, until they have either found, or themselves made, a clean surface.

They will be very right, he said.

Having effected this, they will proceed to trace an outline of the constitution?

No doubt.

And when they are filling in the work, as I conceive, they will often turn their eyes upwards and downwards: I mean that they will first look at absolute justice and beauty and temperance, and again at the human copy; and will mingle and temper the various elements of life into the image of a man; and thus they will conceive according to that other image, which, when existing among men, Homer calls the form and likeness of God.

Very true, he said.

And one feature they will erase, and another they will put in, until they have made the ways of men, as far as possible, agreeable to the ways of God?

Indeed, he said, in no way could they make a fairer picture.

And now, I said, are we beginning to persuade those whom you described as rushing at us with might and main, that the painter of constitutions is such an one as we are praising;

at whom they were so very indignant because to his hands we committed the State; and are they growing a little calmer at what they have just heard?

Much calmer, if there is any sense in them.

Why, where can they still find any ground for objection? Will they doubt that the philosopher is a lover of truth and being?

They would not be so unreasonable.

Or that his nature, being such as we have delineated, is akin to the highest good?

Neither can they doubt this.

But again, will they tell us that such a nature, placed under favourable circumstances, will not be perfectly good and wise if any ever was? Or will they prefer those whom we have rejected?

Surely not.

Then will they still be angry at our saying, that, until philosophers bear rule, States and individuals will have no rest from evil, nor will this our imaginary State ever be realised?

I think that they will be less angry.

Shall we assume that they are not only less angry but quite gentle, and that they have been converted and for very shame, if for no other reason, cannot refuse to come to terms?

By all means, he said.

Then let us suppose that the reconciliation has been effected. Will any one deny the other point, that there may be sons of kings or princes who are by nature philosophers?

Surely no man, he said.

And when they have come into being will any one say that they must of necessity be destroyed; that they can hardly be saved is not denied even by us; but that in the whole course of ages no single one of them can escape—who will venture to affirm this?

Who indeed!

But, said I, one is enough; let there be one man who has a city obedient to his will, and he might bring into existence the ideal polity about which the world is so incredulous.

Yes, one is enough.

The ruler may impose the laws and institutions which we have been describing, and the citizens may possibly be willing to obey them?

Certainly.

And that others should approve, of what we approve, is no miracle or impossibility?

I think not.

But we have sufficiently shown, in what has preceded, that all this, if only possible, is assuredly for the best.

We have.

And now we say not only that our laws, if they could be enacted, would be for the best, but also that the enactment of them, though difficult, is not impossible.

Very good.

And so with pain and toil we have reached the end of one subject, but more remains to be discussed;—how and by what studies and pursuits will the saviours of the constitution be created, and at what ages are they to apply themselves to their several studies?

Certainly.

I omitted the troublesome business of the possession of women, and the procreation of children, and the appointment of the rulers, because I knew that the perfect State would be eyed with jealousy and was difficult of attainment; but that piece of cleverness was not of much service to me, for I had to discuss them all the same. The women and children are now disposed of, but the other question of the rulers must be investigated from the very beginning. We were saying, as you will remember, that they were to be lovers of their country, tried by the test of pleasures and pains, and neither in hardships, nor in dangers, nor at any other critical moment were to lose their patriotism—he was to be rejected who failed, but he who always came forth pure, like gold tried in the refiner's fire, was to be made a ruler, and to receive honours and rewards in life and after death. This was the sort of thing which was being said, and then the argument turned aside and veiled her face; not liking to stir the question which has now arisen.

I perfectly remember, he said.

Yes, my friend, I said, and I then shrank from hazarding the bold word; but now let me dare to say—that the perfect guardian must be a philosopher.

Yes, he said, let that be affirmed.

And do not suppose that there will be many of them; for the gifts which were deemed by us to be essential rarely grow together; they are mostly found in shreds and patches.

What do you mean? he said.

You are aware, I replied, that quick intelligence, memory, sagacity, cleverness, and similar qualities, do not often grow together, and that persons who possess them and are at the same time high-spirited and magnanimous are not so constituted by nature as to live orderly and in a peaceful and settled manner; they are driven any way by their impulses, and all solid principle goes out of them.

Very true, he said.

On the other hand, those steadfast natures which can better be depended upon, which in a battle are impregnable to fear and immovable, are equally immovable when there is anything to be learned; they are always in a torpid state, and are apt to yawn and go to sleep over any intellectual toil.

Quite true.

And yet we were saying that both qualities were necessary in those to whom the higher education is to be imparted, and who are to share in any office or command.

Certainly, he said.

And will they be a class which is rarely found?

Yes, indeed.

Then the aspirant must not only be tested in those labours and dangers and pleasures which we mentioned before, but there is another kind of probation which we did not mention—he must be exercised also in many kinds of knowledge, to see whether the soul will be able to endure the highest of all, or will faint under them, as in any other studies and exercises.

Yes, he said, you are quite right in testing him. But what do you mean by the highest of all knowledge?

You may remember, I said, that we divided the soul into three parts; and distinguished the several natures of justice, temperance, courage, and wisdom?

Indeed, he said, if I had forgotten, I should not deserve to hear more.

And do you remember the word of caution which preceded the discussion of them?

To what do you refer?

We were saying, if I am not mistaken, that he who wanted to see them in their perfect beauty must take a longer and more circuitous way, at the end of which they would appear; but that we could add on a popular exposition of them on a level with the discussion which has preceded. And you replied that such an exposition would be enough for you, and so the enquiry was continued in what to me seemed to be a very inaccurate manner; whether you were satisfied or not, it is for you to say.

Yes, he said, I thought and the others thought that you gave us a fair measure of truth.

But, my friend, I said, a measure of such things which in any degree falls short of the whole truth is not fair measure; for nothing imperfect is the measure of anything, although persons are too apt to be contented and think that they need search no further.

Not an uncommon case when people are indolent.

Yes, I said; and there cannot be any worse fault in a guardian of the State and of the laws.

True.

The guardian then, I said, must be required to take the longer circuit, and toil at learning as well as at gymnastics, or he will never reach the highest knowledge of all which, as we were just now saying, is his proper calling.

What, he said, is there a knowledge still higher than this—higher than justice and the other virtues?

Yes, I said, there is. And of the virtues too we must behold not the outline merely, as at present—nothing short of the most finished picture should satisfy us. When little things are elaborated with an infinity of pains, in order that they may appear in their full beauty and utmost clearness, how ridiculous that we should not think the highest truths worthy of attaining the highest accuracy!

A right noble thought; but do you suppose that we shall refrain from asking you what is this highest knowledge?

Nay, I said, ask if you will; but I am certain that you have heard the answer many times, and now you either do not understand me or, as I rather think, you are disposed to be troublesome; for you have often been told that the idea of good is the highest knowledge, and that all other things become useful and advantageous only by their use of this. You can hardly be ignorant that of this I was about to speak, concerning which, as you have often heard me say, we know so little; and, without which, any other knowledge or possession of any kind will profit us nothing. Do you think that the possession of all other things is of any value if we do not possess the good? or the knowledge of all other things if we have no knowledge of beauty and goodness?

Assuredly not.

You are further aware that most people affirm pleasure to be the good, but the finer sort of wits say it is knowledge?

Yes.

And you are aware too that the latter cannot explain what they mean by knowledge, but are obliged after all to say knowledge of the good?

How ridiculous!

Yes, I said, that they should begin by reproaching us with our ignorance of the good, and then presume our knowledge of it—for the good they define to be knowledge of the good, just as if we understood them when they use the term "good"—this is of course ridiculous.

Most true, he said.

And those who make pleasure their good are in equal perplexity; for they are compelled to admit that there are bad pleasures as well as good.

Certainly.

And therefore to acknowledge that bad and good are the same?

True.

There can be no doubt about the numerous difficulties in which this question is involved.

There can be none.

Further, do we not see that many are willing to do or to have or to seem to be what is just and honourable without the reality; but no one is satisfied with the appearance of good—the reality is what they seek; in the case of the good, appearance is despised by every one.

Very true, he said.

Of this then, which every soul of man pursues and makes the end of all his actions, having a presentiment that there is such an end, and yet hesitating because neither knowing the nature nor having the same assurance of this as of other things, and therefore losing whatever good there is in other things,—of a principle such and so great as this ought the best men in our State, to whom everything is entrusted, to be in the darkness of ignorance?

Certainly not, he said.

I am sure, I said, that he who does not know how the beautiful and the just are likewise good will be but a sorry guardian of them; and I suspect that no one who is ignorant of the good will have a true knowledge of them.

That, he said, is a shrewd suspicion of yours.

And if we only have a guardian who has this knowledge our State will be perfectly ordered?

Of course, he replied; but I wish that you would tell me whether you conceive this supreme principle of the good to be knowledge or pleasure, or different from either?

Aye, I said, I knew all along that a fastidious gentleman like you would not be contented with the thoughts of other people about these matters.

True, Socrates; but I must say that one who like you has passed a lifetime in the study of philosophy should not be always repeating the opinions of others, and never telling his own.

Well, but has any one a right to say positively what he does not know?

Not, he said, with the assurance of positive certainty; he has no right to do that: but he may say what he thinks, as a matter of opinion.

And do you not know, I said, that all mere opinions are bad, and the best of them blind? You would not deny that those who have any true notion without intelligence are only like blind men who feel their way along the road?

Very true.

And do you wish to behold what is blind and crooked and base, when others will tell you of brightness and beauty?

Still, I must implore you, Socrates, said Glaucon, not to turn away just as you are reaching the goal; if you will only give such an explanation of the good as you have already given of justice and temperance and the other virtues, we shall be satisfied.

Yes, my friend, and I shall be at least equally satisfied, but I cannot help fearing that I shall fail, and that my indiscreet zeal will bring ridicule upon me. No, sweet sirs, let us not at present ask what is the actual nature of the good, for to reach what is now in my thoughts would be an effort too great for me. But of the child of the good who is likest him, I would fain speak, if I could be sure that you wished to hear—otherwise, not.

By all means, he said, tell us about the child, and you shall remain in our debt for the account of the parent.

I do indeed wish, I replied, that I could pay, and you receive, the account of the parent, and not, as now, of the offspring only; take, however, this latter by way of interest, and at the same time have a care that I do not render a false account, although I have no intention of deceiving you.

Yes, we will take all the care that we can: proceed.

Yes, I said, but I must first come to an understanding with you, and remind you of what I have mentioned in the course of this discussion, and at many other times.

What?

The old story, that there is a many beautiful and a many good, and so of other things which we describe and define; to all of them "many" is applied.

True, he said.

And there is an absolute beauty and an absolute good, and of other things to which the term "many" is applied there is an absolute; for they may be brought under a single idea, which is called the essence of each.

Very true.

Book VII

. . . Did you never observe the narrow intelligence flashing from the keen eye of a clever rogue—how eager he is, how clearly his paltry soul sees the way to his end; he is the reverse of blind, but his keen eyesight is forced into the service of evil, and he is mischievous in proportion to his cleverness?

Very true, he said.

But what if there had been a circumcision of such natures in the days of their youth; and they had been severed from those sensual pleasures, such as eating and drinking, which, like leaden weights, were attached to them at their birth, and which drag them down and turn the vision of their souls upon the things that are below—if, I say, they had been released from these impediments and turned in the opposite direction, the very same faculty in them would have seen the truth as keenly as they see what their eyes are turned to now.

Very likely.

Yes, I said; and there is another thing which is likely, or rather a necessary inference from what has preceded, that neither the uneducated and uninformed of the truth, nor yet those who never make an end of their education, will be able ministers of State; not the former, because they have no single aim of duty which is the rule of all their actions, private as well as public; nor the latter, because they will not act at all except upon compulsion, fancying that they are already dwelling apart in the islands of the blest.

Very true, he replied.

Then, I said, the business of us who are the founders of the State will be to compel the best minds to attain that knowledge which we have already shown to be the greatest of all— they must continue to ascend until they arrive at the good; but when they have ascended and seen enough we must not allow them to do as they do now.

What do you mean?

I mean that they remain in the upper world: but this must not be allowed; they must be made to descend again among the prisoners in the den, and partake of their labours and honours, whether they are worth having or not.

But is not this unjust? he said; ought we to give them a worse life, when they might have a better?

You have again forgotten, my friend, I said, the intention of the legislator, who did not aim at making any one class in the State happy above the rest; the happiness was to be in the whole State, and he held the citizens together by persuasion and necessity, making them benefactors of the State, and therefore benefactors of one another; to this end he created them, not to please themselves, but to be his instruments in binding up the State.

True, he said, I had forgotten.

Observe, Glaucon, that there will be no injustice in compelling our philosophers to have a care and providence of others; we shall explain to them that in other States, men of their class are not obliged to share in the toil of politics: and this is reasonable, for they grow up at their own sweet will, and the government would rather not have them. Being self-taught, they cannot be expected to show any gratitude for a culture which they have never received. But we have brought you into the world to be rulers of the hive, kings of yourselves and of the other citizens, and have educated you far better and more perfectly than they have been educated, and you are better able to share in the double duty. Wherefore each of you, when his turn comes, must go down to the general underground abode, and get the habit of seeing in the dark. When you have acquired the habit, you will see ten thousand times better than the inhabitants of the den, and you will know what the several images are, and what they represent, because you have seen the beautiful and just and good in their truth. And thus our State which is also yours will be a reality, and not a dream only, and will be administered in a spirit unlike that of other States, in which men fight with one another about shadows only and are distracted in the struggle for power, which in their eyes is a great good. Whereas the truth is that the State in which the rulers are most reluctant to govern is always the best and most quietly governed, and the State in which they are most eager, the worst.

Quite true, he replied.

And will our pupils, when they hear this, refuse to take their turn at the toils of State, when they are allowed to spend the greater part of their time with one another in the heavenly light?

Impossible, he answered; for they are just men, and the commands which we impose upon them are just; there can be no doubt that every one of them will take office as a stern necessity, and not after the fashion of our present rulers of State.

Yes, my friend, I said; and there lies the point. You must contrive for your future rulers another and a better life than that of a ruler, and then you may have a well-ordered State; for only in the State which offers this, will they rule who are truly rich, not in silver and gold, but in virtue and wisdom, which are the true blessings of life. Whereas if they go to the administration of public affairs, poor and hungering after their own private advantage, thinking that hence they are to snatch the chief good, order there can never be; for they will be fighting about office, and the civil and domestic broils which thus arise will be the ruin of the rulers themselves and of the whole State.

Most true, he replied.

And the only life which looks down upon the life of political ambition is that of true philosophy. Do you know of any other?

Indeed, I do not, he said.

And those who govern ought not to be lovers of the task? For, if they are, there will be rival lovers, and they will fight.

No question.

Who then are those whom we shall compel to be guardians? Surely they will be the men who are wisest about affairs of State, and by whom the State is best administered, and who at the same time have other honours and another and a better life than that of politics?

They are the men, and I will choose them, he replied.

And now shall we consider in what way such guardians will be produced, and how they are to be brought from darkness to light,—as some are said to have ascended from the world below to the gods?

By all means, he replied.

The process, I said, is not the turning over of an oyster-shell, but the turning round of a soul passing from a day which is little better than night to the true day of being, that is, the ascent from below, which we affirm to be true philosophy?

Quite so.

And should we not enquire what sort of knowledge has the power of effecting such a change?

Certainly.

What sort of knowledge is there which would draw the soul from becoming to being? And another consideration has just occurred to me: You will remember that our young men are to be warrior athletes?

Yes, that was said.

Then this new kind of knowledge must have an additional quality?

What quality?

Usefulness in war.

Yes, if possible.

There were two parts in our former scheme of education, were there not?

Just so.

There was gymnastic which presided over the growth and decay of the body, and may therefore be regarded as having to do with generation and corruption?

True.

Then that is not the knowledge which we are seeking to discover?

No.

But what do you say of music, which also entered to a certain extent into our former scheme?

Music, he said, as you will remember, was the counterpart of gymnastic, and trained the guardians by the influences of habit, by harmony making them harmonious, by rhythm rhythmical, but not giving them science; and the words, whether fabulous or possibly true, had kindred elements of rhythm and harmony in them. But in music there was nothing which tended to that good which you are now seeking.

You are most accurate, I said, in your recollection; in music there certainly was nothing of the kind. But what branch of knowledge is there, my dear Glaucon, which is of the desired nature; since all the useful arts were reckoned mean by us?

Undoubtedly; and yet if music and gymnastic are excluded, and the arts are also excluded, what remains?

Well, I said, there may be nothing left of our special subjects; and then we shall have to take something which is not special, but of universal application.

What may that be?

A something which all arts and sciences and intelligences use in common, and which every one first has to learn among the elements of education.

What is that?

The little matter of distinguishing one, two, and three—in a word, number and calculation:—do not all arts and sciences necessarily partake of them?

Yes.

Then the art of war partakes of them?

To be sure.

Then Palamedes, whenever he appears in tragedy, proves Agamemnon ridiculously unfit to be a general. Did you never remark how he declares that he had invented number, and had numbered the ships and set in array the ranks of the army at Troy; which implies that they had never been numbered before, and Agamemnon must be supposed literally to have been incapable of counting his own feet—how could he if he was ignorant of number? And if that is true, what sort of general must he have been?

I should say a very strange one, if this was as you say.

Can we deny that a warrior should have knowledge of arithmetic?

Certainly he should, if he is to have the smallest understanding of military tactics, or indeed, I should rather say, if he is to be a man at all.

I should like to know whether you have the same notion which I have of this study?

What is your notion?

It appears to me to be a study of the kind which we are seeking, and which leads naturally to reflection, but never to have been rightly used; for the true use of it is simply to draw the soul towards being.

Will you explain your meaning? he said.

I will try, I said; and I wish you would share the enquiry with me, and say "yes" or "no" when I attempt to distinguish in my own mind what branches of knowledge have this attracting power, in order that we may have clearer proof that arithmetic is, as I suspect, one of them.

Explain, he said.

I mean to say that objects of sense are of two kinds; some of them do not invite thought because the sense is an adequate judge of them; while in the case of other objects sense is so untrustworthy that further enquiry is imperatively demanded.

You are clearly referring, he said, to the manner in which the senses are imposed upon by distance, and by painting in light and shade.

No, I said, that is not at all my meaning.

Then what is your meaning?

When speaking of uninviting objects, I mean those which do not pass from one sensation to the opposite; inviting objects are those which do; in this latter case the sense coming upon the object, whether at a distance or near, gives no more vivid idea of anything in particular than of its opposite. An illustration will make my meaning clearer:—here are three fingers—a little finger, a second finger, and a middle finger.

Very good.

You may suppose that they are seen quite close: And here comes the point.

What is it?

Each of them equally appears a finger, whether seen in the middle or at the extremity, whether white or black, or thick or thin—it makes no difference; a finger is a finger all the same. In these cases a man is not compelled to ask of thought the question, what is a finger? for the sight never intimates to the mind that a finger is other than a finger.

True.

And therefore, I said, as we might expect, there is nothing here which invites or excites intelligence.

There is not, he said.

But is this equally true of the greatness and smallness of the fingers? Can sight adequately perceive them? and is no difference made by the circumstance that one of the fingers is in the middle and another at the extremity? And in like manner does the touch adequately perceive the qualities of thickness or thinness, or softness or hardness? And so of the other senses; do they give perfect intimations of such matters? Is not their mode of operation on this wise—the sense which is concerned with the quality of hardness is necessarily concerned also with the quality of softness, and only intimates to the soul that the same thing is felt to be both hard and soft?

Your are quite right, he said.

And must not the soul be perplexed at this intimation which the sense gives of a hard which is also soft? What, again, is the meaning of light and heavy, if that which is light is also heavy, and that which is heavy, light?

Yes, he said, these intimations which the soul receives are very curious and require to be explained.

Yes, I said, and in these perplexities the soul naturally summons to her aid calculation and intelligence, that she may see whether the several objects announced to her are one or two.

True.

And if they turn out to be two, is not each of them one and different?

Certainly.

And if each is one, and both are two, she will conceive the two as in a state of division, for if they were undivided they could only be conceived of as one?

True.

The eye certainly did see both small and great, but only in a confused manner; they were not distinguished.

Yes.

Whereas the thinking mind, intending to light up the chaos, was compelled to reverse the process, and look at small and great as separate and not confused.

Very true.

Was not this the beginning of the enquiry "What is great?" and "What is small?"

Exactly so.

And thus arose the distinction of the visible and the intelligible.

Most true.

This was what I meant when I spoke of impressions which invited the intellect, or the reverse—those which are simultaneous with opposite impressions, invite thought; those which are not simultaneous do not.

I understand, he said, and agree with you.

And to which class do unity and number belong?

I do not know, he replied.

Think a little and you will see that what has preceded will supply the answer; for if simple unity could be adequately perceived by the sight or by any other sense, then, as we were saying in the case of the finger, there would be nothing to attract towards being; but when there is some contradiction always present, and one is the reverse of one and involves the conception of plurality, then thought begins to be aroused within us, and the soul perplexed and wanting to arrive at a decision asks "What is absolute unity?" This is the way in which the study of the one has a power of drawing and converting the mind to the contemplation of true being.

And surely, he said, this occurs notably in the case of one; for we see the same thing to be both one and infinite in multitude?

Yes, I said; and this being true of one must be equally true of all number?

Certainly.

And all arithmetic and calculation have to do with number?

Yes.

And they appear to lead the mind towards truth?

Yes, in a very remarkable manner.

Then this is knowledge of the kind for which we are seeking, having a double use, military and philosophical; for the man of war must learn the art of number or he will not know how to array his troops, and the philosopher also, because he has to rise out of the sea of change and lay hold of true being, and therefore he must be an arithmetician.

That is true.

And our guardian is both warrior and philosopher?

Certainly.

Then this is a kind of knowledge which legislation may fitly prescribe; and we must endeavour to persuade those who are to be the principal men of our State to go and learn arithmetic, not as amateurs, but they must carry on the study until they see the nature of numbers with the mind only; nor again, like merchants or retail-traders, with a view to buying or selling, but for the sake of their military use, and of the soul herself; and because this will be the easiest way for her to pass from becoming to truth and being.

That is excellent, he said.

Yes, I said, and now having spoken of it, I must add how charming the science is! and in how many ways it conduces to our desired end, if pursued in the spirit of a philosopher, and not of a shopkeeper!

How do you mean?

I mean, as I was saying, that arithmetic has a very great and elevating effect, compelling the soul to reason about abstract number, and rebelling against the introduction of visible or tangible objects into the argument. You know how steadily the masters of the art repel and ridicule any one who attempts to divide absolute unity when he is calculating, and if you divide, they multiply, taking care that one shall continue one and not become lost in fractions.

That is very true.

Now, suppose a person were to say to them: O my friends, what are these wonderful numbers about which you are reasoning, in which, as you say, there is a unity such as you demand, and each unit is equal, invariable, indivisible,—what would they answer?

They would answer, as I should conceive, that they were speaking of those numbers which can only be realised in thought.

Then you see that this knowledge may be truly called necessary, necessitating as it clearly does the use of the pure intelligence in the attainment of pure truth?

Yes; that is a marked characteristic of it.

And have you further observed, that those who have natural talent for calculation are generally quick at every other kind of knowledge; and even the dull, if they have had an arithmetical training, although they may derive no other advantage from it, always become much quicker than they would otherwise have been.

Very true, he said.

And indeed, you will not easily find a more difficult study, and not many as difficult.

You will not.

And, for all these reasons, arithmetic is a kind of knowledge in which the best natures should be trained, and which must not be given up.

I agree.

Let this then be made one of our subjects of education. And next, shall we enquire whether the kindred science also concerns us?

You mean geometry?

Exactly so.

Clearly, he said, we are concerned with that part of geometry which relates to war; for in pitching a camp, or taking up a position, or closing or extending the lines of an army, or any other military manoeuvre, whether in actual battle or on a march, it will make all the difference whether a general is or is not a geometrician.

Yes, I said, but for that purpose a very little of either geometry or calculation will be enough; the question relates rather to the greater and more advanced part of geometry—whether that tends in any degree to make more easy the vision of the idea of good; and thither, as I was saying, all things tend which compel the soul to turn her gaze towards that place, where is the full perfection of being, which she ought, by all means, to behold.

True, he said.

Then if geometry compels us to view being, it concerns us; if becoming only, it does not concern us?

Yes, that is what we assert.

Yet anybody who has the least acquaintance with geometry will not deny that such a conception of the science is in flat contradiction to the ordinary language of geometricians.

How so?

They have in view practice only, and are always speaking, in a narrow and ridiculous manner, of squaring and extending and applying and the like—they confuse the necessities of geometry with those of daily life; whereas knowledge is the real object of the whole science.

Certainly, he said.

Then must not a further admission be made?

What admission?

That the knowledge at which geometry aims is knowledge of the eternal, and not of aught perishing and transient.

That, he replied, may be readily allowed, and is true.

Then, my noble friend, geometry will draw the soul towards truth, and create the spirit of philosophy, and raise up that which is now unhappily allowed to fall down.

Nothing will be more likely to have such an effect.

Then nothing should be more sternly laid down than that the inhabitants of your fair city should by all means learn geometry. Moreover the science has indirect effects, which are not small.

Of what kind? he said.

There are the military advantages of which you spoke, I said; and in all departments of knowledge, as experience proves, any one who has studied geometry is infinitely quicker of apprehension than one who has not.

Yes indeed, he said, there is an infinite difference between them.

Then shall we propose this as a second branch of knowledge which our youth will study?

Let us do so, he replied.

And suppose we make astronomy the third—what do you say?

I am strongly inclined to it, he said; the observation of the seasons and of months and years is as essential to the general as it is to the farmer or sailor.

I am amused, I said, at your fear of the world, which makes you guard against the appearance of insisting upon useless studies; and I quite admit the difficulty of believing that in every man there is an eye of the soul which, when by other pursuits lost and dimmed, is by these purified and re-illumined; and is more precious far than ten thousand bodily eyes, for by it alone is truth seen. Now there are two classes of persons: one class of those who will agree with you and will take your words as a revelation; another class to whom they will be utterly unmeaning, and who will naturally deem them to be idle tales, for they see no sort of profit which is to be obtained from them. And therefore you had better decide at once with which of the two you are proposing to argue. You will very likely say with neither, and that your chief aim in carrying on the argument is your own improvement; at the same time you do not grudge to others any benefit which they may receive.

I think that I should prefer to carry on the argument mainly on my own behalf.

Then take a step backward, for we have gone wrong in the order of the sciences.

What was the mistake? he said.

After plane geometry, I said, we proceeded at once to solids in revolution, instead of taking solids in themselves; whereas after the second dimension the third, which is concerned with cubes and dimensions of depth, ought to have followed.

That is true, Socrates; but so little seems to be known as yet about these subjects.

Why, yes, I said, and for two reasons:—in the first place, no government patronises them; this leads to a want of energy in the pursuit of them, and they are difficult; in the second place, students cannot learn them unless they have a director. But then a director can hardly be found, and even if he could, as matters now stand, the students, who are very conceited, would not attend to him. That, however, would be otherwise if the whole State became the director of these studies and gave honour to them; then disciples would want to come, and there would be continuous and earnest search, and discoveries would be made; since even now, disregarded as they are by the world, and maimed of their fair proportions, and although none of their votaries can tell the use of them, still these studies force their way by their natural charm, and very likely, if they had the help of the State, they would some day emerge into light.

Yes, he said, there is a remarkable charm in them. But I do not clearly understand the change in the order. First you began with a geometry of plane surfaces?

Yes, I said.

And you placed astronomy next, and then you made a step backward?

Yes, and I have delayed you by my hurry; the ludicrous state of solid geometry, which, in natural order, should have followed, made me pass over this branch and go on to astronomy, or motion of solids.

True, he said.

Then assuming that the science now omitted would come into existence if encouraged by the State, let us go on to astronomy, which will be fourth.

The right order, he replied. And now, Socrates, as you rebuked the vulgar manner in which I praised astronomy before, my praise shall be given in you own spirit. For every one, as I think, must see that astronomy compels the soul to look upwards and leads us from this world to another.

Every one but myself, I said; to every one else this may be clear, but not to me.

And what then would you say?

I should rather say that those who elevate astronomy into philosophy appear to me to make us look downwards and not upwards.

What do you mean? he asked.

You, I replied, have in your mind a truly sublime conception of our knowledge of the things above. And I dare say that if a person were to throw his head back and study the fretted ceiling, you would still think that his mind was the percipient, and not his eyes. And you are very likely right, and I may be a simpleton: but, in my opinion, that knowledge only which is of being and of the unseen can make the soul look upwards, and whether a man gapes at the heavens or blinks on the ground, seeking to learn some particular of sense, I would deny that he can learn, for nothing of that sort is matter of science; his soul is looking downwards, not upwards, whether his way to knowledge is by water or by land, whether he floats, or only lies on his back.

I acknowledge, he said, the justice of your rebuke. Still, I should like to ascertain how astronomy can be learned in any manner more conducive to that knowledge of which we are speaking?

I will tell you, I said: The starry heaven which we behold is wrought upon a visible ground, and therefore, although the fairest and most perfect of visible things, must necessarily be deemed inferior far to the true motions of absolute swiftness and absolute slowness, which are relative to each other, and carry with them that which is contained in them, in the true number and in every true figure. Now, these are to be apprehended by reason and intelligence, but not by sight.

True, he replied.

The spangled heavens should be used as a pattern and with a view to that higher knowledge; their beauty is like the beauty of figures or pictures excellently wrought by the hand of Daedalus, or some other great artist, which we may chance to behold; any geometrician who saw them would appreciate the exquisiteness of their workmanship, but he would never dream of thinking that in them he could find the true equal or the true double, or the truth of any other proportion.

No, he replied, such an idea would be ridiculous.

And will not a true astronomer have the same feeling when he looks at the movements of the stars? Will he not think that heaven and the things in heaven are framed by the Creator of them in the most perfect manner? But he will never imagine that the proportions of night and day, or of both to the month, or of the month to the year, or of the stars to these and to one another, and any other things that are material and visible can also be eternal and subject to no deviation—that would be absurd; and it is equally absurd to take so much pains in investigating their exact truth.

I quite agree, though I never thought of this before.

Then, I said, in astronomy, as in geometry, we should employ problems, and let the heavens alone if we would approach the subject in the right way and so make the natural gift of reason to be of any real use.

That, he said, is a work infinitely beyond our present astronomers.

Yes, I said; and there are many other things which must also have a similar extension given to them, if our legislation is to be of any value. But can you tell me of any other suitable study?

No, he said, not without thinking.

Motion, I said, has many forms, and not one only; two of them are obvious enough even to wits no better than ours; and there are others, as I imagine, which may be left to wiser persons.

But where are the two?

There is a second, I said, which is the counterpart of the one already named.

And what may that be?

The second, I said, would seem relatively to the ears to be what the first is to the eyes; for I conceive that as the eyes are designed to look up at the stars, so are the ears to hear harmonious motions; and these are sister sciences—as the Pythagoreans say, and we, Glaucon, agree with them?

Yes, he replied.

But this, I said, is a laborious study, and therefore we had better go and learn of them; and they will tell us whether there are any other applications of these sciences. At the same time, we must not lose sight of our own higher object.

What is that?

There is a perfection which all knowledge ought to reach, and which our pupils ought also to attain, and not to fall short of, as I was saying that they did in astronomy. For in the science of harmony, as you probably know, the same thing happens. The teachers of harmony compare the sounds and consonances which are heard only, and their labour, like that of the astronomers, is in vain.

Yes, by heaven! he said; and 'tis as good as a play to hear them talking about their condensed notes, as they call them; they put their ears close alongside of the strings like persons catching a sound from their neighbour's wall—one set of them declaring that they distinguish an intermediate note and have found the least interval which should be the unit of measurement; the others insisting that the two sounds have passed into the same—either party setting their ears before their understanding.

You mean, I said, those gentlemen who tease and torture the strings and rack them on the pegs of the instrument: I might carry on the metaphor and speak after their manner of the blows which the plectrum gives, and make accusations against the strings, both of backwardness and forwardness to sound; but this would be tedious, and therefore I will only say that these are not the men, and that I am referring to the Pythagoreans, of whom I was just now proposing to enquire about harmony. For they too are in error, like the astronomers; they investigate the numbers of the harmonies which are heard, but they never attain to problems—that is to say, they never reach the natural harmonies of number, or reflect why some numbers are harmonious and others not.

That, he said, is a thing of more than mortal knowledge.

A thing, I replied, which I would rather call useful; that is, if sought after with a view to the beautiful and good; but if pursued to any other spirit, useless.

Very true, he said.

Now, when all these studies reach the point of inter-communion and connection with one another, and come to be considered in their mutual affinities, then, I think, but not till then, will the pursuit of them have a value for our objects; otherwise there is no profit in them.

I suspect so; but you are speaking, Socrates, of a vast work.

What do you mean? I said; the prelude or what? Do you not know that all this is but the prelude to the actual strain which we have to learn? For you surely would not regard the skilled mathematician as a dialectician?

Assuredly not, he said; I have hardly ever known a mathematician who was capable of reasoning.

But do you imagine that men who are unable to give and take a reason will have the knowledge which we require of them?

Neither can this be supposed.

And so, Glaucon, I said, we have at last arrived at the hymn of dialectic. This is that strain which is of the intellect only, but which the faculty of sight will nevertheless be found to imitate; for sight, as you may remember, was imagined by us after a while to behold the real animals and stars, and last of all the sun himself. And so with dialectic; when a person starts on the discovery of the absolute by the light of reason only, and without any assistance of sense, and perseveres until by pure intelligence he arrives at the perception of the absolute good, he at last finds himself at the end of the intellectual world, as in the case of sight at the end of the visible.

Exactly, he said.

Then this is the progress which you call dialectic?

True.

But the release of the prisoners from chains, and their translation from the shadows to the images and to the light, and the ascent from the underground den to the sun, while in his presence they are vainly trying to look on animals and plants and the light of the sun, but are able to perceive even with their weak eyes the images in the water [which are divine], and are the shadows of true existence (not shadows of images cast by a light of fire, which compared with the sun is only an image)—this power of elevating the highest principle in the soul to the contemplation of that which is best in existence, with which we may compare the raising of that faculty which is the very light of the body to the sight of that which is brightest in the material and visible world—this power is given, as I was saying, by all that study and pursuit of the arts which has been described.

I agree in what you are saying, he replied, which may be hard to believe, yet, from another point of view, is harder still to deny. This, however, is not a theme to be treated of in passing only, but will have to be discussed again and again. And so, whether our conclusion be true or false, let us assume all this, and proceed at once from the prelude or preamble to the chief strain, and describe that in like manner. Say, then, what is the nature and what are the divisions of dialectic, and what are the paths which lead thither; for these paths will also lead to our final rest?

Dear Glaucon, I said, you will not be able to follow me here, though I would do my best, and you should behold not an image only but the absolute truth, according to my notion. Whether what I told you would or would not have been a reality I cannot venture to say; but you would have seen something like reality; of that I am confident.

Doubtless, he replied.

But I must also remind you, that the power of dialectic alone can reveal this, and only to one who is a disciple of the previous sciences.

Of that assertion you may be as confident as of the last.

And assuredly no one will argue that there is any other method of comprehending by any regular process all true existence or of ascertaining what each thing is in its own nature; for the arts in general are concerned with the desires or opinions of men, or are cultivated with a view to production and construction, or for the preservation of such productions and constructions; and as to the mathematical sciences which, as we were saying, have some apprehension of true being—geometry and the like—they only dream about being, but never can they behold the waking reality so long as they leave the hypotheses which they use unexamined, and are unable to give an account of them. For when a man knows not his own first principle, and when the conclusion and intermediate steps are also constructed out of he knows not what, how can he imagine that such a fabric of convention can ever become science?

Impossible, he said.

Then dialectic, and dialectic alone, goes directly to the first principle and is the only science which does away with hypotheses in order to make her ground secure; the eye of the soul, which is literally buried in an outlandish slough, is by her gentle aid lifted upwards; and she uses as handmaids and helpers in the work of conversion, the sciences which we have been discussing. Custom terms them sciences, but they ought to have some other name, implying greater clearness than opinion and less clearness than science: and this, in our previous sketch, was called understanding. But why should we dispute about names when we have realities of such importance to consider?

Why indeed, he said, when any name will do which expresses the thought of the mind with clearness?

At any rate, we are satisfied, as before, to have four divisions; two for intellect and two for opinion, and to call the first division science, the second understanding, the third belief, and the fourth perception of shadows, opinion being concerned with becoming, and intellect with being; and so to make a proportion:—

As being is to becoming, so is pure intellect to opinion. And as intellect is to opinion, so is science to belief, and understanding to the perception of shadows.

PARMENIDES

What is your meaning, Zeno? Do you maintain that if being is many, it must be both like and unlike, and that this is impossible, for neither can the like be unlike, nor the unlike like—is that your position?

Just so, said Zeno.

And if the unlike cannot be like or the like unlike, then, according to you, being could not be many; for this would involve an impossibility. In all that you say have you any other purpose except to disprove the being of the many? and is not each division of your treatise intended to furnish a separate proof of this, there being in all as many proofs of the not-being of the many as you have composed arguments? Is that your meaning, or have I misunderstood you?

No, said Zeno; you have correctly understood my general purpose.

I see, Parmenides, said Socrates, that Zeno would like to be not only one with you in friendship but your second self in his writings too; he puts what you say in another way, and would fain make believe that he is telling us something which is new. For you in your poems say "The All is one," and of this you adduce excellent proofs; and he on the other hand says that it is not many, and on behalf of this he offers overwhelming evidence. You affirm unity, he denies plurality. And so you deceive the world into believing that you are saying different things when really you are saying much the same. This is a strain of art beyond the reach of most of us.

Yes, Socrates, said Zeno. But although you are as keen as a Spartan hound in pursuing the track, you do not fully apprehend the true motive of the composition, which is not really such an artificial work as you imagine; for what you speak of was an accident—there was no pretence of a great purpose, nor any serious intention of deceiving the world. The truth is, that these writings of mine were meant to protect the arguments of Parmenides against those who make fun of him and seek to show the many ridiculous and contradictory

From "Parmenides," in *The Dialogues of Plato*, trans. B. Jowett (Oxford: Clarendon Press, 1892).

results which they suppose to follow from the affirmation of the one. My answer is addressed to the partisans of the many, whose attack I return with interest by retorting upon them that their hypothesis of the being of many, if followed out, appears to be still more ridiculous than the hypothesis of the being of one. Zeal for my master led me to write the book in the days of my youth, but someone stole the copy, and therefore I had no choice whether it should be published or not; the motive, however, of writing was not the ambition of an elder man, but the pugnacity of a young one. This you do not seem to see, Socrates; though in other respects, as I was saying, your notion is a very just one.

I understand, said Socrates, and quite accept your account. But tell me, Zeno, do you not further think that there is an idea of likeness, detached and existing by itself, and an opposite idea, which is the essence of unlikeness, and that in these two you and I and all other things to which we apply the term may participate—things which participate in likeness become in that degree and manner like; and so far as they participate in unlikeness become in that degree unlike; or again are both like and unlike in the degree in which they participate in both? And even though all things partake of both opposites, and be both like and unlike to themselves by reason of this participation, where is the wonder? Now if a person could prove the absolute like to become unlike, or the absolute unlike to become like, that, in my opinion, would indeed be a wonder; but there is nothing extraordinary, Zeno, in showing that the things which only partake of likeness and unlikeness experience both. Nor, again, if a person were to show that all is one by partaking of unity, and at the same time many by partaking of plurality, would that be very astonishing. But if he were to show me that the absolute one was many, or the absolute many one, I should be truly amazed. And so of all the rest: I should be surprised to hear that the natures or ideas themselves had these opposite qualities; but not if a person wanted to prove of me that I was many and also one. When he wanted to show I was many he would say that I have a right and a left side, and a front and a back, and an upper and a lower half, for I cannot deny that I partake of multitude; when, on the other hand, he wants to prove that I am one, he will say that we who are here assembled are seven, and that I am one man and partake of unity. In both instances he proves his case. So again, if a person sets out to show that such things as wood, stones, and the like, being many are also one, we shall say that he is proving that something is at once one and many, but not that unity is many, or plurality one; and that he is uttering not a paradox but a truism. If, however, someone were to begin by setting apart the ideas in such instances as I was just now mentioning—like, unlike, one, many, rest, motion, and all similar ideas—and then to show that these admit of admixture with and separation from one another, I should be very much astonished. This part of your argument appears to be treated by you, Zeno, in a very spirited manner; but, as I was saying, I should be far more amazed if anyone found in the ideas themselves which are apprehended by reason, the same puzzle and entanglement which you have shown to exist in visible objects.

While Socrates was speaking, Pythodorus thought that Parmenides and Zeno were not altogether pleased at the successive steps of the argument; but still they gave the closest attention, and often looked at one another, and smiled as if in admiration of him. When he had finished, Parmenides expressed their feelings in the following words:—

Socrates, he said, I admire the bent of your mind towards philosophy; tell me now, was this your own distinction between ideas in themselves and the things which partake of them? and do you think that there is an idea of likeness apart from the likeness which we possess, and of the one and many, and of the other things which Zeno mentioned?

I think that there are such ideas, said Socrates.

Parmenides proceeded: And would you also make absolute ideas of the just and the beautiful and the good, and of all that class?

Yes, he said, I should.

And would you make an idea of man apart from us and from all other human creatures, or of fire and water?

I am often undecided, Parmenides, as to whether I ought to include them or not.

And would you feel equally undecided, Socrates, about things of which the mention may provoke a smile?—I mean such things as hair, mud, dirt, or anything else which is vile and paltry; is it hard to decide whether each of these has an idea distinct from the actual objects with which we come into contact, or not?

Certainly not, said Socrates; visible things like these are such as they appear to us, and I am afraid that there would be an absurdity in assuming any idea of them, although I sometimes get disturbed, and begin to think that there is nothing without an idea; but then again, when I have taken up this position, I run away, because I am afraid that I may fall into a bottomless pit of nonsense, and perish; and so I return to the ideas of which I was just now speaking, and occupy myself with them.

Yes, Socrates, said Parmenides; that is because you are still young; the time will come, if I am not mistaken, when philosophy will have a firmer grasp of you, and then you will not despise even the meanest things; at your age, you are too much disposed to regard the opinions of men. But I should like to know whether you mean that there are certain ideas of which all other things partake, and from which they derive their names; that similars, for example, become similar, because they partake of similarity; and great things become great, because they partake of greatness; and that just and beautiful things become just and beautiful, because they partake of justice and beauty?

Yes, certainly, said Socrates, that is my meaning.

Then each individual partakes either of the whole of the idea or else of a part of the idea? Can there be any other mode of participation?

There cannot be, he said.

Then do you think that the whole idea is one, and yet, being one, is in each one of the many?

What objection is there, Parmenides? said Socrates.

The result will be that one and the same thing will exist as a whole at the same time in many separate individuals, and will therefore be in a state of separation from itself.

Nay, but the idea may be like the day which is one, and the same in many places at once, and yet continuous with itself; in this way each idea may be one and the same in all at the same time.

I like your way, Socrates, of making one in many places at once. You mean to say, that if I were to spread out a sail and cover a number of men, there would be one whole including many—is not that your meaning?

I think so.

And would you say that the whole sail includes each man, or a part of it only, and different parts different men?

The latter.

Then, Socrates, the ideas themselves will be divisible, and things which participate in them will have a part of them only and not the whole idea existing in each of them?

That seems to follow.

Then would you like to say, Socrates, that the one idea is really divisible and yet remains one?

Certainly not, he said.

Suppose that you divide absolute greatness, and that of the many great things each one is great in virtue of a portion of greatness less than absolute greatness—is that conceivable? No.

Or will each equal thing, if possessing some small portion of equality less than absolute equality, be equal to some other thing by virtue of that portion only?

Impossible.

Or suppose one of us to have a portion of smallness; this is but a part of the small, and therefore the absolutely small will be greater; while that to which the abstracted part of the small is added will be smaller and not greater than before.

That, indeed, can scarcely be.

Then in what way, Socrates, will all things participate in the ideas, if they are unable to participate in them either as parts or wholes?

Indeed, he said, you have asked a question which is not easily answered.

Well, said Parmenides, and what do you say of another question?

What question?

I imagine that your reason for assuming one idea of each kind is as follows:—Whenever a number of objects appear to you to be great there doubtless seems to you to be one and the same idea (or nature) visible in them all; hence you conceive of greatness as one.

Very true, said Socrates.

But now, if you allow your mind in like manner to embrace in one view this real greatness and those other great things, will not one more greatness arise, being required to account for the semblance of greatness in all these?

It would seem so.

Then another idea of greatness, now comes into view over and above absolute greatness and the individuals which partake of it; and then another, over and above all these, by virtue of which they will all be great, and so you will be left not with a single idea in every case, but with an infinite number.

But may not the ideas, asked Socrates, be thoughts only, and have no proper existence except in our minds, Parmenides? For in that case each idea may still be one, and not experience this infinite multiplication.

Tell me, then: can each thought have its own definite nature, and yet be a thought of nothing?

Impossible, he said.

The thought must be of something?

Yes.

Of something which is or which is not?

Of something which is.

Must it not be of a single something, which the thought recognizes as attaching to all, being a single form or nature?

Yes.

And will not the something, which is apprehended as one and the same in all, be an idea?

From that, again, there is no escape.

Then, said Parmenides, if you say that everything else must participate in the ideas, must you not say either that everything is made up of thoughts, and that all things think; or that they are thoughts but have no thought?

So this view, Parmenides, is no more rational than the previous one. In my opinion the ideas are, as it were, patterns fixed in nature, and other things are like them and resemblances of them—what is meant by the participation of other things in the ideas, is really assimilation to them.

But if, said he, the individual is like the idea, is it possible that the idea should not be like the copy, in so far as this has been fashioned in resemblance of the idea? That which is like, cannot be conceived of as other than the like of like.

Impossible.

And when two things are alike, must they not partake of the same idea?

They must.

And will not that, by partaking in which like things are alike, be the idea itself?

Certainly.

Then the idea cannot be like the individual, or the individual like the idea; for if they are alike, some further idea of likeness will always be coming to light, and if that be like anything else, another; and new ideas will be always arising, if the idea resembles that which partakes of it?

Quite true.

The theory, then, that other things participate in the ideas by resemblance, has to be given up, and some other mode of participation devised?

It would seem so.

Do you see then, Socrates, how great is the difficulty of making this distinction of ideas (or classes) existing by themselves?

Yes, indeed.

And, further, let me say that as yet you only understand a small part of the difficulty which is involved if you make of each thing a single idea, parting it off from other things.

What difficulty? he said.

There are many, but the greatest of all is this:—If an opponent argues that these ideas, being such as we say they ought to be, must remain unknown, no one can prove to him that he is wrong, unless he who denies their existence be a man of great natural ability and experience, and is willing to follow a long and laborious demonstration; he will remain unconvinced, and still insist that they cannot be known.

What do you mean, Parmenides? said Socrates.

In the first place, I think, Socrates, that you, or anyone who maintains the existence of absolute essences, will admit that they cannot exist in us.

No, said Socrates; for then they would be no longer absolute.

True, he said; and therefore when ideas are what they are in relation to one another, their essence is determined by a relation among themselves, and has nothing to do with the resemblances, or whatever they are to be termed, which are in our sphere, and from which we receive this or that name when we partake of them. And the things which are within our sphere and have the same names with them, are likewise only relative to one another, and not to the ideas which have the same names with them, but belong to themselves and not to them.

What do you mean? said Socrates.

I may illustrate my meaning in this way, said Parmenides. Suppose a man to be a master or a slave—he is obviously not a slave of the abstract idea of a master, or a master of the abstract idea of a slave; the relation is one of man to man. The idea of mastership in the abstract must be defined by relation to the idea of slavery in the abstract, and vice versa. But the things familiar to us are not empowered to act on those ideas, nor the ideas to act upon familiar things; but, as I have said, the ideas belong to and stand in relation to each other, as also do the things in our familiar world. Do you see my meaning?

Yes, said Socrates, I quite see your meaning.

And will not knowledge—I mean absolute knowledge—answer to absolute truth?

Certainly.

And each kind of absolute knowledge will answer to each kind of absolute being?

Yes.

But the knowledge which we have, will answer to the truth which we have; and again, each kind of knowledge which we have, will be a knowledge of each kind of being which we have?

Certainly.

But the ideas themselves, as you admit, we have not, and cannot have?

No, we cannot.

And the absolute natures or kinds are known severally by the absolute idea of knowledge?

Yes.

And we have not got the idea of knowledge?

No.

Then none of the ideas are known, at least by us, because we have no share in absolute knowledge?

I suppose not.

Then the nature of the beautiful in itself, and of the good in itself, and all other ideas which we suppose to exist absolutely, are unknown to us?

It would seem so.

Observe that there is a stranger consequence still.

What is it?

Would you, or would you not, say that absolute knowledge, if there is such a thing, must be a far more exact knowledge than our knowledge; and the same of beauty and of the rest?

Yes.

And no one is more likely than God to have this most exact knowledge, if other things can share in it at all?

Certainly.

But then, will God, having the true knowledge, also be capable of knowledge of human things?

Why not?

Because, Socrates, said Parmenides, we have admitted that the ideas are not valid in relation to human things; nor human things in relation to them; the relations of either are limited to their respective spheres.

Yes, that has been admitted.

And if God has this perfect authority and perfect knowledge, his authority cannot rule us, nor his knowledge know us or any human thing; just as our authority does not extend to the gods, nor our knowledge know anything which is divine, so by parity of reason they, being gods, are not our masters, neither do they know the things of men.

Yet, surely, said Socrates, to deprive God of knowledge is monstrous.

These, Socrates, said Parmenides, are a few and only a few of the difficulties in which we are involved if ideas really are and we determine each of them to be an absolute unity. He who hears what may be said against them will deny the very existence of them—and even if they do exist, he will say that they must of necessity be unknown to man; and he will seem to have reason on his side, and as we were remarking just now, will be very difficult to convince; a man must be gifted with very considerable ability before he can learn that everything has a class and an absolute essence; and still more remarkable will he be who discovers all these things for himself, and having thoroughly investigated them is able to teach them to others.

I agree with you, Parmenides, said Socrates; and what you say is very much to my mind.

And yet, Socrates, said Parmenides, if a man, fixing his attention on these and the like difficulties, does away with ideas of things and will not admit that every individual thing has its own determinate idea which is always one and the same, he will have nothing on which his mind can rest; and so he will utterly destroy the power of reasoning, as you seem to me to have particularly noted.

Very true, he said.

But then, what is to become of philosophy? Whither shall we turn, if the ideas are unknown?

I certainly do not see my way at present.

Yes, said Parmenides; and I think that this arises, Socrates, out of your attempting to define the beautiful, the just, the good, and the ideas generally, without sufficient previous training. I noticed your deficiency, when I heard you talking here with your friend Aristoteles, the day before yesterday. The impulse that carries you towards philosophy is assuredly noble and divine; but there is an art which is called by the vulgar idle talking, and which is often imagined to be useless; in that you must train and exercise yourself, now that you are young, or truth will elude your grasp.

PHILEBUS

SOCRATES: The awe which I always feel, Protarchus, in mentioning the gods by name is not a mere human sentiment, but goes far beyond the greatest fear. So now I give to Aphrodite any name that may be pleasing to that goddess. But I am quite aware that pleasure is a Proteus that assumes many aspects; and, as I said, if we begin with her we are bound to consider well and see what kind of nature she has. For though Pleasure is, so far as mere name goes, abstractedly one, yet we all know that it takes forms many and varied, and in some sense, unlike to each other. For observe: we talk of the *pleasures* of the dissolute man; the *pleasure* that a sober man takes in the mere fact of his soberness; the *pleasures* of one who talks nonsense, and is brimful of nonsensical notions and hopes; the *pleasures* again that the Thinker takes in the act of thinking; and if we venture to say that these two classes of pleasures are like each other, surely we shall justly be thought to have very little sense ourselves.

PROTARCHUS: Very true, Socrates; but that is because these pleasures that you enumerate come from things that are opposite; yet it does not follow that the plea-

From *Philebus of Plato,* trans. F. A. Paley (Cambridge, England: Deighton, Bell & Co., 1873).

sures themselves are opposed to each other. For how can pleasure be anything else than as like as possible to pleasure,—the thing itself to itself?

SOC.: Well, my good friend, so is colour as like as possible to colour; so far as
the mere fact is concerned, there will be no difference as to its being all
colour. But we all know that black, besides being different from, is also
most directly opposed to white. And so indeed is shape most like to shape,
for the matter of that. It is all one *in kind;* but, parts compared with parts,
some of them are most directly opposite to each other, and others, we
know, have a very wide difference. Many other things too we shall find
in the same position; so that you must not too far trust this kind of argument, which classes all the most opposite things under one head. I am
afraid, indeed, that we shall find some pleasures to stand in direct opposition to others.

PROT.: Perhaps so; but what harm will that do to our argument?

SOC.: Because, we shall reply, you call them, as being unlike, by a wrong name.
You assert that all that is pleasant is also good. Now, that things pleasant
are pleasant, no reasoner denies; but, though some of them,—the greater
part, I fear,—are bad, and some, as we admit, good, you call them all
"good," though you are willing to allow that the pleasures themselves are
unlike, if one should press you hard in the argument. What one condition
or quality, then, is there in the bad and the good pleasures alike, that
makes you say all pleasures are a good?

PROT.: What, Socrates! Do you think any man would grant, when he has taken as
his axiom that "Pleasure is the Chief Good,"—I say, do you suppose that
any one will tolerate your assertion, that *some* pleasures only are good, and
that there are some others which are bad?

SOC.: Well, you will at least allow that pleasures are unlike each other, and some
even contrary.

PROT.: No, not in so far as they are *pleasures.*

SOC.: We come back to the same assertion, my Protarchus. For if so, we must
say that neither is pleasure different from pleasure, but all are alike; and
the instances just cited do not affect us at all. Thus we shall have to bear a
defeat from making random assertions, like the weakest and most inexperienced of reasoners.

PROT.: What do you mean?

SOC.: Why, if I, following your example, and determined to fight it out, venture
to assert that nothing is so like its opposite as what is most unlike it, I
shall be able to avail myself of your argument of "it's all the same." And
thus we shall prove ourselves to be rather too young, and our reasoning
will drift out of its course and be lost. So let us beat back, and perhaps if
we start again from the point we began with, we may hope to come to an
understanding with each other.

PROT.: Tell me how you mean.

SOC.: Conceive me again questioned by you, Protarchus.

PROT.: On what point?

SOC.: Whether intellect, exact knowledge, mind, and all those qualities which I at first assumed in my thesis as "good," when I was asked what "The Good" can be,—will not be open to the very same conclusions as your argument about pleasure.

PROT.: How so?

SOC.: All the kinds of knowledge, taken together, will seem so many, that some of them must be unlike to each other. And if some are even in some way opposed, surely I should not deserve the name of a sound reasoner on the present occasion, if through fear of this result of "contraries," I were to assert that no one kind of knowledge is unlike another, and so were to let this argument be lost, as if it were mere idle talk, and we ourselves were to get safe to the shore on the plank of a paradox.

PROT.: Well, certainly *that* must not happen,—except indeed the getting off safe. However, I like the fairness of terms presented by your argument and mine. Granted that pleasures are many and unlike, and the kinds of knowledge many and diverse.

SOC.: This diversity then, Protarchus, in the good which you and I respectively advocate, I propose that we should try not to disguise or conceal. Let us rather bring it forward to the notice of all, and not shrink from the conclusion, if our arguments on being examined should give evidence to show conclusively whether we ought to call Pleasure "The Good," or Intellect, or some other third thing. For now, of course, we are not contending with this object, that *my* view, or your view, shall be the winner; both of us, I suppose, are bound to aid that cause which is the truest.

PROT.: Undoubtedly.

SOC.: Then let us put this proposition on a still firmer footing by coming to an agreement upon it.

PROT.: What proposition?

SOC.: One which causes much trouble to all, whether they like or (as is sometimes the case with some people) dislike it.

PROT.: Express yourself more clearly.

SOC.: I mean, a proposition which has just now presented itself, by a kind of chance, to our notice, and the nature of which is very strange; for it *is* strange, when so stated, that "Many are One," and "One is Many"; and it is easy to argue against any one who takes either as his thesis.

PROT.: Is this then your meaning,—when somebody says that I, Protarchus, who am by nature one, am also on the other hand several, thus assuming that there are ever so many *me*'s, and some of them even contrary to each other,—the tall and the little, and the heavy and the light, in one and the same individual, and so on in numerous other relations?

SOC.: What you have mentioned, Protarchus, is only the popular notion of the marvellous on the subject of the "One and Many." Such a notion now-a-days it is allowed, one might say, by all, that we ought not to take up; they regard it as puerile and obvious, and rather a hindrance than a help to argument. Indeed, they tell us that we should not entertain even such questions as this,—as when some one separately specifies the members or other parts of a particular thing, and then gets another to admit that all these members together form that original "One"; since he only laughs at him as he proves that he has been forced to make the portentous statements, that the One is many and infinite, and the Many but one!

PROT.: And pray what other kinds of "One and Many" are there, which have *not* as yet been given up or become hackneyed on this same subject?

SOC.: When, my son, we apply this doctrine of Unity not to things that are born and die, as in the case we just now took,—for in this instance, and in Unity of this sort, as I just now said, it is generally admitted that we should not take up such a subject for inquiry;—but when one essays to view Man as One, or Ox, or Beauty or Goodness, it is about these and suchlike unities that all the pains are taken, with careful subdivision, and all the real difficulty is felt.

PROT.: In what respect?

SOC.: In the first place, whether we must conceive that any such units have a *real* existence at all; in the next, in what sense, if each of these is One and ever the same, (that is, not admitting of either birth or destruction), we can conceive it still in the most unchangeable manner to remain this One and no other; then, whether we are to assume such a unit as separated into many parts and dispersed through the infinity of things created, or existing as a whole outside of itself,—which, of course, would seem the greatest impossibility of all, that what is One and the same should at the same time be in One and in Many. These, Protarchus, are the cases of "One and Many," viz. in abstracts, and not in those others, the concretes, which are the causes of all perplexity, if not carefully defined and understood, and on the other hand, if they are so, a source of great facility and convenience.

PROT.: If so, Socrates, it is our duty first to work out this argument thoroughly in our present discussion.

SOC.: I should myself certainly be inclined to say so.

PROT.: Then take it for granted that all of us, the present company, are willing to accept your views on these subjects. As for Philebus, indeed, it is best perhaps not to rouse him by putting any question, since he is well out of the discussion.

SOC.: Very well, then. Where shall one take up the fight that has raged so long and with such different results on the matters in dispute? . . . We say, if I mistake not, that this same "One and Many," called into being by discussions, goes the round of every subject of conversation, whether new or old. And as this did not begin in our time, so there is no chance of its ever ceasing; but something of this sort, as it seems to me, is an unfailing and eternal property of the subjects themselves that arises in our minds. And when any of our young men on any occasion has first tried it, he is as delighted with it as if he had discovered a treasury of wisdom, nay, he is transported with pleasure, and would fain allow no subject to rest, at one time giving it a turn in this direction, and lumping it together into one, at another, pulling it to pieces again and separating it into parts, thus perplexing himself first and principally, and next, whoever happens to be near him at the time, whether younger or older or of the same age with himself. And in doing this he spares neither father nor mother nor any other of his hearers,—I might almost say, of the animals in general, and not merely the human kind. For, of course, he would not be likely to spare any of the foreign people, if he could but get some one to make them understand him.

PROT.: Do you not see, Socrates, how many we are, and that all of us are young? Have you no fear lest we should set upon you with Philebus, if you go on abusing us thus? However, we know what you mean; and if there is any way or any shift by which the confusion we are now in would good-naturedly go and leave the argument to ourselves, or if we could find any better way than this for discovering the truth, do you take up the cause with zeal, and we will go with you to the best of our power. For the subject before us is no trifling one, Socrates.

SOC.: Indeed it is not, my dear boys, as Philebus styles you in his address. There is, however, no better way, nor is there ever likely to be, than the one of which I have ever been an ardent admirer, though many a time 'ere now it has escaped from me and left me friendless and forlorn.

PROT.: What way is this? Only let us hear it.

SOC.: It is one which it is not very difficult to make intelligible to you, but which it is very hard indeed to adopt. It is one by which all the discoveries that were ever made in art have become known to us. Now mind what way I am speaking of.

PROT.: Only tell us.

SOC.: It was a gift of the gods to men, as it seems to me, that was flung down from some store-house in heaven by one Prometheus, together with very bright fire. And our forefathers,—better men than ourselves, and in closer converse with the gods,—have handed down to us this tradition, that all things which are said by us to *be,* are composed of both One and Many, and have in them the finite and the infinite as part of their nature. With this constitution then of things before us, it became our duty in all cases to propose to ourselves some one general view for investigation, since we are sure to find it at the bottom of every subject. When we have got hold of this, after *one* we should consider *two,* should there be two, or if not, then three, or some other number, and again each of these units in the same way, till we have clearly perceived the true nature of the original one, viz. not only that it is One and Many, and contains an indefinite number of parts, but also *how many* that can be counted up. But the note or character of infinity we must not apply to plurality, till one has fully seen all the number that plurality has between the original one and infinity. *Then* we may let each unit in them all pass into infinity, and concern ourselves no further with it. The gods then, as I said, so taught us to consider, to learn, and to inform each other. But the present degenerate race of philosophers arrive at the One and the Many too quickly and superficially; for after the One they immediately get to the Infinite, and take no account of intervening numbers. But it is in these very numbers that the difference consists between our conversing with each other like logicians, or on the other hand, like mere disputants.

PROT.: Some of these views of yours I think, Socrates, that I begin to understand; but on other points I should like to hear more plainly what you mean.

SOC.: Well, what I mean is clear enough, surely, in the letters of the alphabet. You may therefore get an idea of it from the very rudiments of your own education.

PROT.: How so?

SOC.: Articulate sound, you will grant, is one, as it proceeds from the mouth; and yet again it is infinite in the number of variations in each and from every individual.

PROT.: Certainly it is.

SOC.: And yet we are not fully informed by knowing either of these facts, viz. that there is Infinity or that there is Oneness in sound. No; it is the knowledge of the number and nature of sounds that makes each of us a grammarian.

PROT.: Most true.

SOC.: And surely what makes a man a musician is this very same knowledge.

PROT.: How so?

SOC.: Sound, we said, according to the former science, is One in itself.

PROT.: Assuredly.

SOC.: Now then let us assume two general kinds, the low-pitch and the high-pitch, and a third, the *homotone,* or note in unison. Is it not so?

PROT.: It is.

SOC.: Well, but you would not as yet be an accomplished musician if you knew only these facts. While, if you did not know them, you would be, one might almost say, good for nothing in musical science.

PROT.: Assuredly so.

SOC.: But when, my friends, you have mastered the number and the nature of the Intervals in sound, in respect of treble and bass, and the limits of these intervals, and the combinations that are made from them,—with a perfect knowledge of all which our predecessors taught us, their followers, to call them "harmonies"; when too, in the various movements of the body, you have discovered that other corresponding effects are produced, (which, numerically measured, they tell us we should call by other terms, "Time" and "Metre";) and when at the same time you begin to perceive that this is the view you ought to take about every "One and Many";—when, I repeat, you have fairly realised all these facts and in this way, then you become an adept; and when, by careful thought, you have apprehended any other truth, so too you are made intelligent in that. But this Infinity of number of and in each subject of thought makes you stray infinitely far from the right view, and does not allow you to become distinguished, or to make a figure in the world, as never having looked to any figures in anything.

PROT.: It seems to me, Philebus, that Socrates has admirably put what he has just now said.

PHIL.: So it seems to me also; as far as *this* subject goes. But why in the world is the argument addressed to *us,* and what is its purport?

SOC.: That indeed, Protarchus, Philebus has very properly asked.

PROT.: He has, in sooth; and therefore do you answer him.

SOC.: I will do so after a few more remarks on the subject itself. For as, when one has taken some one genus, he ought not, according to our view, to look at once to the nature of the Infinite, but to some number; so conversely, when one is obliged to take the Infinite first, he ought not to look to One immediately, but in this case too to a certain number containing in each term a certain plurality, and so try to take in that view, thus ending in *One* from *all.* But let us again illustrate our meaning by taking the case of letters.

SOC.: When *Voice* was found to be unlimited,—whether it was a god who perceived this first or some god-like man, as there is a tradition in Egypt which says that it was Theuth; for he seems to have been the first to notice the vowel-sounds in that infinite, not as a One, but as a plurality, and again, other sounds, not of the vowel-kind, yet partaking of the nature of voice, and to observe that these too had a certain number of their own; when moreover he had distinguished a third kind of letters which we now call *mutes,*—he next proceeded to class by themselves the consonants and the mutes, so far as to make each class One, and the vowels and the medials in the same way, until he had ascertained their precise number, and so gave the name of "letter" to each and all the primary sounds. Seeing however that none of us would ever comprehend any one genus of sound by itself, and without them all, he again considered this group or combination as One, and as making all these various sounds One, and so sounded the praise of one art by calling it Grammar.

PHIL.: I understand this more clearly than your former remarks, Protarchus, to compare the statements themselves with each other. But the same defect seems to present itself in the argument as I felt some time ago.

SOC.: Mean you, Philebus, again to ask, What has this to do with the subject?

PHIL.: Aye, that is what Protarchus and I have been asking ourselves for some time.

SOC.: And yet you have been all the time close to what you say you have long been trying to find.

PHIL.: How is that?

SOC.: Was it not Intellectuality and pleasure that we first undertook to discuss, in order to decide which of them we should prefer?

PHIL.: Certainly it was.

SOC.: But we affirm, I think, that each of these is a One in itself.

PHIL.: We do.

SOC.: Well then, this is the very point that our former argument requires us to determine; first, *how* each of them is at the same time One and Many; next, how it is that they do not pass at once into infinity, but what number of parts each of them has, before they become infinite in their forms or manifestations.

TIMAEUS

TIMAEUS: Let me tell you then why the creator made this world of generation. He was good, and the good can never have any jealousy of anything. And being free from jealousy, he desired that all things should be as like himself as they could be. This is in the truest sense the origin of creation and of the world, as we shall do well in believing on the testimony of wise men: God desired that all things should be good and nothing bad, so far as this was attainable. Wherefore also finding the whole visible sphere not at rest, but moving in an irregular and disorderly fashion, out of disorder he brought order, considering that this was in every way better than the other. Now the deeds of the best could never be or have been other than the fairest; and the creator, reflecting on the things which are by nature visible, found that no unintelligent creature taken as a whole was fairer than the intelligent taken as a whole; and that intelligence could not be present in anything which was devoid of soul. For which reason, when he was framing the universe, he put intelligence in soul, and soul in body, that he might be the creator of a work which was by nature fairest and best. Wherefore, using the language of probability, we may say that the world became a living creature truly endowed with soul and intelligence by the providence of God.

This being supposed, let us proceed to the next stage: In the likeness of what animal did the Creator make the world? It would be an unworthy thing to liken it to any nature which exists as a part only; for nothing can be beautiful which is like any imperfect thing; but let us suppose the world to be the very image of that whole of which all other animals both individually and in their tribes are portions. For the original of the universe contains in itself all intelligible beings, just as this world comprehends us and all other visible creatures. For the Deity, intending to make this world like the fairest and most perfect of intelligible beings, framed one visible animal comprehending within itself all other animals of a kindred nature. Are we right in saying that there is one world, or that they are many and infinite? There must be one only, if the

From "Timaeus," in *The Dialogues of Plato,* trans. B. Jowett (Oxford: Clarendon Press, 1892).

created copy is to accord with the original. For that which includes all other intelligible creatures cannot have a second or companion; in that case there would be need of another living being which would include both, and of which they would be parts, and the likeness would be more truly said to resemble not them, but that other which included them. In order then that the world might be solitary, like the perfect animal, the creator made not two worlds or an infinite number of them; but there is and ever will be one only-begotten and created heaven. . . .

When the father and creator saw the creature which he had made moving and living, the created image of the eternal gods, he rejoiced, and in his joy determined to make the copy still more like the original; and as this was eternal, he sought to make the universe eternal, so far as might be. Now the nature of the ideal being was everlasting, but to bestow this attribute in its fulness upon a creature was impossible. Wherefore he resolved to have a moving image of eternity, and when he set in order the heaven, he made this image eternal but moving according to number, while eternity itself rests in unity; and this image we call time. For there were no days and nights and months and years before the heaven was created, but when he constructed the heaven he created them also. They are all parts of time, and the past and future are created species of time, which we unconsciously but wrongly transfer to the eternal essence; for we say that he "was," he "is," he "will be," but the truth is that "is" alone is properly attributed to him, and that "was" and "will be" are only to be spoken of becoming in time, for they are motions, but that which is immovably the same cannot become older or younger by time, nor ever did or has become, or hereafter will be, older or younger, nor is subject at all to any of those states which affect moving and sensible things and of which generation is the cause. These are the forms of time, which imitates eternity and revolves according to a law of number. Moreover, when we say that what has become *is* become and what becomes *is* becoming, and that what will become *is* about to become and that the non-existent *is* non-existent,—all these are inaccurate modes of expression. But perhaps this whole subject will be more suitable discussed on some other occasion. . . .

Thus far in what we have been saying, with small exceptions, the works of intelligence have been set forth; and now we must place by the side of them in our discourse the things which come into being through necessity—for the creation is mixed, being made up of necessity and mind. Mind, the ruling power, persuaded necessity to bring the greater part of created things to perfection, and thus and after this manner in the beginning, when the influence of reason got the better of necessity, the universe was created. But if a person will truly tell of the way in which the work was accomplished, he must include the other influence of the variable cause as well. Wherefore, we must return again and find another suitable beginning, as about the former matters, so also about these. To which end we must consider the nature of fire, and water, and air, and earth, such as they were prior to the creation of the heaven, and what was happening to them in this previous state; for no one has as yet explained the manner of their generation, but we speak of fire and the rest of them, whatever they mean, as though men knew their natures, and we maintain them to be the first principles and letters or elements of the whole, when they cannot reasonably be compared by a man of any sense even to syllables or first compounds. And let me say thus much: I will not now speak of the first principle or principles of all things, of by whatever name they are to be called, for this reason,—because it is difficult to set forth my opinion according to the method of discussion which we are at present employing. Do not imagine, any more than I can bring myself to imagine, that I should be right in undertaking so great and difficult a task. Remembering what I said at first about probability, I will do my best to give as probable an explanation as any other,—or rather, more probable; and I will first go back to the beginning and try to speak of each thing and of all. Once more, then, at the commencement of my discourse, I call upon God, and beg him to be our saviour out of a strange and unwonted enquiry, and to bring us to the haven of probability. So now let us begin again.

This new beginning of our discussion of the universe requires a fuller division than the former; for then we made two classes, now a third must be revealed. The two sufficed for the former discussion: one, which we assumed, was a pattern intelligible and always the same; and the second was only the imitation of the pattern, generated and visible. There is also a third kind which we did not distinguish at the time, conceiving that the two would be enough. But now the argument seems to require that we should set forth in words another kind, which is difficult of explanation and dimly seen. What nature are we to attribute to this new kind of being? We reply, that it is the receptacle, and in a manner the nurse, of all generation. I have spoken the truth; but I must express myself in clearer language, and this will be an arduous task for many reasons, and in particular because I must first raise questions concerning fire and the other elements, and determine what each of them is; for to say, with any probability or certitude, which of them should be called water rather than fire, and which should be called any of them rather than all or some one of them, is a difficult matter.

ARISTOTLE

384–322 B.C.E.

Plato was sixty years old and running his Academy when Aristotle came to study with him, at the age of seventeen, from Stagira, in Macedon, a Greek colonial town settled by the Ionians. Aristotle had been sent by the Macedonian king, Amyntas, because he was his personal physician's son. The king had wanted to do a favor for his doctor; little did anyone suspect that Aristotle would become Plato's most prodigious pupil.

Aristotle quickly mastered the most difficult aspects of Plato's philosophy. At the time, Plato was in his final period of philosophical creativity, trying to further and further divide the Ideas until he reached the *infima species,* the final and indivisible unit of division. This became the focal point of Aristotle's own early work, in which he developed his own metaphysics and logic. He then went on to develop a method for systemizing knowledge and wrote on virtually every subject, including physics, astronomy, meteorology, taxonomy, psychology, biology, ethics, politics, aesthetics, metaphysics, and logic.

The main philosophical difference between Plato and Aristotle is a fundamental one. For Plato, the world of appearances is an illusion. He sought knowledge in the realm of pure reason. Such knowledge could in Plato's view be communicated only abstractly using myths and metaphors. While Aristotle agreed that knowledge acquired through the senses is not sufficient in itself, this nevertheless is the true and only path to wisdom.

Although Plato and Aristotle remained friends until Plato's death at age eighty-one, they continued to disagree about the primacy of reason versus the primacy of experience. Consequently, they each took a different view of the nature of ideas, and their debate has continued into the twentieth century. Plato, still under Pythagoras's influence, relied on the notion of geometrical forms and the abstract rules of numbers in his theory of Ideas, and his philosophical method aligned itself closely with mathematics. Aristotle, on the other hand, aligned himself with the methods of natural science, especially, with his classifications of genera and species, toward organic biology and the study of physiology. According to Aristotle, the purpose and function of science is to determine the underlying causes of everything. His method for attaining knowledge of these causes is deductive logic, the syllogistic deduction from premises known to be certain.

Aristotle's logical method is a marked contrast to the other two prevailing methods of discourse at the time, the dialectic method, which starts from probable premises, and the eristic method, whose purpose is rhetorical victory, not truth. Aristotle used his method to explain change: what first has only potential being is transformed, through its ideal form, into actual being, which he called *entelechy*. Existence itself is thus conceived in Aristotle's philosophy as a dynamic evolutionary system within which change is not illusory but real, spontaneous, continuous, and teleological. Change is itself the product of discoverable causes.

When King Philip of Macedon asked Aristotle to tutor his thirteen-year-old crown prince, Alexander, Aristotle agreed. Only six years later, Alexander became known as Alexander the Great, conqueror of the whole ancient world from Greece to India.

Upon his return to Athens, Aristotle set up his own school, the Lyceum, called the Peripatos (hence Aristotelians are often called "Peripatetics"). Like Plato's Academy, it too lasted many centuries—over eight hundred years. While Plato's Academy led in the development of mathematics and geometry, Aristotle's Lyceum centered on applied scientific research in the natural sciences. Not being an Athenian citizen, however, Aristotle had to rent the land on which the Lyceum operated. Although he was widely regarded as one of the greatest minds of the time, many Athenians resented him for having trained the Macedonian who had become their conqueror. So, when in 323 B.C.E. Alexander suddenly died and the Macedonians were ousted from power, the Athenians turned against Aristotle. Ironically, Plato's greatest pupil, like Plato's teacher, Socrates, ended up being arrested by the Athenian government and charged—like Socrates before him—with atheism and impiety. Sentenced to death or exile, Aristotle—unlike Socrates—chose exile. A year later, he died on the island of Euboea.

Like Plato, Aristotle was prolific. Although only fragments remain of his published writings, his unpublished writings have survived in the form of lecture notes or texts used by his students. Our first selection is from his *Metaphysics*. Here Aristotle presents his dynamic theory of change, according to which individual beings exist as composites of Ideas and substance. The famous opening passage, "All men by nature desire to know," says that we desire knowledge not through education but through our own natures. That is, our desire for knowledge is *innate*, we are born with it. He suggests, as did Plato, that we are seduced away from our natural desire to know. Nor is it merely practical knowledge that we want. The human mind craves knowledge for its own sake. Aristotle gives the example of our senses, which are of course very useful, but there is also the "delight we take in our senses; for even apart from their usefulness they are loved for themselves." Thus the highest levels of knowledge are like beauty, having not instrumental but intrinsic value. That is, ultimate knowledge has value in and of itself. Although there are different levels of knowledge, the highest form of knowledge is wisdom.

Wisdom, in Aristotle's view, as in Plato's, requires us to see beyond sense experience, to learn about the underlying *first principles and causes* of things, which give us knowledge not merely of the appearances but of that which is behind the appearances and makes them as they are. In many ways, the search for wisdom is the central goal of Aristotelian metaphysics, to construct beyond the Socratic-Platonic conceptual philosophy a theory explaining the phenomenal (mental) world of the appearances. Plato's philosophy tries to explain, for instance, the relationship between the conceptual reality of the Ideas and the perceptual reality of perceived objects using allegories like that of the cave: the perceived objects are but shadows of the Ideas, or reflections, mere representations. But this theory in no way explains why experience is as it is in terms of Aristotle's *first principles*. It does not explain the causes of such phenomena.

The ultimate purpose of Aristotle's metaphysics is to discover those first principles from which all the other various sciences are derived. This is the goal of what Aristotle calls *first philosophy,* or *metaphysics,* which he deems the most abstract and, at the same time, the most exact of all the sciences. "Secondary" sciences like physics ask what things are and why they are as they are. Metaphysics—the primary science, the first philosophy—asks far more general types of questions, such as What does it *mean* to be anything whatsoever? What is it to *be?* Metaphysics is thus "the science of any existent, as existent."

Aristotle argues that Plato's theory of Ideas cannot explain the existence of empirical facts (such as that presently you see a book in front of you). Nor can Ideas explain their own existence: Why are there any Ideas to begin with? To claim the Ideas are eternal is hardly sufficient: *Why* are they eternal? What causes the Ideas to be eternal rather than ephemeral? To suppose that the Ideas exist as a higher level of being, even to think of them in theological terms, such as being God-made entities, would hardly satisfy Aristotle. Regardless of whether God exists, the metaphysical problem is exactly the same. The problem is with being itself, *any* being. Aristotle's solution is to claim that the world of Plato's Ideas is but a conceptual and unnecessary duplication of the empirical, phenomenal world of the appearances. Plato's big mistake, according to Aristotle, is to distinguish these as the two different realities, one which is more fundamental and more real than the other. There is but one reality, one world: the world of Ideas and the world of sense experience are one and the same world. Ultimately, in Aristotle's view, Plato's theory of Ideas fails to explain anything, and Plato cannot prove their existence.

In his *Categories,* the second selection, Aristotle criticizes Plato's theory of Ideas by arguing that universals, like "man" or "blueness," do not exist independently of particular individuals. Each individual thing in the world is a "primary substance" whose species and genera are "secondary substances" that make the thing what it is rather than some other thing.

It should be kept in mind that the actual word used by Aristotle, *ouisa*—usually translated as "substance"—can also be, and sometimes is, translated as "reality." Thus to argue that particular individuals are a type of primary substance is to claim that they are themselves primary *realities.* This of course contradicts Plato's theory that the objects of sense experience are, at best, only partly real reflections of the Ideas. Thus, instead of the a priori analysis of Ideas that Plato envisioned as the true function of the philosopher, Aristotle focuses on an empirical study of the structure of the objects that appear as such in the sensible world of ordinary experience.

In the *Phaedo* Plato had argued that the soul is eternal and immortal and that like the eternal, Ideas, the soul can exist without the body. Indeed, the mind, or soul, is according to Plato more real than the body. In the third selection, taken from *On the Soul,* Aristotle argues to the contrary. First, the soul is not an entity existing separately from the body. The soul cannot ever exist apart from the body. The soul is but the formal principle of life, "the primary actualization of a natural organic body." Souls are individuated from one another by the variety and complexity of their functions, which in turn correspond to individuating differences in the organic structures that embody them. Fundamental functions, common to all living things including plants and animals, are nutrition, growth, and reproduction. At the next level are sensations, desires, and locomotion. Finally, at the highest level, unique to human beings, is the most important function of the soul: rationality.

Rationality, in turn, has several faculties. The most important is perception, which is the faculty of receiving the sensible form of outward objects without their matter. These are the phenomena. Aristotle also coined the term *common sense,* meaning a sense common not among people but within an individual person. It is the unifying sense common to the five senses of perception. It is this "common sense" that makes possible the unity of data by the five separate senses into a single apperception. The common sense also accounts for the soul's awareness of its own activity of perception and all its other states. Hence it is the common sense that is directly responsible for consciousness. Reason, as a separate faculty from perception, allows the soul to apprehend the universals and first principles necessary for all knowledge, but it is useless without sense perception. Reason is not limited to what can be experienced but can, through the faculty of the understanding, grasp the universal and ideal.

The *Nicomachean Ethics,* our fourth selection, is named after Aristotle's son Nicomachus (himself named after Aristotle's father). It is generally regarded as one of the greatest works ever written on moral philosophy. In it, Aristotle extends his teleological view of the world (according to which each and every thing exists for some purpose toward which it tends by its own special and unique nature) to the meaning of life. The final end, or good, of human life is, according to Aristotle, the fulfillment of human nature. He defines the good life using his concept of essence as the unique defining characteristic of something which, for humanity, is the rational faculty of the soul. Rationality is the essence of human life because rationality is unique to humans. The highest good for human life therefore, in Aristotle's view, consists in the improvement and actualization of rationality and rational behavior.

Like Plato, Aristotle defines a good human character in terms of moderation, justice, virtue, and courage, and he claims that knowledge of what is good can be attained through rational means. He too says that the good and virtuous person will be an essentially happy person. The key difference between their approach to ethics stems from Aristotle's rejection of Plato's theory of Ideas: unlike Plato, Aristotle claims that absolute knowledge in the moral realm can never be attained. He describes human virtue in terms of various traits that help us to achieve happiness and live well. This cannot be achieved unless there is a rational harmony within the larger human community. Aristotle thus claims that social institutions are a necessary ingredient to human happiness. Indeed, in his view moral individuals as such cannot exist independently of their political and social setting. It is the society at large that enables individuals to develop virtues for the good and happy life. But he is careful to distinguish between moral virtues and intellectual virtues. Whereas intellectual virtues can be taught, moral virtues must be learned through living.

In the fifth selection, taken from his *Politics,* Aristotle argues, following Plato, that only those who are sufficiently intelligent or well educated—the "natural masters"—should govern the rest—the "natural slaves." The good life, however, is not defined by the political life nor by any other type of practical activity, such as the arts. Rather, the good life consists in theoretical inquiry and contemplation of impartial, disinterested truth for its own sake. Only this endeavor can bring complete happiness because this alone is the proper activity of the highest and noblest part of the soul, that which is least dependent on the external world: namely, intuitive reason, or *nous.* In such rational and theoretic contemplation of the first principle, the human mind participates directly in the activity of pure thought constituting the eternal perfection of the divine soul.

In the sixth selection, taken from his *Poetics,* Aristotle gives his views on poetry, drama, and literary criticism. Unlike Plato, who took a dim view of art, Aristotle claims that poetry "is something more philosophic and of greater import than history, since its statements are of the nature rather of universals, whereas those of history are singulars." For Plato, art was but the cheap imitation of illusory appearances, at best three times removed from reality: a painting of Socrates, for instance, is a copy of Socrates who is himself but a copy of an Idea.

Since according to Aristotle the Ideas themselves exist in particular things, by studying and imitating nature the artist is communing directly with the Ideas, which he can then communicate to others by rendering them more vividly in his work, thereby expressing and illuminating the universal truths hidden in the particulars.

METAPHYSICS

BOOK A

All men by nature desire to know. An indication of this is the delight we take in our senses; for even apart from their usefulness they are loved for themselves; and above all others the sense of sight. For not only with a view to action, but even when we are not going to do anything, we prefer seeing (one might say) to everything else. The reason is that this, most of all the senses, makes us know and brings to light many differences between things.

By nature animals are born with the faculty of sensation, and from sensation memory is produced in some of them, though not in others. And therefore the former are more intelligent and apt at learning than those which cannot remember; those which are incapable of hearing sounds are intelligent though they cannot be taught, e.g. the bee, and any other race of animals that may be like it; and those which besides memory have this sense of hearing can be taught.

The animals other than man live by appearances and memories, and have but little of connected experience; but the human race lives also by art and reasonings. Now from memory experience is produced in men; for the several memories of the same thing produce finally the capacity for a single experience. And experience seems pretty much like science and art, but really science and art come to men *through* experience; for "experience made art," as Polus says, "but inexperience luck." Now art arises when from many notions gained by experience one universal judgement about a class of objects is produced. For to have a judgement that when Callias was ill of this disease this did him good, and similarly in the case of Socrates and in many individual cases, is a matter of experience; but to judge that it has done good to all persons of a certain constitution, marked off in one class, when they were ill of this disease, e.g. to phlegmatic or bilious people when burning with fever,—this is a matter of art.

With a view to action experience seems in no respect inferior to art, and men of experience succeed even better than those who have theory without experience. (The reason is that experience is knowledge of individuals, art of universals, and actions and productions are all concerned with the individual; for the physician does not cure *man*, except in an incidental way, but Callias or Socrates or some other called by some such individual name, who happens to be a man. If, then, a man has the theory without the experience, and

From Aristotle, *Metaphysics,* trans. W. D. Ross (London: Oxford University Press, 1908).

recognizes the universal but does not know the individual included in this, he will often fail to cure; for it is the individual that is to be cured.) But yet we think that *knowledge* and *understanding* belong to art rather than to experience, and we suppose artists to be wiser than men of experience (which implies that Wisdom depends in all cases rather on knowledge); and this because the former know the cause, but the latter do not. For men of experience know that the thing is so, but do not know why, while the others know the "why" and the cause. Hence we think also that the master-workers in each craft are more honourable and know in a truer sense and are wiser than the manual workers, because they know the causes of the things that are done (we think the manual workers are like certain lifeless things which act indeed, but act without knowing what they do, as fire burns,—but while the lifeless things perform each of their functions by a natural tendency, the labourers perform them through habit); thus we view them as being wiser not in virtue of being able to act, but of having the theory for themselves and knowing the causes. And in general it is a sign of the man who knows and of the man who does not know, that the former can teach, and therefore we think art more truly knowledge than experience is; for artists can teach, and men of mere experience cannot.

Again, we do not regard any of the senses as Wisdom; yet surely these give the most authoritative knowledge of particulars. But they do not tell us the "why" of anything—e.g. why fire is hot; they only say *that* it is hot.

At first he who invented any art whatever that went beyond the common perceptions of man was naturally admired by men, not only because there was something useful in the inventions, but because he was thought wise and superior to the rest. But as more arts were invented, and some were directed to the necessities of life, others to recreation, the inventors of the latter were naturally always regarded as wiser than the inventors of the former, because their branches of knowledge did not aim at utility. Hence when all such inventions were already established, the sciences which do not aim at giving pleasure or at the necessities of life were discovered, and first in the places where men first began to have leisure. This is why the mathematical arts were founded in Egypt; for there the priestly caste was allowed to be at leisure.

We have said in the *Ethics* what the difference is between art and science and the other kindred faculties; but the point of our present discussion is this, that all men suppose what is called Wisdom to deal with the first causes and the principles of things; so that, as has been said before, the man of experience is thought to be wiser than the possessors of any sense-perception whatever, the artist wiser than the men of experience, the master-worker than the mechanic, and the theoretical kinds of knowledge to be more of the nature of Wisdom than the productive. Clearly then Wisdom is knowledge about certain principles and causes.

Since we are seeking this knowledge, we must inquire of what kind are the causes and the principles, the knowledge of which is Wisdom. If one were to take the notions we have about the wise man, this might perhaps make the answer more evident. We suppose first, then, that the wise man knows all things, as far as possible, although he has not knowledge of each of them in detail; secondly, that he who can learn things that are difficult, and not easy for man to know, is wise (sense-perception is common to all, and therefore easy and no mark of Wisdom); again, that he who is more exact and more capable of teaching the causes is wiser, in every branch of knowledge; and that of the sciences, also, that which is desirable on its own account and for the sake of knowing it is more of the nature of Wisdom than that which is desirable on account of its results, and the superior science is more of the nature of Wisdom than the ancillary; for the wise man must not be ordered but must order, and he must not obey another, but the less wise must obey *him*.

Such and so many are the notions, then, which we have about Wisdom and the wise. Now of these characteristics that of knowing all things must belong to him who has in the highest degree universal knowledge; for he knows in a sense all the instances that fall under the universal. And these things, the most universal, are on the whole the hardest for men to know; for they are farthest from the senses. And the most exact of the sciences are those which deal most with first principles; for those which involve fewer principles are more exact than those which involve additional principles, e.g. arithmetic than geometry. But the science which investigates causes is also *instructive,* in a higher degree, for the people who instruct us are those who tell the causes of each thing. And understanding and knowledge pursued for their own sake are found most in the knowledge of that which is most knowable (for he who chooses to know for the sake of knowing will choose most readily that which is most truly knowledge, and such is the knowledge of that which is most knowable); and the first principles and the causes are most knowable; for by reason of these, and from these, all other things come to be known, and not these by means of the things subordinate to them. And the science which knows to what end each thing must be done is the most authoritative of the sciences, and more authoritative than any ancillary science; and this end is the good of that thing, and in general the supreme good in the whole of nature. Judged by all the tests we have mentioned, then, the name in question falls to the same science; this must be a science that investigates the first principles and causes; for the good, i.e. the end, is one of the causes.

That it is not a science of production is clear even from the history of the earliest philosophers. For it is owing to their wonder that men both now begin and at first began to philosophize; they wondered originally at the obvious difficulties, then advanced little by little and stated difficulties about the greater matters, e.g. about the phenomena of the moon and those of the sun and of the stars, and about the genesis of the universe. And a man who is puzzled and wonders thinks himself ignorant (whence even the lover of myth is in a sense a lover of Wisdom, for the myth is composed of wonders); therefore since they philosophized in order to escape from ignorance, evidently they were pursuing science in order to know, and not for any utilitarian end. And this is confirmed by the facts; for it was when almost all the necessities of life and the things that make for comfort and recreation had been secured, that such knowledge began to be sought. Evidently then we do not seek it for the sake of any other advantage; but as the man is free, we say, who exists for his own sake and not for another's, so we pursue this as the only free science, for it alone exists for its own sake.

Hence also the possession of it might be justly regarded as beyond human power; for in many ways human nature is in bondage, so that according to Simonides "God alone can have this privilege," and it is unfitting that man should not be content to seek the knowledge that is suited to him. If, then, there is something in what the poets say, and jealousy is natural to the divine power, it would probably occur in this case above all, and all who excelled in this knowledge would be unfortunate. But the divine power cannot be jealous (nay, according to the proverb, "bards tell many a lie"), nor should any other science be thought more honourable than one of this sort. For the most divine science is also most honourable; and this science alone must be, in two ways, most divine. For the science which it would be most meet for God to have is a divine science, and so is any science that deals with divine objects; and this science alone has both these qualities; for (1) God is thought to be among the causes of all things and to be a first principle, and (2) such a science either God alone can have, or God above all others. All the sciences, indeed, are more necessary than this, but none is better.

Yet the acquisition of it must in a sense end in something which is the opposite of our original inquiries. For all men begin, as we said, by wondering that things are as they are, as they do about self-moving marionettes, or about the solstices or the incommensurability of the diagonal of a square with the side; for it seems wonderful to all who have not yet seen the reason, that there is a thing which cannot be measured even by the smallest unit. But we must end in the contrary and, according to the proverb, the better state, as is the case in these instances too when men learn the cause; for there is nothing which would surprise a geometer so much as if the diagonal turned out to be commensurable.

We have stated, then, what is the nature of the science we are searching for, and what is the mark which our search and our whole investigation must reach.

Evidently we have to acquire knowledge of the original causes (for we say we know each thing only when we think we recognize its first cause), and causes are spoken of in four senses. In one of these we mean the substance, i.e. the essence (for the "why" is reducible finally to the definition, and the ultimate "why" is a cause and principle); in another the matter of substratum, in a third the source of the change, and in a fourth the cause opposed to this, the purpose and the good (for this is the end of all generation and change). We have studied these causes sufficiently in our work on nature, but yet let us call to our aid those who have attacked the investigation of being and philosophized about reality before us. For obviously they too speak of certain principles and causes; to go over their views, then, will be of profit to the present inquiry, for we shall either find another kind of cause, or be more convinced of the correctness of those which we now maintain.

Of the first philosophers, then, most thought the principles which were of the nature of matter were the only principles of all things. That of which all things that are consist, the first from which they come to be, the last into which they are resolved (the substance remaining, but changing in its modifications), this they say is the element and this the principle of things, and therefore they think nothing is either generated or destroyed, since this sort of entity is always conserved, as we say Socrates neither comes to be absolutely when he comes to be beautiful or musical, nor ceases to be when he loses these characteristics, because the substratum, Socrates himself, remains. Just so they say nothing else comes to be or ceases to be; for there must be some entity—either one or more than one—from which all other things come to be, it being conserved.

Yet they do not all agree as to the number and the nature of these principles. Thales, the founder of this type of philosophy, says the principle is water (for which reason he declared that the earth rests on water), getting the notion perhaps from seeing that the nutriment of all things is moist, and that heat itself is generated from the moist and kept alive by it (and that from which they come to be is a principle of all things). He got his notion from this fact, and from the fact that the seeds of all things have a moist nature, and that water is the origin of the nature of moist things.

Some think that even the ancients who lived long before the present generation, and first framed accounts of the gods, had a similar view of nature; for they made Ocean and Tethys the parents of creation, and described the oath of the gods as being by water, to which they give the name of Styx; for what is oldest is most honourable, and the most honourable thing is that by which one swears. It may perhaps be uncertain whether this opinion about nature is primitive and ancient, but Thales at any rate is said to have declared himself thus about the first cause. Hippo no one would think fit to include among these thinkers, because of the paltriness of his thought.

Anaximenes and Diogenes make air prior to water, and the most primary of the simple bodies, while Hippasus of Metapontium and Heraclitus of Ephesus say this of fire, and Empedocles says it of the four elements (adding a fourth—earth—to those which have been named); for these, he says, always remain and do not come to be, except that they come to be more or fewer, being aggregated into one and segregated out of one.

Anaxagoras of Clazomenae, who, though older than Empedocles, was later in his philosophical activity, says the principles are infinite in number; for he says almost all the things that are made of parts like themselves, in the manner of water or fire, are generated and destroyed in this way, only by aggregation and segregation, and are not in any other sense generated or destroyed, but remain eternally.

From these facts one might think that the only cause is the so-called material cause; but as men thus advanced, the very facts opened the way for them and joined in forcing them to investigate the subject. However true it may be that all generation and destruction proceed from some one or (for that matter) from more elements, why does this happen and what is the cause? For at least the substratum itself does not make itself change; e.g. neither the wood nor the bronze causes the change of either of them, nor does the wood manufacture a bed and the bronze a statue, but something else is the cause of the change. And to seek this is to seek the second cause, as *we* should say,—that from which comes the beginning of the movement. Now those who at the very beginning set themselves to this kind of inquiry, and said the substratum was one, were not at all dissatisfied with themselves; but some at least of those who maintain it to be one—as though defeated by this search for the second cause—say the one and nature as a whole is unchangeable not only in respect of generation and destruction (for this is a primitive belief, and all agreed in it), but also of all other change; and this view is peculiar to them. Of those who said the universe was one, then, none succeeded in discovering a cause of this sort, except perhaps Parmenides, and he only inasmuch as he supposes that there is not only one but also in some sense two causes. But for those who make more elements it is more possible to state the second cause, e.g. for those who make hot and cold, or fire and earth, the elements; for they treat fire as having a nature which fits it to move things, and water and earth and such things they treat in the contrary way.

When these men and the principles of this kind had had their day, as the latter were found inadequate to generate the nature of things men were again forced by the truth itself, as we said, to inquire into the next kind of cause. For it is not likely either that fire or earth or any such element should be the reason why things manifest goodness and beauty both in their being and in their coming to be, or that those thinkers, should have supposed it was; nor again could it be right to entrust so great a matter to spontaneity and chance. When one man said, then, that reason was present—as in animals, so throughout a nature—as the cause of order and of all arrangement, he seemed like a sober man in contrast with the random talk of his predecessors. We know that Anaxagoras certainly adopted these views, but Hermotimus of Clazomenae is credited with expressing them earlier. Those who thought thus stated that there is a principle of things which is at the same time the cause of beauty, and that sort of cause from which things acquire movement.

One might suspect that Hesiod was the first to look for such a thing—or some one else who put love or desire among existing things as a principle, as Parmenides, too, does; for he, in constructing the genesis of the universe, says:—

Love first of all the Gods she planned.

And Hesiod says:—

First of all things was chaos made, and then
Broad-breasted earth, . . .
And love, 'mid all the gods pre-eminent,

which implies that among existing things there must be from the first a cause which will move things and bring them together. How these thinkers should be arranged with regard to priority of discovery let us be allowed to decide later; but since the contraries of the various forms of good were also perceived to be present in nature—not only order and the beautiful, but also disorder and the ugly, and bad things in greater number than good, and ignoble things than beautiful—therefore another thinker introduced friendship and strife, each of the two the cause of one of these two sets of qualities. For if we were to follow out the view of Empedocles, and interpret it according to its meaning and not to its lisping expression, we should find that friendship is the cause of good things, and strife of bad. Therefore, if we said that Empedocles in a sense both mentions, and is the first to mention, the bad and the good as principles, we should perhaps be right, since the cause of all goods is the good itself.

These thinkers, as we say, evidently grasped, and to this extent, two of the causes which we distinguished in our work on nature—the matter and the source of the movement— vaguely, however, and with no clearness, but as untrained men behave in fights; for they go round their opponents and often strike fine blows, but they do not fight on scientific principles, and so too these thinkers do not seem to know what they say; for it is evident that, as a rule, they make no use of their causes except to a small extent. For Anaxagoras uses reason as a *deus ex machina* for the making of the world, and when he is at a loss to tell from what cause something necessarily is, then he drags reason in, but in all other cases ascribes events to anything rather than to reason. And Empedocles, though he uses the causes to a greater extent than this, neither does so sufficiently nor attains consistency in their use. At least, in many cases he makes love segregate things, and strife aggregate them. For whenever the universe is dissolved into its elements by strife, fire is aggregated into one, and so is each of the other elements; but whenever again under the influence of love they come together into one, the parts must again be segregated out of each element.

Empedocles, then, in contrast with his predecessors, was the first to introduce the dividing of this cause, not positing one source of movement, but different and contrary sources. Again, he was the first to speak of four material elements; yet he does not *use* four, but treats them as two only; he treats fire by itself, and its opposites—earth, air, and water—as one kind of thing. We may learn this by study of his verses.

This philosopher then, as we say, has spoken of the principles in this way, and made them of this number. Leucippus and his associate Democritus say that the full and the empty are the elements, calling the one being and the other non-being—the full and solid being being, the empty non-being (whence they say being no more is than non-being, because the solid no more is than the empty); and they make these the material causes of things. And as those who make the underlying substance one generate all other things by its modifications, supposing the rare and the dense to be the sources of the modifications, in the same way these philosophers say the differences in the elements are the causes of all other qualities. These differences, they say, are three—shape and order and position. For they say the real is differentiated only by "rhythm" and "intercontact" and "turning"; and of these rhythm is shape, inter-contact is order, and turning is position; for A differs from N in shape, AN from NA in order, ☰ from H in position. The question of movement—whence or how it is to belong to things—these thinkers, like the others, lazily neglected.

Regarding the two causes, then, as we say, the inquiry seems to have been pushed thus far by the early philosophers.

Contemporaneously with these philosophers and before them, the so-called Pythagoreans, who were the first to take up mathematics, not only advanced this study, but also having been brought up in it they thought its principles were the principles of all things. Since of these principles numbers are by nature the first, and in numbers they seemed to see many resemblances to the things that exist and come into being—more than in fire and earth and water (such and such a modification of numbers being justice, another being soul and reason, another being opportunity—and similarly almost all other things being numerically expressible); since, again, they saw that the modifications and the ratios of the musical scales were expressible in numbers;—since, then, all other things seemed in their whole nature to be modelled on numbers, and numbers seemed to be the first things in the whole of nature, they supposed the elements of numbers to be the elements of all things, and the whole heaven to be a musical scale and a number. And all the properties of numbers and scales which they could show to agree with the attributes and parts and the whole arrangement of the heavens, they collected and fitted into their scheme; and if there was a gap anywhere, they readily made additions so as to make their whole theory coherent. E.g. as the number 10 is thought to be perfect and to comprise the whole nature of numbers, they say that the bodies which move through the heavens are ten, but as the visible bodies are only nine, to meet this they invent a tenth—the "counter-earth." We have discussed these matters more exactly elsewhere.

But the object of our review is that we may learn from these philosophers also what they suppose to be the principles and how these fall under the causes we have named. Evidently, then, these thinkers also consider that number is the principle both as matter for things and as forming both their modifications and their permanent states, and hold that the elements of number are the even and the odd, and that of these the latter is limited, and the former unlimited; and that the One proceeds from both of these (for it is both even and odd), and number from the One; and that the whole heaven, as has been said, is numbers.

Other members of this same school say there are ten principles, which they arrange in two columns of cognates—limit and unlimited, odd and even, one and plurality, right and left, male and female, resting and moving, straight and curved, light and darkness, good and bad, square and oblong. In this way Alcmaeon of Croton seems also to have conceived the matter, and either he got this view from them or they got it from him; for he expressed himself similarly to them. For he says most human affairs go in pairs, meaning not definite contrarieties such as the Pythagoreans speak of, but any chance contrarieties, e.g. white and black, sweet and bitter, good and bad, great and small. He threw out indefinite suggestions about the other contrarieties, but the Pythagoreans declared both how many and which their contrarieties are.

From both these schools, then, we can learn this much, that the contraries are the principles of things; and how many these principles are and which they are, we can learn from one of the two schools. But how these principles can be brought together under the causes we have named has not been clearly and articulately stated by them; they seem, however, to range the elements under the head of matter; for out of these as immanent parts they say substance is composed and moulded.

From these facts we may sufficiently perceive the meaning of the ancients who said the elements of nature were more than one; but there are some who spoke of the universe as if it were one entity, though they were not all alike either in the excellence of their statement or in its conformity to the facts of nature. The discussion of them is in no way appropriate to our present investigation of causes, for they do not, like some of the natural philosophers, assume being to be one and yet generate it out of the one as out of matter, but they speak in another way; those others add change, since they generate the universe, but these thinkers say the universe is unchangeable. Yet *this* much is germane to the present inquiry: Parmenides seems to fasten on that which is one in definition, Melissus on that which is one in matter, for which reason the former says that it is limited, the latter that it is unlimited; while Xenophanes, the first of these partisans of the One (for Parmenides is said to have been his pupil), gave no clear statement, nor does he seem to have grasped the nature of either of these causes, but with reference to the whole material universe he says the One is God. Now these thinkers, as we said, must be neglected for the purposes of the present inquiry—two of them entirely, as being a little too naïve, viz. Xenophanes and Melissus; but Parmenides seems in places to speak with more insight. For, claiming that, besides the existent, nothing non-existent exists, he thinks that of necessity one thing exists, viz. the existent and nothing else (on this we have spoken more clearly in our work on nature), but being forced to follow the observed facts, and supposing the existence of that which is one in definition, but more than one according to our sensations, he now posits two causes and two principles, calling them hot and cold, i.e. fire and earth; and of these he ranges the hot with the existent, and the other with the non-existent.

From what has been said, then, and from the wise men who have now sat in council with us, we have got thus much—on the one hand from the earliest philosophers, who regard the first principle as corporeal (for water and fire and such things are bodies), and of whom some suppose that there is one corporeal principle, others that there are more than one, but both put these under the head of matter; and on the other hand from some who posit both this cause and besides this the source of movement, which we have got from some as single and from others as twofold.

Down to the Italian school, then, and apart from it, philosophers have treated these subjects rather obscurely, except that, as we said, they have in fact used two kinds of cause, and one of these—the source of movement—some treat as one and others as two. But the Pythagoreans have said in the same way that there are two principles, but added this much, which is peculiar to them, that they thought that finitude and infinity were not attributes of certain other things, e.g. of fire or earth or anything else of this kind, but that infinity itself and unity itself were the substance of the things of which they are predicated. This is why number was the substance of all things. On this subject, then, they expressed themselves thus; and regarding the question of essence they began to make statements and definitions, but treated the matter too simply. For they both defined superficially and thought that the first subject of which a given definition was predicable was the substance of the thing defined, as if one supposed that "double" and "2" were the same, because 2 is the first thing of which "double" is predicable. But surely to be double and to be 2 are not the same; if they are, one thing will be many—a consequence which they actually drew. From the earlier philosophers, then, and from their successors we can learn thus much.

After the systems we have named came the philosophy of Plato, which in most respects followed these thinkers, but had peculiarities that distinguished it from the philosophy of the Italians. For, having in his youth first become familiar with Cratylus and with the Heraclitean doctrines (that all sensible things are ever in a state of flux and there is no knowledge about them), these views he held even in later years. Socrates, however, was busying himself about ethical matters and neglecting the world of nature as a whole but seeking the universal in these ethical matters, and fixed thought for the first time on definitions; Plato accepted his teaching, but held that the problem applied not to sensible things but to entities of another kind—for this reason, that the common definition could not be a definition of any sensible thing, as they were always changing. Things of this other sort, then, he called Ideas, and sensible things, he said, were all named after these, and in virtue of a relation to these; for the many existed by participation in the Ideas that have the same name as they. Only the name "participation" was new; for the Pythagoreans say that things exist by "imitation" of numbers, and Plato says they exist by participation, changing the name. But what the participation or the imitation of the Ideas could be they left an open question.

Further, besides sensible things and Ideas he says there are the objects of mathematics, which occupy an intermediate position, differing from sensible things in being eternal and unchangeable, from Forms in that there are many alike, while the Idea itself is in each case unique.

Since the Ideas were the causes of all other things, he thought their elements were the elements of all things. As matter, the great and the small were principles; as essential reality, the One; for from the great and the small, by participation in the One, come the Numbers.

But he agreed with the Pythagoreans in saying that the One is substance and not a predicate of something else; and in saying that the Numbers are the causes of the reality of other things he agreed with them; but positing a dyad and constructing the infinite out of great and small, instead of treating the infinite as one, is peculiar to him; and so is his view that the Numbers exist apart from sensible things, while *they* say that the things themselves are Numbers, and do not place the objects of mathematics between Ideas and sensible things. His divergence from the Pythagoreans in making the One and the Numbers separate from things, and his introduction of the Ideas, were due to his inquiries in the region of definitions (for the earlier thinkers had no tincture of dialectic), and his making the other entity besides the One a dyad was due to the belief that the numbers, except those which were prime, could be neatly produced out of the dyad as out of some plastic material.

Yet what *happens* is the contrary; the theory is not a reasonable one. For they make many things out of the matter, and the form generates only once, but what we observe is that one table is made from one matter, while the man who applies the idea, though he is one, makes many tables. And the relation of the male to the female is similar; for the latter is impregnated by one copulation, but the male impregnates many females; yet these are analogues of those first principles.

Plato, then, declared himself thus on the points in question; it is evident from what has been said that he has used only two causes, that of the essence and the material cause (for the Ideas are the causes of the essence of all other things, and the One is the cause of the essence of the Ideas); and it is evident what the underlying matter is, of which the Ideas are predicated in the case of sensible things, and the One in the case of Ideas, viz. that this is a dyad, the great and the small. Further, he has assigned the cause of good and that of evil to the elements, one to each of the two, as we say some of his predecessors sought to do, e.g. Empedocles and Anaxagoras.

Our review of those who have spoken about first principles and reality and of the way in which they have spoken, has been concise and summary; but yet we have learnt *this* much from them, that of those who speak about "principle" and "cause" no one has mentioned any principle except those which have been distinguished in our work on nature, but all evidently have some inkling of *them,* though only vaguely. For some speak of the first principle as matter, whether they suppose one or more first principles, and whether they suppose this to be a body or to be incorporeal; e.g. Plato spoke of the great and the small, the Italians of the infinite, Empedocles of fire, earth, water, and air, Anaxagoras of the infinity of things composed of similar parts. These, then, have all had a notion of this kind of cause, and so have all who speak of air or fire or water, or something denser than fire and rarer than air; for some have said the prime element is of this kind.

These thinkers grasped this cause only; but certain others have mentioned the source of movement, e.g. those who make friendship and strife, or reason, or love, a principle.

The essence, i.e. the substantial reality, no one has expressed distinctly. It is hinted at chiefly by those who believe in the Ideas; for they do not suppose either that the Ideas are the matter of sensible things, and the One the matter of the Ideas, or that they are the source of movement (for they say these are causes rather of immobility and of being at rest), but they furnish the Ideas as the essence of every other thing, and the One as the essence of the Ideas.

That for whose sake actions and changes and movements take place, they assert to be a cause in a way, but not in this way, i.e. not in the way in which it is its *nature* to be a cause. For those who speak of reason or friendship class these causes as goods; they do not speak, however, as if anything that exists either existed or came into being for the sake of these, but as if movements started from these. In the same way those who say the One or the existent is the good, say that it is the cause of substance, but not that substance either is or comes to be for the sake of this. Therefore it turns out that in a sense they both say and do not say the good is a cause; for they do not call it a cause *qua* good but only incidentally.

All these thinkers, then, as they cannot pitch on another cause, seem to testify that we have determined rightly both how many and of what sort the causes are. Besides this it is plain that when the causes are being looked for, either all four must be sought thus or they must be sought in one of these four ways. Let us next discuss the possible difficulties with regard to the way in which each of these thinkers has spoken, and with regard to his situation relatively to the first principles.

Those, then, who say the universe is one and posit one kind of thing as a matter, and as corporeal matter which has spatial magnitude, evidently go astray in many ways. For they posit the elements of bodies only, not of incorporeal things, though there are also incorporeal things. And in trying to state the causes of generation and destruction, and in giving a physical account of all things, they do away with the cause of movement. Further, they err in not positing the substance, i.e. the essence, as the cause of anything, and besides this in lightly calling any of the simple bodies except earth the first principle, without inquiring how they are produced out of one another,—I mean fire, water, earth, and air. For some things are produced out of each other by combination, others by separation, and this makes the greatest difference to their priority and posteriority. For (1) in a way the property of being most elementary of all would seem to belong to the first thing from which they are produced by combination, and *this* property would belong to the most fine-grained and subtle of bodies. For this reason those who make fire the principle would be most in agreement with this argument. But each of the other thinkers agrees that the element of corporeal things is of this sort. At least none of those who named one element claimed that earth was the element, evidently because of the coarseness of its grain. (Of the other three elements each has found some judge on its side; for some maintain that fire, others that water, others that air is the element. Yet why, after all, do they not name earth also, as most men do? For people say all things are earth. And Hesiod says earth was produced first of corporeal things; so primitive and popular has the opinion been.) According to this argument, then, no one would be right who either says the first principle is any of the elements other than fire, or supposes it to be denser than air but rarer than water. But (2) if that which is later in generation is prior in nature, and that which is concocted and compounded is later in generation, the contrary of what we have been saying must be true,—water must be prior to air, and earth to water.

So much, then, for those who posit one cause such as we mentioned; but the same is true if one supposes more of these, as Empedocles says the matter of things is four bodies. For he too is confronted by consequences some of which are the same as have been mentioned, while others are peculiar to him. For we see these bodies produced from one another, which implies that the same body does not always remain fire or earth (we have spoken about this in our works on nature); and regarding the cause of movement and the question whether we must posit one or two, he must be thought to have spoken neither correctly nor altogether plausibly. And in general, change of quality is necessarily done away with for those who speak thus, for on their view cold will not come from hot nor hot from cold. For if it did there would be something that accepted the contraries themselves, and there would be some one entity that became fire and water, which Empedocles denies.

As regards Anaxagoras, if one were to suppose that he said there were two elements, the supposition would accord thoroughly with an argument which Anaxagoras himself did not state articulately, but which he must have accepted if any one had led him on to it. True, to say that in the beginning all things were mixed is absurd both on other grounds and because it follows that they must have existed before in an unmixed form, and because nature does not allow any chance thing to be mixed with any chance thing, and also because on this view modifications and accidents could be separated from substances (for the same things which are mixed can be separated); yet if one were to follow him up, piecing together what he means, he would perhaps be seen to be somewhat modern in his views. For when nothing was separated out, evidently nothing could be truly asserted of the substance that then existed. I mean, e.g. that it was neither white nor black, nor grey nor any other colour, but of necessity colourless; for if it had been coloured, it would have had one of these colours. And similarly, by this same argument, it was flavourless, nor had it any similar attribute; for it could not be either of any quality or of any size, nor could it be any definite kind of thing. For if it were, one of the particular forms would have belonged to it, and this is impossible, since all were mixed together; for the particular form would necessarily have been already separated out, but he says all were mixed except reason, and this alone was unmixed and pure. From this it follows, then, that he must say the principles are the One (for this is simple and unmixed) and the Other, which is of such a nature as we suppose the indefinite to be before it is defined and partakes of some form. Therefore, while expressing himself neither rightly nor clearly, he means something like what the later thinkers say and what is now more clearly seen to be the case.

But these thinkers are, after all, at home only in arguments about generation and destruction and movement; for it is practically only of this sort of substance that they seek the principles and the causes. But those who extend their vision to all things that exist, and of existing things suppose some to be perceptible and others not perceptible, evidently study both classes, which is all the more reason why one should devote some time to seeing what is good in their views and what bad from the standpoint of the inquiry we have now before us.

The "Pythagoreans" treat of principles and elements stranger than those of the physical philosophers (the reason is that they got the principles from non-sensible things, for the objects of mathematics, except those of astronomy, are of the class of things without movement); yet their discussions and investigations are all about nature; for they generate the heavens, and with regard to their parts and attributes and functions they observe the phenomena, and use up the principles and the causes in explaining these, which implies that they agree with the others, the physical philosophers, that the *real* is just all that which is perceptible and contained by the so-called "heavens." But the causes and the principles which they mention are, as we said, sufficient to act as steps even up to the higher realms of reality, and are more suited to these than to theories about nature. They do not tell us at all, however, how there can be movement if limit and unlimited and odd and even are the only things assumed, or how without movement and change there can be generation and destruction, or the bodies that move through the heavens can do what they do.

Further, if one either granted them that spatial magnitude consists of these elements, or this were proved, still how would some bodies be light and others have weight? To judge from what they assume and maintain they are speaking no more of mathematical bodies than of perceptible; hence they have said nothing whatever about fire or earth or the other bodies of this sort, I suppose because they have nothing to say which applies *peculiarly* to perceptible things.

Further, how are we to combine the beliefs that the attributes of number, and number itself, are causes of what exists and happens in the heavens both from the beginning and now, and that there is no other number than this number out of which the world is composed? When in one particular region they place opinion and opportunity, and, a little above or below, injustice and decision or mixture, and allege, as proof, that each of these is a number, and that there happens to be already in this place a plurality of the extended bodies composed of numbers, because these attributes of number attach to the various places,—this being so, is this number, which we must suppose each of these abstractions to be, the same number which is exhibited in the material universe, or is it another than this? Plato says it is different; yet even he thinks that both these bodies and their causes are numbers, but that the *intelligible* numbers are causes, while the others are *sensible*.

Let us leave the Pythagoreans for the present; for it is enough to have touched on them as much as we have done. But as for those who posit the Ideas as causes, firstly, in seeking to grasp the causes of the things around us, they introduced others equal in number to these, as if a man who wanted to count things thought he would not be able to do it while they were few, but tried to count them when he had added to their number. For the Ideas are practically equal to—or not fewer than—the things, in trying to explain which these thinkers proceeded from them to the Ideas. For to each thing there answers an entity which has the same name and exists apart from the substances, and so also in the case of all other groups there is a one over many, whether the many are in this world or are eternal.

Further, of the ways in which we prove that the Ideas exist, none is convincing; for from some no inference necessarily follows, and from some arise Ideas even of things of which we think there are no Ideas. For according to the arguments from the existence of the sciences there will be Ideas of all things of which there are sciences, and according to the "one over many" argument there will be Ideas even of negations, and according to the argument that there is an object for thought even when the thing has perished, there will be Ideas of perishable things; for we have an image of these. Further, of the more accurate arguments, some lead to Ideas of relations, of which we say there is no independent class, and others introduce the "third man."

And in general the arguments for the Ideas destroy the things for whose existence we are more zealous than for the existence of the Ideas; for it follows that not the dyad but number is first, i.e. that the relative is prior to the absolute,—besides all the other points on which certain people by following out the opinions held about the Ideas have come into conflict with the principles of the theory.

Further, according to the assumption on which our belief in the Ideas rests, there will be Ideas not only of substances but also of many other things (for the concept is single not only in the case of substances but also in the other cases, and there are sciences not only of substance but also of other things, and a thousand other such difficulties confront them). But according to the necessities of the case and the opinions held about the Ideas, if Ideas can be shared in there must be Ideas of substances only. For they are not shared in incidentally, but a thing must share in its Idea as in something not predicated of a subject (by "being shared in incidentally" I mean that e.g. if a thing shares in "double itself," it shares also in "eternal," but incidentally; for "eternal" happens to be predicable of the "double"). Therefore the Ideas will be substance; but the same terms indicate substance in this and in the ideal world (or what will be the meaning of saying that there is something apart from the particulars—the one over many?). And if the Ideas and the particulars that share in them have the same form, there will be something common to these; for why should "2" be one and the same in the perishable 2's or in those which are many but eternal, and not the same in the "2 itself" as in the particular 2? But if they have not the same form, they must have only the name in common, and it is as if one were to call both Callias and a wooden image a "man," without observing any community between them.

Above all one might discuss the question what on earth the Ideas contribute to sensible things, either to those that are eternal or to those that come into being and cease to be. For they cause neither movement nor any change in them. But again they help in no wise either towards the knowledge of the other things (for they are not even the substance of these, else they would have been in them), or towards their being, if they are not *in* the particulars which share in them; though if they were, they might be thought to be causes, as white causes whiteness in a white object by entering into its composition. But this argument, which first Anaxagoras and later Eudoxus and certain others used, is very easily upset; for it is not difficult to collect many insuperable objections to such a view.

But, further, all other things cannot come from the Ideas in any of the usual senses of "from." And to say that they are patterns and the other things share in them is to use empty words and poetical metaphors. For what is it that works, looking to the Ideas? And anything can either be, or become, like another without being copied from it, so that whether Socrates exists or not a man like Socrates might come to be; and evidently this might be so even if Socrates were eternal. And there will be several patterns of the same thing, and therefore several Ideas; e.g. "animal" and "two-footed" and also "man himself" will be Ideas of man. Again, the Ideas are patterns not only of sensible things, but of Ideas themselves also; i.e. the genus, as genus of various species, will be so; therefore the same thing will be pattern and copy.

Again, it would seem impossible that the substance and that of which it is the substance should exist apart; how, therefore, could the Ideas, being the substances of things, exist apart? In the *Phaedo* the case is stated in this way—that the Ideas are causes both of being and of becoming, yet when the Ideas exist, still the things that share in them do not come into being, unless there is something to originate movement; and many other things come into being (e.g. a house or a ring) of which we say there are no Ideas. Clearly, therefore, even the other things can both be and come into being owing to such causes as produce the things just mentioned.

Again, if the Ideas are numbers, how can they be causes? Is it because existing things are other numbers, e.g. one number is man, another is Socrates, another Callias? Why then are the one set of numbers causes of the other set? It will not make any difference even if the former are eternal and the latter are not. But if it is because things in this sensible world (e.g. harmony) are ratios of numbers, evidently the things between which they are ratios are some one class of things. If, then, this—the matter—is some definite thing, evidently the numbers themselves too will be ratios of something to something else. E.g. if Callias is a numerical ratio between fire and earth and water and air, his Idea also will be a number of certain other underlying things; and man-himself, whether it is a number in a sense or not, will still be a numerical ratio of certain things and not a number proper, nor will it be a kind of number merely because it is a numerical ratio.

Again, from many numbers one number is produced, but how can one Idea come from many Ideas? And if the number comes not from the many numbers themselves but from the units in them, e.g. in 10,000, how is it with the units? If they are specifically alike, numerous absurdities will follow, and also if they are not alike (neither the units in one number being themselves like one another nor those in other numbers being all like to all); for in what will they differ, as they are without quality? This is not a plausible view, nor is it consistent with our thought on the matter.

Further, they must set up a second kind of number (with which arithmetic deals), and all the objects which are called "intermediate" by some thinkers; and how do these exist or from what principles do they proceed? Or why must they be intermediate between the things in this sensible world and the things-themselves?

Further, the units in 2 must each come from a prior 2; but this is impossible.

Further, why is a number, when taken all together, one?

Again, besides what has been said, if the units are *diverse* the Platonists should have spoken like those who say there are four, or two, elements; for each of these thinkers gives the name of element not to that which is common, e.g. to body, but to fire and earth, whether there is something common to them, viz. body, or not. But in fact the Platonists speak as if the One were *homogeneous* like fire or water; and if this is so, the numbers will not be substances. Evidently, if there is a One-itself and this is a first principle, "one" is being used in more than one sense; for otherwise the theory is impossible.

When we wish to reduce substances to their principles, we state that lines come from the short and long (i.e. from a kind of small and great), and the plane from the broad and narrow, and body from the deep and shallow. Yet how then can either the plane contain a line, or the solid a line or a plane? For the broad and narrow is a different class from the deep and shallow. Therefore, just as number is not present in these, evidently no other of the higher classes will be present in the lower. But again the broad is not a genus which includes the deep, for then the solid would have been a species of plane. Further, from what principle will the presence of the *points* in the line be derived? Plato even used to object to this class of things as being a geometrical fiction. He gave the name of principle of the line—and this he often posited—to the indivisible lines. Yet these must have a limit; therefore the argument from which the existence of the line follows proves also the existence of the point.

In general, though philosophy seeks the cause of perceptible things, we have given this up (for we say nothing of the cause from which change takes its start), but while we fancy we are stating the substance of perceptible things, we assert the existence of a second class of substances, while our account of the way in which they are the substances of perceptible things is empty talk; for "sharing," as we said before, means nothing.

Nor have the Ideas any connection with what we see to be the cause in the case of the arts, that for whose sake both all mind and the whole of nature are operative,—with this cause which we assert to be one of the first principles; but mathematics has come to be identical with philosophy for modern thinkers, though they say that it should be studied for the sake of other things.

Further, one might suppose that the substance which according to them underlies as matter is too mathematical, and is a predicate and differentia of the substance, i.e. of the matter, rather than matter itself; i.e. the great and the small are like the rare and the dense which the physical philosophers speak of, calling these the primary differentiae of the substratum; for these are a kind of excess and defect. And regarding movement, if the great and the small are to *be* movement, evidently the Ideas will be moved; but if they are not to be movement, whence did movement come? The whole study of nature has been annihilated.

And what is thought to be easy—to show that all things are one—is not done; for what is proved by the method of setting out instances is not that all things are one but that there is a One-itself,—if we grant all the assumptions. And not even this follows, if we do not grant that the universal is a genus; and this in some cases it cannot be.

Nor can it be explained either how the lines and planes and solids that come after the numbers exist or can exist, or what significance they have; for these can neither be Forms (for they are not numbers), nor the intermediates (for those are the objects of mathematics), nor the perishable things. This is evidently a distinct fourth class.

In general, if we search for the elements of existing things without distinguishing the many senses in which things are said to exist, we cannot find them, especially if the search for the elements of which things are made is conducted in this manner. For it is surely impossible to discover what "acting" or "being acted on," or "the straight," is made of, but if elements can be discovered at all, it is only the elements of substances; therefore either to seek the elements of all existing things or to think one has them is incorrect.

And how could we *learn* the elements of all things? Evidently we cannot start by knowing anything before. For as he who is learning geometry, though he may know other things before, knows none of the things with which the science deals and about which he is to learn, so it is in all other cases. Therefore if there is a science of all things, such as some assert to exist, he who is learning this will know nothing before. Yet all learning is by means of premises which are (either all or some of them) known before,—whether the learning be by demonstration or by definitions; for the elements of the definition must be known before and be familiar; and learning by induction proceeds similarly. But again, if the science were actually innate, it were strange that we are unaware of our possession of the greatest of sciences.

Again, how is one to *come to know* what all things are made of, and how is this to be made *evident?* This also affords a difficulty; for there might be a conflict of opinion, as there is about certain syllables; some say *za* is made out of *s* and *d* and *a*, while others say it is a distinct sound and none of those that are familiar.

Further, how could we know the objects of sense without having the sense in question? Yet we ought to, if the elements of which all things consist, as complex sounds consist of the elements proper to sound, are the same.

It is evident, then, even from what we have said before, that all men seem to seek the causes named in the *Physics,* and that we cannot name any beyond these; but they seek these vaguely; and though in a sense they have all been described before, in a sense they have not been described at all. For the earliest philosophy is, on all subjects, like one who lisps, since it is young and in its beginnings. For even Empedocles says bone exists by virtue of the ratio in it. Now this is the essence and the substance of the thing. But it is similarly necessary that flesh and each of the other tissues should be the ratio of its elements, or that not one of them should; for it is on account of this that both flesh and bone and everything else will exist, and not on account of the matter, which *he* names,—fire and earth and water and air. But while he would necessarily have agreed if another had said this, he has not said it clearly.

On these questions our views have been expressed before; but let us return to enumerate the difficulties that might be raised on these same points; for perhaps we may get from them some help towards our later difficulties.

BOOK α

The investigation of the truth is in one way hard, in another easy. An indication of this is found in the fact that no one is able to attain the truth adequately, while, on the other hand, we do not collectively fail, but every one says something true about the nature of things, and while individually we contribute little or nothing to the truth, by the union of all a considerable amount is amassed. Therefore, since the truth seems to be like the proverbial door, which no one can fail to hit, in this respect it must be easy, but the fact that we can have a whole truth and not the particular part we aim at shows the difficulty of it.

Perhaps, too, as difficulties are of two kinds, the cause of the present difficulty is not in the facts but in us. For as the eyes of bats are to the blaze of day, so is the reason in our soul to the things which are by nature most evident of all.

It is just that we should be grateful, not only to those with whose views we may agree, but also to those who have expressed more superficial views; for these also contributed something, by developing before us the powers of thought. It is true that if there had been no Timotheus we should have been without much of our lyric poetry; but if there had been no Phrynis there would have been no Timotheus. The same holds good of those who have expressed views about the truth; for from some thinkers we have inherited certain opinions, while the others have been responsible for the appearance of the former.

It is right also that philosophy should be called knowledge of the truth. For the end of theoretical knowledge is truth, while that of practical knowledge is action (for even if they consider how things are, practical men do not study the eternal, but what is relative and in the present). Now we do not know a truth without its cause; and a thing has a quality in a higher degree than other things if in virtue of it the similar quality belongs to the other things as well (e.g. fire is the hottest of things; for it is the cause of the heat of all other things); so that that which causes derivative truths to be true is most true. Hence the principles of eternal things must be always most true (for they are not merely sometimes true, nor is there any cause of their being, but they themselves are the cause of the being of other things), so that as each thing is in respect of being, so is it in respect of truth.

But evidently there *is* a first principle, and the causes of things are neither an infinite series nor infinitely various in kind. For (1) neither can one thing proceed from another, as from matter, *ad infinitum* (e.g. flesh from earth, earth from air, air from fire, and so on without stopping), nor can the sources of movement form an endless series (man for instance being acted on by air, air by the sun, the sun by Strife, and so on without limit). Similarly the final causes cannot go on *ad infinitum*,—walking being for the sake of health, this for the sake of happiness, happiness for the sake of something else, and so one thing always for the sake of another. And the case of the essence is similar. For in the case of intermediates, which have a last term and a term prior to them, the prior must be the cause of the later terms. For if we had to say which of the three is the cause, we should say the first; surely not the last, for the final term is the cause of none; nor even the intermediate, for it is the cause only of one. (It makes no difference whether there is one intermediate or more, nor whether they are infinite or finite in number.) But of series which are infinite in this way, and of the infinite in general, all the parts down to that now present are alike intermediates; so that if there is no first there is no cause at all.

Nor can there be an infinite process downwards, with a beginning in the upward direction, so that water should proceed from fire, earth from water, and so always some other kind should be produced. For one thing comes *from* another in two ways—not in the sense in which "from" means "after" (as we say "from the Isthmian games come the Olympian"), but either (i) as the man comes from the boy, by the boy's changing, or (ii) as air comes from water. By "as the man comes from the boy" we mean "as that which has come to be from that which is coming to be, or as that which is finished from that which is being achieved" (for as becoming is between being and not being, so that which is becoming is always between that which is and that which is not; for the learner is a man of science in the making, and this is what is meant when we say that *from* a learner a man of science is being made); on the other hand, coming from another thing as water comes from air implies the destruction of the other thing. This is why changes of the former kind are not reversible, and the boy does not come from the man (for it is not that which comes to be something that comes to be as a result of coming to be, but that which exists after the coming to be; for it is thus that the day, too, comes from the morning—in the sense that it comes after the morning; which is the reason why the morning cannot come from the day); but changes of the other kind are reversible. But in both cases it is impossible that the number of terms should be infinite. For terms of the former kind, being intermediates, must have an end, and terms of the latter kind change back into *one another;* for the destruction of either is the generation of the other.

At the same time it is impossible that the first cause, being eternal, should be destroyed; for since the process of becoming is not infinite in the upward direction, that which is the first thing by whose destruction something came to be must be non-eternal.

Further, the *final cause* is an end, and that sort of end which is not for the sake of something else, but for whose sake everything else is; so that if there is to be a last term of this sort, the process will not be infinite; but if there is no such term, there will be no final cause, but those who maintain the infinite series eliminate the Good without knowing it (yet no one would try to do anything if he were not going to come to a limit); nor would there be reason in the world; the reasonable man, at least, always acts for a purpose, and this is a limit; for the end is a limit.

But the *essence,* also, cannot be reduced to another definition which is fuller in expression. For the original definition is always more of a definition, and not the later one; and in a series in which the first term has not the required character, the next has not it either.— Further, those who speak thus destroy science; for it is not possible to have this till one comes to the unanalysable terms. And knowledge becomes impossible; for how can one apprehend things that are infinite in this way? For this is not like the case of the line, to whose divisibility there is no stop, but which we cannot think if we do not make a stop (for which reason one who is tracing the infinitely divisible line cannot be counting the possibilities of section), but the whole line also must be apprehended by something in us that does not move from part to part.—Again, nothing infinite can exist; and if it could, at least the notion of infinity is not infinite.

But (2) if the *kinds* of causes had been infinite in number, then also knowledge would have been impossible; for we think we know, only when we have ascertained the causes, but that which is infinite by addition cannot be gone through in a finite time.

The effect which lectures produce on a hearer depends on his habits; for we demand the language we are accustomed to, and that which is different from this seems not in keeping but somewhat unintelligible and foreign because of its unwontedness. For it is the customary that is intelligible. The force of habit is shown by the laws, in which the legendary and childish elements prevail over our knowledge about them, owing to habit. Thus some people do not listen to a speaker unless he speaks mathematically, others unless he gives instances, while others expect him to cite a poet as witness. And some want to have everything done accurately, while others are annoyed by accuracy, either because they cannot follow the connection of thought or because they regard it as pettifoggery. For accuracy has something of this character, so that as in trade so in argument some people think it mean. Hence one must be already trained to know how to take each sort of argument, since it is absurd to seek at the same time knowledge and the way of attaining knowledge; and it is not easy to get even one of the two.

The minute accuracy of mathematics is not to be demanded in all cases, but only in the case of things which have no matter. Hence its method is not that of natural science; for presumably the whole of nature has matter. Hence we must inquire first what nature is: for thus we shall also see what natural science treats of [and whether it belongs to one science or to more to investigate the causes and the principles of things].

CATEGORIES

Things are said to be named "equivocally" when, though they have a common name, the definition corresponding with the name differs for each. Thus, a real man and a figure in a picture can both lay claim to the name "animal"; yet these are equivocally so named, for, though they have a common name, the definition corresponding with the name differs for each. For should any one define in what sense each is an animal, his definition in the one case will be appropriate to that case only.

On the other hand, things are said to be named "univocally" which have both the name and the definition answering to the name in common. A man and an ox are both "animal," and these are univocally so named, inasmuch as not only the name, but also the definition, is the same in both cases: for if a man should state in what sense each is an animal, the statement in the one case would be identical with that in the other.

From "Categories," trans. E. M. Edghill, in *The Oxford Translation of Aristotle,* ed. W. D. Ross (Oxford: Clarendon Press, 1928). Reprinted with permission of the publishers.

Things are said to be named "derivatively," which derive their name from some other name, but differ from it in termination. Thus the grammarian derives his name from the word "grammar," and the courageous man from the word "courage."

Forms of speech are either simple or composite. Examples of the latter are such expressions as "the man runs," "the man wins"; of the former "man," "ox," "runs," "wins."

Of things themselves some are predicable of a subject, and are never present in a subject. Thus "man" is predicable of the individual man, and is never present in a subject.

By being "present in a subject" I do not mean present as parts are present in a whole, but being incapable of existence apart from the said subject.

Some things, again, are present in a subject, but are never predicable of a subject. For instance, a certain point of grammatical knowledge is present in the mind, but is not predicable of any subject; or again, a certain whiteness may be present in the body (for colour requires a material basis), yet it is never predicable of anything.

Other things, again, are both predicable of a subject and present in a subject. Thus while knowledge is present in the human mind, it is predicable of grammar.

There is, lastly, a class of things which are neither present in a subject nor predicable of a subject, such as the individual man or the individual horse. But, to speak more generally, that which is individual and has the character of a unit is never predicable of a subject. Yet in some cases there is nothing to prevent such being present in a subject. Thus a certain point of grammatical knowledge is present in a subject.

When one thing is predicated of another, all that which is predicable of the predicate will be predicable also of the subject. Thus, "man" is predicated of the individual man; but "animal" is predicated of "man"; it will, therefore, be predicable of the individual man also: for the individual man is both "man" and "animal."

If genera are different and co-ordinate, their differentiae are themselves different in kind. Take as an instance the genus "animal" and the genus "knowledge." "With feet," "two-footed," "winged," "aquatic," are differentiae of "animal"; the species of knowledge are not distinguished by the same differentiae. One species of knowledge does not differ from another in being "two-footed."

But where one genus is subordinate to another, there is nothing to prevent their having the same differentiae: for the greater class is predicated of the lesser, so that all the differentiae of the predicate will be differentiae also of the subject.

Expressions which are in no way composite signify substance, quantity, quality, relation, place, time, position, state, action, or affection. To sketch my meaning roughly, examples of substance are "man" or "the horse," of quantity, such terms as "two cubits long" or "three cubits long," of quality, such attributes as "white," "grammatical." "Double," "half," "greater," fall under the category of relation; "in the market place," "in the Lyceum," under that of place; "yesterday," "last year," under that of time. "Lying," "sitting," are terms indicating position; "shod," "armed," state; "to lance," "to cauterize," action; "to be lanced," "to be cauterized," affection.

No one of these terms, in and by itself, involves an affirmation; it is by the combination of such terms that positive or negative statements arise. For every assertion must, as is admitted, be either true or false, whereas expressions which are not in any way composite, such as "man," "white," "runs," "wins," cannot be either true or false.

Substance, in the truest and primary and most definite sense of the word, is that which is neither predicable of a subject nor present in a subject; for instance, the individual man or horse. But in a secondary sense those things are called substances within which, as species, the primary substances are included; also those which, as genera, include the species.

For instance, the individual man is included in the species "man," and the genus to which the species belongs is "animal"; these, therefore—that is to say, the species "man" and the genus "animal"—are termed secondary substances.

It is plain from what has been said that both the name and the definition of the predicate must be predicable of the subject. For instance, "man" is predicated of the individual man. Now in this case the name of the species "man" is applied to the individual, for we use the term "man" in describing the individual; and the definition of "man" will also be predicated of the individual man, for the individual man is both man and animal. Thus, both the name and the definition of the species are predicable of the individual.

With regard, on the other hand, to those things which are present in a subject, it is generally the case that neither their name nor their definition is predicable of that in which they are present. Though, however, the definition is never predicable, there is nothing in certain cases to prevent the name being used. For instance, "white" being present in a body is predicated of that in which it is present, for a body is called white: the definition, however, of the colour "white" is never predicable of the body.

Everything except primary substances is either predicable of a primary substance or present in a primary substance. This becomes evident by reference to particular instances which occur. "Animal" is predicated of the species "man," therefore of the individual man, for if there were no individual man of whom it could be predicated, it could not be predicated of the species "man" at all. Again, colour is present in body, therefore in individual bodies, for if there were no individual body in which it was present, it could not be present in body at all. Thus everything except primary substances is either predicated of primary substances, or is present in them, and if these last did not exist, it would be impossible for anything else to exist.

Of secondary substances, the species is more truly substance than the genus, being more nearly related to primary substance. For if any one should render an account of what a primary substance is, he would render a more instructive account, and one more proper to the subject, by stating the species than by stating the genus. Thus, he would give a more instructive account of an individual man by stating that he was man than by stating that he was animal, for the former description is peculiar to the individual in a greater degree, while the latter is too general. Again, the man who gives an account of the nature of an individual tree will give a more instructive account by mentioning the species "tree" than by mentioning the genus "plant."

Moreover, primary substances are most properly called substances in virtue of the fact that they are the entities which underlie everything else, and that everything else is either predicated of them or present in them. Now the same relation which subsists between primary substance and everything else subsists also between the species and the genus: for the species is to the genus as subject is to predicate, since the genus is predicated of the species, whereas the species cannot be predicated of the genus. Thus we have a second ground for asserting that the species is more truly substance than the genus.

Of the species themselves, except in the case of such as are genera, no one is more truly substance than another. We should not give a more appropriate account of the individual man by stating the species to which he belonged, than we should of an individual horse by adopting the same method of definition. In the same way, of primary substances, no one is more truly substance than another; an individual man is not more truly substance than an individual ox.

It is, then, with good reason that of all that remains, when we exclude primary substances, we concede to species and genera alone the name "secondary substance," for these alone of all the predicates convey a knowledge of primary substance. For it is by stating the species or the genus that we appropriately define any individual man; and we shall make our definition more exact by stating the former than by stating the latter. All other things that we state, such as that he is white, that he runs, and so on, are irrelevant to the definition. Thus it is just that these alone, apart from primary substances, should be called substances.

Further, primary substances are most properly so called, because they underlie and are the subjects of everything else. Now the same relation that subsists between primary substance and everything else subsists also between the species and the genus to which the primary substance belongs, on the one hand, and every attribute which is not included within these, on the other. For these are the subject of all such. If we call an individual man "skilled in grammar," the predicate is applicable also to the species and to the genus to which he belongs. This law holds good in all cases.

It is a common characteristic of all substance that it is never present in a subject. For primary substance is neither present in a subject nor predicated of a subject; while, with regard to secondary substances, it is clear from the following arguments (apart from others) that they are not present in a subject. For "man" is predicated of the individual man, but is not present in any subject: for manhood is not present in the individual man. In the same way, "animal" is also predicated of the individual man, but is not present in him. Again, when a thing is present in a subject, though the name may quite well be applied to that in which it is present, the definition cannot be applied. Yet of secondary substances, not only the name, but also the definition, applies to the subject: we should use both the definition of the species and that of the genus with reference to the individual man. Thus substance cannot be present in a subject.

Yet this is not peculiar to substance, for it is also the case that differentiae cannot be present in subjects. The characteristics "terrestrial" and "two-footed" are predicated of the species "man," but present in it. For they are not *in* man. Moreover, the definition of the differentia may be predicated of that of which the differentia itself is predicated. For instance, if the characteristic "terrestrial" is predicated of the species "man," the definition also of that characteristic may be used to form the predicate of the species "man": for "man" is terrestrial.

The fact that the parts of substances appear to be present in the whole, as in a subject, should not make us apprehensive lest we should have to admit that such parts are not substances: for in explaining the phrase "being present in a subject," we stated that we meant "otherwise than as parts in a whole."

It is the mark of substances and of differentiae that, in all propositions of which they form the predicate, they are predicated univocally. For all such propositions have for their subject either the individual or the species. It is true that, inasmuch as primary substance is not predicable of anything, it can never form the predicate of any proposition. But of secondary substances, the species is predicated of the individual, the genus both of the species and of the individual. Similarly the differentiae are predicated of the species and of the individuals. Moreover, the definition of the species and that of the genus are applicable to the primary substance, and that of the genus to the species. For all that is predicated of the predicate will be predicated also of the subject. Similarly, the definition of the differentiae will be applicable to the species and to the individuals. But it was stated above that the word "univocal" was applied to those things which had both name and definition in common. It is, therefore, established that in every proposition, of which either substance or a differentia forms the predicate, these are predicated univocally.

All substance appears to signify that which is individual. In the case of primary substance this is indisputably true, for the thing is a unit. In the case of secondary substances, when we speak, for instance, of "man" or "animal," our form of speech gives the impression that we are here also indicating that which is individual, but the impression is not strictly true; for a secondary substance is not an individual, but a class with a certain qualification; for it is not one and single as a primary substance is; the words "man," "animal," are predicable of more than one subject.

Yet species and genus do not merely indicate quality, like the term "white"; "white" indicates quality and nothing further, but species and genus determine the quality with reference to a substance: they signify substance qualitatively differentiated. The determinate qualification covers a larger field in the case of the genus than in that of the species: he who uses the word "animal" is herein using a word of wider extension than he who uses the word "man."

Another mark of substance is that it has no contrary. What could be the contrary of any primary substance, such as the individual man or animal? It has none. Nor can the species or the genus have a contrary. Yet this characteristic is not peculiar to substance, but is true of many other things, such as quantity. There is nothing that forms the contrary of "two cubits long" or of "three cubits long," or of "ten," or of any such term. A man may contend that "much" is the contrary of "little," or "great" of "small," but of definite quantitative terms no contrary exists.

Substance, again, does not appear to admit of variation of degree. I do not mean by this that one substance cannot be more or less truly substance than another, for it has already been stated that this is the case; but that no single substance admits of varying degrees within itself. For instance, one particular substance, "man," cannot be more or less man either than himself at some other time or than some other man. One man cannot be more than another, as that which is white may be more or less white than some other white object, or as that which is beautiful may be more or less beautiful than some other beautiful object. The same quality, moreover, is said to subsist in a thing in varying degrees at different times. A body, being white, is said to be whiter at one time than it was before, or, being warm, is said to be warmer or less warm than at some other time. But substance is not said to be more or less that which it is: a man is not more truly a man at one time than he was before, nor is anything, if it is substance, more or less what it is. Substance, then, does not admit of variation of degree.

The most distinctive mark of substance appears to be that, while remaining numerically one and the same, it is capable of admitting contrary qualities. From among things other than substance, we should find ourselves unable to bring forward any which possessed this mark. Thus, one and the same colour cannot be white and black. Nor can the same one action be good and bad: this law holds good with everything that is not substance. But one and the self-same substance, while retaining its identity, is yet capable of admitting contrary qualities. The same individual person is at one time white, at another black, at one time warm, at another cold, at one time good, at another bad. This capacity is found nowhere else, though it might be maintained that a statement or opinion was an exception to the rule. The same statement, it is agreed, can be both true and false. For if the statement "he is sitting" is true, yet, when the person in question has risen, the same statement will be false. The same applies to opinions. For if any one thinks truly that a person is sitting, yet, when that person has risen, this same opinion, if still held, will be false. Yet although this exception may be allowed, there is, nevertheless, a difference in the manner in which the thing takes place. It is by themselves changing that substances admit contrary qualities. It is thus that that which was hot becomes cold, for it has entered into a different state. Similarly that which was white becomes black, and that which was bad good, by a process of change; and in the same way in all other cases it is by changing that substances are capable of admitting contrary qualities. But statements and opinions themselves remain unaltered in all respects: it is by the alteration in the facts of the case that the contrary quality comes to be theirs. The statement "he is sitting" remains unaltered, but it is at one time true, at another false, according to circumstances. What has been said of statements applies also to opinions. Thus, in respect of the manner in which the thing takes place, it is the peculiar mark of substance that it should be capable of admitting contrary qualities; for it is by itself changing that it does so.

If, then, a man should make this exception and contend that statements and opinions are capable of admitting contrary qualities, his contention is unsound. For statements and opinions are said to have this capacity, not because they themselves undergo modification, but because this modification occurs in the case of something else. The truth or falsity of a statement depends on facts, and not on any power on the part of the statement itself of admitting contrary qualities. In short, there is nothing which can alter the nature of statements and opinions. As, then, no change takes place in themselves, these cannot be said to be capable of admitting contrary qualities.

But it is by reason of the modification which takes place within the substance itself that a substance is said to be capable of admitting contrary qualities; for a substance admits within itself either disease or health, whiteness or blackness. It is in this sense that it is said to be capable of admitting contrary qualities.

To sum up, it is a distinctive mark of substance, that, while remaining numerically one and the same, it is capable of admitting contrary qualities, the modification taking place through a change in the substance itself.

Let these remarks suffice on the subject of substance.

ON THE SOUL

Now there is one class of existent things which we call substance, including under the term, firstly, matter, which in itself is not this or that; secondly, shape or form, in virtue of which the term this or that is at once applied; thirdly, the whole made up of matter and form. Matter is identical with potentiality, form with actuality. And there are two meanings of actuality: knowledge illustrates the one, exercise of knowledge the other. Now bodies above all things are held to be substances, particularly such bodies as are the work of nature; for to these all the rest owe their origin. Of natural bodies some possess life and some do not: where by life we mean the power of self-nourishment and of independent growth and decay. Consequently every natural body possessed of life must be substance, and substance of the composite order. And since in fact we have here body with a certain attribute, namely, the possession of life, the body will not be the soul: for the body is not an attribute of a subject, it stands rather for a subject of attributes, that is, matter. It must follow, then, that soul is

From "On the Soul," trans. R. D. Hicks, in *Aristotle: De Anima* (Cambridge: Cambridge University Press, 1907).

substance in the sense that it is the form of a natural body having in it the capacity of life. Such substance is actuality. The soul, therefore, is the actuality of the body above described. But the term "actuality" is used in two senses; in the one it answers to knowledge, in the other to the exercise of knowledge. Clearly in this case it is analogous to knowledge: for sleep, as well as waking, implies the presence of soul; and, whilst waking is analogous to the exercise of knowledge, sleep is analogous to the possession of knowledge without its exercise; and in the same individual the possession of knowledge comes in order of time before its exercise. Hence soul is the first actuality of a natural body having in it the capacity of life. And a body which is possessed of organs answers to this description. We may note that the parts of plants, as well as those of animals, are organs, though of a very simple sort: for instance, a leaf is the sheath of the pod and the pod of the fruit. The roots, again, are analogous to the mouths of animals, both serving to take in nourishment. If, then, we have to make a general statement touching soul in all its forms, the soul will be the first actuality of a natural body furnished with organs. Hence there is no need to enquire whether soul and body are one, any more than whether the wax and the imprint are one; or, in general, whether the matter of a thing is the same with that of which it is the matter. For, of all the various meanings borne by the terms unity and being, actuality is the meaning which belongs to them by the fullest right.

It has now been stated in general terms what soul is, namely, substance as notion or form. And this is the quiddity of such and such a body. Suppose, for example, that any instrument, say, an axe, were a natural body, its axeity would be its substance, would in fact be its soul. If this were taken away, it would cease, except in an equivocal sense to be an axe. But the axe is after all an axe. For it is not of a body of this kind that the soul is the quiddity, that is, the notion or form, but of a natural body of a particular sort, having in itself the origination of motion and rest.

Further, we must view our statement in the light of the parts of the body. For, if the eye were an animal, eyesight would be its soul, this being the substance as notion or form of the eye. The eye is the matter of eyesight, and in default of eyesight it is no longer an eye, except equivocally, like an eye in stone or in a picture. What has been said of the part must be understood to apply to the whole living body; for, as the sensation of a part of the body is to that part, so is sensation as a whole to the whole sentient body as such. By that which has in it the capacity of life is meant not the body which has lost its soul, but that which possesses it. Now the seed in animals, like the fruit in plants, is that which is potentially such and such a body. As, then, the cutting of the axe or the seeing of the eye is full actuality, so, too, is the waking state; while the soul is actuality in the same sense as eyesight and the capacity of the instrument. The body, on the other hand, is simply that which is potentially existent. But, just as in the one case the eye means the pupil in conjunction with the eyesight, so in the other soul and body together constitute the animal.

Now it needs no proof that the soul—or if it is divisible into parts, certain of its parts—cannot be separated from the body, for there are cases where the actuality belongs to the parts themselves. There is, however, no reason why some parts should not be separated, if they are not the actualities of any body whatever. Again, it is not clear whether the soul may not be the actuality of the body as the sailor is of the ship. This, then, may suffice for an outline or provisional sketch of soul.

But, as it is from the things which are naturally obscure, though more easily recognized by us, that we proceed to what is clear and, in the order of thought, more knowable, we must employ this method in trying to give a fresh account of soul. For it is not enough that the defining statement should set forth the fact, as most definitions do; it should also contain and present the cause: whereas in practice what is stated in the definition is usually no more than a conclusion. For example, what is quadrature? The construction of an equilateral rectangle equal in area to a given oblong. But such a definition expresses merely the conclusion. Whereas, if you say that quadrature is the discovery of a mean proportional, then you state the reason.

We take, then, as our starting-point for discussion that it is life which distinguishes the animate from the inanimate. But the term life is used in various senses; and, if life is present in but a single one of these senses, we speak of a thing as living. Thus there is intellect, sensation, motion from place to place and rest, the motion concerned with nutrition and, further, decay and growth. Hence it is that all plants are supposed to have life. For apparently they have within themselves a faculty and principle whereby they grow and decay in opposite directions. For plants do not grow upwards without growing downwards; they grow in both directions equally, in fact in all directions, as many as are constantly nourished and therefore continue to live, so long as they are capable of absorbing nutriment. This form of life can be separated from the others, though in mortal creatures the others cannot be separated from it. In the case of plants the fact is manifest: for they have no other faculty of soul at all.

It is, then, in virtue of this principle that all living things live, whether animals or plants. But it is sensation primarily which constitutes the animal. For, provided they have sensation, even those creatures which are devoid of movement and do not change their place are called animals and are not merely said to be alive. Now the primary sense in all animals is touch. But, as the nutritive faculty may exist without touch or any form of sensation, so also touch may exist apart from the other senses. By nutritive faculty we mean the part of the soul in which even plants share. Animals, however, are found universally to have the sense of touch: why this is so in each of the two cases will be stated hereafter.

For the present it may suffice to say that the soul is the origin of the functions above enumerated and is determined by them, namely, by capacities of nutrition, sensation, thought, and by motion. But whether each one of these is a soul or part of a soul and, if a part, whether it is only logically distinct or separable in space also is a question, the answer to which is in some cases not hard to see: other cases present difficulties. For, just as in the case of plants some of them are found to live when divided and separated from each other (which implies that the soul in each plant, though actually one, is potentially several souls), so, too, when insects or annelida are cut up, we see the same thing happen with other varieties of soul: I mean, each of the segments has sensation and moves from place to place, and, if it has sensation, it has also imagination and appetency. For, where there is sensation, there is also pleasure and pain: and, where these are, desire also must of necessity be present. But as regards intellect and the speculative faculty the case is not yet clear. It would seem, however, to be a distinct species of soul, and it alone is capable of separation from the body, as that which is eternal from that which is perishable. The remaining parts of the soul are, as the foregoing consideration shows, not separable in the way that some allege them to be: at the same time it is clear that they are logically distinct. For the faculties of sensation and of opinion taken in the abstract are distinct, since to have sensation and to opine are distinct. And so it is likewise with each of the other faculties above mentioned. Again, while some animals possess all these functions, others have only some of them, others only one. It is this which will differentiate animal from animal. The reason why this is so must be investigated hereafter. The case is similar with the several senses: some animals have all of them, others some of them, others again only one, the most indispensable, that is, touch.

Now "that by which we live and have sensation" is a phrase with two meanings, answering to the two meanings of "that by which we know" (the latter phrase means, firstly, knowledge and, secondly, soul, by either of which we say we know). Similarly that by which we have health means either health itself or a certain part, if not the whole, of the body. Now of these knowledge and health are the shape and in some sort form, the notion and virtual activity, of that which is capable of receiving in the one case knowledge, in the other health: that is to say, it is in that which is acted upon or conditioned that the activity of the causal agencies would seem to take effect. Now the soul is that whereby primarily we live, perceive, and have understanding: therefore it will be a species of notion or form, not matter or substratum. Of the three meanings of substance mentioned above, form, matter and the whole made up of these two, matter is potentiality and form is actuality. And, since the whole made up of the two is endowed with soul, the body is not the actuality of soul, but soul the actuality of a particular body. Hence those are right who regard the soul as not independent of body and yet at the same time as not itself a species of body. It is not body, but something belonging to body, and therefore resides in body and, what is more, in such and such a body. Our predecessors were wrong in endeavouring to fit the soul into a body without further determination of the nature and qualities of that body: although we do not even find that of any two things taken at random the one will admit the other. And this result is what we might expect. For the actuality of each thing comes naturally to be developed in the potentiality of each thing: in other words, in the appropriate matter. From these considerations, then, it is manifest that soul is a certain actuality, a notion or form, of that which has the capacity to be endowed with soul.

NICHOMACHEAN ETHICS

BOOK I

Every art and every inquiry, and similarly every action and pursuit, is thought to aim at some good; and for this reason the good has rightly been declared to be that at which all things aim. But a certain difference is found among ends; some are activities, others are products apart from the activities that produce them. Where there are ends apart from the actions, it is the nature of the products to be better than the activities. Now, as there are many actions, arts, and sciences, their ends also are many; the end of the medical art is health, that of shipbuilding a vessel, that of strategy victory, that of economics wealth. But where such arts fall under a single capacity—as bridle-making and the other arts concerned with the equipment of horses fall under the art of riding, and this and every military action under strategy, in the same way other arts fall under yet others—in all of these the ends of the master arts are to be preferred to all the subordinate ends; for it is for the sake of the

From Aristotle, *Nichomachean Ethics,* trans. W. D. Ross (London: Oxford University Press, 1915).

former that the latter are pursued. It makes no difference whether the activities themselves are the ends of the actions, or something else apart from the activities, as in the case of the sciences just mentioned.

If, then there is some end of the things we do, which we desire for its own sake (everything else being desired for the sake of this), and if we do not choose everything for the sake of something else (for at that rate the process would go on to infinity, so that our desire would be empty and vain), clearly this must be the good and the chief good. Will not the knowledge of it, then, have a great influence on life? Shall we not, like archers who have a mark to aim at, be more likely to hit upon what is right? If so, we must try, in outline at least, to determine what it is, and of which of the sciences or capacities it is the object. It would seem to belong to the most authoritative art and that which is most truly the master art. And politics appears to be of this nature; for it is this that ordains which of the sciences should be studied in a state, and which each class of citizens should learn and up to what point they should learn them; and we see even the most highly esteemed of capacities to fall under this, e.g. strategy, economics, rhetoric; now, since politics uses the rest of the sciences, and since, again, it legislates as to what we are to do and what we are to abstain from, the end of this science must include those of the others, so that this end must be the good for man. For even if the end is the same for a single man and for a state, that of the state seems at all events something greater and more complete whether to attain or to preserve; though it is worthwhile to attain the end merely for one man, it is finer and more godlike to attain it for a nation or for city-states. These, then, are the ends at which our inquiry aims, since it is political science, in one sense of that term. . . .

Let us resume our inquiry and state, in view of the fact that all knowledge and every pursuit aims at some good, what it is that we say political science aims at and what is the highest of all goods achievable by action. Verbally there is very general agreement; for both the general run of men and people of superior refinement say that it is happiness, and identify living well and doing well with being happy; but with regard to what happiness is they differ, and the many do not give the same account as the wise. For the former think it is some plain and obvious thing, like pleasure, wealth, or honour; they differ, however, from one another—and often even the same man identifies it with different things, with health when he is ill, with wealth when he is poor; but, conscious of their ignorance, they admire those who proclaim some great ideal that is above their comprehension. Now some thought that apart from these many goods there is another which is self-subsistent and causes the goodness of all these as well. To examine all the opinions that have been held were perhaps somewhat fruitless; enough to examine those that are most prevalent or that seem to be arguable. . . .

To judge from the lives that men lead, most men, and men of the most vulgar type, seem (not without some ground) to identify the good, or happiness, with pleasure; which is the reason why they love the life of enjoyment. For there are, we may say, three prominent types of life—that just mentioned, the political, and thirdly the contemplative life. Now the mass of mankind are evidently quite slavish in their tastes, preferring a life suitable to beasts, but they get some ground for their view from the fact that many of those in high places share the tastes of Sardanapallus. A consideration of the prominent types of life shows that people of superior refinement and of active disposition identify happiness with honour; for this is, roughly speaking, the end of the political life. But it seems too superficial to be what we are looking for, since it is thought to depend on those who bestow honour rather than on him who receives it, but the good we divine to be something proper to a man and not easily taken from him. Further, men seem to pursue honour in order that they may be assured of their goodness; at least it is by men of practical wisdom that they seek to be honoured, and among those who know them, and on the ground of their virtue; clearly, then, according to them, at any rate, virtue is better. And perhaps one might even suppose this to be, rather than honour, the end of the political life. But even this appears somewhat incomplete; for possession of virtue seems actually compatible with being asleep, or with lifelong inactivity, and, further, with the greatest sufferings and misfortunes; but a man who was living so no one would call happy, unless he were maintaining a thesis at all costs. But enough of this; for the subject has been sufficiently treated even in the current discussions. Third comes the contemplative life, which we shall consider later.

The life of money-making is one undertaken under compulsion, and wealth is evidently not the good we are seeking; for it is merely useful and for the sake of something else. And so one might rather take the aforenamed objects to be ends; for they are loved for themselves. But it is evident that not even these are ends; yet many arguments have been thrown away in support of them. . . .

Let us again return to the good we are seeking, and ask what it can be. It seems different in different actions and arts; it is different in medicine, in strategy, and in the other arts likewise. What then is the good of each? Surely that for whose sake everything else is done. In medicine this is health, in strategy victory, in architecture a house, in any other sphere something else, and in every action and pursuit the end; for it is for the sake of this that all men do whatever else they do. Therefore, if there is an end for all that we do, this will be the good achievable by action, and if there are more than one, these will be the goods achievable by action.

So the argument has by a different course reached the same point; but we must try to state this even more clearly. Since there are evidently more than one end, and we choose some of these (e.g. wealth, flutes, and in general instruments) for the sake of something else, clearly not all ends are final ends; but the chief good is evidently something final. Therefore, if there is only one final end, this will be what we are seeking, and if there are more than one, the most final of these will be what we are seeking. Now we call that which is in itself worthy of pursuit more final than that which is worthy of pursuit for the sake of something else, and that which is never desirable for the sake of something else more final than the things that are desirable both in themselves and for the sake of that other thing, and therefore we call final without qualification that which is always desirable in itself and never for the sake of something else.

Now such a thing happiness, above all else, is held to be; for this we choose always for itself and never for the sake of something else, but honour, pleasure, reason, and every virtue we choose indeed for themselves (for if nothing resulted from them we should still choose each of them), but we choose them also for the sake of happiness, judging that by means of them we shall be happy. Happiness, on the other hand, no one chooses for the sake of these, nor, in general, for anything other than itself.

From the point of view of self-sufficiency the same result seems to follow; for the final good is thought to be self-sufficient. Now by self-sufficient we do not mean that which is sufficient for a man by himself, for one who lives a solitary life, but also for parents, children, wife, and in general for his friends and fellow citizens, since man is born for citizenship. But some limit must be set to this; for if we extend our requirement to ancestors and descendants and friends' friends we are in for an infinite series. Let us examine this question, however, on another occasion; the self-sufficient we now define as that which when isolated makes life desirable and lacking in nothing; and such we think happiness to be; and further we think it most desirable of all things, without being counted as one good thing among others—if it were so counted it would clearly be made more desirable by the addition of even the least of goods; for that which is added becomes an excess of goods, and of goods the greater is always more desirable. Happiness, then, is something final and self-sufficient, and is the end of action.

Presumably, however, to say that happiness is the chief good seems a platitude, and a clearer account of what it is is still desired. This might perhaps be given, if we could first ascertain the function of man. For just as for a flute-player, a sculptor, or any artist, and, in general, for all things that have a function or activity, the good and the "well" is thought to reside in the function, so would it seem to be for man, if he has a function. Have the carpenter, then, and the tanner certain functions or activities, and has man none? Is he born without a function? Or as eye, hand, foot, and in general each of the parts evidently has a function, may one lay it down that man similarly has a function apart from all these? What then can this be? Life seems to be common even to plants, but we are seeking what is peculiar to man. Let us exclude, therefore, the life of nutrition and growth. Next there would be a life of perception, but *it* also seems to be common even to the horse, the ox, and every animal. There remains, then, an active life of the element that has a rational principle; of this, one part has such a principle in the sense of being obedient to one, the other in the sense of possessing one and exercising thought. And, as "life of the rational element" also has two meanings, we must state that life in the sense of activity is what we mean; for this seems to be the more proper sense of the term. Now if the function of man is an activity of soul which follows or implies a rational principle, and if we say "a so-and-so" and "a good so-and-so" have a function which is the same in kind, e.g. a lyre-player and a good lyre-player, and so without qualification in all cases, eminence in respect of goodness being added to the name of the function (for the function of a lyre-player is to play the lyre, and that of a good lyre-player is to do so well): if this is the case, [and we state the function of man to be a certain kind of life, and this to be an activity or actions of the soul implying a rational principle, and the function of a good man to be the good and noble performance of these, and if any action is well performed when it is performed in accordance with the appropriate excellence: if this is the case,] human good turns out to be activity of soul in accordance with virtue, and if there are more than one virtue, in accordance with the best and most complete.

But we must add "in a complete life." For one swallow does not make a summer, nor does one day; and so too one day, or a short time, does not make a man blessed and happy. . . .

Since happiness is an activity of soul in accordance with perfect virtue, we must consider the nature of virtue; for perhaps we shall thus see better the nature of happiness. . . .

But clearly the virtue we must study is human virtue; for the good we were seeking was human good and the happiness human happiness. By human virtue we mean not that of the body but that of the soul. . . .

BOOK II

Virtue, then, being of two kinds, intellectual and moral, intellectual virtue in the main owes both its birth and its growth to teaching (for which reason it requires experience and time), while moral virtue comes about as a result of habit, whence also its name (ἠθική) is one that is formed by a slight variation from the word ἔθος (habit). From this it is also plain that none of the moral virtues arises in us by nature; for nothing that exists by nature can form a habit contrary to its nature. For instance the stone which by nature moves downwards cannot be habituated to move upwards, not even if one tries to train it by throwing it up ten thousand times; nor can fire be habituated to move downwards, nor can anything else that by nature behaves in one way be trained to behave in another. Neither by nature, then, nor contrary to nature do the virtues arise in us; rather we are adapted by nature to receive them, and are made perfect by habit.

Again, of all the things that come to us by nature we first acquire the potentiality and later exhibit the activity (this is plain in the case of the senses; for it was not by often seeing or often hearing that we got these senses, but on the contrary we had them before we used them, and did not come to have them by using them); but the virtues we get by first exercising them, as also happens in the case of the arts as well. For the things we have to learn before we can do them, we learn by doing them, e.g. men become builders by building and lyre-players by playing the lyre; so too we become just by doing just acts, temperate by doing temperate acts, brave by doing brave acts.

This is confirmed by what happens in states; for legislators make the citizens good by forming habits in them, and this is the wish of every legislator, and those who do not effect it miss their mark, and it is in this that a good constitution differs from a bad one.

Again, it is from the same causes and by the same means that every virtue is both produced and destroyed, and similarly every art; for it is from playing the lyre that both good and bad lyre-players are produced. And the corresponding statement is true of builders and of all the rest; men will be good or bad builders as a result of building well or badly. For if this were not so, there would have been no need of a teacher, but all men would have been born good or bad at their craft. This, then, is the case with the virtues also; by doing the acts that we do in our transactions with other men we become just or unjust, and by doing the acts that we do in the presence of danger, and being habituated to feel fear or confidence, we become brave or cowardly. The same is true of appetites and feelings of anger; some men become temperate and good-tempered, others self-indulgent and irascible, by behaving in one way or the other in the appropriate circumstances. Thus, in one word, states of character arise out of like activities. This is why the activities we exhibit must be a certain kind; it is because the states of character correspond to the differences between these. It makes no small difference, then, whether we form habits of one kind or of another from our very youth; it makes a very great difference, or rather *all* the difference.

Since, then, the present inquiry does not aim at theoretical knowledge like the others (for we are inquiring not in order to know what virtue is, but in order to become good, since otherwise our inquiry would have been of no use), we must examine the nature of actions, namely how we ought to do them; for these determine also the nature of the states of character that are produced, as we have said. Now, that we must act according to the right rule is a common principle and must be assumed—it will be discussed later, i.e. both what the right rule is, and how it is related to the other virtues. But this must be agreed upon beforehand, that the whole account of matters of conduct must be given in outline and not precisely, as we said at the very beginning that the accounts we demand must be in accordance with the subject-matter; matters concerned with conduct and questions of what is good for us have no fixity, any more than matters of health. The general account being of this nature, the account of particular cases is yet more lacking in exactness; for they do not fall under any art or precept but the agents themselves must in each case consider what is appropriate to the occasion, as happens also in the art of medicine or of navigation.

But though our present account is of this nature we must give what help we can. First, then, let us consider this, that it is the nature of such things to be destroyed by defect and excess, as we see in the case of strength and of health (for to gain light on things imperceptible we must use the evidence of sensible things); both excessive and defective exercise destroys the strength, and similarly drink or food which is above or below a certain amount destroys the health, while that which is proportionate both produces and increases and preserves it. So too is it, then, in the case of temperance and courage and the other virtues. For the man who flies from and fears everything and does not stand his ground against anything becomes a coward, and the man who fears nothing at all but goes to meet every danger becomes rash; and similarly the man who indulges in every pleasure and abstains from none becomes self-indulgent, while the man who shuns every pleasure, as boors do, becomes in a way insensible; temperance and courage, then, are destroyed by excess and defect, and preserved by the mean.

But not only are the sources and causes of their origination and growth the same as those of their destruction, but also the sphere of their actualization will be the same; for this is also true of the things which are more evident to sense, e.g. of strength; it is produced by taking much food and undergoing much exertion, and it is the strong man that will be most able to do these things. So too is it with the virtues; by abstaining from pleasures we become temperate, and it is when we have become so that we are most able to abstain from them; and similarly too in the case of courage; for by being habituated to despise things that are terrible and to stand our ground against them we become brave, and it is when we have become so that we shall be most able to stand our ground against them.

We must take as a sign of states of character the pleasure or pain that ensues on acts; for the man who abstains from bodily pleasures and delights in this very fact is temperate, while the man who is annoyed at it is self-indulgent, and he who stands his ground against things that are terrible and delights in this or at least is not pained is brave, while the man who is pained is a coward. For moral excellence is concerned with pleasures and pains; it is on account of the pleasure that we do bad things, and on account of the pain that we abstain from noble ones. Hence we ought to have been brought up in a particular way from our very youth, as Plato says, so as both to delight in and to be pained by the things that we ought; for this is the right education. . . .

The question might be asked, what we mean by saying that we must become just by doing just acts, and temperate by doing temperate acts; for if men do just and temperate acts, they are already just and temperate, exactly as, if they do what is in accordance with the laws of grammar and of music, they are grammarians and musicians.

Or is this not true even of the arts? It is possible to do something that is in accordance with the laws of grammar, either by chance or at the suggestion of another. A man will be a grammarian, then, only when he has both done something grammatical and done it grammatically; and this means doing it in accordance with the grammatical knowledge in himself.

Again, the case of the arts and that of the virtues are not similar; for the products of the arts have their goodness in themselves, so that it is enough that they should have a certain character, but if the acts that are in accordance with the virtues have themselves a certain character it does not follow that they are done justly or temperately. The agent also must be in a certain condition when he does them; in the first place he must have knowledge, secondly he must choose the acts, and choose them for their own sakes, and thirdly his action must proceed from a firm and unchangeable character. These are not reckoned in as conditions of the possession of the arts, except the bare knowledge; but as a condition of the possession of the virtues knowledge has little or no weight, while the other conditions count not for a little but for everything, i.e. the very conditions which result from often doing just and temperate acts.

Actions, then, are called just and temperate when they are such as the just or the temperate man would do; but it is not the man who does these that is just and temperate, but the man who also does them *as* just and temperate men do them. It is well said, then, that it is by doing just acts that the just man is produced, and by doing temperate acts the temperate man; without doing these no one would have even a prospect of becoming good.

But most people do not do these, but take refuge in theory and think they are being philosophers and will become good in this way, behaving somewhat like patients who listen attentively to their doctors, but do none of the things they are ordered to do. As the latter will not be made well in body by such a course of treatment, the former will not be made well in soul by such a course of philosophy.

Next we must consider what virtue is. Since things that are found in the soul are of three kinds—passions, faculties, states of character, virtue must be one of these. By passions I mean appetite, anger, fear, confidence, envy, joy, friendly feeling, hatred, longing, emulation, pity, and in general the feelings that are accompanied by pleasure or pain; by faculties the things in virtue of which we are said to be capable of feeling these, e.g. of becoming angry or being pained or feeling pity; by states of character the things in virtue of which we stand well or badly with reference to the passions, e.g. with reference to anger we stand badly if we feel it violently or too weakly, and well if we feel it moderately; and similarly with reference to the other passions.

Now neither the virtues nor the vices are *passions,* because we are not called good or bad on the ground of our passions, but are so called on the ground of our virtues and our vices, and because we are neither praised nor blamed for our passions (for the man who feels fear or anger is not praised, nor is the man who simply feels anger blamed, but the man who feels it in a certain way), but for our virtues and our vices we *are* praised or blamed.

Again, we feel anger and fear without choice, but the virtues are modes of choice or involve choice. Further, in respect of the passions we are said to be moved, but in respect of the virtues and the vices we are said not to be moved but to be disposed in a particular way.

For these reasons also they are not *faculties;* for we are neither called good nor bad, nor praised nor blamed, for the simple capacity of feeling the passions; again, we have the faculties by nature, but we are not made good or bad by nature; we have spoken of this before.

If, then, the virtues are neither passions nor faculties, all that remains is that they should be *states of character.*

Thus we have stated what virtue is in respect of its genus.

We must, however, not only describe virtue as a state of character, but also say what sort of state it is. We may remark, then, that every virtue or excellence both brings into good condition the thing of which it is the excellence and makes the work of that thing be done well; e.g. the excellence of the eye makes both the eye and its work good; for it is by the excellence of the eye that we see well. Similarly the excellence of the horse makes a horse both good in itself and good at running and at carrying its rider and at awaiting the attack of the enemy. Therefore, if this is true in every case, the virtue of man also will be the state of character which makes a man good and which makes him do his own work well.

How this is to happen we have stated already, but it will be made plain also by the following consideration of the specific nature of virtue. In everything that is continuous and divisible it is possible to take more, less, or an equal amount, and that either in terms of the thing itself or relatively to us; and the equal is an intermediate between excess and defect. By the intermediate in the object I mean that which is equidistant from each of the extremes, which is one and the same for all men; by the intermediate relatively to us that which is neither too much nor too little—and this is not one, nor the same for all. For instance, if ten is many and two is few, six is the intermediate, taken in terms of the object; for it exceeds and is exceeded by an equal amount; this is intermediate according to arithmetical proportion. But the intermediate relatively to us is not to be taken so; if ten pounds are too much for a particular person to eat and two too little, it does not follow that the trainer will order six pounds; for this also is perhaps too much for the person who is to take it, or too little—too little for Milo, too much for the beginner in athletic exercises. The same is true of running and wrestling. Thus a master of any art avoids excess and defect, but seeks the intermediate and chooses this—the intermediate not in the object but relatively to us.

If it is thus, then, that every art does its work well—by looking to the intermediate and judging its works by this standard (so that we often say of good works of art that it is not possible either to take away or to add anything, implying that excess and defect destroy the goodness of works of art, while the mean preserves it; and good artists, as we say, look to this in their work), and if, further, virtue is more exact and better than any art, as nature also is, then virtue must have the quality of aiming at the intermediate. I mean moral virtue; for it is this that is concerned with passions and actions, and in these there is excess, defect, and the intermediate. For instance, both fear and confidence and appetite and anger and pity and in general pleasure and pain may be felt both too much and too little, and in both cases not well; but to feel them at the right times, with reference to the right objects, towards the right people, with the right motive, and in the right way, is what is both intermediate and best, and this is characteristic of virtue. Similarly with regard to actions also there is excess, defect, and the intermediate. Now virtue is concerned with passions and actions, in which excess is a form of failure, and so is defect, while the intermediate is praised and is a form of success; and being praised and being successful are both characteristics of virtue. Therefore virtue is a kind of mean, since, as we have seen, it aims at what is intermediate.

Again, it is possible to fail in many ways (for evil belongs to the class of the unlimited, as the Pythagoreans conjectured, and good to that of the limited), while to succeed is possible only in one way (for which reason also one is easy and the other difficult—to miss the mark easy, to hit it difficult); for these reasons also, then, excess and defect are characteristic of vice, and the mean of virtue;

For men are good in but one way, but bad in many.

Virtue, then, is a state of character concerned with choice, lying in a mean, i.e. the mean relative to us, this being determined by a rational principle, and by that principle by which the man of practical wisdom would determine it. Now it is a mean between two vices, that which depends on excess and that which depends on defect; and again it is a mean because the vices respectively fall short of or exceed what is right in both passions and actions, while virtue both finds and chooses that which is intermediate. Hence in respect of its substance and the definition which states its essence virtue is a mean, with regard to what is best and right an extreme.

But not every action nor every passion admits of a mean; for some have names that already imply badness, e.g. spite, shamelessness, envy, and in the case of actions adultery, theft, murder; for all of these and suchlike things imply by their names that they are themselves bad, and not the excesses or deficiencies of them. It is not possible, then, ever to be right with regard to them; one must always be wrong. Nor does goodness or badness with regard to such things depend on committing adultery with the right woman, at the right time, and in the right way, but simply to do any of them is to go wrong. It would be equally absurd, then, to expect that in unjust, cowardly, and voluptuous action there should be a mean, an excess, and a deficiency; for at that rate there would be a mean of excess and of deficiency, an excess of excess, and a deficiency of deficiency. But as there is no excess and deficiency of temperance and courage because what is intermediate is in a sense an extreme, so too of the actions we have mentioned there is no mean nor any excess and deficiency, but however they are done they are wrong; for in general there is neither a mean of excess and deficiency, nor excess and deficiency of a mean. . . .

There are also three other means, which have a certain likeness to one another, but differ from one another: for they are all concerned with intercourse in words and actions, but differ in that one is concerned with truth in this sphere, the other two with pleasantness; and of this one kind is exhibited in giving amusement, the other in all the circumstances of life. We must therefore speak of these too, that we may the better see that in all things the mean is praiseworthy, and the extremes neither praiseworthy nor right, but worthy of blame. Now most of these states also have no names, but we must try, as in the other cases, to invent names ourselves so that we may be clear and easy to follow. With regard to truth, then, the intermediate is a truthful sort of person and the mean may be called truthfulness, while the pretence which exaggerates is boastfulness and the person characterized by it a boaster, and that which understates is mock modesty and the person characterized by it mock-modest. With regard to pleasantness in the giving of amusement the intermediate person is ready-witted and the disposition ready wit, the excess is buffoonery and the person characterized by it a buffoon, while the man who falls short is a sort of boor and his state is boorishness. With regard to the remaining kind of pleasantness, that which is exhibited in life in general, the man who is pleasant in the right way is friendly and the mean is friendliness, while the man who exceeds is an obsequious person if he has no end in view, a flatterer if he is aiming at his own advantage, and the man who falls short and is unpleasant in all circumstances is a quarrelsome and surly sort of person.

There are also means in the passions and concerned with the passions; since shame is not a virtue, and yet praise is extended to the modest man. For even in these matters one man is said to be intermediate, and another to exceed, as for instance the bashful man who is ashamed of everything; while he who falls short or is not ashamed of anything at all is shameless, and the intermediate person is modest. Righteous indignation is a mean between envy and spite, and these states are concerned with the pain and the pleasure that are felt at the fortunes of our neighbours; the man who is characterized by righteous indignation is pained at undeserved good fortune, the envious man, going beyond him, is pained at all good fortune, and the spiteful man falls so far short of being pained that he even rejoices. But these states there will be an opportunity of describing elsewhere; with regard to justice, since it has not one simple meaning, we shall, after describing the other states, distinguish its two kinds and say how each of them is a mean; and similarly we shall treat also of the rational virtues.

There are three kinds of disposition, then, two of them vices, involving excess and deficiency respectively, and one a virtue, viz. the mean, and all are in a sense opposed to all; for the extreme states are contrary both to the intermediate state and to each other, and the intermediate to the extremes; as the equal is greater relatively to the less, less relatively to the greater, so the middle states are excessive relatively to the deficiencies, deficient relatively to the excesses, both in passions and in actions. For the brave man appears rash relatively to the coward, and cowardly relatively to the rash man; and similarly the temperate man appears self-indulgent relatively to the insensible man, insensible relatively to the self-indulgent, and the liberal man prodigal relatively to the mean man, mean relatively to the prodigal. Hence also the people at the extremes push the intermediate man each over to the other, and the brave man is called rash by the coward, cowardly by the rash man, and correspondingly in the other cases.

These states being thus opposed to one another, the greatest contrariety is that of the extremes to each other, rather than to the intermediate; for these are further from each other than from the intermediate, as the great is further from the small and the small from the great than both are from the equal. Again, to the intermediate some extremes show a certain likeness, as that of rashness to courage and that of prodigality to liberality; but the extremes show the greatest unlikeness to each other; now contraries are defined as the things that are furthest from each other, so that things that are further apart are more contrary.

To the mean in some cases the deficiency, in some the excess is more opposed; e.g. it is not rashness, which is an excess, but cowardice, which is a deficiency, that is more opposed to courage, and not insensibility, which is a deficiency, but self-indulgence, which is an excess, that is more opposed to temperance. This happens from two reasons, one being drawn from the thing itself; for because one extreme is nearer and liker to the intermediate, we oppose not this but rather its contrary to the intermediate. E.g., since rashness is thought liker and nearer to courage, and cowardice more unlike, we oppose rather the latter to courage; for things that are further from the intermediate are thought more contrary to it. This, then, is one cause, drawn from the thing itself; another is drawn from ourselves; for the things to which we ourselves more naturally tend seem more contrary to the intermediate. For instance, we ourselves tend more naturally to pleasures, and hence are more easily carried away towards self-indulgence than towards propriety. We describe as contrary to the mean, then, rather the directions in which we more often go to great lengths; and therefore self-indulgence, which is an excess, is the more contrary to temperance.

That moral virtue is a mean, then, and in what sense it is so, and that it is a mean between two vices, the one involving excess, the other deficiency, and that it is such because its character is to aim at what is intermediate in passions and in actions, has been sufficiently stated. Hence also it is no easy task to be good. For in everything it is no easy task to find the middle, e.g. to find the middle of a circle is not for every one but for him who knows; so, too, any one can get angry—that is easy—or give or spend money; but to do this to the right person, to the right extent, at the right time, with the right motive, and in the right way, *that* is not for every one, nor is it easy; wherefore goodness is both rare and laudable and noble.

Hence he who aims at the intermediate must first depart from what is the more contrary to it, as Calypso advises—

Hold the ship out beyond that surf and spray.

For of the extremes one is more erroneous, one less so; therefore, since to hit the mean is hard in the extreme, we must as a second best, as people say, take the least of the evils; and this will be done best in the way we describe.

But we must consider the things towards which we ourselves also are easily carried away; for some of us tend to one thing, some to another; and this will be recognizable from the pleasure and the pain we feel. We must drag ourselves away to the contrary extreme; for we shall get into the intermediate state by drawing well away from error, as people do in straightening sticks that are bent.

Now in everything the pleasant or pleasure is most to be guarded against; for we do not judge it impartially. We ought, then, to feel towards pleasure as the elders of the people felt towards Helen, and in all circumstances repeat their saying; for if we dismiss pleasure thus we are less likely to go astray. It is by doing this, then, (to sum the matter up) that we shall best be able to hit the mean.

But this is no doubt difficult, and especially in individual cases; for it is not easy to determine both how and with whom and on what provocation and how long one should be angry; for we too sometimes praise those who fall short and call them good-tempered, but sometimes we praise those who get angry and call them manly. The man, however, who deviates little from goodness is not blamed, whether he do so in the direction of the more or of the less, but only the man who deviates more widely; for *he* does not fail to be noticed. But up to what point and to what extent a man must deviate before he becomes blame-worthy it is not easy to determine by reasoning, any more than anything else that is per-ceived by the senses; such things depend on particular facts, and the decision rests with perception. So much, then, is plain, that the intermediate state is in all things to be praised, but that we must incline sometimes towards the excess, sometimes towards the deficiency; for so shall we most easily hit the mean and what is right.

BOOK X

After this discussion of the kinds of virtue and friendship and pleasure it remains to give a sketch of happiness, since we defined happiness as the end of human things. We shall shorten our account of it if we begin by recapitulating our previous remarks.

We said that happiness is not a moral state; for, if it were, it would be predicable of one who spends his whole life in sleep, living the life of a vegetable, or of one who is utterly miserable. If then we cannot accept this view if we must rather define happiness as an activity of some kind, as has been said before, and if activities are either necessary and desirable as a means to something else or desirable in themselves, it is clear that we must define happiness as belonging to the class of activities which are desirable in themselves, and not desirable as means to something else; for happiness has no want, it is self-sufficient.

Again, activities are desirable in themselves, if nothing is expected from them beyond the activity. This seems to be the case with virtuous actions, as the practice of what is noble and virtuous is a thing desirable in itself. It seems to be the case also with such amusements as are pleasant, we do not desire them as means to other things; for they often do us harm rather than good by making us careless about our persons and our property. Such pastimes are generally the resources of those whom the world calls happy. Accordingly people who are clever at such pastimes are generally popular in the courts of despots, as they make themselves pleasant to the despot in the matters which are the objects of his desire, and what he wants is to pass the time pleasantly.

The reason why these things are regarded as elements of happiness is that people who occupy high positions devote their leisure to them. But such people are not, I think, a criterion. For a high position is no guarantee of virtue or intellect, which are the sources on which virtuous activities depend. And if these people, who have never tasted a pure and liberal pleasure, have recourse to the pleasures of the body, it must not be inferred that these pleasures are preferable; for even children suppose that such things as are valued or hon-oured among them are best. It is only reasonable then that, as men and children differ in their estimate of what is honourable, so should good and bad people.

As has been frequently said, therefore, it is the things which are honourable and pleasant to the virtuous man that are really honourable and pleasant. But everybody feels the activity

From *Nichomachean Ethics of Aristotle*, trans. J. E. C. Welldon (London: Macmillan, 1908).

which accords with his own moral state to be most desirable, and accordingly the virtuous man regards the activity in accordance with virtue as most desirable.

Happiness then does not consist in amusement. It would be paradoxical to hold that the end of human life is amusement, and that we should toil and suffer all our life for the sake of amusing ourselves. For we may be said to desire all things as means to something else except indeed happiness, as happiness is the end *or perfect state.*

It appears to be foolish and utterly childish to take serious trouble and pains for the sake of amusement. But to amuse oneself with a view to being serious seems to be right, as Anacharsis says; for amusement is a kind of relaxation, and it is because we cannot work for ever that we need relaxation.

Relaxation then is not an end. We enjoy it as a means to activity; but it seems that the happy life is a life of virtue, and such a life is serious, it is not one of mere amusement. We speak of serious things too (*for serious things are virtuous*) as better than things which are ridiculous and amusing, and of the activity of the better part of man's being or of the better man as always the more virtuous. But the activity of that which is better is necessarily higher and happier. Anybody can enjoy bodily pleasures, a slave can enjoy them as much as the best of men; but nobody would allow that a slave is capable of happiness unless he is capable of life; for happiness consists not in such pastimes as I have been speaking of, but in virtuous activities, as has been already said.

If happiness consists in virtuous activity, it is only reasonable to suppose that it is the activity of the highest virtue, or in other words, of the best part of our nature. Whether it is the reason or something else which seems to exercise rule and authority by a natural right, and to have a conception of things noble and divine, either as being itself divine or as relatively the most divine part of our being, it is the activity of this part in accordance with its proper virtue which will be the perfect happiness.

It has been already stated that it is a speculative activity, *i.e. an activity which takes the form of contemplation.* This is a conclusion which would seem to agree with our previous arguments and with the truth itself; for the speculative is the highest activity, as the intuitive reason is the highest of our faculties, and the objects with which the intuitive reason is concerned are the highest of things that can be known. It is also the most continuous; for our speculation can more easily be continuous than any kind of action. We consider too that pleasure is an essential element of happiness, and it is admitted that there is no virtuous activity so pleasant as the activity of wisdom or philosophic reflexion; at all events it appears that philosophy possesses pleasures of wonderful purity and certainty, and it is reasonable to suppose that people who possess knowledge pass their time more pleasantly than people who are seekers after truth.

Self-sufficiency too, as it is called, is preeminently a characteristic of the speculative activity; for the wise man, the just man, and all others, need the necessaries of life; but when they are adequately provided with these things, the just man needs people to whom and with whom he may do justice, so do the temperate man, the courageous man and everyone else; but the wise man is capable of speculation by himself, and the wiser he is, the more capable he is of such speculation. It is perhaps better for him in his speculation to have fellow-workers; but nevertheless he is in the highest degree self-sufficient.

It would seem too that the speculative is the only activity which is loved for its own sake as it has no result except speculation, whereas from all moral actions we gain something more or less besides the action itself.

Again, happiness, it seems, requires leisure; for the object of our business is leisure, as the object of war is the enjoyment of peace. Now the activity of the practical virtues is displayed in politics or war, and actions of this sort seem incompatible with leisure. This is absolutely true of military actions, as nobody desires war, or prepares to go to war, for its own sake. A person would be regarded as absolutely bloodthirsty if he were to make enemies of his friends for the mere sake of fighting and bloodshed. But the activity of the statesman too is incompatible with leisure. It aims at securing something beyond and apart from politics, viz. the power and honour or at least the happiness of the statesman himself and his fellow citizens, which is different from the political activity and is proved to be different by our search for it *as something distinct.*

If then political and military actions are preeminent among virtuous actions in beauty and grandeur, if they are incompatible with leisure and aim at some end, and are not desired for their own sakes, if the activity of the intuitive reason seems to be superior in seriousness as being speculative, and not to aim at any end beyond itself, and to have its proper pleasure, and if this pleasure enhances the activity, it follows that such self-sufficiency and power of leisure and absence of fatigue as are possible to a man and all other attributes of felicity are found to be realized in this activity. This then will be the perfect happiness of Man, if a perfect length of life is given it, for there is no imperfection in happiness. But such a life will be too good for Man. He will enjoy such a life not in virtue of his humanity but in virtue of some divine element within him, and the superiority of this activity to the activity of any other virtue will be proportionate to the superiority of this divine element in man to his composite *or material* nature.

If then the reason is divine in comparison with *the rest of* Man's nature, the life which accords with reason will be divine in comparison with human life in general. Nor is it right to follow the advice of people who say that the thoughts of men should not be too high for humanity or the thoughts of mortals too high for mortality; for a man, as far as in him lies, should seek immortality and do all that is in his power to live in accordance with the highest part of his nature, as, although that part is insignificant in size, yet in power and honour it is far superior to all the rest.

It would seem too that this is the true self of everyone, if a man's true self is his supreme or better part. It would be absurd then that a man should desire not the life which is properly his own but the life which properly belongs to some other being. The remark already made will be appropriate here. It is what is proper to everyone that is in its nature best and pleasantest for him. It is the life which accords with reason then that will be best and pleasantest for Man, as a man's reason is in the highest sense himself. This will therefore be also the happiest life.

It is only in a secondary sense that the life which accords with other, *i.e. non-speculative,* virtue can be said to be happy; for the activities of such virtue are human, *they have no divine element.* Our just or courageous actions or our virtuous actions of any kind we perform in relation to one another, when we observe the law of propriety in contracts and mutual services and the various moral actions and in our emotions. But all these actions appear to be human affairs. It seems too that moral virtue is in some respects actually the result of physical organization and is in many respects closely associated with the emotions. Again, prudence is indissolubly linked to moral virtue, and moral virtue to prudence, since the principles of prudence are determined by the moral virtues, and moral rectitude is determined by prudence. But the moral virtues, as being inseparably united with the emotions, must have to do with the composite *or material* part *of our nature,* and the virtues of the composite part *of our nature* are human, *and not divine,* virtues. So too therefore is the life which accords with these virtues; so too is the happiness *which accords with them.*

But the happiness *which consists in the exercise* of the reason is separated *from these emo-*

tions. It must be enough to say so much about it; for to discuss it in detail would take us beyond our present purpose. It would seem too to require external resources only to a small extent or to a less extent than moral virtue. It may be granted that both will require the necessaries of life and will require them equally, even if the politician devotes more trouble to his body and his bodily welfare than the philosopher; for the difference will not be important. But there will be a great difference in respect of their activities. The liberal man will want money for the practice of liberality, and the just man for the requital of services which have been done him; for our wishes, *unless they are manifested in actions,* must always be obscure, and even people who are not just pretend that it is their wish to act justly. The courageous man too will want physical strength if he is to perform any virtuous action, and the temperate man liberty, as otherwise it will be impossible for him or for anybody else to show his character.

But if the question be asked whether it is the purpose or the performance that is the surer determinant of virtue, as virtue implies both, it is clear that both are necessary to perfection. But action requires various conditions, and the greater and nobler the action, the more numerous will the conditions be.

In speculation on the other hand there is no need of such conditions, at least for its activity; it may rather be said that they are actual impediments to speculation. It is as a human being and as living in society that a person chooses to perform virtuous actions. Such conditions then will be requisite if he is to live as a man.

That perfect happiness is a species of speculative activity will appear from the following consideration among others. Our conception of the Gods is that they are preeminently happy and fortunate. But what kind of actions do we properly attribute to them? Are they just actions? But it would make the Gods ridiculous to suppose that they form contracts, restore deposits, and so on. Are they then courageous actions? Do the Gods endure dangers and alarms for the sake of honour? Or liberal actions? But to whom should they give money? It would be absurd to suppose that they have a currency or anything of the kind. Again, what will be the nature of their temperate actions? Surely to praise the gods for temperance is to degrade them; they are exempt from low desires. We may go through the whole category of virtues, and it will appear that whatever relates to moral action is petty and unworthy of the Gods.

Yet the Gods are universally conceived as living and therefore as displaying activity; they are certainly not conceived as sleeping like Endymion. If then action and still more production is denied to one who is alive, what is left but speculation? It follows that the activity of God being preeminently blissful will be speculative, and if so then the human activity which is most nearly related to it will be most capable of happiness.

It is an evidence of this truth that the other animals, as being perfectly destitute of such activity, do not participate in happiness; for while the whole life of the God is fortunate or blessed, the life of men is blessed in so far as it possesses a certain resemblance to their speculative activity. But no other animal is happy, as no other animal participates at all in speculation.

We conclude then that happiness is coextensive with speculation, and that the greater a person's power of speculation, the greater will be his happiness, not as an accidental fact but in virtue of the speculation, as speculation is honourable in itself. Hence happiness must be a kind of speculation.

Man, as being human, will require external prosperity. His nature is not of itself sufficient for speculation, it needs bodily health, food, and care of every kind. It must not however be supposed that, because it is impossible to be fortunate without external goods, a great variety of such goods will be necessary to happiness. For neither self-sufficiency nor moral action consists in excess; it is possible to do noble deeds without being lord of land and sea, as moderate means will enable a person to act in accordance with virtue. We may clearly see that it is so; for it seems that private persons practise virtue not less but actually more than persons in high place. It is enough that such a person should possess as much as is requisite for virtue; his life will be happy if he lives in the active exercise of virtue. Solon was right perhaps in his description of the happy man as one "who is moderately supplied with external goods, and yet has performed the noblest actions,"—such was his opinion— "and had lived a temperate life," for it is possible to do one's duty with only moderate means. It seems too that Anaxagoras did not conceive of the happy man as possessing wealth or power when he said that he should not be surprised if the happy man proved a puzzle in the eyes of the world; for the world judges by externals alone, it has no perception of anything that is not external.

The opinions of philosophers then seem to agree with our theories. Such opinions, it is true, possess a sort of authority; but it is the facts of life that are the tests of truth in practical matters, as they possess a supreme authority. It is right then to consider the doctrines which have been already advanced in reference to the facts of life, to accept them if they harmonize with those facts, and to regard them as mere theories if they disagree with them.

Again, he whose activity is directed by reason and who cultivates reason, and is in the best, *i.e. the most rational,* state of mind is also, as it seems, the most beloved of the Gods. For if the Gods care at all for human things, as is believed, it will be only reasonable to hold that they delight in what is best and most related to themselves, i.e. in reason, and that they require with kindness those who love and honour it above all else, as caring for what is dear to themselves and performing right and noble actions.

It is easy to see that these conditions are found preeminently in the wise man. He will therefore be most beloved of the Gods. We may fairly suppose too that he is most happy; and if so, this is another reason for thinking that the wise man is preeminently happy.

Suppose then that our sketch of these subjects and of the virtues, and of friendship too, and pleasure, has been adequate, are we to regard our object as achieved? Or are we to say in the old phrase that in practical matters the end is not speculation and knowledge but action? It is not enough to know the nature of virtue; we must endeavour to possess it, and to exercise it, and to use whatever other means are necessary for becoming good.

Now, if theories were sufficient of themselves to make men good, they would deserve to receive any number of handsome rewards, as Theognis said, and it would have been our duty to provide them. But it appears in fact that, although they are strong enough to inspire the mass of men to chivalrous action; for it is not the nature of such men to obey honour but terror, nor to abstain from evil for fear of disgrace but for fear of punishment. For, as their life is one of emotion, they pursue their proper pleasures and the means of gaining these pleasures, and eschew the pains which are opposite to them. But of what is noble and truly pleasant they have not so much as a conception, because they have never tasted it. Where is the theory or argument which can reform such people as these? It is difficult to change by argument the settled features of character. We must be content perhaps if, when we possess all the means by which we are thought to become virtuous, we gain some share of virtue.

Some people think that men are made good by nature, others by habit, others again by teaching.

Now it is clear that the gift of Nature is not in our own power, but is bestowed through some divine providence upon those who are truly fortunate. It is probably true also that reason and teaching are not universally efficacious; the soul of the pupil must first have been cultivated by habit to a right spirit of pleasure and aversion, like the earth that is to nourish the seed. For he whose life is governed by emotion would not listen to the dissuasive voice of reason, or even comprehend it, and if this is his state, how is it possible to convert him? Emotion, it seems, never submits to reason but only to force. It is necessary then to presuppose a character which is in a sense akin to virtue, which loves what is noble and dislikes what is dishonourable. But it is difficult for one to receive from his early days a right inclination to virtue, unless he is brought up under virtuous laws; for a life of temperance and steadfastness is not pleasant to most people, least of all to the young. It follows that the nurture and pursuits *of the young* should be regulated by law, as they will not be painful, if he becomes used to them.

But it is not enough, I think, that we should receive a right nurture and control in youth; we must practise what is right and get the habit of doing it when we have come to man's estate. We shall need laws then to teach us what is right, and so to teach us all the duty of life; for most people are moved by necessity rather than by reason, and by the fear of punishment rather than by the love of nobleness.

Accordingly it is sometimes held that legislators should on the one hand invite and exhort men to pursue virtue because it is so noble, as they who have been already trained in virtue will pay heed to them, and on the other hand, if they are disobedient and degenerate, should inflict punishments and chastisements on them and utterly expel them, if they are incurable; for so the good man who lives by the rule of honour will obey reason, and the bad man whose aim is pleasure must be chastened by pain like a beast of burden. Hence too it is said that the pains ought to be such as are most opposed to a person's favourite pleasures.

If then, as has been said, he who is to be a good man should receive a noble nurture and training and then should live accordingly in virtuous pursuits and never voluntarily or involuntarily do evil, this result will only be attained if we live, so to say, in accordance with reason and right order resting upon force.

Now the authority of a father does not possess such force or compulsion, nor indeed does that of any individual, unless he is a king or some such person. But the law has a compulsory power, as being itself in a sense the outcome of prudence and reason; and whereas we hate people who oppose our inclinations, even if they are right in so doing, we do not feel the law to be grievous in its insistence upon virtue.

It is only in the state of Lacedaemon and a few other states that the legislator seems to have undertaken to control the nurture and pursuits of the citizens. In the great majority of states there is an absolute neglect of such matters, and everybody lives as he chooses, "being lawgiver of wife and children" like the Cyclops.

It is best then that the state should undertake the control of these matters and should exercise it rightly and should have the power of giving effect to its command. But if the state altogether neglects it, it would seem to be the duty of every citizen to further the cause of virtue in his own children and friends, or at least to set before himself the purpose of furthering it. It would seem too from what has been said that he will be best able to do this, if he has learnt the principles of legislation; for the control of the state is clearly exercised through the form of laws, and is good if the laws are virtuous. Whether they are written or unwritten laws, and whether they are suited to the education of an individual or of a number of people is apparently a matter of indifference, as it is in music or gymnastic or other studies. For as in a state it is law and custom which are supreme, so in a household it is the paternal precepts and customs, and all the more because of the father's relationship to the members of his family, and of the benefits which he had conferred upon them; for the members of a family are naturally affectionate and obedient to the father from the first.

Again, there is a superiority in the individual as against the general methods of education; it is much the same as in medicine where, although it is the general rule that a feverish patient needs to be kept quiet and to take no food, there may perhaps be some exceptions. Nor does a teacher of boxing teach all his pupils to box in the same style.

It would seem then that a study of individual character is the best way of perfecting the education of the individual, as then everyone has a better chance of receiving such treatment as is suitable. Still the individual case may best be treated, whether in medicine or in gymnastic or in any other subject, by one who knows the general rule applicable to all people or to people of a particular kind; for the sciences are said to deal, and do deal, with general laws. At the same time there is no reason why even without scientific knowledge a person should not be successful in treating a particular case if he has made an accurate, although empirical, observation of the results which follow from a particular course of treatment, as there are some doctors who seem to be excellent doctors in their own cases, although they would be unable to relieve anybody else.

Nevertheless if a person wishes to succeed in art or speculation, it is, I think, his duty to proceed to a universal principle and to make himself acquainted with it as far as possible; for sciences, as has been said, deal with universals. Also it is the duty of any one who wishes to elevate people, whether they be few or many, by his treatment, to try to learn the principles of legislation, if it is laws that are the natural means of making us good. So in education it is not everybody—it is at the most only the man of science—who can create a noble disposition in all who come to him as patients, as it is in medicine or in any other art which demands care and prudence.

Is it not then our next step to consider the sources and means of learning the principles of legislation? It may be thought that here as elsewhere we must look *to the persons who practise the principles, i.e.* to statesmen; for legislation, as we saw, is apparently a branch of politics. But there is this difference between politics and all other sciences and faculties. In these it is the same people who are found to teach the faculties and to make practical use of them, e.g. doctors and painters; whereas in politics it is the sophists who profess to teach, but it is never they who practise. The practical people are the active statesmen who would seem to be guided in practical life by a kind of faculty or experience rather than by intelligence; for we see that they never write or speak on these subjects, although it is perhaps a nobler task than the composition of forensic or parliamentary speeches, nor have they ever made their own sons or any other people whom they care for into statesmen. Yet it might be expected that they should do so, if it were in their power, for they could not have bequeathed any better legacy to their state, nor is there anything which they would have preferred for themselves or their dearest friends to such a faculty. Still it must be admitted that experience does much good; otherwise people could not be made statesmen by familiarity with politics. It follows that, if people desire to understand politics, they need experience as well as theory.

These sophists however who are lavish in their professions appear to be far from teaching *statesmanship;* in fact they are absolutely ignorant of the sphere or nature of statesmanship. If it were not so they would not have made statesmanship identical with, or inferior to, rhetoric; they would not have thought it easy work to form a legislative code by merely collecting such laws are held in high repute; they would not have supposed that all they have to do is to make a selection of the best laws, as if the selection itself did not demand intelligence, and as if a right judgment were not a thing of the greatest difficulty in legislation no less than in music. For it is only such persons as possess experience of particular arts who can form a correct judgment of artistic works, and understand the means and manner of executing them, and the harmony of particular combinations. Inexperienced persons on the other hand are only too glad if they are alive to the fact that a work has been well or badly executed, as in painting. But laws are like the artistic works of political science. How then should *a mere collection of* laws make a person capable of legislating, or of deciding upon the best laws? It does not appear that *the study* of medical books makes people good doctors; yet medical books affect not only to state methods of treatment, but to state the way of curing people, and the proper method of treating particular cases by classifying the various states of health. But all this, although it seems useful to the experienced, is useless to those who are ignorant of medical science. It may be supposed then that collections of laws and politics would be useful to those who are capable of considering and deciding what is right or wrong, and what is suitable to particular cases; but if people who examine such questions have not *the proper* frame of mind, they will find it impossible to form a right judgment unless indeed by accident, although they may gain a more intelligent appreciation of them.

As previous writers have failed to investigate the subject of legislation, it will perhaps be better to examine it ourselves, and indeed to examine the whole subject of politics, in order that the philosophy of human life may be made as complete as possible.

Let us try then, first of all, to recount such particular opinions as have been rightly expressed by our predecessors, then, in view of the polities which we have collected, to consider the preservatives and destructives of states and of particular polities, and the reasons why some polities are good and others bad. For when we have considered these, it will perhaps be easier to see what kind of polity is best, and what is the best way of ordering it and what are its laws and customs.

POLITICS

I

Every state is a community of some kind, and every community is established with a view to some good; for mankind always act in order to obtain that which they think good. But, if all communities aim at some good, the state or political community, which is the highest of all, and which embraces all the rest, aims, and in a greater degree than any other, at the highest good.

Now there is an erroneous opinion that a statesman, king, householder, and master are the same, and that they differ, not in kind, but only in the number of their subjects. For example, the ruler over a few is called a master; over more, the manager of a household; over a still larger number, a statesman or king, as if there were no difference between a great

From Aristotle, *The Politics*, trans. B. Jowett (London: Oxford University Press, 1885).

household and a small state. The distinction which is made between the king and statesman is as follows: When the government is personal, the ruler is a king; when, according to the principles of the political science, the citizens rule and are ruled in turn, then he is called a statesman.

But all this is a mistake; for governments differ in kind, as will be evident to any one who considers the matter according to the method which has hitherto guided us. As in other departments of science, so in politics, the compound should always be resolved into the simple elements or least parts of the whole. We must therefore look at the elements of which the state is composed, in order that we may see in what they differ from one another, and whether any scientific distinction can be drawn between the different kinds of rule.

II

He who thus considers things in their first growth and origin, whether a state or anything else, will obtain the clearest view of them. In the first place (1) there must be a union of those who cannot exist without each other; for example, of male and female, that the race may continue; and this is a union which is formed, not of deliberate purpose, but because, in common with other animals and with plants, mankind have a natural desire to leave behind them an image of themselves. And (2) there must be a union of natural ruler and subject, that both may be preserved. For he who can foresee with his mind is by nature intended to be lord and master, and he who can work with his body is a subject, and by nature a slave; hence master and slave have the same interest. Nature, however, has distinguished between the female and the slave. For she is not niggardly, like the smith who fashions the Delphian knife for many uses; she makes each thing for a single use, and every instrument is best made when intended for one and not for many uses. But among barbarians no distinction is made between women and slaves, because there is no natural ruler among them: they are a community of slaves, male and female. Wherefore the poets say,—

It is meet that Hellenes should rule over barbarians;

as if they thought that the barbarian and the slave were by nature one.

Out of these two relationships between man and woman, master and slave, the family first arises, and Hesiod is right when he says,—

First house and wife and an ox for the plough,

for the ox is the poor man's slave. The family is the association established by nature for the supply of men's every-day wants, and the members of it are called by Charondas "companions of the cupboard," and by Epimenides the Cretan, "companions of the manger." But when several families are united, and the association aims at something more than the supply of daily needs, then comes into existence the village. And the most natural form of the village appears to be that of a colony from the family, composed of the children and grandchildren, who are said to be "suckled with the same milk." And this is the reason why Hellenic states were originally governed by kings; because the Hellenes were under royal rule before they came together, as the barbarians still are. Every family is ruled by the eldest, and therefore in the colonies of the family the kingly form of government prevailed because they were of the same blood. As Homer says [of the Cyclopes]:—

Each one gives law to his children and to his wives.

For they lived dispersedly, as was the manner in ancient times. Wherefore men say that the Gods have a king, because they themselves either are or were in ancient times under the rule of a king. For they imagine, not only the forms of the Gods, but their ways of life to be like their own.

When several villages are united in a single community, perfect and large enough to be nearly or quite self-sufficing, the state comes into existence, originating in the bare needs of life, and continuing in existence for the sake of a good life. And therefore, if the earlier forms of society are natural, so is the state, for it is the end of them, and the [completed] nature is the end. For what each thing is when fully developed, we call its nature, whether we are speaking of a man, a horse, or a family. Besides, the final cause and end of a thing is the best, and to be self-sufficing is the end and the best.

Hence it is evident that the state is a creation of nature, and that man is by nature a political animal. And he who by nature and not by mere accident is without a state, is either above humanity, or below it; he is the

Tribeless, lawless, heartless one,

whom Homer denounces—the outcast who is a lover of war; he may be compared to an unprotected piece in the game of draughts.

Now the reason why man is more of a political animal than bees or any other gregarious animals is evident. Nature, as we often say, makes nothing in vain, and man is the only animal whom she has endowed with the gift of speech. And whereas mere sound is but an indication of pleasure or pain, and is therefore found in other animals (for their nature attains to the perception of pleasure and pain and the intimation of them to one another, and no further), the power of speech is intended to set forth the expedient and inexpedient, and likewise the just and the unjust. And it is a characteristic of man that he alone has any sense of good and evil, of just and unjust, and the association of living beings who have this sense makes a family and a state.

Thus the state is by nature clearly prior to the family and to the individual, since the whole is of necessity prior to the part; for example, if the whole body be destroyed, there will be no foot or hand, except in an equivocal sense, as we might speak of a stone hand; for when destroyed the hand will be no better. But things are defined by their working and power; and we ought not to say that they are the same when they are no longer the same, but only that they have the same name. The proof that the state is a creation of nature and prior to the individual is that the individual, when isolated, is not self-sufficing; and therefore he is like a part in relation to the whole. But he who is unable to live in society, or who has no need because he is sufficient for himself, must be either a beast or a god: he is no part of a state. A social instinct is implanted in all men by nature, and yet he who first founded the state was the greatest of benefactors. For man, when perfected, is the best of animals, but when separated from law and justice, he is the worst of all; since armed injustice is the more dangerous, and he is equipped at birth with the arms of intelligence and with moral qualities which he may use for the worst ends. Wherefore, if he have not virtue, he is the most unholy and the most savage of animals, and the most full of lust and gluttony. But justice is the bond of men in states, and the administration of justice, which is the determination of what is just, is the principle of order in political society.

III

Seeing then that the state is made up of households, before speaking of the state we must speak of the management of the household. The parts of the household are the persons who compose it, and a complete household consists of slaves and freemen. Now we should begin by examining everything in its least elements; and the first and least parts of a family are master and slave, husband and wife, father and children. We have therefore to consider what each of these three relations is and ought to be:—I mean the relation of master and servant, of husband and wife, and thirdly of parent and child. . . . And there is another element of a household, the so-called art of money-making, which, according to some, is identical with household management, according to others, a principal part of it; the nature of this art will also have to be considered by us.

Let us first speak of master and slave, looking to the needs of practical life and also seeking to attain some better theory of their relation than exists at present. For some are of opinion that the rule of a master is a science, and that the management of a household, and the mastership of slaves, and the political and royal rule, as I was saying at the outset, are all the same. Others affirm that the rule of a master over slaves is contrary to nature, and that the distinction between slave and freeman exists by law only, and not by nature; and being an interference with nature is therefore unjust.

IV

Property is a part of the household, and therefore the art of acquiring property is a part of the art of managing the household; for no man can live well, or indeed live at all, unless he be provided with necessaries. And as in the arts which have a definite sphere the workers must have their own proper instruments for the accomplishment of their work, so it is in the management of a household. Now, instruments are of various sorts; some are living, others lifeless; in the rudder, the pilot of a ship has a lifeless, in the look-out man, a living instrument; for in the arts the servant is a kind of instrument. Thus, too, a possession is an instrument for maintaining life. And so, in the arrangement of the family, a slave is a living possession, and property a number of such instruments; and the servant is himself an instrument, which takes precedence of all other instruments. For if every instrument could accomplish its own work, obeying or anticipating the will of others, like the statues of Daedalus, or the tripods of Hephaestus, which, says the poet,

> *of their own accord entered the assembly of the Gods;*

if, in like manner, the shuttle would weave and the plectrum touch the lyre without a hand to guide them, chief workmen would not want servants, nor masters slaves. Here, however, another distinction must be drawn: the instruments commonly so called are instruments of production, whilst a possession is an instrument of action. The shuttle, for example, is not only of use, but something else is made by it, whereas of a garment or of a bed there is only the use. Further, as production and action are different in kind, and both require instruments, the instruments which they employ must likewise differ in kind. But life is action and not production, and therefore the slave is the minister of action [for he ministers to his master's life]. Again, a possession is spoken of as a part is spoken of; for the part is not only a part of something else, but wholly belongs to it; and this is also true of a possession. The master is only the master of the slave; he does not belong to him, whereas the slave is not only the slave of his master, but wholly belongs to him. Hence we see what is the nature and office of a slave; he who is by nature not his own but another's and yet a man, is by nature a slave; and he may be said to belong to another who, being a human being, is also a possession. And a possession may be defined as an instrument of action, separable from the possessor.

V

But is there any one thus intended by nature to be a slave, and for whom such a condition is expedient and right, or rather is not all slavery a violation of nature?

There is no difficulty in answering this question, on grounds both of reason and of fact. For that some should rule and others be ruled is a thing, not only necessary, but expedient; from the hour of their birth, some are marked out for subjection, others for rule.

And whereas there are many kinds both of rulers and subjects, that rule is the better which is exercised over better subjects—for example, to rule over men is better than to rule over wild beasts. The work is better which is executed by better workmen; and where one man rules and another is ruled, they may be said to have a work. In all things which form a composite whole and which are made up of parts, whether continuous or discrete, a distinction between the ruling and the subject elements comes to light. Such a duality exists in living creatures, but not in them only; it originates in the construction of the universe; even in things which have no life, there is a ruling principle, as in musical harmony. But we are wandering from the subject. We will, therefore, restrict ourselves to the living creature which, in the first place, consists of soul and body: and of these two, the one is by nature the ruler, and the other the subject. But then we must look for the intentions of nature in things which retain their nature, and not in things which are corrupted. And therefore we must study the man who is in the most perfect state both of body and soul, for in him we shall see the true relation of the two; although in bad or corrupted natures the body will often appear to rule over the soul, because they are in an evil and unnatural condition. First then we may observe in living creatures both a despotical and a constitutional rule; for the soul rules the body with a despotical rule, whereas the intellect rules the appetites with a constitutional and royal rule. And it is clear that the rule of the soul over the body, and of the mind and the rational element over the passionate is natural and expedient; whereas the equality of the two or the rule of the inferior is always hurtful. The same holds good of animals as well as of men; for tame animals have a better nature than wild, and all tame animals are better off when they are ruled by man; for then they are preserved. Again, the male is by nature superior, and the female inferior; and the one rules, and other is ruled; this principle, of necessity, extends to all mankind. Where then there is such a difference as that between soul and body, or between men and animals (as in the case of those whose business is to use their body, and who can do nothing better), the lower sort are by nature slaves, and it is better for them as for all inferiors that they should be under the rule of a master. For he who can be, and therefore is another's, and he who participates in reason enough to apprehend, but not to have, reason, is a slave by nature. Whereas the lower animals cannot even apprehend reason; they obey their instincts. And indeed the use made of slaves and of tame animals is not very different; for both with their bodies minister to the needs of life. Nature would like to distinguish between the bodies of freemen and slaves, making the one strong for servile labour, the other upright, and although useless for such services, useful for political life in the arts both of war and peace. But this does not hold universally: for some slaves have the souls and others have the bodies of freemen. And doubtless if men differed from one another in the mere forms of their bodies as much as the statutes of the Gods do from men, all would acknowledge that the inferior class should be slaves of the superior. And if there is a difference in the body, how much more in the soul! But the beauty of the body is seen, whereas the beauty of the soul is not seen. It is clear, then, that some men are by nature free, and others slaves, and that for these latter slavery is both expedient and right. . . .

But that those who take the opposite view have in a certain way right on their side, may be easily seen. For the words slavery and slave are used in two senses. There is a slave or slavery by law as well as by nature. The law of which I speak is a sort of convention, according to which whatever is taken in war is supposed to belong to the victors. But this right many jurists impeach, as they would an orator who brought forward an unconstitutional measure: they detest the notion that, because one man has the power of doing violence and is superior in brute strength, another shall be his slave and subject. Even among philosophers there is a difference of opinion. The origin of the dispute, and the reason why the arguments cross, is as follows: Virtue, when furnished with means, may be deemed to have the greatest power of doing violence: and as superior power is only found where there is superior excellence of some kind, power is thought to imply virtue. But does it likewise imply justice?—that is the question. And, in order to make a distinction between them, some assert that justice is benevolence: to which others reply that justice is nothing more than the rule of a superior. If the two views are regarded as antagonistic and exclusive [i.e. if the notion that justice is benevolence excludes the idea of a just rule of a superior], the alternative [viz. that no one should rule over others] has no force or plausibility, because it implies that not even the superior in virtue ought to rule, or be master. Some, clinging, as they think, to a principle of justice (for law and custom are a sort of justice), assume that slavery in war is justified by law, but they are not consistent. For what if the cause of the war be unjust? No one would ever say that he is a slave who is unworthy to be a slave. Were this the case, men of the highest rank would be slaves and the children of slaves if they or their parents chance to have been taken captive and sold. Wherefore Hellenes do not like to call themselves slaves, but confine the term to barbarians. Yet, in using this language, they really mean the natural slave of whom we spoke at first; for it must be admitted that some are slaves everywhere, others nowhere. The same principle applies to nobility. Hellenes regard themselves as noble everywhere, and not only in their own country, but they deem the barbarians noble only when at home, thereby implying that there are two sorts of nobility and freedom, the one absolute, the other relative. The Helen of Theodectes says:

> Who would presume to call me servant who am on both sides sprung from the stem of
> the Gods?

What does this mean but that they distinguish freedom and slavery, noble and humble birth, by the two principles of good and evil? They think that as men and animals beget men and animals, so from good men a good man springs. But this is what nature, though she may intend it, cannot always accomplish.

We see then there is some foundation for this difference of opinion, and that all are not either slaves by nature or freemen by nature, and also that there is in some cases a marked distinction between the two classes, rendering it expedient and right for the one to be slaves and the others to be masters: the one practising obedience, the others exercising the authority which nature intended them to have. The abuse of this authority is injurious to both; for the interests of part and whole, of body and soul, are the same, and the slave is a part of the master, a living but separated part of his bodily frame. Where the relation between them is natural they are friends and have a common interest, but where it rests merely on law and force the reverse is true. . . .

But a state exists for the sake of a good life, and not for the sake of life only: if life only were the object, slaves and brute animals might form a state, but they cannot, for they have no share in happiness or in a life of free choice. Nor does a state exist for the sake of alliance and security from injustice, nor yet for the sake of exchange and mutual intercourse; for then the Tyrrhenians an the Carthaginians, and all who have commercial treaties with one another, would be the citizens of one state. True, they have agreements about imports, and engagements that they will do no wrong to one another, and written articles of alliance. But there are no magistracies common to the contracting parties who will enforce their engagements; different states have each their own magistracies. Nor does one state take care that the citizens of the other are such as they ought to be, nor see that those who come under the terms of the treaty do no wrong or wickedness at all, but only that they do no injustice to one another. Whereas, those who care for good government take into consideration (the larger question of) virtue and vice in states. Whence it may be further inferred that virtue must be the serious care of a state which truly deserves the name: for (without this ethical end) the community becomes a mere alliance which differs only in place from alliances of which the members live apart; and law is only a convention, a surety to one another of justice, as the sophist Lycophron says, and has no real power to make the citizens good and just.

This is obvious; for suppose distinct places, such as Corinth and Megara, to be united by a wall, still they would not be one city, not even if the citizens had the right to intermarry, which is one of the rights peculiarly characteristic of states. Again, if men dwelt at a distance from one another, but not so far off as to have no intercourse, and there were laws among them that they should not wrong each other in their exchanges, neither would this be a state. Let us suppose that one man is a carpenter, another a husbandman, another a shoe-maker, and so on, and that their number is ten thousand: nevertheless, if they have nothing in common but exchange, alliance, and the like, that would not constitute a state. Why is this? Surely not because they are at a distance from one another: for even supposing that such a community were to meet in one place, and that each man had a house of his own, which was in a manner his state, and that they made alliance with one another, but only against evil-doers; still an accurate thinker would not deem this to be a state, if their intercourse with one another was of the same character after as before their union. It is clear then that a state is not a mere society, having a common place, established for the prevention of crime and for the sake of exchange. These are conditions without which a state cannot exist; but all of them together do not constitute a state, which is a community of well-being in families and aggregations of families, for the sake of a perfect and self-sufficing life. Such a community can only be established among those who live in the same place and inter-marry. Hence arise in cities family connections, brotherhoods, common sacrifices, amuse-ments, which draw men together. They are created by friendship, for friendship is the motive of society. The end is the good life, and these are the means towards it. And the state is the union of families and villages having for an end a perfect and self-sufficing life, by which we mean a happy and honourable life.

Our conclusion, then, is that political society exists for the sake of noble actions, and not of mere companionship. And they who contribute most to such a society have a greater share in it than those who have the same or a greater freedom or nobility of birth but are inferior to them in a political virtue; or than those who exceed them in wealth but are surpassed by them in virtue. . . .

He who would enquire into the nature and various kinds of government must first of all determine "What is a state?" At present this is a disputed question. Some say that the state has done a certain act; others, no, not the state, but the oligarchy or the tyrant. And the legislator or statesman is concerned entirely with the state; a constitution or government being an arrangement of the inhabitants of a state. But a state is composite, and, like any other whole, made up of many parts;—these are the citizens, who compose it. It is evident, therefore, that we must begin by asking, Who is the citizen, and what is the meaning of the term? For here again there may be a difference of opinion. He who is a citizen in a democracy will often not be a citizen in an oligarchy. Leaving out of consideration those who have been made citizens, or who have obtained the name of citizen in any other accidental manner, we may say, first, that a citizen is not a citizen because he lives in a certain place, for resident aliens and slaves share in the place; nor is he a citizen who has no legal right except that of suing and being sued; for this right may be enjoyed under the provisions of a treaty. Even resident aliens in many places possess such rights, although in an imperfect form; for they are obliged to have a patron. Hence they do but imperfectly participate in citizenship, and we call them citizens only in a qualified sense, as we might apply the term to children who are too young to be on the register, or to old men who have been relieved from state duties. Of these we do not say simply that they are citizens, but add in the one case that they are not of age, and in the other, that they are past the age, or something of that sort; the precise expression is immaterial, for our meaning is clear. Similar difficulties to those which I have mentioned may be raised and answered about deprived citizens and about exiles. But the citizen, whom we are seeking to define, is a citizen in the strictest sense, against whom no such exception can be taken, and his special characteristic is that he shares in the administration of justice, and in offices. . . .

There is a point nearly allied to the preceding: Whether the virtue of a good man and a good citizen is the same or not. But, before entering on this discussion, we must first obtain some general notion of the virtue of the citizen. Like the sailor, the citizen is a member of a community. Now, sailors have different functions, for one of them is a rower, another a pilot, a third a look-out man, and a fourth is described by some similar term; and while the precise definition of each individual's virtue applies exclusively to him, there is, at the same time, a common definition applicable to them all. For they have all of them a common object, which is safety in navigation. Similarly, one citizen differs from another, but the salvation of the community is the common business of them all. This community is the state; the virtue of the citizen must therefore be relative to the constitution of which he is a member. If, then, there are many forms of government, it is evident that the virtue of the good citizen cannot be the one perfect virtue. But we say that the good man is he who has perfect virtue. Hence it is evident that the good citizen need not of necessity possess the virtue which makes a good man.

The same question may also be approached by another road, from a consideration of the perfect state. If the state cannot be entirely composed of good men, and each citizen is expected to do his own business well, and must therefore have virtue inasmuch as all the citizens cannot be alike, the virtue of the citizen and of the good man cannot coincide. All must have the virtue of the good citizen—thus, and thus only, can the state be perfect; but they will not have the virtue of a good man, unless we assume that in the good state all the citizens must be good.

Again, the state may be compared to the living being; as the first elements into which the living being is resolved are soul and body, as the soul is made up of reason and appetite, the family of husband and wife, property of master and slave, so out of all these, as well as other dissimilar elements, the state is composed; and, therefore, the virtue of all the citizens cannot possibly be the same, any more than the excellence of the leader of a chorus is the same as that of the performer who stands by his side. I have said enough to show why the two kinds of virtue cannot be absolutely and always the same.

But will there then be no case in which the virtue of the good citizen and the virtue of the good man coincide? To this we answer (not that the good citizen, but) that the good ruler is a good and wise man, and that he who would be a statesman must be a wise man. And some persons say that even the education of the ruler should be of a special kind; for are not the children of kings instructed in riding and military exercises? As Euripides says:

No subtle arts for me, but what the state requires.

As though there were a special education needed by a ruler. If then the virtue of a good ruler is the same as that of a good man, and we assume further that the subject is a citizen as well as the ruler, the virtue of the good citizen and the virtue of the good man cannot be always the same, although in some cases (i.e. in the perfect state) they may; for the virtue of a ruler differs from that of a citizen. It was the sense of this difference which made Jason say that "he felt hungry when he was a tyrant," meaning that he could not endure to live in a private station. But, on the other hand, it may be argued that men are praised for knowing both how to rule and how to obey, and he is said to be a citizen of approved virtue who is able to do both. Now if we suppose the virtue of a good man to be that which rules, and the virtue of the citizen to include ruling and obeying, it cannot be said that they are equally worthy of praise. Since then, it is occasionally held that the ruler and the ruled should learn different things and not the same things, and that the citizen must know and share in both; the inference is obvious. There is, indeed, the rule of a master which is concerned with menial offices,—the master need not know how to perform these, but may employ others in the execution of them: anything else would be degrading; and by anything else I mean the menial duties which vary much in character and are executed by various classes of slaves, such, for example, as handicraftsmen, who, as their name signifies, live by the labour of their hands:—under these the mechanic is included. Hence in ancient times, and among some nations, the working classes had no share in the government—a privilege which they only acquired under the extreme democracy. Certainly the good man and the statesman and the good citizen ought not to learn the crafts of inferiors except for their own occasional use; if they habitually practise them, there will cease to be a distinction between master and slave.

This is not the rule of which we are speaking; but there is a rule of another kind, which is exercised over freemen and equals by birth—a constitutional rule, which the ruler must learn by obeying, as he would learn the duties of a general of cavalry by being under the orders of a general of cavalry, or the duties of a general of infantry by being under the orders of a general of infantry, or by having had the command of a company or brigade. It has been well said that "he who has never learned to obey cannot be a good commander." The two are not the same, but the good citizen ought to be capable of both; he should know how to govern like a freeman, and how to obey like a freeman—these are the virtues of a citizen. And, although the temperance and justice of a ruler are distinct from those of a subject, the virtue of a good man will include both; for the good man, who is free and also a subject, will not have one virtue only, say justice, but he will have distinct kinds of virtue, the one qualifying him to rule, the other to obey, and differing as the temperance and courage of men and women differ. For a man would be thought coward if he had no more courage than a courageous woman, and a woman would be thought loquacious if she imposed no more restraint on her conversation than the good man; and indeed their part in the management of the household is different, for the duty of the one is to acquire, and of the other to preserve. Practical wisdom only is characteristic of the ruler: it would seem that all other virtues must equally belong to ruler and subject. The virtue of the subject is certainly not wisdom, but only true opinion; he may be compared to the maker of the flute, while his master is like the flute-player or user of the flute.

From these considerations may be gathered the answer to the question, whether the virtue of the good man is the same as that of the good citizen, or different, and how far the same, and how far different. . . .

Since every political society is composed of rulers and subjects, let us consider whether the relations of one to the other should interchange or be permanent. For the education of the citizens will necessarily vary with the answer given to this question. Now, if some men excelled others in the same degree in which gods and heroes are supposed to excel mankind in general, having in the first place a great advantage even in their bodies, and secondly in their minds, so that the superiority of the governors over their subjects was patent and undisputed, it would clearly be better that once for all the one class should rule and the others serve. But since this is unattainable, and kings have no marked superiority over their subjects, such as Scylax affirms to be found among the Indians, it is obviously necessary on many grounds that all the citizens alike should take their turn of governing and being governed. Equality consists in the same treatment of similar persons, and no government can stand which is not founded upon justice. For (if the government be unjust) every one in the country unites with the governed in the desire to have a revolution, and it is an impossibility that the members of the government can be so numerous as to be stronger than all their enemies put together. Yet that governors should excel their subjects is undeniable. How all this is to be effected, and in what way they will respectively share in the government, the legislator has to consider. The subject has been already mentioned. Nature herself has given the principle of choice when she made a difference between old and young (though they are really the same in kind), of whom she fitted the one to govern and the others to be governed. No one takes offence at being governed when he is young, nor does he think himself better than his governors, especially if he will enjoy the same privilege when he reaches the required age.

We conclude that from one point of view governors and governed are identical, and from another different. And therefore their education must be the same and also different. For he who would learn to command well must, as men say, first of all learn to obey. As I observed in the first part of this treatise, there is one rule which is for the sake of the rulers and another rule which is for the sake of the ruled; the former is a despotic, the latter a free government. Some commands differ not in the thing commanded, but in the intention with which they are imposed. Wherefore, many apparently menial offices are an honour to the free youth by whom they are performed; for actions do not differ as honourable or dishonourable in themselves so much as in the end and intention of them. But since we say that the virtue of the citizen and ruler is the same as that of the good man, and that the same person must first be a subject and then a ruler, the legislator has to see that they become good men, and by what means this may be accomplished, and what is the end of the perfect life.

POETICS

Having thus distinguished the parts, let us now consider the proper construction of the Fable or Plot, as that is at once the first and the most important thing in Tragedy. We have laid it down that a tragedy is an imitation of an action that is complete in itself, as a whole of some magnitude; for a whole may be of no magnitude to speak of. Now a whole is that which has beginning, middle, and end. A beginning is that which is not itself necessarily after anything else, and which has naturally something else after it; an end is that which is naturally after something itself, either as its necessary or usual consequent, and with nothing else after it; and a middle, that which is by nature after one thing and has also another after it. A well-constructed Plot, therefore, cannot either begin or end at any point one likes; beginning and end in it must be of the forms just described. Again: to be beautiful, a living creature, and every whole made up of parts, must not only present a certain order in its arrangement of parts, but also be of a certain definite magnitude. Beauty is a matter of size and order, and therefore impossible either (1) in a very minute creature, since our perception becomes indistinct as it approaches instantaneity; or (2) in a creature of vast size—one, say, 1000 miles long—as in that case, instead of the object being seen all at once, the unity and wholeness of it is lost to the beholder. Just in the same way, then, as a beautiful whole made up of parts, or a beautiful living creature, must be of some size, a size to be taken in by the eye, so a story or Plot must be of some length, but of a length to be taken in by the memory. As for the limit of its length, so far as that is relative to public performances and spectators, it does not fall within the theory of poetry. If they had to perform a hundred tragedies, they would be timed by water-clocks, as they are said to have been at one period. The limit, however, set by the actual nature of the thing is this: the longer the story, consistently with its being comprehensible as a whole, the finer it is by reason of its magnitude. As a rough general formula, "a length which allows of the hero passing by a series of probable or necessary stages from misfortune to happiness, or from happiness to misfortune," may suffice as a limit for the magnitude of the story.

The Unity of a Plot does not consist, as some suppose, in its having one man as its subject. An infinity of things befall that one man, some of which it is impossible to reduce to unity; and in like manner there are many actions of one man which cannot be made to form one action. One sees, therefore, the mistake of all the poets who have written a *Heracleid*, a *Theseid*, or similar poems; they suppose that, because Heracles was one man, the story also of Heracles must be one story. Homer, however, evidently understood this point quite well, whether by art or instinct, just in the same way as he excels the rest in every other respect. In writing an *Odyssey*, he did not make the poem cover all that ever befell his hero—it befell him, for instance, to get wounded on Parnassus and also to feign madness at the time of the call to arms, but the two incidents had no probable or necessary connection with one another—instead of doing that, he took an action with a Unity of the kind we are describing as the subject of the *Odyssey*, as also of the *Iliad*. The truth is that, just as in the other imitative arts one imitation is always of one thing, so in poetry the story, as an

From "Poetics," trans. I. Bywater, in *Aristotle, On the Art of Poetry* (Oxford: Clarendon Press, 1909).

imitation of action, must represent one action, a complete whole, with its several incidents so closely connected that the transposal or withdrawal of any one of them will disjoin and dislocate the whole. For that which makes no perceptible difference by its presence or absence is no real part of the whole.

From what we have said it will be seen that the poet's function is to describe, not the thing that has happened, but a kind of thing that might happen, i.e. what is possible as being probable or necessary. The distinction between historian and poet is not in the one writing prose and the other verse—you might put the work of Herodotus into verse, and it would still be a species of history; it consists really in this, that the one describes the thing that has been, and the other a kind of thing that might be. Hence poetry is something more philosophic and of graver import than history, since its statements are of the nature rather of universals, whereas those of history are singulars. By a universal statement I mean one as to what such or such a kind of man will probably or necessarily say or do—which is the aim of poetry, though it affixes proper names to the characters; by a singular statement, one as to what, say, Alcibiades did or had done to him. In Comedy this has become clear by this time; it is only when their plot is already made up of probable incidents that they give it a basis of proper names, choosing for the purpose any names that may occur to them, instead of writing like the old iambic poets about particular persons. In Tragedy, however, they still adhere to the historic names; and for this reason: what convinces is the possible; now whereas we are not yet sure as to the possibility of that which has not happened, that which has happened is manifestly possible, else it would not have come to pass. Nevertheless even in Tragedy there are some plays with but one or two known names in them, the rest being inventions; and there are some without a single known name, e.g. Agathon's *Antheus,* in which both incidents and names are of the poet's invention; and it is no less delightful on that account. So that one must not aim at a rigid adherence to the traditional stories on which tragedies are based. It would be absurd, in fact, to do so, as even the known stories are only known to a few, though they are a delight none the less to all.

It is evident from the above that the poet must be more the poet of his stories or Plots than of his verses, inasmuch as he is a poet by virtue of the imitative element in his work, and it is actions that he imitates. And if he should come to take a subject from actual history, he is none the less a poet for that; since some historic occurrences may very well be in the probable and possible order of things; and it is in that aspect of them that he is their poet.

Of simple Plots and actions the episodic are the worst. I call a Plot episodic when there is neither probability nor necessity in the sequence of its episodes. Actions of this sort bad poets construct through their own fault, and good ones on account of the players. His work being for public performance, a good poet often stretches out a Plot beyond its capabilities, and is thus obliged to twist the sequence of incident.

Tragedy, however, is an imitation not only of a complete action, but also of incidents arousing pity and fear. Such incidents have the very greatest effect on the mind when they occur unexpectedly and at the same time in consequence of one another; there is more of the marvelous in them then than if they happened of themselves or by mere chance. Even matters of chance seem most marvelous if there is an appearance of design as it were in them; as for instance the statue of Mitys at Argos killed the author of Mitys' death by falling down on him when a looker-on at a public spectacle; for incidents like that we think to be not without a meaning. A Plot, therefore, of this sort is necessarily finer than others.

Plots are either simple or complex, since the actions they represent are naturally of this twofold description. The action, proceeding in the way defined, as one continuous whole, I call simple, when the change in the hero's fortunes takes place without Peripety or Discovery; and complex, when it involves one or the other, or both. These should each of them arise out of the structure of the Plot itself, so as to be the consequence, necessary or probable, of the antecedents. There is a great difference between a thing happening *propter hoc* and *post hoc.*

A Peripety is the change from one state of things within the play to its opposite of the kind described, and that too in the way we are saying, in the probable or necessary sequence of events; as it is for instance in *Oedipus:* here the opposite state of things is produced by the Messenger, who, coming to gladden Oedipus and to remove his fears as to his mother, reveals the secret of his birth. And in *Lynceus:* just as he is being led off for execution, with Danaus at his side to put him to death, the incidents preceding this bring it about that he is saved and Danaus put to death. A Discovery is, as the very word implies, a change from ignorance to knowledge, and thus to either love or hate, in the personages marked for good or evil fortune. The finest form of Discovery is one attended by Peripeties, like that which goes with the Discovery in *Oedipus.* There are no doubt other forms of it; what we have said may happen in a way in reference to inanimate things, even things of a very casual kind; and it is also possible to discover whether some one has done or not done something. But the form most directly connected with the Plot and the action of the piece is the first-mentioned. This, with a Peripety, will arouse either pity or fear—actions of that nature being what Tragedy is assumed to represent; and it will also serve to bring about the happy or unhappy ending. The Discovery, then, being of persons, it may be that of one party only to the other, the latter being already known; or both the parties may have to discover themselves. Iphigenia, for instance, was discovered to Orestes by sending the letter; and another Discovery was required to reveal him to Iphigenia.

Two parts of the Plot, then, Peripety and Discovery, are on matters of this sort. A third part is Suffering; which we may define as an action of a destructive or painful nature, such as murders on the stage, tortures, woundings, and the like. The other two have been already explained.

The parts of Tragedy to be treated as formative elements in the whole were mentioned . . . (previously). From the point of view, however, of its quantity, i.e. the separate sections into which it is divided, a tragedy has the following parts: Prologue, Episode, Exode, and a choral portion, distinguished into Parode and Stasimon; these two are common to all tragedies, whereas songs from the stage and *Commoe* are only found in some. The Prologue is all that precedes the Parode of the chorus; an Episode all that comes in between two whole choral songs; the Exode all that follows after the last choral song. In the choral portion the Parode is the whole first statement of the chorus; a Stasimon, a song of the chorus without anapaests or trochees; a *Commos,* a lamentation sung by chorus and actor in concert. The parts of Tragedy to be used as formative elements in the whole we have already mentioned; the above are its parts from the point of view of its quantity, or the separate sections into which it is divided.

The next points after what we have said above will be these: (1) What is the poet to aim at, and what is he to avoid, in constructing his Plots? and (2) What are the conditions on which the tragic effect depends?

We assume that, for the finest form of Tragedy, the Plot must be not simple but complex; and further, that it must imitate actions arousing pity and fear, since that is the distinctive function of this kind of imitation. It follows, therefore, that there are three forms of Plot to be avoided. (1) A good man must not be seen passing from happiness to misery, or (2) a bad man from misery to happiness. The first situation is not fear-inspiring or piteous, but simply odious to us. The second is the most untragic that can be; it has no one of the requisites of Tragedy; it does not appeal either to the human feeling in us, or to our pity, or to our fears. Nor on the other hand should (3) an extremely bad man be seen falling from happiness into misery. Such a story may arouse the human feeling in us, but it will not move us to either pity or fear; pity is occasioned by undeserved misfortune, and fear by that of one like ourselves; so that there will be nothing either piteous or fear-inspiring in the situation. There remains, then, the intermediate kind of personage, a man not pre-eminently virtuous and just, whose misfortune, however, is brought upon him not by vice and depravity but by some error of judgement, of the number of those in the enjoyment of great reputation and prosperity; e.g. Oedipus, Thyestes, and the men of note of similar families. The perfect Plot, accordingly, must have a single, and not (as some tell us) a double issue; the change in the hero's fortunes must be not from misery to happiness, but on the contrary from happiness to misery; and the cause of it must lie not in any depravity, but in some great error on his part; the man himself being either such as we have described, or better, not worse, than that. Fact also confirms our theory. Though the poets began by accepting any tragic story that came to hand, in these days the finest tragedies are always on the story of some few houses, on that of Alcmeon, Oedipus, Orestes, Meleager, Thyestes, Telephus, or any others that may have been involved, as either agents or sufferers, in some deed of horror. The theoretically best tragedy, then, has a Plot of this description. The critics, therefore, are wrong, who blame Euripides for taking this line in his tragedies, and giving many of them an unhappy ending. It is, as we have said, the right line to take. The best proof is this: on the stage, and in the public performances, such plays, properly worked out, are seen to be the most truly tragic; and Euripides, even if his execution be faulty in every other point, is seen to be nevertheless the most tragic certainly of the dramatists. After this comes the construction of Plot which some rank first, one with a double story (like the *Odyssey*) and an opposite issue for the good and the bad personages. It is ranked as first only through the weakness of the audiences; the poets merely follow their public, writing as its wishes dictate. But the pleasure here is not that of Tragedy. It belongs rather to Comedy, where the bitterest enemies in the piece (e.g. Orestes and Aegisthus) walk off good friends at the end, with no slaying of any one by any one.

The tragic fear and pity may be aroused by the Spectacle; but they may also be aroused by the very structure and incidents of the play—which is the better way and shows the better poet. The Plot in fact should be so framed that, even without seeing the things take place, he who simply hears the account of them shall be filled with horror and pity at the incidents; which is just the effect that the mere recital of the story in *Oedipus* would have on one. To produce this same effect by means of the Spectacle is less artistic, and requires extraneous aid. Those, however, who make use of the Spectacle to put before us that which is merely monstrous and not productive of fear, are wholly out of touch with Tragedy; not every kind of pleasure should be required of a tragedy, but only its own proper pleasure.

The tragic pleasure is that of pity and fear, and the poet has to produce it by a work of imitation; it is clear, therefore, that the causes should be included in the incidents of his story. Let us see, then, what kinds of incident strike one as horrible, or rather as piteous. In a deed of this description the parties must necessarily be either friends, or enemies, or indifferent to one another. Now when enemy does it on enemy, there is nothing to move us to pity either in his doing or in his meditating the deed, except so far as the actual pain of the sufferer is concerned; and the same is true when the parties are indifferent to one another. Whenever the tragic deed, however, is done within the family—when murder or the like is done or meditated by brother on brother, by son on father, by mother on son, or son on mother—these are the situations the poet should seek after. The traditional stories, accordingly, must be kept as they are, e.g. the murder of Clytaemnestra by Orestes and of Eriphyle by Alcmeon. At the same time even with these there is something left to the poet himself; it is for him to devise the right way of treating them. Let us explain more clearly what we mean by "the right way." The deed of horror may be done by the doer knowingly and consciously, as in the old poets, and in Medea's murder of her children in Euripides. Or he may do it, but in ignorance of his relationship, and discover that afterwards, as does the Oedipus in Sophocles. Here the deed is outside the play; but it may be within it, like the act of the Alcmeon in Astydamas, or that of the Telegonus in *Ulysses Wounded.* A third possibility is for one meditating some deadly injury to another, in ignorance of his relationship, to make the discovery in time to draw back. These exhaust the possibilities, since the deed must necessarily be either done or not done, and either knowingly or unknowingly.

The worst situation is when the personage is with full knowledge on the point of doing the deed, and leaves it undone. It is odious and also (through the absence of suffering) untragic; hence it is that no one is made to act thus except in some few instances, e.g. Haemon and Creon in *Antigone.* Next after this comes the actual perpetration of the deed meditated. A better situation than that, however, is for the deed to be done in ignorance, and the relationship discovered afterwards, since there is nothing odious in it, and the Discovery will serve to astound us. But the best of all is the last; what we have in *Cresphontes,* for example, where Merope, on the point of slaying her son, recognizes him in time; in *Iphigenia,* where sister and brother are in a like position; and in *Helle,* where the son recognizes his mother, when on the point of giving her up to her enemy.

This will explain why our tragedies are restricted (as we said just now) to such a small number of families. It was accident rather than art that led the poets in quest of subjects to embody this kind of incident in their Plots. They are still obliged, accordingly, to have recourse to the families in which such horrors have occurred.

On the construction of the Plot, and the kind of Plot required for Tragedy, enough has now been said.

EPICTETUS

55–135 C.E.[1]

Epictetus was born a Roman slave in Hierop-
olis, in Asia Minor (the peninsula comprising most of modern Turkey). While still a slave,
he began studying with the Stoic Musonius Rufus. Shortly after his master freed him,
Epictetus founded his own school in Nicopolis, Epirus. Like Socrates, Epictetus wrote
nothing. His teaching, based on early rather than late Stoic doctrines, has been preserved
by one of his students, Arrian (known also for writing the history of Alexander the Great),
in the *Enchiridion,* or *Manual,* and the *Discourses,* which are transcriptions of Epictetus's
lectures. In the *Enchiridion,* from which the first selection is taken, Epictetus argues that
both happiness and unhappiness are completely under our control. He relies on the Stoic
distinction between what is within our power—"the use of the phenomena of existence"—
and what is not, namely the phenomena of existence themselves. In other words, although
we have no control over the objects of existence, we can to a limited extent control their *use*
because we have the power to view objects as we choose, to form opinions about them, and
to fear or desire them. This control can be achieved only if we learn "how it is possible to
employ desire and aversion without hindrance."

The main purpose of philosophy, according to Epictetus, is to help us achieve inner
peace through a proper understanding of the world. Like most Stoics, he had a Heraclitan
philosophy of nature, according to which change, the fundamental force of the universe, is
governed by *logos,* or reason. Inner peace comes from conforming to the way the world is
rather than to our own prejudice and then following reason in three stages: master your
desires, perform your duties, and think correctly about yourself and the world.

In the second selection, taken from the *Discourses,* Epictetus begins by arguing, following
Plato, that you cannot make yourself believe something simply by wishing it. For instance,
if you try to make yourself believe on a bright day that it is the middle of the night, you
will fail. Or try to make yourself believe that right now as you are reading this book there
are exactly 1,720 other people reading this book (there might be—you don't know). Still,
you can't do it. In other words, our beliefs and ideas about ourselves and the world are not
of our own conscious choosing. We cannot simply believe what we wish, nor can we wish
whatever ideas we want into our own minds. We therefore, according to Epictetus, are not

---

1. Common Era, which corresponds to and replaces the locution "A.D."

responsible for the way the world is nor for our own ideas. All that we are responsible for is reduced by Epictetus to the *use* we make of the ideas that present themselves to our minds: "Two maxims we must ever bear in mind—that apart from the will there is nothing good or bad, and that we must not try to anticipate or to direct events, but merely to accept them with intelligence."

Lame and physically weak from the time he had been a slave, Epictetus worked arduously in making his views known. He developed a large following, even among early Christians, and in 90 C.E. the emperor Domitian expelled him from Rome along with many other philosophers whose teachings he saw as dangerous to his tyranny. In the latter part of the selection from the *Discourses*, you will find Epictetus's powerful and ironical polemic against the illusion of freedom, no doubt inspired by his own experience of having been "freed" from slavery and then attaining fame and even power. Thinking that because you are not a slave you are free can be especially deceptive, he says, because unlike the slave who knows he is not the master of his own life, a "free" man is in the even graver danger of being a slave without even knowing it.

ENCHIRIDION

Of things, some are in our power and others not. In our power are opinion, pursuit, desire, aversion, and, in one word, whatever are our own actions. Not in our power are body, property, reputation, command, and, in one word, whatever are not our own actions.

Now, the things in our power are by nature free, unrestrained, unhindered; but those not in our power, weak, slavish, restrained, belonging to others. Remember, then, that if you suppose things by nature slavish to be free, and what belongs to others your own, you will be hindered; you will lament; you will be disturbed; you will find fault both with gods and men. But if you suppose that only to be your own which is your own, and what belongs to others such as it really is, no one will ever compel you; no one will restrain you; you will find fault with no one; you will accuse no one; you will do no one thing against your will; no one will hurt you; you will not have an enemy, for you will suffer no harm. . . .

Study therefore to be able to say to every harsh appearance, "You are but an appearance, and not absolutely the thing you appear to be." And then examine it by those rules which you have, and first, and chiefly, by this: whether it concerns the things which are in our own power, or those which are not; and, if it concerns anything not in our power, be prepared to say that it is nothing to you.

Remember that desire promises the attainment of that of which you are desirous; and aversion promises the avoiding of that to which you are averse; that he who fails of the object of his desire is disappointed, and he who incurs the object of his aversion wretched. If, then, you confine your aversion to those objects only which are contrary to the natural use of your faculties, which you have in your own power, you will never incur anything to which you are averse. But if you are averse to sickness, or death, or poverty, you will be

From *The Moral Discourses of Epictetus*, trans. Elizabeth Carter (London: J. M. Dent, 1910).

wretched. Remove aversion, then, from all things that are not in our power, and transfer it to things contrary to the nature of what is in our power. But, for the present, totally suppress desire: for, if you desire any of the things not in our own power, you must necessarily be disappointed; and of those which are, and which it would be laudable to desire, nothing is yet in your possession. Use only [the requisite acts] of pursuit and avoidance; and even these lightly, and with gentleness and reservation. . . .

Men are disturbed, not by things, but by the principles and notions which they form concerning things. Death, for instance, is not terrible, else it would have appeared so to Socrates. But the terror consists in our notion of death that it is terrible. When therefore we are hindered, or disturbed, or grieved, let us never impute it to others, but to ourselves; that is, to our own principles. It is the action of an uninstructed person to lay the fault of his own bad condition upon others; of one entering upon instruction to lay the fault on himself; and of one perfectly instructed, neither on others nor on himself.

Be not elated on any excellence not your own. If a horse should be elated and say, "I am handsome," it would be supportable. But when you are elated, and say, "I have a handsome horse," know that you are elated on what is, in fact, only the good of the horse. What, then is your own? The use of the appearances of things. So that when you behave conformably to nature in the use of these appearances, you will be elated with reason; for you will be elated on some good of your own. . . .

Require not things to happen as you wish, but wish them to happen as they do happen, and you will go on well.

Never say of anything, "I have lost it"; but, "I have restored it." Is your child dead? It is restored. Is your wife dead? She is restored. Is your estate taken away? Well, and is not that likewise restored? "But he who took it away is a bad man." What is it to you by whose hands he, who gave it, has demanded it back again? While he gives you to possess it, take care of it; but as of something not your own, as passengers do of an inn.

If you wish your children, and your wife, and your friends to live for ever, you are stupid; for you wish things to be in your power which are not so, and what belongs to others to be your own. So likewise, if you wish your servant to be without fault, you are a fool; for you wish vice not to be vice, but something else. But, if you wish to have your desires undisappointed, this is in your own power. Exercise, therefore, what is in your power. He is the master of every other person who is able to confer or remove whatever that person wishes either to have or to avoid. Whoever, then, would be free, let him wish nothing, let him decline nothing, which depends on others else he must necessarily be a slave.

Remember that you must behave [in life] as at an entertainment. Is anything brought round to you? Put out your hand and take your share with moderation. Does it pass by you? Do not stop it. Is it not yet come? Do not stretch forth your desire towards it, but wait till it reaches you. Thus do with regard to children, to a wife, to public posts, to riches, and you will be some time or other a worthy partner of the feasts of the gods. And if you do not so much as take the things which are set before you, but are able even to despise them, then you will not only be a partner of the feasts of the gods, but of their empire also. For, by thus doing, Diogenes and Heraclitus, and others like them, deservedly became, and were called, divine.

When you see any one weeping for grief, either that his son is gone abroad, or dead, or that he has suffered in his affairs, take heed that the appearance may not hurry you away with it. But immediately make the distinction within your own mind, and have it ready to say, "It is not the accident that distresses this person, for it does not distress another man; but the judgment which he forms concerning it." As far as words go, however, do not disdain to condescend to him, and even, if it should so happen, to groan with him. Take heed, however, not to groan inwardly too.

Remember that you are an actor in a drama, of such a kind as the author pleases to make it. If short, of a short one; if long, of a long one. If it be his pleasure you should act a poor man, a cripple, a governor, or a private person, see that you act it naturally. For this is your business, to act well the character assigned you; to choose it is another's.

If you have an earnest desire of attaining to philosophy, prepare yourself from the very first to be laughed at, to be sneered by the multitude, to hear them say, "He is returned to us a philosopher all at once," and "Whence this supercilious look?" Now, for your part, do not have a supercilious look indeed; but keep steadily to those things which appear best to you as one appointed by God to this station. For remember that, if you adhere to the same point, those very persons who at first ridiculed will afterwards admire you. But if you are conquered by them, you will incur a double ridicule.

If you ever happen to turn your attention to externals, so as to wish to please any one, be assured that you have ruined your scheme of life. Be contented, then, in everything with being a philosopher; and, if you wish to be thought so likewise by any one, appear so to yourself, and it will suffice you.

Never call yourself a philosopher, nor talk a great deal among the unlearned about theorems, but act conformably to them. Thus, at an entertainment, do not talk how persons ought to eat, but eat as you ought. For remember that in this manner Socrates also universally avoided all ostentation. And when persons came to him and desired to be recommended by him to philosophers, he took and recommended them, so well did he bear being overlooked. So that if ever any talk should happen among the unlearned concerning philosophic theorems, be you, for the most part, silent. For there is great danger in immediately throwing out what you have not digested. And, if any one tells you that you know nothing, and you are not nettled at it, then you may be sure that you have begun your business. For sheep do not throw up the grass to show the shepherds how much they have eaten; but, inwardly digesting their food, they outwardly produce wool and milk. Thus, therefore, do you likewise not show theorems to the unlearned, but the actions produced by them after they have been digested.

DISCOURSES

THAT WE ARE NOT TO BE ANGRY WITH MANKIND

What is the cause of assent to anything?

Its appearing to be true.

It is not possible, therefore, to assent to what happens to be not true.

From *The Moral Discourses of Epictetus,* trans. Elizabeth Carter (London: J. M. Dent, 1910). With emendations by Daniel Kolak.

Why?

Because it is the very nature of the understanding to agree to truth, to be dissatisfied with falsehood, and to suspend its belief in doubtful cases.

What is the proof of this?

Persuade yourself, if you can, that it is now night.

Impossible.

Unpersuade yourself that it is day.

Impossible.

Persuade yourself that the stars are, or are not, even.

Impossible.

When any one, then, assents to what is false, be assured that he does not willfully assent to it as false (for, as Plato affirms, the soul is never voluntarily deprived of truth); but what is false appears to him to be true. Well, then, have we, in actions, anything correspondent to true and false in propositions?

Duty, and contrary to duty: advantageous, and disadvantageous: suitable, and unsuitable; and the like.

A person, then, cannot think a thing advantageous to him, and not choose it.

He cannot. . . .

Whoever, therefore, duly remembers that the appearance of things to the mind is the standard of every action to man: that this is either right or wrong: and, if right, he is without fault, if wrong, he himself bears the punishment; for that one man cannot be the person deceived, and another the sufferer: will not be outrageous and angry at any one; will not revile, or reproach, or hate, or quarrel with any one.

So, then, have all the great and dreadful deeds that have been done in the world no other original than appearance?

Absolutely no other. The *Iliad* consists of nothing but the appearances and the use of those appearances. It appeared to Paris to carry off the wife of Menelaus. It appeared to Helen to follow him. If, then, it had appeared to Menelaus to persuade himself that it was an advantage to be robbed of such a wife, what would have happened? Not only the *Iliad* had been lost, but the *Odyssey* too.

Do these great events, then, depend on so small a cause?

What are these events which you call great?

Wars and seditions, the destruction of numbers of men, and the overthrow of cities.

And what great matter is there in all this? Nothing. What great matter is there in the death of numbers of oxen, numbers of sheep, or in the burning or pulling down numbers of nests of storks or swallows?

Are these like cases, then?

Perfectly like. The bodies of men are destroyed, and the bodies of sheep and oxen. The houses of men are burnt, and the nests of storks. What is there great or dreadful in all this? Pray, show me what difference there is between the house of a man, and the nest of a stork, so far as it is a habitation, excepting that houses are built with beams and tiles and bricks; and nests with sticks and clay?

What, then, is a stork and a man a like thing? What do you mean?

With regard to body, extremely like.

Is there no difference, then, between a man and a stork?

Yes, surely; but not in these things. . . .

WHAT THE BEGINNING OF PHILOSOPHY IS

The beginning of philosophy, at least to such as enter upon it in a proper way, and by the door, is a consciousness of our own weakness, and inability in necessary things. For we came into the world without any natural idea of a right-angled triangle, of a diesis or a hermitone in music; but we learn each of these things by some instruction of art. Hence, they who do not understand them do not form any conceit of understanding them. But whoever came into the world without an innate idea of good and evil, fair and base, becoming and unbecoming, happiness and misery, proper and improper, what ought to be done and what not to be done? Hence we all make use of the names, and endeavour to apply our pre-conceptions to particular cases. . . . Now, since you think that you make a suitable application of your pre-conceptions to particular cases, tell me whence you derive this.

From its seeming so to me.

But it does not seem so to another, and does not he too form a conceit that he makes a right application?

He does.

Is it possible, then, that each of you should apply your pre-conceptions right, on the very subjects about which you have contradictory opinions?

It is not.

Have you anything to show us, then, for this application, preferable to its seeming so to you? And does a madman act any other way than seems to him right? Is this, then, a sufficient criterion to him too?

It is not.

Come, therefore, to something preferable to what seems.

What is that?

The beginning of philosophy is this: The being sensible of the disagreement of men with each other; an inquiry into the cause of this disagreement, and a disapprobation and distrust of what merely seems; a certain examination into what seems, whether it seems rightly, and an invention of some rule, like a balance for the determination of weights, like a square for straight and crooked.

Is this the beginning of philosophy, that all things which seem right to all persons are so?

Why, is it possible that contradictions can be right?

Well, then, not all things; but all that seem so to us.

And why more to you than to the Syrians, or Egyptians? Than to me, or to any other man?

Not at all more.

Therefore merely what seems to each man is not sufficient to determine the reality of a thing. For even in weights or measures we are not satisfied with the bare appearance; but for everything we find some rule. And is there in the present case, then, no rule preferable to what seems? Is it possible that what is of the greatest necessity in human life should be left incapable of determination and discovery?

There is, then, some rule.

And why do we not seek and discover it; and when we have discovered, make use of it, without fail, ever after, so as not even to move a finger without it? For this, I conceive, is what, when found, will cure those of their madness who make use of no other measure but their own perverted way of thinking. That afterwards, beginning from certain known and determinate points, we may make use of pre-conceptions properly applied to particulars. What is the subject that falls under our inquiry?

Pleasure.

Bring it to the rule. Throw it into the scale. Must good be something in which it is fit to confide, and to which we may trust?

Yes.

Is it fit to trust to anything unsteady?

No.

Is pleasure, then, a steady thing?

No.

Take it, then, and throw it out of the scale, and drive it far distant from the place of good things. But, if you are not quick-sighted, and one balance is insufficient, bring another. Is it fit to be elated by good?

Yes.

Is it fit, then, to be elated by a present pleasure? See that you do not say it is; otherwise I shall not think you so much as worthy to use a scale. Thus are things judged, and weighed, when we have the rules ready. This is the part of philosophy, to examine and fix the rules; and to make use of them when they are known is the business of a wise and good man.

OF FREEDOM

He is free who lives as he likes; who is not subject either to compulsion, to restraint, or to violence; whose pursuits are unhindered, his desires successful, his aversions unincurred. Who, then, would wish to lead a wrong course of life?—"No one." Who would live deceived, prone to mistake, unjust, dissolute, discontented, dejected?—"No one." No wicked man, then, lives as he likes; therefore neither is he free. And who would live in sorrow, fear, envy, pity; with disappointed desires, and incurred aversions?—"No one." Do we then find any of the wicked exempt from sorrow, fear, disappointed desires, incurred aversions?— "Not one." Consequently, then, not free.

If a person who has been twice consul should hear this, provided you add, "But you are a wise man; this is nothing to you," he will forgive you. But if you tell him the truth—that in point of slavery he does not differ from those who have been thrice sold—what must you expect but to be beaten? "For how," says he, "am I a slave? My father was free, my mother free. Besides, I am a senator, too, and the friend of Caesar, and have been twice consul, and have myself many slaves." In the first place, most worthy sir, perhaps your father too was a slave of the same kind, and your mother, and your grandfather, and all your ancestors successively. But even if they were ever so free, what is that to you? For what if they were of a generous, you of a mean spirit; they brave, and you a coward; they sober, and you dissolute? . . .

Consider in animals what is our idea of freedom. Some keep tame lions, and feed and even carry them about with them; and who will say that any such lion is free? Nay, does he not live the more slavishly the more he lives at ease? And who, that had sense and reason, would wish to be one of those lions? Again, how much do birds, which are taken and kept in a cage, suffer by trying to fly away? Nay, some of them starve with hunger rather than undergo such a life; then, as many of them as are saved, it is scarcely and with difficulty and in a pining condition, and the moment they find any hole, out they hop. Such a desire have they of natural freedom, and to be at their own disposal and unrestrained.—"And what harm does this confinement do you?"—"What say you? I was born to fly where I please, to live in the open air, to sing when I please. You deprive me of all this, and say, What harm does it do you?"

Hence we will allow those only to be free who do not endure captivity; but, as soon as they are taken, die, and escape. Thus Diogenes somewhere says, that the only way to freedom is to die with ease. And he writes to the Persian king, "You can no more enslave the Athenians than you can fish."—"How? What, shall not I take them?"—"If you do take them," says he, "they will leave you, and be gone like fish. For take a fish, and it dies. And, if the Athenians too die as soon as you have taken them, of what use are your warlike preparations?" This is the voice of a free man, who had examined the matter in earnest, and, as it might be expected, found it out. But, if you seek it where it is not, what wonder if you never find it?

A slave wishes to be immediately set free. Think you it is because he is desirous to pay his fine to the officer? No; but because he fancies that, for want of acquiring his freedom, he has hitherto lived under restraint and unprosperously. "If I am once set free," says he, "it is all prosperity; I care for no one, I speak to all as their equal, and on a level with them. I go where I will, I come when and how I will." He is at last made free; and presently, having nowhere to eat, he seeks whom he may flatter, with whom he may sup. He then either submits to the basest and most infamous prostitution, and, if he can obtain admission to some great man's table, falls into a slavery much worse than the former; or, if the creature, void of sense and right taste, happens to acquire an affluent fortune, he dotes upon some girl, laments, and is unhappy, and wishes for slavery again. "For what harm did it do me? Another clothed me, another shod me, another fed me, another took care of me when I was sick. It was but in a few things, by way of return, I used to serve him. But now, miserable wretch! what do I suffer in being a slave to many instead of one! Yet, if I can obtain the equestrian rings, I shall live with the utmost prosperity and happiness." In order to obtain them he first suffers what he deserves, and, as soon as he has obtained them, it is all the same again. "But, then," says he, "if I do but get a military command, I shall be delivered from all my troubles." He gets a military command. He suffers as much as the vilest rogue of a slave; and, nevertheless, he asks for a second command, and a third; and, when he has put the finishing hand and is made a senator, then he is a slave indeed. When he comes into the assembly, it is then that he undergoes his finest and most splendid slavery. . . .

Since, then, neither they who are called kings, nor the friends of kings, live as they like, who, after all, are free? Seek, and you will find; for you are furnished by nature with means for discovering the truth. But, if you are not able by these alone to find the consequence, hear them who have sought it. What do they say? Do you think freedom a good?—"The greatest." Can any one then who attains the greatest good be unhappy or unsuccessful in his affairs?—"No." As many, therefore, as you see unhappy, lamenting, unprosperous, confidently pronounce them not free.—"I do." Henceforth then we have done with buying and selling, and suchlike stated conditions of becoming slaves. For, if you have made these concessions properly, whether a great or a little king, a consular, or one twice a consul, be unhappy, he is not free.—"Agreed."

Further, then, answer me this: Do you think freedom to be something great and noble and valuable?—"How should I not?" Is it possible, then, that he who acquires anything so great and valuable and noble should be of an abject spirit?—"It is not." Whenever, then, you see any one subject to another, and flattering him, contrary to his own opinion, confidently say that he too is not free; and not only if he does it for a supper, but even if it be for a government, nay, a consulship; but call those indeed little slaves who act thus for the sake of little things, and the others, as they deserve, great slaves.—"Be this, too, agreed." Well, do you think freedom to be something independent and self-determined?—"How can it be otherwise?" Him, then, whom it is in the power of another to restrain or to compel, affirm confidently to be not free. And do not mind his grandfathers, or great-grandfathers, or inquire whether he has been bought or sold; but if you hear him say from his heart, and with emotion, My master, though twelve lictors should march before him, call him a slave. And if you should hear him say, Wretch that I am, what do I suffer! call him a slave. In short, if you see him wailing, complaining, unprosperous, call him a slave in purple. "Suppose, then, he does nothing of all this?"—Do not yet say he is free, but learn whether his principles are liable to compulsion, to restraint, or disappointment, and, if you find this to be the case, call him a slave. . . . "Have we so many masters, then?"—We have. For, prior to all such, we have the things themselves for our masters; now they are many, and it is through these that it becomes necessary that such as have the disposal of them should be our masters too. For no one fears Caesar himself, but death, banishment, loss of goods, prison, disgrace. Nor does any one love Caesar, unless he be a person of great worth; but we love riches, the tribunate, the praetorship, the consulship. When we love and hate and fear these things, they who have the disposal of them must necessarily be our masters. Hence we even worship them as gods. . . .

"What is it, then, that makes a man free and independent? For neither riches, nor consulship, nor command of provinces, or kingdoms, make him so; but something else must be found." What is it that preserves any one from being hindered and restrained in writing? —"The science of writing." In music?—"The science of music." Therefore, in life, too, the science of living. As you have heard it in general, then, consider it likewise in particulars. Is it possible for him to be unrestrained who desires any of those things that are in the power of others?—"No." Can he avoid being hindered?—"No." Therefore neither can he be free. Consider, then, whether we have nothing, or all, in our own power alone; or whether some things are in our own power, and some in that of others.—"What do you mean?" When you would have your body perfect, is it in your own power, or is it not?—"It is not." When you would be healthy?—"Nor this." When you would be handsome?—"Nor this." Live, or die?—"Nor this." Body, then, is not our own, but subject to everything stronger than itself.—"Agreed." Well, is it in your own power to have an estate when you please?—"No." Slaves?—"No." Clothes?—"No." A house?—"No." Horses?—"Indeed none of these." Well, if you would ever so fain have your children live, or your wife, or your brother, or your friends, is it in your own power?—"No, nor this." Will you say, then, that there is nothing independent which is in your own power alone, and unalienable? See, then, if you have anything of this sort.—"I do not know." But, consider it thus: Can any one make you assent to a falsehood?—"No one." In the topic of assent, then, you are unrestrained and unhindered.—"Agreed." Well, and can any one compel you to exert your pursuits towards what you do not like?—"He can. For when he threatens me with death, or fetters, he compels me to exert them." If, then, you were to despise dying, or being fettered, would you any longer regard him?—"No." Is despising death, then, an action in our power, or is it not?—"It is." Is it, therefore, in your power also to exert your pursuits towards anything, or is it not?—"Agreed that it is. But in whose power is my avoiding anything?" This, too, is in your own.—"What then, if, when I am exerting myself to walk, any one should restrain me?" What part of you can he restrain? Can he restrain your assent?—"No, but my body." Ay, as he may a stone.—"Be it so. But still I walk no more." And who told you that walking was an action of your own that cannot be restrained? For I only said that your exerting yourself towards it could not be restrained. But where there is need of body and its assistance, you have already heard that nothing is in your power.—"Be this, too, agreed." And can any one compel you to desire against your will?—"No one." Or to propose or intend, or, in short, not to make use of the appearances which present themselves to you?— "Nor this. But when I desire anything, he will restrain me from obtaining what I desire." If you desire anything that is your own, and that cannot be restrained, how can he restrain you?—"By no means." And pray who tells you that he who desires what depends on another cannot be restrained?—"May not I desire health, then?" By no means, nor anything else that depends on another; for what is not in your own power, either to procure or to preserve when you will, that belongs to another. Keep off not only your hands from it, but, far prior to these, your desires. Otherwise you have given yourself up a slave, you have put your neck under the yoke, if you admire any of the things not your own, but subject and mortal, to whichsoever of them you are attached.—"Is not my hand my own?" It is a part of you, but it is by nature clay, liable to restraint, to compulsion, a slave to everything stronger than itself. And why do I say your hand? You ought to possess your whole body as a paltry ass with a pack-saddle on, as long as may be, as long as it is allowed you. But if there should come a press and a soldier should lay hold on it, let it go. Do not resist or murmur, otherwise you will be first beat, and lose the ass after all. And, since you are to consider the body itself in this manner, think what remains to do concerning those things which are provided for the sake of the body. If that be an ass, the rest are bridles, pack-saddles, shoes, oats, hay, for the ass. Let these go too. Quit them more easily and expeditiously than the ass. And when you are thus prepared and thus exercised to distinguish what belongs to others from your own; what is liable to restraint from what is not; to esteem your own property, the other not; to keep your desire, to keep your aversion carefully turned to this point; whom have you any longer to fear?—"No one." For about what should you be afraid? About what is your own, in which consists the essence of good and evil? And who has any power over this? Who can take it away? Who can hinder you? No more than God [can be hindered]. But are you afraid for body, for possessions, for what belongs to others, for what is nothing to you? And what have you been studying all this while, but to distinguish between your own and not your own; what is in your power and what is not in your power; what is liable to restraint and what is not? And for what purpose have you applied to the philosophers? That you might be nevertheless disappointed and unfortunate? No doubt you will be exempt from fear and perturbation! And what is grief to you? For nothing but what we fear when expected, affects us with grief when present. And what will you any longer passionately wish for? For you have a temperate and steady desire of things dependent on choice, as they are good, and present; and you have no desire of things independent on choice, so as to leave room for that irrational and impetuous and immoderately hasty passion.

Since, then, you are thus affected with regard to things, what man can any longer be formidable to you? What has man formidable to man, either in appearance or speech or mutual intercourse? No more than horse to horse, or dog to dog, or bee to bee. But things are formidable to every one; and whenever any person can either confer or take away these from another, he becomes formidable too. "How, then, is the citadel" [the seat of tyranny] "to be destroyed?"—Not by sword or fire, but by principle. For if we should demolish that which is in the town, shall we have demolished also that of a fever, of pretty girls, in short, the citadel within ourselves; and turned out the tyrants, to whom we are subject upon all occasions every day, sometimes the same, sometimes others? From hence we must begin, from hence demolish the citadel, turn out the tyrants; give up body, its parts, riches, power, fame, magistracies, honours, children, brothers, friends; esteem all these as belonging to others. And, if the tyrants be turned out from hence, why should I besides demolish the [external] citadel; at least, on my own account? For what does it do to me by standing? Why should I turn out the guards? For in what point do they affect me? It is against others they direct their fasces, their staves, and their swords. Have I ever been restrained from what I willed? Or compelled against my will? Indeed, how is this possible? I have ranged my pursuits under the direction of God. Is it his will that I should have a fever? It is my will too. Is it his will that I should pursue anything? It is my will too. Is it his will that I should desire? It is my will too. Is it his will that I should obtain anything? It is mine too. Is it not his will? It is not mine. Is it his will that I should be tortured? Then it is my will to be tortured. Is it his will that I should die? Then it is my will to die. Who can any longer restrain or compel me contrary to my own opinion? No more than Jupiter [can be restrained]. It is thus that cautious travellers act. Does any one hear that the road is beset by robbers? He does not set out alone, but waits for the retinue of an ambassador or questor, or a pro-consul; and, when he has joined himself to their company, goes along in safety. Thus does the prudent man act in the world. There are many robberies, tyrants, storms, distresses, losses of things the most dear. Where is there any refuge? How can he go along unattacked? What retinue can he wait for to go safely through his journey? To what company join himself? To some rich man? To some consular senator? And what good will that do me? He is stripped himself; groans and laments. And what if my fellow-traveller himself should turn against me, and rob me? What shall I do? I will be the friend of Caesar. While I am his companion, no one will injure me. Yet, before I can become illustrious enough for this, what must I bear and suffer! How often, and by how many, must I be robbed! And then, if I do become the friend of Caesar, he too is mortal; and, if by any accident he should become my enemy, where can I best retreat? To a desert? Well, and does not a fever come there? What can be done, then? Is it not possible to find a fellow-traveller, safe, faithful, brave, incapable of being surprised? A person who reasons thus understands and considers that, if he joins himself to God, he shall go safely through his journey—"How do you mean, join himself?" That whatever is the will of God may be his will too; whatever is not the will of God may not be his. "How, then, can this be done?"—Why, how otherwise than by considering the exertions of God's power, and his administration? What has he given me, my own, and independent? What has he reserved to himself? He has given me whatever depends upon choice. The things in my power he has made incapable of hindrance or restraint. But how could he make a body of clay incapable of hindrance? Therefore he has subjected possessions, furniture, house, children, wife, to the revolution of the universe. Why, then, do I fight against God? Why do I will to retain what depends not on will? What is not granted absolutely; but how? In such a manner and for such a time as was thought proper. But he who gave, takes away. Why, then, do I resist? Not to say that I shall be a fool in contending with a stronger than myself; what is a prior consideration, I shall be unjust. For whence had I these things when I came into the world? My father gave them to me. And who gave them to him? And who made the sun? Who the fruits? Who the seasons? Who their connection and relation to each other? And, after you have received all, and even your very self, from another, are you angry with the giver, and complain if he takes anything away from you? Who are you, and for what purpose did you come? Was it not he who brought you here? Was it not he who showed you the light? Has not he given you assistants? Has not he given you senses? Has not he given you reason? And as whom did he bring you here? Was it not as a mortal? Was it not as one to live, with a little portion of flesh, upon earth, and to see his administration; to behold the spectacle with him, and partake of the festival for a short time? After having beheld the spectacle, and the solemnity, then, as long as it is permitted you, will you not depart when he leads you out, adoring and thankful for what you have heard and seen?—"No, but I would enjoy the feast still longer." So would the initiated, too, be longer in their initiation; so perhaps would the spectators at Olympia see more combatants. But the solemnity is over. Go away. Depart like a grateful and modest person; make room for others. Others too must be born, as you were, and when they are born must have a place and habitations and necessaries. But if the first do not give way, what room is there left? Why are you insatiable? Why are you unconscionable? Why do you crowd the world?—"Ay, but I would have my wife and children with me too." Why, are they yours? Are they not the giver's? Are they not his who made you also? Will you not quit what belongs to another, then? Will you not yield to your superior?—"Why, then, did he bring me into the world upon these conditions?" Well, if it is not worth your while, depart. He has no need of a discontented spectator. He wants such as may share the festival, make part of the chorus, who may rather extol, applaud, celebrate the solemnity; he will not be displeased to see the wretched and fearful dismissed from it. For when they were present, they did not behave as at a festival, nor fill a proper place, but lamented, found fault with the deity, fortune, their companions; insensible both of their advantage and their powers, which they received for contrary purposes, the powers of magnanimity, nobleness of spirit, fortitude, and the subject of present inquiry, freedom.—"For what purpose then have I received these things?"—To use them. "How long?"—As long as he who lent them pleases. If, then, they are not necessary, do not attach yourself to them, and they will not be so; do not tell yourself that they are necessary, and they are not.

This should be our study from morning till night, beginning from the least and frailest things, from an earthen vessel, from a glass. Afterwards, proceed to a suit of clothes, a dog, a horse, an estate; from thence to your self, body, parts of the body, children, wife, brothers. Look everywhere around you, and throw them from yourself. Correct your principles. See that nothing cleave to you which is not your own; nothing grow to you that may give you pain when it is torn away. And say, when you are daily exercising yourself as you do here, not that you act the philosopher (admit this to be an insolent title), but that you are asserting your freedom. For this is true freedom. . . .

MARCUS AURELIUS

121–180

Marcus Aurelius was born to a prominent Spanish family in Rome. After the death of his parents, while he was still a boy, he devoted himself to a life of study. By the age of twelve Marcus was mastering geometry, music, mathematics, painting, and literature. Under the mentorship of private tutors, he learned fluent Greek and Latin and the whole of philosophy from the ancients through the Stoics, whom he most admired. At age fourteen he received the *toga virilis,* the white robe signifying adulthood and full citizenship in Rome. He showed so much promise and talent that when the emperor Hadrian picked Marcus's uncle Antoninus as his successor, he specified that Antoninus should designate Marcus to be the next emperor. Thus, by the age of seventeen Marcus Aurelius became the heir apparent to the imperial throne of Rome.

According to Plato, "philosophers must become kings or kings must become philosophers before the world will have peace." As the fourteenth Roman emperor (from 161 to 180), Marcus Aurelius was probably the closest thing to a philosopher king the world has ever known. Already by the time he became emperor at thirty-nine, he had earned a reputation as a great statesman and philosophical visionary. During his nineteen-year reign, he brought about more political, social, educational, and economic reforms than any other emperor. He championed the poor and, because of his own experience as an orphan, initiated many programs to aid young children. He brought about many reforms that improved the condition of slaves. He resisted what he saw as the corrupting trappings of power, remaining a sincere and simple human being capable of great kindness but a powerful and resolute leader.

As the commander-in-chief of the Roman legions, Marcus Aurelius successfully defended Rome against more invasions than any other emperor: he fought back invasions from Syria, Spain, Egypt, Britain, Italy, and the Germanic tribes along the Rhine-Danube frontier. Today there still stands, in Piazza Colonna in Rome, a column erected to his memory. Its spiral frieze contains dramatic, brutally realistic depictions of the Danube wars.

Marcus Aurelius regarded Christians as the most subversive and dangerous elements within the Roman Empire and violently persecuted them, warning that if Christianity were allowed to corrupt the intellects and souls of the citizens the entire Roman Empire would fall, destroyed in the end not by physical assault from external enemies but from within, ruined by the mental deterioration of its own people. In Athens he financed all four great philosophical schools: the Academy, the Lyceum, the Garden, and the Stoa.

The *Meditations,* written during military campaigns, is a twelve-volume compendium of Marcus Aurelius's ruminations on life. Written not in Roman but in Greek, it reveals the mind of a Stoic philosopher of great eloquence, laying out his own path of self-discovery and enlightenment; he rejects, for instance, the Stoic doctrine of absolute truth, holding instead that we can at best have *probable* knowledge and that therefore to be virtuous we must always keep an open mind. His overarching theme throughout the *Meditations* is that there is but one activity that can keep the "daemon within you free" through the tumultuous trials and tribulations of life: philosophy. The work itself is a unique window into the mind of an enlightened Roman emperor who tried to integrate wisdom into the sphere of human politics. Most historians believe the work was written for his own eyes only, to inspire him and to keep alive within himself the Stoic philosophy that was his lifelong allegiance.

MEDITATIONS

Begin the morning by saying to yourself, I shall meet with the busybody, the ungrateful, arrogant, deceitful, envious, unsocial. All these things happen to them by reason of their ignorance of what is good and evil. But I who have seen the nature of the good that it is beautiful, and of the bad that it is ugly, and the nature of him who does wrong, that it is akin to me, not only of the same blood or seed, but that it participates in the same intelligence and the same portion of the divinity. I can neither be injured by any of them, for no one can fix on me what is ugly, nor can I be angry with my kinsman, nor hate him. For we are made for co-operation, like feet, like hands, like eyelids, like the rows of the upper and lower teeth. To act against one another then is contrary to nature; and it is acting against one another to be vexed and to turn away. . . .

This you must always bear in mind, what is the nature of the whole, and what is my nature, and how this is related to that, and what kind of a part it is of what kind of a whole; and that there is no one who hinders thee from always doing and saying the things which are according to the nature of which thou are a part.

We do violence to ourselves, first of all, when we become an abscess and, as it were, a tumor on the universe. For to be vexed at anything which happens is a separation of ourselves from nature, in some part of which the natures of all other things are contained. In the next place, we do violence to ourselves when we turn anyone away from or even move closer with the intention of injuring, such as do they who are angry. In the third place, we do violence to ourselves when we are overpowered by pleasure or by pain. Fourthly, when

From *The Meditations of Marcus Aurelius Antoninus,* trans. George Long (New York: C. P. Putnam's Sons, 1862). With emendations by Daniel Kolak.

we play a part, and do or say anything insincerely and untruly. Fifthly, when we allow any act of our own and any movement to be without an aim, and do anything thoughtlessly and without considering what it is, it being right that even the smallest things be done with reference to an end; and the end of rational animals is to follow the reason and the law of the most ancient city and polity.

Of human life the time is a point, and the substance is in a flux, and the perception dull, and the composition of the whole body subject to putrefaction, and the mind a whirl, and fortune hard to divine, and fame a thing devoid of judgment. And, to say all in a word, everything which belongs to the body is a stream, and what belongs to the mind is a dream and vapour, and life is a warfare and a stranger's sojourn, and after-fame is oblivion. What then is that which is able to conduct us? One thing and only one, philosophy. But this consists in keeping the daemon within you free from violence and unharmed, superior to pains and pleasures, doing nothing without a purpose, nor yet falsely and with hypocrisy, not feeling the need of another person's doing or not doing anything; and besides, accepting all that happens, and all that it allotted, as coming from thence, wherever it is, from whence you yourself came; and, finally, waiting for death with a cheerful mind, as being nothing else than a dissolution of the elements of which every living being is compounded. But if there is no harm to the elements themselves in each continually changing into another, why should you have any apprehension about the change and dissolution of all the elements? For it is according to nature, and nothing is evil which is according to nature.

If our intellectual part is common, the reason also, in respect of which we are rational beings, is common: if this is so, common also is the reason which commands us what to do, and what not to do; if this is so, there is a common law also; if this is so, we are fellow-citizens; if this is so, we are members of some political community; if this is so, the world is in a manner a state. For of what other common political community will anyone say that the whole human race are members? And from thence, from this common political community comes also our very intellectual faculty and reasoning faculty and our capacity for law; or whence do they come? For as my earthly part is a portion given to me from certain earth, and that which is watery from another element, and that which is hot and fiery from some peculiar source (for nothing comes out of that which is nothing, as nothing also returns to non-existence), so also the intellectual part comes from some source.

Everything harmonizes with me, which is harmonious to you, O Universe. Nothing for me is too early nor too late, which is in due time for you. Everything is fruit to me which your seasons bring, O Nature: from you are all things, in you are all things, to you all things return.

Do not despise death, but be well content with it, since this too is one of those things which nature wills. For such as it is to be young and to grow old, and to increase and to reach maturity, and to have teeth and beard and grey hairs, and to beget, and to be pregnant and to bring forth, and all the other natural operations which the seasons of thy life bring, such also is dissolution. This, then, is consistent with the character of a reflecting person, to be neither careless nor impatient nor contemptuous with respect to death, but to wait for it as one of the operations of nature.

SEXTUS EMPIRICUS

175–225

The so-called Pyrrhonian skeptics are named after Pyrrhon of Elis (367–275 B.C.E.), according to whom it is absolutely impossible to attain knowledge about anything. He argued that we should, at best, suspend judgment about whether any statement is true or false. This includes the statement "It is absolutely impossible to attain knowledge about anything." Such a suspension of belief, according to Pyrrhon, leads not to insecurity and anxiety but rather to a tranquil, liberating state of indifference about the world.

Much like the early Sophists and their successor Socrates, who in the *Apology* declares, "All that I know is that I know nothing," the Pyrrhonian skeptics claimed that before you should accept anything as true, you must subject it to careful, rigorous scrutiny, seeking proof based on clear and undoubtable evidence. Such strict adherence to absolute certainty as a necessary condition for knowledge led the Pyrrhonian skeptics to extremely negative views about the possibility of absolute knowledge.

As a philosophical method, the Pyrrhonian movement grew out of the form of skepticism that had developed in Plato's Academy under its leaders Arcesilas (315–241 B.C.E.) and Carneades (213–219 B.C.E.), who presented a series of devastating arguments designed to show why nothing can be known except that nothing can be known; one ought therefore to live only by probabilities—a principle the Pyrrhonists regarded as too dogmatic, arguing that even the previous skeptical position that "nothing can be known" itself cannot be known. The Pyrrhonians were thus led to suspend judgment about everything, never affirming or denying anything. Things appear a certain way to the Pyrrhonian skeptic, who accepts this at face value without knowing whether the appearances are as they seem. The Pyrrhonian suspends judgment about everything that is not immediately evident and lives by following the laws and customs of society, with peace of mind that comes from not having ever to judge anything—much in the same manner as Socrates did.

None of the writings of the Pyrhonnian skeptics have survived, except the work of Sextus Empiricus. Trained not as a philosopher but as a medical doctor and teacher, he became the last leader of the Pyrrhonian movement. His written works are viewed by most historians as copies of lectures consisting of arguments worked out by previous skeptics. *Against the Mathematicians* and *Against the Dogmatists* contain detailed arguments against each area of knowledge: the liberal arts (grammar, rhetoric, geometry, arithmetic, astronomy, and music), and what then were the three branches of philosophy—logic, physics, and ethics. Ironically, these writings are two of our most important sources of knowledge about the early history of astronomy, geometry, grammar, and the prevailing Stoic theology of the time.

Our selection is from Sextus Empiricus's *Outlines of Pyrrhonism*. A general summary of the various Pyrrhonian arguments, it is organized into a specific and precise philosophical method. Just as doctors use varying remedies of different strengths to cure the sick, depending on the severity of their illness, so the skeptical philosopher must use arguments of appropriate strength to cure the ills of dogmatic belief. The more entrenched you are in your beliefs, the stronger the skeptical argument should be applied to you until you see that you don't really know what you think you know. He thus distinguishes the Pyrrhonian position both from the dogmatists, such as Aristotle and Epicurus who think they have discovered the truth, and from those who think truth cannot be found. The purpose of his skeptical arguments is to cure people of both types of dogmatism—the dogmatism of those who believe they have attained knowledge and the dogmatism of those who believe that knowledge cannot be attained. The philosophically healthy position is never to draw final conclusions; the healthy philosopher must always keep seeking.

OUTLINES OF PYRRHONISM

CHAPTER IV
What skepticism is

Skepticism is an ability, or mental attitude, which opposes appearances to judgments in any way whatsoever, with the result that, owing to the balance of the objects and reasons thus opposed, we are brought firstly to a state of mental suspense and next to a state of "unperturbedness" or quietude. Now we call it an "ability" not in any subtle sense, but simply in respect of its "being able." By "appearances" we now mean the objects of sense-perception, whence we contrast them with the objects of thought or "judgments." . . .

The originating cause of skepticism is, we say, the hope of attaining quietude. Men of talent, who were perturbed by the contradictions in things and in doubts as to which of the alternatives they ought to accept, were led on to inquire what is true in things and what false, hoping by the settlement of this question to attain quietude. The main basic principle of the skeptic system is that of opposing to every proposition an equal proposition; for we believe that as a consequence of this we end by ceasing to dogmatize.

When we say that the skeptic refrains from dogmatizing we do not use the term "dogma," as some do, in the broader sense of "approval of a thing" (for the skeptic gives assent to the feelings which are the necessary results of sense-impressions, and he would not, for

From Sextus Empiricus, *Outlines of Pyrrhonism*, trans. R. G. Bury.

example, say when feeling hot or cold "I believe that I am not hot or cold"); but we say that "he does not dogmatize" using "dogma" in the sense, which some give it, of "assent to one of the non-evident objects of scientific inquiry"; for the Pyrrhonein philosopher assents to nothing that is non-evident. Moreover, even in the act of enunciating the skeptic formulae concerning things non-evident—such as the formula "No more (one thing than another)," or the formula "I determine nothing," or any of the others which we shall presently mention,—he does not dogmatize. For whereas the dogmatizer posits the things about which he is said to be dogmatizing as really existent, the skeptic does not posit these formulae in any absolute sense; for he conceives that, just as the formula "All things are false" asserts the falsity of itself as well as of everything else, as does the formula "Nothing is true," so also the formula "No more" asserts that itself, like all the rest, is "No more (this than that)," and thus cancels itself along with the rest. And of the other formulae we say the same. If then, while the dogmatizer posits the matter of his dogma as substantial truth, the skeptic enunciates his formulae so that they are virtually canceled by themselves, he should not be said to dogmatize in his enunciation of them. And, most important of all, in his enunciation of these formulae he states what appears to himself and announces his own impression in an undogmatic way, without making any positive assertion regarding the external realities. . . .

That we adhere to appearances is plain from what we say about the Criterion of the Skeptic School. The word "Criterion" is used in two senses: in the one it means "the standard regulating belief in reality or unreality," (and this we shall discuss in our refutation); in the other it denotes the standard of action by conforming to which in the conduct of life we perform some actions and abstain from others; and it is of the latter that we are now speaking. The criterion, then, of the skeptic school is, we say, the appearance, giving this name to what is virtually the sense-presentation. For since this lies in feeling and involuntary affection, it is not open to question. Consequently, no one, I suppose, disputes that the underlying object has this or that appearances; the point in dispute is whether the object is in reality such as it appears to be.

Adhering, then, to appearances we live in accordance with the normal rules of life, undogmatically, seeing that we cannot remain wholly inactive. And it would seem that this regulation of life is fourfold, and that one part of it lies in the guidance of nature, another in the constraint of the passions, another in the instruction of the arts. Nature's guidance is that by which we are naturally capable of sensation and thought; constraint of the passions is that whereby hunger drives us to food and thirst to drink; tradition of customs and laws, that whereby we regard piety in the conduct of life as good, but impiety as evil; instruction of the arts, that whereby we are not inactive in such arts as we adopt. But we make all these statements undogmatically.

Our next subject will be the end of the skeptic system. Now an "end" is "that for which all actions or reasonings are undertaken, while it exists for the sake of none"; or, otherwise, "the ultimate object of appetency." We assert still that the skeptic's end is quietude in respect of matters of opinion and moderate feeling in respect of things unavoidable. For the skeptic, having set out to philosophize with the object of passing judgment on the sense-impressions and ascertaining which of them are true and which false, so as to attain quietude thereby, found himself involved in contradictions of equal weight, and being unable to decide between them suspended judgment; and as he was thus in suspense there followed, as it happened, the state of quietude in respect of matters of opinion. For the man who opines that anything is by nature good or bad is for ever being disquieted: when he is without the things which he deems good he believes himself to be tormented by things naturally bad and he pursues after the things which are, as he thinks, good; which when he has obtained he keeps falling into still more perturbations because of his irrational and immoderate elation, and in his dread of a change of fortune he uses every endeavour to avoid losing the things which he deems good. On the other hand, the man who determines nothing as to what is naturally good or bad neither shuns nor pursues anything eagerly; and, in consequence, he is unperturbed.

The skeptic, in fact, had the same experience which is said to have befallen the painter Apelles. Once, they say, when he was painting a horse and wished to represent in the painting the horse's foam, he was so unsuccessful that he gave up the attempt and flung at the picture the sponge on which he used to wipe the paints off his brush, and the mark of the sponge produced the effects of the horse's foam. So, too, the skeptics were in hopes of gaining quietude by means of a decision regarding the disparity of the objects of sense and thought, and being unable to effect this they suspended judgment; and they found that quietude, as if by chance, followed upon their suspense, even as a shadow follows its substance. We do not, however, suppose that the skeptic is wholly untroubled; but we say that he is troubled by things unavoidable; for we grant that he is old at times and thirsty, and suffers various affections of that kind. But even in these cases, whereas ordinary people are afflicted by two circumstances—namely, by the affections themselves and in no less degree, by the belief that these conditions are evil by nature—the skeptic, by his rejection of the added belief in the natural badness of all these conditions, escapes here too with less discomfort. Hence we say that, in regard to matters of opinion the skeptics end is quietude, in regard to things unavoidable it is "moderate affection." But some notable skeptics have added the further definition "suspension of judgment in investigations."

Now that we have been saying that tranquillity follows on the suspension of judgment, it will be our next task to explain how we arrive at this suspension. Speaking generally, one may say that it is the result of setting things in opposition. We oppose either appearances to appearances or objects of thought to objects of thought or *alternando.* For instance, we oppose appearances to appearances when we say "The same tower appears round from a distance, but square from close at hand"; and thoughts to thoughts, when in answer to him who argues the existence of providence from the order of the heavenly bodies we oppose the fact that often the good fare ill and the bad fare well, and draw from this the inference that providence does not exist. And thoughts we oppose to appearances, as when Anaxagoras countered the notion that snow is white with the argument, "Snow is frozen water, and water is black; therefore snow also is black." With a different idea we oppose things present sometimes to things present, as in the foregoing examples, and sometimes to things past or future, as, for instance, when someone propounds to us a theory which we are unable to refute, we say to him in reply, "Just as, before the birth of the founder of the school to which you belong, the theory it holds was not as yet apparent as a sound theory, although it was really in existence, so likewise it is possible that the opposite theory to that which you now propound is already really existent, though not yet apparent to us, so that we ought not as yet to yield assent to this theory which at the moment seems to be valid."

PLOTINUS

205–270

Born and raised in Egypt, Plotinus studied philosophy in Alexandria. He joined the Roman expedition in 244 against the Persians with the idea that he could learn about Eastern philosophies. After settling in Rome, he single-handedly tried to revive the classical Hellenic philosophy as an antidote to the ruin and misery of the crumbling world around him. Because it was based on the views of Plato, the philosophical movement that Plotinus founded came to be called Neoplatonism. Under the auspices of the emperor, Plotinus became extremely influential throughout the Roman Empire, and for a time it seemed as if his mission would succeed. At one point the emperor agreed to let him build a second city near Rome, based on Plato's *Republic,* to be called Platonopolis. It would have been the center for the new philosophical revival. But then, suddenly, for reasons unknown, the emperor withdrew the offer.

Plotinus's works stand at the crossroads between the Greek tradition spanning the seven centuries from Thales to Sextus Empiricus and the beginning of Christendom. Although he did not begin writing until he was forty-nine, his works, edited posthumously by his student Porphyry into fifty-four books called the *Enneads,* covered every major branch of philosophy except politics. In them, under the influence of all the ancient thinkers, especially Parmenides and Pythagoras, Plotinus tried to resurrect Plato's philosophy. He used Plato's ideas to attack what he saw as the materialism of the Stoics and atomists, as well as to argue against the whole of Epicurean philosophy. He thought that, for all their practical wisdom, the Epicureans were incapable of dealing with the base instincts driving the superstitious beliefs that suddenly seemed to be making philosophy irrelevant.

Catholic theology after the end of the Roman Empire and throughout the subsequent Christian era of the Middle Ages was importantly influenced by the works of Plotinus, especially by his distinction among three levels of reality, which became the avatar for Christian views of the Holy Trinity. The Parmenidean One, in Plotinus's view, is equated not only with "God" but also with Plato's *good.* Although the One precedes the good, always the One is essentially undefinable and therefore no predicates can be attributed to it. All we can say about this highest level of reality is that "it is."

At the second level, below the One, is its image, *nous,* variously translated as mind, spirit, or intellectual principle. *Nous* exists because the One, in its quest to understand itself, attains the power of seeing, or vision; in a sense, *nous* is the "light" by which the One sees itself. Finally, the third and lowest level of reality is the soul, which in Plotinus's view is the creator of all living things, including the sun, moon, and stars, and the visible world itself. The three metaphysical levels—the One, the *nous,* and the soul—correspond to three distinct levels of consciousness: discursive thought, intuitive thought, and mystical awareness—the soul, the *nous,* and the One, respectively.

In the following passages, Plotinus raises for the first time in a formal manner the question of why the mind is not aware of itself. He asks: why is the soul oblivious to itself? In saying that without the soul there is no sun, he is of course relying on the idealist world view that began with Plato and will find its culmination among the modern British philosophers in Berkeley; among the Germans in Hegel, Fichte, and Schelling; and among the nineteenth-century American idealists, such as Royce.

ENNEADS

II

It has appeared to us that the nature of *the good* is simple and the first; for every thing which is not the first is not simple; and since it has nothing in itself, but is one alone, and the nature of what is called *the one,* is the same with *the good;* for it is not first something else, and afterwards one,—not is *the good* something else, and afterwards *the good;* this being the case, when we say *the one,* and when we say *the good,* it is necessary to think that we speak of one and the same nature; not predicating any thing of it, but manifesting it to ourselves as much as possible. It is also called *the first,* because it is most simple; and sufficient to itself, because it does not consist of many things. For if it did, it would be suspended from the things of which it consists. It likewise is not in any thing else, because every thing which is in another, is also derived from another. If, therefore, it is neither from, not in another, and has not any composition in its nature, it is necessary that there should not be any thing superior to it. Hence, it is not necessary to proceed to other principles, but having admitted this, and next to this intellect which is primarily intellect, we ought afterwards to place souls as the next in rank. For this is the order according to nature, neither to admit more, nor fewer than these in the intelligible. For those who admit fewer than these, must either say that soul and intellect are the same, or that intellect and that which is first are the same. It has, however, been frequently demonstrated by us, that these are different from each other.

It remains, therefore, that we should consider at present, if there are more than these three, what the natures are which exist besides these. For since the principle of all things subsists in the way we have shown, it is not possible for any one to find a more simple and elevated principle. For they will not say that there is one principle in capacity, but another in energy; since it is ridiculous in things which are in energy, and immaterial, to make many

From *Select Works of Plotinus,* trans. T. Taylor (London: George Bell & Sons, 1895). With emendations by Daniel Kolak.

natures by dividing into capacity and energy. But neither in the natures posterior to these, is it to be supposed that there is a certain intellect established in quiet, but that another is as it were moved. For what is the quiet of intellect, what the motion and language of it? And what will be the leisure of one intellect, and the work of the other? For intellect always possesses an invariable sameness of subsistence, being constituted in a stable energy. But motion directed to, and subsisting about it, is now the employment of soul. Reason also proceeding from intellect into soul, causes soul to be intellectual, and does not produce a certain other nature between intellect and soul. Moreover, neither, is it necessary to make many intellects on this account, that one of them perceives intellectually, but another sees that it sees intellectually. For if in these, to perceive intellectually is one thing, but another to perceive that it sees intellectually, yet there must be one intuitive perception in these which is not insensible of its own energies. For it would be ridiculous to form any other conception than this of true intellect. But the intellect will be entirely the same, which perceives intellectually, and which sees that it sees intellectually. For if this were not the case, the one would be alone intelligent but the other would perceive that it was intelligent, and the former would be different from the latter. If, however, they say that these two differ from each other in conceptions, in the first place indeed, they will be deprived of many hypostases; and in the next place it is necessary to consider, whether any conception of ours can admit the subsistence of an intellect which is alone intelligent, and which does not perceive that it sees intellectually. For when a thing of this kind happens to us who are always attentive to impulses and cogitations, if we are moderately worthy, it becomes the cause to us of folly.

When, therefore, that which is truly intellect intellectually perceives itself in its intellections, and the intelligible of it is not externally posited, but intellect itself is also the intelligible, it necessarily follows that in intellectual perception it possesses itself, and sees itself. But seeing itself, it perceives itself not to be void of intelligence, but intelligent. So that in primarily energizing intellectually, it will also have a perception that it sees intellectually, both being as one; nor can there be any conception of duplicity there. If, likewise, always perceiving intellectually it is that which it is, what place can there be for the conception which separates intellectual perception from the perceiving that it sees intellectually? If, however, some one should introduce a third conception to the second, which asserts that it perceives that it sees intellectually, and should say that it understands (*i.e.,* sees intellectually), that what understands understands, the absurdity is still more apparent. And why may not assertions of this kind be made to infinity? The reason, likewise, proceeding from intellect which may be adduced, and from which afterwards another reason is generated in the soul, so as to become a medium between intellect and soul, deprives the soul of intellectual perception, if it does not derive this reason from intellect, but from some other intermediate nature. Hence it would possess an image of reason, but not reason itself. And in short, it would not have a knowledge of intellect, nor would it be intelligent.

Hence it must not be admitted that there are more principles than these, nor must these superfluous conceptions be adopted, which have no place there; but it must be said that there is one intellect always subsisting with invariable sameness, and in every respect without fluctuation, which imitates as much as possible its father; and with respect to our soul, that one part of it always abides on high, that another part of it is conversant with sensibles, and that another has a subsistence in the middle of these. For as there is one nature in many powers, at one time the whole soul tends upward in conjunction with the most excellent part, of itself, and of the universe, but at another time, the worst part being drawn down, draws together with itself the middle part. For it is not lawful that the whole of it should be drawn downward. This passion also happens to the soul, because it did not abide in that which is most beautiful, where the soul which does not rank as a part abiding, and of which we are not a part, imparts to the whole body of the universe, as much as it is able to receive from it. At the same time also, this soul remains free from all solicitude, not governing the world by the discursive energy of reason, nor correcting any thing but by the vision of that which is prior to itself, adorning the universe with an admirable power. For the more it looks to itself, the more beautiful and powerful it becomes, and possessing these excellencies from the intelligible world, it imparts them to that which is posterior to itself, and as it is always illuminated, it always illuminates.

Being therefore always illuminated, and continually possessing light, it imparts it to the natures that are in a consequent order. And these are always contained and irrigated by this light, and enjoy life through it, as far as they are able. Just as if a fire being placed in a certain middle, whatever is capable of receiving heat, should be heated by it as much as possible; though the fire is limited by measure. But when the powers not being measured, are never-failing, how is it possible that they should have an existence, and yet nothing should participate of them? It is, however, necessary that every thing should impart itself to something else; or *the good* will not be good, nor intellect be intellect, nor soul be soul; unless after that which lives primarily, there is also that which has a secondary life, as long as that exists which is primarily vital. Hence it is necessary that all things should be perpetually linked to each other, and should be generated by other things, because they depend on others for their subsistence. Things therefore that are said to be generated, were not generated at a certain time, but were and will be rising into existence; nor will they be corrupted, those things excepted which they contain, into which they may be resolved. But that which has nothing into which it can be resolved, will not be corrupted. If, however, some one should say that things which are in generation may be resolved into matter, we reply, and why may not matter also be dissolved? But if it is said that matter may be dissolved, we ask what necessity there was that it should be generated? If they say it was necessary, and therefore it was generated, we reply, and it is also now necessary. But if it should be left alone, divine natures would not be every where, but would be circumscribed in a certain place, as if surrounded with a wall. If, however, this is impossible, matter is perpetually illuminated . . .

III

Let us, however, again return in the first place, to the subject matter, and afterwards to the things which are said to be in matter, from which it will be known that matter itself has no existence, and that it is impassive. It is therefore incorporeal, since body is a later production, and is a composite, and matter in conjunction with another thing produces body. Thus it is included among the incorporeal, because both being and matter are different from bodies. Since, however, matter is neither soul nor intellect, nor life, nor form, nor reason, nor bound; for it is infinite; nor power; for what can it effect; but falls off from all these, neither can it rightly receive the title of being. But it may deservedly be called non-being. Yet it is not non-being in the same manner as motion is, or permanency; but it is truly non-being, the image and phantasm of mass, and the desire of subsistence. And it stands, indeed, but not in that which is permanent, is of itself invisible, and flies from him who wishes to behold it. When, likewise, some one does not see it, then it is present; but is not perceived by him who strives intently to behold it. Add too, that contraries are always apparent in it; the small and the great, the less and the more, the deficient and the exceeding, being an image neither able to remain, nor yet to fly away. For it has not even power to effect this, as receiving no strength from intellect, but subsisting in the defect of all being. Hence its every utterance is a lie; so that if it should appear to be great, it is small; if more, it is less; and the being which we meet with in the imagination of it, is non-being, and as it were a flying mockery. Hence, also, the things which appear to be ingenerated in it, are tricks, and images in an image, just as in a mirror, where a thing which is situated in one place appears to be in another. It likewise seems to be full and to be all things, and yet has nothing. But the things which enter into and depart from matter, are imitations and images of beings, flowing about a formless resemblance; and on account of its formless nature are seen within it. They also appear, indeed, to effect something in it, but effect nothing; for they are vain and debile, and have no resisting power. And since matter, likewise, is void of resistance, they pervade without dividing it, like images in water, or as if some one should send as it were forms into the void. For again, if the things which are beheld in matter were such as those from which they proceeded into it, perhaps a certain power of these might be ascribed to material forms, and matter might be supposed to suffer by them. But now, since the things which are represented are of one kind, and those that are beheld in matter of another, from these also we may learn that the passion of matter is false; that which is seen in it being false, and in no respect possessing any similitude to its maker. Hence, being feeble and false, projected into a falsity, as in a dream, or in water, or a mirror, it necessarily permits matter to be impassive, though in the things which have been just mentioned, there is a similitude between the representations in them, and the originals of which they are the resemblances.

V

What is the reason that souls become oblivious of divinity, being ignorant both of themselves and him, though their allotment is from thence, and they in short partake of God? The principle therefore of evil to them is audacity, generation, the first difference, and the wish to exercise an unrestrained freedom of the will. [The five genera of being are, essence, sameness, *difference,* motion and permanency. This *difference,* therefore, which ranks as the first, and which is the source of all diversity, causes souls by predominating in them to be forgetful of deity, and themselves.] When, therefore, souls began to be delighted with this unbounded liberty, abundantly employing the power of being moved from themselves, they ran in a direction contrary to their origin, and thus becoming most distant from their source, they were at length ignorant that they were thence derived. Just as children who are immediately torn from their parents, and have for a long time been nurtured at a great distance from them, become ignorant both of themselves and their parents. Hence, souls neither seeing their father, nor themselves, despise themselves through ignorance of their race, but honour other things, and admiring every thing rather than themselves, being vehemently astonished about, and adhering to sensible natures, they as much as possible hurl themselves and thus despise the beings from which they have become estranged. Hence, the honour which they play to sensible objects, and the contempt of themselves, happen to be the causes of their complete ignorance. For at the same time they pursue and admire something else, and acknowledge themselves to be inferior to that which they admire and pursue. But the soul admitting that it is something subordinate to ephemeral things and apprehending that it is the most ignoble and mortal of every thing which it honours, neither believes in the nature nor power of God. . . .

Every soul, therefore, ought to consider in the first place, that soul produced all animals, and inspired them with life; viz. those animals which the earth and sea nourish, those which live in the air, and the divine stars contained in the heavens. Soul also made the sun; soul made and adorned this mighty heaven. Soul, too, circumvolves it in an orderly course, being of a nature different from the things which it adorns, which it moves, and causes to live, and is necessarily more honourable than these. For these are corrupted when soul deserts them, and generated when it supplies them with life. But soul always exists, because it never deserts itself. . . .

Hence, as the soul is so honourable and divine a thing, now confiding in a cause of this kind, ascend with it to divinity. For you will not be very distant from him; nor are the intermediate natures many. In this, therefore, which is divine, receive that part which is more divine, viz. the vicinity of the soul to that which is supernal, to which the soul is posterior, and from which it proceeds. For though it is so great a thing as we have demonstrated it to be, yet it is a certain image of intellect. And, just as external discourse is an image of the discursive energy within the soul, after the same manner, soul, and the whole of its energy, are the discourse of intellect, and a life which it emits in order to the hypostasis of another thing; just as in fire, the inherent heat of it is one thing, and the heat which it imparts another. It is necessary, however, to assume there, not a life flowing forth, but partly abiding in intellect, and partly giving subsistence to another life. Hence, since soul is derived from intellect, it is intellectual, and the intellect of soul is conversant with discursive energies. And again, the perfection of soul is from intellect, as from a father that nourishes it, who generated soul, as with reference to himself, not perfect. This hypostasis, therefore, is from intellect, and is also reason in energy when it perceives intellect. For when it looks to intellect, it possesses internally, and appropriately, the things which it understands, and the energies which it performs. And it is necessary to call those energies alone the energies of the soul, which are intellectual and dwell with it. But its subordinate energies have an external source, and are the passions of a soul of this kind. Intellect, therefore, causes the soul to be more divine, both because it is the father of it, and because it is present with it. For there is nothing between them, except the difference of one with reference to the other, soul being successive to, and the recipient of intellect; but intellect subsisting as form. The matter also of intellect is beautiful, since it has the form of intellect, and is simple. The great excellence, however, of intellect, is manifest from this, that though soul is such as we have described it to be, yet it is surpassed by intellect. . . . And it is itself truly eternity, which time running round soul imitates, omitting some things, but applying itself to others. For other and again other things are about soul; since at one time the form of Socrates, and at another the form of horse present themselves to its view; and always one certain thing among the number of beings. But intellect has all things. Hence, it possesses in the same all things established in the same. It likewise alone *is,* and *is* always, but is never *future;* for when the future arrives, it then also *is;* nor is it the *past.* For nothing there has passed away, but all things abide in the present *now;* since they are things of such a kind, as to be satisfied with themselves thus subsisting. But each of them is intellect and being. And the whole is every intellect, and every being. Intellect, therefore, derives its subsistence as intellect, from the intellection of being. But being subsists as being, through becoming the object of intellectual perception to intellect, and through imparting to it, intellection and existence. There is, however, another cause of intellection, which is also the cause of existence to being. Of both therefore at once, there is another cause. For both these are con-subsistent, and never desert each other. But being two, this one thing is at once intellect; and is being, intellective, and intelligible. It is intellect, indeed, so far as it is intellective; but being, so far as it is intelligible. For intellectual perception could not subsist, difference and sameness not existing. Intellect, therefore, being, difference and sameness, are the first of things. But it is likewise necessary to assume together with these, motion and permanency. And motion, indeed, is necessary if being intellectually perceives; but permanency in order that it may remain the same; and difference, in order that it may be intellective and intelligible. For if you take away difference from it, then becoming one it will be perfectly silent. It is necessary, however, that intellective natures should be different from each other; and that they should also be the same with each other, since they subsist in the same thing, and there is something common in all of them. Diversity, likewise, is *otherness.* But these becoming many produce number and quantity. And the peculiarity of each of these produces quality, from all which, as principles, other things proceed.

This exuberant God, therefore, exists in the soul which is here, being conjoined to him by things of this kind, unless it wishes to depart from him. Approaching therefore to, and as it were becoming one with him, it enquires as follows: Who is he that, being simple and prior to a multitude of this kind, generated this God? Who is the cause of his existence, and of his being exuberant, and by whom number was produced? For number is not the first of things; since *the one* is prior to the duad. But the duad is the second thing, and being generated by *the one,* is defined by it. The duad, however, is of itself indefinite. But when it is defined, it is now number. And it is number as essence. Soul also is number. For neither corporeal masses nor magnitudes are the first of things. For these gross substances which sense fancies to be beings, are things of a posterior nature. Nor is the moisture which is in seeds honourable, but that contained in them, which is not visible. But this is number and reason. What are said therefore to be number and the duad in the intelligible world, are reasons and intellect. But the duad indeed is indefinite, when it is assumed as analogous to a subject. Number, however, which proceeds from it and *the one,* is each form of things; intellect being as it were formed by the species of things which are generated in it. But it is formed in one manner from *the one,* and in another from itself, in the same manner as sight which is in energy. For intelligence is sight perceiving, both being one.

How, therefore, does intelligence see; what does it see; and, in short, how does it subsist; and how is it generated from *the one,* so that it may see? For now indeed the mind perceives the necessity of the existence of these things. It desires, however, to understand this which is so much spoken of by the wise men of antiquity, viz. how from *the one* being such as we have said it is, each thing has its subsistence, whether it be multitude, or the duad, or number; and why *the one* did not abide in itself, but so great a multitude flowed from it, as is seen to have an existence, and which we think should be referred to *the one.* We must say, therefore, as follows, *invoking God himself, not with external speech, but with the soul itself, extending ourselves in prayer to him, since we shall then be able to pray to him properly, when we approach by ourselves alone to the alone.* It is necessary, therefore, that the beholder of him, being in himself as if in the interior part of a temple, and quietly abiding in an eminence beyond all things, should survey the statues as it were which are established outwardly, or rather that statue which first shines forth to the view, and after the following manner behold that which is naturally adapted to be beheld. With respect to every thing that is moved, it is necessary there should be something to which it is moved. For if there is nothing of this kind, we should not admit that it is moved. But if any thing is generated posterior to that to which the moveable nature tends, it is necessary that it should always be generated in consequence of that prior cause being converted to itself. Let, however, the generation which is in time be now removed form us who are discoursing about eternal beings. And if in the course of the discussion we attribute generation to things which exist eternally, let it be considered as indicative of cause and order. Hence, that which is from thence generated, must be said to be generated, the cause not being moved. For if something was generated in consequence of that cause being moved, the thing generated after the motion would be the third, and not the second from the cause. It is necessary, therefore, the cause being immoveable, that if any thing secondary subsists after it, this second nature should be produced, without the cause either verging to it, or consulting, or in short being moved. How, therefore, and what is it necessary to conceive about that abiding cause? We must conceive a surrounding splendour, proceeding indeed from this cause, but from it in a permanent state, like a light from the sun shining, and as it were running round it, and being generated from it, the cause itself always abiding in the same immoveable condition. All beings, likewise, as long as they remain, necessarily produce from their own essence, about themselves, and externally from the power which is present with them, a nature whose hypostasis is suspended from them, and which is as it were an image of the archetype from which it proceeded. Thus fire emits from itself indeed heat, and snow not only retains cold within itself but imparts it to other things. This, however, such things as are fragrant especially testify. For as long as they exist, something proceeds from them, of which whatever is near them partakes. All such things, likewise, as are now perfect generate; but that which is always perfect, always generates, and that which it produces is perpetual. It also generates something less than itself. What, therefore, is it requisite to say of that which is most perfect? Shall we say that nothing proceeds from it; or rather that the greatest things posterior to it are its progeny? But the greatest thing posterior to it, and the second, is intellect. For intellect sees it, and is in want of it alone. But this most perfect nature is not in want of intellect. It is also necessary that the thing generated from that which is better than intellect, should be intellect. And intellect is superior to all things after the first, because other things are posterior to it. Thus, for instance, soul is the reason of intellect, and a certain energy of it, just as intellect of that first God. But the reason of soul is indeed obscure. For as it is the image of intellect, on this account it is necessary that it should look to intellect. After the same manner also, it is necessary that intellect should look to the highest God, in order that it may be intellect. It sees him, however, not separated from him, but because it is after him, and there is nothing between; as neither is there any thing between soul and intellect. But every thing desires its generator. This also it loves, and especially when that which is generated and the generator are alone. When, however, that which generates is the most excellent of things, the thing begotten is necessarily present with it in such a manner, as to be separated by *otherness* alone.

But we say that intellect is the image of this most excellent nature. For it is necessary to speak more clearly. In the first place, indeed, it is necessary that intellect should in a certain respect be generated, and preserve much of its generator; and also that it should have such a similitude to it, as light has to the sun. Its generator, however, is not intellect. How therefore did he generate intellect? May we not say, because intellect, by conversion, looks to him? But the vision itself is intellect. For that which apprehends another thing, is either sense or intellect. And sense indeed may be compared to a line, but the other knowing powers of the soul to a circle. A circle, however, of this kind is as it were partible. But this is not the case with intellect. Or may we not say that this also is one? But the one here is the power of all things. Hence intelligence surveys those things of which it is the power, divided as it were from the power; for otherwise it would not be intellect. For intellect now possesses from itself a co-sensation as it were of the great extent of its power; in which power, its essence, consists. Intellect, therefore, through itself defines its own being, by a power derived from the first God, and perceives that essence is as it were one of the parts of and from him, and that it is corroborated by him, and perfected by and from him into essence. It sees, however, itself derived as something which is as it were partible from that which is impartible; and not only itself, but life, and intellection, and all things, because the first God is nothing of all things. For on this account all things are from him, because he is not detained by a certain form. For he is one alone. And intellect, indeed, in the order of beings is all things. But he on this account is none of the things which are in intellect; and all things which have a subsistence among beings are derived from him. Hence also these are essences. For they are now definite, and each possesses as it were a form. Being, however, ought not to be surveyed in that which is as it were indefinite, but as fixed by bound and permanency. But permanency in intelligibles is circumscription and form, in which also they receive their hypostasis. This intellect, therefore, which deserves the appellation of the most pure intellect, and which is of the genus of intelligibles, originates from no other source than the first principle. And being now generated, it generates together with itself beings, all the beauty of ideas, and all the intelligible Gods. . . .

It has been shown, however, as far as it is possible to demonstrate about things of this kind, that it is requisite to think that beyond being there is *the one,* such as reason wishes to unfold; that next to this, being and intellect subsist; and that, in the third place, follows the nature of soul. But, as in the nature of things there are these three hypostases, so likewise it is proper to think, that the above mentioned three subsist with us. I do not mean to assert that they are to be found in sensibles; for they have a separate subsistence; but that they are external to sensibles, and external after the same manner in man also, as the three which we have been considering are external to all heaven. This, however, is such a man as Plato calls the inward man. Our soul, therefore, is likewise something divine, and of a nature different from sensibles, such as is the whole nature of soul. But the soul is perfect which possesses intellect. With respect to intellect, however, one kind is a reasoning intellect, but another imparts the power of reasoning. He, therefore, will not err who places in the intelligible order of things this reasoning intellect of the soul, which is not in want of any corporeal organ to the subsistence of its discursive energy, but which possesses the energy of itself in purity, in order that it may reason purely, in as great perfection as possible. For we must not inquire after a place where we may establish it, but it must be arranged external to all place. For thus that which is from itself, the external, and the immaterial subsist, when they are alone, and have nothing from a corporeal nature. On this account, also, Plato in the Timaeus says, "that the Demiurgus surrounded the body of the universe with soul," indicating that part of the mundane soul which abides in the intelligible. Concerning our soul, likewise, concealing his meaning, he says, in the Phaedrus, that it sometimes hides its head in the heavens, and sometimes elevates it beyond them. The exhortation, too, in the Phaedo, to separate the soul from the body, does not relate to a local separation, which is effected by nature, but insinuates that the soul should not verge to imaginations, and to an alienation from itself, by a tendency to body. He also indicates that we should elevate the remaining [*i.e.* the irrational] form of the soul, and lead it on high together with the superior part of it; and that the part which is established in the sensible region, and is alone the fabricator and plastic maker of body, should likewise be engaged in an employment of this kind.

Since, therefore, the soul reasons about things just and beautiful, and inquires by a reasoning process whether this thing is just, and that is beautiful, it is necessary there should be something stably just, from which the reasoning of the soul originates; or how could it reason? And if the soul at one time reasons about these things, but at another time not, it is necessary there should be an intellect in us, which does not reason about, but always possesses the just. It is likewise necessary that we should contain the principle and cause of intellect, and God; the latter of these not being divisible, but abiding, yet not in place, and again being surveyed in each of the multitude of things that are able to receive him. They receive him, however, as something different from themselves; just as the centre of a circle is in itself, but each of the lines in the circle has its summit terminating in the centre, and the several lines tend with their peculiarity to this. For by a thing of this kind which is in us, we also touch, associate with, and are suspended from deity. But we are established in it more or less according as we converge to it in a greater or less degree.

How, therefore, does it happen, since we possess things of such great dignity, that we do not apprehend them, but for the most part are sluggish with respect to such like energies? And there are some who do not energize about them at all. Intellect, indeed, and that which, prior to intellect, is always in itself, are always employed in their own energies. Soul, likewise, is thus that which is always moved. For not every thing which is in the soul is now sensible; but it arrives to us when it proceeds as far as to sense. When, however, each thing in us energizing, does not impart itself to the sensitive power, it does not yet proceed through the whole soul. Hence we have not yet any knowledge of the energy, because we exist in conjunction with the sensitive power, and are not a part of the soul, but the whole soul. And farther still, each of the psychical animals in us, always energizes essentially according to its peculiarity; but we then only recognize the energy, when there is a participation and apprehension of it. It is necessary, therefore, in order that there may be an apprehension of things which are thus present, that the animadversive power should be converted to the interior of the soul, and there fix its attention. Just as if some one waiting to hear a voice which is pleasing to him, should separate himself from other voices, and excite his hearing to the perception of the more excellent sound, when it approaches. Thus, also, here it is necessary to dismiss sensible auditions, except so far as is necessary, and to preserve the animadversive power of the soul pure, and prepared to hear supernal sounds.

IV

We must examine how soul enters the body. The mode in which the soul enters into the body is twofold. For one of these modes takes place, when the soul being in one body changes it for another, and from an aerial or fiery form becomes situated in a terrestrial body; which some do not call a transmigration, because that from which the insertion originates is immanifest. But the other mode is a transition from an incorporeal essence to any body whatever; which also will be the first communion of the soul with the body. It will be right, therefore, to consider respecting this communion, what the passion arising from this conjunction then is, when the soul being entirely pure from body, becomes surrounded with the nature of body. Let us, however, first consider how this is effected in the soul of the universe; for perhaps it is proper, or rather is necessary, to begin from hence. Notice that to explain clearly, we must use words such as "entry" and "transmigration," even though the soul of the universe is eternal, never did body exist without soul, never soul without body; we separate in order to understand. We may legitimately sunder, verbally and mentally, things that are in fact co-existent. For by this method we may analyze every composition. The truth then is as follows: Without body, the soul could not go forth, since there is not any other place, where it is naturally adapted to be. If, however, soul intends to go forth, it will generate for itself a place, so that it will generate body. The stability of soul, however, being as it were corroborated in permanency itself, and soul also resembling a brilliant light, a darkness was in the mean time generated in the very extremity of the light, which soul perceiving, gave form to it, since it was likewise the cause of its subsistence. For it was not lawful for any things proximate to soul, to be destitute of form. Hence, by this obscure nature which was generated by soul, that which is called obscure was received. The universe therefore, being generated like a certain beautiful and various edifice, is not sepa-rated from the soul, nor yet is mingled with it; but the whole of it is every where considered by its maker as deserving a providential attention. It is advantageous, therefore, both to its existence and its beauty, to participate as much as possible of its maker; and to the latter this participation is not injurious. For it governs, abiding on high. And the universe is animated after such a manner, that it cannot with so much propriety be said to have a soul of its own, as to have a soul presiding over it; being subdued by, and not subduing it, and being possessed, and not possessing. For it lies in soul which sustains it, and no part of it is without soul; being moistened with life, like a net in water. It is not, however, able to become that in which it lies; but the sea being now extended, the net is also co-extended with it, as far as it is able. For each of the parts is incapable of existing in any other situation than where each is placed. But soul is naturally so great, because it is without quantity. Hence every body is comprehended by one and the same thing. And wherever body is extended, there also soul is. Unless, however, body existed, the attention of soul would not be at all directed to magnitude. For it is of itself that which it is. For the world is so greatly extended, through soul being present with the whole of it. And the extension of the world is bounded, so far as in its progression it has soul for its saviour. The magnitude of the shadow, likewise, is as great as the reason which is suspended from soul. But the reason was of such a kind as to be able to produce as great a magnitude as the form of it wished might be produced. . . .

AUGUSTINE

354–430

Augustine was born at Thagaste, near Carthage in North Africa. He studied and then taught rhetoric in Carthage, Rome, and Milan. As a teenager he joined the Manichaean religion, a synthesis of Christianity and Zoroastrianism that had spread throughout the Roman Empire and rivaled the growing Christian religion. Its founder, Mani (Greek *Manes*, Latinized *Manichaeus*), converted to Christianity from Zoroastrianism, an Indo-Iranian movement based on the teachings of Zarathustra, an ancient figure from the sixth century B.C.E. According to Zarathustra, the human struggle between good and evil is a manifestation of a cosmic duel between the divine forces of light and the demonic forces of darkness. Individual human spirits must, according to Zarathustra, fight personal battles between light and darkness, truth and falsehood, moral right and wrong, in order to gain either the salvation of eternal bliss or eternal agony. Mani synthesized Zoroastrian ideas with Christianity, claiming that Christ was an incarnation of the same spirit as Buddha and Zarathustra, the original soul of the first man created by the "mother of light" to help the rest of humanity become a major force in combating the overpowering darkness.

Augustine finally rejected Manichaeanism when he came under the influence of the Skeptics, and for a brief time he turned to Skepticism. When he discovered Plotinus, however, he became a devout Neoplatonist, arguing on behalf of Plotinus's semireligious interpretation of Plato, which he embellished with Zoroastrian and Manichaean ideas about the human struggle between good and evil, sin and salvation. These ideas remained a central aspect of Augustine's thought even after his conversion to Christianity so that through his writings they became a central aspect of later Christian dogma. In 387, at age thirty-two, he formally converted to Christianity and returned to Africa, where he established many monasteries. He became a priest in 391 and in 396 was appointed bishop of Hippo, a city near Carthage.

Just as the history of philosophy contains variations on the themes of Plato and Aristotle, so the history of Christian thought consists in the variations on the themes of Augustine and Aquinas. Aquinas was primarily an Aristotelian and Augustine was primarily a Platonist, and thus the influence of Plato and Aristotle has remained central. In some ways, Augustine's philosophy is a return to the Socratic tradition in which metaphysics and epistemology are studied not for their own sake but as a way of enlightening the individual soul. The purpose of philosophy is salvation from suffering and the attainment of happiness, not just in this world but in the next world as well. Influenced by the Epicureans, Stoics, and Skeptics, as well as by Plotinus and the Neoplatonists, Augustine's philosophy became the foundation for subsequent Christianity. He gave a Christian reinterpretation to the Neoplatonic view that knowledge can be obtained only by the select few individuals who have been preordained to have a mystical intuition with God.

In his own dramatic conversion experience, Augustine sees the key role the desire for happiness plays in the mind's desire to know. Influenced by the Manichaean doctrine that final salvation comes through ascetic living itself derived from the views of the Stoics and Skeptics, Augustine argues that the path to salvation lies in turning away from the worldly pleasures—but not through the abstract detachment of the Stoics or the belief-free disinterestedness of the Skeptics. Augustine's answer is predicated on the understanding, provided in the philosophies of his Platonic predecessors, that what we call "the world" is not the real world but only an idea. Likewise, what you call your "self" is merely an idea within your own mind, and not your real soul. It is the ability to see beyond both the external and internal world of appearances that allows one to attain knowledge of ultimate reality, which Augustine calls *God.*

Under the philosophical influence of Plato and distinctly *unlike* much of the Christianity of today, Augustine's view is grounded, he claims, in reason.[1] Faith[2] plays a subordinate but important role. According to Augustine, no one can believe in the true God without first willing it. This is because no amount of rational argument can affect the will. Self-centeredness corrupts us away from truth and the "true reality" (the "true God") so that we fashion reality in our own image. Only when we are touched by "Divine Grace" can we will the true God—true reality—to be God—real for *us.* In other words, the true reality can be understood as real only when we understand what we take to be true reality—the world of appearances, for instance—to be false.

Augustine's view, then, is that the sort of inner, transcendental revelation of truth, which he calls "faith," cannot be approached by reason. Rather, one must start with inner insights and reason from them to the truth (this is exactly the procedure Descartes will later use). One cannot reason *to* faith, one must reason *from* faith. The cornerstone of Augustine's position is the famous dictum "I believe in order to understand." This view of religion replaced the previous theology and dominated subsequent Christian thought for over nine centuries, until the advent of Aquinas's scholastic philosophy.

The first selection is from his *Confessions.* Written in 400 when he was forty-three, it begins with a description of the events of his life that led to his conversion. He raises the following philosophical question: "When I think of God, *what is the object of my thought?*" Suppose I am thinking about my death. You ask me, "What is the object of your thought?" This would be an analogous puzzle to what Augustine is here raising.[3] My death—like God—is not an object present before my mind the way a table or a chair is. It's not even so much a question of what I am thinking *of* or *about* as it is a question of what, exactly, is present to my mind at the moment when my thinking *about that* is going on. *God* is not

---

1. That is *not* to say that rationality is somehow par for the course in philosophy or even essential to it. We shall see many examples of philosophers who have argued, asserted, or even just expressed (without any rational argument) that *nothing* can be argued for rationally, that *everything*—not just one's views of God—rests on faith.

2. There are many different meanings of this word, too, as used in different systems of thought.

3. We shall see Josiah Royce raise this question in exactly the same way, even using similar examples (see Chapter 46).

present (at least not the way the chair is) any more than *death* (my own death) is present. What, then *is* present? A concept? An idea? Whatever *these* are, they are present before the mind. Thus, the mind is thereby engaging with a concept or an idea, each of which are present to consciousness (they are at that moment the "objects" of consciousness), of a something *beyond* consciousness (in the case of both God and death). Like most philosophers from Thales to Plato, Augustine seeks to understand what *ultimate,* or *absolute* reality is. Augustine's God is the age-old quest for the ultimate ground, or source, of Being.

The passages from his *Confessions* highlight the way in which Augustine *argues* for the existence of God (i.e., the existence of some supreme, higher being of which this reality is only an image or imperfect representation). His main philosophical concern is with what *faculty* of the mind we can know God. This question is not just about a religious concept per se, but about how it could be possible that the mind can reach out beyond itself, either via its percepts or its concepts, to gain access to what is beyond the mind. In this way Augustine enters upon what is probably the first introspective psychological analysis ever of the nature and function of awareness, consciousness, language, and memory, from both an analytic and phenomenological perspective, to see what it is about the mind's own structures that allows it by inner extension to reach out beyond itself and thereby apprehend structures as they exist in themselves, outside the mind's own *actual* reach. That this is even possible will be denied by many idealist philosophers, and so here we see that Augustine is squarely a *realist,* a position from which all subsequent Christian thought, even post-Thomistic (after Aquinas) has never veered.

The second selection is from his *Against the Manichaeans.* It contains his criticism of the Manichaean version of Zoroastrianism to which he had once belonged. Augustine argues that we have no choice but to accept the existence of forces and powers beyond the grasp of the conscious mind and the intellect. And this he calls God. But why, then, is the world so imperfect? Why is there evil, pain, and suffering? One way to respond would be to claim that God is evil, that the purpose of existence is itself negative. Some medieval theologians believed this to be the case and traveled through the land inflicting pain on others and each other, thinking that this is what God wants.[4] Or one could claim that what we take to be evil, pain, and suffering is but an elaborate illusion. Augustine does not take either of these ways out. He claims, instead, that evil and suffering are themselves necessary tools by which God carries out God's plan.

In the next selection, taken from the *Enchiridion,* Augustine claims that while God is perfectly good, not all the things God creates—such as human beings—are perfectly good. God created us knowing we would sometimes choose evil so that, through our evil acts, God's perfectly good will could be fulfilled in ways that we, in our finite wisdom, cannot understand. The subtle implication is that God needs human beings because we can do what God cannot; we are, ourselves, a necessary ingredient in the fabric of reality. We make it possible for God to carry out what otherwise God could not achieve. This aspect of Augustine's theology was largely an attempt to respond to critics who had claimed that the weakening of the Roman Empire was—as Marcus Aurelius had warned—directly brought about by Christianity. Many religious thinkers of Augustine's time claimed that belief in Christ had brought the vengeance of the "pagan" gods, whereas secular philosophers claimed that Christian belief in otherworldliness had ruined the minds of the citizens and weakened their hold on practical reality. Indeed, more than fifteen hundred years later, the

---

4. Ingmar Bergman's film *The Seventh Seal* is a classic that poignantly explores this theme.

same charge is echoed by Bertrand Russell in his *History of Western Philosophy;* speaking of Jerome, Ambrose, and Augustine, he writes: "It is no wonder that the Empire fell into ruin when all the best and most vigorous minds of the age were so completely remote from secular concerns." Russell does, however, acknowledge the powerful emotional appeal of Augustine: "On the other hand, if ruin was inevitable, the Christian outlook was admirably fitted to give men fortitude, and to enable them to preserve their religious hopes when earthly hopes seemed vain. The expression of this point of view . . . was the supreme merit of Saint Augustine."

In the last selection, *The Three-Fold Nature of Mind,* Augustine displays his philosophical gifts in a context where his ideas can be viewed outside the religious framework of most of the rest of his writings. Turning to the difficult question of how self-knowledge is possible and why it is so difficult to attain, he claims that most of the mind's own beliefs about itself are false. Arguing against the Skeptics, according to whom we cannot know ourselves with certainty, he points out that even if one is a Skeptic and doubts everything, the act of doubting itself requires thought and a thinker and therefore affirms the existence of the self. Augustine thus anticipates Descartes's famous argument of more than a thousand years later that the proposition "I think, therefore I am," can be known with absolute certainty. Indeed, these passages were so influential to the thinking of Descartes that studying them gives us a unique opportunity to understand firsthand the source of much subsequent thinking about the relationship between our minds and world and the nature of knowledge.

Augustine answers the question raised by Plotinus in the previous chapter about why the soul is not fully aware of itself. According to Augustine, the reason the mind is not readily known to itself is because in order to function properly in the world the mind must have images of things and take them to be not images but things; hence, through deceiving itself into taking its own representations as being not of its own self but of things in the world, the mind must operate under a false view of its own operations. To become aware of its own existence, the mind must detach itself, in the manner of the Buddhist, Stoic, and Skeptic, from both its own perceptions and the things to which it is attracted to by desire. The mind must make itself aware of the seductive power of its own images. This process of enlightenment requires that the mind become aware of three separately functioning faculties within itself, each of which, according to Augustine, is a direct image of the Holy Trinity. These three divine faculties reflected in the human spirit are memory, understanding, and the will.

CONFESSIONS

What then have I to do with men, that they should hear my confessions—as if they could *heal all my infirmities*—a race, curious to know the lives of others, slothful to amend their own? Why seek they to hear from me what I am; who will not hear from Thee what them-

From *The Confessions of St. Augustine,* trans. E. B. Pusey (New York: Collier and Son, 1909). With emendations by Daniel Kolak.

selves are? And how know they, when from myself they hear of myself, whether I say true; seeing *no man knows what is in man, but the spirit of man which is in him?* But if they hear from Thee themselves, they cannot say, "The Lord lies." For what is it to hear from Thee of themselves, but to know themselves? and who knows and says, "It is false," unless himself lies? But because *charity believes all things* (that is, among those whom knitting unto itself it makes one), I also, O Lord, will in such wise confess unto Thee, that men may hear, to whom I cannot demonstrate whether I confess truly; yet they believe me, whose ears charity opens unto me. . . .

With what objective, then, O Lord my God, to Whom my conscience daily confesses, trusting more in the hope of Thy mercy than in her own innocency, with what objective, I pray, do I by this book confess to men also in Thy presence what I now am, not what I have been? For that other objective I have seen and spoken of. But what I now am, at the very time of making these confessions, diverse desire to know, who have or have not known me, who have heard from me or of me; but their ear is not at my heart, where I am, whatever I am. They wish then to hear me confess what I am within; whither neither their eye, nor ear, nor understanding can reach; they wish it, as ready to believe—but will they know? For charity, whereby they are good, tells them that in my confessions I lie not; and she in them, believes me. . . .

This is the objective of my confessions of what I am, not of what I have been, to confess this, not before Thee only, in a secret *exultation with trembling,* and a secret sorrow with hope; but in the ears also of the believing sons of men, sharers of my joy, and partners in my mortality, my fellow-citizens, and fellow-pilgrims, who are gone before, or are to follow on, companions on my way. . . .

But what do I love, when I love Thee? not beauty of bodies, nor the fair harmony of time, nor the brightness of the light, so beautiful to our eyes, nor sweet melodies of varied songs, nor the fragrant smell of flowers, and ointments, and spices, not manna and honey, not limbs acceptable to embracements of flesh. None of these I love, when I love my God; and yet I love a kind of light, and melody, and fragrance, and meat, and embracement when I love my God, the light, melody, fragrance, meat, embracement of my inner man: where there shines unto my soul what space cannot contain and there sounds what time bears not away, and there smells what breathing disperses not, and there tastes what eating diminishes not, and there clings what satiety divorces not. This is it which I love when I love my God.

And what is this? I asked the earth, and it answered me, "I am not He"; and whatsoever are in it confessed the same. I asked the sea and the depths, and the living creeping things, and they answered, "We are not Thy God, seek above us." I asked the moving air; and the whole air with his inhabitants answered, "Anaximenes was deceived, I am not God." I asked the heavens, sun, moon, stars, "Nor (say they) are we the God whom thou seeks." And I replied unto all the things which encompass the door of my flesh: "You have told me of my God, that you are not He; tell me something of Him." And they cried out with a loud voice, "He made us." My questioning them, was my thoughts on them: and their form of beauty gave the answer. And I turned myself unto myself, and said to myself, "Who are you?" And I answered, "A man." And behold, in me there present themselves to my soul, and body, one without, the other within. By which of these ought I to seek my God? I had sought Him in the body from earth to heaven, so far as I could send messengers, the beams of mine eyes. But the better is the inner, for to it as presiding and judging, all the bodily messengers reported the answers of heaven and earth, and all things therein, who said, "We are not God, but He made us." These things did my inner man know by the ministry of the outer: I the inner knew them; I, the mind, through the senses of my body. I asked the whole frame of the world about my God; and it answered me, "I am not He, but He made me."

Is not this corporeal figure apparent to all whose senses are perfect? why then speaks it not the same to all? Animals small and great see it but they cannot ask it: because no reason is set over their senses to judge on what they report. But men ask, so that *the invisible things of God are clearly seen, being understood by the things that are made;* but by love of them, they are made subject unto them: and subjects cannot judge. Nor yet do the creatures answer such as ask, unless they can judge: nor yet do they change their voice (*i.e.,* their appearance), if one man only sees, another seeing asks, so as to appear one way to this man, another way to that; but appearing the same way to both, it is dumb to this, speaks to that; rather it speaks to all; but they only understand, who compare its voice received from without, with the truth within. For truth says to me, "Neither heaven, nor earth, nor any other body is your God." This, their very nature says to him that sees them: "They are a mass; a mass is less in a part thereof than in the whole." Now to you I speak, O my soul, you are my better part: for you quickens the mass of my body, giving it life, which no body can give to a body: but your God is even unto you the Life of your life.

What then do I love, when I love my God? who is He above the head of my soul? By my very soul will I ascend to Him. I will pass beyond that power whereby I am united to my body, and fill its whole frame with life. Nor can I by that power find my God; for so *horse and mule that have no understanding,* might find Him; seeing it is the same power, whereby even their bodies live. But another power there is, not that only whereby I animate, but that too whereby I imbue with sense my flesh, which the Lord has framed for me: commanding the eye not to hear, and the ear not to see; but the eye, that through it I should see, and the ear, that through it I should hear; and to the other senses severally, what is to each their own peculiar seats and offices; which, being diverse, I the one mind, do through them enact. I will pass beyond this power of mine also; for this also have the horse and mule, for they also perceive through the body.

I will pass then beyond this power of my nature also, rising by degrees unto Him who made me. And I come to the fields and spacious palaces of my memory, where are the treasures of innumerable images, brought into it from things of all sorts perceived by the senses. There is stored up, whatsoever besides we think, either by enlarging or diminishing, or any other way varying those things which the sense has come to; and whatever else has been committed and laid up, which forgetfulness has not yet swallowed up and buried. When I enter there, I require what I will to be brought forth, and something instantly comes; others must be longer sought after, which are fetched, as it were, out of some inner receptacle; others rush out in troops, and while one thing is desired and required, they start forth, as who should say, "Is it perchance I?" These I drive away with the hand of my heart, from the face of my remembrance; until what I wish for is unveiled, and appears in sight, out of its secret place. Other things come up readily, in unbroken order, as they are called for; those in front making way for the following; and as they make way, they are hidden from sight, ready to come when I will. All which takes place when I repeat a thing by heart.

There are all things preserved distinctly and under general heads, each having entered by its own avenue: as light, and all colours and forms of bodies by the eyes; by the ears all sorts of sounds; all smells by the avenue of the nostrils; all tastes by the mouth; and by the sensation of the whole body, what is hard or soft; hot or cold; smooth or rugged; heavy or light; either outwardly or inwardly to the body. All these does that great harbour of the memory receive in her numberless secret and inexpressible windings, to be forthcoming, and brought out at need; each entering in by his own gate, and there laid up. Nor yet do the things themselves enter in; only the images of the things perceived are there in readiness, for thought to recall. Which images, how they are formed, who can tell, though it does plainly appear by which sense each has been brought in and stored up? For even while I dwell in darkness and in silence, in my memory I can produce colours, if I will, and discern between black and white, and what others I will: nor yet do sounds break in and disturb the image drawn in by my eyes, which I am reviewing, though they also are there, lying dormant, and laid up, as it were, apart. For these too I call for, and they appear. And though my tongue be still, and my throat mute, so can I sing as much as I will; nor do those images of colours, which notwithstanding be there, intrude themselves and interrupt, when another store is called for, which flowed in by the ears. So the other things, piled in and up by the other senses, I recall at my pleasure. Yea, I discern the breath of lilies from violets, though smelling nothing; and I prefer honey to sweet wine, smooth before rugged, at the time neither tasting nor handling, but remembering only.

These things do I within, in that vast court of my memory. For there are present with me, heaven, earth, sea, and whatever I could think on therein, besides what I have forgotten. There also meet I with myself, and recall myself, and when, where, and what I have done, and under what feelings. There be all which I remember, either on my own experience, or others' credit. Out of the same store do I myself with the past continually combine fresh and fresh likenesses of things which I have experienced, or, from what I have experienced, have believed: and then again infer future actions, events and hopes, and all these again I reflect on, as present. "I will do this or that," say I to myself, in that great receptacle of my mind, stored with the images of things so many and so great, "and this or that will follow." "O that this or that might be!" "God avert this or that!" So speak I to myself: and when I speak, the images of all I speak of are present, out of the same treasury of memory; nor would I speak of any thereof, were the images wanting.

Great is this force of memory, excessive great, O my God; a large and boundless chamber! who ever sounded the bottom thereof? yet is this a power of mine, and belongs unto my nature; nor do I myself comprehend all that I am. Therefore is the mind too strait to contain itself. And where should that be, which it contained not of itself? Is it without it, and not within? how then does it not comprehend itself? A wonderful admiration surprises me, amazement seizes me upon this. And men go abroad to admire the heights of mountains, the mighty billows of the sea, the broad tides of rivers, the compass of the ocean, and the circuits of the stars, and pass themselves by; nor wonder that when I spoke of all these things, I did not see them with my eyes, yet could not have spoken of them, unless I then actually saw the mountains, billows, rivers, stars which I had seen, and that ocean which I believe to be, inwardly in my memory, and that, with the same vast spaces between, as if I saw them abroad. Yet did not I by seeing draw them into myself, when with my eyes I beheld them; nor are they themselves with me, but their images only. And I know by what sense of the body each was impressed upon me. . . .

Lord, I truly, toil therein, yea and toil in myself; I am become a heavy soil requiring over much *sweat of the brow.* For we are not now searching out the regions of heaven, or measuring the distances of the stars, or enquiring the balancings of the earth. It is I myself who remember, I the mind. It is not so wonderful, if what I myself am not, be far from me. But what is nearer to me than myself? And lo, the force of my own memory is not understood by me; though I cannot so much as name myself without it.

AGAINST THE MANICHAEANS

Happiness is in the enjoyment of man's chief good. Two conditions of the chief good: 1st, nothing is better than it; 2d, it cannot be lost against the will.

How then, according to reason, ought man to live? We all certainly desire to live happily; and there is no human being but assents to this statement almost before it is made. But the title happy cannot, in my opinion, belong either to him who has not what he loves, whatever it may be, or to him who has what he loves if it is hurtful, or to him who does not love what he has, although it is good in perfection. For one who seeks what he cannot obtain suffers torture, and one who has got what is not desirable is cheated, and one who does not seek for what is worth seeking for is diseased. Now in all these cases the mind cannot but be unhappy, and happiness and unhappiness cannot reside at the same time in one man: so in none of these cases can the man be happy. I find, then, a fourth case, where the happy life exists—when that which is man's chief good is both loved and possessed. For what do we call enjoyment but having at hand the objects of love? And no one can be happy who does not enjoy what is man's chief good, nor is there any one who enjoys this who is not happy. We must then have at hand our chief good, if we think of living happily.

We must now inquire what is man's chief good, which of course cannot be anything inferior to man himself. For whoever follows after what is inferior to himself, becomes himself inferior. But every man is bound to follow what is best. Wherefore man's chief good is not inferior to man. Is it then something similar to man himself? It must be so, if there is nothing above man which he is capable of enjoying. But if we find something which is both superior to man, and can be possessed by the man who loves it, who can doubt that in seeking for happiness man should endeavor to reach that which is more excellent than the being who makes the endeavor. For if happiness consists in the enjoyment of a good than which there is nothing better, which we call the chief good, how can a man be properly called happy who has not yet attained to his chief good? or how can that be the chief good beyond which something better remains for us to arrive at? Such, then, being the chief good, it must be something which cannot be lost against the will. For no one can feel confident regarding a good which he knows can be taken from him, although he wishes to keep and cherish it. But if a man feels no confidence regarding the good which he enjoys, how can he be happy while in such fear of losing it?

Man—what?

Let us then see what is better than man. This must necessarily be hard to find, unless we first ask and examine what man is. I am not now called upon to give a definition of man. The question here seems to me to be—since almost all agree, or at least, which is enough, those I have now to do with are of the same opinion with me, that we are made up of soul and body—What is man? Is he both of these? or is he the body only, or the soul only? For although the things are two, soul and body, and although neither without the other could

From Augustine, in *The Writings against the Manichaens and against the Donatists* (a Select Library of the Nicene and post-Nicene Fathers), First Series, ed. Philip Schaff, vol. 4 (New York: Christian Literature Publishing Co., 1886–1890).

be called man (for the body would not be man without the soul, nor again would the soul be man if there were not a body animated by it), still it is possible that one of these may be held to be man, and may be called so. What then do we call man? Is he soul and body, as in a double harness, or like a centaur? Or do we mean the body only, as being in the service of the soul which rules it, as the word lamp denotes not the light and the case together, but only the case, yet it is on account of the light that it is so called? Or do we mean only the mind, and that on account of the body which it rules, as horseman means not the man and the horse, but the man only, and that as employed in ruling the horse? This dispute is not easy to settle; or, if the proof is plain, the statement requires time. This is an expenditure of time and strength which we need not incur. For whether the name man belongs to both, or only to the soul, the chief good of man is not the chief good of the body; but what is the chief good either of both soul and body, or of the soul only, that is man's chief good.

Man's chief good is not the chief good of the body only, but the chief good of the soul.

Now if we ask what is the chief good of the body, reason obliges us to admit that it is that by means of which the body comes to be in its best state. But of all the things which invigorate the body, there is nothing better or greater than the soul. The chief good of the body, then, is not bodily pleasure, not absence of pain, not strength, not beauty, not swiftness, or whatever else is usually reckoned among the goods of the body, but simply the soul. For all the things mentioned the soul supplies to the body by its presence, and, what is above them all, life. Hence I conclude that the soul is not the chief good of man, whether we give the name of man to soul and body together, or to the soul alone. For as, according to reason, the chief good of the body is that which is better than the body and from which the body receives vigor and life, so whether the soul itself is man, or soul and body both, we must discover whether there is anything which goes before the soul itself, in following which the soul comes to the perfection of good of which it is capable in its own kind. If such a thing can be found, all uncertainty must be at an end, and we must pronounce this to be really and truly the chief good of man.

If, again, the body is man, it must be admitted that the soul is the chief good of man. But clearly, when we treat of morals—when we inquire what manner of life must be held in order to obtain happiness—it is not the body to which the precepts are addressed, it is not bodily discipline which we discuss. In short, the observance of good *customs* belongs to that part of us which inquires and learns, which are the prerogatives of the soul; so, when we speak of attaining to virtue, the question does not regard the body. But if it follows, as it does, that the body which is ruled over by a soul possessed of virtue is ruled both better and more honorably, and is in its greatest perfection in consequence of the perfection of the soul which rightfully governs it, that which gives perfection to the soul will be man's chief good, though we call the body man. For if my coachman, in obedience to me, feeds and drives the horses he has charge of in the most satisfactory manner, himself enjoying the more of my bounty in proportion to his good conduct, can any one deny that the good condition of the horses, as well as that of the coachman, is due to me? So the question seems to me to be not, whether soul and body is man, or the soul only, or the body only, but what gives perfection to the soul; for when this is obtained, a man cannot but be either perfect, or at least much better than in the absence of this one thing. . . .

God is the chief good, whom we are to seek after with supreme affection.

Let us see how the Lord Himself in the gospel has taught us to live; how, too, Paul the apostle—for the Manichaeans dare not reject these Scriptures. Let us hear, O Christ, what chief end Thou dost prescribe to us; and that is evidently the chief end after which we are told to strive with supreme affection. "Thou shalt love," He says, "the Lord thy God." Tell me also, I pray Thee, what must be the measure of love; for I fear lest the desire enkindled in my heart should exceed or come short in fervor. "With all thy heart," He says. Nor is that enough. "With all thy soul." Nor is it enough yet. "With all thy mind." What do you wish more? I might, perhaps, wish more if I could see the possibility of more. What does Paul say on this? "We know," he says, "that all things issue in good to them that love God." Let him, too, say what is the measure of love. "Who then," he says, "shall separate us from the love of Christ? shall tribulation, or distress, or persecution, or famine, or nakedness, or peril, or the sword?" We have heard, then, what and how much we must love; this we must strive after, and to this we must refer all our plans. The perfection of all our good things and our perfect good is God. We must neither come short of this nor go beyond it: the one is dangerous, the other impossible. . . .

That in all natures, of every kind and rank, God is glorified.

All natures, then, inasmuch as they are, and have therefore a rank and species of their own, and a kind of internal harmony, are certainly good. And when they are in the places assigned to them by the order of their nature, they preserve such being as they have received. And those things which have received everlasting being, are altered for better or for worse, so as to suit the wants and notions of those things to which the Creator's law has made them subservient; and thus they tend in the divine providence to that end which is embraced in the general scheme of the government of the universe. So that, though the corruption of transitory and perishable things brings them to utter destruction, it does not prevent their producing that which was designed to be their result. And this being so, God, who supremely is, and who therefore created every being which has not supreme existence (for that which was made of nothing could not be equal to Him, and indeed could not be at all had He not made it), is not to be found fault with on account of the creature's faults, but is to be praised in view of the natures He has made. . . .

That we ought not to expect to find any efficient cause of the evil will.

Let no one, therefore, look for an efficient cause of the evil will; for it is not efficient, but deficient, as the will itself is not an effecting of something, but a defect. For defection from that which supremely is, to that which has less of being—this is to begin to have an evil will. Now, to seek to discover the causes of these defections—causes, as I have said, not efficient, but deficient—is as if someone sought to see darkness, or hear silence. Yet both of these are known by us, and the former by means only of the eye, the latter only by the ear; but not by their positive actuality, but by their want of it. Let no one, then seek to know from me what I know that I do not know; unless he perhaps wishes to learn to be ignorant of that of which all we know is, that it cannot be known. For those things which are known not by their actuality, but by their want of it, are known, if our expression may be allowed and understood, by not knowing them, that by knowing them they may be not known. For when the eyesight surveys objects that strike the sense, it nowhere sees darkness but where it begins not to see. And so no other sense but the ear can perceive silence, and yet it is only perceived by not hearing. Thus, too, our mind perceives intelligible forms by understanding them; but when they are deficient, it knows them by not knowing them; for who can understand defects?

Of the misdirected love whereby the will fell away from the immutable to the mutable good.

This I do know, that the nature of God can never, nowhere, nowise be defective, and that natures made of nothing can. These latter, however, the more being they have, and the more good they do (for then they do something positive), the more they have efficient causes; but in so far as they are defective in being, and consequently do evil (for then what is their work but vanity?) they have deficient causes. And I know likewise, that the will could not become evil, were it unwilling to become so; and therefore its failings are justly punished, being not necessary, but voluntary. For its defections are not to evil things, but are themselves evil; that is to say, are not toward things that are naturally and in themselves evil, but the defection of the will is evil, because it is contrary to the order of nature, and an abandonment of that which has supreme being for that which has less. For avarice is not a fault inherent in gold, but in the man who inordinately loves gold, to the detriment of justice, which ought to be held in incomparably higher regard than gold. Neither is luxury the fault of lovely and charming objects, but of the heart that inordinately loves sensual pleasures, to the neglect of temperance, which attaches us to objects more lovely in their spirituality, and more delectable by their incorruptibility. Nor yet is boasting the fault of human praise but of the soul that is inordinately fond of the applause of men, and that makes light of the voice of conscience. Pride, too, is not the fault of him who delegates power, nor of power itself, but of the soul that is inordinately enamored of its own power, and despises the more just dominion of a higher authority. Consequently he who inordinately loves the good which any nature possesses, even though he obtain it, himself becomes evil in the good, and wretched because deprived of a greater good. . . .

That even the fierceness of war and all the disquietude of men make towards this one end of peace, which every nature desires.

Whoever gives even moderate attention to human affairs and to our common nature, will recognize that if there is no man who does not wish to be joyful, neither is there any one who does not wish to have peace. For even they who make war desire nothing but victory—desire, that is to say, to attain to peace with glory. For what else is victory than the conquest of those who resist us? and when this is done there is peace. It is therefore with the desire for peace that wars are waged, even by those who take pleasure in exercising their warlike nature in command and battle. And hence it is obvious that peace is the end sought for by war. For every man seeks peace by waging war, but no man seeks war by making peace. For even they who intentionally interrupt the peace in which they are living have no hatred of peace, but only wish it changed into a peace that suits them better. They do not, therefore, wish to have no peace, but only one more to their mind. And in the case of sedition, when men have separated themselves from the community, they yet do not effect what they wish, unless they maintain some kind of peace with their fellow-conspirators. And therefore even robbers take care to maintain peace with their comrades, that they may with greater effect and greater safety invade the peace of other men. And if an individual happens to be of such unrivalled strength, and to be so jealous of partnership, that he trusts himself with no comrades, but makes his own plots, and commits depredations and murders on his own account, yet he maintains some shadow of peace with such persons as he is unable to kill, and from whom he wishes to conceal his deeds. In his own home, too, he makes it his aim to be at peace with his wife and children, and any other members of his household; for unquestionably their prompt obedience to his every look is a source of pleasure to him.

And if this be not rendered, he is angry, he chides and punishes; and even by this storm he secures the calm peace of his own home, as occasion demands. For he sees that peace cannot be maintained unless all the members of the same domestic circle be subject to one head, such as he himself is in his own house. And therefore if a city or nation offered to submit itself to him, to serve him in the same style as he had made his household serve him, he would no longer lurk in a brigand's hiding-places, but lift his head in open day as a king, though the same coveteousness and wickedness should remain in him. And thus all men desire to have peace with their own circle whom they wish to govern as suits themselves. For even those whom they make war against they wish to make their own, and impose on them the laws of their own peace.

But let us suppose a man such as poetry and mythology speak of—a man so insociable and savage as to be called rather a semi-man than a man. Although, then, his kingdom was the solitude of a dreary cave, and he himself was so singularly bad-hearted that he was named Kaxos, which is the Greek word for *bad;* though he had no wife to soothe him with endearing talk, no children to play with, no sons to do his bidding, no friend to enliven him with intercourse, not even his father Vulcan (though in one respect he was happier than his father, not having begotten a monster like himself); although he gave to no man, but took as he wished whatever he could, from whomsoever he could, when he could; yet in that solitary den, the floor of which, as Virgil says, was always reeking with recent slaughter, there was nothing else than peace sought, a peace in which no one should molest him, or disquiet him with any assault or alarm. With his own body he desired to be at peace, and he was satisfied only in proportion as he had this peace. For he ruled his members, and they obeyed him; and for the sake of pacifying his mortal nature, which rebelled when it needed anything, and of allaying the sedition of hunger which threatened to banish the soul from the body, he made forays, slew, and devoured, but used the ferocity and savageness he displayed in these actions only for the preservation of his own life's peace. So that, had he been willing to make with other men the same peace which he made with himself in his own cave, he would neither have been called bad, nor a monster, nor a semi-man. Or if the appearance of his body and his vomiting smoky fires frightened men from having any dealings with him, perhaps his fierce ways arose not from a desire to do mischief, but from the necessity of finding a living. But he may have had no existence, or, at least, he was not such as the poets fancifully describe him, for they had to exalt Hercules, and did so at the expense of Cacus. It is better, then, to believe that such a man or semi-man never existed, and that this, in common with many other fancies of the poets, is mere fiction. For the most savage animals (and he is said to have been almost a wild beast) encompass their own species with a ring of protecting peace. They cohabit, beget, produce, suckle, and bring up their young, though very many of them are not gregarious, but solitary—not like sheep, deer, pigeons, starlings, bees, but such as lions, foxes, eagles, bats. For what tigress does not gently purr over her cubs, and lay aside her ferocity to fondle them? What kite, solitary as he is when circling over his prey, does not seek a mate, build a nest, hatch the eggs, bring up the young birds, and maintain with the mother of his family as peaceful a domestic alliance as he can? How much more powerfully do the laws of man's nature move him to hold fellowship and maintain peace with all men so far as in him lies, since even wicked men wage war to maintain the peace of their own circle, and wish that, if possible, all men belonged to them, that all men and things might serve but one head, and might, either through love or fear, yield themselves to peace with him! It is thus that pride in its perversity apes God. It abhors equality with other men under Him; but, instead of His rule, it seeks to impose a rule of its own upon its equals. It abhors, that is to say, the just peace of God, and loves its own unjust peace; but it cannot help loving peace of one kind or other. For there is no vice so clean contrary to nature that it obliterates even the faintest traces of nature.

He, then, who prefers what is right to what is wrong, and what is well-ordered to what is perverted, sees that the peace of unjust men is not worthy to be called peace in comparison with the peace of the just. And yet even what is perverted must of necessity be in harmony with, and in dependence on, and in some part of the order of things, for otherwise it would have no existence at all. Suppose a man hangs with his head downwards, this is certainly a perverted attitude of body and arrangement of its members; for that which nature requires to be above is beneath, and *vice versa*. This perversity disturbs the peace of the body, and is therefore painful. Nevertheless the spirit is at peace with its body, and labors for its preservation, and hence the suffering; but if it is banished from the body by its pains, then, so long as the bodily framework holds together, there is in the remains a kind of peace among the members, and hence the body remains suspended. And inasmuch as the earthly body tends towards the earth, and rests on the bond by which it is suspended, it tends thus to its natural peace, and the voice of its own weight demands a place for it to rest; and though now lifeless and without feeling, it does not fall from the peace that is natural to its place in creation, whether it already has it, or is tending towards it. For if you apply embalming preparations to prevent the bodily frame from mouldering and dissolving, a kind of peace still unites part to part, and keeps the whole body in a suitable place on the earth— in other words, in a place that is at peace with the body. If, on the other hand, the body receive no such care, but be left to the natural course, it is disturbed by exhalations that do not harmonize with one another, and that offend our senses; for it is this which is perceived in putrefaction until it is assimilated to the elements of the world, and particle by particle enters into peace with them. Yet throughout this process the laws of the most high Creator and Governor are strictly observed, for it is by Him the peace of the universe is administered. For although minute animals are produced from the carcass of a larger animal, all these little atoms, by the law of the same Creator, serve the animals they belong to in peace. And although the flesh of dead animals be eaten by others, no matter where it be carried, nor what it be brought into contact with, nor what it be converted and changed into, it still is ruled by the same laws which pervade all things for the conservation of every mortal race, and which bring things that fit one another into harmony.

Of the universal place which the law of nature preserves through all disturbances, and by which every one reaches his desert in a way regulated by the just judge.

The peace of the body then consists in the duly proportioned arrangement of its parts. The peace of the irrational soul is the harmonious repose of the appetites, and that of the rational soul the harmony of knowledge and action. The peace of body and soul is the well-ordered and harmonious life and health of the living creature. Peace between man and God is the well-ordered obedience of faith to eternal law. Peace between man and man is well-ordered concord. Domestic peace is the well-ordered concord between those of the family who rule and those who obey. Civil peace is a similar concord among the citizens. The peace of the celestial city is the perfectly ordered and harmonious enjoyment of God, and of one another in God. The peace of all things is the tranquility of order. Order is the distribution which allots things equal and unequal, each to its own place. And hence, though the miserable, in so far as they are such, do certainly not enjoy peace, but are severed from that tranquillity of order in which there is no disturbance, nevertheless, inasmuch as they are deservedly and justly miserable, they are by their very misery connected with order. They are not, indeed, conjoined with the blessed, but they are disjoined from them by the law of order. And though they are disquieted, their circumstances are notwithstanding adjusted to them, and consequently they have some tranquillity of order, and therefore some peace. But they are wretched because, although not wholly miserable, they are not in that place where any mixture of misery is impossible. They would, however, be more wretched if they had not that peace which arises from being in harmony with the natural order of things. When they suffer, their peace is in so far disturbed; but their peace continues in so far as they do not suffer, and in so far as their nature continues to exist. As, then, there may be life without pain, while there cannot be pain without some kind of life, so there may be peace without war, but there cannot be war without some kind of peace, because war supposes the existence of some natures to wage it, and these natures cannot exist without peace of one kind or other.

And therefore there is a nature in which evil does not or even cannot exist; but there cannot be a nature in which there is no good. Hence not even the nature of the devil himself is evil, in so far as it is nature, but it was made evil by being perverted. . . .

ENCHIRIDION

What is called evil in the universe is but the absence of good: . . . In the bodies of animals, disease and wounds mean nothing but the absence of health; for when a cure is effected, that does not mean that the evils which were present—namely, the diseases and wounds— go away from the body and dwell elsewhere: they altogether cease to exist; for the wound or disease is not a substance, but a defect in the fleshly substance—the flesh itself being a substance, and therefore something good, of which those evils—that is, privations of the good which we call health—are accidents. Just in the same way, what are called vices in the soul are nothing but privations of natural good. And when they are cured, they are not transferred elsewhere: when they cease to exist in the healthy soul, they cannot exist anywhere else.

All beings were made good, but not being made perfectly good, are liable to corruption: All things that exist, therefore, seeing that the Creator of them all is supremely good, are themselves good. But because they are not, like their Creator, supremely and unchangeably good, their good may be diminished and increased. But for good to be diminished is an evil, although, however much it may be diminished, it is necessary, if the being is to continue, that some good should remain to constitute the being. For however small or of whatever kind the being may be, the good which makes it a being cannot be destroyed without destroying the being itself. An uncorrupted nature is justly held in esteem. But if, still further, it be incorruptible, it is undoubtedly considered of still higher value. When it is corrupted, however, its corruption is an evil, because it is deprived of some sort of good. For if it be deprived of no good, it receives no injury; but it does receive injury, therefore it

From Saint Augustine, *Enchiridion,* trans. J. F. Shaw, in *The Works of Aurelius Augustine,* ed. M. Dods (Edinburgh: T. & T. Clark, 1892).

is deprived of good. Therefore, so long as a being is in process of corruption, there is in it some good of which it is being deprived; and if a part of the being should remain which cannot be corrupted, this will certainly be an incorruptible being, and accordingly the process of corruption will result in the manifestation of this great good. But if it does not cease to be corrupted, neither can it cease to possess good of which corruption may deprive it. But if it should be thoroughly and completely consumed by corruption, there will then be no good left, because there will be no being. Wherefore corruption can consume the good only by consuming the being. Every being, therefore, is a good; a great good, if it cannot be corrupted; a little good, if it can; but in any case, only the foolish or ignorant will deny that it is a good. And if it be wholly consumed by corruption, then the corruption itself must cease to exist, as there is no being left in which it can dwell. . . .

The omnipotent God does well even in the permission of evil: Nor can we doubt that God does well even in the permission of what is evil. For He permits it only in the justice of His judgment. And surely all that is just is good. Although, therefore, evil, insofar as it is evil, is not a good; yet the fact that evil as well as good exists, is a good. For if it were not a good that evil should exist, its existence would not be permitted by the omnipotent God, who without doubt can as easily refuse to permit what He does not wish, as bring about what He does wish. And if we do not believe this, the very first sentence of our creed is endangered, wherein we profess to believe in God the Father Almighty. For He is not truly called Almighty if He cannot do whatsoever He pleases, or if the power of His almighty will is hindered by the will of any creature whatsoever. . . .

The will of God is never defeated, though much is done that is contrary to His will: These are the great works of the Lord, sought out according to all His pleasure, and so wisely sought out, that when the intelligent creation, both angelic and human, sinned, doing not His will but their own, He used the very will of the creature which was working in opposition to the Creator's will as an instrument for carrying out His will, the supremely Good thus turning to good account even what is evil, to the condemnation of those whom in His justice He has predestined to punishment, and to the salvation of those whom in His mercy He has predestined to grace. For, as far as relates to their own consciousness, these creatures did what God wished not to be done: but in view of God's omnipotence, they could in no wise effect their purpose. For in the very fact that they acted in opposition to His will, His will concerning them was fulfilled. And hence it is that "the works of the Lord are great, sought out according to all His pleasure," because in a way unspeakably strange and wonderful, even what is done in opposition to His will does not defeat His will. For it would not be done did He not permit it (and of course His permission is not unwilling, but willing); nor would a Good Being permit evil to be done that in His omnipotence He can turn evil into good.

The will of God, which is always good, is sometimes fulfilled through the evil will of man: Sometimes, however, a man in the goodness of his will desires something that God does not desire, even though God's will is also good, nay, much more fully and more surely good (for His will never can be evil): for example, if a good son is anxious that his father should live, when it is God's goodwill that he should die. Again, it is possible for a man with evil will to desire what God wills in His goodness: for example, if a bad son wishes his father to die, when this is also the will of God. It is plain that the former wishes what God does not wish, and that the latter wishes what God does wish; and yet the filial love of the former is more in harmony with the goodwill of God, though its desire is different from God's, than the want of filial affection of the latter, though its desire is the same as God's. So necessary is it, in determining whether a man's desire is one to be approved or disapproved, to consider what it is proper for man, and what it is proper for God, to desire, and what is in each case the real motive of the will. For God accomplishes some of His purposes, which of course are all good, through the evil desires of wicked men.

THE THREE-FOLD NATURE OF MIND

BOOK X

Chapter 6: The Opinion which the mind has of itself is deceitful.

But the mind errs, when it so lovingly and intimately connects itself with these images, as even to consider itself to be something of the same kind. For so it is conformed to them to some extent, not by being this, but by thinking it is so: not that it thinks itself to be an image, but outright that very thing itself of which it entertains the image. For there still lives in it the power of distinguishing the corporeal thing which it leaves without, from the image of that corporeal thing which it contains therefrom within itself; except when these images are so projected as if felt without and not thought within, as in the case of people who are asleep, or mad, or in a trance.

Chapter 7: The opinions of philosophers respecting the substance of the soul. The error of those who are of opinion that the soul is corporeal, does not arise from defective knowledge of the soul, but from their adding thereto something foreign to it. What is meant by finding.

When, therefore, it thinks itself to be something of this kind, it thinks itself to be a corporeal thing; and since it is perfectly conscious of its own superiority, by which it rules the body, it has hence come to pass that the question has been raised what part of the body has the greater power in the body; and the opinion has been held that this is the mind, nay, that it is even the whole soul altogether. And some accordingly think it to be the blood, others the brain, others the heart; not as the Scripture says, "I will praise Thee, O Lord, with my whole heart"; and, "Thou shalt love the Lord thy God with all thine heart"; for this word by misapplication or metaphor is transferred from the body to the soul; but they have simply thought it to be that small part itself of the body, which we see when the inward parts are rent asunder. Others, again, have believed the soul to be made up of very minute and individual corpuscles, which they call atoms, meeting in themselves and cohering. Others have said that its substance is air, others fire. Others have been of opinion that it is no substance at all, since they could not think any substance unless it is body, and they did not find that the soul was body; but it was in their opinion the tempering together itself of our body, or the combining together of the elements, by which that flesh is as it were conjoined. And hence all of these have held the soul to be mortal; since, whether it were body, or some combination of body, certainly it could not in either case continue always without death. But they who have held its substance to be some kind of life the reverse of corporeal, since

From *History of the Christian Church,* Vol. III: *Nicene and Post-Nicene Fathers,* ed. Philip Schaff (New York: Charles Scribner's Sons, 1884).

they have found it to be a life that animates and quickens every living body, have by consequence striven also, according as each was able, to prove it immortal, since life cannot be without life.

For as to that fifth kind of body, I know not what, which some have added to the four well-known elements of the world, and have said that the soul was made of this, I do not think we need spend time in discussing it in this place. For either they mean by body what we mean by it, *viz.,* that of which a part is less than the whole in extension of place, and they are to be reckoned among those who have believed the mind to be corporeal: or if they call either all substance, or all changeable substance, body, whereas they know that not all substance is contained in extension of place by any length and breadth and height, we need not contend with them about a question of words.

Now, in the case of all these opinions, any one who sees that the nature of the mind is at once substance, and yet not corporeal,—that is, that it does not occupy a less extension of place with a less part of itself, and a greater with a greater,—must needs see at the same time that they who are of opinion that it is corporeal, do not err from defect of knowledge concerning mind, but because they associate with it qualities without which they are not able to conceive any nature at all. For if you bid them conceive of existence that is without corporeal phantasms, they hold it merely nothing. And so the mind would not seek itself, as though wanting to itself. For what is so present to knowledge as that which is present to the mind? Or what is so present to the mind as the mind itself? And hence what is called "invention," if we consider the origin of the word, what else does it mean, unless that to find out (*invenire*) is to "come into" that which is sought? Those things accordingly which come into the mind as it were of themselves, are not usually said to be found out (*inventa*), although they may be said to be known; since we did not endeavor by seeking to come into them, that is, to invent or find them out. And therefore, as the mind itself really seeks those things which are sought by the eyes or by any other sense of the body (for the mind directs even the carnal sense, and then finds out or invents, when that sense comes to the things which are sought); so, too, it finds out or invents other things which it ought to know, not with the medium of corporeal sense, but through itself, when it "comes into" them; and this, whether in the case of the higher substance that is in God, or of the other parts of the soul; just as it does when it judges of bodily images themselves; for it finds these within, in the soul, impressed through the body.

Chapter 8: How the soul inquires into itself. Whence comes the error of the soul concerning itself.

It is then a wonderful question, in what manner the soul seeks and finds itself; at what it aims in order to seek, or whither it comes, that it may come into or find out. For what is so much in the mind as the mind itself? But because it is *in* those things which it thinks of with love, and is wont to be in sensible, that is, in corporeal things with love, it is unable to be in itself without the images of those corporeal things. And hence shameful error arises to block its way, whilst it cannot separate from itself the images of sensible things, so as to see itself alone. For they have marvellously cohered with it by the close adhesion of love. And herein consists its uncleanness; since, while it strives to think of itself alone, it fancies itself to be that, without which it cannot think of itself. When, therefore, it is bidden to become acquainted with itself, let it not seek itself as though it were withdrawn from itself; but let it withdraw that which it has added to itself. For itself lies more deeply within not only than those sensible things, which are clearly without, but also than the images of them; which are indeed in some part of the soul, *viz.,* that which beasts also have, although these want understanding, which is proper to the mind. As therefore the mind is within, it goes forth in some sort from itself, when it exerts the affection of love towards these, as it were, footprints of many acts of attention. And these footprints are, as it were, imprinted on the memory, at the time when the corporeal things which are without are perceived in such way, that even when those corporeal things are absent, yet the images of them are at hand to those who think of them. Therefore let the mind become acquainted with itself, and not seek itself as if it were absent; but fix upon itself the act of [voluntary] attention, by which it was wandering among other things, and let it think of itself. So it will see that at no time did it ever not love itself, at no time did it ever not know itself; but by loving another thing together with itself it has confounded itself with it, and in some sense has grown one with it. And so, while it embraces diverse things, as though they were one, it has come to think those things to be one which are diverse.

Chapter 9: The mind knows itself, by the very act of understanding the precept to know itself.

Let it not therefore seek to discern itself as though absent, but take pains to discern itself as present. Nor let it take knowledge of itself as if it did not know itself, but let it distinguish itself from that which it knows to be another. For how will it take pains to obey that very precept which is given it, "Know thyself," if it knows not either what "know" means or what "thyself" means? But if it knows both, then it knows also itself. Since "know thyself" is not so said to the mind as is "Know the cherubim and the seraphim"; for they are absent, and we believe concerning them, and according to that belief they are declared to be certain celestial powers. Nor yet again as it is said, Know the will of that man: for this it is not within our reach to perceive at all, either by sense or understanding, unless by corporeal signs actually set forth; and this in such a way that we rather believe than understand. Nor again as it is said to a man, Behold thy own face; which he can only do in a looking-glass. For even our own face itself is out of the reach of our own seeing it; because it is not there where our look can be directed. But when it is said to the mind, Know thyself; then it knows itself by that very act by which it understands the word "thyself"; and this for no other reason than that it is present to itself. But if it does not understand what is said, then certainly it does not do as it is bid to do. And therefore it is bidden to do that thing which it does do, when it understands the very precept that bids it.

Chapter 10: Every mind knows certainly three things concerning itself—that it understands, that it is, and that it lives.

Let it not then add anything to that which it knows itself to be, when it is bidden to know itself. For it knows, at any rate, that this is said to itself; namely, to the self that is, and that lives, and that understands. But a dead body also is, and cattle live; but neither a dead body nor cattle understand. Therefore it so knows that it so is, and that it so lives, as an understanding is and lives. When, therefore, for example's sake, the mind thinks itself air, it thinks that air understands; it knows, however, that itself understands, but it does not know itself to be air, but only thinks so. Let it separate that which it thinks itself; let it discern that which it knows; let this remain to it, about which not even have they doubted who have thought the mind to be this corporeal thing or that. For certainly every mind does not consider itself to be air; but some think themselves fire, others the brain, and some one kind of corporeal thing, others another, as I have mentioned before; yet all know that they themselves understand, and are, and live; but they refer understanding to that which they understand, but to be, and to live, to themselves. And no one doubts, either that no one understands who does not live, or that no one lives of whom it is not true that he is; and that therefore by consequence that which understands both is and lives; not as a dead body is which does not live, nor as a soul lives which does not understand, but in some proper and more excellent manner. Further, they know that they will, and they equally know that no one can will who is not and who does not live; and they also refer that will itself to something which they will with that will. They know also that they remember; and they know at the same time that nobody could remember, unless he both was and lived; but we refer memory itself also to something, in that we remember those things. Therefore the knowledge and science of many things are contained in two of these three, memory and understanding; but will must be present, that we may enjoy or use them. For we enjoy things known, in which things themselves the will finds delight for their own sake, and so reposes; but we use those things, which we refer to some other thing which we are to enjoy. Neither is the life of man vicious and culpable in any other way, than as wrongly using and wrongly enjoying. But it is no place here to discuss this.

But since we treat of the nature of the mind, let us remove from our consideration all knowledge which is received from without, through the senses of the body, and attend more carefully to the position which we have laid down, that all minds know and are certain concerning themselves. For men certainly have doubted whether the power of living, of remembering, of understanding, of willing, of thinking, of knowing, of judging, be of air, or of fire, or of the brain, or of the blood, or of atoms, or besides the usual four elements of a fifth kind of body, I know not what; or whether the combining or tempering together of this our flesh itself has power to accomplish these things. And one has attempted to establish this, and another to establish that. Yet who ever doubts that he himself lives, and remembers, and understands, and wills, and thinks, and knows, and judges? Seeing that even if he doubts, he lives; if he doubts, he remembers why he doubts; if he doubts, he understands that he doubts; if he doubts, he wishes to be certain; if he doubts, he thinks; if he doubts, he knows that he does not know; if he doubts, he judges that he ought not to assent rashly. Whosoever therefore doubts about anything else, ought not to doubt of all these things; which if they were not, he would not be able to doubt of anything.

They who think the mind to be either a body or the combination or tempering of the body, will have all these things to seem to be in a subject, so that the substance is air, or fire, or some other corporeal thing, which they think to be the mind; but that the understanding (*intelligentia*) is *in* this corporeal thing as its quality, so that this corporeal thing is the subject, but the understanding is in the subject: *viz.* that the mind is the subject, which they judge to be a corporeal thing, but the understanding [intelligence], or any other of those things which we have mentioned as certain to us, is in that subject. They also hold nearly the same opinion who deny the mind itself to be body, but think it to be the combination or tempering together of the body; for there is this difference, that the former say that the mind itself is the substance, in which the understanding [intelligence] is, as in a subject; but the latter say that the mind itself is in a subject, *viz.* in the body. of which it is the combination or tempering together. And hence, by consequence, what else can they think, except that the understanding also is in the same body as in a subject?

And all these do not perceive that the mind knows itself, even when it seeks for itself, as we have already shown. But nothing is at all rightly said to be known while its substance is not known. And therefore, when the mind knows itself, it knows its own substance. But it is certain about itself, as those things which are said above prove convincingly; although it is not at all certain whether itself is air, or fire, or some body, or some function of body. Therefore it is not any of these. And to the whole which is bidden to know itself, belongs this, that it is certain that it is not any of those things of which it is uncertain, and is certain that it is that only, which only it is certain that it is. For it thinks in this way of fire, or air, and whatever else of the body it thinks of. Neither can it in any way be brought to pass that it should so think that which itself is, as it thinks that which itself is not. Since it thinks all these things through an imaginary phantasy, whether fire, or air, or this or that body or that part or combination and tempering together of the body: nor assuredly is it said to be all those things, but some one of them. But if it were any one of them, it would think this one in a different manner from the rest, *viz.* not through an imaginary phantasy, as absent things are thought, which either themselves or some of like kind have been touched by the bodily sense; but by some inward, not feigned, but true presence (for nothing is more present to it than itself); just as it thinks that itself lives, and remembers, and understands, and wills. For it knows these things in itself, and does not imagine them as though it had touched them by the sense outside itself, as corporeal things are touched. And if it attaches nothing to itself from the thought of these things, so as to think itself to be something of the kind, then whatsoever remains to it from itself, that alone is itself.

Chapter 11: In memory, understanding [or intelligence], and will, we have to note ability, learning, and use. Memory, understanding, and will are one essentially, and three relatively.

Putting aside, then, for a little while all other things, of which the mind is certain concerning itself, let us especially consider and discuss these three—memory, understanding, will. For we may commonly discern in these three the character of the abilities of the young also; since the more tenaciously and easily a boy remembers, and the more acutely he understands, and the more ardently he studies, the more praiseworthy is he in point of ability. But when the question is about any one's learning, then we ask not how solidly and easily he remembers, or how shrewdly he understands; but what it is that he remembers, and what it is that he understands. And because the mind is regarded as praiseworthy, not only as being learned, but also as being good, one gives heed not only to what he remembers and what he understands, but also to what he wills (*velit*); not how ardently he wills, but first, what it is he wills, and then how greatly he wills it. For the mind that loves eagerly is then to be praised, when it loves that which ought to be loved eagerly. Since then, we speak of these three—ability, knowledge, use—the first of these is to be considered under the three heads, of what a man can do in memory, and understanding, and will. The second of them is to be considered in regard to that which any one has in his memory and in his understanding, which he has attained by a studious will. But the third, *viz.* use, lies in the will, which handles those things that are contained in the memory and understanding, whether it refer them to anything further, or rest satisfied with them as an end. For to use, is to take up something into the power of the will; and to enjoy, is to use with joy, not any longer of hope, but of the actual thing. Accordingly, every one who enjoys, uses; for he takes up something into the power of the will, wherein he also is satisfied as with an end. But not every one who uses, enjoys, if he has sought after that, which he takes up into the power of the will, not on account of the thing itself, but on account of something else.

Since, then, these three, memory, understanding, will, are not three lives, but one life, nor three minds, but one mind; it follows certainly that neither are they three substances, but one substance. Since memory, which is called life, and mind, and substance, is so called in respect to itself; but it is called memory, relatively to something. And I should say the same also of understanding and of will, since they are called understanding and will, relatively to something; but each in respect to itself is life, and mind, and essence. And hence these three are one, in that they are one life, one mind, one essence; and whatever else they are severally called in respect to themselves, they are called also together, not plurally, but in the singular number. But they are three, in that wherein they are mutually referred to each other; and if they were not equal, and this not only each to each, but also each to all, they certainly could not mutually contain each other; for not only is each contained by each, but also all by each. For I remember that I have memory and understanding, and will; and I understand that I understand, and will, and remember; and I will that I will, and remember, and understand; and I remember together my whole memory, and understanding, and will. For that of my memory which I do not remember, is not in my memory; and nothing is so much in the memory as memory itself. Therefore I remember the whole memory. Also, whatever I understand I know that I understand, and I know that I will whatever I will; but whatever I know I remember. Therefore I remember the whole of my understanding, and the whole of my will. Likewise, when I understand these three things, I understand them together as a whole. For there is none of things intelligible which I do not understand, except what I do not know; but what I do not know, I neither remember, nor will. Therefore, whatever of things intelligible I do not understand, it follows also that I neither remember nor will. And whatever of things intelligible I remember and will, it follows that I understand. My will also embraces my whole understanding and my whole memory, whilst I use the whole that I understand and remember. And, therefore, while all are mutually comprehended by each, and as wholes, each as a whole is equal to each as a whole, and each as a whole at the same time to all as wholes; and these three are one, one life, one mind, one essence.

Chapter 12. The mind is an image of the trinity in its own memory, and understanding, and will.

Are we, then, now to go upward, with whatever strength of purpose we may, to that chiefest and highest essence, of which the human mind is an inadequate image, yet an image? Or are these same three things to be yet more distinctly made plain in the soul, by means of those things which we receive from without, through the bodily sense, wherein the knowledge of corporeal things is impressed upon us in time? Since we found the mind itself to be such in its own memory, and understanding, and will, that since it was understood always to know and always to will itself, it was understood also at the same time always to remember itself, always to understand and love itself, although not always to think of itself as *separate* from those things which are not itself; and hence its memory of itself, and understanding of itself, are with difficulty discerned in it. For in this case, where these two things are very closely conjoined, and one is not preceded by the other by any time at all, it looks as if they were not two things, but one called by two names; and love itself is not so plainly felt to exist when the sense of need does not disclose it, since what is loved is always at hand. And hence these things may be more lucidly set forth, even to men of duller minds, if such topics are treated of as are brought within reach of the mind in time, and happen to it in time; while it remembers what it did not remember before, and sees what it did not see before, and loves what it did not love before. But this discussion demands now another beginning, by reason of the measure of the present book.

ANSELM
1033–1109

Anselm was born to a noble family in Piedmont (Aosta), a town in the Italian Alps. His father had prepared him for a political career, but instead he joined a Benedictine monastery at Bec, Normandy, to study philosophy and theology. After graduating, he became the abbott. In 1093 he became the archbishop. Besides his three main theological works, *Monologion, Proslogion,* and *Cur Deus homo?* (Why God and man?), he wrote studies on semantics (*De grammatico*), truth (*De veritate*), and freedom (*De libertate arbitrii*). In his final, unfinished work, called *On Power and Powerlessness, Possibility and Impossibility, Necessity and Liberty,* Anselm tried to unravel the mystery of how a soul could come into existence. Upon learning that he would soon die, he wrote, "If it is His will I shall gladly obey, but if He should prefer me to stay with you just long enough to solve the question of the origin of the soul which I have been turning over in my mind, I would gratefully accept the chance, for I doubt whether anybody else will solve it when I am gone."[1]

Anselm's philosophy and theology, highly influenced by Greek rationality, helped build a foundation for scholasticism, a method and system of thought based primarily on the works of Plato and Aristotle and embracing all the intellectual, artistic, philosophical, and theological activities carried on in various medieval schools as taught by its proponents. But unlike ancient Greek philosophy, which was essentially the work of individuals, scholasticism was an attempt to build philosophy as part of a "Christian society" whose purpose in turn was to transcend both individuals and nations. As the corporate product of social thought, scholastic reasoning depended on obedience to authority as espoused by the traditional forms of thought codified within the supposedly "revealed" Christian religion under the auspices of the church. As a result, philosophy was subjugated to theology and rigidly controlled by the authoritarian hierarchy of the church.

Anselm was one of the first to use a formal linguistic analysis to "solve" philosophical problems. In his *De veritate* (On truth), for instance, he shows that there are different senses of the concept of "truth," which are abused by various thinkers to achieve false ends. In *De*

---

1. M. Charlesworth, *St. Anselm's Proslogion* (Oxford: Oxford University Press, 1965), p. 21.

libertate arbitrii (On free will), he tries to identify the necessary and sufficient conditions for the concept of free will, a technique that will reappear in twentieth-century analytic philosophy. In *De casu diaboli* (On the devil's fall), he uses the idea of the fall from grace by a God-created Satan to argue that the existence of evil is compatible with the existence of an all-good God.

In his most famous work, *Proslogion,* from which our selection is taken, Anselm relies on Aristotelian logic as developed by Boethius, along with a variety of Neoplatonic ideas, to create his famous ontological argument for the existence of God. Later thinkers divided over it vehemently. Philosophers such as Descartes, Spinoza, Leibniz, and Hegel, inclined toward a Platonic or Neoplatonic realism about universals in which the role of essences is emphasized over materialism, each accepted some form of the ontological argument as valid and profound. Others, most notably Aquinas, Hume, and Kant, under the influence of Aristotelian nominalism, rejected the argument as mere verbal trickery.

In an attempt to equate the denial of God with a self-contradiction, Anselm quotes from Psalms 14:1, "The fool has said in his heart: There is no God." He tries to derive God's existence from the meaning of the word "God": the greatest conceivable being a greater than which cannot be conceived. Anselm then claims that since existence is greater than nonexistence, to say that "God does not exist" is tantamount to saying something like, "A being that cannot be conceived as anything other than existing does not exist," or "A being that exists necessarily does not exist," which is self-contradictory. Crucial to understanding Anselm's thinking is the distinction between an idea that exists in reality—*in re*—and an idea that exists only in conception—*in intellectu.* Anselm's argument is that if an idea is the greatest, then it must exist *in re,* not just *in intellectu,* since it is greater to exist in reality than merely in the conception. That is why any supreme or perfect idea, such as Being, exists *in re,* why reality itself has existence not just in concept (for instance, merely *in intellectu* in the mind of God). This line of argument, based on Plato's realistic metaphysics and buttressed by Augustine's Neoplatonic reinterpretation of Christian dogma, was inspired by a question that had puzzled many medieval Christian thinkers, namely, why God would have to create a world at all. If God is perfect, there would be no need for God to add to the realm of His own being. Anselm's ontological argument is followed by objections from another Benedictine monk, Gaunilon, from the Abbey of Marmoutier near Tours. Gaunilon claims, on behalf of "the fool," that Anselm's proof is bogus for two main reasons: first, we cannot properly form the concept of a necessarily existent being since there is nothing in experience on which to base such a concept; second, we can imagine a lot of perfect things defined as "perfect" but that in fact do not exist. For instance, why not argue for the existence of the perfect island or the perfect unicorn?

PROSLOGION

. . . I began to ask myself whether there might be found a single argument which would require no other for its proof than itself alone; and alone would suffice to demonstrate that God truly exists, and that there is a supreme good requiring nothing else, which all other things require for their existence and well-being; and whatever we believe regarding the divine Being.

Although I often and earnestly directed my thought to this end, and at some times that which I sought seemed to be just within my reach, while again it wholly evaded my mental vision, at last in despair I was about to cease, as if from the search for a thing which could not be found. But when I wished to exclude this thought altogether, lest, by busying my mind to no purpose, it should keep me from other thoughts, in which I might be successful; then more and more, though I was unwilling and shunned it, it began to force itself upon me, with a kind of importunity. So, one day, when I was exceedingly wearied with resisting its importunity, in the very conflict of my thoughts, the proof of which I had despaired offered itself, so that I eagerly embraced the thoughts which I was strenuously repelling. . . .

And so Lord, do thou, who does give understanding to faith, give me, so far as thou knowest it to be profitable, to understand that thou art as we believe; and that thou art that which we believe. And, indeed, we believe that thou art a being than which nothing greater can be conceived. Or is there no such nature, since the fool hath said in his heart, there is no God? But, at any rate, this very fool, when he hears of this being of which I speak—a being than which nothing greater can be conceived—understands what he hears, and what he understands is in his understanding; although he does not understand it to exist.

For, it is one thing for an object to be in the understanding, and another to understand that the object exists. When a painter first conceives of what he will afterwards perform, he has it in his understanding, but he does not yet understand it to be, because he has not yet performed it. But after he has made the painting, he both has it in his understanding, and he understands that it exists, because he has made it.

Hence, even the fool is convinced that something exists in the understanding, at least, than which nothing greater can be conceived. For, when he hears of this, he understands it. And whatever is understood, exists in the understanding. And assuredly that, than which nothing greater can be conceived, cannot exist in the understanding alone. For, suppose it exists in the understanding alone: then it can be conceived to exist in reality; which is greater.

Therefore, if that, than which nothing greater can be conceived, exists in the understanding alone, the very being, than which nothing greater can be conceived, is one, than which a greater can be conceived. But obviously this is impossible. Hence, there is no doubt that there exists a being, than which nothing greater can be conceived, and it exists both in the understanding and in reality. . . .

And it assuredly exists so truly, that it cannot be conceived not to exist. For, it is possible

From the *Proslogium* trans. Sidney Norton Deane (Open Court, 1903).

to conceive of a being which cannot be conceived not to exist, and this is greater than one which can be conceived not to exist. Hence, if that, than which nothing greater can be conceived, can be conceived not to exist, it is not that, than which nothing greater can be conceived. But this is an irreconcilable contradiction. There is, then, so truly a being than which nothing greater can be conceived to exist, that it cannot even be conceived not to exist; and this being thou art, O Lord, our God.

So truly, therefore, dost thou exist, O Lord, my God, that thou canst not be conceived not to exist; and rightly. For if a mind could conceive of a being better than thee, the creature would rise above the Creator; and this is most absurd. And, indeed, whatever else there is, except thee alone, can be conceived not to exist. To thee alone, therefore, it belongs to exist more truly than all other beings, and hence in a higher degree than all others. For, whatever else exists does not exist so truly, and hence in a less degree it belongs to it to exist. Why, then, has the fool said in his heart, there is no God, since it is so evident, to a rational mind, that thou dost exist in the highest degree of all? Why, except that he is dull and a fool? . . .

ON BEHALF OF THE FOOL
An answer to the argument of Anselm by Gaunilon, a monk of Marmoutier

. . . if it should be said that a being which cannot be even conceived in terms of any fact, is in the understanding, I do not deny that this being is, accordingly, in my understanding. But since through this fact it can in no wise attain to real existence also, I do not yet concede to it that existence at all, until some certain proof of it shall be given.

For he who says that this being exists, because otherwise the being which is greater than all will not be greater than all, does not attend strictly to what he is saying. For I do not yet say, no, I even deny or doubt that this being is greater than any real object. Nor do I concede to it any other existence than this (if it should be called existence) which it has when the mind, according to a word merely heard, tries to form the image of an object absolutely unknown to it.

How, then, is the veritable existence of that being proved to me from the assumption, by hypothesis, that it is greater than all other beings? For I should still deny this, or doubt your demonstration of it, to this extent, that I should not admit that this being is in my understanding and concept even in the way in which many objects whose real existence is uncertain and doubtful, are in my understanding and concept. For it should be proved first that this being itself really exists somewhere; and then, from the fact that it is greater than all, we shall not hesitate to infer that it also subsists in itself.

For example: it is said that somewhere in the ocean is an island, which, because of the difficulty, or rather the impossibility, of discovering what does not exist, is called the lost island. And they say that this island has an inestimable wealth of all manner of riches and delicacies in greater abundance than is told of the Islands of the Blest; and that having no owner or inhabitant, it is more excellent than all other countries, which are inhabited by mankind, in the abundance with which it is stored.

Now if someone should tell me that there is such an island, I should easily understand his words, in which there is no difficulty. But suppose that he went on to say, as if by a logical inference: "You can no longer doubt that this island which is more excellent than all lands exists somewhere, since you have no doubt that it is in your understanding. And since it is more excellent not to be in the understanding alone, but to exist both in the understanding and in reality, for this reason it must exist. For if it does not exist, any land which really exists will be more excellent than it; and so the island already understood by you to be more excellent will not be more excellent."

If a man should try to prove to me by such reasoning that this island truly exists, and that its existence should no longer be doubted, either I should believe that he was jesting, or I know not which I ought to regard as the greater fool: myself, supposing that I should allow this proof; or him, if he should suppose that he had established with any certainty the existence of this island. For he ought to show first that the hypothetical excellence of this island exists as a real and indubitable fact, and in no wise as any unreal object, or one whose existence is uncertain, in my understanding.

ANSELM'S REPLY

But, you say, it is as if one should suppose an island in the ocean, which surpasses all lands in its fertility, and which, because of the difficulty, or rather the impossibility, of discovering what does not exist, is called a lost island; and should say that there can be no doubt that this island truly exists in reality, for this reason, that one who hears it described easily understands what he hears.

Now I promise confidently that if any man shall devise anything existing either in reality or in concept alone (except that than which a greater cannot be conceived) to which he can adapt the sequence of my reasoning, I will discover that thing, and will give him his lost island, not to be lost again.

But it now appears that this being than which a greater is inconceivable cannot be conceived not to be, because it exists on so assured a ground of truth; for otherwise it would not exist at all.

Hence, if any one says that he conceives this being not to exist, I say that at the time when he conceives of this either he conceives of a being than which a greater is inconceivable, or he does not conceive at all. If he does not conceive, he does not conceive of the nonexistence of that of which he does not conceive. But if he does conceive, he certainly conceives of a being which cannot be even conceived not to exist. For if it could be conceived not to exist, it could be conceived to have a beginning and an end. But this is impossible.

He, then, who conceives of this being conceives of a being which cannot be even conceived not to exist; but he who conceives of this being does not conceive that it does not exist; else he conceives what is inconceivable. The nonexistence, then, of that than which a greater cannot be conceived is inconceivable.

AVERROES (IBN RUSHD)

1126–1198

After the fall of the Roman Empire, with Christianity in full swing, the philosophical schools of Athens were closed by Justinian in 529 C.E. The books were burned and Greek learning, denounced by papal authorities as pagan heresies punishable by death, virtually disappeared from Europe. Many philosophers escaped to Persia where Greek works, translated first into Syriac and then Arabic, had already begun to exert wide influence among Islamic and Jewish thinkers. Thus the Platonic and Aristotelian systems not only survived the five hundred years of the Dark Ages of Christendom in Europe, but continued to evolve on the other side of the Mediterranean.

Schools in Alexandria, Syria, and Persia became centers for the translation and study of Greek texts. After the Arab conquest of Spain, philosophy migrated back from across North Africa into Europe through Spain, where in Toledo and Cordova a group of brilliant Islamic philosophers rekindled the flame of the golden age of Greece within Christendom. Among them were Avicenna (Ibn Sina, 980–1037) and Averroes. Both are considered followers solely of Aristotle, due in part to a confusion of Platonic and Aristotelian ideas as espoused in an influential work of the time, the *Theology of Aristotle,* a Neoplatonic work that was really a compilation of Plotinus's *Enneads.*

Averroes (Mohammed Ibn Rushd) saw Avicenna's interpretations of Aristotle as colored on the one hand by religion and, on the other, by Stoic and Neoplatonic influences. He tried to purge these influences from his own interpretations of Aristotle, whom he regarded not only as the greatest of all philosophers but as the "model of human perfection." He was born in Europe, in Cordova, Spain, the son of a *qadi* (judge). He studied theology, law, medicine, mathematics, and philosophy, which under Islamic protection centered on the masterworks of Plato and Aristotle as preserved by an evolving series of lengthy and often innovative commentators, ideas that by then had been banned for centuries and virtually forgotten in the adjoining Holy Roman Empire.

Averroes began his career as a judge, first in Seville and then Cordova. But his main interest was philosophy. According to legend, one night he and Prince Abu Ya'qub Yusuf were arguing over the origin of the world and the nature of mind. Supposedly, Averroes's ruminations on Aristotle's account of existence and the nature of the soul so impressed the prince that he commissioned Averroes to write an entire set of commentaries. Then, a few years later, the same prince appointed Averroes as his personal physician so that he would no longer have to be a judge. Averroes thus spent the rest of his life writing commentaries on virtually all of Aristotle's works.

Averroes wrote detailed and original reconstructive commentaries on Aristotle's *Metaphysics, Physics, Posterior Analytics, De caelo,* and *De anima,* as well as Plato's *Republic.* His main concern was not with subtle reinterpretations of ancient Greek wisdom according to then-current religious tenets (to which most previous Islamic commentators, and most subsequent Christian commentators were prone), but rather to "reawaken philosophy's slumbering soul." Indeed, he argues that previous commentators such as Avicenna had completely misunderstood and corrupted Aristotle's ideas with theological concerns.

After the prince died, Averroes's enemies accused him of promoting the "pagan" philosophy of the ancients instead of following the accepted Muslim faith. He spent the last years of his life in exile, first outside Cordova and then in Morocco. Ironically, just as five centuries earlier Justinian and the Christians had burned the philosophy books, so now the Caliph al-Mansur burned all available books on logic and metaphysics. He published an edict that anyone who believed that truth can be known by unaided reason, independently of divine revelation, would be sentenced by God to Hell.

After the Christian-Muslim wars pushed the Muslims out of Spain, the censorship of Averroes by the Islamic rulers marked the end of Muslim philosophy. Banished from the Mohammedan world, it was replaced by a rigid orthodoxy. And just as the Islam authorities once welcomed works banned by their Christian enemies, the conquering Christians were quick to seize works banned by the Muslims. Thus, in one of the greatest historical ironies, philosophy managed to pass hands from one opposing religion to another and then back again.

Averroes defended Aristotelian philosophy and "purified" it of its Stoic and Neoplatonic elements so well that scholastic writers called him "*The* Commentator." Thomas Aquinas, for instance, will use Averroes as a source while writing his own commentaries on Aristotle and the *Summa contra Gentiles.* During his lifetime, Averroes defended philosophy from various assaults by the Mohammedan orthodoxy. For instance, when al-Ghazali, a famous theologian of the time, published *Destruction of the Philosophers,* claiming that because all necessary truth is revealed in the Koran, philosophical speculation is completely unnecessary, Averroes responded by publishing *Destruction of the Destruction,* showing that religious dogmas are at best philosophical truths presented in allegorical form and amenable to an Aristotelian interpretation. Likewise, Averroes's *Ta-hafut al-Tahafut* (The incoherence of the incoherence) was a response to al-Ghazali's *The Incoherence of the Philosophers.* Al-Ghazali had criticized philosophers, especially Avicenna, for advocating views incompatible with religious faith. In his defense of the philosophers, Averroes attacks al-Ghazali's book without himself having to deny any of the doctrines of Islam.

Averroes does this by evoking a distinction which many later medieval philosophers would rely on to avoid direct conflict with the Christian counterparts of the orthodox Muslim authorities, the distinction between "revealed" theology and "natural" theology. The idea is that philosophy and theology each have a legitimate but distinct function based on a three-tiered class division of human beings, much like the Golden Lie espoused by Plato in the *Republic* about the three different classes of souls ("gold," "silver," and "bronze"). Like Plato's cave-dwellers, the lowest class of people—the vast majority—live by imagination, not reason. Unable to comprehend philosophy, they need the security of religious answers forced by obedience to an orthodox dogma into which they must be indoctrinated by eloquent or charismatic priests. The next, slightly higher, class—much smaller than the first—lives by the same sorts of beliefs as the lowest class but with more intelligence. They do not merely accept dogma because it is taught but try to establish intellectual justification for their beliefs. Theologians come from this class. However, since they too are ultimately prejudiced (they seek justification only for commonly accepted beliefs), they can never attain the truth, which requires complete impartiality from all orthodoxy. The third, highest level of intelligence, found in but a few extraordinary individuals who can discover directly for themselves the awesome truths that the rational theologians and the irrational believers can only go on seeking, allows one to see that religion does not and cannot ever provide a connection to truth. This highest level of intelligence is found only among the philosophers.

According to Averroes, philosophers know that to know the truth you must know it not by faith nor by rationalization from premises accepted as true by faith, but directly on the basis of premises first tested by experience and justified by careful and logical reasoning. The most difficult of all truths, known by only a select few philosophers, is one that in a way contradicts all that has just been said about the three different levels of intelligence: namely, that the active part of the mind of each human being is not a distinct and separately existing individual but is the same, numerically identical unity. The greatest of all truths, hidden in the tradition passed down to us from Plato and Aristotle as revealed through Averroes's commentaries, is that each individual mind is numerically identical with all other individual minds, identical to the Agent Intellect, the mind of God. Like Avicenna before him, Averroes claims that the individual human intellect, activated from without by the Agent Intellect (God), is itself the emanation of the Agent Intellect (God). But it has both an active and a passive part. The passive intellect, brought into existence through interaction with the Agent Intellect via the active intellect, does not survive the body. Only the active intellect, which is immortal, survives. It is this active intellect that is numerically identical (one and the same entity) within all sentient beings. The active intellect, described in the selection presented from Averroes's *Commentary on "On the Soul,"* is not a personal faculty but is numerically identical to the Agent Intellect, the One that individuates itself into the Many by illuminating the passive intellects within each individual human being.

Averroes's monopsychism cut deeply against both Christian dogma and the Mohammedan theology within which Averroes presented it. His response to his own rulers was to claim that while reason compelled him to assert the unity of the intellect among all human beings, the belief in separate individual human intelligences could be accepted by faith. But he persisted in arguing that the ultimate culmination of reason led to what he took to be Aristotle's secret teaching as passed down through his cryptic remarks in *On the Soul:* the intellectual unity of all mankind.

Islamic theologians tried to reinterpret their understanding of Greek philosophy away from Averroes's monopsychism. Lacking any good argument, they simply banned it as a Muslim heresy. This brought it to the attention of Christians. Secular thinkers in northern Europe took interest, until a philosophical movement arose in the thirteenth century known as the "Averroists" or "integral Aristotelians." Their main proponents were members of the faculty in Paris. These philosophers argued, following Averroes, that the ultimate conclusion of reason and the correct understanding of Plato and Aristotle leads to the same inexorable truth: the numerical unity of the active intelligences of all conscious beings. Christian theologians of the time, notably St. Albert and St. Thomas, saw in this idea the end not just of Islam but of Christianity as well and so, like their Islam counterparts, united as a front against Averroism until monopsychism was proclaimed a Christian heresy as well and condemned by the church in Paris in 1270—the same year as the publication of Thomas's *On the Unity of the Intellect Against the Averroists*—and formally added to the list of "forbidden propositions." Thus Averroes's monopsychism had the added distinction of being declared heresy in two opposing religions. Although the Averroists continued to teach in secret what they took to be the only correct understanding of the ancient Greek wisdom—the unity of the active intellect within all minds—the idea became successfully repressed from Western philosophy until the present day.[1]

COMMENTARY ON "ON THE SOUL"

BOOK III

TEXT 4

It is necessary, therefore, that, if the intellect understands all things, it be not mixed, as Anaxagoras has said, in order that it may dominate, that is in order that it may understand. For if something were to appear in it, that which appears would prevent something foreign from appearing in it, since it is something other.

COMMENTARY

After Aristotle has set down that the material, receiving intellect must belong to the genus of passive powers, and, that in spite of this, it is not altered by the reception of that which it receives, for it is neither a body nor a power within a body, he provides a demonstration for this. And he says: *It is necessary, therefore, that, if the intellect understands,* etc. That is, it is necessary, therefore, that, if the intellect understands all those things which exist outside the soul, it be described—prior to its understanding—as belonging to the genus of passive, not active, powers, and it is necessary that it be not mixed with bodies, that is, that it be neither a body nor a power within a body, be it a natural or animate power, as Anaxagoras has said. Thereafter Aristotle says: *in order that it may understand* etc. That is, it is necessary that it be not mixed, in order that it may understand all things and receive them. For if it were mixed, then it would be either a body or a power within a body, and if it were one of these, it would have a form proper to itself, which form would prevent it from receiving some foreign form.

This is what he has in mind when he says: *For if something were to appear in it* etc. That is, if the passive intellect were to have a form proper to itself, then that form would prevent it from receiving the various external forms, which are different from it. Thus, one must inquire into those propositions by means of which Aristotle shows these two things about the intellect, namely [1] that it belongs to the genus of passive powers, and [2] that it is not

1. Daniel Kolak, *I Am You: A Philosophical Explanation of the Possibility That We Are All the Same Person* (Ann Arbor, Mich.: UMI, 1986).

From Averroes, "Long Commentary on De Anima," trans. A. Hyman, in *Philosophy in the Middle Ages,* ed. A. Hyman and J. Walsh (New York: Harper & Row, 1967). Copyright Arthur Hyman. Used by permission.

alterable, since it is neither a body nor a power within a body. For these two [propositions] are the starting point of all those things which are said about the intellect. As Plato said, the most extensive discussion must take place in the beginning; for the slightest error in the beginning is the cause of the greatest error in the end, as Aristotle says.

We say: That conception by the intellect belongs in some way to a passive power, just as in the case of a sensory power perception by a sense belongs to a passive power, becomes clear through the following considerations. Now, the passive powers are moveable by that to which they are related, while active powers move that to which they are related. And since it is the case that something moves something else only insofar as it exists in actuality and something is moved insofar as it exists in potentiality, it follows necessarily, that since the forms of things exist in actuality outside the soul, they move the rational soul insofar as it understands them, just as in the case of sensible things it is necessary that they move the senses insofar as they are things existing in actuality and that the senses are moved by them. Therefore, the rational soul must consider the forms which are in the imaginative faculty, just as the senses must inspect sensible things. And since it appears that the forms of external things move this power in such a way that the mind abstracts these forms from material things and thereby makes them the first intelligibles in actuality, after they had been intelligibles in potentiality—it appears from this that this soul [the intellect] is also active, not only passive. For insofar as the intelligibles move [the intellect], it is passive, but insofar as they are moved by it, it is active. For this reason Aristotle states subsequently that it is necessary to posit in the rational soul the following two distinct powers, namely, an active power and a passive power. And he states clearly that each one of the rational soul's parts is neither generable nor corruptible. In the present discussion, however, he begins to describe the nature of this passive power, to the extent to which it is necessary in this exposition. Therefore he states that this distinct power, namely, that which is passive and receptive, exists in the rational faculty.

That the substance which receives these forms can not be a body or a power in a body, becomes clear from the propositions of which Aristotle makes use in this discussion. One of these is that this substance [the material intellect] receives all material forms, and this is something well known about this intellect. The other is that everything which receives something else must necessarily be devoid of the nature of that which it receives and that its essence is not the same in species as the essence of that which it receives. For, if that which receives is of the same nature as that which is received, then something would receive itself and that which moves would be the same as that which is moved. Wherefore it is necessary that the sense which receives color lacks color and the sense which receives sound lacks sound. And this proposition is necessarily true and there is no doubt about it. From these two propositions it follows that the substance which is called the material intellect does not have any of the material forms in its nature. And since the material forms are either a body or forms in a body, it is evident that the substance which is called the material intellect is not a body or a form in a body. For this reason it is not mixed with matter in any way at all. And you should know that what he states is necessarily so, namely that, since it [the material intellect] is a substance, and since it receives the forms of material things or material forms, it does not have in itself a material form, that is, it is not composed of matter and form. Nor is it some one of the material forms, for the material forms are not separable from bodies. Nor, again, is it one of the first simple forms since these are separable from bodies, but it [the material intellect] does not . . . receive forms except as differentiated and insofar as they are intelligible in potentiality, not in actuality, that is, it must be related to the body in some way. Therefore it is something different from form and from matter and from that which is composed of these. But whether this substance [the material intellect] has a proper form which is different in its being from the material forms has not yet been explained in this discussion. For the proposition which states that that which receives must be devoid of the nature of that which it receives is understood as referring to the nature of the species, not to the nature of its genus, and even less to the nature of something remote, and still less to the nature of something which is predicated according to equivocation. Thus we say that in the sense of touch there exists something intermediate between the two contraries which it perceives, for contraries differ in species from intermediate things. Since this is the disposition of the material intellect, namely, that it is some existing thing, and that it is a power separate from body, and that it has no material form, it is clear that it is not passive [in the sense of being alterable] (for passive things, that is things which are alterable, are like material forms), and that it is simple, and separable from body, as Aristotle says. The nature of the material intellect is understood by Aristotle in this manner. We shall speak subsequently about the questions which he raised.

TEXT 5

And thus [the material intellect] has no other nature but that which is possible. Therefore that part of the soul which is called intellect (and I call intellect that part by means of which we distinguish and think) is not something existing in actuality before it thinks.

COMMENTARY

After Aristotle has shown that the material intellect does not possess any of the forms of material things, he begins to define it in the following manner. And he says that it has no nature but the nature of the possibility for receiving the material intelligible forms. And he states: *And thus the material intellect has no other nature,* etc. That is, that part of the soul which is called the material intellect has no nature and essence through which it exists (*constituatur*) insofar as it is material but the nature of possibility, for it is devoid of all material and intelligible forms.

Thereafter he says: *and I call intellect,* etc. That is, and I intend by *intellect* that faculty of the soul which is truly called intellect, not that faculty which is called intellect in a general sense, that is, the imaginative faculty (in the Greek language), but I intend that faculty by means of which we distinguish speculative things and by means of which we think about things to be done in the future. Thereafter he says: *it is not something existing in actuality before it thinks.* That is, it is the definition of the material intellect that it is that which is in potentiality all the concepts (*intentiones*) of the universal material forms and it is not something in actuality before it understands them.

Since this is the definition of the material intellect, it is clear that it differs in respect to itself from prime matter in that it is in potentiality all the concepts of the universal material forms, while prime matter is in potentiality all these sensible forms, not as knowing and comprehending. And the reason why this nature, that is, the material intellect, distinguishes and knows, while prime matter does not distinguish or know, is that prime matter receives differentiated, that is, individual and particular forms, while the material intellect receives universal forms. And from this it is clear that this nature, that is, the material intellect, is not some individual thing, either a body or a power in a body, for if it were, it would receive the forms insofar as they are differentiated and particular, and if this were the case, then the forms existing in the material intellect would be intelligible in potentiality and thus this intellect would not distinguish the nature of the forms insofar as they are forms, and the case would be the same as that of a disposition for individual forms, whether they are spiritual or corporeal. Therefore, if this nature, which is called intellect, receives forms, it is necessary that it receives these forms in a manner of reception different from that according to which these matters receive the forms whose determination in prime matter is the determination of prime matter in respect to them. Therefore it is not necessary that there belong to the genus of those matters by which the form is determined as particular anything but prime matter. For if there were other matters in this genus, then the reception of forms in these matters would be of the same genus, for diversity in the nature of the receptacle produces a diversity in the nature of that which is received. This consideration moved Aristotle to affirm that this nature, that is, the material intellect, differs from the nature of matter and from the nature of form and from the nature of the composite.

All these things being as they are, it seems to me proper to write down what appears to me to be correct concerning this subject. And if that which appears to me to be correct will not be complete, let it be the starting point for something which can be completed. Now, I beg those brethren who see what has been written, that they write down their questions and perhaps in this way that which is true about this subject will be discovered, if I should not have discovered it. But should I have discovered what is true, as I think I have, then this truth will become clear through these questions. For truth, as Aristotle says, agrees with itself and bears witness to itself in every way.

As for the question stating: in what way are the speculative intelligibles generable and corruptible, while the intellect producing them and that receiving them are eternal (and what need would there be to posit an agent intellect and a receiving intellect were there not something that is generated)—this question would not arise would there not exist something which is the cause of the generation of the speculative intelligibles. But what has been said concerning the fact that these [speculative] intelligibles consists of two [principles], one of which is generated, the other of which is not generated is according to the course of nature. For, since conception by the intellect, as Aristotle says, is like perception by the senses—but perception by a sense is accomplished through two principles, one of which is that object through which sense perception becomes true (and this is the sensible outside the soul), and the other is that subject through which sense perception is an existing form (and this is the first actuality of the sense organ), it is likewise necessary that the intelligibles in actuality have two principles, one of which is the object through which they are true, namely, the forms which are the true images, the other one of which is that subject through which the intelligibles are one of the things existing in the world, and this is the material intellect. But there is no difference between sense and intellect except that the object through which sense-perception is true exists outside the soul, while the object through which conception by the intellect is true exists within the soul. As will be seen subsequently, this is what was said by Aristotle about this intellect.

This similarity exists in an even more perfect manner between the visible object which moves the sense of sight and the intelligible object which moves the intellect. For just as the visible object, which is color, moves the sense of sight only when through the presence of light it was made color in actuality after it had been color in potentiality, so also the imaginative forms move the material intellect only when they are made intelligibles in actuality after they had been intelligibles in potentiality. And for this reason (as will be seen later) it was necessary for Aristotle to posit an agent intellect, and this is the intellect which brings the imaginative forms from potentiality into actuality. Thus, just as the color which exists in potentiality is not the first actuality of that color which is the perceived form, while the subject which is actualized by this color is the sense of sight, so also the subject which is actualized by the intelligible object is not the imaginative forms which are intelligible in potentiality, but the material intellect is that subject which is actualized by the intelligibles. And the relation of the intelligible forms to the material intellect is as the relation of the form of color to the faculty of sight.

All these matters being as we have related, it is only necessary that the intelligibles in actuality, that is the speculative intelligibles, are generable according to the object through which they are true, that is, according to the imaginative forms, but not according to that subject through which they are one of the existing things, that is, according to the material intellect.

But the second question which states: in what way is the material intellect numerically one in all individual human beings, not generable nor corruptible, while the intelligibles existing in it in actuality (and this is the speculative intellect) are numbered according to the numeration of individual human beings, and generable and corruptible through the generation and corruption of individual human beings—this question is extremely difficult and one that has the greatest ambiguity.

If we posit that this material intellect is numbered according to the numeration of individual human beings, it follows that it is some individual thing, either a body or a power in a body. And if it were some individual thing, it would be the intelligible form in potentiality. But the intelligible form in potentiality is an object which moves the receiving intellect, not a subject which is moved. For, if the receiving subject were assumed to be some individual thing, it would follow, as we have said, that something receives itself, and this is impossible.

Even if we were to admit that it receives itself, it would necessarily follow that it receives itself insofar as it is diverse. And thus the intellectual faculty would be the same as the sensory faculty, and there would be no distinction between the existence of the form outside the soul and in the soul. For this individual matter receives the forms only as particulars and individuals. And this is one of the arguments which provide evidence that Aristotle was of the opinion that the material intellect is not an individual form.

On the other hand, were we to assert that the material intellect is not numbered according to the numeration of individual human beings, it would follow that its relation to all individual human beings who possess its ultimate perfection through generation would be the same. Whence it would be necessary that if one of these individual human beings acquires some knowledge, this knowledge would be acquired by all of them. For, if the conjunction of these individual human beings with what is known occurs because of the conjunction of the material intellect with them, just as the conjunction of a human being with the sensory form occurs because of the conjunction of the first perfection of the sense organ with him who receives the sensory form (but the conjunction of the material intellect with all human beings who exist in actuality in their ultimate perfection at some given time must be one and the same conjunction, for there is nothing which would produce any difference in the relation of conjunction between the two who are conjoined)—if, I say, this is the case, it is necessary that if you acquire some knowledge, I will acquire the same knowledge, which is absurd.

And regardless whether you assert that the ultimate perfection which is generated in some individual human being—that is, that perfection through which the material intellect is joined to human beings and through which it is as a form separable from the subject to which it is joined—inheres in the intellect, if something like that should be the case, or whether you assert that this perfection belongs to one of the faculties of the soul or to one of the faculties of the body, each of these assumptions leads to an absurd conclusion.

Therefore one must be of the opinion that if there exist some beings having a soul whose first perfection is a substance existing in separation from their subjects, as it is thought about the celestial bodies, it is impossible that there exist in each of their species more than one individual. For if there would exist in these, that is, in each of their species more than one individual, for example, in the body moved by the same mover, then the existence of these individuals would be unnecessary and superfluous, since their motion would result from the form which is one in number. For example, it is unnecessary that one sailor [captain] should have more than one ship at the same time, and it is likewise unnecessary that one artisan should have more than one instrument of the same kind.

This is the meaning of what was said in the first book of *De caelo,* namely that, if there existed another world, there would have to exist another celestial body corresponding to a celestial body in this world. And if there existed another celestial body, it would have to have a motive force numerically different from the motive force of this celestial body, that is, the one existing in this world. If this were the case, then the motive force of the celestial body would be material and numbered through the numeration of the celestial bodies, since it is impossible that a motive force which is one in number should belong to two bodies which are different in number. Therefore, a craftsman does not use more than one instrument when only one action proceeds from him. And it is generally thought that necessarily absurd conclusions will follow from the assertion we have made, namely, that the intellect *in habitu* is one in number. Avempace enumerated most of these absurd conclusions in his Letter which he called *The Conjunction of the Intellect with Man.* Since this is so, of what sort is the road toward the solution of this difficult question?

We say that it is evident that a man is thinking in actuality only because of the conjunction of the intelligible in actuality with him. It is also evident that matter and form are joined to one another in such a way that something which is composed of them is a unitary thing and this is especially evident in the case of the conjunction of the material intellect and the intelligible form in actuality. For that which is composed of these [the material intellect and the intelligible form] is not some third thing different from them as is the case in respect to other beings composed of matter and form. Hence the conjunction of the intelligible with man is only possible through the conjunction of one of these two parts with him, namely, that part which belongs to it [the intelligible] as matter or that part which belongs to it (namely, the intelligible) as form.

Since it is clear from the previously mentioned difficulties that it is impossible that the intelligible be joined to each individual human being and that it be numbered according their numeration through that part which is to it as matter, that is, through the material intellect, it remains that the conjunction of the intelligibles with us human beings takes place through the conjunction of the intelligible forms (and they are the imaginative forms) with us, that is, through that part which is in us in respect to them in some way like a form. And therefore the statement that a boy is potentially thinking can be understood in two ways. One of these is insofar as the imaginative forms which exist in him are intelligible in potentiality; the other is insofar as the material intellect, to whose nature it belongs to receive the concept of this imaginative form, is receptive in potentiality and joined to us in potentiality.

It is clear, therefore, that the first perfection of the intellect differs from the first perfection of the other faculties of the soul and that the term *perfection* is predicated of them in an equivocal fashion, and this is the opposite of what Alexander [of Aphrodisias] thought.

For this reason Aristotle said in his definition of the soul that the soul is the first perfection of a natural organic body, for it is not yet clear whether a body is perfected by all faculties in the same way, or whether there is among them some faculty by which a body is not perfected, or, if it is perfected by it, it will be perfected in some other way.

Now the predisposition of the intelligibles which exists in the imaginative faculty is similar to the predispositions which exist in the other faculties of the soul, namely, the predisposition for the first perfections of the other faculties of the soul, insofar as each of these predispositions is generated through the generation of the individual in which it exists and destroyed through the destruction of this individual and, generally, this predisposition is numbered according to the numeration of that individual.

But the two kinds of predisposition differ in that the first kind, namely, the predisposition which exists in the imaginative forms, is a predisposition in a moving principle, while the second kind, namely that predisposition which exists for the first perfections of the other parts of the soul, is a predisposition in a recipient.

Because of the similarity between these two kinds of predispositions Avempace thought that the only predisposition for the production of the intelligible concept is the predisposition existing in the imaginative forms. But these two predispositions differ as earth and heaven. For one of them is a predisposition in a moving principle insofar as it is a moving principle, while the other is a predisposition in something moved insofar as it is moved and is a recipient.

Thus one should hold the opinion which has already become clear to us from Aristotle's discussion, namely, that there are two kinds of intellect in the soul. One of these is the receiving intellect whose existence has been shown here, the other is the agent intellect and this is the one which causes the forms which are in the imaginative faculty to move the material intellect in actuality, after they had only moved it potentially, as will be clear further on from Aristotle's discussion. And these two kinds of intellect are not generable or corruptible. And the agent intellect is to the receiving intellect as form to matter, as will be shown later on.

Now Themistius was of the opinion that we are the agent intellect, and that the speculative intellect is nothing but the conjunction of the agent intellect with the material intellect. And it is not as he thought, but one must be of the opinion that there are three kinds of intellect in the soul. One of these is the receiving intellect, the second is the producing [agent] intellect, and the third is the produced [speculative] intellect. Two of these intellects are eternal, namely, the agent and receiving intellects, the third, however, is generable and corruptible in one way, eternal in another way.

Since as a result of this discussion we are of the opinion that the material intellect is a single one for all human beings and since we are also of the opinion that the human species is eternal, as has been shown in other places, it follows that the material intellect is never devoid of the natural principles which are common to the whole human species, namely, the first propositions and individual concepts which are common to all. For these intelligibles are one according to the recipient [the material intellect], and many according to the received form [the imaginative form].

Hence according to the manner in which they are one, they are necessarily eternal, for existence does not depart from the received object, namely, the moving principle which is the form of the imaginative forms, and there is nothing on part of the recipient which prevents its reception. For generation and corruption belongs to them only according to the multitude which befalls them, not according to the manner according to which they are one. Therefore, when in respect to some individual human being, some knowledge of the things first known is destroyed through the destruction of the object through which it is joined to us and through which it is true, that is the imaginative form, it does not follow that this knowledge is destroyed absolutely, but it is only destroyed in respect to some individual human being. Because of this we can say that the speculative intellect is one in all human beings.

If one considers these intelligibles insofar as they exist absolutely, not in respect to some individual human being, they are truly said to be eternal, and it is not the case that they are known at one time and not known at another time, but they are known always. And that existence belongs to them as intermediate between absence of existence and permanent existence. For in accordance with the quantitative difference [literally: according to the increase and decrease] which comes to the intelligibles from the ultimate perfection of human beings they are generable and corruptible, while insofar as they are one in number they are eternal.

This will be the case if it is not set down that the disposition in respect to the ultimate perfection in man is as the disposition in respect to the intelligibles which are common to all men, that is, that the world [literally: worldly existence] is not devoid of such an individual existence. That this should be impossible is not obvious, but someone who affirms this must have an adequate reason and one that puts the mind at rest. For if knowledge belongs in some proper fashion to human beings, just as the various kinds of crafts belong in some proper fashions to human beings, one should think that it is impossible that philosophy should be without any abode, just as one must be of the opinion that it is impossible that all the natural crafts should be without any abode. For if some part of the earth lacks them, that is, these crafts, for example, the northern quarter of the earth, the other quarters will not lack them, since it is clear that they can have an abode in the southern part, just as in the northern.

Thus, perhaps, philosophy comes to be in the major portion of the subject at all times, just as man comes to be from man and horse from horse. According to this mode of existence the speculative intellect is neither generable nor corruptible.

In general, the case of the agent intellect which produces the intelligibles is the same as the case of the intellect which distinguishes and receives the intelligibles. For just as the agent intellect never ceases from generating and producing intelligibles in an absolute manner, even though some particular subject may be removed from this generation, so is it with the intellect that distinguishes.

Aristotle indicated this in the first treatise of this book [*De anima*] when he said: *Conception and consideration by the intellect are differentiated, so that within the intellect something other is destroyed, while the intellect itself is not subject to destruction.* Aristotle intends by *something other* the human imaginative forms. And he intends by *conception by the intellect* the reception which exists always in the material intellect, about which he intends to raise questions in the present treatise as well as in the former when he says: *And when it [the intellect] is set free . . . we do not remember, since this intellect is not passive, but the passive intellect is corruptible, and without it nothing thinks.*

And by the *passive intellect* he intends the imaginative faculty, as will be shown later. Generally, this meaning seems to be remote, namely, that the soul, that is, the speculative intellect, should be immortal.

For this reason Plato said that the universals are neither generable nor corruptible and that they exist outside the mind. This statement is true in the sense that the intelligibles inhering in the speculative intellect are immortal, but false according to the sound of his words (and this is the sense which Aristotle labored to destroy in the *Metaphysics*). In general, in regard of the nature of the soul, there is something true in the probable propositions which attribute to the soul both kinds of existence, namely mortal and immortal, since it is impossible that probable propositions should be completely false. The Ancients give an account of this and all the religious laws agree in this account.

The third question (namely, in what way is the material intellect some existing thing, while it is not one of the material forms nor prime matter) is answered as follows. One should be of the opinion that there are four kinds of existence. For just as sensible being is divided into form and matter, so also must intelligible being be divided into principles similar to these, that is into something similar to form and something similar to matter. This distinction is necessary for every incorporeal intellect which understands another, for if this distinction did not apply there would be no multiplicity in regard to the incorporeal forms. It has been shown in *First Philosophy* [that is in the *Metaphysics*] that there exists no form absolutely free from potentiality except the first form which does not think anything outside itself, but its existence is its quiddity, but other forms are differentiated in respect to quiddity and existence in some way. Were there not this genus of beings which we know in the science of the soul, we could not think of multiplicity in the case of incorporeal beings, just as we would not know that incorporeal motive forces must be intellect, if we would not know the nature of the intellect.

This escaped many modern philosophers, so that they deny what Aristotle said in the eleventh treatise of the *First Philosophy,* namely, that it is necessary, that the incorporeal forms which move the celestial bodies are numbered according to the number of the celestial bodies. Therefore, knowledge about the soul is necessary for the knowledge of First Philosophy. It is necessary that the receiving intellect knows the intellect which exists in actuality. For if this intellect understands the material forms, it is more fitting that it understands immaterial forms, and that which it knows of the incorporeal forms, for example, of the agent intellect, does not hinder it from knowing the material forms.

But the proposition which states that a recipient must not have anything in actuality insofar as it receives is not said in an absolute fashion, but with the provision, that it is not necessary that the receiving intellect be not anything whatsoever in actuality, but only that it is not something in actuality in respect to that which it receives, as we have stated previously. Indeed, you should know that the relation of the agent intellect to the receiving intellect is as the relation of light to the transparent medium, and that the relation of the material forms to the receiving intellect is as the relation of color to the transparent medium. For just as light is the perfection of the transparent medium, so is the agent intellect the perfection of the material intellect. And just as the transparent medium is only moved by color and receives it when it is illuminated, so also the material intellect only receives the intelligibles which exist in it when the material intellect is perfected by the agent intellect and illuminated by it. And just as light makes color in potentiality exist in actuality, as a result of which it [color] can move the transparent medium, so also the agent intellect makes the intelligible forms in potentiality exist in actuality, as a result of which the material intellect receives them. In this manner one must understand about the material and agent intellect.

When the material intellect becomes joined insofar as it is perfected through the agent intellect, then we are joined with the agent intellect. And this disposition is called *acquisition* and *acquired intellect,* as will be seen later. The manner in which we have described the essence of the material intellect answers all the questions arising about our statement that this intellect is one and many. For if something which is known by me and by you were one in all respects, it would follow that, if I know something, you would also know it, and many other absurdities would also follow. And if we were to assert that the material intellect is many, it would follow that something known by me and by you is one in respect to species and two in respect to individual, and thus something known would possess something else known and this would go on to infinity. Thus it will be impossible that a student learns from a teacher if the knowledge which exists in the teacher is not a force generating and producing the knowledge which is in the student, in the same manner as one fire produces another fire alike to it in species, which is absurd. The fact that something known by the teacher and the student is the same in this manner made Plato believe that learning is remembering. But if we assert that something known by me and by you is many in respect to that object according to which it is true, that is in respect to the imaginative forms, and one in respect to the subject through which it is an existing intellect (and this is the material intellect), these questions are resolved completely.

MAIMONIDES (MOSES BEN MAIMON)

1135–1204

L̲ike Averroes, Moses Maimonides was born in Cordova, Spain, while Averroes was still a boy. Unfortunately, the two never met. Maimonides came from a prominent Jewish family. In 1148 the Almohads conquered Cordova and life became very difficult for the Jews, and his family escaped first to Morocco, then Palestine. They finally settled in Fostat (old Cairo), Egypt.

Maimonides became both a physician and a rabbi. He was such a good doctor that he was appointed royal physician to the king of Egypt. And as rabbi he became *nagid,* or head of the Egyptian Jewish community in Fostat. While still a young man, he began to publish widely read books, such as *Sharh al-Mishnah* (Commentary on the Mishnah), also known as *Siraj* (Luminary), in 1168; *Mishnah Torah* (Code of Jewish law), in 1178; and *Treatise on Resurrection,* in 1191. Maimonides' most famous work, however, is now generally regarded as one of the greatest philosophical works of the Middle Ages: *Dalalat al-Ha'rin* (Guide for the perplexed, 1190). In it, he tries to bring Judaism in line with Neoplatonic Aristotelianism as taught by al-Farabi (Abu Nasr, 870–950) and Avicenna. Written in Arabic for philosophers and theologians, not the general public, it is often deliberately obscure.

Maimonides argues that metaphysics is the supreme level of human activity, attainable only by those with a sufficiently high intellect. Unlike Averroes, however, who implied that the different classes of intellectual ability among people were predetermined, Maimonides offers a pedagogy by which individuals can evolve through the different stages of intellectual ability up to the highest level. This requires careful guidance through education. The work had tremendous influence over both Jewish and Christian scholasticism, especially Albertus Magnus and Thomas Aquinas, as well as, over subsequent centuries, Spinoza, Mendelssohn, and Leibniz. Maimonides' development of John Scotus Erigena's (810–877) method *via negativa* ("the negative way") was also deeply influential. The idea is to provide a method of finding out what something is even if it cannot directly be experienced. You can't do it by stating the thing's attributes, since the thing cannot be experienced. So instead of getting at the essence in positive terms, you try to find out what is left over after all positive statements about the essence of the unexperiencable thing are exhausted. The *via negativa* method can be used, according to Maimonides, to transcend the limitations of the human mind and attain knowledge of things beyond the direct reach of the senses or the intellect, such as God. The idea is that by stating all the things that God is not, we are in a position to intuit what God actually is.

The first part of the *Guide for the Perplexed* deals with problems of biblical anthropomorphism and application of the *via negativa* method to discovering the divine attributes of God, along with criticisms of the Muslim scholastic theology according to the method of *kalam,* in which philosophical proof is used to justify religious propositions already accepted in advance to be true. The second part offers proofs of God's existence, an Aristotelian analysis of the relationship between matter and form, and an explanation of the role of prophecy. The third part contains studies of the problems of free will and determinism, evil, the nature of rationality, and an original defense of how to reconcile reason with divine revelation. If on some point the Old Testament is perfectly clear and no obvious philosophical arguments can be adduced to the contrary, we ought to accept the word of the Bible. If, on the other hand, the point seems dubious and a contrary philosophical argument easily presents itself, the biblical statement ought to be reinterpreted according to the dictates of rationality so as to be understood only in allegorical terms. This was an extremely revolutionary idea, and it paved the way for subsequent Jewish philosophers who wanted to emphasize reason over revealed scripture. It has had a lasting influence on the rational process central to rabbinical theology.

Our selection from the *Guide for the Perplexed* begins with an explanation of why one ought not to begin with the study of metaphysics. There are certain things that the undisciplined mind cannot accurately represent to itself, neither as a perception nor as a concept. Trying to do so without the proper training is like trying to lift too heavy a weight or running too far before one is in the proper physical condition. The highest form of knowledge consists in the truths of metaphysics, but these cannot be comprehended by unaided perception or unaided reason without causing psychological and intellectual harm.

According to Maimonides, there can be no relation between any aspect of the world, including the human intellect, with the absolute unity of God. People who think they have a relationship with God are utterly deluded. There can be no such relationship between the relative world of potentiality and the absolute actuality. Even to say of God that "God exists" or that "God is One" must, according to Maimonides, be tempered with the knowledge that God exists without having the attribute of existence and that God is One without having the attribute of unity. The idea is that God has no positive attributes at all. Yet God is not nothing. And in some mysterious way the universe does not exist independently of God but ultimately is itself a reflection of God.

GUIDE FOR THE PERPLEXED

Know that for the human mind there are certain objects of perception which are within the scope of its nature and capacity; on the other hand, there are, amongst things which actually exist, certain objects which the mind can in no way and by no means grasp: the gates of perception are closed against it. Further, there are things of which the mind understands one part, but remains ignorant of the other; and when man is able to comprehend certain things, it does not follow that he must be able to comprehend everything. This also applies to the senses: they are able to perceive things, but not at every distance; and all other powers of the body are limited in a similar way. . . .

All this is applicable to the intellectual faculties of man. There is a considerable difference between one person and another as regards these faculties, as is well known to philosophers. While one man can discover a certain thing by himself, another is never able to understand it, even if taught by means of all possible expressions and metaphors, and during a long period; his mind can in no way grasp it, his capacity is insufficient for it. This distinction is not unlimited. A boundary is undoubtedly set to the human mind which it cannot pass. There are things (beyond that boundary) which are acknowledged to be inaccessible to human understanding, and man does not show any desire to comprehend them, being aware that such knowledge is impossible, and that there are no means of overcoming the difficulty; e.g., we do not know the number of stars in heaven, whether the number is even or odd; we do not know the number of animals, minerals, or plants, and the like. There are other things, however, which man very much desires to know, and strenuous efforts to examine and to investigate them have been made by thinkers of all classes, and at all times. They differ and disagree, and constantly raise new doubts with regard to them, because their minds are bent on comprehending such things, that is to say, they are moved by desire; and every one of them believes that he has discovered the way leading to a true knowledge of the thing, although human reason is entirely unable to demonstrate the fact by convincing evidence.—For a proposition which can be proved by evidence is not subject to dispute, denial, or rejection; none but the ignorant would contradict it, and such contradiction is called "denial of a demonstrated proof." Thus you find men who deny the spherical form of the earth, or the circular form of the line in which the stars move, and the like; such men are not considered in this treatise. This confusion prevails mostly in metaphysical subjects, less in problems relating to physics, and is entirely absent from the exact sciences. Alexander Aphrodisius said that there are three causes which prevent men from discovering the exact truth; first, arrogance and vainglory; secondly, the subtlety, depth, and difficulty of any subject which is being examined; thirdly, ignorance and want of capacity to comprehend what might be comprehended. These causes are enumerated by Alexander. At the present time there is a fourth cause not mentioned by him, because it did not then prevail, namely, habit and training. We naturally like what we have been accustomed to, and are attracted towards it. . . .

From Maimonides, *Guide for the Perplexed,* trans. M. Friedländer (London: Routledge & Kegan Paul, 1904).

The same is the case with those opinions of man to which he has been accustomed from his youth; he likes them, defends them, and shuns the opposite views. This is likewise one of the causes which prevent men from finding truth, and which make them cling to their habitual opinions. . . .

You must consider, when reading this treatise, that mental perception, because connected with matter, is subject to conditions similar to those to which physical perception is subject. That is to say, if your eye looks around, you can perceive all that is within the range of your vision; if, however, you overstrain your eye, exerting it too much by attempting to see an object which is too distant for your eye, or to examine writings or engravings too small for your sight, and forcing it to obtain a correct perception of them, you will not only weaken your sight with regard to that special object, but also for those things which you otherwise are able to perceive: your eye will have become too weak to perceive what you were able to see before you exerted yourself and exceeded the limits of your vision.

The same is the case with the speculative faculties of one who devotes himself to the study of any science. If a person studies too much and exhausts his reflective powers, he will be confused, and will not be able to apprehend even that which had been within the power of his apprehension. For the powers of the body are all alike in this respect.

The mental perceptions are not exempt from a similar condition. If you admit the doubt, and do not persuade yourself to believe that there is a proof for things which cannot be demonstrated, or to try at once to reject and positively to deny an assertion the opposite of which has never been proved or attempt to perceive things which are beyond your perception, then you have attained the highest degree of human perfection. . . . If, on the other hand, you attempt to exceed the limit of your intellectual power, or at once to reject things as impossible which have never been proved to be impossible, or which are in fact possible, though their possibility be very remote, then you will . . . not only fail to become perfect, but you will become exceedingly imperfect. Ideas founded on mere imagination will prevail over you, you will incline toward defects, and toward base and degraded habits, on account of the confusion which troubles the mind, and of the dimness of its light, just as weakness of sight causes invalids to see many kinds of unreal images, especially when they have looked for a long time at dazzling or at very minute objects.

Respecting this it has been said, "Hast thou found honey? eat so much as is sufficient for thee, lest thou be filled therewith, and vomit it" (Prov. xxv. 16).

How excellent is this simile! In comparing knowledge to food, . . . the author of Proverbs mentions the sweetest food, namely, honey, which has the further property of irritating the stomach, and of causing sickness. He thus fully describes the nature of knowledge. Though great, excellent, noble and perfect, it is injurious if not kept within bounds or not guarded properly; it is like honey which gives nourishment and is pleasant, when eaten in moderation, but is totally thrown away when eaten immoderately. Therefore, it is not said "lest thou be filled and loathe it," but "lest thou vomit it." . . .

It was not the object of the Prophets and our Sages in these utterances to close the gate of investigation entirely, and to prevent the mind from comprehending what is within its reach, as is imagined by simple and idle people, whom it suits better to put forth their ignorance and incapacity as wisdom and perfection, and to regard the distinction and wisdom of others as irreligion and imperfection, thus taking darkness for light and light for darkness. The whole object of the Prophets and the Sages was to declare that a limit is set to human reason where it must halt. . . .

You must know that it is very injurious to begin with this branch of philosophy, viz., Metaphysics; or to explain the sense of the similes occurring in prophecies, and interpret the metaphors which are employed in historical accounts and which abound in the writings of the Prophets. On the contrary, it is necessary to initiate the young and to instruct the less intelligent according to their comprehension; those who appear to be talented and to have capacity for the higher method of study, i.e., that based on proof and on true logical argument, should be gradually advanced towards perfection, either by tuition or by self-instruction. He, however, who begins with Metaphysics, will not only become confused in matters of religion, but will fall into complete infidelity. I compare such a person to an infant fed with wheaten bread, meat and wine; it will undoubtedly die, not because such food is naturally unfit for the human body, but because of the weakness of the child, who is unable to digest the food, and cannot derive benefit from it. The same is the case with the true principles of science. They were presented in enigmas, clad in riddles, and taught by all wise men in the most mysterious way that could be devised, not because they contain some secret evil, or are contrary to the fundamental principles of the Law (as fools think who are only philosophers in their own eyes), but because of the incapacity of man to comprehend them at the beginning of his studies: only slight allusions have been made to them to serve for the guidance of those who are capable of understanding them. These sciences were, therefore, called Mysteries (*sodoth*), and Secrets of the Law (*sitre torah*), as we shall explain.

This also is the reason why "the Torah speaks the language of man," as we have explained, for it is the object of the Torah to serve as a guide for the instruction of the young, of women, and of the common people; and as all of them are incapable to comprehend the true sense of the words, tradition was considered sufficient to convey all truths which were to be established; and as regards ideals, only such remarks were made as would lead towards a knowledge of their existence, though not to a comprehension of their true essence. When a man attains to perfection, and arrives at a knowledge of the "Secrets of the Law," either through the assistance of a teacher or by self-instruction, being led by the understanding of one part to the study of the other, he will belong to those who faithfully believe in the true principles, either because of conclusive proof, where proof is possible, or by forcible arguments, where argument is admissible; he will have a true notion of those things which he previously received in similes and metaphors, and he will fully understand their sense. We have frequently mentioned in this treatise the principle of our Sages "not to discuss the *Ma'aseh Mercabah* even in the presence of one pupil, except he be wise and intelligent; and then only the headings of the chapters are to be given to him." We must, therefore, begin with teaching these subjects according to the capacity of the pupil, and on two conditions, first, that he be wise, i.e., that he should have successfully gone through the preliminary studies, and secondly that he be intelligent, talented, clear-headed, and of quick perception, that is, "have a mind of his own" (*mebin midda'ato*), as our Sages termed it.

I will now proceed to explain the reasons why we should not instruct the multitude in pure metaphysics, or begin with describing to them the true essence of things, or with showing them that a thing must be as it is, and cannot be otherwise. This will form the subject of the next chapter; and I proceed to say—

There are five reasons why instruction should not begin with Metaphysics, but should at first be restricted to pointing out what is fitted for notice and what may be made manifest to the multitude.

First Reason.—The subject itself is difficult, subtle and profound, "Far off and exceeding deep, who can find it out?" (Eccles. vii. 24). The following words of Job may be applied to it: "Whence then cometh wisdom? and where is the place of understanding?" (Job xxviii. 20). Instruction should not begin with abstruse and difficult subjects. In one of the similes contained in the Bible, wisdom is compared to water, and amongst other interpretations given by our Sages of this simile, occurs the following: He who can swim may bring up pearls from the depth of the sea, he who is unable to swim will be drowned, therefore only such persons as have had proper instruction should expose themselves to the risk.

Second Reason.—The intelligence of man is at first insufficient; for he is not endowed with perfection at the beginning, but at first possesses perfection only *in potentiâ*, not in fact. Thus it is said, "And man is born a wild ass" (Job xi. 12). If a man possesses a certain faculty *in potentiâ*, it does not follow that it must become in him a reality. He may possibly remain deficient either on account of some obstacle, or from want of training in practices which would turn the possibility into a reality. Thus it is distinctly stated in the Bible, "Not many are wise" (*ib.,* xxxii. 9); also our Sages say, "I noticed how few were those who attained to a higher degree of perfection" (B. T. Succah 45*a*). There are many things which obstruct the path to perfection, and which keep man away from it. Where can he find sufficient preparation and leisure to learn all that is necessary in order to develop that perfection which he has *in potentiâ?*

Third Reason.—The preparatory studies are of long duration, and man, in his natural desire to reach the goal, finds them frequently too wearisome, and does not wish to be troubled by them. Be convinced that, if man were able to reach the end without preparatory studies, such studies would not be preparatory but tiresome and utterly superfluous. Suppose you awaken any person, even the most simple, as if from sleep, and you say to him, Do you not desire to know what the heavens are, what is their number and their form; what beings are contained in them; what the angels are; how the creation of the whole world took place; what is its purpose, and what is the relation of its various parts to each other; what is the nature of the soul; how it enters the body; whether it has an independent existence, and if so, how it can exist independently of the body; by what means and to what purpose, and similar problems. He would undoubtedly say "Yes," and show a natural desire for the true knowledge of these things; but he will wish to satisfy that desire and to attain to that knowledge by listening to a few words from you. Ask him to interrupt his usual pursuits for a week, till he learns all this, he would not do it, and would be satisfied and contented with imaginary and misleading notions; he would refuse to believe that there is anything which requires preparatory studies and persevering research. . . .

The majority of scholars, that is to say, the most famous in science, are afflicted with this failing, viz., that of hurrying at once to the final results, and of speaking about them, without treating of the preliminary disciplines. Led by folly or ambition to disregard those preparatory studies, for the attainment of which they are either incapable or too idle, some scholars endeavour to prove that these are injurious or superfluous. On reflection the truth will become obvious.

The Fourth Reason is taken from the physical constitution of man. It has been proved that moral conduct is a preparation for intellectual progress, and that only a man whose character is pure, calm and steadfast, can attain to intellectual perfection; that is, acquire correct conceptions. Many men are naturally so constituted that all perfection is impossible; e.g., he whose heart is very warm and is himself very powerful, is sure to be passionate, though he tries to counteract that disposition by training; he whose testicles are warm, humid, and vigorous, and the organs connected therewith are surcharged, will not easily refrain from sin, even if he makes great efforts to restrain himself. You also find persons of

great levity and rashness, whose excited manners and wild gestures prove that their constitution is in disorder, and their temperament so bad that it cannot be cured. Such persons
can never attain to perfection; it is utterly useless to occupy oneself with them on such a
subject [as Metaphysics]. For this science is, as you know, different from the science of
Medicine and of Geometry, and, from the reason already mentioned, it is not every person
who is capable of approaching it. It is impossible for a man to study it successfully without
moral preparation; he must acquire the highest degree of uprightness and integrity, "for the
froward is an abomination to the Lord, but His secret is with the righteous" (Prov. iii. 32).
Therefore it was considered inadvisable to teach it to young men; nay, it is impossible for
them to comprehend it, on account of the heat of their blood and the flame of youth, which
confuses their minds; that heat, which causes all the disorder, must first disappear; they
must have become moderate and settled, humble in their hearts, and subdued in their
temperament; only then will they be able to arrive at the highest degree of the perception
of God, i.e., the study of Metaphysics. . . .

Fifth Reason.—Man is disturbed in his intellectual occupation by the necessity of looking after the material wants of the body, especially if the necessity of providing for wife and
children be superadded; much more so if he seeks superfluities in addition to his ordinary
wants, for by custom and bad habits these become a powerful motive. Even the perfect man
to whom we have referred, if too busy with these necessary things, much more so if busy
with unnecessary things, and filled with a great desire for them—must weaken or altogether
lose his desire for study, to which he will apply himself with interruption, lassitude, and
want of attention. He will not attain to that for which he is fitted by his abilities, or he will
acquire imperfect knowledge, a confused mass of true and false ideas. For these reasons it
was proper that the study of Metaphysics should have been exclusively cultivated by privileged persons, and not entrusted to the common people. It is not for the beginner, and he
should abstain from it, as the little child has to abstain from taking solid food and from
carrying heavy weights.

Know that many branches of science relating to the correct solution of these problems,
were once cultivated by our forefathers, but were in the course of time neglected, especially
in consequence of the tyranny which barbarous nations exercised over us. Besides, speculative studies were not open to all men, as we have already stated (Introd. p. 2 and I.
chap. xxxi.), only the subjects taught in the Scriptures were accessible to all. Even the traditional Law, as you are well aware, was not originally committed to writing, in conformity
with the rule to which our nation generally adhered, "Things which I have communicated
to you orally, you must not communicate to others in writing." With reference to the Law,
this rule was very opportune; for while it remained in force it averted the evils which happened subsequently, viz., great diversity of opinion, doubts as to the meaning of written
words, slips of the pen, dissensions among the people, formation of new sects, and confused
notions about practical subjects. The traditional teaching was in fact, according to the
words of the Law, entrusted to the Great Tribunal, as we have already stated in our works
on the Talmud.

Care having been taken, for the sake of obviating injurious influences, that the Oral Law
should not be recorded in a form accessible to all, it was but natural that no portion of "the
secrets of the Law" (i.e., metaphysical problems) would be permitted to be written down or
divulged for the use of all men. These secrets, as has been explained, were orally communicated by a few able men to others who were equally distinguished. Hence the principle
applied by our teachers, "The secrets of the Law can only be entrusted to him who is a
councillor, a cunning artificer, etc." The natural effect of this practice was that our nation

lost the knowledge of those important disciplines. Nothing but a few remarks and allusions are to be found in the Talmud and the Midrashim, like a few kernels enveloped in such a quantity of husk, that the reader is generally occupied with the husk, and forgets that it encloses a kernel. . . .

Know that this Universe, in its entirety, is nothing else but one individual being; that is to say, the outermost heavenly sphere, together with all included therein, is as regards individuality beyond all question a single being like Said and Omar. The variety of its substances—I mean the substances of that sphere and all its component parts—is like the variety of the substances of a human being: just as, e.g., Said is one individual, consisting of various solid substances, such as flesh, bones, sinews, of various humours, and of various spiritual elements. . . .

The living being as such is one through the action of its heart, although some parts of the body are devoid of motion and sensation, as, e.g., the bones, the cartilage, and similar parts. The same is the case with the entire universe; although it includes many beings without motion and without life, it is a single being living through the motion of the sphere, which may be compared to the heart of an animated being. You must therefore consider the entire globe as one individual being which is endowed with life, motion, and a soul. This mode of considering the universe is, as will be explained, indispensable, that is to say, it is very useful for demonstrating the unity of God; it also helps to elucidate the principle that He who is One has created only *one* being.

Again, it is impossible that any of the members of a human body should exist by themselves, not connected with the body, and at the same time should actually be organic parts of that body, that is to say, that the liver should exist by itself, the heart by itself, or the flesh by itself. In like manner, it is impossible that one part of the Universe should exist independently of the other parts in the existing order of things as here considered. . . .

In man there is a certain force which unites the members of the body, controls them, and gives to each of them what it requires for the conservation of its condition, and for the repulsion of injury—the physicians distinctly call it the leading force in the body of the living being; sometimes they call it "nature." The Universe likewise possesses a force which unites the several parts with each other, protects the species from destruction, maintains the individuals of each species as long as possible, and endows some individual beings with permanent existence. Whether this force operates through the medium of the sphere or otherwise remains an open question. . . .

* * *

. . . [T]hese subjects belong to the mysteries of the Law. You are well aware how our Sages blame those who reveal these mysteries, and praise the merits of those who keep them secret, although they are perfectly clear to the philosopher. In this sense they explain the passage, "Her merchandise shall be for them that dwell before the Lord, to eat sufficiently" (Isa. xxiii. 18), which concludes in the original with the words *ve-li-me-kasseh 'atik,* i.e., that these blessings are promised to him who hides things which the Eternal has revealed [to him], viz., the mysteries of the Law (Babyl. Talmud, *Pesaḥim* 119a). If you have understanding you will comprehend that which our Sages pointed out. They have clearly stated that the Divine Chariot includes matters too deep and too profound for the ordinary intellect. It has been shown that a person favoured by Providence with reason to understand these mysteries is forbidden by the Law to teach them except *viva voce,* and on condition that the pupil possess certain qualifications, and even then only the heads of the sections may be communicated. This has been the cause why the knowledge of this mystery has entirely disappeared from our nation, and nothing has remained of it. This was unavoidable, for the explanation of these mysteries was always communicated *viva voce,* it was never committed to writing. Such being the case, how can I venture to call your attention to such portions of it as may be known, intelligible, and perfectly clear to me? But if, on the other hand, I were to abstain from writing on this subject, according to my knowledge of it, when I die, as I shall inevitably do, that knowledge would die with me, and I would thus inflict great injury on you and all those who are perplexed [by these theological problems]. I would then be guilty of withholding the truth from those to whom it ought to be communicated, and of jealously depriving the heir of his inheritance. I should in either case be guilty of gross misconduct.

To give a full explanation of the mystic passages of the Bible is contrary to the Law and to reason; besides, my knowledge of them is based on reasoning, not on divine inspiration [and is therefore not infallible]. I have not received my belief in this respect from any teacher, but it has been formed by what I learnt from Scripture and the utterances of our Sages, and by the philosophical principles which I have adopted. It is therefore possible that my view is wrong, and that I misunderstood the passages referred to. . . . Those, however, for whom this treatise has been composed, will, on reflecting on it and thoroughly examining each chapter, obtain a perfect and clear insight into all that has been clear and intelligible to me. This is the utmost that can be done in treating this subject so as to be useful to all without fully explaining it. . . .

AQUINAS

1225–1274

Thomas Aquinas was born in Italy near Aquino, between Rome and Naples. He was first educated at the Benedictine abbey at Monte Cassino and then went to the University of Naples. When in 1244 he joined the Dominican order of mendicant (begging) friars, his father, the count of Aquino, was outraged. The Dominicans espoused complete poverty and traveled the country spreading the gospel as living examples of Jesus' teaching. His father had fully expected him to join the more respectable Benedictines, a powerful order founded by great corporate wealth. As a result, he locked young Aquinas in the family castle. Legend has it that his father offered him all sorts of bribes, including a beautiful prostitute, to join the Benedictines.

To his father's great dismay, Aquinas supposedly refused even the prostitute and escaped to Paris. He went on to study philosophy and theology in Cologne under Albertus Magnus (1200–1280), a Dominican philosopher and theologian known as "Doctor Universalis" and "Albert the Great" because of his immense knowledge. From Magnus, Aquinas learned Greek and Islamic philosophy, and the natural sciences.

At the time, the Paris Dominicans were under suspicion by the church and the conservative university authorities because of their "heretical sympathy" with Averroist doctrine about the unity of the active intellect in all human beings. Recall that according to Averroes, it is not the human personality as exemplified by the individual soul that is immortal but only the active intellect, which is numerically identical in all sentient beings. It was Aquinas who helped defend the Dominicans with his Averroist arguments that there are two different sorts of truths—one based on reason and the other based on revelation—and that only through revelation could one know the "real" truth. Since Christian dogma is foundationally embedded in views antithetical to Averroes's monopsychism, its truths must therefore supercede the cosmic unity of all mankind as espoused by the internal Aristotelian philosophers of the Averroist school.

Conservative Christian theologians feared that Plato and Aristotle, whose works had disappeared from non-Arabic Europe, would now return to the philosophical scene, especially since the Islamic philosophers might have put their own spins and interpretations on the Greek works through the commentaries. The church therefore viewed the Greek works as a pagan and infidel threat to Christian dogma. Aquinas boldly took the opposite approach. He saw Aristotle not just as the greatest of all philosophers—he even called him "*The* Philosopher"—but as an opportunity to put Christian doctrine on a solid intellectual foundation.

Aquinas argued that Aristotle's metaphysics, cosmology, and epistemology could provide the solid theoretical framework for Christianity, provided that an account could be given of how the soul can preserve the individual human ego, personality intact, after death. In all his early work, Aquinas tried to put the conservative theologians' fears to rest by showing various ways that Aristotelian philosophy could be made consistent with Christian belief. Often he ended up simply rejecting whatever parts of Aristotle's philosophy did not fit Christian dogma. Whenever he saw insoluble contradictions between the two views, he tried to prove that reason could force neither conclusion. The implication was that one needed faith to decide—a position that would be used again and again by conflicting systems, including that of Copernicus. For instance, on the question of whether God created the universe, as it was written in the Bible, or whether the universe is eternal and uncreated, as Aristotle had argued, Aquinas said that there is no way to tell: neither the creation of the universe nor the eternity of the universe can be confirmed or denied by reason. His conclusion is that we need *revelation* to know the truth. In the same way, instead of simply declaring Averroist monopsychism to be a false heresy or banning the heretical proposition, Aquinas argued that whether the individual human soul is mortal or immortal cannot be settled by reason. Such truths can be known only through revelation, and studying the "forbidden" philosophies is itself a way of strengthening the dogmatic theology.

Likewise, Aquinas enabled the study of Aristotle's argument against the immortality of the soul; such study can, according to Aquinas, only help make the point that without divine revelation there can be no knowledge. This brilliant and perhaps philosophically covert line of thought so pleased church leaders that they made the arguments of the philosophers against the very things that they held sacred part of the church's "proof" of the need for nonphilosophical ways of knowing truth! It is philosophy itself that establishes the necessity of revelation. Thus, whether advertently or inadvertently, Aquinas managed to appease the conservative critics of philosophy and revive Greek philosophy within the Christian domain.

Aquinas's early work, like that of his antithesis Averroes, consisted of commentaries on Aristotle. The most famous are the *Analytics, De anima, De caelo, Ethics, De interpretatione, Metaphysics, Physics,* and *Politics.* Among his best original writings are *De ente et essentia,* which explores the nature of being and essence. But it is not until *De principiis naturae,* on the principles and causes of change in nature, and *De unitate intellectus,* that he explicitly argues against the Averroist position that all human beings share one and the same, numerically identical, intellect.

Aquinas's two most important works are the encyclopedic *Summa contra Gentiles* and *Summa Theologica.* The former, written between 1259 and 1264, attempts to speak to readers who are not already believing Christians and uses arguments without assuming, in advance, that Christianity is true. Our selection is from the latter. In it Aquinas offers his famous five proofs for the existence of God. It was written between 1265 and 1274.

After being appointed a regent master (full professor) at the University of Paris, in subsequent years Aquinas served under the popes at Orvieto, Rome, and Vitergo in Italy. He continued teaching in Paris and Naples until his death.

SUMMA THEOLOGICA

THE FIRST WAY
The argument from change

The existence of God can be shown in five ways. The first and clearest is taken from the idea of motion. (1) Now it is certain, and our senses corroborate it, that some things in this world are in motion. (2) But everything which is in motion is moved by something else. (3) For nothing is in motion except in so far as it is in potentiality in relation to that towards which it is in motion. (4) Now a thing causes movement in so far as it is in actuality. For to cause movement is nothing else than to bring something from potentiality to actuality; but a thing cannot be brought from potentiality to actuality except by something which exists in actuality, as, for example, that which is hot in actuality, like fire, makes wood, which is only hot in potentiality, to be hot in actuality, and thereby causes movement in it and alters it. (5) But it is not possible that the same thing should be at the same time in actuality and potentiality in relation to the same thing, but only in relation to different things; for what is hot in actuality cannot at the same time be hot in potentiality, though it is at the same time cold in potentiality. (6) It is impossible, therefore, that in relation to the same thing and in the same way anything should both cause movement and be caused, or that it should cause itself to move. (7) Everything therefore that is in motion must be moved by something else. If therefore the thing which causes it to move be in motion, this too must be moved by something else, and so on. (8) But we cannot proceed to infinity in this way, because in that case there would be no first mover, and in consequence, neither would there be any other mover; for secondary movers do not cause movement except they be moved by a first mover, as, for example, a stick cannot cause movement unless it is moved by the hand. Therefore it is necessary to stop at some first mover which is moved by nothing else. And this is what we all understand God to be.

THE SECOND WAY
The argument from causation

The Second Way is taken from the idea of the Efficient Cause. (1) For we find that there is among material things a regular order of efficient causes. (2) But we do not find, nor indeed is it possible, that anything is the efficient cause of itself, for in that case it would be prior to itself, which is impossible. (3) Now it is not possible to proceed to infinity in efficient causes. (4) For if we arrange in order all efficient causes, the first is the cause of the intermediate, and the intermediate the cause of the last, whether the intermediate be many or only one. (5) But if we remove a cause the effect is removed; therefore, if there is no *first* among efficient causes, neither will there be a last or an intermediate. (6) But if we proceed

From *Summa Theologica,* trans. Laurence Shapcote (London: O. P. Benziger Brothers, 1911).

to infinity in efficient causes there will be no first efficient cause, and thus there will be no ultimate effect, nor any intermediate efficient causes, which is clearly false. Therefore it is necessary to suppose the existence of some first efficient cause, and this men call God.

THE THIRD WAY
The argument from contingency

The Third Way rests on the idea of the "contingent" and the "necessary" and is as follows: (1) Now we find that there are certain things in the Universe which are capable of existing and of not existing, for we find that some things are brought into existence and then destroyed, and consequently are capable of being or not being. (2) But it is impossible for all things which exist to be of this kind, because anything which is capable of not existing, at some time or other does not exist. (3) If therefore *all* things are capable of not existing, there was a time when nothing existed in the Universe. (4) But if this is true there would also be nothing in existence now; because anything that does not exist cannot begin to exist except by the agency of something which has existence. If therefore there was once nothing which existed, it would have been impossible for anything to begin to exist, and so nothing would exist now. (5) This is clearly false. Therefore all things are not contingent, and there must be something which is necessary in the Universe. (6) But everything which is necessary either has or has not the cause of its necessity from an outside source. Now it is not possible to proceed to infinity in necessary things which have a cause of their necessity, as has been proved in the case of efficient causes. Therefore it is necessary to suppose the existence of something which is necessary in itself, not having the cause of its necessity from any outside source, but which is the cause of necessity in others. And this "something" we call God.

THE FOURTH WAY
The argument from degrees of excellence

The Fourth Way is taken from the degrees which are found in things. (1) For among different things we find that one is more or less good or true or noble; and likewise in the case of other things of this kind. (2) But the words "more" or "less' are used of different things in proportion as they approximate in their different ways to something which has the particular quality in the highest degree—e.g., we call a thing hotter when it approximates more nearly to that which is hot in the highest degree. There is therefore something which is true in the highest degree, good in the highest degree and noble in the highest degree; (3) and consequently there must be also something which has being in the highest degree. For things which are true in the highest degree also have being in the highest degree (see Aristotle, *Metaphysics,* 2). (4) But anything which has a certain quality of any kind in the highest degree is also the cause of all the things of that kind, as, for example, fire which is hot in the highest degree is the cause of all hot things (as is said in the same book). (5) Therefore there exists something which is the cause of being, and goodness, and of every perfection in all existing things; and this we call God.

THE FIFTH WAY
The argument from harmony

The Fifth Way is taken from the way in which nature is governed. (1) For we observe that certain things which lack knowledge, such as natural bodies, work for an End. This is obvious, because they always, or at any rate very frequently, operate in the same way so as to attain the best possible result. (2) Hence it is clear that they do not arrive at their goal by chance, but by purpose. (3) But those things which have no knowledge do not move towards a goal unless they are guided by someone or something which does possess knowledge and intelligence—e.g., an arrow by an archer. Therefore, there does exist something which possesses intelligence by which all natural things are directed to their goal; and this we call God.

21

BACON

1561–1626

Born in London to a family of high-ranking civil servants, Francis Bacon studied law at Trinity College, Cambridge. After an illustrious political and legal career, he became lord chancellor (attorney general) under King James I. A prolific and brilliant writer, Bacon produced a body of highly revolutionary philosophical works that made him a pivotal figure in the ensuing transition from medieval to modern philosophy and influenced subsequent British empiricist philosophers Locke, Berkeley, Hume, Mill, and Russell. Indeed, his philosophical works shifted the entire focus of the knowledge-seeking enterprise away from the medieval concerns with predominantly religious themes. He provided a model for a new way of gathering scientific knowledge that bares the name "Baconian method," in which one moves from particular facts to more general knowledge of forms using experimentally discovered laws.

Bacon shunned what he saw as a vain craving for psychological satisfaction under the guise of a search for truth: "I find that even those that have sought knowledge for itself, and not for benefit or ostentation, or any practical enablement in the course of their life, have nevertheless propounded to themselves a wrong mark, namely satisfaction (which men call Truth) and not operation." According to Bacon, knowledge has nothing to do with personal happiness or satisfaction. The sole purpose of knowledge should be the technological mastery of nature. Philosophers should avoid the sort of abstract contemplations about the ultimate natures of things that so interested medieval theologians, give up the Socratic search for enlightenment, and avoid the inner tranquillity sought by the Stoics and ancients. All of these are wrongheaded. What philosophy should do instead is "endow the condition and life of man with new powers or works" and "extend more widely the limits of the power and greatness of man." Philosophers must stop "prostituting" themselves by supporting or establishing religious or even scientific dogma and by seeking inner bliss or any other manner of "delight only and not of discovery."

Baconian philosophy is thus a shift away from metaphysical abstraction and psychological satiation toward a concrete, practical, utilitarian conception of wisdom. Bacon is as critical of skeptics who claim that knowledge is impossible as he is of the dogmatists who claim that knowledge must be based on the authority of ancient Greek learning. He wants to find a balanced, middle ground. His method, the so-called Baconian method, is designed to be used by those seeking sound judgments who wish to find out the truth for themselves. It is a purely mechanical procedure for attaining knowledge, openly available to anyone.

The idea is that just as a person untrained in geometry could use a pair of compasses to construct a circle, anyone could use Bacon's method to construct knowledge. Before you can use this method, however, or even learn it, you must first clear your mind of all the falsehoods you have been conditioned to believe.

Our selection is from his most celebrated work, the *Novum Organum*. In it, Bacon tries to shed light on the psychological motives and covert personal interests behind the previous philosophers. These stand in the way of real philosophical progress and must be removed before real learning can take place. These fallacies come in four types. According to Bacon, these four intellectual and emotional idolatries, as the main obstacles to objective knowledge, have kept humanity in the dark for centuries. He urges people to dispense with them so that they can apply his new method and thereby pave the way for new thinking. Once freed of these old fallacies, humanity would be free to establish a natural philosophy, which he divides into theoretical and practical, physical and metaphysical. This leads him to his concept of forms, the central aspect of his theory that is supposed to solve both the theoretical and practical problems of science.

In the concluding part of the work, he gives a description of a method that would come to be called the "Baconian method" of induction. This method stipulates that we must always begin with as clear and unambiguous description of the facts as possible and then all generalizations from these facts must be checked by a search for (1) positive instances of the phenomenon in question, (2) negative instances of its absence, and (3) instances of its presence in varying degrees. We must then eliminate whatever is not directly connected with the phenomenon under investigation. (1), (2), and (3) are essentially an anticipation of the methods of agreement, the joint method and the method of concomitant variations as used in modern science.

Bacon's influence on the subsequent revolution in modern thought has been pivotal and often unappreciated. Early twentieth-century philosopher John Dewey (Chapter 48), inspired by Bacon's views as summed up in the aphorism "Knowledge is power" to invent the philosophy known as American pragmatism, wrote, "Francis Bacon of the Elizabethan age is the great forerunner of the spirit of modern life [who as] a prophet of new tendencies . . . hardly receives his due as the real founder of modern thought."

NOVUM ORGANUM

THE IDOLS

Man, being the servant and interpreter of nature, can do and understand so much and so much only as he has observed in fact or in thought of the course of nature: beyond this he neither knows anything nor can do anything.

From *The Philosophical Works of Francis Bacon,* ed. R. L. Ellis and J. Spedding and trans. J. Spedding. With emendations by Daniel Kolak.

Neither the naked hand nor the understanding left to itself can effect much. It is by instruments and aids that the work is done, which are as much wanted for the understanding as for the hand. And as the instruments of the hand either give motion or guide it, so the instruments of the mind supply either suggestions for the understanding or cautions.

Human knowledge and human power meet in one; for where the cause is not known the effect cannot be produced. Nature to be commanded must be obeyed; and that which in contemplation is as the cause is in operation as the rule.

Towards the affecting of works, all that man can do is to put together or put asunder natural bodies. The rest is done by nature working within.

The study of nature with a view to works is engaged in by the mechanic, the mathematician, the physician, the alchemist, and the magician; but by all (as things now are) with laziness and scanty success.

It would be an unsound fancy and self-contradictory to expect that things which have never yet been done can be done except by means which have never yet been tried.

The productions of the mind and hand seem very numerous in books and manufactures. But all this variety lies in an exquisite subtlety and derivations from a few things already known; not in the number of axioms.

Moreover the works already known are due to chance and experiment rather than to sciences; for the sciences we now possess are merely systems for the nice ordering and setting forth of things already invented; not methods of invention or directions for new works.

The cause and root of nearly all evils in the sciences is this—that while we falsely admire and extol the powers of the human mind we neglect to seek for its true aids.

The subtlety of nature is greater many times over than the subtlety of the senses and understanding; so that all those specious meditations, speculations, and glosses in which men indulge are quite useless, only there is no one there to notice.

As the sciences which we now have do not help us in finding out new works, so neither does the logic which we now have help us in finding out new sciences.

The logic now in use serves rather to fix and give stability to the errors which have their foundation in commonly received notions than to help the search after truth. So it does more harm than good.

The syllogism is not applied to the first principles of sciences, and is applied in vain to middle axioms; being no match for the subtlety of nature. It commands assent therefore to the proposition, but does not take hold of the thing.

The syllogism consists of propositions, propositions consist of words, words are symbols of notions. Therefore if the notions themselves (which is the root of the matter) are confused and over-hastily abstracted from the facts, there can be no firmness in the superstructure. Our only hope therefore lies in a true induction.

There is no soundness in our notions whether logical or physical. Substance, Quality, Action, Passion, Essence itself, are not sound notions: much less are Heavy, Light, Dense, Rare, Moist, Dry, Generation, Corruption, Attraction, Repulsion, Element, Matter, Form, and the like; but all are fantastical and ill defined.

Our notions of less general species, as Man, Dog, Dove, and of the immediate perceptions of the sense, as Hot, Cold, Black, White, do not materially mislead us; yet even these are sometimes confused by the flux and alteration of matter and the mixing of one thing with another. All the others which men have hitherto adopted are but idle speculations, not being abstracted and formed from things by proper methods.

Nor is there less of wilfulness and wandering in the construction of axioms than in the formations of ideas; not excepting even those very principles which are obtained by common induction; but much more in the axioms and lower propositions inferred by the syllogism.

The discoveries which have hitherto been made in the sciences are superficial, scarcely beneath the surface. In order to penetrate into the inner and further recesses of nature, it is necessary that both notions and axioms be derived from things by a more sure and careful way; and that a method of intellectual operation be introduced altogether better and more certain.

There are and can be only two ways of searching into and discovering truth. The one flies from the senses and particulars to the most general axioms, and from these principles, the truth of which it takes for settled and immovable, proceeds to judgment and to the discovery of middle axioms. And this way is now in fashion. The other derives axioms from the senses and particulars, rising by a gradual and unbroken ascent, so that it arrives at the most general axioms last of all. This is the correct way, but as yet untried.

The understanding left to itself takes the same course (namely, the former) which it takes in accordance with logical order. For the mind longs to spring up to positions of higher generality, that it may find rest there; and so after a little while wearies of experiment. But this evil is increased by logic, because of the order and solemnity of its arguments.

The understanding left to itself, in a sober, patient, and serious mind, especially if it be not hindered by received doctrines, tries a little that other way, which is the right one, but with little progress; since the understanding, unless directed and assisted, is a thing unequal, and quite unfit to contend with the obscurity of things.

Both ways set out from the senses and particulars, and rest in the highest generalities; but the difference between them is infinite. For the one just glances at experiment and particulars in passing, the other dwells duly and orderly among them. The one, again, begins at once by establishing certain abstract and useless generalities, the other rises by gradual steps to that which is prior and better known in the order of nature.

There is a great difference between the Idols of the human mind and the Ideas of the divine. That is to say, between certain empty dogmas, and the true signatures and marks set upon the works of creation as they are found in nature.

It cannot be that axioms established by argumentation should avail for the discovery of new works; since the subtlety of nature is greater many times over than the subtlety of argument. But axioms duly and orderly formed from particulars easily discover the way to new particulars, and thus render sciences active.

The axioms now in use, having been suggested by a scanty and deceptive experience and a few particulars of most general occurrence, are made for the most part just large enough to fit and take these in: and therefore it is no wonder if they do not lead to new particulars. And if some opposite instance, not observed or not known before, chance to come in the way, the axiom is rescued and preserved by some frivolous distinction; whereas the truer course would be to correct the axiom itself.

The conclusions of human reason as ordinarily applied in matter of nature, I call for the sake of distinction *Preconceptions of Nature* (as a thing rash or premature). That reason which is elicited from facts by a just and methodical process, I call *Interpretation of Nature*.

Preconceptions are a ground sufficiently firm for consent; for even if men went mad all after the same fashion, they might agree one with another well enough.

For the winning of assent, indeed, preconceptions are far more powerful than interpretations; because being collected from a few instances, and those for the most part of familiar occurrence, they straightway touch the understanding and fill the imagination; whereas interpretations on the other hand, being gathered here and there from very various and widely dispersed facts, cannot suddenly strike the understanding; and therefore they must seem harsh and out of tune with the opinions of the time, much as the mysteries of faith do.

In sciences founded on opinions and dogmas, the use of preconceptions and logic is good; for in them the object is to command assent to the proposition, not to master the thing.

Though all the wits of all the ages should meet together and combine and transmit their labours, yet will no great progress ever be made in science by means of preconceptions; because radical errors in the first concoction of the mind are not to be cured by the excellence of functions and remedies subsequent.

It is idle to expect any great advancement in science from the superinducing and engrafting of new things upon old. We must begin anew from the very foundations, unless we would revolve forever in a circle with mean and contemptible progress.

The honour of the ancient authors, and indeed of all, remains untouched; since the comparison I challenge is not of wits or faculties, but of ways and methods, and the part I take upon myself is not that of a judge, but of a guide.

This must be plainly avowed: no judgment can be rightly formed either of my method or of the discoveries to which it leads, by means of preconceptions (that is to say, of the reasoning which is now in use); since I cannot be called on to abide by the sentence of a tribunal which is itself on its trial.

Even to deliver and explain what I bring forward is no easy matter; for things in themselves new will yet be apprehended with reference to what is old. . . .

One method of delivery alone remains to us; which is simply this: we must lead men to the particulars themselves, and their series and order; while men on their side must force themselves for awhile to lay their notions by and begin to familiarise themselves with facts.

The doctrine of those who have denied that certainly could be attained at all, has some agreement with my way of proceeding at the first setting out; but they end in being infinitely separated and opposed. For the holders of that doctrine assert simply that nothing can be known; I also assert that not much can be known in nature by the way which is now in use. But then they go on to destroy the authority of the senses and understanding; whereas I proceed to devise and supply helps for the same.

The idols and false notions which are now in possession of the human understanding, and have taken deep root therein, not only so beset men's minds that truth can hardly find entrance, but even after entrance obtained, they will again in the sciences meet and trouble us, unless men being forewarned of the danger fortify themselves as far as may be against their assaults.

There are four classes of Idols which beset men's minds. To these for distinction's sake I have assigned names,—calling the first class *Idols of the Tribe;* the second, *Idols of the Cave;* the third, *Idols of the Market-place;* the fourth, *Idols of the Theatre.*

The formation of ideas and axioms by true induction is no doubt the proper remedy to be applied for the keeping off and clearing away of idols. To point them out, however, is of great use; for the doctrine of Idols is to the Interpretation of Nature what the doctrine of the refutation of Sophisms is to common Logic.

The Idols of the Tribe have their foundation in human nature itself, and in the tribe or race of men. For it is a false assertion that the sense of man is the measure of things. On the contrary, all perceptions as well of the sense as of the mind are according to the measure of the individual and not according to the measure of the universe. And the human understanding is like a false mirror, which, receiving rays irregularly, distorts and discolours the nature of things by mingling its own nature with it.

The Idols of the Cave are the idols of the individual man. For every one (besides the errors common to human nature in general) has a cave or den of his own, which refracts and discolours the light of nature; owing either to his own proper and peculiar nature; or to his education and conversation with others; or to the reading of books, and the authority of those whom he esteems and admires; or to the differences of impressions, accordingly as they take place in a mind preoccupied and predisposed or in a mind indifferent and settled; or the like. So that the spirit of man (according as it is meted out to different individuals) is in fact a thing variable and full of perturbation, and governed as it were by chance. Whence it was well observed by Heraclitus that men look for sciences in their own lesser worlds, and not in the greater or common world.

There are also Idols formed by the intercourse and association of men with each other, which I call Idols of the Market-place, on account of the commerce and consort of men there. For it is by discourse that men associate; and words are imposed according to the apprehension of the naive. And therefore the ill and unfit choice of words wonderfully obstructs the understanding. Nor do the definitions or explanations wherewithin some things learned men are wont to guard and defend themselves, by any means set the matter right. But words plainly force and overrule the understanding, and throw all into confusion, and lead men away into numberless empty controversies and idle fancies.

Lastly, there are Idols which have immigrated into men's minds from the various dogmas of philosophies, and also from wrong laws of demonstration. These I call Idols of the Theatre; because in my judgment all the received systems are but so many stage-plays, representing worlds of their own creation after an unreal and scenic fashion. Nor is it only of the systems now in vogue, or only of the ancient sects and philosophies, that I speak; for many more plays of the same kind may yet be composed and in like artificial manner set forth; seeing that errors the most widely different have nevertheless causes for the most part alike. Neither again do I mean this only of entire systems, but also of many principles and axioms in science, which by tradition, credulity, and negligence have come to be received. . . .

Idols of the Theatre, or of Systems, are many, and there can be and perhaps will be yet many more. For were it not that now for many ages men's minds have been busied with religion and theology; and were it not that civil governments, especially monarchies, have been averse to such novelties, even in matters speculative; so that men labour therein to the peril and harming of their fortunes,—not only unrewarded, but exposed also to contempt and envy; doubtless there would have arisen many other philosophical sects like to those which in great variety flourished once among the Greeks. For as on the phenomena of the heavens many hypotheses may be constructed, so likewise (and more also) many various dogmas may be set up and established on the phenomena of philosophy. And in the plays of this philosophical theatre you may observe the same thing which is found in the theatre of the poets, that stories invented for the stage are more compact and elegant, and more as one would wish them to be, than true stories out of history.

In general however there is taken for the material of philosophy either a great deal out of a few things, or a very little out of many things; so that on both sides philosophy is based on too narrow a foundation of experiment and natural history, and decides on the authority of too few cases. For the Rational School of philosophers snatches from experience a variety of common instances, neither duly ascertained nor diligently examined and weighed, and leaves all the rest to meditation and agitation of wit.

There is also another class of philosophers, who having bestowed much diligent and careful labour on a few experiments, have thus made bold to infer and construct systems; wresting all other facts in a strange fashion to conformity therewith.

And there is yet a third class, consisting of those who out of faith and veneration mix their philosophy with theology and traditions; among whom the vanity of some has gone so far aside as to seek the origin of sciences among gods and geniuses. So that this parent stock of errors—this false philosophy—is of three kinds: the Sophistical, the Empirical, and the Superstitious.

The most conspicuous example of the first class was Aristotle, who corrupted natural philosophy by his logic: fashioning the world out of categories; assigning to the human soul, the noblest of substances, a genus from words of the second intention; doing the business of density and rarity (which is to make bodies of greater or less dimensions, that is, occupy greater or less spaces), by the frigid distinction of act and power; asserting that single bodies have each a single and proper motion, and that if they participate in any other, then this results from an external cause and imposing countless other arbitrary restrictions on the nature of things; being always more solicitous to provide an answer to the question and affirm something positive in words, than about the inner truth of things; a failing best shown when his philosophy is compared with other systems of note among the Greeks. For the Homoeomera of Anaxagoras; the Atoms of Leucippus and Democritus; the Heaven and Earth of Parmenides; the Strife and Friendship of Empedocles; Heraclitus's doctrine how bodies are resolved into the indifferent nature of fire, and remoulded into solids; have all of them some taste of the natural philosopher,—some savour of the nature of things, and experience, and bodies; whereas in the physics of Aristotle you hear hardly anything but the words of logic; which in his metaphysics also, under a more imposing name, and more forsooth as a realist than a nominalist, he has handled over again. Nor let any weight be given to the fact, that in his books on animals and his problems, and other of his treatises, there is frequent dealing with experiments. For he had come to his conclusion before; he did not consult experience, as he should have done, in order to the framing of his decisions and axioms: but having first determined the question according to his will, he then resorts to experience, and bending her into conformity with his beliefs leads her about like a captive in a procession; so that even on this count he is more guilty than his modern followers, the schoolmen, who have abandoned experience altogether.

But the Empirical school of philosophy gives birth to dogmas more deformed and monstrous than the Sophistical or Rational school. For it has its foundations not in the light of common notions (which though it be a faint and superficial light, is yet in a manner universal, and has reference to many things) but in the narrowness and darkness of a few experiments. To those therefore who are daily busied with these experiments, and have infected their imagination with them, such a philosophy seems probable and all but certain; to all men else incredible and vain. Of this there is a notable instance in the alchemists and their dogmas; though it is hardly to be found elsewhere in these times, except perhaps in the philosophy of Gilbert. Nevertheless with regard to philosophies of this kind there is one caution not to be omitted; for I foresee that if ever men are roused by my admonitions to betake themselves seriously to experiment and bid farewell to sophistical doctrines, then indeed through the premature hurry of the understanding to leap or fly to universals and principles of things, great danger may be apprehended from philosophies of this kind; against which evil we ought even now to prepare.

But the corruption of philosophy by superstition and an admixture of theology is far more widely spread, and does the greatest harm, whether to entire systems or to their parts. For the human understanding is obnoxious to the influence of the imagination no less than to the influence of common notions. For the contentious and sophistical kind of philosophy ensnares the understanding; but this kind, being fanciful and tumid and half poetical, misleads it more by flattery. For there is in man an ambition of the understanding, no less than of the will, especially in high and lofty spirits.

Of this kind we have among the Greeks a striking example in Pythagoras, though he united with it a coarser and more cumbersome superstition; another in Plato and his school, more dangerous and subtle. It shows itself likewise in parts of other philosophies, in the introduction of abstract forms and final causes and first causes, with the omission in most cases of causes intermediate, and the like. Upon this point the greatest caution should be used. For nothing is so mischievous as the apotheosis of error; and it is a very plague of the understanding for vanity to become the object of veneration. Yet in this vanity some of the moderns have with extreme levity indulged so far as to attempt to found a system of natural philosophy on the first chapter of Genesis, on the book of Job, and other parts of the sacred writings; seeking for the dead among the living; which also makes the inhibition and re-pression of it the more important, because from this unwholesome mixture of things human and divine there arises not only a fantastic philosophy but also an heretical religion. We must therefore be sober-minded, and give to faith that only which is faith's. . . .

So much concerning the several classes of Idols, and their equipage: all of which must be renounced and put away with a fixed and solemn determination, and the understanding thoroughly freed and cleansed; the entrance into the kingdom of man, founded on the sciences, being not much other than the entrance into the kingdom of heaven, whereinto none may enter except as a little child.

But vicious demonstrations are as the strongholds and defences of Idols; and those we have in logic do little else than make the world the bond-slave of human thought, and human thought the bond-slave of words. Demonstrations truly are in effect the philoso-phies themselves and the sciences. For such as *they* are, well or ill established, such are the systems of philosophy and the contemplations which follow. Now in the whole of the pro-cess which leads from the sense and objects to axioms and conclusions, the demonstrations which we use are deceptive and incompetent. This process consists of four parts, and has as many faults. In the first place, the impressions of the sense itself are faulty; for the sense both fails us and deceives us. But its short-comings are to be supplied, and its deceptions to be corrected. Secondly, notions are ill drawn from the impression of the senses, and are indefinite and confused, whereas they should be definite and distinctly bounded. Thirdly, the induction is amiss which infers the principles of sciences by simple enumeration, and does not, as it ought, employ exclusions and solutions (or separations) of nature. Lastly, that method of discovery and proof according to which the most general principles are first established, and then intermediate axioms are tried and proved by them, is the parent of error and the curse of all science. Of these things, however, which now I do but touch upon, I will speak more largely, when, having performed these expiations and purgings of the mind, I come to set forth the true way for the interpretation of nature.

INDUCTION

Those who have handled sciences have been either men of experiment or men of dogmas. The men of experiment are like the ant; they only collect and use: the reasoners resemble spiders, who make cobwebs out of their own substance. But the bee takes a middle course; it gathers its material from the flowers of the garden and of the field, but transforms and digests it by a power of its own. Not unlike this is the true business of philosophy; for it neither relies solely or chiefly on the powers of the mind, nor does it take the matter which it gathers from natural history and mechanical experiments and lay it up in the memory whole, as it finds it; but lays it up in the understanding altered and digested. Therefore from a closer and purer league between these two faculties, the experimental and the rational (such as has never yet been made), much may be hoped.

We have as yet no natural philosophy that is pure; all is tainted and corrupted; in Aristotle's school by logic; in Plato's by natural theology; in the second school of Platonists, such as Proclus and others, by mathematics, which ought only to give definiteness to natural philosophy, not to generate or give it birth. From a natural philosophy pure and unmixed, better things are to be expected.

No one has yet been found so firm of mind and purpose as resolutely to compel himself to sweep away all theories and common notions, and to apply the understanding, thus made fair and even, to a fresh examination of particulars. Thus it happens that human knowledge, as we have it, is a mere medley and ill-digested mass, made up of much credulity and much accident, and also of the childish notions which we at first imbibed.

Now for grounds of experience—since to experience we must come—we have as yet had either none or very weak ones; no search has been made to collect a store of particular observations sufficient either in number, or in kind, or in certainty, to inform the understanding, or in any way adequate. On the contrary, men of learning, but easy withal and idle, have taken for the construction or for the confirmation of their philosophy certain rumours and vague fames or airs of experience, and allowed to these the weight of lawful evidence. And just as if some kingdom or state were to direct its counsels and affairs, not by letters and reports from ambassadors and trustworthy messengers, but by the gossip of the streets; such exactly is the system of management introduced into philosophy with relation to experience. Nothing duly investigated, nothing verified, nothing counted, weighed, or measured, is to be found in natural history; and what in observation is loose and vague, is in information deceptive and treacherous. And if any one thinks that this is a strange thing to say, and something like an unjust complaint, seeing that Aristotle, himself so great a man, and supported by the wealth of so great a king, has composed so accurate a history of animals; and that others with greater diligence, though less pretence, have made many additions; while others, again, have compiled copious histories and descriptions of metals, plants, and fossils; it seems that he does not rightly apprehend what it is that we are now about. For a natural history which is composed for its own sake is not like one that is collected to supply the understanding with information for the building up of philosophy. They differ in many ways, but especially in this; that the former contains the variety of natural species only, and not experiment of the mechanical arts. For even as in the business of life a man's disposition and the secret workings of his mind and affections are better discovered when he is in trouble than at other times; so likewise the secrets of Nature reveal themselves more readily under artificial conditions than when they go on their own way. Good hopes may therefore be conceived of natural philosophy, when natural history, which is the basis and foundation of it, has been drawn up on a better plan; but not till then.

Again, even in the great plenty of mechanical experiments, there is yet a great scarcity of those which are of most use for the information of the understanding. For the mechanic, not troubling himself with the investigation of truth, confines his attention to those things which bear upon his particular work, and will not either raise his mind or stretch out his hand for anything else. But then only will there be good ground of hope for the further advance of knowledge, when there shall be received and gathered together into natural history a variety of experiments, which are of no use in themselves, but simply serve to discover causes and axioms; which I call *"Experimenta lucifera,"* experiments of *light,* to distinguish them from those which I call *"fructifera,"* experiments of *fruit.*

Now experiments of this kind have one admirable property and condition; they never miss or fail. For since they are applied, not for the purpose of producing any particular effect, but only of discovering the natural cause of some effect, they answer the end equally well which ever way they turn out; for they settle the question. . . .

The understanding must not however be allowed to jump and fly from particulars to remote axioms and of almost the highest generality (such as the first principles, as they are called, of arts and things), and taking stand upon them as truths that cannot be shaken, proceed to prove and frame the middle axioms by reference to them; which has been the practice hitherto; the understanding being not only carried that way by a natural impulse, but also by the use of syllogistic demonstration trained and inured to it. But then, and then only, may we hope well of the sciences, when in a just scale of ascent, and by successive steps not interrupted or broken, we rise from particulars to lesser axioms; and then to middle axioms, one above the other; and last of all to the most general. For the lowest axioms differ but slightly from bare experience, while the highest and most general (which we now have) are notional and abstract and without solidity. But the middle are the true and solid and living axioms, on which depend the affairs and fortunes of men; and above them again, last of all, those which are indeed the most general; such I mean as are not abstract, but of which those intermediate axioms are really limitations.

The understanding must not therefore be supplied with wings, but rather hung with weights, to keep it from leaping and flying. Now this has never yet been done; when it is done, we may entertain better hopes of the sciences.

In establishing axioms, another form of induction must be devised than has hitherto been employed; and it must be used for proving and discovering not first principles (as they are called) only, but also the lesser axioms, and the middle, and indeed all. For the induction which proceeds by simple enumeration is childish; its conclusions are precarious, and exposed to peril from a contradictory instance; and it generally decides on too small a number of facts, and on those only which are at hand. But the induction which is to be available for the discovery and demonstration of sciences and arts, must analyse nature by proper rejections and exclusions; and then, after a sufficient number of negatives, come to a conclusion on the affirmative instances: which has not yet been done or even attempted, save only by Plato, who does indeed employ this form of induction to a certain extent for the purpose of discussing definitions and ideas. But in order to furnish this induction or demonstration well and duly for its work, very many things are to be provided which no mortal has yet thought of; insomuch that greater labour will have to be spent in it than has hitherto been spent on the syllogism. And this induction must be used not only to discover axioms, but also in the formation of notions. And it is in this induction that our chief hope lies.

But in establishing axioms by this kind of induction, we must also examine and try whether the axiom so established be framed to the measure of those particulars only from which it is derived, or whether it be larger and wider. And if it be larger and wider, we must observe whether by indicating to us new particulars it confirm that wideness and largeness as by a collateral security; that we may not either stick fast in things already known, or loosely grasp at shadows and abstract form; not at things solid and realised in matter. And when this process shall have come into use, then at last shall we see the dawn of a solid hope.

22

BRUNO

1548–1600

Giordano Bruno was born in Nola, Italy. At the age of fourteen he went to Naples to study with G. V. de Colle ("il Sarnasse"), a leading member of the secret Averroist circle of philosophers that had continued teaching the Averroist view that all human beings are one, numerically identical intellect (see Chapter 18), which they did in spite of the ban against such teaching by the list of "forbidden propositions." After joining up with an Augustinian friar to study logic, Bruno continued his studies in 1565 at the Neapolitan convent of San Domenico Maggiore.

Bruno became a Dominican and got into trouble for having anti-ascetic and anti-Christian views. In 1576 he came under suspicion of heresy and fled to Rome. Things did not work out much better there; he got involved in a murder case and once again had to flee. This time he went to Liguria and ended up in Venice. In 1578 he was forced out of the Dominican order. He fled across the Alps to Geneva and there made a humble living as a proofreader. Trying to improve his standing, he converted to Calvinism, but as soon as he was in favor with the new authorities he published a devastating criticism of leading Calvinist Antoine de la Faye.

By now Bruno had become one of the most controversial and certainly the most persecuted of the late Renaissance philosophers. He was charged with both impiety and heresy and was sent off to prison. He retracted his views and after his release moved to Toulouse, France. He earned the degree master of arts and finally managed to secure a lecturing position in philosophy.

Interestingly enough, most philosophers who have been accused of impiety and heresy—from Socrates onward (even the case of Galileo[1])—were *not* accused of being atheists. As the church authorities saw it, atheism was not the problem. Rather, the problem was that these philosophers claimed to be able to know God, or ultimate reality, themselves, without having to rely on the orthodox authority of the church. They claimed to be able to have knowledge on the basis of their own reason or experience. Spinoza too, as we shall see, will find himself in the same predicament. Bruno is no exception. What got him in trouble was what the church considered to be a most heretical and dangerous idea: pantheism. This

---

1. See the chapter "The Church vs. Galileo" in Daniel Kolak, *In Search of God: The Language and Logic of Belief* (Belmont, Calif.: Wadsworth, 1994).

is the view that the universe is the living God and that everything in it is a manifestation of God. Bruno's own version of pantheism was founded on the metaphysics of Averroes. He conceived of God in ways that church officials saw as the most heretical of all and which they feared even more than atheism: the identification of God with the world.

According to Bruno, "God" and "world" are two names for the same being. As God, *natura naturans,* the universe is one unified whole, transcendent and ineffable; as *natura naturata* it is the infinity of worlds, things, and events. The idea is that Being, which is a cosmic, Parmenidean unity, divides itself into a Many so as to display all infinite potentialities of the One. This leads to an eternal process of outgoing creative activity into the Many and a return into the One, the divine unity. The supreme achievement of this activity is the human mind, whose search for the One within the Many, unity among diversity, simplicity in complexity, the changeless within the eternal, and so on, is the expression of the divine mind returning to itself. In Bruno's philosophy the human mind functions as the fulcrum of the cosmic process of existence, which is in many ways suggestive of the philosophy of Hegel (Chapter 34).

Despite warnings from the authorities, Bruno continued teaching and publishing his controversial views. Just when he was in danger of being arrested, French king Henry III read his works and was so impressed he offered Bruno his protection, brought him to Paris, and appointed him official court lecturer. Two years later Bruno got into trouble again, this time at Oxford, for his unorthodox views about the immortality of the soul and the unity of the intellect among all human beings.

During his stay in England he published *Ars Reminiscendi* (1583) and *La Cena de le Ceneri* (1584), in which he accepts Copernicus's view of the solar system and argues for an infinite universe composed of an infinite number of worlds; in addition, the works criticize English society in general and the Oxford philosophers and theologians as unenlightened pedants. His *De la Causa, Principio et Uno* (Concerning the cause, the principle, and the one, 1585), from which the following selection is taken, is an Averroes-inspired attempt to demonstrate the fundamental unity of all substances including, and especially, the human intellect. He begins by relating the world *as it appears to us* as described within the current scholastic terminology and the traditional Aristotelian distinctions: form and matter, cause and principle, final and efficient cause, and *potentia* (possibility) and *actus* (actuality). By *divine substance,* Bruno means things in themselves as they actually are—the originating cause of all the things we see: the ultimate reality of which the appearances are merely a secondary affect. In calling it a "divine" substance, he is as much claiming that it is *transcendental* to experience (rather than immanent) as he is claiming that it is God. On both the "thing in itself" and the "transcendental" nature of the divine substance, Kant, as we shall see, will agree.

In his ethical writings, Bruno urges social reforms along anti-Christian lines, with obvious parallels to his metaphysics: treat others as yourself *because they are you.* The church, which held as sacred the division of human beings into good and evil, sinners and saved, considered this idea an assault on its authority. The church argued that if Bruno is right, then everyone has the same relationship to God and, in a very important sense, *is* God. The person who follows obediently the rules of the church is no closer to God than the person who rebels against them; they are equally close, they are one. In the end, because Bruno refused to recant his views, the order was put forth to burn him at the stake.

He returned to Paris and continued his criticisms of Aristotle in his *Fuguratio Aristotelici Physici Auditus* (1586). He then came out with more of his heretical views and was again forced to leave. Only Wittenberg, Germany, allowed him a place to teach, and there he continued to publish until the Calvinists came to power. Once again Bruno was exiled, and for a brief time he found safe haven in Prague, Czechoslovakia. Among his written works from this period, the greatest is *De Immenso* (1588). Here his monopsychism is presented in full force, along with its Averroist foundation, and he explicitly argues for the single-identity view of the human intellect.

Upon reading this work, the local Protestant church excommunicated him. He fled to Frankfurt and was immediately denounced. Next he fled to Venice under the protection of a Venetian nobleman who soon himself, after hearing Bruno's arguments, denounced him to the Inquisition and helped bring him to Rome. After seven years in prison and a long trial for heresy, Bruno refused to take back any part of his views. He continued to espouse the unity of the universal world-form and of the numerical identity each human being has with the world-soul—that, ultimately, we are all the same person. In the end he was burned at the stake, with great pomp and circumstance. His dying words were, "Why do you burn yourself? Why?" to which a heckler responded: "Why do you?"

CONCERNING THE CAUSE, THE PRINCIPLE, AND THE ONE

Personages:
Aurelius Dixon
Theophilus
Gervasius
Polyhymnius

DIXON: Have the kindness, Master Polyhymnius, and you too, Gervasius, not to interrupt our discourse further.

POLYHYMNIUS: So be it.

GERVASIUS: If he who is the master speaks, surely I shall be unable to keep silence.

DIX.: Then you say, Theophilus, that everything which is not a first principle and a first cause, has such a principle and such a cause?

THEOPHILUS: Without doubt, and without the least controversy.

DIX.: Do you believe, accordingly, that whoever knows the things thus caused and originated must know the ultimate cause and principle?

THEO.: Not easily the proximate cause or the proximate principle; it would be extremely difficult to recognize even the traces of an ultimate cause and creative principle.

Translated from the Italian by Josiah Royce and Katherine Royce (London: Routledge, 1902).

DIX.: Then how do you think that those things which have a first and a proximate cause and principle can be really known, if their efficient cause
(which is one of the things which contribute to the true cognition of
things) is hidden?

THEO.: I grant you that it is easy to set forth the theory of proof, but the proof
itself is difficult. It is very practicable to set forth the causes, circumstances, and methods of sciences; but afterward our method-makers and
analytical scholars can use but awkwardly their *organum,* the principles
of their methods, and their arts of arts.

GERV.: Like those who know how to make fine swords, but do not know how to
use them.

POLY.: Aye, aye.

GERV.: May your eyes be closed so that you may never be able to open them.

THEO.: I should say, then, that one should not expect the natural philosopher to
make plain all causes and principles; but only the physical, and only the
principal and most essential of these. And although these, depend upon
the first cause and first principle, and can be said to possess such a cause
and principle, this is, in any case, not such a necessary relation that from
the knowledge of the one the knowledge of the other would follow; and
therefore one should not expect that in the same science both should be
set forth.

DIX.: How is that?

THEO.: Because from the cognition of all dependent things, we are unable to infer other knowledge of first cause and principle, than by the somewhat
inefficacious method of traces. All things are, indeed, derived from the
Creator's will or goodness, which is the principle of His works, and from
which proceeds the universal effect. The same consideration arises in the
case of works of art, in so much as he who sees the statue does not see the
sculptor; he who sees the portrait of Helen does not see Apelles: but he
sees only the result of the work which comes from the merit and genius
of Apelles. This work is entirely an effect of the accidents and circumstances of the substance of that man, who, as to his absolute essence, is
not in the least known.

DIX.: So that to know the universe is like knowing nothing of the being and
substance of the first principle, because it is like knowing the accidents of
the accidents. . . .
    Behold, then, of the divine substance, as well because it is infinite as
because it is extremely remote from its effects (while these effects are the
furthest boundary of the source of our reasoning faculties), we can know
nothing,—unless through the means of traces, as the Platonists say, of
remote effects, as the Peripatetic philosophers say, of the dress or outer
covering, as say the Cabalists, of the mere shoulders and back, as the Tal-
mudists say, or of the mirror, the shadow, the enigma, as the Apocalyptic
writers say.

THEO.:   All the more is this the case because we do not see perfectly this universe whose substance and principle are so difficult of comprehension. And thus it follows that with far less ground can we know the first principle and cause through its effect, than Apelles may be known through the statue he has made. For the statue all may see and examine, part by part; but not so the grand and infinite effect of the Divine Power. Therefore our simile should be understood not as a matter of close comparison.

DIX.:   Since, then, we have come to an understanding concerning the difference between those things, I wish you to devote your attention first to the Causes and then to the Principles. And as to the Causes, I desire first to know about the first efficient cause, about the formal cause, which you say is conjoined to the efficient; and, lastly, about the final cause, which is understood to be the power which moves this.

THEO.:   The order of discourse which you propose pleases me much. Now as to the efficient cause: I assert that the universal physical efficient cause is the universal Intellect, which is the first and principal faculty of the world-soul and which is the universal form of the Cosmos.

DIX.:   Your thought appears to me to be not only in agreement with that of Empedocles, but more certain, more distinct, and more explicit, and also (in so far as I can see from the above) more profound, yet you will give me pleasure if you will explain the whole more in detail, beginning by informing me just what is that universal intellect.

THEO.:   The universal intellect is the most intimate, real, and essential faculty and effective part of the world-soul. This is one and the same thing which fills the whole, illumines the universe and directs nature to produce the various species as is fitting, and has the same relation to the production of natural things as our intellect to the parallel production of our general ideas.* This is called by the Pythagoreans the moving spirit and propelling power of the universe; as saith the poet, "Infused through the members, mind vitalizes the whole mass and is mingled with the whole body." This is called by the Platonic philosophers the world-builder. This builder (they say) proceeds from the higher world (which is, in fact, one) to this world of sense, which is divided into many, and in which not only harmony but also discord reigns, because it is sundered into parts. This intellect, infusing and extending something of its own into matter, restful and moveless in itself, produces all things. By the Magi this intelligence is called most fruitful of seeds, or even the seed-sower since it is He who impregnates matter with all its forms, and according to type and condition of these succeeds in shaping, forming, and arranging all in such admirable order, as cannot be attributed to chance, or to any principle which cannot distinguish or arrange. Orpheus calls this Intellect the

---

* The reference is to a well-known scholastic parallel of the universals present *in things* and the universals present *in our minds* when we form our ideas of natural classes. The universal Intellect is related to the production of natural forms, or species, as our mind is related to the production of our ideas of these species.

eye of the world, because it sees all natural objects, both within and without, in order that all things may succeed in producing and maintaining themselves in their proper symmetry, not only intrinsically but also extrinsically. By Empedocles it is called the Distinguisher, since it never wearies of unfolding the confused forms within the breast of matter or of calling forth the birth of one thing from the corruption of another. Plotinus calls it the father and progenitor, because it distributes seeds throughout the field of nature, and is the proximate dispenser of forms. By us this Intellect is called the inner artificer, because it forms and shapes material objects from within, as from within the seed or the root is sent forth and unfolded the trunk, from within the trunk are put forth the branches, from within the branches the finished twigs, and from within the twigs unfurl the buds, and there within are woven like nerves, leaves, flowers and fruits; and inversely, at certain times the sap is recalled from the flowers and fruits to the twigs, from the twigs to the branches, from the branches to the trunk, and from the trunk to the root. Just so it is with animals; its work proceeding from the original seed, and from the center of the heart, to the external members, and from these finally gathering back to the heart the unfolded powers, it behaves as it is again knotting together spun-out threads. Now, since we believe that even inanimate works, such as we know how to produce with a certain order, imitatively working on the surface of matter, are not produced without forethought and mind,—as when, cutting and sculpturing a piece of wood, we bring forth the effigy of a horse: how much greater must we believe is that creative intelligence which, from the interior of the germinal matter, brings forth the bones, extends the cartilage, hollows out the arteries, breathes into the pores, weaves the fibres, forms the branching nerves, and with such admirable mastery arranges the whole? I say, how much greater an artificer is He who is not restricted to one sole part of the material world, but operates continually throughout the whole. . . .

DIX.: You show me the seemingly true way in which the opinion of Anaxagoras may be maintained, who held that all things are in all things. For since spirit, or soul, or universal form, exists in all things, all may be produced from all.

THEO.: I do not say seemingly true, but true. For spirit is found in all things, those which are not living creatures are still vitalized, if not according to the perceptible presence of animation and life, yet they are animate according to the principle and, as it were, primal being of animation and life.

. . . On other occasions, I shall be able to discuss more at length the mind, the spirit, the soul, the life, which penetrates all, is in all, and moves all matter, fills the lap of that matter and dominates it rather than is dominated by it. For the spiritual substance cannot be overpowered by the material, but rather embraces it.

DIX.: That appears to me to conform not only to the sense of Pythagoras, whose opinion the Poet rehearses when he says,—

In the beginning the sky, the earth and the fields of the waters,
Glistening orb of the moon, and also the radiant sunlight,
All is inspired with life, and trembling through every member,
Mind vitalizes the mass, and with the whole body is mingled.

VIRGIL'S *Aeneid,* VI 724

but also it conforms to the Theologian who says, "The spirit rules over and fills the earth, and that it is which contains all things." And another, speaking perchance of the dealings of form with matter and with potentiality, says that the latter is dominated by actuality and by form.

THEO.: If then, spirit, mind, life, is found in all things, and in various degrees fills all matter, it must certainly follow, that it is the true actuality, and the true form of all things. The soul of the world, then, is the formal, constitutive principle of the universe, and of that which is contained within it. I say that if life is found in all things, the soul must be the form of all things; that which through everything presides over matter, holds sway over composite things, effects the composition and consistency of their parts. And therefore such form is no less enduring than matter. This I understand to be One in all things, which, however, according to the diversity of the disposition of matter, and according to the power of the material principle, both active and passive, comes to produce diverse configurations, and to effect different faculties, sometimes showing the effects of life without sense, sometimes the effects of life and sensation without intellect, and sometimes it appears that all the faculties are suppressed or repressed either by weakness, or by other conditions of matter. While this form thus changes place and circumstance, it is impossible that it should be annulled; because the spiritual substance is not less real than the material. Then only external forms can change and even be annulled, because they are not things but of things; they are not substances, they are accidents and circumstances.

DIX.: Then you approve, in some sort, the opinion of Anaxagoras who calls the particular forms of Nature latent, and in a sense that of Plato who deduces them from ideas, and in a manner that of Empedocles who makes them proceed from intelligence, and in some sort that of Aristotle who makes them, as it were, issue from the potentiality of matter?

THEO.: Yes. Because, as we have said, where there is form, there is, in a certain manner, everything. Where there is soul, spirit, life, there is everything, for the creator of ideal forms and varieties is intellect. And even if it does not obtain forms from matter, it nevertheless does not go begging for them outside of matter, because this spirit fills the whole.

. . . Know, then, in brief, that the Soul of the world, and the Divinity are not omnipresent through all and through every part, in the way in which material things could be there: because this is impossible to any sort of body, and to any sort of spirit; but in a manner which is not easy to explain to you if not in this way. You should take notice that if the Soul of the World and the universal form are said to be everywhere, we do not mean *corporeally* and *dimensionally,* because such things cannot be; and just so they cannot be in any part. But they are *spiritually* present in everything—as, for example (perhaps a rough one), you can imagine a voice which is throughout a whole room and in every part of the room; because, through all, it is completely heard: just as these words which I utter are heard completely by all, even were there a thousand present, and my voice, could it reach throughout the whole world, would be everywhere through everything. I tell you then, Master Polyhymnius, that the soul is not indivisible like a point, but in some sort like the voice. And I answer you, Gervasius, that the Divinity is not everywhere in the sense that the God of Grandazzo was in the whole of the chapel, because, although he was present throughout the church, yet all of him was not present everywhere, but his head was in one part, his feet in another, his arms and his chest in yet other parts. But that other is in its entirety in even, part, as my voice is heard completely in every part of this room.

CHAPTER

23

❧❧❧

HOBBES
1588–1679

Thomas Hobbes, Jr., was born near Malmesbury, England. His father, the vicar of Westport and Charlton, enrolled him at the age of four in the church school at Westport, intending for his son to follow in his footsteps. A few years later his father got into a vicious fight at the church door and then disappeared, leaving his three children to be brought up by their uncle, a glover in Malmesbury. When Hobbes turned fourteen, his uncle sent him to Magden Hall of Oxford University. Bored and even repulsed by the prevailing Oxfordian scholasticism, Hobbes spent most of his time reading travel books and studying charts and maps.

Three events seem to have been pivotal in Hobbes's extremely gradual awakening to philosophy. The first of these occurred when after graduating at age twenty, he was hired by the noble Cavendish family as a sort of travel companion and tutor to a young man only a few years his junior, William Cavendish, who would later become the second earl of Devonshire. The two took the opportunity to travel throughout continental Europe, and there Hobbes was surprised to find himself defending the Oxfordian philosophy which, much to his surprise, was treated with great contempt especially by the French, Germans, and Italians. This experience inspired him, upon their return, to study more carefully the philosophy that before had not in the least bit stirred his interest.

The second event came as a stroke of luck when between 1622 and 1625 he was hired by Francis Bacon (Chapter 21) to transcribe Bacon's lectures and oral notes and to translate some of his *Essays* into Latin. Thus, though Hobbes was already in his late thirties, by coincidence and almost without his own will he happened to become a personal student of one of the greatest living philosophers of the time. This further stoked his growing interest in philosophy and science that culminated with the third event, his discovery of geometry at age forty-two. Having recently been disheartened in his growing study of the classics by all the disagreements among the various philosophers and the completely different systems developed by the various schools, one day in the library he happened to come across an open copy of Euclid's *Elements*. He read the Pythagorean theorem, which seemed to him probably false and certainly undemonstrable. Yet he followed the proof to its inexorable conclusion. Profoundly moved by seeing how the power of reason could attain absolute certainty in geometry, Hobbes suddenly began thinking about how—and whether—one could achieve the same level of certainty within philosophy. Thus armed with an avid aversion to the religiously tainted views of his immediate philosophical predecessors and a mathematical model of knowledge, he set out to purge philosophy of its scholastic influence and to develop a method for attaining absolutely certain knowledge to which end all the subsequent modern philosophers aspired. Nevertheless, certain strong medieval influences remained, particularly the paradigm of understanding the world in its entirety and as a unity. Thus what now really began to perplex Hobbes most of all was this: if the world was ultimately all one substance, could there ever be a distinction between one thing and another, and how could there even be perception (in addition to the thing perceived)?

It is with this burning question that Hobbes approached some of the leading thinkers of the time. His support from the Cavendish family continued after William died and Hobbes remained tutor to William Cavendish, Jr. It was during their travels to France and Italy that Hobbes met with Marin Mersenne's[1] circle in Paris, and in Florence with Galileo. He was so impressed by Galileo's mechanics that he saw in his method a key to developing a new system, and it became an overwhelming passion. Everything could be explained in terms of the motion of bodies, even sense perception. Yet, unlike the experimentalists, Hobbes was equally moved by his insights into geometry and so developed a purely a priori mathematical system in sharp contrast with the prevailing inductive approaches based on the methods of Francis Bacon. He thus formulated the major philosophical insight that would propel his thinking on all subjects for the rest of his life, namely, that all things must be understood just as the ancient Greek Democritus has once supposed, in terms of bodies in motion. He embarked on a philosophical trilogy that would explain everything. In *De Corpore* he showed that all physical phenomena could be explained using geometry and mechanics. In *De Homine* he showed that specific bodily motions are the specific causes of all human mental activity, including thinking and willing. In *De Cive* he explained how the ideal human society should be formed and sustained to be in harmony with the way the world is.

Upon his return to England, however, Hobbes found that instead of embarking on his philosophical quest he had to deal with the political turmoil of civil war. Having just turned fifty, he thought he should give up his philosophical dream and help his country and so used his knowledge and growing influence to heal the two sides that had begun to fight over the divine right of kings versus the rule of constitutional government. His views, however, ended up antagonizing both sides; those loyal to the king saw him as a traitor for arguing that the sovereignty of law ought to be based on the social contract, while the parliamentarians were threatened by his advocacy of the rule of many by one single individual. In 1440 he was thus forced to flee to Paris, and during the next eleven years spent in exile he not only began work on his trilogy but joined the Mersenne circle where by lucky coincidence there happened to be circulating a new and unpublished work that would become one of the most influential documents in the history of philosophy, the *Meditations* by René Descartes (Chapter 24). Hobbes wrote brilliant objections to the *Meditations*. The work looked to him so derivative of Plato, that his first response was, "I am sorry that so excellent an author of new speculations should publish this old stuff." Descartes published all of Hobbes's objections, along with Descartes's rebuttal, in his edition of the *Meditations* (see the selection in the next chapter). But Hobbes's continued criticisms so angered Des-

---

1. Descartes's friend, who organized the publication of the *Meditations*.

cartes that after several exchanges Descartes refused to have anything more to do with "the Englishman."

Because of the political turmoil across Europe stemming from the beginning of the end of the great monarchies, *De Cive* (1642) was the first of Hobbes's trilogy to appear. In 1651 he published his masterpiece, from which our selection is taken, *Leviathan, or the Matter, Form and Power of a Commonwealth, Ecclesiastical and Civil.* At the end of that year, though still exiled from the British court and now under suspicion by Paris authorities for his attack on the papacy, Hobbes returned to London and made peace with the new regime. Now sixty-three he began work on *De Corpore* (1655). He had by now further alienated the philosophers at Oxford for his attack in *Leviathan* of the university system as functioning mainly to covertly sustain papal against civil authority and to confound the people by their adherence to "old learning." He completed his *De Homine* in 1658, which presents a new theory of vision and an account of psychology.

From his seventies on, Hobbes enjoyed the protection and patronage of the new King Charles II, who as it turned out had been a pupil of Hobbes while Hobbes was in exile in Paris. Thus, while Hobbes was widely regarded as a freethinker and, for his attacks on the church, as a subversive atheist against all religion, the king bequeathed to him a lifelong pension and much enjoyed his presence in court precisely because it scandalized the bishops. The only proviso King Charles made was that in the interest of not further inflaming the public Hobbes would not be allowed to publish anything in England that related to human conduct.

In the selection from the *Leviathan* that follows, knowledge is considered as fundamentally empirical in nature, but the appropriate method for inferring causes of things from their effects and vice versa had to be done via an a priori mathematical method. By carefully analyzing the elements of experience, one finds the concepts of matter and motion to be the least common denominators, and that is why Hobbes claims that physical bodies and their movements, as understood by geometrical laws, are the only valid subject matter of philosophy.

Although *Leviathan* was supposed to be mainly a treatise on the philosophy of politics, it remains a fundamental work in metaphysics and epistemology, as well as on the philosophy of language and philosophical psychology. Paramount to both aspects is Hobbes's distinction between two different functions of the mind. On the one hand there is sense, imagination, and the movements arising from them; on the other, there is ratiocination—calculation, using words looking into the causes of phenomena. The former is natural, the latter artificial in that it depends on the manipulation of language and the naming of things; philosophy's main concern is with the latter. Following Galileo and the emerging physical science of the time, which involved a new synthesis of empiricism and mathematics, in *Leviathan* Hobbes develops in precise modern terms the ancient Democritan and Epicurean atomistic materialist philosophy according to which everything that exists reduces ultimately to physical particles moving in accordance with physical laws. Thus, for instance, the first law of motion appears in every body as a tendency toward self—preservation and self-assertion, which become a natural *right*. On this basis he argues that all organic as well as inorganic bodies exist in the primary condition of collision, conflict, and war. Similarly, the second law of motion manifests itself in organic things and impels us to relinquish a portion of our natural rights in purely self-interested acts in return for being guaranteed that others will do the same. This is how the antagonistic forces of diverse individual wills can exist in harmony through a social contract that forms the basis of the political state.

LEVIATHAN

PART I: OF MAN

CHAPTER I: OF SENSE

Concerning the thoughts of man, I will consider them first singly, and afterwards in train, or dependence upon one another. Singly, they are every one a *representation* or *appearance,* of some quality, or other accident of a body without us, which is commonly called an *object.* Which object works on the eyes, ears, and other parts of a man's body; and by diversity of working, produces diversity of appearances.

The original of them all, is that which we call SENSE, for there is no conception in a man's mind, which has not at first, totally or by parts, been begotten upon the organs of sense. The rest are derived from that original. . . .

The cause of sense, is the external body, or object, which presses the organ proper to each sense, either immediately, as in the taste and touch; or mediately, as in seeing, hearing, and smelling; which pressure, by the mediation of the nerves, and other strings and membranes of the body, continued inwards to the brain and heart, causes there a resistance, or counterpressure or endeavour of the heart to deliver itself, which endeavour, because *outward,* seems to be some matter without. And this *seeming,* or *fancy,* is that which men call *sense;* and consists, as to the eye, in a *light,* or *colour figured;* to the ear, in a *sound;* to the nostril, in an *odour;* to the tongue and palate, in a *savour;* and to the rest of the body, in *heat, cold, hardness, softness,* and such other qualities as we discern by *feeling.* All which qualities, called *sensible,* are in the object, that causes them, but so many several motions of the matter, by which it presses our organs diversely. Neither in us that are pressed, are they anything else, but diverse motions; for motion produces nothing but motion. But their appearance to us is fancy, the same waking, that dreaming. And as pressing, rubbing, or striking the eye, makes us fancy a light; and pressing the ear, produces a din; so do the bodies also we see, or hear, produce the same by their strong, though unobserved action. For if those colours and sounds were in the bodies, or objects that cause them, they could not be severed from them, as by glasses, and in echoes by reflection, we see they are; where we know the thing we see is in one place, the appearance in another. And though at some certain distance, the real and very object seem invested with the fancy it begets in us; yet still the object is one thing, the image or fancy is another. So that sense, in all cases, is nothing else but original fancy, caused, as I have said, by the pressure, that is, by the motion, of external things upon our eyes, ears, and other organs thereunto ordained.

But the philosophy-schools, through all the universities of Christendom, grounded upon certain texts of Aristotle, teach another doctrine, and say, for the cause of *vision,* that the thing seen, sends forth on every side a *visible species,* in English, a *visible show, apparition,* or *aspect,* or *a being seen;* the receiving whereof into the eye is *seeing.* And for the cause of *hearing,* that the thing heard, sends forth an *audible species,* that is an *audible aspect,* or

Leviathan, first edition, London, 1651. From Hobbes's *English Works,* collected and edited by Sir William Molesworth, London, 1839, vol. iii. With emendations by Daniel Kolak.

audible being seen; which entering at the ear, makes *hearing.* Nay, for the cause of *understanding* also, they say the thing understood, sends forth an *intelligible species,* that is, an *intelligible being seen;* which, coming into the understanding, makes us understand. I say not this, as disproving the use of universities; but because I am to speak hereafter of their office in a commonwealth, I must let you see on all occasions by the way, what things would be amended in them; amongst which the frequency of insignificant speech is one.

CHAPTER II: OF IMAGINATION

That when a thing lies still, unless somewhat else stir it, it will lie still for ever, is a truth that no man doubts of. But that when a thing is in motion, it will eternally be in motion, unless somewhat else stay it, though the reason be the same, namely, that nothing can change itself, is not so easily assented to. For men measure, not only other men, but all other things, by themselves; and because they find themselves subject after motion to pain, and lassitude, think everything else grows weary of motion, and seeks repose of its own accord; little considering, whether it be not some other motion, wherein that desire of rest they find in themselves, consists. From hence it is, that the schools say, heavy bodies fall downwards, out of an appetite to rest, and to conserve their nature in that place which is most proper for them; ascribing appetite, and knowledge of what is good for their conservation, which is more than man has, to things inanimate, absurdly.

When a body is once in motion, it moves, unless something else hinder it, eternally; and whatsoever hinders it, cannot in an instant, but in time, and by degrees, quite extinguish it; and as we see in the water, though the wind cease, the waves give not over rolling for a long time after: so also it happens in that motion, which is made in the internal parts of a man, then, when he sees, dreams, etc. For after the object is removed, or the eye shut, we still retain an image of the thing seen, though more obscure than when we see it. And this is it, the Latins call *imagination,* from the image made in seeing; and apply the same, though improperly, to all the other senses. But the Greeks call it *fancy;* which signifies *appearance,* and is as proper to one sense, as to another. IMAGINATION, therefore, is nothing but *decaying sense;* and is found in men, and many other living creatures, as well sleeping, as waking.

The decay of sense in men waking, is not the decay of the motion made in sense; but an obscuring of it, in such manner as the light of the sun obscures the light of the stars; which stars do no less exercise their virtue, by which they are visible, in the day than in the night. But because amongst many strokes, which our eyes, ears, and other organs receive from external bodies, the predominant only is sensible; therefore, the light of the sun being predominant, we are not affected with the action of the stars. And any object being removed from our eyes, though the impression it made in us remain, yet other objects more present succeeding, and working on us, the imagination of the past is obscured, and made weak, as the voice of a man is in the noise of the day. From whence it follows, that the longer the time is, after the sight or sense of any object, the weaker is the imagination. For the continual change of man's body destroys in time the parts which in sense were moved: so that distance of time, and of place, has one and the same effect in us. For as at a great distance of place, that which we look at appears dim, and without distinction of the smaller parts; and as voices grow weak, and inarticulate; so also, after great distance of time, our imagination of the past is weak; and we lose, for example, of cities we have seen, many particular streets, and of actions, many particular circumstances. This *decaying sense,* when we would express the thing itself, I mean *fancy* itself, we call *imagination*, as I said before: but when we would express the decay, and signify that the sense is fading, old, and past, it is called *memory*. So that imagination and memory are but one thing, which for diverse considerations has diverse names.

Much memory, or memory of many things, is called *experience*. Again, imagination being only of those things which have been formerly perceived by sense, either all at once, or by parts at several times, the former, which is the imagining the whole object as it was presented to the sense, is *simple* imagination, as when one imagines a man, or horse, which he has seen before. The other is *compounded;* as when, from the sight of a man at one time, and of a horse at another, we conceive in our mind a Centaur. So when a man compounds the image of his own person with the image of the actions of another man, as when a man imagines himself a Hercules or an Alexander, which happens often to them that are much taken with reading of romances, it is a compound imagination, and properly but a fiction of the mind. There be also other imaginations that rise in men, though waking, from the great impression made in sense: as from gazing upon the sun, the impression leaves an image of the sun before our eyes a long time after; and from being long and vehemently attent upon geometrical figures, a man shall in the dark, though awake, have the images of lines and angles before his eyes; which kind of fancy has no particular name, as being a thing that does not commonly fall into men's discourse.

The imaginations of them that sleep are those we call *dreams*. And these also, as also all other imaginations, have been before, either totally or by parcels, in the sense. And because in sense, the brain and nerves, which are the necessary organs of sense, are so benumbed in sleep as not easily to be moved by the action of external objects, there can happen in sleep no imagination, and therefore no dream, but what proceeds from the agitation of the inward parts of man's body; which inward parts, for the connection they have with the brain, and other organs, when they be distempered, do keep the same in motion; whereby the imaginations there formerly made appear as if a man were waking; saving that the organs of sense being now benumbed, so as there is no new object, which can master and obscure them with a more vigorous impression, a dream must needs be more clear, in this silence of sense, than our waking thoughts. And hence it comes to pass, that it is a hard matter, and by many thought impossible, to distinguish exactly between sense and dreaming. For my part, when I consider that in dreams I do not often nor constantly think of the same persons, places, objects, and actions, that I do waking; nor remember so long a train of coherent thoughts, dreaming, as at other times; and because waking I often observe the absurdity of dreams, but never dream of the absurdities of my waking thoughts; I am well satisfied, that being awake, I know I dream not, though when I dream I think myself awake.

And seeing dreams are caused by the distemper of some of the inward parts of the body, diverse distempers must needs cause different dreams. And hence it is that lying cold breeds dreams of fear, and raises the thought and image of some fearful object, the motion from the brain to the inner parts and from the inner parts to the brain being reciprocal; and that as anger causes heat in some parts of the body when we are awake, so when we sleep the overheating of the same parts causes anger, and raises up in the brain the imagination of an enemy. In the same manner, as natural kindness, when we are awake, causes desire, and desire makes heat in certain other parts of the body; so also too much heat in those parts, while we sleep, raises in the brain an imagination of some kindness shown. In sum, our dreams are the reverse of our waking imaginations; the motion when we are awake beginning at one end, and when we dream at another. . . .

CHAPTER III: OF THE CONSEQUENCE OR TRAIN OF IMAGINATIONS

By *Consequence,* or TRAIN of thoughts, I understand that succession of one thought to another which is called, to distinguish it from discourse in words, *mental discourse.*

When a man thinks on anything whatsoever, his next thought after is not altogether so casual as it seems to be. Not every thought to every thought succeeds indifferently. But as we have no imagination, whereof we have not formerly had sense, in whole, or in parts, so we have no transition from one imagination to another, whereof we never had the like before in our senses. The reason is this. All fancies are motions within us, relics of those made in the sense; and those motions that immediately succeeded one another in the sense continue also together after sense; insomuch as the former coming again to take place and be predominant, the latter follows, by coherence of the matter moved, in such manner as water upon a plane table is drawn which way any one part of it is guided by the finger. But because in sense, to one and the same thing perceived, sometimes one thing, sometimes another succeeds, it comes to pass in time, that in the imagining of anything, there is no certainty what we shall imagine next; only this is certain, it shall be something that succeeded the same before, at one time or another.

This train of thoughts, or mental discourse, is of two sorts. The first is *unguided, without design,* and inconstant; wherein there is no passionate thought to govern and direct those that follow, to itself, as the end and scope of some desire, or other passion: in which case the thoughts are said to wander, and seem impertinent one to another, as in a dream. Such are commonly the thoughts of men, that are not only without company, but also without care of anything; though even then their thoughts are as busy as at other times, but without harmony; as the sound which a lute out of tune would yield to any man, or in tune to one that could not play. And yet in this wild ranging of the mind, a man may oft-times perceive the way of it, and the dependence of one thought upon another. For in a discourse of our present civil war, what could seem more impertinent than to ask, as one did, what was the value of a Roman penny? Yet the coherence to me was manifest enough. For the thought of the war, introduced the thought of the delivering up the king to his enemies; the thought of that, brought in the thought of the delivering up of Christ; and that again the thought of the thirty pence, which was the price of that treason; and thence easily followed that malicious question, and all this in a moment of time; for thought is quick.

The second is more constant, as being *regulated* by some desire, and design. For the impression made by such things as we desire, or fear, is strong and permanent, or, if it cease for a time, of quick return: so strong it is sometimes, as to hinder and break our sleep. From desire, arises the thought of some means we have seen produce the like of that which we aim at; and from the thought of that, the thought of means to that means; and so continually till we come to some beginning within our own power. And because the end, by the greatness of the impression, comes often to mind, in case our thoughts begin to wander, they are quickly again reduced into the way: which observed by one of the seven wise men, made him give men this precept, which is now worn out, *Respice finem;* that is to say, in all your actions, look often upon what you would have as the thing that directs all your thoughts in the way to attain it.

The train of regulated thoughts is of two kinds: one, when of an effect imagined we seek the causes, or means that produce it; and this is common to man and beast. The other is, when imagining anything whatsoever, we seek all the possible effects that can by it be produced; that is to say, we imagine what we can do with it, when we have it. Of which I have not at any time seen any sign, but in man only; for this is a curiosity hardly incident to the nature of any living creature that has no other passion but sensual, such as are hunger, thirst, lust, and anger. In sum, the discourse of the mind, when it is governed by design, is nothing but *seeking,* or the faculty of invention, which the Latins called *sagacitas,* and *solertia;* a hunting out of the causes of some effect, present or past; or of the effects of some present or past cause. Sometimes a man seeks what he has lost; and from that place and time wherein he misses it, his mind runs back, from place to place, and time to time, to find where, and when he had it; that is to say, to find some certain and limited time and place, in which to begin a method of seeking. Again, from thence his thoughts run over the same places and times, to find what action or other occasion might make him lose it. This we call *remembrance,* or calling to mind: the Latins call it *reminiscentia,* as it were a *re-conning* of our former actions. . . .

There is no other act of man's mind, that I can remember, naturally planted in him, so as to need no other thing, to the exercise of it, but to be born a man and live with the use of his five senses. Those other faculties, of which I shall speak by and by, and which seem proper to man only, are acquired and increased by study and industry, and of most men learned by instruction, and discipline, and proceed all from the invention of words, and speech. For besides sense, and thoughts, and the train of thoughts, the mind of man has no other motion; though by the help of speech and method, the same faculties may be improved to such a height, as to distinguish men from all other living creatures.

Whatsoever we imagine is *finite.* Therefore there is no idea, or conception of any thing we call *infinite.* No man can have in his mind an image of infinite magnitude, nor conceive infinite swiftness, infinite time, or infinite force, or infinite power. When we say any thing is infinite, we signify only that we are not able to conceive the ends, and bounds of the things named, having no conception of the thing, but of our own inability. And therefore the name of God is used, not to make us conceive him, for he is incomprehensible, and his greatness, and power are unconceivable; but that we may honour him. Also because, whatsoever, as I said before, we conceive has been perceived first by sense, either all at once, or by parts; a man can have no thought, representing any thing, not subject to sense. No man therefore can conceive any thing, but he must conceive it in some place, and indued with some determinate magnitude, and which may be divided into parts; nor that any thing is all in this place and all in another place at the same time; nor that two or more things can be in one and the same place at once: for none of these things ever have nor can be incident to sense; but are absurd speeches, taken upon credit, without any signification at all, from deceived philosophers, and deceived, or deceiving schoolmen. . . .

CHAPTER IV: OF SPEECH

The invention of *printing,* though ingenious, compared with the invention of *letters,* is no great matter. But who was the first that found the use of letters, is not known. He that first brought them into Greece, men say was Cadmus, the son of Agenor, king of Phoenicia. A profitable invention for continuing the memory of time passed, and the conjunction of mankind, dispersed into so many, and distant regions of the earth; and withal difficult, as proceeding from a watchful observation of the diverse motions of the tongue, palate, lips, and other organs of speech; whereby to make as many differences of characters, to remember them. But the most noble and profitable invention of all other, was that of SPEECH, consisting of *names* or *appellations,* and their connection; whereby men register their thoughts; recall them when they are past; and also declare them one to another for mutual utility and conversation; without which, there had been amongst men, neither commonwealth, nor society, nor contract, nor peace, no more than amongst lions, bears and wolves. . . .

The general use of speech, is to transfer our mental discourse, into verbal: or the train of our thoughts, into a train of words; and that for two commodities, whereof one is the registering of the consequences of our thoughts; which being apt to slip out of our memory and put us to a new labour, may again be recalled, by such words as they were marked by. So that the first use of names is to serve for *marks*, or *notes* of remembrance. Another is, when many use the same words, to signify, by their connection and order, one to another, what they conceive, or think of each matter; and also what they desire, fear, or have any other passion for. And for this use they are called *signs*. Special uses of speech are these: first, to register, what by cogitation, we find to be the cause of anything, present or past; and what we find things present or past may produce, or effect; which in sum, is acquiring of arts. Secondly, to show to others that knowledge which we have attained, which is, to counsel and teach one another. Thirdly, to make known to others our wills and purposes, that we may have the mutual help of one another. Fourthly, to please and delight ourselves and others, by playing with our words, for pleasure or ornament, innocently.

To these uses, there are also four correspondent abuses. First, when men register their thoughts wrong, by the inconstancy of the signification of their words; by which they register for their conception, that which they never conceived, and so deceive themselves. Secondly, when they use words metaphorically; that is, in other sense than that they are ordained for; and thereby deceive others. Thirdly, by words, when they declare that to be their will, which is not. Fourthly, when they use them to grieve one another; for seeing nature has armed living creatures, some with teeth, some with horns, and some with hands, to grieve an enemy, it is but an abuse of speech, to grieve him with the tongue, unless it be one whom we are obliged to govern; and then it is not to grieve, but to correct and amend.

The manner how speech serves to the remembrance of the consequence of causes and effects, consists in the imposing of *names*, and the *connection* of them.

Of names, some are *proper*, and singular to one only thing, as *Peter, John, this man, this tree*; and some are *common* to many things, as *man, horse, tree*; every of which, though but one name, is nevertheless the name of diverse particular things; in respect of all which together, it is called an *universal*; there being nothing in the world universal but names; for the things named are every one of them individual and singular.

One universal name is imposed on many things, for their similitude in some quality, or other accident; and whereas a proper name brings to mind one thing only, universals recall any one of those many.

And of names universal, some are of more, and some of less extent; the larger comprehending the less large; and some again of equal extent, comprehending each other reciprocally. As for example, the name *body* is of larger signification than the word *man*, and comprehends it; and the names *man* and *rational* are of equal extent, comprehending mutually one another. But here we must take notice, that by a name is not always understood, as in grammar, one only word; but sometimes, by circumlocution, many words together. For all these words, *he that in his actions observes the laws of his country*, make but one name, equivalent to this one word, *just*.

By this imposition of names, some of larger, some of stricter signification, we turn the reckoning of the consequences of things imagined in the mind, into a reckoning of the consequences of appellations. For example: a man that has no use of speech at all, such as is born and remains perfectly deaf and dumb, if he set before his eyes a triangle, and by it two right angles, such as are the corners of a square figure, he may, by meditation, compare and find, that the three angles of that triangle, are equal to those two right angles that stand by it. But if another triangle be shown him, different in shape from the former, he cannot know, without a new labour, whether the three angles of that also be equal to the same. But he that has the use of words, when he observes, that such quality was consequent, not to the length of the sides, nor to any other particular thing in his triangle; but only to this, that the sides were straight, and the angles three; and that that was all, for which he named it a triangle; will boldly conclude universally, that such equality of angles is in all triangles whatsoever; and register his invention in these general terms, *every triangle has its three angles equal to two right angles*. And thus the consequence found in one particular, comes to be registered and remembered, as a universal rule, and discharges our mental reckoning, of time and place, and delivers us from all labour of the mind, saving the first, and makes that which was found true *here*, and *now*, to be true in *all times* and *places*.

But the use of words in registering our thoughts is in nothing so evident as in numbering. A natural fool that could never learn by heart the order of numeral words, as *one, two,* and *three*, may observe every stroke of the clock, and nod to it, or say *one, one, one*, but can never know what hour it strikes. And it seems, there was a time when those names of number were not in use; and men were fain to apply their fingers of one or both hands, to those things they desired to keep account of; and that thence it proceeded, that now our numeral words are but ten, in any nation, and in some but five; and then they begin again. And he that can tell ten, if he recite them out of order, will lose himself, and not know when he has done. Much less will he be able to add, and subtract, and perform all other operations of arithmetic. So that without words there is no possibility of reckoning of numbers; much less of magnitudes, of swiftness, of force, and other things, the reckonings whereof are necessary to the being, or well-being of mankind.

When two names are joined together into a consequence, or affirmation, as thus, *a man is a living creature;* or thus, *if he be a man, he is a living creature;* if the latter name, *living creature,* signify all that the former name *man* signifies, then the affirmation, or consequence, is *true;* otherwise *false.* For *true* and *false* are attributes of speech, not of things. And where speech is not, there is neither *truth* nor *falsehood; error* there may be, as when we expect that which shall not be, or suspect what has not been; but in neither case can a man be charged with untruth.

Seeing then that truth consists in the right ordering of names in our affirmations, a man that seeks precise truth had need to remember what every name he uses stands for, and to place it accordingly, or else he will find himself entangled in words, as a bird in lime twigs, the more he struggles the more belimed. And therefore in geometry, which is the only science that it has pleased God hitherto to bestow on mankind, men begin at settling the significations of their words; which settling of significations they call *definitions,* and place them in the beginning of their reckoning.

By this it appears how necessary it is for any man that aspires to true knowledge, to examine the definitions of former authors; and either to correct them, where they are negligently set down, or to make them himself. For the errors of definitions multiply themselves according as the reckoning proceeds, and lead men into absurdities, which at last they see, but cannot avoid, without reckoning anew from the beginning, in which lies the foundation of their errors. From whence it happens, that they which trust to books do as they that cast up many little sums into a greater, without considering whether those little sums were rightly cast up or not; and at last finding the error visible, and not mistrusting their first grounds, know not which way to clear themselves, but spend time in fluttering over their books; as birds that entering by the chimney, and finding themselves enclosed in a chamber, flutter at the false light of a glass window, for want of wit to consider which way they came in. So that in the right definition of names lies the first use of speech; which is the acquisition of science: and in wrong, or no definitions, lies the first abuse; from which proceed all false and senseless tenets; which make those men that take their instruction from the authority of books, and not from their own meditation, to be as much below the condition of ignorant men, as men endued with true science are above it. For between true science and erroneous doctrines, ignorance is in the middle. Natural sense and imagination are not subject to absurdity. Nature itself cannot err; and as men abound in copiousness of language, so they become more wise, or more mad than ordinary. Nor is it possible without letters for any man to become either excellently wise, or, unless his memory be hurt by disease or ill constitution of organs, excellently foolish. For words are wise men's counters, they do but reckon by them; but they are the money of fools, that value them by the authority of an Aristotle, a Cicero, or a Thomas, or any other doctor whatsoever, if but a man.

Subject to names is whatsoever can enter into or be considered in an account, and be added one to another to make a sum, or subtracted one from another and leave a remainder. The Latins called accounts of money *rationes,* and accounting *ratiocinatio;* and that which we in bills or books of account call *items,* they call *nomina,* that is *names;* and thence it seems to proceed, that they extended the word *ratio* to the faculty of reckoning in all other things. The Greeks have but one word, λόγος for both *speech* and *reason;* not that they thought there was no speech without reason, but no reasoning without speech: and the act of reasoning they called *syllogism,* which signifies summing up of the consequences of one saying to another. And because the same thing may enter into account for diverse accidents, their names are, to show that diversity, diversely wrested and diversified. This diversity of names may be reduced to four general heads.

First, a thing may enter into account for *matter* or *body;* as *living, sensible, rational, hot, cold, moved, quiet;* with all which names the word *matter,* or *body,* is understood; all such being names of matter.

Secondly, it may enter into account, or be considered, for some accident or quality which we conceive to be in it; as for *being moved,* for *being so long,* for *being hot,* etc.; and then, of the name of the thing itself, by a little change or wresting, we make a name for that accident, which we consider; and for *living* put into the account *life;* for *moved, motion;* for *hot, heat;* for *long, length;* and the like; and all such names are the names of the accidents and properties by which one matter and body is distinguished from another. These are called *names abstract,* because severed, not from matter, but from the account of matter.

Thirdly, we bring into account the properties of our own bodies whereby we make such distinction; as when anything is seen by us, we reckon not the thing itself, but the sight, the colour, the idea of it in the fancy: and when anything is heard, we reckon it not, but the hearing or sound only, which is our fancy or conception of it by the ear; and such are names of fancies.

Fourthly, we bring into account, consider, and give names, to *names* themselves, and to *speech:* for *general, universal, special, equivocal,* are names of names. And *affirmation, interrogation, commandment, narration, syllogism, sermon, oration,* and many other such, are names of speeches. And this is all the variety of names *positive;* which are put to mark somewhat which is in nature, or may be feigned by the mind of man, as bodies that are, or may be conceived to be; or of bodies, the properties that are, or may be feigned to be; or words and speech.

There be also other names, called *negative,* which are notes to signify that a word is not the name of the thing in question as these words, *nothing, no man, infinite, indocible, three want four,* and the like; which are nevertheless of use in reckoning, or in correcting of reckoning, and call to mind our past cogitations, though they be not names of anything, because they make us refuse to admit of names not rightly used.

All other names are but insignificant sounds; and those of two sorts. One when they are new, and yet their meaning not explained by definition; whereof there have been abundance coined by schoolmen, and puzzled philosophers.

Another, when men make a name of two names, whose significations are contradictory and inconsistent; as this name, an *incorporeal body,* or, which is all one, an *incorporeal substance,* and a great number more. For whensoever any affirmation is false, the two names of which it is composed, put together and made one, signify nothing at all. For example, if it be a false affirmation to say *a quadrangle is round,* the word *round quadrangle* signifies nothing, but is a mere sound. So likewise, if it be false to say that virtue can be poured, or blown up and down, the words, *impoured virtue, inblown virtue,* are as absurd and insignificant as a *round quadrangle.* . . .

When a man, upon the hearing of any speech, hath those thoughts which the words of that speech and their connection were ordained and constituted to signify, then he is said to understand it; *understanding* being nothing else but conception caused by speech. And therefore if speech be peculiar to man, as for ought I know it is, then is understanding peculiar to him also. And therefore of absurd and false affirmations, in case they be universal, there can be no understanding; though many think they understand then, when they do but repeat the words softly, or con them in their mind. . . .

And therefore in reasoning a man must take heed of words; which besides the signification also of the nature, disposition, and interest of the speaker; such as are the names of virtue and vices; for one man calls *wisdom,* what another calls *fear;* and one *cruelty,* what another *justice;* one *prodigalty,* what another *magnanimity;* and one *gravity,* what another *stupidity,* etc. And therefore such names can never be true grounds of any ratiocination. No more can metaphors, and tropes of speech; but these are less dangerous, because they profess their inconstancy; which the other do not.

CHAPTER V: OF REASON AND SCIENCE

When a man *reasons,* he does nothing else but conceive a sum total, from *addition* of parcels; or conceive a remainder, from *subtraction* of one sum from another; which, if it be done by words, is conceiving of the consequence of the names of all the parts, to the name of the whole; or from the names of the whole and one part, to the name of the other part. And though in some things, as in numbers, besides adding and subtracting, men name other operations, as *multiplying* and *dividing,* yet they are the same; for multiplication is but adding together of things equal; and division, but subtracting of one thing, as often as we can. These operations are not incident to numbers only, but to all manner of things that can be added together, and taken one out of another. For as arithmeticians teach to add and subtract in *numbers;* so the geometricians teach the same in *lines, figures,* solid and superficial, *angles, proportions, times,* degrees of *swiftness, force, power,* and the like; the logicians teach the same in *consequences of words;* adding together two *names* to make an *affirmation,* and two *affirmations* to make a *syllogism;* and *many syllogisms* to make a *demonstration;* and from the *sum,* or *conclusion* of a *syllogism,* they subtract one *proposition* to find the other. Writers of politics add together *pactions* to find men's *duties;* and lawyers, *laws and facts,* to find what is *right* and *wrong* in the actions of private men. In sum, in what matter soever there is place for *addition* and *subtraction,* there also is place for *reason;* and where these have no place, there *reason* has nothing at all to do.

Out of all which we may define, that is to say determine, what that is, which is meant by this word *reason,* when we reckon it amongst the faculties of the mind. For REASON in this sense is nothing but *reckoning,* that is adding and subtracting, of the consequences of general names agreed upon for the *marking* and *signifying* of our thoughts; I say *marking* them when we reckon by ourselves; and *signifying,* when we demonstrate or approve our reckonings to other men.

And, as in arithmetic, unpractised men must, and professors themselves may often, err, and cast up false; so also in any other subject of reasoning; the ablest, most attentive, and most practised men may deceive themselves, and infer false conclusions; not but that reason itself is always right reason, as well as arithmetic is a certain and infallible art: but no one man's reason, nor the reason of any one number of men, makes the certainty; no more than an account is therefore well cast up, because a great many men have unanimously approved it. And therefore, as when there is a controversy in an account, the parties must by their own accord, set up, for right reason, the reason of some arbitrator, or judge, to whose sentence they will both stand, or their controversy must either come to blows, or be undecided, for want of a right reason constituted by nature; so it is also in all debates of what kind so-ever. And when men that think themselves wiser than all others, clamour and demand right reason for judge, yet seek no more but that things should be determined by no other men's reason but their own, it is as intolerable in the society of men, as it is in play after trump is turned, to use for trump on every occasion, that suite whereof they have most in their hand. For they do nothing else, that will have every of their passions, as it comes to bear sway in them, to be taken for right reason, and that in their own controversies: betraying their want of right reason, by the claim they lay to it.

The use and end of reason is not the finding of the sum and truth of one, or a few consequences, remote from the first definitions, and settled significations of names, but to begin at these, and proceed from one consequence to another. For there can be no certainty of the last conclusion, without a certainty of all those affirmations and negations, on which it was grounded and inferred. As when a master of a family, in taking an account, casts up the sums of all the bills of expense into one sum, and not regarding how each bill is summed up, by those that give them in account; nor what it is he pays for; he advantages himself no more, than if he allowed the account in gross, trusting to every of the accountants' skill and honesty: so also in reasoning of all other things, he that takes up conclusions on the trust of authors, and does not fetch them from the first items in every reckoning, which are the significations of names settled by definitions, loses his labour; and does not know anything, but only believes.

When a man reckons without the use of words, which may be done in particular things, as when upon the sight of any one thing, we conjecture what was likely to have preceded, or is likely to follow upon it; if that which he thought likely to follows, not, or that which he thought likely to have preceded it, has not preceded it, this is called *error;* to which even the most prudent men are subject. But when we reason in words of general signification, and fall upon a general inference which is false, though it be commonly called *error,* it is indeed an *absurdity,* or senseless speech. For error is but a deception, in presuming that somewhat is passed, or to come; of which, though it were not past, or not to come, yet there was no impossibility discoverable. But when we make a general assertion, unless it be a true one, the possibility of it is inconceivable. And words whereby we conceive nothing but the sound, are those we call *absurd, insignificant,* and *nonsense.* And therefore if a man should talk to me of a *round quadrangle;* or, *accidents of bread in cheese;* or, *immaterial substances;* or of *a free subject; a free will;* or any *free,* but free from being hindered by opposition, I should not say he were in an error, but that his words were without meaning, that is to say, absurd.

I have said before, in the second chapter, that a man did excel all other animals in this faculty, that when he conceived any thing whatsoever, he was apt to enquire the consequences of it, and what effects he could do with it. And now I add this other degree of the same excellence, that he can by words reduce the consequences he finds to general rules, called *theorems,* or *aphorisms;* that is, he can reason, or reckon, not only in number, but in all other things, whereof one may be added unto, or subtracted from another.

But this privilege is allayed by another; and that is, by the privilege of absurdity; to which no living creature is subject, but man only. And of men, those are of all most subject to it, that profess philosophy. For it is most true that Cicero says of them somewhere; that there can be nothing so absurd; but may be found in the books of philosophers. And the reason is manifest. For there is not one of them that begins his ratiocination from the definitions, or explications of the names they are to use; which is a method that has been used only in geometry; whose conclusions have thereby been made indisputable.

I. The first cause of absurd conclusions I ascribe to the want of method; in that they begin not their ratiocination from definitions; that is, from settled significations of their words: as if they could cast account, without knowing the value of the numeral words, *one, two,* and *three.*

And whereas all bodies enter into account upon diverse considerations, which I have mentioned in the precedent chapter; these considerations being diversely named, diverse absurdities proceed from the confusion, and unfit connection of their names into assertions. And therefore,

II. The second cause of absurd assertions, I ascribe to the giving of names of *bodies* to *accidents;* or of *accidents* to *bodies;* as they do, that say, *faith is infused,* or *inspired;* when nothing can be *poured,* or *breathed* into anything, but body; and that, *extension is body;* that *phantasms* are *spirits,* etc.

III. The third I ascribe to the giving of the names of the *accidents* of *bodies without us,* to the *accidents* of our *own bodies;* as they do that say, *the colour is in the body; the sound is in the air,* etc.

IV. The fourth, to the giving of the names of *bodies* to *names,* or *speeches;* as they do that say, that *there be things universal;* that *a living creature is genus,* or *a general thing,* etc.

V. The fifth, to the giving of the names of *accidents* to *names* and *speeches;* as they do that say, *the nature of a thing is its definition; a man's command is his will;* and the like.

VI. The sixth, to the use of metaphors, tropes, and other rhetorical figures, instead of words proper. For though it be lawful to say, for example, in common speech, *the way goes, or leads here, or there; the proverb says this or that,* whereas ways cannot go, nor proverbs speak; yet in reckoning, and seeking of truth, such speeches are not to be admitted.

VII. The seventh, to names that signify nothing; but are taken up, and learned by rote from the schools, as *hypostatical, transubstantiate, consubstantiate, eternal-now,* and the like canting of schoolmen.

To him that can avoid these things it is not easy to fall into any absurdity, unless it be by the length of an account; wherein he may perhaps forget what went before. For all men by nature reason alike, and well, when they have good principles. For who is so stupid, as both to mistake in geometry, and also to persist in it, when another detects his error to him?

But this it appears that reason is not, as sense and memory, born with us; nor gotten by experience only, as prudence is; but attained by industry; first in apt imposing of names; and secondly by getting a good and orderly method in proceeding from the elements, which are names, to assertions made by connection of one of them to another; and so to syllogisms, which are the connections of one assertion to another, till we come to a knowledge of all the consequences of names appertaining to the subject in hand; and that is it, men call SCIENCE. And whereas sense and memory are but knowledge of fact, which is a thing past and irrevocable. *Science* is the knowledge of consequences, and dependence of one fact upon another: by which, out of that we can presently do, we know how to do something else when we will, or the like another time; because when we see how anything comes about, upon what causes, and by what manner; when the like causes come into our power, we see how to make it produce the like effects.

Children therefore are not endowed with reason at all, till they have attained the use of speech; but are called reasonable creatures, for the possibility apparent of having the use of reason in time to come. And the most part of men, though they have the use of reasoning a little way, as in numbering to some degree; yet it serves them to little use in common life; in which they govern themselves, some better, some worse, according to their differences of experience, quickness of memory, and inclinations to several ends; but specially according to good or evil fortune, and the errors of one another. For as for *science*, or certain rules of their actions, they are so far from it, they know not what it is. Geometry they have thought conjuring; but for other sciences, they who have not been taught the beginnings and some progress in them, that they may see how they be acquired and generated, are in this point like children, that having no thought of generation, are made believe by the women that their brothers and sisters are not born, but found in the garden.

But yet they that have no *science* are in better, and nobler condition, with their natural prudence; than men, that by misreasoning, or by trusting them that reason wrong, fall upon false and absurd general rules. For ignorance of causes, and of rules, does not set men so far out of their way, as relying on false rules, and taking for causes of what they aspire to, those that are not so, but rather causes of the contrary.

To conclude, the light of human minds is perspicuous words, but by exact definitions first snuffed, and purged from ambiguity; *reason* is the *pace;* increase of *science,* the *way;* and the benefit of mankind, the *end.* And, on the contrary, metaphors, and senseless and ambiguous words, are like *ignes fatui* [ignitors of foolishness], and reasoning upon them is wandering amongst innumerable absurdities; and their end, contention and sedition, or contempt.

As, much experience, is *prudence;* so, is much science, *sapience.* For though we usually have one name of wisdom for them both; yet the Latins did always distinguish between *prudentia* and *sapientia;* ascribing the former to experience, the later to science. But to make their difference appear more clearly, let us suppose one man endowed with an excellent natural use, and dexterity in handling his arms; and another to have added to that dexterity, an acquired science, of where he can offend, or be offended by his adversary, in every possible posture, or guard: The ability of the former would be to the ability of the later, as *prudence* to *sapience;* both useful; but the later infallible. But they that trusting only to the authority of books, ignitors of foolishness follow the blind blindly, are like him that trusting to the false rules of a master of fence, ventures presumptuously upon an adversary, that either kills, or disgraces him.

The signs of science are some, certain and infallible; some, uncertain. Certain, when he that pretends the science of any thing, can teach the same; that is to say, demonstrate the truth thereof perspicuously to another: Uncertain, when only some particular events answer to his pretense, and upon many occasions prove so as he says they must. Signs of prudence are all uncertain; because to observe by experience, and remember all circumstances that may alter the success, is impossible. But in any business whereof a man has not infallible science to proceed by, to forsake his own natural judgment, and be guided by general sentences read in authors, and subject to many exceptions, is a sign of folly, and generally scorned by the name of pedantry. And even of those men themselves, that in Councels of the Common-wealth love to show their reading of politics and history, very few do it in their domestic affairs, where their particular interest is concerned; having prudence enough for their private affairs: but in public they study more the reputation of their own wit, than the success of another's business.

CHAPTER VI: OF THE INTERIOR BEGINNINGS OF VOLUNTARY MOTIONS; COMMONLY CALLED THE PASSIONS

There be in animals, two sorts of *motions* peculiar to them: one called *vital;* begun in generation, and continued without interruption through their whole life; such as are the *course* of the *blood,* the *pulse,* the *breathing,* the *concoction, nutrition, excretion,* etc., to which motions there needs no help of imagination: the other is *animal motion,* otherwise called *voluntary motion;* as to *go,* to *speak,* to *move* any of our limbs in such manner as is first fancied in our minds. That sense is motion in the organs and interior parts of man's body, caused by the action of the things we see, hear, etc.; and that fancy is but the relics of the same motion, remaining after sense, has been already said in the first and second chapters. And because *going, speaking,* and the like voluntary motions, depend always upon a precedent thought of *whither, which way,* and *what;* it is evident that the imagination is the first internal beginning of all voluntary motion. And although unstudied men do not conceive any motion at all to be there, where the thing moved is invisible; or the space it is moved in is, for the shortness of it, insensible; yet that does not hinder but that such motions are. For let a space be never so little, that which is moved over a greater space, whereof that little one is part, must first be moved over that. These small beginnings of motion, within the body of man, before they appear in walking, speaking, striking, and other visible actions, are commonly called ENDEAVOUR.

This endeavour, when it is toward something which causes it, is called APPETITE, or DESIRE; the latter being the general name; and the other oftentimes restrained to signify the desire of food, namely *hunger* and *thirst.* And when the endeavour is away from something, it is generally called AVERSION. These words, *appetite* and *aversion,* we have from the Latins, and they both of them signify the motions, one of approaching, the other of retiring. So also do the Greek words for the same, which are ὁρμὴ and ἀφορμὴ. For nature itself does often press upon men those truths, which afterwards, when they look for somewhat beyond nature, they stumble at. For the Schools find in mere appetite to go, or move, no actual motion at all: but because some motion they must acknowledge, they call it metaphorical motion; which is but an absurd speech: for though words may be called metaphorical, bodies and motions can not.

That which men desire, they are also said to LOVE, and to HATE those things for which they have aversion. So that desire and love are the same thing; save that by desire, we always signify the absence of the object; by love, most commonly the presence of the same. So also by aversion, we signify the absence; and by hate, the presence of the object.

Of appetites and aversions, some are born with men; as appetite of food, appetite of excretion, and exoneration, which may also and more properly be called aversions, from somewhat they feel in their bodies; and some other appetites, not many. The rest, which are appetites of particular things, proceed from experience, and trial of their effects upon themselves or other men. For of things we know not at all, or believe not to be, we can have no further desire than to taste and try. But aversion we have for things, not only which we know have hurt us, but also that we do not know whether they will hurt us, or not.

Those things which we neither desire, nor hate, we are said to *contemn;* CONTEMPT being nothing else but an immobility, or contumacy of the heart, in resisting the action of certain things; and proceeding from that the heart is already moved otherwise, by other more potent objects; or from want of experience of them.

And because the constitution of a man's body is in continual mutation, it is impossible that all the same things should always cause in him the same appetites and aversions: much less can all men consent, in the desire of almost any one and the same object.

But whatsoever is the object of any man's appetite or desire, that is it which he for his part calls *good:* and the object of his hate and aversion, *evil;* and of his contempt, *vile* and *inconsiderable.* For these words of good, evil, and contemptible, are ever used with relation to the person that uses them: there being nothing simply and absolutely so; nor any common rule of good and evil, to be taken from the nature of the objects themselves; but from the person of the man, where there is no commonwealth; or, in a commonwealth, from the person that represents it; or from an arbitrator or judge, whom men disagreeing shall by consent set up, and make his sentence the rule thereof.

The Latin tongue has two words, whose significations approach to those of good and evil; but are not precisely the same; and those are *pulchrum* and *turpe.* Whereof the former signifies that, which by some apparent signs promises good; and the latter, that which promises evil. But in our tongue we have not so general names to express them by. But for *pulchrum* we say in some things, *fair;* in others, *beautiful,* or *handsome,* or *gallant,* or *honourable,* or *comely,* or *amiable;* and for *turpe, foul, deformed, ugly, base, nauseous,* and the like, as the subject shall require; all which words, in their proper places, signify nothing else but the *mien* or countenance, that promises good and evil. So that of good there be three kinds; good in the promise, that is *pulchrum;* good in effect, as the end desired, which is called *jucundum, delightful;* and good as the means, which is called *utile, profitable;* and as many of evil: for *evil* in promise, is that they call *turpe;* evil in effect, and end, is *molestum, unpleasant, troublesome;* and evil in the means, *inutile, unprofitable, hurtful.*

As, in sense, that which is really within us, is, as I have said before, only motion, caused by the action of external objects, but in appearance; to the sight, light and colour; to the ear, sound; to the nostril, odour, etc.: so, when the action of the same object is continued from the eyes, ears, and other organs to the heart, the real effect there is nothing but motion, or endeavour; which consists in appetite, or aversion, to or from the object moving. But the appearance, or sense of that motion, is that we either call *delight* or *trouble of mind.*

This motion, which is called appetite, and for the appearance of it *delight* and *pleasure,* seems to be a corroboration of vital motion, and a help thereunto; and therefore such things as caused delight were not improperly called *jucunda, à juvando,* from helping or fortifying; and the contrary *molesta, offensive,* from hindering, and troubling the motion vital.

Pleasure, therefore, or *delight* is the appearance, or sense of good; and *molestation* or *displeasure,* the appearance or sense of evil. And consequently all appetite, desire, and love, is accompanied with some delight more or less; and all hatred and aversion, with more or less displeasure and offence.

Of pleasures or delights, some arise from the sense of an object present; and those may be called *pleasure of sense;* the word *sensual,* as it is used by those only that condemn them, having no place till there be laws. Of this kind are all onerations and exonerations of the body; as also all that is pleasant, in the *sight, hearing, smell, taste,* or *touch.* Others arise from the expectation that proceeds from foresight of the end, or consequence of things; whether those things in the sense please or displease. And these are *pleasures of the mind* of him that draws those consequences, and are generally called JOY. In the like manner, displeasures are some in the sense, and called PAIN; others in the expectation of consequences, and are called GRIEF.

These simple passions called *appetite, desire, love, aversion, hate, joy,* and *grief,* have their names for diverse considerations diversified. As first, when they one succeed another, they are diversely called from the opinion men have of the likelihood of attaining what they desire. Secondly, from the object loved or hated. Thirdly, from the consideration of many of them together. Fourthly, from the alteration or succession itself. . . .

CHAPTER XIII: OF THE NATURAL CONDITION OF MANKIND AS CONCERNING THEIR FELICITY AND MISERY

Nature has made men so equal, in the faculties of the body, and mind; as that though there be found one man sometimes manifestly stronger in body, or of quicker mind than another, yet when all is reckoned together, the difference between man and man is not so considerable, as that one man can thereupon claim to himself any benefit to which another may not pretend, as well as he. For as to the strength of body, the weakest has strength enough to kill the strongest, either by secret machination, or by confederacy with others, that are in the same danger with himself.

And as to the faculties of the mind, setting aside the arts grounded upon words, and especially that skill of proceeding upon general and infallible rules, called science; which very few have, and but in few things; as being not a native faculty born with us; nor attained, as prudence, while we look after somewhat else, I find yet a greater equality amongst men than that of strength. For prudence is but experience; which equal time, equally bestows on all men, in those things they equally apply themselves unto. That which may perhaps make such equality incredible is but a vain conceit of one's own wisdom, which almost all men think they have in a greater degree than the vulgar; that is, than all men but themselves, and a few others, whom by fame, or for concurring with themselves, they approve. For such is the nature of men, that howsoever they may acknowledge many others to be more witty, or more eloquent, or more learned: yet they will hardly believe there be many so wise as themselves; for they see their own wit at hand, and other men's at a distance. But this proves rather that men are in that point equal, than unequal. For there is not ordinarily a greater sign of the equal distribution of anything, than that every man is contented with his share.

From this equality of ability, arises equality of hope in the attaining of our ends. And therefore if any two men desire the same thing, which nevertheless they cannot both enjoy, they become enemies; and in the way to their end, which is principally their own conservation, and sometimes their delectation only, endeavour to destroy or subdue one another. And from hence it comes to pass, that where an invader hath no more to fear, than another man's single power; if one plant, sow, build, or possess a convenient seat, others may probably be expected to come prepared with forces united, to dispossess, and deprive him, not only of the fruit of his labour, but also of his life or liberty. And the invader again is in the like danger of another.

And from this diffidence of one another, there is no way for any man to secure himself, so reasonable as anticipation; that is, by force, or wiles, to master the persons of all men he can, so long, till he see no other power great enough to endanger him: and this is no more than his own conservation requires, and is generally allowed. Also because there be some, that taking pleasure in contemplating their own power in the acts of conquest, which they pursue farther than their security requires; if others, that otherwise would be glad to be at east within modest bounds, should not by invasion increase their power, they would not be able, long time, by standing only on their defence, to subsist. And by consequence, such augmentation of dominion over men being necessary to a man's conservation, it ought to be allowed him.

Again, men have no pleasure, but on the contrary a great deal of grief, in keeping company, where there is no power able to overawe them all. For every man looks that his companion should value him, at the same rate he sets upon himself: and upon all signs of contempt, or undervaluing, naturally endeavours as far as he dares (which amongst them that have no common power to keep them in quiet, is far enough to make them destroy each other), to extort a greater value from his contemners, by damage; and from others, by the example.

So that in the nature of man, we find three principal causes of quarrel. First, competition; secondly, diffidence; thirdly, glory.

The first makes men invade for gain; the second, for safety; and the third, for reputation. The first use violence, to make themselves masters of other men's persons, wives, children, and cattle; the second, to defend them; the third, for trifles, as a word, a smile, a different opinion, and any other sign of undervalue, either direct in their persons, or by reflection in their kindred, their friends, their nation, their profession, or their name.

Hereby it is manifest, that during the time men live without a common power to keep them all in awe, they are in that condition which is called war; and such a war, as is of every man, against every man. For WAR consists not in battle only, or the act of fighting; but in a tract of time, wherein the will to contend by battle is sufficiently known: and therefore the notion of *time* is to be considered in the nature of war, as it is in the nature of weather. For as the nature of foul weather, lieth not in a shower or two of rain, but in an inclination thereto of many days together; so the nature of war consists not in actual fighting, but in the known disposition thereto, during all the time there is no assurance to the contrary. All other time is PEACE.

Whatsoever therefore is consequent to a time of war, where every man is enemy to every man, the same is consequent to the time wherein men live without other security, than what their own strength, and their own invention shall furnish them withal. In such condition, there is no place for industry, because the fruit thereof is uncertain, and consequently no culture of the earth; no navigation, nor use of the commodities that may be imported by sea; no commodious building; no instruments of moving, and removing, such things as require much force; no knowledge of the face of the earth; no account of time; no arts; no letters; no society; and, which is worst of all, continual fear, and danger of violent death; and the life of man, solitary, poor, nasty, brutish, and short.

It may seem strange to some man, that has not well weighed these things, that Nature should thus dissociate, and render men apt to invade and destroy one another: and he may therefore, not trusting to this inference made from the passions, desire perhaps to have the same confirmed by experience. Let him therefore consider with himself, when taking a journey, he arms himself, and seeks to go well accompanied; when going to sleep he locks his doors; when even in his house, he locks his chests; and this when he knows there be laws, and public officers, armed, to avenge all injuries shall be done him; what opinion he has of his fellow-subjects, when he rides armed; of his fellow-citizens, when he locks his doors; and of his children and servants, when he locks his chests. Does he not there as much accuse mankind by his actions, as I do by my words? But neither of us accuse man's nature in it. The desires, and other passions of man, are in themselves no sin. No more are the actions, that proceed from those passions, till they know a law that forbids them: which till laws be made they cannot know, nor can any law be made, till they have agreed upon the person that shall make it.

It may peradventure be thought, there was never such a time nor condition of war as this; and I believe it was never generally so, over all the world: but there are many places where they live so now. For the savage people in many places of America, except the government of small families, the concord whereof depends on natural lust, have no government at all, and live at this day in that brutish manner, as I said before. Howsoever, it may be perceived what manner of life there would be, where there were no common power to fear, by the manner of life, which men that have formerly lived under a peaceful government, use to degenerate into, in a civil war.

But though there had never been any time, wherein particular men were in a condition of war one against another; yet in all times, kings, and persons of sovereign authority, because of their independency, are in continual jealousies, and in the state and posture of gladiators; having their weapons pointing, and their eyes fixed on one another; that is, their forts, garrisons, and guns upon the frontiers of their kingdoms; and continual spies upon their neighbours; which is a posture of war. But because they uphold thereby, the industry of their subjects; there does not follow from it that misery, which accompanies the liberty of particular men.

To this war of every man, against every man, this also is consequent; that nothing can be unjust. The notions of right and wrong, justice and injustice, have there no place. Where there is no common power, there is no law: where no law, no injustice. Force, and fraud, are in war the two cardinal virtues. Justice and injustice are none of the faculties neither of the body nor mind. If they were, they might be in a man that were alone in the world, as well as his senses, and passions. They are qualities, that relate to men in society, not in solitude. It is consequent also to the same condition, that there be no propriety, no dominion, no *mine* and *thine* distinct; but only that to be every man's, that he can get; and for so long, as he can keep it. And thus much for the ill condition, which man by mere nature is actually placed in; though with a possibility to come out of it, consisting partly in the passions, partly in his reason.

The passions that incline men to peace, are fear of death; desire of such things as are necessary to commodious living; and a hope by their industry to obtain them. And reason suggests convenient articles of peace, upon which men may be drawn to agreement. These articles, are they, which otherwise are called the Laws of Nature: whereof I shall speak more particularly, in the two following chapters.

CHAPTER XIV: OF THE FIRST AND SECOND NATURAL LAWS, AND OF CONTRACTS

The RIGHT OF NATURE, which writers commonly call *jus naturale,* is the liberty each man has, to use his own power, as he will himself, for the preservation of his own nature; that is to say, of his own life; and consequently, of doing anything which in his own judgment and reason he shall conceive to be the aptest means thereunto.

By LIBERTY is understood, according to the proper signification of the word, the absence of external impediments: which impediments, may oft take away part of a man's power to do what he would; but cannot hinder him from using the power left him, according as his judgment and reason shall dictate to him.

A LAW OF NATURE, *lex naturalis,* is a precept or general rule, found out by reason, by which a man is forbidden to do that, which is destructive of his life, or takes away the means of preserving the same; and to omit that, by which he thinks it may be best preserved. For though they that speak of this subject use to confound *jus* and *lex, right* and *law:* yet they ought to be distinguished; because RIGHT consists in liberty to do, or to forbear; where LAW, determines, and binds to one of them: so that law, and right, differ as much as obligation, and liberty; which in one and the same matter are inconsistent.

And because the condition of man, as has been declared in the precedent chapter, is a condition of war of every one against every one; in which case every one is governed by his own reason; and there is nothing he can make use of, that may not be a help unto him in preserving his life against his enemies; it follows, that in such a condition, every man has a right to everything; even to one another's body. And therefore, as long as this natural right of every man to everything endures, there can be no security to any man, how strong or wise soever he be, of living out the time which Nature ordinarily allows men to live. And consequently it is a precept, or general rule of reason, *that every man ought to endeavour peace, as far as he has hope of obtaining it; and when he cannot obtain it, that he may seek, and use, all helps and advantages of war.* The first branch of which rule contains the first and fundamental law of Nature; which is *to seek peace, and follow it.* The second, the sum of the right of Nature: which is, *by all means we can, to defend ourselves.*

From this fundamental law of Nature, by which men are commanded to endeavour peace, is derived this second law; *that a man be willing, when others are so too, as far-forth, as for peace, and defence of himself he shall think it necessary to lay down this right to all things; and be contented with so much liberty against other men as he would allow other men against himself.* For as long as every man holds this right of doing anything he likes; so long are all men in the condition of war. But if other men will not lay down their right, as well as he; then there is no reason for any one to divest himself of his: for that were to expose himself to prey, which no man is bound to, rather than to dispose himself to peace. This is that law of the Gospel; *whatsoever you require that others should do to you, that do ye to them.* And that law of all men, *quod tibi fieri non vis, alteri ne feceris.*

To *lay down* a man's *right* to anything is to *divest* himself of the *liberty* of hindering another of the benefit of his own right to the same. For he that renounces, or passes away his right, gives not to any other man a right which he had not before; because there is nothing to which every man had not right by Nature: but only stands out of his way, that he may enjoy his own original right, without hindrance from him; not without hindrance from another. So that the effect which redounds to one man, by another man's defect of right is but so much diminution of impediments to the use of his own right original.

Right is laid aside, either by simply renouncing it; or by transferring it to another. By *simply* RENOUNCING; when he cares not to whom the benefit thereof redounds. By TRANS-FERRING; when he intends the benefit thereof to some certain person or persons. And when a man has in either manner abandoned, or granted away his right; then is he said to be OBLIGED, or BOUND, not to hinder those, to whom such right is granted, or abandoned, from the benefit of it: and that he *ought*, and it is his DUTY, not to make void that voluntary act of his own: and that such hindrance is INJUSTICE, and INJURY, as being *sine jure;* the right being before renounced, or transferred. So that *injury,* or *injustice,* in the controversies of the world is somewhat like to that, which in the disputations of scholars is called *ab-surdity.* For as it is there called an absurdity, to contradict what one maintained in the beginning: so in the world it is called injustice, and injury, voluntarily to undo that, which from the beginning he had voluntarily done. The way by which a man either simply re-nounces, or transfers his right, is a declaration, or signification, by some voluntary and sufficient sign, or signs, that he does so renounce, or transfer; or has so renounced, or transferred the same, to him that accepts it. And these signs are either words only, or actions only: or, as it happens most often, both words and actions. And the same are the BONDS, by which men are bound, and obliged: bonds that have their strength, not from their own nature, for nothing is more easily broken than a man's word, but from fear of some evil consequence upon the rupture.

Whensoever a man transfers his right, or renounces it; it is either in consideration of some right reciprocally transferred to himself; or for some other good he hopes for thereby. For it is a voluntary act; and of the voluntary acts of every man, the object is some *good to himself.* And therefore there be some rights, which no man can be understood by any words, or other signs, to have abandoned, or transferred. As first a man cannot lay down the right of resisting them, that assault him by force, to take away his life; because he cannot be understood to aim thereby, at any good to himself. The same may be said of wounds, and chains, and imprisonment; both because there is no benefit consequent to such patience; as there is to the patience of suffering another to be wounded, or imprisoned: as also because a man cannot tell, when he sees men proceed against him by violence, whether they intend his death or not. And lastly the motive and end for which this renouncing and transferring of right is introduced, is nothing else but the security of a man's person, in his life, and in the means of so preserving life, as not to be weary of it. And therefore if a man by words, or other signs, seems to despoil himself of the end, for which those signs were intended; he is not to be understood as if he meant it, or that it was his will; but that he was ignorant of how such words and actions were to be interpreted.

The mutual transferring of right is that which men call CONTRACT.

There is difference between transferring of right to the thing and transferring, or tradi-tion, that is delivery of the thing itself. For the thing may be delivered together with the translation of the right; as in buying and selling with ready-money; or exchange of goods, or lands; and it may be delivered some time after.

Again, one of the contractors may deliver the thing contracted for on his part, and leave the other to perform his part at some determinate time after, and in the meantime be trusted; and then the contract on his part is called PACT, or COVENANT: or both parts may contract now, to perform hereafter; in which cases, he that is to perform in time to come, being trusted, his performance is called *keeping of promise,* or faith; and the failing of per-formance, if it be voluntary, *violation of faith.*

When the transferring of right is not mutual: but one of the parties transfers, in hope to gain thereby friendship, or service from another, or from his friends; or in hope to gain the reputation of charity; or magnanimity; or to deliver his mind from the pain of compassion; or in hope of reward in heaven; this is not contract, but GIFT, FREE GIFT, GRACE: which words signify one and the same thing. . . .

CHAPTER XV: OF OTHER LAWS OF NATURE

From that law of Nature, by which we are obliged to transfer to another, such rights, as being retained, hinder the peace of mankind, there follows a third; which is this, *that men perform their covenants made:* without which, covenants are in vain, and but empty words; and the right of all men to all things remaining, we are still in the condition of war.

And in this law of Nature consists the fountain and original of JUSTICE. For where no covenant has preceded, there has no right been transferred, and every man has right to everything; and consequently, no action can be unjust. But when a covenant is made, then to break it is *unjust:* and the definition of INJUSTICE is no other than *the not performance of covenant.* And whatsoever is not unjust is *just.*

But because covenants of mutual trust, where there is a fear of not performance on either part, as has been said in the former chapter, are invalid; though the original of justice be the making of covenants; yet injustice actually there can be none, till the cause of such fear be taken away; which while men are in the natural condition of war, cannot be done. Therefore before the names of just and unjust can have place, there must be some coercive power, to compel men equally to the performance of their covenants, by the terror of some punishment, greater than the benefit they expect by the breach of their covenant; and to make good that propriety, which by mutual contract men acquire, in recompense of the universal right they abandon: and such power there is none before the erection of a commonwealth. And this is also to be gathered out of the ordinary definition of justice in the Schools: for they say, that *justice is the constant will of giving to every man his own.* And therefore where there is no *own,* that is no propriety, there is no injustice; and where there is no coercive power erected, that is, where there is no commonwealth, there is no propriety; all men having right to all things: therefore where there is no commonwealth, there nothing is unjust. So that the nature of justice consists in keeping of valid covenants: but the validity of covenants begins not but with the constitution of a civil power, sufficient to compel men to keep them; and then it is also that propriety begins. . . .

As justice depends on antecedent covenant; so does GRATITUDE depend on antecedent grace; that is to say, antecedent free gift: and is the fourth law of Nature; which may be conceived in this form, *that a man which receives benefit from another of mere grace, endeavour that he which gives it, have no reasonable cause to repent him of his good will.* For no man gives, but with intention of good to himself; because gift is voluntary; and of all voluntary acts, the object is to every man his own good; of which if men see they shall be frustrated, there will be no beginning of benevolence, or trust, nor consequently of mutual help; nor of reconciliation of one man to another; and therefore they are to remain still in the condition of *war;* which is contrary to the first and fundamental law of Nature, which commands men to *seek peace.* The breach of this law is called *ingratitude,* and has the same relation to grace, that injustice has to obligation by covenant.

A fifth law of Nature is COMPLAISANCE; that is to say, *that every man strive to accommodate himself to the rest.* For the understanding whereof, we may consider, that there is in men's aptness to society, a diversity of nature, rising from their diversity of affections; not unlike to that we see in stones brought together for building of an edifice. For as that stone which by the asperity, and irregularity of figure, takes more room from others than itself fills; and for the hardness, cannot be easily made plain, and thereby hinders the building, is by the builders cast away as unprofitable and troublesome: so also, a man that by asperity of nature, will strive to retain those things which to himself are superfluous, and to others necessary; and for the stubbornness of his passions, cannot be corrected, is to be left, or cast out of society, as cumbersome thereunto. For seeing every man, not only by right, but also by necessity of nature, is supposed to endeavour all he can, to obtain that which is necessary for his conservation; he that shall oppose himself against it, for things superfluous, is guilty of the war that thereupon is to follow; and therefore does that, which is contrary to the fundamental law of Nature, which commands *to seek peace.* The observers of this law may be called SOCIABLE, the Latins call them *commodi;* the contrary, *stubborn, insociable, froward, intractable.*

A sixth law of Nature is this, *that upon caution of the future time, a man ought to pardon the offences past of them that repenting, desire it.* For PARDON is nothing but granting of peace; which though granted to them that persevere in their hostility, be not peace, but fear; yet not granted to them that give caution of the future time, is sign of an aversion to peace; and therefore contrary to the law of Nature.

A seventh is, *that in revenges,* that is, retribution of evil for evil, *men look not at the greatness of the evil past, but the greatness of the good to follow.* Whereby we are forbidden to inflict punishment with any other design, than for correction of the offender, or direction of others. For this law is consequent to the next before it, that commands pardon, upon security of the future time. Besides, revenge, without respect to the example, and profit to come, is a triumph or glorying in the hurt of another, tending to no end; for the end is always somewhat to come; and glorying to no end, is vain-glory, and contrary to reason, and to hurt without reason, tends to the introduction of war; which is against the law of Nature; and is commonly styled by the name of *cruelty.*

And because all signs of hatred, or contempt, provoke to fight; insomuch as most men choose rather to hazard their life, than not to be avenged; we may in the eighth place, for a law of nature, set down this precept, *that no man by deed, word, countenance, or gesture, declare hatred, or contempt of another.* The breach of which law is commonly called *contumely.*

The question who is the better man has no place in the condition of mere nature; where, as has been shown before, all men are equal. The inequality that now is, has been introduced by the laws civil. I know that Aristotle in the first book of his *Politics,* for a foundation of his doctrine, makes men by nature, some more worthy to command, meaning the wiser sort, such as he thought himself to be for his philosophy; others to serve, meaning those that had strong bodies, but were not philosophers as he; as if master and servant were not introduced by consent of men, but by difference of wit; which is not only against reason, but also against experience. For there are very few so foolish, that had not rather govern themselves, than be governed by others: nor when the wise in their own conceit, contend by force, with them who distrust their own wisdom, do they always, or often, or almost at any time, get the victory. If Nature therefore have made them equal, that equality is to be acknowledged: or if nature have made men unequal; yet because men that think themselves equal, will not enter into conditions of peace, but upon equal terms, such equality must be admitted. And therefore for the ninth law of Nature, I put this, *that every man acknowledge another for his equal by nature.* The breach of this precept is *pride.*

On this law depends another, *that at the entrance into conditions of peace, no man require to reserve to himself any right, which he is not content should be reserved to every one of the rest.* As it is necessary for all men that seek peace to lay down certain rights of nature; that is to say, not to have liberty to do all they list: so is it necessary for man's life, to retain some, as right to govern their own bodies; enjoy air, water, motion, ways to go from place to place; and all things else, without which a man cannot live, or not live well. If in this case, at the making of peace, men require for themselves that which they would not have to be granted to others, they do contrary to the precedent law, that commands the acknowledgment of natural equality, and therefore also against the law of Nature. The observers of this law are those we call *modest,* and the breakers *arrogant men.* The Greeks call the violation of this law πλεονεξία, that is, a desire for more than their share.

Also if *a man be trusted to judge between man and man,* it is a precept of the law of Nature, *that he deal equally between them.* For without that, the controversies of men cannot be determined but by war. He therefore that is partial in judgment, doth what in him lies, to deter men from the use of judges and arbitrators; and consequently, against the fundamental law of Nature, is the cause of war.

The observance of this law, from the equal distribution to each man, of that which in reason belongs to him, is called EQUITY, and, as I have said before, distributive justice: the violation, *acception of persons,* προσωποληψία.

And from this follows another law, *that such things as cannot be divided, be enjoyed in common, if it can be; and if the quantity of the thing permit, without stint; otherwise proportionably to the number of them that have right.* For otherwise the distribution is unequal, and contrary to equity.

But some things there be, that can neither be divided, nor enjoyed in common. Then, the law of Nature, which prescribes equity, requires *that the entire right, or else, making the use alternate, the first possession, be determined by lot.* For equal distribution, is of the law of Nature, and other means of equal distribution cannot be imagined.

Of *lots* there be two sorts, *arbitrary,* and *natural.* Arbitrary is that which is agreed on by the competitors: natural is either *primogeniture,* which the Greeks call κληρονομία, which signifies *given by lot;* or *first seizure.*

And therefore those things which cannot be enjoyed in common, nor divided, ought to be adjudged to the first possessor; and in some cases to the first born, as acquired by lot.

It is also a law of Nature, *that all men that mediate peace, be allowed safe conduct.* For the law that commands peace, as the *end,* commands intercession, as the *means;* and to intercession the means is safe conduct.

And because, though men be never so willing to observe these laws, there may nevertheless arise questions concerning a man's action; first, whether it were done, or not done; secondly, if done, whether against the law, or not against the law; the former whereof, is called a question *of fact;* the latter a question *of right,* therefore unless the parties to the question covenant mutually to stand to the sentence of another, they are as far from peace as ever. This other to whose sentence they submit is called an ARBITRATOR. And therefore it is of the law of Nature, *that they that are at controversy, submit their right to the judgment of an arbitrator.*

And seeing every man is presumed to do all things in order to his own benefit, no man is a fit arbitrator in his own cause; and if he were never so fit; yet equity allowing to each party equal benefit, if one be admitted to be judge, the other is to be admitted also; and so the controversy, that is, the cause of war, remains against the law of Nature.

For the same reason no man in any cause ought to be received for arbitrator, to whom greater profit, or honour, or pleasure apparently arises out of the victory of one party than of the other: for he has taken, though an unavoidable bribe, yet a bribe; and no man can be obliged to trust him. And thus also the controversy, and the condition of war remains, contrary to the law of Nature.

And in a controversy of *fact,* the judge being to give no more credit to one than to the other, if there be no other arguments, must give credit to a third; or to a third and fourth; or more: for else the question is undecided, and left to force, contrary to the law of Nature.

These are the laws of Nature, dictating peace, for a means of the conservation of men in multitudes; and which only concern the doctrine of civil society. There be other things tending to the destruction of particular men; as drunkenness, and all other parts of intemperance; which may therefore also be reckoned amongst those things which the law of Nature has forbidden; but are not necessary to be mentioned, nor are pertinent enough to this place.

And though this may seem too subtle a deduction of the laws of Nature to be taken notice of by all men; whereof the most part are too busy in getting food, and the rest too negligent to understand; yet to leave all men inexcusable, they have been contracted into one easy sum, intelligible even to the meanest capacity; and that is, *Do not that to another, which thou would not have done to thyself;* which shows him, that he has no more to do in learning the laws of nature, but, when weighing the actions of other men with his own, they seem too heavy, to put them into the other part of the balance, and his own into their place, that his own passions, and self-love, may add nothing to the weight; and then there is none of these laws of Nature that will not appear unto him very reasonable.

The laws of Nature oblige *in foro interno;* that is to say, they bind to a desire they should take place: but *in foro externo;* that is, to the putting them in act, not always. For he that should be modest, and tractable, and perform all he promises, in such time and place where no man else should do so, should but make himself a prey to others, and procure his own certain ruin, contrary to the ground of all laws of Nature, which tend to nature's preservation. And again, he that having sufficient security, that others shall observe the same laws towards him, observes them not himself, seeks not peace, but war; and consequently the destruction of his nature by violence.

And whatsoever laws bind *in foro interno,* may be broken, not only by a fact contrary to the law, but also by a fact according to it, in case a man think it contrary. For though his action in this case be according to the law, yet his purpose was against the law; which, where the obligation is *in foro interno,* is a breach.

The laws of Nature are immutable and eternal; for injustice, ingratitude, arrogance, pride, iniquity, acception if persons, and the rest, can never be made lawful. For it can never be that war shall preserve life, and peace destroy it.

The same laws, because they oblige only to a desire and endeavour, I mean an unfeigned and constant endeavour, are easy to be observed. For in that they require nothing but endeavour, he that endeavours their performance, fulfills them; and he that fulfills the law, is just.

And the science of them is the true and only moral philosophy. For moral philosophy is nothing else but the science of what is *good,* and *evil,* in the conversation and society of mankind. *Good,* and *evil,* are names that signify our appetites, and aversions; which in different tempers, customs, and doctrines of men, are different: and diverse men, differ not only in their judgment, on the senses of what is pleasant, and unpleasant to the taste, smell, hearing, touch, and sight; but also of what is conformable or disagreeable to reason, in the actions of common life. Nay, the same man, in diverse times, differs from himself; and one time praises, that is, calls good, what another time he dispraises, and calls evil, from whence arise disputes, controversies, and at last war. And therefore so long as man is in the condition of mere nature, which is a condition of war, as private appetite is the measure of good and evil: and consequently all men agree on this, that peace is good, and therefore also the way or means of peace, which, as I have showed before, are *justice, gratitude, modesty, equity, mercy,* and the rest of the laws of Nature, are good; that is to say, *moral virtues;* and their contrary *vices,* evil. Now the science of virtue and vice, is moral philosophy; and therefore the true doctrine of the laws of Nature is the true moral philosophy. But the writers of moral philosophy, though they acknowledge the same virtues and vices; yet not seeing wherein consisted their goodness; nor that they come to be praised, as the means of peaceable, sociable, and comfortable living, place them in a mediocrity of passions: as if not the cause, but the degree of daring, made fortitude; or not the cause, but the quantity of a gift, made liberality.

These dictates of reason, men used to call by the name of laws, but improperly: for they are but conclusions, or theorems concerning what conduces to the conservation and defence of themselves; whereas law, properly, is the word of him that by right has command over others. But yet if we consider the same theorems, as delivered in the word of God, that by right commands all things; then are they properly called laws.

PART II: OF COMMONWEALTH
CHAPTER XVII: OF THE CAUSES, GENERATION, AND DEFINITION OF A COMMONWEALTH

The final cause, end, or design of men, who naturally love liberty, and dominion over others, in the introduction of that restraint upon themselves, in which we see them live in commonwealths, is the foresight of their own preservation, and of a more contented life thereby; that is to say, of getting themselves out from that miserable condition of war, which is necessarily consequent, as has been shown in chapter xiii, to the natural passions of men, when there is no visible power to keep them in awe, and tie them by fear of punishment to the performance of their covenants, and observation of those laws of Nature set down in the fourteenth and fifteenth chapters.

For the laws of Nature, as *justice, equity, modesty, mercy,* and, in sum, *doing to others, as we would be done to,* of themselves, without the terror of some power, to cause them to be observed, are contrary to our natural passions, that carry us to partiality, pride, revenge, and the like. And covenants, without the sword, are but words, and of no strength to secure a man at all. Therefore notwithstanding the laws of nature, which every one has then kept, when he has the will to keep them, when he can do it safely, if there be no power erected, or not great enough for our security, every man will, and may lawfully rely on his own strength and art, for caution against all other men. And in all places, where men have lived by small families, to rob and spoil one another, has been a trade, and so far from being reputed against the law of Nature, that the greater spoils they gained, the greater was their honour; and men observed no other laws therein, but the laws of honour; that is, to abstain from cruelty, leaving to men their lives, and instruments of husbandry. And as small families did then; so now do cities and kingdoms, which are but greater families, for their own security, enlarge their dominions, upon all pretences of danger, and fear of invasion, or assistance that may be given to invaders, and endeavour as much as they can, to subdue, or weaken their neighbours, by open force and secret arts, for want of other caution, justly; and are remembered for it in after ages with honour.

Nor is it the joining together of a small number of men, that gives them this security;

because in small numbers, small additions on the one side or the other, make the advantage of strength so great, as is sufficient to carry the victory; and therefore gives encouragement to an invasion. The multitude sufficient to confide in for our security, is not determined by any certain number, but by comparison with the enemy we fear; and is then sufficient when the odds of the enemy is not of so visible and conspicuous moment, to determine the event of war, as to move him to attempt.

And be there never so great a multitude; yet if their actions be directed according to their particular judgments, and particular appetites, they can expect thereby no defence, nor protection, neither against a common enemy, nor against the injuries of one another. For being distracted in opinions concerning the best use and application of their strength, they do not help but hinder one another; and reduce their strength by mutual opposition to nothing: whereby they are easily, not only subdued by a very few that agree together; but also when there is no common enemy, they make war upon each other, for their particular interests. For if we could suppose a great multitude of men to consent in the observation of justice, and other laws of Nature, without a common power to keep them all in awe; we might as well suppose all mankind to do the same; and then there neither would be, nor need to be any civil government or commonwealth at all; because there would be peace without subjection.

Nor is it enough for the security, which men desire should last all the time of their life, that they be governed, and directed by one judgment, for a limited time; as in one battle, or one war. For though they obtain a victory by their unanimous endeavour against a foreign enemy; yet afterwards, when either they have no common enemy, or he that by one part is held for an enemy, is by another part held for a friend, they must needs by the difference of their interests dissolve, and fall again into a war amongst themselves.

It is true that certain living creatures, as bees and ants, live sociably one with another, which are therefore by Aristotle numbered amongst political creatures; and yet have no other direction, than their particular judgments and appetites; nor speech, whereby one of them can signify to another, what he thinks expedient for the common benefit: and therefore some man may perhaps desire to know, why mankind cannot do the same. To which I answer,

First, that men are continually in competition for honour and dignity, which these creatures are not; and consequently amongst men there arises on that ground, envy and hatred, and finally war; but amongst these not so.

Secondly, that amongst these creatures, the common good differs not from the private; and being by nature inclined to their private, they procure thereby the common benefit. But man, whose joy consists in comparing himself with other men, can relish nothing but what is eminent.

Thirdly, that these creatures, having not, as man, the use of reason, do not see, nor think they see any fault, in the administration of their common business; whereas amongst men, there are very many that think themselves wiser, and abler to govern the public, better than the rest; and these strive to reform and innovate, one this way, another that way; and thereby bring it into distraction and civil war.

Fourthly, that these creatures, though they have some use of voice, in making known to one another their desires and other affections; yet they want that art of words, by which some men can represent to others, that which is good, in the likeness of evil; and evil, in the likeness of good; and augment, or diminish the apparent greatness of good and evil; discontenting men, and troubling their peace at their pleasure.

Fifthly, irrational creatures cannot distinguish between *injury,* and *damage;* and therefore as long as they be at ease, they are not offended with their fellows: whereas man is then most troublesome, when he is most at ease; for then it is that he loves to show his wisdom, and control the actions of them that govern the commonwealth.

Lastly, the agreement of these creatures is natural; that of men is by covenant only, which is artificial; and therefore it is no wonder if there be somewhat else required, besides covenant, to make their agreement constant and lasting; which is a common power, to keep them in awe, and to direct their actions to the common benefit.

The only way to erect such a common power, as may be able to defend them from the invasion of foreigners, and the injuries of one another, and thereby to secure them in such sort, as that by their own industry, and by the fruits of the earth, they may nourish themselves, and live contentedly; is to confer all their power and strength upon one man, or upon one assembly of men, that may reduce all their wills, by plurality of voices, unto one will: which is as much as to say, to appoint one man, or assembly of men, to bear their person; and every one to own, and acknowledge himself to be author of whatsoever he that so bears their person, shall act, or cause to be acted, in those things which concern the common peace and safety; and therein to submit their wills, every one to his will, and their judgments, to his judgment. This is more than consent, or concord; it is a real unity of them all, in one and the same person, made by covenant of every man with every man, in such manner, as if every man should say to every man, *I authorize and give up my right of governing myself, to this man, or to this assembly of men, on this condition, that thou give up thy right to him, and authorize all his actions in like manner.* This done, the multitude so united in one person is called a COMMONWEALTH, in Latin CIVITAS. This is the generation of that great LEVIATHAN, or rather, to speak more reverently, of that *mortal god,* to which we owe under the *immortal God,* our peace and defence. For by this authority, given him by every particular man in the Commonwealth, he has the use of so much power and strength conferred on him, that by terror thereof, he is enabled to perform the wills of them all, to peace at home, and mutual aid against their enemies abroad. And in him consists the essence of the Commonwealth; which, to define it, is *one person, of whose acts a great multitude, by mutual covenants one with another, have made themselves every one the author, to the end he may use the strength and means of them all, as he shall think expedient, for their peace and common defence.*

And he that carries this person is called SOVEREIGN, and said to have *sovereign power;* and every one besides, his SUBJECT.

The attaining to this sovereign power is by two ways. One, by natural force; as when a man makes his children to submit themselves, and their children, to his government, as being able to destroy them if they refuse; or by war subdues his enemies to his will, giving them their lives on that condition. The other is when men agree amongst themselves to submit to some man or assembly of men, voluntarily, on confidence to be protected by him against all others. This latter may be called a political commonwealth, or commonwealth by *institution;* and the former, a commonwealth by *acquisition.*

24

DESCARTES

1596–1650

René Descartes's mother died not long after he was born in La Haye in Touraine, France, and he was raised by his father, a councilor of the *parlement* of Rennes in Brittany. At the age of eight he enrolled in the celebrated Jesuit college La Flèche, where he studied science, philosophy, literature, and mathematics. Legend has it that he refused to get up in the morning, complaining of ill health, but his teachers allowed him to study in bed until noon. He continued the practice for the rest of his life.

By the close of the sixteenth century the Catholic Counter-Reformation was in full swing. Catholic theologians began using the newly rediscovered Pyrrhonian skepticism against their Protestant, Calvinist, and Lutheran opponents, arguing that they could not use reason to come to know what they professed to know. Skepticism had thus aligned itself with religion exactly in the way it once opposed it. There was grave doubt about whether any of the scholastic teachings of science, philosophy, and mathematics were infallible. These developments had a notable effect on Descartes.

Instead of pursuing his studies he turned to gambling, fencing, and horsemanship, and had numerous love affairs, one of which ended up in a duel with the woman's husband. Although Descartes was a French citizen, he fought as a soldier in the Netherlands, and in Bavaria.

In Paris, Descartes joined an illustrious and influential group of thinkers headed by Marin Mersenne, his best friend from La Flèche, who would one day oversee the publication of the *Meditations.* They urged Descartes to publish his views right away, convinced that here was a new method for doing philosophy. But, instead, he quit the group and went into hiding, keeping his residence a secret, and refused to publish. Then, in 1629, disillusioned with "the book of the world," Descartes fled to Holland where he began writing *Le Monde,* a work divided into two parts, "Light" and "Man." When his old friend, now Father Mersenne, happened to read it, once again he urged Descartes to publish. The popular historical account has it that the reason Descartes again refused is because he had just heard about the condemnation of Galileo (in 1632). But Mersenne had shown the *Meditations* to the faculty of theology in Paris, and they already had approved it. In fact, it wasn't until twenty-two years after Descartes's death that the Roman Catholic Church first put the *Meditations* on the *Index Librorum Prohibitorum,* the list of books considered dangerous to read that was begun by Pope Pius V in 1571. This was then approved by the Council of Trent,[1] and the people were forbidden to read the work.

Only fragments of *Le Monde* were published in Descartes's lifetime. But he did publish the ground-breaking *Discourse on the Method of Properly Guiding the Reason in the Search for Truth in the Sciences* (1637). Here he states, "The greatest minds, as they are capable of the highest excellencies, are open likewise to the greatest aberrations; and those who travel very slowly may yet make far greater progress, provided they keep always to the straight road, than those who, while they run, forsake it." His purpose in this work is to correct the "aberrations of the mind." Inspired by Francis Bacon's proposition that "the entire work of the understanding must be begun afresh, and the mind itself be, from the start, not left to take its own course, but be guided step by step," Descartes says the straight road must be followed without ever veering from it.

Descartes rejects scholastic Aristotelianism in favor of a type of classical Platonism. He formulates his system of universal knowledge on undoubtable premises. As in mathematics, he proceeds with straightforward deductions in which each step is as clear as the starting proposition. His attempt to construct a universal mathematics as a complete system of absolute validity includes not just numbers and figures but the whole world. In the process, he discovered a way to link geometry and algebra and thereby invented an entirely new branch of mathematics still practiced today and known as analytic geometry.

Descartes wrote a manual outlining his method in perfect detail for anyone who should wish to follow in his footsteps. Called *Rules for the Direction of the Mind*, it was written in 1628 but not published until 1701, half a century after his death. In it, he offers clear and explicit rules that, he claims, have the power to lead to similar, far-reaching results in any-one who applies them. *The key is to study and learn everything you can about as many different, even nonconnected, areas, teaching yourself the skills in those areas even if they seem completely unrelated.* Descartes formulates in explicit detail such rules for philosophical thought designed to lead to clear and distinct ideas via a method modeled on the precision of mathematical thought. The purpose is not mathematical theory per se but the foundation of a perfect and complete understanding of ourselves and the world. Descartes thus echoes Plato's warning, placed above the Academy, "Let no one ignorant of mathematics enter here."

Descartes claims that *anyone* can know everything there is to know. This of course would, on the views of other philosophers such as Bruno and Averroes, be possible through mystical intuitions, unity with the divine, the transcendental self, and so on; it does not require divine grace or genius or any sort of special talent. What makes it possible for the mind to attain such knowledge is explained in Descartes's first rule, in which he claims that one of the greatest mistakes we make is to limit the mind in the ways that we limit the physical body.

Descartes's *Meditations on First Philosophy, in Which the Existence of God and the Distinction between Mind and Body Are Demonstrated* (1641; 2nd ed., 1642) is among the most influential philosophical works of all time. By "first philosophy," Descartes means the same as Aristotle's *first principles of things,* or metaphysics. "Thus the whole of philosophy," he wrote, "is like a tree; the roots are metaphysics, the trunk is physics, and the branches that

---

1. The Council of Trent, the Roman Catholic Church council created to deal with the crisis created by the Protestant Reformation, started the Catholic Counter-Reformation and the *Index* was one of its main tools.

rise from the trunk are all the other sciences." The work has been reprinted more times than just about any other work of philosophy.

In the *Meditations,* Descartes dispenses with the foundations laid by all previous philosophical and scientific systems built on external authority. He attempts instead to reconstruct philosophy and the entire knowledge-seeking enterprise. Many philosophers at the time objected furiously to the *Meditations,* whereas others praised it as a great intellectual achievement. Instead of ignoring his worst critics, Descartes published in the same volume all the most prominent objections and criticisms, including those of Pierre Gassendi, Antoine Arnauld, and Hobbes (Chapter 23).

Descartes begins the *Meditations* by taking stock of all his acquired opinions. He asks himself, *how do I know that all these things that I believe to be true, are true?* He wonders how he came to his beliefs. He notices that, while it would be impossible to examine each of his beliefs individually, there are only a few *methods* by which his beliefs were acquired. Most of his beliefs come about through conditioning by various religious, political, and educational authorities. Descartes now asks: *have I ever been deceived by any of these methods?* If so, then I must throw out all beliefs derived from that method. His method, in other words, is to find the general method or principles on the basis of which some set of beliefs is acquired, and then to test not the individual beliefs but the principles on which they are based—the method by which they were acquired. If the principles and methods are bad, any beliefs thus acquired are not knowledge.

Descartes offers a brilliant solution to the problem of skepticism. Just as Archimedes showed how, if only he had a firm place to put his fulcrum, he could move the entire Earth, Descartes finds a firm place to put his absolutely undoubtable proposition, which he shall then use to move the whole of philosophy. After doubting everything that can be doubted and throwing out anything which can be doubted, he finds solid ground: he realizes that even if he is dreaming, even if an evil demon is deceiving him into having the experiences he is now having, *nobody, not even God, could deceive him into believing falsely that he exists.* Why? Because even if he is always and forever being deceived, *deception* is going on. So there is at least the fact that something, someone, is being deceived. And so this deceived entity cannot be deceived into thinking, falsely, that it exists. Even a deception is something, even a false thought is a thought.

So there is one undoubtable proposition: "I think, therefore I am." It occurs as an insight at the end of a series of apparently endless doubts: I doubt that the world is what it appears, that there is a God, that external objects exist, that I have a body, that twice two is four (even *that* can be doubted!). But it is impossible for me to doubt that I myself, who am involved in this activity of doubting, exist. So here is this one single point at which the apparently endless series of doubts comes to an abrupt end: at the doubter, at the self-existence of the thinker who thinks such thoughts. I can doubt everything except that I doubt and that, in thus doubting, I am. This, then, is the absolute point of departure necessary for knowledge, found in the *self-certitude of the thinking ego* (the Latin *ego* means "I"). In other words, from the fact that I doubt—that is, from the fact that I think—it follows not as a logical deduction that I, the doubter, the thinker, am, but as an *insight* or philosophical *realization.* Thus, Descartes's Latin phrase, *Cogito, ergo sum*—"Thinking, therefore existing"—is the most certain of all truths.

Cartesian doubt thus raises a question that will be a major preoccupation for many subsequent philosophers and which has continued to this day: is knowledge attained through rational intuition or by sense experience? Descartes's answer lays the foundation for Kant's critique of dogmatic metaphysics and paves the way for idealism with the Cartesian argument that we know our own minds more immediately than we know our bodies and the material world.

The *Meditations* attracted a wide following among philosophers, scientists, artists, and leading intellectuals of the time. When the daughter of the titular king of Bohemia, Princess Elizabeth, began writing Descartes, he wrote back that her understanding of both his *Discourse* and his *Meditations* was "incomparable." In 1649, Queen Christina of Sweden invited him to Sweden. She wanted Descartes to be her private tutor. He accepted the offer, but when he arrived in Stockholm the queen requested her lessons at 5:00 A.M. Accustomed to sleeping until noon, in less than four months Descartes caught pneumonia and died.

He was found clutching an unfinished letter,[2] which he had begun to pen to his friend Marin Mersenne:

> February 11, 1650
> Dear Marin,
>   I just woke up from a . . .

His friend had died two years earlier.

DISCOURSE ON METHOD

PART I

Good sense is, of all things among men, the most equally distributed; for every one thinks himself so abundantly provided with it, that those even who are the most difficult to satisfy in everything else, do not usually desire a larger measure of this quality than they already possess. And in this it is not likely that all are mistaken: the conviction is rather to be held as testifying that the power of judging aright and of distinguishing Truth from Error, which is properly what is called Good Sense or Reason, is by nature equal in all men; and that the diversity of our opinions, consequently, does not arise from some being endowed with a larger share of Reason than others, but solely from this, that we conduct our thoughts along different ways, and do not fix our attention on the same objects. For to be possessed of a vigorous mind is not enough; the prime requisite is rightly to apply it. The greatest minds, as they are capable of the highest excellencies, are open likewise to the greatest aberrations; and those who travel very slowly may yet make far greater progress, provided they keep always to the straight road, than those who, while they run, forsake it. . . .

But like one walking alone and in the dark, I resolved to proceed so slowly and with such circumspection, that if I did not advance far, I would at least guard against falling. I

---

2. See Daniel Kolak, *In Search of Self: Life, Death, and Personal Identity* (Belmont, Calif.: Wadsworth, 1998).

From René Descartes, *Discourse on Method,* trans. John Veitch (Open Court, 1902).

did not even choose to dismiss summarily any of the opinions that had crept into my belief without having been introduced by Reason, but first of all took sufficient time carefully to satisfy myself of the general nature of the task I was setting myself, and ascertain the true Method by which to arrive at the knowledge of whatever lay within the compass of my powers.

Among the branches of Philosophy, I had, at an earlier period, given some attention to Logic, and among those of the Mathematics to Geometrical Analysis and Algebra,—three Arts or Sciences which ought, as I conceived, to contribute something to my design. But, on examination, I found that, as for Logic, its syllogisms and the majority of its other precepts are of avail rather in the communication of what we already know, or even as the Art of Lully, in speaking without judgment of things of which we are ignorant, than in the investigation of the unknown; and although this Science contains indeed a number of correct and very excellent precepts, there are, nevertheless, so many others, and these either injurious or superfluous, mingled with the former, that it is almost quite as difficult to effect a severance of the true from the false as it is to extract a Diana or a Minerva from a rough block of marble. Then as to the Analysis of the ancients and the Algebra of the moderns, besides that they embrace only matters highly abstract, and, to appearance, of no use, the former is so exclusively restricted to the consideration of figures, that it can exercise the Understanding only on condition of greatly fatiguing the Imagination; and, in the latter, there is so complete a subjection to certain rules and formulas, that there results an art full of confusion and obscurity calculated to embarrass, instead of a science fitted to cultivate the mind. By these considerations I was induced to seek some other Method which would comprise the advantages of the three and be exempt from their defects. And as a multitude of laws often only hampers justice, so that a state is best governed when, with few laws, these are rigidly administered; in like manner, instead of the great number of precepts of which Logic is composed, I believed that the four following would prove perfectly sufficient for me, provided I took the firm and unwavering resolution never in a single instance to fail in observing them.

The *first* was never to accept anything for true which I did not clearly know to be such; that is to say, carefully to avoid precipitancy and prejudice, and to comprise nothing more in my judgment than what was presented to my mind so clearly and distinctly as to exclude all ground of doubt.

The *second*, to divide each of the difficulties under examination into as many parts as possible, and as might be necessary for its adequate solution.

The *third*, to conduct my thoughts in such order that, by commencing with objects the simplest and easiest to know, I might ascend by little and little, and, as it were, step by step, to the knowledge of the more complex; assigning in thought a certain order even to those objects which in their own nature do not stand in a relation of antecedence and sequence.

And the *last*, in every case to make enumerations so complete, and reviews so general, that I might be assured that nothing was omitted.

The long chains of simple and easy reasonings by means of which geometers are accustomed to reach the conclusions of their most difficult demonstrations, had led me to imagine that all things, to the knowledge of which man is competent, are mutually connected in the same way, and that there is nothing so far removed from us as to be beyond our reach, or so hidden that we cannot discover it, provided only we abstain from accepting the false for the true, and always preserve in our thoughts the order necessary for the deduction of one truth from another. And I had little difficulty in determining the objects with which it was necessary to commence, for I was already persuaded that it must be with the simplest and easiest to know, and, considering that of all those who have hitherto sought truth in the sciences, the mathematicians alone have been able to find any demonstrations, that is, any certain and evident reasons, I did not doubt but that such must have been the rule of their investigations. I resolved to commence, therefore, with the examination of the simplest objects, not anticipating, however, from this any other advantage than that to be found in accustoming my mind to the love and nourishment of truth, and to a distaste for all such reasonings as were unsound. But I had no intention on that account of attempting to master all the particular Sciences commonly denominated Mathematics: but observing that, however different their objects, they all agree in considering only the various relations or proportions subsisting among those objects, I thought it best for my purpose to consider these proportions in the most general form possible, without referring them to any objects in particular, except such as would most facilitate the knowledge of them, and without by any means restricting them to these, that afterwards I might thus be the better able to apply them to every other class of objects to which they are legitimately applicable. Perceiving further, that in order to understand these relations I should sometimes have to consider them one by one, and sometimes only to bear them in mind, or embrace them in the aggregate, I thought that, in order the better to consider them individually, I should view them as subsisting between straight lines, than which I could find no objects more simple, or capable of being more distinctly represented to my imagination and senses; and on the other hand, that in order to retain them in the memory, or embrace an aggregate of many, I should express them by certain characters the briefest possible. In this way I believed that I could borrow all that was best both in Geometrical Analysis and in Algebra, and correct all the defects of the one by help of the other.

And, in point of fact, the accurate observance of these few precepts gave me, I take the liberty of saying, such ease in unravelling all the questions embraced in these two sciences, that in the two or three months I devoted to their examination, not only did I reach solutions of questions I had formerly deemed exceedingly difficult, but even as regards questions of the solution of which I continued ignorant, I was enabled, as it appeared to me, to determine the means whereby, and the extent to which, a solution was possible; results attributable to the circumstance that I commenced with the simplest and most general truths, and that thus each truth discovered was a rule available in the discovery of subsequent ones. Nor in this perhaps shall I appear too vain, if it be considered that, as the truth on any particular point is one, whoever apprehends the truth, knows all that on that point can be known. The child, for example, who has been instructed in the elements of Arithmetic, and has made a particular addition, according to rule, may be assured that he has found, with respect to the sum of the numbers before him, all that in this instance is within the reach of human genius. Now, in conclusion, the Method which teaches adherence to the true order, and an exact enumeration of all the conditions of the thing sought includes all that gives certitude to the rules of Arithmetic.

But the chief ground of my satisfaction with this Method, was the assurance I had of thereby exercising my reason in all matters, if not with absolute perfection, at least with the greatest attainable by me: besides, I was conscious that by its use my mind was becoming gradually habituated to clearer and more distinct conceptions of its objects; and I hoped also, from not having restricted this Method to any particular matter, to apply it to the difficulties of the other Sciences, with not less success than to those of Algebra. I should not, however, on this account have ventured at once on the examination of all the difficulties of the Sciences which presented themselves to me, for this would have been contrary to the order prescribed in the Method, but observing that the knowledge of such is dependent on principles borrowed from Philosophy, in which I found nothing certain, I thought it necessary first of all to endeavour to establish its principles. And because I observed, besides, that an inquiry of this kind was of all others of the greatest moment, and one in which precipitancy and anticipation in judgment were most to be dreaded, I thought that I ought not to approach it till I had reached a more mature age, (being at that time but twenty-three), and had first of all employed much of my time in preparation for the work, as well by eradicating from my mind all the erroneous opinions I had up to that moment accepted, as by amassing variety of experience to afford materials for my reasonings, and by continually exercising myself in my chosen Method with a view to increased skill in its application.

RULES FOR THE DIRECTION OF THE MIND

Rule I: The end of study should be to direct the mind towards the enunciation of sound and correct judgments on all matters that come before it.

Whenever men notice some similarity between two things, they are wont to ascribe to each, even in those respects in which the two differ, what they have found to be true of the other. Thus they erroneously compare the sciences, which entirely consist in the cognitive exercise of the mind, with the arts, which depend upon an exercise and disposition of the body. They see that not all the arts can be acquired by the same man, but that he who restricts himself to one, most readily becomes the best executant, since it is not so easy for the same hand to adapt itself both to agricultural operations and to harp-playing, or to the performance of several such tasks as to one alone. Hence they have held the same to be true of the sciences also, and distinguishing them from one another according to their subject matter, they have imagined that they ought to be studied separately, each in isolation from all the rest. But this is certainly wrong. For since the sciences taken all together are identical with human wisdom, which always remains one and the same, however applied to different subjects, and suffers no more differentiation proceeding from them than the light of the sun experiences from the variety of the things which it illumines, there is no need for minds to be confined at all within limits; for neither does the knowing of one truth have an effect like that of the acquisition of one art and prevent us from finding out another, it rather aids us to do so. Certainly it appears to me strange that so many people should investigate human customs with such care, the virtues of plants, the motions of the stars, the transmutations of metals, and the objects of similar sciences, while at the same time practically none bethink themselves about good understanding, or universal Wisdom, though nevertheless all other studies are to be esteemed not so much for their own value as because they contribute something to this. Consequently we are justified in bringing forward this as the first rule of all, since there is nothing more prone to turn us aside from the correct way of

From René Descartes, *Rules for the Direction of the Mind,* trans. Elizabeth S. Haldane and G. R. T. Ross (Cambridge: Cambridge University Press, 1911).

seeking out truth than this directing of our inquiries, not towards their general end, but towards certain special investigations. I do not here refer to perverse and censurable pursuits like empty glory or base gain; obviously counterfeit reasonings and quibbles suited to vulgar understanding open up a much more direct route to such a goal than does a sound apprehension of the truth. But I have in view even honourable and laudable pursuits, because these mislead us in a more subtle fashion. For example take our investigations of those sciences conducive to the conveniences of life or which yield that pleasure which is found in the contemplation of truth, practically the only joy in life that is complete and untroubled with any pain. There we may indeed expect to receive the legitimate fruits of scientific inquiry; but if, in the course of our study, we think of them, they frequently cause us to omit many facts which are necessary to the understanding of other matters, because they seem to be either of slight value or of little interest. Hence we must believe that all the sciences are so inter-connected, that it is much easier to study them all together than to isolate one from all the others. If, therefore, anyone wishes to search out the truth of things in serious earnest, he ought not to select one special science; for all the sciences are conjoined with each other and interdependent: he ought rather to think how to increase the natural light of reason, not for the purpose of resolving this or that difficulty of scholastic type, but in order that his understanding may light his will to its proper choice in all the contingencies of life. In a short time he will see with amazement that he has made much more progress than those who are eager about particular ends, and that he has not only obtained all that they desire, but even higher results than fall within his expectation.

Rule II: Only those objects should engage our attention, to the sure and indubitable knowledge of which our mental powers seem to be adequate.

Science in its entirety is true and evident cognition. He is no more learned who has doubts on many matters than the man who has never thought of them; nay he appears to be less learned if he has formed wrong opinions on any particulars. Hence it were better not to study at all than to occupy one's self with objects of such difficulty, that, owing to our inability to distinguish true from false, we are forced to regard the doubtful as certain; for in those matters any hope of augmenting our knowledge is exceeded by the risk of diminishing it. Thus in accordance with the above maxim we reject all such merely probable knowledge and make it a rule to trust only what is completely known and incapable of being doubted. No doubt men of education may persuade themselves that there is but little of such certain knowledge, because, forsooth, a common failing of human nature has made them deem it too easy and open to everyone, and so led them to neglect to think upon such truths; but I nevertheless announce that there are more of these than they think—truths which suffice to give a rigorous demonstration of innumerable propositions, the discussion of which they have hitherto been unable to free from the element of probability. Further, because they have believed that it was unbecoming for a man of education to confess ignorance on any point, they have so accustomed themselves to trick out their fabricated explanations, that they have ended by gradually imposing on themselves and thus have issued them to the public as genuine.

But if we adhere closely to this rule we shall find left but few objects of legitimate study. For there is scarce any question occurring in the sciences about which talented men have not disagreed. But whenever two men come to opposite decisions about the same matter one of them at least must certainly be in the wrong, and apparently there is not even one of them who knows; for if the reasoning of the second was sound and clear he would be able so to lay it before the other as finally to succeed in convincing *his* understanding also. Hence apparently we cannot attain to a perfect knowledge in any such case of probable opinion, for it would be rashness to hope for more than others have attained to. Consequently if we reckon correctly, of the sciences already discovered, Arithmetic and Geometry alone are left, to which the observance of this rule reduces us.

Yet we do not therefore condemn that method of philosophizing which others have already discovered and those weapons of the schoolmen, probable syllogisms, which are so well suited for polemics. They indeed give practice to the wits of youths and, producing emulation among them, act as a stimulus; and it is much better for their minds to be moulded by opinions of this sort, uncertain though they appear, as being objects of controversy among the learned, than to be left entirely to their own devices. For thus through lack of guidance they might stray into some abyss; but as long as they follow in their masters' footsteps, though they may diverge at times from the truth, they will yet certainly find a path which is at least in this respect safer, that it has been approved of by more prudent people. We ourselves rejoice that we in earlier years experienced this scholastic training; but now, being released from that oath of allegiance which bound us to our old masters, and since, as becomes our riper years, we are no longer subject to the ferule, if we wish in earnest to establish for ourselves those rules which shall aid us in scaling the heights of human knowledge, we must admit assuredly among the primary members of our catalogue that maxim which forbids us to abuse our leisure as many do, who neglect all easy quests and take up their time only with difficult matters; for they, though certainly making all sorts of subtle conjectures and elaborating most plausible arguments with great ingenuity, frequently find too late that after all their labours they have only increased the multitude of their doubts, without acquiring any knowledge whatsoever.

But now let us proceed to explain more carefully our reasons for saying, as we did a little while ago, that of all the sciences known as yet, Arithmetic and Geometry alone are free from any taint of falsity or uncertainty. We must note then that there are two ways by which we arrive at the knowledge of facts, viz. by experience and by deduction. We must further observe that while our inferences from experience are frequently fallacious, deduction, or the pure illation of one thing from another, though it may be passed over, if it is not seen through, cannot be erroneous when performed by an understanding that is in the least degree rational. And it seems to me that the operation is profited but little by those constraining bonds by means of which the Dialecticians claim to control human reason, though I do not deny that that discipline may be serviceable for other purposes. My reason for saying so is that none of the mistakes which men can make (men, I say, not beasts) are due to faulty inference; they are caused merely by the fact that we found upon a basis of poorly comprehended experiences, or that propositions are posited which are hasty and groundless.

This furnishes us with an evident explanation of the great superiority in certitude of Arithmetic and Geometry to other sciences. The former alone deal with an object so pure and uncomplicated, that they need make no assumptions at all which experience renders uncertain, but wholly consist in the rational deduction of consequences. They are on that account much the easiest and clearest of all, and possess an object such as we require, for in them it is scarce humanly possible for anyone to err except by inadvertence. And yet we should not be surprised to find that plenty of people of their own accord prefer to apply their intelligence to other studies, or to Philosophy. The reason for this is that every person permits himself the liberty of making guesses in the matter of an obscure subject with more confidence than in one which is clear, and that it is much easier to have some vague notion about any subject, no matter what, than to arrive at the real truth about a single question however simple that may be.

But one conclusion now emerges out of these considerations, viz. not, indeed, that Arithmetic and Geometry are the sole sciences to be studied, but only that in our search for the direct road towards truth we should busy ourselves with no object about which we cannot attain a certitude equal to that of the demonstrations of Arithmetic and Geometry.

Rule III: In the subjects we propose to investigate, our inquiries should be directed, not to what others have thought, nor to what we ourselves conjecture, but to what we can clearly and perspicuously behold and with certainty deduce; for knowledge is not won in any other way.

To study the writings of the ancients is right, because it is a great boon for us to be able to make use of the labours of so many men; and we should do so, both in order to discover what they have correctly made out in previous ages, and also that we may inform ourselves as to what in the various sciences is still left for investigation. But yet there is a great danger lest in a too absorbed study of these works we should become infected with their errors, guard against them as we may. For it is the way of writers, whenever they have allowed themselves rashly and credulously to take up a position in any controverted matter, to try with the subtlest of arguments to compel us to go along with them. But when, on the contrary, they have happily come upon something certain and evident, in displaying it they never fail to surround it with ambiguities, fearing, it would seem, lest the simplicity of their explanation should make us respect their discovery less, or because they grudge us an open vision of the truth.

Further, supposing now that all were wholly open and candid, and never thrust upon us doubtful opinions as true, but expounded every matter in good faith, yet since scarce anything has been asserted by any one man the contrary of which has not been alleged by another, we should be eternally uncertain which of the two to believe. It would be no use to total up the testimonies in favour of each, meaning to follow that opinion which was supported by the greater number of authors; for if it is a question of difficulty that is in dispute, it is more likely that the truth would have been discovered by few than by many. But even though all these men agreed among themselves, what they teach us would not suffice for us. For we shall not, e.g. all turn out to be mathematicians though we know by heart all the proofs that others have elaborated, unless we have an intellectual talent that fits us to resolve difficulties of any kind. Neither, though we have mastered all the arguments of Plato and Aristotle, if yet we have not the capacity for passing a solid judgment on these matters, shall we become Philosophers; we should have acquired the knowledge not of a science, but of history.

I lay down the rule also, that we must wholly refrain from ever mixing up conjectures with our pronouncements on the truth of things. This warning is of no little importance. There is no stronger reason for our finding nothing in the current Philosophy which is so evident and certain as not to be capable of being controverted, than the fact that the learned, not content with the recognition of what is clear and certain, in the first instance hazard the assertion of obscure and ill-comprehended theories, at which they have arrived merely by probable conjecture. Then afterwards they gradually attach complete credence to them, and mingling them promiscuously with what is true and evident, they finish by being unable to deduce any conclusion which does not appear to depend upon some proposition of the doubtful sort, and hence is not uncertain.

But lest we in turn should slip into the same error, we shall here take note of all those mental operations by which we are able, wholly without fear of illusion, to arrive at the knowledge of things. Now I admit only two, viz. intuition and induction.

By *intuition* I understand, not the fluctuating testimony of the senses, nor the misleading judgment that proceeds from the blundering constructions of imagination, but the conception which an unclouded and attentive mind gives us so readily and distinctly that we are wholly freed from doubt about that which we understand. Or, what comes to the same thing, *intuition* is the undoubting conception of an unclouded and attentive mind, and springs from the light of reason alone; it is more certain than deduction itself, in that it is simpler, though deduction, as we have noted above, cannot by us be erroneously conducted. Thus each individual can mentally have intuition of the fact that he exists, and that he thinks; that the triangle is bounded by three lines only, the sphere by a single radius, and so on. Facts of such a kind are far more numerous than many people think, disdaining as they do to direct their attention upon such simple matters.

But in case anyone may be put out by this new use of the term intuition and of other terms which in the following pages I am similarly compelled to dissever from their current meaning, I here make the general announcement that I pay no attention to the way in which particular terms have of late been employed in the schools, because it would have been difficult to employ the same terminology while my theory was wholly different. All that I take note of is the meaning of the Latin of each word, when, in cases where an appropriate term is lacking, I wish to transfer to the vocabulary that expresses my own meaning those that I deem most suitable.

This evidence and certitude, however, which belongs to intuition, is required not only in the enunciation of propositions, but also in discursive reasoning of whatever sort. For example consider this consequence: 2 and 2 amount to the same as 3 and 1. Now we need to see intuitively not only that 2 and 2 make 4, and that likewise 3 and 1 make 4, but further that the third of the above statement is a necessary conclusion from these two.

Hence now we are in a position to raise the question as to why we have, besides intuition, given this supplementary method of knowing, viz. knowing by *deduction,* by which we understand all necessary inference from other facts that are known with certainty. This, however, we could not avoid, because many things are known with certainty, though not by themselves evident, but only deduced from true and known principles by the continuous and uninterrupted action of a mind that has a clear vision of each step in the process. It is in a similar way that we know that the last link in a long chain is connected with the first, even though we do not take in by means of one and the same act of vision all the intermediate links on which that connection depends, but only remember that we have taken them successively under review and that each single one is united to its neighbour, from the first even to the last. Hence we distinguish this mental intuition from deduction by the fact that into the conception of the latter there enters a certain movement or succession, into that of the former there does not. Further deduction does not require an immediately presented evidence such as intuition possesses; its certitude is rather conferred upon it in some way by memory. The upshot of the matter is that it is possible to say that those propositions indeed which are immediately deduced from first principles are known now by intuition, now by deduction, i.e. in a way that differs according to our point of view. But the first principles themselves are given by intuition alone, while, on the contrary, the remote conclusions are furnished only by deduction.

These two methods are the most certain routes to knowledge, and the mind should admit no others. All the rest should be rejected as suspect of error and dangerous. But this does not prevent us from believing matters that have been divinely revealed as being more certain than our surest knowledge, since belief in these things, as all faith in obscure matters, is an action not of our intelligence, but of our will. They should be heeded also since, if they have any basis in our understanding, they can and ought to be, more than all things else, discovered by one or other of the ways above-mentioned, as we hope perhaps to show at greater length on some future opportunity.

Rule IV: There is need of a method for finding out the truth.

So blind is the curiosity by which mortals are possessed, that they often conduct their minds along unexplored routes, having no reason to hope for success, but merely being willing to risk the experiment of finding whether the truth they seek lies there. As well might a man burning with an unintelligent desire to find treasure, continuously roam the streets, seeking to find something that a passerby might have chanced to drop. This is the way in which most Chemists, many Geometricians, and Philosophers not a few prosecute their studies. I do not deny that sometimes in these wanderings they are lucky enough to find something true. But I do not allow that this argues greater industry on their part, but only better luck. But however that may be, it were far better never to think of investigating truth at all, than to do so without a method. For it is very certain that unregulated inquiries and confused reflections of this kind only confound the natural light and blind our mental powers. Those who so become accustomed to walk in darkness weaken their eye-sight so much that afterwards they cannot bear the light of day. This is confirmed by experience; for how often do we not see that those who have never taken to letters, give a sounder and clearer decision about obvious matters than those who have spent all their time in the schools? Moreover by a method I mean certain and simple rules, such that, if a man observe them accurately, he shall never assume what is false as true, and will never spend his mental efforts to no purpose, but will always gradually increase his knowledge and so arrive at a true understanding of all that does not surpass his powers.

These two points must be carefully noted, viz. never to assume what is false as true, and to arrive at a knowledge which takes in all things. For, if we are without the knowledge of any of the things which we are capable of understanding, that is only because we have never perceived any way to bring us to this knowledge, or because we have fallen into the contrary error. But if our method rightly explains how our mental vision should be used, so as not to fall into the contrary error, and how deduction should be discovered in order that we may arrive at the knowledge of all things, I do not see what else is needed to make it complete; for I have already said that no science is acquired except by mental intuition or deduction. There is besides no question of extending it further in order to show how these said operations ought to be effected, because they are the most simple and primary of all. Consequently, unless our understanding were already able to employ them, it could comprehend none of the precepts of that very method, not even the simplest. But as for the other mental operations, which Dialectic does its best to direct by making use of these prior ones, they are quite useless here; rather they are to be accounted impediments, because nothing can be added to the pure light of reason which does not in some way obscure it.

Since then the usefulness of this method is so great that without it study seems to be harmful rather than profitable, I am quite ready to believe that the greater minds of former ages had some knowledge of it, nature even conducting them to it. For the human mind has in it something that we may call divine, wherein are scattered the first germs of useful modes of thought. Consequently it often happens that however much neglected and choked by interfering studies they bear fruit of their own accord. Arithmetic and Geometry, the simplest sciences, give us an instance of this; for we have sufficient evidence that the ancient Geometricians made use of a certain analysis which they extended to the resolution of all problems, though they grudged the secret to posterity. At the present day also there flourishes a certain kind of Arithmetic, called Algebra, which designs to effect, when dealing with numbers, what the ancients achieved in the matter of figures. These two methods are nothing else than the spontaneous fruit sprung from the inborn principles of the discipline here in question; and I do not wonder that these sciences with their very simple subject matter should have yielded results so much more satisfactory than others in which greater obstructions choke all growth. But even in the latter case, if only we take care to cultivate them assiduously, fruits will certainly be able to come to full maturity.

This is the chief result which I have had in view in writing this treatise. For I should not think much of these rules, if they had no utility save for the solution of the empty problems with which Logicians and Geometers have been wont to beguile their leisure; my only achievement thus would have seemed to be an ability to argue about trifles more subtly than others. Further, though much mention is here made of numbers and figures, because no other sciences furnish us with illustrations of such self-evidence and certainty, the reader who follows my drift with sufficient attention will easily see that nothing is less in my mind than ordinary Mathematics and that I am expounding quite another science, of which these illustrations are rather the outer husk than the constituents. Such a science should contain the primary rudiments of human reason, and its province ought to extend to the eliciting of true results in every subject. To speak freely, I am convinced that it is a more powerful instrument of knowledge than any other that has been bequeathed to us by human agency, as being the source of all others. But as for the outer covering I mentioned, I mean not to employ it to cover up and conceal my method for the purpose of warding off the vulgar; rather I hope so to clothe and embellish it that I may make it more suitable for presentation to the human mind.

When first I applied my mind to Mathematics I read straight away most of what is usually given by the mathematical writers, and I paid special attention to Arithmetic and Geometry, because they were said to be the simplest and so to speak the way to all the rest. But in neither case did I then meet with authors who fully satisfied me. I did indeed learn in their works many propositions about numbers which I found on calculation to be true. As to figures, they in a sense exhibited to my eyes a great number of truths and drew conclusions from certain consequences. But they did not seem to make it sufficiently plain to the mind itself why those things are so, and how they discovered them. Consequently I was not surprised that many people, even of talent and scholarship, should, after glancing at these sciences, have either given them up as being empty and childish or, taking them to be very difficult and intricate, been deterred at the very outset from learning them. For really there is nothing more futile than to busy one's self with bare numbers and imaginary figures in such a way as to appear to rest content with such trifles, and so to resort to those superficial demonstrations, which are discovered more frequently by chance than by skill, and are a matter more of the eyes and the imagination than of the understanding, that in a sense one ceases to make use of one's reason. I might add that there is no more intricate task than that of solving by this method of proof new difficulties that arise, involved as they are with numerical confusions. But when I afterwards bethought myself how it could be that the earliest pioneers of Philosophy in bygone ages refused to admit to the study of wisdom any one who was not versed in Mathematics, evidently believing that this was the easiest and most indispensable mental exercise and preparation for laying hold of other more important sciences, I was confirmed in my suspicion that they had knowledge of a species of Mathematics very different from that which passes current in our time. I do not indeed imagine that they had a perfect knowledge of it, for they plainly show how little advanced they were by the insensate rejoicings they display and the pompous thanksgivings they offer for the most trifling discoveries. I am not shaken in my opinion by the fact that historians make a great deal of certain machines of theirs. Possibly these machines were quite simple, and yet the ignorant and wonder-loving multitude might easily have lauded them as miraculous. But I am convinced that certain primary germs of truth implanted by nature in human minds—though in our case the daily reading and hearing of innumerable diverse errors stifle them—had a very great vitality in that rude and unsophisticated age of the ancient world. Thus the same mental illumination which let them see that virtue was to be preferred to pleasure, an honour to utility, although they knew not why this was so, made them recognize true notions in Philosophy and Mathematics, although they were not yet able thoroughly to grasp these sciences. Indeed I seem to recognize certain traces of this true Mathematics in Pappus and Diophantus, who though not belonging to the earliest age, yet lived many centuries before our own times. But my opinion is that these writers then with a sort of low cunning, deplorable indeed, suppressed this knowledge. Possibly they acted just as many inventors are known to have done in the case of their discoveries, i.e. they feared that their method being so easy and simple would become cheapened on being divulged, and they preferred to exhibit in its place certain barren truths, deductively demonstrated with show enough of ingenuity, as the results of their art, in order to win from us our admiration for these achievements, rather than to disclose to us that method itself which would have wholly annulled the admiration accorded. Finally there have been certain men of talent who in the present age have tried to revive this same art. For it seems to be precisely that science known by the barbarous name Algebra, if only we could extricate it from that vast array of numbers and inexplicable figures by which it is overwhelmed, so that it might display the clearness and simplicity which, we imagine, ought to exist in a genuine Mathematics. It was these reflections that recalled me from the particular studies of Arithmetic and Geometry to a general investigation of Mathematics, and thereupon I sought to determine what precisely was universally meant by that term, and why not only the above mentioned sciences, but also Astronomy, Music, Optics, Mechanics and several others are styled parts of Mathematics. Here indeed it is not enough to look to the origin of the word; for since the name "Mathematics" means exactly the same thing as "scientific study," these other branches could, with as much right as Geometry itself, be called Mathematics. Yet we see that almost anyone who has had the slightest schooling, can easily distinguish what relates to Mathematics in any question from that which belongs to the other sciences. But as I considered the matter carefully it gradually came to light that all those matters only were referred to Mathematics in which order and measurement are investigated, and that it makes no difference whether it be in numbers, figures, stars, sounds or any other object that the question of measurement arises. I saw consequently that there must be some general science to explain that element as a whole which gives rise to problems about order and measurement, restricted as these are to no special subject matter. This, I perceived, was called "Universal Mathematics," not a far fetched designation, but one of long standing which has passed into current use, because in this science is contained everything on account of which the others are called parts of Mathematics. We can see how much it excels in utility and simplicity the sciences subordinate to it, by the fact that it can deal with all the objects of which they have cognizance and many more besides, and that any difficulties it contains are found in them as well, added to the fact that in them fresh difficulties arise due to their special subject matter which in it do not exist. But now how comes it that though everyone knows the name of this science and understands what is its province even without studying it attentively, so many people laboriously pursue the other dependent sciences, and no one cares to master this one? I should marvel indeed were I not aware that everyone thinks it to be so very easy, and had I not long since observed that the human mind passes over what it thinks it can easily accomplish, and hastens straight away to new and more imposing occupations.

I, however, conscious as I am of my inadequacy, have resolved that in my investigation into truth I shall follow obstinately such an order as will require me first to start with what is simplest and easiest, and never permit me to proceed farther until in the first sphere there seems to be nothing further to be done. This is why up to the present time to the best of my ability I have made a study of this universal Mathematics; consequently I believe that when I go on to deal in their turn with more profound sciences, as I hope to do soon, my efforts will not be premature. But before I make this transition I shall try to bring together and arrange in an orderly manner, the facts which in my previous studies I have noted as being more worthy of attention. Thus I hope both that at a future date, when through advancing years my memory is enfeebled, I shall, if need be, conveniently be able to recall them by looking in this little book, and that having now disburdened my memory of them I may be free to concentrate my mind on my future studies.

Rule V: Method consists entirely in the order and disposition of the objects towards which our mental vision must be directed if we would find out any truth. We shall comply with it exactly if we reduce involved and obscure propositions step by step to those that are simpler, and then starting with the intuitive apprehension of all those that are absolutely simple, attempt to ascend to the knowledge of all others by precisely similar steps.

In this alone lies the sum of all human endeavour, and he who would approach the investigation of truth must hold to this rule as closely as he who enters the labyrinth must follow the thread which guided Theseus. But many people either do not reflect on the precept at all, or ignore it altogether, or presume not to need it. Consequently they often investigate the most difficult questions with so little regard to order, that, to my mind, they act like a man who should attempt to leap with one bound from the base to the summit of a house, either making no account of the ladders provided for his ascent or not noticing them. It is thus that all Astrologers behave, who, though in ignorance of the nature of the heavens, and even without having made proper observations of the movements of the heavenly bodies, expect to be able to indicate their effects. This is also what many do who study Mechanics apart from Physics, and rashly set about devising new instruments for producing motion. Along with them go also those Philosophers who, neglecting experience, imagine that truth will spring from their brain like Pallas from the head of Zeus.

Now it is obvious that all such people violate the present rule. But since the order here required is often so obscure and intricate that not everyone can make it out, they can scarcely avoid error unless they diligently observe what is laid down in the following proposition.

Rule VI: In order to separate out what is quite simple from what is complex, and to arrange these matters methodically, we ought, in the case of every series in which we have deduced certain facts the one from the other, to notice which fact is simple, and to mark the interval, greater, less, or equal, which separates all the others from this.

Although this proposition seems to teach nothing very new, it contains, nevertheless, the chief secret of method, and none in the whole of this treatise is of greater utility. For it tells us that all facts can be arranged in certain series, not indeed in the sense of being referred to some ontological genus such as the categories employed by Philosophers in their classification, but in so far as certain truths can be known from others; and thus, whenever a difficulty occurs we are able at once to perceive whether it will be profitable to examine certain others first, and which, and in what order.

Further, in order to do that correctly, we must note first that for the purpose of our procedure, which does not regard things as isolated realities, but compares them with one another in order to discover the dependence in knowledge of one upon the other, all things can be said to be either absolute or relative.

I call that absolute which contains within itself the pure and simple essence of which we are in quest. Thus the term will be applicable to whatever is considered as being independent, or a cause, or simple, universal, one, equal, like, straight, and so forth; and the absolute I call the simplest and the easiest of all, so that we can make use of it in the solution of questions.

But the relative is that which, while participating in the same nature, or at least sharing in it to some degree which enables us to relate it to the absolute and to deduce it from that by a chain of operations, involves in addition something else in its concept which I call relativity. Examples of this are found in whatever is said to be dependent, or an effect, composite, particular, many, unequal, unlike, oblique, etc. These relatives are the further removed from the absolute, in proportion as they contain more elements of relativity subordinate the one to the other. We state in this rule that these should all be distinguished and their correlative connection and natural order so observed, that we may be able by traversing all the intermediate steps to proceed from the most remote to that which is in the highest degree absolute.

Herein lies the secret of this whole method, that in all things we should diligently mark that which is most absolute. For some things are from one point of view more absolute than others, but from a different standpoint are more relative. Thus though the universal is more absolute than the particular because its essence is simpler, yet it can be held to be more relative than the latter, because it depends upon individuals for its existence, and so on. Certain things likewise are truly more absolute than others, but yet are not the most absolute of all. Thus relatively to individuals, species is something absolute, but contrasted with genus it is relative. So too, among things that can be measured, extension is something absolute, but among the various aspects of extension it is length that is absolute, and so on. Finally also, in order to bring out more clearly that we are considering here not the nature of each thing taken in isolation, but the series involved in knowing them, we have purposely enumerated cause and equality among our absolutes, though the nature of these terms is really relative. For though Philosophers make cause and effect correlative, we find that here even, if we ask what the effect is, we must first know the cause and not conversely. Equals too mutually imply one another, but we can know unequals only by comparing them with equals and not *per contra*.

Secondly we must note that there are but few pure and simple essences, which either our experiences or some sort of light innate in us enable us to behold as primary and existing *per se,* not as depending on any others. These we say should be carefully noticed, for they are just those facts which we have called the simplest in any single series. All the others can only be perceived as deductions from these, either immediate and proximate, or not to be attained save by two or three or more acts of inference. The number of these acts should be noted in order that we may perceive whether the facts are separated from the primary and simplest proposition by a greater or smaller number of steps. And so pronounced is everywhere the inter-connection of ground and consequence, which gives rise, in the objects to be examined, to those series to which every inquiry must be reduced, that it can be investigated by a sure method. But because it is not easy to make a review of them all, and besides, since they have not so much to be kept in the memory as to be detected by a sort of mental penetration, we must seek for something which will so mould our intelligence as to let it perceive these connected sequences immediately whenever it needs to do so. For this purpose I have found nothing so effectual as to accustom ourselves to turn our attention with a sort of penetrative insight on the very minutest of the facts which we have already discovered.

Finally we must in the third place note that our inquiry ought not to start with the investigation of difficult matters. Rather, before setting out to attack any definite problem, it behoves us first, without making any selection, to assemble those truths that are obvious as they present themselves to us, and afterwards, proceeding step by step, to inquire whether any others can be deduced from these, and again any others from these conclusions and so on, in order. This done, we should attentively think over the truths we have discovered and mark with diligence the reasons why we have been able to detect some more easily than others, and which these are. Thus, when we come to attack some definite problem we shall be able to judge what previous questions it were best to settle first. For example, if it comes into my thought that the number 6 is twice 3, I may then ask what is twice 6, viz. 12; again, perhaps I seek for the double of this, viz. 24, and again of this, viz. 48. Thus I may easily deduce that there is the same proportion between 3 and 6, as between 6 and 12, and likewise 12 and 24, and so on, and hence that the numbers 3, 6, 12, 24, 48, etc. are in continued proportion. But though these facts are all so clear as to seem almost childish, I am now able by attentive reflection to understand what is the form involved by all questions that can be propounded about the proportions or relations of things, and the order in which they should be investigated; and this discovery embraces the sum of the entire science of Pure Mathematics.

For first I perceive that it was not more difficult to discover the double of six than that of three; and that equally in all cases, when we have found a proportion between any two magnitudes, we can find innumerable others which have the same proportion between them. So too there is no increase of difficulty, if three, or four, or more of such magnitudes are sought for, because each has to be found separately and without any relation to the others. But next I notice that though, when the magnitudes 3 and 6 are given, one can easily find a third in continued proportion, viz. 12, it is yet not equally easy, when the two extremes, 3 and 12, are given, to find the mean proportional, viz. 6. When we look into the reason for this, it is clear that here we have a type of difficulty quite different from the former; for, in order to find the mean proportional, we must at the same time attend to the two extremes and to the proportion which exists between these two in order to discover a new ratio by dividing the previous one; and this is a very different thing from finding a third term in continued proportion with two given numbers. I go forward likewise and examine whether, when the numbers 3 and 24 were given, it would have been equally easy to determine one of the two intermediate proportionals, viz. 6 and 12. But here still another sort of difficulty arises more involved than the previous ones, for on this occasion we have to attend not to one or two things only but to three, in order to discover the fourth. We may go still further and inquire whether if only 3 and 48 had been given it would have been still more difficult to discover one of the three mean proportionals, viz. 6, 12, and 24. At the first blush this indeed appears to be so; but immediately afterwards it comes to mind that this difficulty can be split up and lessened, if first of all we ask only for the mean proportional between 3 and 48, viz. 12, and then seek for the other mean proportional between 3 and 12, viz. 6, and the other between 12 and 48, viz. 24. Thus we have reduced the problem to the difficulty of the second type shown above.

These illustrations further lead me to note that the quest for knowledge about the same thing can traverse different routes, the one much more difficult and obscure than the other.

Thus to find these four continued proportionals, 3, 6, 12, and 24, if two consecutive numbers be assumed, e.g. 3 and 6, or 6 and 12, or 12 and 24, in order that we may discover the others, our task will be easy. In this case we shall say that the proposition to be discovered is directly examined. But if the two numbers given are alternates, like 3 and 12, or 6 and 24, which are to lead us to the discovery of the others, then we shall call this an indirect investigation of the first mode. Likewise if we are given two extremes like 3 and 24, in order to find out from these the intermediates 6 and 12, the investigation will be indirect and of the second mode. Thus I should be able to proceed further and deduce many other results from this example; but these will be sufficient, if the reader follows my meaning when I say that a proposition is directly deduced, or indirectly, and will reflect that from a knowledge of each of these matters that are simplest and primary, much may be discovered in other sciences by those who bring to them attentive thought and a power of sagacious analysis.

Rule VII: If we wish our science to be complete, those matters which promote the end we have in view must one and all be scrutinized by a movement of thought which is continuous and nowhere interrupted; they must also be included in an enumeration which is both adequate and methodical.

It is necessary to obey the injunctions of this rule if we hope to gain admission among the certain truths for those which, we have declared above, are not immediate deductions from primary and self-evident principles. For this deduction frequently involves such a long series of transitions from ground to consequent that when we come to the conclusion we have difficulty in recalling the whole of the route by which we have arrived at it. This is why I say that there must be a continuous movement of thought to make good this weakness of the memory. Thus, e.g. if I have first found out by separate mental operations what the relation is between the magnitudes A and B, then what between B and C, between C and D, and finally between D and E, that does not entail my seeing what the relation is between A and E, nor can the truths previously learned give me a precise knowledge of it unless I recall them all. To remedy this I would run them over from time to time, keeping the imagination moving continuously in such a way that while it is intuitively perceiving each fact it simultaneously passes on to the next; and this I would do until I had learned to pass from the first to the last so quickly, that no stage in the process was left to the care of the memory, but I seemed to have the whole in intuition before me at the same time. This method will both relieve the memory, diminish the sluggishness of our thinking, and definitely enlarge our mental capacity.

But we must add that this movement should nowhere be interrupted. Often people who attempt to deduce a conclusion too quickly and from remote principles do not trace the whole chain of intermediate conclusions with sufficient accuracy to prevent them from passing over many steps without due consideration. But it is certain that wherever the smallest link is left out the chain is broken and the whole of the certainty of the conclusion falls to the ground.

Here we maintain that an enumeration [of the steps in a proof] is required as well, if we wish to make our science complete. For resolving most problems other precepts are profitable, but enumeration alone will secure our always passing a true and certain judgment on whatsoever engages our attention; by means of it nothing at all will escape us, but we shall evidently have some knowledge of every step.

This enumeration or induction is thus a review or inventory of all those matters that have a bearing on the problem raised, which is so thorough and accurate that by its means we can clearly and with confidence conclude that we have omitted nothing by mistake.

Consequently as often as we have employed it, if the problem defies us, we shall at least be wiser in this respect, viz. that we are quite certain that we know of no way of resolving it. If it chance, as often it does, that we have been able to scan all the routes leading to it which lie open to the human intelligence, we shall be entitled boldly to assert that the solution of the problem lies outside the reach of human knowledge.

Furthermore we must note that by adequate enumeration or induction is only meant that method by which we may attain surer conclusions than by any other type of proof, with the exception of simple intuition. But when the knowledge of some matter cannot be reduced to this, we must cast aside all syllogistic fetters and employ induction, the only method left us, but one in which all confidence should be reposed. For whenever single facts have been immediately deduced the one from the other, they have been already reduced, if the inference was evident, to a true intuition. But if we infer any single thing from various and disconnected facts, often our intellectual capacity is not so great as to be able to embrace them all in a single intuition; in which case our mind should be content with the certitude attaching to this operation. It is in precisely similar fashion that though we cannot with one single gaze distinguish all the links of a lengthy chain, yet if we have seen the connection of each with its neighbour, we shall be entitled to say that we have seen how the first is connected with the last.

I have declared that this operation ought to be adequate, because it is often in danger of being defective and consequently exposed to error. For sometimes, even though in our enumeration we scrutinize many facts which are highly evident, yet if we omit the smallest step the chain is broken and the whole of the certitude of the conclusion falls to the ground. Sometimes also, even though all the facts are included in an accurate enumeration, the single steps are not distinguished from one another, and our knowledge of them all is thus only confused.

Further, while now the enumeration ought to be complete, now distinct, there are times when it need have neither of these characters; it was for this reason that I said only that it should be adequate. For if I want to prove by enumeration how many genera there are of corporeal things, or of those that in any way fall under the senses, I shall not assert that they are just so many and no more, unless I previously have become aware that I have included them all in my enumeration, and have distinguished them each separately from all the others. But if in the same way I wish to prove that the rational soul is not corporeal, I do not need a complete enumeration; it will be sufficient to include all bodies in certain collections in such a way as to be able to demonstrate that the rational soul has nothing to do with any of these. If, finally, I wish to show by enumeration that the area of a circle is greater than the area of all other figures whose perimeter is equal, there is no need for me to call in review all other figures; it is enough to demonstrate this of certain others in particular, in order to get thence by induction the same conclusion about all the others.

I added also that the enumeration ought to be methodical. This is both because we have no more serviceable remedy for the defects already instanced, than to scan all things in an orderly manner; and also because it often happens that if each single matter which concerns the quest in hand were to be investigated separately, no man's life would be long enough for the purpose, whether because they are far too many, or because it would chance that the same things had to be repeated too often. But if all these facts are arranged in the best order, they will for the most part be reduced to determinate classes, out of which it will be sufficient to take one example for exact inspection, or some one feature in a single case, or certain things rather than others, or at least we shall never have to waste our time in traversing the same ground twice. The advantage of this course is so great that often many particulars can, owing to a well devised arrangement, be gone over in a short space of time and with little trouble, though at first view the matter looked immense.

But this order which we employ in our enumerations can for the most part be varied and depends upon each man's judgment. For this reason, if we would elaborate it in our thought with greater penetration, we must remember what was said in our fifth proposition. There are also many of the trivial things of man's devising, in the discovery of which the whole method lies in the disposal of this order. Thus if you wish to construct a perfect anagram by the transposition of the letters of a name, there is no need to pass from the easy to the difficult, nor to distinguish absolute from relative. Here there is no place for these operations; it will be sufficient to adopt an order to be followed in the transpositions of the letters which we are to examine, such that the same arrangements are never handled twice over. The total number of transpositions should, e.g. be split up into definite classes, so that it may immediately appear in which there is the best hope of finding what is sought. In this way the task is often not tedious but merely child's play.

However, these three propositions should not be separated, because for the most part we have to think of them together, and all equally tend towards the perfecting of our method. There was no great reason for treating one before the other, and we have expounded them but briefly here. The reason for this is that in the rest of the treatise we have practically nothing else left for consideration. . . .

MEDITATIONS ON THE FIRST PHILOSOPHY

In Which the Existence of God, and the Real Distinction of Mind and Body, Are Demonstrated

MEDITATION I
Of the things of which we may doubt

Several years have now elapsed since I first became aware that I had accepted, even from my youth, many false opinions for true, and that consequently what I afterwards based on such principles was highly doubtful; and from that time I was convinced of the necessity of undertaking once in my life to rid myself of all the opinions I had adopted, and of commencing anew the work of building from the foundation, if I desired to establish a firm and abiding superstructure in the sciences. But as this enterprise appeared to me to be one of great magnitude, I waited until I had attained an age so mature as to leave me no hope that at any stage of life more advanced I should be better able to execute my design. On this account, I have delayed so long that I should henceforth consider I was doing wrong were I still to consume in deliberation any of the time that now remains for action. To-day, then,

Translated by John Veitch.

since I have opportunely freed my mind from all cares, [and am happily disturbed by no passions], and since I am in the secure possession of leisure in a peaceable retirement, I will at length apply myself earnestly and freely to the general overthrow of all my former opinions. But, to this end, it will not be necessary for me to show that the whole of these are false—a point, perhaps, which I shall never reach; but as even now my reason convinces me that I ought not the less carefully to withhold belief from what is not entirely certain and indubitable, than from what is manifestly false, it will be sufficient to justify the rejection of the whole if I shall find in each some ground for doubt. Nor for this purpose will it be necessary even to deal with each belief individually, which would be truly an endless labour; but, as the removal from below of the foundation necessarily involves the downfall of the whole edifice, I will at once approach the criticism of the principles on which all my former beliefs rested.

All that I have, up to this moment, accepted as possessed of the highest truth and certainty, I received either from or through the senses. I observed, however, that these sometimes misled us; and it is the part of prudence not to place absolute confidence in that by which we have even once been deceived.

But it may be said, perhaps, that, although the senses occasionally mislead us respecting minute objects, and such as are so far removed from us as to be beyond the reach of close observation, there are yet many other of their informations (presentations), of the truth of which it is manifestly impossible to doubt; as for example, that I am in this place, seated by the fire, clothed in a winter dressing-gown, that I hold in my hands this piece of paper, with other intimations of the same nature. But how could I deny that I possess these hands and this body, and withal escape being classed with persons in a state of insanity, whose brains are so disordered and clouded by dark bilious vapours as to cause them pertinaciously to assert that they are monarchs when they are in the greatest poverty; or clothed [in gold] and purple when destitute of any covering; or that their head is made of clay, their body of glass, or that they are gourds? I should certainly be not less insane than they, were I to regulate my procedure according to examples so extravagant.

Though this be true, I must nevertheless here consider that I am a man, and that, consequently, I am in the habit of sleeping, and representing to myself in dreams those same things, or even sometimes others less probable, which the insane think are presented to them in their waking moments. How often have I dreamt that I was in these familiar circumstances—that I was dressed, and occupied this place by the fire, when I was lying undressed in bed? At the present moment, however, I certainly look upon this paper with eyes wide awake; the head which I now move is not asleep; I extend this hand consciously and with express purpose, and I perceive it; the occurrences in sleep are not so distinct as all this. But I cannot forget that, at other times, I have been deceived in sleep by similar illusions; and, attentively considering those cases, I perceive so clearly that there exist no certain marks by which the state of waking can ever be distinguished from sleep, that I feel greatly astonished; and in amazement I almost persuade myself that I am now dreaming.

Let us suppose, then, that we are dreaming, and that all these particulars—namely, the opening of the eyes, the motion of the head, the forth-putting of the hands—are merely illusions; and even that we really possess neither an entire body nor hands such as we see. Nevertheless, it must be admitted at least that the objects which appear to us in sleep are, as it were, painted representations which could not have been formed unless in the likeness of realities; and, therefore, that those general objects, at all events,—namely, eyes, a head, hands, and an entire body—are not simply imaginary, but really existent. For, in truth, painters themselves, even when they study to represent sirens and satyrs by forms the most fantastic and extraordinary, cannot bestow upon them natures absolutely new, but can only make a certain medley of the members of different animals; or if they chance to imagine something so novel that nothing at all similar has ever been seen before, and such as is, therefore, purely fictitious and absolutely false, it is at least certain that the colours of which this is composed are real.

And on the same principle, although these general objects, viz. a body, eyes, a head, hands, and the like, be imaginary, we are nevertheless absolutely necessitated to admit the reality at least of some other objects still more simple and universal than these, of which, just as of certain real colours, all those images of things, whether true and real, or false and fantastic, that are found in our consciousness (*cogitatio*), are formed.

To this class of objects seem to belong corporeal nature in general and its extension; the figure of extended things, their quantity or magnitude, and their number, as also the place in, and the time during, which they exist, and other things of the same sort. We will not, therefore, perhaps reason illegitimately if we conclude from this that Physics, Astronomy, Medicine, and all the other sciences that have for their end the consideration of composite objects, are indeed of a doubtful character; but that Arithmetic, Geometry, and the other sciences of the same class, which regard merely the simplest and most general objects, and scarcely inquire whether or not these are really existent, contain somewhat that is certain and indubitable: for whether I am awake or dreaming, it remains true that two and three make five, and that a square has but four sides; nor does it seem possible that truths so apparent can ever fall under a suspicion of falsity [or incertitude].

Nevertheless, the belief that there is a God who is all-powerful, and who created me, such as I am, has, for a long time, obtained steady possession of my mind. How, then, do I know that he has not arranged that there should be neither earth, nor sky, nor any extended thing, nor figure, nor magnitude, nor place, providing at the same time, however, for [the rise in me of the perceptions of all these objects, and] the persuasion that these do not exist otherwise than as I perceive them? And further, as I sometimes think that others are in error respecting matters of which they believe themselves to possess a perfect knowledge, how do I know that I am not also deceived each time I add together two and three, or number the sides of a square, or form some judgment still more simple, if more simple indeed can be imagined? But perhaps Deity has not been willing that I should be thus deceived, for He is said to be supremely good. If, however, it were repugnant to the goodness of Deity to have created me subject to constant deception, it would seem likewise to be contrary to his goodness to allow me to be occasionally deceived; and yet it is clear that this is permitted. Some, indeed, might perhaps be found who would be disposed rather to deny the existence of a Being so powerful than to believe that there is nothing certain. But let us for the present refrain from opposing this opinion, and grant that all which is here said of a Deity is fabulous; nevertheless in whatever way it be supposed that I reached the state in which I exist, whether by fate, or chance, or by an endless series of antecedents and consequents, or by any other means, it is clear (since to be deceived and to err is a certain defect) that the probability of my being so imperfect as to be the constant victim of deception, will be increased exactly in proportion as the power possessed by the cause, to which they assign my origin, is lessened. To these reasonings I have assuredly nothing to reply, but am constrained at last to avow that there is nothing of all that I formerly believed to be true of which it is impossible to doubt, and that not through thoughtlessness or levity, but from cogent and maturely considered reasons; so that henceforward, if I desire to discover anything certain, I ought not the less carefully to refrain from assenting to those same opinions than to what might be shown to be manifestly false.

But it is not sufficient to have made these observations; care must be taken likewise to keep them in remembrance. For those old and customary opinions perpetually recur—long and familiar usage giving them the right of occupying my mind, even almost against my will, and subduing my belief; nor will I lose the habit of deferring to them and confiding in them so long as I shall consider them to be what in truth they are, viz., opinions to some extent doubtful, as I have already shown, but still highly probable, and such as it is much more reasonable to believe than deny. It is for this reason I am persuaded that I shall not be doing wrong, if, taking an opposite judgment of deliberate design, I become my own deceiver, by supposing, for a time, that all those opinions are entirely false and imaginary, until at length, having thus balanced my old by my new prejudices, my judgment shall no longer be turned aside by perverted usage from the path that may conduct to the perception of truth. For I am assured that, meanwhile, there will arise neither peril nor error from this course, and that I cannot for the present yield too much to distrust, since the end I now seek is not action but knowledge.

I will suppose, then, not that Deity, who is sovereignly good and the fountain of truth, but that some malignant demon, who is at once exceedingly potent and deceitful, has employed all his artifice to deceive me; I will suppose that the sky, the air, the earth, colours, figures, sounds, and all external things, are nothing better than the illusions of dreams, by means of which this being has laid snares for my credulity; I will consider myself as without hands, eyes, flesh, blood, or any of the senses, and as falsely believing that I am possessed of these; I will continue resolutely fixed in this belief, and if indeed by this means it be not in my power to arrive at the knowledge of truth, I shall at least do what is in my power, viz., [suspend my judgment], and guard with settled purpose against giving my assent to what is false, and being imposed upon by this deceiver, whatever be his power and artifice.

But this undertaking is arduous, and a certain indolence insensibly leads me back to my ordinary course of life; and just as the captive, who, perchance, was enjoying in his dreams an imaginary liberty, when he begins to suspect that it is but a vision, dreads awakening, and conspires with the agreeable illusions that the deception may be prolonged; so I, of my own accord, fall back into the train of my former beliefs, and fear to arouse myself from my slumber, lest the time of laborious wakefulness that would succeed this quiet rest, in place of bringing any light of day, should prove inadequate to dispel the darkness that will arise from the difficulties that have now been raised.

MEDITATION II
Of the nature of the human mind; and that it is more easily known than the body

The Meditation of yesterday has filled my mind with so many doubts, that it is no longer in my power to forget them. Nor do I see, meanwhile, any principle on which they can be resolved; and, just as if I had fallen all of a sudden into very deep water, I am so greatly disconcerted as to be unable either to plant my feet firmly on the bottom or sustain myself by swimming on the surface. I will, nevertheless, make an effort, and try anew the same path on which I had entered yesterday, that is, proceed by casting aside all that admits of the slightest doubt, not less than if I had discovered it to be absolutely false; and I will continue always in this track until I shall find something that is certain, or at least, if I can do nothing more, until I shall know with certainty that there is nothing certain. Archimedes, that he might transport the entire globe from the place it occupied to another, demanded only a point that was firm and immoveable; so also, I shall be entitled to entertain the highest expectations, if I am fortunate enough to discover only one thing that is certain and indubitable.

I suppose, accordingly, that all the things which I see are false (fictitious); I believe that none of those objects which my fallacious memory represents ever existed; I suppose that I possess no senses; I believe that body, figure, extension, motion, and place are merely fictions of my mind. What is there, then, that can be esteemed true? Perhaps this only, that there is absolutely nothing certain.

But how do I know that there is not something different altogether from the objects I have now enumerated, of which it is impossible to entertain the slightest doubt? Is there not a God, or some being, by whatever name I may designate him, who causes these thoughts to arise in my mind? But why suppose such a being, for it may be I myself am capable of producing them? Am I, then, at least not something? But I before denied that I possessed senses or a body; I hesitate, however, for what follows from that? Am I so dependent on the body and the senses that without these I cannot exist? But I had the persuasion that there was absolutely nothing in the world, that there was no sky and no earth, neither minds nor bodies; was I not, therefore, at the same time, persuaded that I did not exist? Far from it; I assuredly existed, since I was persuaded. But there is I know not what being, who is possessed at once of the highest power and the deepest cunning, who is constantly employing all his ingenuity in deceiving me. Doubtless, then, I exist, since I am deceived; and, let him deceive me as he may, he can never bring it about that I am nothing, so long as I shall be conscious that I am something. So that it must, in fine, be maintained, all things being maturely and carefully considered, that this proposition (*pronunciatum*) I am, I exist, is necessarily true each time it is expressed by me, or conceived in my mind.

But I do not yet know with sufficient clearness what I am, though assured that I am; and hence, in the next place, I must take care, lest perchance I inconsiderately substitute some other object in room of what is properly myself, and thus wander from truth, even in that knowledge (cognition) which I hold to be of all others the most certain and evident. For this reason, I will now consider anew what I formerly believed myself to be, before I entered on the present train of thought; and of my previous opinion I will retrench all that can in the least be invalidated by the grounds of doubt I have adduced, in order that there may at length remain nothing but what is certain and indubitable. What then did I formerly think I was? Undoubtedly I judged that I was a man. But what is a man? Shall I say a rational animal? Assuredly not; for it would be necessary forthwith to inquire into what is meant by animal, and what by rational, and thus, from a single question, I should insensibly glide into others, and these more difficult than the first; nor do I now possess enough of leisure to warrant me in wasting my time amid subtleties of this sort. I prefer here to attend to the thoughts that sprang up of themselves in my mind, and were inspired by my own nature alone, when I applied myself to the consideration of what I was. In the first place, then, I thought that I possessed a countenance, hands, arms, and all the fabric of members that appears in a corpse, and which I called by the name of body. It further occurred to me that I was nourished, that I walked, perceived, and thought, and all those actions I referred to the soul; but what the soul itself was I either did not stay to consider, or, if I did, I imagined that it was something extremely rare and subtle, like wind, or flame, or ether, spread through my grosser parts. As regarded the body, I did not even doubt of its nature, but thought I distinctly knew it, and if I had wished to describe it according to the notions I then entertained, I should have explained myself in this manner: By body I understand all that can be terminated by a certain figure; that can be comprised in a certain place, and so fill a certain space as therefrom to exclude every other body; that can be perceived either by touch, sight, hearing, taste, or smell; that can be moved in different ways, not indeed of itself, but by something foreign to it by which it is touched [and from which it receives the impression]; for the power of self-motion, as likewise that of perceiving and thinking, I held as by no means pertaining to the nature of body; on the contrary, I was somewhat astonished to find such faculties existing in some bodies.

But [as to myself, what can I now say that I am], since I suppose there exists an extremely powerful, and, if I may so speak, malignant being, whose whole endeavours are directed towards deceiving me? Can I affirm that I possess any one of all those attributes of which I have lately spoken as belonging to the nature of body? After attentively considering them in my own mind, I find none of them that can properly be said to belong to myself. To recount them were idle and tedious. Let us pass, then, to the attributes of the soul. The first mentioned were the powers of nutrition and walking; but, if it be true that I have no body, it is true likewise that I am capable neither of walking nor of being nourished. Perception is another attribute of the soul; but perception too is impossible without the body: besides, I have frequently, during sleep, believed that I perceived objects which I afterwards observed I did not in reality perceive. Thinking is another attribute of the soul; and here I discover what properly belongs to myself. This alone is inseparable from me. I am—I exist: this is certain; but how often? As often as I think; for perhaps it would even happen, if I should wholly cease to think, that I should at the same time altogether cease to be. I now admit nothing that is not necessarily true: I am therefore, precisely speaking, only a thinking thing, that is, a mind (*mens sive animus*), understanding, or reason,—terms whose signification was before unknown to me. I am, however, a real thing, and really existent; but what thing? The answer was, a thinking thing. The question now arises, am I aught besides? I will stimulate my imagination with a view to discovering whether I am not still something more than a thinking being. Now it is plain I am not the assemblage of members called the human body; I am not a thin and penetrating air diffused through all these members, or wind, or flame, or vapour, or breath, or any of all the things I can imagine; for I supposed that all these were not, and, without changing the supposition, I find that I still feel assured of my existence.

But it is true, perhaps, that those very things which I suppose to be non-existent, because they are unknown to me, are not in truth different from myself whom I know. This is a point I cannot determine, and do not now enter into any dispute regarding it. I can only judge of things that are known to me: I am conscious that I exist, and I who know that I exist inquire into what I am. It is, however, perfectly certain that the knowledge of my existence, thus precisely taken, is not dependent on things, the existence of which is as yet unknown to me: and consequently it is not dependent on any of the things I can feign in imagination. Moreover, the phrase itself, I frame an image (*effingo*), reminds me of my error; for I should in truth frame one if I were to imagine myself to be anything, since to imagine is nothing more than to contemplate the figure or image of a corporeal thing; but I already know that I exist, and that it is possible at the same time that all those images, and in general all that relates to the nature of body, are merely dreams [or chimeras]. From this I discover that it is not more reasonable to say, I will excite my imagination that I may know more distinctly what I am, than to express myself as follows: I am now awake, and perceive something real; but because my perception is not sufficiently clear, I will of express purpose go to sleep that my dreams may represent to me the object of my perception with more truth and clearness. And, therefore, I know that nothing of all that I can embrace in imagination belongs to the knowledge which I have of myself, and that there is need to recall with the utmost care the mind from this mode of thinking, that it may be able to know its own nature with perfect distinctness.

But what, then, am I? A thinking thing, it has been said. But what is a thinking thing? It is a thing that doubts, understands, [conceives], affirms, denies, wills, refuses, that imagines also, and perceives. Assuredly it is not little, if all these properties belong to my nature. But why should they not belong to it? Am I not that very being who now doubts of almost everything; who, for all that, understands and conceives certain things; who affirms one alone as true, and denies the others; who desires to know more of them, and does not wish to be deceived; who imagines many things, sometimes even despite his will; and is likewise percipient of many, as if through the medium of the senses. Is there nothing of all this as true as that I am, even although I should be always dreaming, and although he who gave me being employed all his ingenuity to deceive me? Is there also any one of these attributes that can be properly distinguished from my thought, or that can be said to be separate from myself? For it is of itself so evident that it is I who doubt, I who understand, and I who desire, that it is here unnecessary to add anything by way of rendering it more clear. And I am as certainly the same being who imagines; for, although it may be (as I before supposed) that nothing I imagine is true, still the power of imagination does not cease really to exist in me and to form part of my thought. In fine, I am the same being who perceives, that is, who apprehends certain objects as by the organs of sense, since, in truth, I see light, hear a noise, and feel heat. But it will be said that these presentations are false, and that I am dreaming. Let it be so. At all events it is certain that I seem to see light, hear a noise, and feel heat; this cannot be false, and this is what in me is properly called perceiving (*sentire*), which is nothing else than thinking. From this I begin to know what I am with somewhat greater clearness and distinctness than heretofore.

But, nevertheless, it still seems to me, and I cannot help believing, that corporeal things, whose images are formed by thought, [which fall under the senses], and are examined by the same, are known with much greater distinctness than that I know not what part of myself which is not imaginable; although, in truth, it may seem strange to say that I know and comprehend with greater distinctness things whose existence appears to me doubtful, that are unknown, and do not belong to me, than others of whose reality I am persuaded, that are known to me, and appertain to my proper nature; in a word, than myself. But I see clearly what is the state of the case. My mind is apt to wander, and will not yet submit to be restrained within the limits of truth. Let us therefore leave the mind to itself once more, and, according to it every kind of liberty, [permit it to consider the objects that appear to it from without], in order that, having afterwards withdrawn it from these gently and opportunely, [and fixed it on the consideration of its being and the properties it finds in itself], it may then be the more easily controlled.

Let us now accordingly consider the objects that are commonly thought to be [the most easily, and likewise] the most distinctly known, viz., the bodies we touch and see; not, indeed, bodies in general, for these general notions are usually somewhat more confused, but one body in particular. Take, for example, this piece of wax; it is quite fresh, having been but recently taken from the bee-hive; it has not yet lost the sweetness of the honey it contained; it still retains somewhat of the odour of the flowers from which it was gathered; its colour, figure, size, are apparent (to the sight); it is hard, cold, easily handled; and sounds when struck upon with the finger. In fine, all that contributes to make a body as distinctly known as possible, is found in the one before us. But, while I am speaking, let it be placed near the fire—what remained of the taste exhales, the smell evaporates, the colour changes, its figure is destroyed, its size increases, it becomes liquid, it grows hot, it can hardly be handled, and, although struck upon, it emits no sound. Does the same wax still remain after this change? It must be admitted that it does remain; no one doubts it, or judges otherwise. What, then, was it I knew with so much distinctness in the piece of wax? Assuredly, it could be nothing of all that I observed by means of the senses, since all the things that fell under taste, smell, sight, touch, and hearing are changed, and yet the same wax remains. It was perhaps what I now think, viz., that this wax was neither the sweetness of honey, the pleasant odour of flowers, the whiteness, the figure, nor the sound, but only a body that a little before appeared to me conspicuous under these forms, and which is now perceived under others. But, to speak precisely, what is it that I imagine when I think of it in this way? Let it be attentively considered, and, retrenching all that does not belong to the wax, let us see what remains. There certainly remains nothing, except something extended, flexible, and movable. But what is meant by flexible and movable? Is it not that I imagine that the piece of wax, being round, is capable of becoming square, or of passing from a square into a triangular figure? Assuredly such is not the case, because I conceive that it admits of an infinity of similar changes; and I am, moreover, unable to compass this infinity by imagination, and consequently this conception which I have of the wax is not the product of the faculty of imagination. But what now is this extension? Is it not also unknown? for it becomes greater when the wax is melted, greater when it is boiled, and greater still when the heat increases; and I should not conceive [clearly and] according to truth, the wax as it is, if I did not suppose that the piece we are considering admitted even of a wider variety of extension than I ever imagined. I must, therefore, admit that I cannot even comprehend by imagination what the piece of wax is, and that it is the mind alone (*mens,* Lat., *entendement,* F.) which perceives it. I speak of one piece in particular; for, as to wax in general, this is still more evident. But what is the piece of wax that can be perceived only by the [understanding or] mind? It is certainly the same which I see, touch, imagine; and, in fine, it is the same which, from the beginning, I believed it to be. But (and this it is of moment to observe) the perception of it is neither an act of sight, of touch, nor of imagination, and never was either of these, though it might formerly seem so, but is simply an intuition (*inspectio*) of the mind, which may be imperfect and confused, as it formerly was, or very clear and distinct, as it is at present, according as the attention is more or less directed to the elements which it contains, and of which it is composed.

But, meanwhile, I feel greatly astonished when I observe [the weakness of my mind, and] its proneness to error. For although, without at all giving expression to what I think, I consider all this in my own mind, words yet occasionally impede my progress, and I am almost led into error by the terms of ordinary language. We say, for example, that we see the same wax when it is before us, and not that we judge it to be the same from its retaining the same colour and figure: whence I should forthwith be disposed to conclude that the wax is known by the act of sight, and not by the intuition of the mind alone, were it not for the analogous instance of human beings passing on in the street below, as observed from a window. In this case I do not fail to say that I see the men themselves, just as I say that I see the wax; and yet what do I see from the window beyond hats and cloaks that might cover artificial machines, whose motions might be determined by springs? But I judge that there are human beings from these appearances, and thus I comprehend, by the faculty of judgment alone which is in the mind, what I believed I saw with my eyes.

The man who makes it his aim to rise to knowledge superior to the common, ought to be ashamed to seek occasions of doubting from the vulgar forms of speech: instead, therefore, of doing this, I shall proceed with the matter in hand, and inquire whether I had a clearer and more perfect perception of the piece of wax when I first saw it, and when I thought I knew it by means of the external sense itself, or, at all events, by the common sense (*sensus communis*), as it is called, that is, by the imaginative faculty; or whether I rather apprehend it more clearly at present, after having examined with greater care, both what it is, and in what way it can be known. It would certainly be ridiculous to entertain any doubt on this point. For what, in that first perception, was there distinct? What did I perceive which any animal might not have perceived? But when I distinguish the wax from its exterior forms, and when, as if I had stripped it of its vestments, I consider it quite naked, it is certain, although some error may still be found in my judgment, that I cannot, nevertheless, thus apprehend it without possessing a human mind.

But, finally, what shall I say of the mind itself, that is, of myself? for as yet I do not admit that I am anything but mind. What, then! I who seem to possess so distinct an apprehension of the piece of wax,—do I not know myself, both with greater truth and certitude, and also much more distinctly and clearly? For if I judge that the wax exists because I see it, it assuredly follows, much more evidently, that I myself am or exist, for the same reason: for it is possible that what I see may not in truth be wax, and that I do not even possess eyes with which to see anything; but it cannot be that when I see, or, which comes to the same thing, when I think I see, I myself who think am nothing. So likewise, if I judge that the wax exists because I touch it, it will still also follow that I am; and if I determine that my imagination, or any other cause, whatever it be, persuades me of the existence of the wax, I will still draw the same conclusion. And what is here remarked of the piece of wax, is applicable to all the other things that are external to me. And further, if the [notion or] perception of wax appeared to me more precise and distinct, after that not only sight and touch, but many other causes besides, rendered it manifest to my apprehension, with how much greater distinctness must I now know myself, since all the reasons that contribute to the knowledge of the nature of wax, or of any body whatever, manifest still better the nature of my mind? And there are besides so many other things in the mind itself that contribute to the illustration of its nature, that those dependent on the body, to which I have here referred, scarcely merit to be taken into account.

But, in conclusion, I find I have insensibly reverted to the point I desired; for, since it is now manifest to me that bodies themselves are not properly perceived by the senses nor by the faculty of imagination, but by the intellect alone; and since they are not perceived because they are seen and touched, but only because they are understood [or rightly comprehended by thought], I readily discover that there is nothing more easily or clearly apprehended than my own mind. But because it is difficult to rid one's self so promptly of an opinion to which one has been long accustomed, it will be desirable to tarry for some time at this stage, that, by long continued meditation, I may more deeply impress upon my memory this new knowledge.

MEDITATION III
Of God: that He exists

I will now close my eyes, I will stop my ears, I will turn away my senses from their objects, I will even efface from my consciousness all the images of corporeal things; or at least, because this can hardly be accomplished, I will consider them as empty and false; and thus, holding converse only with myself, and closely examining my nature, I will endeavour to obtain by degrees a more intimate and familiar knowledge of myself. I am a thinking (conscious) thing, that is, a being who doubts, affirms, denies, knows a few objects, and is ignorant of many,—[who loves, hates], wills, refuses,—who imagines likewise, and perceives; for, as I before remarked, although the things which I perceive or imagine are perhaps nothing at all apart from me [and in themselves], I am nevertheless assured that those modes of consciousness which I call perceptions and imaginations, in as far only as they are modes of consciousness, exist in me. And in the little I have said I think I have summed up all that I really know, or at least all that up to this time I was aware I knew. Now, as I am endeavouring to extend my knowledge more widely, I will use circumspection, and consider with care whether I can still discover in myself anything further which I have not yet hitherto observed. I am certain that I am a thinking thing; but do I not therefore likewise know what is required to render me certain of a truth? In this first knowledge, doubtless, there is nothing that gives me assurance of its truth except the clear and distinct perception of what I affirm, which would not indeed be sufficient to give me the assurance that what I say is true, if it could ever happen that anything I thus clearly and distinctly perceived should prove false; and accordingly it seems to me that I may now take as a general rule, that all that is very clearly and distinctly apprehended (conceived) is true.

Nevertheless I before received and admitted many things as wholly certain and manifest, which yet I afterwards found to be doubtful. What, then, were those? They were the earth, the sky, the stars, and all the other objects which I was in the habit of perceiving by the senses. But what was it that I clearly [and distinctly] perceived in them? Nothing more than that the ideas and the thoughts of those objects were presented to my mind. And even now I do not deny that these ideas are found in my mind. But there was yet another thing which I affirmed, and which, from having been accustomed to believe it, I thought I clearly perceived, although, in truth, I did not perceive it at all; I mean the existence of objects external to me, from which those ideas proceeded, and to which they had a perfect resemblance; and it was here I was mistaken, or if I judged correctly, this assuredly was not to be traced to any knowledge I possessed (the force of my perception, Lat.).

But when I considered any matter in arithmetic and geometry, that was very simple and easy, as, for example, that two and three added together make five, and things of this sort, did I not view them with at least sufficient clearness to warrant me in affirming their truth? Indeed, if I afterwards judged that we ought to doubt of these things, it was for no other reason than because it occurred to me that a God might perhaps have given me such a nature as that I should be deceived, even respecting the matters that appeared to me the most evidently true. But as often as this preconceived opinion of the sovereign power of a God presents itself to my mind, I am constrained to admit that it is easy for him, if he wishes it, to cause me to err, even in matters where I think I possess the highest evidence; and, on the other hand, as often as I direct my attention to things which I think I apprehend with great clearness, I am so persuaded of their truth that I naturally break out into expressions such as these: Deceive me who may, no one will yet ever be able to bring it about that I am not, so long as I shall be conscious that I am, or at any future time cause it to be true that I have never been, it being now true that I am, or make two and three more or less than five, in supposing which, and other like absurdities, I discover a manifest contradiction.

And in truth, as I have no ground for believing that Deity is deceitful, and as, indeed, I have not even considered the reasons by which the existence of a Deity of any kind is established, the ground of doubt that rests only on this supposition is very slight, and, so to speak, metaphysical. But, that I may be able wholly to remove it, I must inquire whether there is a God, as soon as an opportunity of doing so shall present itself; and if I find that there is a God, I must examine likewise whether he can be a deceiver: for, without the knowledge of these two truths, I do not see that I can ever be certain of anything. And that I may be enabled to examine this without interrupting the order of meditation I have proposed to myself [which is, to pass by degrees from the notions that I shall find first in my mind to those I shall afterwards discover in it], it is necessary at this stage to divide all my thoughts into certain classes, and to consider in which of these classes truth and error are, strictly speaking, to be found.

Of my thoughts some are, as it were, images of things, and to these alone properly belongs the name *idea;* as when I think [represent to my mind] a man, a chimera, the sky, an angel, or God. Others, again, have certain other forms; as when I will, fear, affirm, or deny, I always, indeed, apprehend something as the object of my thought, but I also embrace in thought something more than the representation of the object; and of this class of thoughts some are called volitions or affections, and others judgments.

Now, with respect to ideas, if these are considered only in themselves, and are not referred to any object beyond them, they cannot, properly speaking, be false; for, whether I imagine a goat or a chimera, it is not less true that I imagine the one than the other. Nor need we fear that falsity may exist in the will or affections; for, although I may desire objects that are wrong, and even that never existed, it is still true that I desire them. There thus only remain our judgments, in which we must take diligent heed that we be not deceived. But the chief and most ordinary error that arises in them consists in judging that the ideas which are in us are like or conformed to the things that are external to us; for assuredly, if we but considered the ideas themselves as certain modes of our thought (consciousness), without referring them to anything beyond, they would hardly afford any occasion of error.

But, among these ideas, some appear to me to be innate, others adventitious, and others to be made by myself (factitious); for, as I have the power of conceiving what is called a thing, or a truth, or a thought, it seems to me that I hold this power from no other source than my own nature; but if I now hear a noise, if I see the sun, or if I feel heat, I have all along judged that these sensations proceeded from certain objects existing out of myself; and, in fine, it appears to me that sirens, hippogryphs, and the like, are inventions of my own mind. But I may even perhaps come to be of opinion that all my ideas are of the class which I call adventitious, or that they are all innate, or that they are all factitious, for I have not yet clearly discovered their true origin; and what I have here principally to do is to consider, with reference to those that appear to come from certain objects without me, what grounds there are for thinking them like these objects.

The first of these grounds is that it seems to me I am so taught by nature; and the second that I am conscious that those ideas are not dependent on my will, and therefore not on myself, for they are frequently presented to me against my will,—as at present, whether I will or not, I feel heat; and I am thus persuaded that this sensation or idea (*sensum vel ideam*) of heat is produced in me by something different from myself, viz., by the heat of the fire by which I sit. And it is very reasonable to suppose that this object impresses me with its own likeness rather than any other thing.

But I must consider whether these reasons are sufficiently strong and convincing. When I speak of being taught by nature in this matter, I understand by the word nature only a certain spontaneous impetus that impels me to believe in a resemblance between ideas and their objects, and not a natural light that affords a knowledge of its truth. But these two things are widely different; for what the natural light shows to be true can be in no degree doubtful, as, for example, that I am because I doubt, and other truths of the like kind: inasmuch as I possess no other faculty whereby to distinguish truth from error, which can teach me the falsity of what the natural light declares to be true, and which is equally trustworthy; but with respect to [seemingly] natural impulses, I have observed, when the question related to the choice of right or wrong in action, that they frequently led me to take the worse part; nor do I see that I have any better ground for following them in what relates to truth and error. Then, with respect to the other reason, which is that because these ideas do not depend on my will, they must arise from objects existing without me, I do not find it more convincing than the former; for, just as those natural impulses, of which I have lately spoken, are found in me, notwithstanding that they are not always in harmony with my will, so likewise it may be that I possess some power not sufficiently known to myself capable of producing ideas without the aid of external objects, and, indeed, it has always hitherto appeared to me that they are formed during sleep, by some power of this nature, without the aid of aught external. And, in fine, although I should grant that they proceeded from those objects, it is not a necessary consequence that they must be like them. On the contrary, I have observed, in a number of instances, that there was a great difference between the object and its idea. Thus, for example, I find in my mind two wholly diverse ideas of the sun; the one, by which it appears to me extremely small, draws its origin from the senses, and should be placed in the class of adventitious ideas; the other, by which it seems to be many times larger than the whole earth, is taken up on astronomical grounds, that is, elicited from certain notions born with me, or is framed by myself in some other manner. These two ideas cannot certainly both resemble the same sun; and reason teaches me that the one which seems to have immediately emanated from it is the most unlike. And these things sufficiently prove that hitherto it has not been from a certain and deliberate judgment, but only from a sort of blind impulse, that I believed in the existence of certain things different from myself, which, by the organs of sense, or by whatever other means it might be, conveyed their ideas or images into my mind [and impressed it with their likenesses].

But there is still another way of inquiring whether, of the objects whose ideas are in my mind, there are any that exist out of me. If ideas are taken in so far only as they are certain modes of consciousness, I do not remark any difference or inequality among them, and all seem, in the same manner, to proceed from myself; but, considering them as images, of which one represents one thing and another a different, it is evident that a great diversity obtains among them. For, without doubt, those that represent substances are something more, and contain in themselves, so to speak, more objective reality [that is, participate by representation in higher degrees of being or perfection], than those that represent only modes or accidents; and again, the idea by which I conceive a God [sovereign], eternal, infinite, [immutable], all-knowing, all-powerful, and the creator of all things that are out of himself,—this, I say, has certainly in it more objective reality than those ideas by which finite substances are represented.

Now, it is manifest by the natural light that there must at least be as much reality in the efficient and total cause as in its effect; for whence can the effect draw its reality if not from its cause? and how could the cause communicate to it this reality unless it possessed it in itself? And hence it follows, not only that what is cannot be produced by what is not, but likewise that the more perfect,—in other words, that which contains in itself more reality,—cannot be the effect of the less perfect: and this is not only evidently true of those effects, whose reality is actual or formal, but likewise of ideas, whose reality is only considered as objective. Thus, for example, the stone that is not yet in existence, not only cannot now commence to be, unless it be produced by that which possesses in itself, formally or eminently, all that enters into its composition, [in other words, by that which contains in itself the same properties that are in the stone, or others superior to them]; and heat can only be produced in a subject that was before devoid of it, by a cause that is of an order [degree or kind], at least as perfect as heat; and so of the others. But further, even the idea of the heat, or of the stone, cannot exist in me unless it be put there by a cause that contains, at least, as much reality as I conceive existent in the heat or in the stone: for, although that cause may not transmit into my idea anything of its actual or formal reality, we ought not on this account to imagine that it is less real; but we ought to consider that, [as every idea is a work of the mind], its nature is such as of itself to demand no other formal reality than that which it borrows from our consciousness, of which it is but a mode, [that is, a manner or way of thinking]. But in order that an idea may contain this objective reality rather than that, it must doubtless derive it from some cause in which is found at least as much formal reality as the idea contains of objective; for, if we suppose that there is found in an idea anything which was not in its cause, it must of course derive this from nothing. But, however imperfect may be the mode of existence by which a thing is objectively [or by representation] in the understanding by its idea, we certainly cannot, for all that, allege that this mode of existence is nothing, nor, consequently, that the idea owes its origin to nothing. Nor must it be imagined that, since the reality which is considered in these ideas is only objective, the same reality need not be formally (actually) in the causes of these ideas, but only objectively: for, just as the mode of existing objectively belongs to ideas by their peculiar nature, so likewise the mode of existing formally appertains to the causes of these ideas (at least to the first and principal), by their peculiar nature. And although an idea may give rise to another idea, this regress cannot, nevertheless, be infinite; we must in the end reach a first idea, the cause of which is, as it were, the archetype in which all the reality [or perfection] that is found objectively [or by representation] in these ideas is contained formally [and in act]. I am thus clearly taught by the natural light that ideas exist in me as pictures or images, which may in truth readily fall short of the perfection of the objects from which they are taken, but can never contain anything greater or more perfect.

And in proportion to the time and care with which I examine all those matters, the conviction of their truth brightens and becomes distinct. But, to sum up, what conclusion shall I draw from it all? It is this;—if the objective reality [or perfection] of any one of my ideas be such as clearly to convince me, that this same reality exists in me neither formally nor eminently, and if, as follows from this, I myself cannot be the cause of it, it is a necessary consequence that I am not alone in the world, but that there is besides myself some other being who exists as the cause of that idea; while, on the contrary, if no such idea be found in my mind, I shall have no sufficient ground of assurance of the existence of any other being besides myself; for, after a most careful search, I have, up to this moment, been unable to discover any other ground.

But, among these my ideas, besides that which represents myself, respecting which there can be here no difficulty, there is one that represents a God; others that represent corporeal and inanimate things; others angels; others animals; and, finally, there are some that represent men like myself. But with respect to the ideas that represent other men, or animals, or angels, I can easily suppose that they were formed by the mingling and composition of the other ideas which I have of myself, of corporeal things, and of God, although there were, apart from myself, neither men, animals, nor angels. And with regard to the ideas of corporeal objects, I never discovered in them anything so great or excellent which I myself did not appear capable of originating; for, by considering these ideas closely and scrutinising them individually, in the same way that I yesterday examined the idea of wax, I find that there is but little in them that is clearly and distinctly perceived. As belonging to the class of things that are clearly apprehended, I recognise the following, viz., magnitude or extension in length, breadth, and depth; figure, which results from the termination of extension; situation, which bodies of diverse figures preserve with reference to each other; and motion or the change of situation; to which may be added substance, duration, and number. But with regard to light, colours, sounds, odours, tastes, heat, cold, and the other tactile qualities, they are thought with so much obscurity and confusion, that I cannot determine even whether they are true or false; in other words, whether or not the ideas I have of these qualities are in truth the ideas of real objects. For although I before remarked that it is only in judgments that formal falsity, or falsity properly so called, can be met with, there may nevertheless be found in ideas a certain material falsity, which arises when they represent what is nothing as if it were something. Thus, for example, the ideas I have of cold and heat are so far from being clear and distinct, that I am unable from them to discover whether cold is only the privation of heat, or heat the privation of cold; or whether they are not real qualities: and since, ideas being as it were images, there can be none that does not seem to us to represent some object, the idea which represents cold as something real and positive will not improperly be called false, if it be correct to say that cold is nothing but a privation of heat; and so in other cases. To ideas of this kind, indeed, it is not necessary that I should assign any author besides myself: for if they are false, that is, represent objects that are unreal, the natural light teaches me that they proceed from nothing; in other words, that they are in me only because something is wanting to the perfection of my nature; but if these ideas are true, yet because they exhibit to me so little reality that I cannot even distinguish the object represented from non-being, I do not see why I should not be the author of them.

With reference to those ideas of corporeal things that are clear and distinct, there are some which, as appears to me, might have been taken from the idea I have of myself, as those of substance, duration, number, and the like. For when I think that a stone is a substance, or a thing capable of existing of itself, and that I am likewise a substance, although I conceive that I am a thinking and non-extended thing, and that the stone, on the contrary, is extended and unconscious, there being thus the greatest diversity between the two concepts,—yet these two ideas seem to have this in common that they both represent substances. In the same way, when I think of myself as now existing, and recollect besides that I existed some time ago, and when I am conscious of various thoughts whose number I know, I then acquire the ideas of duration and number, which I can afterwards transfer to as many objects as I please. With respect to the other qualities that go to make up the ideas of corporeal objects, viz., extension, figure, situation, and motion, it is true that they are not formally in me, since I am merely a thinking being; but because they are only certain modes of substance, and because I myself am a substance, it seems possible that they may be contained in me eminently.

There only remains, therefore, the idea of God, in which I must consider whether there is anything that cannot be supposed to originate with myself. By the name God, I understand a substance infinite, [eternal, immutable], independent, all-knowing, all-powerful, and by which I myself, and every other thing that exists, if any such there be, were created. But these properties are so great and excellent, that the more attentively I consider them the less I feel persuaded that the idea I have of them owes its origin to myself alone. And thus it is absolutely necessary to conclude, from all that I have before said, that God exists: for though the idea of substance be in my mind owing to this, that I myself am a substance, I should not, however, have the idea of an infinite substance, seeing I am a finite being, unless it were given me by some substance in reality infinite.

And I must not imagine that I do not apprehend the infinite by a true idea, but only by the negation of the finite, in the same way that I comprehend repose and darkness by the negation of motion and light: since, on the contrary, I clearly perceive that there is more reality in the infinite substance than in the finite, and therefore that in some way I possess the perception (notion) of the infinite before that of the finite, that is, the perception of God before that of myself, for how could I know that I doubt, desire, or that something is wanting to me, and that I am not wholly perfect, if I possessed no idea of a being more perfect than myself, by comparison of which I knew the deficiencies of my nature?

And it cannot be said that this idea of God is perhaps materially false, and consequently that it may have arisen from nothing, [in other words, that it may exist in me from my imperfection], as I before said of the ideas of heat and cold, and the like: for, on the contrary, as this idea is very clear and distinct, and contains in itself more objective reality than any other, there can be no one of itself more true, or less open to the suspicion of falsity.

The idea, I say, of a being supremely perfect, and infinite, is in the highest degree true; for although, perhaps, we may imagine that such a being does not exist, we cannot, nevertheless, suppose that his idea represents nothing real, as I have already said of the idea of cold. It is likewise clear and distinct in the highest degree, since whatever the mind clearly and distinctly conceives as real or true, and as implying any perfection, is contained entire in this idea. And this is true, nevertheless, although I do not comprehend the infinite, and although there may be in God an infinity of things that I cannot comprehend, nor perhaps even compass by thought in any way; for it is of the nature of the infinite that it should not be comprehended by the finite; and it is enough that I rightly understand this, and judge that all which I clearly perceive, and in which I know there is some perfection, and perhaps also an infinity of properties of which I am ignorant, are formally or eminently in God, in order that the idea I have of him may become the most true, clear, and distinct of all the ideas in my mind.

But perhaps I am something more than I suppose myself to be, and it may be that all those perfections which I attribute to God, in some way exist potentially in me, although they do not yet show themselves, and are not reduced to act. Indeed, I am already conscious that my knowledge is being increased [and perfected] by degrees; and I see nothing to prevent it from thus gradually increasing to infinity, nor any reason why, after such increase and perfection, I should not be able thereby to acquire all the other perfections of the Divine nature; nor, in fine, why the power I possess of acquiring those perfections, if it really now exist in me, should not be sufficient to produce the ideas of them. Yet, on looking more closely into the matter, I discover that this cannot be; for, in the first place, although it were true that my knowledge daily acquired new degrees of perfection, and although there were potentially in my nature much that was not as yet actually in it, still all these excellences make not the slightest approach to the idea I have of the Deity, in whom there is no perfection merely potentially [but all actually] existent; for it is even an unmistakable token of imperfection in my knowledge, that it is augmented by degrees. Further, although my knowledge increase more and more, nevertheless I am not, therefore, induced to think that it will ever be actually infinite, since it can never reach that point beyond which it shall be incapable of further increase. But I conceive God as actually infinite, so that nothing can be added to his perfection. And, in fine, I readily perceive that the objective being of an idea cannot be produced by a being that is merely potentially existent, which, properly speaking, is nothing, but only by a being existing formally or actually.

And, truly, I see nothing in all that I have now said which it is not easy for any one, who shall carefully consider it, to discern by the natural light; but when I allow my attention in some degree to relax, the vision of my mind being obscured, and, as it were, blinded by the images of sensible objects, I do not readily remember the reason why the idea of a being more perfect than myself, must of necessity have proceeded from a being in reality more perfect. On this account I am here desirous to inquire further, whether I, who possess this idea of God, could exist supposing there were no God. And I ask, from whom could I, in that case, derive my existence? Perhaps from myself, or from my parents, or from some other causes less perfect than God; for anything more perfect, or even equal to God, cannot be thought or imagined. But if I [were independent of every other existence, and] were myself the author of my being, I should doubt of nothing, I should desire nothing, and, in fine, no perfection would be awanting to me; for I should have bestowed upon myself every perfection of which I possess the idea, and I should thus be God. And it must not be imagined that what is now wanting to me is perhaps of more difficult acquisition than that of which I am already possessed; for, on the contrary, it is quite manifest that it was a matter of much higher difficulty that I, a thinking being, should arise from nothing, than it would be for me to acquire the knowledge of many things of which I am ignorant, and which are merely the accidents of a thinking substance; and certainly, if I possessed of myself the greater perfection of which I have now spoken, [in other words, if I were the author of my own existence], I would not at least have denied to myself things that may be more easily obtained, [as that infinite variety of knowledge of which I am at present destitute]. I could not, indeed, have denied to myself any property which I perceive is contained in the idea of God, because there is none of these that seems to me to be more difficult to make or acquire; and if there were any that should happen to be more difficult to acquire, they would certainly appear so to me (supposing that I myself were the source of the other things I possess), because I should discover in them a limit to my power. And though I were to suppose that I always was as I now am, I should not, on this ground, escape the force of these reasonings, since it would not follow, even on this supposition, that no author of my existence needed to be sought after. For the whole time of my life may be divided into an infinity of parts, each of which is in no way dependent on any other; and, accordingly, because I was in existence a short time ago, it does not follow that I must now exist, unless in this moment some cause create me anew as it were,—that is, conserve me. In truth, it is perfectly clear and evident to all who will attentively consider the nature of duration, that the conservation of a substance, in each moment of its duration, requires the same power and act that would be necessary to create it, supposing it were not yet in existence; so that it is manifestly a dictate of the natural light that conservation and creation differ merely in respect of our mode of thinking [and not in reality]. All that is here required, therefore, is that I interrogate myself to discover whether I possess any power by means of which I can bring it about that I, who now am, shall exist a moment afterwards; for, since I am merely a thinking thing (or since, at least, the precise question, in the meantime, is only of that part of myself), if such a power resided in me, I should, without doubt, be conscious of it; but I am conscious of no such power, and thereby I manifestly know that I am dependent upon some being different from myself.

But perhaps the being upon whom I am dependent, is not God, and I have been produced either by my parents, or by some causes less perfect than Deity. This cannot be: for, as I before said, it is perfectly evident that there must at least be as much reality in the cause as in its effect; and accordingly, since I am a thinking thing, and possess in myself an idea of God, whatever in the end be the cause of my existence, it must of necessity be admitted that it is likewise a thinking being, and that it possesses in itself the idea and all the perfections I attribute to Deity. Then it may again be inquired whether this cause owes its origin and existence to itself, or to some other cause. For if it be self-existent, it follows, from what

I have before laid down, that this cause is God; for, since it possesses the perfection of self-existence, it must likewise, without doubt, have the power of actually possessing every perfection of which it has the idea,—in other words, all the perfections I conceive to belong to God. But if it owe its existence to another cause than itself, we demand again, for a similar reason, whether this second cause exists of itself or through some other, until, from stage to stage, we at length arrive at an ultimate cause, which will be God. And it is quite manifest that in this matter there can be no infinite regress of causes, seeing that the question raised respects not so much the cause which once produced me, as that by which I am at this present moment conserved.

Nor can it be supposed that several causes concurred in my production, and that from one I received the idea of one of the perfections I attribute to Deity, and from another the idea of some other, and thus that all those perfections are indeed found somewhere in the universe, but do not all exist together in a single being who is God; for, on the contrary, the unity, the simplicity or inseparability of all the properties of Deity, is one of the chief perfections I conceive him to possess; and the idea of this unity of all the perfections of Deity could certainly not be put into my mind by any cause from which I did not likewise receive the ideas of all the other perfections; for no power could enable me to embrace them in an inseparable unity, without at the same time giving me the knowledge of what they were [and of their existence in a particular mode].

Finally, with regard to my parents [from whom it appears I sprung], although all that I believed respecting them be true, it does not, nevertheless, follow that I am conserved by them, or even that I was produced by them, in so far as I am a thinking being. All that, at the most, they contributed to my origin was the giving of certain dispositions (modifications) to the matter in which I have hitherto judged that I or my mind, which is what alone I now consider to be myself, is enclosed; and thus there can here be no difficulty with respect to them, and it is absolutely necessary to conclude from this alone that I am, and possess the idea of a being absolutely perfect, that is, of God, that his existence is most clearly demonstrated.

There remains only the inquiry as to the way in which I received this idea from God; for I have not drawn it from the senses, nor is it even presented to me unexpectedly, as is usual with the ideas of sensible objects, when these are presented or appear to be presented to the external organs of the senses; it is not even a pure production or fiction of my mind, for it is not in my power to take from or add to it; and consequently there but remains the alternative that it is innate, in the same way as is the idea of myself. And, in truth, it is not to be wondered at that God, at my creation, implanted this idea in me, that it might serve, as it were, for the mark of the workman impressed on his work; and it is not also necessary that the mark should be something different from the work itself; but considering only that God is my creator, it is highly probable that he in some way fashioned me after his own image and likeness, and that I perceive this likeness, in which is contained the idea of God, by the same faculty by which I apprehend myself,—in other words, when I make myself the object of reflection, I not only find that I am an incomplete, [imperfect] and dependent being, and one who unceasingly aspires after something better and greater than he is; but, at the same time, I am assured likewise that he upon whom I am dependent possesses in himself all the goods after which I aspire, [and the ideas of which I find in my mind], and that not merely indefinitely and potentially, but infinitely and actually, and that he is thus God. And the whole force of the argument of which I have here availed myself to establish the existence of God, consists in this, that I perceive I could not possibly be of such a nature as I am, and yet have in my mind the idea of a God, if God did not in reality exist,—this same God, I say, whose idea is in my mind—that is, a being who possesses all those lofty perfections, of which the mind may have some slight conception, without, however, being able fully to comprehend them—and who is wholly superior to all defect, [and has nothing that marks imperfection]: whence it is sufficiently manifest that he cannot be a deceiver, since it is a dictate of the natural light that all fraud and deception spring from some defect.

But before I examine this with more attention, and pass on to the consideration of other truths that may be evolved out of it, I think it proper to remain here for some time in the contemplation of God himself—that I may ponder at leisure his marvellous attributes— and behold, admire, and adore the beauty of this light so unspeakably great, as far, at least, as the strength of my mind, which is to some degree dazzled by the sight, will permit. For just as we learn by faith that the supreme felicity of another life consists in the contempla- tion of the Divine majesty alone, so even now we learn from experience that a like medita- tion, though incomparably less perfect, is the source of the highest satisfaction of which we are susceptible in this life.

MEDITATION IV
Of truth and error

I have been habituated these bygone days to detach my mind from the senses, and I have accurately observed that there is exceedingly little which is known with certainty respecting corporeal objects,—that we know much more of the human mind, and still more of God himself. I am thus able now without difficulty to abstract my mind from the contemplation of [sensible of] imaginable objects, and apply it to those which, as disengaged from all matter, are purely intelligible. And certainly the idea I have of the human mind in so far as it is a thinking thing, and not extended in length, breadth, and depth, and participating in none of the properties of body, is incomparably more distinct than the idea of any corporeal object; and when I consider that I doubt, in other words, that I am an incomplete and dependent being, the idea of a complete and independent being, that is to say of God, occurs to my mind with so much clearness and distinctness,—and from the fact alone that this idea is found in me, or that I who possess it exist, the conclusions that God exists, and that my own existence, each moment of its continuance, is absolutely dependent upon him, are so manifest,—as to lead me to believe it impossible that the human mind can know anything with more clearness and certitude. And now I seem to discover a path that will conduct us from the contemplation of the true God, in whom are contained all the treasures of science and wisdom, to the knowledge of the other things in the universe.

For, in the first place, I discover that it is impossible for him ever to deceive me, for in all fraud and deceit there is a certain imperfection: and although it may seem that the ability to deceive is a mark of subtlety or power, yet the will testifies without doubt of malice and weakness; and such, accordingly, cannot be found in God. In the next place, I am conscious that I possess a certain faculty of judging [or discerning truth from error], which I doubtless received from God, along with whatever else is mine; and since it is impossible that he should will to deceive me, it is likewise certain that he has not given me a faculty that will ever lead me into error, provided I use it aright.

And there would remain no doubt on this head, did it not seem to follow from this, that I can never therefore be deceived; for if all I possess be from God, and if he planted in me no faculty that is deceitful, it seems to follow that I can never fall into error. Accordingly, it is true that when I think only of God (when I look upon myself as coming from God, Fr.), and turn wholly to him, I discover [in myself] no cause of error or falsity: but immediately thereafter, recurring to myself, experience assures me that I am nevertheless subject to innumerable errors. When I come to inquire into the cause of these, I observe that there is not only present to my consciousness a real and positive idea of God, or of a being supremely perfect, but also, so to speak, a certain negative idea of nothing,—in other words, of that which is at an infinite distance from every sort of perfection, and that I am, as it were, a mean between God and nothing, or placed in such a way between absolute existence and non-existence, that there is in truth nothing in me to lead me into error, in so far as an absolute being is my creator; but that, on the other hand, as I thus likewise participate in some degree of nothing or of non-being, in other words, as I am not myself the supreme Being, and as I am wanting in many perfections, it is not surprising I should fall into error. And I hence discern that error, so far as error is not something real, which depends for its existence on God, but is simply defect; and therefore that, in order to fall into it, it is not necessary God should have given me a faculty expressly for this end, but that my being deceived arises from the circumstance that the power which God has given me of discerning truth from error is not infinite.

Nevertheless this is not yet quite satisfactory; for error is not a pure negation, [in other words, it is not the simple deficiency or want of some knowledge which is not due], but the privation or want of some knowledge which it would seem I ought to possess. But, on considering the nature of God, it seems impossible that he should have planted in his creature any faculty not perfect in its kind, that is, wanting in some perfection due to it: for if it be true, that in proportion to the skill of the maker the perfection of his work is greater, what thing can have been produced by the supreme Creator of the universe that is not absolutely perfect in all its parts? And assuredly there is no doubt that God could have created me such as that I should never be deceived; it is certain, likewise, that he always wills what is best; is it better, then, that I should be capable of being deceived than that I should not?

Considering this more attentively, the first thing that occurs to me is the reflection that I must not be surprised if I am not always capable of comprehending the reasons why God acts as he does; nor must I doubt of his existence because I find, perhaps, that there are several other things besides the present respecting which I understand neither why nor how they were created by him; for, knowing already that my nature is extremely weak and limited, and that the nature of God, on the other hand, is immense, incomprehensible, and infinite, I have no longer any difficulty in discerning that there is an infinity of things in his power whose causes transcend the grasp of my mind: and this consideration alone is sufficient to convince me, that the whole class of final causes is of no avail in physical [or natural] things; for it appears to me that I cannot, without exposing myself to the charge of temerity, seek to discover the [impenetrable] ends of Deity.

It further occurs to me that we must not consider only one creature apart from the others, if we wish to determine the perfection of the works of Deity, but generally all his creatures together; for the same object that might perhaps, with some show of reason, be deemed highly imperfect if it were alone in the world, may for all that be the most perfect possible, considered as forming part of the whole universe: and although, as it was my purpose to doubt of everything, I only as yet know with certainty my own existence and that of God, nevertheless, after having remarked the infinite power of Deity, I cannot deny that he may have produced many other objects, or at least that he is able to produce them, so that I may occupy a place in the relation of a part to the great whole of his creatures.

Whereupon, regarding myself more closely, and considering what my errors are (which alone testify to the existence of imperfection in me), I observe that these depend on the concurrence of two causes, viz., the faculty of cognition which I possess, and that of election or the power of free choice,—in other words, the understanding and the will. For by the understanding alone, I [neither affirm nor deny anything, but] merely apprehend (*percipio*) the ideas regarding which I may form a judgment; nor is any error, properly so called, found in it thus accurately taken. And although there are perhaps innumerable objects in the world of which I have no idea in my understanding, it cannot, on that account, be said that I am deprived of those ideas [as of something that is due to my nature], but simply that I do not possess them, because, in truth, there is no ground to prove that Deity ought to have endowed me with a larger faculty of cognition than he has actually bestowed upon me; and however skilful a workman I suppose him to be, I have no reason, on that account, to think that it was obligatory on him to give to each of his works all the perfections he is able to bestow upon some. Nor, moreover, can I complain that God has not given me freedom of choice, or a will sufficiently ample and perfect, since, in truth, I am conscious of will so ample and extended as to be superior to all limits. And what appears to me here to be highly remarkable is that, of all the other properties I possess, there is none so great and perfect as that I do not clearly discern it could be still greater and more perfect. For, to take an example, if I consider the faculty of understanding which I possess, I find that it is of very small extent, and greatly limited, and at the same time I form the idea of another faculty of the same nature, much more ample and even infinite; and seeing that I can frame the idea of it, I discover, from this circumstance alone, that it pertains to the nature of God. In the same way, if I examine the faculty of memory or imagination, or any other faculty I possess, I find none that is not small and circumscribed, and in God immense [and infinite]. It is the faculty of will only, or freedom of choice, which I experience to be so great that I am unable to conceive the idea of another that shall be more ample and extended; so that it is chiefly my will which leads me to discern that I bear a certain image and similitude of Deity. For although the faculty of will is incomparably greater in God than in myself, as well in respect of the knowledge and power that are conjoined with it, and that render it stronger and more efficacious, as in respect of the object, since in him it extends to a greater number of things, it does not, nevertheless, appear to me greater, considered in itself formally and precisely: for the power of will consists only in this, that we are able to do or not to do the same thing (that is, to affirm or deny, to pursue or shun it), or rather in this alone, that in affirming or denying, pursuing or shunning, what is proposed to us by the understanding, we so act that we are not conscious of being determined to a particular action by any external force. For, to the possession of freedom, it is not necessary that I be alike indifferent towards each of two contraries; but, on the contrary, the more I am inclined towards the one, whether because I clearly know that in it there is the reason of truth and goodness, or because God thus internally disposes my thought, the more freely do I choose and embrace it; and assuredly divine grace and natural knowledge, very far from diminishing liberty, rather augment and fortify it. But the indifference of which I am conscious when I am not impelled to one side rather than to another for want of a reason, is the lowest grade of liberty, and manifests defect or negation of knowledge rather than perfection of will; for if I always clearly knew what was true and good, I should never have any difficulty in determining what judgment I ought to come to, and what choice I ought to make, and I should thus be entirely free without ever being indifferent.

From all this I discover, however, that neither the power of willing, which I have received from God, is of itself the source of my errors, for it is exceedingly ample and perfect in its kind; nor even the power of understanding, for as I conceive no object unless by means of the faculty that God bestowed upon me, all that I conceive is doubtless rightly conceived by me, and it is impossible for me to be deceived in it.

Whence, then, spring my errors? They arise from this cause alone, that I do not restrain the will, which is of much wider range than the understanding, within the same limits, but extend it even to things I do not understand, and as the will is of itself indifferent to such, it readily falls into error and sin by choosing the false in room of the true, and evil instead of good.

For example, when I lately considered whether aught really existed in the world, and found that because I considered this question, it very manifestly followed that I myself existed, I could not but judge that what I so clearly conceived was true, not that I was forced to this judgment by any external cause, but simply because great clearness of the understanding was succeeded by strong inclination in the will; and I believed this the more freely and spontaneously in proportion as I was less indifferent with respect to it. But now I not only know that I exist, in so far as I am a thinking being, but there is likewise presented to my mind a certain idea of corporeal nature; hence I am in doubt as to whether the thinking nature which is in me, or rather which I myself am, is different from that corporeal nature, or whether both are merely one and the same thing, and I here suppose that I am as yet ignorant of any reason that would determine me to adopt the one belief in preference to the other: whence it happens that it is a matter of perfect indifference to me which of the two suppositions I affirm or deny, or whether I form any judgment at all in the matter.

This indifference, moreover, extends not only to things of which the understanding has no knowledge at all, but in general also to all those which it does not discover with perfect clearness at the moment the will is deliberating upon them; for, however probable the conjectures may be that dispose me to form a judgment in a particular matter, the simple knowledge that these are merely conjectures, and not certain and indubitable reasons, is sufficient to lead me to form one that is directly the opposite. Of this I lately had abundant experience, when I laid aside as false all that I had before held for true, on the single ground that I could in some degree doubt of it. But if I abstain from judging of a thing when I do not conceive it with sufficient clearness and distinctness, it is plain that I act rightly, and am not deceived; but if I resolve to deny or affirm, I then do not make a right use of my free will; and if I affirm what is false, it is evident that I am deceived: moreover, even although I judge according to truth, I stumble upon it by chance, and do not therefore escape the imputation of a wrong use of my freedom; for it is a dictate of the natural light, that the knowledge of the understanding ought always to precede the determination of the will.

And it is this wrong use of the freedom of the will in which is found the privation that constitutes the form of error. Privation, I say, is found in the act, in so far as it proceeds from myself, but it does not exist in the faculty which I received from God, nor even in the act, in so far as it depends on him; for I have assuredly no reason to complain that God has not given me a greater power of intelligence or more perfect natural light than he has actually bestowed, since it is of the nature of a finite understanding not to comprehend many things, and of the nature of a created understanding to be finite; on the contrary, I have every reason to render thanks to God, who owed me nothing, for having given me all the perfections I possess, and I should be far from thinking that he has unjustly deprived me of, or kept back, the other perfections which he has not bestowed upon me.

I have no reason, moreover, to complain because he has given me a will more ample than my understanding, since, as the will consists only of a single element, and that indivisible, it would appear that this faculty is of such a nature that nothing could be taken from it [without destroying it]: and certainly, the more extensive it is, the more cause I have to thank the goodness of him who bestowed it upon me.

And, finally, I ought not also to complain that God concurs with me in forming the acts of this will, or the judgments in which I am deceived, because those acts are wholly true and good, in so far as they depend on God; and the ability to form them is a higher degree of perfection in my nature than the want of it would be. With regard to privation, in which alone consists the formal reason of error and sin, this does not require the concurrence of Deity, because it is not a thing [or existence], and if it be referred to God as to its cause, it ought not to be called privation, but negation, [according to the signification of these words in the schools]. For in truth it is no imperfection in Deity that he has accorded to me the power of giving or withholding my assent from certain things of which he has not put a clear and distinct knowledge in my understanding; but it is doubtless an imperfection in me that I do not use my freedom aright, and readily give my judgment on matters which I only obscurely and confusedly conceive.

I perceive, nevertheless, that it was easy for Deity so to have constituted me as that I should never be deceived, although I still remained free and possessed of a limited knowledge, viz., by implanting in my understanding a clear and distinct knowledge of all the objects respecting which I should ever have to deliberate; or simply by so deeply engraving on my memory the resolution to judge of nothing without previously possessing a clear and distinct conception of it, that I should never forget it. And I easily understand that, in so far as I consider myself as a single whole, without reference to any other being in the universe, I should have been much more perfect than I now am, had Deity created me superior to error; but I cannot therefore deny that it is not somehow a greater perfection in the universe, that certain of its parts are not exempt from defect, as others are, than if they were all perfectly alike.

And I have no right to complain because God, who placed me in the world, was not willing that I should sustain that character which of all others is the chief and most perfect; I have even good reason to remain satisfied on the ground that, if he has not given me the perfection of being superior to error by the first means I have pointed out above, which depends on a clear and evident knowledge of all the matters regarding which I can deliberate, he has at least left in my power the other means, which is, firmly to retain the resolution never to judge where the truth is not clearly known to me: for, although I am conscious of the weakness of not being able to keep my mind continually fixed on the same thought, I can nevertheless, by attentive and oft-repeated meditation, impress it so strongly on my memory that I shall never fail to recollect it as often as I require it, and I can acquire in this way the habitude of not erring; and since it is in being superior to error that the highest and chief perfection of man consists, I deem that I have not gained little by this day's meditation, in having discovered the source of error and falsity.

And certainly this can be no other than what I have now explained: for as often as I so restrain my will within the limits of my knowledge, that it forms no judgment except regarding objects which are clearly and distinctly represented to it by the understanding, I can never be deceived; because every clear and distinct conception is doubtless something, and as such cannot owe its origin to nothing, but must of necessity have God for its author—God, I say, who, as supremely perfect, cannot, without a contradiction, be the cause of any error; and consequently it is necessary to conclude that every such conception [or judgment] is true. Nor have I merely learned to-day what I must avoid to escape error, but also what I must do to arrive at the knowledge of truth; for I will assuredly reach truth if I only fix my attention sufficiently on all the things I conceive perfectly, and separate these from others which I conceive more confusedly and obscurely: to which for the future I shall give diligent heed.

MEDITATION V
Of the essence of material things; and, again, of God; that He exists

Several other questions remain for consideration respecting the attributes of God and my own nature or mind. I will, however, on some other occasion perhaps resume the investigation of these. Meanwhile, as I have discovered what must be done and what avoided to arrive at the knowledge of truth, what I have chiefly to do is to essay to emerge from the state of doubt in which I have for some time been, and to discover whether anything can be known with certainty regarding material objects. But before considering whether such objects as I conceive exist without me, I must examine their ideas in so far as these are to be found in my consciousness, and discover which of them are distinct and which confused.

In the first place, I distinctly imagine that quantity which the philosophers commonly call continuous, or the extension in length, breadth, and depth that is in this quantity, or rather in the object to which it is attributed. Further, I can enumerate in it many diverse parts, and attribute to each of these all sorts of sizes, figures, situations, and local motions; and, in fine, I can assign to each of these motions all degrees of duration. And I not only distinctly know these things when I thus consider them in general; but besides, by a little attention, I discover innumerable particulars respecting figures, numbers, motion, and the like, which are so evidently true, and so accordant with my nature, that when I now discover them I do not so much appear to learn anything new, as to call to remembrance what I before knew, or for the first time to remark what was before in my mind, but to which I had not hitherto directed my attention. And what I here find of most importance is, that I discover in my mind innumerable ideas of certain objects, which cannot be esteemed pure negations, although perhaps they possess no reality beyond my thought, and which are not framed by me though it may be in my power to think, or not to think them, but possess true and immutable natures of their own. As, for example, when I imagine a triangle, although there is not perhaps and never was in any place in the universe apart from my thought one such figure, it remains true nevertheless that this figure possesses a certain determinate nature, form, or essence, which is immutable and eternal, and not framed by me, nor in any degree dependent on my thought; as appears from the circumstance, that diverse properties of the triangle may be demonstrated, viz., that its three angles are equal to two right, that its greatest side is subtended by its greatest angle, and the like, which, whether I will or not, I now clearly discern to belong to it, although before I did not at all think of them, when, for the first time, I imagined a triangle, and which accordingly cannot be said to have been invented by me. Nor is it a valid objection to allege, that perhaps this idea of a triangle came into my mind by the medium of the senses, through my having seen bodies of a triangular figure; for I am able to form in thought an innumerable variety of figures with regard to which it cannot be supposed that they were ever objects of sense, and I can nevertheless demonstrate diverse properties of their nature no less than of the triangle, all of which are assuredly true since I clearly conceive them: and they are therefore something, and not mere negations; for it is highly evident that all that is true is something, [truth being identical with existence]; and I have already fully shown the truth of the principle, that whatever is clearly and distinctly known is true. And although this had not been demonstrated, yet the nature of my mind is such as to compel me to assent to what I clearly conceive while I so conceive it; and I recollect that even when I still strongly adhered to the objects of sense, I reckoned among the number of the most certain truths those I clearly conceived relating to figures, numbers, and other matters that pertain to arithmetic and geometry, and in general to the pure mathematics.

But now if because I can draw from my thought the idea of an object, it follows that all I clearly and distinctly apprehend to pertain to this object, does in truth belong to it, may I not from this derive an argument for the existence of God? It is certain that I no less find the idea of a God in my consciousness, that is, the idea of a being supremely perfect, than that of any figure or number whatever: and I know with not less clearness and distinctness that an [actual and] eternal existence pertains to his nature than that all which is demonstrable of any figure or number really belongs to the nature of that figure or number; and, therefore, although all the conclusions of the preceding Meditations were false, the existence of God would pass with me for a truth at least as certain as I ever judged any truth of mathematics to be, although indeed such a doctrine may at first sight appear to contain more sophistry than truth. For, as I have been accustomed in every other matter to distinguish between existence and essence, I easily believe that the existence can be separated from the essence of God, and that thus God may be conceived as not actually existing. But, nevertheless, when I think of it more attentively, it appears that the existence can no more be separated from the essence of God, than the idea of a mountain from that of a valley, or the equality of its three angles to two right angles, from the essence of a [rectilineal] triangle; so that it is not less impossible to conceive a God, that is, a being supremely perfect, to whom existence is awanting, or who is devoid of a certain perfection, than to conceive a mountain without a valley.

But though, in truth, I cannot conceive a God unless as existing, any more than I can a mountain without a valley, yet, just as it does not follow that there is any mountain in the world merely because I conceive a mountain with a valley, so likewise, though I conceive God as existing, it does not seem to follow on that account that God exists; for my thought imposes no necessity on things; and as I may imagine a winged horse, though there be none such, so I could perhaps attribute existence to God, though no God existed. But the cases are not analogous, and a fallacy lurks under the semblance of this objection: for because I cannot conceive a mountain without a valley, it does not follow that there is any mountain or valley in existence, but simply that the mountain or valley, whether they do or do not exist, are inseparable from each other; whereas, on the other hand, because I cannot conceive God unless as existing, it follows that existence is inseparable from him, and therefore that he really exists: not that this is brought about by my thought, or that it imposes any necessity on things, but, on the contrary, the necessity which lies in the thing itself, that is, the necessity of the existence of God, determines me to think in this way: for it is not in my power to conceive a God without existence, that is, a being supremely perfect, and yet devoid of an absolute perfection, as I am free to imagine a horse with or without wings.

Nor must it be alleged here as an objection, that it is in truth necessary to admit that God exists, after having supposed him to possess all perfections, since existence is one of them, but that my original supposition was not necessary; just as it is not necessary to think that all quadrilateral figures can be inscribed in the circle, since, if I supposed this, I should be constrained to admit that the rhombus, being a figure of four sides, can be therein inscribed, which, however, is manifestly false. This objection is, I say, incompetent; for although it may not be necessary that I shall at any time entertain the notion of Deity, yet each time I happen to think of a first and sovereign being, and to draw, so to speak, the idea of him from the storehouse of the mind, I am necessitated to attribute to him all kinds of perfections, though I may not then enumerate them all, nor think of each of them in particular. And this necessity is sufficient, as soon as I discover that existence is a perfection, to cause me to infer the existence of this first and sovereign being: just as it is not necessary that I should ever imagine any triangle, but whenever I am desirous of considering a rectilineal figure composed of only three angles, it is absolutely necessary to attribute those properties to it from which it is correctly inferred that its three angles are not greater than two right angles, although perhaps I may not then advert to this relation in particular. But when I consider what figures are capable of being inscribed in the circle, it is by no means necessary to hold that all quadrilateral figures are of this number; on the contrary, I cannot even imagine such to be the case, so long as I shall be unwilling to accept in thought aught that I do not clearly and distinctly conceive: and consequently there is a vast difference between false suppositions, as is the one in question, and the true ideas that were born with me, the first and chief of which is the idea of God. For indeed I discern on many grounds that this idea is not factitious, depending simply on my thought, but that it is the representation of a true and immutable nature: in the first place, because I can conceive no other being, except God, to whose essence existence [necessarily] pertains; in the second, because it is impossible to conceive two or more gods of this kind; and it being supposed that one such God exists, I clearly see that he must have existed from all eternity, and will exist to all eternity; and finally, because I apprehend many other properties in God, none of which I can either diminish or change.

But, indeed, whatever mode of probation I in the end adopt, it always returns to this, that it is only the things I clearly and distinctly conceive which have the power of completely persuading me. And although, of the objects I conceive in this manner, some, indeed, are obvious to every one, while others are only discovered after close and careful investigation; nevertheless, after they are once discovered, the latter are not esteemed less certain than the former. Thus, for example, to take the case of a right-angled triangle, although it is not so manifest at first that the square of the base is equal to the squares of the other two sides, as that the base is opposite to the greatest angle; nevertheless, after it is once apprehended, we are as firmly persuaded of the truth of the former as of the latter. And, with respect to God, if I were not pre-occupied by prejudices, and my thought beset on all sides by the continual presence of the images of sensible objects, I should know nothing sooner or more easily than the fact of his being. For is there any truth more clear than the existence of a Supreme Being, or of God, seeing it is to his essence alone that [necessary and eternal] existence pertains? And although the right conception of this truth has cost me much close thinking, nevertheless at present I feel not only as assured of it as of what I deem most certain, but I remark further that the certitude of all other truths is so absolutely dependent on it, that without this knowledge it is impossible ever to know anything perfectly.

For although I am of such a nature as to be unable, while I possess a very clear and distinct apprehension of a matter, to resist the conviction of its truth, yet because my constitution is also such as to incapacitate me from keeping my mind continually fixed on the same object, and as I frequently recollect a past judgment without at the same time being able to recall the grounds of it, it may happen meanwhile that other reasons are presented to me which would readily cause me to change my opinion, if I did not know that God existed; and thus I should possess no true and certain knowledge, but merely vague and vacillating opinions. Thus, for example, when I consider the nature of the [rectilineal] triangle, it most clearly appears to me, who have been instructed in the principles of geometry, that its three angles are equal to two right angles, and I find it impossible to believe other-wise, while I apply my mind to the demonstration; but as soon as I cease from attending to the process of proof, although I still remember that I had a clear comprehension of it, yet I may readily come to doubt of the truth demonstrated, if I do not know that there is a God: for I may persuade myself that I have been so constituted by nature as to be sometimes deceived, even in matters which I think I apprehend with the greatest evidence and certi-tude, especially when I recollect that I frequently considered many things to be true and certain which other reasons afterwards constrained me to reckon as wholly false.

But after I have discovered that God exists, seeing I also at the same time observed that all things depend on him, and that he is no deceiver, and thence inferred that all which I clearly and distinctly perceive is of necessity true: although I no longer attend to the grounds of a judgment, no opposite reason can be alleged sufficient to lead me to doubt of its truth, provided only I remember that I once possessed a clear and distinct comprehension of it. My knowledge of it thus becomes true and certain. And this same knowledge extends like-wise to whatever I remember to have formerly demonstrated, as the truths of geometry and the like: for what can be alleged against them to lead me to doubt of them? Will it be that my nature is such that I may be frequently deceived? But I already know that I cannot be deceived in judgments of the grounds of which I possess a clear knowledge. Will it be that I formerly deemed things to be true and certain which I afterwards discovered to be false? But I had no clear and distinct knowledge of any of those things, and, being as yet ignorant of the rule by which I am assured of the truth of a judgment, I was led to give my assent to them on grounds which I afterwards discovered were less strong than at the time I imagined them to be. What further objection, then, is there? Will it be said that perhaps I am dream-ing (an objection I lately myself raised), or that all the thoughts of which I am now con-scious have no more truth than the reveries of my dreams? But although, in truth, I should be dreaming, the rule still holds that all which is clearly presented to my intellect is indis-putably true.

And thus I very clearly see that the certitude and truth of all science depends on the knowledge alone of the true God, insomuch that, before I knew him, I could have no perfect knowledge of any other thing. And now that I know him, I possess the means of acquiring a perfect knowledge respecting innumerable matters, as well relative to God him-self and other intellectual objects as to corporeal nature, in so far as it is the object of pure mathematics [which do not consider whether it exists or not].

MEDITATION VI
Of the existence of material things, and of the real distinction between the mind and body of man

There now only remains the inquiry as to whether material things exist. With regard to this question, I at least know with certainty that such things may exist, in as far as they constitute the object of the pure mathematics, since, regarding them in this aspect, I can conceive them clearly and distinctly. For there can be no doubt that God possesses the power of producing all the objects I am able distinctly to conceive, and I never considered anything impossible to him, unless when I experienced a contradiction in the attempt to conceive it aright. Further, the faculty of imagination which I possess, and of which I am conscious that I make use when I apply myself to the consideration of material things, is sufficient to persuade me of their existence: for, when I attentively consider what imagination is, I find that it is simply a certain application of the cognitive faculty (*facultas cognoscitiva*) to a body which is immediately present to it, and which therefore exists.

And to render this quite clear, I remark, in the first place, the difference that subsists between imagination and pure intellection [or conception]. For example, when I imagine a triangle I not only conceive (*intelligo*) that it is a figure comprehended by three lines, but at the same time also I look upon (*intueor*) these three lines as present by the power and internal application of my mind (*acie mentis*), and this is what I call imagining. But if I desire to think of a chiliogon, I indeed rightly conceive that it is a figure composed of a thousand sides, as easily as I conceive that a triangle is a figure composed of only three sides; but I cannot imagine the thousand sides of a chiliogon as I do the three sides of a triangle, nor, so to speak, view them as present [with the eyes of my mind]. And although, in accordance with the habit I have of always imagining something when I think of corporeal things, it may happen that, in conceiving a chiliogon, I confusedly represent some figure to myself, yet it is quite evident that this is not a chiliogon, since it in no wise differs from that which I would represent to myself, if I were to think of a myriogon, or any other figure of many sides; nor would this representation be of any use in discovering and unfolding the properties that constitute the difference between a chiliogon and other polygons. But if the question turns on a pentagon, it is quite true that I can conceive its figure, as well as that of a chiliogon, without the aid of imagination; but I can likewise imagine it by applying the attention of my mind to its five sides, and at the same time to the area which they contain. Thus I observe that a special effort of mind is necessary to the act of imagination, which is not required to conceiving or understanding (*ad intelligendum*); and this special exertion of mind clearly shows the difference between imagination and pure intellection (*imaginatio et intellectio pura*). I remark, besides, that this power of imagination which I possess, in as far as it differs from the power of conceiving, is in no way necessary to my [nature or] essence, that is, to the essence of my mind; for although I did not possess it, I should still remain the same that I now am, from which it seems we may conclude that it depends on something different from the mind. And I easily understand that, if some body exists, with which my mind is so conjoined and united as to be able, as it were, to consider it when it chooses, it may thus imagine corporeal objects; so that this mode of thinking differs from pure intellection only in this respect, that the mind in conceiving turns in some way upon itself, and considers some one of the ideas it possesses within itself; but in imagining it turns towards the body, and contemplates in it some object conformed to the idea which it either of itself conceived or apprehended by sense. I easily understand, I say, that imagination may be thus formed, if it is true that there are bodies; and because I find no other obvious mode of explaining it, I thence, with probability, conjecture that they exist, but only with probability; and although I carefully examine all things, nevertheless I do not find that, from the distinct idea of corporeal nature I have in my imagination, I can necessarily infer the existence of any body.

But I am accustomed to imagine many other objects besides that corporeal nature which is the object of the pure mathematics, as, for example, colours, sounds, tastes, pain ,and the like, although with less distinctness; and, inasmuch as I perceive these objects much better by the senses, through the medium of which and of memory, they seem to have reached the imagination, I believe that, in order the more advantageously to examine them, it is proper I should at the same time examine what sense-perception is, and inquire whether from those ideas that are apprehended by this mode of thinking (consciousness), I cannot obtain a certain proof of the existence of corporeal objects.

And, in the first place, I will recall to my mind the things I have hitherto held as true, because perceived by the senses, and the foundations upon which my belief in their truth rested; I will, in the second place, examine the reasons that afterwards constrained me to doubt of them; and, finally, I will consider what of them I ought now to believe.

Firstly, then, I perceived that I had a head, hands, feet, and other members composing that body which I considered as part, or perhaps even as a whole, of myself. I perceived further, that that body was placed among many others, by which it was capable of being affected in diverse ways, both beneficial and hurtful; and what was beneficial I remarked by a certain sensation of pleasure, and what was hurtful by a sensation of pain. And, besides this pleasure and pain, I was likewise conscious of hunger, thirst, and other appetites, as well as certain corporeal inclinations towards joy, sadness, anger, and similar passions. And, out of myself, besides the extension, figure, and motions of bodies, I likewise perceived in them hardness, heat, and the other tactile qualities, and, in addition, light, colours, odours, tastes, and sounds, the variety of which gave me the means of distinguishing the sky, the earth, the sea, and generally all the other bodies, from one another. And certainly, considering the ideas of all these qualities, which were presented to my mind, and which alone I properly and immediately perceived, it was not without reason that I thought I perceived certain objects wholly different from my thought, namely, bodies from which those ideas proceeded; for I was conscious that the ideas were presented to me without my consent being required, so that I could not perceive any object, however desirous I might be, unless it were present to the organ of sense; and it was wholly out of my power not to perceive it when it was thus present. And because the ideas I perceived by the senses were much more lively and clear, and even, in their own way, more distinct than any of those I could of myself frame by meditation, or which I found impressed on my memory, it seemed that they could not have proceeded from myself, and must therefore have been caused in me by some other objects; and as of those objects I had no knowledge beyond what the ideas themselves gave me, nothing was so likely to occur to my mind as the supposition that the objects were similar to the ideas which they caused. And because I recollected also that I had formerly trusted to the senses, rather than to reason, and that the ideas which I myself formed were not so clear as those I perceived by sense, and that they were even for the most part composed of parts of the latter, I was readily persuaded that I had no idea in my intellect which had not formerly passed through the senses. Nor was I altogether wrong in likewise believing that that body which, by a special right, I called my own, pertained to me more properly and strictly than any of the others; for in truth, I could never be separated from it as from other bodies: I felt in it and on account of it all my appetites and affections, and in fine I was affected in its parts by pain and the titillation of pleasure, and not in the parts of the other bodies that were separated from it. But when I inquired into the reason why, from this I know not what sensation of pain, sadness of mind should follow, and why from the sensation of pleasure joy should arise, or why this indescribable twitching of the stomach, which I call hunger, should put me in mind of taking food, and the parchedness of the throat of drink, and so in other cases, I was unable to give any explanation, unless that I was so taught by nature; for there is assuredly no affinity, at least none that I am able to comprehend, between this irritation of the stomach and the desire of food, any more than between the perception of an object that causes pain and the consciousness of sadness which springs from the perception. And in the same way it seemed to me that all the other judgments I had formed regarding the objects of sense, were dictates of nature; because I remarked that those judgments were formed in me, before I had leisure to weight and consider the reasons that might constrain me to form them.

But, afterwards, a wide experience by degrees sapped the faith I had reposed in my senses; for I frequently observed that towers, which at a distance seemed round, appeared square when more closely viewed, and that colossal figures, raised on the summits of these towers, looked like small statues, when viewed from the bottom of them; and, in other instances without number, I also discovered error in judgments founded on the external senses; and not only in those founded on the external, but even in those that rested on the internal senses; for is there aught more internal than pain? and yet I have sometimes been informed by parties whose arm or leg had been amputated, that they still occasionally seemed to feel pain in that part of the body which they had lost,—a circumstance that led me to think that I could not be quite certain even that any one of my members was affected when I felt pain in it. And to these grounds of doubt I shortly afterwards also added two others of very wide generality: the first of them was that I believed I never perceived anything when awake which I could not occasionally think I also perceived when asleep, and as I do not believe that the ideas I seem to perceive in my sleep proceed from objects external to me, I did not any more observe any ground for believing this of such as I seem to perceive when awake; the second was that since I was as yet ignorant of the author of my being, or at least supposed myself to be so, I saw nothing to prevent my having been so constituted by nature as that I should be deceived even in matters that appeared to me to possess the greatest truth. And, with respect to the ground on which I had before been persuaded of the existence of sensible objects, I had no great difficulty in finding suitable answers to them; for as nature seemed to incline me to many things from which reason made me averse, I thought that I ought not to confide much in its teachings. And although the perceptions of the senses were not dependent on my will, I did not think that I ought on that ground to conclude that they proceeded from things different from myself, since perhaps there might be found in me some faculty, though hitherto unknown to me, which produced them.

But now that I begin to know myself better, and to discover more clearly the author of my being, I do not, indeed, think that I ought rashly to admit all which the senses seem to teach, nor, on the other hand, is it my conviction that I ought to doubt in general of their teachings.

And, firstly, because I know that all which I clearly and distinctly conceive can be produced by God exactly as I conceive it, it is sufficient that I am able clearly and distinctly to conceive one thing apart from another, in order to be certain that the one is different from the other, seeing they may at least be made to exist separately, by the omnipotence of God; and it matters not by what power this separation is made, in order to be compelled to judge them different; and, therefore, merely because I know with certitude that I exist, and because, in the meantime, I do not observe that aught necessarily belongs to my nature or essence beyond my being a thinking thing, I rightly conclude that my essence consists only in my being a thinking thing, [or a substance whose whole essence or nature is merely thinking]. And although I may, or rather, as I will shortly say, although I certainly do possess a body with which I am very closely conjoined; nevertheless, because, on the one hand, I have a clear and distinct idea of myself, in as far as I am only a thinking and unextended thing, and as, on the other hand, I possess a distinct idea of body, in as far as it is only an extended and unthinking thing, it is certain that I, [that is, my mind, by which I am what I am], is entirely and truly distinct from my body, and may exist without it.

Moreover, I find in myself diverse faculties of thinking that have each their special mode: for example, I find I possess the faculties of imagining and perceiving, without which I can indeed clearly and distinctly conceive myself as entire, but I cannot reciprocally conceive them without conceiving myself, that is to say, without an intelligent substance in which they reside, for [in the notion we have of them, or to use the terms of the schools] in their formal concept, they comprise some sort of intellection; whence I perceive that they are distinct from myself as modes are from things. I remark likewise certain other faculties, as the power of changing place, of assuming diverse figures, and the like, that cannot be conceived and cannot therefore exist, any more than the preceding, apart from a substance in which they inhere. It is very evident, however, that these faculties, if they really exist, must belong to some corporeal or extended substance, since in their clear and distinct concept there is contained some sort of extension, but no intellection at all. Farther, I cannot doubt but that there is in me a certain passive faculty of perception, that is, of receiving and taking knowledge of the ideas of sensible things; but this would be useless to me, if there did not also exist in me, or in some other thing, another active faculty capable of forming and producing those ideas. But this active faculty cannot be in me [in as far as I am but a thinking thing], seeing that it does not presuppose thought, and also that those ideas are frequently produced in my mind without my contributing to it in any way, and even frequently contrary to my will. This faculty must therefore exist in some substance different from me, in which all the objective reality of the ideas that are produced by this faculty, is contained formally or eminently, as I before remarked; and this substance is either a body, that is to say, a corporeal nature in which is contained formally [and in effect] all that is objectively [and by representation] in those ideas; or it is God himself, or some other creature, of a rank superior to body, in which the same is contained eminently. But as God is no deceiver, it is manifest that he does not of himself and immediately communicate those ideas to me, nor even by the intervention of any creature in which their objective reality is not formally, but only eminently, contained. For as he has given me no faculty whereby I can discover this to be the case, but, on the contrary, a very strong inclination to believe that those ideas arise from corporeal objects, I do not see how he could be vindicated from the charge of deceit, if in truth they proceeded from any other source, or were produced by other causes than corporeal things: and accordingly it must be concluded, that corporeal objects exist. Nevertheless they are not perhaps exactly such as we perceive by the senses, for their comprehension by the senses is, in many instances, very obscure and confused; but it is at least necessary to admit that all which I clearly and distinctly conceive as in them, that is, generally speaking, all that is comprehended in the object of speculative geometry, really exists external to me.

But with respect to other things which are either only particular, as, for example, that the sun is of such a size and figure, etc., or are conceived with less clearness and distinctness, as light, sound, pain, and the like, although they are highly dubious and uncertain, nevertheless on the ground alone that God is no deceiver, and that consequently he has permitted no falsity in my opinions which he has not likewise given me a faculty of correcting, I think I may with safety conclude that I possess in myself the means of arriving at the truth. And, in the first place, it cannot be doubted that in each of the dictates of nature there is some truth: for by nature, considered in general, I now understand nothing more than God himself, or the order and disposition established by God in created things; and by my nature in particular I understand the assemblage of all that God has given me.

But there is nothing which that nature teaches me more expressly [or more sensibly] than that I have a body which is ill affected when I feel pain, and stands in need of food and drink when I experience the sensations of hunger and thirst, etc. And therefore I ought not to doubt but that there is some truth in these informations.

Nature likewise teaches me by these sensations of pain, hunger, thirst, etc., that I am not only lodged in my body as a pilot in a vessel, but that I am besides so intimately conjoined, and as it were intermixed with it, that my mind and body compose a certain unity. For if this were not the case, I should not feel pain when my body is hurt, seeing I am merely a thinking thing, but should perceive the wound by the understanding alone, just as a pilot perceives by sight when any part of his vessel is damaged; and when my body has need of food or drink, I should have a clear knowledge of this, and not be made aware of it by the confused sensations of hunger and thirst; for, in truth, all these sensations of hunger, thirst, pain, etc., are nothing more than certain confused modes of thinking, arising from the union and apparent fusion of mind and body.

Besides this, nature teaches me that my own body is surrounded by many other bodies, some of which I have to seek after, and others to shun. And indeed, as I perceive different sorts of colours, sounds, odours, tastes, heat, hardness, etc., I safely conclude that there are in the bodies from which the diverse perceptions of the senses proceed, certain varieties corresponding to them, although, perhaps, not in reality like them; and since, among these diverse perceptions of the senses, some are agreeable, and others disagreeable, there can be no doubt that my body, or rather my entire self, in as far as I am composed of body and mind, may be variously affected, both beneficially and hurtfully, by surrounding bodies.

But there are many other beliefs which, though seemingly the teaching of nature, are not in reality so, but which obtained a place in my mind through a habit of judging inconsiderately of things. It may thus easily happen that such judgments shall contain error: thus, for example, the opinion I have that all space in which there is nothing to affect [or make an impression on] my senses is void; that in a hot body there is something in every respect similar to the idea of heat in my mind; that in a white or green body there is the same whiteness or greenness which I perceive; that in a bitter or sweet body there is the same taste, and so in other instances; that the stars, towers, and all distant bodies, are of the same size and figure as they appear to our eyes, etc. But that I may avoid everything like indistinctness of conception, I must accurately define what I properly understand by being taught by nature. For nature is here taken in a narrower sense than when it signifies the sum of all the things which God has given me; seeing that in that meaning the notion comprehends much that belongs only to the mind [to which I am not here to be understood as referring when I use the term nature]; as, for example, the notion I have of the truth, that what is done cannot be undone, and all the other truths I discern by the natural light [without the aid of the body]; and seeing that it comprehends likewise much besides that belongs only to body, and is not here any more contained under the name nature, as the quality of heaviness, and the like, of which I do not speak,—the term being reserved exclusively to designate the things which God has given to me as a being composed of mind and body. But nature, taking the term in the sense explained, teaches me to shun what causes in me the sensation of pain, and to pursue what affords me the sensation of pleasure, and other things of this sort; but I do not discover that it teaches me, in addition to this, from these diverse perceptions of the senses, to draw any conclusions respecting external objects without a previous [careful and mature] consideration of them by the mind; for it is, as appears to me, the office of the mind alone, and not of the composite whole of mind and body, to discern the truth in those matters. Thus, although the impression a star makes on my eye is not larger than that from the flame of a candle, I do not, nevertheless, experience any real or positive impulse determining me to believe that the star is not greater than the flame; the true account of the matter being merely that I have so judged from my youth without any rational ground. And, though on approaching the fire I feel heat, and even pain on approaching it too closely, I have, however, from this no ground for holding that something resembling the heat I feel is in the fire, any more than that there is something similar to the pain; all that I have ground for believing is, that there is something in it, whatever it may be, which excites in me those sensations of heat or pain. So also, although there are spaces in which I find nothing to excite and affect my senses, I must not therefore conclude that those spaces contain in them no body; for I see that in this, as in many other similar matters, I have been accustomed to pervert the order of nature, because these perceptions of the senses, although given me by nature merely to signify to my mind what things are beneficial and hurtful to the composite whole of which it is a part, and being sufficiently clear and distinct for that purpose, are nevertheless used by me as infallible rules by which to determine immediately the essence of the bodies that exist out of me, of which they can of course afford me only the most obscure and confused knowledge.

But I have already sufficiently considered how it happens that, notwithstanding the supreme goodness of God, there is falsity in my judgments. A difficulty, however, here presents itself, respecting the things which I am taught by nature must be pursued or avoided, and also respecting the internal sensations in which I seem to have occasionally detected error, [and thus to be directly deceived by nature]: thus, for example, I may be so deceived by the agreeable taste of some viand with which poison has been mixed, as to be induced to take the poison. In this case, however, nature may be excused, for it simply leads me to desire the viand for its agreeable taste, and not the poison, which is unknown to it; and thus we can infer nothing from this circumstance beyond that our nature is not omniscient; at which there is assuredly no ground for surprise, since, man being of a finite nature, his knowledge must likewise be of limited perfection. But we also not unfrequently err in that to which we are directly impelled by nature, as is the case with invalids who desire drink or food that would be hurtful to them. It will here, perhaps, be alleged that the reason why such persons are deceived is that their nature is corrupted; but this leaves the difficulty untouched, for a sick man is not less really the creature of God than a man who is in full health; and therefore it is as repugnant to the goodness of God that the nature of the former should be deceitful as it is for that of the latter to be so. And, as a clock, composed of wheels and counter weights, observes not the less accurately all the laws of nature when it is ill made, and points out the hours incorrectly, than when it satisfies the desire of the maker in every respect; so likewise if the body of man be considered as a kind of machine, so made up and composed of bones, nerves, muscles, veins, blood, and skin, that although there were in it no mind, it would still exhibit the same motions which it at present manifests involuntarily, and therefore without the aid of the mind, [and simply by the dispositions of its organs], I easily discern that it would also be as natural for such a body, supposing it dropsical, for example, to experience the parchedness of the throat that is usually accompanied in the mind by the sensation of thirst, and to be disposed by this parchedness to move its nerves and its other parts in the way required for drinking, and thus increase its malady and do itself harm, as it is natural for it, when it is not indisposed to be stimulated to drink for its good by a similar cause; and although looking to the use for which a clock was destined by its maker, I may say that it is deflected from its proper nature when it incorrectly indicates the hours, and on the same principle, considering the machine of the human body as having been formed by God for the sake of the motions which it usually manifests, although I may likewise have ground for thinking that it does not follow the order of its nature when the throat is parched and drink does not tend to its preservation, nevertheless I yet plainly discern that this latter acceptation of the term nature is very different from the other; for this is nothing more than a certain denomination, depending entirely on my thought, and hence called extrinsic, by which I compare a sick man and an imperfectly constructed clock with the idea I have of a man in good health and a well made clock; while by the other acceptation of nature is understood something which is truly found in things, and therefore possessed of some truth.

But certainly, although in respect of a dropsical body, it is only by way of exterior denomination that we say its nature is corrupted, when, without requiring drink, the throat is parched; yet, in respect of the composite whole, that is, of the mind in its union with the body, it is not a pure denomination, but really an error of nature, for it to feel thirst when drink would be hurtful to it: and, accordingly, it still remains to be considered why it is that the goodness of God does not prevent the nature of man thus taken from being fallacious.

To commence this examination accordingly, I here remark, in the first place, that there is a vast difference between mind and body, in respect that body, from its nature, is always divisible, and that mind is entirely indivisible. For in truth, when I consider the mind, that is, when I consider myself in so far only as I am a thinking thing, I can distinguish in myself no parts, but I very clearly discern that I am somewhat absolutely one and entire; and although the whole mind seems to be united to the whole body, yet, when a foot, an arm, or any other part is cut off, I am conscious that nothing has been taken from my mind; nor can the faculties of willing, perceiving, conceiving, etc., properly be called its parts, for it is the same mind that is exercises [all entire] in willing, in perceiving, and in conceiving, etc. But quite the opposite holds in corporeal or extended things; for I cannot imagine any one of them [how small soever it may be], which I cannot easily sunder in thought, and which, therefore, I do not know to be divisible. This would be sufficient to teach me that the mind or soul of man is entirely different from the body, if I had not already been apprised of it on other grounds.

I remark, in the next place, that the mind does not immediately receive the impression from all the parts of the body, but only from the brain, or perhaps even from one small part of it, viz., that in which the common sense (*sensus communis*) is said to be, which as often as it is affected in the same way, gives rise to the same perception in the mind, although meanwhile the other parts of the body may be diversely disposed, as is proved by innumerable experiments, which it is unnecessary here to enumerate.

I remark, besides, that the nature of body is such that none of its parts can be moved by another part a little removed from the other, which cannot likewise be moved in the same way by any one of the parts that lie between those two, although the most remote part does not act at all. As, for example, in the cord A, B, C, D, [which is in tension], if its last part D, be pulled, the first part A, will not be moved in a different way than it would be were one of the intermediate parts B or C to be pulled, and the last part D meanwhile to remain fixed. And in the same way, when I feel pain in the foot, the science of physics teaches me that this sensation is experienced by means of the nerves dispersed over the foot, which, extending like cords from it to the brain, when they are contracted, in the foot, contract at the same time the inmost parts of the brain in which they have their origin, and excite in these parts a certain motion appointed by nature to cause in the mind a sensation of pain, as if existing in the foot: but as these nerves must pass through the tibia, the leg, the loins, the back, and neck, in order to reach the brain, it may happen that although their extremities in the foot are not affected, but only certain of their parts that pass through the loins or neck, the same movements, nevertheless, are excited in the brain by this motion as would have been caused there by a hurt received in the foot, and hence the mind will necessarily feel pain in the foot, just as if it had been hurt; and the same is true of all the other perceptions of our senses.

I remark, finally, that as each of the movements that are made in the part of the brain by which the mind is immediately affected, impresses it with but a single sensation, the most likely supposition in the circumstances is, that this movement causes the mind to experience, among all the sensations which it is capable of impressing upon it, that one which is the best fitted, and generally the most useful for the preservation of the human body when it is in full health. But experience shows us that all the perceptions which nature has given us are of such a kind as I have mentioned; and accordingly, there is nothing found in them that does not manifest the power and goodness of God. Thus, for example, when the nerves of the foot are violently or more than usually shaken, the motion passing through the medulla of the spine to the innermost parts of the brain affords a sign to the mind on which it experiences a sensation, viz., of pain, as if it were in the foot, by which the mind is admonished and excited to do its utmost to remove the cause of it as dangerous and hurtful to the foot. It is true that God could have so constituted the nature of man as that the same motion in the brain would have informed the mind of something altogether different: the motion might, for example, have been the occasion on which the mind became conscious of itself, in so far as it is in the brain, or in so far as it is in some place intermediate between the foot and the brain, or, finally, the occasion on which it perceived some other object quite different, whatever that might be; but nothing of all this would have so well contributed to the preservation of the body as that which the mind actually feels. In the same way, when we stand in need of drink, there arises from this want a certain parchedness in the throat that moves its nerves, and by means of them the internal parts of the brain; and this movement affects the mind with the sensation of thirst, because there is nothing on that occasion which is more useful for us than to be made aware that we have need of drink for the preservation of our health; and so in other instances.

Whence it is quite manifest that, notwithstanding the sovereign goodness of God, the nature of man, in so far as it is composed of mind and body, cannot but be sometimes fallacious. For, if there is any cause which excites, not in the foot, but in some one of the parts of the nerves that stretch from the foot to the brain, or even in the brain itself, the same movement that is ordinarily created when the foot is ill affected, pain will be felt, as it were, in the foot, and the sense will thus be naturally deceived; for as the same movement in the brain can but impress the mind with the same sensation, and as this sensation is much more frequently excited by a cause which hurts the foot than by one acting in a different quarter, it is reasonable that it should lead the mind to feel pain in the foot rather than in any other part of the body. And if it sometimes happens that the parchedness of the throat does not arise, as is usual, from drink being necessary for the health of the body, but from quite the opposite cause, as is the case with the dropsical, yet it is much better that it should be deceitful in that instance, than if, on the contrary, it were continually fallacious when the body is well-disposed; and the same holds true in other cases.

And certainly this consideration is of great service, not only in enabling me to recognize the errors to which my nature is liable, but likewise in rendering it more easy to avoid or correct them: for, knowing that all my senses more usually indicate to me what is true than what is false, in matters relating to the advantage of the body, and being able almost always to make use of more than a single sense in examining the same object, and besides this, being able to use my memory in connecting present with past knowledge, and my understanding which has already discovered all the causes of my errors, I ought no longer to fear that falsity may be met with in what is daily presented to me by the senses. And I ought to reject all the doubts of those bygone days, as hyperbolical and ridiculous, especially the general uncertainty respecting sleep, which I could not distinguish from the waking state: for I now find a very marked difference between the two states, in respect that our memory can never connect our dreams with each other and with the course of life, in the way it is in the habit of doing with events that occur when we are awake. And, in truth, if some one, when I am awake, appeared to me all of a sudden and as suddenly disappeared, as do the images I see in sleep, so that I could not observe either whence he came or whither he went, I should not without reason esteem it either a spectre or phantom formed in my brain, rather than a real man. But when I perceive objects with regard to which I can distinctly determine both the place whence they come, and that in which they are, and the time at which they appear to me, and when, without interruption, I can connect the perception I have of them with the whole of the other parts of my life, I am perfectly sure that what I thus perceive occurs while I am awake and not during sleep. And I ought not in the least degree to doubt of the truth of those presentations, if, after having called together all my senses, my memory, and my understanding for the purpose of examining them, no deliverance is given by any one of these faculties which is repugnant to that of any other: for since God is no deceiver, it necessarily follows that I am not herein deceived. But because the necessities of action frequently oblige us to come to a determination before we have had leisure for so careful an examination, it must be confessed that the life of man is frequently obnoxious to error with respect to individual objects; and we must, in conclusion, acknowledge the weakness of our nature.

PASCAL

1623–1662

Born at Clermont in Auvergne, France, Blaise Pascal was educated by his father, a high government official. In his youth he converted to Jansenism, a Calvinistic religion that stressed God's free grace and individual moral conscience. As a mathematician and physicist he did pioneering work in hydrodynamics and the theory of probability; his advancement of conic sections anticipated modern projective geometry. His work on the cycloid apparently suggested the infinitesimal calculus to Leibniz. He also designed the first mechanical calculating machine.

A prolific writer with a clear and direct writing style, Pascal had a great influence on subsequent French thought, especially those philosophers who argued that the human mind could not understand itself and the world by using reason. In his own work, he evolved from mathematics and logical philosophy to a blend of mysticism and Cartesianism. The Port-Royal *Logic* (*The Art of Thinking*, 1662), was based on one of Pascal's early treatises. He was most influenced by Descartes, Montaigne, and Epictetus. Although Pascal, like Plato and Descartes, believed mathematics to be the queen of the sciences, he concluded that mathematics is ultimately useless in our trying to understand nature because mathematics can deal with infinity only in artificial ways. Indeed, like some of the earlier Pythagoreans who also had a mystical bent, Pascal decided that mathematics in particular and reason in general obscures the mystery of existence. Mathematics is in the end deceptive because it cannot reveal the true infinite nature of existence, the whole without which the parts are unintelligible.

In 1654, at age thirty-one, Pascal had a mystical experience that turned his attentions exclusively to writing about God and the paradoxical nature of human existence. His *Pensées* (Thoughts; 1670), from which the following selection is taken, is a compilation made from his notes. Central to the work is his original view, contrary to both the empiricists and rationalists, of the "heart" (that is, the emotions instead of the intellect) as a source of knowledge.

THOUGHTS

MATHEMATICS, INTUITION

True eloquence makes light of eloquence, true morality makes light of morality; that is to say, the morality of the judgment, which has no rules, makes light of the morality of the intellect.

For it is to judgment that perception belongs, as science belongs to intellect. Intuition is the part of judgment, mathematics of intellect.

To make light of philosophy is to be a true philosopher.

MAN'S DISPROPORTION

Let man then contemplate the whole of nature in her full and grand majesty, and turn his vision from the low objects which surround him. Let him gaze on that brilliant light, set like an eternal lamp to illumine the universe; let the earth appear to him a point in comparison with the vast circle described by the sun; and let him wonder at the fact that this vast circle is itself but a very fine point in comparison with that described by the stars in their revolution round the firmament. But if our view be arrested there, let our imagination pass beyond; it will sooner exhaust the power of conception than nature that of supplying material for conception. The whole visible world is only an imperceptible atom in the ample bosom of nature. No idea approaches it. We may enlarge our conceptions beyond all imaginable space; we only produce atoms in comparison with the reality of things. It is an infinite sphere, the center of which is everywhere, the circumference nowhere. In short it is the greatest sensible mark of the almighty power of God, that imagination loses itself in that thought.

Returning to himself, let man consider what he is in comparison with all existence; let him regard himself as lost in this remote corner of nature; and from the little cell in which he finds himself lodged, I mean the universe, let him estimate at their true value the earth, kingdoms, cities, and himself. What is a man in the Infinite?

But to show him another prodigy equally astonishing, let him examine the most delicate things he knows. Let a mite be given him, with its minute body and parts incomparably more minute, limbs with their joints, veins in the limbs, blood in the veins, humors in the blood, drops in the humors, vapors in the drops. Dividing these last things again, let him exhaust his powers of conception, and let the last object at which he can arrive be now that of our discourse. Perhaps he will think that here is the smallest point in nature. I will let him see therein a new abyss. I will paint for him not only the visible universe, but all that he can conceive of nature's immensity in the womb of this abridged atom. Let him see therein an infinity of universes, each of which has its firmament, its planets, its earth, in the same proportion as in the visible world; in each earth animals, and in the last mites, in which he will find again all that the first had, finding still in these others the same thing

From *Pensées*, trans. W. F. Trotter, (New York: E. P. Dutton, and London: J. M. Dent and Sons, 1904).

without end and without cessation. Let him lose himself in wonders as amazing in their littleness as the others in their vastness. For who will not be astounded at the fact that our body, which a little while ago was imperceptible in the universe, itself imperceptible in the bosom of the whole, is now a colossus, a world, or rather a whole, in respect of the nothingness which we cannot reach? He who regards himself in this light will be afraid of himself, and observing himself sustained in the body given him by nature between those two abysses of the Infinite and Nothing, will tremble at the sight of these marvels; and I think that, as his curiosity changes into admiration, he will be more disposed to contemplate them in silence than to examine them with presumption.

For in fact what is man in nature? A Nothing in comparison with the Infinite, an All in comparison with the Nothing, a mean between nothing and everything. Since he is infinitely removed from comprehending the extremes, the end of things and their beginning are hopelessly hidden from him in an impenetrable secret; he is equally incapable of seeing the Nothing from which he was made, and the Infinite in which he is swallowed up.

What will he do then, but perceive the appearance of the middle of things, in an eternal despair of knowing either their beginning or their end. All things proceed from the Nothing, and are borne towards the Infinite. Who will follow these marvelous processes? The Author of these wonders understands them. None others can do so.

Through failure to contemplate these Infinites, men have rashly rushed into the examination of nature, as though they bore some proportion to her. It is strange that they have wished to understand the beginnings of things, and thence to arrive at the knowledge of the whole, with a presumption as infinite as their object. For surely this design cannot be formed without presumption or without a capacity infinite like nature.

If we are well informed, we understand that, as nature has graven her image and that of her Author on all things, they almost all partake of her double infinity. Thus we see that all the sciences are infinite in the extent of their researches. For who doubts that geometry, for instance, has an infinite infinity of problems to solve? They are also infinite in the multitude and fineness of their premises; for it is clear that those which are put forward as ultimate are not self-supporting, but are based on others which, again having others for their support, do not permit of finality. But we represent some as ultimate for reason, in the same way as in regard to material objects we call that an indivisible point beyond which our senses can no longer perceive anything, although by its nature it is infinitely divisible.

Of these two Infinites of science, that of greatness is the most palpable, and hence a few persons have pretended to know all things. "I will speak of the whole," said Democritus.

But infinitely little is the least obvious. Philosophers have much oftener claimed to have reached it, and it is here they have all stumbled. This has given rise to such common titles as *First Principles, Principles of Philosophy,* and the like, as ostentatious in fact, though not in appearance, as that one which blinds us, *De omni scibili.*

We naturally believe ourselves far more capable of reaching the center of things than of embracing their circumference. The visible extent of the world visibly exceeds us; but as we exceed little things, we think ourselves more capable of knowing them. And yet we need no less capacity for attaining the Nothing than the All. Infinite capacity is required for both, and it seems to me that whoever shall have understood the ultimate principles of being might also attain to the knowledge of the Infinite. The one depends on the other, and one leads to the other. These extremes meet and reunite by force of distance, and find each other in God, and in God alone.

Let us then take our compass; we are something, and we are not everything. The nature of our existence hides from us the knowledge of first beginnings which are born of the Nothing; and the littleness of our being conceals from us the sight of the Infinite.

Our intellect holds the same position in the world of thought as our body occupies in the expanse of nature.

Limited as we are in every way, this state which holds the mean between two extremes is present in all our impotence. Our senses perceive no extreme. Too much sound deafens us; too much light dazzles us; too great distance or proximity hinders our view. Too great length and too great brevity of discourse tends to obscurity; too much truth is paralyzing (I know some who cannot understand that to take four from nothing leaves nothing). First principles are too self-evident for us; too much pleasure disagrees with us. Too many concords are annoying in music; too many benefits irritate us; we wish to have the wherewithal to over-pay our debts. . . . We feel neither extreme heat nor extreme cold. Excessive qualities are prejudicial to us and not perceptible by the senses; we do not feel but suffer them. Extreme youth and extreme age hinder the mind, as also too much and too little education. In short, extremes are for us as though they were not, and we are not within their notice. They escape us, or we them.

This is our true state; this is what makes us incapable of certain knowledge and of absolute ignorance. We sail within a vast sphere, ever drifting in uncertainty, driven from end to end. When we think to attach ourselves to any point and to fasten to it, it wavers and leaves us; and if we follow it, it eludes our grasp, slips past us, and vanishes for ever. Nothing stays for us. This is our natural condition, and yet most contrary to our inclination; we burn with desire to find solid ground and an ultimate sure foundation whereon to build a tower reaching to the Infinite. But our whole groundwork cracks, and the earth opens to abysses.

Let us therefore not look for certainty and stability. Our reason is always deceived by fickle shadows; nothing can fix the finite between the two Infinites, which both enclose and fly from it.

If this be well understood, I think that we shall remain at rest, each in the state wherein nature has placed him. As this sphere which has fallen to us as our lot is always distant from either extreme, what matters it that man should have a little more knowledge of the universe? If he has it, he but gets a little higher. Is he not always infinitely removed from the end, and is not the duration of our life equally removed from eternity, even if it lasts ten years longer?

In comparison with these Infinites all finites are equal, and I see no reason for fixing our imagination on one more than on another. The only comparison which we make of ourselves to the finite is painful to us.

If man made himself the first object of study, he would see how incapable he is of going further. How can a part know the whole? But he may perhaps aspire to know at least the parts to which he bears some proportion. But the parts of the world are all so related and linked to one another, that I believe it impossible to know one without the other and without the whole.

Man, for instance, is related to all he knows. He needs a place wherein to abide, time through which to live, motion in order to live, elements to compose him, warmth and food to nourish him, air to breathe. He sees light; he feels bodies; in short, he is in a dependent alliance with everything. To know man, then, it is necessary to know how it happens that he needs air to live, and, to know the air, we must know how it is thus related to the life of man, etc. Flame cannot exist without air; therefore to understand the one, we must understand the other.

Since everything then is cause and effect, dependent and supporting, mediate and immediate, and all is held together by a natural though imperceptible chain, which binds together things most distant and most different, I hold it equally impossible to know the parts without knowing the whole, and to know the whole without knowing the parts in detail.

And what completes our incapability of knowing things, is the fact that they are simple, and that we are composed of two opposite natures, different in kind, soul and body. For it is impossible that our rational part should be other than spiritual; and if any one maintain that we are simply corporeal, this would far more exclude us from the knowledge of things, there being nothing so inconceivable as to say that matter knows itself. It is impossible to imagine how it should know itself.

So if we are simply material, we can know nothing at all; and if we are composed of mind and matter, we cannot know perfectly things which are simple, whether spiritual or corporeal. Hence it comes that almost all philosophers have confused ideas of things, and speak of material things in spiritual terms, and of spiritual things in material terms. For they say boldly that bodies have a tendency to fall, that they seek after their center, that they fly from destruction, that they fear the void, that they have inclinations, sympathies, antipathies, all of which attributes pertain only to mind. And in speaking of minds, they consider them as in a place, and attribute to them movement from one place to another; and these are qualities which belong only to bodies.

Instead of receiving the ideas of these things in their purity, we color them with our own qualities, and stamp with our composite being all the simple things which we contemplate.

Who would not think, seeing us compose all things of mind and body, but that this mixture would be quite intelligible to us? Yet it is the very thing we least understand. Man is to himself the most wonderful object in nature; for he cannot conceive what the body is, still less what the mind is, and least of all how a body should be united to a mind. This is the consummation of his difficulties, and yet it is his very being. . . .

Thought constitutes the greatness of man.

Man is but a reed, the most feeble thing in nature; but he is a thinking reed. The entire universe need not arm itself to crush him. A vapor, a drop of water suffices to kill him. But, if the universe were to crush him, man would still be more noble than that which killed him, because he knows that he dies and the advantage which the universe has over him; the universe knows nothing of this.

All our dignity consists, then, in thought. By it we must elevate ourselves, and not by space and time which we cannot fill. Let us endeavor, then, to think well; this is the principle of morality.

A THINKING REED

It is not from space that I must seek my dignity, but from the government of my thought. I shall have no more if I possess worlds. By space the universe encompasses and swallows me like an atom; by thought I comprehend the world. . . .

SKEPTICISM

Each thing here is partly true and partly false. Essential truth is not so; it is altogether pure and altogether true. This mixture dishonors and annihilates it. Nothing is purely true, and thus nothing is true, meaning by that pure truth. You will say it is true that homicide is wrong. Yes; for we know well the wrong and the false. But what will you say is good? Chastity? I say no; for the world would come to an end. Marriage? No; continence is better. Not to kill? No; for lawlessness would be horrible, and the wicked would kill all the good. To kill? No; for that destroys nature. We possess truth and goodness only in part, and mingled with falsehood and evil.

If we dreamt the same thing every night, it would affect us as much as the objects we see every day. And if an artisan were sure to dream every night for twelve hours' duration that he was a king I believe he would be almost as happy as a king who should dream every night for twelve hours on end that he was an artisan.

If we were to dream every night that we were pursued by enemies, and harassed by these painful phantoms, or that we passed every day in different occupations, as in making a voyage, we should suffer almost as much as if it were real, and should fear to sleep, as we fear to wake when we dread in fact to enter on such mishaps. And, indeed, it would cause pretty nearly the same discomforts as the reality.

But since dreams are all different, and each single one is diversified, what is seen in them affects us much less than what we see when awake, because of its continuity, which is not, however, so continuous and level as not to change too; but it changes less abruptly, except rarely, as when we travel, and then we say, "It seems to me I am dreaming." For life is a dream a little less inconstant.

The greatness of man is great in that he knows himself to be miserable. A tree does not know itself to be miserable. It is then being miserable to know oneself to be miserable; but it is also being great to know that one is miserable.

All these same miseries prove man's greatness. They are the miseries of a great lord, of a deposed king. . . .

Men are so necessarily mad that not to be mad would amount to another form of madness. . . .

This twofold nature of man is so evident that some have thought that we had two souls. A single subject seemed to them incapable of such sudden variations from unmeasured presumption to a dreadful dejection of heart.

It is dangerous to make man see too clearly his equality with the brutes without showing him his greatness. It is also dangerous to make him see his greatness too clearly, apart from his vileness. It is still more dangerous to leave him in ignorance of both. But it is very advantageous to show him both. Man must not think that he is on a level either with the brutes or with the angels, nor must he be ignorant of both sides of his nature; but he must know both.

I will not allow man to depend upon himself, or upon another, to the end that being without a resting-place and without repose. . . .

If he exalt himself, I humble him; if he humble himself, I exalt him; and I always contradict him, till he understands that he is an incomprehensible monster.

The chief arguments of the skeptics—I pass over the lesser ones—are that we have no certainty of the truth of these principles apart from faith and revelation, except in so far as we naturally perceive them in ourselves. Now this natural intuition is not a convincing proof of their truth; since, having no certainty, apart from faith, whether man was created by a good God, or by a wicked demon, or by chance, it is doubtful whether these principles given to us are true, or false, or uncertain, according to our origin. Again, no person is certain, apart from faith, whether he is awake or sleeps, seeing that during sleep we believe that we are awake as firmly as we do when we *are* awake; we believe that we see space, figure, and motion; we are aware of the passage of time, we measure it; and in fact we act as if we were awake. So that half of our life being passed in sleep, we have on our own admission no idea of truth, whatever we may imagine. As all our intuitions are then illusions, who knows whether the other half of our life, in which we think we are awake, is not another sleep a little different from the former, from which we awake when we suppose ourselves asleep?

And who doubts that, if we dreamed in company, and the dreams chanced to agree, which is common enough, and if we were always alone when awake, we should believe that matters were reversed? In short, as we often dream that we dream, heaping dream upon dream, may it not be that this half of our life, wherein we think ourselves awake, is itself only a dream on which the others are grafted, from which we wake at death, during which we have as few principles of truth and good as during natural sleep, these different thoughts which disturb us being perhaps only illusions like the flight of time and the vain fancies of our dreams?

These are the chief arguments on one side and the other.

I omit minor ones, such as the skeptical talk against the impressions of custom, education, manners, country, and the like. Though these influence the majority of common folk, who dogmatize only on shallow foundations, they are upset by the least breath of the skeptics. We have only to see their books if we are not sufficiently convinced of this, and we shall very quickly become so, perhaps too much.

I notice the only strong point of the dogmatists, namely, that, speaking in good faith and sincerely, we cannot doubt natural principles. Against this the skeptics set up in one word the uncertainty of our origin, which includes that of our nature. The dogmatists have been trying to answer this objection ever since the world began.

So there is open war among men, in which each must take a part, and side either with dogmatism or skepticism. For he who thinks to remain neutral is above all a skeptic. The neutrality is the essence of the sect; he who is not against them is essentially for them. [In this appears their advantage.] They are not for themselves; they are neutral, indifferent, in suspense as to all things, even themselves being no exception.

What then shall man do in this state? Shall he doubt everything? Shall he doubt whether he is awake, whether he is being pinched, or whether he is being burned? Shall he doubt whether he doubts? Shall he doubt whether he exists? We cannot go so far as that; and I lay it down as a fact that there never has been a real complete skeptic. Nature sustains our feeble reason, and prevents it raving to this extent.

Shall he then say, on the contrary, that he certainly possesses truth—he who, when pressed ever so little, can show no title to it, and is forced to let go his hold?

What a chimera then is man! What a novelty! What a monster, what a chaos, what a contradiction, what a prodigy! Judge of all things, imbecile worm of the earth; depositary of truth, a sink of uncertainty and error; the pride and refuse of the universe!

Who will unravel this tangle? Nature confutes the skeptics, and reason confutes the dogmatists. What then will you become, O men! who try to find out by your natural reason what is your true condition? You cannot avoid one of these sects, nor adhere to one of them.

Know then, proud man, what a paradox you are to yourself. Humble yourself, weak reason; be silent, foolish nature; learn that man infinitely transcends man, and learn from your Master your true condition, of which you are ignorant. Hear God.

SPINOZA

1632–1677

Baruch Spinoza came from a family of Jewish merchants that had escaped to Holland from their native Portugal to avoid persecution. In Amsterdam he attended the local school for Jewish boys. Known for arguing with his fellow students and teachers, he got into trouble for claiming that the Bible itself is no evidence whatsoever for God and that its authors were as ignorant about physics as they were about fine points of theology. The rabbis and teachers tried to silence him but were unsuccessful. In 1656 he was banished from Amsterdam and excommunicated by the Jewish community.

Spinoza supported himself by grinding and polishing lenses. Privately, however, he began work on a vast, new metaphysical system. In 1670 he published his *Tractatus Theologico-Politicus* (Treatise on theology and politics). Christian theologians quickly banned it, calling it a work "forged in Hell by a renegade Jew and the devil." Spinoza thus has the distinction of being banned by both Christian and Jewish theologians. As a result, his masterpiece, the *Ethics,* never appeared in print during his lifetime.

Influenced by the new Cartesian method and the sudden success of mathematics and geometry in physics, Spinoza's *Ethics* is designed according to a strictly rational geometrical system with definitions, axioms, and propositions arranged in a deductive system. It begins with a discussion of God's nature, from which the rest of existence, even our understanding of existence, is derived. It should be noted that Spinoza's conception of God is anything but the traditional theistic one. Spinoza's God is not something separate and distinct from the world but is the world itself. God, and whatever is true of God, is to some extent true in each and every existent thing in the world.

Spinoza's pantheistic conception of God is an elaboration of a Parmenidean view of the world in which there exists but one substance. Mind and matter, thought and extension, are themselves but attributes of the one infinite and universal substance, God. You and I do not have separate identities, nor are we individual beings. We are each one of us but aspects of the one infinite being, God. Spinoza argues that what makes it possible to see the truth of this idea is the sort of rational introspection begun by Descartes.

Spinoza takes the Cartesian definition of substance as that which is absolutely independent and then shows why there can be only one such substance; essentially, the idea is that if there were two such substances this would be logically impossible, for the two would limit each other's independence. Thus the Cartesian "mind-body" problem is solved; the assumed interaction between mind and body is as unnecessary as it is impossible. Body and mind do not need to act on each other because they are not two things but one thing. What explains the apparent duality, according to Spinoza, is that when the one universal substance (reality) is viewed from the perspective of its attribute of extension, it becomes *body,* whereas when it is viewed from the perspective of its attribute of thought, it becomes mind. Thus, there is only one, infinite, Parmenidean substance. This is the centerpiece of Spinoza's system. Material and spiritual being form but two sides of one and the same world: particular extended beings and particular thinking beings are but the emphemeral and transitory states of the eternal, unified world-being; they are its *modes.* All multiplicity, the apparent self-substance of particular objects, free will, and evolution are mere illusions. Philosophy allows us to see the truth behind the illusion.

Spinoza lived out his life in exile in The Hague in south Holland, in virtual anonymity. Ironically, in 1676—the year before his death, his lungs having been destroyed by years of inhaling glass from the grinding of lenses—he had a visitor: Leibniz. But the reason he came to Spinoza was not to learn his philosophy but to learn his techniques for grinding lenses!

Leibniz had been told that Spinoza was one of the greatest lens makers in Europe. He had sent Spinoza one of his own research articles on optics; in his reply, Spinoza had included the *Tractatus Theologico-Politicus.* This worked later influenced Leibniz's own philosophical development. From that point on, Leibniz, according to his own account, "conversed with him often and at great length."

THE ETHICS

PART I: CONCERNING GOD

DEFINITIONS

I. By that which is *self-caused,* I mean that of which the essence involves existence, or that of which the nature is only conceivable as existent.

II. A thing is called *finite after its kind,* when it can be limited by another thing of the same nature; for instance, a body is called finite because we always conceive another greater body. So, also, a thought is limited by another thought, but a body is not limited by thought, nor a thought by body.

III. By *substance,* I mean that which is in itself, and is conceived through itself: in other words, that of which a conception can be formed independently of any other conception.

IV. By *attribute,* I mean that which the intellect perceives as constituting the essence of substance.

V. By *mode,* I mean the modifications of substance, or that which exists in, and is conceived through, something other than itself.

From *The Chief Works of Benedict de Spinoza,* trans. R. H. M. Elwes (London: G. Bell and Sons, 1883–84).

VI. By *God,* I mean a being absolutely infinite—that is, a substance consisting in infinite attributes, of which each expresses eternal and infinite essentiality.

Explanation.—I say absolutely infinite, not infinite after its kind: for, of a thing infinite only after its kind, infinite attributes may be denied; but that which is absolutely infinite, contains in its essence whatever expresses reality, and involves no negation.

VII. That thing is called free, which exists solely by the necessity of its own nature, and of which the action is determined by itself alone. On the other hand, that thing is necessary, or rather constrained, which is determined by something external to itself to a fixed and definite method of existence or action.

VIII. By *eternity,* I mean existence itself, in so far as it is conceived necessarily to follow solely from the definition of that which is eternal.

Explanation.—Existence of this kind is conceived as an eternal truth, like the essence of a thing, and, therefore, cannot be explained by means of continuance or time, though continuance may be conceived without a beginning or end.

AXIOMS

I. Everything which exists, exists either in itself or in something else.

II. That which cannot be conceived through anything else must be conceived through itself.

III. From a given definite cause an effect necessarily follows; and, on the other hand, if no definite cause be granted, it is impossible that an effect can follow.

IV. The knowledge of an effect depends on and involves the knowledge of a cause.

V. Things which have nothing in common cannot be understood, the one by means of the other; the conception of one does not involve the conception of the other.

VI. A true idea must correspond with its ideate or object.

VII. If a thing can be conceived as non-existing, its essence does not involve existence.

PROPOSITIONS

PROP. I. *Substance is by nature prior to its modifications.*

Proof.—This is clear from Deff. iii. and v.

PROP. II. *Two substances, whose attributes are different, have nothing in common.*

Proof.—Also evident from Def. iii. For each must exist in itself, and be conceived through itself; in other words, the conception of one does not imply the conception of the other.

PROP. III. *Things which have nothing in common cannot be one the cause of the other.*

Proof.—If they have nothing in common, it follows that one cannot be apprehended by means of the other (Ax. v.), and, therefore, one cannot be the cause of the other (Ax. iv.). *Q.E.D.*

PROP. IV. *Two or more distinct things are distinguished one from the other, either by the difference of the attributes of the substances, or by the difference of their modifications.*

Proof.—Everything which exists, exists either in itself or in something else (Ax. i.),—that is (by Deff. iii. and v.), nothing is granted in addition to the understanding, except substance and its modifications. Nothing is, therefore, given besides the understanding, by which several things may be distinguished one from the other, except the substances, or, in other words (see Ax. iv.), their attributes and modifications. *Q.E.D.*

PROP. V. *There cannot exist in the universe two or more substances having the same nature or attribute.*

Proof.—If several distinct substances be granted, they must be distinguished one from the other, either by the difference of their attributes, or by the difference of their modifications (Prop. iv.). If only by the difference of their attributes, it will be granted that there cannot be more than one with an identical attribute. If by the difference of their modifications—as substance is naturally prior to its modifications (Prop. i.),—it follows that setting the modifications aside, and considering substance in itself, that is truly, (Deff. iii. and vi.), there cannot be conceived one substance different from another,—that is (by Prop. iv.), there cannot be granted several substances, but one substance only. *Q.E.D.*

PROP. VI. *One substance cannot be produced by another substance.*

Proof.—It is impossible that there should be in the universe two substances with an identical attribute, *i.e.* which have anything common to them both (Prop. ii.), and, therefore (Prop. iii.), one cannot be the cause of another, neither can one be produced by the other. *Q.E.D.*

Corollary.—Hence it follows that a substance cannot be produced by anything external to itself. For in the universe nothing is granted, save substances and their modifications (as appears from Ax. i. and Deff. iii. and v.). Now (by the last Prop.) substance cannot be produced by another substance, therefore it cannot be produced by anything external to itself. *Q.E.D.* This is shown still more readily by the absurdity of the contradictory. For, if substance be produced by an external cause, the knowledge of it would depend on the knowledge of its cause (Ax. iv.), and (by Def. iii.) it would itself not be substance.

PROP. VII. *Existence belongs to the nature of substance.*

Proof.—Substance cannot be produced by anything external (Corollary, Prop. vi.); it must, therefore, be its own cause—that is, its essence necessarily involves existence, or existence belongs to its nature.

PROP. VIII. *Every substance is necessarily infinite.*

Proof.—There can only be one substance with an identical attribute, and existence follows from its nature (Prop. vii.); its nature, therefore, involves existence, either as finite or infinite. It does not exist as finite, for (by Def. ii.) it would then be limited by something else of the same kind, which would also necessarily exist (Prop. vii.); and there would be two substances with an identical attribute, which is absurd (Prop. v.). It therefore exists as infinite. *Q.E.D.*

Note I.—As finite existence involves a partial negation, and infinite existence is the absolute affirmation of the given nature, it follows (solely from Prop. vii.) that every substance is necessarily infinite.

Note II.—No doubt it will be difficult for those who think about things loosely, and have not been accustomed to know them by their primary causes, to comprehend the demonstration of Prop. vii.: for such persons make no distinction between the modifications of substances and the substances themselves, and are ignorant of the manner in which things are produced; hence they attribute to substances the beginning which they observe in natural objects. Those who are ignorant of true causes, make complete confusion—think that trees might talk just as well as men—that men might be formed from stones as well as from seed; and imagine that any form might be changed into any other. So, also, those who confuse the two natures, divine and human, readily attribute human passions to the deity, especially so long as they do not know how passions originate in the mind. But, if people would consider the nature of substance, they would have no doubt about the truth of Prop. vii. In fact, this proposition would be a universal axiom, and accounted a truism. For, by substance, would be understood that which is in itself, and is conceived through itself—that is, something of which the conception requires not the conception of anything else; whereas modifications exist in something external to themselves, and a conception of them is formed by means of a conception of the thing in which they exist. Therefore, we may have true ideas of non-existent modifications; for, although they may have no *actual* existence apart from the conceiving intellect, yet their essence is so involved in something external to themselves that they may through it be conceived. Whereas the only truth substances can have, external to the intellect, must consist in their existence, because they are conceived through themselves. Therefore, for a person to say that he has a clear and distinct—that is, a true—idea of a substance, but that he is not sure whether such substance exists, would be the same as if he said that he had a true idea, but was not sure whether or no it was false (a little consideration will make this plain); or if anyone affirmed that substance is created, it would be the same as saying that a false idea was true—in short, the height of absurdity. It must, then, necessarily be admitted that the existence of substance as its essence is an eternal truth. And we can hence conclude by another process of reasoning—that there is but one such substance. I think that this may profitably be done at once; and, in order to proceed regularly with the demonstration, we must premise:—

1. The true definition of a thing neither involves nor expresses anything beyond the nature of the thing defined. From this it follows that—

2. No definition implies or expresses a certain number of individuals, inasmuch as it expresses nothing beyond the nature of the thing defined. For instance, the definition of a triangle expresses nothing beyond the actual nature of a triangle: it does not imply any fixed number of triangles.

3. There is necessarily for each individual existent thing a cause why it should exist.

4. This cause of existence must either be contained in the nature and definition of the thing defined, or must be postulated apart from such definition.

It therefore follows that, if a given number of individual things exist in nature, there must be some cause for the existence of exactly that number, neither more nor less. For example, if twenty men exist in the universe (for simplicity's sake, I will suppose them existing simultaneously, and to have had no predecessors), and we want to account for the existence of these twenty men, it will not be enough to show the cause of human existence in general; we must also show why there are exactly twenty men, neither more nor less: for a cause must be assigned for the existence of each individual. Now this cause cannot be contained in the actual nature of man, for the true definition of man does not involve any consideration of the number twenty. Consequently, the cause for the existence of these twenty men, and, consequently, of each of them, must necessarily be sought externally to each individual. Hence we may lay down the absolute rule, that everything which may consist of several individuals must have an external cause. And, as it has been shown already that existence appertains to the nature of substance, existence must necessarily be included in its definition; and from its definition alone existence must be deducible. But from its definition (as we have shown, Notes ii., iii.), we cannot infer the existence of several substances; therefore it follows that there is only one substance of the same nature. *Q.E.D.*

PROP. IX. *The more reality or being a thing has the greater the number of its attributes* (Def. iv.).

Prop. X. *Each particular attribute of the one substance must be conceived through itself.*

Proof.—An attribute is that which the intellect perceives of substance, as constituting its essence (Def. iv.), and, therefore, must be conceived through itself (Def. iii.). *Q.E.D.*

Note.—It is thus evident that, though two attributes are, in fact, conceived as distinct— that is, one without the help of the other—yet we cannot, therefore, conclude that they constitute two entities, or two different substances. For it is the nature of substance that each of its attributes is conceived through itself, inasmuch as all the attributes it has have always existed simultaneously in it, and none could be produced by any other; but each expresses the reality or being of substance. It is, then, far from an absurdity to ascribe several attributes to one substance: for nothing in nature is more clear than that each and every entity must be conceived under some attribute, and that its reality or being is in proportion to the number of its attributes expressing necessity or eternity and infinity. Consequently it is abundantly clear, that an absolutely infinite being must necessarily be defined as consisting in infinite attributes, each of which expresses a certain eternal and infinite essence.

If anyone now ask, by what sign shall he be able to distinguish different substances, let him read the following propositions, which show that there is but one substance in the universe, and that it is absolutely infinite, wherefore such a sign would be sought for in vain.

Prop. XI. *God, or substance, consisting of infinite attributes, of which each expresses eternal and infinite essentiality, necessarily exists.*

Proof.—If this be denied, conceive, if possible, that God does not exist: then his essence does not involve existence. But this (by Prop. vii.) is absurd. Therefore God necessarily exists.

Another proof.—Of everything whatsoever a cause or reason must be assigned, either for its existence, or for its non-existence—*e.g.* if a triangle exists, a reason or cause must be granted for its existence; if, on the contrary, it does not exist, a cause must also be granted, which prevents it from existing, or annuls its existence. This reason or cause must either be contained in the nature of the thing in question, or be external to it. For instance, the reason for the non-existence of a square circle is indicated in its nature, namely, because it would involve a contradiction. On the other hand, the existence of substance follows also solely from its nature, inasmuch as its nature involves existence. (See Prop. vii.)

But the reason for the existence of a triangle or a circle does not follow from the nature of those figures, but from the order of universal nature in extension. From the latter it must follow, either that a triangle necessarily exists, or that it is impossible that it should exist. So much is self-evident. It follows therefrom that a thing necessarily exists, if no cause or reason be granted which prevents its existence.

If, then, no cause or reason can be given, which prevents the existence of God, or which destroys his existence, we must certainly conclude that he necessarily does exist. If such a reason or cause should be given, it must either be drawn from the very nature of God, or be external to him—that is, drawn from another substance of another nature. For if it were of the same nature, God, by that very fact, would be admitted to exist. But substance of another nature could have nothing in common with God (by Prop. ii.), and therefore would be unable either to cause or to destroy his existence.

As, then, a reason or cause which would annul the divine existence cannot be drawn from anything external to the divine nature, such cause must perforce, if God does not exist, be drawn from God's own nature, which would involve a contradiction. To make such an affirmation about a being absolutely infinite and supremely perfect, is absurd; therefore, neither in the nature of God, nor externally to his nature, can a cause or reason be assigned which would annul his existence. Therefore, God necessarily exists. *Q.E.D.*

Another proof.—The potentiality of non-existence is a negation of power, and contrariwise the potentiality of existence is a power, as is obvious. If, then, that which necessarily exists is nothing but finite beings, such finite beings are more powerful than a being absolutely infinite, which is obviously absurd; therefore, either nothing exists, or else a being absolutely infinite necessarily exists also. Now we exist either in ourselves, or in something else which necessarily exists (see Axiom i. and Prop. vii.). Therefore a being absolutely infinite—in other words, God (Def. vi.)—necessarily exists. *Q.E.D.*

Note.—In this last proof, I have purposely shown God's existence *a posteriori,* so that the proof might be more easily followed, not because, from the same premises, God's existence does not follow *a priori.* For, as the potentiality of existence is a power, it follows that, in proportion as reality increases in the nature of a thing, so also will it increase its strength for existence. Therefore a being absolutely infinite, such as God, has from himself an absolutely infinite power of existence, and hence he does absolutely exist. Perhaps there will be many who will be unable to see the force of this proof, inasmuch as they are accustomed only to consider those things which flow from external causes. Of such things, they see that those which quickly come to pass—that is, quickly come into existence—quickly also disappear; whereas they regard as more difficult of accomplishment—that is, not so easily brought into existence—those things which they conceive as more complicated.

However, to do away with this misconception, I need not here show the measure of truth in the proverb, "What comes quickly, goes quickly," nor discuss whether, from the point of view of universal nature, all things are equally easy, or otherwise: I need only remark, that I am not here speaking of things, which come to pass through causes external to themselves, but only of substances which (by Prop. vi.) cannot be produced by any external cause. Things which are produced by external causes, whether they consist of many parts or few, owe whatsoever perfection or reality they possess solely to the efficacy of their external cause, and therefore their existence arises solely from the perfection of their external cause, not from their own. Contrariwise, whatsoever perfection is possessed by substance is due to no external cause; wherefore the existence of substance must arise solely from its own nature, which is nothing else but its essence. Thus, the perfection of a thing does not annul its existence, but, on the contrary, asserts it. Imperfection, on the other hand, does annul it; therefore we cannot be more certain of the existence of anything, than of the existence of a being absolutely infinite or perfect—that is, of God. For inasmuch as his essence excludes all imperfection, and involves absolute perfection, all cause for doubt concerning his existence is done away, and the utmost certainty on the question is given. This, I think, will be evident to every moderately attentive reader.

PROP. XII. *No attribute of substance can be conceived from which it would follow that substance can be divided.*

Proof.—The parts into which substance as thus conceived would be divided, either will retain the nature of substance, or they will not. If the former, then (by Prop. viii.) each part will necessarily be infinite, and (by Prop. vi.) self-caused, and (by Prop. v.) will perforce consist of a different attribute, so that, in that case, several substances could be formed out of one substance, which (by Prop. vi.) is absurd. Moreover, the parts (by Prop. ii.) would have nothing in common with their whole, and the whole (by Def. iv. and Prop. x.) could both exist and be conceived without its parts, which everyone will admit to be absurd. If we adopt the second alternative—namely, that the parts will not retain the nature of substance—then, if the whole substance were divided into equal parts, it would lose the nature of substance, and would cease to exist, which (by Prop. vii.) is absurd.

PROP. XIII. *Substance absolutely infinite is indivisible.*

Proof.—If it could be divided, the parts into which it was divided would either retain the nature of absolutely infinite substance, or they would not. If the former, we should have several substances of the same nature, which (by Prop. v.) is absurd. If the latter, then (by Prop. vii.) substance absolutely infinite could cease to exist, which (by Prop. xi.) is also absurd.

Corollary.—It follows, that no substance, and consequently no extended substance, in so far as it is substance, is divisible.

Note.—The indivisibility of substance may be more easily understood as follows. The nature of substance can only be conceived as infinite, and by a part of substance, nothing else can be understood than finite substance, which (by Prop. viii.) involves a manifest contradiction.

PROP. XIV. *Besides God no substance can be granted or conceived.*

Proof.—As God is a being absolutely infinite, of whom no attribute that expresses the essence of substance can be denied (by Def. vi.), and he necessarily exists (by Prop. xi.); if any substance besides god were granted, it would have to be explained by some attribute of God, and thus two substances with the same attribute would exist, which (by Prop. v.) is absurd; therefore, besides God no substance can be granted, or, consequently, be conceived. If it could be conceived, it would necessarily have to be conceived as existent; but this (by the first part of this proof) is absurd. Therefore, besides God no substance can be granted or conceived. *Q.E.D.*

Corollary I.—Clearly, therefore: 1. God is one, that is (by Def. vi.) only one substance can be granted in the universe, and that substance is absolutely infinite, as we have already indicated (in the note to Prop. x.).

Corollary II.—It follows: 2. That extension and thought are either attributes of God or (by Ax. i.) accidents (*affectiones*) of the attributes of God.

PROP. XV. *Whatsoever is, is in God, and without God nothing can be, or be conceived.*

Proof.—Besides God, no substance is granted or can be conceived (by Prop. xiv.) that is (by Def. iii.) nothing which is in itself and is conceived through itself. But modes (by Def. v.) can neither be, nor be conceived without substance; wherefore they can only be in the divine nature, and can only through it be conceived. But substances and modes form the sum total of existence (by Ax. i.), therefore, without God nothing can be, or be conceived. *Q.E.D.*

Note.—Some assert that God, like a man, consists of body and mind, and is susceptible of passions. How far such persons have strayed from the truth is sufficiently evident from what has been said. But these I pass over. For all who have in any way reflected on the divine nature deny that God has a body. Of this they find excellent proof in the fact that we understand by body a definite quantity, so long, so broad, so deep, bounded by a certain shape, and it is the height of absurdity to predicate such a thing of God, a being absolutely infinite. But meanwhile by the other reasons with which they try to prove their point, they show that they think corporeal or extended substance wholly apart from the divine nature, and say it was created by God. Wherefrom the divine nature can have been created, they are wholly ignorant; thus they clearly show, that they do not know the meaning of their own words. I myself have proved sufficiently clearly, at any rate in my own judgment (Coroll. Prop. vi., and Note 2, Prop. viii.), that no substance can be produced or created by anything other than itself. Further, I showed (in Prop. xiv.), that besides God no substance can be granted or conceived. Hence we drew the conclusion that extended substance is one of the infinite attributes of God. However, in order to explain more fully, I will refute the arguments of my adversaries, which all start from the following points:—

Extended substance, in so far as it is substance, consists, as they think, in parts, wherefore they deny that it can be infinite, or, consequently, that it can appertain to God. This they illustrate with many examples, of which I will take one or two. If extended substance, they say, is infinite, let it be conceived to be divided into two parts; each part will then be either finite or infinite. If the former, then infinite substance is composed of two finite parts, which is absurd. If the latter, then one infinite will be twice as large as another infinite, which is also absurd.

Further, if an infinite line be measured out in foot lengths, it will consist of an infinite number of such parts; it would equally consist of an infinite number of parts, if each part measured only an inch: therefore, one infinity would be twelve times as great as the other.

Lastly, if from a single point there be conceived to be drawn two diverging lines which at first are at a definite distance apart, but are produced to infinity, it is certain that the distance between the two lines will be continually increased, until at length it changes from definite to indefinable. As these absurdities follow, it is said, from considering quantity as infinite, the conclusion is drawn, that extended substance must necessarily be finite, and, consequently, cannot appertain to the nature of God.

The second argument is also drawn from God's supreme perfection. God, it is said, inasmuch as he is a supremely perfect being, cannot be passive; but extended substance, in so far as it is divisible, is passive. It follows, therefore, that extended substance does not appertain to the essence of God.

Such are the arguments I find on the subject in writers, who by them try to prove that extended substance is unworthy of the divine nature, and cannot possibly appertain thereto. However, I think an attentive reader will see that I have already answered their propositions; for all their arguments are founded on the hypothesis that extended substance is composed of parts, and such a hypothesis I have shown (Prop. xii., and Coroll. Prop. xiii.) to be absurd. Moreover, anyone who reflects will see that all these absurdities (if absurdities they be, which I am not now discussing), from which it is sought to extract the conclusion that extended substance is finite, do not at all follow from the notion of an infinite quantity, but merely from the notion that an infinite quantity is measurable, and composed of finite parts: therefore, the only fair conclusion to be drawn is that infinite quantity is not measurable, and cannot be composed of finite parts. This is exactly what we have already proved (in Prop. xii.). Wherefore the weapon which they aimed at us has in reality recoiled upon themselves. If, from this absurdity of theirs, they persist in drawing the conclusion that extended substance must be finite, they will in good sooth be acting like a man who asserts that circles have the properties of squares, and, finding himself thereby landed in absurdities, proceed to deny that circles have any centre, from which all lines drawn to the circumference are equal. For, taking extended substance, which can only be conceived as infinite, one, and indivisible (Props. viii., v., xii.) they assert, in order to prove that it is finite, that it is composed of finite parts, and that it can be multiplied and divided.

So, also, others, after asserting that a line is composed of points, can produce many arguments to prove that a line cannot be infinitely divided. Assuredly it is not less absurd to assert that extended substance is made up of bodies or parts, than it would be to assert that a solid is made up of surfaces, a surface of lines, and a line of points. This must be admitted by all who know clear reason to be infallible, and most of all by those who deny the possibility of a vacuum. For if extended substance could be so divided that its parts were really separate, why should not one part admit of being destroyed, the others remaining joined together as before? And why should all be so fitted into one another as to leave no vacuum? Surely in the case of things, which are really distinct one from the other, one can exist without the other, and can remain in its original condition. As, then, there does not exist a vacuum in nature (of which anon), but all parts are bound to come together to prevent it, it follows from this also that the parts cannot be really distinguished, and that extended substance in so far as it is substance cannot be divided.

If anyone asks me the further question, Why are we naturally so prone to divide quantity? I answer, that quantity is conceived by us in two ways; in the abstract and superficially, as we imagine it; or as substance, as we conceive it solely by the intellect. If, then, we regard quantity as it is represented in our imagination, which we often and more easily do, we shall find that it is finite, divisible, and compounded of parts; but if we regard it as it is represented in our intellect, and conceive it as substance, which it is very difficult to do, we shall then, as I have sufficiently proved, find that it is infinite, one, and indivisible. This will be plain enough to all, who make a distinction between the intellect and the imagination, especially if it be remembered, that matter is everywhere the same, that its parts are not distinguishable, except in so far as we conceive matter as diversely modified, whence its parts are distinguished, not really, but modally. For instance, water, in so far as it is water, we conceive to be divided, and its parts to be separated one from the other; but not in so far as it is extended substance; from this point of view it is neither separated nor divisible. Further, water, in so far as it is water, is produced and corrupted; but, in so far as it is substance, it is neither produced nor corrupted.

I think I have now answered the second argument; it is, in fact, founded on the same assumption as the first—namely, that matter, in so far as it is substance, is divisible, and composed of parts. Even if it were so, I do not know why it should be considered unworthy of the divine nature, inasmuch as besides God (by Prop. xiv.) no substance can be granted, wherefrom it could receive its modifications. All things, I repeat, are in God, and all things which come to pass, come to pass solely through the laws of the infinite nature of God, and follow (as I will shortly show) from the necessity of his essence. Wherefore it can in no way be said, that God is passive in respect to anything other than himself, or that extended substance is unworthy of the Divine nature, even if it be supposed divisible, so long as it is granted to be infinite and eternal. But enough of this for the present. . . .

PART II: OF THE NATURE AND ORIGIN OF THE MIND
PROPOSITIONS

PROP. XLIV. *It is not in the nature of reason to regard things as contingent, but as necessary.*

Proof.—It is in the nature of reason to perceive things truly (II. xli.), namely (I. Ax. vi.), as they are in themselves—that is (I. xxix.), not as contingent, but as necessary. *Q.E.D.*

Corollary I.—Hence it follows, that it is only through our imagination that we consider things, whether in respect to the future or the past, as contingent.

Note.—How this way of looking at things arises, I will briefly explain. We have shown above (II. xvii. and Coroll.) that the mind always regards things as present to itself, even though they be not in existence, until some causes arise which exclude their existence and presence. Further (II. xviii.), we showed that, if the human body has once been affected by two external bodies simultaneously, the mind, when it afterwards imagines one of the said external bodies, will straightway remember the other—that is, it will regard both as present to itself, unless there arise causes which exclude their existence and presence. Further, no one doubts that we imagine time, from the fact that we imagine bodies to be moved some more slowly than others, some more quickly, some at equal speed. Thus, let us suppose that a child yesterday saw Peter for the first time in the morning, Paul at noon, and Simon in the evening; then, that to-day he again sees Peter in the morning. It is evident, from II. Prop. xviii., that, as soon as he sees the morning light, he will imagine that the sun will traverse the same parts of the sky, as it did when he saw it on the preceding day; in other words, he will imagine a complete day, and, together with his imagination of the morning, he will imagine Peter; with noon, he will imagine Paul; and with evening, he will imagine Simon—that is, he will imagine the existence of Paul and Simon in relation to a future time; on the other hand, if he sees Simon in the evening, he will refer Peter and Paul to a past time, by imagining them simultaneously with the imagination of a past time. If it should at any time happen, that on some other evening the child should see James instead of Simon, he will, on the following morning, associate with his imagination of evening sometimes Simon, sometimes James, not both together: for the child is supposed to have seen, at evening, one or other of them, not both together. His imagination will therefore waver; and, with the imagination of future evenings, he will associate first one, then the other—that is, he will imagine them in the future, neither of them as certain, but both as contingent. This wavering of the imagination will be the same, if the imagination be concerned with things which we thus contemplate, standing in relation to time past or time present: consequently, we may imagine things as contingent, whether they be referred to time present, past, or future.

Corollary II.—It is in the nature of reason to perceive things under a certain form of eternity (*sub quâdam oeternitatis specie*).

Proof.—It is in the nature of reason to regard things, not as contingent, but as necessary (II. xliv.). Reason perceives this necessity of things (II. xli.) truly—that is (I. Ax. vi.), as it is in itself. But (I. xvi.) this necessity of things is the very necessity of the eternal nature of God; therefore, it is in the nature of reason to regard things under this form of eternity. We may add that the bases of reason are the notions (II. xxxviii.), which answer to things common to all, and which (II. xxxvii.) do not answer to the essence of any particular thing: which must therefore be conceived without any relation to time, under a certain form of eternity.

PROP. XLV. *Every idea of every body, or of every particular thing actually existing, necessarily involves the eternal and infinite essence of God.*

Proof.—The idea of a particular thing actually existing necessarily involves both the existence and the essence of the said thing (II. viii.). Now particular things cannot be conceived without God (I. xv.); but, inasmuch as (II. vi.) they have God for their cause, in so far as he is regarded under the attribute of which the things in question are modes, their ideas must necessarily involve (I. Ax. iv.) the conception of the attribute of those ideas— that is (I. vi.), the eternal and infinite essence of God. Q.E.D.

Note.—By existence I do not here mean duration—that is, existence in so far as it is conceived abstractedly, and as a certain form of quantity. I am speaking of the very nature of existence, which is assigned to particular things, because they follow in infinite numbers and in infinite ways from the eternal necessity of God's nature (I. xvi.). I am speaking, I repeat, of the very existence of particular things, in so far as they are in God. For although each particular thing be conditioned by another particular thing to exist in a given way, yet the force whereby each particular thing perseveres in existing follows from the eternal necessity of God's nature (cf. I. xxiv. Coroll.).

PROP. XLVI. *The knowledge of the eternal and infinite essence of God which every idea involves is adequate and perfect.*

Proof.—The proof of the last proposition is universal; and whether a thing be considered as a part or a whole, the idea thereof, whether of the whole or of a part (by the last Prop.), will involve God's eternal and infinite essence. Wherefore, that, which gives knowledge of the eternal and infinite essence of God, is common to all, and is equally in the part and in the whole; therefore (II. xxxviii.) this knowledge will be adequate. *Q.E.D.*

PROP. XLVII. *The human mind has an adequate knowledge of the eternal and infinite essence of God.*

Proof.—The human mind has ideas (II. xxii.), from which (II. xxiii.) it perceives itself and its own body (II. xix.) and external bodies (II. xvi. Coroll. I. and II. xvii.) as actually existing; therefore (II. xlv. xlvi.) it has an adequate knowledge of the eternal and infinite essence of God. *Q.E.D.*

Note.—Hence we see, that the infinite essence and the eternity of God are known to all. Now as all things are in God, and are conceived through God, we can from this knowledge infer many things, which we may adequately know, and we may form that third kind of knowledge of which we spoke in the note to II. xl., and of the excellence and use of which we shall have occasion to speak in Part V. Men have not so clear a knowledge of God as they have of general notions, because they are unable to imagine God as they do bodies, and also because they have associated the name God with images of things that they are in the habit of seeing, as indeed they can hardly avoid doing, being, as they are, men, and continually affected by external bodies. Many errors, in truth, can be traced to this head, namely, that we do not apply names to things rightly. For instance, when a man says that the lines drawn from the centre of a circle to its circumference are not equal, he then, at all events, assuredly attaches a meaning to the word circle different from that assigned by mathematicians. So again, when men make mistakes in calculation, they have one set of figures in their mind, and another on the paper. If we could see into their minds, they do not make a mistake; they seem to do so, because we think, that they have the same numbers in their mind as they have on the paper. If this were not so, we should not believe them to be in error, any more than I thought that a man was in error, whom I lately heard exclaiming that his entrance hall had flown into a neighbour's hen, for his meaning seemed to me sufficiently clear. Very many controversies have arisen from the fact, that men do not rightly explain their meaning, or do not rightly interpret the meaning of others. For, as a matter of fact, as they flatly contradict themselves, they assume now one side, now another, of the argument, so as to oppose the opinions, which they consider mistaken and absurd in their opponents.

PROP. XLVIII. *In the mind there is no absolute or free will; but the mind is determined to wish this or that by a cause, which has also been determined by another cause, and this last by another cause, and so on to infinity.*

Proof.—The mind is a fixed and definite mode of thought (II. xi.), therefore it cannot be the free cause of its actions (I. xvii. Coroll. ii.); in other words, it cannot have an absolute faculty of positive or negative volition; but (by I. xxviii.) it must be determined by a cause, which has also been determined by another cause, and this last by another, etc. *Q.E.D.*

Note.—In the same way it is proved, that there is in the mind no absolute faculty of understanding, desiring, loving, etc. Whence it follows, that these and similar faculties are either entirely fictitious, or are merely abstract or general terms, such as we are accustomed to put together from particular things. Thus the intellect and the will stand in the same relation to this or that idea, or this or that volition, as "lapidity" to this or that stone, or as "man" to Peter and Paul. The cause which leads men to consider themselves free has been set forth in the Appendix to Part I. But, before I proceed further, I would here remark that, by the will to affirm and decide, I mean the faculty, not the desire. I mean, I repeat, the faculty, whereby the mind affirms or denies what is true or false, not the desire, wherewith the mind wishes for or turns away from any given thing. After we have proved, that these faculties of ours are general notions, which cannot be distinguished from the particular instances on which they are based, we must inquire whether volitions themselves are anything besides the ideas of things. We must inquire, I say, whether there is in the mind any affirmation or negation beyond that, which the idea, in so far as it is an idea, involves. On which subject see the following proposition, and II. Def. iii., lest the idea of pictures should suggest itself. For by ideas I do not mean images such as are formed at the back of the eye, or in the midst of the brain, but the conceptions of thought.

PROP. XLIX. *There is in the mind no volition or affirmation and negation, save that which an idea, inasmuch as it is an idea, involves.*

Proof.—There is in the mind no absolute faculty of positive or negative volition, but only particular volitions, namely, this or that affirmation, and this or that negation. Now let us conceive a particular volition, namely, the mode of thinking whereby the mind affirms, that the three interior angles of a triangle are equal to two right angles. This affirmation involves the conception or idea of a triangle, that is, without the idea of a triangle it cannot be conceived. It is the same thing to say, that the concept A must involve the concept B, as it is to say, that A cannot be conceived without B. Further, this affirmation cannot be made (II. Ax. iii.) without the idea of a triangle. Therefore, this affirmation can neither be nor be conceived, without the idea of a triangle. Again, this idea of a triangle must involve this same affirmation, namely, that its three interior angles are equal to two right angles. Wherefore, and *vice versa,* this idea of a triangle can neither be nor be conceived without this affirmation, therefore, this affirmation belongs to the essence of the idea of a triangle, and is nothing besides. What we have said of this volition (inasmuch as we have selected it at random) may be said of any other volition, namely, that it is nothing but an idea. *Q.E.D.*

Corollary.—Will and understanding are one and the same.

Proof.—Will and understanding are nothing beyond the individual volitions and ideas (II. xlviii. and note). But a particular volition and a particular idea are one and the same (by the foregoing Prop.); therefore, will and understanding are one and the same. *Q.E.D.*

Note.—We have thus removed the cause which is commonly assigned for error. For we have shown above, that falsity consists solely in the privation of knowledge involved in ideas which are fragmentary and confused. Wherefore, a false idea, inasmuch as it is false, does not involve certainty. When we say, then, that a man acquiesces in what is false, and that he has no doubts on the subject, we do not say that he is certain, but only that he does not doubt, or that he acquiesces in what is false, inasmuch as there are no reasons, which should cause his imagination to waver (see II. xliv. note). Thus, although the man be assumed to acquiesce in what is false, we shall never say that he is certain. For by certainty we mean something positive (II. xliii. and note), not merely the absence of doubt.

However, in order that the foregoing proposition may be fully explained, I will draw attention to a few additional points, and I will furthermore answer the objections which may be advanced against our doctrine. Lastly, in order to remove every scruple, I have thought it worth while to point out some of the advantages, which follow therefrom. I say "some," for they will be better appreciated from what we shall set forth in the fifth part.

I begin, then, with the first point, and warn my readers to make an accurate distinction between an idea, or conception of the mind, and the images of things which we imagine. It is further necessary that they should distinguish between idea and words, whereby we signify things. These three—namely, images, words, and ideas—are by many persons either entirely confused together, or not distinguished with sufficient accuracy or care, and hence people are generally in ignorance, how absolutely necessary is a knowledge of this doctrine of the will, both for philosophic purposes and for the wise ordering of life. Those who think that ideas consist in images which are formed in us by contact with external bodies, persuade themselves that the ideas of those things, whereof we can form no mental picture, are not ideas, but only figments, which we invent by the free decree of our will; they thus regard ideas as though they were inanimate pictures on a panel, and, filled with this misconception, do not see that an idea, inasmuch as it is an idea, involves an affirmation or negation. Again, those who confuse words with ideas, or with the affirmation which an idea involves, think that they can wish something contrary to what they feel, affirm, or deny. This misconception will easily be laid aside by one, who reflects on the nature of knowledge, and seeing that it in no way involves the conception of extension, will therefore clearly understand, that an idea (being a mode of thinking) does not consist in the image of anything, nor in words. The essence of words and images is put together by bodily motions, which in no way involve the conception of thought.

These few words on this subject will suffice: I will therefore pass on to consider the objections, which may be raised against our doctrine. Of these, the first is advanced by those, who think that the will has a wider scope than the understanding, and that therefore it is different therefrom. The reason for their holding the belief, that the will has wider scope than the understanding, is that they assert, that they have no need of an increase in their faculty of assent, that is of affirmation or negation, in order to assent to an infinity of things which we do not perceive, but that they have need of an increase in their faculty of understanding. The will is thus distinguished from the intellect, the latter being finite and the former infinite. Secondly, it may be objected that experience seems to teach us especially clearly, that we are able to suspend our judgment before assenting to things which we perceive; this is confirmed by the fact that no one is said to be deceived, in so far as he perceives anything, but only in so far as he assents or dissents.

For instance, he who feigns a winged horse, does not therefore admit that a winged horse exists; that is, he is not deceived, unless he admits in addition that a winged horse does exist. Nothing therefore seems to be taught more clearly by experience, than that the will or faculty of assent is free and different from the faculty of understanding. Thirdly, it may be objected that one affirmation does not apparently contain more reality than another; in other words, that we do not seem to need for affirming, that what is true is true, any greater power than for affirming, that what is false is true. We have, however, seen that one idea has more reality or perfection than another, for as objects are some more excellent than others, so also are the ideas of them some more excellent than others; this also seems to point to a difference between the understanding and the will. Fourthly, it may be objected, if man does not act from free will, what will happen if the incentives to action are equally balanced, as in the case of Buridan's ass? Will he perish of hunger and thirst? If I say that he would, I shall seem to have in my thoughts an ass or the statue of a man rather than an actual man. If I say that he would not, he would then determine his own action, and would consequently possess the faculty of going and doing whatever he liked. Other objections might also be raised, but, as I am not bound to put in evidence everything that anyone may dream, I will only set myself to the task of refuting those I have mentioned, and that as briefly as possible.

To the *first* objection I answer, that I admit that the will has a wider scope than the understanding, if by the understanding be meant only clear and distinct ideas; but I deny that the will has a wider scope than the perceptions, and the faculty of forming conceptions;

nor do I see why the faculty of volition should be called infinite, any more than the faculty of feeling: for, as we are able by the same faculty of volition to affirm an infinite number of things (one after the other, for we cannot affirm an infinite number simultaneously), so also can we, by the same faculty of feeling, feel or perceive (in succession) an infinite number of bodies. If it be said that there is an infinite number of things which we cannot perceive, I answer, that we cannot attain to such things by any thinking, nor, consequently, by any faculty of volition. But, it may still be urged, if God wished to bring it about that we should perceive them, he would be obliged to endow us with a greater faculty of perception, but not a greater faculty of volition than we have already. This is the same as to say that, if God wished to bring it about that we should understand an infinite number of other entities, it would be necessary for him to give us a greater understanding, but not a more universal idea of entity than that which we have already, in order to grasp such infinite entities. We have shown that will is a universal entity or idea, whereby we explain all particular volitions—in other words, that which is common to all such volitions.

As, then, our opponents maintain that this idea, common or universal to all volitions, is a faculty, it is little to be wondered at that they assert, that such a faculty extends itself into the infinite, beyond the limits of the understanding: for what is universal is predicated alike of one, of many, and of an infinite number of individuals.

To the *second* objection I reply by denying, that we have a free power of suspending our judgment: for, when we say that anyone suspends his judgment, we merely mean that he sees, that he does not perceive the matter in question adequately. Suspension of judgment is, therefore, strictly speaking, a perception, and not free will. In order to illustrate the point, let us suppose a boy imagining a horse, and perceiving nothing else. Inasmuch as this imagination involves the existence of the horse (II. xvii. Coroll.), and the boy does not perceive anything which would exclude the existence of the horse, he will necessarily regard the horse as present: he will not be able to doubt of its existence, although he be not certain thereof. We have daily experience of such a state of things in dreams; and I do not suppose that there is anyone, who would maintain that, while he is dreaming, he has the free power of suspending his judgment concerning the things in his dream, and bringing it about that he should not dream those things, which he dreams that he sees; yet it happens, notwithstanding, that even in dreams we suspend our judgment, namely, when we dream that we are dreaming.

Further, I grant that no one can be deceived, so far as actual perception extends—that is, I grant that the mind's imaginations, regarded in themselves, do not involve error (II. xvii., note); but I deny, that a man does not, in the act of perception, make any affirmation. For what is the perception of a winged horse, save affirming that a horse has wings? If the mind could perceive nothing else but the winged horse, it would regard the same as present to itself: it would have no reasons for doubting its existence, nor any faculty of dissent, unless the imagination of a winged horse be joined to an idea which precludes the existence of the said horse, or unless the mind perceives that the idea which it possesses of a winged horse is inadequate, in which case it will either necessarily deny the existence of such a horse, or will necessarily be in doubt on the subject.

I think that I have anticipated my answer to the *third* objection, namely, that the will is something universal which is predicated of all ideas, and that it only signifies that which is common to all ideas, namely, an affirmation, whose adequate essence must, therefore, in so far as it is thus conceived in the abstract, be in every idea, and be, in this respect alone, the same in all, not in so far as it is considered as constituting the idea's essence: for, in this respect, particular affirmations differ one from the other, as much as do ideas. For instance, the affirmation which involves the idea of a circle, differs from that which involves the idea of a triangle, as much as the idea of a circle differs from the idea of a triangle.

Further, I absolutely deny, that we are in need of an equal power of thinking, to affirm that that which is true is true, and to affirm that that which is false is true. These two affirmations, if we regard the mind, are in the same relation to one another as being and not-being; for there is nothing positive in ideas, which constitutes the actual reality of falsehood (II. xxxv. note, and xlvii. note).

We must therefore conclude, that we are easily deceived, when we confuse universals with singulars, and the entities of reason and abstractions with realities. As for the *fourth* objection, I am quite ready to admit, that a man placed in the equilibrium described (namely, as perceiving nothing but hunger and thirst, a certain food and a certain drink, each equally distant from him) would die of hunger and thirst. If I am asked, whether such a one should not rather be considered an ass than a man; I answer, that I do not know, neither do I know how a man should be considered, who hangs himself, or how we should consider children, fools, madmen, etc.

It remains to point out the advantages of a knowledge of this doctrine as bearing on conduct, and this may be easily gathered from what has been said. The doctrine is good,

1. Inasmuch as it teaches us to act solely according to the decree of God, and to be partakers in the Divine nature, and so much the more, as we perform more perfect actions and more and more understand God. Such a doctrine not only completely tranquilizes our spirit, but also shows us where our highest happiness or blessedness is, namely, solely in the knowledge of God, whereby we are led to act only as love and piety shall bid us. We may thus clearly understand, how far astray from a true estimate of virtue are those who expect to be decorated by God with high rewards for their virtue, and their best actions, as for having endured the direst slavery; as if virtue and the service of God were not in itself happiness and perfect freedom.

2. Inasmuch as it teaches us, how we ought to conduct ourselves with respect to the gifts of fortune, or matters which are not in our own power, and do not follow from our nature. For it shows us, that we should await and endure fortune's smiles or frowns with an equal mind, seeing that all things follow from the eternal decree of God by the same necessity, as it follows from the essence of a triangle, that the three angles are equal to two right angles.

3. This doctrine raises social life, inasmuch as it teaches us to hate no man, neither to despise, to deride, to envy, or to be angry with any. Further, as it tells us that each should be content with his own, and helpful to his neighbour, not from any womanish pity, favour, or superstition, but solely by the guidance of reason, according as the time and occasion demand, as I will show in Part III.

4. Lastly, this doctrine confers no small advantage on the commonwealth; for it teaches how citizens should be governed and led, not so as to become slaves, but so that they may freely do whatsoever things are best.

I have thus fulfilled the promise made at the beginning of this note, and I thus bring the second part of my treatise to a close. I think I have therein explained the nature and properties of the human mind at sufficient length, and, considering the difficulty of the subject, with sufficient clearness. I have laid a foundation, whereon may be raised many excellent conclusions of the highest utility and most necessary to be known, as will, in what follows, be partly made plain.

PART IV: OF HUMAN BONDAGE,
OR THE STRENGTH OF THE EMOTIONS

PREFACE

Human infirmity in moderating and checking the emotions I name bondage: for, when a man is a prey to his emotions, he is not his own master, but lies at the mercy of fortune: so much so, that he is often compelled, while seeing that which is better for him, to follow that which is worse. Why this is so, and what is good or evil in the emotions, I propose to show in this part of my treatise. But, before I begin, it would be well to make a few prefatory observations on perfection and imperfection, good and evil.

When a man has purposed to make a given thing, and has brought it to perfection, his work will be pronounced perfect, not only by himself, but by everyone who rightly knows, or thinks that he knows, the intention and aim of its author. For instance, suppose anyone sees a work (which I assume to be not yet completed), and knows that the aim of the author of that work is to build a house, he will call the work imperfect; he will, on the other hand, call it perfect, as soon as he sees that it is carried through to the end, which its author had purposed for it. But if a man sees a work, the like whereof he has never seen before, and if he knows not the intention of the artificer, he plainly cannot know, whether that work be perfect or imperfect. Such seems to be the primary meaning of these terms.

But after men began to form general ideas, to think out types of houses, buildings, towers, etc. and to prefer certain types to others, it came about, that each man called perfect that which he saw agree with the general idea he had formed of the thing in question, and called imperfect that which he saw agree less with his own preconceived type, even though it had evidently been completed in accordance with the idea of its artificer. This seems to be the only reason for calling natural phenomena, which, indeed, are not made with human hands, perfect or imperfect: for men are wont to form general ideas of things natural, no less than of things artificial, and such ideas they hold as types, believing that Nature (who they think does nothing without an object) has them in view, and has set them as types before herself. Therefore, when they behold something in Nature, which does not wholly conform to the preconceived type which they have formed of the thing in question, they say that Nature has fallen short or has blundered, and has left her work incomplete. Thus we see that men are wont to style natural phenomena perfect or imperfect rather from their own prejudices, than from true knowledge of what they pronounce upon.

Now we showed in the Appendix to Part I., that nature does not work with an end in view. For the eternal and infinite Being, which we call God or Nature, acts by the same necessity as that whereby it exists. For we have shown, that by the same necessity of its nature, whereby it exists, it likewise works (I. xvi.). The reason or cause why God or Nature exists, and the reason why he acts, are one and the same. Therefore, as he does not exist for the sake of an end, so neither does he act for the sake of an end; of his existence and of his action there is neither origin nor end. Wherefore, a cause which is called final is nothing else but human desire, in so far as it is considered as the origin or cause of anything. For example, when we say that to be inhabited is the final cause of this or that house, we mean nothing more than that a man, conceiving the conveniences of household life, had a desire to build a house. Wherefore, the being inhabited, in so far as it is regarded as a final cause, is nothing else but this particular desire, which is really the efficient cause; it is regarded as the primary cause, because men are generally ignorant of the causes of their desires. They are, as I have often said already, conscious of their own actions and appetites, but ignorant of the causes whereby they are determined to any particular desire. Therefore, the common saying that Nature sometimes falls short, or blunders, and produces things which are imperfect, I set down among the glosses treated of in the Appendix to Part I. Perfection and imperfection, then, are in reality merely modes of thinking, or notions which we form from a comparison among one another of individuals of the same species; hence I said above (II. Def. vi.), that by reality and perfection I mean the same thing. For we are wont to refer all the individual things in nature to one genus, which is called the highest genus, namely, to the category of Being, whereto absolutely all individuals in nature belong. Thus, in so far as we refer the individuals in nature to this category, and comparing them one with another, find that some possess more of being or reality than others, we, to this extent, say that some are more perfect than others. Again, in so far as we attribute to them anything implying negation—as term, end, infirmity, etc.,—we, to this extent, call them imperfect, because they do not affect our mind so much as the things which we call perfect, not because they have any intrinsic deficiency, or because Nature has blundered. For nothing lies within the scope of a thing's nature, save that which follows from the necessity of the nature of its efficient cause, and whatsoever follows from the necessity of the nature of its efficient cause necessarily comes to pass.

As for the terms *good* and *bad,* they indicate no positive quality in things regarded in themselves, but are merely modes of thinking, or notions which we form from the comparison of things one with another. Thus one and the same thing can be at the same time good, bad, and indifferent. For instance, music is good for him that is melancholy, bad for him that mourns; for him that is deaf, it is neither good nor bad.

Nevertheless, though this be so, the terms should still be retained. For, inasmuch as we desire to form an idea of man as a type of human nature which we may hold in view, it will be useful for us to retain the terms in question, in the sense I have indicated.

In what follows, then, I shall mean by "good" that which we certainly know to be a means of approaching more nearly to the type of human nature, which we have set before ourselves; by "bad," that which we certainly know to be a hindrance to us in approaching the said type. Again, we shall say that men are more perfect, or more imperfect, in proportion as they approach more or less nearly to the said type. For it must be specially remarked that, when I say that a man passes from a lesser to a greater perfection, or *vice versa,* I do not mean that he is changed from one essence or reality to another; for instance, a horse would be as completely destroyed by being changed into a man, as by being changed into an insect. What I mean is, that we conceive the thing's power of action, in so far as this is understood by its nature, to be increased or diminished. Lastly, by perfection in general I shall, as I have said, mean reality—in other words, each thing's essence, in so far as it exists, and operates in a particular manner, and without paying any regard to its duration. For no given thing can be said to be more perfect, because it has passed a longer time in existence. The duration of things cannot be determined by their essence, for the essence of things involves no fixed and definite period of existence; but everything, whether it be more perfect or less perfect, will always be able to persist in existence with the same force wherewith it began to exist; wherefore, in this respect, all things are equal

DEFINITIONS

I. By *good* I mean that which we certainly know to be useful to us.

II. By *evil* I mean that which we certainly know to be a hindrance to us in the attainment of any good.

(Concerning these terms see the foregoing preface towards the end.)

III. Particular things I call *contingent* in so far as, while regarding their essence only, we find nothing therein, which necessarily asserts their existence or excludes it.

IV. Particular things I call *possible* in so far as, while regarding the causes whereby they must be produced, we know not, whether such causes be determined for producing them.

(In I. xxxiii. note i., I drew no distinction between possible and contingent, because there was in that place no need to distinguish them accurately.)

V. By *conflicting emotions* I mean those which draw a man in different directions, though they are of the same kind, such as luxury and avarice, which are both species of love, and are contraries, not by nature, but by accident.

VI. What I mean by emotion felt towards a thing, future, present, and past, I explained in III. xviii., notes i. and ii., which see.

(But I should here also remark, that we can only distinctly conceive distance of space or time up to a certain definite limit; that is, all objects distant from us more than two hundred feet, or whose distance from the place where we are exceeds that which we can distinctly conceive, seem to be an equal distance from us, and all in the same plane; so also objects, whose time of existing is conceived as removed from the present by a longer interval than we can distinctly conceive, seem to be all equally distant from the present, and are set down, as it were, to the same moment of time.)

VII. By an *end,* for the sake of which we do something, I mean a desire.

VIII. By *virtue* (*virtus*) and *power* I mean the same thing; that is (III. vii.), virtue, in so far as it is referred to man, is a man's nature or essence, in so far as it has the power of effecting what can only be understood by the laws of that nature. . . .

PROPOSITIONS

Prop. XXXI. *In so far as a thing is in harmony with our nature, it is necessarily good.*

Proof.—In so far as a thing is in harmony with our nature, it cannot be bad for it. It will therefore necessarily be either good or indifferent. If it be assumed that it be neither good nor bad, nothing will follow from its nature (IV. Def. i.), which tends to the preservation of our nature, that is (by the hypothesis), which tends to the preservation of the thing itself; but this (III. vi.) is absurd; therefore, in so far as a thing is in harmony with our nature, it is necessarily good. *Q.E.D.*

Corollary.—Hence it follows, that, in proportion as a thing is in harmony with our nature, so is it more useful or better for us, and *vice versa,* in proportion as a thing is more useful for us, so is it more in harmony with our nature. For, in so far as it is not in harmony with our nature, it will necessarily be different therefrom or contrary thereto. If different, it can neither be good nor bad (IV. xxix.); if contrary, it will be contrary to that which is in harmony with our nature, that is, contrary to what is good—in short, bad. Nothing, therefore, can be good, except in so far as it is in harmony with our nature; and hence a thing is useful, in proportion as it is in harmony with our nature, and *vice versa. Q.E.D.*

Prop. XXXII. *In so far as men are a prey to passion, they cannot, in that respect, be said to be naturally in harmony.*

Proof.—Things, which are said to be in harmony naturally, are understood to agree in power (III. vii.), not in want of power or negation, and consequently not in passion (III. iii. note); wherefore men, in so far as they are a prey to their passions, cannot be said to be naturally in harmony. *Q.E.D.*

Note.—This is also self-evident; for, if we say that white and black only agree in the fact that neither is red, we absolutely affirm that they do not agree in any respect. So, if we say that a man and a stone only agree in the fact that both are finite—wanting in power, not existing by the necessity of their own nature, or, lastly, indefinitely surpassed by the power of external causes—we should certainly affirm that a man and a stone are in no respect alike; therefore, things which agree only in negation, or in qualities which neither possess, really agree in no respect.

PROP. XXXIII. *Men can differ in nature, in so far as they are assailed by those emotions, which are passions, or passive states; and to this extent one and the same man is variable and inconstant.*

Proof.—The nature or essence of the emotions cannot be explained solely through our essence or nature (III. Deff. i. ii.), but it must be defined by the power, that is (III. vii.), by the nature of external causes in comparison with our own; hence it follows, that there are as many kinds of each emotion as there are external objects whereby we are affected (III. lvi.), and that men may be differently affected by one and the same object (III. li.), and to this extent differ in nature; lastly, that one and the same man may be differently affected towards the same object, and may therefore be variable and inconstant. Q.E.D.

PROP. XXXIV. *In so far as men are assailed by emotions which are passions, they can be contrary one to another.*

Proof.—A man, for instance Peter, can be the cause of Paul's feeling pain, because he (Peter) possesses something similar to that which Paul hates (III. xvi.), or because Peter has sole possession of a thing which Paul also loves (III. xxxii. and note), or for other causes (of which the chief are enumerated in III. lv. note); it may therefore happen that Paul should hate Peter (Def. of Emotions, vii.), consequently it may easily happen also, that Peter should hate Paul in return, and that each should endeavour to do the other an injury (III. xxxix.), that is (IV. xxx.), that they should be contrary one to another. But the emotion of pain is always a passion or passive state (III. lix.); hence men, in so far as they are assailed by emotions which are passions, can be contrary one to another. Q.E.D.

Note.—I said that Paul may hate Peter, because he conceives that Peter possesses something which he (Paul) also loves; from this it seems, at first sight, to follow, that these two men, through both loving the same thing, and, consequently, through agreement of their respective natures, stand in one another's way; if this were so, Props. xxx. and xxxi. of this Part would be untrue. But if we give the matter our unbiased attention, we shall see that the discrepancy vanishes. For the two men are not in one another's way in virtue of the agreement of their natures, that is, through both loving the same thing, but in virtue of one differing from the other. For, in so far as each loves the same thing, the love of each is fostered thereby (III. xxxi.), that is (Def. of the Emotions, vi.) the pleasure of each is fostered thereby. Wherefore it is far from being the case, that they are at variance through both loving the same thing, and through the agreement in their natures. The cause for their opposition lies, as I have said, solely in the fact that they are assumed to differ. For we assume that Peter has the idea of the loved object as already in his possession, while Paul has the idea of the loved object as lost. Hence the one man will be affected with pleasure, the other will be affected with pain, and thus they will be at variance one with another. We can easily show in like manner, that all other causes of hatred depend solely on differences, and not on the agreement between men's natures.

PROP. XXXV. *In so far only as men live in obedience to reason, do they always necessarily agree in nature.*

Proof.—In so far as men are assailed by emotions that are passions, they can be different in nature (IV. xxxiii.), and at variance one with another. But men are only said to be active, in so far as they act in obedience to reason (III. iii.); therefore, whatsoever follows from human nature in so far as it is defined by reason must (III. Def. ii.) be understood solely through human nature as its proximate cause. But, since every man by the laws of his nature desires that which he deems good, and endeavours to remove that which he deems bad (IV. xix.); and further, since that which we, in accordance with reason, deem good or bad, necessarily is good or bad (II. xli.); it follows that men, in so far as they live in obedience to reason, necessarily do only such things as are necessarily good for human nature, and consequently for each individual man (IV. xxxi. Coroll.); in other words, such things as are in harmony with each man's nature. Therefore, men in so far as they live in obedience to reason, necessarily live always in harmony one with another. *Q.E.D.*

Corollary I.—There is no individual thing in nature, which is more useful to man, than a man who lives in obedience to reason. For that thing is to man most useful, which is most in harmony with his nature (IV. xxxi. Coroll.); that is, obviously, man. But man acts absolutely according to the laws of his nature, when he lives in obedience to reason (III. Def. ii.), and to this extent only is always necessarily in harmony with the nature of another man (by the last Prop.); wherefore among individual things nothing is more useful to man, than a man who lives in obedience to reason. *Q.E.D.*

Corollary II.—As every man seeks most that which is useful to him, so are men most useful one to another. For the more a man seeks what is useful to him and endeavours to preserve himself, the more is he endowed with virtue (IV. xx.), or, what is the same thing (IV. Def. viii.), the more is he endowed with power to act according to the laws of his own nature, that is to live in obedience to reason. But men are most in natural harmony, when they live in obedience to reason (by the last Prop.); therefore (by the foregoing Coroll.) men will be most useful one to another, when each seeks most that which is useful to him. *Q.E.D.*

Note.—What we have just shown is attested by experience so conspicuously, that it is in the mouth of nearly everyone: "Man is to man a God." Yet it rarely happens that men live in obedience to reason, for things are so ordered among them, that they are generally envious and troublesome one to another. Nevertheless they are scarcely able to lead a solitary life, so that the definition of man as a social animal has met with general assent; in fact, men do derive from social life much more convenience than injury. Let satirists then laugh their fill at human affairs, let theologians rail, and let misanthropes praise to their utmost the life of untutored rusticity, let them heap contempt on men and praises on beasts; when all is said, they will find that men can provide for their wants much more easily by mutual help, and that only by uniting their forces can they escape from the dangers that on every side beset them: not to say how much more excellent and worthy of our knowledge it is, to study the actions of men than the actions of beasts. But I will treat of this more at length elsewhere.

Prop. XXXVI. *The highest good of those who follow virtue is common to all, and therefore all can equally rejoice therein.*

Proof.—To act virtuously is to act in obedience with reason (IV. xxiv.), and whatsoever we endeavour to do in obedience to reason is to understand (IV. xxvi.); therefore (IV. xxviii.) the highest good for those who follow after virtue is to know God; that is (II. xlvii. and note) a good which is common to all and can be possessed by all men equally, in so far as they are of the same nature. *Q.E.D.*

Note.—Someone may ask how it would be, if the highest good of those who follow after virtue were not common to all? Would it not then follow, as above (IV. xxxiv.), that men living in obedience to reason, that is (IV. xxxv.), men in so far as they agree in nature, would be at variance one with another? To such an inquiry I make answer, that it follows not accidentally but from the very nature of reason, that man's highest good is common to all, inasmuch as it is deduced from the very essence of man, in so far as defined by reason; and that a man could neither be, nor be conceived without the power of taking pleasure in this highest good. For it belongs to the essence of the human mind (II. xlvii.), to have an adequate knowledge of the eternal and infinite essence of God. . . .

27

LOCKE

1632–1704

Born in Somerset, England, John Locke attended the famous Westminster School. He studied philosophy and medicine at Oxford University, where he learned the new experimental science of Robert Boyle. As a member of the Royal Society, he worked with and got to know Isaac Newton. Although he became a medical doctor, Locke turned his full attention to philosophy after reading Descartes's *Meditations* and seeing how a method might be worked out that could accommodate the progress being made in the newly emerging sciences.

Descartes, Spinoza, and Leibniz were rationalists who, like Plato, held that knowledge must be attained by the light of reason. Locke was an empiricist who claimed that all knowledge comes from experience. However, he fully agreed with Descartes that the mind and our ideas are more directly and better known than physical objects, which are known only indirectly. In many ways, Locke's *Essay Concerning Human Understanding* (1690) is a critical response to, and further development of, Descartes's views, only in a different direction. Locke attacks the idea of innate knowledge, arguing that all ideas in the mind can be accounted for through experience—via either sensation (mental events derived from the outer senses) or reflection (mental events evoked through introspection).

Locke distinguishes simple ideas like red, cold, and salty, which are atomic in that they cannot be further divided, from complex ideas, put together by the mind, which do not correspond to the real world (like fictional objects). He explains the origin of all our ideas by analyzing complex ideas into simpler ones. In the first book of his *Essay,* he paves the way for his account of the nature and origin of the mind and our ideas. The second book, from which our first selection is taken, begins with a criticism of the commonsense distinction between our perceptions and our ideas. For Locke, as for Descartes, *having ideas* and *having perceptions* are one and the same thing. Although anything that occurs in the mind—all mental events—are ideas, perceptions too are mental events.

With what do you apprehend the perceptions? Obviously, your mind. But what exactly is it within your mind that makes seeing, as a visual event, possible? What until Locke had been only implicit is now made explicit. The all-important mental faculty, as Locke defines it, is *the faculty of the understanding.* In Locke's view, understanding is to perception as eyes are to things out there in the world. Further, just as the eyes are "transparent" to themselves—the looking eye does not see itself, the eye, looking—so too the understanding does not notice itself.

Locke claims that the mind at birth is exactly what Leibniz claimed it was *not,* namely, a *tabula rasa,* a blank slate. This is the so-called empirical view of knowledge as something acquired from the "external world," "through the senses," according to which the newborn mind knows nothing and is thereby ready to learn anything and everything, which it can do only through experience.

Locke goes on to give a detailed account of the history and origin of our ideas on which our understanding of ourselves and the world is based. Just as the eye cannot actively choose how it reacts to the light hitting upon it but instead is passive, so too the understanding is completely passive. Thus, "the mind is forced to receive the impressions"; nor can the mind "avoid the perception of those ideas that are annexed to them." What causes impressions and the subsequent perceptions based on them is that objects out there in the world have *qualities,* by which Locke means the *power* of objects to affect our minds. Ideas (that is, perceptions) in the mind are the effect; the qualities of objects are the cause. Ideas of primary qualities, which resemble objects out there in the world, are solidity, extension, figure, mobility, and number. Ideas of secondary qualities, which do not resemble objects out there in the world, exist only in the mind, giving rise to complex ideas (such as colors, smells, and textures).

According to Locke, our perceptions do not render an accurate and perfect picture of the world; rather, our perceptions are imperfect representations of reality. What allows us to have knowledge to the extent that we do have it is that all our simple ideas are real: the mind cannot create them but receives them, passively, from the primary qualities in the things themselves that exist out there independently of the mind. Ideas of secondary qualities are also real. But in these ideas the things out there existing beyond the mind are represented only partially and imperfectly.

The second selection is from the second of Locke's *Two Treatises on Government* (1690), an important work on political philosophy published the same year as his *Essay Concerning Human Understanding.* Though motivated in part to justify the ascendancy of King William after the Glorious Revolution of 1688, it is widely regarded as among the greatest political works of modern times. In it, Locke begins, as did Hobbes, with an analysis of the "state of nature" as it existed prior to the formation of a political state. But Locke takes a much less pessimistic view than Hobbes. According to Locke, all human beings are created equal "within the bounds of the law of nature," which is *reason* itself: "reason, which is that law, teaches all mankind who will but consult it, that, being all equal and independent, no one ought to harm another in his life, health, liberty or possessions." Since in Locke's view empirical inquiry furnishes no certain universal knowledge and since assumptions such as that like bodies will in the same circumstances have like effects is only a conjecture from analogy, natural science in the strict sense does not exist. Both mathematics and ethics, however, belong in the sphere of the demonstrative knowledge of relations. Thus the principles of ethics are according to Locke as capable of exact demonstration as are those of arithmetic and geometry, although their underlying ideas are more complex, more involved, and hence more exposed to misunderstanding. Further, though lacking the visible symbols of mathematics, these principles should be made explicit through careful and strictly consistent definitions. Moral principles such as "where there is no property there is no injustice" and "no government allows absolute liberty" are as certain as any propositions in Euclid.

Locke thus constructs one of the most influential political philosophies of all time, in which exactly those propositions that are usually taken to be most subjective and least certain become the most incontrovertible and best known; what is brewing in such a new and revolutionary philosophy, in part, is the idea that society can be constructed in such a way that its functioning can become an absolute arbiter not just of justice but of truth and knowledge as well. A just political system must be constructed so as to reflect and amplify the natural state of the world. Majority rule, the separation of church and state, the right of a people to change governments, the natural right of a people to overthrow unjust governments, the separation of powers within a government, are all ideas central to Locke's system.

Locke championed the idea that all people are born free and with like capacities and rights. Each person is free to preserve his or her own interests, but without injuring those of others. The right to be treated by everyone as a rational being holds even prior to the founding of the state; but then there is no authoritative power to decide conflicts. The state of nature is not in itself a state of war, but it would lead to war if each person attempted to exercise the right of self-protection. To prevent such acts of violence, the civil community is constructed based on a free contract to which all individual members transfer their natural freedom and power. Submission to the authority of the state is thus defined by Locke as a free act; by this "contract" natural rights are not destroyed but guarded. Political freedom is thus an obedience to self-imposed law, the subordination to the common will expressing itself in the majority. Political power should therefore be neither tyrannical, since arbitrary rule is no better than the state of nature, nor paternal, since rulers and their subjects are equally rational, which is not the case in a parent-child relationship.

The supreme political power is the legislative branch, entrusted by the community to its chosen representatives, whose laws should aim at the general good. Subordinate to the legislative power, and to be kept separate from it, come the two executing powers, which are best united in a single hand under a king or monarch: the executive power (administrative and judicial), which carries the laws into effect, and the federative power, which defends the community against external enemies. The ruler is subject to the same law as the citizens; if the government, through violation of the law, has become unworthy of the power entrusted to it, sovereign authority reverts to the source from which it was derived: the people, who then must decide whether their representatives and leader have deserved the confidence placed in them. The people then have the right to depose their leaders. The sworn obedience of the subjects is to the law alone, not to the ruler; so a ruler who acts contrary to the law has lost the right to govern. Revolution is then necessary.

Locke had a great and lasting influence on political philosophy in the eighteenth century, not just in Europe but also among the founders of a new, revolutionary country called the United States.

AN ESSAY CONCERNING HUMAN UNDERSTANDING

BOOK II

INTRODUCTION

Since it is the *understanding* that sets man above the rest of sensible beings, and gives him all the advantage and dominion which he has over them; it is certainly a subject, even for its nobleness, worth our labour to inquire into. The understanding, like the eye, whilst it makes us see and perceive all other things, takes no notice of itself; and it requires art and pains to set it at a distance and make it its own object. But whatever be the difficulties that lie in the way of this inquiry; whatever it be that keeps us so much in the dark to ourselves; sure I am that all the light we can let in upon our minds, all the acquaintance we can make with our own understandings, will not only be very pleasant, but bring us great advantage, in directing our thoughts in the search of other things.

This, therefore, being my purpose—to inquire into the original, certainty, and extent of *human knowledge,* together with the grounds and degrees of *belief, opinion,* and *assent;*—I shall not at present meddle with the physical consideration of the mind; or trouble myself to examine wherein its essence consists; or by what motions of our spirits or alterations of our bodies we come to have any *sensation* by our organs, or any *ideas* in our understandings; and whether those ideas do in their formation, any or all of them, depend on matter or not. These are speculations which, however curious and entertaining, I shall decline, as lying out of my way in the design I am now upon. It shall suffice to my present purpose, to consider the discerning faculties of a man, as they are employed about the objects which they have to do with. And I shall imagine I have not wholly misemployed myself in the thoughts I shall have on this occasion, if, in this historical, plain method, I can give any account of the ways whereby our understandings come to attain those notions of things we have; and can set down any measures of the certainty of our knowledge; or the grounds of those persuasions which are to be found amongst men, so various, different, and wholly contradictory; and yet asserted somewhere or other with such assurance and confidence, that he that shall take a view of the opinions of mankind, observe their opposition, and at the same time consider the fondness and devotion wherewith they are embraced, the resolution and eagerness wherewith they are maintained, may perhaps have reason to suspect, that either there is no such thing as truth at all, or that mankind hath no sufficient means to attain a certain knowledge of it.

It is therefore worth while to search out the bounds between opinion and knowledge; and examine by what measures, in things whereof we have no certain knowledge, we ought to regulate our assent and moderate our persuasion. In order whereunto I shall pursue this following method:—

From John Locke, *An Essay Concerning Human Understanding,* ed. A. C. Fraser (Oxford: Clarendon Press, 1894).

First, I shall inquire into the original of those *ideas,* notions, or whatever else you please to call them, which a man observes, and is conscious to himself he has in his mind; and the ways whereby the understanding comes to be furnished with them.

Secondly, I shall endeavour to show what *knowledge* the understanding hath by those ideas; and the certainty, evidence, and extent of it.

Thirdly, I shall make some inquiry into the nature and grounds of *faith* or *opinion:* whereby I mean that assent which we give to any proposition as true, of whose truth yet we have no certain knowledge. And here we shall have occasion to examine the reasons and degrees of *assent.*

If by this inquiry into the nature of the understanding, I can discover the powers thereof; how far they reach; to what things they are in any degree proportionate; and where they fail us, I suppose it may be of use to prevail with the busy mind of man to be more cautious in meddling with things exceeding its comprehension; to stop when it is at the utmost extent of its tether; and to sit down in a quiet ignorance of those things which, upon examination, are found to be beyond the reach of our capacities. We should not then perhaps be so forward, out of an affectation of an universal knowledge, to raise questions, and perplex ourselves and others with disputes about things to which our understandings are not suited; and of which we cannot frame in our minds any clear or distinct perceptions, or whereof (as it has perhaps too often happened) we have not any notions at all. If we can find out how far the understanding can extend its view; how far it has faculties to attain certainty; and in what cases it can only judge and guess, we may learn to content ourselves with what is attainable by us in this state.

For though the comprehension of our understandings comes exceeding short of the vast extent of things, yet we shall have cause enough to magnify the bountiful Author of our being, for that proportion and degree of knowledge he has bestowed on us, so far above all the rest of the inhabitants of this our mansion. Men have reason to be well satisfied with what God hath thought fit for them, since he hath given them (as St. Peter says). . . whatsoever is necessary for the conveniences of life and information of virtue; and has put within the reach of their discovery, the comfortable provision for this life, and the way that leads to a better. How short soever their knowledge may come of an universal or perfect comprehension of whatsoever is, it yet secures their great concernments, that they have light enough to lead them to the knowledge of their Maker, and the sight of their own duties. Men may find matter sufficient to busy their heads, and employ their hands with variety, delight, and satisfaction, if they will not boldly quarrel with their own constitution, and throw away the blessings their hands are filled with, because they are not big enough to grasp everything. We shall not have much reason to complain of the narrowness of our minds, if we will but employ them about what may be of use to us; for of that they are very capable. And it will be an unpardonable, as well as childish peevishness, if we undervalue the advantages of our knowledge, and neglect to improve it to the ends for which it was given us, because there are some things that are set out of the reach of it. It will be no excuse to an idle and untoward servant, who would not attend his business by candle light, to plead that he had not broad sunshine. The Candle that is set up in us shines bright enough for all our purposes. The discoveries we can make with this ought to satisfy us; and we shall then use our understandings right, when we entertain all objects in that way and proportion that they are suited to our faculties, and upon those grounds they are capable of being proposed to us; and not peremptorily or intemperately require demonstration, and demand certainty, where probability only is to be had, and which is sufficient to govern all our concernments. If we will disbelieve everything, because we cannot certainly know all things, we shall do muchwhat as wisely as he who would not use his legs, but sit still and perish, because he had no wings to fly.

When we know our own strength, we shall the better know what to undertake with hopes of success; and when we have well surveyed the *powers* of our own minds, and made some estimate what we may expect from them, we shall not be inclined either to sit still, and not set our thoughts on work at all, in despair of knowing anything; nor on the other side, question everything, and disclaim all knowledge, because some things are not to be understood. It is of great use to the sailor to know the length of his line, though he cannot with it fathom all the depths of the ocean. It is well he knows that it is long enough to reach the bottom, at such places as are necessary to direct his voyage, and caution him against running upon shoals that may ruin him. Our business here is not to know all things, but those which concern our conduct. If we can find out those measures, whereby a rational creature, put in that state in which man is in this world, may and ought to govern his opinions, and actions depending thereon, we need not to be troubled that some other things escape our knowledge.

This was that which gave the first rise to this *Essay* concerning the understanding. For I thought that the first step towards satisfying several inquiries the mind of man was very apt to run into, was, to take a survey of our own understandings, examine our own powers, and see to what things they were adapted. Till that was done I suspected we began at the wrong end, and in vain sought for satisfaction in a quiet and sure possession of truths that most concerned us, whilst we let loose our thoughts into the vast ocean of Being; as if all that boundless extent were the natural and undoubted possession of our understandings, wherein there was nothing exempt from its decisions, or that escaped its comprehension. Thus men, extending their inquiries beyond their capacities, and letting their thoughts wander into those depths where they can find no sure footing, it is no wonder that they raise questions and multiply disputes, which, never coming to any clear resolution, are proper only to continue and increase their doubts, and to confirm them at last in perfect scepticism. Whereas, were the capacities of our understandings well considered, the extent of our knowledge once discovered, and the horizon found which sets the bounds between the enlightened and dark parts of things; between what is and what is not comprehensible by us, men would perhaps with less scruple acquiesce in the avowed ignorance of the one, and employ their thoughts and discourse with more advantage and satisfaction in the other.

Thus much I thought necessary to say concerning the occasion of this Inquiry into human Understanding. But, before I proceed on to what I have thought on this subject, I must here in the entrance beg pardon of my reader for the frequent use of the word *idea*, which he will find in the following treatise. It being that term which, I think, serves best to stand for whatsoever is the *object* of the understanding when a man thinks, I have used it to express whatever is meant by *phantasm, notion, species,* or *whatever it is which the mind can be employed about in thinking;* and I could not avoid frequently using it.

I presume it will be easily granted me, that there are such *ideas* in men's minds: every one is conscious of them in himself; and men's words and actions will satisfy him that they are in others.

Our first inquiry then shall be,—how they come into the mind.

CHAPTER I
Of Ideas in General, and Their Origin

Every man being conscious to himself that he thinks; and that which his mind is applied about whilst thinking being the *ideas* that are there, it is past doubt that men have in their minds several ideas,—such as are those expressed by the words *whiteness, hardness, sweetness, thinking, motion, man, elephant, army, drunkenness,* and others: it is in the first place then to be inquired, *How he comes by them?*

I know it is a received doctrine, that men have native ideas, and original characters, stamped upon their minds in their very first being. This opinion I have at large examined already; and, I suppose what I have said in the foregoing Book will be much more easily admitted, when I have shown whence the understanding may get all the ideas it has; and by what ways and degrees they may come into the mind;—for which I shall appeal to every one's own observation and experience.

Let us then suppose the mind to be, as we say, white paper, void of all characters, without any ideas:—How comes it to be furnished? Whence comes it by that vast store which the busy and boundless fancy of man has painted on it with an almost endless variety? Whence has it all the materials of reason and knowledge? To this I answer, in one word, from EXPERIENCE. In that all our knowledge is founded; and from that it ultimately derives itself. Our observation employed either, about external sensible objects, or about the internal operations of our minds perceived and reflected on by ourselves, is that which supplies our understandings with all the *materials* of thinking. These two are the fountains of knowledge, from whence all the ideas we have, or can naturally have, do spring.

First, our Senses, conversant about particular sensible objects, do convey into the mind several distinct perceptions of things, according to those various ways wherein those objects do affect them. And thus we come by those *ideas* we have of *yellow, white, heat, cold, soft, hard, bitter, sweet,* and all those which we call sensible qualities; which when I say the senses convey into the mind, I mean, they from external objects convey into the mind what produces there those perceptions. This great source of most of the ideas we have, depending wholly upon our senses, and derived by them to the understanding, I call SENSATION.

Secondly, the other fountain from which experience furnishes the understanding with ideas is,—the perception of the operations of our own mind within us, as it is employed about the ideas it has got;—which operations, when the soul comes to reflect on and consider, do furnish the understanding with another set of ideas, which could not be had from things without. And such are *perception, thinking, doubting, believing, reasoning, knowing, willing,* and all the different actings of our own minds;—which we being conscious of, and observing in ourselves, do from these receive into our understandings as distinct ideas as we do from bodies affecting our senses. This source of ideas every man has wholly in himself; and though it be not sense, as having nothing to do with external objects, yet it is very like it, and might properly enough be called *internal sense*. But as I call the other Sensation, so I call this REFLECTION, the ideas it affords being such only as the mind gets by reflecting on its own operations within itself. By reflection then, in the following part of this discourse, I would be understood to mean, that notice which the mind takes of its own operations, and the manner of them, by reason whereof there come to be ideas of these operations in the understanding. These two, I say, viz. external material things, as the objects of SENSATION, and the operations of our own minds within, as the objects of REFLECTION, are to me the only originals from whence all our ideas take their beginnings. The term *operations* here I use in a large sense, as comprehending not barely the actions of the mind about its ideas, but some sort of passions arising sometimes from them, such as is the satisfaction or uneasiness arising from any thought.

The understanding seems to me not to have the least glimmering of any ideas which it doth not receive from one of these two. *External objects* furnish the mind with the ideas of sensible qualities, which are all those different perceptions they produce in us; and *the mind* furnishes the understanding with ideas of its own operations.

These, when we have taken a full survey of them, and their several modes, [combinations, and relations,] we shall find to contain all our whole stock of ideas; and that we have nothing in our minds which did not come in one of these two ways. Let any one examine his own thoughts, and thoroughly search into his understanding; and then let him tell me, whether all the original ideas he has there, are any other than of the objects of his senses, or of the operations of his mind, considered as objects of his reflection. And how great a mass of knowledge soever he imagines to be lodged there, he will, upon taking a strict view, see that he has not any idea in his mind but what one of these two have imprinted;—though perhaps, with infinite variety compounded and enlarged by the understanding, as we shall see hereafter.

He that attentively considers the state of a child, at his first coming into the world, will have little reason to think him stored with plenty of ideas, that are to be the matter of his future knowledge. It is *by degrees* he comes to be furnished with them. And though the ideas of obvious and familiar qualities imprint themselves before the memory begins to keep a register of time or order, yet it is often so late before some unusual qualities come in the way, that there are few men that cannot recollect the beginning of their acquaintance with them. And if it were worth while, no doubt a child might be so ordered as to have but a very few, even of the ordinary ideas, till he were grown up to a man. But all that are born into the world, being surrounded with bodies that perpetually and diversely affect them, variety of ideas, whether care be taken of it or not, are imprinted on the minds of children. Light and colours are busy at hand everywhere, when the eye is but open; sounds and some tangible qualities fail not to solicit their proper senses, and force an entrance to the mind;—but yet, I think, it will be granted easily, that if a child were kept in a place where he never saw any other but black and white till he were a man, he would have no more ideas of scarlet or green, than he that from his childhood never tasted an oyster, or a pine-apple, has of those particular relishes.

Men then come to be furnished with fewer or more simple ideas from without, according as the objects they converse with afford greater or less variety; and from the operations of their minds within, according as they more or less reflect on them. For, though he that contemplates the operations of his mind, cannot but have plain and clear ideas of them; yet, unless he turn his thoughts that way, and considers them *attentively,* he will no more have clear and distinct ideas of all the operations of his mind, and all that may be observed therein, than he will have all the particular ideas of any landscape, or of the parts and motions of a clock, who will not turn his eyes to it, and with attention heed all the parts of it. The picture, or clock may be so placed, that they may come in his way every day; but yet he will have but a confused idea of all the parts they are made up of, till he applies himself with attention, to consider them each in particular.

And hence we see the reason why it is pretty late before most children get ideas of the operations of their own minds; and some have not any very clear or perfect ideas of the greatest part of them all their lives. Because, though they pass there continually, yet, like floating visions, they make not deep impressions enough to leave in their mind clear, distinct, lasting ideas, till the understanding turns inward upon itself, reflects on its own operations, and makes them the objects of its own contemplation. Children when they come first into it, are surrounded with a world of new things, which, by a constant solicitation of their senses, draw the mind constantly to them; forward to take notice of new, and apt to be delighted with the variety of changing objects. Thus the first years are usually employed and diverted in looking abroad. Men's business in them is to acquaint themselves with what is to be found without; and so growing up in a constant attention to outward sensations, seldom make any considerable reflection on what passes within them, till they come to be of riper years; and some scarce ever at all.

To ask, at what *time* a man has first any ideas, is to ask, when he begins to perceive;—*having ideas,* and *perception,* being the same thing. I know it is an opinion, that the soul always thinks, and that it has the actual perception of ideas in itself constantly, as long as it exists; and that actual thinking is as inseparable from the soul as actual extension is from the body; which if true, to inquire after the beginning of a man's ideas is the same as to inquire after the beginning of his soul. For, by this account, soul and its ideas, as body and its extension, will begin to exist both at the same time.

But whether the soul be supposed to exist antecedent to, or coeval with, or some time after the first rudiments of organization, or the beginnings of life in the body, I leave to be disputed by those who have better thought of that matter. I confess myself to have one of those dull souls, that does not perceive itself always to contemplate ideas; nor can conceive it any more necessary for the soul always to think, than for the body always to move: the perception of ideas being (as I conceive) to the soul, what motion is to the body; not its essence, but one of its operations. And therefore, though thinking be supposed never so much the proper action of the soul, yet it is not necessary to suppose that it should be always thinking, always in action. That, perhaps, is the privilege of the infinite Author and Preserver of all things, who "never slumbers nor sleeps"; but is not competent to any finite being, at least not to the soul of man. We know certainly, by experience, that we *sometimes* think; and thence draw this infallible consequence,—that there is something in us that has a power to think. But whether that substance *perpetually* thinks or no, we can be no further assured than experience informs us. For, to say that actual thinking is essential to the soul, and inseparable from it, is to beg what is in question, and not to prove it by reason;—which is necessary to be done, if it be not a self-evident proposition. But whether this, "That the soul always thinks," be a self-evident proposition, that everybody assents to at first hearing, I appeal to mankind. It is doubted whether I thought at all last night or no. The question being about a matter of fact, it is begging it to bring, as a proof for it, an hypothesis, which is the very thing in dispute: by which way one may prove anything, and it is but supposing that all watches, whilst the balance beats, think, and it is sufficiently proved, and past doubt, that my watch thought all last night. But he that would not deceive himself, ought to build his hypothesis on matter of fact, and make it out by sensible experience, and not presume on matter of fact, because of his hypothesis, that is, because he supposes it to be so; which way of proving amounts to this, that I must necessarily think all last night, because another supposes I always think, though I myself cannot perceive that I always do so.

But men in love with their opinions may not only suppose what is in question, but allege wrong matter of fact. How else could any one make it an inference of mine, that a thing is not, because we are not sensible of it in our sleep? I do not say there is no *soul* in a man, because he is not sensible of it in his sleep; but I do say, he cannot *think* at any time, waking or sleeping, without being sensible of it. Our being sensible of it is not necessary to anything but to our thoughts; and to them it is; and to them it always will be necessary, till we can think without being conscious of it.

I grant that the soul, in a waking man, is never without thought, because it is the condition of being awake. But whether sleeping without dreaming be not an affection of the whole man, mind as well as body, may be worth a waking man's consideration; it being hard to conceive that anything should think and not be conscious of it. If the soul does think in a sleeping man without being conscious of it, I ask whether, during such thinking, it has any pleasure or pain, or be capable of happiness or misery? I am sure the man is not; no more than the bed or earth he lies on. For to be happy or miserable without being conscious of it, seems to me utterly inconsistent and impossible. Or if it be possible that the *soul* can, whilst the body is sleeping, have its thinking, enjoyments, and concerns, its pleasures or pain, apart, which the *man* is not conscious of nor partakes in,—it is certain that Socrates asleep and Socrates awake is not the same person; but his soul when he sleeps, and Socrates the man, consisting of body and soul, when he is waking, are two persons: since waking Socrates has no knowledge of, or concernment for that happiness or misery of his soul, which it enjoys alone by itself whilst he sleeps, without perceiving anything of it; no more than he has for the happiness or misery of a man in the Indies, whom he knows not. For, if we take wholly away all consciousness of our actions and sensations, especially of pleasure and pain, and the concernment that accompanies it, it will be hard to know wherein to place personal identity.

The soul, during sound sleep, thinks, say these men. Whilst it thinks and perceives, it is capable certainly of those of delight or trouble, as well as any other perceptions; and *it* must necessarily be *conscious* of its own perceptions. But it has all this apart: the sleeping *man,* it is plain, is conscious of nothing of all this. Let us suppose, then, the soul of Castor, while he is sleeping, retired from his body; which is no impossible supposition for the men I have here to do with, who so liberally allow life, without a thinking soul, to all other animals. These men cannot then judge it impossible, or a contradiction, that the body should live without the soul; nor that the soul should subsist and think, or have perception, even perception of happiness or misery, without the body. Let us then, I say, suppose the soul of Castor separated during his sleep from his body, to think apart. Let us suppose, too, that it chooses for its scene of thinking the body of another man, v.g. Pollux, who is sleeping without a soul. For, if Castor's soul can think, whilst Castor is asleep, what Castor is never conscious of, it is no matter what *place* it chooses to think in. We have here, then, the bodies of two men with only one soul between them, which we will suppose to sleep and wake by turns; and the soul still thinking in the waking man, whereof the sleeping man is never conscious, has never the least perception. I ask, then, whether Castor and Pollux, thus with only one soul between them, which thinks and perceives in one what the other is never conscious of, nor is concerned for, are not two as distinct *persons* as Castor and Hercules, or as Socrates and Plato were? And whether one of them might not be very happy, and the other very miserable? Just by the same reason, they make the soul and the man two persons, who make the soul think apart what the man is not conscious of. For, I suppose nobody will make identity of persons to consist in the soul's being united to the very same numerical particles of matter. For if that be necessary to identity, it will be impossible, in that constant flux of the particles of our bodies, that any man should be the same person two days, or two moments, together.

Thus, methinks, every drowsy nod shakes their doctrine, who teach that the soul is always thinking. Those, at least, who do at any time *sleep without dreaming,* can never be convinced that their thoughts are sometimes for four hours busy without their knowing of it; and if they are taken in the very act, waked in the middle of that sleeping contemplation, can give no manner of account of it.

It will perhaps be said,—That the soul thinks even in the soundest sleep, but the *memory* retains it not. That the soul in a sleeping man should be this moment busy thinking, and the next moment in a waking man not remember nor be able to recollect one jot of all those thoughts, is very hard to be conceived, and would need some better proof than bare assertion to make it be believed. For who can without any more ado, but being barely told so, imagine that the greatest part of men do, during all their lives, for several hours every day, think of something, which if they were asked, even in the middle of these thoughts, they could remember nothing at all of? Most men, I think, pass a great part of their sleep without dreaming. I once knew a man that was bred a scholar, and had no bad memory, who told me he had never dreamed in his life, till he had that fever he was then newly recovered of, which was about the five or six and twentieth year of his age. I suppose the world affords more such instances: at least every one's acquaintance will furnish him with examples enough of such as pass most of their nights without dreaming.

To think often, and never to retain it so much as one moment, is a very useless sort of thinking; and the soul, in such a state of thinking, does very little, if at all, excel that of a looking-glass, which constantly receives variety of images, or ideas, but retains none; they disappear and vanish, and there remain no footsteps of them; the looking-glass is never the better for such ideas, nor the soul for such thoughts. Perhaps it will be said, that in a waking *man* the materials of the body are employed, and made use of, in thinking; and that the memory of thoughts is retained by the impressions that are made on the brain, and the traces there left after such thinking; but that in the thinking of the *soul,* which is not per-ceived in a sleeping man, there the soul thinks apart, and making no use of the organs of the body, leaves no impressions on it, and consequently no memory of such thoughts. Not to mention again the absurdity of two distinct persons, which follows from this supposition, I answer, further,—That whatever ideas the mind can receive and contemplate without the help of the body, it is reasonable to conclude it can retain without the help of the body too; or else the soul, or any separate spirit, will have but little advantage by thinking. If it has no memory of its own thoughts; if it cannot lay them up for its own use, and be able to recall them upon occasion; if it cannot reflect upon what is past, and make use of its former experiences, reasonings, and contemplations, to what purpose does it think? They who make the soul a thinking thing, at this rate, will not make it a much more noble being than those do whom they condemn, for allowing it to be nothing but the subtilist parts of matter. Characters drawn on dust, that the first breath of wind effaces; or impressions made on a heap of atoms, or animal spirits, are altogether as useful, and render the subject as noble, as the thoughts of a soul that perish in thinking; that, once out of sight, are gone for ever, and leave no memory of themselves behind them. Nature never makes excellent things for mean or no uses: and it is hardly to be conceived that our infinitely wise Creator should make so admirable a faculty as the power of thinking, that faculty which comes nearest the excellency of his own incomprehensible being, to be so idly and uselessly employed, at least a fourth part of its time here, as to think constantly, without remembering any of those thoughts, without doing any good to itself or others, or being any way useful to any other part of the creation. If we will examine it, we shall not find, I suppose, the motion of dull and senseless matter, any where in the universe, made so little use of and so wholly thrown away.

It is true, we have sometimes instances of perception whilst we are asleep, and retain the memory of those thoughts: but how extravagant and incoherent for the most part they are; how little conformable to the perfection and order of a rational being, those who are acquainted with dreams need not be told. This I would willingly be satisfied in,—whether the soul, when it thinks thus apart, and as it were separate from the body, acts less rationally than when conjointly with it, or no. If its separate thoughts be less rational, then these men must say, that the soul owes the perfection of rational thinking to the body: if it does not, it is a wonder that our dreams should be, for the most part, so frivolous and irrational; and that the soul should retain none of its more rational soliloquies and meditations.

Those who so confidently tell us that the soul always actually thinks, I would they would also tell us, what those ideas are that are in the soul of a child, before or just at the union with the body, before it hath received any by sensation. The dreams of sleeping men are, as I take it, all made up of the waking man's ideas; though for the most part oddly put together. It is strange, if the soul has ideas of its own that it derived not from sensation or reflection, (as it must have, if it thought before it received any impressions from the body,) that it should never, in its private thinking, (so private, that the man himself perceives it not,) retain any of them the very moment it wakes out of them, and then make the man glad with new discoveries. Who can find it reason that the soul should, in its retirement during sleep, have so many hours' thoughts, and yet never light on any of those ideas it borrowed not from sensation or reflection; or at least preserve the memory of none but such, which, being occasioned from the body, must needs be less natural to a spirit? It is strange the soul should never once in a man's whole life recall over any of its pure native thoughts, and those ideas it had before it borrowed anything from the body; never bring into the waking man's view any other ideas but what have a tang of the cask, and manifestly derive their original from that union. If it always thinks, and so had ideas before it was united, or before it received any from the body, it is not to be supposed but that during sleep it recollects its native ideas; and during that retirement from communicating with the body, whilst it thinks by itself, the ideas it is busied about should be, sometimes at least, those more natural and congenial ones which it had in itself, underived from the body, or its own operations about them: which, since the waking man never remembers, we must from this hypothesis conclude either that the soul remembers something that the man does not; or else that memory belongs only to such ideas as are derived from the body, or the mind's operations about them.

I would be glad also to learn from these men who so confidently pronounce that the human soul, or, which is all one, that a man always thinks, how they come to know it; nay, how they come to know that they themselves think, when they themselves do not perceive it. This, I am afraid, is to be sure without proofs, and to know without perceiving. It is, I suspect, a confused notion, taken up to serve an hypothesis; and none of those clear truths, that either their own evidence forces us to admit, or common experience makes it impudence to deny. For the most that can be said of it is, that it is possible the soul may always think, but not always retain it in memory. And I say, it is as possible that the soul may not always think; and much more probable that it should sometimes not think, than that it should often think, and that a long while together, and not be conscious to itself, the next moment after, that it had thought.

To suppose the soul to think, and the man not to perceive it, is, as has been said, to make two persons in one man. And if one considers well these men's way of speaking, one should be led into a suspicion that they do so. For they who tell us that the *soul* always thinks, do never, that I remember, say that a *man* always thinks. Can the soul think, and not the man? Or a man think, and not be conscious of it? This, perhaps, would be suspected of jargon in others. If they say the man thinks always, but is not always conscious of it, they may as well say his body is extended without having parts. For it is altogether as intelligible to say that a body is extended without parts, as that anything thinks without being conscious of it, or perceiving that it does so. They who talk thus may, with as much reason, if it be necessary to their hypothesis, say that a man is always hungry, but that he does not always feel it; whereas hunger consists in that very sensation, as thinking consists in being conscious that one thinks. If they say that a man is always conscious to himself of thinking, I ask, How they know it? Consciousness is the perception of what passes in a man's own mind. Can another man perceive that I am conscious of anything, when I perceive it not myself? No man's knowledge here can go beyond his experience. Wake a man out of a sound sleep, and ask him what he was that moment thinking of. If he himself be conscious of nothing he then thought on, he must be a notable diviner of thoughts that can assure him that he has thinking. May he not, with more reason, assure him he was not asleep? This is something beyond philosophy; and it cannot be less than revelation, that discovers to another thoughts in my mind, when I can find none there myself. And they must needs have a penetrating sight who can certainly see that I think, when I cannot perceive it myself, and when I declare that I do not; and yet can see that dogs or elephants do not think, when they give all the demonstration of it imaginable, except only telling us that they do so. This some may suspect to be a step beyond the Rosicrucians; it seeming easier to make one's self invisible to others, than to make another's thoughts visible to me, which are not visible to himself. But it is but defining the soul to be "a substance that always thinks," and the business is done. If such definition be of any authority, I know not what it can serve for but to make many men suspect that they have no souls at all; since they find a good part of their lives pass away without thinking. For no definitions that I know, no suppositions of any sect, are of force enough to destroy constant experience; and perhaps it is the affectation of knowing beyond what we perceive, that makes so much useless dispute and noise in the world.

I see no reason, therefore, to believe that the soul thinks before the senses have furnished it with ideas to think on; and as those are increased and retained so it comes, by exercise, to improve its faculty of thinking in the several parts of it; as well as, afterwards, by compounding those ideas, and reflecting on its own operations, it increases its stock, as well as facility in remembering, imagining, reasoning, and other modes of thinking.

He that will suffer himself to be informed by observation and experience, and not make his own hypothesis the rule of nature, will find few signs of a soul accustomed to much thinking in a new-born child, and much fewer of any reasoning at all. And yet it is hard to imagine that the rational soul should think so much, and not reason at all. And he that will consider that infants newly come into the world spend the greatest part of their time in sleep, and are seldom awake but when either hunger calls for the teat, or some pain (the most importunate of all sensations), or some other violent impression on the body, forces the mind to perceive and attend to it;—he, I say, who considers this, will perhaps find reason to imagine that a *foetus* in the mother's womb differs not much from the state of a vegetable, but passes the greatest part of its time without perception or thought; doing very little but sleep in a place where it needs not seek for food, and is surrounded with liquor, always equally soft, and near of the same temper; where the eyes have no light, and the ears so shut up are not very susceptible of sounds; and where there is little or no variety, or change of objects, to move the senses.

Follow a child from its birth, and observe the alterations that time makes and you shall find, as the mind by the senses comes more and more to be furnished with ideas, it comes to be more and more awake; thinks more, the more it has matter to think on. After some time it begins to know the objects which, being most familiar with it, have made lasting impressions. Thus it comes by degrees to know the persons it daily converses with, and distinguishes them from strangers; which are instances and effects of its coming to retain and distinguish the ideas the senses convey to it. And so we may observe how the mind, *by degrees*, improves in these; and *advances* to the exercise of those other faculties of enlarging, compounding, and abstracting its ideas, and of reasoning about them, and reflecting upon all these; of which I shall have occasion to speak more hereafter.

If it shall be demanded then, *when* a man *begins* to have any ideas, I think the true answer is,—*when he first has any sensation*. For, since there appear not to be any ideas in the mind before the senses have conveyed any in, I conceive that ideas in the understanding are coeval with *sensation; which is such an impression or motion made in some part of the body, as produces some perception in the understanding*. It is about these impressions made on our senses by outward objects that the mind seems *first* to employ itself, in such operations as we call perception, remembering, consideration, reasoning, &c.

In time the mind comes to reflect on its own operations about the ideas got by sensation, and thereby stores itself with a new set of ideas, which I call ideas of reflection. These are the impressions that are made on our senses by outward objects that are extrinsic to the mind; and its own operations, proceeding from powers intrinsical and proper to itself, which, when reflected on by itself, become also objects of its contemplation—are, as I have said, the original of all knowledge. Thus the first capacity of human intellect is,—that the mind is fitted to receive the impressions made on it; either through the senses by outward objects, or by its own operations when it reflects on them. This is the first step a man makes towards the discovery of anything, and the groundwork whereon to build all those notions which ever he shall have naturally in this world. All those sublime thoughts which tower above the clouds, and reach as high as heaven itself, take their rise and footing here: in all that great extent wherein the mind wanders, in those remote speculations it may seem to be elevated with, it stirs not one jot beyond those ideas which *sense* or *reflection* have offered for its contemplation.

In this part the understanding is merely passive; and whether or no it will have these beginnings, and as it were materials of knowledge, is not in its own power. For the objects of our senses do, many of them, obtrude their particular ideas upon our minds whether we will or not; and the operations of our minds will not let us be without, at least, some obscure notions of them. No man can be wholly ignorant of what he does when he thinks. These simple ideas, when offered to the mind, the understanding can no more refuse to have, nor alter when they are imprinted, nor blot them out and make new ones itself, than a mirror can refuse, alter, or obliterate the images or ideas which the objects set before it do therein produce. As the bodies that surround us do diversely affect our organs, the mind is forced to receive the impressions; and cannot avoid the perception of those ideas that are annexed to them.

CHAPTER II
Of Simple Ideas

The better to understand the nature, manner, and extent of our knowledge, one thing is carefully to be observed concerning the ideas we have; and that is, that some of them are *simple* and some *complex*.

Though the qualities that affect our senses are, in the things themselves, so united and blended, that there is no separation, no distance between them; yet it is plain, the ideas they produce in the mind enter by the senses simple and unmixed. For, though the sight and touch often take in from the same object, at the same time, different ideas;—as a man sees at once motion and colour; the hand feels softness and warmth in the same piece of wax: yet the simple ideas thus united in the same subject, are as perfectly distinct as those that come in by different senses. The coldness and hardness which a man feels in a piece of ice being as distinct ideas in the mind as the smell and whiteness of a lily; or as the taste of sugar, and smell of a rose. And there is nothing can be plainer to a man than the clear and distinct perception he has of those simple ideas; which, being each in itself uncompounded, contains in it nothing but *one uniform appearance, or conception in the mind,* and is not distinguishable into different ideas.

These simple ideas, the materials of all our knowledge, are suggested and furnished to the mind only by those two ways above mentioned, viz. sensation and reflection. When the understanding is once stored with these simple ideas, it has the power to repeat, compare, and unite them, even to an almost infinite variety, and so can make at pleasure new complex ideas. But it is not in the power of the most exalted wit, or enlarged understanding, by any quickness or variety of thought, to *invent* or *frame* one new simple idea in the mind, not taken in by the ways before mentioned: nor can any force of the understanding *destroy* those that are there. The dominion of man, in this little world of his own understanding being muchwhat the same as it is in the great world of visible things; wherein his power, however managed by art and skill, reaches no farther than to compound and divide the materials that are made to his hand; but can do nothing towards the making the least particle of new matter, or destroying one atom of what is already in being. The same inability will every one find in himself, who shall go about to fashion in his understanding one simple idea, not received in by his senses from external objects, or by reflection from the operations of his own mind about them. I would have any one try to fancy any taste which had never affected his palate; or frame the idea of a scent he had never smelt: and when he can do this, I will also conclude that a blind man has ideas of colours, and a deaf man true distinct notions of sounds.

This is the reason why—though we cannot believe it impossible to God to make a creature with other organs, and more ways to convey into the understanding the notice of corporeal things than those five, as they are usually counted, which he has given to man— yet I think it is not possible for any *man* to imagine any other qualities in bodies, howsoever constituted, whereby they can be taken notice of, besides sounds, tastes, smells, visible and tangible qualities. And had mankind been made but with four senses, the qualities then which are the objects of the fifth sense had been as far from our notice, imagination, and conception, as now any belonging to a sixth, seventh, or eighth sense can possibly be;— which, whether yet some other creatures, in some other parts of this vast and stupendous universe, may not have, will be a great presumption to deny. He that will not set himself proudly at the top of all things, but will consider the immensity of this fabric, and the great variety that is to be found in this little and inconsiderable part of it which he has to do with, may be apt to think that, in other mansions of it, there may be other and different intelligent beings, of whose faculties he has as little knowledge or apprehension as a worm shut up in one drawer of a cabinet has of the senses or understanding of a man; such variety and excellency being suitable to the wisdom and power of the Maker. I have here followed the common opinion of man's having but five senses; though, perhaps, there may be justly counted more;—but either supposition serves equally to my present purpose.

CHAPTER III
Of Simple Ideas of Sense

The better to conceive the ideas we receive from sensation, it may not be amiss for us to consider them, in reference to the different ways whereby they make their approaches to our minds, and make themselves perceivable by us.

First, then, There are some which come into our minds *by one sense only.*

Secondly, There are others that convey themselves into the mind *by more senses than one.*

Thirdly, Others that are had from *reflection only.*

Fourthly, There are some that make themselves way, and are suggested to the mind *by all the ways of sensation and reflection.*

We shall consider them apart under these several heads.

There are some ideas which have admittance only through one sense, which is peculiarly adapted to receive them. Thus light and colours, as white, red, yellow, blue; with their several degrees or shades and mixtures, as green, scarlet, purple, sea-green, and the rest, come in only by the eyes. All kinds of noises, sounds, and tones, only by the ears. The several tastes and smells, by the nose and palate. And if these organs, or the nerves which are the conduits to convey them from without to their audience in the brain,—the mind's presence-room (as I may so call it)—are any of them so disordered as not to perform their functions, they have no postern to be admitted by; no other way to bring themselves into view, and be perceived by the understanding.

The most considerable of those belonging to the touch, are heat and cold, and solidity: all the rest, consisting almost wholly in the sensible configuration, as smooth and rough; or else, more or less firm adhesion of the parts, as hard and soft, tough and brittle, are obvious enough.

I think it will be needless to enumerate all the particular simple ideas belonging to each sense. Nor indeed is it possible if we would; there being a great many more of them belonging to most of the senses than we have names for. The variety of smells, which are as many almost, if not more, than species of bodies in the world, do most of them want names. Sweet and stinking commonly serve our turn for these ideas, which in effect is little more than to call them pleasing or displeasing; though the smell of a rose and violet, both sweet, are certainly very distinct ideas. Nor are the different tastes, that by our palates we receive ideas of, much better provided with names. Sweet, bitter, sour, harsh, and salt are almost all the epithets we have to denominate that numberless variety of relishes, which are to be found distinct, not only in almost every sort of creatures, but in the different parts of the same plant, fruit, or animal. The same may be said of colours and sounds. I shall, therefore, in the account of simple ideas I am here giving, content myself to set down only such as are most material to our present purpose, or are in themselves less apt to be taken notice of though they are very frequently the ingredients of our complex ideas; amongst which, I think I may well account solidity, which therefore I shall treat of in the next chapter.

CHAPTER IV
Idea of Solidity

The idea of *solidity* we receive by our touch: and it arises from the resistance which we find in body to the entrance of any other body into the place it possesses, till it has left it. There is no idea which we receive more constantly from sensation than solidity. Whether we move or rest, in what posture soever we are, we always feel something under us that supports us, and hinders our further sinking downwards; and the bodies which we daily handle make us perceive that, whilst they remain between them, they do, by an insurmountable force, hinder the approach of the parts of our hands that press them. *That which thus hinders the approach of two bodies, when they are moved one towards another, I call solidity.* I will not dispute whether this acceptation of the word solid be nearer to its original signification than that which mathematicians use it in. It suffices that I think the common notion of solidity will allow, if not justify, this use of it; but if any one think it better to call it *impenetrability,* he has my consent. Only I have thought the term solidity the more proper to express this idea, not only because of its vulgar use in that sense, but also because it carries something more of positive in it than impenetrability; which is negative, and is perhaps more a consequence of solidity, than solidity itself. This, of all other, seems the idea most intimately connected with, and essential to body; so as nowhere else to be found or imagined, but only in matter. And though our senses take no notice of it, but in masses of matter, of a bulk sufficient to cause a sensation in us: yet the mind, having once got this idea from such grosser sensible bodies, traces it further, and considers it, as well as figure, in the minutest particle of matter that can exist; and finds it inseparably inherent in body, wherever or however modified.

This is the idea which belongs to body, whereby we conceive it to fill space. The idea of which filling of space is,—that where we imagine any space taken up by a solid substance, we conceive it so to possess it, that it excludes all other solid substances; and will for ever hinder any other two bodies, that move toward one another in a straight line, from coming to touch one another, unless it removes from between them in a line not parallel to that which they move in. This idea of it, the bodies which we ordinarily handle sufficiently furnish us with.

This resistance, whereby it keeps other bodies out of the space which it possesses, is so great, that no force, how great soever, can surmount it. All the bodies in the world, pressing a drop of water on all sides, will never be able to overcome the resistance which it will make, soft as it is, to their approaching one another, till it be removed out of their way: whereby our idea of solidity is distinguished both from pure space, which is capable neither of resistance nor motion; and from the ordinary idea of hardness. For a man may conceive two bodies at a distance, so as they may approach one another, without touching or displacing any solid thing, till their superficies come to meet; whereby, I think, we have the clear idea of space without solidity. For (not to go so far as annihilation of any particular body) I ask, whether a man cannot have the idea of the motion of one single body alone, without any other succeeding immediately into its place? I think it is evident he can: the idea of motion in one body no more including the idea of motion in another, than the idea of a square figure in one body includes the idea of a square figure in another. I do not ask, whether bodies do so *exist,* that the motion of one body cannot really be without the motion of another. To determine this either way, is to beg the question for or against a *vacuum.* But my question is,—whether one cannot have the *idea* of one body moved, whilst others are at rest? And I think this no one will deny. If so, then the place it deserted gives us the idea of pure space without solidity; whereinto any other body may enter, without either resistance or protrusion of anything. When the sucker in a pump is drawn, the space it filled in the tube is certainly the same whether any other body follows the motion of the sucker or not: nor does it imply a contradiction that, upon the motion of one body, another that is only contiguous to it should not follow it. The necessity of such a motion is built only on the supposition that the world is full; but not on the distinct *ideas* of space and solidity, which are as different as resistance and not resistance, protrusion and not protrusion. And that men have ideas of space without a body, their very disputes about a vacuum plainly demonstrate, as is shown in another place.

Solidity is hereby also differenced from hardness, in that solidity consists in repletion, and so an utter exclusion of other bodies out of the space it possesses: but hardness, in a firm cohesion of the parts of matter, making up masses of a sensible bulk, so that the whole does not easily change its figure. And indeed, hard and soft are names that we give to things only in relation to the constitutions of our own bodies; that being generally called hard by us, which will put us to pain sooner than change figure by the pressure of any part of our bodies; and that, on the contrary, soft, which changes the situation of its parts upon an easy and unpainful touch.

But this difficulty of changing the situation of the sensible parts amongst themselves, or of the figure of the whole, gives no more solidity to the hardest body in the world than to the softest; nor is an adamant one jot more solid than water. For, though the two flat sides of two pieces of marble will more easily approach each other, between which there is nothing but water or air, than if there be a diamond between them; yet it is not that the parts of the diamond are more solid than those of water, or resist more; but because the parts of water, being more easily separable from each other, they will, by a side motion, be more easily removed, and give way to the approach of the two pieces of marble. But if they could be kept from making place by that side motion, they would eternally hinder the approach of these two pieces of marble, as much as the diamond; and it would be as impossible by any force to surmount their resistance, as to surmount the resistance of the parts of a diamond. The softest body in the world will as invincibly resist the coming together of any other two bodies, if it be not put out of the way, but remain between them, as the hardest that can be found or imagined. He that shall fill a yielding soft body well with air or water, will quickly find its resistance. And he that thinks that nothing but bodies that are hard can keep his hands from approaching one another, may be pleased to make a trial, with the air inclosed in a football. The experiment, I have been told, was made at Florence, with a hollow globe of gold filled with water, and exactly closed; which further shows the solidity of so soft a body as water. For the golden globe thus filled, being put into a press, which was driven by the extreme force of screws, the water made itself way through the pores of that very close metal, and finding no room for a nearer approach of its particles within, got to the outside, where it rose like a dew, and so fell in drops, before the sides of the globe could be made to yield to the violent compression of the engine that squeezed it.

By this idea of solidity is the extension of body distinguished from the extension of space:—the extension of body being nothing but the cohesion or continuity of solid, separable, movable parts; and the extension of space, the continuity of unsolid, inseparable, and immovable parts. Upon the solidity of bodies also depend their mutual impulse, resistance, and protrusion. Of pure space then, and solidity, there are several (amongst which I confess myself one) who persuade themselves they have clear and distinct ideas; and that they can think on space, without anything in it that resists or is protruded by body. This is the idea of pure space, which they think they have as clear as any idea they can have of the extension of body: the idea of the distance between the opposite parts of a concave superficies being equally as clear without as with the idea of any solid parts between: and on the other side, they persuade themselves that they have, distinct from that of pure space, the idea of *some-*

thing that fills space, that can be protruded by the impulse of other bodies, or resist their motion. If there be others that have not these two ideas distinct, but confound them, and make but one of them, I know not how men, who have the same idea under different names, or different ideas under the same name, can in that case talk with one another; any more than a man who, not being blind or deaf, has distinct ideas of the colour of scarlet and the sound of a trumpet, could discourse concerning scarlet colour with the blind man I mentioned in another place, who fancied that the idea of scarlet was like the sound of a trumpet.

If any one asks me, *What this solidity is,* I send him to his senses to inform him. Let him put a flint or a football between his hands, and then endeavour to join them, and he will know. If he thinks this not a sufficient explication of solidity, what it is, and wherein it consists; I promise to tell him what it is, and wherein it consists, when he tells me what thinking is, or wherein it consists; or explains to me what extension or motion is, which perhaps seems much easier. The simple ideas we have, are such as experience teaches them us; but if, beyond that, we endeavour by words to make them clearer in the mind, we shall succeed no better than if we went about to clear up the darkness of a blind man's mind by talking; and to discourse into him the ideas of light and colours. The reason of this I shall show in another place.

CHAPTER V
Of Simple Ideas of Divers Senses

The ideas we get by more than one sense are, of *space* or *extension, figure, rest,* and *motion.* For these make perceivable impressions, both on the eyes and touch; and we can receive and convey into our minds the ideas of the extension, figure, motion, and rest of bodies, both by seeing and feeling. But having occasion to speak more at large of these in another place, I here only enumerate them.

CHAPTER VI
Of Simple Ideas of Reflection

The mind receiving the ideas mentioned in the foregoing chapters from without, when it turns its view inward upon itself, and observes its own actions about those ideas it has, takes from thence other ideas, which are as capable to be the objects of its contemplation as any of those it received from foreign things.

The two great and principal actions of the mind, which are most frequently considered, and which are so frequent that every one that pleases may take notice of them in himself, are these two:—

> *Perception,* or *Thinking;* and
> *Volition,* or *Willing.*

The power of thinking is called the *Understanding,* and the power of volition is called the *Will;* and these two powers or abilities in the mind are denominated faculties.

Of some of the *modes* of these simple ideas of reflection, such as are *remembrance, discerning, reasoning, judging, knowledge, faith,* &c., I shall have occasion to speak hereafter.

CHAPTER VII
Of Simple Ideas of Both Sensation and Reflection

There be other simple ideas which convey themselves into the mind by all the ways of sensation and reflection, viz. *pleasure* or *delight,* and its opposite, *pain,* or *uneasiness; power; existence; unity.*

Delight or uneasiness, one or other of them, join themselves to almost all our ideas both of sensation and reflection: and there is scarce any affection of our senses from without, any retired thought of our mind within, which is not able to produce in us pleasure or pain. By pleasure and pain, I would be understood to signify, whatsoever delights or molests us; whether it arises from the thoughts of our minds, or anything operating on our bodies. For, whether we call it satisfaction, delight, pleasure, happiness, &c., on the one side, or uneasiness, trouble, pain, torment, anguish, misery, &c., on the other, they are still but different degrees of the same thing, and belong to the ideas of pleasure and pain, delight or uneasiness; which are the names I shall most commonly use for those two sorts of ideas.

The infinite wise Author of our being, having given us the power over several parts of our bodies, to move or keep them at rest as we think fit; and also, by the motion of them, to move ourselves and other contiguous bodies, in which consist all the actions of our body: having also given a power to our minds, in several instances, to choose, amongst its ideas, which it will think on, and to pursue the inquiry of this or that subject with consideration and attention, to excite us to these actions of thinking and motion that we are capable of,— has been pleased to join to several thoughts, and several sensations a perception of delight. If this were wholly separated from all our outward sensations, and inward thoughts, we should have no reason to prefer one thought or action to another; negligence to attention, or motion to rest. And so we should neither stir our bodies, nor employ our minds, but let our thoughts (if I may so call it) run adrift, without any direction or design, and suffer the ideas of our minds, like unregarded shadows, to make their appearances there, as it happened, without attending to them. In which state man, however furnished with the faculties of understanding and will, would be a very idle, inactive creature, and pass his time only in a lazy, lethargic dream. It has therefore pleased our wise Creator to annex to several objects, and the ideas which we receive from them, as also to several of our thoughts, a concomitant pleasure, and that in several objects, to several degrees, that those faculties which he had endowed us with might not remain wholly idle and unemployed by us.

Pain has the same efficacy and use to set us on work that pleasure has, we being as ready to employ our faculties to avoid that, as to pursue this: only this is worth our consideration, that pain is often produced by the same objects and ideas that produce pleasure in us. This their near conjunction, which makes us often feel pain in the sensations where we expected pleasure, gives us new occasion of admiring the wisdom and goodness of our Maker, who, designing the preservation of our being, has annexed pain to the application of many things to our bodies, to warn us of the harm that they will do, and as advices to withdraw from them. But he, not designing our preservation barely, but the preservation of every part and organ in its perfection, hath in many cases annexed pain to those very ideas which delight us. Thus heat, that is very agreeable to us in one degree, by a little greater increase of it proves no ordinary torment: and the most pleasant of all sensible objects, light itself, if there be too much of it, if increased beyond a due proportion to our eyes, causes a very painful sensation. Which is wisely and favourably so ordered by nature, that when any object does, by the vehemency of its operation, disorder the instruments of sensation, whose structures cannot but be very nice and delicate, we might, by the pain, be warned to withdraw, before the organ be quite put out of order, and so be unfitted for its proper function for the future. The consideration of those objects that produce it may well persuade us, that this is the end or use of pain. For, though great light be insufferable to our eyes, yet the highest degree of darkness does not at all disease them: because that, causing no disorderly motion in it, leaves that curious organ unarmed in its natural state. But yet excess of cold as well as heat pains us: because it is equally destructive to that temper which is necessary to the preservation of life, and the exercise of the several functions of the body, and which consists in a moderate degree of warmth; or, if you please, a motion of the insensible parts of our bodies, confined within certain bounds.

Beyond all this, we may find another reason why God hath scattered up and down several degrees of pleasure and pain, in all the things that environ and affect us; and blended them together in almost all that our thoughts and senses have to do with;—that we, finding imperfection, dissatisfaction, and want of complete happiness, in all the enjoyments which the creatures can afford us, might be led to seek it in the enjoyment of Him with whom there is fullness of joy, and at whose right hand are pleasures for evermore.

Though what I have here said may not, perhaps, make the ideas of pleasure and pain clearer to us than our own experience does, which is the only way that we are capable of having them; yet the consideration of the reason why they are annexed to so many other ideas, serving to give us due sentiments of the wisdom and goodness of the Sovereign Disposer of all things, may not be unsuitable to the main end of these inquiries: the knowledge and veneration of him being the chief end of all our thoughts, and the proper business of all understandings.

Existence and *Unity* are two other ideas that are suggested to the understanding by every object without, and every idea within. When ideas are in our minds, we consider them as being actually there, as well as we consider things to be actually without us;—which is, that they exist, or have existence. And whatever we can consider as one thing, whether a real being or idea, suggests to the understanding the idea of unity.

Power also is another of those simple ideas which we receive from sensation and reflection. For, observing in ourselves that we do and can think, and that we can at pleasure move several parts of our bodies which were at rest; the effects, also, that natural bodies are able to produce in one another, occurring every moment to our senses,—we both these ways get the idea of power.

Besides these there is another idea, which, though suggested by our senses, yet is more constantly offered to us by what passes in our minds; and that is the idea of *succession.* For if we look immediately into ourselves, and reflect on what is observable there, we shall find our ideas always, whilst we are awake, or have any thought, passing in train, one going and another coming, without intermission.

These, if they are not all, are at least (as I think) the most considerable of those simple ideas which the mind has, and out of which is made all its other knowledge; all which it receives only by the two forementioned ways of sensation and reflection.

Nor let any one think these too narrow bounds for the capacious mind of man to expatiate in, which takes its flight further than the stars, and cannot be confined by the limits of the world; that extends its thoughts often even beyond the utmost expansion of Matter, and makes excursions into that incomprehensible Inane. I grant all this, but desire any one to assign any *simple idea* which is not received from one of those inlets before mentioned, or any *complex idea* not made out of those simple ones. Nor will it be so strange to think these few simple ideas sufficient to employ the quickest thought, or largest capacity; and to furnish the materials of all that various knowledge, and more various fancies and opinions of all mankind, if we consider how many words may be made out of the various composition of twenty-four letters; or if, going one step further, we will but reflect on the variety of combinations that may be made with barely one of the above-mentioned ideas, viz. number, whose stock is inexhaustible and truly infinite: and what a large and immense field does extension alone afford the mathematicians?

CHAPTER VIII
Some Further Considerations Concerning Our Simple Ideas of Sensation

Concerning the simple ideas of Sensation, it is to be considered,—that whatsoever is so constituted in nature as to be able, by affecting our senses, to cause any perception in the mind, does thereby produce in the understanding a simple idea; which, whatever be the external cause of it, when it comes to be taken notice of by our discerning faculty, it is by the mind looked on and considered there to be a real positive idea in the understanding, as much as any other whatsoever; though, perhaps, the cause of it be but a privation of the subject.

Thus the ideas of heat and cold, light and darkness, white and black, motion and rest, are equally clear and positive ideas in the mind; though, perhaps, some of the causes which produce them are barely privations, in those subjects from whence our senses derive those ideas. These the understanding, in its view of them, considers all as distinct positive ideas, without taking notice of the causes that produce them: which is an inquiry not belonging to the idea, as it is in the understanding, but to the nature of the things existing without us. These are two very different things, and carefully to be distinguished; it being one thing to perceive and know the idea of white or black, and quite another to examine what kind of particles they must be, and how ranged in the superficies, to make any object appear white or black.

A painter or dyer who never inquired into their causes has the ideas of white and black, and other colours, as clearly, perfectly, and distinctly in his understanding, and perhaps more distinctly, than the philosopher who has busied himself in considering their natures, and thinks he knows how far either of them is, in its cause, positive or privative; and the idea of black is no less positive in his mind than that of white, however the cause of that colour in the external object may be only a privation.

If it were the design of my present undertaking to inquire into the natural causes and manner of perception, I should offer this as a reason why a privative cause might, in some cases at least, produce a positive idea; viz. that all sensation being produced in us only by different degrees an modes of motion in our animal spirits, variously agitated by external objects, the abatement of any former motion must as necessarily produce a new sensation as the variation or increase of it; and so introduce a new idea, which depends only on a different motion of the animal spirits in that organ.

But whether this be so or not I will not here determine, but appeal to every one's own experience, whether the shadow of a man, though it consists of nothing but the absence of light (and the more the absence of light is, the more discernible is the shadow) does not, when a man looks on it, cause as clear and positive idea in his mind, as a man himself, though covered over with clear sunshine? And the picture of a shadow is a positive thing. Indeed, we have negative names, which stand not directly for positive ideas, but for their absence, such as *insipid, silence, nihil,* &c.; which words denote positive ideas, v.g. *taste, sound, being,* with a signification of their absence.

And thus one may truly be said to see darkness. For, supposing a hole perfectly dark, from whence no light is reflected, it is certain one may see the figure of it, or it may be painted; or whether the ink I write with makes any other idea, is a question. The privative causes I have here assigned of positive ideas are according to the common opinion; but, in truth, it will be hard to determine whether there be really any ideas from a privative cause, till it be determined, whether rest be any more a privation than motion.

To discover the nature of our *ideas* the better, and to discourse of them intelligibly, it will be convenient to distinguish them *as they are ideas or perceptions in our minds;* and as they are modifications of matter in the bodies that cause such perceptions in us: that so we may not think (as perhaps usually is done) that they are exactly the images and resemblances of something inherent in the subject; most of those of sensation being in the mind no more the likeness of something existing without us, than the names that stand for them are the likeness of our ideas, which yet upon hearing they are apt to excite in us.

Whatsoever the mind perceives *in itself,* or is the immediate object of perception, thought, or understanding, that I call *idea;* and the power to produce any idea in our mind, I call *quality* of the subject wherein that power is. Thus a snowball having the power to produce in us the ideas of white, cold, and round,—the power to produce those ideas in us, as they are in the snowball, I call qualities; and as they are sensations or perceptions in our understandings, I call them ideas; which *ideas,* if I speak of sometimes as in the things themselves, I would be understood to mean those qualities in the objects which produce them in us.

Qualities thus considered in bodies are,

First, such as are utterly inseparable from the body, in what state soever it be; and such as in all the alterations and changes it suffers, all the force can be used upon it, it constantly keeps; and such as sense constantly finds in every particle of matter which has bulk enough to be perceived; and the mind finds inseparable from every particle of matter, though less than to make itself singly be perceived by our senses: v.g. Take a grain of wheat, divide it into two parts; each part has still solidity, extension, figure, and mobility: divide it again, and it retains still the same qualities; and so divide it on, till the parts become insensible; they must retain still each of them all those qualities. For division (which is all that a mill, or pestle, or any other body, does upon another, in reducing it to insensible parts) can never take away either solidity, extension, figure, or mobility from any body, but only makes two or more distinct separate masses of matter, of that which was but one before; all which distinct masses, reckoned as so many distinct bodies, after division, make a certain number. These I call *original* or *primary qualities* of body, which I think we may observe to produce simple ideas in us, viz. solidity, extension, figure, motion or rest, and number.

Secondly, such qualities which in truth are nothing in the objects themselves but powers to produce various sensations in us by their primary qualities, i.e. by the bulk, figure, texture, and motion of their insensible parts, as colours, sounds, tastes, &c. These I call *secondary qualities.* To these might be added a *third* sort, which are allowed to be barely powers; though they are as much real qualities in the subject as those which I, to comply with the common way of speaking, call qualities, but for distinction, secondary qualities. For the power in fire to produce a new colour, or consistency, in *wax* or *clay,*—by its primary qualities, is as much a quality in fire, as the power it has to produce in *me* a new idea or sensation of warmth or burning, which I felt not before,—by the same primary qualities, viz. the bulk, texture, and motion of its insensible parts.

The next thing to be considered is, how bodies produce ideas in us; and that is manifestly by impulse, the only way which we can conceive bodies to operate in.

If then external objects be not united to our minds when they produce ideas therein; and yet we perceive these *original* qualities in such of them as singly fall under our senses, it is evident that some motion must be thence continued by our nerves, or animal spirits, by some parts of our bodies, to the brains or the seat of sensation, there to produce in our minds the particular ideas we have of them. And since the extension, figure, number, and motion of bodies of an observable bigness, may be perceived at a distance by the sight, it is evident some singly imperceptible bodies must come from them to the eyes, and thereby convey to the brain some motion; which produces these ideas which we have of them in us.

After the same manner that the ideas of these original qualities are produced in us, we may conceive that the ideas of *secondary* qualities are also produced, viz. by the operation of insensible particles on our senses. For, it being manifest that there are bodies and good store of bodies, each whereof are so small, that we cannot by any of our senses discover either their bulk, figure, or motion,—as is evident in the particles of the air and water, and others extremely smaller than those; perhaps as much smaller than the particles of air and water, as the particles of air and water are smaller than peas or hail-stones;—let us suppose at present that the different motions and figures, bulk and number, of such particles, affecting the several organs of our senses, produce in us those different sensations which we have from the colours and smells of bodies; v.g. that a violet, by the impulse of such insensible particles of matter, of peculiar figures and bulks, and in different degrees and modifications of their motions, causes the ideas of the blue colour, and sweet scent of that flower to be produced in our minds. It being no more impossible to conceive that God should annex such ideas to such motions, with which they have no similitude, than that he should annex the idea of pain to the motion of a piece of steel dividing our flesh, with which that idea has no resemblance.

What I have said concerning colours and smells may be understood also of tastes and sounds, and other the like sensible qualities; which, whatever reality we by mistake attribute to them, are in truth nothing in the objects themselves, but powers to produce various sensations in us; and depend on those primary qualities, viz. bulk, figure, texture, and motion of parts.

From whence I think it easy to draw this observation,—that the ideas of primary qualities of bodies are resemblances of them, and their patterns do really exist in the bodies themselves, but the ideas produced in us by these secondary qualities have no resemblance of them at all. There is nothing like our ideas, existing in the bodies themselves. They are, in the bodies we denominate from them, only a power to produce those sensations in us: and what is sweet, blue, or warm in idea, is but the certain bulk, figure, and motion of the insensible parts, in the bodies themselves, which we call so.

Flame is denominated hot and light; snow, white and cold; and manna, white and sweet, from the ideas they produce in us. Which qualities are commonly thought to be the same in those bodies that those ideas are in us, the one the perfect resemblance of the other, as they are in a mirror, and it would by most men be judged very extravagant if one should say otherwise. And yet he that will consider that the same fire that, at one distance produces in us the sensation of warmth, does, at a nearer approach, produce in us the far different sensation of pain, ought to bethink himself what reason he has to say—that this idea of warmth, which was produced in him by the fire, is *actually in the fire;* and this idea of pain, which the same fire produced in him the same way, is *not* in the fire. Why are whiteness and coldness in snow, and pain not, when it produces the one and the other idea in us; and can do neither, but by the bulk, figure, number, and motion of its solid parts?

The particular bulk, number, figure, and motion of the parts of fire or snow are really in them,—whether any one's senses perceive them or no: and therefore they may be called *real* qualities, because they really exist in those bodies. But light, heat, whiteness, or coldness, are no more really in them than sickness or pain is in manna. Take away the sensation of them; let not the eyes see light or colours, nor the ears hear sounds; let the palate not taste, nor the nose smell, and all colours, tastes, odours, and sounds, *as they are such particular ideas,* vanish and cease, and are reduced to their causes, i.e. bulk, figure, and motion of parts.

A piece of manna of a sensible bulk is able to produce in us the idea of a round or square figure; and by being removed from one place to another, the idea of motion. This idea of motion represents it as it really is in manna moving: a circle or square are the same, whether in idea or existence, in the mind or in the manna. And this, both motion and figure, are really in the manna, whether we take notice of them or no: this everybody is ready to agree to. Besides, manna, by the bulk, figure, texture, and motion of its parts, has a power to produce the sensations of sickness, and sometimes of acute pains or gripings in us. That these ideas of sickness and pain are *not* in the manna, but effects of its operations on us, and are nowhere when we feel them not; this also every one readily agrees to. And yet men are hardly to be brought to think that sweetness and whiteness are not really in manna; which are but the effects of the operations of manna, by the motion, size, and figure of its particles, on the eyes and palate: as the pain and sickness caused by manna are confessedly nothing but the effects of its operations on the stomach and guts, by the size, motion, and figure of its insensible parts, (for by nothing else can a body operate, as has been proved): as if it could not operate on the eyes and palate, and thereby produce in the mind particular distinct ideas, which in itself it has not, as well as we allow it can operate on the guts and stomach, and thereby produce distinct ideas, which in itself it has not. These ideas, being all effects of the operations of manna on several parts of our bodies, by the size, figure, number, and motion of its parts;—why those produced by the eyes and palate should rather be thought to be really in the manna, than those produced by the stomach and guts; or why the pain and sickness, ideas that are the effect of manna, should be thought to be nowhere when they are not felt; and yet the sweetness and whiteness, effects of the same manna on other parts of the body, by ways equally as unknown, should be thought to exist in the manna, when they are not seen or tasted, would need some reason to explain.

Let us consider the red and white colours in porphyry. Hinder light from striking on it, and its colours vanish; it no longer produces any such ideas in us: upon the return of light it produces these appearances on us again. Can any one think any real alterations are made in the porphyry by the presence or absence of light; and that those ideas of whiteness and redness are really in porphryry in the light, when it is plain *it has no colour in the dark?* It has, indeed, such a configuration of particles, both night and day, as are apt, by the rays of light rebounding from some parts of that hard stone, to produce in us the idea of redness, and from others the idea of whiteness; but whiteness or redness are not in it at any time, but such a texture that hath the power to produce such a sensation in us.

Pound an almond, and the clear white colour will be altered into a dirty one, and the sweet taste into an oily one. What real alteration can the beating of the pestle make in any body, but an alteration of the texture of it?

Ideas being thus distinguished and understood, we may be able to give an account how the same water, at the same time, may produce the idea of cold by one hand and of heat by the other: whereas it is impossible that the same water, if those ideas were really in it, should at the same time be both hot and cold. For, if we imagine *warmth,* as it is in our hands, to be nothing but a certain sort and degree of motion in the minute particles of our nerves or animal spirits, we may understand how it is possible that the same water may, at the same time, produce the sensations of heat in one hand and cold in the other; which yet *figure* never does, that never producing the idea of a square by one hand which has produced the idea of a globe by another. But if the sensation of heat and cold be nothing but the increase or diminution of the motion of the minute parts of our bodies, caused by the corpuscles of any other body, it is easy to be understood, that if that motion be greater in one hand than in the other; if a body be applied to the two hands, which has in its minute particles a greater motion than in those of one of the hands, and a less than in those of the other, it will increase the motion of the one hand and lessen it in the other; and so cause the different sensations of heat and cold that depend thereon.

I have in what just goes before been engaged in physical inquiries a little further than perhaps I intended. But, it being necessary to make the nature of sensation a little understood; and to make the difference between the *qualities* in bodies, and the *ideas* produced by them in the mind, to be distinctly conceived, without which it were impossible to discourse intelligibly of them;—I hope I shall be pardoned this little excursion into natural philosophy; it being necessary in our present inquiry to distinguish the *primary* and *real* qualities of bodies, which are always in them (viz. solidity, extension, figure, number, and motion, or rest, and are sometimes perceived by us, viz. when the bodies they are in are big enough singly to be discerned), from those *secondary* and *imputed* qualities, which are but the powers of several combinations of those primary ones, when they operate without being distinctly discerned;—whereby we may also come to know what ideas are, and what are not, resemblances of something really existing in the bodies we denominate from them.

The qualities, then, that are in bodies, rightly considered, are of three sorts:—

First, The bulk, figure, number, situation, and motion or rest of their solid parts. Those are in them, whether we perceive them or not; and when they are of that size that we can discover them, we have by these an idea of the thing as it is in itself; as is plain in artificial things. These I call *primary qualities.*

Secondly, The power that is in any body, by reason of its insensible primary qualities, to operate after a peculiar manner on any of our senses, and thereby produce in *us* the different ideas of several colours, sounds, smells, tastes, &c. These are usually called *sensible qualities.*

Thirdly, The power that is in any body, by reason of the particular constitution of its primary qualities, to make such a change in the bulk, figure, texture, and motion of *another body,* as to make it operate on our senses differently from what it did before. Thus the sun has a power to make wax white, and fire to make lead fluid. These are usually called *powers.*

The first of these, as has been said, I think may be properly called real, original, or primary qualities; because they are in the things themselves, whether they are perceived or not: and upon their different modifications it is that the secondary qualities depend.

The other two are only powers to act differently upon other things: which powers result from the different modifications of those primary qualities.

But, though the two latter sorts of qualities are powers barely, and nothing but powers, relating to several other bodies, and resulting from the different modifications of the original qualities, yet they are generally otherwise thought of. For the *second* sort, viz. the powers to produce several ideas in us, by our senses, are looked upon as real qualities in the things thus affecting us: but the *third* sort are called and esteemed barely powers. v.g. The idea of heat or light, which we receive by our eyes, or touch, from the sun, are commonly thought real qualities existing in the sun, and something more than mere powers in it. But when we consider the sun in reference to wax, which it melts or blanches, we look on the whiteness and softness produced in the wax, not as qualities in the sun, but effects produced by powers in it. Whereas, if rightly considered, these qualities of light and warmth, which are perceptions in me when I am warmed or enlightened by the sun, are no otherwise in the sun, than the changes made in the wax, when it is blanched or melted, are in the sun. They are all of them equally *powers in the sun, depending on its primary qualities;* whereby it is able, in the one case, so to alter the bulk, figure, texture, or motion of some of the insensible parts of my eyes or hands, as thereby to produce in me the idea of light or heat; and in the other, it is able so to alter the bulk, figure, texture, or motion of the insensible parts of the wax, as to make them fit to produce in me the distinct ideas of white and fluid.

The reason why the one are ordinarily taken for real qualities, and the other only for bare powers, seems to be, because the ideas we have of distinct colours, sounds, &c., containing nothing at all in them of bulk, figure, or motion, we are not apt to think them the effects of these primary qualities; which appear not, to our senses, to operate in their production, and with which they have not any apparent congruity or conceivable connection. Hence it is that we are so forward to imagine, that those ideas are the resemblances of something really existing in the objects themselves: since sensation discovers nothing of bulk, figure, or motion of parts in their production; nor can reason show how bodies, *by their bulk, figure, and motion,* should produce in the mind the ides of blue or yellow, &c. But, in the other case, in the operations of bodies changing the qualities one of another, we plainly discover that the quality produced has commonly no resemblance with anything in the thing producing it; wherefore we look on it as a bare effect of power. For, through receiving the idea of heat or light from the sun, we are apt to think *it* is a perception and resemblance of such a quality in the sun; yet when we see wax, or a fair face, receive change of colour from the sun, we cannot imagine *that* to be the reception or resemblance of anything in the sun, because we find not those different colours in the sun itself. For, our senses being able to observe a likeness or unlikeness of sensible qualities in two different external objects, we forwardly enough conclude the production of any sensible quality in any subject to be an effect of bare power, and not the communication of any quality which was really in the efficient, when we find no such sensible quality in the thing that produced it. But our senses, not being able to discover any unlikeness between the idea produced in us, and the quality of the object producing it, we are apt to imagine that our ideas are resemblances of something in the objects, and not the effects of certain powers placed in the modification of their primary qualities, with which primary qualities the ideas produced in us have no resemblance.

To conclude. Beside those before-mentioned primary qualities in bodies, viz. bulk, figure, extension, number, and motion of their solid parts; all the rest, whereby we take notice of bodies, and distinguish them one from another, are nothing else but several powers in them, depending on those primary qualities; whereby they are fitted, either by immediately operating on our bodies to produce several different ideas in us; or else, by operating on other bodies, so to change their primary qualities as to render them capable of producing ideas in us different from what before they did. The former of these, I think, may be called secondary qualities *immediately perceivable:* the latter, secondary qualities, *mediately perceivable.*

SECOND TREATISE ON GOVERNMENT

VII. OF THE BEGINNING OF POLITICAL SOCIETIES

Men being, as has been said, by nature all free, equal, and independent, no one can be put out of his estate and subjected to the political power of another without his own consent, which is done by agreeing with other men, to join and unite into a community for their comfortable, safe, and peaceable living, one amongst another, in a secure enjoyment of their properties, and a greater security against any that are not of it. This any number of men may do, because it injures not the freedom of the rest; they are left, as they were, in the liberty of the state of nature. When any number of men have so consented to make one community or government, they are thereby presently incorporated, and make one body politic, wherein the majority have a right to act and conclude the rest.

For, when any number of men have, by the consent of every individual, made a community, they have thereby made that community one body, with a power to act as one body, which is only by the will and determination of the majority. For that which acts any community, being only the consent of the individuals of it, and it being one body, must move one way, it is necessary the body should move that way whither the greater force carries it, which is the consent of the majority, or else it is impossible it should act or continue one body, one community, which the consent of every individual that united into it agreed that it should; and so everyone is bound by that consent to be concluded by the majority. And therefore we see that in assemblies enpowered to act by positive laws where no number is set by that positive law which empowers them, the act of the majority passes for the act of the whole, and of course determines as having, by the law of nature and reason, the power of the whole.

And thus every man, by consenting with others to make one body politic under one government, puts himself under an obligation to everyone of that society to submit to the determination of the majority, and to be concluded by it; or else this original compact, whereby he with others incorporates into one society, would signify nothing, and be no compact if he be left free and under no other ties than he was in before in the state of nature. For what appearance would there be of any compact? What new engagement if he were no farther tied by any decrees of the society than he himself thought fit and did actually consent to? This would be still as great a liberty as he himself had before his compact, or anyone else in the state of nature has, who may submit himself and consent to any acts of it if the thinks fit.

For if the consent of the majority shall not in reason be received as the act of the whole, and conclude every individual, nothing but the consent of every individual can make any thing to be the act of the whole, which, considering the infirmities of health and avocations of business, which in a number though much less than that of a commonwealth, will necessarily keep many away from the public assembly; and the variety of opinions and contrariety of interests which unavoidably happen in all collections of men, 'tis next impossible

First published in 1690.

ever to be had. And, therefore, if coming into society be upon such terms, it will be only like Cato's coming into the theatre, *tantum ut exiret*. Such a constitution as this would make the mighty *Leviathan* of a shorter duration than the feeblest creatures, and not let it outlast the day it was born in, which cannot be supposed till we can think that rational creatures should desire and constitute societies only to be dissolved. For where the majority cannot conclude the rest, there they cannot act as one body, and consequently will be immediately dissolved again.

Whosoever therefore out of a state of nature unite into a community, must be understood to give up all the power necessary to the ends for which they unite into society to the majority of the community, unless they expressly agreed in any number greater than the majority. And this is done by barely agreeing to unite into one political society, which is all the compact that is, or needs be, between the individuals that enter into or make up a commonwealth. And thus, that which begins and actually constitutes any political society is nothing but the consent of any number of freemen capable of a majority, to unite and incorporate into such a society. And this is that, and that only, which did or could give beginning to any lawful government in the world. . . .

Every man being, as has been showed, naturally free, and nothing being able to put him into subjection to any earthly power, but only his own consent, it is to be considered what shall be understood to be a sufficient declaration of a man's consent to make him subject to the laws of any government. There is a common distinction of an express and a tacit consent, which will concern our present case. No body doubts but an express consent of any man, entering into any society, makes him a perfect member of that society, a subject of that government. The difficulty is, what ought to be looked upon as a tacit consent, and how far it binds, i.e., how far anyone shall be looked on to have consented, and thereby submitted to any government, where he has made no expressions of it at all. And to this I say, that every man that has any possession of enjoyment of any part of the dominions of any government does thereby give his tacit consent, and is as far forth obliged to obedience to the laws of that government, during such enjoyment, as any one under it, whether this his possession be of land to him and his heirs for ever, or a lodging only for a week; or whether it be barely travelling freely on the highway; and, in effect, it reaches as far as the very being of anyone within the territories of that government.

To understand this the better, it is fit to consider that every man when he at first incorporates himself into any commonwealth, he, by his uniting himself thereunto, annexes also, and submits to the community those possessions which he has, or shall acquire, that do not already belong to any other government. For it would be a direct contradiction for anyone to enter into society with others for the securing and regulating of property, and yet to suppose his land, whose property is to be regulated by the laws of the society, should be exempt from the jurisdiction of that government to which he himself, the proprietor of the land, is subject. By the same act, therefore, whereby anyone unites his person, which was before free, to any commonwealth, by the same he unites his possessions, which were before free, to it also; and they become, both of them, person and possession, subject to the government and dominion of that commonwealth as long as it has a being. Whoever therefore, from thenceforth, by inheritance, purchase, permission, or otherwise enjoys any part of the land so annexed to, and under the government of that commonwealth, must take it with the condition it is under; that is, of submitting to the government of the commonwealth, under whose jurisdiction it is, as far forth as any subject of it.

But since the government has a direct jurisdiction only over the land and reaches the possessor of it (before he has actually incorporated himself in the society) only as he dwells upon and enjoys that, the obligation anyone is under by virtue of such enjoyment to submit to the government begins and ends with the enjoyment; so that whenever the owner, who has given nothing but such a tacit consent to the government, will, by donation, sale or otherwise, quit the said possession, he is at liberty to go and incorporate himself into any other commonwealth, or agree with others to begin a new one *in vacuis locis,* in any part of the world they can find free and unpossessed; whereas he that has once, by actual agreement and any express declaration, given his consent to be of any commonweal, is perpetually and indispensably obliged to be, and remain unalterably a subject to it, and can never be again in the liberty of the state of nature, unless by any calamity the government he was under comes to be dissolved; or else by some public act cuts him off from being any longer a member of it.

But submitting to the laws of any country, living quietly, and enjoying privileges and protection under them, makes not a man a member of that society; this is only a local protection and homage due to and from all those who, not being in a state of war, come within the territories belonging to any government, to all parts whereof the force of its law extends. But this no more makes a man a member of that society, a perpetual subject of that commonwealth, than it would make a man a subject to another in whose family he found it convenient to abide for some time, though, whilst he continued in it, he were obliged to comply with the laws and submit to the government he found there. And thus we see that foreigners, by living all their lives under another government, and enjoying the privileges and protection of it, though they are bound, even in conscience, to submit to its administration as far forth as any denizen, yet do not thereby come to be subjects or members of that commonwealth. Nothing can make any man so but his actually entering into it by positive engagement and express promise and compact. This is that which I think, concerning the beginning of political societies, and that consent which makes anyone a member of any commonwealth.

IX. OF THE ENDS OF POLITICAL SOCIETY AND GOVERNMENT

If man in the state of nature be so free as has been said; if he be absolute lord of his own person and possessions; equal to the greatest and subject to no body, why will he part with his freedom? Why will he give up this empire, and subject himself to the dominion and control of any other power? To which 'tis obvious to answer, that though in the state of nature he has such a right, yet the enjoyment of it is very uncertain and constantly exposed to the invasion of others; for all being kings as much as he, every man his equal, and the greater part no strict observers of equity and justice, the enjoyment of the property he has in this state is very unsafe, very unsecure. This makes him willing to quit this condition which, however free, is full of fears and continual dangers; and 'tis not without reason that he seeks out and is willing to join in society with others who are already united, or have a mind to unite for the mutual preservation of their lives, liberties, and estates, which I call by the general name, property.

The great and chief end therefore, of men's uniting into commonwealths, and putting themselves under government, is the preservation of their property; to which in the state of nature there are many things wanting.

First, There wants an established, settled, known law, received and allowed by common consent to be the standard of right and wrong, and the common measure to decide all controversies between them. For though the law of nature be plain and intelligible to all rational creatures, yet men, being biased by their interest, as well as ignorant for want of study of it, are not apt to allow of it as a law binding to them in the application of it to their particular cases.

Secondly, In the state of nature there wants a known and indifferent judge, with authority to determine all differences according to the established law. For everyone in that state being both judge and executioner of the law of nature, men being partial to themselves, passion and revenge is very apt to carry them too far, and with too much heat in their own cases, as well as negligence and unconcernedness, make them too remiss in other men's.

Thirdly, In the state of nature there often wants power to back and support the sentence when right, and to give it due execution. They who by any injustice offended, will seldom fail where they are able by force to make good their injustice. Such resistance many times makes the punishment dangerous, and frequently destructive to those who attempt it.

Thus mankind, notwithstanding all the privileges of the state of nature, being but in an ill condition while they remain in it, are quickly driven into society. Hence it comes to pass, that we seldom find any number of men live any time together in this state. The inconveniences that they are therein exposed to by the irregular and uncertain exercise of the power every man has of punishing the transgressions of others, make them take sanctuary under the established laws of government, and therein seek the preservation of their property. 'Tis this makes them so willingly give up every one his single power of punishing to be exercised by such alone as shall be appointed to it amongst them, and by such rules as the community, or those authorized by them to that purpose, shall agree on. And in this we have the original right and rise of both the legislative and executive power as well as of the governments and societies themselves.

For in the state of nature to omit the liberty he has of innocent delights, a man has two powers.

The first is to do whatsoever he thinks fit for the preservation of himself and others within the permission of the law of nature; by which law, common to them all, he and all the rest of mankind are one community, make up one society distinct from all other creatures and were it not for the corruption and viciousness of degenerate men, there would be no need of any other, no necessity that men should separate from this great and natural community, and associate into less combinations.

The other power a man has in the state of nature is the power to punish the crimes committed against that law. Both these he gives up when he joins in a private, if I may so call it, or particular political society, and incorporates into any commonwealth separate from the rest of mankind.

The first power, *viz.* of doing whatsoever he thought fit for the preservation of himself and the rest of mankind, he gives up to be regulated by laws made by the society, so far forth as the preservation of himself and the rest of that society shall require; which laws of the society in many things confine the liberty he had by the law of nature.

Secondly, the power of punishing he wholly gives up, and engages his natural force (which he might before employ in the execution of the law of nature, by his own single authority, as he thought fit) to assist the executive power of the society as the law thereof shall require. For being now in a new state, wherein he is to enjoy many conveniences from the labour, assistance, and society of others in the same community, as well as protection from its whole strength, he is to part also with as much of his natural liberty, in providing for himself, as the good, prosperity, and safety of the society shall require, which is not only necessary but just, since the other members of the society do the like.

But though men when they enter into society give up the equality, liberty, and executive power they had in the state of nature into the hands of the society, to be so far disposed of by the legislative as the good of the society shall require, yet it being only with an intention in everyone the better to preserve himself, his liberty and property (for no rational creature can be supposed to change his condition with an intention to be worse), the power of the society or legislative constituted by them can never be supposed to extend farther than the common good, but is obliged to secure everyone's property by providing against those three defects above-mentioned that made the state of nature so unsafe and uneasy. And so, who-ever has the legislative or supreme power of any commonwealth, is bound to govern by established standing laws, promulgated and known to the people, and not by extemporary decrees, by indifferent and upright judges, who are to decide controversies by those laws; and to employ the force of the community at home only in the execution of such laws, or abroad to prevent or redress foreign injuries and secure the community from inroads and invasion. And all this to be directed to no other end but the peace, safety, and public good of the people. . . .

XI. OF THE EXTENT OF THE LEGISLATIVE POWER

These are the bounds which the trust that is put in them by the society and the law of God and nature have set to the legislative power of every commonwealth, in all forms of government.

First, They are to govern by promulgated established laws, not to be varied in particular cases, but to have one rule for rich and poor, for the favourite at Court, and the countryman at plough.

Secondly, These laws also ought to be designed for no other end ultimately but the good of the people.

Thirdly, They must not raise taxes on the property of the people without the consent of the people given by themselves or their deputies. And this properly concerns only such governments where the legislative is always in being, or at least where the people have not reserved any part of the legislative to deputies, to be from time to time chosen by themselves.

Fourthly, The legislative neither must nor can transfer the power of making laws to anybody else, or place it anywhere but where the people have. . . .

XIX. OF THE DISSOLUTION OF GOVERNMENT

He that will with any clearness speak of the dissolution of government, ought in the first place to distinguish between the dissolution of the society and the dissolution of the gov-ernment. That which makes the community, and brings men out of the loose state of nature into one politic society, is the agreement which every one has with the rest to incorporate and act as one body, and so be one distinct commonwealth. The usual, and almost only way whereby this union is dissolved, is the inroad of foreign force making a conquest upon them. For in that case (not being able to maintain and support themselves as one entire and independent body) the union belonging to that body which consisted therein, must neces-sarily cease, and so every one return to the state he was in before, with a liberty to shift for himself and provide for his own safety, as he thinks fit, in some other society. Whenever the society is dissolved, 'tis certain the government of that society cannot remain. Thus conquerors' swords often cut up governments by the roots, and mangle societies to pieces, separating the subdued or scattered multitude from the protection of and dependence on that society which ought to have preserved them from violence. The world is too well instructed in, and too forward to allow of this way of dissolving of governments, to need any more to be said of it; and there wants not much argument to prove that where the society is dissolved, the government cannot remain; that being as impossible as for the frame of an house to subsist when the materials of it are scattered and dissipated by a whirlwind, or jumbled into a confused heap by an earthquake.

Besides this overturning from without, governments are dissolved from within,

First, When the legislative is altered, civil society being a state of peace amongst those who are of it, from whom the state of war is excluded by the umpirage which they have provided in their legislative for the ending all differences that may arise amongst any of them. 'Tis in their legislative that the members of a commonwealth are united and combined together into one coherent living body. This is the soul that gives form, life, and unity to the commonwealth. From hence the several members have their mutual influence, sympathy, and connection. And therefore when the legislative is broken, or dissolved, dissolution and death follows. For the essence and union of the society consisting in having one will, the legislative, when once established by the majority has the declaring and, as it were, keeping of that will. The constitution of the legislative is the first and fundamental act of society, whereby provision is made for the continuation of their union under the direction of persons and bonds of laws, made by persons authorized thereunto, by the consent and appointment of the people, without which no one man, or number of men, amongst them can have authority of making laws that shall be binding to the rest. When any one, or more, shall take upon them to make laws whom the people have not appointed so to do, they make laws without authority, which the people are not therefore bound to obey; by which means they come again to be out of subjection, and may constitute to themselves a new legislative, as they think best, being in full liberty to resist the force of those who, without authority, would impose any thing upon them. Every one is at the disposure of his own will, when those who had, by the delegation of the society, the declaring of the public will, are excluded from it, and others usurp the place who have no such authority or delegation. . . .

There is therefore Secondly another way whereby governments are dissolved, and that is, when the legislative, or the prince, either of them act contrary to their trust.

First, The legislative acts against the trust reposed in them when they endeavour to invade the property of the subject, and to make themselves, or any part of the community, masters or arbitrary disposers of the lives, liberties, or fortunes of the people.

The reason why men enter into society is the preservation of their property; and the end why they choose and authorize a legislative is that there may be laws made, and rules set, as guards and fences to the properties of all the members of the society, to limit the power and moderate the dominion of every part and member of the society. For since it can never be supposed to be the will of the society that the legislative should have a power to destroy that which every one designs to secure by entering into society, and for which the people submitted themselves to legislators of their own making: whenever the legislators endeavour to take away and destroy the property of the people, or to reduce them to slavery under arbitrary power, they put themselves into a state of war with the people, who are thereupon absolved from any farther obedience, and are left to the common refuge which God has provided for all men against force and violence. Whensoever therefore the legislative shall transgress this fundamental rule of society, and either by ambition, fear, folly, or corruption, endeavour to grasp themselves, or put into the hands of any other, an absolute power over the lives, liberties, and estates of the people, by this breach of trust they forfeit the power the people had put into their hands for quite contrary ends, and it devolves to the people; who have a right to resume their original liberty, and by the establishment of a new legislative (such as they shall think fit), provide for their own safety and security, which is the end for which they are in society. What I have said here concerning the legislative in general holds true also concerning the supreme executor, who having a double trust put in him, both to have a part in the legislative and the supreme execution of the law, acts against both, when he goes about to set up his own arbitary will as the law of the society. He acts also contrary to his trust when he employs the force, treasure, and offices of the society to corrupt the representatives and gain them to his purposes, when he openly preengages the electors, and prescribes, to their choice, such whom he has, by solicitations, threats, promises, or otherwise, won to his designs, and employs them to bring in such who have promised beforehand what to vote and what to enact. Thus to regulate candidates and electors, and new model the ways of election, what is it but to cut up the government by the roots, and poison the very fountain of public security? For the people having reserved to themselves the choice of their representatives as the fence to their properties, could to it for no other end but that they might always be freely chosen, and so chosen, freely act and advise as the necessity of the commonwealth and the public good should, upon examination and mature debate, be judged to require. This, those who give their votes before they hear the debate, and have weighed the reasons on all sides, are not capable of doing. To prepare such an assembly as this, and endeavour to set up the declared abettors of his own will, for the true representatives of the people, and the law-makers of the society, is certainly as great a breach of trust, and as perfect a declaration of a design to subvert the government, as is possible to be met with. To which, if one shall add rewards and punishments visibly employed to the same end, and all the arts of perverted law made use of to take off and destroy all that stand in the way of such a design, and will not comply and consent to betray the liberties of their country, 'twill be past doubt what is doing. What power they ought to have in the society who thus employ it contrary to the trust went along with it in its first institution, is easy to determine; and one cannot but see that he who has once attempted any such thing as this cannot any longer be trusted.

To this, perhaps, it will be said, that the people being ignorant and always discontented, to lay the foundation of government in the unsteady opinion and uncertain humor of the people, is to expose it to certain ruin; and no government will be able long to subsist if the people may set up a new legislative whenever they take offence at the old one. To this I answer, quite the contrary. People are not so easily got out of their old forms as some are apt to suggest. They are hardly to be prevailed with to amend the acknowledged faults in the frame they have been accustomed to. And if there be any original defects, or adventitious ones introduced by time or corruption, 'tis not an easy thing to get them changed, even when all the world sees there is an opportunity for it. This slowness and aversion in the people to quit their old constitutions has in the many revolutions (that) have been seen in this kingdom, in this and former ages, still kept us to, or after some interval of fruitless attempts, still brought us back again to our old legislative of king, lords and commons; and whatever provocations have made the crown be taken from some of our princes' heads, they never carried the people so far as to place it in another line.

But 'twill be said, this hypothesis lays a ferment for frequent rebellion. To which I answer:

First, No more than any other hypothesis. For when the people are made miserable, and find themselves exposed to the ill usage of arbitrary power; cry up their governors as much as you will for sons of *Jupiter,* let them be sacred and divine, descended or authorized from Heaven; given them out for whom or what you please, the same will happen. The people generally ill treated, and contrary to right, will be ready upon any occasion to ease themselves of a burden that sits heavy upon them. They will wish and seek for the opportunity, which in the change, weakness, and accidents of humane affairs, seldom delays long to offer itself. He must have lived but a little while in the world, who has not seen examples of this in his time; and he must have read very little who cannot produce examples of it in all sorts of governments in the world.

Secondly, I answer, such revolutions happen not upon every little mismanagement in public affairs. Great mistakes in the ruling part, many wrong and inconvenient laws, and all the slips of human frailty will be born by the people without mutiny or murmur. But if a long train of abuses, prevarications, and artifices, all tending the same way, make the design visible to the people, and they cannot but feel what they lie under, and see whither they are going, 'tis not to be wondered that they should then rouse themselves, and endeavour to put the rule into such hands which may secure to them the ends for which government was at first erected, and without which, ancient names and specious forms are so far from being better, that they are much worse than the state of nature or pure anarchy; the inconveniences being all as great and as near, but the remedy farther off and more difficult.

Thirdly, I answer, That this power in the people of providing for their safety anew by a new legislative when their legislators have acted contrary to their trust by invading their property, is the best fence against rebellion, and the probablest means to hinder it. For rebellion being an opposition, not to persons, but authority, which is founded only in the constitutions and laws of the government; those, whoever they be, who by force break through, and by force justify their violation of them, are truly and properly rebels. For when men, by entering into society and civil government, have excluded force, and introduced laws for the preservation of property, peace, and unity amongst themselves; those who set up force again in opposition to the laws, do *rebellare*—that is, bring back again the state of war, and are properly rebels, which they who are in power, by the pretence they have to authority, the temptation of force they have in their hands, and the flattery of those about them being likeliest to do, the properest way to prevent the evil is to shew them the danger and injustice of it who are under the greatest temptation to run into it. . . .

In both the fore-mentioned cases, when either the legislative is changed or the legislators act contrary to the end for which they were constituted, those who are guilty are guilty of rebellion. For if anyone by force takes away the established legislative of any society, and the laws by them made pursuant to their trust, he thereby takes away the umpirage which everyone had consented to for a peaceable decision of all their controversies, and a bar to the state of war amongst them. They who remove or change the legislative, take away their decisive power, which nobody can have but by the appointment and consent of the people, and so destroying the authority which the people did, and nobody else can, set up; and introducing a power which the people has not authorised, actually introduce a state of war which is that of force without authority. And thus by removing the legislative established by the society (in whose decisions the people acquiesced and united as to that of their own will), they untie the knot and expose the people anew to the state of war. And if those who by force take away the legislative are rebels, the legislators themselves, as have been shown, can be no less esteemed so, when they who were set up for the protection and preservation of the people, their liberties and properties, shall by force invade and endeavour to take them away; and so they, putting themselves into a state of war with those who made them the protectors and guardians of their peace, are properly and with the greatest aggravation *rebellants* (rebels).

But if they who say it lays a foundation for rebellion mean that it may occasion civil wars or intestine broils, to tell the people they are absolved from obedience when illegal attempts are made upon their liberties or properties, and may oppose the unlawful violence of those who were their magistrates when they invade their properties contrary to the trust put in them and that therefore this doctrine is not to be allowed, being so destructive to the peace of the world: they may as well say upon the same ground that honest men may not oppose robbers or pirates because this may occasion disorder or bloodshed. If any mischief comes in such cases, it is not to be charged upon him who defends his own right, but on him that invades his neighbour's. If the innocent honest man must quietly quit all he has for peace's sake to him who will lay violent hands upon it, I desire it may be considered what a kind of peace there will be in the world which consists only in violence and rapine, and which is to be maintained only for the benefit of robbers and oppressors. Who would not think it an admirable peace betwixt the mighty and the mean when the lamb without resistance yielded his throat to be torn by the imperious wolf? Polyphemus's den gives us a perfect pattern of such a peace and such a government, wherein Ulysses and his companions had nothing to do but quietly to suffer themselves to be devoured. And no doubt Ulysses, who was a prudent man, preached up passive obedience, and exhorted them to a quiet submission by representing to them of what concernment peace was to mankind, and by showing the inconveniences which might happen if they should offer to resist Polyphemus, who had now the power over them.

The end of government is the good of mankind, and which is best for mankind, that the people should be always exposed to the boundless will of tyranny, or that the rulers should be sometimes liable to be opposed when they grow exorbitant in the use of their power, and employ it for the destruction and not the preservation of the properties of their people?

Nor let anyone say that mischief can arise from hence, as often as it shall please a busy head or turbulent spirit to desire the alteration of the government. It is true such men may stir whenever they please, but it will be only to their own just ruin and perdition. For till the mischief be grown general, and the ill-designs of the rulers become visible, or their attempts sensible to the greater part, the people who are more disposed to suffer than right themselves by resistance are not apt to stir. The examples of particular injustice or oppression of here and there an unfortunate man, move them not. But if they universally have a persuasion grounded upon manifest evidence that designs are carrying on against their liberties, and the general course and tendency of things cannot but given them strong suspicions of the evil intention of their governors, who is to be blamed for it? Who can help it if they who might avoid it bring themselves into this suspicion? Are the people to be blamed, if they have the sense of rational creatures, and can think of things no otherwise than as they find and feel them? And is it not rather their fault who put things into such a posture, that they would not have them thought to be as they are? I grant that the pride, ambition, and turbulency of private men have sometimes caused great disorders in commonwealths, and factions have been fatal to states and kingdoms. But whether the mischief has oftener begun in the people's wantonness, and a desire to cast off the lawful authority of their rulers, or in the ruler's insolence, and endeavours to get and exercise an arbitrary power over their people; whether oppression or disobedience gave the first rise to the disorder, I leave it to impartial history to determine. This I am sure, whoever, either ruler or subject, by force goes about to invade the rights of either prince or people, and lays the foundation for overturning the constitution and fame of any just government, he is guilty of the greatest crime I think a man is capable of, being to answer for all those mischiefs of blood, rapine, and desolation, which the breaking to pieces of governments brings on a country. And he who does it is justly to be esteemed the common enemy and pest of mankind, and is to be treated accordingly. . . .

To conclude, the power that every individual gave the society when he entered into it, can never revert to the individuals again as long as the society lasts, but will always remain in the community, because without this there can be no community, no commonwealth, which is contrary to the original agreement; so also when the society has placed the legislative in any assembly of men to continue in them and their successors, with direction and authority for providing such successors, the legislative can never revert to the people whilst that government lasts, because having provided a legislative with power to continue for ever, they have given up their political power to the legislative and cannot resume it. But if they have set limits to the duration of their legislative, and made this supreme power in any person or assembly only temporary; or else when by the miscarriages of those in authority it is forfeited; upon the forfeiture, or at the determination of the time set, it reverts to the society, and the people have a right to act as supreme, and continue the legislative in themselves; or place it in a new form, or new hands as they think good.

LEIBNIZ

1646–1716

Gottfried Wilhelm Leibniz was born in Leipzig, Germany. He went to the University of Leipzig to study law, but under the guidance of a neo-Aristotelian philosophy professor named Jakob Thomasius, he devoted most of his time to studying the philosophical works of Bacon, Kepler, Galileo, and Descartes. His undergraduate thesis, written when he was only seventeen, *De Principio Individui* (1663) presented a nominalistic view of individuation and identity. After getting his doctorate in law, Leibniz worked for the elector of Mainz in Frankfurt.

In 1672 Leibniz went to Paris, where he met Melebranche, Arnauld, and Huygens. On his way home he visited Spinoza at The Hague. He was soon hired in Hanover at the House of Brunswick, to work as a librarian and historian. He held a series of other jobs, including diplomat, alchemist, and even engineer (he worked on draining the Harz mountains). As an inventor he made designs of an express coach and something that would have to await construction for several centuries: a computer. Like Descartes, Leibniz invented an entirely new branch of mathematics: the differential and integral calculus, which he published several years before Newton published his. At one time he actively corresponded with more than 1,000 people, among them many courtesans and princes. In Berlin he directed the founding of the Academy of Sciences and served as its first college president. During his life he continued trying to apply philosophy and mathematics to everyday affairs. For instance, he once tried to demonstrate, using logic and mathematics, why a German candidate should succeed the Polish monarchy, and he used his calculus to try to make peace between Catholic and Protestant theologies.

The last years of Leibniz's life were tormented by the controversy over whether he or Isaac Newton had first invented the calculus. By then Leibniz had already fallen out of favor with the princes of Brunswick, who viewed his philosophy and academic propaganda as impractical and no longer useful. Unlike most great philosophers, he left no single great work, not even, like Spinoza, one that was published posthumously. Some of Leibniz's original and powerful writing can be found in his two main books, *New Essays on the Human Understanding* (1705) and *Theodicy* (1710), but his most important contributions lie in his many shorter works, most of which were not published until this century and many of which for reasons not quite understood still exist only in manuscript form. But he died a famous and often lampooned figure, one of the most influential of the eighteenth century. The character of Pangloss in Voltaire's *Candide* is supposedly based on Leibniz.

Reality according to Leibniz consists not of one substance, as Spinoza and other types of monists had believed, nor in some finite number of different substances, such as Descartes and other mind/body dualists believed, but in an *infinite* number of individual substances.[1] As the ultimate constituents of the whole of reality, these individual substances (realities), which Leibniz called *monads,* are—like the Parmenidean whole—simple (without parts); "What is not truly *one* being," he wrote in his letter to Arnauld in 1687, "is not truly one *being.*"

The monads are neither created nor destroyable; viewed abstractly, they are like physical points but, being unextended (nonspatial), their only essential attribute is *thought.* Following the Cartesian argument that substances cannot interact, Leibniz held that monads cannot interact with each other nor can they be causally related; each monad exists in a preestablished harmony with all other monads. Each monad is a "windowless" mirror of the entire universe. Monads form a hierarchy according to the clearness and distinctness with which they mirror the universe. Thus it should in principle be possible to deduce all knowledge about all aspects of the universe from within a single monad. In other words, not only is knowledge of the whole universe possible, it is possible to attain such knowledge of the whole from any of its constituent parts.

Every monad thus represents all others in itself, a concentrated all, the universe in miniature. Each individual monad contains an infinity in itself. A supreme intelligence, for which every obscure idea would at once become distinct, would be able to read in a single monad the whole universe and its entire history—all that is, has been, or will be. For the past has left its traces behind in the monad, and the future will bring nothing not founded in the present: the monad is the bearer of the past and the forbearer of the future. Each monad represents that which is near at hand distinctly and that which is distant confusedly. Since all monads reflect the same content or object, their difference consists only in the energy or degree of clearness in their representations. Every monad is thus a mirror of the universe. And it is a *living* mirror, meaning that it generates the images of things by its own activity or develops them from within itself. All monads represent the same universe, but each one represents it differently, that is, from its particular point of view.

Starting thus with his concept of representation, Leibniz ends with the harmony of the universe. The representations are multiplicity in unity; the harmony is unity in multiplicity. All monads represent the same universe. But each one mirrors it differently. The unity, as well as the difference, could not be greater than it is; every possible degree of distinctness of representation is present in each single monad, and yet there is a single harmonic accord in which the infinite tones unite. This total unity is none other than God.

In the *Monadology,* from which our second selection is taken, Leibniz puts forth the thesis that unless the ultimate constituents of the world are themselves living minds, minds as we know them could never emerge into existence as such. But what does it mean to say that the world consists not of lifeless, immaterial atoms but rather of monads each of which is a living individual mind? Starting with composites of simple substances, he distinguishes *natural automata,* or divine machines, which is what we are, from *artificial automata,* that

---

1. "Substances" can be thought of as "realities"; thus Leibniz was the first thinker to conceive of a many-worlds view of the world, an infinity of existences each of which is equally and fully real.

is, artificial machines such as those made by us; the difference is that we, unlike the machines we make, *are an infinity of machines within machines, forever.*

Leibniz argues that this is the best of all possible worlds. Everything has a necessary reason for being as it is rather than some other way; this is his *principle of sufficient reason.* It is impossible, according to this principle, that something could exist without any explanation, cause, or reason; this is the main principle of his metaphysical rationality. It may be the case that only God's perspective can clearly and distinctly reveal all the reasons until the necessity itself is made explicit, but the inquiry into the reasons is in principle open to human scientific inquiry.

There must according to Leibniz be some reason the universe in its totality and everything in it exists at all. Why is there something at all rather than nothing? Because everything exists of necessity. Like Thomas Aquinas, whom he greatly admired, Leibniz's answer to this biggest question of all time is in terms of an uncaused cause, an all-perfect being whose being is itself necessary. This Leibniz calls "God." But, unlike Spinoza's God, Leibniz's God is free, except not in any ordinary sense. God must act so as to create the maximum amount of existence—metaphysical perfection—and the maximum amount of possible activity— moral perfection. But God is free in the absolute sense—that is, in that the absolute necessities that are world-independent come into existence with the actual world, realized by God through "free choice."

DISCOURSE ON METAPHYSICS

VIII. In order to distinguish between the activities of God and the activities of created things we must explain the conception of an individual substance.

It is quite difficult to distinguish God's actions from those of his creatures. Some think that God does everything; others imagine that he only conserves the force that he has given to created things. How far can we say either of these opinions is right?

In the first place since activity and passivity pertain properly to individual substances (*actiones sunt suppositorum*) it will be necessary to explain what such a substance is. It is indeed true that when several predicates are attributes of a single subject and this subject is not an attribute of another, we speak of it as an individual substance, but this is not enough, and such an explanation is merely nominal. We must therefore inquire what it is to be an attribute in reality of a certain subject. Now it is evident that every true predication has some basis in the nature of things, and even when a proposition is not identical, that is, when the predicate is not expressly contained in the subject, it is still necessary that it be virtually contained in it, and this is what the philosophers call *in-esse,* saying thereby that the predicate is in the subject. Thus the content of the subject must always include that of

From *Leibniz: Discourse on Metaphysics,* trans. G. R. Montgomery (Open Court, 1902).

the predicate in such a way that if one understands perfectly the concept of the subject, he will know that the predicate appertains to it also. This being so, we are able to say that this is the nature of an individual substance or of a complete being, namely, to afford a conception so complete that the concept shall be sufficient for the understanding of it and for the deduction of all the predicates of which the substance is or may become the subject. Thus the quality of king, which belonged to Alexander the Great, an abstraction from the subject, is not sufficiently determined to constitute an individual, and does not contain the other qualities of the same subject, nor everything which the idea of this prince includes. God, however, seeing the individual concept, or haecceity, of Alexander, sees there at the same time the basis and the reason of all the predicates which can be truly uttered regarding him; for instance that he will conquer Darius and Porus, even to the point of knowing *a priori* (and not by experience) whether he died a natural death or by poison,—facts which we can learn only through history. When we carefully consider the connection of things we see also the possibility of saying that there was always in the soul of Alexander marks of all that had happened to him and evidences of all that would happen to him and traces even of everything which occurs in the universe, although God alone could recognize them all.

IX. That every individual substance expresses the whole universe in its own manner and that in its full concept is included all its experiences together with all the attendant circumstances and the whole sequence of exterior events.

There follow from these considerations several noticeable paradoxes; among others that it is not true that two substances may be exactly alike and differ only numerically, *solo numero,* and that what St. Thomas says on this point regarding angels and intelligences (*quod ibi omne individuum sit species infima*) is true of all substances, provided that the specific difference is understood as Geometers understand it in the case of figures; again that a substance will be able to commence only through creation and perish only through annihilation; that a substance cannot be divided into two nor can one be made out of two, and that thus the number of substances neither augments nor diminishes through natural means, although they are frequently transformed. Furthermore every substance is like an entire world and like a mirror of God, or indeed of the whole world which it portrays, each one in its own fashion; almost as the same city is variously represented according to the various situations of him who is regarding it. Thus the universe is multiplied in some sort as many times as there are substances, and the glory of God is multiplied in the same way by as many wholly different representations of his works. It can indeed be said that every substance bears in some sort the character of God's infinite wisdom and omnipotence, and imitates him as much as it is able to; for it expresses, although confusedly, all that happens in the universe, past, present and future, deriving thus a certain resemblance to an infinite perception or power of knowing. And since all other substances express this particular substance and accommodate themselves to it, we can say that it exerts its power upon all the others in imitation of the omnipotence of the creator.

X. That the belief in substantial forms has a certain basis in fact, but that these forms effect no changes in the phenomena and must not be employed for the explanation of particular events.

It seems that the ancients, able men, who were accustomed to profound meditations and taught theology and philosophy for several centuries and some of whom recommend themselves to us on account of their piety, had some knowledge of that which we have just said and this is why they introduced and maintained the substantial forms so much decried to-day. But they were not so far from the truth nor so open to ridicule as the common run of our new philosophers imagine. I grant that the consideration of these forms is of no service in the details of physics and ought not to be employed in the explanation of particular phenomena. In regard to this last point, the schoolmen were at fault, as were also the physicians of times past who followed their example, thinking they had given the reason for the properties of a body in mentioning the forms and qualities without going to the trouble of examining the manner of operation; as if one should be content to say that a clock had a certain amount of clockness derived from its form, and should not inquire in what that clockness consisted. This is indeed enough for the man who buys it, provided he surrenders the care of it to someone else. The fact, however, that there was this misunderstanding and misuse of the substantial forms should not bring us to throw away something whose recognition is so necessary in metaphysics. Since without these we will not be able, I hold, to know the ultimate principles nor to lift our minds to the knowledge of the incorporeal natures and of the marvels of God. Yet as the geometer does not need to encumber his mind with the famous puzzle of the composition of the continuum, and as no moralist, and still less a jurist or a statesman has need to trouble himself with the great difficulties which arise in conciliating free will with the providential activity of God, (since the geometer is able to make all his demonstrations and the statesman can complete all his deliberations without entering into these discussions which are so necessary and important in Philosophy and Theology), so in the same way the physicist can explain his experiments, now using simpler experiments already made, now employing geometrical and mechanical demonstrations without any need of the general considerations which belong to another sphere, and if he employs the co-operation of God, or perhaps of some soul or animating force, or something else of a similar nature, he goes out of his path quite as much as that man who, when facing an important practical question would wish to enter into profound argumentations regarding the nature of destiny and of our liberty; a fault which men quite frequently commit without realizing it when they cumber their minds with considerations regarding fate, and thus they are even sometimes turned from a good resolution or from some necessary provision.

XI. That the opinions of the theologians and of the so-called scholastic philosophers are not to be wholly despised.

I know that I am advancing a great paradox in pretending to resuscitate in some sort the ancient philosophy, and to recall *postliminio* the substantial forms almost banished from our modern thought. But perhaps I will not be condemned lightly when it is known that I have long meditated over the modern philosophy and that I have devoted much time to experiments in physics and to the demonstrations of geometry and that I, too, for a long time was persuaded of the baselessness of those "beings" which, however, I was finally obliged to take up again in spite of myself and as though by force. The many investigations which I carried on compelled me to recognize that our moderns do not do sufficient justice to Saint Thomas and to the other great men of that period and that there is in the theories of the scholastic philosophers and theologians far more solidity than is imagined, provided that these theories are employed *à propos* and in their place. I am persuaded that if some careful and meditative mind were to take the trouble to clarify and direct their thoughts in the manner of analytic geometers, he would find a great treasure of very important truths, wholly demonstrable.

XII. That the conception of the extension of a body is in a way imaginary and does not constitute the substance of the body.

But to resume the thread of our discussion, I believe that he who will meditate upon the nature of substance, as I have explained it above, will find that the whole nature of bodies is not exhausted in their extension, that is to say, in their size, figure and motion, but that we must recognize something which corresponds to soul, something which is commonly called substantial form, although these forms effect no change in the phenomena, any more than do the souls of beasts, that is if they have souls. It is even possible to demonstrate that the ideas of size, figure and motion are not so distinctive as is imagined, and that they stand for something imaginary relative to our preceptions as do, although to a greater extent, the ideas of color, heat, and the other similar qualities in regard to which we may doubt whether they are actually to be found in the nature of the things outside of us. This is why these latter qualities are unable to constitute "substance" and if there is no other principle of identity in bodies than that which has just been referred to a body would not subsist more than for a moment.

The souls and the substance-forms of other bodies are entirely different from intelligent souls which alone know their actions, and not only do not perish through natural means but indeed always retain the knowledge of what they are; a fact which makes them alone open to chastisement or recompense, and makes them citizens of the republic of the universe whose monarch is God. Hence it follows that all the other creatures should serve them, a point which we shall discuss more amply later.

XIII. As the individual concept of each person includes once for all everything which can ever happen to him, in it can be seen, *a priori* the evidences or the reasons for the reality of each event, and why one happened sooner than the other. But these events, however certain, are nevertheless contingent, being based on the free choice of God and of his creatures. It is true that their choices always have their reasons, but they incline to the choices under no compulsion of necessity.

But before going further it is necessary to meet a difficulty which may arise regarding the principles which we have set forth in the preceding. We have said that the concept of an individual substance includes once for all everything which can ever happen to it and that in considering this concept one will be able to see everything which can truly be said concerning the individual, just as we are able to see in the nature of a circle all the properties which can be derived from it. But does it not seem that in this way the difference between contingent and necessary truths will be destroyed, that there will be no place for human liberty, and that an absolute fatality will rule as well over all our actions as over all the rest of the events of the world? To this I reply that a distinction must be made between that which is certain and that which is necessary. Every one grants that future contingencies are assured since God foresees them, but we do not say just because of that that they are necessary. But it will be objected, that if any conclusion can be deduced infallibly from some definition or concept, it is necessary; and now since we have maintained that everything which is to happen to anyone is already virtually included in his nature or concept, as all the properties are contained in the definition of a circle, therefore, the difficulty still remains. In order to meet the objection completely, I say that the connection or sequence is of two kinds; the one, absolutely necessary, whose contrary implies contradiction, occurs in the eternal verities like the truths of geometry; the other is necessary only *ex hypothesi*, and so to speak by accident, and in itself it is contingent since the contrary is not implied. This latter sequence is not founded upon ideas wholly pure and upon the pure understanding of God, but upon his free decrees and upon the processes of the universe. Let us give an example. Since Julius Caesar will become perpetual Dictator and master of the Republic and will overthrow the liberty of Rome, this action is contained in his concept, for we have supposed that it is the nature of such a perfect concept of a subject to involve everything, in fact so that the predicate may be included in the subject *ut possit inesse subjecto*. We may say that it is not in virtue of this concept or idea that he is obliged to perform this action, since it pertains to him only because God knows everything. But it will be insisted in reply that his nature or form responds to this concept, and since God imposes upon him this personality, he is compelled henceforth to live up to it. I could reply by instancing the similar case of the future contingencies which as yet have no reality save in the understanding and will of God, and which, because God has given them in advance this form, must needs correspond to it. But I prefer to overcome a difficulty rather than to excuse it by instancing other difficulties, and what I am about to say will serve to clear up the one as well as the other. It is here that must be applied the distinction in the kind of relation, and I say that that which happens conformably to these decrees is assured, but that it is not therefore necessary, and if anyone did the contrary, he would do nothing impossible in itself, although it is impossible *ex hypothesi* that that other happen. For if anyone were capable of carrying out a complete demonstration by virtue of which he could prove this connection of the subject, which is Caesar, with the predicate, which is his successful enterprise, he would bring us to see in fact that the future dictatorship of Caesar had its basis in his concept or nature, so that one would see there a reason why he resolved to cross the Rubicon rather than to stop, and why he gained instead of losing the day at Pharsalus, and that it was reasonable and by consequence assured that this would occur, but one would not prove that it was necessary in itself, nor that the contrary implied a contradiction, almost in the same way in which it is reasonable and assured that God will always do what is best although that which is less perfect is not thereby implied. For it would be found that this demonstration of this predicate as belonging to Caesar is not as absolute as are those of numbers or of geometry, but that this predicate supposes a sequence of things which God has shown by his free will. This sequence is based on the first free decree of God which was to do always that which is the most perfect and upon the decree which God made following the first one, regarding human nature, which is that men should always do, although freely, that which appears to be the best. Now every truth which is founded upon this kind of decree is contingent, although certain, for the decrees of God do not change the possibilities of things and, as I have already said, although God assuredly chooses the best, this does not prevent that which is less perfect from being possible in itself. Although it will never happen, it is not its impossibility but its imperfection which causes him to reject it. Now nothing is necessitated whose opposite is possible. One will then be in a position to satisfy these kinds of difficulties, however great they may appear (and in fact they have not been less vexing to all other thinkers who have ever treated this matter), provided that he considers well that all contingent propositions have reasons why they are thus, rather than otherwise, or indeed (what is the same thing) that they have proof *a priori* of their truth, which render them certain and show that the connection of the subject and predicate in these propositions has its basis in the nature of the one and of the other, but he must further remember that such contingent propositions have not the demonstrations of necessity, since their reasons are founded only on the principle of contingency or of the existence of things, that is to say, upon that which is, or which appears to be the best among several things equally possible. Necessary truths, on the other hand, are founded upon the principle of contradiction, and upon the possibility or impossibility of the essences themselves, without regard here to the free will of God or of creatures.

XXVI. Ideas are all stored up within us. Plato's doctrine of reminiscence.

In order to see clearly what an idea is, we must guard ourselves against a misunderstanding. Many regard the idea as the form or the differentiation of our thinking, and according to this opinion we have the idea in our mind, in so far as we are thinking of it, and each separate time that we think of it anew we have another idea although similar to the preceding one. Some, however, take the idea as the immediate object of thought, or as a permanent form which remains even when we are no longer contemplating it. As a matter of fact our soul has the power of representing to itself any form or nature whenever the occasion comes for thinking about it, and I think that this activity of our soul is, so far as it expresses some nature, form or essence, properly the idea of the thing. This is in us, and is always in us, whether we are thinking of it or no. (Our soul expresses God and the universe and all essences as well as all existences.) This position is in accord with my principles that naturally nothing enters into our minds from outside.

It is a bad habit we have of thinking as though our minds receive certain messengers, as it were, or as if they had doors or windows. We have in our minds all those forms for all periods of time because the mind at every moment expresses all its future thoughts and already thinks confusedly of all that of which it will ever think distinctly. Nothing can be taught us of which we have not already in our minds the idea. This idea is as it were the material out of which the thought will form itself. This is what Plato has excellently brought out in his doctrine of reminiscence, a doctrine which contains a great deal of truth, provided that it is properly understood and purged of the error of pre-existence, and provided that one does not conceive of the soul as having already known and thought at some other time what it learns and thinks now. Plato has also confirmed his position by a beautiful experiment. He introduces a small boy, whom he leads by short steps, to extremely difficult truths of geometry bearing on incommensurables, all this without teaching the boy anything, merely drawing out replies by a well arranged series of questions. This shows that the soul virtually knows those things, and needs only to be reminded (animadverted) to recognize the truths. Consequently it possesses at least the idea upon which those truths depend. We may say even that it already possesses those truths, if we consider them as the relations of the ideas.

XXVII. In what respect our souls can be compared to blank tablets and how conceptions are derived from the senses.

Aristotle preferred to compare our souls to blank tablets prepared for writing, and he maintained that nothing is in the understanding which does not come through the senses. This position is in accord with the popular conceptions as Aristotle's positions usually are. Plato thinks more profoundly. Such tenets or practicologies are nevertheless allowable in ordinary use somewhat in the same way as those who accept the Copernican theory still continue to speak of the rising and setting of the sun. I find indeed that these usages can be given a real meaning containing no error, quite in the same way as I have already pointed out that we may truly say particular substances act upon one another. In this same sense we may say that knowledge is received from without through the medium of the senses because certain exterior things contain or express more particularly the causes which determine us to certain thoughts. Because in the ordinary uses of life we attribute to the soul only that which belongs to it most manifestly and particularly, and there is no advantage in going further. When, however, we are dealing with the exactness of metaphysical truths, it is important to recognize the powers and independence of the soul which extend infinitely further than is commonly supposed. In order, therefore, to avoid misunderstandings it would be well to choose separate terms for the two. These expressions which are in the soul whether one is conceiving of them or not may be called ideas, while those which one conceives of or constructs may be called conceptions, *conceptus.* But whatever terms are used, it is always false to say that all our conceptions come from the so-called external senses, because those conceptions which I have of myself and of my thoughts, and consequently of being, of substance, of action, of identity, and of many others came from an inner experience.

XXVIII. The only immediate object of our perceptions which exists outside of us is God, and in him alone is our light.

In the strictly metaphysical sense no external cause acts upon us excepting God alone, and he is in immediate relation with us only by virtue of our continual dependence upon him. Whence it follows that there is absolutely no other external object which comes into contact with our souls and directly excites perceptions in us. We have in our souls ideas of everything, only because of the continual action of God upon us, that is to say, because every effect expresses its cause and therefore the essences of our souls are certain expressions, imitations or images of the divine essence, divine thought and divine will, including all the ideas which are there contained. We may say, therefore, that God is for us the only immediate external object, and that we see things through him. For example, when we see the sun or the stars, it is God who gives to us and preserves in us the ideas and whenever our senses are affected according to his own laws in a certain manner, it is he, who by his continual concurrence, determines our thinking. God is the sun and the light of souls, *lumen illuminans omnem hominem venientem in hunc mundum,* although this is not the current conception. I think I have already remarked that during the scholastic period many believed God to be the light of the soul, *intellectus agens animae rationalis,* following in this the Holy Scriptures and the fathers who were always more Platonic than Aristotelian in their mode of thinking. The Averroists misused this conception, but others, among whom were several mystic theologians, and William of Saint Amour, also I think, understood this conception in a manner which assured the dignity of God and was able to raise the soul to a knowledge of its welfare.

XXIX. Yet we think directly by means of our own ideas and not through God's.

Nevertheless I cannot approve of the position of certain able philosophers who seem to hold that our ideas themselves are in God and not at all in us. I think that in taking this position they have neither sufficiently considered the nature of substance, which we have just explained, nor the entire extension and independence of the soul which includes all that happens to it, and expresses God, and with him all possible and actual beings in the same way that an effect expresses its cause. It is indeed inconceivable that the soul should think using the ideas of something else. The soul when it thinks of anything must be affected effectively in a certain manner, and it must needs have in itself in advance not only the passive capacity of being thus affected, a capacity already wholly determined, but it must have besides an active power by virtue of which it has always had in its nature the marks of the future production of this thought, and the disposition to produce it at its proper time. All of this shows that the soul already includes the idea which is comprised in any particular thought.

XXXIII. Explanation of the relation between the soul and the body, a matter which has been regarded as inexplicable or else as miraculous; concerning the origin of confused perceptions.

We can also see the explanation of that great mystery "the union of the soul and the body," that is to say how it comes about that the passions and actions of the one are accompanied by the actions and passions or else the appropriate phenomena of the other. For it is not possible to conceive how one can have an influence upon the other and it is unreasonable to have recourse at once to the extraordinary intervention of the universal cause in an ordinary and particular case. The following, however, is the true explanation. We have said that everything which happens to a soul or to any substance is a consequence of its concept; hence the idea itself or the essence of the soul brings it about that all of its appearances or perceptions should be born out of its nature and precisely in such a way that they correspond of themselves to that which happens in the universe at large, but more particularly and more perfectly to that which happens in the body associated with it, because it is in a particular way and only for a certain time according to the relation of other bodies to its own body that the soul expresses the state of the univese. This last fact enables us to see how our body belongs to us, without, however, being attached to our essence. I believe that those who are careful thinkers will decide favorably for our principles because of this single reason, viz., that they are able to see in what consists the relation between the soul and the body, a parallelism which appears inexplicable in any other way. We can also see that the perceptions of our senses even when they are clear must necessarily contain certain confused elements, for as all the bodies in the universe are in sympathy, ours receives the impressions of all the others, and while our senses respond to everything, our soul cannot pay attention to every particular. That is why our confused sensations are the result of a variety of perceptions. This variety is infinite. It is almost like the confused murmuring which is heard by those who approach the shore of a sea. It comes from the continual beatings of innumerable waves. If now, out of many perceptions which do not at all fit together to make one, no particular one perception surpasses the others, and if they make impressions about equally strong or equally capable of holding the attention of the soul, they can be perceived only confusedly.

XXXIV. Concerning the difference between spirits and other substances, souls or substantial forms; that the immortality which men desire includes memory.

Supposing that the bodies which constitute a *unum per se,* as human bodies, are substances, and have substantial forms, and supposing that animals have souls, we are obliged to grant that these souls and these substantial forms cannot entirely perish, any more than can the atoms or the ultimate elements of matter, according to the position of other philosophers; for no substance perishes, although it may become very different. Such substances also express the whole universe, although more imperfectly than do spirits. The principle difference, however, is that they do not know that they are, nor what they are. Consequently, not being able to reason, they are unable to discover necessary and universal truths. It is also because they do not reflect regarding themselves that they have no moral qualities, whence it follows that undergoing a thousand transformations, as we see a caterpillar change into a butterfly, the result from a moral or practical standpoint is the same as if we said that they perished in each case, and we can indeed say it from the physical standpoint in the same way that we say bodies perish in their dissolution. But the intelligent soul, knowing that it is and having the ability to say that word "I" so full of meaning, not only continues and exists, metaphysically far more certainly than do the others, but it remains the same from the moral standpoint, and constitutes the same personality, for it is its memory or knowledge of this ego which renders it open to punishment and reward. Also the immortality which is required in morals and in religion does not consist merely in this perpetual existence, which pertains to all substances, for if in addition there were no remembrance of what one had been, immortality would not be at all desirable. Suppose that some individual could suddenly become King of China on condition, however, of forgetting what he had been, as though being born again, would it not amount to the same practically, or as far as the effects could be perceived, as if the individual were annihilated, and a king of China were the same instant created in his place? The individual would have no reason to desire this.

XXXV. The excellence of spirits; that God considers them preferable to other creatures; that the spirits express God rather than the world, while other simple substances express the world rather than God.

In order, however, to prove by natural reasons that God will preserve forever not only our substance, but also our personality, that is to say the recollection and knowledge of what we are (although the distinct knowledge is sometimes suspended during sleep and in swoons) it is necessary to join to metaphysics moral considerations. God must be considered not only as the principle and the cause of all substances and of all existing things, but also as the chief of all persons or intelligent substances, as the absolute monarch of the most perfect city or republic, such as is constituted by all the spirits together in the universe, God being the most complete of all spirits at the same time that he is greatest of all beings. For assuredly the spirits are the most perfect of substances and best express the divinity. Since all the nature, purpose, virtue and function of substances is, as has been sufficiently explained, to express God and the universe, there is no room for doubting that those substances which give the expression, knowing what they are doing and which are able to understand the great truths about God and the universe, do express God and the universe incomparably better than do those natures which are either brutish and incapable of recognizing truths, or are wholly destitute of sensation and knowledge. The difference between intelligent substances and those which are not intelligent is quite as great as between a mirror and one who sees. As God is himself the greatest and wisest of spirits it is easy to understand that the spirits with which he can, so to speak, enter into conversation and even into social relations by communicating to them in particular ways his feelings and his will so that they are able to know and love their benefactor, must be much nearer to him than the rest of created things which may be regarded as the instruments of spirits. In the same way we see that all wise persons consider far more the condition of a man than of anything else however precious it may be; and it seems that the greatest satisfaction which a soul, satisfied in other respects, can have is to see itself loved by others. However, with respect to God there is this difference that his glory and our worship can add nothing to his satisfaction, the recognition of creatures being nothing but a consequence of his sovereign and perfect felicity and being far from contributing to it or from causing it even in part. Nevertheless, that which is reasonable in finite spirits is found eminently in him and as we praise a king who prefers to preserve the life of a man before that of the most precious and rare of his animals, we should not doubt that the most enlightened and most just of all monarchs has the same preference.

MONADOLOGY

1. The Monad, of which we will speak here, is nothing else than a simple substance, which goes to make up composites; by simple, we mean without parts.

2. There must be simple substances because there are composites; for a composite is nothing else than a collection or *aggregatum* of simple substances.

3. Now, where there are no constituent parts there is possible neither extension, nor form, nor divisibility. These Monads are the true Atoms of nature, and, in fact, the Elements of things.

4. Their dissolution, therefore, is not to be feared and there is no way conceivable by which a simple substance can perish through natural means.

5. For the same reason there is no way conceivable by which a simple substance might, through natural means, come into existence, since it can not be formed by composition.

6. We may say then, that the existence of Monads can begin or end only all at once, that is to say, the Monad can begin only through creation and end only through annihilation. Composites, however, begin or end gradually.

7. There is also no way of explaining how a Monad can be altered or changed in its inner being by any other created thing, since there is no possibility of transposition within it, nor can we conceive of any internal movement which can be produced, directed, increased or diminished there within the substance, such as can take place in the case of composites where a change can occur among the parts. The Monads have no windows through which anything may come in or go out. The Attributes are not liable to detach themselves and make an excursion outside the substance, as could *sensible species* of the Schoolmen. In the same way neither substance nor attribute can enter from without into a Monad.

8. Still Monads must needs have some qualities, otherwise they would not even be existences. And if simple substances did not differ at all in their qualities, there would be no means of perceiving any change in things. Whatever is in a composite can come into it only through its simple elements and the Monads, if they were without qualities, since they do not differ at all in quantity, would be indistinguishable one from another. For instance, if we imagine *a plenum* or completely filled space, where each part receives only the equivalent of its own previous motion, one state of things would not be distinguishable from another.

9. Each Monad, indeed, must be different from every other. For there are never in nature two beings which are exactly alike, and in which it is not possible to find a difference either internal or based on an intrinsic property.

10. I assume it as admitted that every created being, and consequently the created Monad, is subject to change, and indeed that this change is continuous in each.

11. It follows from what has just been said, that the natural changes of the Monad come from an internal principle, because an external cause can have no influence upon its inner being.

12. Now besides this principle of change there must also be in the Monad a manifoldness which changes. This manifoldness constitutes, so to speak, the specific nature and the variety of the simple substances.

From Leibniz, *Monadology,* trans. George Montgomery (Open Court, 1902).

13. This manifoldness must involve a multiplicity in the unity or in that which is simple. For since every natural change takes place by degrees, there must be something which changes and something which remains unchanged, and consequently there must be in the simple substance a plurality of conditions and relations, even though it has no parts.

14. The passing condition which involves and represents a multiplicity in the unity, or in the simple substance, is nothing else than what is called Perception. This should be carefully distinguished from Apperception or Consciousness, as will appear in what follows. In this matter the Cartesians have fallen into a serious error, in that they treat as nonexistent those perceptions of which we are not conscious. It is this also which has led them to believe that spirits alone are Monads and that there are no souls of animals or other Entelechies, and it has led them to make the common confusion between a protracted period of unconsciousness and actual death. They have thus adopted the Scholastic error that souls can exist entirely separated from bodies, and have even confirmed ill-balanced minds in the belief that souls are mortal.

15. The action of the internal principle which brings about the change or the passing from one perception to another may be called Appetition. It is true that the desire (*l'appetit*) is not always able to attain to the whole of the perception which it strives for, but it always attains a portion of it and reaches new perceptions.

16. We, ourselves, experience a multiplicity in a simple substance, when we find that the most trifling thought of which we are conscious involves a variety in the object. Therefore all those who acknowledge that the soul is a simple substance ought to grant this multiplicity in the Monad, and Monsieur Bayle should have found no difficulty in it, as he has done in his *Dictionary,* article "Rorarius."

17. It must be confessed, however, that Perception, and that which depends upon it, are inexplicable by mechanical causes, that is to say, by figures and motions. Supposing that there were a machine whose structure produced thought, sensation, and perception, we could conceive of it as increased in size with the same proportions until one was able to enter into its interior, as he would into a mill. Now, on going into it he would find only pieces working upon one another, but never would he find anything to explain Perception. It is accordingly in the simple substance, and not in the composite nor in a machine that the Perception is to be sought. Furthermore, there is nothing besides perceptions and their changes to be found in the simple substance. And it is in these alone that all the internal activities of the simple substance can consist.

18. All simple substances or created Monads may be called Entelechies, because they have in themselves a certain perfection. . . . There is in them a sufficiency . . . which makes them the source of their internal activities, and renders them, so to speak, incorporeal Automatons.

19. If we wish to designate as soul everything which has perceptions and desires in the general sense that I have just explained, all simple substances or created Monads could be called souls. But since feeling is something more than a mere perception I think that the general name of Monad or Entelechy should suffice for simple substances which have only perception, while we may reserve the term Soul for those whose perception is more distinct and is accompanied by memory.

20. We experience in ourselves a state where we remember nothing and where we have no distinct perception, as in periods of fainting, or when we are overcome by a profound, dreamless sleep. In such a state the soul does not sensibly differ at all from a simple Monad. As this state, however, is not permanent and the soul can recover from it, the soul is something more.

21. Nevertheless it does not follow at all that the simple substance is in such a state without perception. This is so because of the reasons given above; for it cannot perish, nor on the other hand would it exist without some affection and the affection is nothing else than its perception. When, however, there are a great number of weak perceptions where nothing stands out distinctively, we are stunned; as when one turns around and around in the same direction, a dizziness comes on, which makes him swoon and makes him able to distinguish nothing. Among animals, death can occasion this state for quite a period.

22. Every present state of a simple substance is a natural consequence of its preceding state, in such a way that its present is big with its future.

23. Therefore, since on awakening after a period of unconsciousness we become conscious of our perceptions, we must, without having been conscious of them, have had perceptions immediately before; for one perception can come in a natural way only from another perception, just as a motion can come in a natural way only from a motion.

24. It is evident from this that if we were to have nothing distinctive, or so to speak prominent, and of a higher flavor in our perceptions, we should be in a continual state of stupor. This is the condition of Monads which are wholly bare.

25. We see that nature has given to animals heightened perceptions, having provided them with organs which collect numerous rays of light or numerous waves of air and thus make them more effective in their combination. Something similar to this takes place in the case of smell, in that of taste and of touch, and perhaps in many other senses which are unknown to us. I shall have occasion very soon to explain how that which occurs in the soul represents that which goes on in the sense-organs.

26. The memory furnishes a sort of consecutiveness which imitates reason but is to be distinguished from it. We see that animals when they have the perception of something which they notice and of which they have had a similar previous perception, are led by the representation of their memory to expect that which was associated in the preceding perception, and they come to have feelings like those which they had before. For instance, if a stick be shown to a dog, he remembers the pain which it has caused him and he whines or runs away.

27. The vividness of the picture, which comes to him or moves him, is derived either from the magnitude or from the number of the previous perceptions. For, oftentimes, a strong impression brings about, all at once, the same effect as a long-continued habit or as a great many re-iterated, moderate perceptions.

28. Men act in like manner as animals, in so far as the sequence of their perceptions is determined only by the law of memory, resembling the *empirical physicians* who practice simply, without any theory, and we are empiricists in three-fourths of our actions. For instance, when we expect that there will be day-light to-morrow, we do so empirically, because it has always happened so up to the present time. It is only the astronomer who uses his reason in making such an affirmation.

29. But the knowledge of eternal and necessary truths is that which distinguishes us from mere animals and gives us reason and the sciences, thus raising us to a knowledge of ourselves and of God. This is what is called in us the Rational Soul or the Mind.

30. It is also through the knowledge of necessary truths and through abstractions from them that we come to perform Reflective Acts, which cause us to think of what is called the I, and to decide that this or that is within us. It is thus, that in thinking upon ourselves we think of *being,* of *substance,* of the *simple* and *composite,* of a *material* thing and of *God* himself, conceiving that what is limited in us is in him without limits. These Reflective Acts furnish the principal objects of our reasonings.

31. Our reasoning is based upon two great principles: first, that of Contradiction, by means of which we decide that to be false which involves contradiction and that to be true which contradicts or is opposed to the false.

32. And second, the principle of Sufficient Reason, in virtue of which we believe that no fact can be real or existing and no statement true unless it has a sufficient reason why it should be thus and not otherwise. Most frequently, however, these reasons cannot be known by us.

33. There are also two kinds of Truths: those of Reasoning and those of Fact. The Truths of Reasoning are necessary, and their opposite is impossible. Those of Fact, however, are contingent, and their opposite is possible. When a truth is necessary, the reason can be found by analysis in resolving it into simpler ideas and into simpler truths until we reach those which are primary.

34. It is thus that with mathematicians the Speculative Theorems and the practical Canons are reduced by analysis to Definitions, Axioms, and Postulates.

35. There are finally simple ideas of which no definition can be given. There are also the Axioms and Postulates or, in a word, the primary principles which cannot be proved and, indeed, have no need of proof. These are identical propositions whose opposites involve express contradictions.

36. But there must be also a sufficient reason for contingent truths or truths of fact; that is to say, for the sequence of the things which extend throughout the universe of created beings, where the analysis into more particular reasons can be continued into greater detail without limit because of the immense variety of the things in nature and because of the infinite division of bodies. There is an infinity of figures and of movements, present and past, which enter into the efficient cause of my present writing, and in its final cause there are an infinity of slight tendencies and dispositions of my soul, present and past.

37. And as all this detail again involves other and more detailed contingencies, each of which again has need of a similar analysis in order to find its explanation, no real advance has been made. Therefore, the sufficient or ultimate reason must needs be outside of the sequence or series of these details of contingencies, however infinite they may be.

38. It is thus that the ultimate reason for things must be a necessary substance, in which the detail of the changes shall be present merely potentially, as in the fountain-head, and this substance we call God.

39. Now, since this substance is a sufficient reason for all the above mentioned details, which are linked together throughout, *there is but one God, and this God is sufficient.*

40. We may hold that the supreme substance, which is unique, universal and necessary with nothing independent outside of it, which is further a pure sequence of possible being, must be incapable of limitation and must contain as much reality as possible.

41. Whence it follows that God is absolutely perfect, perfection being understood as the magnitude of positive reality in the strict sense, when the limitations or the bounds of those things which have them are removed. There where there are no limits, that is to say, in God, perfection is absolutely infinite.

42. It follows also that created things derive their perfections through the influence of God, but their imperfections come from their own natures, which cannot exist without limits. It is in this latter that they are distinguished from God. An example of this original imperfection of created things is to be found in the natural inertia of bodies.

43. It is true, furthermore, that in God is found not only the source of existences, but also that of essences, in so far as they are real. In other words, he is the source of whatever

there is real in the possible. This is because the Understanding of God is in the region of eternal truths or of the ideas upon which they depend, and because without him there would be nothing real in the possibilities of things, and not only would nothing be existent, nothing would be even possible.

44. For it must needs be that if there is a reality in essences or in possibilities or indeed in the eternal truths, this reality is based upon something existent and actual, and, consequently, in the existence of the necessary Being in whom essence includes existence or in whom possibility is sufficient to produce actuality.

45. Therefore God alone (or the Necessary Being) has this prerogative that if he be possible he must necessarily exist, and, as nothing is able to prevent the possibility of that which involves no bounds, no negation, and consequently, no contradiction, this alone is sufficient to establish *a priori* his existence. We have, therefore, proved his existence through the reality of eternal truths. But a little while ago we also proved it *a posteriori,* because contingent beings exist which can have their ultimate and sufficient reason only in the necessary being which, in turn, has the reason for existence in itself.

46. Yet we must not think that the eternal truths being dependent upon God are therefore arbitrary and depend upon his will, as Descartes seems to have held, and after him M. Poiret. This is the case only with contingent truths which depend upon fitness or the choice of the greatest good; necessarily truths on the other hand depend solely upon his understanding and are the inner objects of it.

47. God alone is the ultimate unity or the original simple substance, of which all created or derivative monads are the products, and arise, so to speak, through the continual outflashings (fulgurations) of the divinity from moment to moment, limited by the receptivity of the creature to whom limitation is an essential.

48. In God are present: power, which is the source of everything; knowledge, which contains the details of the ideas; and, finally, will, which changes or produces things in accordance with the principle of the greatest good. To these correspond in the created monad, the subject or basis, the faculty of perception, and the faculty of appetition. In God these attributes are absolutely infinite or perfect, while in the created monads or in the entelechies (*perfectihabies,* as Hermolaus Barbarus translates this word), they are imitations approaching him in proportion to the perfection.

49. A created thing is said to act outwardly in so far as it has perfection, and to be acted upon by another in so far as it is imperfect. Thus action is attributed to the monad in so far as it has distinct perceptions, and passion or passivity is attributed in so far as it has confused perceptions.

50. One created thing is more perfect than another when we find in the first that which gives an *a priori* reason for what occurs in the second. This is why we say that one acts upon the other.

51. In the case of simple substances, the influence which one monad has upon another is only ideal. It can have its effect only through the mediation of God, in so far as in the ideas of God each monad can rightly demand that God, in regulating the others from the beginning of things, should have regarded it also. For since one created monad cannot have a physical influence upon the inner being of another, it is only through the primal regulation that one can have dependence upon another.

52. It is thus that among created things action and passivity are reciprocal. For God, in comparing two simple substances, finds in each one reasons obliging him to adapt the other to it; and consequently what is active in certain respects is passive from another point of

view, active in so far as what we distinctly know in it serves to give a reason for what occurs in another, and passive in so far as the reason for what occurs in it is found in what is distinctly known in another.

53. Now as there are an infinity of possible universes in the ideas of God, and but one of them can exist, there must be a sufficient reason for the choice of God which determines him to select one rather than another.

54. And this reason is to be found only in the fitness or in the degree of perfection which these worlds possess, each possible thing having the right to claim existence in proportion to the perfection which it involves.

55. This is the cause for the existence of the greatest good; namely, that the wisdom of God permits him to know it, his goodness causes him to choose it, and his power enables him to produce it.

56. Now this interconnection, relationship, or this adaptation of all things to each particular one, and of each one to all the rest, brings it about that every simple substance has relations which express all the others and that it is consequently a perpetual living mirror of the universe.

57. And as the same city regarded from different sides appears entirely different, and is, as it were multiplied respectively, so, because of the infinite number of simple substances, there are a similar infinite number of universes which are, nevertheless, only the aspects of a single one as seen from the special point of view of each monad.

58. Through this means has been obtained the greatest possible variety, together with the greatest order that may be; that is to say, through this means has been obtained the greatest possible perfection.

59. This hypothesis, moreover, which I venture to call demonstrated, is the only one which fittingly gives proper prominence to the greatness of God. M. Bayle recognized this when in his dictionary (article "Rorarius") he raised objections to it; indeed, he was inclined to believe that I attributed too much to God, and more than it is possible to attribute to him: But he was unable to bring forward any reason why this universal harmony which causes every substance to express exactly all others through the relation which it has with them is impossible.

60. Besides, in what has just been said can be seen the *a priori* reasons why things cannot be otherwise than they are. It is because God, in ordering the whole, has had regard to every part and in particular to each monad; and since the monad is by its very nature *representative,* nothing can limit it to represent merely a part of things. It is nevertheless true that this representation is, as regards the details of the whole universe, only a confused representation, and is distinct only as regards a small part of them, that is to say, as regards those things which are nearest or greatest in relation to each monad. If the representation were distinct as to the details of the entire universe, each monad would be a Deity. It is not in the object represented that the monads are limited, but in the modifications of their knowledge of the object. In a confused way they reach out to infinity or to the whole, but are limited and differentiated in the degree of their distinct perceptions.

61. In this respect composites are like simple substances, for all space is filled up; therefore, all matter is connected. And in a plenum or filled space every movement has an effect upon bodies in proportion to this distance, so that not only is every body affected by those which are in contact with it and responds in some way to whatever happens to them, but also by means of them the body responds to those bodies adjoining them, and their intercommunication reaches to any distance whatsoever. Consequently every body responds to all that happens in the universe, so that he who saw all could read in each one what is hap-

pening everywhere, and even what has happened and what will happen. He can discover in the present what is distant both as regards space and as regards time; "All things conspire" as Hippocrates said. A soul can, however, read in itself only what is there represented distinctly. It cannot all at once open up all its folds, because they extend to infinity.

62. Thus although each created monad represents the whole universe, it represents more distinctly the body which specially pertains to it and of which it constitutes the entelechy. And as this body expresses all the universe through the interconnection of all matter in the plenum, the soul also represents the whole universe in representing this body, which belongs to it in a particular way.

63. The body belonging to a monad, which is its entelechy or soul, constitutes together with the entelechy what may be called a *living being,* and with a soul what is called an *animal.* Now this body of a living being or of an animal is always organic, because every monad as a mirror of the universe is regulated with perfect order there must needs be order also in what represents it, that is to say in the perceptions of the soul and consequently in the body through which the universe is represented in the soul.

64. Therefore every organic body of a living being is a kind of divine machine or natural automaton, infinitely surpassing all artificial automatons. Because a machine constructed by man's skill is not a machine in each of its parts; for instance, the teeth of a brass wheel have parts or bits which to us are not artificial products and contain nothing in themselves to show the use to which the wheel was destined in the machine. The machines of nature, however, that is to say, living bodies, are still machines in their smallest parts *ad infinitum.* Such is the difference between nature and art, that is to say, between divine art and ours.

65. The author of nature has been able to employ this divine and infinitely marvelous artifice, because each portion of matter is not only, as the ancients recognized, infinitely divisible, but also because it is really divided without end, every part into other parts, each one of which has its own proper motion. Otherwise it would be impossible for each portion of matter to express all the universe.

66. Whence we see that there is a world of created things, of living beings, of animals, of entelechies, of souls, in the minutest particle of matter.

67. Every portion of matter may be conceived as like a garden full of plants and like a pond full of fish. But every branch of a plant, every member of an animal, and every drop of the fluids within it, is also such a garden or such a pond.

68. And although the ground and air which lies between the plants of the garden, and the water which is between the fish in the pond, are not themselves plants or fish, yet they nevertheless contain these, usually so small however as to be imperceptible to us.

69. There is, therefore, nothing uncultivated, or sterile or dead in the universe, no chaos, no confusion, save in appearance; somewhat as a pond would appear at a distance when we could see in it a confused movement, and so to speak, a swarming of the fish, without however discerning the fish themselves.

70. It is evident, then, that every living body has a dominating entelechy, which in animals is the soul. The parts, however, of this living body are full of other living beings, plants and animals, which in turn have each one its entelechy or dominating soul.

71. This does not mean, as some who have misunderstood my thought have imagined, that each soul has a quantity or portion of matter appropriated to it or attached to itself for ever, and that it consequently owns other inferior living beings destined to serve it always; because all bodies are in a state of perpetual flux like rivers, and the parts are continually entering in or passing out.

72. The soul, therefore, changes its body only gradually and by degrees, so that it is

never deprived all at once of all its organs. There is frequently a metamorphosis in animals, but never metempsychosis or a transmigration of souls. Neither are there souls wholly separate from bodies, not bodiless spirits. God alone is without body.

73. This is also why there is never absolute generation or perfect death in the strict sense, consisting in the separation of the soul from the body. What we call generation is development and growth, and what we call death is envelopment and diminution.

74. Philosophers have been much perplexed in accounting for the origin of forms, entelechies, or souls. To-day, however, when it has been learned through careful investigations made in plant, insect and animal life, that the organic bodies of nature are never the product of chaos or putrefaction, but always come from seeds in which there was without doubt some preformation, it has been decided that not only is the organic body already present before conception, but also a soul in this body, in a word, the animal itself; and it has been decided that, by means of conception the animal is merely made ready for a great transformation, so as to become an animal of another sort. We can see cases somewhat similar outside of generation when grubs become flies and caterpillars butterflies.

75. These little animals, some of which by conception become large animals, may be called spermatic. Those among them which remain in their species, that is to say, the greater part, are born, multiply, and are destroyed, like the larger animals. There are only a few chosen ones which come out upon a greater stage.

76. This, however, is only half the truth. I believe, therefore, that if the animal never actually commences by natural means, no more does it by natural means come to an end. Not only is there no generation, but also there is no entire destruction or absolute death. These reasonings, carried on *a posteriori* and drawn from experience, accord perfectly with the principles which I have above deduced *a priori*.

77. Therefore we may say that not only the soul (the mirror of the indestructible universe) is indestructible, but also the animal itself is, although its mechanism is frequently destroyed in parts and although it puts off and takes on organic coatings.

78. These principles have furnished me the means of explaining on natural grounds the union, or rather the conformity between the soul and the organic body. The soul follows its own laws, and the body likewise follows its own laws. They are fitted to each other in virtue of the preestablished harmony between all substances, since they are all representations of one and the same universe.

79. Souls act in accordance with the laws of final causes through their desires, ends and means. Bodies act in accordance with the laws of efficient causes or of motion. The two realms, that of efficient causes and that of final causes, are in harmony, each with the other.

80. Descartes saw that souls cannot at all impart force to bodies, because there is always the same quantity of force in matter. Yet he thought that the soul could change the direction of bodies. This was, however, because at that time the law of nature which affirms also that conservation of the same total direction in the motion of matter was not known. If he had known that law, he would have fallen upon my system of preestablished harmony.

81. According to this system bodies act as if (to suppose the impossible) there were no souls at all, and souls act as if there were no bodies, and yet both body and soul act as if the one were influencing the other.

82. Although I find that essentially the same thing is true of all living things and animals, which we have just said (namely, that animals and souls begin from the very commencement of the world and that they no more come to an end than does the world) nevertheless, rational animals have this peculiarity, that their little spermatic animals, as long as they remain such, have only ordinary or sensuous souls, but those of them which are, so to speak,

elected, attain by actual conception to human nature, and their sensuous souls are raised to the rank of reason and to the prerogative of spirits.

83. Among the differences that there are between ordinary souls and spirits, some of which I have already instanced, there is also this, that while souls in general are living mirrors or images of the universe of created things, spirits are also images of the Deity himself or of the author of nature. They are capable of knowing the system of the universe, and of imitating some features of it by means of artificial models, each spirit being like a small divinity in its own sphere.

84. Therefore, spirits are able to enter into a sort of social relationship with God, and with respect to them he is not only what an inventor is to his machine (as in his relation to the other created things), but he is also what a prince is to his subjects, and even what a father is to his children.

85. Whence it is easy to conclude that the totality of all spirits must compose the city of God, that is to say, the most perfect state that is possible under the most perfect monarch.

86. This city of God, this truly universal monarchy, is a moral world within the natural world. It is what is noblest and most divine among the works of God. And in it consists in reality the glory of God, because he would have no glory were not his greatness and goodness known and wondered at by spirits. It is also in relation to this divine city that God properly has goodness. His wisdom and his power are shown everywhere.

87. As we established above that there is a perfect harmony between the two natural realms of efficient and final causes, it will be in place here to point out another harmony which appears between the physical realm of nature and the moral realm of grace, that is to say, between God considered as the architect of the mechanism of the world and God considered as the monarch of the divine city of spirits.

88. This harmony brings it about that things progress of themselves toward grace along natural lines, and that this earth, for example, must be destroyed and restored by natural means at those times when the proper government of spirits demands it, for chastisement in the one case and for a reward in the other.

89. We can say also that God, the Architect, satisfies in all respects God the Law-Giver, that therefore sins will bring their own penalty with them through the order of nature, and because of the very structure of things, mechanical though it is. And in the same way the good actions will attain their rewards in mechanical way through their relation to bodies, although this cannot and ought not always to take place without delay.

90. Finally, under this perfect government, there will be no good action unrewarded and no evil action unpunished; everything must turn out for the well-being of the good; that is to say, of those who are not disaffected in this great state, who, after having done their duty, trust in Providence and who love and imitate, as is meet, the Author of all Good, delighting in the contemplation of his perfections according to the nature of that genuine, pure love which finds pleasure in the happiness of those who are loved. It is for this reason that wise and virtuous persons work in behalf of everything which seems conformable to presumptive or antecedent will of God, and are, nevertheless, content with what God actually brings to pass through his secret, consequent and determining will, recognizing that if we were able to understand sufficiently well the order of the universe, we should find that it surpasses all the desires of the wisest of us, and that it is impossible to render it better than it is, not only for all in general, but also for each one of us in particular, provided that we have the proper attachment for the author of all, not only as the Architect and the efficient cause of our being, but also as our Lord and the Final Cause, who ought to be the whole goal of our will, and who alone can make us happy.

BERKELEY

1685–1753

George Berkeley was born in Kilkenny, Ireland. He went to Trinity College in Dublin, where he studied Locke, Newton, and Malebranche, as well as earlier philosophers such as Bacon, Descartes, Hobbes, and Leibniz. He also became an expert in mathematics, physics, and optics from the works of Kepler, Descartes, and Newton. Unlike most of his contemporaries, Berkeley saw the scientific revolution of his day as the starting symptoms of the decline of the philosophical mind. In his view, both science and mathematics were ultimately on par with religion. For instance, in his criticism of the calculus of Newton and Leibniz, he wrote, "He who can digest a second or third fluxion[1] . . . need not, methinks, be squeamish about any point in divinity."

Berkeley produced most of his most important works at a young age: *Essays Towards a New Theory of Vision* (1709), *Three Dialogues between Hylas and Philonous* (1713), and *A Treatise Concerning Human Knowledge* (1710), written when he was only twenty-five. However, all these works were ignored by the reading public and vehemently disliked by most philosophers, scientists, and mathematicians. Nearly everyone, even the theologians, regarded his views as absurd. His books having, in his eyes, failed, Berkeley journeyed to the American colonies with the idea of founding a new university in the style of Plato's Academy. "The savage Americans," he wrote, "if they are in a state purely natural and unimproved by education, they are also unencumbered with all that rubbish of superstition and prejudice, which is the effect of a wrong one."

At Newport, Rhode Island, Berkeley awaited the monetary support he had been promised so that he could go to Bermuda and there establish his academy. But the money never arrived. He gave up the project and returned to London, where eventually he received a position as bishop of Cloyne.

During his remaining years Berkeley continued to write, but his works continued to fall mostly on deaf ears. Subsequent philosophers, however, have held him in great esteem. His pioneering work on the nature of the mind, particularly his analysis of the complex, bundled nature of our ideas and his elaborate argument against the existence of abstract ideas, David Hume called "one of the greatest and most valuable discoveries that has been

---

1. In today's terminology, *fluxion* means "derivative."

made of late years in the republic of letters." American idealists considered Berkeley their founder, including Josiah Royce at Harvard who developed his own brand of absolute idealism. The American pragmatist Charles Sanders Peirce claimed Berkeley paved the way for the development of pragmatism. Immanuel Kant, though supposedly a critic of Berkeley's idealism, relied heavily on Berkeley's views, especially his criticism of materialism; Kant's transcendental idealism incorporates Berkeley's famous dictum, *esse is percipi,* "to be is to be perceived," tailored according to Kant's transcendental philosophy. Arthur Schopenhauer credited Berkeley as being the first to put forth the view that the world is but an idea in the mind. Ernst Mach, influential physicist and philosopher of the nineteenth century, claims to have been guided in his criticisms of absolute space, time, and motion by the work of Berkeley, which led him toward laying the foundations for the revolutionary idea in physics that the conscious observer plays a fundamental role in structuring reality.

Berkeley developed his philosophy in part as a reaction to Locke. Locke had shown that secondary qualities exist only in the mind, leaving the primary qualities in the things themselves. Berkeley argued that even primary qualities exist only in the mind. Locke's mistake, he claimed, is that he derived the objective existence of extension, hardness, weight, motion, and the other primary qualities of sensible objects, through the (bogus) principle of abstraction. That is, Locke according to Berkeley mistakenly thinks he has an abstract idea of substance and extension—matter—as a something "I know not what" to which the mind adheres the secondary qualities of color, texture, and so on. A closer scrutiny of such notions and careful inspection of the actual contents of the mind, along with an analysis of language—the "curtain of words" that deceive us—reveals, Berkeley argues, that there really are no such things as abstract ideas. If we do not allow ourselves to be deceived by our language and analyze the actual notions themselves, we shall see that the mind contains only *particular* ideas. What Locke called the "primary qualities" of sensible objects thus have no existence beyond the conscious mind. Each and every property of a sensible object exists only as a sensation within the perception of a conscious being.

In Berkeley's view, the entire universe, and all things within it, cannot exist without being perceived by a mind. Once we realize the truth about the nature of perception and the inner working of the mind we will see that, as he says in his *Treatise,* "all the choir of heaven and furniture of the earth, in a word, all those bodies which compose the mighty frame of the world, have not any subsistence without a mind—that their *being* is to be perceived or know, that, consequently so long as they are not actually perceived by me or do not exist in my mind or that of any other created spirit, they must either have no existence at all or else subsist in the mind of some eternal spirit."

Of the things that do exist, Berkeley says, "Their *esse is percipi.*" You will find this phrase quoted again and again in various places, translated, now world famously, as "to be is to be perceived." But that all-important first word is usually, and notoriously, left out. Without the *their* as a reference point, the phrase becomes exactly the sort of abstraction that Berkeley's philosophy was designed to eradicate from the enlightened mind. He derives the principle without reference to science or experience or experiment, a priori. In fact, though this may be a gross oversimplification, what Berkeley is saying is actually a tautology, a logically necessary truth that cannot possibly be false: "That which is mental is mental" or "Events in the mind are events in the mind." He doesn't just stay with that, any more than Descartes stays with his *cogito,* "I think therefore I am." Like Descartes, Berkeley attempts to erect a whole philosophy upon the certainty of his true statement.

But what then keeps everything from disappearing? If to be is to be perceived, what happens when there is no perception of, say, the chair in my study? According to the commonly received view, it's the stuff out there in the world that persists over time, even when we are not looking at it. According to Berkeley, that objects persist the way they do is evidence not for matter but for "some *other* will," which ultimately he identifies with God. God is the absolute "other" whose *will* runs the world, whose continual presence keeps everything from vanishing into a void of utter insubstantiality, into *nothing*.

A TREATISE CONCERNING THE PRINCIPLES OF HUMAN KNOWLEDGE
Wherein the Chief Causes of Error and Difficulty in the Sciences, with the Grounds of Skepticism, Atheism, and Irreligion, Are Inquired into

PREFACE

What I here make public has, after a long and scrupulous inquiry, seemed to me evidently true and not unuseful to be known—particularly to those who are tainted with skepticism or want a demonstration of the existence and immateriality of God or the natural immortality of the soul. Whether it be so or no, I am content the reader should impartially examine, since I do not think myself any further concerned for the success of what I have written than as it is agreeable to truth. But to the end this may not suffer I make it my request that the reader suspend his judgment till he has once at least read the whole through with that degree of attention and thought which the subject matter shall seem to deserve. For as there are some passages that, taken by themselves, are very liable (nor could it be remedied) to gross misinterpretation, and to be charged with most absurd consequences which, nevertheless, upon an entire perusal will appear not to follow from them, so likewise, though the whole should be read over, yet, if this be done transiently, it is very probable my sense may be mistaken; but to a thinking reader, I flatter myself, it will be throughout clear and obvious. As for the characters of novelty and singularity which some of the following notions may seem to bear, it is, I hope, needless to make any apology on that account. He must surely be either very weak or very little acquainted with the sciences who shall reject a truth that is capable of demonstration for no other reason but because it is newly known and contrary to the prejudices of mankind. Thus much I thought fit to premise in order to prevent, if possible, the hasty censures of a sort of men who are too apt to condemn an opinion before they rightly comprehend it.

From *The Works of George Berkeley*, ed. A. C. Fraser (Oxford: Clarendon Press, 1901).

INTRODUCTION

1. Philosophy being nothing else but the study of wisdom and truth, it may with reason be expected that those who have spent most time and pains in it should enjoy a greater calm and serenity of mind, a greater clearness and evidence of knowledge, and be less disturbed with doubts and difficulties than other men. Yet so it is, we see the illiterate bulk of mankind that walk the high road of plain common sense, and are governed by the dictates of nature, for the most part easy and undisturbed. To them nothing that is familiar appears unaccountable or difficult to comprehend. They complain not of any want of evidence in their senses, and are out of all danger of becoming skeptics. But no sooner do we depart from sense and instinct to follow the light of a superior principle, to reason, meditate, and reflect on the nature of things, but a thousand scruples spring up in our minds concerning those things which before we seemed fully to comprehend. Prejudices and errors of sense do from all parts discover themselves to our view; and, endeavoring to correct these by reason, we are insensibly drawn into uncouth paradoxes, difficulties, and inconsistencies, which multiply and grow upon us as we advance in speculation, till at length, having wandered through many intricate mazes, we find ourselves just where we were, or, which is worse, sit down in a forlorn skepticism.

2. The cause of this is thought to be the obscurity of things, or the natural weakness and imperfection of our understandings. It is said the faculties we have are few and those designed by nature for the support and comfort of life, and not to penetrate into the inward essence and constitution of things. Besides, the mind of man being finite, when it treats of things which partake of infinity it is not to be wondered at if it run into absurdities and contradictions, out of which it is impossible it should ever extricate itself, it being of the nature of infinite not to be comprehended by that which is finite.

3. But, perhaps, we may be too partial to ourselves in placing the fault originally in our faculties and not rather in the wrong use we make of them. It is a hard thing to suppose that right deductions from true principles should ever end in consequences which cannot be maintained or made consistent. We should believe that God has dealt more bountifully with the sons of men than to give them a strong desire for that knowledge which he had placed quite out of their reach. This were not agreeable to the wonted, indulgent methods of Providence, which, whatever appetites it may have implanted in the creatures, does usually furnish them with such means as, if rightly made use of, will not fail to satisfy them. Upon the whole, I am inclined to think that the far greater part, if not all, of those difficulties which have hitherto amused philosophers and blocked up the way to knowledge, are entirely owing to ourselves—that we have first raised a dust and then complain we cannot see.

4. My purpose therefore is to try if I can discover what those principles are which have introduced all that doubtfulness and uncertainty, those absurdities and contradictions, into the several sects of philosophy—insomuch that the wisest men have thought our ignorance incurable, conceiving it to arise from the natural dullness and limitation of our faculties. And surely it is a work well deserving our pains to make a strict inquiry concerning the first principles of human knowledge, to sift and examine them on all sides, especially since there may be some grounds to suspect that those lets and difficulties which stay and embarrass the mind in its search after truth do not spring from any darkness and intricacy in the objects or natural defect in the understanding so much as from false principles which have been insisted on, and might have been avoided.

5. How difficult and discouraging soever this attempt may seem when I consider how many great and extraordinary men have gone before me in the same designs, yet I am not without some hopes—upon the consideration that the largest views are not always the clearest, and that he who is shortsighted will be obliged to draw the object nearer, and may, perhaps, by a close and narrow survey discern that which had escaped far better eyes.

6. In order to prepare the mind of the reader for the easier conceiving what follows, it is proper to premise somewhat, by way of introduction, concerning the nature and abuse of language. But the unraveling this matter leads me in some measure to anticipate my design by taking notice of what seems to have had a chief part in rendering speculation intricate and perplexed and to have occasioned innumerable errors and difficulties in almost all parts of knowledge. And that is the opinion that the mind has a power of framing *abstract ideas* or notions of things. He who is not a perfect stranger to the writings and disputes of philosophers must needs acknowledge that no small part of them are spent about abstract ideas. These are in a more especial manner thought to be the object of those sciences which go by the name of logic and metaphysics, and of all that which passes under the notion of the most abstracted and sublime learning, in all which one shall scarce find any question handled in such a manner as does not suppose their existence in the mind, and that it is well acquainted with them.

7. It is agreed on all hands that the qualities or modes of things do never really exist each of them apart by itself and separated from all others, but are mixed, as it were, and blended together, several in the same object. But we are told the mind, being able to consider each quality singly, or abstracted from those other qualities with which it is united, does by that means frame to itself abstract ideas. For example, there is perceived by sight an object extended, colored, and moved: this mixed or compound idea the mind, resolving into its simple, constituent parts and viewing each by itself, exclusive of the rest, does frame the abstract ideas of extension, color, and motion. Not that it is possible for color or motion to exist without extension, but only that the mind can frame to itself by *abstraction* the idea of color exclusive of extension, and of motion exclusive of both color and extension.

8. Again, the mind having observed that in the particular extensions perceived by sense there is something common and alike in all, and some other things peculiar, as this or that figure or magnitude, which distinguish them one from another, it considers apart or singles out by itself that which is common, making thereof a most abstract idea of extension, which is neither line, surface, nor solid, nor has any figure or magnitude, but is an idea entirely prescinded from all these. So likewise the mind, by leaving out of the particular colors perceived by sense that which distinguishes them one from another, and retaining that only which is common to all, makes an idea of color in abstract, which is neither red, nor blue, nor white, nor any other determinate color. And, in like manner, by considering motion abstractedly not only from the body moved, but likewise from the figure it describes, and all particular directions and velocities, the abstract idea of motion is framed, which equally corresponds to all particular motions whatsoever that may be perceived by sense.

9. And as the mind frames to itself abstract ideas of qualities or modes, so does it, by the same precision or mental separation, attain abstract ideas of the more compounded beings which include several coexistent qualities. For example, the mind, having observed that Peter, James, and John resemble each other in certain common agreements of shape and other qualities, leaves out of the complex or compounded idea it has of Peter, James, and any other particular man that which is peculiar to each, retaining only what is common to all, and so makes an abstract idea wherein all the particulars equally partake—abstracting entirely from and cutting off all those circumstances and differences which might determine

it to any particular existence. And after this manner it is said we come by the abstract idea of *man* or, if you please, humanity, or human nature; wherein it is true there is included color, because there is no man but has some color, but then it can be neither white, nor black, nor any particular color, because there is no one particular color wherein all men partake. So likewise there is included stature, but then it is neither tall stature, nor low stature, nor yet middle stature, but something abstracted from all these. And so of the rest. Moreover, there being a great variety of other creatures that partake in some parts, but not all, of the complex idea of man, the mind, leaving out those parts which are peculiar to men, and retaining those only which are common to all the living creatures, frames the idea of *animal,* which abstracts not only from all particular men, but also all birds, beasts, fishes, and insects. The constituent parts of the abstract idea of animal are body, life, sense, and spontaneous motion. By "body" is meant body without any particular shape or figure, there being no one shape or figure common to all animals, without covering, either of hair, or feathers, or scales, etc., nor yet naked: hair, feathers, scales, and nakedness being the distinguishing properties of particular animals, and for that reason left out of the *abstract idea.* Upon the same account the spontaneous motion must be neither walking, nor flying, nor creeping; it is nevertheless a motion, but what that motion is it is not easy to conceive.

10. Whether others have this wonderful faculty of abstracting their ideas, they best can tell; for myself I find indeed I have a faculty of imagining, or representing to myself, the ideas of those particular things I have perceived, and of various compounding and dividing them. I can imagine a man with two heads, or the upper parts of a man joined to the body of a horse. I can consider the hand, the eye, the nose, each by itself abstracted or separated from the rest of the body. But then whatever hand or eye I imagine, it must have some particular shape and color. Likewise the idea of man that I frame to myself must be either of a white, or a black, or a tawny, a straight, or a crooked, a tall, or a low, or a middle-sized man. I cannot by any effort of thought conceive the abstract idea above described. And it is equally impossible for me to form the abstract idea of motion distinct from the body moving, and which is neither swift nor slow, curvilinear nor rectilinear; and the like may be said of all other abstract general ideas whatsoever. To be plain, I own myself able to abstract in one sense, as when I consider some particular parts or qualities separated from others, with which, though they are united in some object, yet it is possible they may really exist without them. But I deny that I can abstract one from another, or conceive separately, those qualities which it is impossible should exist so separated; or that I can frame a general notion by abstracting from particulars in the manner aforesaid—which two last are the two proper acceptations of "abstraction." And there are grounds to think most men will acknowledge themselves to be in my case. The generality of men which are simple and illiterate never pretend to abstract notions. It is said they are difficult and not to be attained without pains and study; we may therefore reasonably conclude that, if such there be, they are confined only to the learned.

11. I proceed to examine what can be alleged in defense of the doctrine of abstraction, and try if I can discover what it is that inclines the men of speculation to embrace an opinion so remote from common sense as that seems to be. There has been a late, deservedly esteemed philosopher [Locke] who, no doubt, has given it very much countenance by seeming to think the having abstract general ideas is what puts the widest difference in point of understanding betwixt man and beast. . . .

I readily agree with this learned author that the faculties of brutes can by no means attain to abstraction. But then if this be made the distinguishing property of that sort of animals, I fear a great many of those that pass for men must be reckoned into their number. The reason that is here assigned why we have no grounds to think brutes have abstract general ideas is that we observe in them no use of words or any other general signs; which is built on this supposition—that the making use of words implies the having general ideas. From which it follows that men who use language are able to abstract or generalize their ideas. That this is the sense and arguing of the author will further appear by his answering the question he in another place puts: "Since all things that exist are only particulars, how come we by general terms?" His answer is: "Words become general by being made the signs of general ideas."—(*Essay on Human Understanding*, Bk. III, chap. 3, sec. 6.) But it seems that a word becomes general by being made the sign, not of an abstract general idea, but of several particular ideas, any one of which it indifferently suggests to the mind. For example, when it is said, "the change of motion is proportional to the impressed force," or that, "whatever has extension is divisible," these propositions are to be understood of motion and extension in general; and nevertheless it will not follow that they suggest to my thoughts an idea of motion without a body moved, or any determinate direction and velocity, or that I must conceive an abstract general idea of extension which is neither line, surface, nor solid, neither great nor small, black, white, nor red, nor of any other determinate color. It is only implied that whatever motion I consider, whether it be swift or slow, perpendicular, horizontal, or oblique, or in whatever object, the axiom concerning it holds equally true. As does the other of every particular extension, it matters not whether line, surface, or solid, whether of this or that magnitude or figure.

12. By observing how ideas become general we may the better judge how words are made so. And here it is to be noted that I do not deny absolutely there are general ideas, but only that there are any *abstract* general ideas; for, in the passages above quoted, wherein there is mention of general ideas, it is always supposed that they are formed by abstraction, after the manner set forth in sections 8 and 9. Now, if we will annex a meaning to our words and speak only of what we can conceive, I believe we shall acknowledge that an idea which, considered in itself, is particular, becomes general by being made to represent or stand for all other particular ideas of the same sort. To make this plain by an example, suppose a geometrician is demonstrating the method of cutting a line in two equal parts. He draws, for instance, a black line of an inch in length: this, which in itself is a particular line, is nevertheless with regard to its signification general, since, as it is there used, it represents all particular lines whatsoever; for that which is demonstrated of it is demonstrated of all lines or, in other words, of a line in general. And, as that *particular* line becomes general by being made a sign, so the *name* "line," which taken absolutely is particular, by being a sign is made general. And as the former owes its generality not to its being the sign of an abstract or general line, but of all particular right lines that may possibly exist, so the latter must be thought to derive its generality from the same cause, namely, the various particular lines which it indifferently denotes.

13. To give the reader a yet clearer view of the nature of abstract ideas, and the uses they are thought necessary to, I shall add one more passage out of the *Essay on Human Understanding*, which is as follows:

> . . . does it not require some pains and skill to form the general idea of a triangle (which is yet none of the most abstract, comprehensive, and difficult); for it must be neither oblique nor rectangle, neither equilateral, equicrural, nor scalenon, but *all and none* of these at once? In effect, it is something imperfect that cannot exist, an idea wherein some parts of several different and *inconsistent* ideas are put together. It is true the mind in this imperfect state has need of such ideas and makes all the haste to them it can, for the convenience of communication and enlargement of

knowledge to both which it is naturally very much inclined. But yet one has reason to suspect such ideas are marks of our imperfection. At least this is enough to show that the most abstract and general ideas are not those that the mind is first and most easily acquainted with, nor such as its earliest knowledge is conversant about.—Bk. IV, chap. 7, sec. 9.

If any man has the faculty of framing in his mind such an idea of a triangle as is here described, it is in vain to pretend to dispute him out of it, nor would I go about it. All I desire is that the reader would fully and certainly inform himself whether he has such an idea or no. And this, methinks, can be no hard task for anyone to perform. What more easy than for anyone to look a little into his own thoughts, and there try whether he has, or can attain to have, an idea that shall correspond with the description that is here given of the general idea of a triangle, which is "neither oblique nor rectangle, equilateral, equicrural nor scalenon, but all and none of these at once"?

14. Much is here said of the difficulty that abstract ideas carry with them, and the pains and skill requisite to the forming them. And it is on all hands agreed that there is need of great toil and labor of the mind to emancipate our thoughts from particular objects and raise them to those sublime speculations that are conversant about abstract ideas. From all which the natural consequence should seem to be, that so difficult a thing as the forming abstract ideas was not necessary for *communication,* which is so easy and familiar to all sorts of men. But, we are told, if they seem obvious and easy to grown men, "it is only because by constant and familiar use they are made so." Now, I would fain know at what time it is men are employed in surmounting that difficulty and furnishing themselves with those necessary helps for discourse. It cannot be when they are grown up, for then it seems they are not conscious of any such painstaking; it remains, therefore, to be the business of their childhood. And surely the great and multiplied labor of framing abstract notions will be found a hard task for that tender age. Is it not a hard thing to imagine that a couple of children cannot prate together of their sugar plums and rattles and the rest of their little trinkets till they have first tacked together numberless inconsistencies and so framed in their minds abstract general ideas and annexed them to every common name they make use of?

15. Nor do I think them a whit more needful for the *enlargement of knowledge* than for *communication.* It is, I know, a point much insisted on, that all knowledge and demonstration are about universal notions, to which I fully agree; but then it does not appear to me that those notions are formed by abstraction in the manner premised—*universality,* so far as I can comprehend, not consisting in the absolute, positive nature or conception of any thing, but in the relation it bears to the particulars signified or represented by it; by virtue whereof it is that things, names, or notions, bring in their own nature *particular,* are rendered *universal.* Thus, when I demonstrate any proposition concerning triangles, it is to be supposed that I have in view the universal idea of a triangle, which ought not to be understood as if I could frame an idea of a triangle which was neither equilateral, nor scalenon, nor equicrural, but only that the particular triangle I consider, whether of this or that sort it matters not, does equally stand for and represent all rectilinear triangles whatsoever, and is in that sense *universal.* All which seems very plain and not to include any difficulty in it.

16. But here it will be demanded how we can know any proposition to be true of all particular triangles, except we have first seen it demonstrated of the abstract idea of a triangle which equally agrees to all? For, because a property may be demonstrated to agree to some one particular triangle, it will not thence follow that it equally belongs to any other triangle which in all respects is not the same with it. For example, having demonstrated that the three angles of an isosceles rectangular triangle are equal to two right ones, I cannot

therefore conclude this affection agrees to all other triangles which have neither a right angle nor two equal sides. It seems therefore that, to be certain this proposition is universally true, we must either make a particular demonstration for every particular triangle, which is impossible, or once for all demonstrate it of the abstract idea of a triangle in which all the particulars do indifferently partake and by which they are all equally represented. To which I answer that, though the idea I have in view whilst I make the demonstration be, for instance, that of an isosceles rectangular triangle whose sides are of a determinate length, I may nevertheless be certain it extends to all other rectilinear triangles, of what sort of bigness soever. And that because neither the right angle, nor the equality, nor determinate length of the sides are at all concerned in the demonstration. It is true the diagram I have in view includes all these particulars, but then there is not the least mention made of them in the proof of the proposition. It is not said the three angles are equal to two right ones, because one of them is a right angle, or because the sides comprehending it are of the same length. Which sufficiently shows that the right angle might have been oblique, and the sides unequal, and for all that the demonstration have held good. And for this reason it is that I conclude that to be true of any obliquangular or scalenon which I had demonstrated of a particular right-angled equicrural triangle, and not because I demonstrated the proposition of the abstract idea of a triangle.

17. It were an endless as well as a useless thing to trace the Schoolmen, those great masters of abstraction, through all the manifold, inextricable labyrinths of error and dispute which their doctrine of abstract natures and notions seems to have led them into. What bickerings and controversies, and what a learned dust have been raised about those matters, and what mighty advantage has been from thence derived to mankind, are things at this day too clearly known to need being insisted on. And it had been well if the ill effects of that doctrine were confined to those only who make the most avowed profession of it. When men consider the great pains, industry, and parts that have for so many ages been laid out on the cultivation and advancement of the sciences, and that notwithstanding all this the far greater part of them remains full of darkness and uncertainty, and disputes that are like never to have an end, and even those that are thought to be supported by the most clear and cogent demonstrations, contain in them paradoxes which are perfectly irreconcilable to the understandings of men, and that, taking all together, a small portion of them does supply any real benefit to mankind, otherwise than by being an innocent diversion and amusement—I say the consideration of all this is apt to throw them into a despondency and perfect contempt of all study. But this may, perhaps, cease upon a view of the false principles that have obtained in the world, amongst all which there is none, methinks, has a more wide influence over the thoughts of speculative men than this of *abstract* general ideas.

18. I come now to consider the *source* of this prevailing notion, and that seems to me to be language. And surely nothing of less extent than reason itself could have been the source of an opinion so universally received. The truth of this appears, as from other reasons, so also from the plain confession of the ablest patrons of abstract ideas, who acknowledge that they are made in order to naming; from which it is a clear consequence that if there had been no such thing as speech or universal signs there never had been any thought of abstraction. See Bk. III, chap. 6, sec. 39, and elsewhere of the *Essay on Human Understanding.* Let us examine the manner wherein words have contributed to the origin of that mistake: First then, it is thought that every name has, or ought to have, one only precise and settled signification, which inclines men to think there are certain abstract, determinate ideas which constitute the true and only immediate signification of each general name; and

that it is by the mediation of these abstract ideas that a general name comes to signify any particular thing. Whereas, in truth, there is no such thing as one precise and definite signification annexed to any general name, they all signifying indifferently a great number of particular ideas. All which does evidently follow from what has been already said, and will clearly appear to anyone by a little reflection. To this it will be objected that every name that has a definition is thereby restrained to one certain signification. For example, a "triangle" is defined to be "a plane surface comprehended by three right lines," by which that name is limited to denote one certain idea and no other. To which I answer that in the definition it is not said whether the surface be great or small, black or white, nor whether the sides are long or short, equal or unequal, nor with what angles they are inclined to each other; in all which there may be great variety, and consequently there is no one settled idea which limits the signification of the word "triangle." It is one thing for to keep a name constantly to the same definition, and another to make it stand everywhere for the same idea; the one is necessary, the other useless and impracticable.

19. But, to give a further account how words came to produce the doctrine of abstract ideas, it must be observed that it is a received opinion that language has no other end but the communicating ideas, and that every significant name stands for an idea. This being so, and it being withal certain that names which yet are not thought altogether insignificant do not always mark out particular conceivable ideas, it is straightway concluded that they stand for abstract notions. That there are many names in use amongst speculative men which do not always suggest to others determinate, particular ideas is what nobody will deny. And a little attention will discover that it is not necessary (even in the strictest reasonings) that significant names which stand for ideas should, every time they are used, excite in the understanding the ideas they are made to stand for—in reading and discoursing, names being for the most part used as letters are in algebra, in which, though a particular quantity be marked by each letter, yet to proceed right it is not requisite that in every step each letter suggest to your thoughts that particular quantity it was appointed to stand for.

20. Besides, the communicating of ideas marked by words is not the chief and only end of language, as is commonly supposed. There are other ends, as the raising of some passion, the exciting to or deterring from an action, the putting the mind in some particular disposition—to which the former is in many cases barely subservient, and sometimes entirely omitted, when these can be obtained without it, as I think does not unfrequently happen in the familiar use of language. I entreat the reader to reflect with himself and see if it does not often happen, either in hearing or reading a discourse, that the passions of fear, love, hatred, admiration, disdain, and the like, arise immediately in his mind upon the perception of certain words, without any idea coming between. At first, indeed, the words might have occasioned ideas that were fit to produce those emotions; but, if I mistake not, it will be found that, when language is once grown familiar, the hearing of the sounds or sight of the characters is oft immediately attended with those passions which at first were wont to be produced by the intervention of ideas that are now quite omitted. May we not, for example, be affected with the promise of a *good thing*, though we have not an idea of what it is? Or is not the being threatened with danger sufficient to excite a dread, though we think not of any particular evil likely to befall us, nor yet frame to ourselves an idea of danger in abstract? If anyone shall join ever so little reflection of his own to what has been said, I believe that it will evidently appear to him that general names are often used in the propriety of language without the speaker's designing them for marks of ideas in his own, which he would have them raise in the mind of the hearer. Even proper names themselves do not seem always spoken with a design to bring into our view the ideas of those individuals that are supposed

to be marked by them. For example, when a Schoolman tells me, "Aristotle has said it," all I conceive he means by it is to dispose me to embrace his opinion with the deference and submission which custom has annexed to that name. And this effect may be so instantly produced in the minds of those who are accustomed to resign their judgment to the authority of that philosopher, as it is impossible any idea either of his person, writings, or reputation should go before. Innumerable examples of this kind may be given, but why should I insist on those things which everyone's experience will, I doubt not, plentifully suggest unto him?

21. We have, I think, shown the impossibility of abstract ideas. We have considered what has been said for them by their ablest patrons, and endeavored to show they are of no use for those ends to which they are thought necessary. And lastly, we have traced them to the source from whence they flow, which appears to be language.—It cannot be denied that words are of excellent use, in that by their means all that stock of knowledge which has been purchased by the joint labors of inquisitive men in all ages and nations may be drawn into the view and made the possession of one single person. But at the same time it must be owned that most parts of knowledge have been strangely perplexed and darkened by the abuse of words, and general ways of speech wherein they are delivered. Since therefore words are so apt to impose on the understanding, whatever ideas I consider, I shall endeavor to take them bare and naked into my view, keeping out of my thoughts so far as I am able those names which long and constant use has so strictly united with them; from which I may expect to derive the following advantages:

22. *First,* I shall be sure to get clear of all controversies purely verbal—the springing up of which weeds in almost all the sciences has been a main hindrance to the growth of true and sound knowledge. *Secondly,* this seems to be a sure way to extricate myself out of that fine and subtle net of *abstract ideas* which has so miserably perplexed and entangled the minds of men; and that with this peculiar circumstance, that by how much the finer and more curious was the wit of any man, by so much the deeper was he likely to be ensnared and faster held therein. *Thirdly,* so long as I confine my thoughts to my own ideas divested of words, I do not see how I can easily be mistaken. The objects I consider I clearly and adequately know. I cannot be deceived in thinking I have an idea which I have not. It is not possible for me to imagine that any of my own ideas are alike or unlike that are not truly so. To discern the agreements or disagreements there are between my ideas, to see what ideas are included in any compound idea and what not, there is nothing more requisite than an attentive perception of what passes in my own understanding.

23. But the attainment of all these advantages does presuppose an entire deliverance from the deception of words, which I dare hardly promise myself—so difficult a thing it is to dissolve a union so early begun and confirmed by so long a habit as that betwixt words and ideas. Which difficulty seems to have been very much increased by the doctrine of *abstraction.* For so long as men thought abstract ideas were annexed to their words, it does not seem strange that they should use words for ideas—it being found an impracticable thing to lay aside the word, and retain the *abstract* idea in the mind, which in itself was perfectly inconceivable.

This seems to me the principal cause why those who have so emphatically recommended to others the laying aside all use of words in their meditations, and contemplating their bare ideas, have yet failed to perform it themselves. Of late many have been very sensible of the absurd opinions and insignificant disputes which grow out of the abuse of words. And, in order to remedy these evils, they advise well, that we attend to the ideas signified, and draw off our attention from the words which signify them. But, how good soever this advice may be they have given others, it is plain they could not have a due regard to it themselves, so long as they thought the only immediate use of words was to signify ideas, and that the immediate signification of every general name was a determinate abstract idea.

24. But, these being known to be mistakes, a man may with greater ease prevent his being imposed on by words. He that knows he has no other than *particular* ideas, will not puzzle himself in vain to find out and conceive the *abstract* idea annexed to any name. And he that knows names do not always stand for ideas will spare himself the labour of looking for ideas where there are none to be had. It were, therefore, to be wished that every one would use his utmost endeavours to obtain a clear view of the ideas he would consider, separating from them all that dress and incumbrance of words which so much contribute to blind the judgment and divide the attention. In vain do we extend our view into the heavens and pry into the entrails of the earth, in vain do we consult the writings of learned men and trace the dark footsteps of antiquity—we need only draw the curtain of words, to behold the fairest tree of knowledge, whose fruit is excellent, and within the reach of our hand.

25. Unless we take care to clear the First Principles of Knowledge from the embarras and delusion of words, we may make infinite reasonings upon them to no purpose; we may draw consequences from consequences, and be never the wiser. The farther we go, we shall only lose ourselves the more irrecoverably, and be the deeper entangled in difficulties and mistakes. Whoever therefore designs to read the following sheets, I entreat him that he would make my words the occasion of his own thinking, and endeavour to attain the same train of thoughts in reading that I had in writing them. By this means it will be easy for him to discover the truth or falsity of what I say. He will be out of all danger of being deceived by my words, and I do not see how he can be led into an error by considering his own naked, undisguised ideas.

OF THE PRINCIPLES OF HUMAN KNOWLEDGE

It is evident to anyone who takes a survey of the *objects* of human knowledge that they are either ideas actually imprinted on the senses, or else such as are perceived by attending to the passions and operations of the mind, or lastly, ideas formed by help of memory and imagination—either compounding, dividing, or barely representing those originally perceived in the aforesaid ways. By sight I have the ideas of light and colors, with their several degrees and variations. By touch I perceive, for example, hard and soft, heat and cold, motion and resistance, and of all these more and less either as to quantity or degree. Smelling furnishes me with odors, the palate with tastes, and hearing conveys sounds to the mind in all their variety of tone and composition. And as several of these are observed to accompany each other, they come to be marked by one name, and so to be reputed as one thing. Thus, for example, a certain color, taste, smell, figure, and consistence having been observed to go together, are accounted one distinct thing signified by the name "apple"; other collections of ideas constitute a stone, a tree, a book, and the like sensible things—which as they are pleasing or disagreeable excite the passions of love, hatred, joy, grief, and so forth.

2. But, besides all that endless variety of ideas or objects of knowledge, there is likewise something which knows or perceives them and exercises diverse operations, as willing, imagining, remembering, about them. This perceiving, active being is what I call "mind, " "spirit," "soul," or "myself." By which words I do not denote any one of my ideas, but a thing entirely distinct from them, wherein they exist or, which is the same thing, whereby they are perceived—for the existence of an idea consists in being perceived.

3. That neither our thoughts, nor passions, nor ideas formed by the imagination exist without the mind is what everybody will allow. And it seems no less evident that the various sensations or ideas imprinted on the sense, however blended or combined together (that is, whatever objects they compose), cannot exist otherwise than in a mind perceiving them.— I think an intuitive knowledge may be obtained of this by anyone that shall attend to what is meant by the term "exist" when applied to sensible things. The table I write on I say exists, that is, I see and feel it; and if I were out of my study I should say it existed—meaning thereby that if I was in my study I might perceive it, or that some other spirit actually does perceive it. There was an odor, that is, it was smelled, there was a sound, that is to say, it was heard; a color or figure, and it was perceived by sight or touch. This is all that I can understand by these and the like expressions. For as to what is said of the absolute existence of unthinking things without any relation to their being perceived, that seems perfectly unintelligible. Their *esse* is *percipi,* nor is it possible they should have any existence out of the minds or thinking things which perceive them.

4. It is indeed an opinion strangely prevailing amongst men that houses, mountains, rivers, and, in a word, all sensible objects have an existence, natural or real, distinct from their being perceived by the understanding. But with how great an assurance and acquiescence soever this principle may be entertained in the world, yet whoever shall find in his heart to call it in question may, if I mistake not, perceive it to involve a manifest contradiction. For what are the forementioned objects but the things we perceive by sense? And what do we perceive besides our own ideas or sensations? And is it not plainly repugnant that any one of these, or any combination of them, should exist unperceived?

5. If we thoroughly examine this tenet it will, perhaps, be found at bottom to depend on the doctrine of *abstract ideas.* For can there be a nicer strain of abstraction than to distinguish the existence of sensible objects from their being perceived, so as to conceive them existing unperceived? Light and colors, heat and cold, extension and figures—in a word, the things we see and feel—what are they but so many sensations, notions, ideas, or impressions on the sense? And is it possible to separate, even in thought, any of these from perception? For my part, I might as easily divide a thing from itself. I may, indeed, divide in my thoughts, or conceive apart from each other, those things which, perhaps, I never perceived by sense so divided. Thus I imagine the trunk of a human body without the limbs, or conceive the smell of a rose without thinking on the rose itself. So far, I will not deny, I can abstract—if that may properly be called "abstraction" which extends only to the conceiving separately such objects as it is possible may really exist or be actually perceived asunder. But my conceiving or imagining power does not extend beyond the possibility of real existence or perception. Hence, as it is impossible for me to see or feel anything without an actual sensation of that thing, so it is impossible for me to conceive in my thoughts any sensible thing or object distinct from the sensation or perception of it.

6. Some truths there are so near and obvious to the mind that a man need only open his eyes to see them. Such I take this important one to be, to wit, that all the choir of heaven and furniture of the earth, in a word, all those bodies which compose the mighty frame of the world, have not any subsistence without a mind—that their *being* is to be perceived or known, that, consequently, so long as they are not actually perceived by me or do not exist in my mind or that of any other created spirit, they must either have no existence at all or else subsist in the mind of some eternal spirit—it being perfectly unintelligible, and involving all the absurdity of abstraction, to attribute to any single part of them an existence independent of a spirit. To be conceived of which, the reader need only reflect, and try to separate in his own thoughts, the *being* of a sensible thing from its *being perceived.*

7. From what has been said it follows there is not any other substance than *spirit,* or that which perceives. But, for the fuller proof of this point, let it be considered the sensible qualities are color, figure, motion, smell, taste, and such like—that is, the ideas perceived by sense. Now, for an idea to exist in an unperceiving thing is a manifest contradiction, for to have an idea is all one as to perceive; that, therefore, wherein color, figure, and the like qualities exist must perceive them; hence it is clear there can be no unthinking substance or *substratum* of those ideas.

8. But, say you, though the ideas themselves do not exist without the mind, yet there may be things like them, whereof they are copies or resemblances, which things exist without the mind in an unthinking substance. I answer, an idea can be like nothing but an idea; a color or figure can be like nothing but another color or figure. If we look but ever so little into our thoughts, we shall find it impossible for us to conceive a likeness except only between our ideas. Again, I ask whether those supposed originals or external things, of which our ideas are the pictures or representations, be themselves perceivable or no? If they are, then they are ideas and we have gained our point; but if you say they are not, I appeal to anyone whether it be sense to assert a color is like something which is invisible; hard or soft, like something which is intangible; and so of the rest.

9. Some there are who make a distinction betwixt primary and secondary qualities. By the former they mean extension, figure, motion, rest, solidity or impenetrability, and number; by the latter they denote all other sensible qualities, as colors, sounds, tastes, and so forth. The ideas we have of these they acknowledge not to be the resemblances of anything existing without the mind, or unperceived, but they will have our ideas of the primary qualities to be patterns or images of things which exist without the mind, in an unthinking substance which they call "matter." By "matter," therefore, we are to understand an inert, senseless substance, in which extension, figure, and motion do actually subsist. But it is evident from what we have already shown that extension, figure, and motion are only ideas existing in the mind, and that an idea can be like nothing but another idea, and that consequently neither they nor their archetypes can exist in an unperceiving substance. Hence it is plain that the very notion of what is called "matter" or "corporeal substance" involves a contradiction in it.

10. They who assert that figure, motion, and the rest of the primary or original qualities do exist without the mind in unthinking substances do at the same time acknowledge that colors, sounds, heat, cold, and suchlike secondary qualities do not—which they tell us are sensations existing in the mind alone, that depend on and are occasioned by the different size, texture, and motion of the minute particles of matter. This they take for an undoubted truth which they can demonstrate beyond all exception. Now, if it be certain that those original qualities are inseparably united with the other sensible qualities, and not, even in thought, capable of being abstracted from them, it plainly follows that they exist only in the mind. But I desire anyone to reflect and try whether he can, by any abstraction of thought, conceive the extension and motion of a body without all other sensible qualities. For my own part, I see evidently that it is not in my power to frame an idea of a body extended and moved, but I must withal give it some color or other sensible quality which is acknowledged to exist only in the mind. In short, extension, figure, and motion, abstracted from all other qualities, are inconceivable. Where therefore the other sensible qualities are, there must these be also, to wit, in the mind and nowhere else.

11. Again, *great* and *small, swift* and *slow* are allowed to exist nowhere without the mind, being entirely relative, and changing as the frame or position of the organs of sense varies. The extension, therefore, which exists without the mind is neither great nor small, the

motion neither swift nor slow; that is, they are nothing at all. But, say you, they are extension in general, and motion in general: thus we see how much the tenet of extended movable substances existing without the mind depends on that strange doctrine of *abstract ideas*. And here I cannot but remark how nearly the vague and indeterminate description of matter or corporeal substance, which the modern philosophers are run into by their own principles, resembles that antiquated and so much ridiculed notion of *materia prima,* to be met with in Aristotle and his followers. Without extension, solidity cannot be conceived; since, therefore, it has been shown that extension exists not in an unthinking substance, the same must also be true of solidity.

12. That number is entirely the creature of the mind, even though the other qualities be allowed to exist without, will be evident to whoever considers that the same thing bears a different denomination of number as the mind views it with different respects. Thus the same extension is one, or three, or thirty-six, according as the mind considers it with reference to a yard, a foot, or an inch. Number is so visibly relative and dependent on men's understanding that it is strange to think how anyone should give it an absolute existence without the mind. We say one book, one page, one line; all these are equally units, though some contain several of the others. And in each instance it is plain the unit relates to some particular combination of ideas arbitrarily put together by the mind.

13. Unity I know some will have to be a simple or uncompounded idea accompanying all other ideas into the mind. That I have any such idea answering the word "unity" I do not find; and if I had, methinks I could not miss finding it; on the contrary, it should be the most familiar to my understanding, since it is said to accompany all other ideas and to be perceived by all the ways of sensation and reflection. To say no more, it is an *abstract idea.*

14. I shall further add that, after the same manner as modern philosophers prove certain sensible qualities to have no existence in matter, or without the mind, the same thing may be likewise proved of all other sensible qualities whatsoever. Thus, for instance, it is said that heat and cold are affections only of the mind, and not at all patterns of real beings existing in the corporeal substances which excite them, for that the same body which appears cold to one hand seems warm to another. Now, why may we not as well argue that figure and extension are not patterns or resemblances of qualities existing in matter, because to the same eye at different stations, or eyes of a different texture at the same station, they appear various and cannot, therefore, be the images of anything settled and determinate without the mind? Again, it is proved that sweetness is not really in the sapid thing, because, the thing remaining unaltered, the sweetness is changed into bitter, as in case of a fever or otherwise vitiated palate. Is it not as reasonable to say that motion is not without the mind, since if the succession of ideas in the mind become swifter, the motion, it is acknowledged, shall appear slower without any alteration in any external object?

15. In short, let anyone consider those arguments which are thought manifestly to prove that colors and tastes exist only in the mind, and he shall find they may with equal force be brought to prove the same thing of extension, figure, and motion. Though it must be confessed this method of arguing does not so much prove that there is no extension or color in an outward object as that we do not know by sense which is the true extension or color of the object. But the arguments foregoing plainly show it to be impossible that any color or extension at all, or other sensible quality whatsoever, should exist in an unthinking subject without the mind, or, in truth, that there should be any such thing as an outward object.

16. But let us examine a little the received opinion.—It is said extension is a mode or accident of matter, and that matter is the *substratum* that supports it. Now I desire that you

would explain what is meant by matter's "supporting" extension. Say you, I have no idea of matter and, therefore, cannot explain it. I answer, though you have no positive, yet, if you have any meaning at all, you must at least have a relative idea of matter; though you know not what it is, yet you must be supposed to know what relation it bears to accidents, and what is meant by its supporting them. It is evident "support" cannot here be taken in its usual or literal sense—as when we say that pillars support a building; in what sense therefore must it be taken?

17. If we inquire into what the most accurate philosophers declare themselves to mean by "material substance," we shall find them acknowledge they have no other meaning annexed to those sounds but the idea of being in general together with the relative notion of its supporting accidents. The general idea of being appears to me the most abstract and incomprehensible of all other; and as for its supporting accidents, this, as we have just now observed, cannot be understood in the common sense of those words; it must, therefore, be taken in some other sense, but what that is they do not explain. So that when I consider the two parts or branches which make the signification of the words "material substance," I am convinced there is no distinct meaning annexed to them. But why should we trouble ourselves any further in discussing this material *substratum* or support of figure and motion and other sensible qualities? Does it not suppose they have an existence without the mind? And is not this a direct repugnancy and altogether inconceivable?

18. But, though it were possible that solid, figured, movable substances may exist without the mind, corresponding to the ideas we have of bodies, yet how is it possible for us to know this? Either we must know it by sense or by reason. As for our senses, by them we have the knowledge only of our sensations, ideas, or those things that are immediately perceived by sense, call them what you will; but they do not inform us that things exist without the mind, or unperceived, like to those which are perceived. This the materialists themselves acknowledge. It remains therefore that if we have any knowledge at all of external things, it must be by reason, inferring their existence from what is immediately perceived by sense. But what reason can induce us to believe the existence of bodies without the mind, from what we perceive, since the very patrons of matter themselves do not pretend there is any necessary connection betwixt them and our ideas? I say it is granted on all hands (and what happens in dreams, frenzies, and the like, puts it beyond dispute) that it is possible we might be affected with all the ideas we have now, though no bodies existed without resembling them. Hence it is evident the supposition of external bodies is not necessary for the producing our ideas; since it is granted they are produced sometimes, and might possibly be produced always in the same order we see them in at present, without their concurrence.

19. But though we might possibly have all our sensations without them, yet perhaps it may be thought easier to conceive and explain the manner of their production by supposing external bodies in their likeness rather than otherwise; and so it might be at least probable there are such things as bodies that excite their ideas in our minds. But neither can this be said, for, though we give the materialists their external bodies, they by their own confession are never the nearer knowing how our ideas are produced, since they own themselves unable to comprehend in what manner body can act upon spirit, or how it is possible it should imprint any idea in the mind. Hence it is evident the production of ideas or sensations in our minds can be no reason why we should suppose matter or corporeal substances, since that is acknowledged to remain equally inexplicable with or without this supposition. If therefore it were possible for bodies to exist without the mind, yet to hold they do so must needs be a very precarious opinion, since it is to suppose, without any reason at all, that

God has created innumerable beings that are entirely useless and serve to no manner of purpose.

20. In short, if there were external bodies, it is impossible we should ever come to know it; and if there were not, we might have the very same reasons to think there were that we have now. Suppose—what no one can deny possible—an intelligence without the help of external bodies, to be affected with the same train of sensations or ideas that you are, imprinted in the same order and with like vividness in his mind. I ask whether that intelligence has not all the reason to believe the existence of corporeal substances, represented by his ideas and exciting them in his mind, that you can possibly have for believing the same thing? Of this there can be no question—which one consideration is enough to make any reasonable person suspect the strength of whatever arguments he may think himself to have for the existence of bodies without the mind.

21. Were it necessary to add any further proof against the existence of matter after what has been said, I could instance several of those errors and difficulties (not to mention impieties) which have sprung from that tenet. It has occasioned numberless controversies and disputes in philosophy, and not a few of far greater moment in religion. But I shall not enter into the detail of them in this place as well because I think arguments a posteriori are unnecessary for confirming what has been, if I mistake not, sufficiently demonstrated a priori, as because I shall hereafter find occasion to speak somewhat of them.

22. I am afraid I have given cause to think me needlessly prolix in handling this subject. For to what purpose is it to dilate on that which may be demonstrated with the utmost evidence in a line or two to anyone that is capable of the least reflection? It is but looking into your own thoughts, and so trying whether you can conceive it possible for a sound, or figure, or motion, or color to exist without the mind or unperceived. This easy trial may make you see that what you contend for is a downright contradiction. Insomuch that I am content to put the whole upon this issue: if you can but conceive it possible for one extended movable substance, or, in general, for any one idea, or anything like an idea, to exist otherwise than in a mind perceiving it, I shall readily give up the cause. And, as for all that compages of external bodies which you contend for, I shall grant you its existence, though you cannot either give me any reason why you believe it exists, or assign any use to it when it is supposed to exist. I say the bare possibility of your opinion's being true shall pass for an argument that it is so.

23. But, say you, surely there is nothing easier than to imagine trees, for instance, in a park, or books existing in a closet, and nobody by to perceive them. I answer you may so, there is no difficulty in it; but what is all this, I beseech you, more than framing in your mind certain ideas which you call books and trees, and at the same time omitting to frame the idea of anyone that may perceive them? But do not you yourself perceive or think of them all the while? This therefore is nothing to the purpose; it only shows you have the power of imagining or forming ideas in your mind; but it does not show that you can conceive it possible the objects of your thought may exist without the mind. To make out this, it is necessary that you conceive them existing unconceived or unthought of, which is a manifest repugnancy. When we do our utmost to conceive the existence of external bodies, we are all the while only contemplating our own ideas. But the mind, taking no notice of itself, is deluded to think it can and does conceive bodies existing unthought of or without the mind, though at the same time they are apprehended by or exist in itself. A little attention will discover to anyone the truth and evidence of what is here said, and make it unnecessary to insist on any other proofs against the existence of *material substance.*

24. It is very obvious, upon the least inquiry into our own thoughts, to know whether

it be possible for us to understand what is meant by "the absolute existence of sensible objects in themselves, or without the mind." To me it is evident those words mark out either a direct contradiction or else nothing at all. And to convince others of this, I know no readier or fairer way than to entreat they would calmly attend to their own thoughts; and if by this attention the emptiness or repugnancy of those expressions does appear, surely nothing more is requisite for their conviction. It is on this, therefore, that I insist, to wit, that "the absolute existence of unthinking things" are words without a meaning, or which include a contradiction. This is what I repeat and inculcate, and earnestly recommend to the attentive thoughts of the reader.

25. All our ideas, sensations, or the things which we perceive, by whatsoever names they may be distinguished, are visibly inactive—there is nothing of power or agency included in them. So that one idea or object of thought cannot produce or make any alteration in another. To be satisfied of the truth of this, there is nothing else requisite but a bare observation of our ideas. For since they and every part of them exist only in the mind, it follows that there is nothing in them but what is perceived; but whoever shall attend to his ideas, whether of sense or reflection, will not perceive in them any power or activity; there is, therefore, no such thing contained in them. A little attention will discover to us that the very being of an idea implies passiveness and inertness in it, insomuch that it is impossible for an idea to do anything or, strictly speaking, to be the cause of anything; neither can it be the resemblance or pattern of any active being, as is evident from sec. 8. Whence it plainly follows that extension, figure, and motion cannot be the cause of our sensations. To say, therefore, that these are the effects of powers resulting from the configuration, number, motion, and size of corpuscles must certainly be false.

26. We perceive a continual succession of ideas, some are anew excited, others are changed or totally disappear. There is, therefore, some cause of these ideas, whereon they depend and which produces and changes them. That this cause cannot be any quality or idea or combination of ideas is clear from the preceding section. It must therefore be a substance; but it has been shown that there is no corporeal or material substance; it remains, therefore, that the cause of ideas is an incorporeal, active substance or spirit.

27. A spirit is one simple, undivided, active being—as it perceives ideas it is called "the understanding," and as it produces or otherwise operates about them it is called "the will." Hence there can be no *idea* formed of a soul or spirit; for all ideas whatever, being passive and inert (*vide* sec. 25), they cannot represent unto us, by way of image or likeness, that which acts. A little attention will make it plain to anyone that to have an idea which shall be like that active principle of motion and change of ideas is absolutely impossible. Such is the nature of *spirit,* or that which acts, that it cannot be of itself perceived, but only by the effects which it produces. If any man shall doubt of the truth of what is here delivered, let him but reflect and try if he can frame the idea of any power or active being, and whether he has ideas of two principal powers marked by the names "will" and "understanding," distinct from each other as well as from a third idea of substance or being in general, with a relative notion of its supporting or being the subject of the aforesaid powers—which is signified by the name "soul" or "spirit." This is what some hold; but, so far as I can see, the words "will," "soul," "spirit" do not stand for different ideas or, in truth, for any idea at all, but for something which is very different from ideas, and which, being an agent, cannot be like unto, or represented by, any idea whatsoever. [Though it must be owned at the same time that we have some notion of soul, spirit, and the operations of the mind, such as willing, loving, hating—in as much as we know or understand the meaning of those words.]

28. I find I can excite ideas in my mind at pleasure, and vary and shift the scene as oft

as I think fit. It is no more than willing, and straightway this or that idea arises in my fancy; and by the same power it is obliterated and makes way for another. This making and unmaking of ideas does very properly denominate the mind active. Thus much is certain and grounded on experience; but when we talk of unthinking agents or of exciting ideas exclusive of volition, we only amuse ourselves with words.

29. But, whatever power I may have over my own thoughts, I find the ideas actually perceived by sense have not a like dependence on my will. When in broad daylight I open my eyes, it is not in my power to choose whether I shall see or no, or to determine what particular objects shall present themselves to my view; and so likewise as to the hearing and other senses; the ideas imprinted on them are not creatures of my will. There is therefore some *other* will or spirit that produces them.

30. The ideas of sense are more strong, lively, and distinct than those of the imagination; they have likewise a steadiness, order, and coherence, and are not excited at random, as those which are the effects of human wills often are, but in a regular train or series, the admirable connection whereof sufficiently testifies the wisdom and benevolence of its Author. Now the set rules or established methods wherein the mind we depend on excites in us the ideas of sense are called "the laws of nature"; and these we learn by experience, which teaches us that such and such ideas are attended with such and such other ideas in the ordinary course of things.

31. This gives us a sort of foresight which enables us to regulate our actions for the benefit of life. And without this we should be eternally at a loss; we could not know how to act anything that might procure us the least pleasure or remove the least pain of sense. That food nourishes, sleep refreshes, and fire warms us; that to sow in the seedtime is the way to reap in the harvest; and in general that to obtain such or such ends, such or such means are conducive—all this we know, not by discovering any necessary connection between our ideas, but only by the observation of the settled laws of nature, without which we should be all in uncertainty and confusion, and a grown man no more know how to manage himself in the affairs of life than an infant just born.

32. And yet this consistent, uniform working which so evidently displays the goodness and wisdom of that Governing Spirit whose Will constitutes the laws of nature, is so far from leading our thoughts to Him that it rather sends them awandering after second causes. For when we perceive certain ideas of sense constantly followed by other ideas, and we know this is not of our own doing, we forthwith attribute power and agency to the ideas themselves and make one the cause of another, than which nothing can be more absurd and unintelligible. Thus, for example, having observed that when we perceive by sight a certain round, luminous figure, we at the same time perceive by touch the idea or sensation called "heat," we do from thence conclude the sun to be the cause of heat. And in like manner perceiving the motion and collision of bodies to be attended with sound, we are inclined to think the latter an effect of the former.

33. The ideas imprinted on the senses by the Author of Nature are called "real things"; and those excited in the imagination, being less regular, vivid, and constant, are more properly termed "ideas" or "images of things" which they copy and represent. But then our sensations, be they never so vivid and distinct, are nevertheless ideas, that is, they exist in the mind, or are perceived by it, as truly as the ideas of its own framing. The ideas of sense are allowed to have more reality in them, that is, to be more strong, orderly, and coherent than the creatures of the mind; but this is no argument that they exist without the mind. They are also less dependent on the spirit, or thinking substance which perceives them, in that they are excited by the will of another and more powerful spirit; yet still they are

ideas; and certainly no idea, whether faint or strong, can exist otherwise than in a mind perceiving it.

34. Before we proceed any further it is necessary to spend some time in answering objections which may probably be made against the principles hitherto laid down. In doing of which, if I seem too prolix to those of quick apprehensions, I hope it may be pardoned, since all men do not equally apprehend things of this nature, and I am willing to be understood by everyone.

First, then, it will be objected that by the foregoing principles all that is real and substantial in nature is banished out of the world, and instead thereof a chimerical scheme of *ideas* takes place. All things that exist, exist only in the mind, that is, they are purely notional. What therefore becomes of the sun, moon, and stars? What must we think of houses, rivers, mountains, trees, stones, nay, even of our own bodies? Are all these but so many chimeras and illusions on the fancy? To all which, and whatever else of the same sort may be objected, I answer that by the principles premised we are not deprived of any one thing in nature. Whatever we see, feel, hear, or anywise conceive or understand remains as secure as ever, and is as real as ever. There is a *rerum natura,* and the distinction between realities and chimeras retains its full force. This is evident from secs. 29, 30, and 33, where we have shown what is meant by "real things" in opposition to "chimeras" or ideas of our own framing; but then they both equally exist in the mind, and in that sense they are alike *ideas.*

35. I do not argue against the existence of any one thing that we can apprehend either by sense or reflection. That the things I see with my eyes and touch with my hands do exist, really exist, I make not the least question. The only thing whose existence we deny is that which philosophers call matter or corporeal substance. And in doing of this there is no damage done to the rest of mankind, who, I dare say, will never miss it. The atheist indeed will want the color of an empty name to support his impiety; and the philosophers may possibly find they have lost a great handle for trifling and disputation.

36. If any man thinks this detracts from the existence or reality of things, he is very far from understanding what has been premised in the plainest terms I could think of. Take here an abstract of what has been said: there are spiritual substances, minds, or human souls, which will or excite ideas in themselves at pleasure, but these are faint, weak, and unsteady in respect of others they perceive by sense—which, being impressed upon them according to certain rules or laws of nature, speak themselves the effects of a mind more powerful and wise than human spirits. These latter are said to have more *reality* in them than the former—by which is meant that they are more affecting, orderly, and distinct, and that they are not fictions of the mind perceiving them. And in this sense the sun that I see by day is the real sun, and that which I imagine by night is the idea of the former. In the sense here given of "reality" it is evident that every vegetable, star, mineral, and in general each part of the mundane system, is as much a *real being* by our principles as by any other. Whether others mean anything by the term "reality" different from what I do, I entreat them to look into their own thought and see.

37. It will be urged that thus much at least is true, to wit, that we take away all corporeal substances. To this my answer is that if the word "substance" be taken in the vulgar sense—for a combination of sensible qualities, such as extension, solidity, weight, and the like—this we cannot be accused of taking away; but if it be taken in a philosophic sense—for the support of accidents or qualities without the mind—then indeed I acknowledge that we take it away, if one may be said to take away that which never had any existence, not even in the imagination.

38. But, say you, it sounds very harsh to say we eat and drink ideas, and are clothed

with ideas. I acknowledge it does so—the word "idea" not being used in common discourse to signify the several combinations of sensible qualities which are called "things"; and it is certain that any expression which varies from the familiar use of language will seem harsh and ridiculous. But this does not concern the truth of the proposition which, in other words, is no more than to say we are fed and clothed with those things which we perceive immediately by our senses. The hardness or softness, the color, taste, warmth, figure, and suchlike qualities, which combined together constitute the several sorts of victuals and apparel, have been shown to exist only in the mind that perceives them; and this is all that is meant by calling them "ideas," which word if it was as ordinarily used as "thing," would sound no harsher nor more ridiculous than it. I am not for disputing about the propriety, but the truth of the expression. If therefore you agree with me that we eat and drink and are clad with the immediate objects of sense, which cannot exist unperceived or without the mind, I shall readily grant it is more proper or conformable to custom that they should be called "things" rather than "ideas."

39. If it be demanded why I make use of the word "idea," and do not rather in compliance with custom call them "things," I answer I do it for two reasons; first, because the term "thing" in contradistinction to "idea" is generally supposed to denote somewhat existing without the mind; secondly, because "thing" has a more comprehensive signification than "idea," including spirits or thinking things as well as ideas. Since therefore the objects of sense exist only in the mind and are withal thoughtless and inactive, I chose to mark them by the word "idea," which implies those properties.

40. But, say what we can, someone perhaps may be apt to reply he will still believe his senses, and never suffer any arguments, how plausible soever, to prevail over the certainty of them. Be it so; assert the evidence of sense as high as you please, we are willing to do the same. That what I see, hear, and feel does exist—that is to say, is perceived by me—I no more doubt than I do of my own being. But I do not see how the testimony of sense can be alleged as a proof for the existence of anything which is not perceived by sense. We are not for having any man turn skeptic and disbelieve his senses; on the contrary, we give them all the stress and assurance imaginable; nor are there any principles more opposite to skepticism than those we have laid down, as shall be hereafter clearly shown.

41. *Secondly*, it will be objected that there is a great difference betwixt real fire, for instance, and the idea of fire, betwixt dreaming or imagining oneself burned, and actually being so. This and the like may be urged in opposition to our tenets. To all which the answer is evident from what has been already said; and I shall only add in this place that if real fire be very different from the idea of fire, so also is the real pain that it occasions very different from the idea of the same pain, and yet nobody will pretend that real pain either is, or can possibly be, in an unperceiving thing, or without the mind, any more than its idea.

42. *Thirdly*, it will be objected that we see things actually without or at a distance from us, and which, consequently, do not exist in the mind, it being absurd that those things which are seen at the distance of several miles should be as near to us as our own thoughts. In answer to this I desire it may be considered that in a dream we do oft perceive things as existing at a great distance off, and yet for all that those things are acknowledged to have their existence only in the mind.

43. But for the fuller clearing of this point it may be worth while to consider how it is that we perceive distance and things placed at a distance by sight. For that we should in truth see external space, and bodies actually existing in it, some nearer, others farther off, seems to carry with it some opposition to what has been said of their existing nowhere without the mind. The consideration of this difficulty it was that gave birth to my *Essay*

Towards a New Theory of Vision, which was published not long since, wherein it is shown that distance or outness is neither immediately of itself perceived by sight, nor yet apprehended or judged of by lines and angles, or anything that has a necessary connection with it; but that it is only suggested to our thoughts by certain visible ideas and sensations attending vision, which in their own nature have no manner of similitude or relation either with distance or things placed at a distance; but by a connection taught us by experience they come to signify and suggest them to us after the same manner that words of any language suggest the ideas they are made to stand for; insomuch that a man born blind and afterwards made to see would not, at first sight, think the things he saw to be without his mind or at any distance from him. See sec. 41 of the forementioned treatise.

44. The ideas of sight and touch make two species entirely distinct and heterogeneous. The former are marks and prognostics of the latter. That the proper objects of sight neither exist without mind, nor are the images of external things, was shown even in that treatise. Though throughout the same the contrary be supposed true of tangible objects—not that to suppose that vulgar error was necessary for establishing the notion therein laid down, but because it was beside my purpose to examine and refute it in a discourse concerning *vision.* So that in strict truth the ideas of sight, when we apprehend by them distance and things placed at a distance, do not suggest or mark out to us things actually existing at a distance, but only admonish us what ideas of touch will be imprinted in our minds at such and such distances of time, and in consequence of such and such actions. It is, I say, evident from what has been said in the foregoing parts of this treatise, and in sec. 147 and elsewhere of the *Essay Concerning Vision,* that visible ideas are the language whereby the Governing Spirit on whom we depend informs us what tangible ideas he is about to imprint upon us in case we excite this or that motion in our own bodies. But for a fuller information in this point I refer to the *Essay* itself.

45. *Fourthly,* it will be objected that from the foregoing principles it follows things are every moment annihilated and created anew. The objects of sense exist only when they are perceived; the trees, therefore, are in the garden, or the chairs in the parlor, no longer than while there is somebody by to perceive them. Upon shutting my eyes all the furniture in the room is reduced to nothing, and barely upon opening them it is again created. In answer to all which I refer the reader to what has been said in secs. 3, 4, etc., and desire he will consider whether he means anything by the actual existence of an idea distinct from its being perceived. For my part, after the nicest inquiry I could make, I am not able to discover that anything else is meant by those words; and I once more entreat the reader to sound his own thoughts and not suffer himself to be imposed on by words. If he can conceive it possible either for his ideas or their archetypes to exist without being perceived, then I give up the cause; but if he cannot, he will acknowledge it is unreasonable for him to stand up in defense of he knows not what and pretend to charge on me as an absurdity the not assenting to those propositions which at bottom have no meaning in them.

46. It will not be amiss to observe how far the received principles of philosophy are themselves chargeable with those pretended absurdities. It is thought strangely absurd that upon closing my eyelids all the visible objects around me should be reduced to nothing; and yet is not this what philosophers commonly acknowledge when they agree on all hands that light and colors, which alone are the proper and immediate objects of sight, are mere sensations that exist no longer than they are perceived? Again, it may to some, perhaps, seem very incredible that things should be every moment creating, yet this very notion is commonly taught in the Schools. For the Schoolmen, though they acknowledge the existence of matter, and that the whole mundane fabric is framed out of it, are nevertheless of

opinion that it cannot subsist without the divine conservation, which by them is expounded to be a continual creation.

47. Further, a little thought will discover to us that though we allow the existence of matter or corporeal substance, yet it will unavoidably follow, from the principles which are now generally admitted, that the particular bodies of what kind soever do none of them exist whilst they are not perceived. For it is evident from sec. 11 and the following sections that the matter philosophers contend for is an incomprehensible somewhat, which has none of those particular qualities whereby the bodies falling under our senses are distinguished one from another. But, to make this more plain, it must be remarked that the infinite divisibility of matter is now universally allowed, at least by the most approved and considerable philosophers, who on the received principles demonstrate it beyond all exception. Hence it follows that there is an infinite number of parts in each particle of matter which are not perceived by sense. The reason, therefore, that any particular body seems to be of a finite magnitude, or exhibits only a finite number of parts to sense, is not because it contains no more, since in itself it contains an infinite number of parts, but because the sense is not acute enough to discern them. In proportion, therefore, as the sense is rendered more acute, it perceives a greater number of parts in the object; that is, the object appears greater, and its figure varies, those parts in its extremities which were before unperceivable appearing now to bound it in very different lines and angles from those perceived by an obtuser sense. And at length, after various changes of size and shape, when the sense becomes infinitely acute, the body shall seem infinite. During all which there is no alteration in the body, but only in the sense. Each body, therefore, considered in itself, is infinitely extended, and consequently void of all shape or figure. From which it follows that, though we should grant the existence of matter to be ever so certain, yet it is withal as certain—the materialists themselves are by their own principles forced to acknowledge—that neither the particular bodies perceived by sense, nor anything like them, exists without the mind. Matter, I say, and each particle thereof, is according to them infinite and shapeless, and it is the mind that frames all that variety of bodies which compose the visible world, any one whereof does not exist longer than it is perceived.

48. If we consider it, the objection proposed in sec. 45 will not be found reasonably charged on the principles we have premised, so as in truth to make any objection at all against our notions. For though we hold indeed the objects of sense to be nothing else but ideas which cannot exist unperceived, yet we may not hence conclude they have no existence except only while they are perceived by us, since there may be some other spirit that perceives them, though we do not. Wherever bodies are said to have no existence without the mind, I would not be understood to mean this or that particular mind, but all minds whatsoever. It does not therefore follow from the foregoing principles that bodies are annihilated and created every moment or exist not at all during the intervals between our perception of them.

49. *Fifthly,* it may perhaps be *objected* that if extension and figure exist only in the mind, it follows that the mind is extended and figured, since extension is a mode or attribute which (to speak with the Schools) is predicated of the *subject* in which it exists. I answer, those qualities are *in the mind* only as they are perceived by it—that is, not by way of *mode* or *attribute,* but only by way of *idea;* and it no more follows the soul or mind is extended, because extension exists in it alone, than it does that it is red or blue, because those colors are on all hands acknowledged to exist in it, and nowhere else. As to what philosophers say of 'subject' and 'mode,' that seems groundless and unintelligible. For instance, in this proposition—'a die is hard, extended and square, they will have it that the word "die"

denotes a subject or substance distinct from the hardness, extension, and figure which are predicated of it, and in which they exist. This I cannot comprehend; to me a die seems to be nothing distinct from those things which are termed its modes or accidents. And to say a die is hard, extended, and square is not to attribute those qualities to a subject distinct from and supporting them, but only an explication of the meaning of the word "die."

50. *Sixthly,* you will say there have been a great many things explained by matter and motion; take away these and you destroy the whole corpuscular philosophy and undermine those mechanical principles which have been applied with so much success to account for the phenomena. In short, whatever advances have been made, either by ancient or modern philosophers, in the study of nature do all proceed on the supposition that corporeal substance or matter does really exist. To this I answer that there is not any one phenomenon explained on that supposition which may not as well be explained without it, as might easily be made appear by an induction of particulars. To explain the phenomena is all one as to show why, upon such and such occasions, we are affected with such and such ideas. But how matter should operate on a spirit, or produce any idea in it, is what no philosopher will pretend to explain; it is therefore evident there can be no use of matter in natural philosophy. Besides, they who attempt to account for things do it not by corporeal substance, but by figure, motion, and other qualities, which are in truth no more than mere ideas and, therefore, cannot be the cause of anything, as has been already shown. See sec. 25.

51. *Seventhly,* it will upon this be demanded whether it does not seem absurd to take away natural causes and ascribe everything to the immediate operation of spirits? We must no longer say, upon these principles, that fire heats, or water cools, but that a spirit heats, and so forth. Would not a man be deservedly laughed at who should talk after this manner? I answer, he would so; in such things we ought to "think with the learned and speak with the vulgar." They who by demonstration are convinced of the truth of the Copernican system do nevertheless say, "the sun rises," "the sun sets," or "comes to the meridian"; and if they affected a contrary style in common talk it would without doubt appear very ridiculous. A little reflection on what is here said will make it manifest that the common use of language would receive no manner of alteration or disturbance from the admission of our tenets.

52. In the ordinary affairs of life, any phrases may be retained so long as they excite in us proper sentiments or dispositions to act in such a manner as is necessary for our well-being, how false soever they may be if taken in a strict and speculative sense. Nay, this is unavoidable, since, propriety being regulated by custom, language is suited to the received opinions, which are not always the truest. Hence it is impossible, even in the most rigid, philosophic reasonings, so far to alter the bent and genius of the tongue we speak, as never to give a handle for cavilers to pretend difficulties and inconsistencies. But a fair and ingenuous reader will collect the sense from the scope and tenor and connection of a discourse, making allowances for those inaccurate modes of speech which use has made inevitable.

53. As to the opinion that there are no corporeal causes, this has been heretofore maintained by some of the Schoolmen, as it is of late by others among the modern philosophers who, though they allow matter to exist, yet will have God alone to be the immediate efficient cause of all things. These men saw that amongst all the objects of sense there was none which had any power or activity included in it, and that by consequence this was likewise true of whatever bodies they supposed to exist without the mind, like unto the immediate objects of sense. But then, that they should suppose an innumerable multitude of created beings which they acknowledge are not capable of producing any one effect in nature, and which therefore are made to no manner of purpose, since God might have done everything

as well without them—this I say, though we should allow it possible, must yet be a very unaccountable and extravagant supposition.

54. In the *eighth* place, the universal concurrent assent of mankind may be thought by some an invincible argument in behalf of matter, or the existence of external things. Must we suppose the whole world to be mistaken? And if so, what cause can be assigned of so widespread and predominant an error? I answer, first, that, upon a narrow inquiry, it will not perhaps be found so many as is imagined do really believe the existence of matter or things without the mind. Strictly speaking, to believe that which involves a contradiction, or has no meaning in it, is impossible; and whether the foregoing expressions are not of that sort, I refer it to the impartial examination of the reader. In one sense, indeed, men may be said to believe that matter exists, that is, they act as if the immediate cause of their sensations, which affects them every moment and is so nearly present to them, were some senseless unthinking being. But that they should clearly apprehend any meaning marked by those words, and form thereof a settled speculative opinion, is what I am not able to conceive. This is not the only instance wherein men impose upon themselves, by imagining they believe those propositions they have often heard, though at bottom they have no meaning in them.

55. But secondly, though we should grant a notion to be ever so universally and stead-fastly adhered to, yet this is but a weak argument of its truth to whoever considers what a vast number of prejudices and false opinions are everywhere embraced with the utmost tenaciousness by the unreflecting (which are the far greater) part of mankind. There was a time when the antipodes and motion of the earth were looked upon as monstrous absurdities even by men of learning; and if it be considered what a small proportion they bear to the rest of mankind, we shall find that at this day those notions have gained but a very inconsiderable footing in the world.

56. But it is demanded that we assign a cause of this prejudice and account for its obtaining in the world. To this I answer that men, knowing they perceived several ideas whereof they themselves were not the authors—as not being excited from within nor de-pending on the operation of their wills—this made them maintain those ideas, or objects of perception, had an existence independent of and without the mind, without ever dream-ing that a contradiction was involved in those words. But philosophers having plainly seen that the immediate objects of perception do not exist without the mind, they in some degree corrected the mistake of the vulgar, but at the same time run into another which seems no less absurd, to wit, that there are certain objects really existing without the mind or having a subsistence distinct from being perceived, of which our ideas are only images or resem-blances, imprinted by those objects on the mind. And this notion of the philosophers owes its origin to the same cause with the former, namely, their being conscious that they were not the authors of their own sensations, which they evidently knew were imprinted from without, and which therefore must have some cause distinct from the minds on which they are imprinted.

57. But why they should suppose the ideas of sense to be excited in us by things in their likeness, and not rather have recourse to *spirit* which alone can act, may be accounted for, first because they were not aware of the repugnancy there is, as well in supposing things like unto our ideas existing without, as in attributing to them power or activity. Secondly, be-cause the supreme spirit which excites those ideas in our minds is not marked out and limited to our view by any particular finite collection of sensible ideas, as human agents are by their size, complexion, limbs, and motions. And thirdly, because His operations are regular and uniform. Whenever the course of nature is interrupted by a miracle, men are

ready to own the presence of a superior agent. But when we see things go on in the ordinary course, they do not excite in us any reflection; their order and concatenation, though it be an argument of the greatest wisdom, power, and goodness in their Creator, is yet so constant and familiar to us that we do not think them the immediate effects of a *free spirit,* especially since inconstancy and mutability in acting, though it be an imperfection, is looked on as a mark of *freedom.*

58. *Tenthly,* it will be objected that the notions we advance are inconsistent with several sound truths in philosophy and mathematics. For example, the motion of the earth is now universally admitted by astronomers as a truth grounded on the clearest and most convincing reasons. But on the foregoing principles there can be no such thing. For, motion being only an idea, it follows that if it be not perceived it exists not; but the motion of the earth is not perceived by sense. I answer, that tenet, if rightly understood, will be found to agree with the principles we have premised, for the question whether the earth moves or no amounts in reality to no more than this, to wit, whether we have reason to conclude, from what has been observed by astronomers, that if we were placed in such and such circumstances, and such or such a position and distance both from the earth and sun, we should perceive the former to move among the choir of the planets, and appearing in all respects like one of them; and this, by the established rules of nature which we have no reason to mistrust, is reasonably collected from the phenomena.

59. We may, from the experience we have had of the train and succession of ideas in our minds, often make, I will not say uncertain conjectures, but sure and well-grounded predictions concerning the ideas we shall be affected with pursuant to a great train of actions, and be enabled to pass a right judgment of what would have appeared to us in case we were placed in circumstances very different from those we are in at present. Herein consists the knowledge of nature, which may preserve its use and certainty very consistently with what has been said. It will be easy to apply this to whatever objections of the like sort may be drawn from the magnitude of the stars or any other discoveries in astronomy or nature.

60. In the *eleventh* place, it will be demanded to what purpose serves that curious organization of plants and the admirable mechanism in the parts of animals; might not vegetables grow and shoot forth leaves and blossoms, and animals perform all their motions as well without as with all that variety of internal parts so elegantly contrives and put together; which, being ideas, have nothing powerful or operative in them, nor have any necessary connection with the effects ascribed to them? If it be a spirit that immediately produces every effect by a fiat or act of his will, we must think all that is fine and artificial in the works, whether of man or nature, to be made in vain. By this doctrine, though an artist has made the spring and wheels, and every movement of a watch, and adjusted them in such a manner as he knew would produce the motions he designed, yet he must think all this done to no purpose, and that it is an Intelligence which directs the index and points to the hour of the day. If so, why may not the Intelligence do it, without his being at the pains of making the movements and putting them together? Why does not an empty case serve as well as another? And how comes it to pass that whenever there is any fault in the going of a watch, there is some corresponding disorder to be found in the movements, which being mended by a skillful hand all is right again? The like may be said of all the clockwork of nature, great part whereof is so wonderfully fine and subtle as scarce to be discerned by the best microscope. In short, it will be asked how, upon our principles, any tolerable account can be given, or any final cause assigned, of an innumerable multitude of bodies and machines, framed with the most exquisite art, which in the common philosophy have very apposite uses assigned them and serve to explain abundance of phenomena?

61. To all which I answer, first, that though there were some difficulties relating to the administration of Providence, and the uses by it assigned to the several parts of nature which I could not solve by the foregoing principles, yet this objection could be of small weight against the truth and certainty of those things which may be proved a priori with the utmost evidence. Secondly, but neither are the received principles free from the like difficulties, for it may still be demanded to what end God should take those roundabout methods of effecting things by instruments and machines which no one can deny might have been effected by the mere command of His will without all that apparatus; nay, if we narrowly consider it, we shall find the objection may be retorted with greater force on those who hold the existence of those machines without the mind, for it has been made evident that solidity, bulk, figure, motion, and the like have no *activity* or *efficacy* in them so as to be capable of producing any one effect in nature. See sec. 25. Whoever, therefore, supposes them to exist (allowing the supposition possible) when they are not perceived does it manifestly to no purpose, since the only use that is assigned to them, as they exist unperceived, is that they produce those perceivable effects which in truth cannot be ascribed to anything but spirit.

62. But, to come nearer the difficulty, it must be observed that though the fabrication of all those parts and organs be not absolutely necessary to the producing any effect, yet it is necessary to the producing of things in a constant regular way according to the laws of nature. There are certain general laws that run through the whole chain of natural effects; these are learned by the observation and study of nature and are by men applied as well to the framing artificial things for the use and ornament of life as to the explaining the various phenomena—which explication consists only in showing the conformity any particular phenomenon has to the general laws of nature or, which is the same thing, in discovering the *uniformity* there is in the production of natural effects, as will be evident to whoever shall attend to the several instances wherein philosophers pretend to account for appearances. That there is a great and conspicuous use in these regular, constant methods of working observed by the Supreme Agent has been shown in sec. 31. And it is no less visible that a particular size, figure, motion, and disposition of parts are necessary, though not absolutely, to the producing any effect, yet to the producing it according to the standing mechanical laws of nature. Thus, for instance, it cannot be denied that God, or the Intelligence which sustains and rules the ordinary course of things, might, if He were minded to produce a miracle, cause all the motions on the dial-plate of a watch, though nobody had ever made the movements and put them in it; but yet, if He will act agreeably to the rules of mechanism by Him for wise ends established and maintained in the Creation, it is necessary that those actions of the watchmaker, whereby he makes the movements and rightly adjusts them, precede the production of the aforesaid motions, as also that any disorder in them be attended with the perception of some corresponding disorder in the movements, which, being once corrected, all is right again.

63. It may indeed on some occasions be necessary that the Author of Nature display His overruling power in producing some appearance out of the ordinary series of things. Such exceptions from the general rules of nature are proper to surprise and awe men into an acknowledgment of the Divine Being; but then they are to be used but seldom, otherwise there is a plain reason why they should fail of that effect. Besides, God seems to choose the convincing our reason of His attributes by the works of nature, which discover so much harmony and contrivance in their make and are such plain indications of wisdom and beneficence in their Author rather than to astonish us into a belief of His being by anomalous and surprising events.

64. To set this matter in a yet clearer light, I shall observe that what has been objected

in sec. 60 amounts in reality to no more than this: ideas are not anyhow and at random produced, there being a certain order and connection between them, like to that of cause and effect; there are also several combinations of them made in a very regular and artificial manner, which seem like so many instruments in the hand of nature that, being hidden, as it were, behind the scenes, have a secret operation in producing those appearances which are seen on the theater of the world, being themselves discernible only to the curious eye of the philosopher. But, since one idea cannot be the cause of another, to what purpose is that connection? And, since those instruments, being barely *inefficacious perceptions* in the mind, are not subservient to the production of natural effects, it is demanded why they are made, or, in other words, what reason can be assigned why God should make us, upon a close inspection into His works, behold so great variety of ideas so artfully laid together, and so much according to rule, it not being credible that He would be at the expense (if one may so speak) of all that art and regularity to no purpose.

65. To all which my answer is, first, that the connection of ideas does not imply the relation of *cause* and *effect,* but only of a mark or *sign* with the thing *signified.* The fire which I see is not the cause of the pain I suffer upon my approaching it, but the mark that forewarns me of it. In like manner, the noise that I hear is not the effect of this or that motion or collision of the ambient bodies, but the sign thereof. Secondly, the reason why ideas are formed into machines, that is, artificial and regular combinations, is the same with that for combining letters into words. That a few original ideas may be made to signify a great number of effects and actions, it is necessary they be variously combined together. And, to the end their use be permanent and universal, these combinations must be made by *rule* and with *wise contrivance.* By this means abundance of information is conveyed unto us concerning what we are to expect from such and such actions and what methods are proper to be taken for the exciting such and such ideas, which in effect is all that I conceive to be distinctly meant when it is said that, by discerning the figure, texture, and mechanism of the inward parts of bodies, whether natural or artificial, we may attain to know the several uses and properties depending thereon, or the nature of the thing.

66. Hence it is evident that those things which, under the notion of a cause cooperating or concurring to the production of effects, are altogether inexplicable and run us into great absurdities may be very naturally explained and have a proper and obvious use assigned to them when they are considered only as marks or signs for our information. And it is the searching after and endeavoring to understand [those signs instituted by] the Author of Nature that ought to be the employment of the natural philosopher, and not the pretending to explain things by corporeal causes, which doctrine seems to have too much estranged the minds of men from that active principle, that supreme and wise Spirit "in whom we live, move, and have our being."

67. In the *twelfth* place, it may perhaps be objected that—though it be clear from what has been said that there can be no such thing as an inert, senseless, extended, solid, figured, movable substance existing without the mind, such as philosophers describe matter—yet, if any man shall leave out of his idea of *matter* the positive ideas of extension, figure, solidity, and motion and say that he means only by what word an inert, senseless substance that exists without the mind or unperceived, which is the occasion of our ideas, or at the presence whereof God is pleased to excite ideas in us—it does not appear but that matter taken in this sense may possibly exist. In answer to which I say, first, that it seems no less absurd to suppose a substance without accidents than it is to suppose accidents without a substance. But secondly, though we should grant this unknown substance may possibly exist, yet where can it be supposed to be? That it exists not in the mind is agreed; and that it exists

not in place is no less certain—since all extension exists only in the mind, as has been already proved. It remains therefore that it exists nowhere at all.

68. Let us examine a little the description that is here given us of *matter*. It neither acts, nor perceives, nor is perceived, for this is all that is meant by saying it is an inert, senseless, unknown substance; which is a definition entirely made up of negatives, excepting only the relative notion of its standing under or supporting. But then it must be observed that it supports nothing at all, and how nearly this comes to the description of a *nonentity* I desire may be considered. But, say you, it is the *unknown occasion* at the presence of which ideas are excited in us by the will of God. Now I would fain know how anything can be present to us which is neither perceivable by sense nor reflection, nor capable of producing any idea in our minds, nor is at all extended, nor has any form, nor exists in any place. The words "to be present," when thus applied, must needs be taken in some abstract and strange meaning, and which I am not able to comprehend.

69. Again, let us examine what is meant by "occasion." So far as I can gather from the common use of language, that word signifies either the agent which produces any effect or else something that is observed to accompany or go before it in the ordinary course of things. But when it is applied to matter as above described, it can be taken in neither of those senses, for matter is said to be passive and inert, and so cannot be an agent or efficient cause. It is also unperceivable, as being devoid of all sensible qualities, and so cannot be the occasion of our perceptions in the latter sense, as when the burning my finger is said to be the occasion of the pain that attends it. What therefore can be meant by calling matter an "occasion"? This term is either used in no sense at all or else in some sense very distant from its received signification.

70. You will perhaps say that matter, though it be not perceived by us, is nevertheless perceived by God, to whom it is the occasion of exciting ideas in our minds. For, say you, since we observe our sensations to be imprinted in an orderly and constant manner, it is but reasonable to suppose there are certain constant and regular occasions of their being produced. That is to say, that there are certain permanent and distinct parcels of matter, corresponding to our ideas, which, though they do not excite them in our minds or anyways immediately affect us, as being altogether passive and unperceivable to us, they are never-theless to God, by whom they are perceived, as it were, so many occasions to remind Him when and what ideas to imprint on our minds that so things may go on in a constant uniform manner.

71. In answer to this I observe that, as the notion of matter is here stated, the question is no longer concerning the existence of a thing distinct from *spirit* and *idea*, from perceiv-ing and being perceived, but whether there are not certain ideas of I know not what sort in the mind of God which are so many marks or notes that direct Him how to produce sensations in our minds in a constant and regular method—much after the same manner as a musician is directed by the notes of music to produce that harmonious train and com-position of sound which is called a "tune," though they who hear the music do not perceive the notes and may be entirely ignorant of them. But this notion of matter seems too extrava-gant to deserve a confutation. Besides, it is in effect no objection against what we have advanced, to wit, that there is no senseless, unperceived substance.

72. If we follow the light of reason we shall, from the constant uniform method of our sensations, collect the goodness and wisdom of the spirit who excites them in our minds; but this is all that I can see reasonably concluded from thence. To me, I say, it is evident that the being of a spirit infinitely wise, good, and powerful is abundantly sufficient to explain all the appearances of nature. But, as for *inert, senseless matter*, nothing that I per-

ceive has any the least connection with it or leads to the thoughts of it. And I would fain see anyone explain any the meanest phenomenon in nature by it or show any manner of reason, though in the lowest rank of probability, that he can have for its existence, or even make any tolerable sense or meaning of that supposition. For as to its being an occasion we have, I think, evidently shown that with regard to us it is no occasion. It remains therefore that it must be, if at all, the occasion to God of exciting ideas in us, and what this amounts to we have just now seen.

73. It is worth while to reflect a little on the motives which induced men to suppose the existence of *material substance;* that so having observed the gradual ceasing and expiration of those motives or reasons, we may proportionably withdraw the assent that was grounded on them. First, therefore, it was thought that color, figure, motion, and the rest of the sensible qualities or accidents did really exist without the mind; and for this reason it seemed needful to suppose some unthinking *substratum* or substance wherein they did exist, since they could not be conceived to exist by themselves. Afterwards, in process of time, men being convinced that colors, sounds, and the rest of the sensible, secondary qualities had no existence without the mind, they stripped this *substratum* or material substance of those qualities, leaving only the primary ones, figure, motion, and suchlike, which they still conceived to exist without the mind, and consequently to stand in need of a material support. But it having been shown that none even of these can possibly exist otherwise than in a spirit or mind which perceives them, it follows that we have no longer any reason to suppose the being of matter; nay, that it is utterly impossible there should be any such thing so long as that word is taken to denote an *unthinking substratum* of qualities or accidents wherein they exist without the mind.

74. But though it be allowed by the materialists themselves that matter was thought of only for the sake of supporting accidents, and, the reason entirely ceasing, one might expect the mind should naturally, and without any reluctance at all, quit the belief of what was solely grounded thereon, yet the prejudice is riveted so deeply in our thoughts that we can scarce tell how to part with it, and are therefore inclined, since the *thing* itself is indefensible, at least to retain the *name,* which we apply to I know not what abstracted and indefinite notions of being, or occasion, though without any show of reason, at least so far as I can see. For what is there on our part, or what do we perceive among all the ideas, sensations, notions which are imprinted on our minds, either by sense or reflection, from whence may be inferred the existence of an inert, thoughtless, unperceived occasion? And, on the other hand, on the part of an all-sufficient Spirit, what can there be that should make us believe or even suspect He is directed by an inert occasion to excite ideas in our minds?

75. It is a very extraordinary instance of the force of prejudice, and much to be lamented, that the mind of man retains so great a fondness, against all the evidence of reason, for a stupid, thoughtless *somewhat,* by the interposition whereof it would as it were screen itself from the Providence of God and remove him farther off from the affairs of the world. But though we do the utmost we can to secure the belief of matter, though, when reason forsakes us, we endeavor to support our opinion on the bare possibility of the thing, and though we indulge ourselves in the full scope of an imagination not regulated by reason to make out that poor possibility, yet the upshot of all is that there are certain *unknown ideas* in the mind of God; for this, if anything, is all that I conceive to be meant by "occasion" with regard to God. And this at the bottom is no longer contending for the thing, but for the name.

76. Whether, therefore, there are such ideas in the mind of God, and whether they may be called by the name "matter," I shall not dispute. But if you stick to the notion of an

unthinking substance or support of extension, motion, and other sensible qualities, then to me it is most evidently impossible there should be any such thing, since it is a plain repugnancy that those qualities should exist in or be supported by an unperceiving substance.

77. But, say you, though it be granted that there is no thoughtless support of extension and the other qualities or accidents which we perceive, yet there may, perhaps, be some inert, unperceiving substance or *substratum* of some other qualities, as incomprehensible to us as colors are to a man born blind, because we have not a sense adapted to them. But if we had a new sense, we should possibly no more doubt of their existence than a blind man made to see does of the existence of light and colors. I answer, first, if what you mean by the word "matter" be only the unknown support of unknown qualities, it is no matter whether there is such a thing or no, since it no way concerns us; and I do not see the advantage there is in disputing about we know not *what,* and we know not *why.*

78. But, secondly, if we have a new sense, it could only furnish us with new ideas or sensations; and then we should have the same reason against their existing in an unperceiving substance that has been already offered with relation to figure, motion, color, and the like. Qualities as has been shown, are nothing else but *sensations* or *ideas,* which exist only in a *mind* perceiving them; and this is true not only of the ideas we are acquainted with at present, but likewise of all possible ideas whatsoever.

79. But, you will insist, what if I have no reason to believe the existence of matter? What if I cannot assign any use to it or explain anything by it, or even conceive what is meant by that word? Yet still it is no contradiction to say that matter exists, and that this matter is in general a *substance,* or *occasion of ideas,* though, indeed, to go about to unfold the meaning or adhere to any particular explication of those words may be attended with great difficulties. I answer, when words are used without a meaning, you may put them together as you please without danger of running into a contradiction. You may say, for example, that twice two is equal to seven, so long as you declare you do not take the words of that proposition in their usual acceptation but for marks of you know not what. And, by the same reason, you may say there is an inert, thoughtless substance without accidents which is the occasion of our ideas. And we shall understand just as much by one proposition as the other.

80. In the *last* place, you will say, What if we give up the cause of material substance and assert that matter is an unknown *somewhat*—neither substance nor accident, spirit nor idea, inert, thoughtless, indivisible, immovable, unextended, existing in no place? For, say you, whatever may be urged against *substance* or *occasion,* or any other positive or relative notion of matter, has no place at all so long as this *negative* definition of matter is adhered to. I answer, You may, if so it shall seem good, use the word "matter" in the same sense as other men use "nothing," and so make those terms convertible in your style. For, after all, this is what appears to me to be the result of that definition, the parts whereof, when I consider with attention, either collectively or separate from each other, I do not find that there is any kind of effect or impression made on my mind different from what is excited by the term "nothing."

81. You will reply, perhaps, that in the foresaid definition is included what does sufficiently distinguish it from nothing—the positive, abstract idea of *quiddity, entity,* or *existence.* I own, indeed, that those who pretend to the faculty of framing abstract general ideas do talk as if they had such an idea, which is, say they, the most abstract and general notion of all; that is, to me, the most incomprehensible of all others. That there are a great variety of spirits of different orders and capacities whose faculties both in number and extent are far exceeding those the Author of my being has bestowed on me, I see no reason to deny. And for me to pretend to determine by my own few, stinted, narrow inlets of perception

what ideas the inexhaustible power of the Supreme Spirit may imprint upon them were certainly the utmost folly and presumption—since there may be, for aught that I know, innumerable sorts of ideas or sensations, as different from one another, and from all that I have perceived, as colors are from sounds. But how ready soever I may be to acknowledge the scantiness of my comprehension with regard to the endless variety of spirits and ideas that might possibly exist, yet for anyone to pretend to a notion of entity or existence, *abstracted* from *spirit* and *idea,* from perceiving and being perceived is, I suspect, a downright repugnancy and trifling with words.—It remains that we consider the objections which may possibly be made on the part of religion.

82. Some there are who think that, though the arguments for the real existence of bodies which are drawn from reason be allowed not to amount to demonstration, yet the Holy Scriptures are so clear in the point as will sufficiently convince every good Christian that bodies do really exist, and are something more than mere ideas, there being in Holy Writ innumerable facts related which evidently suppose the reality of timber and stone, mountains and rivers, and cities, and human bodies. To which I answer that no sort of writings whatever, sacred or profane, which use those and the like words in the vulgar acceptation, or so as to have a meaning in them, are in danger of having their truth called in question by our doctrine. That all those things do really exist, that there are bodies, even corporeal substances, when taken in the vulgar sense, has been shown to be agreeable to our principles; and the difference betwixt *things* and *ideas, realities* and *chimeras* has been distinctly explained. See secs. 29, 30, 33, 36, etc. And I do not think that either what philosophers call "matter," or the existence of objects without the mind, is anywhere mentioned in Scripture.

83. Again, whether there be or be not external things, it is agreed on all hands that the proper use of words is the marking out conceptions, or things only as they are known and perceived by us; whence it plainly follows that in the tenets we have laid down there is nothing inconsistent with the right use and significance of *language,* and that discourse, of what kind soever, so far as it is intelligible, remains undisturbed. But all this seems so very manifest, from what has been set forth in the premises, that it is needless to insist any further on it.

84. But it will be urged that miracles do, at least, lose much of their stress and import by our principles. What must we think of Moses' rod? Was it not *really* turned into a serpent, or was there only a change of *ideas* in the minds of the spectators? And can it be supposed that our Saviour did no more at the marriage-feast in Cana than impose on the sight and smell and taste of the guests, so as to create in them the appearance or idea only of wine? The same may be said of all other miracles, which, in consequence of the foregoing principles, must be looked upon only as so many cheats or illusions of fancy. To this I reply that the rod was changed into a real serpent, and the water into real wine. That this does not in the least contradict what I have elsewhere said will be evident from secs. 34 and 35. But this business of *real* and *imaginary* has been already so plainly and fully explained, and so often referred to, and the difficulties about it are so easily answered from what has gone before, that it were an affront to the reader's understanding to resume the explication of it in this place. I shall only observe that if at table all who were present should see, and smell, and taste, and drink wine, and find the effects of it, with me there could be no doubt of its reality, so that at bottom the scruple concerning real miracles has no place at all on ours, but only on the received principles, and consequently makes rather for than against what has been said.

85. Having done with the objections, which I endeavored to propose in the clearest

light, and gave them all the force and weight I could, we proceed in the next place to take a view of our tenets in their consequences. Some of these appear at first sight—as that several difficult and obscure questions, on which abundance of speculation has been thrown away, are entirely banished from philosophy: whether corporeal substance can think; whether matter be infinitely divisible; and how it operates on spirit—these and the like inquiries have given infinite amusement to philosophers in all ages, but, depending on the existence of matter, they have no longer any place on our principles. Many other advantages there are, as well with regard to religion as the sciences, which it is easy for anyone to deduce from what has been premised; but this will appear more plainly in the sequel.

86. From the principles we have laid down it follows human knowledge may naturally be reduced to two heads—that of *ideas* and that of *spirits*. Of each of these I shall treat in order.

And, *first*, as to ideas or unthinking things. Our knowledge of these has been very much obscured and confounded, and we have been led into very dangerous errors, by supposing a twofold existence of the objects of sense—the one *intelligible* or in the mind, the other *real* and without the mind, whereby unthinking things are thought to have a natural subsistence of their own distinct from being perceived by spirits. This, which, if I mistake not, has been shown to be a most groundless and absurd notion, is the very root of skepticism, for so long as men thought that real things subsisted without the mind, and that their knowledge was only so far forth *real* as it was conformable to *real things*, it follows they could not be certain they had any real knowledge at all. For how can it be known that the things which are perceived are conformable to those which are not perceived or exist without the mind?

87. Color, figure, motion, extension, and the like, considered only as so many *sensations* in the mind, are perfectly known, there being nothing in them which is not perceived. But if they are looked on as notes or images, referred to *things* or *archetypes* existing without the mind, then are we involved all in skepticism. We see only the appearances, and not the real qualities of things. What may be the extension, figure, or motion of anything really and absolutely, or in itself, it is impossible for us to know, but only the proportion or the relation they bear to our senses. Things remaining the same, our ideas vary, and which of them, or even whether any of them at all, represent the true quality really existing in the thing, it is out of our reach to determine. So that, for aught we know, all we see, hear, and feel may be only phantom and vain chimera, and not at all agree with the real things existing in *rerum natura*. All this skepticism follows from our supposing a difference between *things* and *ideas*, and that the former have a subsistence without the mind or unperceived. It were easy to dilate on this subject and show how the arguments urged by skeptics in all ages depend on the supposition of external objects.

88. So long as we attribute a real existence to unthinking things, distinct from their being perceived, it is not only impossible for us to know with evidence the nature of any real unthinking being, but even that it exists. Hence it is that we see philosophers distrust their senses and doubt of the existence of heaven and earth, of everything they see or feel, even of their own bodies. And after all their labor and struggle of thought, they are forced to own we cannot attain to any self-evident or demonstrative knowledge of the existence of sensible things. But all this doubtfulness which so bewilders and confounds the mind and makes philosophy ridiculous in the eyes of the world vanishes if we annex a meaning to our words and do not amuse ourselves with the terms "absolute," "external," "exist," and suchlike, signifying we know not what. I can as well doubt of my own being as of the being of those things which I actually perceive by sense; it being a manifest contradiction that any

sensible object should be immediately perceived by sight or touch and at the same time have no existence in nature, since the very *existence* of an unthinking being consists in *being perceived.*

89. Nothing seems of more importance toward erecting a firm system of sound and real knowledge, which may be proof against the assaults of skepticism, than to lay the beginning in a distinct explication of what is meant by "thing," "reality," "existence"; for in vain shall we dispute concerning the real existence of things or pretend to any knowledge thereof, so long as we have not fixed the meaning of those words. "Thing" or "being" is the most general name of all; it comprehends under it two kinds entirely distinct and heterogeneous, and which have nothing common but the name, to wit, *spirits* and *ideas.* The former are active, indivisible substances; the latter are inert, fleeting, dependent beings which subsist not by themselves, but are supported by or exist in minds or spiritual substances.

90. Ideas imprinted on the senses are real things, or do really exist—this we do not deny, but we deny they can subsist without the minds which perceive them, or that they are resemblances of any archetypes existing without the mind, since the very being of a sensation or idea consists in being perceived, and an idea can be like nothing but an idea. Again, the things perceived by sense may be termed "external" with regard to their origin— in that they are not generated from within by the mind itself, but imprinted by a spirit distinct from that which perceives them. Sensible objects may likewise be said to be "without the mind" in another sense, namely, when they exist in some other mind; thus, when I shut my eyes, the things I saw may still exist, but it must be in another mind.

91. It were a mistake to think that what is here said derogates in the least from the reality of things. It is acknowledged, on the received principles, that extension, motion, and, in a word, all sensible qualities have need of a support, as not being able to subsist by themselves. But the objects perceived by sense are allowed to be nothing but combinations of those qualities, and consequently cannot subsist by themselves. Thus far it is agreed on all hands. So that in denying the things perceived by sense an existence independent of a substance or support wherein they may exist, we detract nothing from the received opinion of their *reality,* and are guilty of no innovation in that respect. All the difference is that, according to us, the unthinking beings perceived by sense have no existence distinct from being perceived, and cannot therefore exist in any other substances than those unextended indivisible substances or *spirits* which act and think and perceive them; whereas philosophers vulgarly hold that the sensible qualities exist in an inert, extended, unperceiving substance which they call "matter," to which they attribute a natural subsistence, exterior to all thinking beings, or distinct from being perceived by any mind whatsoever, even the eternal mind of the Creator, wherein they suppose only ideas of the corporeal substances created by him, if indeed they allow them to be at all created.

92. For as we have shown the doctrine of matter or corporeal substance to have been the main pillar and support of skepticism, so likewise, upon the same foundation, have been raised all the impious schemes of atheism and irreligion. Nay, so great a difficulty has it been thought to conceive matter produced out of nothing that the most celebrated among the ancient philosophers, even of these who maintained the being of a God, have thought matter to be uncreated and coeternal with Him. How great a friend *material substance* has been to atheists in all ages were needless to relate. All their monstrous systems have so visible and necessary a dependence on it that, when this cornerstone is once removed, the whole fabric cannot choose but fall to the ground, insomuch that it is no longer worth while to bestow a particular consideration on the absurdities of every wretched sect of atheists.

93. That impious and profane persons should readily fall in with those systems which

favor their inclinations by deriding immaterial substance and supposing the soul to be divisible and subject to corruption as the body, which exclude all freedom, intelligence, and design from the formation of things, and instead thereof make a self-existent, stupid, unthinking substance the root and origin of all beings; that they should hearken to those who deny a Providence, or inspection of a Superior Mind over the affairs of the world, attributing the whole series of events either to blind chance or fatal necessity arising from the impulse of one body or another—all this is very natural. And, on the other hand, when men of better principles observe the enemies of religion lay so great a stress on *unthinking matter,* and all of them use so much industry and artifice to reduce everything to it, methinks they should rejoice to see them deprived of their grand support and driven from that only fortress without which your Epicureans, Hobbists, and the like, have not even the shadow of a pretense, but become the most cheap and easy triumph in the world.

94. The existence of matter, or bodies unperceived, has not only been the main support of atheists and fatalists, but on the same principle does idolatry likewise in all its various forms depend. Did men but consider that the sun, moon, and stars, and every other object of the senses are only so many sensations in their minds, which have no other existence but barely being perceived, doubtless they would never fall down and worship their own *ideas,* but rather address their homage to that Eternal Invisible Mind which produces and sustains all things.

95. The same absurd principle, by mingling itself with the articles of our faith, has occasioned no small difficulties to Christians. For example, about the resurrection, how many scruples and objections have been raised by Socinians and others? But do not the most plausible of them depend on the supposition that a body is denominated "the same," with regard not to the form or that which is perceived by sense, but the material substance, which remains the same under several forms? Take away this *material substance,* about the identity whereof all the dispute is, and mean by "body" what every plain, ordinary person means by that word, to wit, that which is immediately seen and felt, which is only a combination of sensible qualities or ideas, and then their most unanswerable objections come to nothing.

96. Matter being once expelled out of nature drags with it so many skeptical and impious notions, such an incredible number of disputes and puzzling questions, which have been thorns in the sides of divines as well as philosophers and made so much fruitless work for mankind, that if the arguments we have produced against it are not found equal to demonstration (as to me they evidently seem), yet I am sure all friends to knowledge, peace, and religion have reason to wish they were.

97. Beside the external existence of the objects of perception, another great source of errors and difficulties with regard to ideal knowledge is the doctrine of *abstract ideas,* such as it has been set forth in the Introduction. The plainest things in the world, those we are most intimately acquainted with and perfectly know, when they are considered in an abstract way, appear strangely difficult and incomprehensible. Time, place, and motion, taken in particular or concrete, are what everybody knows, but, having passed through the hands of a metaphysician, they become too abstract and fine to be apprehended by men of ordinary sense. Bid your servant meet you at such a *time* in such a *place,* and he shall never stay to deliberate on the meaning of those words; in conceiving that particular time and place, or the motion by which he is to get thither, he finds not the least difficulty. But if *time* be taken exclusive of all those particular actions and ideas that diversify the day, merely for the continuation of existence or duration in abstract, then it will perhaps gravel even a philosopher to comprehend it.

98. Whenever I attempt to frame a simple idea of *time*, abstracted from the succession of ideas in my mind, which flows uniformly and is participated by all beings, I am lost and embrangled in inextricable difficulties. I have no notion of it at all, only I hear others say it is infinitely divisible, and speak of it in such a manner as leads me to entertain odd thoughts of my existence; since that doctrine lays one under an absolute necessity of thinking, either that he passes away innumerable ages without a thought or else that he is annihilated every moment of his life, both which seem equally absurd. Time therefore being nothing, abstracted from the succession of ideas in our minds, it follows that the duration of any finite spirit must be estimated by the number of ideas or actions succeeding each other in that same spirit or mind. Hence, it is a plain consequence that the soul always thinks; and in truth whoever shall go about to divide in his thoughts or abstract the *existence* of a spirit from its *cogitation* will, I believe, find it no easy task.

99. So likewise when we attempt to abstract extension and motion from all other qualities, and consider them by themselves, we presently lose sight of them, and run into great extravagances. All which depend on a twofold abstraction; first, it is supposed that extension, for example, may be abstracted from all other sensible qualities; and secondly, that the entity of extension may be abstracted from its being perceived. But whoever shall reflect, and take care to understand what he says, will, if I mistake not, acknowledge that all sensible qualities are alike *sensations* and alike *real*; that where the extension is, there is the color, too, to wit, in his mind, and that their archetypes can exist only in some other *mind*; and that the objects of sense are nothing but those sensations combined, blended, or (if one may so speak) concreted together; none of all which can be supposed to exist unperceived.

100. What it is for a man to be happy, or an object good, everyone may think he knows. But to frame an abstract idea of happiness, prescinded from all particular pleasure, or of goodness from everything that is good, this is what few can pretend to. So likewise a man may be just and virtuous without having precise ideas of justice and virtue. The opinion that those and the like words stand for general notions, abstracted from all particular persons and actions, seems to have rendered morality difficult, and the study thereof of less use to mankind. And in effect the doctrine of *abstraction* has not a little contributed toward spoiling the most useful parts of knowledge.

101. The two great provinces of speculative science conversant about ideas received from sense and their relations are natural philosophy and mathematics; with regard to each of these I shall make some observations. And first I shall say somewhat of natural philosophy. On this subject it is that the skeptics triumph. All that stock of arguments they produce to depreciate our faculties and make mankind appear ignorant and low are drawn principally from this head, to wit, that we are under an invincible blindness as to the *true* and *real* nature of things. This they exaggerate, and love to enlarge on. We are miserably bantered, say they, by our senses, and amused only with the outside and show of things. The real essence, the internal qualities and constitution of every the meanest object, is hidden from our view; something there is in every drop of water, every grain of sand, which it is beyond the power of human understanding to fathom or comprehend. But it is evident from what has been shown that all this complaint is groundless, and that we are influenced by false principles to that degree as to mistrust our senses and think we know nothing of those things which we perfectly comprehend.

102. One great inducement to our pronouncing ourselves ignorant of the nature of things is the current opinion that everything includes within itself the cause of its properties; or that there is in each object an inward essence which is the source whence its discernible qualities flow, and whereon they depend. Some have pretended to account for appearances

by occult qualities, but of late they are mostly resolved into mechanical causes, to wit, the figure, motion, weight, and suchlike qualities of insensible particles; whereas, in truth, there is no other agent or efficient cause than *spirit,* it being evident that motion, as well as all other *ideas,* is perfectly inert. See sec. 25. Hence, to endeavor to explain the production of colors or sounds by figure, motion, magnitude, and the like, must needs be labor in vain. And accordingly we see the attempts of that kind are not at all satisfactory. Which may be said in general of those instances wherein one idea or quality is assigned for the cause of another. I need not say how many hypotheses and speculations are left out, and how much the study of nature is abridged by this doctrine.

103. The great mechanical principle now in vogue is *attraction.* That a stone falls to the earth, or the sea swells toward the moon, may to some appear sufficiently explained thereby. But how are we enlightened by being told this is done by attraction? Is it that that word signifies the manner of the tendency, and that it is by the mutual drawing of bodies instead of their being impelled or protruded toward each other? But nothing is determined of the manner or action, and it may as truly (for aught we know) be termed "impulse," or "protrusion," as "attraction." Again, the parts of steel we see cohere firmly together, and this also is accounted for by attraction; but, in this as in the other instances, I do not perceive that anything is signified besides the effect itself; for as to the manner of the action whereby it is produced, or the cause which produces it, these are not so much as aimed at.

104. Indeed, if we take a view of the several phenomena and compare them together, we may observe some likeness and conformity between them. For example, in the falling of a stone to the ground, in the rising of the sea toward the moon, in cohesion and crystallization, there is something alike, namely, a union or mutual approach of bodies. So that any one of these or the like phenomena may not seem strange or surprising to a man who has nicely observed and compared the effects of nature. For that only is thought so which is uncommon, or a thing by itself, and out of the ordinary course of our observation. That bodies should tend toward the center of the earth is not thought strange, because it is what we perceive every moment of our lives. But, that they should have a like gravitation toward the center of the moon may seem odd and unaccountable to most men, because it is discerned only in the tides. But a philosopher, whose thoughts take in a larger compass of nature, having observed a certain similitude of appearances, as well in the heavens as the earth, that argue innumerable bodies to have a mutual tendency toward each other, which he denotes by the general name "attraction," whatever can be reduced to that he thinks justly accounted for. Thus he explains the tides by the attraction of the terraqueous globe toward the moon, which to him does not appear odd or anomalous, but only a particular example of a general rule or law of nature.

105. If therefore we consider the difference there is betwixt natural philosophers and other men with regard to their knowledge of the phenomena, we shall find it consists not in an exacter knowledge of the efficient cause that produces them—for that can be no other than the *will of a spirit*—but only in a greater largeness of comprehension, whereby analogies, harmonies, and agreements are discovered in the works of nature, and the particular effects explained, that is, reduced to general rules, see sec. 62, which rules, grounded on the analogy and uniformness observed in the production of natural effects, are most agreeable and sought after by the mind; for that they extend our prospect beyond what is present and near to us, and enable us to make very probable conjectures touching things that may have happened at very great distances of time and place, as well as to predict things to come; which sort of endeavor toward omniscience is much affected by the mind.

106. But we should proceed warily in such things, for we are apt to lay too great a stress on analogies, and, to the prejudice of truth, humor that eagerness of the mind whereby it is carried to extend its knowledge into general theorems. For example, gravitation or mutual attraction, because it appears in many instances, some are straightway for pronouncing "universal"; and that to attract and be attracted by every other body is an essential quality inherent in all bodies whatsoever. Whereas it appears the fixed stars have no such tendency toward each other; and so far is that gravitation from being *essential* to bodies that in some instances a quite contrary principle seems to show itself; as in the perpendicular growth of plants, and the elasticity of the air. There is nothing necessary or essential in the case, but it depends entirely on the will of the governing spirit, who causes certain bodies to cleave together or tend toward each other according to various laws, while he keeps others at a fixed distance; and to some he gives a quite contrary tendency to fly asunder just as he sees convenient.

107. After what has been premised, I think we may lay down the following conclusions. First, it is plain philosophers amuse themselves in vain when they inquire for any natural efficient cause distinct from a *mind* or *spirit*. Secondly, considering the whole creation is the workmanship of a *wise and good agent*, it should seem to become philosophers to employ their thoughts (contrary to what some hold) about the final causes of things; and I must confess I see no reason why pointing out the various ends to which natural things are adapted, and for which they were originally with unspeakable wisdom contrived, should not be thought one good way of accounting for them, and altogether worthy a philosopher. Thirdly, from what has been premised no reason can be drawn why the history of nature should not still be studied, and observations and experiments made; which, that they are of use to mankind, and enable us to draw any general conclusions, is not the result of any immutable habitudes or relations between things themselves, but only of God's goodness and kindness to men in the administration of the world. See secs. 30 and 31. Fourthly, by a diligent observation of the phenomena within our view, we may discover the general laws of nature, and from them deduce the other phenomena; I do not say "demonstrate," for all deductions of that kind depend on a supposition that the Author of Nature always operates uniformly and in a constant observance of those rules we take for principles, which we cannot evidently know.

108. Those men who frame general rules from the phenomena and afterwards derive the phenomena from those rules seem to consider signs rather than causes. A man may well understand natural signs without knowing their analogy, or being able to say by what rule a thing is so or so. And, as it is very possible to write improperly, through too strict an observance of general grammar rules; so, in arguing from general rules of nature, it is not impossible we may extend the analogy too far, and by that means run into mistakes.

109. As, in reading other books, a wise man will choose to fix his thoughts on the sense and apply it to use, rather than lay them out in grammatical remarks on the language, so, in perusing the volume of nature, it seems beneath the dignity of the mind to affect an exactness in reducing each particular phenomenon to general rules, or showing how it follows from them. We should propose to ourselves nobler views, such as to recreate and exalt the mind with a prospect of the beauty, order, extent, and variety of natural things: hence, by proper inferences, to enlarge our notions of the grandeur, wisdom, and beneficence of the Creator; and lastly, to make the several parts of the Creation, so far as in us lies, subservient to the ends they were designed for—God's glory and the sustentation and comfort of ourselves and fellow creatures.

110. The best key for the aforesaid analogy or natural science will be easily acknowl-edged to be a certain celebrated treatise of *mechanics.** In the entrance of which justly ad-mired treatise, time, space, and motion are distinguished into *absolute* and *relative, true* and *apparent, mathematical* and *vulgar;* which distinction, as it is at large explained by the au-thor, does suppose these quantities to have an existence without the mind; and that they are ordinarily conceived with relation to sensible things, to which nevertheless in their own nature they bear no relation at all.

111. As for "time," as it is there taken in an absolute or abstracted sense, for the duration or perseverance of the existence of things, I have nothing more to add concerning it after what has been already said on that subject. Secs. 97 and 98. For the rest, this celebrated author holds there is an *absolute space,* which, being unperceivable to sense, remains in itself similar and immovable; and relative space to be the measure thereof, which, being movable and defined by its situation in respect of sensible bodies, is vulgarly taken for immovable space. "Place" he defines to be that part of space which is occupied by any body; and according as the space is absolute or relative, so also is the place. "Absolute motion" is said to be the translation of a body from absolute place to absolute place, as relative motion is from one relative place to another. And, because the parts of absolute space do not fall under our senses, instead of them we are obliged to use their sensible measures, and so define both place and motion with respect to bodies which we regard as immovable. But it is said in philosophical matters we must abstract from our senses, since it may be that none of those bodies which seem to be quiescent are truly so, and the same thing which is moved relatively may be really at rest; as likewise one and the same body may be in relative rest and motion, or even moved with contrary relative motions at the same time, according as its place is variously defined. All which ambiguity is to be found in the apparent motions, but not at all in the true or absolute, which should therefore be alone regarded in philosophy. And the true we are told are distinguished from apparent or relative motions by the follow-ing properties.—First, in true or absolute motion all parts which preserve the same position with respect to the whole partake of the motions of the whole. Secondly, the place being moved, that which is placed therein is also moved; so that a body moving in a place which is in motion does participate in the motion of its place. Thirdly, true motion is never gen-erated or changed otherwise than by force impressed on the body itself. Fourthly, true motion is always changed by force impressed on the body moved. Fifthly, in circular mo-tion, barely relative, there is no centrifugal force which, nevertheless, in that which is true or absolute, is proportional to the quantity of motion.

112. But, notwithstanding what has been said, it does not appear to me that there can be any motion other than *relative;* so that to conceive motion there must be at least con-ceived two bodies, whereof the distance or position in regard to each other is varied. Hence, if there was one only body in being it could not possibly be moved. This seems evident, in that the idea I have of motion does necessarily include relation.

113. But, though in every motion it be necessary to conceive more bodies than one, yet it may be that one only is moved, namely, that on which the force causing the change of distance is impressed, or, in other words, that to which the action is applied. For, however some may define relative motion, so as to term that body "moved" which changes its dis-tance from some other body, whether the force or action causing that change were applied to it or no, yet as relative motion is that which is perceived by sense, and regarded in the

*Isaac Newton's *Philosophiae Naturalis Principia Mathematica* (London, 1687).

ordinary affairs of life, it should seem that every man of common sense knows what it is as well as the best philosopher. Now I ask anyone whether, in his sense of motion as he walks along the streets, the stones he passes over may be said to *move,* because they change distance with his feet? To me it seems that though motion includes a relation of one thing to another, yet it is not necessary that each term of the relation be denominated from it. As a man may think of somewhat which does not think, so a body may be moved to or from another body which is not therefore itself in motion.

114. As the place happens to be variously defined, the motion which is related to it varies. A man in a ship may be said to be quiescent with relation to the sides of the vessel, and yet move with relation to the land. Or he may move eastward in respect of the one, and westward in respect of the other. In the common affairs of life, men never go beyond the earth to define the place of any body; and what is quiescent in respect of that is accounted *absolutely* to be so. But philosophers, who have a greater extent of thought, and juster notions of the system of things, discover even the earth itself to be moved. In order therefore to fix their notions, they seem to conceive the corporeal world as finite, and the utmost unmoved walls or shell thereof to be the place whereby they estimate true motions. If we sound our own conceptions, I believe we may find all the absolute motion we can frame an idea of to be at bottom no other than relative motion thus defined. For, as has been already observed, absolute motion, exclusive of all external relation, is incomprehensible; and to this kind of relative motion all the above-mentioned properties, causes, and effects ascribed to absolute motion will, if I mistake not, be found to agree. As to what is said of the centrifugal force, that it does not at all belong to circular relative motion, I do not see how this follows from the experiment which is brought to prove it. See *Philosophiae Naturalis Principia Mathematica, in Schol. Def. VIII.* For the water in the vessel at that time wherein it is said to have the greatest relative circular motion, has, I think, no motion at all; as is plain from the foregoing section.

115. For, to denominate a body "moved" it is requisite, first, that it change its distance or situation with regard to some other body; and secondly, that the force or action occasioning that change be applied to it. If either of these be wanting, I do not think that, agreeably to the sense of mankind, or the propriety of language, a body can be said to be in motion. I grant indeed that it is possible for us to think a body which we see change its distance from some other to be moved, though it have no force applied to it (in which sense there may be apparent motion), but then it is because the force causing the change of distance is imagined by us to be applied or impressed on that body thought to move; which indeed shows we are capable of mistaking a thing to be in motion which is not, and that is all.

116. From what has been said, it follows that the philosophic consideration of motion does not imply the being of an *absolute space,* distinct from that which is perceived by sense and related to bodies; which that it cannot exist without the mind is clear upon the same principles that demonstrate the like of all other objects of sense. And perhaps, if we inquire narrowly, we shall find we cannot even frame an idea of *pure space* exclusive of all body. This I must confess seems impossible, as being a most abstract idea. When I excite a motion in some part of my body, if it be free or without resistance, I say there is *space;* but if I find a resistance, then I say there is *body;* and in proportion as the resistance to motion is lesser or greater, I say the space is more or less *pure.* So that when I speak of pure or empty space, it is not to be supposed that the word "space" stands for an idea distinct from or conceivable without body and motion—though indeed we are apt to think every noun substantive stands for a distinct idea that may be separated from all others; which has occasioned infinite mistakes. When, therefore, supposing all the world to be annihilated besides my own body,

I say there still remains *pure space,* thereby nothing else is meant but only that I conceive it possible for the limbs of my body to be moved on all sides without the least resistance; but if that, too, were annihilated, then there could be no motion, and consequently no space. Some, perhaps, may think the sense of seeing does furnish them with the idea of pure space; but it is plain from what we have elsewhere shown, that the ideas of space and distance are not obtained by that sense. See the *Essay Concerning Vision.*

117. What is here laid down seems to put an end to all those disputes and difficulties that have sprung up amongst the learned concerning the nature of *pure space.* But the chief advantage arising from it is that we are freed from that dangerous dilemma to which several who have employed their thoughts on this subject imagine themselves reduced, to wit, of thinking either that real space is God, or else what there is something besides God which is eternal, uncreated, infinite, indivisible, immutable. Both which may justly be thought pernicious and absurd notions. It is certain that not a few divines, as well as philosophers of great note, have, from the difficulty they found in conceiving either limits or annihilation of space, concluded it must be divine. And some of late have set themselves particularly to show that the incommunicable attributes of God agree to it. Which doctrine, how unworthy soever it may seem of the Divine Nature, yet I do not see how we can get clear of it so long as we adhere to the received opinions.

118. Hitherto of natural philosophy: we come now to make some inquiry concerning the other great branch of speculative knowledge, to wit, mathematics. These, how celebrated soever they may be for their clearness and certainty of demonstration, which is hardly anywhere else to be found, cannot nevertheless be supposed altogether free from mistakes, if in their principles there lurks some secret error which is common to the professors of those sciences with the rest of mankind. Mathematicians, though they deduce their theorems from a great height of evidence, yet their first principles are limited by the consideration of quantity; and they do not ascend into any inquiry concerning those transcendental maxims which influence all the particular sciences, each part whereof, mathematics not excepted, does consequently participate of the errors involved in them. That the principles laid down by mathematicians are true, and their way of deduction from those principles clear and incontestable, we do not deny; but we hold there may be certain erroneous maxims of greater extent than the object of mathematics, and for that reason not expressly mentioned, though tacitly supposed throughout the whole progress of that science; and that the ill effects of those secret, unexamined errors are diffused through all the branches thereof. To be plain, we suspect the mathematicians are as well as other men concerned in the errors arising from the doctrine of abstract general ideas and the existence of objects without the mind.

119. Arithmetic has been thought to have for its object abstract ideas of *number;* of which to understand the properties and mutual habitudes is supposed no mean part of speculative knowledge. The opinion of the pure and intellectual nature of numbers in abstract has made them in esteem with those philosophers who seem to have affected an uncommon fineness and elevation of thought. It has set a price on the most trifling numerical speculations which in practice are of no use but serve only for amusement, and has therefore so far infected the minds of some that they have dreamed of mighty mysteries involved in numbers and attempted the explication of natural things by them. But, if we inquire into our own thoughts and consider what has been premised, we may perhaps entertain a low opinion of those high flights and abstractions, and look on all inquiries about numbers only as so many *difficiles nugae,* so far as they are not subservient to practice and promote the benefit of life.

120. Unity in abstract we have before considered in sec. 13, from which and what has been said in the Introduction, it plainly follows there is not any such idea. But, number being defined a "collection of units," we may conclude that, if there be no such thing as unity or unit in abstract, there are no ideas of number in abstract denoted by the numerical names and figures. The theories therefore in arithmetic, if they are abstracted from the names and figures, as likewise from all use and practice, as well as from the particular things numbered, can be supposed to have nothing at all for their object; hence we may see how entirely the science of numbers is subordinate to practice, and how jejune and trifling it becomes when considered as a matter of mere speculation.

121. However, since there may be some who, deluded by the specious show of discovering abstracted verities, waste their time in arithmetical theorems and problems which have not any use, it will not be amiss if we more fully consider and expose the vanity of that pretense; and this will plainly appear by taking a view of arithmetic in its infancy, and observing what it was that originally put men on the study of that science, and to what scope they directed it. It is natural to think that at first, men, for ease of memory and help of computation, made use of counters, or in writing of single strokes, points, or the like, each whereof was made to signify a unit, that is, some one thing of whatever kind they had occasion to reckon. Afterwards they found out the more compendious ways of making one character stand in place of several strokes or points. And, lastly, the notation of the Arabians or Indians came into use, wherein, by the repetition of a few characters or figures, and varying the signification of each figure according to the place it obtains, all numbers may be most aptly expressed; which seems to have been done in imitation of language, so that an exact analogy is observed betwixt the notation by figures and names, the nine simple figures answering the nine first numeral names and places in the former, corresponding to denominations in the latter. And agreeably to those conditions of the simple and local value of figures were contrived methods of finding, from the given figures or marks of the parts, what figures and how placed are proper to denote the whole, or vice versa. And having found the sought figures, the same rule or analogy being observed throughout, it is easy to read them into words; and so the number becomes perfectly known. For then the number of any particular things is said to be known, when we know the name or figures (with their due arrangement) that according to the standing analogy belong to them. For, these signs being known, we can by the operations of arithmetic know the signs of any part of the particular sums signified by them; and, thus computing in signs (because of the connection established betwixt them and the distinct multitudes of things whereof one is taken for a unit), we may be able rightly to sum up, divide, and proportion the things themselves that we intend to number.

122. In arithmetic, therefore, we regard not the *things,* but the *signs,* which nevertheless are not regarded for their own sake, but because they direct us how to act with relation to things, and dispose rightly of them. Now, agreeable to what we have before observed of words in general (sec. 19, Introd.) it happens here likewise that abstract ideas are thought to be signified by numeral names or characters, while they do not suggest ideas of particular things to our minds. I shall not at present enter into a more particular dissertation on this subject, but only observe that it is evident from what has been said, those things which pass for abstract truths and theorems concerning numbers are in reality conversant about no object distinct from particular numerable things, except only names and characters which originally came to be considered on no other account but their being signs, or capable to represent aptly whatever particular things men had need to compute. Whence it follows that to study them for their own sake would be just as wise, and to as good purpose as if a

man, neglecting the true use or original intention and subservience of language, should spend his time in impertinent criticisms upon words, or reasonings and controversies purely verbal.

123. From numbers we proceed to speak of *extension,* which, considered as relative, is the object of geometry. The *infinite* divisibility of *finite* extension, though it is not expressly laid down either as an axiom or theorem in the elements of that science, yet is throughout the same everywhere supposed and thought to have so inseparable and essential a connection with the principles and demonstrations in geometry that mathematicians never admit it into doubt, or make the least question of it. And, as this notion is the source from whence do spring all those amusing geometrical paradoxes which have such a direct repugnancy to the plain common sense of mankind, and are admitted with so much reluctance into a mind not yet debauched by learning; so is it the principal occasion of all that nice and extreme subtlety which renders the study of mathematics so difficult and tedious. Hence, if we can make it appear that no finite extension contains innumerable parts, or is infinitely divisible, it follows that we shall at once clear the science of geometry from a great number of difficulties and contradictions which have ever been esteemed a reproach to human reason, and withal make the attainment thereof a business of much less time and pains than it hitherto has been.

124. Every particular finite extension which may possibly be the object of our thought is an *idea* existing only in the mind, and consequently each part thereof must be perceived. If, therefore, I cannot perceive innumerable parts in any finite extension that I consider, it is certain they are not contained in it; but it is evident that I cannot distinguish innumerable parts in any particular line, surface, or solid, which I either perceive by sense, or figure to myself in my mind: wherefore I conclude they are not contained in it. Nothing can be plainer to me than that the extensions I have in view are no other than my own ideas; and it is no less plain that I cannot resolve any one of my ideas into an infinite number of other ideas, that is, that they are not infinitely divisible. If by "finite extension" be meant something distinct from a finite idea, I declare I do not know what that is, and so cannot affirm or deny anything of it. But if the terms "extension," "parts," and the like, are taken in any sense conceivable, that is, for ideas, then to say a finite quantity or extension consists of parts infinite in number is so manifest a contradiction that everyone at first sight acknowledges it to be so; and it is impossible it should ever gain the assent of any reasonable creature who is not brought to it by gentle and slow degrees, as a converted gentile to the belief of transubstantiation. Ancient and rooted prejudices do often pass into principles; and those propositions which once obtain the force and credit of a *principle* are not only themselves, but likewise whatever is deducible from them, thought privileged from all examination. And there is no absurdity so gross which, by this means, the mind of man may not be prepared to swallow.

125. He whose understanding is prepossessed with the doctrine of abstract general ideas may be persuaded that (whatever be thought of the ideas of sense) extension in *abstract* is infinitely divisible. And one who thinks the objects of sense exist without the mind will perhaps in virtue thereof be brought to admit that a line but an inch long may contain innumerable parts—really existing, though too small to be discerned. These errors are grafted as well in the minds of geometricians as of other men, and have a like influence on their reasonings; and it were no difficult thing to show how the arguments from geometry made use of to support the infinite divisibility of extension are bottomed on them. At present we shall only observe in general whence it is that the mathematicians are all so fond and tenacious of this doctrine.

126. It has been observed in another place that the theorems and demonstrations in geometry are conversant about universal ideas (sec. 15, Introd.); where it is explained in what sense this ought to be understood, to wit, that the particular lines and figures included in the diagram are supposed to stand for innumerable others of different sizes; or, in other words, the geometer considers them abstracting from their magnitude—which does not imply that he forms an abstract idea, but only that he cares not what the particular magnitude is, whether great or small, but looks on that as a thing indifferent to the demonstration. Hence it follows that a line in the scheme but an inch long must be spoken of as though it contained ten thousand parts, since it is regarded not in itself, but as it is universal; and it is universal only in its signification, whereby it represents innumerable lines greater than itself, in which may be distinguished ten thousand parts or more, though there may not be above an inch in it. After this manner, the properties of the lines signified are (by a very usual figure) transferred to the sign, and thence, through mistake, thought to appertain to it considered in its own nature.

127. Because there is no number of parts so great but it is possible there may be a line containing more, the inch-line is said to contain parts more than any assignable number; which is true, not of the inch taken absolutely, but only for the things signified by it. But men, not retaining that distinction in their thoughts, slide into a belief that the small particular line described on paper contains in itself parts innumerable. There is no such thing as the ten thousandth part of an inch; but there is of a mile or diameter of the earth, which may be signified by that inch. When therefore I delineate a triangle on paper, and take one side not above an inch, for example, in length to be the radius, this I consider as divided into ten thousand or one hundred thousand parts of more; for, though the ten thousandth part of that line considered in itself is nothing at all, and consequently may be neglected without any error or inconvenience, yet these described lines, being only marks standing for greater quantities, whereof it may be the ten thousandth part is very considerable, it follows that, to prevent notable errors in practice, the radius must be taken of ten thousand parts or more.

128. From what has been said the reason is plain why, to the end any theorem may become universal in its use, it is necessary we speak of the lines described on paper as though they contained parts which really they do not. In doing of which, if we examine the matter thoroughly, we shall perhaps discover that we cannot conceive an inch itself as consisting of, or being divisible into, a thousand parts, but only some other line which is far greater than an inch, and represented by it; and that when we say a line is "infinitely divisible" we must mean a line which is infinitely great. What we have here observed seems to be the chief cause why to suppose the infinite divisibility of finite extension has been thought necessary in geometry.

129. The general absurdities and contradictions which flowed from this false principle might, one would think, have been esteemed so many demonstrations against it. But, by I know not what logic, it is held that proofs a posteriori are not to be admitted against propositions relating to infinity, as though it were not impossible even for an infinite mind to reconcile contradictions; or as if anything absurd and repugnant could have a necessary connection with truth or flow from it. But whoever considers the weakness of this pretense will think it was contrived on purpose to humor the laziness of the mind which had rather acquiesce in an indolent skepticism than be at the pains to go through with a severe examination of those principles it has ever embraced for true.

130. Of late the speculations about infinites have run so high, and grown to such strange notions, as have occasioned no small scruples and disputes among the geometers of the

present age. Some there are of great note who, not content with holding that finite lines may be divided into an infinite number of parts, do yet further maintain that each of those infinitesimals is itself subdivisible into an infinity of other parts or infinitesimals of a second order, and so on ad infinitum. These, I say, assert there are infinitesimals of infinitesimals of infinitesimals, without ever coming to an end: so that according to them an inch does not barely contain an infinite number of parts, but an infinity of an infinity of an infinity ad infinitum of parts. Others there be who hold all orders of infinitesimals below the first to be nothing at all; thinking it with good reason absurd to imagine there is any positive quantity or part of extension which, though multiplied infinitely, can ever equal the smallest given extension. And yet on the other hand it seems no less absurd to think the square, cube, or other power of a positive real root should itself be nothing at all; which they who hold infinitesimals of the first order, denying all of the subsequent orders, are obliged to maintain.

131. Have we not therefore reason to conclude that they are *both* in the wrong, and that there is in effect no such thing as parts infinitely small, or an infinite number of parts contained in any finite quantity? But you will say that if this doctrine obtains it will follow the very foundations of geometry are destroyed, and those great men who have raised that science to so astonishing a height have been all the while building a castle in the air. To this it may be replied that whatever is useful in geometry and promotes the benefit of human life does still remain firm and unshaken on our principles; that science considered as practical will rather receive advantage than any prejudice from what has been said. But to set this in a due light may be the subject of a distinct inquiry. For the rest, though it should follow that some of the more intricate and subtle parts of speculative mathematics may be pared off without any prejudice to truth, yet I do not see what damage will be thence derived to mankind. On the contrary, it were highly to be wished that men of great abilities and obstinate application would draw off their thoughts from those amusements, and employ them in the study of such things as lie nearer the concerns of life, or have a more direct influence on the manners.

132. If it be said that several theorems undoubtedly true are discovered by methods in which infinitesimals are made use of, which could never have been if their existence included a contradiction in it, I answer that upon a thorough examination it will not be found that in any instance it is necessary to make use of or conceive infinitesimal parts of finite lines, or even quantities less than the *minimum sensible;* nay, it will be evident this is never done, it being impossible.

133. By what we have premised it is plain that very numerous and important errors have taken their rise from those false principles which were impugned in the foregoing parts of this treatise; and the opposites of those erroneous tenets at the same time appear to be most fruitful principles, from whence do flow innumerable consequences highly advantageous to true philosophy, as well as to religion. Particularly *matter,* or *the absolute existence of corporeal objects,* has been shown to be that wherein the most avowed and pernicious enemies of all knowledge, whether human or divine, have ever placed their chief strength and confidence. And surely, if by distinguishing the real existence of unthinking things from their being perceived, and allowing them a subsistence of their own out of the minds of spirits, no one thing is explained in nature, but, on the contrary, a great many inexplicable difficulties arise; if the supposition of matter is barely precarious, as not being grounded on so much as one single reason; if its consequences cannot endure the light of examination and free inquiry, but screen themselves under the dark and general pretense of "infinites being incomprehensible"; if withal the removal of this *matter* be not attended with the least evil consequence;

if it be not even missed in the world, but everything as well, nay, much easier conceived without it; if, lastly, both skeptics and atheists are forever silenced upon supposing only spirits and ideas, and this scheme of things is perfectly agreeable both to reason and religion: methinks we may expect it should be admitted and firmly embraced, though it were proposed only as a *hypothesis,* and the existence of matter had been allowed possible, which yet I think we have evidently demonstrated that it is not.

134. True it is that, in consequence of the foregoing principles, several disputes and speculations which are esteemed no mean parts of learning are rejected as useless. But, how great a prejudice soever against our notions this may give to those who have already been deeply engaged and made large advances in studies of that nature, yet by others we hope it will not be thought any just ground of dislike to the principles and tenets herein laid down that they abridge the labor of study, and make human sciences more clear, compendious, and attainable than they were before.

135. Having dispatched what we intended to say concerning the knowledge of *ideas,* the method we proposed leads us in the next place to treat of *spirits*—with regard to which, perhaps, human knowledge is not so deficient as is vulgarly imagined. The great reason that is assigned for our being thought ignorant of the nature of spirits is our not having an *idea* of it. But surely it ought not to be looked on as a defect in a human understanding that it does not perceive the idea of spirit if it is manifestly impossible there should be any such idea. And this, if I mistake not, has been demonstrated in section 27; to which I shall here add that a spirit has been shown to be the only substance or support wherein the unthinking beings or ideas can exist; but that this *substance* which supports or perceives ideas should itself be an idea or like an idea is evidently absurd.

136. It will perhaps be said that we want a sense (as some have imagined) proper to show substances withal, which, if we had, we might know our own soul as we do a triangle. To this I answer, that, in case we had a new sense bestowed upon us, we could only receive thereby some new sensations or ideas of sense. But I believe nobody will say that what he means by the terms "soul" and "substance" is only some particular sort of idea or sensation. We may therefore infer, that all things duly considered, it is not more reasonable to think our faculties defective in that they do not furnish us with an idea of spirit or active thinking substance than it would be if we should blame them for not being able to comprehend a *round square.*

137. From the opinion that spirits are to be known after the manner of an idea or sensation have risen many absurd and heterodox tenets, and much skepticism about the nature of the soul. It is even probable that this opinion may have produced a doubt in some whether they had any soul at all distinct from their body, since upon inquiry they could not find they had an idea of it. That an *idea* which is inactive, and the existence whereof consists in being perceived, should be the image or likeness of an agent subsisting by itself seems to need no other refutation than barely attending to what is meant by those words. But perhaps you will say that though an idea cannot resemble a spirit in its thinking, acting, or subsisting by itself, yet it may in some other respects; and it is not necessary that an idea or image be in all respects like the original.

138. I answer, if it does not in those mentioned, it is impossible it should represent it in any other thing. Do but leave out the power of willing, thinking, and perceiving ideas, and there remains nothing else wherein the idea can be like a spirit. For by the word "spirit" we mean only that which thinks, wills, and perceives; this, and this alone, constitutes the signification of that term. If therefore it is impossible that any degree of those powers should be represented in an idea, it is evident there can be no idea of a spirit.

139. But it will be objected that, if there is no idea signified by the terms "soul," "spirit," and "substance," they are wholly insignificant or have no meaning in them. I answer, those words do mean or signify a real thing, which is neither an idea nor like an idea, but that which perceives ideas, and wills, and reasons about them. What I am myself, that which I denote by the term "I," is the same with what is meant by "soul," or "spiritual substance." If it be said that this is only quarreling at a word, and that, since the immediate significations of other names are by common consent called "ideas," no reason can be assigned why that which is signified by the name "spirit" or "soul" may not partake in the same appellation. I answer, all the unthinking objects of the mind agree in that they are entirely passive, and their existence consists only in being perceived; whereas a soul or spirit is an active being whose existence consists, not in being perceived, but in perceiving ideas and thinking. It is therefore necessary, in order to prevent equivocation and confounding natures perfectly disagreeing and unlike, that we distinguish between *spirit* and *idea*. See sec. 27.

140. In a large sense, indeed, we may be said to have an idea [or rather a notion] of *spirit;* that is, we understand the meaning of the word, otherwise we could not affirm or deny anything of it. Moreover, as we conceive the ideas that are in the minds of other spirits by means of our own, which we suppose to be resemblances of them, so we know other spirits by means of our own soul—which in that sense is the image or idea of them; it having a like respect to other spirits that blueness or heat by me perceived has to those ideas perceived by another.

141. It must not be supposed that they who assert the natural immortality of the soul are of opinion that it is absolutely incapable of annihilation even by the infinite power of the Creator who first gave it being, but only that it is not liable to be broken or dissolved by the ordinary laws of nature or motion. They indeed who hold the soul of man to be only a thin vital flame, or system of animal spirits, make it perishing and corruptible as the body; since there is nothing more easily dissipated than such a being, which it is naturally impossible should survive the ruin of the tabernacle wherein it is enclosed. And this notion has been greedily embraced and cherished by the worst part of mankind, as the most effectual antidote against all impressions of virtue and religion. But it has been made evident that bodies, of what frame or texture soever, are barely passive ideas in the mind, which is more distant and heterogeneous from them than light is from darkness. We have shown that the soul is indivisible, incorporeal, unextended, and it is consequently incorruptible. Nothing can be plainer than that the motions, changes, decays, and dissolutions which we hourly see befall natural bodies (and which is what we mean by "the course of nature") cannot possibly affect an active, simple, uncompounded substance; such a being therefore is indissoluble by the force of nature; that is to say, the soul of man is naturally immortal.

142. After what has been said, it is, I suppose, plain that our souls are not to be known in the same manner as senseless, inactive objects, or by way of *idea*. *Spirits* and *ideas* are things so wholly different that when we say "they exist," "they are known," or the like, these words must not be thought to signify anything common to both natures. There is nothing alike or common in them: and to expect that by any multiplication or enlargement of our faculties we may be enabled to know a spirit as we do a triangle seems as absurd as if we should hope to see a sound. This is inculcated because I imagine it may be of moment toward clearing several important questions and preventing some very dangerous errors concerning the nature of the soul. We may not, I think, strictly be said to have an *idea* of an active being, or of an action, although we may be said to have a *notion* of them. I have some knowledge or notion of my mind, and its acts about ideas, inasmuch as I know or understand what is meant by those words. What I know, that I have some notion of. I will

not say that the terms "idea" and "notion" may not be used convertibly, if the world will have it so; but yet it conduces to clearness and propriety that we distinguish things very different by different names. It is also to be remarked that, all relations including an act of the mind, we cannot so properly be said to have an idea, but rather a notion of the relations or habitudes between things. But if, in the modern way, the word "idea" is extended to spirits, and relations, and acts, this is, after all, an affair of verbal concern.

143. It will not be amiss to add that the doctrine of *abstract ideas* has had no small share in rendering those sciences intricate and obscure which are particularly conversant about spiritual things. Men have imagined they could frame abstract notions of the powers and acts of the mind and consider them prescinded as well from the mind or spirit itself as from their respective objects and effects. Hence a great number of dark and ambiguous terms, presumed to stand for abstract notions, have been introduced into metaphysics and morality, and from these have grown infinite distractions and disputes amongst the learned.

144. But nothing seems more to have contributed toward engaging men in controversies and mistakes with regard to the nature and operations of the mind than the being used to speak of those things in terms borrowed from sensible ideas. For example, the will is termed "the motion of the soul": this infuses a belief that the mind of man is as a ball in motion, impelled and determined by the objects of sense, as necessarily as that is by the stroke of a racket. Hence arise endless scruples and errors of dangerous consequence in morality. All which, I doubt not, may be cleared, and truth appear plain, uniform, and consistent, could but philosophers be prevailed on to retire into themselves, and attentively consider their own meaning.

145. From what has been said it is plain that we cannot know the existence of other spirits otherwise than by their operations, or the ideas by them excited in us. I perceive several motions, changes, and combinations of ideas that inform me there are certain particular agents, like myself, which accompany them and concur in their production. Hence, the knowledge I have of other spirits is not immediate, as is the knowledge of my ideas, but depending on the intervention of ideas, by me referred to agents or spirits distinct from myself, as effects or concomitant signs.

146. But though there be some things which convince us human agents are concerned in producing them, yet it is evident to everyone that those things which are called "the works of nature," that is, the far greater part of the ideas or sensations perceived by us, are not produced by, or dependent on, the wills of men. There is therefore some other spirit that causes them; since it is repugnant that they should subsist by themselves. See sec. 29. But, if we attentively consider the constant regularity, order, and concatenation of natural things, the surprising magnificence, beauty, and perfection of the larger, and the exquisite contrivance of the smaller parts of the creation, together with the exact harmony and correspondence of the whole, but above all the never-enough-admired laws of pain and pleasure, and the instincts or natural inclinations, appetites, and passions of animals; I say if we consider all these things, and at the same time attend to the meaning and import of the attributes: one, eternal, infinitely wise, good, and perfect, we shall clearly perceive that they belong to the aforesaid spirit, "who works all in all," and "by whom all things consist."

147. Hence it is evident that God is known as certainly and immediately as any other mind or spirit whatsoever distinct from ourselves. We may even assert that the existence of God is far more evidently perceived than the existence of men; because the effects of nature are infinitely more numerous and considerable than those ascribed to human agents. There is not any one mark that denotes a man, or effect produced by him, which does not more strongly evince the being of that spirit who is the Author of Nature. For it is evident that in

affecting other persons the will of man has no other object than barely the motion of the limbs of his body; but that such a motion should be attended by, or excite any idea in the mind of another, depends wholly on the will of the Creator. He alone it is who, "upholding all things by the word of his power," maintains that intercourse between spirits whereby they are able to perceive the existence of each other. And yet this pure and clear light which enlightens everyone is itself invisible.

148. It seems to be a general pretense of the unthinking herd that they cannot *see* God. Could we but see him, say they, as we see a man, we should believe that he is, and, believing, obey his commands. But alas, we need only open our eyes to see the sovereign Lord of all things, with a more full and clear view than we do any one of our fellow creatures. Not that I imagine we see God (as some will have it) by a direct and immediate view; or see corporeal things, not by themselves, but by seeing that which represents them in the essence of God, which doctrine is, I must confess, to me incomprehensible. But I shall explain my meaning: a human spirit or person is not perceived by sense, as not being an idea; when therefore we see the color, size, figure, and motions of a man, we perceive only certain sensations or ideas excited in our own minds; and these being exhibited to our view in sundry distinct collections, serve to mark out unto us the existence of finite and created spirits like ourselves. Hence it is plain we do not see a man—if by "man" is meant that which lives, moves, perceives, and thinks as we do—but only such a certain collection of ideas as directs us to think there is a distinct principle of thought and motion, like to ourselves, accompanying and represented by it. And after the same manner we see God; all the difference is that, whereas some one finite and narrow assemblage of ideas denotes a particular human mind, whithersoever we direct our view, we do at all times and in all places perceive manifest tokens of the divinity: everything we see, hear, feel, or anywise perceive by sense, being a sign or effect of the power of God; as is our perception of those very motions which are produced by men.

149. It is therefore plain that nothing can be more evident to anyone that is capable of the least reflection than the existence of God, or a spirit who is intimately present to our minds, producing in them all that variety of ideas or sensations which continually affect us, on whom we have an absolute and entire dependence, in short "in whom we live, and move, and have our being." That the discovery of this great truth, which lies so near and obvious to the mind, should be attained to by the reason of so very few, is a sad instance of the stupidity and inattention of men who, though they are surrounded with such clear manifestations of the Deity, are yet so little affected by them that they seem, as it were, blinded with excess of light.

150. But you will say, has nature no share in the production of natural things, and must they be all ascribed to the immediate and sole operation of God? I answer, if by "nature" is meant only the visible *series* of effects or sensations imprinted on our minds, according to certain fixed and general laws, then it is plain that nature, taken in this sense, cannot produce anything at all. But, if by "nature" is meant some being distinct from God, as well as from the laws of nature, and things perceived by sense, I must confess that word is to me an empty sound without any intelligible meaning annexed to it. Nature, in this acceptation, is a vain chimera, introduced by those heathens who had not just notions of the omnipresence and infinite perfection of God. But it is more unaccountable that it should be received among Christians, professing belief in the Holy Scriptures, which constantly ascribe those effects to the immediate hand of God that heathen philosophers are wont to impure to nature. "The Lord he causeth the vapours to ascend; he maketh lightnings with rain; he bringeth forth the wind out of his treasures." Jerem. 10:13. "He turneth the shadow of

death into the morning, and maketh the day dark with night." Amos 5:8. "He visiteth the earth, and maketh it soft with showers: He blesseth the springing thereof, and crowneth the year with his goodness; so that the pastures are clothed with flocks, and the valleys are covered over with corn." See Psalm 65. But notwithstanding that this is the constant language of Scripture, yet we have I know not what aversion from believing that God concerns himself so nearly in our affairs. Fain would we suppose him at a great distance off, and substitute some blind, unthinking deputy in his stead, though (if we may believe Saint Paul) "he be not far from every one of us."

151. It will, I doubt not, be objected that the slow and gradual methods observed in the production of natural things do not seem to have for their cause the immediate hand of an Almighty Agent. Besides, monsters, untimely births, fruits blasted in the blossom, rains failing in desert places, miseries incident to human life, and the like, are so many arguments that the whole frame of nature is not immediately actuated and superintended by a spirit of infinite wisdom and goodness. But the answer to this objection is in a good measure plain from sec. 62; it being visible that the aforesaid methods of nature are absolutely necessary, in order to working by the most simple and general rules, and after a steady and consistent manner; which argues both the wisdom and goodness of God. Such is the artificial contrivance of this mighty machine of nature that, whilst its motions and various phenomena strike on our senses, the hand which actuates the whole is itself unperceivable to men of flesh and blood. "Verily" (says the prophet) "thou art a God that hidest thyself." Isaiah 45: 15. But, though God conceal himself from the eyes of the sensual and lazy, who will not be at the least expense of thought, yet to an unbiased and attentive mind nothing can be more plainly legible than the intimate presence of an all-wise Spirit, who fashions, regulates, and sustains the whole system of being. It is clear, from what we have elsewhere observed, that the operating according to general and stated laws is so necessary for our guidance in the affairs of life, and letting us into the secret of nature, that without it all reach and compass of thought, all human sagacity and design, could serve to no manner of purpose; it were even impossible there should be any such faculties or powers in the mind. See sec. 31. Which one consideration abundantly outbalances whatever particular inconveniences may thence arise.

152. We should further consider that the very blemishes and defects of nature are not without their use, in that they make an agreeable sort of variety and augment the beauty of the rest of the creation, as shades in a picture serve to set off the brighter and more enlightened parts. We would likewise do well to examine whether our taxing the waste of seeds and embryos, and accidental destruction of plants and animals, before they come to full maturity, as an imprudence in the Author of Nature, be not the effect of prejudice contracted by our familiarity with impotent and saving mortals. In man indeed a thrifty management of those things which he cannot procure without much pains and industry may be esteemed wisdom. But we must not imagine that the inexplicably fine machine of an animal or vegetable costs the great Creator any more pains or trouble in its production than a pebble does; nothing being more evident than that an omnipotent spirit can indifferently produce everything by a mere fiat or act of his will. Hence, it is plain that the splendid profusion of natural things should not be interpreted weakness or prodigality in the agent who produces them, but rather be looked on as an argument of the riches of his power.

153. As for the mixture of pain or uneasiness which is in the world, pursuant to the general laws of nature, and the actions of finite, imperfect spirits, this, in the state we are in at present, is indispensably necessary to our well-being. But our prospects are too narrow. We take, for instance, the idea of some one particular pain into our thoughts, and account

it *evil;* whereas, if we enlarge our view, so as to comprehend the various ends, connections, and dependencies of things, on what occasions and in what proportions we are affected with pain and pleasure, the nature of human freedom, and the design with which we are put into the world; we shall be forced to acknowledge that those particular things which, considered in themselves, appear to be evil, have the nature of good, when considered as linked with the whole system of beings.

154. From what has been said, it will be manifest to any considering person, that it is merely for want of attention and comprehensiveness of mind that there are any favorers of atheism or the Manichaean heresy to be found. Little and unreflecting souls may indeed burlesque the works of Providence the beauty and order whereof they have not capacity, or will not be at the pains to comprehend; but those who are masters of any justness and extent of thought, and are withal used to reflect, can never sufficiently admire the divine traces of wisdom and goodness that shine throughout the economy of nature. But what truth is there which shines so strongly on the mind that by an aversion of thought, a willful shutting of the eyes, we may not escape seeing it? Is it therefore to be wondered at if the generality of men, who are ever intent on business or pleasure, and little used to fix or open the eye of their mind, should not have all that conviction and evidence of the being of God which might be expected in reasonable creatures?

155. We should rather wonder that men can be found so stupid as to neglect, than that neglecting they should be unconvinced of such an evident and momentous truth. And yet it is to be feared that too many of parts and leisure, who live in Christian countries, are, merely through a supine and dreadful negligence, sunk into a sort of atheism. Since it is downright impossible that a soul pierced and enlightened with a thorough sense of the omnipresence, holiness, and justice of that Almighty Spirit should persist in a remorseless violation of his laws. We ought, therefore, earnestly to meditate and dwell on those important points; that so we may attain conviction without all scruple "that the eyes of the Lord are in every place beholding the evil and the good; that he is with us and keepth us in all places whither we go, and giveth us bread to eat and raiment to put on"; that he is present and conscious to our innermost thoughts; and that we have a most absolute and immediate dependence on him. A clear view of which great truths cannot choose but fill our hearts with an awful circumspection and holy fear, which is the strongest incentive to *virtue* and the best guard against *vice.*

156. For, after all, what deserves the first place in our studies is the consideration of God and our duty; which to promote, as it was the main drift and design of my labors, so shall I esteem them altogether useless and ineffectual if, by what I have said, I cannot inspire my readers with a pious sense of the presence of God; and, having shown the falseness or vanity of those barren speculations which make the chief employment of learned men, the better dispose them to reverence and embrace the salutary truths of the Gospel, which to know and to practice is the highest perfection of human nature.

CHAPTER

30

HUME

1711–1776

Born in Edinburgh, Scotland, David Hume began his studies in law until he discovered the writings of the philosophers. To support himself he worked in a merchant's office in Bristol, then moved to La Flèche, France, and attended Descartes's old school. There he began writing his monumental *Treatise of Human Nature*. Three years later he published it in England, but the work was completely ignored. In his own words, "It fell dead-born from the press."

Hume tried, and failed, to get a teaching position in philosophy. To make matters worse, those who had read the *Treatise* accused him of heresy and atheism. Hume tried to support himself by tutoring a marquess, then became a secretary, first to a general and then to an ambassador. After failing yet again in 1752 to get hired as a philosopher in Glasgow, he got a job as head librarian at the Advocates' library at Edinburgh, where he continued to write and further develop his views.

Hume rewrote much of Book I of the *Treatise* and used it as the basis for his *Enquiry Concerning Human Understanding* (1748). The material from Book III was incorporated into his *Enquiry Concerning the Principles of Morals* (1751). Finally, by the time he was in his late forties, these reworkings of his original views began attracting a steadily growing audience, so that by 1762, James Boswell declared Hume to be "the greatest writer in Britain." Hume had a tremendous influence on nearly all philosophers who came after him. He inspired Auguste Comte in his development of positivism, an antitheological and antimetaphysical system of scientific knowledge. His moral philosophy influenced Jeremy Bentham and John Stuart Mill. Immanuel Kant claimed that Hume awoke him from his "dogmatic slumbers."

Hume pushed Locke's and Berkeley's empiricism to its logical conclusion. Whereas Locke's views were tempered by commonsense notions of reality, often inconsistently, and Berkeley made an exception to his empiricist principles by relying on the concept of a transcendental other—God—Hume refused to make his philosophy bow either to common sense—for which he was criticized by Thomas Reid (1710–1796)—or to transcendental metaphysics. He wanted to create a fully consistent but purely empirical philosophy. Bertrand Russell, a sympathetic critic of Hume, remarked that by making the empirical philosophy of Berkeley and Locke consistent, Hume "made it incredible." Indeed, not only does Hume deny the existence of a Berkeleyian or Cartesian self, he also provides devastating empirical criticisms of many metaphysical concepts, such as causation, morality, space, time, and freedom, formulating skeptical objections to all inferences that go beyond immediate experience. Even impressions of the "external" senses exist only in the sensing mind, and he rejects all attempts to argue from the senses to the existence of a continuing physical substance outside the mind.

Hume develops Berkeley's criticism of abstract ideas and general entities to their extreme and ends up dissolving the idea of a continuously existing mental substance. He replaces the notion of a unified, continuously existing soul with the famous "bundle theory" of the mind that has so influenced twentieth-century personal identity theorists. According to Hume, the mind is an aggregate, or bundle, of discrete and discontinuous experiences; our minds only seem continuous to us because our imaginations smooth out the borders, bumps, and ceaseless changes. Hume claims that he will be applying Newton's experimental method to the human mind in an effort to develop a "science of man." In his *Enquiry Concerning Human Understanding,* obviously with reference to Locke's *Essay Concerning Human Understanding,* Hume analyzes the mind into a bundle of perceptions, of which there are but two kinds: *impressions* and *ideas,* thereby restoring "the word, idea, to its original sense, from which Mr. Locke had perverted it, in making it stand for all our perceptions."

In Hume's view, there is no causality among perceptions. Hume will conclude that there is no need whatsoever for the supposition that there must be something underlying the various perceived qualities: he will thereby deny substantiality to immaterial as well as to material beings. All that is real are the *impressions* and the *ideas.* Impressions are perceptions that enter most immediately and vividly by way of the senses, whereas ideas are perceptions that are dim facsimiles of impressions. All ideas originate from impressions, each of which is distinct, exists only for a brief moment, and is disconnected from any other impression; how, then, can we justify all our beliefs that reach beyond the contents of our present consciousness? Ultimately, we can't, which will bring us to Hume's problem of induction.

Thus far, then, Hume has analyzed the mind into *perceptions.* He then further analyzes the perceptions into impressions and ideas. Next, he proceeded to the stage of *synthesis,* that is, putting these impressions and ideas together by offering an explanation in terms of the *principles* that bind these elements together into a fully functioning mind. He finds that all the elements of the mind are conjoined, or bound together, by various principles of *association.* There are three principles of association among our ideas: (1) *resemblance,* (2) *contiguity,* and (3) *cause and effect.* Just as Newton's theory of universal gravity governs the elements of the entire physical universe, so the "gentle force" of association governs the entire mind. It is, according to Hume, "a kind of Attraction, which in the mental world will be found to have as extraordinary effects as in the natural, and to show itself in as many as various forms."

Why, for instance, do we all believe in the uniformity of nature? Here is Hume's answer: the "reason" why we all believe as we do is not, itself, a *reason.* It is, itself, just a *fact.* This answer goes contrary to just about all previous philosophies, both Platonic and Aristotelian, which assumed that the universe and the mind each function according to certain laws of cause and effect. Under the sharp knife of Hume's analysis, however, cause and effect dissolve into a psychological construction based on habit: it is a fiction without any reason or evidence behind it. We can never, even in principle, reach beyond the fleeting, momentary, chaotic experience of the present moment to infer truths about the world that reach beyond the tiny duration of brief instants: neither experience, which is fleeting, nor reason—which is but a psychological sense of seeming connections where there are none—can reach beyond experience. Since the relation of cause and effect is the foundation of all our beliefs about everything that we are not right now at this instant of our lives experiencing, the entire world built up by common sense as well as by science *is a construction, an elaborate fiction, without any reason behind it.* All the traditions have just gone up in Pyrrhonian flames; hence the devastating conclusion with which our selection from his *Enquiry* ends.

A section of Hume's *Treatise of Human Nature* titled "Of Personal Identity," our second selection, contains his famous denial of the self. It contains passages that are among the most often quoted in the whole of philosophy. Hume is not merely proving the nonexistence of the self; he is making the much more radical claim that *we do not even have any idea of such a thing!* It is an empty word, like "God," whose reference is to nothing. Thus, technically speaking, Hume is not so much *denying* the existence of the self as he is claiming that to affirm or to deny the existence of the self is to speak utter nonsense. To see why he felt this is nonsense, we must understand Hume claims that there is no impression that corresponds to the (imaginary, fictive) idea of the self. He is applying his own introspective method of paying close attention to the phenomena of his own experience without theorizing about it or framing any hypothesis that goes beyond the immediate data of his experience. All he finds are individual sensations, emotions, and thoughts. There is no unity at a time because of the disjoint cascade of individual impressions flickering in and out of existence; there is no identity at a time because these individual flickerings do not last very long, their duration is "unimaginably brief," not even a few seconds. Thus in the case of "I am cold," the reference of the word *I* is, at best, directed to a bundle of perceptions. There is not even an *idea* corresponding to a self. There are only the *impressions.* There may be qualitative similarity but there is no numerical identity between one impression and another, even if they are exactly similar (that one was *then and there,* this one is *here and now*). So there is no personal identity over time.

In his *Dialogues Concerning Natural Religion,* from which our third selection is taken, Hume mounts a detailed and searing attack on all the major arguments for the existence of God and presents a devastating version of the argument from evil against God's existence. Fearing that his *Dialogues* would again get him into trouble with church authorities, he left instructions to his nephew to publish them posthumously, which he did in 1777.

AN ENQUIRY CONCERNING HUMAN UNDERSTANDING

SECTION II
Of the Origin of Ideas

Every one will readily allow, that there is a considerable difference between the perceptions of the mind, when a man feels the pain of excessive heat, or the pleasure of moderate

From David Hume, *An Enquiry Concerning Human Understanding,* ed. L. A. Selby-Bigge (Oxford: Clarendon Press, 1902).

warmth, and when he afterwards recalls to his memory this sensation, or anticipates it by his imagination. These faculties may mimic or copy the perceptions of the senses; but they never can entirely reach the force and vivacity of the original sentiment. The utmost we say of them, even when they operate with greatest vigour, is, that they represent their object in so lively a manner, that we could *almost* say we feel or see it. But, except the mind be disordered by disease or madness, they never can arrive at such a pitch of vivacity, as to render these perceptions altogether undistinguishable. All the colours of poetry, however splendid, can never paint natural objects in such a manner as to make the description be taken for a real landskip. The most lively thought is still inferior to the dullest sensation.

We may observe a like distinction to run through all the other perceptions of the mind. A man in a fit of anger, is actuated in a very different manner from one who only thinks of that emotion. If you tell me, that any person is in love, I easily understand your meaning, and form a just conception of his situation; but never can mistake that conception for the real disorders and agitations of the passion. When we reflect on our past sentiments and affections, our thought is a faithful mirror, and copies its objects truly; but the colours which it employs are faint and dull, in comparison of those in which our original perceptions were clothed. It requires no nice discernment or metaphysical head to mark the distinction between them.

Here therefore we may divide all the perceptions of the mind into two classes or species, which are distinguished by their different degrees of force and vivacity. The less forcible and lively are commonly denominated *Thoughts* or *Ideas*. The other species want a name in our language, and in most others; I suppose, because it was not requisite for any but philosophical purposes, to rank them under a general term or appellation. Let us, therefore, use a little freedom, and call them *Impressions;* employing that word in a sense somewhat different from the usual. By the term *impression,* then, I mean all our more lively perceptions, when we hear, or see, or feel, or love, or hate, or desire, or will. And the impressions are distinguished from ideas, which are the less lively perceptions, of which we are conscious, when we reflect on any of those sensations or movements above mentioned.

Nothing, at first view, may seem more unbounded than the thought of man, which not only escapes all human power and authority, but is not even restrained within the limits of nature and reality. To form monsters, and join incongruous shapes and appearances, costs the imagination no more trouble than to conceive the most natural and familiar objects. And while the body is confined to one planet, along which it creeps with pain and difficulty; the thought can in an instant transport us into the most distant regions of the universe; or even beyond the universe, into the unbounded chaos, where nature is supposed to lie in total confusion. What never was seen, or heard of, may yet be conceived; nor is any thing beyond the power of thought, except what implies an absolute contradiction.

But though our thought seems to possess this unbounded liberty, we shall find, upon a nearer examination, that it is really confined within very narrow limits, and that all this creative power of the mind amounts to no more than the faculty of compounding, transposing, augmenting, or diminishing the materials afforded us by the senses and experience. When we think of a golden mountain, we only join two consistent ideas, *gold,* and *mountain,* with which we were formerly acquainted. A virtuous horse we can conceive; because, from our own feeling, we can conceive virtue; and this we may unite to the figure and shape of a horse, which is an animal familiar to us. In short, all the materials of thinking are derived either from our outward or inward sentiment: The mixture and composition of these belongs alone to the mind and will. Or, to express myself in philosophical language, all our ideas or more feeble perceptions are copies of our impressions or more lively ones.

To prove this, the two following arguments will, I hope, be sufficient. First, when we analyze our thoughts or ideas, however compounded or sublime, we always find that they resolve themselves into such simple ideas as were copied from a precedent feeling or sentiment. Even those ideas, which, at first view, seem the most wide of this origin, are found, upon a nearer scrutiny, to be derived from it. The idea of God, as meaning an infinitely intelligent, wise, and good Being, arises from reflecting on the operations of our own mind, and augmenting, without limit, those qualities of goodness and wisdom. We may prosecute this enquiry to what length we please; where we shall always find, that every idea which we examine is copied from a similar impression. Those who would assert that this position is not universally true nor without exception, have only one, and that an easy method of refuting it; by producing that idea, which, in their opinion, is not derived from this source. It will then be incumbent on us, if we would maintain our doctrine, to produce the impression, or lively perception, which corresponds to it.

Secondly. If it happen, from a defect of the organ, that a man is not susceptible of any species of sensation, we always find that he is as little susceptible of the correspondent ideas. A blind man can form no notion of colours; a deaf man of sounds. Restore either of them that sense in which he is deficient; by opening this new inlet for his sensations, you also open an inlet for the ideas; and he finds no difficulty in conceiving these objects. The case is the same, if the object, proper for exciting any sensation, has never been applied to the organ. A Laplander or Negro has no notion of the relish of wine. And though there are few or no instances of a like deficiency in the mind, where a person has never felt or is wholly incapable of a sentiment or passion that belongs to his species; yet we find the same observation to take place in a less degree. A man of mild manners can form no idea of inveterate revenge or cruelty; nor can a selfish heart easily conceive the heights of friendship and generosity. It is readily allowed, that other beings may possess many senses of which we can have no conception; because the ideas of them have never been introduced to us in the only manner by which an idea can have access to the mind, to wit, by the actual feeling and sensation.

There is, however, one contradictory phenomenon, which may prove that it is not absolutely impossible for ideas to arise, independent of their correspondent impressions. I believe it will readily be allowed, that the several distinct ideas of colour, which enter by the eye, or those of sound, which are conveyed by the ear, are really different from each other; though, at the same time, resembling. Now if this be true of different colours, it must be no less so of the different shades of the same colour; and each shade produces a distinct idea, independent of the rest. For if this should be denied, it is possible, by the continual gradation of shades, to run a colour insensibly into what is most remote from it; and if you will not allow any of the means to be different, you cannot, without absurdity, deny the extremes to be the same. Suppose, therefore, a person to have enjoyed his sight for thirty years, and to have become perfectly acquainted with colours of all kinds except one particular shade of blue, for instance, which it never has been his fortune to meet with. Let all the different shades of that colour, except that single one, be placed before him, descending gradually from the deepest to the lightest; it is plain that he will perceive a blank, where that shade is wanting, and will be sensible that there is a greater distance in that place between the contiguous colours than in any other. Now I ask, whether it be possible for him, from his own imagination, to supply this deficiency, and raise up to himself the idea of that particular shade, though it had never been conveyed to him by his senses? I believe there are few but will be of opinion that he can: and this may serve as a proof that the simple ideas are not always, in every instance, derived from the correspondent impressions; though this instance is so singular, that it is scarcely worth our observing, and does not merit that for it alone we should alter our general maxim.

Here, therefore, is a proposition, which not only seems, in itself, simple and intelligible; but, if a proper use were made of it, might render every dispute equally intelligible, and banish all that jargon, which has so long taken possession of metaphysical reasonings, and drawn disgrace upon them. All ideas, especially abstract ones, are naturally faint and obscure: the mind has but a slender hold of them: they are apt to be confounded with other resembling ideas; and when we have often employed any term, though without a distinct meaning, we are apt to imagine it has a determinate idea annexed to it. On the contrary, all impressions, that is, all sensations, either outward or inward, are strong and vivid: The limits between them are more exactly determined: nor is it easy to fall into any error or mistake with regard to them. When we entertain, therefore, any suspicion that a philosophical term is employed without any meaning or idea (as is but too frequent), we need but enquire, *from what impression is that supposed idea derived?* And if it be impossible to assign any, this will serve to confirm our suspicion. By bringing ideas into so clear a light we may reasonably hope to remove all dispute, which may arise, concerning their nature and reality.

SECTION III
Of the Association of Ideas

It is evident, that there is a principle or connection between the different thoughts or ideas of the mind, and that, in their appearance to the memory or imagination, they introduce each other with a certain degree of method and regularity. In our more serious thinking or discourse this is so observable that any particular thought, which breaks in upon the regular tract or chain of ideas, is immediately remarked and rejected. And even in our wildest and most wandering reveries, nay in our very dreams, we shall find, if we reflect, that the imagination ran not altogether at adventures, but that there was still a connection upheld among the different ideas, which succeeded each other. Were the loosest and freest conversation to be transcribed there would immediately be observed something which connected it in all its transitions. Or where this is wanting, the person who broke the thread of discourse might still inform you, that there had secretly revolved in his mind a succession of thought, which had gradually led him from the subject of conversation. Among different languages, even where we cannot suspect the least connection or communication, it is found, that the words, expressive of ideas, the most compounded, do yet nearly correspond to each other: a certain proof, that the simple ideas, comprehended in the compound ones, were bound together by some universal principle, which had an unequal influence on all mankind.

Though it be too obvious to escape observation, that different ideas are connected together; I do not find that any philosopher has attempted to enumerate or class all the principles of association; a subject, however, that seems worthy of curiosity. To me, there appear to be only three principles of connection among ideas, namely, *Resemblance, Contiguity* in time or place, and *Cause* or *Effect.*

That these principles serve to connect ideas will not, I believe, be much doubted. A picture naturally leads our thoughts to the original: the mention of one apartment in a building naturally introduces an enquiry or discourse concerning the others: and if we think of a wound, we can scarcely forbear reflecting on the pain which follows it. But that this enumeration is complete, and that there are no other principles of association except these, may be difficult to prove to the satisfaction of the reader, or even to a man's own satisfaction.

All we can do, in such cases, is to run over several instances, and examine carefully the principle which binds the different thoughts to each other, never stopping till we render the principle as general as possible. The more instances we examine, and the more care we employ, the more assurance shall we acquire, that the enumeration, which we form from the whole, is complete and entire.

SECTION IV
Sceptical Doubts Concerning the Operations of the Understanding

PART I

All the objects of human reason or enquiry may naturally be divided into two kinds, to wit, *Relations of Ideas,* and *Matters of Fact.* Of the first kind are the sciences of Geometry, Algebra, and Arithmetic; and in short, every affirmation which is either intuitively or demonstratively certain. *That the square of the hypothenuse is equal to the squares of the two sides,* is a proposition which expresses a relation between these figures. *That three times five is equal to the half of thirty,* expresses a relation between these numbers. Propositions of this kind are discoverable by the mere operation of thought, without dependence on what is anywhere existent in the universe. Though there never were a circle or triangle in nature, the truths demonstrated by Euclid would for ever retain their certainty and evidence.

Matters of fact, which are the second objects of human reason, are not ascertained in the same manner; nor is our evidence of their truth, however great, of a like nature with the foregoing. The contrary of every matter of fact is still possible; because it can never imply a contradiction, and is conceived by the mind with the same facility and distinctness, as if ever so conformable to reality. *That the sun will not rise to-morrow* is no less intelligible a proposition, and implies no more contradiction than the affirmation, *that it will rise.* We should in vain, therefore, attempt to demonstrate its falsehood. Were it demonstratively false, it would imply a contradiction, and could never be distinctly conceived by the mind.

It may, therefore, be a subject worthy of curiosity, to enquire what is the nature of that evidence which assures us of any real existence and matter of fact, beyond the present testimony of our senses, or the records of our memory. This part of philosophy, it is observable, has been little cultivated, either by the ancients or moderns; and therefore our doubts and errors, in the prosecution of so important an enquiry, may be the more excusable; while we march through such difficult paths without any guide or direction. They may even prove useful, by exciting curiosity, and destroying that implicit faith and security, which is the bane of all reasoning and free enquiry. The discovery of defects in the common philosophy, if any such there be, will not, I presume, be a discouragement, but rather an incitement, as is usual, to attempt something more full and satisfactory than has yet been proposed to the public.

All reasonings concerning matter of fact seem to be founded on the relation of *Cause and Effect.* By means of that relation alone we can go beyond the evidence of our memory and senses. If you were to ask a man, why he believes any matter of fact, which is absent; for instance, that his friend is in the country, or in France; he would give you a reason; and this reason would be some other fact; as a letter received from him, or the knowledge of his former resolutions and promises. A man finding a watch or any other machine in a desert island, would conclude that there had once been men in that island. All our reasonings concerning fact are of the same nature. And here it is constantly supposed that there is a connection between the present fact and that which is inferred from it. Were there nothing to bind them together, the inference would be entirely precarious. The hearing of an articulate voice and rational discourse in the dark assures us of the presence of some person: Why? because these are the effects of the human make and fabric, and closely connected with it. If we anatomize all the other reasonings of this nature, we shall find that they are founded on the relation of cause and effect, and that this relation is either near or remote, direct or collateral. Heat and light are collateral effects of fire, and the one effect may justly be inferred from the other.

If we would satisfy ourselves, therefore, concerning the nature of that evidence, which assures us of matters of fact, we must enquire how we arrive at the knowledge of cause and effect.

I shall venture to affirm, as a general proposition, which admits of no exception, that the knowledge of this relation is not, in any instance, attained by reasonings *a priori;* but arises entirely from experience, when we find that any particular objects are constantly conjoined with each other. Let an object be presented to a man of ever so strong natural reason and abilities; if that object be entirely new to him, he will not be able, by the most accurate examination of its sensible qualities, to discover any of its causes or effects. Adam, though his rational faculties be supposed, at the very first, entirely perfect, could not have inferred from the fluidity and transparency of water that it would suffocate him, or from the light and warmth of fire that it would consume him. No object ever discovers, by the qualities which appear to the senses, either the causes which produced it, or the effects which will arise from it; nor can our reason, unassisted by experience, ever draw any inference concerning real existence and matter of fact.

This proposition, *that causes and effects are discoverable, not by reason but by experience,* will readily be admitted with regard to such objects, as we remember to have once been altogether unknown to us; since we must be conscious of the utter inability, which we then lay under, of foretelling what would arise from them. Present two smooth pieces of marble to a man who has no tincture of natural philosophy; he will never discover that they will adhere together in such a manner as to require great force to separate them in a direct line, while they make so small a resistance to a lateral pressure. Such events, as bear little analogy to the common course of nature, are also readily confessed to be known only by experience; nor does any man imagine that the explosion of gunpowder, or the attraction of a loadstone, could ever be discovered by arguments *a priori*. In like manner, when an effect is supposed to depend upon an intricate machinery or secret structure of parts, we make no difficulty in attributing all our knowledge of it to experience. Who will assert that he can give the ultimate reason, why milk or bread is proper nourishment for a man, not for a lion or a tiger?

But the same truth may not appear, at first sight, to have the same evidence with regard to events, which have become familiar to us from our first appearance in the world, which bear a close analogy to the whole course of nature, and which are supposed to depend on the simple qualities of objects, without any secret structure of parts. We are apt to imagine that we could discover these effects by the mere operation of our reason, without experience. We fancy, that were we brought on a sudden into this world, we could at first have inferred that one Billiard-ball would communicate motion to another upon impulse; and that we needed not to have waited for the event, in order to pronounce with certainty concerning it. Such is the influence of custom, that, where it is strongest, it not only covers our natural ignorance, but even conceals itself, and seems not to take place, merely because it is found in the highest degree.

But to convince us that all the laws of nature, and all the operations of bodies without exception, are known only by experience, the following reflections may, perhaps, suffice. Were any object presented to us, and were we required to pronounce concerning the effect, which will result from it, without consulting past observation; after what manner, I beseech you, must the mind proceed in this operation? It must invent or imagine some event, which it ascribes to the object as its effect; and it is plain that this invention must be entirely arbitrary. The mind can never possibly find the effect in the supposed cause, by the most accurate scrutiny and examination. For the effect is totally different from the cause, and consequently can never be discovered in it. Motion in the second Billiard-ball is a quite distinct event from motion in the first; nor is there anything in the one to suggest the smallest hint of the other. A stone or piece of metal raised into the air, and left without any support, immediately falls: but to consider the matter *a priori*, is there anything we discover in this situation which can beget the idea of a downward, rather than an upward, or any other motion, in the stone or metal?

And as the first imagination or invention of a particular effect, in all natural operations, is arbitrary, where we consult not experience; so must we also esteem the supposed tie or connection between the cause and effect, which binds them together, and renders it impossible that any other effect could result from the operation of that cause. When I see, for instance, a Billiard-ball moving in a straight line towards another; even suppose motion in the second ball should by accident be suggested to me, as the result of their contact or impulse; may I not conceive, that a hundred different events might as well follow from that cause? May not both these balls remain at absolute rest? May not the first ball return in a straight line, or leap off from the second in any line or direction? All these suppositions are consistent and conceivable. Why then should we give the preference to one, which is no more consistent or conceivable than the rest? All our reasonings *a priori* will never be able to show us any foundation for this preference.

In a word, then, every effect is a distinct event from its cause. It could not therefore, be discovered in the cause, and the first invention or conception of it, *a priori*, must be entirely arbitrary. And even after it is suggested, the conjunction of it with the cause must appear equally arbitrary; since there are always many other effects, which, to reason, must seem fully as consistent and natural. In vain, therefore, should we pretend to determine any single event, or infer any cause or effect, without the assistance of observation and experience.

Hence we may discover the reason why no philosopher, who is rational and modest, has ever pretended to assign the ultimate cause of any natural operation, or to show distinctly the action of that power, which produces any single effect in the universe. It is confessed, that the utmost effort of human reason is to reduce the principles, productive of natural phenomena, to a greater simplicity, and to resolve the many particular effects into a few general causes, by means of reasonings from analogy, experience, and observation. But as to the causes of these general causes, we should in vain attempt their discovery; nor shall we ever be able to satisfy ourselves, by any particular explication of them. These ultimate springs and principles are totally shut up from human curiosity and enquiry. Elasticity, gravity, cohesion of parts, communication of motion by impulse; these are probably the ultimate causes and principles which we ever discover in nature; and we may esteem ourselves sufficiently happy, if, by accurate enquiry and reasoning, we can trace up the particular phenomena to, or near to, these general principles. The most perfect philosophy of the natural kind only staves off our ignorance a little longer: as perhaps the most perfect philosophy of the moral or metaphysical kind serves only to discover larger portions of it. Thus the observation of human blindness and weakness is the result of all philosophy, and meets us at every turn, in spite of our endeavours to elude or avoid it.

Nor is geometry, when taken into the assistance of natural philosophy, even able to remedy this defect, or lead us into the knowledge of ultimate causes, by all that accuracy of reasoning for which it is so justly celebrated. Every part of mixed mathematics proceeds upon the supposition that certain laws are established by nature in her operations; and abstract reasonings are employed, either to assist experience in the discovery of these laws, or to determine their influence in particular instances, where it depends upon any precise degree of distance and quantity. Thus, it is a law of motion, discovered by experience, that the moment or force of any body in motion is in the compound ratio or proportion of its solid contents and its velocity; and consequently, that a small force may remove the greatest obstacle or raise the greatest weight, if, by any contrivance or machinery, we can increase the velocity of that force, so as to make it an overmatch for its antagonist. Geometry assists us in the application of this law, by giving us the just dimensions of all the parts and figures which can enter into any species of machine; but still the discovery of the law itself is owing merely to experience, and all the abstract reasonings in the world could never lead us one step towards the knowledge of it. When we reason *a priori,* and consider merely any object or cause, as it appears to the mind, independent of all observation, it never could suggest to us the notion of any distinct object, such as its effect; much less, show us the inseparable and inviolable connection between them. A man must be very sagacious who could discover by reasoning that crystal is the effect of heat, and ice of cold, without being previously acquainted with the operation of these qualities.

PART II

But we have not yet attained any tolerable satisfaction with regard to the question first proposed. Each solution still gives rise to a new question as difficult as the foregoing, and leads us on to farther enquiries. When it is asked, *What is the nature of all our reasonings concerning matter of fact?* the proper answer seems to be, that they are founded on the relation of cause and effect. When again it is asked, *What is the foundation of all our reasonings and conclusions concerning that relation?* it may be replied in one word, Experience. But if we still carry on our sifting humour, and ask, *What is the foundation of all conclusions from experience?* this implies a new question, which may be of more difficult solution and explication. Philosophers, that give themselves airs of superior wisdom and sufficiency, have a hard task when they encounter persons of inquisitive dispositions, who push them from every corner to which they retreat, and who are sure at last to bring them to some dangerous dilemma. The best expedient to prevent this confusion, is to be modest in our pretentions; and even to discover the difficulty ourselves before it is objected to us. By this means, we may make a kind of merit of our very ignorance.

I shall content myself, in this section, with an easy task, and shall pretend only to give a negative answer to the question here proposed. I say then, that, even after we have experience of the operations of cause and effect, our conclusions from that experience are *not* founded on reasoning, or any process of the understanding. This answer we must endeavour both to explain and to defend.

It must certainly be allowed, that nature has kept us at a great distance from all her secrets, and has afforded us only the knowledge of a few superficial qualities of objects; while she conceals from us those powers and principles on which the influence of those objects entirely depends. Our senses inform us of the colour, weight, and consistence of bread; but neither sense nor reason can ever inform us of those qualities which fit it for the nourishment and support of a human body. Sight or feeling conveys an idea of the actual motion of bodies; but as to that wonderful force or power, which would carry on a moving body for ever in a continued change of place, and which bodies never lose but by communicating it to others; of this we cannot form the most distant conception. But notwithstanding this ignorance of natural powers and principles, we always presume, when we see like sensible qualities, that they have like secret powers, and expect that effects, similar to those which we have experienced, will follow from them. If a body of like colour and consistence with that bread, which we have formerly eaten, be presented to us, we make no scruple of repeating the experiment, and foresee, with certainty, like nourishment and support. Now this is a process of the mind or thought, of which I would willingly know the foundation. It is allowed on all hands that there is no known connection between the sensible qualities and the secret powers; and consequently, that the mind is not led to form such a conclusion concerning their constant and regular conjunction, by anything which it knows of their nature. As to past *Experience,* it can be allowed to give *direct* and *certain* information of those precise objects only, and that precise period of time, which fell under its cognizance: but why this experience should be extended to future times, and to other objects, which, for aught we know, may be only in appearance similar; this is the main question on which I would insist. The bread, which I formerly eat, nourished me; that is, a body of such sensible qualities was, at that time, endued with such secret powers: but does it follow, that other bread must also nourish me at another time, and that like sensible qualities must always be attended with like secret powers? The consequence seems nowise necessary. At least, it must be acknowledged that there is here a consequence drawn by the mind; that there is a certain step taken; a process of thought, and an inference, which wants to be explained. These two propositions are far from being the same, *I have found that such an object has always been attended with such an effect,* and *I foresee, that other objects, which are, in appearance, similar, will be attended with similar effects.* I shall allow, if you please, that the one proposition may justly be inferred from the other: I know, in fact, that it always is inferred. But if you insist that the inference is made by a chain of reasoning, I desire you to produce that reasoning. The connection between these propositions is not intuitive. There is required a medium, which may enable the mind to draw such an inference, if indeed it be drawn by reasoning and argument. What that medium is, I must confess, passes my comprehension; and it is incumbent on those to produce it, who assert that it really exists, and is the origin of all our conclusions concerning matter of fact.

This negative argument must certainly, in process of time, become altogether convincing, if many penetrating and able philosophers shall turn their enquiries this way and no one be ever able to discover any connecting proposition or intermediate step, which supports the understanding in this conclusion. But as the question is yet new, every reader may not trust so far to his own penetration, as to conclude, because an argument escapes his enquiry, that therefore it does not really exist. For this reason it may be requisite to venture upon a more difficult task; and enumerating all the branches of human knowledge, endeavour to show that none of them can afford such an argument.

All reasonings may be divided into two kinds, namely, demonstrative reasoning, or that concerning relations of ideas, and moral reasoning, or that concerning matter of fact and existence. That there are no demonstrative arguments in the case seems evident; since it implies no contradiction that the course of nature may change, and that an object, seemingly like those which we have experienced, may be attended with different or contrary effects. May I not clearly and distinctly conceive that a body, falling from the clouds, and which, in all other respects, resembles snow, has yet the taste of salt or feeling of fire? Is there any more intelligible proposition than to affirm, that all the trees will flourish in December and January, and decay in May and June? Now whatever is intelligible, and can be distinctly conceived, implies no contradiction, and can never be proved false by any demonstrative argument or abstract reasoning *a priori*.

If we be, therefore, engaged by arguments to put trust in past experience, and make it the standard of our future judgement, these arguments must be probable only, or such as regard matter of fact and real existence, according to the division above mentioned. But that there is no argument of this kind, must appear, if our explication of that species of reasoning be admitted as solid and satisfactory. We have said, that all arguments concerning existence are founded on the relation of cause and effect; that our knowledge of that relation is derived entirely from experience; and that all our experimental conclusions proceed upon the supposition that the future will be conformable to the past. To endeavour, therefore, the proof of this last supposition by probable arguments, or arguments regarding existence, must be evidently going in a circle, and taking that for granted, which is the very point in question.

In reality, all arguments from experience are founded on the similarity which we discover among natural objects, and by which we are induced to expect effects similar to those which we have found to follow from such objects. And though none but a fool or madman will ever pretend to dispute the authority of experience, or to reject that great guide of human life, it may surely be allowed a philosopher to have so much curiosity at least as to examine the principle of human nature, which gives this mighty authority to experience, and makes us draw advantage from that similarity which nature has placed among different objects. From causes which appear *similar* we expect similar effects. This is the sum of all our experimental conclusions. Now it seems evident that, if this conclusion were formed by reason, it would be as perfect at first, and upon one instance, as after ever so long a course of experience. But the case is far otherwise. Nothing so like as eggs; yet no one, on account of this appearing similarity, expects the same taste and relish in all of them. It is only after a long course of uniform experiments in any kind, that we attain a firm reliance and security with regard to a particular event. Now where is that process of reasoning which, from one instance, draws a conclusion, so different from that which it infers from a hundred instances that are nowise different from that single one? This question I propose as much for the sake of information, as with an intention of raising difficulties. I cannot find, I cannot imagine any such reasoning. But I keep my mind still open to instruction, if any one will vouchsafe to bestow it on me.

Should it be said, that, from a number of uniform experiments, we *infer* a connection between the sensible qualities and the secret powers; this, I must confess, seems the same difficulty, couched in different terms. The question still recurs, on what process of argument this *inference* is founded? Where is the medium, the interposing ideas, which join propositions so very wide of each other? It is confessed that the colour, consistence, and other sensible qualities of bread appear not, of themselves, to have any connection with the secret powers of nourishment and support. For otherwise we could infer these secret powers from the first appearance of these sensible qualities, without the aid of experience; contrary to the sentiment of all philosophers, and contrary to plain matter of fact. Here, then, is our natural state of ignorance with regard to the powers and influence of all objects. How is this remedied by experience? It only shows us a number of uniform effects, resulting from certain objects, and teaches us that those particular objects, at that particular time, were endowed with such powers and forces. When a new object, endowed with similar sensible qualities, is produced, we expect similar powers and forces, and look for a like effect. From a body of like colour and consistence with bread we expect like nourishment and support.

But this surely is a step or progress of the mind, which wants to be explained. When a man says, *I have found, in all past instances, such sensible qualities conjoined with such secret powers,* and when he says, *Similar sensible qualities will always be conjoined with similar secret powers,* he is not guilty of a tautology, nor are these propositions in any respect the same. You say that the one proposition is an inference from the other. But you must confess that the inference is not intuitive; neither is it demonstrative. Of what nature is it, then? To say it is experimental, is begging the question. For all inferences from experience suppose, as their foundation, that the future will resemble the past, and that similar powers will be conjoined with similar sensible qualities. If there be any suspicion that the course of nature may change, and that the past may be no rule for the future, all experience becomes useless, and can give rise to no inference or conclusion. It is impossible, therefore, that any arguments from experience can prove this resemblance of the past to the future; since all these arguments are founded on the supposition of that resemblance. Let the course of things be allowed hitherto ever so regular; that alone, without some new argument or inference, proves not that, for the future, it will continue so. In vain do you pretend to have learned the nature of bodies from your past experience. Their secret nature, and consequently all their effects and influence, may change, without any change in their sensible qualities. This happens sometimes, and with regard to some objects; why may it not happen always, and with regard to all objects? What logic, what process of argument secures you against this supposition? My practice, you say, refutes my doubts. But you mistake the purport of my question. As an agent, I am quite satisfied in the point; but as a philosopher, who has some share of curiosity, I will not say scepticism, I want to learn the foundation of this inference. No reading, no enquiry has yet been able to remove my difficulty, or give me satisfaction in a matter of such importance. Can I do better than propose the difficulty to the public, even though, perhaps, I have small hopes of obtaining a solution? We shall, at least, by this means, be sensible of our ignorance, if we do not augment our knowledge.

I must confess that a man is guilty of unpardonable arrogance who concludes, because an argument has escaped his own investigation, that therefore it does not really exist. I must also confess that, though all the learned, for several ages, should have employed themselves in fruitless search upon any subject, it may still, perhaps, be rash to conclude positively that the subject must, therefore, pass all human comprehension. Even though we examine all the sources of our knowledge, and conclude them unfit for such a subject, there may still remain a suspicion, that the enumeration is not complete, or the examination not accurate. But with regard to the present subject, there are some considerations which seem to remove all this accusation of arrogance or suspicion of mistake.

It is certain that the most ignorant and stupid peasants, nay infants, nay even brute beasts, improve by experience, and learn the qualities of natural objects, by observing the effects which result from them. When a child has felt the sensation of pain from touching the flame of a candle, he will be careful not to put his hand near any candle; but will expect a similar effect from a cause which is similar in its sensible qualities and appearance. If you assert, therefore, that the understanding of the child is led into this conclusion by any process of argument or ratiocination, I may justly require you to produce that argument; nor have you any pretense to refuse so equitable a demand. You cannot say that the argument is abstruse, and may possibly escape your enquiry; since you confess that it is obvious to the capacity of a mere infant. If you hesitate, therefore, a moment, or if, after reflection, you produce any intricate or profound argument, you, in a manner, give up the question, and confess that it is not reasoning which engages us to suppose the past resembling the future, and to expect similar effects from causes which are, to appearance, similar. This is the proposition which I intended to enforce in the present section. If I be right, I pretend not to have made any mighty discovery. And if I be wrong, I must acknowledge myself to be indeed a very backward scholar; since I cannot now discover an argument which, it seems was perfectly familiar to me long before I was out of my cradle.

SECTION VII
Of the Idea of Necessary Connection

PART I

The great advantage of the mathematical sciences above the moral consists in this, that the ideas of the former, being sensible, are always clear and determinate, the smallest distinction between them is immediately perceptible, and the same terms are still expressive of the same ideas, without ambiguity or variation. An oval is never mistaken for a circle, nor an hyperbola for an ellipsis. The isosceles and scalenum are distinguished by boundaries more exact than vice and virtue, right and wrong. If any term be defined in geometry, the mind readily, of itself, substitutes, on all occasions, the definition for the term defined. Or even when no definition is employed, the object itself may be presented to the senses, and by that means be steadily and clearly apprehended. But the finer sentiments of the mind, the operations of the understanding, the various agitations of the passions, though really in themselves distinct, easily escape us, when surveyed by reflection; nor is it in our power to recall the original object, as often as we have occasion to contemplate it. Ambiguity, by this means, is gradually introduced into our reasonings; similar objects are readily taken to be the same; and the conclusion becomes at last very wide of the premises.

One may safely, however, affirm, that, if we consider these sciences in a proper light, their advantages and disadvantages nearly compensate each other, and reduce both of them to a state of equality. If the mind, with greater facility, retains the ideas of geometry clear and determinate, it must carry on a much longer and more intricate chain of reasoning, and compare ideas much wider of each other, in order to reach the abstruser truths of that science. And if moral ideas are apt, without extreme care, to fall into obscurity and confusion, the inferences are always much shorter in these disquisitions, and the intermediate steps, which lead to the conclusion, much fewer than in the sciences which treat of quantity and number. In reality, there is scarcely a proposition in Euclid so simple, as not to consist of more parts, than are to be found in any moral reasoning which runs not into chimera and conceit. Where we trace the principles of the human mind through a few steps, we may be very well satisfied with our progress; considering how soon nature throws a bar to all our enquiries concerning causes, and reduces us to an acknowledgment of our ignorance. The chief obstacle, therefore, to our improvement in the moral or metaphysical sciences is the obscurity of the ideas, and ambiguity of the terms. The principal difficulty in the mathematics is the length of inferences and compass of thought, requisite to the forming of any conclusion. And, perhaps, our progress in natural philosophy is chiefly retarded by the want of proper experiments and phenomena, which are often discovered by chance, and cannot always be found, when requisite, even by the most diligent and prudent enquiry. As moral philosophy seems hitherto to have received less improvement than either geometry or physics, we may conclude, that, if there be any difference in this respect among these sciences, the difficulties, which obstruct the progress of the former, require superior care and capacity to be surmounted.

There are no ideas, which occur in metaphysics, more obscure and uncertain, than those of *power, force, energy* or *necessary connection,* of which it is every moment necessary for us to treat in all our disquisitions. We shall, therefore, endeavour, in this section, to fix, if possible, the precise meaning of these terms, and thereby remove some part of that obscurity, which is so much complained of in this species of philosophy.

It seems a proposition, which will not admit of much dispute, that all our ideas are nothing but copies of our impressions, or, in other words, that it is impossible for us to *think* of any thing, which we have not antecedently *felt,* either by our external or internal senses. I have endeavoured to explain and prove this proposition, and have expressed my hopes, that, by a proper application of it, men may reach a greater clearness and precision in philosophical reasonings, than what they have hitherto been able to attain. Complex ideas may, perhaps, be well known by definition, which is nothing but an enumeration of those parts or simple ideas, that compose them. But when we have pushed up definitions to the most simple ideas, and find still some ambiguity and obscurity; what resource are we then possessed of? By what invention can we throw light upon these ideas, and render them altogether precise and determinate to our intellectual view? Produce the impressions or original sentiments, from which the ideas are copied. These impressions are all strong and sensible. They admit not of ambiguity. They are not only placed in a full light themselves, but may throw light on their correspondent ideas, which lie in obscurity. And by this means, we may, perhaps, attain a new microscope or species of optics, by which, in the moral sciences, the most minute and most simple ideas may be so enlarged as to fall readily under our apprehension, and be equally known with the grossest and most sensible ideas, that can be the object of our enquiry.

To be fully acquainted, therefore, with the idea of power or necessary connection, let us examine its impression; and in order to find the impression with greater certainty, let us search for it in all the sources, from which it may possibly be derived.

When we look about us towards external objects, and consider the operation of causes, we are never able, in a single instance, to discover any power or necessary connection; any quality, which binds the effect to the cause, and renders the one an infallible consequence of the other. We only find, that the one does actually, in fact, follow the other. The impulse of one billiard-ball is attended with motion in the second. This is the whole that appears to the *outward* senses. The mind feels no sentiment or *inward* impression from this succession of objects: consequently there is not, in any single, particular instance of cause and effect, any thing which can suggest the idea of power or necessary connection.

From the first appearance of an object, we never can conjecture what effect will result from it. But were the power or energy of any cause discoverable by the mind, we could foresee the effect, even without experience; and might, at first, pronounce with certainty concerning it, by mere dint of thought and reasoning.

In reality, there is no part of matter, that does ever, by its sensible qualities, discover any power or energy, or give us ground to imagine, that it could produce any thing, or be followed by any other object, which we could denominate its effect. Solidity, extension, motion; these qualities are all complete in themselves, and never point out any other event which may result from them. The scenes of the universe are continually shifting, and one object follows another in an uninterrupted succession; but the power of force, which actuates the whole machine, is entirely concealed from us, and never discovers itself in any of the sensible qualities of body. We know, that, in fact, heat is a constant attendant of flame; but what is the connection between them, we have no room so much as to conjecture or imagine. It is impossible, therefore, that the idea of power can be derived from the contemplation of bodies, in single instances of their operation; because no bodies ever discover any power, which can be the original of this idea.

Since, therefore, external objects as they appear to the senses, give us no idea of power or necessary connection, by their operation in particular instances, let us see, whether this idea be derived from reflection on the operations of our own minds, and be copied from any internal impression. It may be said, that we are every moment conscious of internal power; while we feel, that, by the simple command of our will, we can move the organs of our body, or direct the faculties of our mind. An act of volition produces motion in our limbs, or raises a new idea in our imagination. This influence of the will we know by consciousness. Hence we acquire the idea of power or energy, and are certain, that we ourselves and all other intelligent beings are possessed of power. This idea, then, is an idea of reflection, since it arises from reflecting on the operations of our own mind, and on the command which is exercised by will, both over the organs of the body and faculties of the soul.

We shall proceed to examine this pretension; and first with regard to the influence of volition over the organs of the body. This influence, we may observe, is a fact, which, like all other natural events, can be known only by experience, and can never be foreseen from any apparent energy or power in the cause, which connects it with the effect, and renders the one an infallible consequence of the other. The motion of our body follows upon the command of our will. Of this we are every moment conscious. But the means, by which this is effected; the energy, by which the will performs so extraordinary an operation; of this we are so far from being immediately conscious, that it must for ever escape our most diligent enquiry.

For *first,* Is there any principle in all nature more mysterious than the union of soul with body; by which a supposed spiritual substance acquires such an influence over a material one, that the most refined thought is able to actuate the grossest matter? Were we empowered, by a secret wish, to remove mountains, or control the planets in their orbit; this extensive authority would not be more extraordinary, nor more beyond our comprehension. But if by consciousness we perceived any power or energy in the will, we must know this power; we must know its connection with the effect; we must know the secret union of soul and body, and the nature of both these substances; by which the one is able to operate, in so many instances, upon the other.

Secondly, We are not able to move all the organs of the body with a like authority; though we cannot assign any reason besides experience, for so remarkable a difference between one and the other. Why has the will an influence over the tongue and fingers, not over the heart and liver? This question would never embarrass us, were we conscious of a power in the former case, not in the latter. We should then perceive, independent of experience, why the authority of will over the organs of the body is circumscribed within such particular limits. Being in that case fully acquainted with the power or force, by which it operates, we should also know, why its influence reaches precisely to such boundaries, and no farther.

A man, suddenly struck with palsy in the leg or arm, or who has newly lost those members, frequently endeavours, at first, to move them, and employ them in their usual offices. Here he is as much conscious of power to command such limbs, as a man in perfect health is conscious of power to actuate any member which remains in its natural state and condition. But consciousness never deceives. Consequently, neither in the one case nor in the other, are we ever conscious of any power. We learn the influence of our will from experience alone. And experience only teaches us, how one event constantly follows another;

without instructing us in the secret connection, which binds them together, and renders them inseparable.

Thirdly, We learn from anatomy, that the immediate object of power in voluntary motion, is not the member itself which is moved, but certain muscles, and nerves, and animal spirits, and, perhaps, something still more minute and more unknown, through which the motion is successfully propagated, ere it reach the member itself whose motion is the immediate object of volition. Can there be a more certain proof that the power, by which this whole operation is performed, so far from being directly and fully known by an inward sentiment or consciousness, is, to the last degree, mysterious and unintelligible? Here the mind wills a certain event; immediately another event, unknown to ourselves, and totally different from the one intended, is produced. This event produces another, equally unknown: till at last, through a long succession, the desired event is produced. But if the original power were felt, it must be known; were it known, its effect also must be known; since all power is relative to its effect. And *vice versa,* if the effect be not known, the power cannot be known nor felt. How indeed can we be conscious of a power to move our limbs, when we have no such power; but only that to move certain animal spirits, which, though they produce at last the motion of our limbs, yet operate in such a manner as is wholly beyond our comprehension?

We may, therefore, conclude from the whole, I hope, without any temerity, though with assurance; that our idea of power is not copied from any sentiment or consciousness of power within ourselves, when we give rise to animal motion, or apply our limbs, to their proper use and office. That their motion follows the command of the will is a matter of common experience, like other natural events; but the power or energy by which this is effected, like that in other natural events, is unknown and inconceivable.

Shall we then assert, that we are conscious of a power or energy in our own minds, when, by an act or command of our will, we raise up a new idea, fix the mind to the contemplation of it, turn it on all sides, and at last dismiss it for some other idea, when we think that we have surveyed it with sufficient accuracy? I believe the same arguments will prove, that even this command of the will gives us no real idea of force or energy.

First, It must be allowed, that, when we know a power, we know that very circumstance in the cause, by which it is enabled to produce the effect; for these are supposed to be synonymous. We must, therefore, know both the cause and effect, and the relation between them. But do we pretend to be acquainted with the nature of the human soul and the nature of an idea, or the aptitude of the one to produce the other? This is a real creation; a production of something out of nothing; which implies a power so great, that it may seem, at first sight, beyond the reach of any being, less than infinite. At least it must be owned, that such a power is not felt, nor known, nor even conceivable by the mind. We only feel the event, namely, the existence of an idea, consequent to a command of the will; but the manner, in which this operation is performed, the power by which it is produced, is entirely beyond our comprehension.

Secondly, The command of the mind over itself is limited, as well as its command over the body; and these limits are not known by reason, or any acquaintance with the nature of cause and effect; but only by experience and observation, as in all other natural events and in the operation of external objects. Our authority over our sentiments and passions is much weaker than that over our ideas; and even the latter authority is circumscribed within very narrow boundaries. Will any one pretend to assign the ultimate reason of these boundaries, or show why the power is deficient in one case, not in another.

Thirdly, This self-command is very different at different times. A man in health possesses more of it than one languishing with sickness. We are more master of our thoughts in the morning than in the evening; fasting, than after a full meal. Can we give any reason for these variations, except experience? Where then is the power, of which we pretend to be conscious? Is there not here, either in a spiritual or material substance, or both, some secret mechanism or structure of parts, upon which the effect depends, and which, being entirely unknown to us, renders the power or energy of the will equally unknown and incomprehensible?

Volition is surely an act of the mind, with which we are sufficiently acquainted. Reflect upon it. Consider it on all sides. Do you find anything in it like this creative power, by which it raises from nothing a new idea, and with a kind of *Fiat,* imitates the omnipotence of its Maker, if I may be allowed so to speak, who called forth into existence all the various scenes of nature? So far from being conscious of this energy in the will, it requires as certain experience as that of which we are possessed, to convince us that such extraordinary effects do ever result from a simple act of volition.

The generality of mankind never find any difficulty in accounting for the more common and familiar operations of nature—such as the descent of heavy bodies, the growth of plants, the generation of animals, or the nourishment of bodies by food. But suppose, that, in all these cases, they perceive the very force or energy of the cause, by which it is connected with its effect, and is for ever infallible in its operation. They acquire, by long habit, such a turn of mind, that, upon the appearance of the cause, they immediately expect with assurance its usual attendant, and hardly conceive it possible that any other event could result from it. It is only on the discovery of extraordinary phenomena, such as earthquakes, pestilence, and prodigies of any kind, that they find themselves at a loss to assign a proper cause, and to explain the manner in which the effect is produced by it. It is usual for men, in such difficulties, to have recourse to some invisible intelligent principle as the immediate cause of that event which surprises them; and which, they think, cannot be accounted for from the common powers of nature. But philosophers, who carry their scrutiny a little farther, immediately perceive that, even in the most familiar events, the energy of the cause is as unintelligible as in the most unusual, and that we only learn by experience the frequent *Conjunction* of objects, without being ever able to comprehend anything like *Connection* between them. Here, then, many philosophers think themselves obliged by reason to have recourse, on all occasions, to the same principle, which the vulgar never appeal to but in cases that appear miraculous and supernatural. They acknowledge mind and intelligence to be, not only the ultimate and original cause of all things, but the immediate and sole cause of every event which appears in nature. They pretend that those objects which are commonly denominated *causes,* are in reality nothing but *occasions;* and that the true and direct principle of every effect is not any power of force in nature, but a volition of the Supreme Being, who wills that such particular objects should for ever be conjoined with each other. Instead of saying that one billiard-ball moves another by a force which it has derived from the author of nature, it is the Deity himself, they say, who, by a particular volition, moves the second ball, being determined to this operation by the impulse of the first ball, in consequence of those general laws which he has laid down to himself in the government of the universe. But philosophers advancing still in their inquiries, discover that, as we are totally ignorant of the power on which depends the mutual operation of bodies, we are no less ignorant of that power on which depends the operation of mind on body, or of body on mind; nor are we able, either from our senses or consciousness, to assign the ultimate principle in one case more than in the other. The same ignorance, therefore, reduces them to the same conclusion. They assert that the Deity is the immediate cause of the union between soul and body; and that they are not the organs of sense, which, being agitated by external objects, produce sensations in the mind: but that it is a particular volition of our omnipotent Maker, which excites such a sensation, in consequence of such a motion in the organ. In like manner, it is not any energy in the will that produces local motion in our members: it is God himself, who is pleased to second our will, in itself impotent, and to command that motion which we erroneously attribute to our own power and efficacy. Nor do philosophers stop at this conclusion. They sometimes extend the same inference to the mind itself, in its internal operations. Our mental vision or conception of ideas is nothing but a revelation made to us by our Maker. When we voluntarily turn our thoughts to any object, and raise up its image in the fancy; it is not the will which creates that idea; it is the universal Creator, who discovers it to the mind, and renders it present to us.

Thus, according to these philosophers, every thing is full of God. Not content with the principle, that nothing exists but by his will, that nothing possesses any power but by his concession, they rob nature, and all created beings, of every power, in order to render their dependence on the Deity still more sensible and immediate. They consider not that, by this theory, they diminish, instead of magnifying, the grandeur of those attributes, which they affect so much to celebrate. It argues surely more power in the Deity to delegate a certain degree of power to inferior creatures, than to produce every thing by his own immediate volition. It argues more wisdom to contrive at first the fabric of the world with such perfect foresight, that, of itself, and by its proper operation, it may serve all the purposes of providence, than if the great Creator were obliged every moment to adjust its parts, and animate by his breath all the wheels of that stupendous machine.

But if we would have a more philosophical confutation of this theory, perhaps the two following reflections may suffice.

First, It seems to me, that this theory of the universal energy and operation of the Supreme Being, is too bold ever to carry conviction with it to a man, sufficiently apprized of the weakness of human reason, and the narrow limits to which it is confined in all its operations. Though the chain of arguments which conduct to it were ever so logical, there must arise a strong suspicion, if not an absolute assurance, that it has carried us quite beyond the reach of our faculties, when it leads to conclusions so extraordinary, and so remote from common life and experience. We are got into fairy land, long ere we have reached the last steps of our theory; and *there* we have no reason to trust our common methods of argument, or to think that our usual analogies and probabilities have any authority. Our line is too short to fathom such immense abysses. And however we may flatter ourselves that we are guided, in every step which we take, by a kind of verisimilitude and experience; we may be assured that this fancied experience has no authority when we thus apply it to subjects that lie entirely out of the sphere of experience. But on this we shall have occasion to touch afterwards.

Secondly, I cannot perceive any force in the arguments on which this theory is founded. We are ignorant, it is true, of the manner in which bodies operate on each other: their force or energy is entirely incomprehensible; but are we not equally ignorant of the manner or force by which a mind, even the supreme mind, operates either on itself or on body? Whence, I beseech you, do we acquire any idea of it? We have no sentiment or consciousness of this power in ourselves. We have no idea of the Supreme Being but what we learn from reflection on our own faculties. Were our ignorance, therefore, a good reason for rejecting any thing, we should be led into that principle of denying all energy in the Supreme

Being as much as in the grossest matter. We surely comprehend as little the operations of one as of the other. Is it more difficult to conceive that motion may arise from impulse than that it may arise from volition? All we know is our profound ignorance in both cases.

PART II

But to hasten to a conclusion of this argument, which is already drawn out to too great a length: we have sought in vain for an idea of power or necessary connection in all the sources from which we could suppose it to be derived. It appears that, in single instances of the operation of bodies, we never can, by our utmost scrutiny, discover any thing but one event following another, without being able to comprehend any force or power by which the cause operates, or any connection between it and its supposed effect. The same difficulty occurs in contemplating the operations of mind on body; where we observe the motion of the latter to follow upon the volition of the former, but are not able to observe or conceive the tie which binds together the motion and volition, or the energy by which the mind produces this effect. The authority of the will over its own faculties and ideas is not a whit more comprehensible: So that, upon the whole, there appears not, throughout all nature, any one instance of connection which is conceivable by us. All events seem entirely loose and separate. One event follows another; but we never can observe any tie between them. They seem *conjoined*, but never *connected*. And as we can have no idea of any thing which never appeared to our outward sense or inward sentiment, the necessary conclusion *seems* to be, that we have no idea of connection or power at all, and that these words are absolutely without any meaning, when employed either in philosophical reasonings or common life.

But there still remains one method of avoiding this conclusion, and one source which we have not yet examined. When any natural object or event is presented, it is impossible for us, by any sagacity or penetration, to discover, or even conjecture, without experience, what event will result from it, or to carry our foresight beyond that object which is immediately present to the memory and senses. Even after one instance or experiment, where we have observed a particular event to follow upon another, we are not entitled to form a general rule, or foretell what will happen in like cases; it being justly esteemed an unpardonable temerity to judge of the whole course of nature from one single experiment, however accurate or certain. But when one particular species of event has always, in all instances, been conjoined with another, we make no longer any scruple of foretelling one upon the appearance of the other, and of employing that reasoning which can alone assure us of any matter of fact or existence. We then call the one object, *Cause*; the other, *Effect*. We suppose that there is some connection between them; some power in the one, by which it infallibly produces the other, and operates with the greatest certainty and strongest necessity.

It appears, then, that this idea of a necessary connection among events arises from a number of similar instances, which occur, of the constant conjunction of these events; nor can that idea ever be suggested by any one of these instances, surveyed in all possible lights and positions. But there is nothing in a number of instances, different from every single instance, which is supposed to be exactly similar; except only, that after a repetition of similar instances, the mind is carried by habit, upon the appearance of one event, to expect its usual attendant, and to believe that it will exist. This connection, therefore, which we *feel* in the mind, this customary transition of the imagination from one object to its usual attendant, is the sentiment or impression from which we form the idea of power or necessary connection. Nothing farther is in the case. Contemplate the subject on all sides; you will never find any other origin of that idea. This is the sole difference between one instance, from which we can never receive the idea of connection, and a number of similar instances, by which it is suggested. The first time a man saw the communication of motion by impulse, as by the shock of two billiard-balls, he could not pronounce that the one event was *connected:* but only that it was *conjoined* with the other. After he has observed several instances of this nature, he then pronounces them to be *connected.* What alteration has happened to give rise to this new idea of connection? Nothing but that he now *feels* these events to be *connected* in his imagination, and can readily foretell the existence of one from the appearance of the other. When we say, therefore, that one object is connected with another, we mean only that they have acquired a connection in our thought, and give rise to this inference, by which they become proofs of each other's existence: a conclusion which is somewhat extraordinary, but which seems founded on sufficient evidence. Nor will its evidence be weakened by any general diffidence of the understanding, or sceptical suspicion concerning every conclusion which is new and extraordinary. No conclusions can be more agreeable to scepticism than such as make discoveries concerning the weakness and narrow limits of human reason and capacity.

And what stronger instance can be produced of the surprising ignorance and weakness of the understanding than the present? For surely, if there be any relation among objects which it imports to us to know perfectly, it is that of cause and effect. On this are founded all our reasonings concerning matter of fact or existence. By means of it alone we attain any assurance concerning objects which are removed from the present testimony of our memory and senses. The only immediate utility of all sciences, is to teach us, how to control and regulate future events by their causes. Our thoughts and enquiries are, therefore, every moment, employed about this relation; yet so imperfect are the ideas which we form concerning it, that it is impossible to give any just definition of cause, except what is drawn from something extraneous and foreign to it. Similar objects are always conjoined with similar. Of this we have experience. Suitably to this experience, therefore, we may define a cause to be *an object, followed by another, and where all the objects, similar to the first, are followed by objects similar to the second.* Or in other words *where, if the first object had not been, the second never had existed.* The appearance of a cause always conveys the mind, by a customary transition, to the idea of the effect. Of this also we have experience. We may, therefore, suitably to this experience, form another definition of cause, and call it, *an object followed by another, and whose appearance always conveys the thought to that other.* But though both these definitions be drawn from circumstances foreign to the cause, we cannot remedy this inconvenience, or attain any more perfect definition, which may point out that circumstance in the cause, which gives it a connection with its effect. We have no idea of this connection; nor even any distinct notion what it is we desire to know, when we endeavour at a conception of it. We say, for instance, that the vibration of this string is the cause of this particular sound. But what do we mean by that affirmation? We either mean, *that this vibration is followed by this sound, and that all similar vibrations have been followed by similar sounds;* or, *that this vibration is followed by this sound, and that upon the appearance of one the mind anticipates the senses, and forms immediately an idea of the other.* We may consider the relation of cause and effect in either of these two lights; but beyond these, we have no idea of it.

To recapitulate, therefore, the reasonings of this section: Every idea is copied from some preceding impression or sentiment; and where we cannot find any impression, we may be certain that there is no idea. In all single instances of the operation of bodies or minds, there is nothing that produces any impression, nor consequently can suggest any idea of power or necessary connection. But when many uniform instances appear, and the same object is always followed by the same event; we then begin to entertain the notion of cause and connection. We then *feel* a new sentiment or impression, to wit, a customary connection in the thought or imagination between one object and its usual attendant; and this sentiment is the original of that idea which we seek for. For as this idea arises from a number of similar instances, and not from any single instance, it must arise from that circumstance, in which the number of instances differ from every individual instance. But this customary connection or transition of the imagination is the only circumstance in which they differ. In every other particular they are alike. The first instance which we saw of motion communicated by the shock of two billiard-balls (to return to this obvious illustration) is exactly similar to any instance that may, at present, occur to us; except only, that we could not, at first, *infer* one event from the other; which we are enabled to do at present, after so long a course of uniform experience. I know not whether the reader will readily apprehend this reasoning. I am afraid that, should I multiply words about it, or throw it into a greater variety of lights, it would only become more obscure and intricate. In all abstract reasonings there is one point of view which, if we can happily hit, we shall go farther towards illustrating the subject than by all the eloquence in the world. This point of view we should endeavour to reach, and reserve the flowers of rhetoric for subjects which are more adapted to them.

SECTION XII
Of the Academical or Sceptical Philosophy
PART III

There is, indeed, a more *mitigated* scepticism or *academical* philosophy, which may be both durable and useful, and which may, in part, be the result of this Pyrrhonism, or *excessive* scepticism, when its undistinguished doubts are, in some measure, corrected by common sense and reflection. The greater part of mankind are naturally apt to be affirmative and dogmatical in their opinions; and while they see objects only on one side, and have no idea of any counterpoising argument, they throw themselves precipitately into the principles, to which they are inclined; nor have they any indulgence for those who entertain opposite sentiments. To hesitate or balance perplexes their understanding, checks their passion, and suspends their action. They are, therefore, impatient till they escape from a state, which to them is so uneasy: and they think, that they could never remove themselves far enough from it, by the violence of their affirmations and obstinacy of their belief. But could such dogmatical reasoners become sensible of the strange infirmities of human understanding, even in its most perfect state, and when most accurate and cautious in its determinations; such a reflection would naturally inspire them with more modesty and reserve, and diminish their fond opinion of themselves, and their prejudice against antagonists. The illiterate may reflect on the disposition of the learned, who, amidst all the advantages of study and reflection, are commonly still diffident in their determinations; and if any of the learned be inclined, from their natural temper, to haughtiness and obstinacy, a small tincture of Pyrrhonism might abate their pride, by showing them, that the few advantages, which they may have attained over their fellows, are but inconsiderable, if compared with the universal perplexity and confusion, which is inherent in human nature. In general, there is a degree of doubt, and caution, and modesty, which, in all kinds of scrutiny and decision, ought for ever to accompany a just reasoner.

Another species of *mitigated* scepticism which may be of advantage to mankind, and which may be the natural result of the Pyrrhonian doubts and scruples, is the limitation of our enquiries to such subjects as are best adapted to the narrow capacity of human understanding. The *imagination* of man is naturally sublime, delighted with whatever is remote and extraordinary, and running, without control, into the most distant parts of space and time in order to avoid the objects, which custom has rendered too familiar to it. A correct *judgment* observes a contrary method, and avoiding all distant and high enquiries, confines itself to common life, and to such subjects as fall under daily practice and experience; leaving the more sublime topics to the embellishment of poets and orators, or to the arts of priests and politicians. To bring us to so salutary a determination, nothing can be more serviceable, than to be once thoroughly convinced of the force of the Pyrrhonian doubt, and of the impossibility, that anything, but the strong power of natural instinct, could free us from it. Those who have a propensity to philosophy, will still continue their researches; because they reflect, that, besides the immediate pleasure, attending such an occupation, philosophical decisions are nothing but the reflections of common life, methodized and corrected. But they will never be tempted to go beyond common life, so long as they consider the imperfection of those faculties which they employ, their narrow reach, and their inaccurate operations. While we cannot give a satisfactory reason, why we believe, after a thousand experiments, that a stone will fall, or fire burn; can we ever satisfy ourselves concerning any determination, which we may form, with regard to the origin of worlds, and the situation of nature, from, and to eternity?

This narrow limitation, indeed, of our enquiries, is, in every respect, so reasonable, that it suffices to make the slightest examination into the natural powers of the human mind and to compare them with their objects, in order to recommend it to us. We shall then find what are the proper subjects of science and enquiry.

It seems to me, that the only objects of the abstract science or of demonstration are quantity and number, and that all attempts to extend this more perfect species of knowledge beyond these bounds are mere sophistry and illusion. As the component parts of quantity and number are entirely similar, their relations become intricate and involved; and nothing can be more curious, as well as useful, than to trace, by a variety of mediums their equality or inequality, through their different appearances. But as all other ideas are clearly distinct and different from each other, we can never advance farther, by our utmost scrutiny, than to observe this diversity, and, by an obvious reflection, pronounce one thing not to be another. Or if there be any difficulty in these decisions, it proceeds entirely from the undeterminate meaning of words, which is corrected by juster definitions. That *the square of the hypothenuse is equal to the squares of the other two sides,* cannot be known, let the terms be ever so exactly defined, without a train of reasoning and enquiry. But to convince us of this proposition, *that where there is no property, there can be no injustice,* it is only necessary to define the terms, and explain injustice to be a violation of property. This proposition is, indeed, nothing but a more imperfect definition. It is the same case with all those pretended syllogistical reasonings, which may be found in every other branch of learning, except the sciences of quantity and number; and these may safely, I think, be pronounced the only proper objects of knowledge and demonstration.

All other enquiries of men regard only matter of fact and existence; and these are evidently incapable of demonstration. Whatever *is* may *not be.* No negation of a fact can involve a contradiction. The non-existence of any being, without exception, is as clear and distinct an idea as its existence. The proposition, which affirms it not to be, however false, is no less conceivable and intelligible, than that which affirms it to be. The case is different with the sciences, properly so called. Every proposition, which is not true, is there confused and unintelligible. That the cube root of 64 is equal to the half of 10, is a false proposition, and can never be distinctly conceived. But that Caesar, or the angel Gabriel, or any being never existed, may be a false proposition, but still is perfectly conceivable, and implies no contradiction.

The existence, therefore, of any being can only be proved by arguments from its cause or its effect; and these arguments are founded entirely on experience. If we reason *a priori,* anything may appear able to produce anything. The falling of a pebble may, for aught we know, extinguish the sun; or the wish of a man control the planets in their orbits. It is only experience, which teaches us the nature and bounds of cause and effect, and enables us to infer the existence of one object from that of another. Such is the foundation of moral reasoning, which forms the greater part of human knowledge, and is the source of all human action and behaviour.

Moral reasonings are either concerning particular or general facts. All deliberations in life regard the former; as also all disquisitions in history, chronology, geography, and astronomy.

The sciences, which treat of general facts, are politics, natural philosophy, physic, chemistry, etc. where the qualities, causes and effects of a whole species of objects are enquired into.

Divinity or Theology, as it proves the existence of a Deity, and the immortality of souls, is composed partly of reasonings concerning particular, partly concerning general facts. It has a foundation in *reason,* so far as it is supported by experience. But its best and most solid foundation is *faith* and divine revelation.

Morals and criticism are not so properly objects of the understanding as of taste and sentiment. Beauty, whether moral or natural, is felt, more properly than perceived. Or if we reason concerning it, and endeavour to fix its standard, we regard a new fact, to wit, the general tastes of mankind, or some such fact, which may be the object of reasoning and enquiry.

When we run over libraries, persuaded of these principles, what havoc must we make? If we take in our hand any volume; of divinity or school metaphysics, for instance; let us ask, *Does it contain any abstract reasoning concerning quantity or number?* No. *Does it contain any experimental reasoning concerning matter of fact and existence?* No. Commit it then to the flames; for it can contain nothing but sophistry and illusion.

OF PERSONAL IDENTITY

There are some philosophers, who imagine we are every moment intimately conscious of what we call our SELF; that we feel its existence and its continuance in existence; and are certain, beyond the evidence of a demonstration, both of its perfect identity and simplicity. The strongest sensation, the most violent passion, say they, instead of distracting us from this view, only fix it the more intensely, and make us consider their influence on *self* either by their pain or pleasure. To attempt a farther proof of this were to weaken its evidence;

From David Hume, *A Treatise of Human Nature,* ed. L. A. Selby-Bigge (Oxford: Clarendon Press, 1888).

since no proof can be derived from any fact, of which we are so intimately conscious; nor is there any thing, of which we can be certain, if we doubt this.

Unluckily all these positive assertions are contrary to that very experience, which is pleaded for them, nor have we any idea of *self,* after the manner it is here explained. For from what impression could this idea be derived? The question 'tis impossible to answer without a manifest contradiction and absurdity; and yet 'tis a question, which must necessarily be answered, if we would have the idea of self pass for clear and intelligible. It must be some one impression, that gives rise to every real idea. But self or person is not any one impression, but that to which our several impressions and ideas are supposed to have a reference. If any impression gives rise to the idea of self, that impression must continue invariably the same, through the whole course of our lives, since self is supposed to exist after that manner. But there is no impression constant and invariable. Pain and pleasure, grief and joy, passions and sensations succeed each other, and never all exist at the same time. It cannot, therefore, be from any of these impressions, or from any other, that the idea of self is derived, and consequently there is no such idea.

But farther, what must become of all our particular perceptions upon this hypothesis? All these are different, and distinguishable, and separable from each other, and may be separately considered, and may exist separately, and have no need of any thing to support their existence. After what manner, therefore, do they belong to self; and how are they connected with it? For my part, when I enter most intimately into what I call *myself,* I always stumble on some particular perception or other, of heat or cold, light or shade, love or hatred, pain or pleasure. I never can catch *myself* at any time without a perception, and never can observe any thing but the perception. When my perceptions are removed for any time, as by sound sleep; so long am I insensible of *myself,* and may truly be said not to exist. And were all my perceptions removed by death, and could I neither think, nor feel, nor see, nor love, nor hate after the dissolution of my body, I should be entirely annihilated, nor do I conceive what is farther requisite to make me a perfect non-entity. If any one upon serious and unprejudiced reflection, thinks he has a different notion of *himself,* I must confess I can reason no longer with him. All I can allow him is, that he may be in the right as well as I, and that we are essentially different in this particular. He may, perhaps, perceive something simple and continued, which he calls *himself;* though I am certain there is no such principle in me.

But setting aside some metaphysicians of this kind, I may venture to affirm of the rest of mankind, that they are nothing but a bundle or collection of different perceptions, which succeed each other with an inconceivable rapidity, and are in a perpetual flux and movement. Our eyes cannot turn in their sockets without varying our perceptions. Our thought is still more variable than our sight; and all our other senses and faculties contribute to this change; nor is there any single power of the soul, which remains unalterably the same, perhaps for one moment. The mind is a kind of theatre, where several perceptions successively make their appearance; pass, re-pass, glide away, and mingle in an infinite variety of postures and situations. There is properly no *simplicity* in it at one time, nor *identity* in different; whatever natural propension we may have to imagine that simplicity and identity. The comparison of the theatre must not mislead us. They are the successive perceptions only, that constitute the mind; nor have we the most distant notion of the place, where these scenes are represented, or of the materials, of which it is composed.

What then gives us so great a propension to ascribe an identity to these successive perceptions, and to suppose ourselves possessed of an invariable and uninterrupted existence through the whole course of our lives? In order to answer this question, we must distinguish betwixt personal identity, as it regards our thought or imagination, as it regards our passions or the concern we take in ourselves. The first is our present subject; and to explain it perfectly we must take the matter pretty deep, and account for that identity, which we attribute to plants and animals; there being a great analogy betwixt it, and the identity of a self or person.

We have a distinct idea of an object, that remains invariable and uninterrupted through a supposed variation of time; and this idea we call that of *identity or sameness*. We have also a distinct idea of several different objects existing in succession, and connected together by a close relation; and this to an accurate view affords as perfect a notion of *diversity*, as if there was no manner of relation among the objects. But though these two ideas of identity, and a succession of related objects be in themselves perfectly distinct, and even contrary, yet 'tis certain, that in our common way of thinking they are generally confounded with each other. That action of the imagination, by which we consider the uninterrupted and invariable object, and that by which we reflect on the succession of related objects, are almost the same to the feeling, nor is there much more effort of thought required in the latter case than in the former. The relation facilitates the transition of the mind from one object to another, and renders its passage as smooth as if it contemplated one continued object. This resemblance is the cause of the confusion and mistake, and makes us substitute the notion of identity, instead of that of related objects. However at one instant we may consider the related succession as variable or interrupted, we are sure the next to ascribe to it a perfect identity, and regard it as invariable and uninterrupted. Our propensity to this mistake is so great from the resemblance above-mentioned that we fall into it before we are aware; and though we incessantly correct ourselves by reflection, and return to a more accurate method of thinking, yet we cannot long sustain our philosophy, or take off this bias from the imagination. Our last resource is to yield to it, and boldly assert that these different related objects are in effect the same, however, interrupted and variable. In order to justify to ourselves this absurdity, we often feign some new and unintelligible principle, that connects the objects together, and prevents their interruption or variation. Thus we feign the continued existence of the perceptions of our senses, to remove the interruption, and run into the notion of a *soul*, and *self*, and *substance,* to disguise the variation. But we may farther observe, that where we do not give rise to such a fiction, our propension to confound identity with relation is so great, that we are apt to imagine something unknown and mysterious, connecting the parts, beside their relation; and this I take to be the case with regard to the identity we ascribe to plants and vegetables. And even when this does not take place, we still feel a propensity to confound these ideas, though we are not able fully to satisfy ourselves in that particular, nor find any thing invariable and uninterrupted to justify our notion of identity.

Thus the controversy concerning identity is not merely a dispute of words. For when we attribute identity, in an improper sense, to variable or interrupted objects, our mistake is not confined to the expression, but is commonly attended with a fiction, either of something invariable and uninterrupted, or of something mysterious and inexplicable, or at least with a propensity to such fictions. What will suffice to prove this hypothesis to the satisfaction of every fair enquirer, is to show from daily experience and observation, that the objects, which are variable or interrupted, and yet are supposed to continue the same, are such only as consist of a succession of parts, connected together by resemblance, contiguity, or causation. For as such a succession answers evidently to our notion of diversity, it can only be by mistake we ascribe to it an identity; and as the relation of parts, which leads us into this mistake, is really nothing but a quality, which produces an association of ideas, and an easy transition of the imagination from one to another, it can only be from the resemblance, which this act of the mind bears to that, by which we contemplate one continued object, that the error arises. Our chief business, then, must be to prove, that all objects, to which we ascribe identity, without observing their invariableness and uninterruptedness, are such as consist of a succession of related objects.

In order to this, suppose any mass of matter, of which the parts are contiguous and connected, to be placed before us; 'tis plain we must attribute a perfect identity to this mass, provided all the parts continue uninterruptedly and invariably the same, whatever motion or change of place we may observe either in the whole or in any of the parts. For suppose some very *small* or *inconsiderable* part to be added to the mass, or substracted from it; though this absolutely destroys the identity of the whole, strictly speaking: yet as we seldom think so accurately, we scruple not to pronounce a mass of matter the same, where we find so trivial an alteration. The passage of the thought from the object before the change to the object after it, is so smooth and easy, that we scarce perceive the transition, and are apt to imagine, that 'tis nothing but a continued survey of the same object.

There is a very remarkable circumstance, that attends this experiment; which is, that though the change of any considerable part in a mass of matter destroys the identity of the whole, yet we must measure the greatness of the part, not absolutely, but by its *proportion* to the whole. The addition or diminution of a mountain would not be sufficient to produce a diversity in a planet; though the change of a very few inches would be able to destroy the identity of some bodies. 'Twill be impossible to account for this, but by reflecting that objects operate upon the mind, and break or interrupt the continuity of its actions not according to their real greatness, but according to their proportion to each other: And therefore, since this interruption makes an object cease to appear the same, it must be the uninterrupted progress of the thought, which constitutes the imperfect identity.

This may be confirmed by another phenomenon. A change in any considerable part of a body destroys its identity; but 'tis remarkable, that where the change is produced *gradually* and *insensibly* we are less apt to ascribe to it the same effect. The reason can plainly be no other, than that the mind, in following the successive changes of the body, feels an easy passage from the surveying its condition in one moment to the viewing of it in another, and at no particular time perceives any interruption in its actions. From which continued perception, it ascribes a continued existence and identity to the object.

But whatever precaution we may use in introducing the changes gradually, and making them proportionable to the whole, 'tis certain, that where the changes are at least observed to become considerable, we make a scruple of ascribing identity to such different objects. There is, however, another artifice, by which we may induce the imagination to advance a step farther; and that is, by producing a reference of the parts to each other, and a combination to some *common end* or purpose. A ship, of which a considerable part has been changed by frequent reparations, is still considered as the same; nor does the difference of the materials hinder us from ascribing an identity to it. The common end, in which the parts conspire, is the same under all their variations, and affords an easy transition of the imagination from one situation of the body to another.

But this is still more remarkable, when we add a *sympathy* of parts to their *common end,* and suppose that they bear to each other, the reciprocal relation of cause and effect in all their actions and operations. This is the case with all animals and vegetables; where not only the several parts have a reference to some general purpose, but also a mutual dependance on, and connection with each other. The effect of so strong a relation is, that though every one must allow, that in a very few years both vegetables and animals endure a *total* change, yet we still attribute identity to them, while their form, size, and substance are entirely altered. An oak, that grows from a small plant to a large tree, is still the same oak; though there be not one particle of matter, or figure of its parts the same. An infant becomes a man, and is sometimes fat, sometimes lean, without any change in his identity.

We may also consider the two following phenomena, which are remarkable in their kind. The first is, that though we commonly be able to distinguish pretty exactly betwixt numerical and specific identity, yet it sometimes happens, that we confound them, and in our thinking and reasoning employ the one for the other. Thus a man, who hears a noise, that is frequently interrupted and renew'd, says, it is still the same noise; though 'tis evident the sounds have only a specific identity or resemblance, and there is nothing numerically the same, but the cause, which produced them. In like manner it may be said without breach of the propriety of language, that such a church, which was formerly of brick, fell to ruin, and that the parish rebuilt the same church of free-stone, and according to modern architecture. Here neither the form nor materials are the same, nor is there any thing common to the two objects, but their relation to the inhabitants of the parish; and yet this alone is sufficient to make us denominate them the same. But we must observe, that in these cases the first object is in a manner annihilated before the second comes into existence; by which means, we are never presented in any one point of time with the idea of difference and multiplicity; and for that reason are less scrupulous in calling them the same.

Secondly, We may remark, that though in a succession of related objects, it be in a manner requisite, that the change of parts be not sudden nor entire, in order to preserve the identity, yet where the objects are in their nature changeable and inconstant, we admit of a more sudden transition, than would otherwise be consistent with that relation. Thus as the nature of a river consists in the motion and change of parts; though in less than four and twenty hours these be totally altered; this hinders not the river from continuing the same during several ages. What is natural and essential to any thing is, in a manner, expected; and what is expected makes less impression, and appears of less moment, than what is unusual and extraordinary. A considerable change of the former kind seems really less to the imagination, than the most trivial alteration of the latter; and by breaking less the continuity of the thought, has less influence in destroying the identity.

We now proceed to explain the nature of *personal identity,* which has become so great a question in philosophy, especially of late years in *England,* where all the abstruser sciences are studied with a peculiar ardour and application. And here 'tis evident, the same method of reasoning must be continued, which has so successfully explained the identity of plants, and animals, and ships, and houses, and of all the compounded and changeable productions either of art or nature. The identity, which we ascribe to the mind of man, is only a fictitious one, and of a like kind with that which we ascribe to vegetables and animal bodies. It cannot, therefore, have a different origin, but must proceed from a like operation of the imagination upon like objects.

But lest this argument should not convince the reader; though in my opinion perfectly decisive; let him weigh the following reasoning, which is still closer and more immediate. 'Tis evident, that the identity, which we attribute to the human mind, however perfect we may imagine it to be, is not able to run the several different perceptions into one, and make them lose their characters of distinction and difference, which are essential to them. 'Tis still true, that every distinct perception, which enters into the composition of the mind, is a distinct existence, and is different, and distinguishable, and separate from every other perception, either contemporary or successive. But, as, notwithstanding this distinction and separability, we suppose the whole train of perceptions to be united by identity, a question naturally arises concerning this relation of identity; whether it be something that really binds our several perceptions together, or only associates their ideas in the imagination. That is, in other words, whether in pronouncing concerning the identity of a person, we observe some real bond among his perceptions, or only feel one among the ideas we form of them. This question we might easily decide, if we would recollect what has been already proved at large, that the understanding never observes any real connection among objects, and that even the union of cause and effect, when strictly examined, resolves itself into a customary association of ideas. For from thence it evidently follows, that identity is nothing really belonging to these different perceptions, and uniting them together; but is merely a quality, which we attribute to them, because of the union of their ideas in the imagination, when we reflect upon them. Now the only qualities, which can give ideas an union in the imagination, are these three relations above-mention'd. These are the uniting principles in the ideal world, and without them every distinct object is separable by the mind, and may be separately considered, and appears not to have any more connection with any other object, than if disjoined by the greatest difference and remoteness. 'Tis, therefore, on some of these three relations of resemblance, contiguity and causation, that identity depends; and as the very essence of these relations consists in their producing an easy transition of ideas, it follows, that our notions of personal identity, proceed entirely from the smooth and uninterrupted progress of the thought along a train of connected ideas, according to the principles above-explained.

The only question, therefore, which remains, is, by what relations this uninterrupted progress of our thought is produced, when we consider the successive existence of a mind or thinking person. And here 'tis evident we must confine ourselves to resemblance and causation, and must drop contiguity, which has little or no influence in the present case.

To begin with *resemblance;* suppose we could see clearly into the breast of another, and observe that succession of perceptions, which constitutes his mind or thinking principle, and suppose that he always preserves the memory of a considerable part of past perceptions; 'tis evident that nothing could more contribute to the bestowing a relation on this succession amidst all its variations. For what is the memory but a faculty, by which we raise up the images of past perceptions? And as an image necessarily resembles its object, must not the frequent placing of these resembling perceptions in the chain of thought, convey the imagination more easily from one link to another, and make the whole seem like the continuance of one object? In this particular, then, the memory not only discovers the identity, but also contributes to its production, by producing the relation of resemblance among the perceptions. The case is the same whether we consider ourselves or others.

As to *causation;* we may observe, that the true idea of the human mind, is to consider it as a system of different perceptions or different existences, which are linked together by the relation of cause and effect, and mutually produce, destroy, influence, and modify each other. Our impressions give rise to their correspondent ideas; and these ideas in their turn produce other impressions. One thought chases another, and draws after it a third, by which it is expelled in its turn. In this respect, I cannot compare the soul more properly to any thing than to a republic or commonwealth, in which the several members are united by the reciprocal ties of government and subordination, and give rise to other persons, who propagate the same republic in the incessant changes of its parts. And as the same individual republic may not only change its members, but also its laws and constitutions; in like manner the same person may vary his character and disposition, as well as his impressions and ideas, without losing his identity. Whatever changes he endures, his several parts are still connected by the relation of causation. And in this view our identity with regard to the passions serves to corroborate that with regard to the imagination, by the making our distant perceptions influence each other, and by giving us a present concern for our past or future pains or pleasures.

As memory alone acquaints us with the continuance and extent of this succession of perceptions, 'tis to be considered, upon that account chiefly, as the source of personal identity. Had we no memory, we never should have any notion of causation, nor consequently of that chain of causes and effects, which constitute our self or person. But having once acquired this notion of causation from the memory, we can extend the same chain of causes, and consequently the identity of our persons beyond our memory, and can comprehend times, and circumstances, and actions, which we have entirely forgot, but suppose in general to have existed. For how few of our past actions are there, of which we have any memory? Who can tell me, for instance, what were his thoughts and actions on the first of *January* 1715, the 11th of *March* 1719, and the 3d of *August* 1733? Or will he affirm, because he has entirely forgot the incidents of these days, that the present self is not the same person with the self of that time; and by that means overturn all the most established notions of personal identity? In this view, therefore, memory does not so much *produce* as *discover* personal identity, by showing us the relation of cause and effect among our different perceptions. 'Twill be incumbent on those, who affirm that memory produces entirely our personal identity, to give a reason why we can thus extend our identity beyond our memory.

The whole of this doctrine leads us to a conclusion, which is of great importance in the present affair, *viz.* that all the nice and subtile questions concerning personal identity can never possibly be decided and are to be regarded rather as grammatical than as philosophical difficulties. Identity depends on the relations of ideas; and these relations produce identity, by means of that easy transition they occasion. But as the relations, and the easiness of the transition may diminish by insensible degrees, we have no just standard, by which we can decide any dispute concerning the time, when they acquire or lose a title to the name of identity. All the disputes concerning the identity of connected objects are merely verbal, except so far as the relation of parts gives rise to some fiction or imaginary principle of union, as we have already observed.

What I have said concerning the first origin and uncertainty of our notion of identity, as applied to the human mind, may be extended with little or no variation to that of *simplicity*. An object, whose different co-existent parts are bound together by a close relation, operates upon the imagination after much the same manner as one perfectly simple and indivisible, and requires not a much greater stretch of thought in order to its conception. From this similarity of operation we attribute a simplicity to it, and feign a principle of union as the support of this simplicity, and the center of all the different parts and qualities of the object.

DIALOGUES CONCERNING NATURAL RELIGION

1. [THE ARGUMENT FOR A FIRST CAUSE]

The argument, replied Demea, which I would insist on is the common one. Whatever exists must have a cause or reason of its existence, it being absolutely impossible for anything to produce itself or be the cause of its own existence. In mounting up, therefore, from effects to causes, we must either go on in tracing an infinite succession, without any ultimate cause at all, or must at last have recourse to some ultimate cause that is *necessarily* existent. Now that the first supposition is absurd may be thus proved. In the infinite chain or succession of causes and effects, each single effect is determined to exist by the power and efficacy of that cause which immediately preceded; but the whole eternal chain or succession, taken together, is not determined or caused by anything, and yet it is evident that it requires a cause or reason, as much as any particular object which begins to exist in time. The question is still reasonable why this particular succession of causes existed from eternity, and not any other succession or no succession at all. If there be no necessarily existent being, any supposition which can be formed is equally possible; nor is there any more absurdity in *nothing's* having existed from eternity than there is in that succession of causes which constitutes the universe. What was it, then, which determined *something* to exist rather than *nothing,* and bestowed being on a particular possibility, exclusive of the rest? *External causes,* there are supposed to be none. *Chance* is a word without a meaning. Was it *nothing?* But that can never produce anything. We must, therefore, have recourse to a necessarily existent Being who carries the *reason* of his existence in himself, and who cannot be supposed not to exist, without an express contradiction. There is, consequently, such a Being—that is, there is a Deity.

I shall not leave it to Philo, said Cleanthes, though I know that the starting objections is his chief delight, to point out the weakness of this metaphysical reasoning. It seems to me so obviously ill-grounded, and at the same time of so little consequence to the cause of true piety and religion, that I shall myself venture to show the fallacy of it.

I shall begin with observing that there is an evident absurdity in pretending to demonstrate a matter of fact, or to prove it by any arguments *a priori.* Nothing is demonstrable unless the contrary implies a contradiction. Nothing that is distinctly conceivable implies a contradiction. Whatever we conceive as existent, we can also conceive as non-existent. There is no being, therefore, whose non-existence implies a contradiction. Consequently there is no being whose existence is demonstrable. I propose this argument as entirely decisive, and am willing to rest the whole controversy upon it.

It is pretended that the Deity is a necessarily existent being; and this necessity of his existence is attempted to be explained by asserting that, if we knew his whole essence or nature, we should perceive it to be as impossible for him not to exist, as for twice two not to be four. But it is evident that this can never happen, while our faculties remain the same

From David Hume, *Dialogues Concerning Natural Religion,* first published in 1779.

as at present. It will still be possible for us, at any time, to conceive the non-existence of what we formerly conceived to exist; nor can the mind ever lie under a necessity of supposing any object to remain always in being; in the same manner as we lie under a necessity of always conceiving twice two to be four. The words, therefore, *necessary existence* have no meaning or, which is the same thing, none that is consistent.

But further, why may not the material universe be the necessarily existent Being, according to this pretended explication of necessity? We dare not affirm that we know all the qualities of matter; and, for aught we can determine, it may contain some qualities which, were they known, would make its non-existence appear as great a contradiction as that twice two is five. I find only one argument employed to prove that the material world is not the necessarily existent Being; and this argument is derived from the contingency both of the matter and the form of the world. "Any particle of matter," it is said, "may be *conceived* to be annihilated, and any form may be *conceived* to be altered. Such an annihilation or alteration, therefore, is not impossible." But it seems a great partiality not to perceive that the same argument extends equally to the Deity, so far as we have any conception of him, and that the mind can at least imagine him to be non-existent or his attributes to be altered. It must be some unknown, inconceivable qualities which can make his non-existence appear impossible or his attributes unalterable; and no reason can be assigned why these qualities may not belong to matter. As they are altogether unknown and inconceivable, they can never be proved incompatible with it.

Add to this that in tracing an eternal succession of objects it seems absurd to inquire for a general cause or first author. How can anything that exists from eternity have a cause, since that relation implies a priority in time and a beginning of existence?

In such a chain, too, or succession of objects, each part is caused by that which preceded it, and causes that which succeeds it. Where then is the difficulty? But the *whole*, you say, wants a cause. I answer that the uniting of these parts into a whole, like the uniting of several distinct countries into one kingdom, or several distinct members into one body, is performed merely by an arbitrary act of the mind, and has no influence on the nature of things. Did I show you the particular causes of each individual in a collection of twenty particles of matter, I should think it very unreasonable should you afterwards ask me what was the cause of the whole twenty. This is sufficiently explained in explaining the cause of the parts.

Though the reasonings which you have urged, Cleanthes, may well excuse me, said Philo, from starting any further difficulties, yet I cannot forbear insisting still upon another topic. It is observed by arithmeticians that the products of 9 compose always either 9 or some lesser product of 9 if you add together all the characters of which any of the former products is composed. Thus, of 18, 27, 36, which are products of 9, you make 9 by adding 1 to 8, 2 to 7, 3 to 6. Thus 369 is a product also of 9; and if you add 3, 6, and 9, you make 18, a lesser product of 9. To a superficial observer so wonderful a regularity may be admired as the effect either of chance or design; but a skilful algebraist immediately concludes it to be the work of necessity, and demonstrates that it must for ever result from the nature of these numbers. Is it not probable, I ask, that the whole economy of the universe is conducted by a like necessity, though no human algebra can furnish a key which solves the difficulty? And instead of admiring the order of natural beings, may it not happen that, could we penetrate into the intimate nature of bodies, we should clearly see why it was absolutely impossible they could ever admit of any other disposition? So dangerous is it to introduce this idea of necessity into the present question! and so naturally does it afford an inference directly opposite to the religious hypothesis!

2. [THE ARGUMENT FROM DESIGN]

Not to lose any time in circumlocutions, said Cleanthes, . . . I shall briefly explain how I conceive this matter. Look round the world, contemplate the whole and every part of it: you will find it to be nothing but one great machine, subdivided into an infinite number of lesser machines, which again admit of subdivisions to a degree beyond what human senses and faculties can trace and explain. All these various machines, and even their most minute parts, are adjusted to each other with an accuracy which ravishes into admiration all men who have ever contemplated them. The curious adapting of means to ends, through-out all nature, resembles exactly, though it much exceeds, the productions of human con-trivance—of human design, thought, wisdom, and intelligence. Since therefore the effects resemble each other, we are led to infer, by all the rules of analogy, that the causes also re-semble, and that the Author of nature is somewhat similar to the mind of man, though possessed of much larger faculties, proportioned to the grandeur of the work which he has executed. By this argument *a posteriori,* and by this argument alone, do we prove at once the existence of a Deity and his similarity to human mind and intelligence.

I shall be so free, Cleanthes, said Demea, as to tell you that from the beginning I could not approve of your conclusion concerning the similarity of the Deity to men, still less can I approve of the mediums by which you endeavor to establish it. What! No demonstration of the Being of God! No abstract arguments! No proofs *a priori!* Are these which have hith-erto been so much insisted on by philosophers all fallacy, all sophism? Can we reach no far-ther in this subject than experience and probability? I will not say that this is betraying the cause of a Deity; but surely, by this affected candor, you give advantages to atheists which they never could obtain by the mere dint of argument and reasoning.

What I chiefly scruple in this subject, said Philo, is not so much that all religious argu-ments are by Cleanthes reduced to experience, as that they appear not to be even the most certain and irrefragable of that inferior kind. That a stone will fall, that fire will burn, that the earth has solidity, we have observed a thousand and a thousand times; and when any new instance of this nature is presented, we draw without hesitation the accustomed infer-ence. The exact similarity of the cases gives us a perfect assurance of a similar event, and a stronger evidence is never desired nor sought after. But wherever you depart, in the least, from the similarity of the cases, you diminish proportionably the evidence, and may at last bring it to a very weak *analogy,* which is confessedly liable to error and uncertainty. After having experienced the circulation of the blood in human creatures, we make no doubt that it takes place in Titius and Maevius; but from its circulation in frogs and fishes it is only a presumption, though a strong one, from analogy that it takes place in men and other ani-mals. The analogical reasoning is much weaker when we infer the circulation of the sap in vegetables from our experience that the blood circulates in animals; and those who hast-ily followed that imperfect analogy are found, by more accurate experiments, to have been mistaken.

If we see a house, Cleanthes, we conclude, with the greatest certainty, that it had an ar-chitect or builder because this is precisely that species of effect which we have experienced to proceed from that species of cause. But surely you will not affirm that the universe bears such a resemblance to a house that we can with the same certainty infer a similar cause, or that the analogy is here entire and perfect. The dissimilitude is so striking that the utmost you can here pretend to is a guess, a conjecture, a presumption concerning a similar cause; and how that pretension will be received in the world, I leave you to consider. . . .

That all inferences, Cleanthes, concerning fact are founded on experience, and that all experimental reasonings are founded on the supposition that similar causes prove similar effects, and similar effects similar causes, I shall not at present much dispute with you. But observe, I entreat you, with what extreme caution all just reasoners proceed in the transferring of experiments to similar cases. Unless the cases be exactly similar, they repose no perfect confidence in applying their past observation to any particular phenomenon. Every alteration of circumstances occasions a doubt concerning the event; and it requires new experiments to prove certainly that the new circumstances are of no moment or importance. A change in bulk, situation, arrangement, age, disposition of the air, or surrounding bodies—any of these particulars may be attended with the most unexpected consequences. And unless the objects be quite familiar to us, it is the highest temerity to expect with assurance, after any of these changes, an event similar to that which before fell under our observation. The slow and deliberate steps of philosophers here, if anywhere, are distinguished from the precipitate march of the vulgar, who, hurried on by the smallest similitude, are incapable of all discernment or consideration.

But can you think, Cleanthes, that your usual phlegm and philosophy have been preserved in so wide a step as you have taken when you compared to the universe houses, ships, furniture, machines, and, from their similarity in some circumstances, inferred a similarity in their causes? Thought, design, intelligence, such as we discover in men and other animals, is no more than one of the springs and principles of the universe, as well as heat or cold, attraction or repulsion, and a hundred others which fall under daily observation. It is an active cause by which some particular parts of nature, we find, produce alterations on other parts. But can a conclusion, with any propriety, be transferred from parts to the whole? Does not the great disproportion bar all comparison and inference? From observing the growth of a hair, can we learn anything concerning the generation of a man? Would the manner of a leaf's blowing, even though perfectly known, afford us any instruction concerning the vegetation of a tree?

But allowing that we were to take the *operations* of one part of nature upon another for the foundation of our judgment concerning the *origin* of the whole (which never can be admitted), yet why select so minute, so weak, so bounded a principle as the reason and design of animals is found to be upon this planet? What peculiar privilege has this little agitation of the brain which we call *thought,* that we must thus make it the model of the whole universe? Our partiality in our own favor does indeed present it on all occasions, but sound philosophy ought carefully to guard against so natural an illusion.

So far from admitting, continued Philo, that the operations of a part can afford us any just conclusion concerning the origin of the whole, I will not allow any one part to form a rule for another part if the latter be very remote from the former. Is there any reasonable ground to conclude that the inhabitants of other planets possess thought, intelligence, reason, or anything similar to these faculties in men? When nature has so extremely diversified her manner of operation in this small globe, can we imagine that she incessantly copies herself throughout so immense a universe? And if thought, as we may well suppose, be confined merely to this narrow corner and has even there so limited a sphere of action, with what propriety can we assign it for the original cause of all things? The narrow views of a peasant who makes his domestic economy the rule for the government of kingdoms is in comparison a pardonable sophism.

But were we ever so much assured that a thought and reason resembling the human were to be found throughout the whole universe, and were its activity elsewhere vastly greater and more commanding than it appears in this globe, yet I cannot see why the operations of a world constituted, arranged, adjusted, can with any propriety be extended to a world which is in its embryo state, and is advancing towards that constitution and arrangement. By observation we know somewhat of the economy, action, and nourishment of a finished animal, but we must transfer with great caution that observation to the growth of a fetus in the womb, and still more to the formation of an animalcule in the loins of its male parent. Nature, we find, even from our limited experience, possesses an infinite number of springs and principles which incessantly discover themselves on every change of her position and situation. And what new and unknown principles would actuate her in so new and unknown a situation as that of the formation of a universe, we cannot, without the utmost temerity, pretend to determine.

A very small part of this great system, during a very short time, is very imperfectly discovered to us; and do we thence pronounce decisively concerning the origin of the whole?

Admirable conclusion! Stone, wood, brick, iron, brass, have not, at this time, in this minute globe of earth, an order or arrangement without human art and contrivance; therefore, the universe could not originally attain its order and arrangement without something similar to human art. But is a part of nature a rule for another part very wide of the former? Is it a rule for the whole? Is a very small part a rule for the universe? Is nature in one situation a certain rule for nature in another situation vastly different from the former?

And can you blame me, Cleanthes, if I here imitate the prudent reserve of Simonides, who, according to the noted story, being asked by Hiero, *What God was?* desired a day to think of it, and then two days more; and after that manner continually prolonged the term, without ever bringing in his definition or description? Could you even blame me if I had answered, at first, *that I did not know,* and was sensible that this subject lay vastly beyond the reach of my faculties? You might cry out sceptic and rallier, as much as you pleased; but, having found in so many other subjects much more familiar the imperfections and even contradictions of human reason, I never should expect any success from its feeble conjectures in a subject so sublime and so remote from the sphere of our observation. When two *species* of objects have always been observed to be conjoined together, I can *infer,* by custom, the existence of one wherever I *see* the existence of the other; and this I call an argument from experience. But how this argument can have place where the objects, as in the present case, are single, individual, without parallel or specific resemblance, may be difficult to explain. And will any man tell me with a serious countenance that an orderly universe must arise from some thought and art like the human because we have experience of it? To ascertain this reasoning it were requisite that we had experience of the origin of worlds; and it is not sufficient, surely, that we have seen ships and cities arise from human art and contrivance. . . .

. . . I shall endeavor to show you, a little more distinctly, the inconveniences of that anthropomorphism which you have embraced, and shall prove that there is no ground to suppose a plan of the world to be formed in the Divine mind, consisting of distinct ideas, differently arranged, in the same manner as an architect forms in his head the plan of a house which he intends to execute.

It is not easy, I own, to see what is gained by this supposition, whether we judge of the matter by *reason* or by *experience.* We are still obliged to mount higher in order to find the cause of this cause which you had assigned as satisfactory and conclusive.

If *reason* (I mean abstract reason derived from inquiries *a priori*) be not alike mute with regard to all questions concerning cause and effect, this sentence at least it will venture to pronounce: that a mental world or universe of ideas requires a cause as much as does a material world or universe of objects, and, if similar in its arrangement, must require a similar cause. For what is there in this subject which should occasion a different conclusion or inference? In an abstract view, they are entirely alike; and no difficulty attends the one supposition which is not common to both of them.

Again, when we will needs force *experience* to pronounce some sentence, even on these subjects which lie beyond her sphere, neither can she perceive any material difference in this particular between these two kinds of worlds, but finds them to be governed by similar principles, and to depend upon an equal variety of causes in their operations. We have specimens in miniature of both of them. Our own mind resembles the one; a vegetable or animal body the other. Let experience, therefore, judge from these samples. Nothing seems more delicate, with regard to its causes, than thought; and as these causes never operate in two persons after the same manner, so we never find two persons who think exactly alike. Nor indeed does the same person think exactly alike at any two different periods of time. A difference of age, of the disposition of his body, of weather, of food, of company, of books, of passions—any of these particulars, or others more minute, are sufficient to alter the curious machinery of thought and communicate to it very different movements and operations. As far as we can judge, vegetables and animal bodies are not more delicate in their motions, nor depend upon a greater variety or more curious adjustment of springs and principles.

How, therefore, shall we satisfy ourselves concerning the cause of that Being whom you suppose the Author of nature, or, according to your system of anthropomorphism, the ideal world into which you trace the material? Have we not the same reason to trace that ideal world into another ideal world or new intelligent principle? But if we stop and go no farther, why go so far? why not stop at the material world? How can we satisfy ourselves without going on *in infinitum?* And, after all, what satisfaction is there in that infinite progression? Let us remember the story of the Indian philosopher and his elephant. It was never more applicable than to the present subject. If the material world rests upon a similar ideal world, this ideal world must rest upon some other, and so on without end. It were better, therefore, never to look beyond the present material world. By supposing it to contain the principle of its order within itself, we really assert it to be God; and the sooner we arrive at that Divine Being, so much the better. When you go one step beyond the mundane system, you only excite an inquisitive humor which it is impossible ever to satisfy.

To say that the different ideas which compose the reason of the Supreme Being fall into order of themselves and by their own nature is really to talk without any precise meaning. If it has a meaning, I would fain know why it is not as good sense to say that the parts of the material world fall into order of themselves and by their own nature. Can the one opinion be intelligible, while the other is not so?

We have, indeed, experience of ideas which fall into order of themselves and without any *known* cause. But, I am sure, we have a much larger experience of matter which does the same, as in all instances of generation and vegetation where the accurate analysis of the cause exceeds all human comprehension. We have also experience of particular systems of thought and of matter which have no order; of the first in madness, of the second in corruption. Why, then, should we think that order is more essential to one than the other? And if it requires a cause in both, what do we gain by your system, in tracing the universe of objects into a similar universe of ideas? The first step which we make leads us on for ever. It were, therefore, wise in us to limit all our inquiries to the present world, without looking farther. No satisfaction can ever be attained by these speculations which so far exceed the narrow bounds of human understanding. . . .

But to show you still more inconveniences, continued Philo, in your anthropomorphism, please to take a new survey of your principles. *Like effects prove like causes.* This is the experimental argument; and this, you say too, is the sole theological argument. . . .

Now, Cleanthes, said Philo, with an air of alacrity and triumph, mark the consequences. *First,* by this method of reasoning you renounce all claim to infinity in any of the attributes of the Deity. For, as the cause ought only to be proportioned to the effect, and the effect, so far as it falls under our cognizance, is not infinite, what pretensions have we, upon your suppositions, to ascribe that attribute to the Divine Being? You will still insist that, by removing him so much from all similarity to human creatures, we give in to the most arbitrary hypothesis, and at the same time weaken all proofs of his existence.

Secondly, you have no reason, on your theory, for ascribing perfection to the Deity, even in his finite capacity, or for supposing him free from every error, mistake, or incoherence, in his undertakings. There are many inexplicable difficulties in the works of nature which, if we allow a perfect author to be proved *a priori,* are easily solved, and become only seeming difficulties from the narrow capacity of man, who cannot trace infinite relations. But according to your method of reasoning, these difficulties become all real, and, perhaps, will be insisted on as new instances of likeness to human art and contrivance. At least, you must acknowledge that it is impossible for us to tell, from our limited views, whether this system contains any great faults or deserves any considerable praise if compared to other possible and even real systems. Could a peasant, if the *Aeneid* were read to him, pronounce that poem to be absolutely faultless, or even assign to it its proper rank among the productions of human wit, he who had never seen any other production?

But were this world ever so perfect a production, it must still remain uncertain whether all the excellences of the work can justly be ascribed to the workman. If we survey a ship, what an exalted idea must we form of the ingenuity of the carpenter who framed so complicated, useful, and beautiful a machine? And what surprise must we feel when we find him a stupid mechanic who imitated others, and copied an art which, through a long succession of ages, after multiplied trials, mistakes, corrections, deliberations, and controversies, had been gradually improving? Many worlds might have been botched and bungled, throughout an eternity, ere this system was struck out; much labor lost, many fruitless trials made, and a slow but continued improvement carried on during infinite ages in the art of world-making. In such subjects, who can determine where the truth, nay, who can conjecture where the probability lies, amidst a great number of hypotheses which may be proposed, and a still greater which may be imagined?

And what shadow of an argument, continued Philo, can you produce from your hypothesis to prove the unity of the Deity? A great number of men join in building a house or ship, in rearing a city, in framing a commonwealth; why may not several deities combine in contriving and framing a world? This is only so much greater similarity to human affairs. By sharing the work among several, we may so much further limit the attributes of each, and get rid of that extensive power and knowledge which must be supposed in one deity, and which, according to you, can only serve to weaken the proof of his existence. And if such foolish, such vicious creatures as man can yet often unite in framing and executing one plan, how much more those deities or demons, whom we may suppose several degrees more perfect! . . . .

It must be a slight fabric, indeed, said Demea, which can be erected on so tottering a foundation. While we are uncertain whether there is one deity or many, whether the deity or deities, to whom we owe our existence, be perfect or imperfect, subordinate or supreme, dead or alive, what trust or confidence can we repose in them? What devotion or worship address to them? What veneration or obedience pay them? To all the purposes of life the theory of religion becomes altogether useless; and even with regard to speculative consequences its uncertainty, according to you, must render it totally precarious and unsatisfactory.

To render it still more unsatisfactory, said Philo, there occurs to me another hypothesis which must acquire an air of probability from the method of reasoning so much insisted on by Cleanthes. That like effects arise from like causes—this principle he supposes the foundation of all religion. But there is another principle of the same kind, no less certain and derived from the same source of experience, that, where several known circumstances are observed to be similar, the unknown will also be found similar. Thus, if we see the limbs of a human body, we conclude that it is also attended with a human head, though hid from us. Thus, if we see, through a chink in a wall, a small part of the sun, we conclude that were the wall removed we should see the whole body. In short, this method of reasoning is so obvious and familiar that no scruple can ever be made with regard to its solidity.

Now, if we survey the universe, so far as it falls under our knowledge, it bears a great resemblance to an animal or organized body, and seems actuated with a like principle of life and motion. A continual circulation of matter in it produces no disorder; a continual waste in every part is incessantly repaired; the closest sympathy is perceived throughout the entire system; and each part or member, in performing its proper offices, operates both to its own preservation and to that of the whole. The world, therefore, I infer, is an animal; and the Deity is the *soul* of the world, actuating it, and actuated by it.

You have too much learning, Cleanthes, to be at all surprised at this opinion which, you know, was maintained by almost all the theists of antiquity, and chiefly prevails in their discourses and reasonings. For though, sometimes, the ancient philosophers reason from final causes, as if they thought the world the workmanship of God, yet it appears rather their favorite notion to consider it as his body whose organization renders it subservient to him. And it must be confessed that, as the universe resembles more a human body than it does the works of human art and contrivance, if our limited analogy could ever, with any propriety, be extended to the whole of nature, the inference seems juster in favor of the ancient than the modern theory.

There are many other advantages, too, in the former theory which recommended it to the ancient theologians. Nothing more repugnant to all their notions, because nothing more repugnant to common experience, than mind without body, a mere spiritual substance which fell not under their senses nor comprehension, and of which they had not observed one single instance throughout all nature. Mind and body they knew because they felt both; an order, arrangement, organization, or internal machinery, in both they likewise knew, after the same manner; and it could not but seem reasonable to transfer this experience to the universe, and to suppose the divine mind and body to be also coeval and to have, both of them, order and arrangement naturally inherent in them and inseparable from them.

Here, therefore, is a new species of anthropomorphism, Cleanthes, on which you may deliberate, and a theory which seems not liable to any considerable difficulties. You are too much superior, surely, to systematical prejudices to find any more difficulty in supposing an animal body to be, originally, of itself or from unknown causes, possessed of order and organization, than in supposing a similar order to belong to mind. But the vulgar prejudice that body and mind ought always to accompany each other ought not, one should think, to be entirely neglected; since it is founded on vulgar experience, the only guide which you profess to follow in all these theological inquiries. And if you assert that our limited experience is an unequal standard by which to judge of the unlimited extent of nature, you entirely abandon your own hypothesis, and must thenceforward adopt our mysticism, as you call it, and admit of the absolute incomprehensibility of the Divine Nature.

This theory, I own, replied Cleanthes, has never before occurred to me, though a pretty natural one; and I cannot readily, upon so short an examination and reflection, deliver any opinion with regard to it. You are very scrupulous, indeed, said Philo; were I to examine any system of yours, I should not have acted with half that caution and reserve, in stating objections and difficulties to it. However, if anything occur to you, you will oblige us by proposing it.

Why then, replied Cleanthes, it seems to me that, though the world does, in many circumstances, resemble an animal body, yet is the analogy also defective in many circumstances the most material: no organs of sense; no seat of thought or reason; no one precise origin of motion and action. In short, it seems to bear a stronger resemblance to a vegetable than to an animal, and your inference would be so far inconclusive in favor of the soul of the world. . . .

But here, continued Philo, in examining the ancient system of the soul of the world there strikes me, all on a sudden, a new idea which, if just, must go near to subvert all your reasoning, and destroy even your first inferences on which you repose such confidence. If the universe bears a greater likeness to animal bodies and to vegetables than to the works of human art, it is more probable that its cause resembles the cause of the former than that of the latter, and its origin ought rather to be ascribed to generation or vegetation than to reason or design. Your conclusion, even according to your own principles, is therefore lame and defective.

Pray open up this argument a little further, said Demea, for I do not rightly apprehend it in that concise manner in which you have expressed it.

Our friend Cleanthes, replied Philo, as you have heard, asserts that, since no question of fact can be proved otherwise than by experience, the existence of a Deity admits not of proof from any other medium. The world, says he, resembles the works of human contrivance; therefore its cause must also resemble that of the other. Here we may remark that the operation of one very small part of nature, to wit, man, upon another very small part, to wit, that inanimate matter lying within his reach, is the rule by which Cleanthes judges of the origin of the whole; and he measures objects, so widely disproportioned, by the same individual standard. But to waive all objections drawn from this topic, I affirm that there are other parts of the universe (besides the machines of human invention) which bear still a greater resemblance to the fabric of the world, and which, therefore, afford a better conjecture concerning the universal origin of this system. These parts are animals and vegetables. The world plainly resembles more an animal or a vegetable than it does a watch or a knitting-loom. Its cause, therefore, it is more probable, resembles the cause of the former. The cause of the former is generation or vegetation. The cause, therefore, of the world we may infer to be something similar or analogous to generation or vegetation.

. . . In this little corner of the world alone, there are four principles, *reason, instinct, generation, vegetation,* which are similar to each other, and are the causes of similar effects. What a number of other principles may we naturally suppose in the immense extent and variety of the universe could we travel from planet to planet, and from system to system, in order to examine each part of this mighty fabric? Any one of these four principles above mentioned (and a hundred others which lie open to our conjecture) may afford us a theory by which to judge of the origin of the world; and it is a palpable and egregious partiality to confine our view entirely to that principle by which our own minds operate. Were this principle more intelligible on that account, such a partiality might be somewhat excusable; but reason, in its internal fabric and structure, is really as little known to us as instinct or vegetation; and perhaps, even that vague, undeterminate word *nature* to which the vulgar refer everything is not at the bottom more inexplicable. The effects of these principles are all known to us from experience; but the principles themselves and their manner of operation are totally unknown; nor is it less intelligible or less conformable to experience to say that the world arose by vegetation, from a seed shed by another world, than to say that it arose from a divine reason or contrivance, according to the sense in which Cleanthes understands it.

But methinks, said Demea, if the world had a vegetative quality and could sow the seeds of new worlds into the infinite chaos, this power would be still an additional argument for design in its author. For whence could arise so wonderful a faculty but from design? Or how can order spring from anything which perceives not that order which it bestows?

You need only look around you, replied Philo, to satisfy yourself with regard to this question. A tree bestows order and organization on that tree which springs from it, without knowing the order; an animal in the same manner on its offspring; a bird on its nest; and instances of this kind are even more frequent in the world than those of order which arise from reason and contrivance. To say that all this order in animals and vegetables proceeds ultimately from design is begging the question; nor can that great point be ascertained otherwise than by proving, *a priori*, both that order is, from its nature, inseparably attached to thought and that it can never of itself or from original unknown principles belong to matter. . . .

I must confess, Philo, replied Cleanthes, that, of all men living, the task which you have undertaken, of raising doubts and objections, suits you best and seems, in a manner, natural and unavoidable to you. So great is your fertility of invention that I am not ashamed to acknowledge myself unable, on a sudden, to solve regularly such out-of-the-way difficulties as you incessantly start upon me, though I clearly see, in general, their fallacy and error. And I question not, but you are yourself, at present, in the same case, and have not the solution so ready as the objection, while you must be sensible that common sense and reason are entirely against you, and that such whimsies as you have delivered may puzzle but never can convince us.

What you ascribe to the fertility of my invention, replied Philo, is entirely owing to the nature of the subject. In subjects adapted to the narrow compass of human reason there is commonly but one determination which carries probability or conviction with it; and to a man of sound judgment all other suppositions but that one appear entirely absurd and chimerical. But in such questions as the present, a hundred contradictory views may preserve a kind of imperfect analogy, and invention has here full scope to exert itself. Without any great effort of thought, I believe that I could, in an instant, propose other systems of cosmogony which would have some faint appearance of truth, though it is a thousand, a million to one if either yours or any one of mine be the true system.

For instance, what if I should revive the old Epicurean hypothesis? This is commonly, and I believe justly, esteemed the most absurd system that has yet been proposed; yet I know not whether, with a few alterations, it might not be brought to bear a faint appearance of probability. Instead of supposing matter infinite, as Epicurus did, let us suppose it finite. A finite number of particles is only susceptible of finite transpositions; and it must happen, in an eternal duration, that every possible order or position must be tried an infinite number of times. This world, therefore, with all its events, even the most minute, has before been produced and destroyed, and will again be produced and destroyed, without any bounds and limitations. No one who has a conception of the powers of infinite, in comparison of finite, will ever scruple this determination.

But this supposes, said Demea, that matter can acquire motion without any voluntary agent or first mover.

And where is the difficulty, replied Philo, of that supposition? Every event, before experience, is equally difficult and incomprehensible; and every event, after experience, is equally easy and intelligible. Motion, in many instances, from gravity, from elasticity, from electricity, begins in matter, without any known voluntary agent; and to suppose always, in these cases, an unknown voluntary agent is mere hypothesis and hypothesis attended with no advantages. The beginning of motion in matter itself is as conceivable *a priori* as its communication from mind and intelligence.

Besides, why may not motion have been propagated by impulse through all eternity, and the same stock of it, or nearly the same, be still upheld in the universe? As much as is lost by the composition of motion, as much is gained by its resolution. And whatever the causes are, the fact is certain that matter is and always has been in continual agitation, as far as human experience or tradition reaches. There is not probably, at present, in the whole universe, one particle of matter at absolute rest.

And this very consideration, too, continued Philo, which we have stumbled on in the course of the argument suggests a new hypothesis of cosmogony that is not absolutely absurd and improbable. Is there a system, an order, an economy of things, by which matter can preserve that perpetual agitation which seems essential to it, and yet maintain a constancy in the forms which it produces? There certainly is such an economy, for this is actually the case with the present world. The continual motion of matter, therefore, in less than infinite transpositions, must produce this economy or order, and, by its very nature, that order, when once established, supports itself for many ages if not to eternity. But wherever matter is so poised, arranged, and adjusted, as to continue in perpetual motion, and yet preserve a constancy in the forms, its situation must, of necessity, have all the same appearance of art and contrivance which we observe at present. All the parts of each form must have a relation to each other and to the whole; and the whole itself must have a relation to the other parts of the universe, to the element in which the form subsists, to the materials with which it repairs its waste and decay, and to every other form which is hostile or friendly. A defect in any of these particulars destroys the form, and the matter of which it is composed is again set loose, and is thrown into irregular motions and fermentations till it unite itself to some other regular form. If no such form be prepared to receive it, and if there be a great quantity of this corrupted matter in the universe, the universe itself is entirely disordered, whether it be the feeble embryo of a world in its first beginnings that is thus destroyed or the rotten carcass of one languishing in old age and infirmity. In either case, a chaos ensues till finite though innumerable revolutions produce, at last, some forms whose parts and organs are so adjusted as to support the forms amidst a continued succession of matter.

Suppose (for we shall endeavor to vary the expression) that matter were thrown into any position by a blind, unguided force; it is evident that this first position must, in all probability, be the most confused and most disorderly imaginable, without any resemblance to those works of human contrivance which, along with a symmetry of parts, discover an adjustment of means to ends and a tendency to self-preservation. If the actuating force cease after this operation, matter must remain for ever in disorder, and continue an immense chaos, without any proportion or activity. But suppose that the actuating force, whatever it be, still continues in matter, this first position will immediately give place to a second which will likewise, in all probability, be as disorderly as the first, and so on through many successions of changes and revolutions. No particular order or position ever continues a moment unaltered. The original force, still remaining in activity, gives a perpetual restlessness to matter. Every possible situation is produced, and instantly destroyed. If a glimpse or dawn of order appears for a moment, it is instantly hurried away and confounded by that never-ceasing force which actuates every part of matter.

Thus the universe goes on for many ages in a continued succession of chaos and disorder. But is it not possible that it may settle at last, so as not to lose its motion and active force (for that we have supposed inherent in it), yet so as to preserve an uniformity of appearance, amidst the continual motion and fluctuation of its parts? This we find to be the case with the universe at present. Every individual is perpetually changing, and every part of every individual; and yet the whole remains, in appearance, the same. May we not hope for such a position or rather be assured of it from the eternal revolutions of unguided matter; and may not this account for all the appearing wisdom and contrivance which is in the universe? Let us contemplate the subject a little, and we shall find that this adjustment, if attained by matter, of a seeming stability in the forms, with a real and perpetual revolution or motion of parts, affords a plausible, if not a true, solution of the difficulty.

It is in vain, therefore, to insist upon the uses of the parts in animals or vegetables, and their curious adjustment to each other. I would fain know how an animal could subsist unless its parts were so adjusted? Do we not find that it immediately perishes whenever this adjustment ceases, and that its matter, corrupting, tries some new form? It happens indeed that the parts of the world are so well adjusted that some regular form immediately lays claim to this corrupted matter; and if it were not so, could the world subsist? Must it not dissolve, as well as the animal, and pass through new positions and situations till in great but finite succession it fall, at last, into the present or some such order?

It is well, replied Cleanthes, you told us that this hypothesis was suggested on a sudden, in the course of the argument. Had you had leisure to examine it, you would soon have perceived the insuperable objections to which it is exposed. No form, you say, can subsist unless it possess those powers and organs requisite for its subsistence; some new order or economy must be tried, and so on, without intermission, till at last some order which can support and maintain itself is fallen upon. But according to this hypothesis, whence arise the many conveniences and advantages which men and all animals possess? Two eyes, two ears are not absolutely necessary for the subsistence of the species. Human race might have been propagated and preserved without horses, dogs, cows, sheep, and those innumerable fruits and products which serve to our satisfaction and enjoyment. If no camels had been created for the use of man in the sandy deserts of Africa and Arabia, would the world have been dissolved? If no loadstone had been framed to give that wonderful and useful direction to the needle, would human society and the human kind have been immediately extinguished? Though the maxims of nature be in general very frugal, yet instances of this kind are far from being rare; and any one of them is a sufficient proof of design—and of a benevolent design—which gave rise to the order and arrangement of the universe.

At least, you may safely infer, said Philo, that the foregoing hypothesis is so far incomplete and imperfect, which I shall not scruple to allow. But can we ever reasonably expect greater success in any attempts of this nature? Or can we ever hope to erect a system of cosmogony that will be liable to no exceptions, and will contain no circumstance repugnant to our limited and imperfect experience of the analogy of nature? Your theory itself cannot surely pretend to any such advantage, even though you have run into *anthropomorphism,* the better to preserve a conformity to common experience. Let us once more put it to trial.

In all instances which we have ever seen, ideas are copied from real objects, and are ectypal, not archetypal, to express myself in learned terms. You reverse this order and give thought the precedence. In all instances which we have ever seen, thought has no influence upon matter except where that matter is so conjoined with it as to have an equal reciprocal influence upon it. No animal can move immediately anything but the members of its own body; and, indeed, the equality of action and reaction seems to be an universal law of nature; but your theory implies a contradiction to this experience. These instances, with many more which it were easy to collect (particularly the supposition of a mind or system of thought that is eternal or, in other words, an animal ingenerable and immortal)—these instances, I say, may teach all of us sobriety in condemning each other, and let us see that as no system of this kind ought ever to be received from a slight analogy, so neither ought any to be rejected on account of a small incongruity. For that is an inconvenience from which we can justly pronounce no one to be exempted.

All religious systems, it is confessed, are subject to great and insuperable difficulties. Each disputant triumphs in his turn, while he carries on an offensive war, and exposes the absurdities, barbarities, and pernicious tenets of his antagonist. But all of them, on the whole, prepare a complete triumph for the *sceptic,* who tells them that no system ought ever to be embraced with regard to such subjects: for this plain reason than no absurdity ought ever to be assented to with regard to any subject. A total suspense of judgment is here our only reasonable resource. And if every attack, as is commonly observed, and no defense among theologians is successful, how complete must be *his* victory who remains always, with all mankind, on the offensive, and has himself no fixed station or abiding city which he is ever, on any occasion, obliged to defend?

31

ROUSSEAU

1712–1778

Jean Jacques Rousseau was born in Geneva, Switzerland. His mother died giving birth and he was raised by his father, a local watchmaker who could not afford to give him a formal education. So Rousseau got his early education from various novels and books, the most influential of which was *Parallel Lives* by Plutarch (46–119). This was the monumental biography of leading Greek and Roman figures, in which Plutarch tried to discover the universal forms of great human character by making formal comparisons between different individuals unified by common deeds, strengths of character, and so on. At the age of ten, however, Rousseau was sent to live with his aunt and uncle, who shipped him off to boarding school. Here, Rousseau would write in his *Confessions,* "we were to learn . . . all the insignificant trash that has obtained the name of education."

Rousseau was apprenticed at a young age to an engraver, which he despised even more than schooling. In 1728 he ran away to France and there met an older noblewoman, Mme. de Warens, who virtually adopted him and eventually became his lover. She tried to have young Rousseau formally educated at various institutions, including the Hospice of the Holy Spirit in Turin (a Lazarist seminary) where he converted from orthodox Calvinism to Catholicism (he would later convert again, to Protestantism), and then the choir school of the cathedral at Annecy. Unhappy with his schooling, Rousseau worked a variety of odd jobs such as engraving, copying music, and giving music lessons.

He ended up being Warens's live-in lover for seven years, during which time he read Plato, Montaigne, Pascal, Virgil, and Horace, and composed music using a new type of musical notation. He wrote poems, operas, plays, and even a ballet, *Les muses galantes,* which was performed at the Paris Opera in 1747, with lukewarm reception. Warens eventually found a younger lover, and Rousseau had a long affair with a hotel servant, with whom he had five children. He eventually married her but sent all of their children into orphanages.

In 1749 the Dijon Academy announced a national essay contest on the following questions: Has the revival of the arts and sciences purified or corrupted morals? The prevailing opinion, as espoused by the Roman Catholic Church, was that humans are by nature sinners who need orthodox institutions to make them good; education therefore was for the edification, purification, and enlightenment of the soul. Rousseau submitted an essay, titled

Discourse on the Arts and Sciences, in which he argued that it is the institutions of learning themselves that make human beings bad. Further, the arts and the sciences are the worst corruptors of humanity because they mold behavior and condition us away from our authentic passions, which we are given by nature. The arts and sciences condition how we speak and think, even what we feel, away from what we really feel and think. Moreover, the artistic and scientific institutions seduce people with promises of wealth and glory, corrupting them into living false, artificial lives.

Rousseau's scathing essay won first prize. Almost overnight, Rousseau became famous throughout Europe as a new philosopher and social critic. Suddenly, within a year, his operetta, *Le devin du village,* was performed before the court of King Louis XV. His comedy, *Narcisse,* played at the prestigious Théâtre Français. One success followed another. Artists, writers, scientists, philosophers, and politicians all freely quoted him, often in openly criticizing their own institutions.

A few years later, in 1755, Rousseau decided to publish a more thorough version of his essay, called *Discourse on What Is the Origin of the Inequality Among Men, and Is It Authorized by Natural Law?* He then authored a brilliant novel, *Julie, ou la nouvelle Héloïse* (1761). Not only did this became the most celebrated novel of the eighteenth century, it also helped launch the romantic movement in literature. A year later he published *Emile,* a fictional account of his provocative new theory of education. His greatest philosophical work was also published that year: *The Social Contract,* from which our selection is taken.

The Social Contract begins with the famous words "Man is born free; and everywhere he is in chains." In it, Rousseau argues that the transition from the original "state of nature," in which all human beings once lived, to the modern "civil state," provided a firm foundation for modern politics. Evident in the work is the influence of Plutarch, who had been initiated in the mystical rites of Dionysus and inspired by the Stoics, Pythagoreans, and Peripatetics. Like Rousseau's other works, *The Social Contract* is vehemently critical not only of Christianity, but of rationality and philosophical skepticism as well. As a consequence, in the end the French authorities decided to take offense. They issued a warrant for Rousseau's arrest.

Instead of facing trial, Rousseau escaped and spent the remaining years of his life as a fugitive condemned by both church and state authorities. It was none other than David Hume who helped him live in exile in England, for over one and a half years. However, still convinced that his enemies were out to get him, Rousseau apparently accused Hume of conspiring against him and once again fled. He returned to France under the pseudonym "M. Renou." Some years later he decided finally to defend himself publicly. He took his own name back. But by then the authorities had decided to drop all charges against him. Shortly before his death he published a candid and brilliant autobiography, *Confessions.*

Many philosophers have regarded Rousseau as not being systematic or rigorous, or criticize his views as being deeply inconsistent. Yet he has wielded a tremendous influence on some of the greatest philosophers. He has been called the originator of the romantic movement, mainly because of the powerful appeal he makes on behalf of the emotions. His emphasis on equality, liberty, and the supremacy of individual citizens inspired the leaders of the French Revolution and the builders of republican democracies. Yet his works were also used to support many authoritarian movements. His arguments to the effect that human beings can realize their true natures only through society and that it is the individuals who control the sovereign, for instance, inspired the Hegelians with the idea of national spirit.

Others have suggested that it is Rousseau who made possible the suppression of freedom in the name of freedom with the idea that what makes freedom possible is a social contract, that is, by trading natural liberty for civil liberty. In doing so, "each of us puts his persona and all his power in common under the supreme direction of the general will, and, in our corporate capacity, we receive each member as an indivisible part of a whole."

Rousseau claims that anyone who does not obey the "general will" must be forced to do so: it is through the social contract that a human being is "forced to be free." Bertrand Russell thus calls Rousseau "the inventor of the political philosophy of pseudo-democratic dictatorships as opposed to traditional absolute monarchies. Ever since his time, those who considered themselves reformers have been divided into two groups, those who followed him and those who followed Locke. . . . At the present time, Hitler is an outcome of Rousseau; Roosevelt and Churchill, of Locke." [1] In Rousseau's view, the will of the political leader is the incarnation of the general will, which reflects the sum of the individual wills of all the citizens.

Immanuel Kant, as we shall see in the next chapter, drew much inspiration from Rousseau. Especially influential was Rousseau's claim that if each individual citizen was given enough information and the freedom to choose, all citizens would, independently of each other—since they are all directed to the same will to do the common good—arrive at the general will for the good of all humankind. In Kant's study, directly above his desk there still hangs a portrait of Jean Jacques Rousseau, whom Kant admired so much that he called him "the Newton of the moral world."

THE SOCIAL CONTRACT

BOOK I

I mean to inquire if, in the civil order, there can be any sure and legitimate rule of administration, men being taken as they are and laws as they might be. In this inquiry I shall endeavor always to unite what right sanctions with what is prescribed by interest, in order that justice and utility may in no case be divided.

I enter upon my task without proving the importance of the subject. I shall be asked if I am a prince or a legislator, to write on politics. I answer that I am neither, and that is why I do so. If I were a prince or a legislator, I should not waste time in saying what wants doing; I should do it, or hold my peace.

As I was born a citizen of a free State, and a member of the Sovereign, I feel that, however feeble the influence my voice can have on public affairs, the right of voting on them makes it my duty to study them: and I am happy, when I reflect upon governments, to find my inquiries always furnish me with new reasons for loving that of my own country.

1. Bertrand Russell, *A History of Western Philosophy* (New York: Simon and Schuster, 1945), pp. 484–85.
From Jean Jacques Rousseau, *The Social Contract,* trans. G. D. H. Cole (New York: E. P. Dutton, 1913).

CHAPTER I
Subject of the First Book

Man is born free; and everywhere he is in chains. One thinks himself the master of others, and still remains a greater slave than they. How did this change come about? I do not know. What can make it legitimate? That question I think I can answer.

If I took into account only force, and the effects derived from it, I should say: "As long as a people is compelled to obey, and obeys, it does well; as soon as it can shake off the yoke, and shakes it off, it does still better; for, regaining its liberty by the same right as took it away, either it is justified in resuming it, or there was no justification for those who took it away." But the social order is a sacred right which is the basis of all rights. Nevertheless, this right does not come from nature, and must therefore be founded on conventions. Before coming to that, I have to prove what I have just asserted.

CHAPTER II
The First Societies

The most ancient of all societies, and the only one that is natural, is the family: and even so the children remain attached to the father only so long as they need him for their preservation. As soon as this need ceases, the natural bond is dissolved. The children, released from the obedience they owed to the father, and the father, released from the care he owed his children, return equally to independence. If they remain united, they continue so no longer naturally, but voluntarily; and the family itself is then maintained only by convention.

This common liberty results from the nature of man. His first law is to provide for his own preservation, his first cares are those which he owes to himself; and, as soon as he reaches years of discretion, he is the sole judge of the proper means of preserving himself, and consequently becomes his own master.

The family then may be called the first model of political societies: the ruler corresponds to the father, and the people to the children; and all, being born free and equal, alienate their liberty only for their own advantage. The whole difference is that, in the family, the love of the father for his children repays him for the care he takes of them, while, in the State, the pleasure of commanding takes the place of the love which the chief cannot have for the peoples under him.

Grotius denies that all human power is established in favor of the governed, and quotes slavery as an example. His usual method of reasoning is constantly to establish right by fact. It would be possible to employ a more logical method, but none could be more favorable to tyrants.

It is then, according to Grotius, doubtful whether the human race belongs to a hundred men, or that hundred men to the human race: and, throughout his book, he seems to incline to the former alternative, which is also the view of Hobbes. On this showing, the human species is divided into so many herds of cattle, each with its ruler, who keeps guard over them for the purpose of devouring them.

As a shepherd is of a nature superior to that of his flock, the shepherds of men, i.e. their rulers, are of a nature superior to that of the peoples under them. Thus, Philo tells us, the Emperor Caligula reasoned, concluding equally well either that kings were gods, or that men were beasts.

The reasoning of Caligula agrees with that of Hobbes and Grotius. Aristotle, before any of them, had said that men are by no means equal naturally, but that some are born for slavery, and others for dominion.

Aristotle was right; but he took the effect for the cause. Nothing can be more certain than that every man born in slavery is born for slavery. Slaves lose everything in their chains, even the desire of escaping from them: they love their servitude, as the comrades of Ulysses loved their brutish condition. If then there are slaves by nature, it is because there have been slaves against nature. Force made the first slaves, and their cowardice perpetuated the condition.

I have said nothing of King Adam, or Emperor Noah, father of the three great monarchs who shared out the universe, like the children of Saturn, whom some scholars have recognized in them. I trust to getting due thanks for my moderation; for, being a direct descendant of one of these princes, perhaps of the eldest branch, how do I know that a verification of titles might not leave me the legitimate king of the human race? In any case, there can be no doubt that Adam was sovereign of the world, as Robinson Crusoe was of his island, as long as he was its only inhabitant; and this empire had the advantage that the monarch, safe on his throne, had no rebellions, wars, or conspirators to fear.

CHAPTER III
The Right of the Strongest

The strongest is never strong enough to be always the master, unless he transforms strength into right, and obedience into duty. Hence the right of the strongest, which, though to all seeming meant ironically, is really laid down as a fundamental principle. But are we never to have an explanation of this phrase? Force is a physical power, and I fail to see what moral effect it can have. To yield to force is an act of necessity, not of will—at the most, an act of prudence. In what sense can it be a duty?

Suppose for a moment that this so-called "right" exists. I maintain that the sole result is a mass of inexplicable nonsense. For, if force creates right, the effect changes with the cause: every force that is greater than the first succeeds to its right. As soon as it is possible to disobey with impunity, disobedience is legitimate; and, the strongest being always in the right, the only thing that matters is to act so as to become the strongest. But what kind of right is that which perishes when force fails? If we must obey perforce, there is no need to obey because we ought; and if we are not forced to obey, we are under no obligation to do so. Clearly, the word "right" adds nothing to force: in this connection, it means absolutely nothing.

Obey the powers that be. If this means yield to force, it is a good precept, but superfluous: I can answer for its never being violated. All power comes from God, I admit; but so does all sickness: does that mean that we are forbidden to call in the doctor? A brigand surprises me at the edge of a wood: must I not merely surrender my purse on compulsion; but, even if I could withhold it, am I in conscience bound to give it up? For certainly the pistol he holds is also a power.

Let us then admit that force does not create right, and that we are obliged to obey only legitimate powers. In that case, my original question recurs.

CHAPTER IV
Slavery

Since no man has a natural authority over his fellow, and force creates no right, we must conclude that conventions form the basis of all legitimate authority among men.

If an individual, says Grotius, can alienate his liberty and make himself the slave of a master, why could not a whole people do the same and make itself subject to a king? There are in this passage plenty of ambiguous words which would need explaining; but let us confine ourselves to the word *alienate*. To alienate is to give or to sell. Now, a man who becomes the slave of another does not give himself; he sells himself, at the least for his subsistence: but for what does a people sell itself? A king is so far from furnishing his subjects with their subsistence that he gets his own only from them; and, according to Rabelais, kings do not live on nothing. Do subjects then give their persons on condition that the king take their goods also? I fail to see what they have left to preserve.

It will be said that the despot assures his subjects civil tranquility. Granted; but what do they gain, if the wars his ambition brings down upon them, his insatiable avidity, and the vexatious conduct of his ministers press harder on them than their own dissensions would have done? What do they gain, if the very tranquillity they enjoy is one of their miseries? Tranquillity is found also in dungeons; but is that enough to make them desirable places to live in? The Greeks imprisoned in the cave of the Cyclops lived there very tranquilly, while they were awaiting their turn to be devoured.

To say that a man gives himself gratuitously, is to say what is absurd and inconceivable; such an act is null and illegitimate, from the mere fact that he who does it is out of his mind. To say the same of a whole people is to suppose a people of madmen; and madness creates no right.

Even if each man could alienate himself, he could not alienate his children: they are born men and free; their liberty belongs to them, and no one but they has the right to dispose of it. Before they come to years of discretion, the father can, in their name, lay down conditions for their preservation and well-being, but he cannot give them irrevocably and without conditions: such a gift is contrary to the ends of nature, and exceeds the rights of paternity. It would therefore be necessary, in order to legitimize an arbitrary government, that in every generation the people should be in a position to accept or reject it; but, were this so, the government would be no longer arbitrary.

To renounce liberty is to renounce being a man, to surrender the rights of humanity and even its duties. For him who renounces everything no indemnity is possible. Such a renunciation is incompatible with man's nature; to remove all liberty from his will is to remove all morality from his acts. Finally, it is an empty and contradictory convention that sets up, on the one side, absolute authority, and, on the other, unlimited obedience. Is it not clear that we can be under no obligation to a person from whom we have the right to exact everything? Does not this condition alone, in the absence of equivalence or exchange, in itself involve the nullity of the act? For what right can my slave have against me, when all that he has belongs to me, and, his right being mine, this right of mine against myself is a phrase devoid of meaning?

Grotius and the rest find in war another origin for the so-called right of slavery. The victor having, as they hold, the right of killing the vanquished, the latter can buy back his life at the price of his liberty; and this convention is the more legitimate because it is to the advantage of both parties.

But it is clear that this supposed right to kill the conquered is by no means deducible from the state of war. Men, from the mere fact that, while they are living in their primitive independence, they have no mutual relations stable enough to constitute either the state of peace or the state of war, cannot be naturally enemies. War is constituted by a relation between things, and not between persons; and, as the state of war cannot arise out of simple personal relations, but only out of real relations, private war, or war of man with man, can exist neither in the state of nature, where there is no constant property, nor in the social state, where everything is under the authority of the laws.

Individual combats, duels, and encounters, are acts which cannot constitute a state; while the private wars, authorized by the Establishments of Louis IX, King of France, and suspended by the Peace of God, are abuses of feudalism, in itself an absurd system if ever there was one, and contrary to the principles of natural right and to all good polity.

War then is a relation, not between man and man, but between State and State, and individuals are enemies only accidentally, not as men, nor even as citizens, but as soldiers; not as members of their country, but as its defenders. Finally, each State can have for enemies only other States, and not men; for between things disparate in nature there can be no real relation.

Furthermore, this principle is in conformity with the established rules of all times and the constant practice of all civilized peoples. Declarations of war are intimations less to powers than to their subjects. The foreigner, whether king, individual, or people, who robs, kills, or detains the subjects, without declaring war on the prince, is not an enemy, but a brigand. Even in real war, a just prince, while laying hands, in the enemy's country, on all that belongs to the public, respects the lives and goods of individuals: he respects rights on which his own are founded. The object of the war being the destruction of the hostile State, the other side has a right to kill its defenders, while they are bearing arms; but as soon as they lay them down and surrender, they cease to be enemies or instruments of the enemy, and become once more merely men, whose life no one has any right to take. Sometimes it is possible to kill the State without killing a single one of its members; and war gives no right which is not necessary to the gaining of its object. These principles are not those of Grotius: they are not based on the authority of poets, but derived from the nature of reality and based on reason.

The right of conquest has no foundation other than the right of the strongest. If war does not give the conqueror the right to massacre the conquered peoples, the right to enslave them cannot be based upon a right which does not exist. No one has a right to kill an enemy except when he cannot make him a slave, and the right to enslave him cannot therefore be derived from the right to kill him. It is accordingly an unfair exchange to make him buy at the price of his liberty his life, over which the victor holds no right. It is not clear that there is a vicious circle in founding the right of life and death on the right of slavery, and the right of slavery on the right of life and death?

Even if we assume this terrible right to kill everybody, I maintain that a slave made in war, or a conquered people, is under no obligation to a master, except to obey him as far as he is compelled to do so. By taking an equivalent for his life, the victor has not done him a favor; instead of killing him without profit, he has killed him usefully. So far then is he from acquiring over him any authority in addition to that of force, that the state of war continues to subsist between them: their mutual relation is the effect of it, and the usage of the right of war does not imply a treaty of peace. A convention has indeed been made; but this convention, so far from destroying the state of war, presupposes its continuance.

So, from whatever aspect we regard the question, the right of slavery is null and void, not only as being illegitimate, but also because it is absurd and meaningless. The words *slave* and *right* contradict each other, and are mutually exclusive. It will always be equally foolish for a man to say to a man or to a people: "I make with you a convention wholly at your expense and wholly to my advantage; I shall keep it as long as I like, and you will keep it as long as I like."

CHAPTER V
That We Must Always Go Back to a First Convention

Even if I granted that all I have been refuting, the friends of despotism would be no better off. There will always be a great difference between subduing a multitude and ruling a society. Even if scattered individuals were successively enslaved by one man, however numerous they might be, I still see no more than a master and his slaves, and certainly not a people and its ruler; I see what may be termed an aggregation, but not an association; there is as yet neither public good nor body politic. The man in question, even if he has enslaved half the world, is still only an individual; his interest, apart from that of others, is still a purely private interest. If this same man comes to die, his empire, after him, remains scattered and without unity, as an oak falls and dissolves into a heap of ashes when the fire has consumed it.

A people, says Grotius, can give itself to a king. Then according to Grotius, a people is a people before it gives itself. The gift is itself a civil act, and implies public deliberation. It would be better, before examining the act by which a people gives itself to a king, to examine that by which it has become a people; for this act, being necessarily prior to the other, is the true foundation of society.

Indeed, if there were no prior convention, where, unless the election were unanimous, would be the obligation on the minority to submit to the choice of the majority? How have a hundred men who wish for a master the right to vote on behalf of ten who do not? The law of majority voting is itself something established by convention, and presupposes unanimity, on one occasion at least.

CHAPTER VI
The Social Contract

I suppose men to have reached the point at which the obstacles in the way of their preservation in the state of nature show their power of resistance to be greater than the resources at the disposal of each individual for his maintenance in that state. That primitive condition can then subsist no longer; and the human race would perish unless it changed its manner of existence.

But, as a men cannot engender new forces, but only unite and direct existing ones, they have no other means of preserving themselves than the formation, by aggregation, of a sum of forces great enough to overcome the resistance. These they have to bring into play by means of a single motive power, and cause to act in concert.

This sum of forces can arise only where several persons come together; but, as the force and liberty of each man are the chief instruments of his self-preservation, how can he pledge them without harming his own interests, and neglecting the care he owes to himself? This difficulty, in its bearing on my present subject, may be stated in the following terms:

"The problem is to find a form of association which will defend and protect with the whole common force the person and goods of each associate, and in which each, while uniting himself with all, may still obey himself alone, and remain as free as before." This is the fundamental problem of which the *Social Contract* provides the solution.

The clauses of this contract are so determined by the nature of the act that the slightest modification would make them vain and ineffective; so that, although they have perhaps never been formally set forth, they are everywhere the same and everywhere tacitly admitted and recognized, until, on the violation of the social compact, each regains his original rights and resumes his natural liberty, while losing the conventional liberty in favor of which he renounced it.

These clauses, properly understood, may be reduced to one—the total alienation of each associate, together with all his rights, to the whole community; for, in the first place, as each gives himself absolutely, the conditions are the same for all; and, this being so, no one has any interest in making them burdensome to others.

Moreover, the alienation being without reserve, the union is as perfect as it can be, and no associate has anything more to demand: for, if the individuals retained certain rights, as there would be no common superior to decide between them and the public, each, being on one point his own judge, would ask to be so on all; the state of nature would thus continue, and the association would necessarily become inoperative or tyrannical.

Finally, each man, in giving himself to all, gives himself to nobody; and as there is no associate over which he does not acquire the same right as he yields others over himself, he gains an equivalent for everything he loses, and an increase of force for the preservation of what he has.

If then we discard from the social compact what is not of its essence, we shall find that it reduces itself to the following terms:

"Each of us puts his person and all his power in common under the supreme direction of the general will, and, in our corporate capacity, we receive each member as an indivisible part of the whole."

At once, in place of the individual personality of each contracting party, this act of association creates a moral and collective body, composed of as many members as the assembly contains voters, and receiving from this act its unity, its common identity, its life, and its will. This public person, so formed by the union of all other persons, formerly took the name of *city,* and now takes that of *Republic* or *body politic;* it is called by its members *State* when passive, *Sovereign* when active, and *Power* when compared with others like itself. Those who are associated in it take collectively the name of *people,* and severally are called *citizens,* as sharing in the sovereign power, and *subjects,* as being under the laws of the State. But these terms are often confused and taken one for another: it is enough to know how to distinguish them when they are being used with precision.

CHAPTER VII
The Sovereign

This formula shows us that the act of association comprises a mutual undertaking between the public and the individuals, and that each individual, in making a contract, as we may say, with himself, is bound in a double capacity; as a member of the Sovereign he is bound to the individuals, and as a member of the State to the Sovereign. But the maxim of civil right, that no one is bound by undertakings made to himself, does not apply in this case; for there is a great difference between incurring an obligation to yourself and incurring one to a whole of which you form a part.

Attention must further be called to the fact that public deliberation, while competent to bind all the subjects to the Sovereign, because of the two different capacities in which each of them may be regarded, cannot, for the opposite reason, bind the Sovereign to itself; and that it is consequently against the nature of the body politic for the Sovereign to impose on itself a law which it cannot infringe. Being able to regard itself in only one capacity, it is in the position of an individual who makes a contract with himself; and this makes it clear that there neither is nor can be any kind of fundamental law binding on the body of the people—not even the social contract itself. This does not mean that the body politic cannot enter into undertakings with others, provided the contract is not infringed by them; for in relation to what is external to it, it becomes a simple being, an individual.

But the body politic or the Sovereign, drawing its being wholly from the sanctity of the contract, can never bind itself, even to an outsider, to do anything derogatory to the original act, for instance, to alienate any part of itself, or to submit to another Sovereign. Violation of the act by which it exists would be self-annihilation; and that which is itself nothing can create nothing.

As soon as this multitude is so united in one body, it is impossible to offend against one of the members without attacking the body, and still more to offend against the body without the members resenting it. Duty and interest therefore equally oblige the two contracting parties to give each other help; and the same men should seek to combine, in their double capacity, all the advantages dependent upon that capacity.

Again, the Sovereign, being formed wholly of the individuals who compose it, neither has nor can have any interest contrary to theirs; and consequently the sovereign power need give no guarantee to its subjects, because it is impossible for the body to wish to hurt all its members. We shall also see later on that it cannot hurt any in particular. The Sovereign, merely by virtue of what it is, is always what it should be.

This, however, is not the case with the relation of the subjects to the Sovereign, which, despite the common interest, would have no security that they would fulfil their undertakings, unless it found means to assure itself of their fidelity.

In fact, each individual, as a man, may have a particular will contrary or dissimilar to the general will which he has as a citizen. His particular interest may speak to him quite differently from the common interest: his absolute and naturally independent existence may make him look upon what he owes to the common cause as a gratuitous contribution, the loss of which will do less harm to others than the payment of it is burdensome to himself; and, regarding the moral person which constitutes the State as a *persona ficta,* because not a man, he may wish to enjoy the rights of citizenship without being ready to fulfil the duties of a subject. The continuance of such an injustice could not but prove the undoing of the body politic.

In order then that the social compact may not be an empty formula, it tacitly includes the undertaking, which alone can give force to the rest, that whoever refuses to obey the general will shall be compelled to do so by the whole body. This means nothing less than that he will be forced to be free; for this is the condition which, by giving each citizen to his country, secures him against all personal dependence. In this lies the key to the working of the political machine; this alone legitimizes civil undertakings, which, without it, would be absurd, tyrannical, and liable to the most frightful abuses.

CHAPTER VIII
The Civil State

The passage from the state of nature to the civil state produces a very remarkable change in man, by substituting justice for instinct in his conduct, and giving his actions the morality they had formerly lacked. Then only, when the voice of duty takes the place of physical impulses and right of appetite, does man, who so far had considered only himself, find that he is forced to act on different principles, and to consult his reason before listening to his inclinations. Although, in this state, he deprives himself of some advantages which he got from nature, he gains in return others so great, his faculties are so stimulated and developed, his ideas so extended, his feelings so ennobled, and his whole soul so uplifted, that, did not the abuses of this new condition often degrade him below that which he left, he would be bound to bless continually the happy moment which took him from it for ever, and, instead of a stupid and unimaginative animal, made him an intelligent being and a man.

Let us draw upon the whole account in terms easily commensurable. What man loses by the social contract is his natural liberty and an unlimited right to everything he tries to get and succeeds in getting; what he gains is civil liberty and the proprietorship of all he possesses. If we are to avoid mistake in weighing one against the other, we must clearly distinguish natural liberty, which is bounded only by the strength of the individual, from civil liberty, which is limited by the general will; and possession, which is merely the effect of force or the right of the first occupier, from property, which can be founded only on a positive title.

We might, over and above all this, add, to what man acquires in the civil state, moral liberty, which alone makes him truly master of himself; for the mere impulse of appetite is slavery, while obedience to a law which we prescribe to ourselves is liberty. But I have already said too much on this head, and the philosophical meaning of the word "liberty" does not now concern us.

CHAPTER IX
Real Property

Each member of the community gives himself to it, at the moment of its foundation, just as he is, with all the resources at his command, including the goods he possesses. This act does not make possession, in changing hands, change its nature, and become property in the hands of the Sovereign; but, as the forces of the city are incomparably greater than those of an individual, public possession is also, in fact, stronger and more irrevocable, without being any more legitimate, at any rate from the point of view of foreigners. For the State, in relation to its members, is master of all their goods by the social contract, which, within the State, is the basis of all rights; but, in relation to other powers, it is so only by the right of the first occupier, which it holds from its members.

The right of the first occupier, though more real than the right of the strongest, becomes a real right only when the right of property has already been established. Every man has naturally a right to everything he needs; but the positive act which makes him proprietor of one thing excludes him from everything else. Having his share, he ought to keep to it, and can have no further right against the community. This is why the right of the first occupier, which in the state of nature is so weak, claims the respect of every man in civil society. In this right we are respecting not so much what belongs to another as what does not belong to ourselves.

In general, to establish the right of the first occupier over a plot of ground, the following conditions are necessary: first, the land must not yet be inhabited; secondly, a man must occupy only the amount he needs for his subsistence; and, in the third place, possession must be taken, not by an empty ceremony, but by labor and cultivation, the only sign of proprietorship that should be respected by others, in default of a legal title.

In granting the right of first occupancy to necessity and labor, are we not really stretching it as far as it can go? Is it possible to leave such a right unlimited? Is it to be enough to set foot on a plot of common ground, in order to be able to call yourself at once the master of it? Is it to be enough that a man has the strength to expel others for a moment, in order to establish his right to prevent them from ever returning? How can a man or a people seize an immense territory and keep it from the rest of the world except by a punishable usurpation, since all others are being robbed, by such an act, of the place of habitation and the means of subsistence which nature gave them in common? When Nuñez Balboa, standing on the seashore, took possession of the South Seas and the whole of South America in the name of the crown of Castile, was that enough to dispossess all their actual inhabitants, and to shut out from them all the princes of the world? On such a showing, these ceremonies are idly multiplied, and the Catholic King need only take possession all at once, from his apartment, of the whole universe, merely making a subsequent reservation about what was already in the possession of other princes.

We can imagine how the lands of individuals, where they were contiguous and came to be united, became the public territory, and how the right of Sovereignty, extending from the subjects over the lands they held, became at once real and personal. The possessors were thus made more dependent, and the forces at their command used to guarantee their fidelity. The advantage of this does not seem to have been felt by ancient monarchs, who called themselves King of the Persians, Scythians, or Macedonians, and seemed to regard themselves more as rulers of men than as masters of a country. Those of the present day more cleverly call themselves Kings of France, Spain, England, etc.: thus holding the land, they are quite confident of holding the inhabitants.

The peculiar fact about this alienation is that, in taking over the goods of individuals, the community, so far from despoiling them, only assures them legitimate possession, and changes usurpation into a true right and enjoyment into proprietorship. Thus the possessors, being regarded as depositaries of the public good, and having their rights respected by all the members of the State and maintained against foreign aggression by all its forces, have, by a cession which benefits both the public and still more themselves, acquired, so to speak, all that they gave up. This paradox may easily be explained by the distinction between the rights which the Sovereign and the proprietor have over the same estate, as we shall see later on.

It may also happen that men begin to unite one with another before they possess anything, and that, subsequently occupying a tract of country which is enough for all, they enjoy it in common, or share it out among themselves, either equally or according to a scale fixed by the Sovereign. However the acquisition be made, the right which each individual has to his own estate is always subordinate to the right which the community has over all: without this, there would be neither stability in the social tie, nor real force in the exercise of Sovereignty.

I shall end this chapter and this book by remarking on a fact on which the whole social system should rest: i.e. that, instead of destroying natural inequality, the fundamental compact substitutes, for such physical inequality as nature may have set up between men, an equality that is moral and legitimate, and that men, who may be unequal in strength or intelligence, become every one equal by convention and legal right.

32

KANT

1724–1804

Onen of the greatest and most influential philosophers of all time, Immanuel Kant never left the town of his birth, Königsberg—what was then in East Prussia and today is part of Russia. He was a first-generation citizen of Scottish descent, his grandfather having emigrated from Scotland. The local school he attended was then strictly Pietist. His mother had no formal education and his father made saddles for a living.

In 1740 his parents enrolled him in the University of Königsberg. At the time, the philosophy of Leibniz and the science of Newton dominated the university. Although the young Kant was studious, he showed no particular flair or originality. His teachers certainly had no idea that he would one day be regarded as one of the most important thinkers of modern times. He graduated with competent grades but got no job offer from the university. For over ten years he had to support himself as a private tutor in science, mathematics, and philosophy. Finally, in 1755, the University of Königsberg offered him a lowly instructor position without any official title. For the next fifteen years Kant dutifully stayed in this post without any promotion. Then, in 1770, at the age of forty-six, Kant was promoted to a formal position as professor of logic and metaphysics.

His personal life was quiet and unassuming. Only one mild controversy occurred; he was reprimanded for the "distortion of many leading and fundamental doctrines of holy writ and Christianity," and by no less than the Prussian king, Frederick William II. When the king ordered Kant not to lecture or write further on such topics, Kant dutifully obeyed the king's orders. But on the day the king died, Kant promptly resumed. He had few friends and he never married. He hardly ever socialized. The only place he ever went was for his daily walk, at half past four. He walked up and down his street exactly eight times. His neighbors considered him a rather eccentric old recluse.

Kant was fifty-seven years old, a quiet professor nearing the end of an unillustrious career, when he published his first philosophy book. It had a strange and mixed reception, at first. Some scholars said it made no sense at all, that it was practically unreadable, or that it was complete nonsense. But then came the surprise: many began to claim that this obscure and unknown old man had just produced the greatest single work of philosophy ever written. It was called the *Critique of Pure Reason*.

There can be no doubt today that Kant's *Critique* is one of the major achievements in the history of philosophy. Published in 1781, it brought Kant great fame. Philosophers all over Europe suddenly began proclaiming themselves "Kantians." It quickly became the book everyone was talking and writing about. And then, as if out of nowhere, only two years later Kant followed with his *Prolegomena to Any Future Metaphysics.* Then came the *Foundations of the Metaphysics of Morals* in 1785, *Metaphysical First Principles of Natural Science* in 1786, a revision of the *Critique of Pure Reason* in 1787, the *Critique of Practical Reason* in 1788, the *Critique of Judgment* in 1790, *Religion Within the Limits of Mere Reason* in 1793, and *Perpetual Peace* in 1795. Philosophy would never be the same.

Kant's writings are among the most difficult philosophical works to understand. One twentieth-century philosopher, Anthony Flew, calls the *Critique of Pure Reason,* our second selection, "one of the greatest masterpieces of philosophy, although also one of the most unreadable." Kant himself called it "dry, obscure, contrary to all ordinary ideas, and on top of that prolix." It is for this reason that Kant wrote his *Prolegomena to Any Future Metaphysics,* our first selection. The idea was to provide a book for students and teachers that would be much shorter than the *Critique* and more accessible. Understanding the central purpose of the *Critique of Pure Reason,* "which discusses the pure faculty of reason in its whole compass and bounds, will remain the foundation, to which the *Prolegomena,* as a preliminary exercise, refer; for critique as a science must first be established as complete and perfect before we can think of letting metaphysics appear on the scene or even have the most distant hope of attaining it."

It is important to understand what Kant means by *metaphysics.* The term as he uses it means the science of knowing reality as it exists independently of our own understanding: knowledge of substance, of "being in itself." Kant chose the title *Critique of Pure Reason* because Descartes, Leibniz, Spinoza, and all the so-called rationalist philosophers believed it was possible to attain such knowledge through pure reason. Indeed, most philosophers assumed this, just as Kant himself did until he read Hume's criticisms of a priori necessary truths found in the domain of "relations of ideas" versus "matters of fact." Hume's point was not that there aren't any such propositions, merely that they are empty tautologies, empty of content. The only possibly real content to a proposition must come, Hume argued, from a posteriori synthetic truths. But these come to the mind in the form of perceptions. Perceptions, Hume showed, exist only as momentary, flickering sensations. So knowledge of things in themselves must be impossible. For Kant, this is the central problem of metaphysics.

Every attempt to solve the problem of metaphysics, Kant argues, had thus far been thwarted not so much by *lack* of available solutions but by the presence of *too many* solutions. That is, for every solution to the problem of metaphysics, philosophers have constructed competing solutions in terms of a completely different method. Moreover, rationalist systems of pure reason, built using a priori analytic truths, have given rise to dogmatic beliefs such as Berkeley's omniperceiving God, Descartes's self, and Descartes's nondeceiving God. Meanwhile, empiricist systems of pure experience, built using a posteriori synthetic truths, give rise to skeptical doubts, such as Hume's no-self, no-God, no-world. So Kant sets out to find an alternative to both empiricism and rationalism as a way of avoiding both dogmatism and skepticism.

Kant agrees with Hume and just about all the other philosophers who argue that you do not directly experience things in themselves. What you experience directly are the objects of your own mind, which Kant says are mere *representations,* but not of *impressions,* as Hume thought. For that leads to Berkeleian idealism, the view that there is no world beyond the mind, since the "representations" are themselves representing mental (phenomenal) objects. That is, to view the phenomenal world (the world of your experience) as consisting in representations of *phenomena* is to be an idealist, pure and simple. Hence Kant claims that Berkeley's "to be is to be perceived" makes knowledge possible by making metaphysics—in the sense of knowing things in themselves as they exist beyond or outside our experience—*unnecessary*. But Berkeley's philosophy requires the dogma of abstract ideas like God or, as Hume points out, the self, which are mere fictions, and so without the weight of metaphysics the idealist system evaporates. Materialist philosophy, on the other hand, requires abstract ideas like cause and effect, or material substance that then leaves an unbridgeable gap between the phenomenal world of appearances and what Kant calls the *noumenal* world of things in themselves.

The noumenal world is the real world as it is in itself, independent of our representations. Kant claims we can know absolutely nothing about the noumenal world *except* that it exists. All we are ever directly aware of is the activity of our own minds. All we ever have access to is our own representations of things, not the things in themselves. So of course it is not possible to know things in themselves. Experience connects us not to things in themselves but to ourselves. How could the mind-independent world of things in themselves ever be *reachable* given that there is no possible path into the mind from such a world? Kant, like Augustine, predicates his elaborate metaphysics on a threefold division of the mind. Kant's three "faculties" are *intuition, understanding,* and *reason*. But Kant does something no other philosopher before him had ever attempted: he performs what he calls a *transcendental analysis* of each faculty.

It is extremely important to understand what Kant means by the word *intuitions,* for this is extremely confusing. What he actually means is the same thing that Hume means by the terms *impressions* and *perceptions*. Thus, for instance, what you presently see are, in Kant's vocabulary, not things in themselves but your own intuitions of things. The problem is that the word *intuition* in its vernacular English sense means something like "hunch" or "thought" or "gut feeling." This is not at all what Kant means. He means "perception." Further, in calling his philosophy "transcendental," Kant does not mean to imply that it is somehow possible to transcend the phenomena and thereby reach the things in themselves. Rather, he means that his critical method of transcendental analysis can be used to transcend phenomena not for the purposes of reaching the noumenal world, which is impossible, but to reach *the three cognitive faculties of the mind*.

Kant's *Foundations of the Metaphysics of Morals* (1785), from which the third selection is taken, gives his widely influential deontological (rule-based) ethical theory which centers on his categorical imperative, "Act only on that maxim which you can at the same time will to become a universal law." As the universal moral test of right principles of action, the categorical imperative according to Kant makes us all duty-bound to obey certain principles in the same way that objects in nature are bound to act according to the laws of nature. Kant distinguishes two kinds of *imperatives*. An imperative is *hypothetical* when it is of the form "If you wish (or want, or would like) *x* in circumstance *y*, do action *a*." The *categorical* imperative, on the other hand, makes no reference to your wishes, wants, or desires. It is independent of any utilitarian concerns having to do with consequences or goals. It simply says, "If you are in circumstance *y*, do *a*." Period. Regardless of what you want, that is what you must do. Kant's reasoning is rather straightforward. Since the moral law is a rule for choosing among rules—that is, a rule for distinguishing between right and wrong rules—it cannot refer to the content of rules. It must therefore refer only to their *form;* that is why it must be a *categorical* rather than hypothetical imperative. The moral law has the same form as scientific laws of nature; that is, it has a *universal form.* It must apply everywhere and at all times; it can have no exceptions. It applies universally. And so Kant's "supreme principle of morality" is this:

> Act only according to that maxim [rule] whereby you can at the same time will that it should become a universal law.

Notice that this principle is synthetic; if you deny it, no contradiction results. Because it has no empirical content, it is a priori. Therefore it is a paradigm of pure reason at work in the moral realm.

PROLEGOMENA TO ANY FUTURE METAPHYSICS

INTRODUCTION

These prolegomena are destined for the use, not of pupils, but of future teachers, and even the latter should not expect that they will be serviceable for the systematic exposition of a ready-made science, but merely for the discovery of the science itself.

There are scholars, to whom the history of philosophy (both ancient and modern) is philosophy itself; for these the present *Prolegomena* are not written. They must wait till those who endeavor to draw from the fountain of reason itself have completed their work; it will then be the historian's turn to inform the world of what has been done. Unfortunately, nothing can be said, which in their opinion has not been said before, and truly the same prophecy applies to all future time; for since the human reason has for many centuries speculated upon innumerable objects in various ways, it is hardly to be expected that we should not be able to discover analogies for every new idea among the old sayings of past ages.

My object is to persuade all those who think metaphysics worth studying, that it is absolutely necessary to pause a moment, and, neglecting all that has been done, to propose first the preliminary question, "Whether such a thing as metaphysics be at all possible?"

If it be a science, how come it cannot, like other sciences, obtain universal and permanent recognition? If not, how can it maintain its pretensions, and keep the human mind in suspense with hopes, never ceasing, yet never fulfilled? Whether then we demonstrate our knowledge or our ignorance in this field, we must come once for all to a definite conclusion respecting the nature of this so-called science, which cannot possibly remain on its present footing. It seems almost ridiculous, while every other science is continually advancing, that in this, which pretends to be wisdom incarnate, for whose oracle every one inquires, we should constantly move round the same spot, without gaining a single step. And so its followers having melted away, we do not find scholars confident of their ability to shine in other sciences venturing their reputation here, where everybody, however ignorant in other

From Immanuel Kant, *Prolegomena to Any Future Metaphysics,* trans. Paul Carus (Open Court, 1902). With emendations by Daniel Kolak.

matters, may deliver a final verdict, as in this domain there is as yet no standard weight and measure to distinguish sound knowledge from shallow talk.

After all it is nothing extraordinary in the elaboration of a science, when we begin to wonder how far it has advanced, that the question should at last occur, whether and how such a science is possible? Human reason so delights in constructions, that it has several times built up a tower, and then razed it to examine the nature of the foundation. It is never too late to become wise; but if the change comes late, there is always more difficulty in starting a reform.

The question whether a science be possible, presupposes a doubt as to its actuality. But such a doubt offends those whose whole possessions consist of this supposed jewel; hence he who raises the doubt must expect opposition from all sides. Some, in the proud consciousness of their possessions, which are ancient, and therefore considered legitimate, will take their metaphysical compendia in their hands, and look down on him with contempt; others, who never see anything except it be identical with what they have seen before, will not understand him, and everything will remain for a time, as if nothing had happened to excite the concern, or the hope, for an impending change.

Nevertheless, I venture to predict that the independent reader of these *Prolegomena* will not only doubt his previous science, but ultimately be fully persuaded, that it cannot exist unless the demands here stated on which its possibility depends, be satisfied; and, as this has never been done, that there is, as yet, no such thing as metaphysics. But as it can never cease to be in demand,—since the interests of common sense are intimately interwoven with it, he must confess that a radical reform, or rather a new birth of the science after an original plan, are unavoidable, however men may struggle against it for a while.

Since the *Essays* of Locke and Leibnitz, or rather since the origin of metaphysics so far as we know its history, nothing has ever happened which was more decisive to its fate than the attack made upon it by David Hume. He threw no light on this species of knowledge, but he certainly struck a spark from which light might have been obtained, had it caught some inflammable substance and had its smouldering fire been carefully nursed and developed.

Hume started from a single but important concept in metaphysics, viz., that of cause and effect (including its derivatives force and action, etc.). He challenges reason, which pretends to have given birth to this idea from herself, to answer him by what right she thinks anything to be so constituted, that if that thing be posited, something else also must necessarily be posited; for this is the meaning of the concept of cause. He demonstrated irrefutably that it was perfectly impossible for reason to think *a priori* and by means of concepts a combination involving necessity. We cannot at all see why, in consequence of the existence of one thing, another must necessarily exist, or how the concept of such a combination can arise *a priori*. Hence he inferred, that reason was altogether deluded with reference to this concept, which she erroneously considered as one of her children, whereas in reality it was nothing but a bastard of imagination, impregnated by experience, which subsumed certain representations under the law of association, and mistook the subjective necessity of habit for an objective necessity arising from insight. Hence he inferred that reason had no power to think such combinations, even generally, because her concepts would then be purely fictitious, and all her pretended *a priori* cognitions nothing but common experiences marked with a false stamp. In plain language there is not, and cannot be, any such thing as metaphysics at all.

However hasty and mistaken Hume's conclusion may appear, it was at least founded upon investigation, and this investigation deserved the concentrated attention of the brighter spirits of his day as well as determined efforts on their part to discover, if possible, a happier solution of the problem in the sense proposed by him, all of which would have speedily resulted in a complete reform of the science.

But Hume suffered the usual misfortune of metaphysicians, of not being understood. It is positively painful to see how utterly his opponents, Reid, Oswald, Beattie, and lastly Priestley, missed the point of the problem; for while they were ever taking for granted that which he doubted, and demonstrating with zeal and often with impudence that which he never thought of doubting, they so misconstrued his valuable suggestion that everything remained in its old condition, as if nothing had happened.

The question was not whether the concept of cause was right, useful, and even indispensable for our knowledge of nature, for this Hume had never doubted; but whether that concept could be thought by reason *a priori,* and consequently whether it possessed an inner truth, independent of all experience, implying a wider application than merely to the objects of experience. This was Hume's problem. It was a question concerning the *origin,* not concerning the *indispensable need* of the concept. Were the former decided, the conditions of the use and the sphere of its valid application would have been determined as a matter of course.

But to satisfy the conditions of the problem, the opponents of the great thinker should have penetrated very deeply into the nature of reason, so far as it is concerned with pure thinking,—a task which did not suit them. They found a more convenient method of being defiant without any insight, viz., the appeal to *common sense.* It is indeed a great gift of God, to possess right, or (as they now call it) plain common sense. But this common sense must be shown practically, by well-considered and reasonable thoughts and words, not by appealing to it as an oracle, when no rational justification can be advanced. To appeal to common sense, when insight and science fail, and no sooner—this is one of the subtile discoveries of modern times, by means of which the most superficial ranter can safely enter the lists with the most thorough thinker, and hold his own. But as long as a particle of insight remains, no one would think of having recourse to this subterfuge. For what is it but an appeal to the opinion of the multitude, of whose applause the philosopher is ashamed, while the popular charlatan glories and confides in it? I should think that Hume might fairly have laid as much claim to common sense as Beattie, and in addition to a critical reason (such as the latter did not possess), which keeps common sense in check and prevents it from speculating, or, if speculations are under discussion restrains the desire to decide because it cannot satisfy itself concerning its own arguments. By this means alone can common sense remain sound. Chisels and hammers may suffice to work a piece of wood, but for steel-engraving we require an engraver's needle. Thus common sense and speculative understanding are each serviceable in their own way, the former in judgments which apply immediately to experience, the latter when we judge universally from mere concepts, as in metaphysics, where sound common sense, so called in spite of the inapplicability of the word, has no right to judge at all.

I openly confess, the suggestion of David Hume was the very thing, which many years ago first awoke me from my dogmatic slumber, and gave my investigations in the field of speculative philosophy quite a new direction. I was far from following him in the conclusions at which he arrived by regarding, not the whole of his problem, but a part, which by itself can give us no information. If we start from a well-founded, but undeveloped, thought, which another has bequeathed to us, we may well hope by continued reflection to advance farther than the acute man, to whom we owe the first spark of light.

I therefore first tried whether Hume's objection could not be put into a general form, and soon found that the concept of the connection of cause and effect was by no means the only idea by which the understanding thinks the connection of things *a priori,* but rather that metaphysics consists altogether of such connections. I sought to ascertain their number, and when I had satisfactorily succeeded in this by starting from a single principle, I proceeded to the deduction of these concepts, which I was now certain were not deduced from experience, as Hume had apprehended, but sprang from the pure understanding. This deduction (which seemed impossible to my acute predecessor, which had never even occurred to any one else, though no one had hesitated to use the concepts without investigating the basis of their objective validity) was the most difficult task ever undertaken in the service of metaphysics; and the worst was that metaphysics, such as it then existed, could not assist me in the least, because this deduction alone can render metaphysics possible. But as soon as I had succeeded in solving Hume's problem not merely in a particular case, but with respect to the whole faculty of pure reason, I could proceed safely, though slowly, to determine the whole sphere of pure reason completely and from general principles, in its circumference as well as in its contents. This was required for metaphysics in order to construct its system according to a reliable method.

But I fear that the execution of Hume's problem in its widest extent (viz., my *Critique of Pure Reason*) will fare as the problem itself fared, when first proposed. It will be misjudged because it is misunderstood, and misunderstood because people choose to skim through the book, and not to think through it—a disagreeable task, because the work is dry, obscure, opposed to all ordinary notions, and moreover long-winded. I confess, however, I did not expect to hear from philosophers complaints of want of popularity, entertainment, and facility, when the existence of a highly prized and indispensable cognition is at stake, which cannot be established otherwise, than by the strictest rules of methodic precision. Popularity may follow, but is inadmissible at the beginning. Yet as regards a certain obscurity, arising partly from the diffuseness of the plan, owing to which the principal points of the investigation are easily lost sight of, the complaint is just, and I intend to remove it by the present *Prolegomena.*

The first-mentioned work, which discusses the pure faculty of reason in its whole compass and bounds, will remain the foundation, to which the *Prolegomena,* as a preliminary exercise, refer; for our critique must first be established as a complete and perfected science, before we can think of letting metaphysics appear on the scene, or even have the most distant hope of attaining it.

We have been long accustomed to seeing antiquated knowledge produced as new by taking it out of its former context, and reducing it to system in a new suit of any fancy pattern under new titles. Most readers will set out by expecting nothing else from the *Critique;* but these *Prolegomena* may persuade him that it is a perfectly new science, of which no one has ever even thought, the very idea of which was unknown, and for which nothing hitherto accomplished can be of the smallest use, except it be the suggestion of Hume's doubts. Yet even he did not suspect such a formal science, but ran his ship ashore, for safety's sake, landing on scepticism, there to let it lie and rot; whereas my object is rather to give it a pilot, who, by means of safe astronomical principles drawn from a knowledge of the globe, and provided with a complete chart and compass, may steer the ship safely.

If in a new science, which is wholly isolated and unique in its kind, we started with the prejudice that we can judge of things by means of our previously acquired knowledge, which is precisely what has first to be called in question, we should only fancy we saw everywhere what we had already known, the expressions, having a similar sound, only that all would appear utterly metamorphosed, senseless and unintelligible, because we should have as a foundation our own notions, made by long habit a second nature, instead of the author's. But the longwindedness of the work, so far as it depends on the subject, and not the exposition, its consequent unavoidable dryness and its scholastic precision are qualities which can only benefit the science, though they may discredit the book.

Few writers are gifted with the subtilty, and at the same time with the grace, of David Hume, or with the depth, as well as the elegance, of Moses Mendelssohn. Yet I flatter myself I might have made my own exposition popular, had my object been merely to sketch out a plan and leave its completion to others, instead of having my heart in the welfare of the science, to which I had devoted myself so long; in truth, it required no little constancy, and even self-denial, to postpone the sweets of an immediate success to the prospect of a slower, but more lasting, reputation.

Making plans is often the occupation of an opulent and boastful mind, which thus obtains the reputation of a creative genius, by demanding what it cannot itself supply; by censuring, what it cannot improve; and by proposing, what it knows not where to find. And yet something more should belong to a sound plan of a general critique of pure reason than mere conjectures, if this plan is to be other than the usual declamations of pious aspirations. But pure reason is a sphere so separate and self-contained, that we cannot touch a part without affecting all the rest. We can therefore do nothing without first determining the position of each part, and its relation to the rest; for, as our judgment cannot be corrected by anything without, the validity and use of every part depends upon the relation in which it stands to all the rest within the domain of reason.

So in the structure of an organized body, the end of each member can only be deduced from the full conception of the whole. It may, then, be said of such a critique that it is never trustworthy except it be perfectly complete, down to the smallest elements of pure reason. In the sphere of this faculty you can determine either everything or nothing.

But although a mere sketch, preceding the *Critique of Pure Reason,* would be unintelligible, unreliable, and useless, it is all the more useful as a sequel. For so we are able to grasp the whole, to examine in detail the chief points of importance in the science, and to improve in many respects our exposition, as compared with the first execution of the work.

After the completion of the work I offer here such a plan which is sketched out after an analytical method, while the work itself had to be executed in the synthetical style, in order that the science may present all its articulations, as the structure of a peculiar cognitive faculty, in their natural combination. But should any reader find this plan, which I publish as the *Prolegomena to Any Future Metaphysics,* still obscure, let him consider that not every one is bound to study metaphysics, that many minds will succeed very well, in the exact and even in deep sciences, more closely allied to practical experience, while they cannot succeed in investigations dealing exclusively with abstract concepts. In such cases men should apply their talents to other subjects. But he who undertakes to judge, or still more, to construct, a system of metaphysics, must satisfy the demands here made, either by adopting my solution, or by thoroughly refuting it, and substituting another. To evade it is impossible.

In conclusion, let it be remembered that this much-abused obscurity (frequently serving as a mere pretext under which people hide their own indolence or dullness) has its uses, since all who in other sciences observe a judicious silence, speak authoritatively in metaphysics and make bold decisions, because their ignorance is not here contrasted with the knowledge of others. Yet it does contrast with sound critical principles, which we may therefore commend in the words of Virgil:

> Ignavum, fucos, pecus a praesepibus arcent. [Bees are defending their hives against drones, those indolent creatures.]

PROLEGOMENA
Preamble on the Peculiarities of All Metaphysical Cognition

§1. OF THE SOURCES OF METAPHYSICS

If it becomes desirable to formulate any cognition as science, it will be necessary first to determine accurately those peculiar features which no other science has in common with it, constituting its characteristics; otherwise the boundaries of all sciences become confused, and none of them can be treated thoroughly according to its nature.

The characteristics of a science may consist of a simple difference of object, or of the sources of cognition, or of the kind of cognition, or perhaps of all three conjointly. On this, therefore, depends the idea of a possible science and its territory.

First, as concerns the sources of metaphysical cognition, its very concept implies that they cannot be empirical. Its principles (including not only its maxims but its basic notions) must never be derived from experience. It must not be physical but metaphysical knowledge, viz., knowledge lying beyond experience. It can therefore have for its basis neither external experience, which is the source of physics proper, nor internal, which is the basis of empirical psychology. It is therefore *a priori* knowledge, coming from pure understanding and pure reason.

But so far metaphysics would not be distinguishable from pure mathematics; it must therefore be called pure philosophical cognition; and for the meaning of this term I refer to the *Critique of Pure Reason* (II. "Method of Transcendentalism," Chap. I, Sec. i), where the distinction between these two employments of the reason is sufficiently explained. So far concerning the sources of metaphysical cognition.

§2. CONCERNING THE KIND OF COGNITION
WHICH CAN ALONE BE CALLED METAPHYSICAL

a. Of the Distinction between Analytical and Synthetical Judgments in General.—The peculiarity of its sources demands that metaphysical cognition must consist of nothing but *a priori* judgments. But whatever be their origin, or their logical form, there is a distinction in judgments, as to their content, according to which they are either merely explicative, adding nothing to the content of the cognition, or expansive, increasing the given cognition: the former may be called analytical, the latter synthetical, judgments.

Analytical judgments express nothing in the predicate but what has been already actually thought in the concept of the subject, though not so distinctly or with the same (full) consciousness. When I say: All bodies are extended, I have not amplified in the least my concept of body, but have only analysed it, as extension was really thought to belong to that concept before the judgment was made, though it was not expressed; this judgment is therefore analytical. On the contrary, this judgment, All bodies have weight, contains in its predicate something not actually thought in the general concept of the body; it amplifies my knowledge by adding something to my concept, and must therefore be called synthetical.

b. The Common Principle of All Analytical Judgments Is the Law of Contradiction.—All analytical judgments depend wholly on the law of contradiction, and are in their nature *a priori* cognitions, whether the concepts that supply them with matter be empirical or not. For the predicate of an affirmative analytical judgment is already contained in the concept of the subject, of which it cannot be denied without contradiction. In the same way its opposite is necessarily denied of the subject in an analytical, but negative, judgment, by the same law of contradiction. Such is the nature of the judgments: all bodies are extended, and no bodies are unextended (i.e., simple).

For this very reason all analytical judgments are *a priori* even when the concepts are empirical, as, for example, gold is a yellow metal; for to know this I require no experience beyond my concept of gold as a yellow metal: it is, in fact, the very concept, and I need only analyse it, without looking beyond it elsewhere.

c. Synthetical Judgments Require a Different Principle from the Law of Contradiction.— There are synthetical *a posteriori* judgments of empirical origin; but there are also others which are proved to be certain *a priori,* and which spring from pure understanding and reason. Yet they both agree in this, that they cannot possibly spring from the principle of analysis, viz., the law of contradiction, alone; they require a quite different principle, though, from whatever they may be deduced, they must be subject to the law of contradiction, which must never be violated, even though everything cannot be deduced from it. I shall first classify synthetical judgments.

1. *Empirical Judgments* are always synthetical. For it would be absurd to base an analytical judgment on experience, as our concept suffices for the purpose without requiring any testimony from experience. That body is extended, is a judgment established *a priori,* and not an empirical judgment. For before appealing to experience, we already have all the conditions of the judgment in the concept, from which we have but to elicit the predicate according to the law of contradiction, and thereby to become conscious of the necessity of the judgment, which experience could not even teach us.

2. *Mathematical Judgments* are all synthetical. This fact seems hitherto to have altogether escaped the observation of those who have analysed human reason; it even seems directly opposed to all their conjectures, though incontestably certain, and most important in its consequences. For as it was found that the conclusions of mathematicians all proceed according to the law of contradiction (as is demanded by all apodeictic[1] certainty), men persuaded themselves that the fundamental principles were known from the same law. This was a great mistake, for a synthetical proposition can indeed be comprehended according to the law of contradiction, but only by presupposing another synthetical proposition from which it follows, but never in itself.

First of all, we must observe that all proper mathematical judgments are *a priori,* and not empirical, because they carry with them necessity, which cannot be obtained from experience. But if this be not conceded to me, very good; I shall confine my assertion to *pure mathematics,* the very notion of which implies that it contains pure *a priori* and not empirical cognitions.

It might at first be thought that the proposition $7 + 5 = 12$ is a mere analytical judg-

---

1. "Certain beyond dispute."

ment, following from the concept of the sum of seven and five, according to the law of contradiction. But on closer examination it appears that the concept of the sum of $7 + 5$ contains merely their union in a single number, without its being at all thought what the particular number is that unites them. The concept of twelve is by no means thought by merely thinking of the combination of seven and five; and analyse this possible sum as we may, we shall not discover twelve in the concept. We must go beyond these concepts, by calling to our aid some concrete image, i.e., either our five fingers, or five points (as Segner has it in his arithmetic), and we must add successively the units of the five, given in some concrete image, to the concept of seven. Hence our concept is really amplified by the proposition $7 + 5 = 12$, and we add to the first a second, not thought in it. Arithmetical judgments are therefore synthetical, and the more plainly according as we take larger numbers; for in such cases it is clear that, however closely we analyse our concepts without calling visual images to our aid, we can never find the sum by such mere dissection.

All principles of geometry are no less analytical. That a straight line is the shortest path between two points, is a synthetical proposition. For my concept of straight contains nothing of quantity, but only a quality. The attribute of shortness is therefore altogether additional, and cannot be obtained by any analysis of the concept. Here, too, visualisation must come to aid us. It alone makes the synthesis possible.

Some other principles, assumed by geometers, are indeed actually analytical, and depend on the law of contradiction; but they only serve, as identical propositions, as a method of concatenation, and not as principles, e.g., $a = a$, the whole is equal to itself, or $a + b > a$, the whole is greater than its part. And yet even these, though they are recognised as valid from mere concepts, are only admitted in mathematics, because they can be represented in some visual form. What usually makes us believe that the predicate of such apodeictic judgments is already contained in our concept, and that the judgment is therefore analytical, is the duplicity of the expression, requesting us to think a certain predicate as of necessity implied in the thought of a given concept, which necessity attaches to the concept. But the question is not what we are requested to join in thought *to* the given concept, but what we actually think together with and in it, though obscurely; and so it appears that the predicate belongs to these concepts necessarily indeed, yet not directly but indirectly by an added visualisation.

§3. A REMARK ON THE GENERAL DIVISION OF JUDGMENTS INTO ANALYTICAL AND SYNTHETICAL

This division is indispensable, as concerns the critique of human understanding, and therefore deserves to be called classical, though otherwise it is of little use, but this is the reason why dogmatic philosophers, who always seek the sources of metaphysical judgments in metaphysics itself, and not apart from it, in the pure laws of reason generally, altogether neglected this apparently obvious distinction. Thus the celebrated Wolf, and his acute follower Baumgarten, came to seek the proof of the principle of sufficient reason, which is clearly synthetical, in the principle of contradiction. In Locke's *Essay*, however, I find an indication of my division. For in the fourth book (chap. iii. §9, seq.), having discussed the various connections of representations in judgments, and their sources, one of which he makes "identity and contradiction" (analytical judgments), and another the coexistence of representations in a subject, he confesses (§10) that our *a priori* knowledge of the latter is very narrow, and almost nothing. But in his remarks on this species of cognition, there is so little of what is definite, and reduced to rules, that we cannot wonder if no one, not even

Hume, was led to make investigations concerning this sort of judgments. For such general and yet definite principles are not easily learned from other men, who have had them obscurely in their minds. We must hit on them first by our own reflection, then we find them elsewhere, where we could not possibly have found them at first, because the authors themselves did not know that such an idea lay at the basis of their observations. People who never think independently have nevertheless the acuteness to discover everything, after it has been once shown them, in what was said long since, though no one ever saw it there before.

§4. THE GENERAL QUESTION OF THE PROLEGOMENA – IS METAPHYSICS AT ALL POSSIBLE?

Were a metaphysics, which could maintain its place as a science, really in existence; could we say, here is metaphysics, learn it, and it will convince you irresistibly and irrevocably of its truth: this question would be useless, and there would only remain that other question (which would rather be a test of our acuteness, than a proof of the existence of the thing itself), "How is the science possible, and how does reason come to attain it?" But human reason has not been so fortunate in this case. There is no single book to which you can point as you do to Euclid, and say: This is metaphysics; here you may find the noblest objects of this science, the knowledge of a highest being, and of a future existence, proved from principles of pure reason. We can be shown indeed many judgments, demonstrably certain, and never questioned; but these are all analytical, and rather concern the materials and the scaffolding for metaphysics, than the extension of knowledge, which is our proper object in studying it (§2). Even supposing you produce synthetical judgments (such as the law of sufficient reason, which you have never proved, as you ought to, from pure reason *a priori,* though we gladly concede its truth), you lapse when they come to be employed for your principal object, into such doubtful assertions, that in all ages one metaphysics has contradicted another, either in its assertions, or their proofs, and thus has itself destroyed its own claim to lasting assent. Nay, the very attempts to set up such a science are the main cause of the early appearance of scepticism, a mental attitude in which reason treats itself with such violence that it could never have arisen save from complete despair of ever satisfying our most important aspirations. For long before men began to inquire into nature methodically, they consulted abstract reason, which had to some extent been exercised by means of ordinary experience; for reason is ever present, while laws of nature must usually be discovered with labor. So metaphysics floated to the surface, like foam, which dissolved the moment it was scooped off. But immediately there appeared a new supply on the surface, to be ever eagerly gathered up by some, while others, instead of seeking in the depths the cause of the phenomenon, thought they showed their wisdom by ridiculing the idle labor of their neighbors.

The essential and distinguishing feature of pure mathematical cognition among all other *a priori* cognitions is, that it cannot at all proceed from concepts, but only by means of the construction of concepts (see *Critique* II., "Method of Transcendentalism," chap. I., sect. 1). As therefore in its judgments it must proceed beyond the concept to that which its corresponding visualisation contains, these judgments neither can, nor ought to, arise analytically, by dissecting the concept, but are all synthetical.

I cannot refrain from pointing out the disadvantage resulting to philosophy from the neglect of this easy and apparently insignificant observation. Hume being prompted (a task worthy of a philosopher) to cast his eye over the whole field of *a priori* cognitions in which human understanding claims such mighty possessions, heedlessly severed from it a whole, and indeed its most valuable, province, viz., pure mathematics; for he thought its nature, or, so to speak, the state-constitution of this empire, depended on totally different principles, namely, on the law of contradiction alone; and although he did not divide judgments in this manner formally and universally as I have done here, what he said was equivalent to this: that mathematics contains only analytical, but metaphysics synthetical, *a priori* judgments. In this, however, he was greatly mistaken, and the mistake had a decidedly injurious effect upon his whole conception. But for this, he would have extended his question concerning the origin of our synthetical judgments far beyond the metaphysical concept of causality, and included in it the possibility of mathematics *a priori* also, for this latter he must have assumed to be equally synthetical. And then he could not have based his metaphysical judgments on mere experience without subjecting the axioms of mathematics equally to experience, a thing which he was far too acute to do. The good company into which metaphysics would thus have been brought, would have saved it from the danger of a contemptuous ill-treatment, for the thrust intended for it must have reached mathematics, which was not and could not have been Hume's intention. Thus that acute writer would have been led into considerations which must needs be similar to those that now occupy us, but which would have gained inestimably by his inimitably elegant style.

Metaphysical judgments, properly so called, are all synthetical. We must distinguish judgments pertaining to metaphysics from metaphysical judgments properly so called. Many of the former are analytical, but they only afford the means for metaphysical judgments, which are the whole end of the science, and which are always synthetical. For if there be concepts pertaining to metaphysics (as, for example, that of substance), the judgments springing from simple analysis of them also pertain to metaphysics, as, for example, substance is that which only exists as subject; and by means of several such analytical judgments, we seek to approach the definition of the concept. But as the analysis of a pure concept of the understanding pertaining to metaphysics, does not proceed in any different manner from the dissection of any other, even empirical, concepts, not pertaining to metaphysics (such as: air is an elastic fluid, the elasticity of which is not destroyed by any known degree of cold), it follows that the concept indeed, but not the analytical judgment, is properly metaphysical. This science has something peculiar in the production of its *a priori* cognitions, which must therefore be distinguished from the features it has in common with other rational knowledge. Thus the judgment, that all the substance in things is permanent, is a synthetical and properly metaphysical judgment.

If the *a priori* principles, which constitute the materials of metaphysics, have first been collected according to fixed principles, then their analysis will be of great value; it might be taught as a particular part, containing nothing but analytical judgments pertaining to metaphysics, and could be treated separately from the synthetical which constitute metaphysics proper. For indeed these analyses are not elsewhere of much value, except in metaphysics, i.e., as regards the synthetical judgments, which are to be generated by these previously analysed concepts.

§4. THE GENERAL QUESTION OF THE PROLEGOMENA –
IS METAPHYSICS AT ALL POSSIBLE?

The conclusion drawn in this section then is, that metaphysics is properly concerned with synthetical propositions *a priori,* and these alone constitute its end, for which it indeed requires various dissections of its concepts, viz., of its analytical judgments, but wherein the procedure is not different from that in every other kind of knowledge, in which we merely seek to render our concepts distinct by analysis. But the generation of *a priori* cognition by concrete images as well as by concepts, in fine of synthetical propositions *a priori* in philosophical cognition, constitutes the essential subject of metaphysics.

Weary therefore as well of dogmatism, which teaches us nothing, as of scepticism, which does not even promise us anything, not even the quiet state of a contented ignorance; disquieted by the importance of knowledge so much needed; and lastly, rendered suspicious by long experience of all knowledge, which we believe we possess, or which offers itself, under the title of pure reason: there remains but one critical question on the answer to which our future procedure depends, viz., *Is metaphysics at all possible?* But this question must be answered not by sceptical objections to the asseverations of some actual system of metaphysics (for we do not as yet admit such a thing to exist), but from the conception, as yet only problematical, of a science of this sort.

In the *Critique of Pure Reason* I have treated this question synthetically, by making inquiries into pure reason itself, and endeavoring in this source to determine the elements as well as the laws of its pure use according to principles. The task is difficult, and requires a resolute reader to penetrate by degrees into a system, based on no data except reason itself, and which therefore seeks, without resting upon any fact, to unfold knowledge from its original germs. *Prolegomena*, however, are designed for preparatory exercises; they are intended rather to point out what we have to do in order if possible to actualise a science, than to propound it. They must therefore rest upon something already known as trustworthy, from which we can set out with confidence, and ascend to sources as yet unknown, the discovery of which will not only explain to us what we knew, but exhibit a sphere of many cognitions which all spring from the same sources. The method of *Prolegomena*, especially of those designed as a preparation for future metaphysics, is consequently analytical.

But it happens fortunately, that though we cannot assume metaphysics to be an actual science, we can say with confidence that certain pure *a priori* synthetical cognitions, pure mathematics and pure physics are actual and given; for both contain propositions, which are thoroughly recognised as apodeictically certain, partly by mere reason, partly by general consent arising from experience, and yet as independent of experience. We have therefore some at least uncontested synthetical knowledge *a priori*, and need not ask *whether* it be possible, for it is actual, but *how* it is possible, in order that we may deduce from the principle which makes the given cognitions possible the possibility of all the rest.

THE GENERAL PROBLEM: HOW IS COGNITION FROM PURE REASON POSSIBLE?

§5. We have above learned the significant distinction between analytical and synthetical judgments. The possibility of analytical propositions was easily comprehended, being entirely founded on the law of contradiction. The possibility of synthetical *a posteriori* judgments, of those which are gathered from experience, also requires no particular explanation; for experience is nothing but a continual synthesis of perceptions. There remain therefore only synthetical propositions *a priori*, of which the possibility must be sought or investigated, because they must depend upon other principles than the law of contradiction.

But here we need not first establish the possibility of such propositions so as to ask whether they are possible. For there are enough of them which indeed are of undoubted certainty, and as our present method is analytical, we shall start from the fact, that such synthetical but purely rational cognition actually exists; but we must now inquire into the reason of this possibility, and ask, *how* such cognition is possible, in order that we may from the principles of its possibility be enabled to determine the conditions of its use, its sphere and its limits. The proper problem upon which all depends, when expressed with scholastic precision, is therefore:

How are Synthetic Propositions a priori possible?

For the sake of popularity I have above expressed this problem somewhat differently, as an inquiry into purely rational cognition, which I could do for once without detriment to the desired comprehension, because, as we have only to do here with metaphysics and its sources, the reader will, I hope, after the foregoing remarks, keep in mind that when we speak of purely rational cognition, we do not mean analytical, but synthetical cognition.

Metaphysics stands or falls with the solution of this problem: its very existence depends upon it. Let any one make metaphysical assertions with ever so much plausibility, let him overwhelm us with conclusions, if he has not previously proved able to answer this question satisfactorily, I have a right to say: this is all vain baseless philosophy and false wisdom. You speak through pure reason, and claim, as it were to create cognitions *a priori* by not only dissecting given concepts, but also by asserting connections which do not rest upon the law of contradiction, and which you believe you conceive quite independently of all experience; how do you arrive at this, and how will you justify your pretensions? An appeal to the consent of the common sense of mankind cannot be allowed; for that is a witness whose authority depends merely upon rumor. Says Horace:

> Quodcunque ostendis mihi sic, incredulus odi. [To all that which thou provest me thus, I refuse to give credence.]

The answer to this question, though indispensable, is difficult; and though the principal reason that it was not made long ago is, that the possibility of the question never occurred to anybody, there is yet another reason, which is this that a satisfactory answer to this one question requires a much more persistent, profound, and painstaking reflection, than the most diffuse work on metaphysics, which on its first appearance promised immortality to its author. And every intelligent reader, when he carefully reflects what this problem requires, must at first be struck with its difficulty, and would regard it as insoluble and even impossible, did there not actually exist pure synthetical cognitions *a priori*. This actually happened to David Hume, though he did not conceive the question in its entire universality as is done here, and as must be done, should the answer be decisive for all Metaphysics. For how is it possible, says that acute man, that when a concept is given me, I can go beyond it and connect with it another, which is not contained in it, in such a manner as if the latter necessarily belonged to the former? Nothing but experience can furnish us with such connections (thus he concluded from the difficulty which he took to be an impossibility), and all that vaunted necessity, or, what is the same thing, all cognition assumed to be *a priori*, is nothing but a long habit of accepting something as true, and hence of mistaking subjective necessity for objective.

Should my reader complain of the difficulty and the trouble which I occasion him in the solution of this problem, he is at liberty to solve it himself in an easier way. Perhaps he will then feel under obligation to the person who has undertaken for him a labor of so profound research, and will rather be surprised at the facility with which, considering the nature of the subject, the solution has been attained. Yet it has cost years of work to solve the problem in its whole universality (using the term in the mathematical sense, viz., for that which is sufficient for all cases), and finally to exhibit it in the analytical form, as the reader finds it here.

All metaphysicians are therefore solemnly and legally suspended from their occupations till they shall have answered in a satisfactory manner the question, "How are synthetic cognitions *a priori* possible?" For the answer contains the only credentials which they must show when they have anything to offer in the name of pure reason. But if they do not possess these credentials, they can expect nothing else of reasonable people, who have been deceived so often, than to be dismissed without further ado.

If they on the other hand desire to carry on their business, not as a science, but as an art of wholesome oratory suited to the common sense of man, they cannot in justice be prevented. They will then speak the modest language of a rational belief, they will grant that they are not allowed even to conjecture, far less to know, anything which lies beyond the bounds of all possible experience, but only to assume (not for speculative use, which they must abandon, but for practical purposes only) the existence of something that is possible and even indispensable for the guidance of the understanding and of the will in life. In this manner alone can they be called useful and wise men, and the more so as they renounce the title of metaphysicians; for the latter profess to be speculative philosophers, and since, when judgments *a priori* are under discussion, poor probabilities cannot be admitted (for what is declared to be known *a priori* is thereby announced as necessary), such men cannot be permitted to play with conjectures, but their assertions must be either science, or are worth nothing at all.

It may be said, that the entire transcendental philosophy, which necessarily precedes all metaphysics, is nothing but the complete solution of the problem here propounded, in systematical order and completeness, and hitherto we have never had any transcendental philosophy; for what goes by its name is properly a part of metaphysics, whereas the former science is intended first to constitute the possibility of the latter, and must therefore precede all metaphysics. And it is not surprising that when a whole science, deprived of all help from other sciences, and consequently in itself quite new, is required to answer a single question satisfactorily, we should find the answer troublesome and difficult, nay even shrouded in obscurity.

As we now proceed to this solution according to the analytical method, in which we assume that such cognitions from pure reasons actually exist, we can only appeal to two sciences of theoretical cognition (which alone is under consideration here), pure mathematics and pure natural science (physics). For these alone can exhibit to us objects in a definite and actualisable form, and consequently (if there should occur in them a cognition *a priori*) can show the truth or conformity of the cognition to the object *in concreto*, that is, its actuality, from which we could proceed to the reason of its possibility by the analytic method. This facilitates our work greatly, for here universal considerations are not only applied to facts, but even start from them, while in a synthetic procedure they must strictly be derived *in abstracto* from concepts.

But, in order to rise from these actual and at the same time well-grounded pure cognitions *a priori* to such a possible cognition of the same as we are seeking, viz., to metaphysics as a science, we must comprehend that which occasions it, I mean the mere natural, though in spite of its truth not unsuspected, cognition *a priori* which lies at the bottom of that science, the elaboration of which without any critical investigation of its possibility is commonly called metaphysics. In a word, we must comprehend the natural conditions of such a science as a part of our inquiry, and thus the transcendental problem will be gradually answered by a division into four questions:

1. *How is pure mathematics possible?*
2. *How is pure natural science possible?*
3. *How is metaphysics in general possible?*
4. *How is metaphysics as a science possible?*

It may be seen that the solution of these problems, though chiefly designed to exhibit the essential matter of the *Critique,* has yet something peculiar, which for itself alone deserves attention. This is the search for the sources of given sciences in reason itself, so that its faculty of knowing something *a priori* may by its own deeds be investigated and measured. By this procedure these sciences gain, if not with regard to their contents, yet as to their proper use, and while they throw light on the higher question concerning their common origin, they give, at the same time, an occasion better to explain their own nature.

FIRST PART OF THE TRANSCENDENTAL PROBLEM
How Is Pure Mathematics Possible?

§6. Here is a great and established branch of knowledge, encompassing even now a wonderfully large domain and promising an unlimited extension in the future. Yet it carries with it thoroughly apodeictical certainty, i.e., absolute necessity, which therefore rests upon no empirical grounds. Consequently it is a pure product of reason, and moreover is thoroughly synthetical. [Here the question arises:]

"How then is it possible for human reason to produce a cognition of this nature entirely *a priori?*"

Does not this faculty [which produces mathematics], as it neither is nor can be based upon experience, presuppose some ground of cognition *a priori,* which lies deeply hidden, but which might reveal itself by these its effects, if their first beginnings were but diligently ferreted out?

§7. But we find that all mathematical cognition has this peculiarity: it must first exhibit its concept in a visual form and indeed *a priori,* therefore in a visual form which is not empirical, but pure. Without this mathematics cannot take a single step; hence its judgments are always visual, viz., "intuitive"; whereas philosophy must be satisfied with discursive judgments from mere concepts, and though it may illustrate its doctrines through a visual figure, can never derive them from it. This observation on the nature of mathematics gives us a clue to the first and highest condition of its possibility, which is, that some nonsensuous visualisation (called pure intuition) must form its basis, in which all its concepts can be exhibited or constructed, *in concreto* and yet *a priori.* If we can find out this pure intuition and its possibility, we may thence easily explain how synthetical propositions *a priori* are possible in pure mathematics, and consequently how this science itself is possible. Empirical intuition [viz., sense-perception] enables us without difficulty to enlarge the concept which we frame of an object of intuition [or sense-perception], by new predicates, which intuition [i.e., sense-perception] itself presents synthetically in experience. Pure intuition [viz., the visualisation of forms in our imagination, from which every thing sensual, i.e., every thought of material qualities, is excluded] does so likewise, only with this difference, that in the latter case the synthetical judgment is *a priori* certain and apodeictical, in the former, only *a posteriori* and empirically certain; because this latter contains only that which occurs in contingent empirical intuition, but the former, that which must necessarily be discovered in pure intuition. Here intuition, being an intuition *a priori,* is *before all experience,* viz., before any perception of particular objects, inseparably conjoined with its concept.

§8. But with this step our perplexity seems rather to increase than to lessen. For the question now is, "How is it possible to intuit [in a visual form] anything *a priori?*" An intuition [viz., a visual sense-perception] is such a representation as immediately depends upon the presence of the object. Hence it seems impossible to intuit from the outset *a priori,* because intuition would in that event take place without either a former or a present object to refer to, and by consequence could not be intuition. Concepts indeed are such, that we can easily form some of them *a priori,* viz., such as contain nothing but the thought of an object in general; and we need not find ourselves in an immediate relation to the object. Take, for instance, the concepts of quantity, of cause, etc. But even these require, in order to make them understood, a certain concrete use—that is, an application to some sense-experience, by which an object of them is given us. But how can the intuition of the object [its visualisation] precede the object itself?

§9. If our intuition [i.e., our sense-experience] were perforce of such a nature as to represent things as they are in themselves, there would not be any intuition *a priori,* but intuition would be always empirical. For I can only know what is contained in the object in itself when it is present and given to me. It is indeed even then incomprehensible how the visualising of a present thing should make me know this thing as it is in itself, as its properties cannot migrate into my faculty of representation. But even granting this possibility, a visualising of that sort would not take place *a priori,* that is, before the object were presented to me; for without this latter fact no reason of a relation between my representation and the object can be imagined, unless it depend upon a direct inspiration.

Therefore in one way only can my intuition anticipate the actuality of the object, and be a cognition *a priori,* viz.: if my intuition contains nothing but the form of sensibility, antedating in my subjectivity all the actual impressions through which I am affected by objects.

For that objects of sense can only be intuited according to this form of sensibility I can know *a priori.* Hence it follows: that propositions, which concern this form of sensuous intuition only, are possible and valid for objects of the senses; as also, conversely, that intuitions which are possible *a priori* can never concern any other things than objects of our senses.

§10. Accordingly, it is only the form of sensuous intuition by which we can intuit things *a priori,* but by which we can know objects only as they *appear* to us (to our senses), not as they are in themselves; and this assumption is absolutely necessary if synthetical propositions *a priori* be granted as possible, or if, in case they actually occur, their possibility is to be comprehended and determined beforehand.

Now, the intuitions which pure mathematics lays at the foundation of all its cognitions and judgments which appear at once apodeictic and necessary are space and time. For mathematics must first have all its concepts in intuition, and pure mathematics in pure intuition, that is, it must construct them. If it proceeded in any other way, it would be impossible to make any headway, for mathematics proceeds, not analytically by dissection of concepts, but synthetically, and if pure intuition be wanting, there is nothing in which the matter for synthetical judgments *a priori* can be given. Geometry is based upon the pure intuition of space. Arithmetic accomplishes its concept of number by the successive addition of units in time; and pure mechanics especially cannot attain its concepts of motion without employing the representation of time. Both representations, however, are only intuitions; for if we omit from the empirical intuitions of bodies and their alterations (motion) everything empirical, or belonging to sensation, space and time still remain, which are therefore pure intuitions that lie *a priori* at the basis of the empirical. Hence they can never be omitted, but at the same time, by their being pure intuitions *a priori,* they prove that they are mere forms of our sensibility, which must precede all empirical intuition, or perception of actual objects, and conformably to which objects can be known *a priori,* but only as they appear to us.

§11. The problem of the present section is therefore solved. Pure mathematics, as synthetical cognition *a priori,* is only possible by referring to no other objects than those of the senses. At the basis of their empirical intuition lies a pure intuition (of space and of time) which is *a priori.* This is possible, because the latter intuition is nothing but the mere form of sensibility, which precedes the actual appearance of the objects, in that it, in fact, makes them possible. Yet this faculty of intuiting *a priori* affects not the matter of the phenomenon (that is, the sense-element in it, for this constitutes that which is empirical), but its form, viz., space and time. Should any person venture to doubt that these are determinations adhering not to things in themselves, but to their relation to our sensibility, I should be glad to know how it can be possible to know the constitution of things *a priori,* viz., before we have any acquaintance with them and before they are presented to us. Such, however, is the case with space and time. But this is quite comprehensible as soon as both count for nothing more than formal conditions of our sensibility, while the objects count merely as phenomena; for then the form of the phenomenon, i.e., pure intuition, can by all means be represented as proceeding from ourselves, that is, *a priori.*

§12. In order to add something by way of illustration and confirmation, we need only watch the ordinary and necessary procedure of geometers. All proofs of the complete congruence of two given figures (where the one can in every respect be substituted for the other) come ultimately to this that they may be made to coincide; which is evidently nothing else than a synthetical proposition resting upon immediate intuition, and this intuition must be pure, or given *a priori,* otherwise the proposition could not rank as apodeictically certain, but would have empirical certainty only. In that case, it could only be said that it is always found to be so, and holds good only as far as our perception reaches. That everywhere space (which [in its entirety] is itself no longer the boundary of another space) has three dimensions, and that space cannot in any way have more, is based on the proposition that not more than three lines can intersect at right angles in one point; but this proposition cannot by any means be shown from concepts, but rests immediately on intuition, and indeed on pure and *a priori* intuition, because it is apodeictically certain. That we can require a line to be drawn to infinity, or that a series of changes (for example, spaces traversed by motion) shall be infinitely continued, presupposes a representation of space and time, which can only attach to intuition, namely, so far as it in itself is bounded by nothing, for from concepts it could never be inferred. Consequently, the basis of mathematics actually are pure intuitions, which make its synthetical and apodeictically valid propositions possible. Hence our transcendental deduction of the notions of space and of time explains at the same time the possibility of pure mathematics. Without some such deduction its truth may be granted, but its existence could by no means be understood, and we must assume "that everything which can be given to our senses (to the external senses in space, to the internal one in time) is intuited by us as it appears to us, not as it is in itself."

§13. Those who cannot yet rid themselves of the notion that space and time are actual qualities inhering in things in themselves, may exercise their acumen on the following paradox. When they have in vain attempted its solution, and are free from prejudices at least for a few moments, they will suspect that the degradation of space and of time to mere forms of our sensuous intuition may perhaps be well founded.

If two things are quite equal in all respects as much as can be ascertained by all means possible, quantitatively and qualitatively, it must follow, that the one can in all cases and under all circumstances replace the other, and this substitution would not occasion the least perceptible difference. This in fact is true of plane figures in geometry; but some spherical figures exhibit, notwithstanding a complete internal agreement, such a contrast in their external relation, that the one figure cannot possibly be put in the place of the other. For instance, two spherical triangles on opposite hemispheres, which have an arc of the equator as their common base, may be quite equal, both as regards sides and angles, so that nothing is to be found in either, if it be described for itself alone and completed, that would not equally be applicable to both; and yet the one cannot be put in the place of the other (being situated upon the opposite hemisphere). Here then is an internal difference between the two triangles, which difference our understanding cannot describe as internal, and which only manifests itself by external relations in space.

But I shall adduce examples, taken from common life, that are more obvious still.

What can be more similar in every respect and in every part more alike to my hand and to my ear, than their images in a mirror? And yet I cannot put such a hand as is seen in the glass in the place of its archetype; for if this is a right hand, that in the glass is a left one, and the image or reflection of the right ear is a left one which never can serve as a substitute for the other. There are in this case no internal differences which our understanding could determine by thinking alone. Yet the differences are internal as the senses teach, for, notwithstanding their complete equality and similarity, the left hand cannot be enclosed in the same bounds as the right one (they are not congruent); the glove of one hand cannot be used for the other. What is the solution? These objects are not representations of things as they are in themselves, and as the pure understanding would cognise them, but sensuous intuitions, that is, appearances, the possibility of which rests upon the relation of certain things unknown in themselves to something else, viz., to our sensibility. Space is the form of the external intuition of this sensibility, and the internal determination of every space is only possible by the determination of its external relation to the whole space, of which it is a part (in other words, by its relation to the external sense). That is to say, the part is only possible through the whole, which is never the case with things in themselves, as objects of the mere understanding, but with appearances only. Hence the difference between similar and equal things, which are yet not congruent (for instance, two symmetric helices), cannot be made intelligible by any concept, but only by the relation to the right and the left hands which immediately refers to intuition.

Remark I

Pure mathematics, and especially pure geometry, can only have objective reality on condition that they refer to objects of sense. But in regard to the latter the principle holds good, that our sense representation is not a representation of things in themselves, but of the way in which they appear to us. Hence it follows, that the propositions of geometry are not the results of a mere creation of our poetic imagination, and that therefore they cannot be referred with assurance to actual objects; but rather that they are necessarily valid of space, and consequently of all that may be found in space, because space is nothing else than the form of all external appearances, and it is this form alone in which objects of sense can be given. Sensibility, the form of which is the basis of geometry, is that upon which the possibility of external appearance depends. Therefore these appearances can never contain anything but what geometry prescribes to them.

It would be quite otherwise if the senses were so constituted as to represent objects as they are in themselves. For then it would not by any means follow from the conception of space, which with all its properties serves to the geometer as an *a priori* foundation, together with what is thence inferred, must be so in nature. The space of the geometer would be considered a mere fiction, and it would not be credited with objective validity, because we cannot see how things must of necessity agree with an image of them, which we make spontaneously and previous to our acquaintance with them. But if this image, or rather this formal intuition, is the essential property of our sensibility, by means of which alone objects are given to us, and if this sensibility represents not things in themselves, but their appearances: we shall easily comprehend, and at the same time indisputably prove, that all external objects of our world of sense must necessarily coincide in the most rigorous way with the propositions of geometry; because sensibility by means of its form of external intuition, viz., by space, the same with which the geometer is occupied, makes those objects at all possible as mere appearances.

It will always remain a remarkable phenomenon in the history of philosophy, that there was a time, when even mathematicians, who at the same time were philosophers, began to doubt, not of the accuracy of their geometrical propositions so far as they concerned space, but of their objective validity and the applicability of this concept itself, and of all its corollaries, to nature. They showed much concern whether a line in nature might not consist of physical points, and consequently that true space in the object might consist of simple [discrete] parts, while the space which the geometer has in his mind [being continuous] cannot be such. They did not recognise that this mental space renders possible the physical space, i.e., the extension of matter; that this pure space is not at all a quality of things in themselves, but a form of our sensuous faculty of representation; and that all objects in space are mere appearances, i.e., not things in themselves but representations of our sensuous intuition. But such is the case, for the space of the geometer is exactly the form of sensuous intuition which we find *a priori* in us, and contains the ground of the possibility of all external appearances (according to their form), and the latter must necessarily and most rigidly agree with the propositions of the geometer, which he draws not from any fictitious concept, but from the subjective basis of all external phenomena, which is sensibility itself. In this and no other way can geometry be made secure as to the undoubted objective reality of its propositions against all the intrigues of a shallow metaphysics, which is surprised at them [the geometrical propositions], because it has not traced them to the sources of their concepts.

Remark II

Whatever is given us as object, must be given us in intuition. All our intuition however takes place by means of the senses only; the understanding intuits nothing, but only reflects. And as we have just shown that the senses never and in no manner enable us to know things in themselves, but only their appearances, which are mere representations of the sensibility, we conclude that "all bodies, together with the space in which they are, must be considered nothing but mere representations in us, and exist nowhere but in our thoughts." You will say: Is not this manifest idealism?

Idealism consists in the assertion, that there are none but thinking beings, all other things, which we think are perceived in intuition, being nothing but representations in the thinking beings, to which no object external to them corresponds in fact. Whereas I say, that things as objects of our senses existing outside us are given, but we know nothing of what they may be in themselves, knowing only their appearances, i.e., the representations which they cause in us by affecting our senses. Consequently I grant by all means that there are bodies without us, that is, things which, though quite unknown to us as to what they are in themselves, we yet know by the representations which their influence on our sensibility procures us, and which we call bodies, a term signifying merely the appearance of the thing which is unknown to us, but not therefore less actual. Can this be termed idealism? It is the very contrary.

Long before Locke's time, but assuredly since him, it has been generally assumed and granted without detriment to the actual existence of external things, that many of their predicates may be said to belong not to the things in themselves, but to their appearances, and to have no proper existence outside our representation. Heat, color, and taste, for instance, are of this kind. Now, if I go farther, and for weighty reasons rank as mere appearances the remaining qualities of bodies also, which are called primary, such as extension, place, and in general space, with all that which belongs to it (impenetrability or materiality, space, etc.)—no one in the least can adduce the reason of its being inadmissible. As little as the man who admits colors not to be properties of the object in itself, but only as modifications of the sense of sight, should on that account be called an idealist, so little can my system be named idealistic, merely because I find that more, nay,

All the properties which constitute the intuition of a body belong merely to its appearance.

The existence of the thing that appears is thereby not destroyed, as in genuine idealism, but it is only shown, that we cannot possibly know it by the senses as it is in itself.

I should be glad to know what my assertions must be in order to avoid all idealism. Undoubtedly, I should say, that the representation of space is not only perfectly conformable to the relation which our sensibility has to objects—that I have said—but that it is quite similar to the object,—an assertion in which I can find as little meaning as if I said that the sensation of red has a similarity to the property of vermilion, which in me excites this sensation.

Remark III

Hence we may at once dismiss an easily foreseen but futile objection, "that by admitting the ideality of space and of time the whole sensible world would be turned into mere sham." At first all philosophical insight into the nature of sensuous cognition was spoiled, by making the sensibility merely a confused mode of representation, according to which we still know things as they are, but without being able to reduce everything in this our representation to a clear consciousness; whereas proof is offered by us that sensibility consists, not in this logical distinction of clearness and obscurity, but in the genetical one of the origin of cognition itself. For sensuous perception represents things not at all as they are, but only the mode in which they affect our senses, and consequently by sensuous perception appearances only and not things themselves are given to the understanding for reflection. After this necessary corrective, an objection rises from an unpardonable and almost intentional misconception, as if my doctrine turned all the things of the world of sense into mere illusion.

When an appearance is given us, we are still quite free as to how we should judge the matter. The appearance depends upon the senses, but the judgment upon the understanding, and the only question is, whether in the determination of the object there is truth or not. But the difference between truth and dreaming is not ascertained by the nature of the representations, which are referred to objects (for they are the same in both cases), but by their connection according to those rules, which determine the coherence of the representations in the concept of an object, and by ascertaining whether they can subsist together in experience or not. And it is not the fault of the appearances if our cognition takes illusion for truth, i.e., if the intuition, by which an object is given us, is considered a concept of the thing or of its existence also, which the understanding can only think. The senses represent to us the paths of the planets as now progressive, now retrogressive, and herein is neither falsehood nor truth, because as long as we hold this path to be nothing but appearance, we do not judge of the objective nature of their motion. But as a false judgment may easily arise when the understanding is not on its guard against this subjective mode of representation being considered objective, we say they appear to move backward; it is not the senses however which must be charged with the illusion, but the understanding, whose province alone it is to give an objective judgment on appearances.

Thus, even if we did not at all reflect on the origin of our representations, whenever we connect our intuitions of sense (whatever they may contain), in space and in time, according to the rules of the coherence of all cognition in experience, illusion or truth will arise according as we are negligent or careful. It is merely a question of the use of sensuous representations in the understanding, and not of their origin. In the same way, if I consider all the representations of the senses, together with their form, space and time, to be nothing but appearances, and space and time to be a mere form of the sensibility, which is not to be met with in objects out of it, and if I make use of these representations in reference to possible experience only, there is nothing in my regarding them as appearances that can lead astray or cause illusion. For all that they can correctly cohere according to rules of truth in experience. Thus all the propositions of geometry hold good of space as well as of all the objects of the senses, consequently of all possible experience, whether I consider space as a mere form of the sensibility, or as something cleaving to the things themselves. In the former case however I comprehend how I can know *a priori* these propositions concerning all the objects of external intuition. Otherwise, everything else as regards all possible experience remains just as if I had not departed from the vulgar view.

But if I venture to go beyond all possible experience with my notions of space and time, which I cannot refrain from doing if I proclaim them qualities inherent in things in themselves (for what should prevent me from letting them hold good of the same things, even though my senses might be different, and unsuited to them?), then a grave error may arise due to illusion, for thus I would proclaim to be universally valid what is merely a subjective condition of the intuition of things and sure only for all objects of sense, viz., for all possible experience; I would refer this condition to things in themselves, and do not limit it to the conditions of experience.

My doctrine of the ideality of space and of time, therefore, far from reducing the whole sensible world to mere illusion, is the only means of securing the application of one of the most important cognitions (that which mathematics propounds *a priori*) to actual objects, and of preventing its being regarded as mere illusion. For without this observation it would be quite impossible to make out whether the intuitions of space and time, which we borrow from no experience, and which yet lie in our representation *a priori*, are not mere phantasms of our brain, to which objects do not correspond, at least not adequately, and consequently, whether we have been able to show its unquestionable validity with regard to all the objects of the sensible world just because they are mere appearances.

Secondly, though these my principles make appearances of the representations of the senses, they are so far from turning the truth of experience into mere illusion, that they are rather the only means of preventing the transcendental illusion, by which metaphysics has hitherto been deceived, leading to the childish endeavor of catching at bubbles, because appearances, which are mere representations, were taken for things in themselves. Here originated the remarkable event of the antimony of reason which I shall mention by and by, and which is destroyed by the single observation, that appearance, as long as it is employed in experience, produces truth, but the moment it transgresses the bounds of experience, and consequently becomes transcendent, produces nothing but illusion.

Inasmuch, therefore, as I leave to things as we obtain them by the senses their actuality, and only limit our sensuous intuition of these things to this, that they represent in no respect, not even in the pure intuitions of space and of time, anything more than mere appearances of those things, but never their constitution in themselves, this is not a sweeping illusion invented for nature by me. My protestation too against all charges of idealism is so valid and clear as even to seem superfluous, were there not incompetent judges, who, while they would have an old name for every deviation from their perverse though common opinion, and never judge of the spirit of philosophic nomenclature, but cling to the letter only, are ready to put their own conceits in the place of well-defined notions, and thereby deform and distort them. I have myself given this my theory the name of transcendental idealism, but that cannot authorise any one to confound it either with the empirical idealism of Descartes, (indeed, his was only an insoluble problem, owing to which he thought every one at liberty to deny the existence of the corporeal world, because it could never be proved satisfactorily), or with the mystical and visionary idealism of Berkeley, against which and other similar phantasms our *Critique* contains the proper antidote. My idealism concerns not the existence of things (the doubting of which, however, constitutes idealism in the ordinary sense), since it never came into my head to doubt it, but it concerns the sensuous representation of things, to which space and time especially belong. Of these [viz., space and time], consequently of all appearances in general, I have only shown, that they are neither things (but mere modes of representation), nor determinations belonging to things in themselves. But the word "transcendental," which with me means a reference of our cognition, i.e., not to things, but only to the cognitive faculty, was meant to obviate this misconception. Yet rather than give further occasion to it by this word, I now retract it, and desire this idealism of mine to be called critical. But if it be really an objectionable idealism to convert actual things (not appearances) into mere representations, by what name shall we call him who conversely changes mere representations to things? It may, I think, be called "dreaming idealism," in contradistinction to the former, which may be called "visionary," both of which are to be refuted by my transcendental, or, better, critical idealism.

SECOND PART OF THE TRANSCENDENTAL PROBLEM
How Is the Science of Nature Possible?

§14. Nature is the existence of things, so far as it is determined according to universal laws. Should nature signify the existence of things in themselves, we could never cognise it either *a priori* or *a posteriori*. Not *a priori*, for how can we know what belongs to things in themselves, since this never can be done by the dissection of our concepts (in analytical judgments)? We do not want to know what is contained in our concept of a thing (for the [concept describes what] belongs to its logical being), but what is in the actuality of the thing superadded to our concept, and by what the thing itself is determined in its existence outside the concept. Our understanding, and the conditions on which alone it can connect the determinations of things in their existence, do not prescribe any rule to things themselves; these do not conform to our understanding, but it must conform itself to them; they must therefore be first given us in order to gather these determinations from them, wherefore they would not be cognised *a priori*.

A cognition of the nature of things in themselves *a posteriori* would be equally impossible. For, if experience is to teach us laws, to which the existence of things is subject, these laws, if they regard things in themselves, must belong to them of necessity even outside our experience. But experience teaches us what exists and how it exists, but never that it must necessarily exist so and not otherwise. Experience therefore can never teach us the nature of things in themselves.

§15. We nevertheless actually possess a pure science of nature in which are propounded, *a priori* and with all the necessity requisite to apodeictical propositions, laws to which nature is subject. I need only call to witness that propaedeutic of natural science which, under the title of the universal science of nature, precedes all physics (which is founded upon empirical principles). In it we have mathematics applied to appearance, and also merely discursive principles (or those derived from concepts), which constitute the philosophical part of the pure cognition of nature. But there are several things in it, which are not quite pure and independent of empirical sources: such as the concept of *motion*, that of *impenetrability* (upon which the empirical concept of matter rests), that of *inertia*, and many others, which prevent its being called a perfectly pure science of nature. Besides, it only refers to objects of the external sense, and therefore does not give an example of a universal science of nature, in the strict sense, for such a science must reduce nature in general, whether it regards the object of the external or that of the internal sense (the object of physics as well as psychology), to universal laws. But among the principles of this universal physics there are a few which actually have the required universality; for instance, the propositions that "substance is permanent," and that "every event is determined by a cause according to constant laws," etc. These are actually universal laws of nature, which subsist completely *a priori*. There is then in fact a pure science of nature, and the question arises, *How is it possible?*

§16. The word "nature" assumes yet another meaning, which determines the object, whereas in the former sense it only denotes the conformity to law of the determinations of the existence of things generally. If we consider it *materialiter* (i.e., in the matter that forms its objects) "nature is the complex of all the objects of experience." And with this only are we now concerned, for besides, things which can never be objects of experience, if they must be cognised as to their nature, would oblige us to have recourse to concepts whose meaning could never be given *in concreto* (by any example of possible experience). Consequently we must form for ourselves a list of concepts of their nature, the reality whereof (i.e., whether they actually refer to objects, or are mere creations of thought) could never be determined. The cognition of what cannot be an object of experience would be hyperphysical, and with things hyperphysical we are here not concerned, but only with the cognition of nature, the actuality of which can be confirmed by experience, though it [the cognition of nature] is possible *a priori* and precedes all experience.

§17. The formal [aspect] of nature in this narrower sense is therefore the conformity to law of all the objects of experience, and so far as it is cognised *a priori*, their necessary conformity. But it has just been shown that the laws of nature can never be cognised *a priori* in objects so far as they are considered not in reference to possible experience, but as things in themselves. And our inquiry here extends not to things in themselves (the properties of which we pass by), but to things as objects of possible experience, and the complex of these is what we properly designate as nature. And now I ask, when the possibility of a cognition of nature *a priori* is in question, whether it is better to arrange the problem thus: How can we cognise *a priori* that things as objects of experience necessarily conform to law? or thus: How is it possible to cognise *a priori* the necessary conformity to law of experience itself as regards all its objects generally?

Closely considered, the solution of the problem, represented in either way, amounts, with regard to the pure cognition of nature (which is the point of the question at issue), entirely to the same thing. For the subjective laws, under which alone an empirical cognition of things is possible, hold good of these things, as objects of possible experience (not as things in themselves, which are not considered here). Either of the following statements means quite the same:

A judgment of observation can never rank as experience, without the law, that "whenever an event is observed, it is always referred to some antecedent, which it follows according to a universal rule."

"Everything, of which experience teaches that it happens, must have a cause."

It is, however, more commendable to choose the first formula. For we can *a priori* and previous to all given objects have a cognition of those conditions, on which alone experience is possible, but never of the laws to which things may in themselves be subject, without reference to possible experience. We cannot therefore study the nature of things *a priori* otherwise than by investigating the conditions and the universal (though subjective) laws, under which alone such a cognition as experience (as to mere form) is possible, and we determine accordingly the possibility of things, as objects of experience. For if I should choose the second formula, and seek the conditions *a priori*, on which nature as an object of experience is possible, I might easily fall into error, and fancy that I was speaking of nature as a thing in itself, and then move round in endless circles, in a vain search for laws concerning things of which nothing is given me.

Accordingly we shall here be concerned with experience only, and the universal conditions of its possibility which are given *a priori*. Thence we shall determine nature as the whole object of all possible experience. I think it will be understood that I here do not mean the rules of the observation of a nature that is already given, for these already presuppose experience. I do not mean how (through experience) we can study the laws of nature; for these would not then be laws *a priori*, and would yield us no pure science of nature; but [I mean to ask] how the conditions *a priori* of the possibility of experience are at the same time the sources from which all the universal laws of nature must be derived.

§18. In the first place we must state that, while all judgments of experience are empirical (i.e., have their ground in immediate sense-perception), *vice versa*, all empirical judgments are not judgments of experience, but, besides the empirical, and in general besides what is given to the sensuous intuition, particular concepts must yet be superadded—concepts which have their origin quite *a priori* in the pure understanding, and under which every perception must be first of all subsumed and then by their means changed into experience.

Empirical judgments, so far as they have objective validity, are **judgments of experience;** but those which are only subjectively valid, I name mere **judgments of perception.** The latter require no pure concept of the understanding, but only the logical connection of perception in a thinking subject. But the former always require, besides the representation of the sensuous intuition, particular *concepts originally begotten in the understanding,* which produce the objective validity of the judgment of experience.

All our judgments are at first merely judgments of perception; they hold good only for us (i.e., for our subject), and we do not till afterwards give them a new reference (to an object), and desire that they shall always hold good for us and in the same way for everybody else; for when a judgment agrees with an object, all judgments concerning the same object must likewise agree among themselves, and thus the objective validity of the judgment of experience signifies nothing else than its necessary universality of application. And conversely when we have reason to consider a judgment necessarily universal (which never depends upon perception, but upon the pure concept of the understanding, under which the perception is subsumed), we must consider it objective also, that is, that it expresses not merely a reference of our perception to a subject, but a quality of the object. For there would be no reason for the judgments of other men necessarily agreeing with mine, if it were not the unity of the object to which they all refer, and with which they accord; hence they must all agree with one another.

§19. Therefore objective validity and necessary universality (for everybody) are equivalent terms, and though we do not know the object in itself, yet when we consider a judgment as universal, and also necessary, we understand it to have objective validity. By this judgment we cognise the object (though it remains unknown as it is in itself) by the universal and necessary connection of the given perceptions. As this is the case with all objects of sense, judgments of experience take their objective validity not from the immediate cognition of the object (which is impossible), but from the condition of universal validity in empirical judgments, which, as already said, never rests upon empirical, or, in short, sensuous conditions, but upon a pure concept of the understanding. The object always remains unknown in itself; but when by the concept of the understanding the connection of the representations of the object, which are given to our sensibility, is determined as universally valid, the object is determined by this relation, and it is the judgment that is objective.

To illustrate the matter: When we say, "the room is warm, sugar sweet, and wormwood bitter,"—we have only subjectively valid judgments. I do not at all expect that I or any other person shall always find it as I now do; each of these sentences only expresses a relation of two sensations to the same subject, to myself, and that only in my present state of perception; consequently they are not valid of the object. Such are judgments of perception. Judgments of experience are of quite a different nature. What experience teaches me under certain circumstances, it must always teach me and everybody; and its validity is not limited to the subject nor to its state at a particular time. Hence I pronounce all such judgments as being objectively valid. For instance, when I say the air is elastic, this judgment is as yet a judgment of perception only—I do nothing but refer two of my sensations to one another. But, if I would have it called a judgment of experience, I require this connection to stand under a condition, which makes it universally valid. I desire therefore that I and everybody else should always connect necessarily the same perceptions under the same circumstances.

§20. We must consequently analyse experience in order to see what is contained in this product of the senses and of the understanding, and how the judgment of experience itself is possible. The foundation is the intuition of which I become conscious, i.e., perception, which pertains merely to the senses. But in the next place, there are acts of judging (which belong only to the understanding). But this judging may be twofold—first, I may merely compare perceptions and connect them in a particular state of my consciousness; or, secondly, I may connect them in consciousness generally. The former judgment is merely a judgment of perception, and of subjective validity only: it is merely a connection of perceptions in my mental state, without reference to the object. Hence it is not, as is commonly imagined, enough for experience to compare perceptions and to connect them in consciousness through judgment; there arises no universality and necessity, for which alone judgments can become objectively valid and be called experience.

Quite another judgment therefore is required before perception can become experience. The given intuition must be subsumed under a concept, which determines the form of judging in general relatively to the intuition, connects its empirical consciousness in consciousness generally, and thereby procures universal validity for empirical judgments. A concept of this nature is a pure *a priori* concept of the understanding, which does nothing but determine for an intuition the general way in which it can be used for judgments. Let the concept be that of cause, then it determines the intuition which is subsumed under it, e.g., that of air, relative to judgments in general, viz., the concept of air serves with regard to its expansion in the relation of antecedent to consequent in a hypothetical judgment. The concept of cause accordingly is a pure concept of the understanding, which is totally disparate from all possible perception, and only serves to determine the representation subsumed under it, relatively to judgments in general, and so to make a universally valid judgment possible.

Before, therefore, a judgment of perception can become a judgment of experience, it is requisite that the perception should be subsumed under some such a concept of the understanding; for instance, air ranks under the concept of causes, which determines our judgment about it in regard to its expansion as hypothetical. Thereby the expansion of the air is represented not as merely belonging to the perception of the air in my present state or in several states of mine, or in the state of perception of others, but as belonging to it necessarily. The judgment, "the air is elastic," becomes universally valid, and a judgment of experience, only by certain judgments preceding it, which subsume the intuition of air under the concept of cause and effect: and they thereby determine the perceptions not merely as regards one another in me, but relatively to the form of judging in general, which is here hypothetical, and in this way they render the empirical judgment universally valid.

If all our synthetical judgments are analysed so far as they are objectively valid, it will be found that they never consist of mere intuitions connected only (as is commonly believed) by comparison into a judgment; but that they would be impossible were not a pure concept of the understanding superadded to the concepts abstracted from intuition, under which concept these latter are subsumed, and in this manner only combined into an objectively valid judgment. Even the judgments of pure mathematics in their simplest axioms are not exempt from this condition. The principle, "a straight line is the shortest between two points," presupposes that the line is subsumed under the concept of quantity, which certainly is no mere intuition, but has its seat in the understanding alone, and serves to determine the intuition (of the line) with regard to the judgments which may be made about it, relatively to their quantity, that is, to plurality. For under them it is understood that in a given intuition there is contained a plurality of homogeneous parts.

§21. To prove, then, the possibility of experience so far as it rests upon pure concepts of the understanding *a priori*, we must first represent what belongs to judgments in general and the various functions of the understanding, in a complete table. For the pure concepts of the understanding must run parallel to these functions, as such concepts are nothing more than concepts of intuitions in general, so far as these are determined by one or other of these functions of judging, in themselves, that is, necessarily and universally. Hereby also the *a priori* principles of the possibility of all experience, as of an objectively valid empirical cognition, will be precisely determined. For they are nothing but propositions by which all

Logical Table of Judgments

1. *As to Quantity*	2. *As to Quality*
Universal	Affirmative
Particular	Negative
Singular	Infinite

3. *As to Relation*	4. *As to Modality*
Categorical	Problematical
Hypothetical	Assertorical
Disjunctive	Apodeictical

Transcendental Table of the Pure Concepts of the Understanding

1. *As to Quantity*	2. *As to Quality*
Unity (the Measure)	Reality
Plurality (the Quantity)	Negation
Totality (the Whole)	Limitation

3. *As to Relation*	4. *As to Modality*
Substance	Possibility
Cause	Existence
Community	Necessity

Pure Physiological Table of the Universal Principles of the Science of Nature

1. Axioms of Intuition	2. Anticipations of Perception
3. Analogies of Experience	4. Postulates of Empirical Thinking Generally

perception is (under certain universal conditions of intuition) subsumed under those pure concepts of the understanding.

§21*a.* In order to comprise the whole matter in one idea, it is first necessary to remind the reader that we are discussing not the origin of experience, but of that which lies in experience. The former pertains to empirical psychology, and would even then never be adequately explained without the latter, which belongs to the critique of cognition, and particularly of the understanding.

Experience consists of intuitions, which belong to the sensibility, and of judgments, which are entirely a work of the understanding. But the judgments, which the understanding forms alone from sensuous intuitions, are far from being judgments of experience. For in the one case the judgment connects only the perceptions as they are given in the sensuous intuition, while in the other the judgments must express what experience in general, and not what the mere perception (which possesses only subjective validity) contains. The judgment of experience must therefore add to the sensuous intuition and its logical connection in a judgment (after it has been rendered universal by comparison) something that determines the synthetical judgment as necessary and therefore as universally valid. This can be nothing else than that concept which represents the intuition as determined in itself with regard to one form of judgment rather than another, viz., a concept of that synthetical unity of intuitions which can only be represented by a given logical function of judgments.

§22. The sum of the matter is this: the business of the senses is to intuit—that of the understanding is to think. But thinking is uniting representations in one consciousness. This union originates either merely relative to the subject, and is accidental and subjective, or is absolute, and is necessary or objective. The union of representations in one consciousness is judgment. Thinking therefore is the same as judging, or referring representations to judgments in general. Hence judgments are either merely subjective, when representations are referred to a consciousness in one subject only, and united in it, or objective, when they are united in a consciousness generally, that is, necessarily. The logical functions of all judgments are but various modes of uniting representations in consciousness. But if they serve for concepts, they are concepts of their necessary union in a consciousness, and so principles of objectively valid judgments. This union in a consciousness is either analytical, by identity, or synthetical, by the combination and addition of various representations one to another. Experience consists in the synthetical connection of phenomena (perceptions) in consciousness, so far as this connection is necessary. Hence the pure concepts of the understanding are those under which all perceptions must be subsumed ere they can serve for judgments of experience, in which the synthetical unity of the perceptions is represented as necessary and universally valid.

§23. Judgments, when considered merely as the condition of the union of given representations in a consciousness, are rules. These rules, so far as they represent the union as necessary, are rules *a priori,* and so far as they cannot be deduced from higher rules, are fundamental principles. But in regard to the possibility of all experience, merely in relation to the form of thinking in it, no conditions of judgments of experience are higher than those which bring the phenomena, according to the various forms of their intuition, under pure concepts of the understanding, and render the empirical judgment objectively valid. These concepts are therefore the *a priori* principles of possible experience.

The principles of possible experience are then at the same time universal laws of nature, which can be cognised *a priori.* And thus the problem in our second question, "How is the pure science of nature possible?" is solved. For the system which is required for the form of a science is to be met with in perfection here, because, beyond the above-mentioned formal conditions of all judgments in general offered in logic, no others are possible, and these constitute a logical system. The concepts grounded thereupon, which contain the *a priori* conditions of all synthetical and necessary judgments, accordingly constitute a transcendental system. Finally the principles, by means of which all phenomena are subsumed under these concepts, constitute a physical system, that is, a system of nature, which precedes all empirical cognition of nature, makes it even possible, and hence may in strictness be denominated the universal and pure science of nature.

§24. The first one of the physiological principles subsumes all phenomena, as intuitions in space and time, under the concept of quantity, and is so far a principle of the application of mathematics to experience. The second one subsumes the empirical element, viz., sensation, which denotes the real in intuitions, not indeed directly under the concept of quantity, because sensation is not an intuition that contains either space or time, though it places the respective object into both. But still there is between reality (sense-representation) and the zero, or total void of intuition in time, a difference which has a quantity. For between every given degree of light and of darkness, between every degree of heat and of absolute cold, between every degree of weight and of absolute lightness, between every degree of occupied space and of totally void space, diminishing degrees can be conceived, in the same manner as between consciousness and total unconsciousness (the darkness of a psychological blank) ever diminishing degrees obtain. Hence there is no perception that can prove an absolute absence of it; for instance, no psychological darkness that cannot be considered as a kind of consciousness, which is only outbalanced by a stronger consciousness. This occurs in all cases of sensation, and so the understanding can anticipate even sensations, which constitute the peculiar quality of empirical representations (appearances), by means of the principle: "that they all have (consequently that what is real in all phenomena has) a degree." Here is the second application of mathematics to the science of nature.

§25. Regarding the relation of appearances in terms of their existence, the determination is not mathematical but dynamical, and can never be objectively valid, consequently never fit for experience, if it does not come under *a priori* principles by which the cognition of experience relative to appearances becomes even possible. Hence appearances must be subsumed under the concept of substance, which is the foundation of all determination of existence, as a concept of the thing itself; or secondly—so far as a succession is found among phenomena, that is, an event—under the concept of an effect with reference to cause; or lastly—so far as coexistence is to be known objectively, that is, by a judgment of experience—under the concept of community (action and reaction). Thus *a priori* principles form the basis of objectively valid, though empirical judgments, that is, of the possibility of experience so far as it must connect objects as existing in nature. These principles are the proper laws of nature, which may be termed dynamical.

Finally the cognition of the agreement and connection not only of appearances among themselves in experience, but of their relation to experience in general, belongs to the judgments of experience. This relation contains either their agreement with the formal conditions, which the understanding cognises, or their coherence with the materials of the senses and of perception, or combines both into one concept. Consequently it contains possibility, actuality, and necessity according to universal laws of nature; and this constitutes the physical doctrine of method, or the distinction of truth and of hypotheses, and the bounds of the certainty of the latter.

§26. The third table of Principles drawn from the nature of the understanding itself after the critical method, shows an inherent perfection, which raises it far above every other table which has hitherto though in vain been tried or may yet be tried by analysing the objects themselves dogmatically. It exhibits all synthetical *a priori* principles completely and according to one principle, viz., the faculty of judging in general, constituting the essence of experience as regards the understanding, so that we can be certain that there are no more such principles, which affords a satisfaction such as can never be attained by the dogmatical method. Yet is this not all: there is a still greater merit in it.

We must carefully bear in mind the proof which shows the possibility of this cognition *a priori,* and at the same time limits all such principles to a condition which must never be lost sight of, if we desire it not to be misunderstood, and extended in use beyond the original sense which the understanding attaches to it. This limit is that they contain nothing but the conditions of possible experience in general so far as it is subjected to laws *a priori.* Consequently I do not say, that things *in themselves* possess a quantity, that their actuality possesses a degree, their existence a connection of accidents in a substance, etc. This nobody can prove, because such a synthetical connection from mere concepts, without any reference to sensuous intuition on the one side, or connection of it in a possible experience on the other, is absolutely impossible. The essential limitation of the concepts in these principles then is: That all things stand necessarily *a priori* under the afore-mentioned conditions, as objects of experience only.

Hence there follows secondly a specifically peculiar mode of proof of these principles: they are not directly referred to appearances and to their relations, but to the possibility of experience, of which appearances constitute the matter only, not the form. Thus they are referred to objectively and universally valid synthetical propositions, in which we distinguish judgments of experience from those of perception. This takes place because appearances, as mere intuitions, occupying a part of space and time, come under the concept of quantity, which unites their multiplicity *a priori* according to rules synthetically. Again, so far as the perception contains, besides intuition, sensibility, and between the latter and nothing (i.e., the total disappearance of sensibility), there is an ever-decreasing transition, it is apparent that that which is in appearances must have a degree, so far as it (viz., the perception) does not itself occupy any part of space or of time. Still the transition to actuality from empty time or empty space is only possible in time; consequently though sensibility, as the quality of empirical intuition, can never be cognised *a priori,* by its specific difference from other sensibilities, yet it can, in a possible experience in general, as a quantity of perception be intensely distinguished from every other similar perception. Hence the application of mathematics to nature, as regards the sensuous intuition by which nature is given to us, becomes possible and is thus determined.

Above all, the reader must pay attention to the mode of proof of the principles which occur under the title of analogies of experience. For these do not refer to the genesis of intuitions, as do the principles of applied mathematics, but to the connection of their existence in experience; and this can be nothing but the determination of their existence in time according to necessary laws, under which alone the connection is objectively valid, and thus becomes experience. The proof therefore does not turn on the synthetical unity in the connection of things in themselves, but merely of perceptions, and of these not in regard to their matter, but to the determination of time and of the relation of their existence in it, according to universal laws. If the empirical determination in relative time is indeed objectively valid (i.e., experience), these universal laws contain the necessary determination of existence in time generally (viz., according to a rule of the understanding *a priori*).

In these *Prolegomena* I cannot further descant on the subject, but my reader (who has probably been long accustomed to consider experience a mere empirical synthesis of perceptions, and hence not considered that it goes much beyond them, as it imparts to empirical judgments universal validity, and for that purpose requires a pure and *a priori* unity of the understanding) is recommended to pay special attention to this distinction of experience from a mere aggregate of perceptions, and to judge the mode of proof from this point of view.

§27. Now we are prepared to remove Hume's doubt. He justly maintains, that we cannot comprehend by reason the possibility of causality, that is, of the reference of the existence of one thing to the existence of another, which is necessitated by the former. I add, that we comprehend just as little the concept of subsistence, that is, the necessity that at the foundation of the existence of things there lies a subject which cannot itself be a predicate of any other thing; nay, we cannot even form a notion of the possibility of such a thing (though we can point out examples of its use in experience). The very same incomprehensibility affects the community of things, as we cannot comprehend how from the state of one thing an inference to the state of quite another thing beyond it, and *vice versa,* can be drawn, and how substances which have each their own separate existence should depend upon one another necessarily. But I am very far from holding these concepts to be derived merely from experience, and the necessity represented in them, to be imaginary and a mere illusion produced in us by long habit. On the contrary, I have amply shown, that they and the theorems derived from them are firmly established *a priori,* or before all experience, and have their undoubted objective value, though only with regard to experience.

§28. Though I have no notion of such a connection of things in themselves, that they can either exist as substances, or act as causes, or stand in community with others (as parts of a real whole), and I can just as little conceive such properties in appearances as such (because those concepts contain nothing that lies in the appearances, but only what the understanding alone must think): we have yet a notion of such a connection of representations in our understanding, and in judgments generally; consisting in this that representations appear in one sort of judgments as subject in relation to predicates, in another as reason in relation to consequences, and in a third as parts, which constitute together a total possible cognition. Besides we cognise *a priori* that without considering the representation of an object as determined in some of these respects, we can have no valid cognition of the object, and, if we should occupy ourselves about the object in itself, there is no possible attribute, by which I could know that it is determined under any of these aspects, that is, under the concept either of substance, or of cause, or (in relation to other substances) of community, for I have no notion of the possibility of such a connection of existence. But the question is not how things in themselves, but how the empirical cognition of things is determined, as regards the above aspects of judgments in general, that is, how things, as objects of experience, can and shall be subsumed under these concepts of the understanding. And then it is clear, that I completely comprehend not only the possibility, but also the necessity of subsuming all phenomena under these concepts, that is, of using them for principles of the possibility of experience.

§29. When making an experiment with Hume's problematical concept, the concept of cause, we have, in the first place, given *a priori,* by means of logic, the form of a conditional judgment in general, i.e., we have one given cognition as antecedent and another as consequence. But it is possible, that in perception we may meet with a rule of relation, which runs thus: that a certain phenomenon is constantly followed by another (though not conversely), and this is a case for me to use the hypothetical judgment, and, for instance, to say, if the sun shines long enough upon a body, it grows warm. Here there is indeed as yet no necessity of connection, or concept of cause. But I proceed and say, that if this proposition, which is merely a subjective connection of perceptions, is to be a judgment of experience, it must be considered as necessary and universally valid. Such a proposition would be, "the sun is by its light the cause of heat." The empirical rule is now considered as a law, and as valid not merely of appearances but valid of them for the purposes of a possible experience which requires universal and therefore necessarily valid rules. I therefore easily comprehend the concept of cause, as a concept necessarily belonging to the mere form of experience, and its possibility as a synthetical union of perceptions in consciousness generally; but I do not at all comprehend the possibility of a thing generally as a cause, because the concept of cause denotes a condition not at all belonging to things, but to experience. It is nothing in fact but an objectively valid cognition of appearances and of their succession, so far as the antecedent can be conjoined with the consequent according to the rule of hypothetical judgments.

§30. Hence if the pure concepts of the understanding do not refer to objects of experience but to things in themselves (*noumena*), they have no signification whatever. They serve, as it were, only to decipher appearances, that we may be able to read them as experience. The principles which arise from their reference to the sensible world, only serve our understanding for empirical use. Beyond this they are arbitrary combinations, without objective reality, and we can neither cognise their possibility *a priori,* nor verify their reference to objects, let alone make it intelligible by any example; because examples can only be borrowed from some possible experience, consequently the objects of these concepts can be found nowhere but in a possible experience.

This complete (though to its originator unexpected) solution of Hume's problem rescues for the pure concepts of the understanding their *a priori* origin, and for the universal laws of nature their validity, as laws of the understanding, yet in such a way as to limit their use to experience, because their possibility depends solely on the reference of the understanding to experience, but with a completely reversed mode of connection which never occurred to Hume, not by deriving them from experience, but by deriving experience from them.

This is therefore the result of all our foregoing inquiries: "All synthetical principles *a priori* are nothing more than principles of possible experience, and can never be referred to things in themselves, but to appearances as objects of experience. And hence pure mathematics as well as a pure science of nature can never be referred to anything more than mere appearances, and can only represent either that which makes experience generally possible, or else that which, as it is derived from these principles, must always be capable of being represented in some possible experience."

§31. And thus we have at last something definite, upon which to depend in all metaphysical enterprises, which have hitherto, boldly enough but always at random, attempted everything without discrimination. That the aim of their exertions should be so near, struck neither the dogmatical thinkers nor those who, confident in their supposed sound common sense, started with concepts and principles of pure reason (which were legitimate and natural, but destined for mere empirical use) in quest of fields of knowledge, to which they neither knew nor could know any determinate bounds, because they had never reflected nor were able to reflect on the nature or even on the possibility of such a pure understanding.

Many a naturalist of pure reason (by which I mean the man who believes he can decide in matters of metaphysics without any science) may pretend, that he long ago by the prophetic spirit of his sound sense, not only suspected, but knew and comprehended, what is here propounded with so much ado, or, if he likes, with prolix and pedantic pomp: "that with all our reason we can never reach beyond the field of experience." But when he is questioned about his rational principles individually, he must grant, that there are many of them which he has not taken from experience, and which are therefore independent of it and valid *a priori.* How then and on what grounds will he restrain both himself and the dogmatist, who makes use of these concepts and principles beyond all possible experience, because they are recognised to be independent of it? And even he, this adept in sound sense, in spite of all his assumed and cheaply acquired wisdom, is not exempt from wandering inadvertently beyond objects of experience into the field of chimeras. He is often deeply enough involved in them, though in announcing everything as mere probability, rational conjecture, or analogy, he gives by his popular language a color to his groundless pretensions.

§32. Since the oldest days of philosophy inquirers into pure reason have conceived, besides the things of sense, or appearances (phenomena), which make up the sensible world, certain creations of the understanding, called noumena, which should constitute an intelligible world. And as appearance and illusion were by those men identified (a thing which we may well excuse in an undeveloped epoch), actuality was only conceded to the creations of thought.

And we indeed, rightly considering objects of sense as mere appearances, confess thereby that they are based upon a thing in itself, though we know not this thing in its internal constitution, but only know its appearances, viz., the way in which our senses are affected by this unknown something. The understanding, therefore, by assuming appearances, grants the existence of things in themselves also, and so far we may say, that the representation of such things as form the basis of phenomena, consequently of mere creations of the understanding, is not only admissible, but unavoidable.

Our critical deduction by no means excludes things of that sort (noumena), but rather limits the principles of the aesthetic (the science of the sensibility) to this, that they shall not extend to all things, as everything would then be turned into mere appearance, but that they shall only hold good of objects of possible experience. Hereby then objects of the understanding are granted, but with the inculcation of this rule which admits of no exception: "that we neither know nor can know anything at all definite of these pure objects of the understanding, because our pure concepts of the understanding as well as our pure intuitions extend to nothing but objects of possible experience, consequently to mere things of sense, and as soon as we leave this sphere these concepts retain no meaning whatever."

§33. There is indeed something seductive in our pure concepts of the understanding, which tempts us to a transcendent use,—a use which transcends all possible experience. Not only are our concepts of substance, of power, of action, of reality, and others, quite independent of experience, containing nothing of sense appearance, and so apparently applicable to things in themselves (noumena), but, what strengthens this conjecture, they contain a necessity of determination in themselves, which experience never attains. The concept of cause implies a rule, according to which one state follows another necessarily; but experience can only show us, that one state of things often, or at most, commonly, follows another, and therefore affords neither strict universality, nor necessity.

Hence the categories seem to have a deeper meaning and import than can be exhausted by their empirical use, and so the understanding inadvertently adds for itself to the house of experience a much more extensive wing, which it fills with nothing but creatures of thought, without ever observing that it has transgressed with its otherwise lawful concepts the bounds of their use.

§34. Two important, and even indispensable, though very dry, investigations had therefore become indispensable in the *Critique of Pure Reason,*—viz., the two chapters "Vom Schematismus der reinen Verstandsbegriffe," and "Vom Grunde der Unterscheidung aller Verstandesbegriffe überhaupt in Phänomena und Noumena." In the former it is shown, that the senses furnish not the pure concepts of the understanding *in concreto,* but only the schedule for their use, and that the object conformable to it occurs only in experience (as the product of the understanding from materials of the sensibility). In the latter it is shown, that, although our pure concepts of the understanding and our principles are independent of experience, and despite of the apparently greater sphere of their use, still nothing whatever can be thought by them beyond the field of experience, because they can do nothing but merely determine the logical form of the judgment relatively to given intuitions. But as there is no intuition at all beyond the field of the sensibility, these pure concepts, as they cannot possibly be exhibited *in concreto,* are void of all meaning; consequently all these noumena, together with their complex, the intelligible world, are nothing but representation of a problem, of which the object in itself is possible, but the solution, from the nature of our understanding, totally impossible. For our understanding is not a faculty of intuition, but of the connection of given intuitions in experience. Experience must therefore contain all the objects for our concepts; but beyond it no concepts have any significance, as there is no intuition that might offer them a foundation.

§35. The imagination may perhaps be forgiven for occasional vagaries, and for not keeping carefully within the limits of experience, since it gains life and vigor by such flights, and since it is always easier to moderate its boldness, than to stimulate its languor. But the understanding which ought to *think* can never be forgiven for indulging in vagaries; for we depend upon it alone for assistance to set bounds, when necessary, to the vagaries of the imagination.

But the understanding begins its aberrations very innocently and modestly. It first elucidates the elementary cognitions, which inhere in it prior to all experience, but yet must always have their application in experience. It gradually drops these limits, and what is there to prevent it, as it has quite freely derived its principles from itself? And then it proceeds first to newly imagined powers in nature, then to beings outside nature; in short to a world, for whose construction the materials cannot be wanting, because fertile fiction furnishes them abundantly, and though not confirmed, is never refuted, by experience. This is the reason that young thinkers are so partial to metaphysics of the truly dogmatical kind, and often sacrifice to it their time and their talents, which might be otherwise better employed.

But there is no use in trying to moderate these fruitless endeavors of pure reason by all manner of cautions as to the difficulties of solving questions so occult, by complaints of the limits of our reason, and by degrading our assertions into mere conjectures. For if their impossibility is not distinctly shown, and reason's cognition of its own essence does not become a true science, in which the field of its right use is distinguished, so to say, with mathematical certainty from that of its worthless and idle use, these fruitless efforts will never be abandoned for good.

§36. HOW IS NATURE ITSELF POSSIBLE?

This question—the highest point that transcendental philosophy can ever reach, and to which, as its boundary and completion, it must proceed—properly contains two questions.

First: How is nature at all possible in the material sense, by intuition, considered as the totality of appearances; how are space, time, and that which fills both—the object of sensation, in general possible? The answer is: By means of the constitution of our sensibility, according to which it is specifically affected by objects, which are in themselves unknown to it, and totally distinct from those phenomena. This answer is given in the *Critique* itself in the transcendental aesthetic, and in these *Prolegomena* by the solution of the first general problem.

Secondly: How is nature possible in the formal sense, as the totality of the rules, under which all phenomena must come, in order to be thought as connected in experience? The answer must be this: It is only possible by means of the constitution of our understanding, according to which all the above representations of the sensibility are necessarily referred to a consciousness, and by which the peculiar way in which we think (viz., by rules), and hence experience also, are possible, but must be clearly distinguished from an insight into the objects in themselves. This answer is given in the *Critique* itself in the transcendental logic, and in these *Prolegomena,* in the course of the solution of the second main problem.

But how this peculiar property of our sensibility itself is possible, or that of our understanding and of the apperception which is necessarily its basis and that of all thinking, cannot be further analysed or answered, because it is of them that we are in need for all our answers and for all our thinking about objects.

There are many laws of nature, which we can only know by means of experience; but conformity to law in the connection of appearances, i.e., in nature in general, we cannot discover by any experience, because experience itself requires laws which are *a priori* at the basis of its possibility.

The possibility of experience in general is therefore at the same time the universal law of nature, and the principles of the experience are the very laws of nature. For we do not know nature but as the totality of appearances, i.e., of representations in us, and hence we can only derive the laws of its connection from the principles of their connection in us, that is, from the conditions of their necessary union in consciousness, which constitutes the possibility of experience.

Even the main proposition expounded throughout this section—that universal laws of nature can be distinctly cognised *a priori*—leads naturally to the proposition: that the highest legislation of nature must lie in ourselves, i.e., in our understanding, and that we must not seek the universal laws of nature in nature by means of experience, but conversely must seek nature, as to its universal conformity to law, in the conditions of the possibility of experience, which lie in our sensibility and in our understanding. For how were it otherwise possible to know *a priori* these laws, as they are not rules of analytical cognition, but truly synthetical extensions of it?

Such a necessary agreement of the principles of possible experience with the laws of the possibility of nature, can only proceed from one of two reasons: either these laws are drawn from nature by means of experience, or conversely nature is derived from the laws of the possibility of experience in general, and is quite the same as the mere universal conformity to law of the latter. The former is self-contradictory, for the universal laws of nature can and must be cognised *a priori* (that is, independent of all experience), and be the foundation of all empirical use of the understanding; the latter alternative therefore alone remains.

But we must distinguish the empirical laws of nature, which always presuppose particular perceptions, from the pure or universal laws of nature, which, without being based on particular perceptions, contain merely the conditions of their necessary union in experience. In relation to the latter, nature and possible experience are quite the same, and as the conformity to law here depends upon the necessary connection of appearances in experience (without which we cannot cognise any object whatever in the sensible world), consequently upon the original laws of the understanding, it seems at first strange, but is not the less certain, to say:

The understanding does not derive its laws (a priori) from, but prescribes them to, nature.

§37. We shall illustrate this seemingly bold proposition by an example, which will show, that laws, which we discover in objects of sensuous intuition (especially when these laws are cognised as necessary), are commonly held by us to be such as have been placed there by the understanding, in spite of their being similar in all points to the laws of nature, which we ascribe to experience.

§38. If we consider the properties of the circle, by which this figure combines so many arbitrary determinations of space in itself, at once in a universal rule, we cannot avoid attributing a constitution to this geometrical thing. Two right lines, for example, which intersect one another and the circle, howsoever they may be drawn, are always divided so that the rectangle constructed with the segments of the one is equal to that constructed with the segments of the other. The question now is: Does this law lie in the circle or in the understanding, that is, Does this figure, independently of the understanding, contain in itself the ground of the law, or does the understanding, having constructed according to its concepts (according to the quality of the radii) the figure itself, introduce into it this law of the chords cutting one another in geometrical proportion? When we follow the proofs of this law, we soon perceive, that it can only be derived from the condition on which the understanding founds the construction of this figure, and which is that of the equality of the radii. But, if we enlarge this concept, to pursue further the unity of various properties of geometrical figures under common laws, and consider the circle as a conic section, which of course is subject to the same fundamental conditions of construction as other conic sections, we shall find that all the chords which intersect within the ellipse, parabola, and hyperbola, always intersect so that the rectangles of their segments are not indeed equal, but always bear a constant ratio to one another. If we proceed still farther, to the fundamental laws of physical astronomy, we find a physical law of reciprocal attraction diffused over all material nature, the rule of which is: "that it decreases inversely as the square of the distance from each attracting point, i.e., as the spherical surfaces increase, over which this force spreads," which law seems to be necessarily inherent in the very nature of things, and hence is usually propounded as cognisable *a priori.* Simple as the sources of this law are, merely resting upon the relation of spherical surfaces of different radii, its consequences are so valuable with regard to the variety of their agreement and its regularity, that not only are all possible orbits of the celestial bodies conic sections, but such a relation of these orbits to each other results, that no other law of attraction, than that of the inverse square of the distance, can be imagined as fit for a cosmical system.

Here accordingly is a nature that rests upon laws which the understanding cognises *a priori,* and chiefly from the universal principles of the determination of space. Now I ask:

Do the laws of nature lie in space, and does the understanding learn them by merely endeavoring to find out the enormous wealth of meaning that lies in space; or do they inhere in the understanding and in the way in which it determines space according to the conditions of the synthetical unity in which its concepts are all centred?

Space is something so uniform and as to all particular properties so indeterminate, that we should certainly not seek a store of laws of nature in it. Whereas that which determines space to assume the form of a circle or the figures of a cone and a sphere, is the understanding, so far as it contains the ground of the unity of their constructions.

The mere universal form of intuition, called space, must therefore be the substratum of all intuitions determinable to particular objects, and in it of course the condition of the possibility and of the variety of these intuitions lies. But the unity of the objects is entirely determined by the understanding, and on conditions which lie in its own nature; and thus the understanding is the origin of the universal order of nature, in that it comprehends all appearances under its own laws, and thereby first constructs, *a priori,* experience (as to its form), by means of which whatever is to be cognised only by experience, is necessarily subjected to its laws. For we are not now concerned with the nature of things in themselves, which is independent of the conditions both of our sensibility and our understanding, but with nature, as an object of possible experience, and in this case the understanding, while it makes experience possible, thereby insists that the sensuous world is either not an object of experience at all, or must be nature [viz., an existence of things, determined according to universal laws].

Appendix to the Pure Science of Nature

§39. OF THE SYSTEM OF THE CATEGORIES

There can be nothing more desirable to a philosopher, than to be able to derive the scattered multiplicity of the concepts or the principles, which had occurred to him in concrete use, from a principle *a priori,* and to unite everything in this way in one cognition. He formerly only believed that those things, which remained after a certain abstraction, and seemed by comparison among one another to constitute a particular kind of cognitions, were completely collected; but this was only an aggregate. Now he knows, that just so many, neither more nor less, can constitute the mode of cognition, and perceives the necessity of his division, which constitutes comprehension; and now only he has attained a *System.*

To search in our daily cognition for the concepts, which do not rest upon particular experience, and yet occur in all cognition of experience, where they as it were constitute the mere form of connection, presupposes neither great reflection nor deeper insight, than to detect in a language the rules of the actual use of words generally, and thus to collect elements for a grammar. In fact both researches are very nearly related, even though we are not able to give a reason why each language has just this and no other formal constitution, and still less why an exact number of such formal determinations in general are found in it.

Aristotle collected ten pure elementary concepts under the name of categories. To these, which are also called predicaments, he found himself obliged afterwards to add five post-predicaments, some of which however are contained in the former; but this random collection must be considered (and commended) as a mere hint for future inquirers, not as a regularly developed idea, and hence it has, in the present more advanced state of philosophy, been rejected as quite useless.

After long reflection on the pure elements of human knowledge (those which contain nothing empirical), I at last succeeded in distinguishing with certainty and in separating the pure elementary notions of the sensibility (space and time) from those of the understanding. Thus the 7th, 8th, and 9th categories had to be excluded from the old list. And the others were of no service to me; because there was no principle [in them], on which the understanding could be investigated, measured in its completion, and all the functions, whence its pure concepts arise, determined exhaustively and with precision.

But in order to discover such a principle, I looked about for an act of the understanding which comprises all the rest, and is distinguished only by various modifications or phases, in reducing the multiplicity, of representation to the unity of thinking in general: I found this act of the understanding to consist in judging. Here then the labors of the logicians were ready at hand, though not yet quite free from defects, and with this help I was enabled to exhibit a complete table of the pure functions of the understanding, which are however undetermined in regard to any object. I finally referred these functions of judging to objects in general, or rather to the condition of determining judgments as objectively valid, and so there arose the pure concepts of the understanding, concerning which I could make certain, that these, and this exact number only, constitute our whole cognition of things from pure understanding. I was justified in calling them by their old name, *categories,* while I reserved for myself the liberty of adding, under the title of "predicables," a complete list of all the concepts deducible from them, by combinations whether among themselves, or with the pure form of the appearance, i.e., space or time, or with its matter, so far as it is not yet empirically determined (viz., the object of sensation in general), as soon as a system of transcendental philosophy should be completed with the construction of which I am engaged in the *Critique of Pure Reason* itself.

Now the essential point in this system of categories, which distinguishes it from the old rhapsodical collection without any principle, and for which alone it deserves to be considered as philosophy, consists in this: that by means of it the true significance of the pure concepts of the understanding and the condition of their use could be precisely determined. For here it became obvious that they are themselves nothing but logical functions, and as such do not produce the least concept of an object, but require some sensuous intuition as a basis. They therefore only serve to determine empirical judgments, which are otherwise undetermined and indifferent as regards all functions of judging, relatively to these functions, thereby procuring them universal validity, and by means of them making judgments of experience in general possible.

Such an insight into the nature of the categories, which limits them at the same time to the mere use of experience, never occurred either to their first author, or to any of his successors; but without this insight (which immediately depends upon their derivation or deduction), they are quite useless and only a miserable list of names, without explanation or rule for their use. Had the ancients ever conceived such a notion, doubtless the whole study of the pure rational knowledge, which under the name of metaphysics has for centuries spoiled many a sound mind, would have reached us in quite another shape, and would have enlightened the human understanding, instead of actually exhausting it in obscure and vain speculations, thereby rendering it unfit for true science.

This system of categories makes all treatment of every object of pure reason itself systematic, and affords a direction or clue how and through what points of inquiry every metaphysical consideration must proceed, in order to be complete; for it exhausts all the possible movements of the understanding, among which every concept must be classed. In like manner the table of principles has been formulated, the completeness of which we can only vouch for by the system of the categories. Even in the division of the concepts, which must go beyond the physical application of the understanding, it is always the very same clue, which, as it must always be determined *a priori* by the same fixed points of the human understanding, always forms a closed circle. There is no doubt that the object of a pure conception either of the understanding or of reason, so far as it is to be estimated philosophically and on *a priori* principles, can in this way be completely cognised. I could not therefore omit to make use of this clue with regard to one of the most abstract ontological divisions, viz., the various distinctions of "the notions of something and of nothing," and to construct accordingly a regular and necessary table of their divisions.

And this system, like every other true one founded on a universal principle, shows its inestimable value in this, that it excludes all foreign concepts, which might otherwise intrude among the pure concepts of the understanding, and determines the place of every cognition. Those concepts, which under the name of "concepts of reflection" have been likewise arranged in a table according to the clue of the categories, intrude, without having any privilege or title to be among the pure concepts of the understanding in Ontology. They are concepts of connection, and thereby of the objects themselves, whereas the former are only concepts of a mere comparison of concepts already given, hence of quite another nature and use. By my systematic division they are saved from this confusion. But the value of my special table of the categories will be still more obvious, when we separate the table of the transcendental concepts of Reason from the concepts of the understanding. The latter being of quite another nature and origin, they must have quite another form than the former. This so necessary separation has never yet been made in any system of metaphysics for, as a rule, these rational concepts all mixed up with the categories, like children of one family, which confusion was unavoidable in the absence of a definite system of categories.

THIRD PART OF THE MAIN TRANSCENDENTAL PROBLEM
How Is Metaphysics in General Possible?

§40. Pure mathematics and pure science of nature had no occasion for such a deduction, as we have made of both, for their own safety and certainty. For the former rests upon its own evidence; and the latter (though sprung from pure sources of the understanding) upon experience and its thorough confirmation. Physics cannot altogether refuse and dispense with the testimony of the latter; because with all its certainty, it can never, as philosophy, rival mathematics. Both sciences therefore stood in need of this inquiry, not for themselves, but for the sake of another science, metaphysics.

Metaphysics has to do not only with concepts of nature, which always find their application in experience, but also with pure rational concepts, which never can be given in any possible experience. Consequently the objective reality of these concepts (viz., that they are not mere chimeras), and the truth or falsity of metaphysical assertions, cannot be discovered or confirmed by any experience. This part of metaphysics however is precisely what constitutes its essential end, to which the rest is only a means, and thus this science is in need of such a deduction for its own sake. The third question now proposed relates therefore as it were to the root and essential difference of metaphysics, i.e., the occupation of reason with itself, and the supposed knowledge of objects arising immediately from this incubation of its own concepts, without requiring, or indeed being able to reach that knowledge through, experience.

Without solving this problem reason never is justified. The empirical use to which reason limits the pure understanding, does not fully satisfy the proper destination of the latter. Every single experience is only a part of the whole sphere of its domain, but the absolute totality of all possible experience is itself not experience. Yet it is a necessary [concrete] problem for reason, the mere representation of which requires concepts quite different from the categories, whose use is only immanent, or refers to experience, so far as it can be given. Whereas the concepts of reason aim at the completeness, i.e., the collective unity of all possible experience, and thereby transcend every given experience. Thus they become *transcendent.*

As the understanding stands in need of categories for experience, reason contains in itself the source of ideas, by which I mean necessary concepts, whose object cannot be given in any experience. The latter are inherent in the nature of reason, as the former are in that of the understanding. While the former carry with them an illusion likely to mislead, the illusion of the latter is inevitable, though it certainly can be kept from misleading us.

Since all illusion consists in holding the subjective ground of our judgments to be objective, a self-knowledge of pure reason in its transcendent (exaggerated) use is the sole preservative from the aberrations into which reason falls when it mistakes its destination, and refers that to the object transcendently, which only regards its own subject and its guidance in all immanent use.

§41. The distinction of ideas, that is, of pure concepts of reason, from categories, or pure concepts of the understanding, as cognitions of a quite distinct species, origin and use, is so important a point in founding a science that is to contain the system of all these *a priori* cognitions, that without this distinction metaphysics is absolutely impossible, or is at best a random, bungling attempt to build a castle in the air without a knowledge of the materials or of their fitness for any purpose. Had the *Critique of Pure Reason* done nothing but first point out this distinction, it had thereby contributed more to clear up our conception of, and to guide our inquiry in, the field of metaphysics, than all the vain efforts which have

hitherto been made to satisfy the transcendent problems of pure reason, without ever sur-
mising that we were in quite another field than that of the understanding, and hence class-
ing concepts of the understanding and those of reason together, as if they were of the
same kind.

§42. All pure cognitions of the understanding have this feature, that their concepts
present themselves in experience, and their principles can be confirmed by it; whereas the
transcendent cognitions of reason cannot, either as ideas, appear in experience, or as propositions ever be confirmed or refuted by it. Hence whatever errors may slip in unawares, can
only be discovered by pure reason itself—a discovery of much difficulty, because this very
reason naturally becomes dialectical by means of its ideas, and this unavoidable illusion
cannot be limited by any objective and dogmatical researches into things, but by a subjective investigation of reason itself as a source of ideas.

§43. In the *Critique of Pure Reason* it was always my greatest care to endeavor not only
carefully to distinguish the several species of cognition, but to derive concepts belonging to
each one of them from their common source. I did this in order that by knowing whence
they originated, I might determine their use with safety, and also have the unanticipated
but invaluable advantage of knowing the completeness of my enumeration, classification
and specification of concepts *a priori,* and therefore according to principles. Without this,
metaphysics is mere rhapsody, in which no one knows whether he has enough, or whether
and where something is still wanting. We can indeed have this advantage only in pure
philosophy, but of this philosophy it constitutes the very essence.

As I had found the origin of the categories in the four logical functions of all the judgments of the understanding, it was quite natural to seek the origin of the ideas in the three
functions of the syllogisms of reason. For as soon as these pure concepts of reason (the
transcendental ideas) are given, they could hardly, except they be held innate, be found
anywhere else, than in the same activity of reason, which, so far as it regards mere form,
constitutes the logical element of the syllogisms of reason; but, so far as it represents judgments of the understanding with respect to the one or to the other form *a priori,* constitutes
transcendental concepts of pure reason.

The formal distinction of syllogisms renders their division into categorical, hypothetical,
and disjunctive necessary. The concepts of reason founded on them contained therefore,
first, the idea of the complete subject (the substantial); secondly, the idea of the complete
series of conditions; thirdly, the determination of all concepts in the idea of a complete
complex of that which is possible. The first idea is psychological, the second cosmological,
the third theological, and, as all three give occasion to dialectics, yet each in its own way,
the division of the whole dialects of pure reason into its paralogism, its antinomy, and its
ideal, was arranged accordingly. Through this deduction we may feel assured that all the
claims of pure reason are completely represented, and that none can be wanting; because
the faculty of reason itself, whence they all take their origin, is thereby completely surveyed.

§44. In these general considerations it is also remarkable that the ideas of reason are
unlike the categories, of no service to the use of our understanding in experience, but quite
dispensable, and become even an impediment to the maxims of a rational cognition of
nature. Yet in another aspect still to be determined they are necessary. Whether the soul is
or is not a simple substance, is of no consequence to us in the explanation of its phenomena.
For we cannot render the notion of a simple being intelligible by any possible experience
that is sensuous or concrete. The notion is therefore quite void as regards all hoped-for
insight into the cause of phenomena, and cannot at all serve as a principle of the explanation
of that which internal or external experience supplies. So the cosmological ideas of the

beginning of the world or of its eternity cannot be of any greater service to us for the explanation of any event in the world itself. And finally we must, according to a right maxim of the philosophy of nature, refrain from all explanations of the design of nature, drawn from the will of a supreme being; because this would not be natural philosophy, but an acknowledgment that we have come to the end of it. The use of these ideas, therefore, is quite different from that of those categories by which (and by the principles built upon which) experience itself first becomes possible. But our laborious analytics of the understanding would be superfluous if we had nothing else in view than the mere cognition of nature as it can be given in experience; for reason does its work, both in mathematics and in the science of nature, quite safely and well without any of this subtle deduction. Therefore our critique of the understanding combines with the ideas of pure reason for a purpose which lies beyond the empirical use of the understanding; but this we have above declared to be in this aspect totally inadmissible, and without any object or meaning. Yet there must be a harmony between that of the nature of reason and that of the understanding, and the former must contribute to the perfection of the latter, and cannot possibly upset it.

The solution of this question is as follows: Pure reason does not in its ideas point to particular objects, which lie beyond the field of experience, but only requires completeness of the use of the understanding in the system of experience. But this completeness can be a completeness of principles only, not of intuitions (i.e., concrete atsights) and of objects. In order however to represent the ideas definitely, reason conceives them after the fashion of the cognition of an object. The cognition is as far as these rules are concerned completely determined, but the object is only an idea invented for the purpose of bringing the cognition of the understanding as near as possible to the completeness represented by that idea.

PREFATORY REMARK TO THE DIALECTICS OF PURE REASON

§45. We have above shown in §§33 and 34 that the purity of the categories from all admixture of sensuous determinations may mislead reason into extending their use, quite beyond all experience, to things in themselves; though as these categories themselves find no intuition which can give them meaning or sense *in concreto,* they, as mere logical functions, can represent a thing in general, but not give by themselves alone a determinate concept of anything. Such hyperbolical objects are distinguished by the appellation of *noumena,* or pure beings of the understanding (or better, beings of thought), such as, for example, "substance," but conceived without permanence in time, or "cause," but not acting in time, etc. Here predicates, that only serve to make the conformity-to-law of experience possible, are applied to these concepts, and yet they are deprived of all the conditions of intuition, on which alone experience is possible, and so these concepts lose all significance.

There is no danger, however, of the understanding spontaneously making an excursion so very wantonly beyond its own bounds into the field of the mere creatures of thought, without being impelled by foreign laws. But when reason, which cannot be fully satisfied with any empirical use of the rules of the understanding, as being always conditioned, requires a completion of this chain of conditions, then the understanding is forced out of its sphere. And then it partly represents objects of experience in a series so extended that no experience can grasp, partly even (with a view to complete the series) it seeks entirely beyond it noumena, to which it can attach that chain, and so, having at last escaped from the conditions of experience, make its attitude as it were final. These are then the transcendental ideas, which, though according to the true but hidden ends of the natural determination of our reason, they may aim not at extravagant concepts, but at an unbounded extension of their empirical use, yet seduce the understanding by an unavoidable illusion to a transcendent use, which, though deceitful, cannot be restrained within the bounds of experience by any resolution, but only by scientific instruction and with much difficulty.

I. THE PSYCHOLOGICAL IDEA

§46. People have long since observed, that in all substances the proper subject, that which remains after all the accidents (as predicates) are abstracted, consequently that which forms the substance of things remains unknown, and various complaints have been made concerning these limits to our knowledge. But it will be well to consider that the human understanding is not to be blamed for its inability to know the substance of things, that is, to determine it by itself, but rather for requiring to cognise it which is a mere idea definitely as though it were a given object. Pure reason requires us to seek for every predicate of a thing its proper subject, and for this subject, which is itself necessarily nothing but a predicate, its subject, and so on indefinitely (or as far as we can reach). But hence it follows, that we must not hold anything, at which we can arrive, to be an ultimate subject, and that substance itself never can be thought by our understanding, however deep we may penetrate, even if all nature were unveiled to us. For the specific nature of our understanding consists in thinking everything discursively, that is, representing it by concepts, and so by mere predicates, to which therefore the absolute subject must always be wanting. Hence all the real properties, by which we cognise bodies, are mere accidents, not excepting impenetrability, which we can only represent to ourselves as the effect of a power of which the subject is unknown to us.

Now we appear to have this substance in the consciousness of ourselves (in the thinking subject), and indeed in an immediate intuition; for all the predicates of an internal sense refer to the *ego,* as a subject, and I cannot conceive myself as the predicate of any other subject. Hence completeness in the reference of the given concepts as predicates to a subject—not merely an idea, but an object—that is, the absolute subject itself, seems to be given in experience. But this expectation is disappointed. For the ego is not a concept, but only the indication of the object of the internal sense, so far as we cognise it by no further predicate. Consequently it cannot be in itself a predicate of any other thing; but just as little can it be a determinate concept of an absolute subject, but is, as in all other cases, only the reference of the internal phenomena to their unknown subject. Yet this idea (which serves very well, as a regulative principle, totally to destroy all materialistic explanations of the internal phenomena of the soul) occasions by a very natural misunderstanding a very specious argument, which, from this supposed cognition of the substance of our thinking being, infers its nature, so far as the knowledge of it falls quite without the complex of experience.

§47. But though we may call this thinking self (the soul) substance, as being the ultimate subject of thinking which cannot be further represented as the predicate of another thing; it remains quite empty and without significance, if permanence—the quality which renders the concept of substances in experience fruitful—cannot be proved of it.

But permanence can never be proved of the concept of a substance, as a thing in itself, but for the purposes of experience only. This is sufficiently shown by the first analogy of experience, and whoever will not yield to this proof may try for himself whether he can succeed in proving, from the concept of a subject which does not exist itself as the predicate of another thing, that its existence is thoroughly permanent, and that it cannot either in itself or by any natural cause originate or be annihilated. These synthetical *a priori* propositions can never be proved in themselves, but only in reference to things as objects of possible experience.

§48. If therefore from the concept of the soul as a substance, we would infer its permanence, this can hold good as regards possible experience only, not [of the soul] as a thing in itself and beyond all possible experience. But life is the subjective condition of all our possible experience, consequently we can only infer the permanence of the soul in life; for the death of man is the end of all experience which concerns the soul as an object of experience, except the contrary be proved, which is the very question in hand. The permanence of the soul can therefore only be proved (and no one cares for that) during the life of man, but not, as we desire to do, after death; and for this general reason, that the concept of substance, so far as it is to be considered necessarily combined with the concept of permanence, can be so combined only according to the principles of possible experience, and therefore for the purposes of experience only.

§49. That there is something real without us which not only corresponds, but must correspond, to our external perceptions, can likewise be proved to be not a connection of things in themselves, but for the sake of experience. This means that there is something empirical, i.e., some phenomenon in space without us, that admits of a satisfactory proof, for we have nothing to do with other objects than those which belong to possible experience; because objects which cannot be given us in any experience, do not exist for us. Empirically without me is that which appears in space, and space, together with all the phenomena which it contains, belongs to the representations, whose connection according to laws of experience proves their objective truth, just as the connection of the phenomena of the internal sense proves the actuality of my soul (as an object of the internal sense). By means of external experience I am conscious of the actuality of bodies, as external phenomena in space, in the same manner as by means of the internal experience I am conscious of the existence of my soul in time, but this soul is only cognised as an object of the internal sense by phenomena that constitute an internal state, and of which the essence in itself, which forms the basis of these phenomena, is unknown. Cartesian idealism therefore does nothing but distinguish external experience from dreaming; and the conformity to law (as a criterion of its truth) of the former, from the irregularity and the false illusion of the latter. In both it presupposes space and time as conditions of the existence of objects, and it only inquires whether the objects of the external senses, which we when awake put in space, are as actually to be found in it, as the object of the internal sense, the soul, is in time; that is, whether experience carries with it sure criteria to distinguish it from imagination. This doubt, however, may easily be disposed of, and we always do so in common life by investigating the connection of phenomena in both space and time according to universal laws of experience, and we cannot doubt, when the representation of external things throughout agrees therewith, that they constitute truthful experience. Material idealism, in which phenomena are considered as such only according to their connection in experience, may accordingly be very easily refuted; and it is just as sure an experience, that bodies exist without us (in space), as that I myself exist according to the representation of the internal sense (in time): for the notion without us, only signifies existence in space. However as the ego in the proposition "I am," means not only the object of internal intuition (in time), but the subject of consciousness, just as body means not only external intuition (in space), but the thing-in-itself, which is the basis of this phenomenon; [as this is the case] the question, whether bodies (as phenomena of the external sense) exist as bodies apart from my thoughts, may without any hesitation be denied in nature. But the question, whether I myself as a phenomenon of the internal sense (the soul according to empirical psychology) exist apart from my faculty of representation in time, is an exactly similar inquiry, and must likewise be answered in the negative. And in this manner everything, when it is reduced to its true meaning, is decided and certain. The formal (which I have also called transcendental) actually abolishes the material, or Cartesian, idealism. For if space be nothing but a form of my sensibility, it is as a representation in me just as actual as I myself am, and nothing but the empirical truth of the representations in it remains for consideration. But, if this is not the case, if space and the phenomena in it are something existing without us, then all the criteria of experience beyond our perception can never prove the actuality of these objects without us.

II. THE COSMOLOGICAL IDEA

§50. This product of pure reason in its transcendent use is its most remarkable curiosity. It serves as a very powerful agent to rouse philosophy from its dogmatic slumber, and to stimulate it to the arduous task of undertaking a *Critique of Pure Reason* itself.

I term this idea cosmological, because it always takes its object only from the sensible world, and does not use any other than those whose object is given to sense, consequently it remains in this respect in its native home, it does not become transcendent, and is therefore so far not mere idea; whereas, to conceive the soul as a simple substance, already means to conceive such an object (the simple) as cannot be presented to the senses. Yet the cosmological idea extends the connection of the conditioned with its condition (whether the connection is mathematical or dynamical) so far, that experience never can keep up with it. It is therefore with regard to this point always an idea, whose object never can be adequately given in any experience.

§51. In the first place, the use of a system of categories becomes here so obvious and unmistakable, that even if there were not several other proofs of it, this alone would sufficiently prove it indispensable in the system of pure reason. There are only four such transcendent ideas, as there are so many classes of categories; in each of which, however, they refer only to the absolute completeness of the series of the conditions for a given conditioned. In analogy to these cosmological ideas there are only four kinds of dialectical assertions of pure reason, which, as they are dialectical, thereby prove, that to each of them, on equally specious principles of pure reason, a contradictory assertion stands opposed. As all the metaphysical art of the most subtle distinction cannot prevent this opposition, it compels the philosopher to recur to the first sources of pure reason itself. This antinomy, not arbitrarily invented, but founded in the nature of human reason, and hence unavoidable and never ceasing, contains the following four theses together with their antitheses:

1. *Thesis:* The world has, as to time and space, a beginning (limit).
   Antithesis: The world is, as to time and space, infinite.

2. *Thesis:* Everything in the world consists of [elements that are] simple.
   Antithesis: There is nothing simple, but everything is composite.

3. *Thesis:* There are in the world causes through freedom.
   Antithesis: There is no liberty, but all is nature.

4. *Thesis:* In the series of the world-causes there is some necessary being.
   Antithesis: There is nothing necessary in the world, but in this series all is incidental.

§52. *a.* Here is the most singular phenomenon of human reason, no other instance of which can be shown in any other use. If we, as is commonly done, represent to ourselves the appearances of the sensible world as things in themselves, if we assume the principles of their combination as principles universally valid of things in themselves and not merely of experience, as is usually, nay without our *Critique,* unavoidably done, there arises an unexpected conflict, which never can be removed in the common dogmatical way; because the thesis, as well as the antithesis, can be shown by equally clear, evident, and irresistible proofs—for I pledge myself as to the correctness of all these proofs—and reason therefore perceives that it is divided with itself, a state at which the sceptic rejoices, but which must make the critical philosopher pause and feel ill at ease.

§52. *b.* We may blunder in various ways in metaphysics without any fear of being detected in falsehood. For we never can be refuted by experience if we but avoid self-contradiction, which in synthetical, though purely fictitious propositions, may be done whenever the concepts, which we connect, are mere ideas, that cannot be given (in their whole content) in experience. For how can we make out by experience, whether the world is from eternity or had a beginning, whether matter is infinitely divisible or consists of simple parts? Such concept cannot be given in any experience, be it ever so extensive, and consequently the falsehood either of the positive or the negative proposition cannot be discovered by this touch-stone.

The only possible way in which reason could have revealed unintentionally its secret dialectics, falsely announced as dogmatics, would be when it were made to ground an assertion upon a universally admitted principle, and to deduce the exact contrary with the greatest accuracy of inference from another which is equally granted. This is actually here the case with regard to four natural ideas of reason, whence four assertions on the one side, and as many counter-assertions on the other arise, each consistently following from universally acknowledged principles. Thus they reveal by the use of these principles the dialectical illusion of pure reason which would otherwise forever remain concealed.

This is therefore a decisive experiment, which must necessarily expose any error lying hidden in the assumptions of reason. Contradictory propositions cannot both be false, except the concept, which is the subject of both, is self-contradictory; for example, the propositions, "a square circle is round, and a square circle is not round," are both false. For, as to the former it is false, that the circle is round, because it is quadrangular; and it is likewise false, that it is not round, that is, angular, because it is a circle. For the logical criterion of the impossibility of a concept consists in this, that if we presuppose it, two contradictory propositions both become false; consequently, as no middle between them is conceivable, nothing at all is thought by that concept.

§52. *c.* The first two antinomies, which I call mathematical, because they are concerned with the addition or division of the homogeneous, are founded on such a self-contradictory concept; and hence I explain how it happens, that both the thesis and antithesis of the two are false.

When I speak of objects in time and in space, it is not of things in themselves, of which I know nothing, but of things in appearance, that is, of experience, as the particular way of cognising objects which is afforded to man. I must not say of what I think in time or in space, that in itself, and independent of these my thoughts, it exists in space and in time; for in that case I should contradict myself; because space and time, together with the appearances in them, are nothing existing in themselves and outside of my representations, but are themselves only modes of representation, and it is palpably contradictory to say, that a mere mode of representation exists without our representation. Objects of the senses therefore exist only in experience; whereas to give them a self-subsisting existence apart from experience or before it, is merely to represent to ourselves that experience actually exists apart from experience or before it.

Now if I inquire after the quantity of the world, as to space and time, it is equally impossible, as regards all my notions, to declare it infinite or to declare it finite. For neither assertion can be contained in experience, because experience either of an infinite space, or of an infinite time elapsed, or again, of the boundary of the world by a void space, or by an antecedent void time, is impossible; these are mere ideas. This quantity of the world, which is determined in either way, should therefore exist in the world itself apart from all experience. This contradicts the notion of a world of sense, which is merely a complex of the appearances whose existence and connection occur only in our representations, that is, in experience, since this latter is not an object in itself, but a mere mode of representation. Hence it follows, that as the concept of an absolutely existing world of sense is self-contradictory, the solution of the problem concerning its quantity, whether attempted affirmatively or negatively, is always false.

The same holds good of the second antinomy, which relates to the division of phenomena. For these are mere representations, and the parts exist merely in their representation, consequently in the division, or in a possible experience where they are given, and the division reaches only as far as this latter reaches. To assume that an appearance, e.g., that of body, contains in itself before all experience all the parts, which any possible experience can ever reach, is to impute to a mere appearance, which can exist only in experience, an existence previous to experience. In other words, it would mean that mere representations exist before they can be found in our faculty of representation. Such an assertion is self-contradictory, as also every solution of our misunderstood problem, whether we maintain, that bodies in themselves consist of an infinite number of parts, or of a finite number of simple parts.

§53. In the first (the mathematical) class of antinomies the falsehood of the assumption consists in representing in one concept something self-contradictory as if it were compatible (i.e., an appearance as an object in itself). But, as to the second (the dynamical) class of antinomies, the falsehood of the representation consists in representing as contradictory what is compatible; so that, as in the former case, the opposed assertions are both false, in this case, on the other hand, where they are opposed to one another by mere misunderstanding, they may both be true.

Any mathematical connection necessarily presupposes homogeneity of what is connected (in the concept of magnitude), while the dynamical one by no means requires the same. When we have to deal with extended magnitudes, all the parts must be homogeneous with one another and with the whole; whereas, in the connection of cause and effect, homogeneity may indeed likewise be found, but is not necessary; for the concept of causality (by means of which something is posited through something else quite different from it), at all events, does not require it.

If the objects of the world of sense are taken for things in themselves, and the above laws of nature for the laws of things in themselves, the contradiction would be unavoidable. So also, if the subject of freedom were, like other objects, represented as mere appearance, the contradiction would be just as unavoidable, for the same predicate would at once be affirmed and denied of the same kind of object in the same sense. But if natural necessity is referred merely to appearances, and freedom merely to things in themselves, no contradiction arises, if we at once assume, or admit both kinds of causality, however difficult or impossible it may be to make the latter kind conceivable.

As appearance every effect is an event, or something that happens in time; it must, according to the universal law of nature, be preceded by a determination of the causality of its cause (a state), which follows according to a constant law. But this determination of the cause as causality must likewise be something that takes place or happens; the cause must have begun to act, otherwise no succession between it and the effect could be conceived. Otherwise the effect, as well as the causality of the cause, would have always existed. Therefore the determination of the cause to act must also have originated among appearances, and must consequently, as well as its effect, be an event, which must again have its cause, and so on; hence natural necessity must be the condition, on which effective causes are determined. Whereas if freedom is to be a property of certain causes of appearances, it must, as regards these, which are events, be a faculty of starting them spontaneously, that is, without the causality of the cause itself, and hence without requiring any other ground to determine its start. But then the cause, as to its causality, must not rank under time-determinations of its state, that is, it cannot be an appearance, and must be considered a thing in itself, while its effects would be only appearances. If without contradiction we can think of the beings of understanding as exercising such an influence on appearances, then natural necessity will attach to all connections of cause and effect in the sensuous world, though on the other hand, freedom can be granted to such cause, as is itself not an appearance (but the foundation of appearance). Nature therefore and freedom can without contradiction be attributed to the very same thing, but in different relations—on one side as a phenomenon, on the other as a thing in itself.

We have in us a faculty, which not only stands in connection with its subjective determining grounds that are the natural causes of its actions, and is so far the faculty of a being that itself belongs to appearances, but is also referred to objective grounds, that are only ideas, so far as they can determine this faculty, a connection which is expressed by the word *ought*. This faculty is called *reason,* and, so far as we consider a being (man) entirely according to this objectively determinable reason, he cannot be considered as a being of sense, but this property is that of a thing in itself, of which we cannot comprehend the possibility—I mean how the *ought* (which however has never yet taken place) should determine its activity, and can become the cause of actions, whose effect is an appearance in the sensible world. Yet the causality of reason would be freedom with regard to the effects in the sensuous world, so far as we can consider objective grounds, which are themselves ideas, as their determinants. For its action in that case would not depend upon subjective conditions, consequently not upon those of time, and of course not upon the law of nature, which serves to determine them, because grounds of reason give to actions the rule universally, according to principles, without the influence of the circumstances of either time or place.

What I adduce here is merely meant as an example to make the thing intelligible, and does not necessarily belong to our problem, which must be decided from mere concepts, independently of the properties which we meet in the actual world.

Now I may say without contradiction: that all the actions of rational beings, so far as they are appearances (occurring in any experience), are subject to the necessity of nature; but the same actions, as regards merely the rational subject and its faculty of acting according to mere reason, are free. For what is required for the necessity of nature? Nothing more than the determinability of every event in the world of sense according to constant laws, that is, a reference to cause in the appearance; in this process the thing in itself at its foundation and its causality remain unknown. But I say, that the law of nature remains, whether the rational being is the cause of the effects in the sensuous world from reason, that is, through freedom, or whether it does not determine them on grounds of reason. For, if the former is the case, the action is performed according to maxims, the effect of which as appearance is always conformable to constant laws; if the latter is the case, and the action not performed on principles of reason, it is subjected to the empirical laws of the sensibility, and in both cases the effects are connected according to constant laws; more than this we do not require or know concerning natural necessity. But in the former case reason is the cause of these laws of nature, and therefore free; in the latter the effects follow according to mere natural laws of sensibility, because reason does not influence it; but reason itself is not determined on that account by the sensibility, and is therefore free in this case too. Freedom is therefore no hindrance to natural law in appearance, neither does this law abrogate the freedom of the practical use of reason, which is connected with things in themselves, as determining grounds.

Thus practical freedom, viz., the freedom in which reason possesses causality according to objectively determining grounds, is rescued and yet natural necessity is not in the least curtailed with regard to the very same effects, as appearances. The same remarks will serve to explain what we had to say concerning transcendental freedom and its compatibility with natural necessity (in the same subject, but not taken in the same reference). For, as to this, every beginning of the action of a being from objective causes regarded as determining grounds, is always a first start, though the same action is in the series of appearances only a subordinate start, which must be preceded by a state of the cause, which determines it, and is itself determined in the same manner by another immediately preceding. Thus we are able, in rational beings, or in beings generally, so far as their causality is determined in them as things in themselves, to imagine a faculty of beginning from itself a series of states, without falling into contradiction with the laws of nature. For the relation of the action to objective grounds of reason is not a time-relation; in this case that which determines the causality does not precede in time the action, because such determining grounds represent not a reference to objects of sense, e.g., to causes in the appearances, but to determining causes, as things in themselves, which do not rank under conditions of time. And in this way the action, with regard to the causality of reason, can be considered as a first start in respect to the series of appearances, and yet also as a merely subordinate beginning. We may therefore without contradiction consider it in the former aspect as free, but in the latter (in so far as it is merely appearance) as subject to natural necessity.

As to the fourth antinomy, it is solved in the same way as the conflict of reason with itself in the third. For, provided the cause *in* the appearance is distinguished from the cause *of* the appearance (so far as it can be thought as a thing in itself), both propositions are perfectly reconcilable: the one, that there is nowhere in the sensuous world a cause (according to similar laws of causality), whose existence is absolutely necessary; the other, that this world is nevertheless connected with a necessary being as its cause (but of another kind and according to another law). The incompatibility of these propositions entirely rests upon the mistake of extending what is valid merely of appearances to things in themselves, and in general confusing both in one concept.

§54. This then is the proposition and this the solution of the whole antinomy, in which reason finds itself involved in the application of its principles to the sensible world. The former alone (the mere proposition) would be a considerable service in the cause of our knowledge of human reason, even though the solution might fail to fully satisfy the reader, who has here to combat a natural illusion, which has been but recently exposed to him, and which he had hitherto always regarded as genuine. For one result at least is unavoidable. As it is quite impossible to prevent this conflict of reason with itself—so long as the objects of the sensible world are taken for things in themselves, and not for mere appearances, which they are in fact—the reader is thereby compelled to examine over again the deduction of all our *a priori* cognition and the proof which I have given of my deduction in order to come to a decision on the question. This is all I require at present; for when in this occupation he shall have thought himself deep enough into the nature of pure reason, those concepts by which alone the solution of the conflict of reason is possible, will become sufficiently familiar to him. Without this preparation I cannot expect an unreserved assent even from the most attentive reader.

III. THE THEOLOGICAL IDEA

§55. The third transcendental idea, which affords matter for the most important, but, if pursued only speculatively, transcendent and thereby dialectical use of reason, is the ideal of pure reason. Reason in this case does not, as with the psychological and the cosmological ideas, begin from experience, and err by exaggerating its grounds, in striving to attain, if possible, the absolute completeness of their series. It rather totally breaks with experience, and from mere concepts of what constitutes the absolute completeness of a thing in general, consequently by means of the idea of a most perfect primal being, it proceeds to determine the possibility and therefore the actuality of all other things. And so the mere presupposition of a being, who is conceived not in the series of experience, yet for the purposes of experience—for the sake of comprehending its connection, order, and unity—i.e., the idea [the notion of it], is more easily distinguished from the concept of the understanding here, than in the former cases. Hence we can easily expose the dialectical illusion which arises from our making the subjective conditions of our thinking objective conditions of objects themselves, and an hypothesis necessary for the satisfaction of our reason, a dogma. As the observations of the *Critique* on the pretensions of transcendental theology are intelligible, clear, and decisive, I have nothing more to add on the subject.

GENERAL REMARK ON THE TRANSCENDENTAL IDEAS

§56. The objects, which are given us by experience, are in many respects incomprehensible, and many questions, to which the law of nature leads us, when carried beyond a certain point (though quite conformably to the laws of nature), admit of no answer; as for example the question: why substances attract one another? But if we entirely quit nature, or in pursuing its combinations, exceed all possible experience, and so enter the realm of mere ideas, we cannot then say that the object is incomprehensible, and that the nature of things proposes to us insoluble problems. For we are not then concerned with nature or in general with given objects, but with concepts, which have their origin merely in our reason, and with mere creations of thought; and all the problems that arise from our notions of them must be solved, because of course reason can and must give a full account of its own procedure. As the psychological, cosmological, and theological ideas are nothing but pure concepts of reason, which cannot be given in any experience, the questions which reason asks us about them are put to us not by the objects, but by mere maxims of our reason for the sake of its own satisfaction. They must all be capable of satisfactory answers, which is done by showing that they are principles which bring our use of the understanding into thorough agreement, completeness, and synthetical unity, and that they so far hold good of experience only, but of experience as a whole.

Although an absolute whole of experience is impossible, the idea of a whole of cognition according to principles must impart to our knowledge a peculiar kind of unity, that of a system, without which it is nothing but piecework, and cannot be used for proving the existence of a highest purpose (which can only be the general system of all purposes), I do not here refer only to the practical, but also to the highest purpose of the speculative use of reason.

The transcendental ideas therefore express the peculiar application of reason as a principle of systematic unity in the use of the understanding. Yet if we assume this unity of the mode of cognition to be attached to the object of cognition, if we regard that which is merely regulative to be constitutive, and if we persuade ourselves that we can by means of these ideas enlarge our cognition transcendently, or far beyond all possible experience, while it only serves to render experience within itself as nearly complete as possible, i.e., to limit its progress by nothing that cannot belong to experience: we suffer from a mere misunderstanding in our estimate of the proper application of our reason and of its principles, and from a dialectic, which both confuses the empirical use of reason, and also sets reason at variance with itself.

Conclusion

ON THE DETERMINATION OF THE BOUNDS OF PURE REASON

§57. Having adduced the clearest arguments, it would be absurd for us to hope that we can know more of any object, than belongs to the possible experience of it, or lay claim to the least atom of knowledge about anything not assumed to be an object of possible experience, which would determine it according to the constitution it has in itself. For how could we determine anything in this way, since time, space, and the categories, and still more all the concepts formed by empirical experience or perception in the sensible world, have and can have no other use, than to make experience possible. And if this condition is omitted from the pure concepts of the understanding, they do not determine any object, and have no meaning whatever.

But it would be on the other hand a still greater absurdity if we conceded no things in themselves, or set up our experience for the only possible mode of knowing things, our way of beholding them in space and in time for the only possible way, and our discursive understanding for the archetype of every possible understanding; in fact if we wished to have the principles of the possibility of experience considered universal conditions of things in themselves.

Our principles, which limit the use of reason to possible experience, might in this way become transcendent, and the limits of our reason be set up as limits of the possibility of things in themselves (as Hume's dialogues may illustrate), if a careful critique did not guard the bounds of our reason with respect to its empirical use, and set a limit to its pretensions. Scepticism originally arose from metaphysics and its licentious dialectics. At first it might, merely to favor the empirical use of reason, announce everything that transcends this use as worthless and deceitful; but by and by, when it was perceived that the very same principles that are used in experience, insensibly, and apparently with the same right, led still further than experience extends, then men began to doubt even the propositions of experience. But here there is no danger; for common sense will doubtless always assert its rights. A certain confusion, however, arose in science which cannot determine how far reason is to be trusted, and why only so far and no further, and this confusion can only be cleared up and all future relapses obviated by a formal determination, on principle, of the boundary of the use of our reason.

We cannot indeed, beyond all possible experience, form a definite notion of what things in themselves may be. Yet we are not at liberty to abstain entirely from inquiring into them;

for experience never satisfies reason fully, but in answering questions, refers us further and further back, and leaves us dissatisfied with regard to their complete solution. This any one may gather from the dialectics of pure reason, which therefore has its good subjective grounds. Having acquired, as regards the nature of our soul, a clear conception of the subject, and having come to the conviction, that its manifestations cannot be explained materialistically, who can refrain from asking what the soul really is, and, if no concept of experience suffices for the purpose, from accounting for it by a concept of reason (that of a simple immaterial being), though we cannot by any means prove its objective reality? Who can satisfy himself with mere empirical knowledge in all the cosmological questions of the duration and of the quantity of the world, of freedom or of natural necessity, since every answer given on principles of experience begets a fresh question, which likewise requires its answer and thereby clearly shows the insufficiency of all physical modes of explanation to satisfy reason? Finally, who does not see in the thorough-going contingency and dependence of all his thoughts and assumptions on mere principles of experience, the impossibility of stopping there? And who does not feel himself compelled, notwithstanding all interdictions against losing himself in transcendent ideas, to seek rest and contentment beyond all the concepts which he can vindicate by experience, in the concept of a being, the possibility of which we cannot conceive, but at the same time cannot be refuted, because it relates to a mere being of the understanding, and without it reason must needs remain forever dissatisfied?

Bounds (in extended beings) always presuppose a space existing outside a certain definite place, and enclosing it; limits do not require this, but are mere negations, which affect a quantity, so far as it is not absolutely complete. But our reason, as it were, sees in its surroundings a space for the cognition of things in themselves, though we can never have definite notions of them, and are limited to appearances only.

As long as the cognition of reason is homogeneous, definite bounds to it are inconceivable. In mathematics and in natural philosophy human reason admits of limits, but not of bounds, viz., that something indeed lies without it, at which it can never arrive, but not that it will at any point find completion in its internal progress. The enlarging of our views in mathematics, and the possibility of new discoveries, are infinite; and the same is the case with the discovery of new properties of nature, of new powers and laws, by continued experience and its rational combination. But limits cannot be mistaken here, for mathematics refers to appearances only, and what cannot be an object of sensuous contemplation, such as the concepts of metaphysics and of morals, lies entirely without its sphere, and it can never lead to them; neither does it require them. It is therefore not a continual progress and an approximation towards these sciences, and there is not, as it were, any point or line of contact. Natural science will never reveal to us the internal constitution of things, which though not appearance, yet can serve as the ultimate ground of explaining appearance. Nor does that science require this for its physical explanations. Nay even if such grounds should be offered from other sources (for instance, the influence of immaterial beings), they must be rejected and not used in the progress of its explanations. For these explanations must only be grounded upon that which as an object of sense can belong to experience, and be brought into connection with our actual perceptions and empirical laws.

But metaphysics leads us towards bounds in the dialectical attempts of pure reason (not undertaken arbitrarily or wantonly, but stimulated thereto by the nature of reason itself). And the transcendental ideas, as they do not admit of evasion, and are never capable of realisation, serve to point out to us actually not only the bounds of the pure use of reason, but also the way to determine them. Such is the end and the use of this natural predisposition of our reason, which has brought forth metaphysics as its favorite child, whose generation, like every other in the world, is not to be ascribed to blind chance, but to an original germ, wisely organised for great ends. For metaphysics, in its fundamental features, perhaps more than any other science, is placed in us by nature itself, and cannot be considered the production of an arbitrary choice or a casual enlargement in the progress of experience from which it is quite disparate.

Reason with all its concepts and laws of the understanding, which suffice for empirical use, i.e., within the sensible world, finds in itself no satisfaction because ever-recurring questions deprive us of all hope of their complete solution. The transcendental ideas, which have that completion in view, are such problems of reason. But it sees clearly, that the sensuous world cannot contain this completion, neither consequently can all the concepts, which serve merely for understanding the world of sense, such as space and time, and whatever we have adduced under the name of pure concepts of the understanding. The sensuous world is nothing but a chain of appearances connected according to universal laws; it has therefore no subsistence by itself; it is not the thing in itself, and consequently must point to that which contains the basis of this experience, to beings which cannot be cognised merely as phenomena, but as things in themselves. In the cognition of them alone reason can hope to satisfy its desire of completeness in proceeding from the conditioned to its conditions.

We have above (§§33, 34) indicated the limits of reason with regard to all cognition of mere creations of thought. Now, since the transcendental ideas have urged us to approach them, and thus have led us, as it were, to the spot where the occupied space (viz., experience) touches the void (that of which we can know nothing, viz., noumena), we can determine the bounds of pure reason. For in all bounds there is something positive (e.g., a surface is the boundary of corporeal space, and is therefore itself a space, a line is a space, which is the boundary of the surface, a point the boundary of the line, but yet always a place in space), whereas limits contain mere negations. The limits pointed out in those paragraphs are not enough after we have discovered that beyond them there still lies something (though we can never cognise what it is in itself). For the question now is, What is the attitude of our reason in this connection of what we know with what we do not, and never shall, know? This is an actual connection of a known thing with one quite unknown (and which will always remain so), and though what is unknown should not become the least more known— which we cannot even hope—yet the notion of this connection must be definite, and capable of being rendered distinct.

We must therefore accept an immaterial being, a world of understanding, and a supreme being (all mere noumena), because in them only, as things in themselves, reason finds that completion and satisfaction, which it can never hope for in the derivation of appearances from their homogeneous grounds, and because these actually have reference to something distinct from them (and totally heterogeneous), as appearances always presuppose an object in itself, and therefore suggest its existence whether we can know more of it or not.

But as we can never cognise these beings of understanding as they are in themselves, that is, definitely, yet must assume them as regards the sensible world, and connect them with it by reason, we are at least able to think this connection by means of such concepts as express their relation to the world of sense. Yet if we represent to ourselves a being of the understanding by nothing but pure concepts of the understanding, we then indeed represent nothing definite to ourselves, consequently our concept has no significance; but if we think it by properties borrowed from the sensuous world, it is no longer a being of understanding, but is conceived as an appearance, and belongs to the sensible world. Let us take an instance from the notion of the supreme being.

Our deistic conception is quite a pure concept of reason, but represents only a thing containing all realities, without being able to determine any one of them; because for that purpose an example must be taken from the world of sense, in which case we should have an object of sense only, not something quite heterogeneous, which can never be an object of sense. Suppose I attribute to the supreme being understanding, for instance; I have no concept of an understanding other than my own, one that must receive its perceptions by the senses, and which is occupied in bringing them under rules of the unity of consciousness. Then the elements of my concept would always lie in the appearance; I should however by the insufficiency of the appearance be necessitated to go beyond them to the concept of a being which neither depends upon appearance, nor is bound up with them as conditions of its determination. But if I separate understanding from sensibility to obtain a pure understanding, then nothing remains but the mere form of thinking without perception, by which form alone I can cognise nothing definite, and consequently no object. For that purpose I should conceive another understanding, such as would directly perceive its objects, but of which I have not the least notion; because the human understanding is discursive, and can [not directly perceive, it can] only cognise by means of general concepts. And the very same difficulties arise if we attribute a will to the supreme being; for we have this concept only by drawing it from our internal experience, and therefore from our dependence for satisfaction upon objects whose existence we require; and so the notion rests upon sensibility, which is absolutely incompatible with the pure concept of the supreme being.

Hume's objections to deism are weak, and affect only the proofs, and not the deistic assertion itself. But as regards theism, which depends on a stricter determination of the concept of the supreme being which in deism is merely transcendent, they are very strong, and as this concept is formed, in certain (in fact in all common) cases irrefutable. Hume always insists, that by the mere concept of an original being, to which we apply only ontological predicates (eternity, omnipresence, omnipotence), we think nothing definite, and that properties which can yield a concept *in concreto* must be superadded; that it is not enough to say, it is cause, but we must explain the nature of its causality, for example, that of an understanding and of a will. He then begins his attacks on the essential point itself, i.e., theism, as he had previously directed his battery only against the proofs of deism, an attack which is not very dangerous to it in its consequences. All his dangerous arguments refer to anthropomorphism, which he holds to be inseparable from theism, and to make it absurd in itself; but if the former be abandoned, the latter must vanish with it, and nothing remain but deism, of which nothing can come, which is of no value, and which cannot serve as any foundation to religion or morals. If this anthropomorphism were really unavoidable, no proofs whatever of the existence of a supreme being, even were they all granted, could determine for us the concept of this being without involving us in contradictions.

If we connect with the command to avoid all transcendent judgments of pure reason, the command (which apparently conflicts with it) to proceed to concepts that lie beyond the field of its immanent (empirical) use, we discover that both can subsist together, but only at the boundary of all lawful use of reason. For this boundary belongs as well to the field of experience, as to that of the creations of thought, and we are thereby taught, as well, how these so remarkable ideas serve merely for marking the bounds of human reason. On the one hand they give warning not boundlessly to extend cognition of experience, as if nothing but world remained for us to cognise, and yet, on the other hand, not to transgress the bounds of experience, and to think of judging about things beyond them, as things in themselves.

But we stop at this boundary if we limit our judgment merely to the relation which the world may have to a being whose very concept lies beyond all the knowledge which we can attain within the world. For we then do not attribute to the supreme being any of the properties in themselves, by which we represent objects of experience, and thereby avoid dogmatic anthropomorphism; but we attribute them to his relation to the world, and allow ourselves a symbolical anthropomorphism, which in fact concerns language only, and not the object itself.

If I say that we are compelled to consider the world, as if it were the work of a supreme understanding and will, I really say nothing more, than that a watch, a ship, a regiment, bears the same relation to the watchmaker, the shipbuilder, the commanding officer, as the world of sense (or whatever constitutes the substratum of this complex of appearances) does to the unknown, which I do not hereby cognise as it is in itself, but as it is for me or in relation to the world, of which I am a part.

§58. Such a cognition is one of analogy, and does not signify (as is commonly understood) an imperfect similarity of two things, but a perfect similarity of relations between two quite dissimilar things. By means of this analogy, however, there remains a concept of the supreme being sufficiently determined *for us,* though we have left out everything that could determine it absolutely or in itself; for we determine it as regards the world and as regards ourselves, and more do we not require. The attacks which Hume makes upon those who would determine this concept absolutely, by taking the materials for so doing from themselves and the world, do not affect us; and he cannot object to us, that we have nothing left if we give up the objective anthropomorphism of the concept of the supreme being.

For let us assume at the outset (as Hume in his dialogues makes Philo grant Cleanthes), as a necessary hypothesis, the deistical concept of the first being, in which this being is thought by the mere ontological predicates of substance, of cause, etc. This must be done, because reason, actuated in the sensible world by mere conditions, which are themselves always conditional, cannot otherwise have any satisfaction, and it therefore can be done without falling into anthropomorphism (which transfers predicates from the world of sense to a being quite distinct from the world), because those predicates are mere categories, which, though they do not give a determinate concept of God, yet give a concept not limited to any conditions of sensibility. Thus nothing can prevent our predicating of this being a causality through reason with regard to the world, and thus passing to theism, without being obliged to attribute to God in himself this kind of reason, as a property inhering in him. For as to the former, the only possible way of prosecuting the use of reason (as regards all possible experience, in complete harmony with itself) in the world of sense to the highest point, is to assume a supreme reason as a cause of all the connections in the world. Such a principle must be quite advantageous to reason and can hurt it nowhere in its application to nature. As to the latter, reason is thereby not transferred as a property to the first being in himself, but only to his relation to the world of sense, and so anthropomorphism is entirely avoided. For nothing is considered here but the cause of the form of reason which is perceived everywhere in the world, and reason is attributed to the supreme being, so far as it contains the ground of this form of reason in the world, but according to analogy only, that is, so far as this expression shows merely the relation, which the supreme cause unknown to us has to the world, in order to determine everything in it conformably to reason in the highest degree. We are thereby kept from using reason as an attribute for the purpose of conceiving God, but instead of conceiving the world in such a manner as is necessary to have the greatest possible use of reason according to principle. We thereby acknowledge that the Supreme Being is quite inscrutable and even unthinkable in any definite way as to what he is in himself. We are thereby kept, on the one hand, from making a transcendent use of the concepts which we have of reason as an efficient cause (by means of the will), in order to determine the divine nature by properties, which are only borrowed from human nature, and from losing ourselves in gross and extravagant notions, and on the other hand from deluging the contemplation of the world with hyperphysical modes of explanation according to our notions of human reason, which we transfer to God, and so losing for this contemplation its proper application, according to which it should be a rational study of mere nature, and not a presumptuous derivation of its appearances from a supreme reason. The expression suited to our feeble notions is, that we conceive the world as if it came, as to its existence and internal plan, from a supreme reason, by which notion we both cognise the constitution, which belongs to the world itself, yet without pretending to determine the nature of its cause in itself, and on the other hand, we transfer the ground of this constitution (of the form of reason in the world) upon the relation of the supreme cause to the world, without finding the world sufficient by itself for that purpose.

Thus the difficulties which seem to oppose theism disappear by combining with Hume's principle—"not to carry the use of reason dogmatically beyond the field of all possible experience"—this other principle, which he quite overlooked: "not to consider the field of experience as one which bounds itself in the eye of our reason." The *Critique of Pure Reason* here points out the true mean between dogmatism, which Hume combats, and skepticism, which he would substitute for it—a mean which is not like other means that we find advisable to determine for ourselves as it were mechanically (by adopting something from one side and something from the other), and by which nobody is taught a better way, but such a one as can be accurately determined on principles.

§59. At the beginning of this annotation I made use of the metaphor of a boundary, in order to establish the limits of reason in regard to its suitable use. The world of sense contains merely appearances, which are not things in themselves, but the understanding must assume these latter ones, viz., noumena. In our reason both are comprised, and the question is, How does reason proceed to set boundaries to the understanding as regards both these fields? Experience, which contains all that belongs to the sensuous world, does not bound itself; it only proceeds in every case from the conditioned to some other equally conditioned object. Its boundary must lie quite without it, and this field is that of the pure beings of the understanding. But this field, so far as the determination of the nature of these beings is concerned, is an empty space for us, and if dogmatically-determined concepts alone are in question, we cannot pass out of the field of possible experience. But as a boundary itself is something positive, which belongs as well to that which lies within, as to the space that lies without the given complex, it is still an actual positive cognition, which reason only acquires by enlarging itself to this boundary, yet without attempting to pass it; because it there finds itself in the presence of an empty space, in which it can conceive forms of things, but not things themselves. But the setting of a boundary to the field of the understanding by something, which is otherwise unknown to it, is still a cognition which belongs to reason even at this standpoint, and by which it is neither confined within the sensible, nor straying without it, but only refers, as befits the knowledge of a boundary, to the relation between that which lies without it, and that which is contained within it.

Natural theology is such a concept at the boundary of human reason, being constrained to look beyond this boundary to the idea of a supreme being (and, for practical purposes to that of an intelligible world also), not in order to determine anything relatively to this pure creation of the understanding, which lies beyond the world of sense, but in order to guide the use of reason within it according to principles of the greatest possible (theoretical as well as practical) unity. For this purpose we make use of the reference of the world of sense to an independent reason, as the cause of all its connections. Thereby we do not purely invent a being, but, as beyond the sensible world there must be something that can only be thought by the pure understanding, we determine that something in this particular way, though only of course according to analogy.

And thus there remains our original proposition, which is the *résumé* of the whole *Critique:* "that reason by all its *a priori* principles never teaches us anything more than objects of possible experience, and even of these nothing more than can be cognised in experience." But this limitation does not prevent reason leading us to the objective boundary of experience, viz., to the reference to something which is not itself an object of experience, but is the ground of all experience. Reason does not however teach us anything concerning the thing in itself; it only instructs us as regards its own complete and highest use in the field of possible experience. But this is all that can be reasonably desired in the present case, and with which we have cause to be satisfied.

§60. Thus we have fully exhibited metaphysics as it is actually given in the natural predisposition of human reason, and in that which constitutes the essential end of its pursuit, according to its subjective possibility. Though we have found, that this merely natural use of such a predisposition of our reason, if no discipline arising only from a scientific critique bridles and sets limits to it, involves us in transcendent, either apparently or really conflicting, dialectical syllogisms; and this fallacious metaphysics is not only unnecessary as regards the promotion of our knowledge of nature, but even disadvantageous to it: there yet remains a problem worthy of solution, which is to find out the natural ends intended by this disposition to transcendent concepts in our reason, because everything that lies in nature must be originally intended for some useful purpose.

Such an inquiry is of a doubtful nature; and I acknowledge, that what I can say about it is conjecture only, like every speculation about the first ends of nature. The question does not concern the objective validity of metaphysical judgments, but our natural predisposition to them, and therefore does not belong to the system of metaphysics but to anthropology.

When I compare all the transcendental ideas, the totality of which constitutes the particular problem of natural pure reason, compelling it to quit the mere contemplation of nature, to transcend all possible experience, and in this endeavor to produce the thing (be it knowledge or fiction) called metaphysics, I think I perceive that the aim of this natural tendency is, to free our notions from the fetters of experience and from the limits of the mere contemplation of nature so far as at least to open to us a field containing mere objects for the pure understanding, which no sensibility can reach, not indeed for the purpose of speculatively occupying ourselves with them (for there we can find no ground to stand on), but because practical principles, which, without finding some such scope for their necessary expectation and hope, could not expand to the universality which reason unavoidably requires from a moral point of view.

So I find that the psychological idea (however little it may reveal to me the nature of the human soul, which is higher than all concepts of experience), shows the insufficiency of these concepts plainly enough, and thereby deters me from materialism, the psychological notion of which is unfit for any explanation of nature, and besides confines reason in practical respects. The cosmological ideas, by the obvious insufficiency of all possible cognition of nature to satisfy reason in its lawful inquiry, serve in the same manner to keep us from naturalism, which asserts nature to be sufficient for itself. Finally, all natural necessity in the sensible world is conditional, as it always presupposes the dependence of things upon others, and unconditional necessity must be sought only in the unity of a cause different from the world of sense. But as the causality of this cause, in its turn, were it merely nature, could never render the existence of the contingent (as its consequent) comprehensible, reason frees itself by means of the theological idea from fatalism, (both as a blind natural necessity in the coherence of nature itself, without a first principle, and as a blind causality of this principle itself), and leads to the concept of a cause possessing freedom, or of a supreme intelligence. Thus the transcendental ideas serve, if not to instruct us positively, at least to destroy the rash assertions of materialism, of naturalism, and of fatalism, and thus to afford scope for the moral ideas beyond the field of speculation. These considerations, I should think, explain in some measure the natural predisposition of which I spoke.

The practical value, which a merely speculative science may have, lies without the bounds of this science, and can therefore be considered as a scholion merely, and like all scholia does not form part of the science itself. This application however surely lies within the bounds of philosophy, especially of philosophy drawn from the pure sources of reason, where its speculative use in metaphysics must necessarily be at unity with its practical use in morals. Hence the unavoidable dialectics of pure reason, considered in metaphysics, as a natural tendency, deserves to be explained not as an illusion merely, which is to be removed, but also, if possible, as a natural provision as regards its end, though this duty, a work of supererogation, cannot justly be assigned to metaphysics proper.

The solutions of these questions which are treated in the chapter on the "Regulative Use of the Ideas of Pure Reason" (*Critique of Pure Reason,* II., chap. III., section 7) should be considered a second scholion which however has a greater affinity with the subject of metaphysics. For there certain rational principles are expounded which determine *a priori* the order of nature or rather of the understanding, which seeks nature's laws through experience. They seem to be constitutive and legislative with regard to experience, though they spring from pure reason, which cannot be considered, like the understanding, as a principle of possible experience. Now whether or not this harmony rests upon the fact, that just as nature does not inhere in appearances or in their source (the sensibility) itself, but only in so far as the latter is in relation to the understanding, as also a systematic unity in applying the understanding to bring about an entirety of all possible experience can only belong to the understanding when in relation to reason; and whether or not experience is in this way mediately subordinate to the legislation of reason: may be discussed by those who desire to trace the nature of reason even beyond its use in metaphysics, into the general principles of a history of nature; I have represented this task as important, but not attempted its solution, in the book itself.

And thus I conclude the analytical solution of the main question which I had proposed: How is metaphysics in general possible? by ascending from the data of its actual use in its consequences, to the grounds of its possibility.

SCHOLIA
Solution of the General Question of the Prolegomena, "How Is Metaphysics Possible as a Science?"

Metaphysics, as a natural disposition of reason, is actual, but if considered by itself alone (as the analytical solution of the third principal question showed), dialectical and illusory.

If we think of taking principles from it, and in using them follow the natural, but on that account not less false, illusion, we can never produce science, but only a vain dialectical art, in which one school may outdo another, but none can ever acquire a just and lasting approbation.

In order that as a science metaphysics may be entitled to claim not mere fallacious plausibility, but insight and conviction, a *Critique of Reason* must itself exhibit the whole stock of *a priori* concepts, their division according to their various sources (Sensibility, Understanding, and Reason), together with a complete table of them, the analysis of all these concepts, with all their consequences, especially by means of the deduction of these concepts, the possibility of synthetical cognition *a priori,* the principles of its application and finally its bounds, all in a complete system. Critique, therefore, and critique alone, contains in itself the whole well-proven and well-tested plan, and even all the means required to accomplish metaphysics, as a science; by other ways and means it is impossible. The question here therefore is not so much how this performance is possible, as how to set it going, and induce men of clear heads to quit their hitherto perverted and fruitless cultivation for one that will not deceive, and how much a union for the common end may best be directed.

This much is certain, that whoever has once tasted *Critique* will be ever after disgusted with all dogmatical twaddle which he formerly put up with, because his reason must have something, and could find nothing better for its support.

Critique stands in the same relation to the common metaphysics of the schools, as chemistry does to alchemy, or as astronomy to the astrology of the fortune-teller. I pledge myself that nobody who has read through and through, and grasped the principles of, the *Critique* even in these *Prolegomena* only, will ever return to that old and sophistical pseudo-science; but will rather with a certain delight look forward to metaphysics which is now indeed in his power, requiring no more preparatory discoveries, and now at last affording permanent satisfaction to reason. For here is an advantage upon which, of all possible sciences, metaphysics alone can with certainty reckon: that it can be brought to such completion and fixity as to be incapable of further change, or of any augmentation by new discoveries; because here reason has the sources of its knowledge in itself, not in objects and their observation, by which latter its stock of knowledge cannot be further increased. When therefore it has exhibited the fundamental laws of its faculty completely and so definitely as to avoid all misunderstanding, there remains nothing for pure reason to cognise *a priori,* nay, there is even no ground to raise further questions. The sure prospect of knowledge so definite and so compact has a peculiar charm, even though we should set aside all its advantages, of which I shall hereafter speak.

All false art, all vain wisdom, lasts its time, but finally destroys itself, and its highest culture is also the epoch of its decay. That this time is come for metaphysics appears from the state into which it has fallen among all learned nations, despite of all the zeal with which other sciences of every kind are prosecuted. The old arrangement of our university studies still preserves its shadow; now and then an academy of science tempts men by offering prizes to write essays on it, but it is no longer numbered among thorough sciences; and let any one judge for himself how a man of genius, if he were called a great metaphysician, would receive the compliment, which may be well-meant, but is scarce envied by anybody.

Yet, though the period of the downfall of all dogmatical metaphysics has undoubtedly arrived, we are yet far from being able to say that the period of its regeneration is come by means of a thorough and complete *Critique of Reason.* All transitions from a tendency to its contrary pass through the stage of indifference, and this moment is the most dangerous for an author, but, in my opinion, the most favorable for the science. For, when party spirit has died out by a total dissolution of former connections, minds are in the best state to listen to several proposals for an organisation according to a new plan.

When I say, that I hope these *Prolegomena* will excite investigation in the field of critique and afford a new and promising object to sustain the general spirit of philosophy, which seems on its speculative side to want sustenance, I can imagine beforehand, that every one, whom the thorny paths of my *Critique* have tired and put out of humor, will ask me, upon what I found this hope. My answer is, upon the irresistible law of necessity.

That the human mind will ever give up metaphysical researches is as little to be expected as that we should prefer to give up breathing altogether, to avoid inhaling impure air. There will therefore always be metaphysics in the world; nay, every one, especially every man of reflection, will have it, and for want of a recognised standard, will shape it for himself after his own pattern. What has hitherto been called metaphysics, cannot satisfy any critical mind, but to forego it entirely is impossible; therefore a *Critique of Pure Reason* itself must now be attempted or, if one exists, investigated, and brought to the full test, because there is no other means of supplying this pressing want, which is something more than mere thirst for knowledge.

Ever since I have come to know critique, whenever I finish reading a book of metaphysical contents, which, by the preciseness of its notions, by variety, order, and an easy style, was not only entertaining but also helpful, I cannot help asking, "Has this author indeed advanced metaphysics a single step?" The learned men, whose works have been useful to me in other respects and always contributed to the culture of my mental powers, will, I hope, forgive me for saying, that I have never been able to find either their essays or my own less important ones (though self-love may recommend them to me) to have advanced the science of metaphysics in the least, and why?

Here is the very obvious reason: metaphysics did not then exist as a science, nor can it be gathered piecemeal, but its germ must be fully preformed in the *Critique*. But in order to prevent all misconception, we must remember what has been already said, that by the analytical treatment of our concepts the understanding gains indeed a great deal, but the science (of metaphysics) is thereby not in the least advanced, because these dissections of concepts are nothing but the materials from which the intention is to carpenter our science. Let the concepts of substance and of accident be ever so well dissected and determined, all this is very well as a preparation for some future use. But if we cannot prove, that in all which exists the substance endures, and only the accidents vary, our science is not the least advanced by all our analyses.

Metaphysics has hitherto never been able to prove *a priori* either this proposition, or that of sufficient reason, still less any more complex theorem, such as belongs to psychology or cosmology, or indeed any synthetical proposition. By all its analysing therefore nothing is affected, nothing obtained or forwarded, and the science, after all this bustle and noise, still remains as it was in the days of Aristotle, though far better preparations were made for it than of old, if the clue to synthetical cognitions had only been discovered.

If any one thinks himself offended, he is at liberty to refute my charge by producing a single synthetical proposition belonging to metaphysics, which he would prove dogmatically *a priori,* for until he has actually performed this feat, I shall not grant that he has truly advanced the science; even should this proposition be sufficiently confirmed by common experience. No demand can be more moderate or more equitable, and in the (inevitably certain) event of its non-performance, no assertion more just, than that hitherto metaphysics has never existed as a science.

But there are two things which, in case the challenge be accepted, I must deprecate: first, trifling about probability and conjecture, which are suited as little to metaphysics, as to geometry; and secondly, a decision by means of the magic wand of common sense, which does not convince every one, but which accommodates itself to personal peculiarities.

For as to the former, nothing can be more absurd, than in metaphysics, a philosophy from pure reason to think of grounding our judgments upon probability and conjecture. Everything that is to be cognised *a priori*, is thereby announced as apodeictically certain, and must therefore be proved in this way. We might as well think of grounding geometry or arithmetic upon conjectures. As to the doctrine of chances in the latter, it does not contain probable, but perfectly certain, judgments concerning the degree of the probability of certain cases, under given uniform conditions, which, in the sum of all possible cases, infallibly happen according to the rule, though it is not sufficiently determined in respect to every single chance. Conjectures (by means of induction and of analogy) can be suffered in an empirical science of nature only, yet even there the possibility at least of what we assume must be quite certain.

The appeal to common sense is even more absurd, when concept and principles are announced as valid, not in so far as they hold with regard to experience, but even beyond the conditions of experience. For what is common sense? It is normal good sense, so far it judges right. But what is normal good sense? It is the faculty of the knowledge and use of rules *in concreto,* as distinguished from the speculative understanding, which is a faculty of knowing rules *in abstracto.* Common sense can hardly understand the rule, "that every event is determined by means of its cause," and can never comprehend it thus generally. It therefore demands an example from experience, and when it hears that this rule means nothing but what it always thought when a pane was broken or a kitchen-utensil missing, it then understands the principle and grants it. Common sense therefore is only of use so far as it can see its rules (though they actually are *a priori*) confirmed by experience; consequently to comprehend them *a priori,* or independently of experience, belongs to the speculative understanding, and lies quite beyond the horizon of common sense. But the province of metaphysics is entirely confined to the latter kind of knowledge, and it is certainly a bad index of common sense to appeal to it as a witness, for it cannot here form any opinion whatever, and men look down upon it with contempt until they are in difficulties, and can find in their speculation neither in nor out.

It is a common subterfuge of those false friends of common sense (who occasionally prize it highly, but usually despise it) to say, that there must surely be at all events some propositions which are immediately certain, and of which there is no occasion to give any proof, or even any account at all, because we otherwise could never stop inquiring into the grounds of our judgments. But if we except the principle of contradiction, which is not sufficient to show the truth of synthetical judgments, they can never adduce, in proof of this privilege, anything else indubitable, which they can immediately ascribe to common sense, except mathematical propositions, such as twice two make four, between two points there is but one straight line, etc. But these judgments are radically different from those of metaphysics. For in mathematics I myself can by thinking construct whatever I represent to myself as possible by a concept: I add to the first two the other two, one by one, and myself make the number four, or I draw in thought from one point to another all manner of lines, equal as well as unequal; yet I can draw one only, which is like itself in all its parts. But I cannot, by all my power of thinking, extract from the concept of a thing the concept of something else, whose existence is necessarily connected with the former, but I must call in experience. And though my understanding furnishes me *a priori* (yet only in reference to possible experience) with the concept of such a connection (i.e., causation), I cannot exhibit it, like the concepts of mathematics, by visualising them, *a priori,* and so show its possibility *a priori.* This concept, together with the principles of its application, always requires, if it shall hold *a priori*—as is requisite in metaphysics—a justification and deduction of its possibility, because we cannot otherwise know how far it holds good, and whether it can be used in experience only or beyond it also.

Therefore in metaphysics, as a speculative science of pure reason, we can never appeal to common sense, but may do so only when we are forced to surrender it, and to renounce all purely speculative cognition, which must always be knowledge, and consequently when we forego metaphysics itself and its instruction, for the sake of adopting a rational faith which alone may be possible for us, and sufficient to our wants, perhaps even more salutary than knowledge itself. For in this case the attitude of the question is quite altered. Metaphysics must be science, not only as a whole, but in all its parts, otherwise it is nothing; because, as a speculation of pure reason, it finds a hold only on general opinions. Beyond its field, however, probability and common sense may be used with advantage and justly, but on quite special principles, of which the importance always depends on the reference to practical life.

This is what I hold myself justified in requiring for the possibility of metaphysics as a science.

CRITIQUE OF PURE REASON

FIRST SECTION OF THE TRANSCENDENTAL AESTHETIC – OF SPACE

By means of our external sense, a property of our mind, we represent to ourselves objects as external or outside ourselves, and all of these in space. It is within space that their form, size, and relative position are fixed or can be fixed. The internal sense by means of which the mind perceives itself or its internal state, does not give an intuition of the soul itself, as an object, but it is nevertheless a fixed form under which alone an intuition of its internal state is possible, so that whatever belongs to its internal determinations must be represented in relations of time. Time cannot be perceived externally, as little as space can be perceived as something within us.

What then are space and time? Are they real beings? Or, if not that, are they determinations or relations of things, but such as would belong to them even if they were not perceived? Or lastly, are they determinations and relations which are inherent in the form of intuition only, and therefore in the subjective nature of our mind, without which such predicates as space and time would never be ascribed to anything?

From Immanuel Kant, *Critique of Pure Reason,* trans. F. Max Müller (London: Macmillan, 1881).

In order to understand this more clearly, let us first consider space.

1. Space is not an empirical concept which has been derived from external experience. For in order that certain sensations should be referred to something outside myself, i.e. to something in a different part of space from that where I am; again, in order that I may be able to represent them as side by side, that is, not only as different, but as in different places, the representation of space must already be there. Therefore the representation of space cannot be borrowed through experience from relations of external phenomena, but, on the contrary, those external phenomena become possible only by means of the representation of space.

2. Space is a necessary representation *a priori,* forming the very foundation of all external intuitions. It is impossible to imagine that there should be no space, though one might very well imagine that there should be space without objects to fill it. Space is therefore regarded as a condition of the possibility of phenomena, not as a determination produced by them; it is a representation *a priori* which necessarily precedes all external phenomena.

3. On this necessity of an *a priori* representation of space rests the apodeictic certainty of all geometrical principles, and the possibility of their construction *a priori.* For if the intuition of space were a concept gained *a posteriori,* borrowed from general external experience, the first principles of mathematical definition would be nothing but perceptions. They would be exposed to all the accidents of perception, and there being but one straight line between two points would not be a necessity, but only something taught in each case by experience. Whatever is derived from experience possesses a relative generality only, based on induction. We should therefore not be able to say more than that, so far as hitherto observed, no space has yet been found having more than three dimensions.

4. Space is not a discursive or so-called general concept of the relations of things in general, but a pure intuition. For, first of all, we can imagine one space only, and if we speak of many spaces, we mean parts only of one and the same space. Nor can these parts be considered as antecedent to the one and all-embracing space and, as it were, its component parts out of which an aggregate is formed, but they can be thought of as existing within it only. Space is essentially one; its multiplicity, and therefore the general concept of spaces in general, arises entirely from limitations. Hence it follows that, with respect to space, an intuition *a priori,* which is not empirical, must form the foundation of all conceptions of space. In the same manner all geometrical principles, e.g. "that in every triangle two sides together are greater than the third," are never to be derived from the general concepts of side and triangle, but from an intuition, and that *a priori,* with apodeictic certainty.

5. Space is represented as an infinite quantity. Now a general concept of space, which is found in a foot as well as in an ell, could tell us nothing in respect to its quantity. If there were not infinity in the progression of intuition, space, as a concept of relations, could never contain the principle of infinity.

Conclusions from the foregoing concepts.

a. Space does not represent any quality of objects by themselves, or objects in their relation to one another; i.e. space does not represent any determination which is inherent in the objects themselves, and would remain, even if all subjective conditions of intuition were removed. For no determination of objects, whether belonging to them absolutely or in relation to others, can enter into our intuition before the actual existence of the objects themselves, that is to say, they can never be intuitions *a priori*.

b. Space is nothing but the form of the phenomena of all external senses; it is a subjective condition of our sensibility, without which no external intuition is possible for us. If then we consider that the receptivity of the subject, its capacity of being affected by objects, must necessarily precede all intuition of objects, we shall understand how the form of all phenomena may be given before all real perceptions, may be, in fact, *a priori* in the soul, and may, as a pure intuition, by which all objects must be determined, contain, prior to all experience, principles regulating their relations.

It is therefore from the human standpoint only that we can speak of space, extended objects, etc. If we drop the subjective condition under which alone we can gain external intuition, according as we ourselves may be affected by objects, the representation of space means nothing. For this predicate is applied to objects only in so far as they appear to us, and are objects of our senses. The constant form of this receptivity, which we call sensibility, is a necessary condition of all relations in which objects, as without us, can be perceived; and, when abstraction is made of these objects, what remains is that pure intuition which we call space. As the peculiar conditions of our sensibility cannot be looked upon as conditions of the possibility of the objects themselves, but only of their appearance as phenomena to us, we may say indeed that space comprehends all things which may appear to us externally, but not all things by themselves, whether perceived by us or not, or any subject whatsoever. We cannot judge whether the intuitions of other thinking beings are subject to the same conditions which determine our intuition, and which for us are generally binding. If we add the limitation of a judgment to a subjective concept, the judgment gains absolute validity. The proposition "all things are beside each other in space," is valid only under the limitation that things are taken as objects of our sensuous intuition. If I add that limitation to the concept and say "all things, as external phenomena, are beside each other in space," the rule obtains universal and unlimited validity. Our discussions teach therefore the reality, i.e. the objective validity, of space with regard to all that can come to us externally as an object, but likewise the *ideality* of space with regard to things, when they are considered in themselves by our reason, and independent of the nature of our senses. We maintain the empirical reality of space, so far as every possible external experience is concerned, but at the same time its transcendental ideality; that is to say, we maintain that space is nothing, if we leave out of consideration the condition of a possible experience, and accept it as something on which things by themselves are in any way dependent.

With the exception of space there is no other subjective representation referring to something external, that would be called *a priori* objective. This subjective condition of all external phenomena cannot therefore be compared to any other. The taste of wine does not belong to the objective determinations of wine, considered as an object, even as a phenomenal object, but to the peculiar nature of the sense belonging to the subject that tastes the wine. Colours are not qualities of a body, though inherent in its intuition, but they are likewise modifications only of the sense of sight, as it is affected in different ways by light. Space, on the contrary, as the very condition of external objects, is essential to their appearance or intuition. Taste and colour are by no means necessary conditions under which alone things can become to us objects of sensuous perception. They are connected with their appearance, as accidentally added effects only of our peculiar organization. They are not therefore representations *a priori*, but are dependent on sensation, nay taste even on an affection of pleasure and pain, which is the result of a sensation. No one can have *a priori,* an idea either of colour or of taste, but space refers to the pure form of intuition only, and involves no kind of sensation, nothing empirical; nay all kinds and determinations of space can and must be represented *a priori,* if concepts of forms and their relations are to arise. Through it alone is it possible that things should become external objects to us.

My object in what I have said just now is only to prevent people from imagining that they can prove the ideality of space by illustrations which are altogether insufficient, such as colour, taste, etc., which should never be considered as qualities of things, but as modifications of the subject, and which therefore may be different with different people. For in this case that which originally is itself a phenomenon only, as for instance, a rose, is taken by the empirical understanding for a thing by itself, which nevertheless, with regard to colour, may appear different to every eye. The transcendental conception, on the contrary, of all phenomena in space, is a critical warning that nothing which is seen in space is a thing by itself, nor space a form of things supposed to belong to them by themselves, but that objects by themselves are not known to us at all, and that what we call external objects are nothing but representations of our senses, the form of which is space, and the true correlative of which, that is the thing by itself, is not known, nor can be known by these representations, nor do we care to know anything about it in our daily experience.

SECOND SECTION OF THE TRANSCENDENTAL AESTHETIC – OF TIME

I. Time is not an empirical concept deduced from any experience, for neither coexistence nor succession would enter into our perception, if the representation of time were not given *a priori.* Only when this representation *a priori* is given, can we imagine that certain things happen at the same time (simultaneously) or at different times (successively).

II. Time is a necessary representation on which all intuitions depend. We cannot take away time from phenomena in general, though we can well take away phenomena out of time. Time therefore is given *a priori.* In time alone is reality of phenomena possible. All phenomena may vanish, but time itself (as the general condition of their possibility) cannot be done away with.

III. On this *a priori* necessity depends also the possibility of apodeictic principles of the relations of time, or of axioms of time in general. Time has one dimension only; different times are not simultaneous, but successive, while different spaces are never successive, but simultaneous. Such principles cannot be derived from experience, because experience could not impart to them absolute universality nor apodeictic certainty. We should only be able to say that common experience teaches us that it is so, but not that it must be so. These principles are valid as rules under which alone experience is possible; they teach us before experience, not by means of experience.

IV. Time is not a discursive, or what is called a general concept, but a pure form of sensuous intuition. Different times are parts only of one and the same time. Representation, which can be produced by a single object only, is called an intuition. The proposition that different times cannot exist at the same time cannot be deduced from any general concept. Such a proposition is synthetical, and cannot be deducted from concepts only. It is contained immediately in the intuition and representation of time.

V. To say that time is infinite means no more than that every definite quantity of time is possible only by limitations of one time which forms the foundation of all times. The original representation of time must therefore be given as unlimited. But when the parts themselves and every quantity of an object can be represented as determined by limitation only, the whole representation cannot be given by concepts (for in that case the partial representations come first), but it must be founded on immediate intuition.

Conclusions from the foregoing concepts.

a. Time is not something existing by itself, or inherent in things as an objective determination of them, something therefore that might remain when abstraction is made of all subjective conditions of intuition. For in the former case it would be something real, without being a real object. In the latter it could not, as a determination or order inherent in things themselves, be antecedent to things as their condition, and be known and perceived by means of synthetical propositions *a priori.* All this is perfectly possible if time is nothing but a subjective condition under which all intuitions take place within us. For in that case this form of internal intuition can be represented prior to the objects themselves, that is, *a priori.*

b. Time is nothing but the form of the internal sense, that is, of our intuition of ourselves, and of our internal state. Time cannot be a determination peculiar to external phenomena. It refers neither to their shape, nor their position, etc., it only determines the relation of representations in our internal state. And exactly because this internal intuition supplies no shape, we try to make good this deficiency by means of analogies, and represent to ourselves the succession of time by a line progressing to infinity, in which the manifold constitutes a series of one dimension only; and we conclude from the properties of this line as to all the properties of time, with one exception, i.e. that the parts of the former are simultaneous, those of the latter successive. From this it becomes clear also, that the representation of time is itself an intuition, because all its relations can be expressed by means of an external intuition.

c. Time is the formal condition, *a priori,* of all phenomena whatsoever. Space, as the pure form of all external intuition, is a condition, *a priori,* of external phenomena only. But, as all representations, whether they have for their objects external things or not, belong by themselves, as determinations of the mind, to our inner state, and as this inner state falls under the formal conditions of internal intuition, and therefore of time, time is a condition, *a priori,* of all phenomena whatsoever, and is so directly as a condition of internal phenomena (of our mind) and thereby indirectly of external phenomena also. If I am able to say, *a priori,* that all external phenomena are in space, and are determined, *a priori,* according to the relations of space, I can, according to the principle of the internal sense, make the general assertion that all phenomena, that is, all objects of the senses, are in time, and stand necessarily in relations of time.

If we drop our manner of looking at ourselves internally, and of comprehending by means of that intuition all external intuitions also within our power of representation, and thus take objects as they may be by themselves, then time is nothing. Time has objective validity with reference to phenomena only, because these are things which we accept as objects of our senses; but time is no longer objective, if we remove the sensuous character of our intuitions, that is to say, that mode of representation which is peculiar to ourselves, and speak of things in general. Time is therefore simply a subjective condition of our (human) intuition (which is always sensuous, that is so far as we are affected by objects), but by itself, apart from the subject, nothing. Nevertheless, with respect to all phenomena, that is, all things which can come within our experience, time is necessarily objective. We cannot say that all things are in time, because, if we speak of things in general, nothing is said about the manner of intuition, which is the real condition under which time enters into our representation of things. If therefore this condition is added to the concept, and if we say that all things as phenomena (as objects of sensuous intuition) are in time, then such a proposition has its full objective validity and *a priori* universality.

What we insist on therefore is the empirical reality of time, that is, its objective validity, with reference to all objects which can ever come before our senses. And as our intuition must at all times be sensuous, no object can ever fall under our experience that does not come under the conditions of time. What we deny is, that time has any claim on absolute reality, so that, without taking into account the form of our sensuous condition, it should by itself be a condition or quality inherent in things; for such qualities which belong to things by themselves can never be given to us through the senses. This is what constitutes the transcendental ideality of time, so that, if we take no account of the subjective conditions of our sensuous intuitions, time is nothing, and cannot be added to the objects by themselves (without their relation to our intuition) whether as subsisting or inherent. This ideality of time, however, as well as that of space, should not be confounded with the deceptions of our sensations, because in their case we always suppose that the phenomenon to which such predicates belong has objective reality, which is not at all the case here, except so far as the phenomenon is purely empirical, that is, so far as the object itself is looked upon as a mere phenomenon.

DEDUCTION OF THE PURE CONCEPTS OF THE UNDERSTANDING
III. Of the Relation of the Understanding to Objects in General, and the Possibility of Knowing Them a *Priori*

What in the preceding section we have discussed singly and separately we shall now try to treat in connection with each other and as a whole. We saw that there are three subjective sources of knowledge on which the possibility of all experience and of the knowledge of all objects depends, namely, *sense, imagination, and apperception.* Each of them may be considered as empirical in its application to given phenomena; all, however, are also elements or grounds *a priori,* which render their empirical application possible. *Sense* represents phenomena empirically in *perception, imagination* in *association* (and reproduction), *apperception* in the *empirical consciousness* of the identity of these reproductive representations with the phenomena by which they were given; therefore in *recognition.*

The whole of our perception rests on pure intuition (if regarded as representation, then on time, as the form of our internal intuition), their association on the pure synthesis of imagination, and our empirical consciousness of them on pure apperception, that is, on the permanent identity of oneself in the midst of all possible representations.

If we wish to follow up the internal ground of this connection of representations to that point towards which they must all converge and where they receive for the first time that unity of knowledge which is requisite for every possible experience, we must begin with pure apperception. Intuitions are nothing to us and do not concern us in the least, if they cannot be received into our consciousness, into which they may enter either directly or indirectly. Knowledge is impossible in any other way. We are conscious *a priori* of our own permanent identity with regard to all representations that can ever belong to our knowledge, as forming a necessary condition of the possibility of all representations (because these could not represent anything in me, unless they belonged with everything else to one consciousness and could at least be connected within it). This principle stands firm *a priori,* and may be called the *transcendental principle of the unity* of all the manifold of our representations (therefore also of intuition). This unity of the manifold in one subject is synthetical; the pure apperception therefore supplies us with a principle of the synthetical unity of the manifold in all possible intuitions.

This synthetical unity, however, presupposes or involves a synthesis, and if that unity is necessary *a priori,* the synthesis also must be *a priori.* The transcendental unity of apperception therefore refers to the pure synthesis of imagination as a condition *a priori* of the possibility of the manifold being united in one knowledge. This can only be the productive synthesis of imagination *a priori,* because the reproductive rests on conditions of experience. The principle therefore of the necessary unity of the pure (productive) synthesis of imagination, before all apperception, constitutes the ground of the possibility of all knowledge, particularly of experience.

The synthesis of the manifold in imagination is called transcendental, if, without reference to intuitions, it affects only the conjunction of the manifold *a priori;* and the unity of that synthesis is called transcendental if, with reference to the original unity of apperception, it is represented as *a priori* necessary. As the possibility of all knowledge depends on the unity of that apperception, it follows that the transcendental unity of the synthesis of imagination is the pure form of all possible knowledge through which all objects of possible experience may be represented *a priori.*

This unity of apperception with reference to the synthesis of imagination is the *understanding,* and the same unity with reference to the transcendental synthesis of the imagination, the *pure understanding.* It must be admitted therefore that there exist in the understanding pure forms of knowledge *a priori,* which contain the necessary unity of the pure synthesis of the imagination in reference to all possible phenomena. These are the categories, that is, the pure concepts of the understanding. The empirical knowledge of man contains therefore by necessity an understanding which refers to all objects of the senses, though by intuition only, and by its synthesis through imagination, and all phenomena, as data of a possible experience, must conform to those categories. As this relation of phenomena to a possible experience is likewise necessary (because, without it, we should receive no knowledge through them and they would not in the least concern us), it follows that the pure understanding constitutes by the means of the categories a formal and synthetical principle of all experience, and that phenomena have thus a necessary relation to the understanding.

We shall now try to place the necessary connection of the understanding with the phenomena by means of the categories more clearly before the reader, by beginning with the beginning, namely, with the empirical.

The first that is given us is the *phenomenon,* which, if connected with consciousness, is called *perception.* Without its relation to an at least possible consciousness, the phenomenon could never become to us an object of knowledge. It would therefore be nothing to us, and because it has no objective reality in itself, but exists only in being known, it would be nothing altogether. As every phenomenon contains a manifold, and different perceptions are found in the mind singly and scattered, a connection of them is necessary, such as they cannot have in the senses by themselves. There exists therefore in us an active power for the synthesis of the manifold which we call imagination, and the function of which, as applied to perceptions, I call *apprehension.* This imagination is meant to change the manifold of intuition into an image, it must therefore first receive the impressions by its own activity, which I call *to apprehend.*

It must be clear, however, that even this apprehension of the manifold could not alone produce a coherence of impressions or an image, without some subjective power of calling one perception from which the mind has gone over to another back to that which follows, and thus forming whole series of perceptions. This is the reproductive faculty of imagination which is and can be empirical only.

If representations, as they happen to meet with one another, could reproduce each other at haphazard, they would have no definite coherence, but would form irregular agglomerations only, and never produce knowledge. It is necessary therefore that their reproduction should be subject to a rule by which one representation connects itself in imagination with a second and not with a third. It is this subjective and empirical ground of reproduction according to rules, which is called the *association* of representations.

If this unity of association did not possess an objective foundation also, which makes it impossible that phenomena should be apprehended by imagination in any other way but under the condition of a possible synthetical unity of that apprehension, it would be a mere accident that phenomena lend themselves to a certain connection in human knowledge. Though we might have the power of associating perceptions, it would still be a matter of uncertainty and chance whether they themselves are associable; and, in case they should not be so, a number of perceptions, nay, the whole of our sensibility, might possibly contain a great deal of empirical consciousness, but in a separate state, nay, without belonging to the *one* consciousness of myself, which however is impossible. Only by ascribing all perceptions to one consciousness (the original apprehension) can I say of all of them that I am conscious of them. It must be therefore an objective ground, that is, one that can be understood as existing *a priori,* and before all empirical laws of imagination, on which alone the possibility, nay, even the necessity of a law can rest, which pervades all phenomena, and which makes us look upon them all, without exception, as data of the senses, being associable by themselves, and subject to general rules of a permanent connection in their reproduction. This objective ground of all association of phenomena I call their *affinity,* and this can nowhere be found except in the principle of the unity of apperception applied to all knowledge which is to belong to me. According to it all phenomena, without exception, must so enter into the mind or be apprehended as to agree with the unity of apperception. This, without a synthetical unity in their connection, which is therefore necessary objectively also, would be impossible.

We have thus seen that the objective unity of all (empirical) consciousness in one consciousness (that of the original apperception) is the necessary condition of all possible perception, while the affinity of all phenomena (near or remote) is a necessary consequence of a synthesis in imagination which is, *a priori,* founded on rules.

Imagination is therefore likewise the power of a synthesis *a priori,* which is the reason why we called it productive imagination, and so far as this aims at nothing but the necessary unity in the synthesis of all the manifold in phenomena, it may be called the transcendental function of imagination. However strange therefore it may appear at first, it must nevertheless have become clear by this time that the affinity of phenomena and with it their association, and through that, lastly, their reproduction also according to laws, that is, the whole of our experience, becomes possible only by means of that transcendental function of imagination, without which no concepts of objects could ever come together in one experience.

It is the permanent and unchanging Ego (of pure apperception) which forms the correlative of all our representations, if we are to become conscious of them, and all consciousness belongs quite as much to such an all-embracing pure apperception as all sensuous intuition belongs, as a representation, to a pure internal intuition, namely, time. This apperception it is which must be added to pure imagination, in order to render its function intelligible. For by itself, the synthesis of imagination, though carried out *a priori*, is always sensuous, and only connects the manifold as it appears in intuition, for instance, the shape of a triangle. But when the manifold is brought into relation with the unity of apperception, concepts which belong to the understanding become possible, but only as related to sensuous intuition through imagination.

We have therefore a pure imagination as one of the fundamental faculties of the human soul, on which all knowledge *a priori* depends. Through it we bring the manifold of intuition on one side in connection with the condition of the necessary unity of pure apperception on the other. These two extreme ends, sense and understanding, must be brought into contact with each other by means of the transcendental function of imagination, because, without it, the senses might give us phenomena, but no objects of empirical knowledge, therefore no experience. Real experience, which is made up of apprehension, association (of reproduction), and lastly recognition of phenomena, contains in this last and highest (among the purely empirical elements of experience) concepts, which render possible the formal unity of experience, and with it, all objective validity (truth) of empirical knowledge. These grounds for the recognition of the manifold, so far as they concern the form only of experience in general, are our categories. On them is founded the whole formal unity in the synthesis of imagination and, through it, of the whole empirical use of them (in recognition, reproduction, association, and apprehension) down to the very phenomena, because it is only by means of those elements of knowledge that the phenomena can belong to our consciousness and therefore to ourselves.

It is we therefore who carry into the phenomena which we call nature, order and regularity, nay, we should never find them in nature, if we ourselves, or the nature of our mind, had not originally placed them there. For the unity of nature is meant to be a necessary and *a priori* certain unity in the connection of all phenomena. And how should we *a priori* have arrived at such a synthetical unity, if the subjective grounds of such unity were not contained *a priori* in the original sources of our knowledge, and if those subjective conditions did not at the same time possess objective validity, as being the grounds on which alone an object becomes possible in our experience?

We have before given various definitions of the understanding, by calling it the spontaneity of knowledge (as opposed to the receptivity of the senses), or the faculty of thinking, or the faculty of concepts or of judgments; all of these explanations, if more closely examined, coming to the same. We may now characterise it as *the faculty of rules*. This characteristic is more significant, and approaches nearer to the essence of the understanding. The senses give us forms (of intuition), the understanding rules, being always busy to examine phenomena, in order to discover in them some kind of rule. Rules, so far as they are objective (therefore necessarily inherent in our knowledge of an object), are called laws. Although experience teaches us many laws, yet these are only particular determinations of higher laws, the highest of them, to which all others are subject, springing *a priori* from the understanding; not being derived from experience, but, on the contrary, imparting to the phenomena their regularity, and thus making experience possible. The understanding therefore is not only a power of making rules by a comparison of phenomena, it is itself the lawgiver of nature, and without the understanding nature, that is, a synthetical unity of the manifold of phenomena, according to rules, would be nowhere to be found, because phenomena, as such, cannot exist without us, but exist in our sensibility only. This sensibility, as an object of our knowledge in any experience, with everything it may contain, is possible only in the unity of apperception, which unity of apperception is the transcendental ground of the necessary order of all phenomena in an experience. The same unity of apperception with reference to the manifold of representations (so as to comprehend it in one) forms what we call the rule, and the faculty of these rules I call the understanding. As possible experience therefore, all phenomena depend in the same way *a priori* on the understanding, and receive their formal possibility from it as, when looked upon as mere intuitions, they depend on sensibility, and become possible through it, so far as their form is concerned.

However exaggerated therefore and absurd it may sound, that the understanding is itself the source of the laws of nature, and of its formal unity, such a statement is nevertheless correct and in accordance with experience. It is quite true, no doubt, that empirical laws, as such, cannot derive their origin from the pure understanding, as little as the infinite manifoldness of phenomena could be sufficiently comprehended through the pure form of sensuous intuition. But all empirical laws are only particular determinations of the pure laws of the understanding, under which and according to which the former become possible, and phenomena assume a regular form, quite as much as all phenomena, in spite of the variety of their empirical form, must always submit to the conditions of the pure form of sensibility.

The pure understanding is therefore in the categories the law of the synthetical unity of all phenomena, and thus makes experience, so far as its form is concerned, for the first time possible. This, and no more than this, we were called upon to prove in the transcendental deduction of the categories, namely, to make the relation of the understanding to our sensibility, and through it to all objects of experience, that is the objective validity of the pure concepts of the understanding, conceivable *a priori,* and thus to establish their origin and their truth.

SUMMARY REPRESENTATION
Of the Correctness and of the Only Possibility of a Deduction of the Pure Concepts of the Understanding

If the objects with which our knowledge has to deal were things by themselves, we could have no concepts *a priori* of them. For where should we take them? If we took them from the object (without asking even the question, how that object could be known to us) our concepts would be empirical only, not concepts *a priori.* If we took them from within ourselves, then that which is within us only, could not determine the nature of an object different from our representations, that is, supply a ground why there should be a thing to which something like what we have in our thoughts really belongs, and why all this representation should not rather be altogether empty. But if, on the contrary, we have to deal with phenomena only, then it becomes not only possible, but necessary, that certain concepts *a priori* should precede our empirical knowledge of objects. For being phenomena, they form an object that is within us only, because a mere modification of our sensibility can never exist outside us. The very idea that all these phenomena, and therefore all objects with which we have to deal, are altogether within me, or determinations of my own identical self, implies by itself the necessity of a permanent unity of them in one and the same apperception. In that unity of a possible consciousness consists also the form of all knowledge of objects, by which the manifold, as belonging to *one* object, is thought. The manner therefore in which the manifold of sensuous representation (intuition) belongs to our consciousness, precedes all knowledge of an object, as its intellectual form, and constitutes a kind of formal knowledge of all objects *a priori,* if they are to be thought (categories). Their synthesis by means of pure imagination, and the unity of all representations with reference to the original apperception, precede all empirical knowledge. Pure concepts of the understanding are therefore *a priori* possible, nay, with regard to experience, necessary, for this simple reason, because our knowledge has to deal with nothing but phenomena, the possibility of which depends on ourselves, and the connection and unity of which (in the representation of an object) can be found in ourselves only, as antecedent to all experience, nay, as first rendering all experience possible, so far as its form is concerned. On this ground, as the only possible one, our deduction of the categories has been carried out.

FOUNDATIONS OF THE METAPHYSICS OF MORALS

PREFACE

As my concern here is with moral philosophy, I limit the question suggested to this: Whether it is not of the utmost necessity to construct a pure moral philosophy, perfectly cleared of everything which is only empirical, and which belongs to anthropology? for that such a philosophy must be possible is evident from the common idea of duty and of the moral laws. Everyone must admit that if a law is to have moral force, *i.e.* to be the basis of an obligation, it must carry with it absolute necessity; that, for example, the precept "Thou shall not lie," is not valid for men alone, as if other rational beings had no need to observe it; and so with all the other moral laws properly so called; that, therefore, the basis of obligation must not be sought in the nature of man, or in the circumstances in the world in which he is placed, but *a priori* simply in the conception of pure reason; and although any other precept which is founded on principles of mere experience may be in certain respects universal, yet in as far as it rests even in the least degree on an empirical basis, perhaps only as to a motive, such a precept, while it may be a practical rule, can never be called a moral law. . . .

THE GOOD WILL

Nothing can possibly be conceived in the world, or even out of it, which can be called good, without qualification, except a Good Will. Intelligence, wit, judgment, and the other *talents* of the mind, however they may be named, or courage, resolution, perseverance, as qualities of temperament, are undoubtedly good and desirable in many respects; but these gifts of

From Immanuel Kant, *The Foundations of the Metaphysics of Morals,* trans. T. K. Abbott (London: Longmans, Green and Co., 1873). With emendations by Daniel Kolak.

nature may also become extremely bad and mischievous if the will which is to make use of them, and which, therefore, constitutes what is called *character,* is not good. It is the same with the *gifts of fortune.* Power, riches, honour, even health, and the general well-being and contentment with one's conditions which is called *happiness,* inspire pride, and often presumption, if there is not a good will to correct the influence of these on the mind, and with this also to rectify the whole principle of acting, and adapt it to its end. The sight of a being who is not adorned with a single feature of a pure and good will, enjoying unbroken prosperity, can never give pleasure to an imperial rational spectator. Thus a good will appears to constitute the indispensable condition even of being worthy of happiness.

There are even some qualities which are of service to this good will itself, and may facilitate its action, yet which have no intrinsic unconditional value, but always presuppose a good will, and this qualifies the esteem that we justly have for them, and does not permit us to regard them as absolutely good. Moderation in the affections and passions, self-control, and calm deliberation are not only good in many respects, but even seem to constitute part of the intrinsic worth of the person; but they are far from deserving to be called good without qualification, although they have been so unconditionally praised by the ancients. For without the principles of a good will, they may become extremely bad; and the coolness of a villain not only makes him far more dangerous, but also directly makes him more abominable in our eyes than he would have been without it.

A good will is good not because of what it performs or effects, not by its aptness for the attainment of some proposed end, but simply by virtue of the volition, that is, it is good in itself, and considered by itself to be esteemed much higher than all that can be brought about by it in favour of any inclination, nay, even of the sum-total of all inclinations. Even if it should happen that, owing to special disfavour of fortune, or the niggardly provision of a step-motherly nature, this will should wholly lack power to accomplish its purpose, if with its greatest efforts it should yet achieve nothing, and there should remain only the good will (not, to be sure, a mere wish, but the summoning of all means in our power), then, like a jewel, it would still shine by its own light, as a thing which has its whole value in itself. Its usefulness or fruitlessness can neither add to nor take away anything from this value. It would be, as it were, only the setting to enable us to handle it the more conveniently in common commerce, or to attract to it the attention of those who are not yet connoisseurs, but not to recommend it to true connoisseurs, or to determine its value.

WHY REASON WAS MADE TO GUIDE THE WILL

There is, however, something so strange in this idea of the absolute value of the mere will, in which no account is taken of its utility, that notwithstanding the thorough assent of even common reason to the idea, yet a suspicion must arise that it may perhaps really be the product of mere high-blown fancy, and that we may have misunderstood the purpose of nature in assigning reason as the governor of our will. Therefore we will examine this idea from this point of view.

In the physical constitution of an organized being, that is, a being adapted suitably to the purposes of life, we assume it as a fundamental principle that no organ for any purpose will be found but what is also the fittest and best adapted for that purpose. Now in a being which has reason and a will, if the proper object of nature were its *conservatism,* its *welfare,* in a word, its *happiness,* then nature would have hit upon a very bad arrangement in selecting the reason of the creature to carry out this purpose. For all the actions which the creature has to perform with a view to this purpose, and the whole rule of its conduct, would be far more surely prescribed to it by instinct, and that end would have been attained thereby much more certainly than it ever can be by reason. Should reason have been communicated to this favoured creature over and above, it must only have served it to contemplate the happy constitution of its nature, to admire it, to congratulate itself thereon, and to feel thankful for it to the beneficent cause, but not that it should subject its desires to that weak and delusive guidance, and meddle bunglingly with the purpose of nature. In a word, nature would have taken care that reason should not break forth into *practical exercise,* nor have the presumption, with its weak insight, to think out for itself the plan of happiness, and of the means of attaining it. Nature would not only have taken on herself the choice of the ends, but also of the means, and with wise foresight would have entrusted both to instinct.

And, in fact, we find that the more a cultivated reason applies itself with deliberate purpose to the enjoyment of life and happiness, so much the more does the man fail of true satisfaction. And from this circumstance there arises in many, if they are candid enough to confess it, a certain degree of *misology,* that is, hatred of reason, especially in the case of those who are most experienced in the use of it, because after calculating all the advantages they derive, I do not say from the invention of all the arts of common luxury, but even from the sciences (which seem to them to be after all only a luxury of the understanding), they find that they have, in fact, only brought more trouble on their shoulders, rather than gained in happiness; and they end by envying, rather than despising, the more common stamp of men who keep closer to the guidance of mere instinct, and do not allow their reason much influence on their conduct. And this we must admit, that the judgment of those who would very much lower the lofty eulogies of the advantages which reason gives us in regard to the happiness and satisfaction of life, or who would even reduce them below zero, is by no means morose or ungrateful to the goodness with which the world is governed, but that there lies at the root of these judgments the idea that our existence has a different and far nobler end, for which, and not for happiness, reason is properly intended, and which must, therefore, be regarded as the supreme condition to which the private ends of man must, for the most part, be postponed.

For as reason is not competent to guide the will with certainty in regard to its objects and the satisfaction of all our wants (which it to some extent even multiplies), this being an end to which an implanted instinct would have led with much greater certainty; and since, nevertheless, reason is imparted to us as a practical faculty, *i.e.* as one which is to have influence on the *will,* therefore, admitting that nature generally in the distribution of her capacities has adapted the means to the end, its true destination must be to produce a *will,* not merely good as a *means* to something else, but *good in itself,* for which reason was absolutely necessary. This will then, though not indeed the sole and complete good, must be the supreme good and the condition of every other, even of the desire of happiness. Under these circumstances, there is nothing inconsistent with the wisdom of nature in the fact that the cultivation of the reason, which is requisite for the first and unconditional purpose, does in many ways interfere, at least in this life, with the attainment of the second, which is always conditional, namely, happiness. Nay, it may even reduce it to nothing, without nature thereby failing in her purpose. For reason recognizes the establishment of a good will as its highest practical destination, and in attaining this purpose is capable only of a satisfaction of its own proper kind, namely, that from the attainment of an end, which end again is determined by reason only, notwithstanding that this may involve many a disappointment to the ends of inclination.

THE FIRST PROPOSITION OF MORALITY

We have then to develop the notion of a will which deserves to be highly esteemed for itself, and is good without a view to anything further, a notion which exists already in the sound natural understanding, requiring rather to be cleared up than to be taught, and which in estimating the value of our actions always takes the first place, and constitutes the condition of all the rest. In order to do this, we will take the notion of duty, which includes that of a good will, although implying certain subjective restrictions and hindrances. These, however, far from concealing it, or rendering it unrecognizable, rather bring it out by contrast, and make it shine forth so much the brighter.

I omit here all actions which are already recognized as inconsistent with duty although they may be useful for this or that purpose, for with these the question whether they are done *from duty* cannot arise at all, since they even conflict with it. I also set aside those actions which really conform to duty, but to which men have *no* direct *inclination,* performing them because they are impelled thereto by some other inclination. For in this case we can readily distinguish whether the action which agrees with duty is done *from duty,* or from a selfish view. It is much harder to make this distinction when the action accords with duty, and the subject has besides a *direct* inclination to it. For example, it is always a matter of duty that a dealer should not overcharge an inexperienced purchaser; and wherever there is much commerce the prudent tradesman does not overcharge, but keeps a fixed price for everyone, so that a child buys of him as well as any other. Men are thus *honestly* served; but this is not enough to make us believe that the tradesman has so acted from duty and from principles of honesty: his own advantage required it; it is out of the question in this case to suppose that he might besides have a direct inclination in favour of the buyers, so that, as it were, from love he should give no advantage to one over another. Accordingly the action was done neither from duty nor from direct inclination, but merely with a selfish view.

On the other hand, it is a duty to maintain one's life; and, in addition, everyone has also a direct inclination to do so. But on this account the often anxious care which most men take for it has no intrinsic worth, and their maxim has no moral import. They preserve their life *as duty requires,* no doubt, but not *because duty requires.* On the other hand, if adversity and hopeless sorrow have completely taken away the relish for life; if the unfortunate one, strong in mind, indignant at his fate rather than desponding or dejected, wishes for death, and yet preserves his life without loving it—not from inclination or fear, but from duty—then his maxim has a moral worth.

To be beneficent when we can is a duty; and besides this, there are many minds so sympathetically constituted that, without any other motive of vanity or self-interest, they find a pleasure in spreading joy around them, and can take delight in the satisfaction of others so far as it is their own work. But I maintain that in such a case an action of this kind, however proper, however amiable it may be, has nevertheless no true moral worth, but is on a level with other inclinations, *e.g.* the inclination to honour, which, if it is happily directed to that which is in fact of public utility and accordant with duty, and consequently honourable, deserves praise and encouragement, but not esteem. For the maxim lacks the moral import, namely, that such actions be done *from duty,* not from inclination. Put the case that the mind of that philanthropist was clouded by sorrow of his own, extinguishing all sympathy with the lot of others, and that while he still has the power to benefit others in distress, he is not touched by their trouble because he is absorbed with his own; and now suppose that he tears himself out of this dead insensibility, and performs the action without any inclination to it, but simply from duty, then first has his action its genuine moral worth. Further still; if nature has put little sympathy in the heart of this or that man; if he, supposed to be an upright man, is by temperament cold and indifferent to the sufferings of others, perhaps because in respect of his own he is provided with the special gift of patience and fortitude, and supposes, or even requires, that others should have the same—and such a man would certainly not be the meanest product of nature—but if nature had not specially framed him for a philanthropist, would he not still find in himself a source from whence to give himself a far higher worth than that of a good-natured temperament could be? Unquestionably. It is just in this that the moral worth of the character is brought out which is incomparably the highest of all, namely, that he is beneficent, not from inclination, but from duty.

To secure one's own happiness is a duty, at least indirectly; for discontent with one's condition, under a pressure of many anxieties and amidst unsatisfied wants, might easily become a great *temptation to transgression of duty.* But here again, without looking to duty, all men have already the strongest and most intimate inclination to happiness, because it is just in this idea that all inclinations are combined in one total. But the precept of happiness is often of such a sort that it greatly interferes with some inclinations, and yet a man cannot form any definite and certain conception of the sum of satisfaction of all of them which is called happiness. It is not then to be wondered at that a single inclination, definite both as to what it promises and as to the time within which it can be gratified, is often able to overcome such a fluctuating idea, and that a gouty patient, for instance, can choose to enjoy what he likes, and to suffer what he may, since, according to his calculation, on this occasion at least, he has [only] not sacrificed the enjoyment of the present moment to a possibly mistaken expectation of a happiness which is supposed to be found in health. But even in this case, if the general desire for happiness did not influence his will, and supposing that in his particular case health was not a necessary element in this calculation, there yet remains in this, as in all other cases, this law, namely, that he should promote his happiness not from inclination but from duty, and by this would his conduct first acquire true moral worth.

It is in this manner, undoubtedly, that we are to understand those passages of Scripture also in which we are commanded to love our neighbour, even our enemy. For love, as an affection, cannot be commanded, but beneficence for duty's sake may; even though we are not impelled to it by any inclination—nay, are even repelled by a natural and unconquerable aversion. This is *practical* love, and not *pathological*—a love which is seated in the will, and not in the propensions of sense—in principles of action and not of tender sympathy; and it is this love alone which can be commanded.

THE SECOND PROPOSITION OF MORALITY

The second proposition is: That an action done from duty derives its moral worth, *not from the purpose* which is to be attained by it, but from the maxim by which it is determined, and therefore does not depend on the realization of the object of the action, but merely on the *principle of volition* by which the action has taken place, without regard to any object of desire. It is clear from what precedes that the purposes which we may have in view in our actions, or their effects regarded as ends and springs of the will, cannot give to actions any unconditional or moral worth. In what, then, can their worth lie, if it is not to consist in the will and in reference to its expected effect? It cannot lie anywhere but in the *principle of the will* without regard to the ends which can be attained by the action. For the will stands between its *a priori principle,* which is formal, and its *a posteriori* spring, which is material, as between two roads, and as it must be determined by something, it follows that it must be determined by the formal principle of volition when an action is done from duty, in which case every material principle has been withdrawn from it.

THE THIRD PROPOSITION OF MORALITY

The third proposition, which is a consequence of the two preceding, I would express thus: *Duty is the necessity of acting from respect for the law.* I may have *inclination* for an object as the effect of my proposed action, but I cannot have *respect* for it, just for this reason, that it is an effect and not an energy of will. Similarly, I cannot have respect for inclination, whether my own or another's; I can at most, if my own, approve it; if another's, sometimes even love it; *i.e.* look on it as favourable to my own interest. It is only what is connected with my will as a principle, by no means as an effect—what does not subserve my inclination, but overpowers it, or at least in case of choice excludes it from its calculation—in other words, simply the law of itself, which can be an object of respect, and hence a command. Now an action done from duty must wholly exclude the influence of inclination, and with it every object of the will, so that nothing remains which can determine the will except objectively the *law,* and subjectively *pure respect* for this practical law, and consequently the maxim that I should follow this law even to the thwarting of all my inclinations.

Thus the moral worth of an action does not lie in the effect expected from it, nor in any principle of action which requires to borrow its motive from this expected effect. For all these effects—agreeableness of one's condition, and even the promotion of the happiness of others—could have been also brought about by other causes, so that for this there would have been no need of the will of a rational being; whereas it is in this alone that the supreme and unconditional good can be found. The pre-eminent good which we call moral can therefore consist in nothing else than *the conception of law* in itself, *which certainly is only possible in a rational being,* in so far as this conception, and not the expected effect, determines the will. This is a good which is already present in the person who acts accordingly, and we have not to wait for it to appear first in the result.

THE SUPREME PRINCIPLE OF MORALITY: THE CATEGORICAL IMPERATIVE

But what sort of law can that be, the conception of which must determine the will, even without paying any regard to the effect expected from it, in order that this will may be called good absolutely and without qualification? As I have deprived the will of every impulse which could arise to it from obedience to any law, there remains nothing but the universal conformity of its actions to law in general, which alone is to serve the will as a principle, *i.e.* I am never to act otherwise than so *that I could also will that my maxim should become a universal law.* Here, now, it is the simple conformity to law in general, without assuming any particular law applicable to certain actions, that serves the will as its principle, and must so serve it, if duty is not to be a vain delusion and a chimerical notion. The common reason of men in its practical judgments perfectly coincides with this, and always has in view the principle here suggested. Let the question be, for example: May I when in distress make a promise with the intention not to keep it? I readily distinguish here between the two significations which the question may have: Whether it is prudent, or whether it is right, to make a false promise? The former may undoubtedly often be the case. I see clearly indeed that it is not enough to extricate myself from a present difficulty by means of this subterfuge, but it must be well considered whether there may not hereafter spring from this lie much greater inconvenience than that from which I now free myself, and as, with all my supposed *cunning*, the consequences cannot be so easily foreseen but that credit once lost may be much more injurious to me than any mischief which I seek to avoid at present, it should be considered whether it would not be more *prudent* to act herein according to a universal maxim, and to make it a habit to promise nothing except with the intention of keeping it. But it is soon clear to me that such a maxim will still only be based on the fear of consequences. Now it is a wholly different thing to be truthful from duty, and to be so from apprehension of injurious consequences. In the first case, the very notion of the action already implies a law for me; in the second case, I must first look about elsewhere to see what results may be combined with it which would affect myself. For to deviate from the principle of duty is beyond all doubt wicked; but to be unfaithful to my maxim of prudence may often be very advantageous to me, although to abide by it is certainly safer. The shortest way, however, and an unerring one, to discover the answer to this question whether a lying promise is consistent with duty, is to ask myself, Should I be content that my maxim (to extricate myself from difficulty by a false promise) should hold good as a universal law, for myself as well as for others? and should I be able to say to myself, "Every one may make a deceitful promise when he finds himself in a difficulty from which he cannot otherwise extricate himself"? Then I presently become aware that while I can will the lie, I can by no means will that lying should be a universal law. For with such a law there would be no promises at all, since it would be in vain to allege my intention in regard to my future actions to those who would not believe this allegation, or if they over-hastily did so, would pay me back in my own coin. Hence my maxim, as soon as it should be made a universal law, would necessarily destroy itself.

I do not, therefore, need any far-reaching penetration to discern what I have to do in order that my will may be morally good. Inexperienced in the course of the world, incapable of being prepared for all its contingencies, I only ask myself: Can you also will that your maxim should be a universal law? If not, then it must be rejected, and that not because of a disadvantage accruing from myself or even to others, but because it cannot enter as a principle into a possible universal legislation, and reason extorts from me immediate respect for such legislation. I do not indeed as yet *discern* on what this respect is based (this the philosopher may inquire), but at least I understand this, that it is an estimation of the worth which far outweighs all worth of what is recommended by inclination, and that the necessity of acting from *pure* respect for the practical law is what constitutes duty, to which every other motive must give place, because it is the condition of a will being good *in itself*, and the worth of such a will is above everything.

Thus, then, without quitting the moral knowledge of common human reason, we have arrived at its principle. And although, no doubt, common men do not conceive it in such an abstract and universal form, yet they always have it really before their eyes, and use it as the standard of their decision. . . .

Nor could anything be more fatal to morality than that we should wish to derive it from examples. For every example of it that is set before me must be first itself tested by principles of morality, whether it is worthy to serve as an original example, *i.e.* as a pattern, but by no means can it authoritatively furnish the conception of morality. Even the Holy One of the Gospels must first be compared with our ideal of moral perfection before we can recognize

Him as such; and so He says of Himself, "Why call ye Me [whom you see] good; none is good [the model of good] but God only [whom ye do not see]." But whence have we the conception of God as the supreme good? Simply from the *idea* of moral perfection, which reason frames *a priori*, and connects inseparably with the notion of a free will. Imitation finds no place at all in morality, and examples serve only for encouragement, *i.e.* they put beyond doubt the feasibility of what the law commands, they make visible that which the practical rule expresses more generally, but they can never authorize us to set aside the true original which lies in reason, and to guide ourselves by examples.

From what has been said, it is clear that all moral conceptions have their seat and origin completely *a priori* in the reason, and that, moreover, in the commonest reason just as truly as in that which is in the highest degree speculative; that they cannot be obtained by abstraction from any empirical, and therefore merely contingent knowledge; that it is just this purity of their origin that makes them worthy to serve as our supreme practical principle, and that just in proportion as we add anything empirical, we detract from their genuine influence, and from the absolute value of actions; that it is not only of the greatest necessity, in a purely speculative point of view, but is also of the greatest practical importance, to derive these notions and laws from pure reason, to present them pure and unmixed, and even to determine the compass of this practical or pure rational knowledge, *i.e.* to determine the whole faculty of pure practical reason; and, in doing so, we must not make its principles dependent on the particular nature of human reason, though in speculative philosophy this may be permitted, or may even at times be necessary; but since moral laws ought to hold good for every rational creature, we must derive them from the general concept of a rational being. In this way, although for its *application* to man morality has need of anthropology, yet, in the first instance, we must treat it independently as pure philosophy, *i.e.* as metaphysic, complete in itself (a thing which in such distinct branches of science is easily done); knowing well that unless we are in possession of this, it would not only be vain to determine the moral element of duty in right actions for purposes of speculative criticism, but it would be impossible to base morals on their genuine principles, even for common practical purposes, especially of moral instruction, so as to produce pure moral dispositions, and to engraft them on men's minds to the promotion of the greatest possible good in the world. . . .

THE RATIONAL GROUND OF THE CATEGORICAL IMPERATIVE

. . . the question, how the imperative of *morality* is possible, is undoubtedly one, the only one, demanding a solution, as this is not at all hypothetical, and the objective necessity which it presents cannot rest on any hypothesis, as is the case with the hypothetical imperatives. Only here we must never leave out of consideration that we *cannot* make out *by any example*, in other words empirically, whether there is such an imperative at all; but it is rather to be feared that all those which seem to be categorical may yet be at bottom hypothetical. For instance, when the precept is: Thou shalt not promise deceitfully; and it is assumed that the necessity of this is not a mere counsel to avoid some other evil, so that it should mean: Thou shalt not make a lying promise, lest if it become known thou shouldst destroy thy credit, but that an action of this kind must be regarded as evil in itself, so that the imperative of the prohibition is categorical; then we cannot show with certainty in any example that the will was determined merely by the law, without any other spring of action, although it may appear to be so. For it is always possible that fear of disgrace, perhaps also obscure dread of other dangers, may have a secret influence on the will. Who can prove by experience the nonexistence of a cause when all that experience tells us is that we do not perceive it? But in such a case the so-called moral imperative, which as such appears to be categorical and unconditional, would in reality be only a pragmatic precept, drawing our attention to our own interests, and merely teaching us to take these into consideration.

We shall therefore have to investigate *a priori* the possibility of a categorical imperative, as we have not in this case the advantage of its reality being given in experience, so that [the elucidation of] its possibility should be requisite only for its explanation, not for its establishment. In the meantime it may be discerned beforehand that the categorical imperative alone has the purport of a practical law: all the rest may indeed be called *principles* of the will but not laws, since whatever is only necessary for the attainment of some arbitrary purpose may be considered as in itself contingent, and we can at any time be free from the precept if we give up the purpose: on the contrary, the unconditional command leaves the will no liberty to choose the opposite; consequently it alone carries with it that necessity which we require in a law.

Secondly, in the case of this categorical imperative or law of morality, the difficulty (of discerning its possibility) is a very profound one. It is an *a priori* synthetical practical proposition; and as there is so much difficulty in discerning the possibility of speculative propositions of this kind, it may readily be supposed that the difficulty will be no less with the practical.

FIRST FORMULATION OF THE CATEGORICAL IMPERATIVE: UNIVERSAL LAW

In this problem we will first inquire whether the mere conception of a categorical imperative may not perhaps supply us also with the formula of it, containing the proposition which alone can be a categorical imperative; for even if we know the tenor of such an absolute command, yet how it is possible will require further special and laborious study, which we postpone to the last section.

When I conceive a hypothetical imperative, in general I do not know beforehand what it will contain until I am given the condition. But when I conceive a categorical imperative, I know at once what it contains. For as the imperative contains besides the law only the necessity that the maxims shall conform to this law, while the law contain no conditions restricting it, there remains nothing but the general statement that the maxim of the action should conform to a universal law, and it is this conformity alone that the imperative properly represents as necessary.

There is therefore but one categorical imperative, namely, this: *Act only on that maxim whereby you can at the same time will that it should become a universal law.*

Now if all imperatives of duty can be deduced from this one imperative as from their principle, then, although it should remain undecided whether what is called duty is not merely a vain notion, yet at least we shall be able to show what we understand by it and what this notion means.

Since the universality of the law according to which effects are produced constitutes what is properly called *nature* in the most general sense (as to form), that is the existence of things so far as it is determined by general laws, the imperative of duty may be expressed thus: *Act as if the maxim of your action were to become by your will a universal law of nature.*

FOUR ILLUSTRATIONS

We will now enumerate a few duties, adopting the usual division of them into duties to ourselves and to others, and into perfect and imperfect duties.

1. A man reduced to despair by a series of misfortunes feels wearied of life, but is still so far in possession of his reason that he can ask himself whether it would not be contrary to his duty to himself to take his own life. Now he inquires whether the maxim of his action could become a universal law of nature. His maxim is: From self-love I adopt it as a principle to shorten my life when its longer duration is likely to bring more evil than satisfaction. It is asked then simply whether this principle founded on self-love can become a universal law of nature. Now we see at once that a system of nature of which it should be a law to destroy life by means of the very feeling whose special nature it is to impel to the improvement of life would contradict itself, and therefore could not exist as a system of nature; hence that maxim cannot possibly exist as a universal law of nature, and consequently would be wholly inconsistent with the supreme principle of all duty.

2. Another finds himself forced by necessity to borrow money. He knows that he will not be able to repay it, but sees also that nothing will be lent to him, unless he promises stoutly to repay it in a definite time. He desires to make this promise, but he has still so much conscience as to ask himself: Is it not unlawful and inconsistent with duty to get out of a difficulty in this way? Suppose, however, that he resolves to do so, then the maxim of his action would be expressed thus: When I think myself in want of money, I will borrow money and promise to repay it, although I know that I never can do so. Now this principle of self-love or of one's own advantage may perhaps be consistent with my whole future welfare; but the question is, Is it right? I change then the suggestion of self-love into a universal law, and state the question thus: How would it be if my maxim were a universal law? Then I see at once that it could never hold as a universal law of nature, but would necessarily contradict itself. For supposing it to be a universal law that everyone when he thinks himself in a difficulty should be able to promise whatever he pleases, with the purpose of not keeping his promise, the promise itself would become impossible, as well as the end that one might have in view in it, since no one would consider that anything was promised to him, but would ridicule all such statements as vain pretenses.

3. A third finds in himself a talent which with the help of some culture might make him a useful man in many respects. But he finds himself in comfortable circumstances, and prefers to indulge in pleasure rather than to take pains in enlarging and improving his happy natural capacities. He asks, however, whether his maxim of neglect of his natural gifts, besides agreeing with his inclination to indulgence, agrees also with what is called duty. He sees then that a system of nature could indeed subsist with such a universal law although men (like the South Sea islanders) should let their talents rest, and resolve to devote their lives merely to idleness, amusement, and propagation of their species—in a word, to enjoyment; but he cannot possibly *will* that this should be a universal law of nature, or be implanted in us as such by a natural instinct. For, as a rational being, he necessarily wills that his faculties be developed, since they serve him, and have been given him, for all sorts of possible purposes.

4. A fourth, who is in prosperity, while he sees that others have to contend with great wretchedness and that he could help them, thinks: What concern is it of mine? Let everyone

be as happy as Heaven pleases, or as he can make himself; I will take nothing from him nor even envy him, only I do not wish to contribute anything to his welfare or to his assistance in distress! Now no doubt if such a mode of thinking were a universal law, the human race might very well subsist, and doubtless even better than in a state in which everyone talks of sympathy and good-will, or even takes care occasionally to put it into practice, but, on the other side, also cheats when he can, betrays the rights of men, or otherwise violates them. But although it is possible that a universal law of nature might exist in accordance with that maxim, it is impossible to *will* that such a principle should have the universal validity of a law of nature. For a will which resolved this would contradict itself, inasmuch as many cases might occur in which one would have need of the love and sympathy of others, and in which, by such a law of nature, sprung from his own will, he would deprive himself of all hope of the aid he desires.

These are a few of the many actual duties, or at least what we regard as such, which obviously fall into two classes on the one principle that we have laid down. We must be *able to will* that a maxim of our action should be a universal law. This is the canon of the moral appreciation of the action generally. Some actions are of such a character that their maxim cannot without contradiction be even *conceived* as a universal law of nature, far from it being possible that we should *will* that it *should* be so. In others this intrinsic impossibility is not found, but still it is impossible to *will* that their maxim should be raised to the universality of a law of nature, since such a will would contradict itself. It is easily seen that the former violate strict or rigorous (inflexible) duty; the latter only laxer (meritorious) duty. Thus it has been completely shown by these examples how all duties depend as regards the nature of the obligation (not the object of the action) on the same principle.

33

FICHTE

1762–1814

Johann Gottlieb Fichte was born in Rammenau, a village in Upper (Saxon) Lusatia. After studying at the Universities of Jena and Leipzig, he worked as a tutor in Zürich. His first work, *Aphorisms on Religion and God* (1790) was highly influenced by Spinoza's philosophy, especially his views on determinism. But of the philosophers then living, it was Kant who exerted the greatest and most lasting influence on Fichte.

When Fichte visited Kant in Königsberg to pay his respects, Kant agreed to read Fichte's next manuscript, *Essay Toward a Critique of All Revelation* (1792). Fichte sent it to him and Kant was so impressed that he sent the manuscript to his publisher on Fichte's behalf. The publisher decided to publish it. However, due to a printer's error, the book appeared without Fichte's name on it and because Kant had written the preface, everyone assumed the book had been written by Kant!

Soon afterward Kant published a retraction stating that the work was Fichte's, not his. He then added, almost in passing, that Fichte's book just happens to solve a major problem with Kant's own system that Kant himself had found insoluble. The problem with his own work, as Kant saw it, was that his *Critique of Pure Reason* puts speculative theology in a completely negative light. Yet his *Critique of Practical Reason* puts the moral law, so central to Kant's thought, as the absolute content, or substance, of any religion. This inconsistency left open the puzzling question as to the conditions under which religious belief is possible.

Fichte's brilliant *Critique of All Revelation* bridges the gap between Kant's two monumental works by showing how the absolute requirements of the moral law supply the necessary conditions that make revealed religion possible. Fichte's reputation was instantly secured. He became professor of philosophy at the University of Jena in 1794 and in the same year published *On the Concept of the Science of Knowledge, or So-called Philosophy* and *Fundamental Principles of the Science of Knowledge,* from which our selection is taken.

Fichte departs from Kant in a direction that paved the way for three related, subsequent, extremely important movements in philosophy: absolute idealism, phenomenology, and existentialism. Fichte's analysis of the ego was especially influential. According to Fichte, the ego is a self-affirming primitive act of consciousness that constructs the objective world not in tandem with "things in themselves," as Kant supposed, but solely out of its own appearances. This process gives rise to an antinomy-like conflict between the inner sense of free will and the external sense that the world is completely determined: "In immediate consciousness, I appear to myself as free; by reflection on the whole of Nature, I discover that freedom is absolutely impossible." And yet, the only knowledge of which any one of us is capable is that of our own minds: "In all perception you perceive only your own state." Thus, in a way that Hume might well have responded to Kant's rebuttal to his argument against causality, the idea of things in themselves is *itself* but a projection of the mind and therefore not something to which consciousness is bound.

The idea is this. For something, say a rock, to be *objectively real* simply means, in Fichte's philosophy, that it consists of all possible experiences that it can generate in the mind of a potential observer. Take the rock apart or don't take it apart, look at it from above and below or not; the point is that you could do these things because the rock is a containing space of all (perhaps infinite) possibilities of relation of that object. Fichte is thus a subjective idealist. Like Berkeley, he believes that everything is made of thought. But what is thought? Thought, according to Fichte,

> has no *being* proper, no subsistence, for this is the result of an interaction and there is nothing . . . with which the intellect could be set to interact [because, for Fichte, there is no noumenal world of the thing in itself]. The intellect, for idealism, is an *act,* and absolutely nothing more; we should not even call it an *active* something, for this expression refers to something subsistent in which activity inheres.

Fichte was recognized in his lifetime as one of the three leading successors to Kant, with Hegel and Schelling being the other two. An extremely dynamic and popular lecturer at Jena, he commanded a large following among his students as well as the public, but this did not work out to his advantage. After a prolonged conflict with the Jena administration over academic freedom, he was forcibly dismissed from his position. Apparently, Fichte's philosophy was regarded as so highly dangerous that he had been asked not to publish his views; he refused, arguing that a philosopher had not only the right but the moral duty to expound his thoughts, including and especially the philosophy of religion (one of the leading bones of contention with both the university and public authorities). After his dismissal, Fichte continued to publish and even increased his public lectures, becoming one of the leading figures in Berlin. There, during the French occupation, shortly after Napoleon had arrived in 1806, Fichte delivered his famous *Addresses to the German Nation* (1807) inspiring his fellow Germans to moral regeneration through national unity and political reform. Four years later, in 1810, Fichte helped found the new University of Berlin. He remained there, teaching his philosophy and writing, until his death.

THE SCIENCE OF KNOWLEDGE

1

Attend to yourself; turn your glance away from all that surrounds you and upon your own innermost self. Such is the first demand which philosophy makes of its disciples. We speak of nothing that is without you, but wholly of yourself.

In the most fleeting self-observation every one must perceive a marked difference between the various immediate determinations of his consciousness, which we may also call representations. Some of them appear entirely dependent upon our freedom, and it is impossible for us to believe that there is anything without us corresponding to them. Our imagination, our will, appears to us as free. Others, however, we refer to a truth, as their model, which is held to be established, independent of us; and in the attempt to determine such representations, we find ourselves conditioned by the necessity of their harmony with this truth. In the knowledge of their contents we do not consider ourselves free. In brief, we can say, some of our representations are accompanied by the feeling of freedom, others by the feeling of necessity.

The question cannot reasonably arise: Why are the representations, which are directly dependent upon our freedom, determined in precisely this manner and not otherwise? For when it is affirmed that they are dependent upon our freedom, all application of the conception of a ground is dismissed; they are thus, because I have so determined them, and if I had determined them otherwise, then they would be different. But it is certainly a question worthy of reflection: What is the ground of the system of those representations which are accompanied by the feelings of necessity and of that feeling of necessity itself? To answer this question is the task of philosophy; and, in my opinion, nothing is philosophy but the science which solves this problem. The system of those representations which are accompanied by the feeling of necessity is also called *experience:* internal as well as external experience. Philosophy has therefore—to express the same thing in other words—to discover the ground of all experience.

Only three distinct objections can be raised against what has here been stated. Some one might deny that representations, accompanied by the feeling of necessity, and referred to a truth determined without our aid, are ever present in our consciousness. Such a person would either make the denial against better knowledge or be differently constituted from other men. In the latter case there would also be nothing for him that he denied, and hence no denial. We could therefore dismiss his protest without further ceremony. Or some one might say: the question raised is entirely unanswerable, we are and must remain in insuperable ignorance concerning it. To enter upon an argument with such a person is wholly superfluous. He is best refuted by an actual answer to the question; then all he can do is to test our attempt and to state where and why it appears to him insufficient. Finally, some one might dispute about the designation, and assert: Philosophy is something else, or at

From *Erste Einleitung in die Wissenschaftslehre,* trans. Benjamin Rand (Berlin: Sämmtlichte Werke, 1845).

least something more, than what you have above stated. It might easily be proved to such a one, that scholars have at all times regarded exactly what has here been stated, to be philosophy, and that whatever else he might set up for it has already another name; that if this word is to signify anything at all, it must mean precisely this particular science.

Since, however, we are unwilling to enter upon any unfruitful controversy about words, we have on our part already abandoned the name of philosophy, and have called the science which has, properly speaking, the solution of the problem here indicated for its object, the *Science of Knowledge.*

2

Only when speaking of something regarded as accidental, that is, which we suppose might also have been otherwise, though it was not determined by freedom, can we inquire concerning a ground. And precisely because of this asking concerning its ground does it become accidental to the inquirer. The problem involved in seeking the ground of anything means to find something else, from the special nature of which it can be seen why the accidental, among the manifold determinations which might have come to it, assumed precisely the one it did. The ground lies, by virtue of the mere thought of a ground, outside of that which is grounded; and both are, in so far as they are the ground and the grounded, opposed to each other, related to each other, and thus the latter is explained from the former.

Now philosophy seeks to discover the ground of all experience; hence its object lies necessarily *beyond all experience.* This proposition applies to all philosophy, and has also actually been so applied, down to the period of the Kantians and their facts of consciousness, that is, of inner experience.

No objection can be raised against the proposition here set forth; for the premise to our conclusion is a mere analysis of the above-stated conception of philosophy and from it the conclusion is drawn. If some one possibly should remind us that the conception of a ground must be differently explained, we certainly could not prevent him from forming another conception of it if he chooses; but we affirm with equal right, that in the above description of philosophy we wish nothing else to be understood by that word but what has been stated. Hence, if this meaning is not permitted, the possibility of philosophy, as we have described it, must be altogether denied; and to such a denial we have already made reply in our first section.

3

The finite intelligence has nothing outside of experience. This it is that yields the entire material of its thinking. The philosopher is subject necessarily to similar conditions, and hence it appears inconceivable how he can raise himself above experience.

But he can abstract; that is to say, he can separate by the freedom of thinking what is united in experience. In experience, *the thing,* or, that which is to be determined independently of our freedom and in accordance with which our knowledge is to shape itself, and *the intelligence,* or that which is to acquire a knowledge of it, are inseparably united. The philosopher may abstract from both, and if he does, he has abstracted from experience and lifted himself above it. If he abstracts from the first, he retains an intelligence *in itself,* that is, abstracted from its relation to experience; if he abstracts from the latter, he retains the thing *in itself,* that is, abstracted from the fact that it occurs in experience. He thus retains either the intelligence in itself, or the thing-in-itself, as the ground of explanation of experience. The former mode of procedure is called *Idealism,* the latter *Dogmatism.*

Only these two philosophical systems (and of that these remarks should convince everybody) are possible. According to the first system, the representations which are accompanied by the feeling of necessity are products of the intelligence, which must be presupposed in their explanation; according to the latter system they are products of a thing in itself, which must be presupposed to explain them. If any one desired to dispute this position, he would have to prove either that there is still another way to transcend experience than by means of abstraction, or that there exist in the consciousness of experience more than the two components just mentioned. Now, in regard to the first, it will appear below that what we have here called intelligence is actually present under another name in consciousness, and therefore is not something entirely produced by abstraction; but it will at the same time be shown that the consciousness of it is conditioned by an abstraction, which is wholly natural to mankind.

It will not be denied that it is possible to frame an entire system from fragments of these dissimilar systems, and that this illogical labor has actually very often been undertaken; but it is denied that more than these two systems are possible in any logical mode of procedure.

4

Between the object (we shall call the explanatory ground of experience affirmed by a philosophy the *object of that philosophy,* since it appears to be only through and for such philosophy) of *idealism* and that of *dogmatism* there is a remarkable distinction in reference to their relation to consciousness. Everything of which I am conscious is called object of consciousness. There are three ways in which the object can be related to consciousness. Either the object appears to have been produced by the representation, or as existing without its aid; and in the latter case, either also as determined in regard to its structure, or as present merely with respect to its existence, but determinable in regard to its structure by the free intelligence.

The first relation applies merely to an imaginary object, whether with or without purpose; the second applies to an object of experience; and the third applies only to an object, which we shall forthwith describe.

I can determine myself by freedom to think this or that; for example, the thing-in-itself of the dogmatist. Now if I abstract from the thought and look simply upon myself, then I myself become the object of a particular representation. That I appear to myself as determined in precisely this manner and not otherwise, *e.g.,* as thinking, and among all possible thoughts as thinking just the thing-in-itself, is in my opinion to depend upon my freedom of self-determination: I have made myself such an object of my own free will. I have not, however, made myself, but I am compelled to presuppose myself as determinable through this self-determination. I am therefore myself my own object, the determinate character of which depends under certain conditions altogether upon intelligence, but the existence of which must always be presupposed.

Now this very I in itself is the object of Idealism. The object of this system does not occur actually as something real in consciousness, as a *thing in itself,*—for then idealism would cease to be what it is, and would be transformed into dogmatism,—but it does appear as *I in itself.* It occurs not as object of experience,—for it is not determined, but is solely determinable through me, and without this determination it would be nothing at all,—but it appears as something raised above all experience.

The object of dogmatism, on the contrary, belongs to the objects of the first class, which are produced wholly by free thinking. The thing-in-itself is a mere invention, and has no reality at all. It does not occur in experience, for the system of experience is nothing else than thinking accompanied by the feeling of necessity; it cannot even be pretended to be anything else by the dogmatist, who, like every philosopher, has to give an explanation of it. The dogmatist, indeed, desires to assure reality to it, through the necessity of thinking it as the ground of all experience; and he would succeed, if he could prove that experience thereby can be, and can thereby only be explained. But this is the very question in dispute, and he cannot presuppose what must first be proved.

The object of idealism thus has the advantage over that of dogmatism, inasmuch as it is not to be deduced as the ground of explanation of experience,—which would be a contradiction and would transform this system itself into a part of experience,—but is nevertheless to be referred to as a part of consciousness. Whereas, the object of dogmatism can assume to be nothing but a mere invention, which attains realization only through the success of the system. This is cited merely to promote a clearer insight into the distinction between the two systems; but not to draw therefrom an argument against the latter system. That the object of every philosophy, as the explanatory ground of experience, must be beyond experience, is demanded by the very nature of philosophy, and is far from being derogatory to a system. But we have as yet discovered no reason why that object should be present also in a particular manner in consciousness.

If anybody should remain unconvinced of the truth of what has just been said, it still would not be impossible to convince him of the truth of the whole system, since the foregoing has only been incidental. Nevertheless, in conformity with our plan, we will also here take into consideration possible objections. Some one might deny the immediate self-consciousness affirmed to be in every free act of the mind. Such a one we have only again to remind of the conditions of it above specified. This self-consciousness neither obtrudes itself, nor comes of its own accord; one must really have a free act, and then abstract from the object and attend entirely to one's self. No one can be compelled to do this, and also if he professes to have done it, one cannot know whether he has proceeded correctly. In a word, this consciousness cannot be proved to any one; but every one must produce it with freedom in himself. Against the second affirmation, that the thing-in-itself is a mere invention, an objection could only be made, because one misunderstood it. Such a one we would refer back to the preceding description of the origin of this conception.

5

Neither of these two systems can directly refute the other; for their controversy is one about the first underivable principle. Each refutes the other, if only you admit its own first principle as established. Each denies everything to the opposite; and they have no point in common whereby they can attain a mutual understanding and reconciliation. Though they appear to agree on the words of a proposition, yet each one takes them in a different sense.

First of all, idealism cannot refute dogmatism. The former system, indeed, has, as we have seen, the advantage over the latter of being able to establish its explanatory ground of experience—the free acting intelligence—as a fact of consciousness. This fact the dogmatist must also concede to him, for otherwise he would render himself incapable of any further dealing with his opponent; but he transformed, however, the ground of explanation by a correct inference from his principle into an appearance and illusion, and thus disqualifies it for becoming an explanatory ground of anything else, since it cannot maintain its own existence in its own philosophy. According to the dogmatist everything that presents itself to our consciousness is a product of a thing-in-itself,—even our pretended determinations by means of freedom, and the belief that we are free. This belief is produced in us by the effect upon ourselves of the Thing and the determinations which we deduced from our freedom are similarly caused by it. Only, we are not aware of it in these instances, and hence ascribe it to no cause, that is, to our freedom. Every consistent dogmatist is necessarily a fatalist; he does not deny the fact of consciousness, that we regard ourselves as free, for this would be against all reason; but he proves from his principle the falsity of this view. He denies the independence of the Ego upon which the idealist builds, and makes it merely a product of the thing, an *accident* of the world; hence the consistent dogmatist is necessarily also a materialist. He can only be refuted by the postulate of the freedom and independence of the ego; but this is directly what he denies.

Even as little can the dogmatist refute the idealist.

The principle of the former, the thing-in-itself, is nothing, and, as the defenders of it must admit, has no reality beyond that which it receives from the fact that experience can only be explained by it. But the idealist destroys this proof by explaining experience in another way, hence by denying precisely what the dogmatist assumes. The thing-in-itself is a complete chimera. There is no further reason why it should be assumed; and with its disappearance the entire structure of dogmatism falls.

From what has just been stated there follows likewise the absolute irreconcilability of the two systems; since the results of the one destroy those of the other. Wherever their union has been attempted the members would not fit into one another, and somewhere an enormous gap has appeared. Any one who would deny the truth of this position must prove the possibility of such a union, that is, of a union which consists in a perpetual transition from matter to spirit, or, what is entirely the same, from necessity to freedom.

Since so far as we can perceive at present both systems appear to have the same speculative value, and since both cannot stand together, nor yet either of the two convince the other, it becomes a very interesting question what induces persons who comprehend this— and it is easily understood—to prefer the one to the other; and why it happens that scepticism, as the total renunciation of a reply to this problem, does not become universal.

The dispute between the idealist and the dogmatist is precisely the question whether the independence of the Ego is to be sacrificed to that of the thing, or *vice versa*. What, then, is it which compels a reasonable man to decide in favor of the one or the other?

The philosopher discovers from the foregoing point of view,—which is one where he must necessarily place himself if he is to be regarded as a philosopher, and which every man, in the progress of thinking, must necessarily sooner or later occupy,—nothing further *than that he must represent to himself* both that he is free, and that there are determined things outside of him. It is, however, impossible for him to stop at this thought; the thought of the mere representation is only a half-thought, a broken fragment of a thought. Something must be thought in addition as corresponding to the representation independent of it. In other words, the representation cannot exist by itself,—it is something only in connection with something else, and in itself it is nothing. It is this necessity of thought which forces one from that point of view to the question, What is the ground of the representations? or, which is entirely the same, What is that which corresponds to them?

Now the representation of the independence of the Ego and that of the thing can exist certainly together; but not the independence itself of both. Only one can be the first, the beginning, the independent; the second, by the very fact of being second, is necessarily dependent upon the first, with which it is to be connected.

Now which of the two is to be made the first? Reason affords no ground for a decision; for the question does not relate to the connecting of one link with another, where alone the grounds of reason extend; but to the beginning of the entire succession, which as an absolute first act is wholly dependent upon the freedom of thinking. The decision is therefore entirely arbitrary; and since the arbitrariness must have a cause, the decision is dependent upon *inclination* and *interest.* The last ground of the distinction between the dogmatist and the idealist is consequently the difference of their interest.

The highest interest, and hence the ground of all other interest, is that *for ourselves.* Thus with the philosopher. Not to lose his Self in his reasoning, but to retain and to assert it, this is the interest which unconsciously guides all his thinking. Now, there exist two grades of mankind; and in the progress of our race, before the last grade has been universally attained, two chief classes of men. The one class consist of those who have not raised themselves to the full feeling of their freedom and of absolute independence, but who are merely conscious of themselves in the representations of outward things. These have only a desultory self-consciousness, bound up with outward objects, and collected from their manifoldness. The image of their Self is reflected to them only from the things, as from a mirror. If the latter be taken from them, then they lose the Self at the same time. For their own sake, they cannot give up the belief in the independence of things, since they exist only together with these things. Whatever they are they have actually become through the external world. Whosoever is only a product of the things will never view himself in any other manner, and he is entirely correct, so long as he speaks merely of himself and of those like him. The principle of the dogmatist is: belief in the things for their own sake; hence, a mediated belief in his own desultory Self, as merely the result of the things.

But whosoever becomes conscious of his self-existence and independence from all outward things—and this one can only become by making something of one's self, by means of one's own self, independently of all external things—needs no longer the things in support of his Self, and cannot use them, because they destroy his self-existence and transform it into an empty appearance. The Ego, which he possesses, and which interests him, destroys that belief in the things; he believes in his independence from inclination, and lays hold of it with affection. His belief in himself is immediate.

From this interest can be explained the various passions which commonly mingle with the defence of these philosophical systems. The dogmatist is actually in peril of losing his Self when his system is attacked; and yet he is not armed against this attack, because there is something in his inmost self which takes the side of the assailant; hence he defends himself with heat and bitterness. The idealist, on the contrary, cannot well refrain from looking down with disesteem upon the dogmatist, who can tell him nothing which he first has not long since known and thrown aside as useless, inasmuch as one arrives at idealism, if not through dogmatism itself, yet at least by the disposition thereto. The dogmatist gets angry, misconstrues, and would persecute, if he had the power; the idealist is cold, and inclined to ridicule the dogmatist.

What kind of a philosophy one chooses depends consequently upon what kind of a man one is; for a philosophical system is not a piece of dead household furniture, which one can use or lay aside at pleasure, but is animated by the soul of the man who has it. A person of a naturally indolent character, or who has become weak-minded and perverted through intellectual slavery, scholarly luxury, and vanity, will never elevate himself to idealism.

You can reveal to the dogmatist the inadequacy and inconsequence of his system; you can confuse and terrify him from all sides; but you cannot convince him, because he is unable quietly and coolly to hear and to examine what he cannot tolerate. If idealism should prove to be the only true philosophy, it will also appear that a man must be born a philosopher, be educated to be one, and educate himself to be one; but that by no human art can one be made a philosopher. Hence this science of knowledge expects few proselytes among men whose mental habits have already been moulded; but its hopes are centred in the rising generation, whose native vigor has not yet been impaired by the intellectual laxness of the present age.

34

HEGEL

1770–1831

Georg Wilhelm Friedrich Hegel was born in Stuttgart, Germany. At the University of Tübingen he made friends with fellow student Schelling (Chapter 35). After graduating he worked as a private tutor until he received his teaching appointment in 1801, as a lecturer, at the University of Jena. He became professor of philosophy in 1805, but a year later Napoleon's troops marched into Jena and Hegel lost his position during the French occupation. He supported himself first as a newspaper editor, then as a school principal in Nuremberg. Ten years later he was reappointed professor of philosophy, first in Heidelberg and then in 1818 at the University of Berlin.

Hegel's philosophy, like Fichte's and Schelling's, developed in opposition to Kant's notion of a nonmental reality, the noumenal world, that is utterly unknowable. According to Kant, the objects of the phenomenal world—all the things you see around you—are actively processed by the faculties of your mind into existence. Since these faculties themselves are in part the effect of the noumenal world, the objects thereby constituted are created partly (and indirectly) by the noumenal reality and partly (and directly) by your own mental faculties. Hegel argues that there is just one world whose objects are created *completely* by the mind *whose own faculties* are created through its own (historical, evolutionary) oppositions against itself.

Hegel's is an idealist metaphysical system in which the mind does not merely structure and regulate reality but wholly generates and constitutes it, up to and including itself. What he calls "the Absolute," the world as it exists in itself, is mind or spirit.[1] That is, the world in itself is a self-thinking thought, such that the entire process of existence in time is the teleological (goal directed) movement[2] of the universe becoming aware of itself, a process of "the Absolute realizing itself." In marked contrast to Kant's transcendental (or critical) idealism and Berkeley's subjective idealism, both of which are pluralistic,[3] Hegel conceives

---

1. There is no word for "mind" in Germanic and Slavic languages; the word Hegel used was *geist,* which has, as its root, the concept of ghost or spirit.

2. The easiest way to understand the Aristotelian concept of teleology is as opposed to mechanism, which explains the present and the future in terms of the past; teleology explains the past and the present in terms of the future.

3. That is, they involve more than one substance: Noumenal and Phenomenal reality for Kant; the human mind and the spiritual mind of God for Berkeley.

of the Absolute in terms of a monistic system in which the whole of existence is one substance that is itself a spirit, or mind. In other words, everything that is, was, or will be is itself an evolving form within the world-mind, where the forces of evolution are driven not by events in the past or present, but by the still uncreated future. In this way, the Kantian noumenal reality, nowhere present among the phenomenal world of appearances, becomes as yet undeveloped domains of future possibility toward which everything evolves.

The history of philosophy according to Hegel is part of this evolution. The events of history are not merely a succession of various physical *things* rearranged into different positions. Nor is history a series of ideas and views each of which turns out to be false when it is replaced by a new view. Rather, historical developments are changes in the way the world realizes itself into existence. In this way, philosophy comes to represent not just some passive intellectual activity as practiced by human beings, but rather the absolute mind going through various stages of the thinking process in its own metaphysical development. The evolution of philosophy is the evolution of the world trying to understand itself. The history of thought does not consist of the intellectual struggles of individual thinkers, but is itself the birthing stages in the evolution of the world's consciousness.

The stages of the development of thought are presented in Hegel's *Encyclopedia of the Philosophical Sciences in Outline* (1817), a manual written for his students in three parts. Our first selection is from the first part, called "Logic," by which Hegel means not formal logic but what he called "the science of thought." Here he argues that since only thought exists, logic should be viewed as metaphysics: logic according to Hegel and the subsequent generation of absolute idealist philosophers is the study of "the idea in and for itself." Thus he would proclaim to his students: "The Living Being is a syllogism whose very moments are syllogisms." The second part of Hegel's *Encyclopedia* is the "Philosophy of Nature," the study of "the idea in its otherness"; and the third part, the "Philosophy of Mind," is the study of "the idea come back to itself out of that otherness."

The first and most difficult of Hegel's systematic works, published in 1807, is *The Phenomenology of Mind,* from which our second selection is taken. It describes the stages consciousness must undergo in its evolution from naive commonsense notions of reality to a truly philosophical, synthetic view and full self-consciousness in which the universe not only fully realizes that it exists but, therein, creates itself through "the consciousness of its own freedom." Starting with the "unhappy consciousness" stage—a subjectively idealistic, abstract, and dualistic view of truth which represents itself in our conscious psychologies as a lonely, religious quest for some remote, "changeless," deified, consciousness—consciousness begins the slow process of awakening into its final, absolute stage. The process of Hegelian enlightenment is thus not just the process of our trying to become lovers of wisdom, though it *is* that. It is also the enlightenment of the world entire, of being itself, through a process whose machinery can be studied. For that process is history.

Out last selection is from Hegel's *Lectures on the Philosophy of History* (published posthumously in 1837), which Hegel delivered between 1822 and 1831 and which were supplemented with two sets of notes by students. In this work Hegel gives an account of "the philosophical history of the world," by which he means not observations on history or the study of records and facts nor even reflections on history but the "universal history" of the evolutionary unfolding of thought itself, the absolute world-mind trying to realize itself. In a sense, the work represents what in Hegel's view is nothing less than the autobiography of the universe.

LOGIC

1. Philosophy misses an advantage enjoyed by the other sciences. It cannot like them rest the existence of its objects on the natural admissions of consciousness, nor can it assume that its method of cognition, either for starting or for continuing, is one already accepted. The objects of philosophy, it is true, are upon the whole the same as those of religion. In both the object is truth, in that supreme sense in which God and God only is the truth. Both in like manner go on to treat of the finite worlds of nature and the human mind, with their relation to each other and to their truth in God. Some *acquaintance* with its objects, therefore, philosophy may and even must presume, that and a certain interest in them to boot, were it for no other reason than this: that in point of time the mind makes general *images* of objects, long before it makes *notions* of them and that it is only through these mental images, and by recourse to them, that the thinking mind rises to know and comprehend *thinkingly*.

But with the rise of this thinking study of things, it soon becomes evident that thought will be satisfied with nothing short of showing the *necessity* of its facts, of demonstrating the existence of its objects, as well as their nature and qualities. Our original acquaintance with them is thus discovered to be inadequate. We can assume nothing, and assert nothing dogmatically: nor can we accept the assertions and assumptions of others. And yet we must make a beginning: and a beginning, as primary and underived, makes an assumption, or rather is an assumption. It seems as if it were impossible to make a beginning at all.

2. This *thinking study of things* may serve, in a general way, as a description of philosophy. But the description is too wide. If it be correct to say, that thought makes the distinction between man and the lower animals, then everything human is human, for the sole and simple reason that it is due to the operation of thought. Philosophy, on the other hand, is a peculiar mode of thinking—a mode in which thinking becomes knowledge, and knowledge through notions. However great therefore may be the identity and essential unity of the two modes of thought, the philosophic mode gets to be different from the more general thought which acts in all that is human, in all that gives humanity its distinctive character. And this difference connects itself with the fact that the strictly human and thought-induced phenomena of consciousness do not originally appear in the form of a thought, but as a feeling, a perception, or mental image—all of which aspects must be distinguished from the form of thought proper.

11. The special conditions which call for the existence of philosophy may be thus described. The mind or spirit, when it is sentient or perceptive, finds its object in something sensuous; when it imagines, in a picture or image; when it wills, in an aim or end. But in contrast to, or it may be only in distinction from, these forms of its existence and of its objects, the mind has also to gratify the cravings of its highest and most inward life. That innermost self is thought. Thus the mind renders thought its object. In the best meaning of the phrase, it comes to itself; for thought is its principle, and its very unadulterated self.

From *The Logic of Hegel,* 2d rev. ed., trans. William Wallace (Oxford: Clarendon Press, 1892). With emendations by Daniel Kolak.

But while thus occupied, thought entangles itself in contradictions, *i.e.* loses itself in the hard-and-fast non-identity of its thoughts, and so, instead of reaching itself, is caught and held in its counterpart. This result, to which honest but narrow thinking leads the mere understanding, is resisted by the loftier craving of which we have spoken. That craving expresses the perseverance of thought, which continues true to itself, even in this conscious loss of its native rest and independence, "that it may overcome" and work out in itself the solution of its own contradictions.

To see that thought in its very nature is dialectical, and that, as understanding, it must fall into contradiction,—the negative of itself, will form one of the main lessons of logic. When thought grows hopeless of ever achieving, by its own means, the solution of the contradiction which it has by its own action brought upon itself, it turns back to those solutions of the question with which the mind had learned to pacify itself in some of its other modes and forms. Unfortunately, however, the retreat of thought has led it, as Plato noticed even in his time, to a very uncalled-for hatred of reason (misology); and it then takes up against its own endeavours that hostile attitude of which an example is seen in the doctrine that "immediate" knowledge, as it is called, is the exclusive form in which we become cognisant of truth.

12. The rise of philosophy is due to these cravings of thought. Its point of departure is experience; including under that name both our immediate consciousness and the inductions from it. Awakened, as it were, by this stimulus, thought is vitally characterised by raising itself above the natural state of mind, above the senses and inferences from the senses into its own unadulterated element, and by assuming, accordingly, at first a stand-aloof and negative attitude towards the point from which it started. Through this state of antagonism to the phenomena of sense its first satisfaction is found in itself, in the idea of the universal essence of these phenomena: an idea (the Absolute, or God) which may be more or less abstract. Meanwhile, on the other hand, the sciences, based on experience, exert upon the mind a stimulus to overcome the form in which their varied contents are presented, and to elevate these contents to the rank of necessary truth. For the facts of science have the aspect of a vast conglomerate, one thing coming side by side with another, as if they were merely given and presented,—as in short devoid of all essential or necessary connection. In consequence of this stimulus thought is dragged out of its unrealised universality and its fancied or merely possible satisfaction, and impelled onwards to a development from itself. On one hand this development only means that thought incorporates the contents of science, in all their specialty of detail as submitted. On the other it makes these contents imitate the action of the original creative thought, and present the aspect of a free evolution determined by the logic of the fact alone.

15. Each of the parts of philosophy is a philosophical whole, a circle rounded and complete in itself. In each of these parts, however, the philosophical idea is found in a particular specificity or medium. The single circle, because it is a real totality, bursts through the limits imposed by its special medium, and gives rise to a wider circle. The whole of philosophy in this way resembles a circle of circles. The idea appears in each single circle, but, at the same time, the whole idea is constituted by the system of these peculiar phases, and each is a necessary member of the organisation.

17. It may seem as if philosophy, in order to start on its course, had, like the rest of the sciences, to begin with a subjective presupposition. The sciences postulate their respective objects, such as space, number, or whatever it be; and it might be supposed that philosophy had also to postulate the existence of thought. But the two cases are not exactly parallel. It

is by the free act of thought that it occupies a point of view, in which it is for its own self, and thus gives itself an object of its own production. Nor is this all. The very point of view, which originally is taken on its own evidence only, must in the course of the science be converted to a result,—the ultimate result in which philosophy returns into itself and reaches the point with which it began. In this manner philosophy exhibits the appearance of a circle which closes with itself, and has no beginning in the same way as the other sciences have. To speak of a beginning of philosophy has a meaning only in relation to a person who proposes to commence the study, and not in relation to the science as science. The same thing may be thus expressed. The notion of science—the notion therefore with which we start—which, for the very reason that it is initial, implies a separation between the thought which is our object, and the subject philosophising which is, as it were, external to the former, must be grasped and comprehended by the science itself. This is in short the one single aim, action, and goal of philosophy—to arrive at the notion of its notion, and thus secure its return and its satisfaction.

18. As the whole science, and only the whole, can exhibit what the idea or system of reason is, it is impossible to give in a preliminary way a general impression of a philosophy. Nor can a division of philosophy into its parts be intelligible, except in connection with the system. A preliminary division, like the limited conception from which it comes, can only be an anticipation. Here however it is premised that the idea turns out to be the thought which is completely identical with itself, and not identical simply in the abstract, but also in its action of setting itself over against itself, so as to gain a being of its own, and yet of being in full possession of itself while it is in this other. Thus philosophy is subdivided into three parts:

I. Logic: the science of the idea in and for itself.

II. The philosophy of nature: the science of the idea in its otherness.

III. The philosophy of mind: the science of the idea come back to itself out of that otherness.

As observed in § 15, the differences between the several philosophical sciences are only aspects or specialisations of the one idea or system of reason, which and which alone is alike exhibited in these different media. In nature nothing else would have to be discerned, except the idea: but the idea has here divested itself of its proper being. In mind, again, the idea has asserted a being of its own, and is on the way to become absolute. Every such form in which the idea is expressed, is at the same time a passing or fleeting stage: and hence each of these subdivisions has not only to know its contents as an object which has being for the time, but also in the same act to expound how these contents pass into their higher circle. To represent the relation between them as a division, therefore, leads to misconception: for it co-ordinates the several parts or sciences one beside another, as if they had no innate development, but were, like so many species, really and radically distinct.

CHAPTER II
Preliminary Notion

19. Logic is the science of the pure idea; pure, that is, because the idea is in the abstract medium of thought.

This definition, and the others which occur in these introductory outlines, are derived from a survey of the whole system, to which accordingly they are subsequent. The same remark applies to all prefatory notions whatever about philosophy.

Logic might have been defined as the science of thought, and of its laws and characteristic forms. But thought, as thought, constitutes only the general medium, or qualifying circumstance, which renders the idea distinctively logical. If we identify the idea with thought, thought must not be taken in the sense of a method or form, but in the sense of the self-developing totality of its laws and peculiar terms. These laws are the work of thought itself, and not a fact which it finds and must submit to.

From different points of view, logic is either the hardest or the easiest of the sciences. Logic is hard, because it has to deal not with perceptions, nor, like geometry, with abstract representations of the senses, but with pure abstractions; and because it demands a force and facility of withdrawing into pure thought, of keeping firm hold on it, and of moving in such an element. Logic is easy, because its facts are nothing but our own thought and its familiar forms or terms: and these are the acmé of simplicity, the a b c of everything else. They are also what we are best acquainted with: such as, "Is" and "Is not"; quality and magnitude; being potential and being actual; one, many, and so on. But such an acquaintance only adds to the difficulties of the study; for while, on the one hand, we naturally think it is not worth our trouble to occupy ourselves any longer with things so familiar, on the other hand, the problem is to become acquainted with them in a new way, quite opposite to that in which we know them already.

The utility of logic is a matter which concerns its bearings upon the student, and the training it may give for other purposes. This logical training consists in the exercise of thinking which the student has to go through (this science is the thinking of thinking): and in the fact that he stores his head with thoughts in their native unalloyed character. It is true that logic, being the absolute form of truth, and another name for the very truth itself, is something more than merely useful. Yet if what is noblest, most liberal and most independent is also most useful, logic has some claim to the latter character. Its utility must then be estimated at another rate than exercise in thought for the sake of the exercise.

. . . .

24. With these explanations and qualifications, thoughts may be termed objective thoughts,—among which are also to be included the forms which are more especially discussed in the common logic, where they are usually treated as forms of conscious thought only. *Logic therefore coincides with metaphysics, the science of things set and held in thoughts,*— thoughts accredited able to express the essential reality of things.

(2) Logic is the study of thought pure and simple, or of the pure thought-forms. In the ordinary sense of the term, by thought we generally represent to ourselves something more than simple and unmixed thought; we mean some thought, the material of which is from experience. Whereas in logic a thought is understood to include nothing else but what depends on thinking and what thinking has brought into existence. It is in these circumstances that thoughts are *pure* thoughts. The mind is then in its own home-element and therefore free: for freedom means that the other thing with which you deal is a second self—so that you never leave your own ground but give the law to yourself. In the impulses or appetites the beginning is from something else, from something which we feel to be external. In this case then we speak of dependence. For freedom it is necessary that we should feel no presence of something else which is not ourselves. The natural man, whose

motions follow the rule only of his appetites, is not his own master. Be he as self-willed as he may, the constituents of his will and opinion are not his own, and his freedom is merely formal. But when we *think,* we renounce our selfish and particular being, sink ourselves in the thing, allow thought to follow its own course,—and, if we add anything of our own, we think ill.

If in pursuance of the foregoing remarks we consider logic to be the system of the pure types of thought, we find that the other philosophical sciences, the philosophy of nature and the philosophy of mind, take the place, as it were, of an applied logic, and that logic is the soul which animates them both. Their problem in that case is only to recognise the logical forms under the shapes they assume in nature and mind,—shapes which are only a particular mode of expression for the forms of pure thought. If for instance we take the syllogism (not as it was understood in the old formal logic, but at its real value), we shall find it gives expression to the law that the particular is the middle term which fuses together the extremes of the universal and the singular. The syllogistic form is a universal form of all things. Everything that exists is a particular, which couples together the universal and the singular. But nature is weak and fails to exhibit the logical forms in their purity. Such a feeble exemplification of the syllogism may be seen in the magnet. In the middle or point of indifference of a magnet, its two poles, however they may be distinguished, are brought into one. Physics also teaches us to see the universal or essence in nature: and the only difference between it and the philosophy of nature is that the latter brings before our mind the adequate forms of the notion in the physical world.

It will now be understood that logic is the all-animating spirit of all the sciences, and its categories the spiritual hierarchy. They are the heart and centre of things: and yet at the same time they are always on our lips, and, apparently at least, perfectly familiar objects. But things thus familiar are usually the greatest strangers. Being, for example, is a category of pure thought: but to make "Is" an object of investigation never occurs to us. Common fancy puts the Absolute far away in a world beyond. The Absolute is rather directly before us, so present that so long as we think, we must, though without express consciousness of it, always carry it with us and always use it. Language is the main depository of these types of thought; and one use of the grammatical instruction which children receive is unconsciously to turn their attention to distinctions of thought.

. . . .

To ask if a category is true or not, must sound strange to the ordinary mind: for a category apparently becomes true only when it is applied to a given object, and apart from this application it would seem meaningless to inquire into its truth. But this is the very question on which everything turns. We must however in the first place understand clearly what we mean by truth. In common life truth means the agreement of an object with our conception of it. We thus pre-suppose an object to which our conception must conform. In the philosophical sense of the word, on the other hand, truth may be described, in general abstract terms, as the agreement of a thought-content with itself. This meaning is quite different from the one given above. At the same time the deeper and philosophical meaning of truth can be partially traced even in the ordinary usage of language. Thus we speak of a true friend; by which we mean a friend whose manner of conduct accords with the notion of friendship. In the same way we speak of a true work of art. Untrue in this sense means the same as bad, or self-discordant. In this sense a bad state is an untrue state; and evil and untruth may be said to consist in the contradiction subsisting between the function or notion and the existence of the object. Of such a bad object we may form a correct representation, but the import of such representation is inherently false. Of these correctnesses, which are at the same time untruths, we may have many in our heads.—God alone is the thorough harmony of notion and reality. All finite things involve an untruth: they have a notion and an existence, but their existence does not meet the requirements of the notion. For this reason they must perish, and then the incompatibility between their notion and their existence becomes manifest. It is in the kind that the individual animal has its notion: and the kind liberates itself from this individuality by death.

The study of truth, or as it is here explained to mean, consistency, constitutes the proper problem of logic. In our everyday mind we are never troubled with questions about the truth of the forms of thought.—We may also express the problem of logic by saying that it examines the forms of thought touching their capability to hold truth. And the question comes to this: What are the forms of the infinite, and what are the forms of the finite? Usually no suspicion attaches to the finite forms of thought; they are allowed to pass unquestioned. But it is from conforming to finite categories in thought and action that all deception originates.

. . . .

CHAPTER VI
Logic Further Defined and Divided

79. In point of form logical doctrine has three sides: (α) the abstract side, or that of understanding; (β) the dialectical, or that of negative reason; (γ) the speculative, or that of positive reason.

These three sides do not make three *parts of logic*, but are stages or "moments" in every logical entity, that is, of every notion and truth whatever. They may all be put under the first stage, that of understanding, and so kept isolated from each other; but this would give an inadequate conception of them.—The statement of the dividing lines and the characteristic aspects of logic is at this point no more than historical and anticipatory.

80. (α) Thought, as *understanding*, sticks to fixity of characters and their distinctness from one another: every such limited abstract it treats as having a subsistence and being of its own.

In our ordinary usage of the term thought and even notion we often have before our eyes nothing more than the operation of understanding. And no doubt thought is primarily an exercise of understanding:—only it goes further, and the notion is not a function of understanding merely. The action of understanding may be in general described as investing its subject-matter with the form of universality. But this universal is an abstract universal: that is to say, its opposition to the particular is so rigorously maintained, that it is at the same time also reduced to the character of a particular again. In this separating and abstracting attitude towards its objects, understanding is the reverse of immediate perception and sensation, which, as such, keep completely to their native sphere of action in the concrete.

It is by referring to this opposition of understanding to sensation or feeling that we must explain the frequent attacks made upon thought for being hard and narrow, and for leading, if consistently developed, to ruinous and pernicious results. The answer to these charges, in so far as they are warranted by their facts, is, that they do not touch thinking in general, certainly not the thinking of reason, but only the exercise of understanding. It must be added however, that the merit and rights of the mere understanding should unhesitatingly be admitted. And that merit lies in the fact, that apart from understanding there is no fixity or accuracy in the region either of theory or of practice.

. . . .

81. (β) In the dialectical stage these finite characterisations or formulae supersede themselves, and pass into their opposites.

(I) But when the dialectical principle is employed by the understanding separately and independently,—especially as seen in its application to philosophical theories, dialectic becomes scepticism; in which the result that ensues from its action is presented as a mere negation.

(II) It is customary to treat dialectic as an adventitious art, which for very wantonness introduces confusion and a mere semblance of contradiction into definite notions. And in that light, the semblance is the nonentity, while the true reality is supposed to belong to the original dicta of understanding. Often, indeed, dialectic is nothing more than a subjective seesaw of arguments *pro* and *con,* where the absence of sterling thought is disguised by the subtlety which gives birth to such arguments. But in its true and proper character, dialectic is the very nature and essence of everything predicated by mere understanding,—the law of things and of the finite as a whole. Dialectic is different from "reflection." In the first instance, reflection is that movement out beyond the isolated predicate of a thing which gives it some reference, and brings out its relativity, while still in other respects leaving it its isolated validity. But by dialectic is meant the in-dwelling tendency outwards by which the one-sidedness and limitation of the predicates of understanding is seen in its true light, and shown to be the negation of them. For anything to be finite is just to suppress itself and put itself aside. Thus understood the dialectical principle constitutes the life and soul of scientific progress, the dynamic which alone gives immanent connection and necessity to the body of science; and, in a word, is seen to constitute the real and true, as opposed to the external, exaltation above the finite.

. . . .

(1) . . . Dialectic, it may be added, is no novelty in philosophy. Among the ancients, Plato is termed the inventor of dialectic and his right to the name rests on the fact, that the Platonic philosophy first gave the free scientific, and thus at the same time the objective, form to dialectic. Socrates, as we should expect from the general character of his philosophising, has the dialectical element in a predominantly subjective shape, that of irony. He used to turn his dialectic, first against ordinary consciousness, and then especially against the Sophists. In his conversations he used to simulate the wish for some clearer knowledge about the subject under discussion, and after putting all sorts of questions with that intent, he drew on those with whom he conversed to the opposite of what their first impressions had pronounced correct. If, for instance, the Sophists claimed to be teachers, Socrates by a series of questions forced the Sophist Protagoras to confess that all learning is only recollection. In his more strictly scientific dialogues Plato employs the dialectical method to show the finitude of all hard and fast terms of understanding. Thus in the Parmenides he deduces the many from the one, and shows nevertheless that the many cannot but define itself as the one. In this grand style did Plato treat dialectic. In modern times it was, more than any other, Kant who resuscitated the name of dialectic, and restored it to its

post of honour. He did it, as we have seen (§ 48), by working out the antinomies of the reason. The problem of these antinomies is no mere subjective piece of work oscillating between one set of grounds and another; it really serves to show that every abstract proposition of understanding, taken precisely as it is given, naturally veers round into its opposite.

. . . .

82. (γ) The Speculative stage, or stage of positive reason, apprehends the unity of terms (propositions) in their opposition,—the affirmative, which is involved in their disintegration and in their transition.

(1) The result of dialectic is positive, because it has a definite content, or because its result is not empty and abstract nothing, but the negation of certain specific propositions which are contained in the result,—for the very reason that it is a resultant and not an immediate nothing. (2) It follows from this that the "reason" result, though it be only a thought and abstract, is still a concrete, being not a plain formal unity, but a unity of distinct propositions. Bare abstractions or formal thoughts are therefore no business of philosophy, which has to deal only with concrete thoughts. (3) The logic of mere understanding is involved in speculative logic, and can at will be elicited from it, by the simple process of omitting the dialectical and "reasonable" element. When that is done, it becomes what the common logic is, a descriptive collection of sundry thought-forms and rules which, finite though they are, are taken to be something infinite.

If we consider only what it contains, and not how it contains it, the true reason-world, so far from being the exclusive property of philosophy, is the right of every human being, on whatever grade of culture or mental growth he may stand; which would justify man's ancient title of rational being. The general mode by which experience first makes us aware of the reasonable order of things is by accepted and unreasoned belief; and the character of the rational, as already noted (§ 45), is to be unconditioned, and thus to be self-contained, self-determining. In this sense man above all things becomes aware of the reasonable order, when he knows of God, and knows him to be the completely self-determined. Similarly, the consciousness a citizen has of his country and its laws is a perception of the reason-world, so long as he looks up to them as unconditioned and likewise universal powers, to which he must subject his individual will. And in the same sense, the knowledge and will of the child is rational, when he knows his parents' will, and wills it.

Now, to turn these rational (of course positively-rational) realities into speculative principles, the only thing needed is that they be *thought.* The expression "speculation" in common life is often used with a very vague and at the same time secondary sense, as when we speak of a matrimonial or a commercial speculation. By this we only mean two things: first, that what is immediately at hand has to be passed and left behind; and secondly, that the subject-matter of such speculations, though in the first place only subjective, must not remain so, but be realised or translated into objectivity.

83. Logic is subdivided into three parts:—

I. The Doctrine of Being
II. The Doctrine of Essence
III. The Doctrine of Notion and Idea

That is, into the Theory of Thought:

I. In its immediacy: the notion implicit and in germ.

II. In its reflection and mediation: the being-for-self and show of the notion.

III. In its return into itself, and its developed abiding by itself: the notion in and for itself.

The division of logic now given, as well as the whole of the previous discussion on the nature of thought, is anticipatory: and the justification, or proof of it, can only result from the detailed treatment of thought itself. For in philosophy, to prove means to show how the subject by and from itself makes itself what it is. The relation in which these three leading grades of thought, or of the logical idea, stand to each other must be conceived as follows. Truth comes only with the notion: or, more precisely, the notion is the truth of being and essence, both of which, when separately maintained in their isolation, cannot but be untrue, the former because it is exclusively immediate, and the latter because it is exclusively mediate. Why then, it may be asked, begin with the false and not at once with the true? To which we answer that truth, to deserve the name, must authenticate its own truth: which authentication, here within the sphere of logic, is given when the notion demonstrates itself to be what is mediated by and with itself, and thus at the same time to be truly immediate. This relation between the three stages of the logical idea appears in a real and concrete shape thus: God, who is the truth, is known by us in his truth, that is, as absolute spirit, only in so far as we at the same time recognise that the world which He created, nature and the finite spirit, are, in their difference from God, untrue.

CHAPTER VII
The Doctrine of Being

84. Being is the notion implicit only: its special forms have the predicate "is"; when they are distinguished they are each of them an "other": and the shape which dialectic takes in them, *i.e.* their further specialisation, is a passing over into another. This further determination, or specialisation, is at once a forthputting and in that way a disengaging of the notion implicit in being; and at the same time the withdrawing of being inwards, its sinking deeper into itself. Thus the explication of the notion in the sphere of being does two things: it brings out the totality of being, and it abolishes the immediacy of being, or the form of being as such.

. . . .

A. QUALITY
(a) Being

86. Pure Being makes the beginning: because it is on one hand pure thought, and on the other immediacy itself, simple and indeterminate; and the first beginning cannot be mediated by anything, or be further determined.

All doubts and admonitions, which might be brought against beginning the science with an abstract empty being, will disappear, if we only perceive what a beginning naturally implies. It is possible to define being as "I = I," "absolute indifference" or identity, and so on. Where it is felt necessary to begin either with what is absolutely certain, *i.e.* the certainty of one's self, or with a definition or intuition of the absolute truth, these and other forms of the kind may be looked on as if they must be the first. But each of these forms contains a mediation, and hence cannot be the real first: for all mediation implies advance made from a first on to a second, and proceeding from something different. If I = I, or even the intellectual intuition, are really taken to mean no more than the first, they are in this mere immediacy identical with being: while conversely, pure being, if abstract no longer, but including in it mediation, is pure thought or intuition.

If we enunciate Being as a predicate of the Absolute, we get the first definition of the latter. The Absolute is Being. This is (in thought) the absolutely initial definition, the most abstract and stinted. It is the definition given by the Eleatics, but at the same time is also the well-known definition of God as the sum of all realities. It means, in short, that we are to set aside that limitation which is in every reality, so that God shall be only the real in all reality, the superlatively real.

. . . .

(2) . . . It is sufficient to mention here, that logic begins where the proper history of philosophy begins. Philosophy began in the Eleatic school, especially with Parmenides. Parmenides, who conceives the absolute as being, says that "Being alone is and nothing is not." Such was the true starting-point of philosophy, which is always knowledge by thought: and here for the first time we find pure thought seized and made an object to itself.

Men indeed thought from the beginning (for thus only were they distinguished from the animals). But thousands of years had to elapse before they came to apprehend thought in its purity, and to see in it the truly objective. The Eleatics are celebrated as daring thinkers. But this nominal admiration is often accompanied by the remark that they went too far, when they made Being alone true, and denied the truth of every other object of consciousness. We must go further than mere being, it is true: and yet it is absurd to speak of the other contents of our consciousness as somewhat as it were outside and beside being, or to say that there are other things, as well as being. The true state of the case is rather as follows. Being, as being, is nothing fixed or ultimate: it yields to dialectic and sinks into its opposite, which, also taken immediately, is Nothing. After all, the point is, that Being is the first pure thought; whatever else you may begin with (the I = I, the absolute indifference, or God himself), you begin with a figure of materialised conception, not a product of thought; and that, so far as its thought-content is concerned, such beginning is merely being.

87. But this mere being, as it is mere abstraction, is therefore the absolutely negative: which, in a similarly immediate aspect, is just NOTHING.

(1) Hence was derived the second definition of the Absolute; the Absolute is the Nought. In fact this definition is implied in saying that the thing-in-itself is the indeterminate, utterly without form and so without content,—or in saying that God is only the supreme being and nothing more; for this is really declaring him to be the same negativity as above. The Nothing which the Buddhists make the universal principle, as well as the final aim and goal of everything, is the same abstraction.

. . . .

The distinction between being and nought is, in the first place, only implicit, and not yet actually made: they only *ought* to be distinguished. A distinction of course implies two things, and that one of them possesses an attribute which is not found in the other. Being however is an absolute absence of attributes, and so is nothing. Hence the distinction between the two is only meant to be; it is a quite nominal distinction, which is at the same time no distinction. In all other cases of difference there is some common point which comprehends both things. Suppose *e.g.* we speak of two different species: the genus forms a common ground for both. Both in the case of mere being and nothing, distinction is without a bottom to stand upon: hence there can be no distinction, both determinations being the same bottomlessness. If it be replied that being and nothing are both of them thoughts, so that thought may be reckoned common ground, the objector forgets that being is not a particular or definite thought, and hence, being quite indeterminate, is a thought not to be distinguished from nothing.—It is natural too for us to represent being as absolute riches, and nothing as absolute poverty. But if when we view the whole world we can only say that everything *is,* and nothing more, we are neglecting all speciality and instead of absolute plenitude, we have absolute emptiness. The same stricture is applicable to those who define God to be mere being; a definition not a whit better than that of the Buddhists, who make God to be nothing, and who from that principle draw the further conclusion that self-annihilation is the means by which man becomes God.

88. Nothing, if it be thus immediate and equal to itself, is also conversely the same as being is. The truth of being and of nothing is accordingly the unity of the two: and this unity is Becoming.

. . . .

(3) It may perhaps be said that nobody can form a notion of the unity of being and nothing. As for that, the notion of the unity is stated in the sections preceding, and that is all: apprehend that, and you have comprehended this unity. What the objector really means by comprehension—by a notion—is more than his language properly implies: he wants a richer and more complex state of mind, a pictorial conception which will propound the notion as a concrete case and one more familiar to the ordinary operations of thought. And so long as incomprehensibility means only the want of habituation for the effort needed to grasp and abstract thought, free from all sensuous admixture, and to seize a speculative truth, the reply to the criticism is, that philosophical knowledge is undoubtedly distinct in kind from the mode of knowledge best known in common life, as well as from that which reigns in the other sciences. But if to have no notion merely means that we cannot represent in imagination the oneness of being and nothing, the statement is far from being true; for every one has countless ways of envisaging this unity. To say that we have no such conception can only mean, that in none of these images do we recognise the notion in question, and that we are not aware that they exemplify it. The readiest example of it is Becoming. Every one has a mental idea of becoming, and will even allow that it is *one* idea: he will further allow that, when it is analysed, it involves the attribute of being, and also what is the very reverse of being, viz. nothing: and that these two attributes lie undivided in the one idea: so that becoming is the unity of being and nothing.—Another tolerably plain example is a beginning. In its beginning, the thing is not yet, but it is more than merely nothing, for its Being is already in the beginning. Beginning is itself a case of Becoming; only the former term is employed with an eye to the further advance.—If we were to adapt logic to the more usual method of the sciences, we might start with the representation of a beginning as abstractly thought, or with beginning as such, and then analyse this representation; and perhaps people would more readily admit, as a result of this analysis, that being and nothing present themselves as undivided in unity.

. . . .

As the first concrete thought-term, becoming is the first adequate vehicle of truth. In the history of philosophy, this stage of the logical idea finds its analogue in the system of

Heraclitus. When Heraclitus says, All is flowing, he enunciates Becoming as the fundamental feature of all existence, whereas the Eleatics, as already remarked, saw the only truth in Being, rigid processless being. Glancing at the principle of the Eleatics, Heraclitus then goes on to say: Being no more is than not-Being: a statement expressing the negativity of abstract Being, and its identity with not-Being, as made explicit in Becoming: both abstractions being alike untenable. This may be looked at as an instance of the real refutation of one system by another. To refute a philosophy is to exhibit the dialectical movement in its principle, and thus reduce it to a constituent member of a higher concrete form of the idea. Even becoming however, taken at its best on its own ground, is an extremely poor term: it needs to grow in depth and weight of meaning. Such deepened force we find *e.g.* in life. Life is a becoming; but that is not enough to exhaust the notion of life. A still higher form is found in mind. Here too is becoming, but richer and more intensive than mere logical becoming. The elements, whose unity constitutes mind, are not the bare abstracts of being and of nothing, but the system of the logical idea and of nature.

B. QUANTITY
(a) Pure Quantity

99. Quantity is pure being, where the mode or character is no longer taken as one with the being itself, but explicitly put as superseded or indifferent.

. . . .

Quantity, of course, is a stage of the idea: and as such it must have its due, first as a logical category, and then in the world of objects, natural as well as spiritual. Still even so, there soon emerges the different importance attaching to the category of quantity according as its objects belong to the natural or to the spiritual world. For in nature, where the form of the idea is to be other than, and at the same time outside, itself, greater importance is for that very reason attached to quantity than in the spiritual world, the world of free inwardness. No doubt we regard even spiritual facts under a quantitative point of view; but it is at once apparent that in speaking of God as a trinity, the number three has by no means the same prominence, as when we consider the three dimensions of space or the three sides of a triangle;—the fundamental feature of which last is just to be a surface bounded by three lines. Even inside the realm of nature we find the same distinction of greater or less importance of quantitative features. In the inorganic world, quantity plays, so to say, a more prominent part than in the organic. Even in organic nature when we distinguish mechanical functions from what are called chemical, and in the narrower sense, physical, there is the same difference. Mechanics is of all branches of science, confessedly, that in which the aid of mathematics can be least dispensed with,—where indeed we cannot take one step without them. On that account mechanics is regarded next to mathematics as the science *par excellence;* which leads us to repeat the remark about the coincidence of the materialist with the exclusively mathematical point of view. After all that has been said, we cannot but hold it, in the interest of exact and thorough knowledge, one of the most hurtful prejudices, to seek all distinction and determinateness of objects merely in quantitative considerations. Mind to be sure is more than nature and the animal is more than the plant: but we know very little of these objects and the distinction between them, if a more and less is enough for us, and if we do not proceed to comprehend them in their peculiar, that is their qualitative character.

. . . .

(b) Quantum (How Much)

101. Quantity, essentially invested with the exclusionist character which it involves, is QUANTUM (or How Much): *i.e.* limited quantity.

Quantum is, as it were, the determinate being of quantity: whereas mere quantity corresponds to abstract being, and the degree, which is next to be considered, corresponds to being-for-self. As for the details of the advance from mere quantity to quantum, it is founded on this: that while in mere quantity the distinction, as a distinction of continuity and discreteness, is at first only implicit, in a quantum the distinction is actually made, so that quantity in general now appears as distinguished or limited. But in this way the quantum breaks up at the same time into an indefinite multitude of quanta or definite magnitudes. Each of these definite magnitudes, as distinguished from the others, forms a unity, while on the other hand, viewed *per se,* it is a many. And, when that is done, the quantum is described as number.

. . . .

103. The limit (in a quantum) is identical with the whole of the quantum itself. As *in itself* multiple, the limit is extensive magnitude; as in itself *simple* determinateness (qualitative simplicity), it is intensive magnitude or DEGREE.

. . . .

104. In degree the notion of quantum is explicitly put. It is magnitude as indifferent on its own account and simple: but in such a way that the character (or modal being) which makes it a quantum lies quite outside it in other magnitudes. In this contradiction, where the *independent* indifferent limit is absolute *externality,* the INFINITE QUANTITATIVE PROGRESSION is made explicit—an immediacy which immediately veers round into its counterpart, into mediation (the passing beyond and over the quantum just laid down), and *vice versa.*

Number is a thought, but thought in its complete self-externalisation. Because it is a thought, it does not belong to perception: but it is a thought which is characterised by the externality of perception.—Not only therefore *may* the quantum be increased or diminished without end: the very notion of quantum is thus to push out and out beyond itself. The infinite quantitative progression is only the meaningless repetition of one and the same contradiction, which attaches to the quantum, both generally and, when explicitly invested with its special character, as degree. Touching the futility of enunciating this contradiction in the form of infinite progression, Zeno, as quoted by Aristotle, rightly says, "It is the same to say a thing once, and to say it for ever."

(1) If we follow the usual definition of the mathematicians, given in § 99, and say that magnitude is what can be increased or diminished, there may be nothing to urge against the correctness of the perception on which it is founded; but the question remains, how we come to assume such a capacity of increase or diminution. If we simply appeal for an answer to experience, we try an unsatisfactory course; because apart from the fact that we should merely have a material image of magnitude, and not the thought of it, magnitude would come out as a bare possibility (of increasing or diminishing) and we should have no key to the necessity for its exhibiting this behaviour. In the way of our logical evolution, on the contrary, quantity is obviously a grade in the process of self-determining thought; and it has been shown that it lies in the very notion of quantity to shoot out beyond itself. In that way, the increase or diminution (of which we have heard) is not merely possible, but necessary.

(2) The quantitative infinite progression is what the reflective understanding usually relies upon when it is engaged with the general question of Infinity. The same thing however holds good of this progression, as was already remarked on the occasion of the qualitatively infinite progression. As was then said, it is not the expression of a true, but of a wrong infinity; it never gets further than a bare "ought," and thus really remains within the limits of finitude. The quantitative form of this infinite progression, which Spinoza rightly calls a mere imaginary infinity (*infinitum imaginationis*), is an image often employed by poets, such as Haller and Klopstock, to depict the infinity, not of Nature merely, but even of God himself. Thus we find Haller, in a famous description of God's infinity, saying:—

> I heap up monstrous numbers, mountains of millions; I pile time upon time, and world on top of world; and when from the awful height I cast a dizzy look towards Thee, all the power of number, multiplied a thousand times, is not yet one part of Thee.

Here then we meet, in the first place, that continual extrusion of quantity, and especially of number, beyond itself, which Kant describes as "eerie." The only really "eerie" thing about it is the wearisomeness of ever fixing, and anon unfixing a limit, without advancing a single step. The same poet, however, well adds to that description of false infinity the closing line:—

> These I remove, and Thou liest all before me.

Which means, that the true infinite is more than a mere world beyond the finite, and that we, in order to become conscious of it, must renounce that *progressus in infinitum.*

. . . .

C. MEASURE

107. Measure is the qualitative quantum, in the first place as immediate,—a quantum, to which a determinate being or a quality is attached.

Measure, where quality and quantity are in one, is thus the completion of Being. Being, as we first apprehend it, is something utterly abstract and characterless: but it is the very essence of Being to characterise itself, and its complete characterisation is reached in measure. Measure, like the other stages of Being, may serve as a definition of the Absolute: God, it has been said, is the measure of all things. It is this idea which forms the ground-note of many of the ancient Hebrew hymns, in which the glorification of God tends in the main to show that He has appointed to everything its bound: to the sea and the solid land, to the rivers and mountains; and also to the various kinds of plants and animals. To the religious sense of the Greeks the divinity of measure, especially in respect of social ethics, was represented by Nemesis. That conception implies a general theory that all human things, riches, honour, and power, as well as joy and pain, have their definite measure, the transgression of which brings ruin and destruction.

. . . .

CHAPTER VIII
The Doctrine of Essence

112. The terms in ESSENCE are always mere pairs of correlatives, and not yet absolutely reflected in themselves: hence in essence the actual unity of the notion is not realised, but

only postulated by reflection. Essence,—which is Being coming into mediation with itself through the negativity of itself—is self-relatedness, only in so far as it is relation to an Other,—this Other however coming to view at first not as something which *is,* but as postulated and hypothesized.—Being has not vanished; but, firstly, essence, as simple self-relation, is Being, and secondly, as regards its one-sided characteristic of immediacy, Being is deposed to a mere negative, to a seeming or reflected light—essence accordingly is Being thus reflecting light into itself.

The Absolute is the essence. This is the same definition as the previous one that the Absolute is Being, in so far as Being likewise is simple self-relation. But it is at the same time higher, because essence is Being that has gone into itself: that is to say, the simple self-relation (in Being) is expressly put as negation of the negative, as immanent self-mediation.—Unfortunately when the Absolute is defined to be the essence, the negativity which this implies is often taken only to mean the withdrawal of all determinate predicates. This negative action of withdrawal or abstraction thus falls outside of the essence—which is thus left as a mere result apart from its premises,—the *caput mortuum* of abstraction. But as this negativity, instead of being external to Being, is its own dialectic, the truth of the latter, viz. essence, will be Being as retired within itself,—immanent Being. That reflection, or light thrown into itself, constitutes the distinction between essence and immediate Being, and is the peculiar characteristic of essence itself.

Any mention of essence implies that we distinguish it from Being: the latter is immediate, and, compared with the essence, we look upon it as mere seeming. But this seeming is not an utter nonentity and nothing at all, but Being superseded and put by. The point of view given by the essence is in general the standpoint of "reflection." This word "reflection" is originally applied, when a ray of light in a straight line impinging upon the surface of a mirror is thrown back from it. In this phenomenon we have two things,—first an immediate fact which is, and secondly the deputed, derivated, or transmitted phase of the same.—Something of this sort takes place when we reflect, or think upon an object; for here we want to know the object, not in its immediacy, but as derivative or mediated. The problem or aim of philosophy is often represented as the ascertainment of the essence of things: a phrase which only means that things instead of being left in their immediacy, must be shown to be mediated by, or based upon, something else. The immediate Being of things is thus conceived under the magic of a rind or curtain behind which the essence lies hidden.

. . . .

A. ESSENCE AS GROUND OF EXISTENCE
(a) The Pure Principles or Categories of Reflection
(α) IDENTITY

115. The essence lights up *in itself* or is mere reflection: and therefore is only self-relation, not as immediate but as reflected. And that reflex relation is SELF-IDENTITY.

This identity becomes an identity in form only, or of the understanding, if it be held hard and fast, quite aloof from difference. Or, rather, abstraction is the imposition of this identity of form, the transformation of something inherently concrete into this form of elementary simplicity. And this may be done in two ways. Either we may neglect a part of the multiple features which are found in the concrete thing (by what is called analysis) and select only one of them; or, neglecting their variety, we may concentrate the multiple characters into one.

If we associate identity with the Absolute, making the Absolute the subject of a proposition, we get: The Absolute is what is identical with itself. However true this proposition may be, it is doubtful whether it be meant in its truth: and therefore it is at least imperfect in the expression. For it is left undecided, whether it means the abstract Identity of understanding,—abstract, that is, because contrasted with the other characteristics of essence, or the identity which is inherently concrete. In the latter case, as will be seen, true identity is first discoverable in the ground, and, with a higher truth, in the notion.

. . . .

Identity is, in the first place, the repetition of what we had earlier as Being, but as *become,* through supersession of its character of immediateness. It is therefore Being as ideality.—It is important to come to a proper understanding on the true meaning of identity: and, for that purpose, we must especially guard against taking it as abstract identity, to the exclusion of all difference. That is the touch-stone for distinguishing all bad philosophy from what alone deserves the name of philosophy. Identity in its truth, as an ideality of what immediately is, is a high category for our religious modes of mind as well as all other forms of thought and mental activity. The true knowledge of God, it may be said, begins when we know him as identity,—as absolute identity. To know so much is to see that all the power and glory of the world sinks into nothing in God's presence, and subsists only as the reflection of His power and His glory. In the same way, identity, as self-consciousness, is what distinguishes man from nature, particularly from the brutes which never reach the point of comprehending themselves as "I," that is, pure self-contained unity. So again, in connection with thought, the main thing is not to confuse the true identity, which contains Being and its characteristics ideally transfigured in it, with an abstract identity, identity of bare form. All the charges of narrowness, hardness, meaninglessness, which are so often directed against thought from the quarter of feeling and immediate perception, rest on the perverse assumption that thought acts only as a faculty of abstract identification. The formal logic itself confirms this assumption by laying down the supreme law of thought (so-called) which has been discussed above. If thinking were no more than an abstract identity, we could not but own it to be a most futile and tedious business, No doubt the notion, and the idea too, are identical with themselves; but identical only in so far as they at the same time involve distinction.

(β) DIFFERENCE

116. Essence is mere identity and reflection in itself only as it is self-relating negativity, and in that way self-repulsion. It contains therefore essentially the characteristic of Difference.

Other-being is here no longer qualitative, taking the shape of the character or limit. It is now in essence, in self-relating essence, and therefore the negation is at the same time a relation,—is, in short, distinction, relativity, mediation.

To ask, "How identity comes to difference," assumes that identity as mere abstract identity is something of itself, and difference also something else equally independent. This supposition renders an answer to the question impossible. If identity is viewed as diverse from difference, all that we have in this way is but difference; and hence we cannot demonstrate the advance to difference, because the person who asks for the how of the progress thereby implies that for him the starting-point is non-existent. The question then when put to the test has obviously no meaning, and its proposer may be met with the question what he means by identity; whereupon we should soon see that he attaches no idea to it at all, and that identity is for him an empty name. As we have seen, besides, Identity is undoubtedly a negative,—not however an abstract empty Nought, but the negation of Being and its characteristics. Being so, identity is at the same time self-relation, and, what is more, negative self-relation; in other words, it draws a distinction between it and itself.

. . . .

(γ) THE GROUND

121. The GROUND is the unity of identity and difference, the truth of what difference and identity have turned out to be,—the reflection-into-self, which is equally a reflection-into-another, and *vice versa*. It is essence put explicitly as a totality.

The maxim of the ground runs thus: Everything has its sufficient ground: that is, the true essentiality of any thing is not the predication of it as identical with itself, or as different (various), or merely positive, or merely negative, but as having its Being in an other, which, being its self-same, is its essence. And to this extent the essence is not abstract reflection into self, but into an other. The ground is the essence in its own inwardness; the essence is intrinsically a ground; and it is a ground only when it is a ground of somewhat, of an other.

We must be careful, when we say that the ground is the unity of identity and difference, not to understand by this unity an abstract identity. Otherwise we only change the name, while we still think the identity (of understanding) already seen to be false. To avoid this misconception we may say that the ground, besides being the unity, is also the difference of identity and difference. In that case in the ground, which promised at first to supersede contradiction, a new contradiction seems to arise. It is however a contradiction which so far from persisting quietly in itself, is rather the expulsion of it from itself. The ground is a ground only to the extent that it affords ground: but the result which thus issued from the ground is only itself. In this lies its formalism. The ground and what is grounded are one and the same content: the difference between the two is the mere difference of form which separates simple self-relation, on the one hand, from mediation or derivativeness on the other. Inquiry into the grounds of things goes with the point of view which, as already noted (note to § 112), is adopted by reflection. We wish, as it were, to see the matter double, first in its immediacy, and secondly in its ground, where it is no longer immediate. This is the plain meaning of the law of sufficient ground, as it is called; it asserts that things should essentially be viewed as mediated. The manner in which formal logic establishes this law of thought, sets a bad example to other sciences. Formal logic asks these sciences not to accept their subject-matter as it is immediately given; and yet herself lays down a law of thought without deducing it,—in other words, without exhibiting its mediation. With the same justice as the logician maintains our faculty of thought to be so constituted that we must ask for the ground of everything, might the physicist, when asked why a man who falls into water is drowned, reply that man happens to be so organised that he cannot live under water; or the jurist, when asked why a criminal is punished, reply that civil society happens to be so constituted that crimes cannot be left unpunished.

Yet even if logic be excused the duty of giving a ground for the law of the sufficient ground, it might at least explain what is to be understood by a ground. The common explanation, which describes the ground as what has a consequence, seems at the first glance more lucid and intelligible than the preceding definition in logical terms. If you ask however what the consequence is, you are told that it is what has a ground; and it becomes obvious that the explanation is intelligible only because it assumes what in our case has been reached as the termination of an antecedent movement of thought. And this is the true business of logic: to show that those thoughts, which as usually employed merely float before consciousness neither understood nor demonstrated, are really grades in the self-determination of thought. It is by this means that they are understood and demonstrated.

B. APPEARANCE

131. The essence must appear or shine forth. Its shining or reflection in it is the suspension and translation of it to immediacy, which, while as reflection-on-self it is matter or subsistence, is also form, reflection-on-something-else, a subsistence which sets itself aside. To show or shine is the characteristic by which essence is distinguished from being,—by which it is essence; and it is this show which, when it is developed, shows itself, and is appearance. Essence accordingly is not something beyond or behind appearance, but just because it is the essence which exists—the existence is APPEARANCE (Forth-shining).

Existence stated explicitly in its contradiction is appearance. But appearance (forth-shining) is not to be confused with a mere show (shining). Show is the proximate truth of Being or immediacy. The immediate, instead of being, as we suppose, something independent, resting on its own self, is a mere show, and as such it is packed or summed up under the simplicity of the immanent essence. The essence is, in the first place, the sum total of the showing itself, shining in itself (inwardly); but, far from abiding in this inwardness, it comes as a ground forward into existence; and this existence being grounded not in itself, but on something else, is just appearance. In our imagination we ordinarily combine with the term appearance or phenomenon the conception of an indefinite congeries of things existing, the being of which is purely relative, and which consequently do not rest on a foundation of their own, but are esteemed only as passing stages. But in this conception it is no less implied that essence does not linger behind or beyond appearance. Rather it is, we may say, the infinite kindness which lets its own show freely issue into immediacy, and graciously allows it the joy of existence. The appearance which is thus created does not stand on its own feet, and has its being not in itself but in something else. God who is the essence, when He lends existence to the passing stages of his own show in himself, may be described as the goodness that creates a world: but He is also the power above it, and the righteousness, which manifests the merely phenomenal character of the content of this existing world, whenever it tries to exist in independence.

Appearance is in every way a very important grade of the logical idea. It may be said to be the distinction of philosophy from ordinary consciousness that it sees the merely phenomenal character of what the latter supposes to have a self-subsistent being. The significance of appearance however must be properly grasped, or mistakes will arise. To say that anything is a *mere* appearance may be misinterpreted to mean that, as compared with what is merely phenomenal, there is greater truth in the immediate, in that which *is*. Now in strict fact, the case is precisely the reverse. Appearance is higher than mere Being,—a richer category because it holds in combination the two elements of reflection-into-self and reflection-into-another: whereas Being (or immediacy) is still mere relationlessness, and apparently rests upon itself alone. Still, to say that anything is *only* an appearance suggests a real flaw, which consists in this, that appearance is still divided against itself and without intrinsic stability. Beyond and above mere appearance comes in the first place actuality, the third grade of essence, of which we shall afterwards speak.

. . . .

C. ACTUALITY

142. Actuality is the unity, become immediate, of essence with existence, or of inward with outward. The utterance of the actual is the actual itself: so that in this utterance it remains just as essential, and only is essential, in so far as it is in immediate external existence.

We have ere this met Being and existence as forms of the immediate. Being is, in general, unreflected immediacy and transition into another. Existence is immediate unity of being and reflection; hence appearance: it comes from the ground, and falls to the ground. In actuality this unity is explicitly put, and the two sides of the relation identified. Hence the actual is exempted from transition, and its externality is its energising. In that energising it is reflected into itself: its existence is only the manifestation of itself, not of another.

Actuality and thought (or idea) are often absurdly opposed. How commonly we hear people saying that, though no objection can be urged against the truth and correctness of a certain thought, there is nothing of the kind to be seen in actuality, or it cannot be actually carried out! People who use such language only prove that they have not properly apprehended the nature either of thought or of actuality. Thought in such a case is, on one hand, the synonym for a subjective conception, plan, intention or the like, just as actuality, on the other, is made synonymous with external and sensible existence. This is all very well in common life, where great laxity is allowed in the categories and the names given to them: and it may of course happen that *e.g.* the plan, or so-called idea, say of a certain method of taxation, is good and advisable in the abstract, but that nothing of the sort is found in so-called actuality, or could possibly be carried out under the given conditions. But when the abstract understanding gets hold of these categories and exaggerates the distinction they imply into a hard and fast line of contrast, when it tells us that in this actual world we must knock ideas out of our heads, it is necessary energetically to protest against these doctrines, alike in the name of science and of sound reason. For on the one hand ideas are not confined to our heads merely, nor is the idea, upon the whole, so feeble as to leave the question of its actualisation or non-actualisation dependent on our will. The idea is rather the absolutely active as well as actual. And on the other hand actuality is not so bad and irrational, as purblind or wrong-headed and muddle-brained would-be reformers imagine. So far is actuality, as distinguished from mere appearance, and primarily presenting a unity of inward and outward, from being in contrariety with reason, that it is rather thoroughly reasonable, and everything which is not reasonable must on that very ground cease to be held actual. The same view may be traced in the usages of educated speech, which declines to give the name of real poet or real statesman to a poet or a statesman who can do nothing really meritorious or reasonable.

143. (α) Viewed as an identity in general, actuality is first of all POSSIBILITY—the reflection-into-self which, as in contrast with the concrete unity of the actual, is taken and made an abstract and unessential essentiality. Possibility is what is essential to reality, but in such a way that it is at the same time only a possibility.

. . . .

144. (β) But the actual in its distinction from possibility (which is reflection-into-self) is itself only the outward concrete, the unessential immediate. In other words, to such extent as the actual is primarily (§ 142) the simple merely immediate unity of inward and outward, it is obviously made an unessential outward, and thus at the same time (§ 140) it is merely inward, the abstraction of reflection-into-self. Hence it is itself characterised as a merely

possible. When thus valued at the rate of a mere possibility, the actual is a CONTINGENT or accidental, and, conversely, possibility is mere accident itself or CHANCE.

145. Possibility and contingency are the two factors of actuality,—inward and outward, put as mere forms which constitute the externality of the actual. They have their reflection-into-self on the body of actual fact, or content, with its intrinsic definiteness which gives the essential ground of their characterisation. The finitude of the contingent and the possible lies, therefore, as we now see, in the distinction of the form-determination from the content: and, therefore, it depends on the content alone whether anything is contingent and possible.

.   .   .   .

147. (γ) When this externality (of actuality) is thus developed into a circle of the two categories of possibility and immediate actuality, showing the intermediation of the one by the other, it is what is called REAL POSSIBILITY. Being such a circle, further, it is the totality, and thus the content, the actual fact or affair in its all-round definiteness. While in like manner, if we look at the distinction between the two characteristics in this unity, it realises the concrete totality of the form, the immediate self-translation of inner into outer, and of outer into inner. This self-movement of the form is ACTIVITY, carrying into effect the fact or affair as a *real* ground which is self-suspended to actuality, and carrying into effect the contingent actuality, the conditions; *i.e.* it is their reflection-in-self, and their self-suspension to another actuality, the actuality of the actual fact. If all the conditions are at hand, the fact (event) *must* be actual; and the fact itself is one of the conditions: for being in the first place only inner, it is at first itself only pre-supposed. Developed actuality, as the coincident alternation of inner and outer, the alternation of their opposite motions combined into a single motion, is NECESSITY.

.   .   .   .

The theory however which regards the world as determined through necessity and the belief in a divine providence are by no means mutually excluding points of view. The intellectual principle underlying the idea of divine providence will hereafter be shown to be the notion. But the notion is the truth of necessity, which it contains in suspension in itself; just as, conversely, necessity is the notion implicit. Necessity is blind only so long as it is not understood. There is nothing therefore more mistaken than the charge of blind fatalism made against the philosophy of history, when it takes for its problem to understand the necessity of every event. The philosophy of history rightly understood takes the rank of a Théodicée; and those, who fancy they honour divine providence by excluding necessity from it, are really degrading it by this exclusiveness to a blind and irrational caprice. In the simple language of the religious mind which speaks of God's eternal and immutable decrees, there is implied an express recognition that necessity forms part of the essence of God. In his difference from God, man, with his own private opinion and will, follows the call of caprice and arbitrary humour, and thus often finds his acts turn out something quite different from what he had meant and willed. But God knows what he wills, is determined in his eternal will neither by accident from within nor from without, and what he wills he also accomplishes, irresistibly.

159. The passage from necessity to freedom, or from actuality into the notion, is the very hardest, because it proposes that independent actuality shall be thought as having all its substantiality in the passing over and identity with the other independent actuality. The

notion, too, is extremely hard, because it is itself just this very identity. But the actual substance as such, the cause, which in its exclusiveness resists all invasion, is *ipso facto* subjected to necessity or the destiny of passing into dependency: and it is this subjection rather where the chief hardness lies. To think necessity, on the contrary, rather tends to melt that hardness. For thinking means that, in the other, one meets with one's self.—It means a liberation, which is not the flight of abstraction, but consists in that which is actual having itself not as something else, but as its own being and creation, in the other actuality with which it is bound up by the force of necessity. As existing in an individual form, this liberation is called I: as developed to its totality, it is free Spirit; as feeling, it is love; and as enjoyment, it is blessedness.—The great vision of substance in Spinoza is only a potential liberation from finite exclusiveness and egoism: but the notion itself realises for its own both the power of necessity and actual freedom.

When, as now, the notion is called the truth of Being and essence, we must expect to be asked, why we do not begin with the notion? The answer is that, where knowledge by thought is our aim, we cannot begin with the truth, because the truth, when it forms the beginning, must rest on mere assertion. The truth when it is thought must as such verify itself to thought. If the notion were put at the head of logic, and defined, quite correctly in point of content, as the unity of Being and essence, the following question would come up: What are we to think under the terms "Being" and "essence," and how do they come to be embraced in the unity of the notion? But if we answered these questions, then our beginning with the notion would be merely nominal. The real start would be made with Being, as we have here done: with this difference, that the characteristics of Being as well as those of essence would have to be accepted uncritically from figurate conception, whereas we have observed Being and essence in their own dialectical development and learned how they lose themselves in the unity of the notion.

CHAPTER IX
The Doctrine of the Notion

160. The NOTION is the principle of freedom, the power of substance self-realised. It is a systematic whole, in which each of its constituent functions is the very total which the notion is, and is put as indissolubly one with it. Thus in its self-identity it has original and complete determinateness.

The position taken up by the notion is that of absolute idealism. Philosophy is a knowledge through notions because it sees that what on other grades of consciousness is taken to have Being, and to be naturally or immediately independent, is but a constituent stage in the idea. In the logic of understanding, the notion is generally reckoned a mere form of thought, and treated as a general conception. It is to this inferior view of the notion that the assertion refers, so often urged on behalf of the heart and sentiment, that notions as such are something dead, empty, and abstract. The case is really quite the reverse. The notion is, on the contrary, the principle of all life, and thus possesses at the same time a character of thorough concreteness. That it is so follows from the whole logical movement up to this point, and need not be here proved. The contrast between form and content, which is thus used to criticise the notion when it is alleged to be merely formal, has, like all the other contrasts upheld by reflection, been already left behind and overcome dialectically or through itself. The notion, in short, is what contains all the earlier categories of thought merged in it. It certainly is a form, but an infinite and creative form, which includes, but at the same time releases from itself, the fulness of all content. And so too the notion may, if it be wished, be styled abstract, if the name concrete is restricted to the concrete facts of sense or of immediate perception. For the notion is not palpable to the touch, and when we are engaged with it, hearing and seeing must quite fail us. And yet, as it was before remarked, the notion is a true concrete; for the reason that it involves Being and essence, and the total wealth of these two spheres with them, merged in the unity of thought.

If, as was said at an earlier point, the different stages of the logical idea are to be treated as a series of definitions of the Absolute, the definition which now results for us is that the Absolute is the notion. That necessitates a higher estimate of the notion, however, than is found in formal conceptualist logic, where the notion is a mere form of our subjective thought, with no original content of its own. But if speculative logic thus attaches a meaning to the term notion so very different from that usually given, it may be asked why the same word should be employed in two contrary acceptations, and an occasion thus given for confusion and misconception. The answer is that, great as the interval is between the speculative notion and the notion of formal logic, a closer examination shows that the deeper meaning is not so foreign to the general usages of language as it seems at first sight. We speak of the deduction of a content from the notion, *e.g.* of the specific provisions of the law of property from the notion of property; and so again we speak of tracing back these material details to the notion. We thus recognise that the notion is no mere form without a content of its own: for if it were, there would be in the one case nothing to deduce from such a form, and in the other case to trace a given body of fact back to the empty form of the notion would only rob the fact of its specific character, without making it understood.

. . . .

162. The doctrine of the notion is divided into three parts. (1) The first is the doctrine of the SUBJECTIVE or FORMAL NOTION. (2) The second is the doctrine of the notion invested with the character of immediacy, or of OBJECTIVITY. (3) The third is the doctrine of the IDEA, the subject-object, the unity of notion and objectivity, the absolute truth.

A. THE SUBJECTIVE NOTION
(a) The Notion as Notion

163. The notion as notion contains the three following "moments" or functional parts. (1) The first is UNIVERSALITY—meaning that it is in free equality with itself in its specific character. (2) The second is PARTICULARITY—that is, the specific character, in which the universal continues serenely equal to itself. (3) The third is INDIVIDUALITY—meaning the reflection-into-self of the specific characters of universality and particularity;—which negative self-unity has complete and original determinateness, without any loss to its self-identity or universality.

. . . .

164. Universality, particularity, and individuality are, taken in the abstract, the same as identity, difference, and ground. But the universal is the self-identical, with the express qualification, that it simultaneously contains the particular and the individual. Again, the particular is the different or the specific character, but with the qualification that it is in itself universal and is as an individual. Similarly the individual must be understood to be a subject or substratum, which involves the genus and species in itself and possesses a substantial existence. Such is the explicit or realised inseparability of the functions of the notion

in their difference (§ 160)—what may be called the clearness of the notion, in which each distinction causes no dimness or interruption, but is quite as much transparent.

No complaint is oftener made against the notion than that it is *abstract.* Of course it is abstract, if abstract means that the medium in which the notion exists is thought in general and not the sensible thing in its empirical concreteness. It is abstract also, because the notion falls short of the idea. To this extent the subjective notion is still formal. This however does not mean that it ought to have or receive another content than its own. It is itself the absolute form, and so is all specific character, but as that character is in its truth. Although it be abstract therefore, it is the concrete, concrete altogether, the subject as such. The absolutely concrete is the mind (see end of § 159)—the notion when it *exists* as notion distinguishing itself from its objectivity, which notwithstanding the distinction still continues to be its own. Everything else which is concrete, however rich it be, is not so intensely identical with itself and therefore not so concrete on its own part,—least of all what is commonly supposed to be concrete, but is only a congeries held together by external influence.—What are called notions, and in fact specific notions, such as man, house, animal, etc., are simply denotations and abstract representations. These abstractions retain out of all the functions of the notion only that of universality; they leave particularity and individuality out of account and have no development in these directions. By so doing they just miss the notion.

165. It is the element of individuality which first explicitly differentiates the elements of the notion. Individuality is the negative reflection of the notion into itself, and it is in that way at first the free differentiating of it as the first negation, by which the specific character of the notion is realised, but under the form of particularity. That is to say, the different elements are in the first place only qualified as the several elements of the notion, and, secondly, their identity is no less explicitly stated, the one being said to be the other. This realised particularity of the notion is the judgment.

· · · · · · · · ·

(b) The Judgment

166. The JUDGMENT is the notion in its particularity, as a connection which is also a distinguishing of its functions, which are put as independent and yet as identical with themselves, not with one another.

One's first impression about the judgment is the independence of the two extremes, the subject and the predicate. The former we take to be a thing or term *per se,* and the predicate a general term outside the said subject and somewhere in our heads. The next point is for us to bring the latter into combination with the former, and in this way frame a judgment. The copula "is" however enunciates the predicate *of* the subject, and so that external subjective subsumption is again put in abeyance, and the judgment taken as a determination of the object itself.—The etymological meaning of the judgment (*Urtheil*) in German goes deeper, as it were declaring the unity of the notion to be primary, and its distinction to be the original partition. And that is what the judgment really is.

· · · · · · · · ·

B. THE OBJECT

194. The OBJECT is immediate being, because insensible to difference, which in it has suspended itself. It is, further, a totality in itself, while at the same time (as this identity is

only the *implicit* identity of its dynamic elements) it is equally indifferent to its immediate unity. It thus breaks up into distinct parts, each of which is itself the totality. Hence the object is the absolute contradiction between a complete independence of the multiplicity, and the equally complete non-independence of the different pieces.

The definition, which states that the Absolute is the object, is most definitely implied in the Leibnitzian monad. The monads are each an object, but an object implicitly "representative," indeed the total representation of the world. In the simple unity of the monad, all difference is merely ideal, not independent or real. Nothing from without comes into the monad, it is the whole notion in itself, only distinguished by its own greater or less development. None the less, this simple totality parts into the absolute multitude of differences, each becoming an independent monad. In the monad of monads, the preestablished harmony of their inward developments, these substances are in like manner again reduced to "ideality" and unsubstantiality. The philosophy of Leibnitz, therefore, represents contradiction in its complete development.

. . . .

(2) Objectivity contains the three forms of mechanism, chemism, and teleology. The object of mechanical type is the immediate and undifferentiated object. No doubt it contains difference, but the different pieces stand, as it were, without affinity to each other, and their connection is only extraneous. In chemism, on the contrary, the object exhibits an essential tendency to differentiation, in such a way that the objects are what they are only by their relation to each other: this tendency to difference constitutes their quality. The third type of objectivity, the teleological relation, is the unity of mechanism and chemism. Design, like the mechanical object, is a self-contained totality, enriched however by the principle of differentiation which came to the fore in chemism, and thus referring itself to the object that stands over against it. Finally, it is the realization of design which forms the transition to the idea.

. . . .

C. THE IDEA

213. The IDEA is truth in itself and for itself,—the absolute unity of the notion and objectivity. Its "ideal" content is nothing but the notion in its detailed terms: its "real" content is only the exhibition which the notion gives itself in the form of external existence, whilst yet, by enclosing this shape in its ideality, it keeps it in its power, and so keeps itself in it.

The definition, which declares the Absolute to be the idea, is itself absolute. All former definitions come back to this. The idea is the truth: for truth is the correspondence of objectivity with the notion:—not of course the correspondence of external things with my conceptions,—for these are only *correct* conceptions held by *me,* the individual person. In the idea we have nothing to do with the individual, nor with figurate conceptions, nor with external things. And yet, again, everything actual, in so far as it is true, is the idea, and has its truth by and in virtue of the idea alone. Every individual being is some one aspect of the idea: for which, therefore, yet other actualities are needed, which in their turn appear to have a self-subsistence of their own. It is only in them altogether and in their relation that the notion is realised. The individual by itself does not correspond to its notion. It is this limitation of its existence which constitutes the finitude and the ruin of the individual.

When we hear the idea spoken of, we need not imagine something far away beyond this mortal sphere. The idea is rather what is completely present: and it is found, however confused and degenerated, in every consciousness. We conceive the world to ourselves as a great totality which is created by God, and so created that in it God has manifested himself to us. We regard the world also as ruled by divine providence: implying that the scattered and divided parts of the world are continually brought back, and made conformable, to the unity from which they have issued. The purpose of philosophy has always been the intellectual ascertainment of the idea; and everything deserving the name of philosophy has constantly been based on the consciousness of an absolute unity where the understanding sees and accepts only separation.—It is too late now to ask for proof that the idea is the truth. The proof of that is contained in the whole deduction and development of thought up to this point. The idea is the result of this course of dialectic. Not that it is to be supposed that the idea is mediate only, *i.e.* mediated through something else than itself. It is rather its own result, and being so, is no less immediate than mediate. The stages hitherto considered, viz. those of Being and essence, as well as those of notion and of objectivity, are not, when so distinguished, something permanent, resting upon themselves. They have proved to be dialectical; and their only truth is that they are dynamic elements of the idea.

214. The idea may be described in many ways. It may be called reason (and this is the proper philosophical signification of reason); subject-object; the unity of the ideal and the real, of the finite and the infinite, of soul and body; the possibility which has its actuality in its own self; that of which the nature can be thought only as existent, etc. All these descriptions apply, because the idea contains all the relations of understanding, but contains them in their infinite self-return and self-identity.

It is easy work for the understanding to show that everything said of the idea is self-contradictory. But that can quite as well be retaliated, or rather in the idea the retaliation is actually made. And this work, which is the work of reason, is certainly not so easy as that of the understanding. Understanding may demonstrate that the idea is self-contradictory: because the subjective is subjective only and is always confronted by the objective,—because being is different from notion and therefore cannot be picked out of it,—because the finite is finite only, the exact antithesis of the infinite, and therefore not identical with it; and so on with every term of the description. The reverse of all this however is the doctrine of logic. Logic shows that the subjective which is to be subjective only, the finite which would be finite only, the infinite which would be infinite only, and so on, have no truth, but contradict themselves, and pass over into their opposites. Hence this transition, and the unity in which the extremes are merged and become factors, each with a merely reflected existence, reveals itself as their truth.

The understanding, which addresses itself to deal with the idea, commits a double misunderstanding. It takes *first* the extremes of the idea (be they expressed as they will, so long as they are in their unity), not as they are understood when stamped with this concrete unity, but as if they remained abstractions outside of it. It no less mistakes the relation between them, even when it has been expressly stated. Thus, for example, it overlooks even the nature of the copula in the judgment, which affirms that the individual, or subject, is after all not individual, but universal. But, in the *second* place, the understanding believes *its* "reflection,"—that the self-identical idea contains its own negative, or contains contradiction,—to be an external reflection which does not lie within the idea itself. But the reflection is really no peculiar cleverness of the understanding. The idea itself is the dialectic which for ever divides and distinguishes the self-identical from the differentiated, the subjective from the objective, the finite from the infinite, soul from body. Only on these terms is it an eternal creation, eternal vitality, and eternal spirit. But while it thus passes or rather translates itself into the abstract understanding, it for ever remains reason. The idea is the dialectic which again makes this mass of understanding and diversity understand its finite nature and the pseudo-independence in its productions, and which brings the diversity back to unity. Since this double movement is not separate or distinct in time, nor indeed in any other way—otherwise it would be only a repetition of the abstract understanding—the idea is the eternal vision of itself in the other,—notion which in its objectivity *has* carried out *itself,*—object which is inward design, essential subjectivity.

The different modes of apprehending the idea as unity of ideal and real, of finite and infinite, of identity and difference, etc., are more or less formal. They designate some one stage of the *specific* notion. Only the notion itself, however, is free and the genuine universal: in the idea, therefore, the specific character of the notion is only the notion itself,—an objectivity, viz., into which it, being the universal, continues itself, and in which it has only its own character, the total character. The idea is the infinite judgment, of which the terms are severally the independent totality; and in which, as each grows to the fulness of its own nature, it has thereby at the same time passed into the other. None of the other specific notions exhibits this totality complete on both its sides as the notion itself and objectivity.

215. The idea is essentially a process, because its identity is the absolute and free identity of the notion, only in so far as it is absolute negativity and for that reason dialectical. It is the round of movement, in which the notion, in the capacity of universality which is individuality, gives itself the character of objectivity and of the antithesis thereto; and this externality which has the notion for its substance, finds its way back to subjectivity through its immanent dialectic.

As the idea is (*a*) a process, it follows that such an expression for the Absolute as *unity* of thought and being, of finite and infinite, etc., is false; for unity expresses an abstract and merely quiescent identity. As the idea is (*b*) subjectivity, it follows that the expression is equally false on another account. That unity of which it speaks expresses a merely virtual or underlying presence of the genuine unity. The infinite would thus seem to be merely *neutralised* by the finite, the subjective by the objective, thought by being. But in the negative unity of the idea, the infinite overlaps and includes the finite, thought overlaps being, subjectivity overlaps objectivity. The unity of the idea is thought, infinity, and subjectivity, and is in consequence to be essentially distinguished from the idea as *substance,* just as this overlapping subjectivity, thought, or infinity is to be distinguished from the one-sided subjectivity, one-sided thought, one-sided infinity to which it descends in judging and defining.

The idea as a process runs through three stages in its development. The first form of the idea is life: that is, the idea in the form of immediacy. The second form is that of mediation or differentiation; and this is the idea in the form of knowledge, which appears under the double aspect of the theoretical and practical idea. The process of knowledge eventuates in the restoration of the unity enriched by difference. This gives the third form of the idea, the Absolute idea: which last stage of the logical idea evinces itself to be at the same time the true first, and to have a being due to itself alone.

. . . .

THE PHENOMENOLOGY OF MIND

In scepticism consciousness learns in truth, that it is divided against itself. And from this experience there is born a new type of consciousness, wherein are linked the two thoughts which scepticism had kept asunder. The thoughtless self-ignorance of scepticism must pass away; for in fact the two attitudes of scepticism express one consciousness. This new type of consciousness is therefore explicitly aware of its own doubleness. It regards itself on the one hand as the deliverer, changeless and self-possessed; on the other hand it regards itself as the absolutely confounded and contrary; and it is the awareness of this its own contra-diction.—In Stoicism the self owns itself in the simplicity of freedom. In scepticism it gives itself embodiment, makes naught of other embodied reality, but, in the very act of so doing, renders itself the rather twofold and is now parted in twain. Hereby the same duplication that was formerly shared between two individuals, the lord and the slave, has now entered into the nature of one individual. The differentiation of the self, which is essential to the notion of mind, is already present, but not as constituting an organic unity, and the un-happy consciousness is this awareness of the self as the divided nature, wherein is only conflict.

This unhappy and broken consciousness, just because the conflict of its nature is known as belonging to one person, must forever, in each of its two forms, have the other also present to it. Whenever, in either form, it seems to have come to victory and unity, it finds no rest there, but is forthwith driven over to the other. Its true home-coming, its true reconciliation with itself, will, however, display to us the nature of the mind, as he will appear when, having come to life, he has entered the world of his manifestation. For it already belongs to the unhappy consciousness to be one undivided soul in the midst of its doubleness. It is in fact the very gazing of one self into another; it is both these selves; it has no nature save in so far as it unites the two. But thus far it knows not yet this its own real essence; it has not entered into possession of this unity.

For the first then, the unhappy consciousness is but the unwon unity of the two selves. To its view the two are not one, but are at war together. And accordingly it regards one of them, viz., the simple, the changeless consciousness, as the true self. The other, the multi-form and fickle, it regards as the false self. The unhappy consciousness finds these two as mutually estranged. For its own part, because it is the awareness of this contradiction, it takes sides with the changeless consciousness, and calls itself the false self. But since it is aware of the changeless, *i.e.* of the true self, its task must be one of self-deliverance, that is, the task of delivering itself from the unreality. For on the one hand it knows itself only as the fickle; and the changeless is far remote from it. And yet the unhappy consciousness is in its genuine selfhood one with the simple and changeless consciousness; for therein lies its own true self. But yet again it knows that it is not in possession of this true self. So long as the unhappy consciousness assigns to the two selves this position, they cannot remain in-different to each other; or, in other words, the unhappy consciousness cannot itself be

From the translation by Josiah Royce in *Modern Classical Philosophers* (Boston: Houghton Mifflin, 1908). With emendations by Daniel Kolak.

indifferent to the changeless. For the unhappy consciousness is, as a fact, of both kinds, and knows the relation of the changeless to the fickle as a relation of truth to falsehood. The falsehood must be turned to naught; but since the unhappy consciousness finds both the false and the true alike necessary to it, and contradictory, there remains to it only the contradictory movement, wherein neither of the opposed elements can find repose in going over to its opponent but must create itself anew in the opponent's very bosom.

To win, then, in this strife against the adversary, is rather to be vanquished. To attain one goal, is rather to lose it in its opposite. The whole life, whatever it be, whatever it do, is aware only of the pain of this being and doing. For this consciousness has no object besides its opposite, the true self, and its own nothingness. In aspiration it strives hence towards the changeless. But this aspiration is itself the unhappy consciousness, and contains forthwith the knowledge of the opposite, namely of its own individuality. The changeless, when it enters consciousness, is sicklied over with individuality, is present therewith; instead of being lost in the consciousness of the changeless, individuality arises ever afresh therein.

But one thing the unhappy consciousness thus learns, namely that individuality is made manifest in the changeless, and that the changeless is made manifest in individuality. It finds that in general individuality belongs to the changeless true self, and that in fact its own individuality also belongs thereto. For the outcome of this process is precisely the unity of this twofold consciousness. This unity, then, comes to light, but for the first only as an unity wherein the diversity of the two aspects plays the chief part. For the unhappy consciousness there thus result three ways in which individuality and the changeless are linked. First, it rediscovers itself as again banished into its opposition to the changeless self; and it is cast back to the beginning of the strife, which latter still remains the element of the entire relationship. In the second place, the unhappy consciousness learns that individuality belongs to the very essence of the changeless, is the incarnation of the changeless; and the latter hereupon assumes the burden of this whole range of phenomena. In the third place, the unhappy consciousness discovers itself to be the individual who dwells in the changeless. In the first stage the changeless appears to consciousness only as the remote self, that condemns individuality. In passing through the second stage, consciousness learns that the changeless is as much an incarnate individual as it is itself; and thus, in the third stage, consciousness reaches the grade of the mind, rejoices to find itself in the mind, and becomes aware that its individuality is reconciled with the universal.

What is here set forth as the character and relationship of the changeless has appeared as the experience that the divided consciousness obtains in its woe. This experience is to be sure not its own one-sided process; for it is itself the changeless consciousness, and the latter is also an individual consciousness; so that the process is all the while a process in the changeless consciousness, belonging to the latter quite as much as to the other. For the changeless consciousness passes through the three stages, being first the changeless as in general opposed to the individual, then becoming an individual over against another individual, and finally being united with the latter. But this observation, in so far as it is made from our own point of view as observers, is here premature; for thus far we have come to know the changeless only in so far as consciousness has defined it. Not, as yet, the true changeless, but the changeless as modified by the duality of consciousness, has come to our sight; and so we know not how the developed and self-possessed changeless will behave. What has resulted from the foregoing is only this, that the mentioned characteristics appear, to the consciousness now under consideration, as belonging to the changeless.

Consequently the changeless consciousness itself also preserves even in its incarnate form the character and principle of separation and isolation as against the individual consciousness. From the latter's point of view, the fact that the changeless takes on the form of individuality appears as something which somehow *comes to pass.* The opposition to the changeless is something, moreover, which the individual consciousness merely finds as a fact. The relation seems to it merely a result of its natural constitution. As for the final reconciliation, the individual consciousness looks upon this as in part its own deed, the result of its own individuality; but it also regards a part of the unity as due, both in origin and in existence, to the changeless. The element of opposition thus remains even in the unity. In fact, in taking on its incarnate form, the changeless has not only retained but actually confirmed its character of remoteness. For although, in assuming a developed and incarnate individuality, it seems on the one hand to have approached the individual, still, on the other hand, it now stands over against him as an opaque fact of sense, with all the stubbornness of the actual about it. The hope that the individual may become one with the changeless must remain but hope, empty and distant; for between hope and fruition stand now the fatal chance and the lifeless indifference which have resulted from that very incarnation wherein lies the foundation of the hope. Because the changeless has thus entered the world of facts, has taken on the garments of actuality, it follows necessarily that in the world of time it has vanished, that in space it is far away, and forever far remains.

If at the outset the mere notion of the divided consciousness demanded that it should undertake the destruction of its individuality, and the growth into the changeless, the present result defines the undertaking thus: That the individual should leave off its relation with the formless ideal, and should come only into relations with the changeless as incarnate. For it is now the fact of the unity of the individual and the changeless which has become the truth and the object for consciousness, as before, in the mere notion, only the abstract and disembodied changeless was the essential object; and consciousness now finds the total separation of the notion as the relation which is to be forgotten. The thing which has now to be reduced to unity is the still external relation to the embodied ideal, in so far as the latter is a foreign actuality.

The process whereby the unreal self seeks to reach this unity is once more threefold, since it will be found to have a threefold relation to its incarnate but remote ideal. In the first place it will appear as the devout consciousness; in the second place, as an individual, whose relation to the actuality will be one of aspiration and of service; in the third place it will reach the consciousness of self-possession. We must now follow these three states of being, to see how they are involved in the general relation, and are determined thereby.

Taking the first state, that of the devout consciousness, one finds indeed that the incarnate changeless, as it appears to this consciousness, seems to be present in all the completeness of its being. But as a fact the fashion of the completed being of the changeless has not yet been developed. Should this completed being be revealed to consciousness, the revelation would be, as it were, rather the deed of the Ideal than the work of the devout consciousness; and thus the revelation would come from one side alone, would be no full and genuine revelation, but would remain burdened with incompleteness and with duality.

Although the unhappy consciousness still lacks the presence of its ideal, it is nevertheless as we see beyond the stage of pure thought, whether such thought were the mere abstract thinking of Stoicism, which forgets all individuality, or the merely restless thinking of scepticism, which in fact embodies individuality in its ignorant contradictions and its ceaseless unrepose. Both of these stages the unhappy consciousness has transcended. It begins the synthesis of pure thought and of individuality and persists therein. But it has not yet risen to the thought which is aware of the reconciliation of the conscious individual with the demands of pure thought. The unhappy consciousness stands between the two extremes, at the place where pure thought and the individual consciousness meet. It is in fact itself this meeting place; it is the unity of pure thought and individuality. It even knows that pure thought, yes the changeless itself, is essentially individual. But what it does not know is that this its object, the changeless, which it regards as having necessarily assumed an incarnate individuality, is identical with its own self, with the very individual as he is in consciousness.

Its attitude, then, in this first form, in which it appears as the devout consciousness, is not one in which it explicitly thinks about its object. It is implicitly indeed the consciousness of a thinking individual, and its object also is a thinking individual. But the relation between these two is still one that defies pure thought. Consciousness accordingly as it were makes but a feint at thinking, and takes the form of adoration. Such thought as it has remains the mere formless tinkling of an altar bell, or the wreathing of warm incense smoke—a thinking in music, such as never reaches an organized notion, wherein alone an inner objectivity could be attained. This limitless and devout inner feeling finds indeed its object, but as something uncomprehended, and so as a stranger. Thus comes to pass the inward activity of the devout soul, which is indeed self-conscious, but only in so far as it possesses the mere feeling of its sorrowful disharmony. This activity is one of ceaseless longing. It possesses the assurance that its true self is just such a pure soul,—pure thought in fact, taking on the form of individuality,—and that this being, who is the object of the devotion, since he possesses the thought of his own individuality, recognizes and approves the worshipper. But at the same time this Being is the unapproachable and remote. As you seize hold upon him he escapes, or rather he has already gone away. He has already gone away; for he is the ideal giving himself in thought the form of an individual and therefore consciousness gets without hindrance its self-fulfilment in him,—gets self-fulfilment, but only to learn that it is the very opposite of this ideal. Instead of seizing hold on the true self, its mere feeling is all. It sinks back into itself. Unable at the moment of union to escape finding itself as the very opposite of the ideal, it has actually seized hold upon its own untruthfulness, not upon the truth. In the true self it has sought to find its own fulfilment; but *its own* means only its isolated individual reality. For the same reason it cannot get hold upon the true self in so far as he is at once an individual and a reality. Where one seeks him, the true self is not to be found; for by definition he is the remote self, and so is to be found nowhere. To seek him in so far as he is an individual is not to look for his universal, his ideal individuality, nor for his presence as the law of life, but merely to seek him as an individual thing, as a fact amongst facts, as something that sense could touch unhindered. But as such an object the ideal exists only as a lost object. What consciousness finds is thus only the sepulchre of its true life. But this sepulchre is now the actuality, and, moreover, one that by its nature forbids any abiding possession; and the presence of this tomb means only the strife of a search that must be fruitless. But consciousness thus learns that there is no real sepulchre which can contain its true lord, the changeless. As lord who has been taken away he is not the true lord. The changeless will no longer be looked for here below, or grasped after as the vanished one. For hereby consciousness learns to look for individuality as a genuine and universal ideal.

In the next place then, the return of the soul to itself is to be defined as its knowledge that in its own individuality it has genuine being. It is the pure heart, which potentially, or from our point of view, has discovered the secret of self-satisfaction. For although in feeling it is sundered from its ideal, still this feeling is in essence a feeling of self-possession. What has been felt is the ideal as expressed in terms of pure feeling; and this ideal is its own very self. It issues from the process then as the feeling of self-possession, and so as an actual and independent being. By this return to itself it has, from our point of view, passed to its second relationship, that of aspiration and service. And in this second stage consciousness confirms itself in the assurance of self-possession (an assurance which we now see it to have attained), by overcoming and feeding upon the true self, which, in so far as it was an independent thing, was estranged. From the point of view of the unhappy consciousness, however, all that yet appears is the aspiration and the service. It knows not yet that in finding these it has the assurance of self-possession as the basis of its existence, and that its feeling of the true self is a self-possessed feeling. Not knowing this, it has still ever within it the fragmentary assurance of itself. Therefore any confirmation which it should receive from toiling and from communion would still be a fragmentary confirmation. Yes, itself it must destroy even this confirmation also, finding therein indeed a confirmation of something, but only of its isolation and its separation.

The actual world wherein the aspiration and the service find their calling, seems to this consciousness no longer an essentially vain world, that is only to be destroyed and consumed, but rather, like the consciousness itself, a world broken in twain, which is only in one aspect vain, while in another aspect it is a sanctified world, wherein the changeless is incarnate. For the changeless has retained the nature of individuality, and being, as changeless, an universal, its individuality has in general the significance of all actuality.

If consciousness were now aware of its independent personality, and if it regarded the actual world as essentially vain, it would get the feeling of its independence in its service and in its communion, since it would be aware of itself as the victory that overcometh the world. But because the world is regarded by it as an embodiment of the ideal, it may not overcome by its own power. It does indeed attain to conquest over the world and to a feasting thereon, but to this end it is essential that the changeless should itself give its own body as the food. And in this respect consciousness appears as a mere matter of fact having no part in the deed; but it also appears inwardly broken in twain, and this doubleness, its division into a self that stands in a genuine relation to itself and to reality, and a self whose life is hidden and undeveloped, is now apparent in the contrast between its service and its communion. As in actual relation to the world, consciousness is a doer of works, and knows itself as such, and this side belongs to its individuality. But it has also its undeveloped reality. This is hidden in the true self, and consists in the talents and virtues of the individual. They are a foreign gift. The changeless grants them to consciousness that they may be used.

In doing its good works, consciousness is, for the first, parted into a relationship between two extremes. On one side stands the toiler in the world here below; on the other side stands the passive actuality in whose midst he toils. Both are related to each other; both however are also referred to the changeless as their source, and have their being hidden therein. From each side, then, there is but a shadowy image let free to enter into play with the other. That term of the relationship which is called the actuality is overcome by the other term, the doer of good works. But the former term, for its part, can only be overcome because its own changeless nature overcomes it, divides itself in twain, and gives over the divided part to be the material for deeds. The power that does the deeds appears as the might that overcometh the world. But for this very reason the present consciousness, which regards its true self as something foreign, must regard this might also, whereby it works, as a thing remote from itself. Instead of winning self-possession from its good works, and becoming thereby sure of itself, consciousness relates all this activity back again to the other member of the relationship, which thus proves itself to be the pure universal, the absolute might, whence flows every form of activity, and wherein lies the truth both of the mutually dissolving terms, as they first appeared, and of their interchanging of relationship.

The changeless consciousness sacrifices its body, and gives it over to be used. On the other hand the individual consciousness renders thanks for the gift, forbids itself the satisfaction of a sense of independence, and refers all its doings to the changeless. In these two aspects of the mutual sacrifice made by both the members of the relation, consciousness does indeed win the sense of its own oneness with the changeless. But at the same time this oneness is still beladen with the separation, and is divided in itself. The opposition between the individual and the universal comes afresh to sight. For consciousness only *seems* to resign selfish satisfaction. As a fact it gets selfish satisfaction. For it still remains longing, activity, and fulfilment. As consciousness it has longed, it has acted, it has been filled. In giving thanks, in acknowledging the other as the true self, in making naught of itself, it has still been doing its own deed. This deed has repaid the deed of the other, has rendered a price for the kindly sacrifice. If the other has offered its own image as a gift, consciousness, for its part, has made its return in thanks, and has herein done actually more than the other, since it has offered its all, namely, its good works, while the other has been parted with its mere image. The entire process returns then back to the side of the individual, and does so not merely in respect of the actual aspiration, service, and communion, but even in respect of the very act of giving thanks, an act that was to attain the opposite result. In giving thanks consciousness is aware of itself as this individual, and refuses to be deceived by its own seeming resignation. What has resulted is only the twofold reference of the process to its two terms; and the result is the renewed division into the conflicting consciousness of the changeless on the one hand, and, on the other hand, the consciousness of the opposed will, activity, and fulfilment, and even of the very resignation itself; for these constitute in general the separated individuality.

Herewith begins the third phase of the process of this consciousness, which follows from the second as a consciousness that in truth, by will and by deed, has proved its independence. In the first phase it was the mere notion of a live consciousness, an inner life that had not yet attained actuality by service and communion. The second phase was the attainment, as outer activity and communion. Returned from this outer activity, consciousness has now reached the stage where it has experienced its own actuality and power, where it knows in truth that it is fully self-possessed. But now the enemy comes to light in his most genuine form. In the struggle of the inner life the individual had existence only as an abstraction, as "passed in music out of sight." In service and in communion, as the realization of this unreal selfhood, it is able in its immediate experience to forget itself, and its consciousness of its own merit in this actual service is turned to humiliation through the act of thankful acknowledgment. But this humiliation is in truth a return of consciousness to itself, and to itself as the possessor of its own actuality.

This third relationship, wherein this genuine actuality is to be one term, is that relationship of the actuality to the universal, wherein the actuality is nevertheless to appear as an unreality; and the process of this relationship is still to be considered.

In the first place, as regards the conflicting relationship of consciousness, wherein its own reality appears to it as an obvious nothingness, the result is that its actual work seems to it a doing of naught, and its satisfaction is but a sense of its misery. Work and satisfaction thus lose all universal content and meaning; for if they had any, then they would involve a full self-possession. Both of them sink to the level of individuality; and consciousness, turning upon this individuality, devotes itself to making naught of it. Consciousness of an actual individual is a consciousness of the mere animal functions of the body. These latter are no longer naïvely carried out as something that is altogether of no moment, and that can have no weight or significance for the spirit; on the contrary, they become the object of earnest concern, and are of the very weightiest moment. The enemy arises anew in his defeat. Consciousness holds him in eye, yet frees itself not from him, but rather dwells upon the sight, and sees constantly its own uncleanness. And because, at the same time, this object of its striving, instead of being significant, is of the most contemptible, instead of being an universal is of the most individual, we therefore behold at this stage only a brooding, unhappy and miserable personality, limited solely to himself and his little deeds.

But all the while this person links both to the sense of his misery and to the worthlessness of his deeds, the consciousness that he is one with the ideal. For the attempted direct destruction of individuality is determined by the thought of the ideal, and takes place for the sake of the Ideal. This relation of dependence constitutes the essence of the negative onslaught upon individuality. But the dependence is as such potentially positive, and will bring consciousness to a sense of its own unity.

This determinate dependence is the rational tie, whereby the individual who at first holds fast by his opposition to the true self, is still linked to the other term, yet only by means of a third element. This mediating element reveals the true self to the false self, which in its turn knows that in the eyes of the true self it has existence only by virtue of the dependence. It is the dependence then which reveals the two terms of the relationship to one another, and which, as mediator, takes the part of each one of the terms in presence of the other. The mediator too is a conscious being, for its work is the production of this consciousness as such. What it brings to pass is that overcoming of individuality which consciousness is undertaking.

Through the mediator, then, consciousness frees itself from regarding its good works and its communion as due to its private merit. It rejects all claim to independence of will. It casts upon the mediator, the intercessor, the burden of its self-will, its freedom of choice, and its sins. The mediator, dwelling in the immediate presence of the ideal, gives counsel as to what is to be done. And what is done, being in submission to the will of another, is no longer one's own act. What is still left to the untrue self is the objective result of the deed, the fruit of the toil, the satisfaction. But this too it refuses to accept as its own, and resigns not only its self-will, but the actual outcome of its service and its satisfaction. It resigns this outcome, first, because the latter would involve an attainment of self-conscious truth and independence (and this consciousness lives in the thought and the speech of a strange and incomprehensible mystery). Secondly, moreover, it resigns the outcome in so far as the latter consists of worldly goods, and so it abandons, in a measure, whatever it has earned by its labor. Thirdly, it resigns all the satisfaction which has fallen to its lot, forbidding itself such satisfaction through fasting and through penance.

By these characteristics, by the surrender of self-will, of property, and of satisfaction, and by the further and positive characteristic of its undertaking of a mysterious task, consciousness does in truth free itself completely from any sense of inner or outer freedom, from any trust in the reality of its independence. It is sure that it has verily surrendered its ego, and has reduced its natural self-consciousness to a mere thing, to a fact amongst facts. Only by such a genuine self-surrender could consciousness prove its own resignation. For only thus does there vanish the deceit that lies in the inner offering of thanks with the heart, with the sentiments, with the lips. Such offering does indeed strip from the individual all independent might, and ascribes all the glory to the heavenly giver. But the individual even when thus stripped, retains his outer self-will, for he abandons not his possessions; and he retains his inner self-will, for he is aware that it is he who undertakes this self-sacrifice, and who has in himself the virtue involved in such an undertaking,—a virtue which he has not exchanged for the mysterious grace that cometh from above.

But in the genuine resignation, when once it has come to pass, consciousness, in laying aside the burden of its own deeds, has also, in effect, laid aside the burden of its grief. Yet that this laying aside has already, in effect, taken place, is due to the deed of the other member of the tie, namely to the essential self. The sacrifice of the unreal self was made not by its own one-sided act, but involved the working of the other's grace. For the resignation of self-will is only in part negative, and on the other hand involves in its very notion, or in its beginning, the positive transformation of the will, and, in particular, its transformation from an individual into an universal will. Consciousness finds this positive meaning of the denial of self-will to consist in the will of the changeless, as this will is done, not by consciousness itself, but through the counsel of the mediator. Consciousness becomes aware, then, that its will is universal and essential, but it does not regard itself as identical with this essential nature. Self-resignation is not seen to be in its very notion identical with the positive work of the universal will. In the same way the abandonment of possession and of satisfaction has only the same negative significance, and the universal that thus comes in sight does not appear to consciousness as its own deed. The unity of truth and of self-possession implied in the notion of this activity, an unity which consciousness accordingly regards as its essence and its reality, is not recognized as implied in this very notion. Nor is the unity recognized by consciousness as its own self-created and immediately possessed object. Rather does consciousness only hear, spoken by the mediator's voice, the still fragile assurance that its own grief is, in the yet hidden truth of the matter, the very reverse, namely the bliss of an activity which rejoices in its tasks, that its own miserable deeds are, in the same hidden truth, the perfect work. And the real meaning of this assurance is that only what is done by an individual is or can be a deed. But for consciousness both activity and its own actual deeds remain miserable. Its satisfaction is its sorrow, and the freedom from this sorrow, in a positive joy, it looks for in another world. But this other world, where its activity and its being are to become, even while they remain its own, real activity and being,—what is this world but the image of REASON,—of the assurance of consciousness that in its individuality it is and possesses all reality?

THE PHILOSOPHY OF HISTORY

The only thought that philosophy brings with it to the contemplation of history, is the simple conception of reason; that reason is the sovereign of the world; that the history of the world, therefore, presents us with a rational process. This conviction and intuition is a

From G. W. F. Hegel, *Philosophy of History*, trans. J. Sibree (London: Citadel Press, 1900). With emendations by Daniel Kolak.

hypothesis in the domain of history as such. In that of philosophy it is no hypothesis. It is there proved by speculative cognition, that reason—and this term may here suffice us, without investigating the relation sustained by the universe to the divine being—is substance, as well as infinite power, its own infinite material underlying all the natural and spiritual life which it originates, as also the infinite form—that which sets this material in motion. On the one hand, reason is the substance of the universe, viz. that by which and in which all reality has its being and subsistence. On the other hand, it is the infinite energy of the universe; since reason is not so powerless as to be incapable of producing anything but a mere ideal, a mere intention—having its place outside reality, nobody knows where; something separate and abstract, in the heads of certain human beings. It is the infinite complex of things, their entire essence and truth. It is its own material which it commits to its own active energy to work up; not needing, as finite action does, the conditions of an external material of given means from which it may obtain its support and the objects of its activity. It supplies its own nourishment, and is the object of its own operations. While it is exclusively its own basis of existence, and absolute final aim, it is also the energizing power realizing this aim; developing it not only in the phenomena of the natural, but also of the mental, universe—the history of the world. That this "idea" or "reason" is the true, the eternal, the absolutely powerful essence, that it reveals itself in the world, and that in that world nothing else is revealed but this and its honor and glory—is the thesis which, as we have said, has been proved in philosophy, and is here regarded as demonstrated.

In those of my hearers who are not acquainted with philosophy, I may fairly presume, at least, the existence of a belief in reason, a desire, a thirst for acquaintance with it, in entering upon this course of lectures. It is, in fact, the wish for rational insight, not the ambition to amass a mere heap of acquirements, that should be presupposed in every case as possessing the mind of the learner in the study of science. If the clear idea of reason is not already developed in our minds, in beginning the study of universal history, we should at least have the firm, unconquerable faith that reason *does* exist there; and that the world of intelligence and conscious volition is not abandoned to chance, but must show itself in the light of the self-aware idea. Yet I am not obliged to make any such preliminary demand upon your faith. What I have said thus provisionally, and what I shall have further to say, is, even in reference to our branch of science, not to be regarded as hypothetical, but as a summary view of the whole; the result of the investigation we are about to pursue; a result which happens to be known to *me,* because I have traversed the entire field. It is only an inference from the history of the world that its development has been a rational process; that the history in question has constituted the rational necessary course of the world-mind—that mind whose nature is always one and the same, but which unfolds this one nature in the phenomena of the world's existence. This must, as before stated, present itself as the ultimate result of history. But we have to take the latter as it is. We must proceed historically—empirically. Among other precautions we must take care not to be misled by professed historians who . . . are chargeable with the very procedure of which they accuse the philosopher—introducing *a priori* inventions of their own into the records of the past. It is, for example, a widely current fiction that there was an original primeval people, taught immediately by God, endowed with perfect insight and wisdom, possessing a thorough knowledge of all natural laws and spiritual truth; that there have been such or such sacerdotal peoples; or, to mention a more specific assertion, that there was a Roman Epos, from which the Roman historians derived the early annals of their city, etc. *A priorities* of this kind we leave to those talented historians by profession, among whom . . . their use is not uncommon. We might then announce it as the first condition to be observed, that we should faithfully adopt all that is historical. But in such general expressions as "faithfully" and "adopt" lies the ambiguity. Even the ordinary, the "impartial" historian, who believes and professes that he maintains a simply receptive attitude, surrendering himself only to the data supplied him, is by no means passive as regards the exercise of his thinking powers. He brings his categories with him, and sees the phenomena presented to his mental vision exclusively through these media. And, especially in all that pretends to the name of science, it is indispensable that reason should not sleep, that reflection should be in full play. To him who looks upon the world rationally, the world in its turn, presents a rational aspect. The relation is mutual. But the various exercises of reflection—the different points of view— the modes of deciding the simple question of the relative importance of events (the first category that occupies the attention of the historian), do not belong to this place.

I will only mention two phases and points of view that concern the generally diffused conviction that reason has ruled, and is still ruling in the world, and consequently in the world's history, because they give us, at the same time, an opportunity for more closely investigating the question that presents the greatest difficulty, and for indicating a branch of the subject that will have to be enlarged on in the sequel.

(1) One of these points is the historical fact that the Greek Anaxagoras was the first to enunciate the doctrine that nous, understanding in general, or reason, governs the world. It is not intelligence as self-conscious reason, not a spirit as such, that is meant; and we must clearly distinguish these from each other. The movement of the solar system takes place according to unchangeable laws. These laws are reason, implicit in the phenomena in question. But neither the sun nor the planets that revolve around it according to these laws can be said to have any consciousness of them.

A thought of this kind—that nature is an embodiment of reason; that it is unchangeably subordinate to universal laws—appears nowise striking or strange to us. We are accustomed to such conceptions, and find nothing extraordinary in them. And I have mentioned this extraordinary occurrence partly to show how history teaches that ideas of this kind, which may seem trivial to us, have not always been in the world; that on the contrary, such a thought marks an epoch in the annals of human intelligence. Aristotle says of Anaxagoras, as the originator of the thought in question, that he appeared as a sober man among the drunken. Socrates adopted the doctrine from Anaxagoras, and it forthwith became the ruling idea in philosophy—except in the school of Epicurus, who ascribed all events to chance. "I was delighted with the sentiment," Plato makes Socrates say, "and hoped I had found a teacher who would show me nature in harmony with reason, who would demonstrate in each particular phenomenon its specific aim, and in the whole, the grand object of the universe. I would not have surrendered this hope for a great deal. But how very much was I disappointed, when, having zealously applied myself to the writings of Anaxagoras, I found that he adduces only external causes, such as air, ether, water, and the like." It is evident that the defect Socrates complains of respecting Anaxagoras' doctrine does not concern the principle itself but the shortcoming of the propounder in applying it to nature in the concrete. Nature is not deduced from that principle: the latter remains in fact a mere abstraction, inasmuch as the former is not comprehended and exhibited as a development of it—an organization produced by and from reason. I wish, at the very outset, to call your attention to the important difference between a conception, a principle, a truth limited to an *abstract* form and its determinate application and concrete development. This distinction affects the whole fabric of philosophy; and among other bearings of it there is one to which we shall have to revert at the close of our view of universal history, in investigating the aspect of political affairs in the most recent period.

(2) We have next to notice the rise of this idea—that reason directs the world—in connection with a further application of it, well known to us: in the form, viz. of the religious truth that the world is not abandoned to chance and external contingent causes, but that a providence controls it. I stated above that I would not make a demand on your faith with regard to the principle announced. Yet I might appeal to your belief in it, in this religious aspect, if, as a general rule, the nature of philosophical science allowed it to attach authority to presuppositions. To put it in another form, this appeal is forbidden, because the science of which we have to treat proposes itself to furnish the proof (not indeed of the abstract truth of the doctrine, but) of its correctness as compared with facts. The truth, then, that a providence (that of God) presides over the events of the world, consorts with the proposition in question; for divine providence is wisdom endowed with an infinite power, which realizes its aim, viz. the absolute rational design of the world. Reason is thought conditioning itself with perfect freedom. But a difference—rather a contradiction—will manifest itself, between this belief and our principle, just as was the case in reference to the demand made by Socrates in the case of Anaxagoras' dictum. For that belief is similarly indefinite; it is what is called a belief in a general providence, and is not followed out into definite application, or displayed in its bearing on the grand total—the entire course of human history. But to *explain* history is to depict the passions of mankind, the genius, the active powers, that play their part on the great stage; and the providentially determined process that these exhibit constitutes what is generally called the "plan" of providence. Yet it is this very plan which is supposed to be concealed from our view: which it is deemed presumption even to wish to recognize. The ignorance of Anaxagoras as to how intelligence reveals itself in actual existence was ingenuous. Neither in his consciousness nor in that of Greece at large had that thought been further expanded. He had not attained the power to apply his general principle to the concrete, so as to deduce the latter from the former. It was Socrates who took the first step in comprehending the union of the concrete with the universal. Anaxagoras, then, did not take up a hostile position towards such an application. The common belief in providence *does;* at least it opposes the use of the principle on the large scale, and denies the possibility of discerning the plan of providence. In isolated cases this plan is supposed to be manifest. Pious persons are encouraged to recognize in particular circumstances something more than mere chance, to acknowledge the guiding hand of God—*e.g.* when help has unexpectedly come to an individual in great perplexity and need. But these instances of providential design are of a limited kind, and concern the accomplishment of nothing more than the desires of the individual in question. But in the history of the world, the individuals we have to do with are peoples, totalities that are states. We cannot, therefore, be satisfied with what we may call this "peddling" view of providence, to which the belief alluded to limits itself. Equally unsatisfactory is the merely abstract, undefined belief in a providence, when that belief is not brought to bear upon the details of the process which it conducts. On the contrary our earnest endeavor must be directed to the recognition of the ways of providence, the means it uses, and the historical phenomena in which it manifests itself; and we must show their connection with the general principle above mentioned. . . .

The enquiry into the essential destiny of reason—as far as it is considered in reference to the world—is identical with the question, what is the ultimate design of the world? And the expression implies that that design is destined to be realized. Two points of consideration suggest themselves: first, the import of this design, its abstract definition, and second, its realization.

It must be observed at the outset that the phenomenon we investigate—universal history—belongs to the realm of mind. The term "world" includes both physical and psychical nature. Physical nature also plays its part in the world's history, and attention will have to be paid to the fundamental natural relations thus involved. But mind, and the course of its development, is our substantial object. Our task does not require us to contemplate nature as a rational system in itself—though in its own proper domain it proves itself such—but simply in its relation to mind. On the stage on which we are observing it—universal history—mind displays itself in its most concrete reality. Notwithstanding this (or rather for the very purpose of comprehending the general principles which this, its form of concrete reality, embodies) we must premise some abstract characteristics of the nature of spirit. Such an explanation, however, cannot be given here under any other form than that of bare assertion. The present is not the occasion for unfolding the idea of mind speculatively; for whatever has a place in an introduction must, as already observed, be taken as simply historical, something assumed as having been explained and proved elsewhere, or whose demonstration awaits the sequel of the science of history itself.

We have therefore to mention here:

1. The abstract characteristics of the nature of mind.
2. The means mind uses in order to realize its idea.
3. The form that the perfect embodiment of mind assumes: the state.

1. FREEDOM AS THE GOAL OF MIND

The nature of mind may be understood by a glance at its direct opposite—matter. As the essence of matter is gravity, so, on the other hand, we may affirm that the essence, the substance, of mind is freedom. All will readily assent to the doctrine that, among other properties, mind is also endowed with freedom; but philosophy teaches that all the qualities of mind exist only through freedom, that all are but means for attaining freedom, that all seek and produce this and this alone. It is a finding of speculative philosophy that freedom is the sole truth of mind. . . .

The destiny of the mental world, and—since this is the substantial world, while the physical remains subordinate to it, or, in the language of speculation, has no truth as against the mental—the final cause of the world at large, we allege to be the consciousness of its own freedom on the part of mind, and *ipso facto* the reality of that freedom. But that this term "freedom," without further qualification, is an indefinite and incalculably ambiguous term, and that, while what it represents is the *ne plus ultra* of attainment, it is liable to an infinity of misunderstandings, confusions and errors, and can become the occasion for all imaginable excesses—has never been more clearly known and felt than in modern times. Yet, for the present, we must content ourselves with the term itself without further definition. Attention was also directed to the importance of the infinite difference between a principle in the abstract and its realization in the concrete. In the process before us, the essential nature of freedom—which involves in it absolute necessity—is to be displayed as coming to a consciousness of itself (for it is in its very nature self-consciousness) and thereby realizing its existence. It is its own object of attainment, and the sole aim of mind. This is the result at which the process of the world's history has been continually aiming, and to which the sacrifices that have ever and anon been laid on the vast altar of the earth, through the long lapse of ages, have been offered. This is the only aim that sees itself realized and fulfilled, the only pole of repose amid the ceaseless change of events and conditions, and the sole efficient principle that pervades them. This final aim is God's purpose with the world; but God is the absolute perfect Being, and can, therefore, will nothing other than himself—his own will. The nature of His will—that is, His nature itself—is what we here call the idea of freedom, translating the language of religion into that of thought. The question, then, which we may next put, is: What means does this principle of freedom use for its realization? This is the second point we have to consider.

2. THE ROLE OF THE INDIVIDUAL

The question of the means by which freedom develops itself into a world conducts us to the phenomenon of history itself. Although freedom is, primarily, an inward idea, the means it uses are external and phenomenal, presenting themselves in history to our sensuous vision. The first glance at history convinces us that the actions of men proceed from their needs, their passions, their characters and talents, and impresses us with the belief that such needs, passions and interests are the sole springs of action—the efficient agents in this scene of activity. Among these may, perhaps, be found aims of a liberal or universal kind, benevolence it may be, or noble patriotism; but such virtues and general views are but insignificant as compared with the world and its doings. We may perhaps see the ideal of reason actualized in those who adopt such aims, and within the sphere of their influence; but they bear only a trifling proportion to the mass of the human race, and the extent of that influence is limited accordingly. Passions, private aims, and the satisfaction of selfish desires, are on the other hand most effective springs of action. Their power lies in the fact that they respect none of the limitations that justice and morality would impose on them, and that these natural impulses have a more direct influence over man than the artificial and tedious discipline that tends to order and self-restraint, law and morality. When we look at this display of passions and the consequences of their violence, the irrationality which is associated not only with them, but even (rather we might say especially) with good designs and righteous aims—when we see the evil, the vice, the ruin that has befallen the most flourishing kingdoms which the mind of man ever created, we can scarce avoid being filled with sorrow at this universal taint of corruption: and, since this decay is not the work of mere nature, but of the human will—a moral embitterment—a revolt of the good mind (if it have a place within us) may well be the result of our reflections. Without rhetorical exaggeration, a simply truthful account of the miseries that have overwhelmed the noblest of nations and polities, and the finest exemplars of private virtue, forms a picture of most fearful aspect, and excites emotions of the profoundest and most hopeless sadness, counter-balanced by no consolatory result. We endure in beholding it a mental torture, allowing no defense or escape but the consideration that what has happened could not be otherwise, that it is a fatality no intervention could alter. And at last we draw back from the intolerable disgust with which these sorrowful reflections threaten us, into the more agreeable environment of our individual life—the present formed by our private aims and interests. In short we retreat into the selfishness that stands on the quiet shore, and thence enjoy in safety the distant spectacle of "wrecks confusedly hurled." But even regarding history as the slaughter-bench at which the happiness of peoples, the wisdom of states, and the virtue of individuals have been made victims, the question involuntarily arises: to what principle, to what final aim these enormous sacrifices have been offered. . . .

The first remark we have to make, one which—though already presented more than once—cannot be too often repeated when the occasion seems to call for it, is that what we call principle, aim, destiny, or the nature and idea of mind, is something merely general and abstract. Principle, plan of existence, law, is a hidden, undeveloped essence, which as such—however true in itself—is not completely real. Aims, principles, etc., have a place in our thoughts, in our subjective design only, but not yet in the sphere of reality. What exists only for itself is a possibility, a potentiality, but has not yet emerged into existence. A second element must be introduced in order to produce actuality—viz. realization, activity whose motive power is the will, the activity of man in the widest sense. It is only by this activity that that idea, or abstract characteristics generally, can be realized, actualized; for of themselves they are powerless. The motive power that puts them in operation, and gives them determinate existence, is the need, instinct, inclination, and passion of man. . . .

We assert then that nothing has been accomplished without interest on the part of the actors; and—if interest be called passion, inasmuch as the whole individuality, to the neglect of all other actual or possible interests and claims, is devoted to an object with every fibre of volition, concentrating all its desires and powers upon it—we may affirm absolutely that nothing great in the world has been accomplished without passion. Two elements, therefore, enter into the object of our investigation: the first the idea, the second the complex of human passions; the one the warp, the other the woof, of the vast tapestry of universal history. The concrete mean and union of the two is liberty, under the conditions of morality in a state. . . .

From this comment on the second essential element in the historical embodiment of an aim, we infer—glancing at the institution of the state in passing—that a state is then well constituted and internally powerful when the private interest of its citizens is one with the common interest of the state, when the one finds its gratification and realization in the other—a proposition in itself very important. But in a state many institutions must be adopted, much political machinery invented, accompanied by appropriate political arrangements, necessitating long struggles of the understanding before what is really appropriate can be discovered—involving, moreover, contentions with private interest and passions, and a tedious discipline of these latter, in order to bring about the desired harmony. The epoch when a state attains this harmonious condition marks the period of its blossoming, its virtue, its vigor, and its prosperity. But the history of mankind does not begin with a conscious aim of any kind, as it is the case with the particular circles into which men form themselves of set purpose. The mere social instinct implies a conscious purpose of security for life and property, and when society has been constituted this purpose becomes more comprehensive. The history of the world begins with its general aim—the realization of the idea of mind—only in an *implicit* form that is, as nature, a hidden (most profoundly hidden) unconscious instinct; and the whole process of history (as already observed) is directed to rendering this unconscious impulse a conscious one. Thus appearing in the form of merely natural existence, natural will—which has been called the subjective side—physical craving, instinct, passion, private interest, as also opinion and subjective conception, spontaneously present themselves at the very start. This vast congeries of volitions, interests and activities, constitutes the instruments and means of the world-mind for attaining its object, bringing it to consciousness, and realizing it. And this aim is none other than finding it-self—coming to itself—and contemplating itself in concrete actuality. But that those manifestations of vitality on the part of individuals and peoples, in which they seek and fulfil their own purposes, are, at the same time, the means and instruments of a higher and broader purpose of which they know nothing, which they realize unconsciously, might be made a matter of question—indeed has been questioned, and in every variety of form denied, decried and condemned as mere dreaming and "philosophy." But on this point I announced my view at the very outset, and asserted our hypothesis—which, however, will appear finally in the form of a legitimate inference—and our belief that reason governs the world and has consequently governed its history. In relation to this independently universal and substantial existence, all else is subordinate, subservient to it, and the means for its development. . . .

He is happy who finds his condition suited to his special character, will, and fancy, and so enjoys himself in that condition. The history of the world is not the theatre of happiness. Periods of happiness are blank pages in it, for they are periods of harmony, periods when the antithesis is in abeyance. Reflection on self—the freedom above described—is abstractly defined as the formal element of the activity of the absolute idea. The realizing *activity* of which we have spoken is the middle term of the syllogism, one of whose extremes is the universal essence, the *idea,* which reposes in the hidden depths of mind, and the other, the complex of external things, objective matter. That activity is the medium by which the universal latent principle is translated into the domain of objectivity.

I will endeavor to make what has been said more vivid and clear by examples.

The building of a house is, in the first instance, a subjective aim and design. On the other hand we have, as means, the several substances required for the work—iron, wood, stones. The elements are made use of in working up this material: fire to melt the iron, wind to blow the fire, water to set wheels in motion, in order to cut the wood, etc. The result is that the wind, which has helped to build the house, is shut out by the house; so also are the violence of rains and floods, and the destructive powers of fire, so far as the house is made fire-proof. The stones and beams obey the law of gravity, press downwards, and so high walls are carried up. Thus the elements are made use of in accordance with their nature, and yet are made to cooperate for a product by which their operation is limited. Thus the passions of men are gratified; they develop themselves and their aims in accordance with their natural tendencies, and build up the edifice of human society, thus fortifying a position for right and order against themselves.

The connection of events above indicated, involves also the fact that in history an additional result is commonly produced by human actions beyond what they aim at and obtain, what they immediately recognize and desire. They gratify their own interest; but something further is thereby accomplished, latent in the actions in question, though not present to their consciousness and not included in their design. An analogous example is the case of a man who, from a feeling of revenge—perhaps not an unjust one, but produced by injury on the other's part—burns that other man's house. A connection is immediately established between the deed itself and a train of circumstances not directly included in it, considered in abstraction. In itself it consisted in merely presenting a small flame to a small portion of a beam. Events not involved in that simple act follow of themselves. The part of the beam that was set fire to is connected with its remote portions; the beam itself is united with the woodwork of the house generally, and this with other houses, so that a wide conflagration ensues, which destroys the goods and chattels of many others besides the man against whom the act of revenge was first directed—perhaps even costs not a few men their lives. This lay neither in the deed considered in itself, nor in the design of the man who committed it. But the action has a further general bearing. In the design of the doer it was only revenge executed against an individual in the destruction of his property, but it is moreover a crime, and that involves punishment also. This may not have been present to the mind of the perpetrator, still less in his intention; but his deed itself—the general principles it calls into play, its substantial content—entails it. By this example I wish only to impress on you the point that in a simple act something further may be implicated than lies in the intention and consciousness of the agent. The example before us involves, however, this additional consideration, that the substance of the act, consequently we may say the act itself, recoils upon the perpetrator—reacts upon him with destructive tendency. This union of the two extremes—the embodiment of a general idea in the form of direct reality, and the elevation of a particularity into connection with universal truth—is brought to pass, at first sight, under the conditions of an utter diversity of nature between the two, and an indifference of the one extreme towards the other. The aims that the agents set before themselves are limited and special; but it must be remarked that the agents themselves are intelligent thinking beings. The purport of their desires is interwoven with general, essential considerations of justice, good, duty, etc.; for mere desire—volition in its rough and savage forms—falls not within the scene and sphere of universal history. Those general considerations, which form at the same time a norm for directing aims and actions, have a determinate purport; for such an abstraction as "good for its own sake" has no place in living reality. If men are to act, they must not only intend the good, but must have decided for themselves whether this or that particular thing is a good. What special course of action, however, is good or not is determined, as regards the ordinary contingencies of private life, by the laws and customs of a state; and here no great difficulty is presented. Each individual has his position; he knows on the whole what a just, honorable course of conduct is. As to ordinary, private relations, the assertion that it is difficult to choose the right and good—regarding it as the mark of an exalted morality to find difficulties and raise scruples on that score—may be set down to an evil or perverse will that seeks to evade duties not in themselves of a perplexing nature, or, at any rate, to an idly reflective habit of mind, where a feeble will affords no sufficient exercise to the faculties, leaving them therefore to find occupation within themselves, and to expend themselves on moral self-adulation.

It is quite otherwise with the comprehensive relations that history has to do with. In this sphere are presented those momentous collisions between existing, acknowledged duties, laws, and rights, and those contingencies which are adverse to this fixed system, which assail and even destroy its foundations and existence, whose tenor may nevertheless seem good, on the whole advantageous—yes, even indispensable and necessary. These contingencies realize themselves in history: they involve a general principle of a different order from that on which depends the permanence of a people or a state. This principle is an essential phase in the development of the creating idea, of truth striving and urging towards itself. Historical men—world-historical individuals—are those in whose aims such a general principle lies.

Caesar—in danger of losing a position, not perhaps at that time of superiority, yet at least of equality with the others who were at the head of the state, and of succumbing to those who were just on the point of becoming his enemies—belongs essentially to this category. These enemies, who were at the same time pursuing *their* personal aims, had the form of the constitution, and the power conferred by an appearance of justice, on their side. Caesar was contending for the maintenance of his position, honor, and safety; and, since the power of his opponents included the sovereignty over the provinces of the Roman Empire, his victory secured for him the conquest of that entire Empire, and he thus became—though leaving the form of the constitution—the autocrat of the state. What secured for him the execution of a design, which in the first instance was of negative import—the autocracy of Rome—was, however, at the same time an independently necessary feature in the history of Rome and of the world. It was not, then, his private gain merely, but an unconscious impulse that occasioned the accomplishment of that for which the time was ripe. Such are all great historical men, whose own particular aims involve those large issues which are the will of the world-mind. They may be called heroes, inasmuch as they have derived their purposes and their vocation, not from the calm, regular course of things, sanctioned by the existing order, but from a concealed fount—one that has not attained to phenomenal, present existence—from that inner mind, still hidden beneath the surface, which, impinging on the outer world as on a shell, bursts it in pieces, because it is a different kernel from that which belongs to that shell. They are men, therefore, who appear to draw the impulse of their life from themselves, and whose deeds have produced a condition of things and a complex of historical relations that appear to be only their interest and their work.

Such individuals have no consciousness of the general idea they were unfolding, while prosecuting those aims of theirs; on the contrary, they were practical, political men. But at the same time they were thinking men, who had an insight into the requirements of the time—what was ripe for development. This was the very truth for their age, for their world, the genus next in order, so to speak, and which was already formed in the womb of time. It was theirs to know this nascent principle, the necessary, directly sequent step in progress that their world was to take, to make this their aim, and to expend their energy in promoting it. World-historical men—the heroes of an epoch—must, therefore, be recognized as its clear-sighted ones; their deeds, their words are the best of that time. Great men have formed purposes to satisfy themselves, not others. Whatever prudent designs and counsels they might have learned from others would be the more limited and inconsistent features in their career, for it was they who best understood affairs, from whom others learned, and whose policy was approved, or at least acquiesced in. For that mind which had taken this fresh step in history is the inmost soul of all individuals, but in a state of unconsciousness which the great men in question awoke. Their fellows therefore follow these soul-leaders, for they feel the irresistible power of their own inner mind thus embodied. If we go on to cast a look at the fate of these world-historical persons whose vocation it was to be the agents of the world-mind, we shall find it to have been no happy one. They attained no calm enjoyment; their whole life was labor and trouble; their whole nature was nothing but their master-passion. When their object is attained they fall off like empty hulls from the kernel. They die early, like Alexander; they are murdered, like Caesar; transported to St. Helena, like Napoleon. This fearful consolation—that historical men have not enjoyed what is called happiness, of which only private life (and this may be passed under very various external circumstances) is capable—this consolation those may draw from history who stand in need of it; and it is craved by envy, vexed at what is great and transcendent, striving, therefore, to belittle it and to find some flaw in it. Thus in modern times it has been demonstrated *ad nauseam* that princes are generally unhappy on their thrones; in consideration of which the possession of a throne is tolerated, and men acquiesce in the fact that not themselves but the personages in question are its occupants. The free man, we may observe, is not envious, but gladly recognizes what is great and exalted, and rejoices that it exists.

It is in the light of those common elements which constitute the interest and therefore the passions of individuals that these historical men are to be regarded. They are great men, because they willed and accomplished something great, not a mere fancy, a mere intention, but what met the case and fell in with the needs of the age. This mode of considering them also excludes the so-called "psychological" view, which—serving the purpose of envy most effectually—contrives to refer all actions to the heart, to bring them under a subjective aspect—so that they appear to have done everything under the impulse of some passion, mean, or grand—some morbid craving—and on account of these passions and cravings to have been not moral men. Alexander of Macedonia partly subdued Greece, and then Asia; therefore he was possessed by a morbid craving for conquest. He is alleged to have acted from greed of fame and conquest; and the proof that these were the impelling motives is that what he did resulted in fame. What pedagogue has not demonstrated of Alexander the Great, of Julius Caesar, that they were moved by such passions, and were consequently immoral men? By which it is implied that he, the pedagogue, is a better man than they, because he has not such passions; a proof of which lies in the fact that he does not conquer Asia, vanquish Darius and Porus, but while he enjoys life himself lets others enjoy it too. These psychologists are particularly fond of contemplating those peculiarities of great historical figures which appertain to them as private persons. Man must eat and drink; he sustains relations to friends and acquaintances; he has passing impulses and ebullitions of temper. "No man is a hero to his valet," is a well-known proverb; I have added—and Goethe repeated it two years later—"but not because the former is no hero, but because the latter is a valet." He takes off the hero's boots, assists him to bed, knows that he prefers champagne, etc. Historical personages waited upon in historical literature by such psychological valets do not make out well; they are brought down by their attendants to a level with—or rather a few degrees below the level of—the morality of such exquisite discerners of spirits. Homer's Thersites, who abuses the kings, is a standing figure for all times. Blows—that is beating with a solid cudgel—he does not get in every age, as in the Homeric one; but his envy, his egotism, is the thorn he has to carry in his flesh; and the undying worm that gnaws him is the tormenting consideration that his excellent views and vituperations remain absolutely without effect in the world. But our satisfaction at the fate of Thersitism also may have its sinister side.

A world-historical individual is not so unwise as to indulge a variety of wishes to divide his regards. He is devoted to the one aim, regardless of all else. It is even possible that such men may treat other great, even sacred, interests inconsiderately—conduct which is indeed obnoxious to moral reprehension. But so mighty a form must trample down many an innocent flower, crush to pieces many an object in its path.

The special interest of passion is thus inseparable from the active development of a general principle: for it is from the special and determinate, and from its negation, that the universal results. Particularity contends with its like, and some loss is involved in the issue. It is not the general idea that is implicated in opposition and combat and that is exposed to danger. It remains in the background, untouched and uninjured. This may be called the cunning of reason—that it sets the passions to work for itself, while what develops its existence through such impulsion pays the penalty, and suffers loss. For it is *phenomenal* being that is so treated, of which part is of no value, part is positive and real. The particular is for the most part of too trifling value as compared with the general: individuals are sacrificed and abandoned. The idea pays the penalty of determinate existence and of corruptibility, not from itself, but from the passions of individuals. . . .

3. THE ROLE OF THE STATE

The third point to be analyzed is, therefore: what object is to be realized by these means, *i.e.* what form it assumes in the realm of reality. We have spoken of means; but in the carrying out of a subjective, limited aim, we have also to take into consideration the material that either is already present or has to be procured. Thus the question would arise: What is the material in which the ideal of reason is wrought out? The primary answer would be: personality itself, human desires, subjectivity generally. In human knowledge and volition, as its material element, reason attains positive existence. We have considered subjective volition where it has an object that is the truth and essence of a reality, viz. where it constitutes a great world-historical passion. As a subjective will, occupied with limited passions, it is dependent, and can gratify its desires only within the limits of this dependence. But the subjective will has also a substantial life, a reality, in which it moves in the region of essential being and has the essential itself as the object of its existence. This essential being is the union of the subjective with the rational will: it is the moral whole, the state, which is that form of reality in which the individual has and enjoys his freedom, but on the condition of his recognizing, believing in, and willing what is common to the whole. And this must not be understood as if the subjective will of the social unit attained its gratification and enjoyment through that common will, as if this were a means provided for its benefit, as if the individual, in his relations to other individuals, thus limited his freedom, in order that this universal limitation—the mutual constraint of all—might secure a small space of liberty for each. Rather, we affirm that law, morality, government, and they alone, are the positive reality and completion of freedom. Freedom of a low and limited order is mere caprice, which finds its exercise in the sphere of particular and limited desires.

Subjective volition, passion, is what sets men in activity, and effects "practical" realization. The idea is the inner spring of action; the state is the actually existing, realized moral life. For it is the unity of the universal essential will with that of the individual; and this is "morality." The individual living in this unity has a moral life, possesses a value that consists in this substantiality alone. Sophocles in his *Antigone,* says, "The divine commands are not of yesterday, nor of today; no, they have an infinite existence, and no one could say whence they came." The laws of morality are not accidental, but are the essentially rational. It is the very purpose of the state that what is essential in the practical activity of men, and in their dispositions, should be duly recognized, that it should have a manifest existence, and maintain its position. It is the absolute interest of reason that this moral whole should exist; and herein lies the justification and merit of heroes who have founded states, however rude these may have been. In the history of the world, only those peoples that form a state can come under our notice. For it must be understood that this latter is the realization of freedom, *i.e.* of the absolute final aim, and that it exists for its own sake. It must further be understood that all the worth the human being possesses, all spiritual reality, he possesses only through the state. For his spiritual reality consists in this, that his own essence—reason—is objectively present to him, that it possesses objective immediate existence for him. Thus only is he fully conscious; thus only is he a partaker of morality, of a just and moral social and political life. For truth is the unity of the universal and subjective will; and the universal is to be found in the state, in its laws, its universal and rational arrangements. The state is the divine idea as it exists on earth. We have in it, therefore, the object of history in a more definite shape than before—that in which freedom obtains objectivity, and lives in the enjoyment of this objectivity. For law is the objectivity of mind, volition in its true form. Only that will which obeys law is free, for it obeys itself—it is independent and so free. When the state, our country, constitutes a community of existence, when the subjective will of man submits to laws, the contradiction between liberty and necessity vanishes. The rational has necessary existence, as being the reality and substance of things, and we are free in recognizing it as law, and following it as the substance of our own being. The objective and the subjective will are then reconciled, and present one identical homogeneous whole.

SCHELLING

1775–1854

Friedrich Wilhelm Von Schelling was born in Leonburg, a small town of Württemberg in Germany. His first education was at the cloister school where his father was chaplain and professor, which got him accepted to the theological seminary at Tübingen. Here he became deeply interested in the philosophy of Spinoza, Kant, and especially Fichte. His friendship with Hegel, a fellow student, led to their editing a philosophy journal. After graduating, he was appointed professor at the University of Jena.

Schelling developed an "objective" version of transcendental idealism, which owed much to the work of Kant, Fichte, and Hegel. Reacting against both continental rationalism and British empiricism, Schelling's philosophy centers on the self, the power of imagination, and the relation of philosophy and theology to art. Generally regarded as the leading romantic of the period, Schelling inspired the great English romantic poets, including Wordsworth and Shelley.

Our selection is from Schelling's main work, *System of Transcendental Idealism,* a treatise on nature, epistemology, and ethics. In it, Schelling tries to unify objective and subjective thought into an objective version of idealism, with his "philosophy of identity." According to Schelling, subject and object coincide in the Absolute, which can be attained through intellectual intuition as a conscious mystical state. In marked contrast to both Kant and Fichte, according to whom the purpose of philosophical thought is morality, for Schelling the ultimate culmination of human experience is in the creative act of artists expressing the special relation of identity between the subjective self and the objective world.

For Schelling, the only immediate object of knowledge is consciousness. Knowledge of the objective world can be attained, however, as a limiting condition of the dynamic evolutionary process from consciousness to self-consciousness. In becoming self-aware as a subject, the relation of subject to object within the Absolute itself becomes intellectually intuited in the subject as an objective state of affairs. And only through art can the mind become fully aware of its own existence. Thus, the ultimate pinnacle of philosophical reflection is the production of objects that are great and profound works of art.

Schelling distinguishes, as does Fichte, between Nature, by which he means the external, objective world, and Spirit, by which he means the mind (the internal, subjective world). The distinction is derived from the concept of a third, higher reality, the Absolute, which is neither conscious nor unconscious. The Absolute owes much to Kant's notion of Noumenal Self, especially that it transcends the categories of thought. For unknown reasons, the Absolute desires to become conscious. It achieves consciousness by positing the existence of a material, inanimate, nonconscious world, as people ordinarily conceive of reality. It then uses this concept of a mind-independent reality to distinguish the *subject* part of itself from the *object* part, thereby creating within the mind a conscious sub-mind. In this way the Absolute, in opposition to its own concept of itself, becomes the relative, phenomenal world.

Schelling claims that there are distinct kinds of knowledge, much in the way that Spinoza did. There is the *philosophical knowledge,* which is of one's own rational faculties, and there is the *confused knowledge* of the imagination. Each gives rise to a different form of existence: the infinite, undivided existence of the absolute, and the finite existence of individual things. The phenomenal world consists of self-developing objects that arise in thought and possess no true reality. These objects appear as separately existing, particular individuals, but this is due—as Leibniz too had supposed—to our inadequate representations of them. Only the enlightened philosopher can view them *sub specie aeternitatis,* in their totality, so that the objects themselves are revealed to be ideas. Having such a philosophical vision allows us, as philosophers, to interpret objects as they truly exist in the totality of the World Soul, wherein all things are a Parmenidean One. From the perspectiveless point of view of the Absolute, which is the sum of the whole of existence, all is absolute, eternal, infinite.

Schelling begins his elaborate *System of Transcendental Idealism* with a Cartesian-like certainty in the proposition "I Am." Like Descartes, he then shows how the transcendental proposition "There are things outside of me" can also be known with the same absolute certainty. For Kant, such a transcendental process reaches beyond the phenomenal world of appearance, *not* to the noumenal world of the thing in itself but only to the cognitive faculties of the mind. According to Schelling, the object reached is the objective, absolute world itself. Thus, in marked contrast with Fichte's subjective idealism, Schelling paves the way for his absolute idealism, which is still idealism but radically different from its previous incarnations, including, and especially, Fichte's:

> Fichte could side with idealism from the point of view of reflection. I, on the other hand, took the viewpoint of production with the principle of idealism. To express this contrast most distinctly, idealism in the subjective sense had to assert, the ego is everything, while conversely idealism in the objective sense had to assert: Everything = ego and nothing exists but what = ego. These are certainly different views, although it will not be denied that both are idealism.

Schelling reverses the traditional religious concept of "the fall." In an absolute act of freedom, the origin of the phenomenal, relative world comes about so that we, as creative agents, can actualize the world through our consciousness. In other words, it is our own individual minds, driven by an unconscious impulse toward self-representation, that add the crucial ingredient which solidifies the worlds from the realm of possibility into actuality.

God in Schelling's view is nothing like Spinoza's deterministic God, but in fact makes choice and freedom possible within the real world through the creation of individual human beings, each of whom is empowered by the self-actualizing, creative force of the Absolute. Unlike the Judeo-Christian God, who creates the world to be inhabited by individual souls, it is we ourselves who are the true artists of reality. Such a view leads Schelling to a conclusion exactly opposite to Plato's view of art, elevating it as the highest branch of philosophy.

SYSTEM OF TRANSCENDENTAL IDEALISM

INTRODUCTION TO IDEALISM

SECTION I: IDEA OF TRANSCENDENTAL PHILOSOPHY

1. All knowledge is based upon the agreement of an objective with a subjective. For we *know* only the true, and the truth is universally held to be the agreement of representations with their objects.

2. The sum of all that is purely objective in our knowledge we may call Nature; whereas the sum of everything subjective may be termed the *Ego,* or Intelligence. These two concepts are mutually opposed. Intelligence is originally conceived as that which solely represents, and nature as that which is merely capable of representation; the former as the conscious—the latter as the unconscious. But in all knowledge there is necessary a mutual agreement of the two—the conscious and the unconscious *per se.* The problem is to explain this agreement.

3. In knowledge itself, in that I know, the objective and subjective are so united that one cannot say which of the two has priority. There is here no first and no second—the two are contemporaneous and one. In any attempt to explain this identity, I must already have resolved it. In order to explain it, inasmuch as there is nothing else given me as a principle of explanation except these two factors of knowledge, I must of necessity place the one before the other, that is to say, must set out from the one in order to arrive at the other. From which of the two I shall set out is not determined by the problem.

4. There are, consequently, only two cases possible:

A. *Either the objective is made first, and the question arises how a subjective agreeing with it is superinduced.*

The idea of the subjective is not contained in the idea of the objective; on the contrary they mutually exclude each other. The subjective must therefore be *superinduced* upon the objective. It forms no part of the conception of Nature that there must be likewise an intelligence to represent it. Nature, to all appearance, would exist even if there were nothing to represent it. The problem may therefore likewise be expressed thus: How is the Intelligent superinduced upon Nature? or, How does Nature come to be represented?

The problem assumes Nature, or the objective, as the first. It is, therefore, undoubtedly the task of natural science, which does the same. That natural science actually, and without knowing it, approximates, at least, to the solution of this problem can here be only briefly shown.

If all knowledge has, as it were, two poles, which mutually presuppose and demand each other, then they must seek each other in all sciences. There must, therefore, of necessity, exist two fundamental sciences; and it must be impossible to set out from one pole without being driven to the other. The necessary tendency of all natural science, therefore, is to proceed from Nature to the intelligent. This, and this alone, lies at the foundation of the effort to bring theory into natural phenomena. The final perfection of natural science would

Translated from the German by Benjamin Rand, 1908. With emendations by Daniel Kolak.

be the complete intellectualization of all the laws of Nature into laws of intuition and of thought. The phenomena, that is, the material, must completely vanish, and leave only the laws,—that is, the formal. Hence it happens that the more the conformity to law is manifested in Nature, so much the more the wrapping disappears—the phenomena themselves become more intellectualized, and at length entirely cease. Optical phenomena are nothing more than a geometry whose lines are drawn by aid of the light; and even this light itself is already of doubtful materiality. In the phenomena of magnetism every trace of matter has already vanished: and of the phenomena of gravitation, which even the natural philosopher believed could be attributed only to direct spiritual influence, there remains nothing but their law, whose performance on a large scale is the mechanism of the heavenly motions. The complete theory of Nature would be that by virtue of which the whole of Nature should be resolved into an intelligence. The dead and unconscious products of Nature are only unsuccessful attempts of Nature to reflect itself, but the so-called dead Nature is merely an unripe Intelligence, hence in its phenomena the intelligent character appears, though still unconscious. Its highest aim, that is of becoming wholly self-objective, Nature does not attain, except in its highest and last reflection, which is none other than man, or more generally what we call reason. By its means Nature first turns completely back upon itself, and thereby it is manifest that Nature is originally identical with what in us is known as intelligent and conscious.

This may suffice to prove that natural science has a necessary tendency to render Nature intelligent. By this very tendency it becomes natural philosophy, which is one of the two necessary fundamental sciences of philosophy.

B. *Or the subjective is made first, and the problem is, how an objective is superinduced agreeing with it.*

If all knowledge is based upon the agreement of these two, then the problem to explain this agreement is undoubtedly the highest for all knowledge; and if, as is generally admitted, philosophy is the highest and loftiest of all sciences, it becomes certainly the chief task of philosophy.

But the problem demands only the explanation of that agreement generally, and leaves it entirely undetermined where the explanation shall begin, what it shall make its first, and what its second. Since also the two opposites are mutually necessary, the result of the operation is the same, from whichever point one sets out. To make the objective the first, and to derive the subjective from it, is, as has just been shown, the task of natural philosophy.

If, therefore, there is a transcendental philosophy, the only direction remaining for it is the opposite, that is: to proceed from the subjective as the first and the absolute, and to deduce the origin of the objective from it. Natural and transcendental philosophy have divided between themselves these two possible directions of philosophy. And if all philosophy must have for an aim to make either an Intelligence out of Nature or a Nature out of Intelligence, then transcendental philosophy, to which this latter problem belongs, is the other necessary fundamental science of philosophy.

SECTION II: COROLLARIES

In the foregoing we have not only deduced the concept of transcendental philosophy, but have at the same time afforded the reader a glance into the whole system of philosophy. It is composed, as has been shown, of two fundamental sciences, which though opposed to one another in principle and direction, reciprocally demand and supplement each other. Not the entire system of philosophy, but only the one fundamental science of it, is here to be set up, and, in the first place, to be more strictly characterized in accordance with the idea of it already deduced.

1. If, for transcendental philosophy, the subjective is the first and only ground of all reality, and the sole principle of explanation of everything else (§ 1), then it necessarily begins with universal doubt regarding the reality of the objective.

As the natural philosopher, wholly intent upon the objective, seeks nothing so much as to exclude every admixture of the subjective in his knowledge, so, on the other hand, the transcendental philosopher seeks nothing so much as the entire exclusion of the objective from the purely subjective principle of knowledge. The means of separation is absolute skepticism—not that partial scepticism which is directed merely against the common prejudices of men and never sees the foundation—but the radical scepticism which aims not at the individual prejudices, but against the fundamental prejudice, with which all others must stand or fall. For beyond the artificial and inculcated prejudices of man, there exist others of deeper origin which have been placed in him not by art or education, but by nature itself. These are regarded by all except the philosopher, as the principles of knowledge, and by the mere thinker of self, as the test of all truth.

The one fundamental prejudice, to which all others may be reduced, is this: that there exist things outside of us. This is an opinion, which, although it rests neither on proofs nor on conclusions (for there is not a single valid proof of it), yet as it cannot be uprooted by any opposite proof (*naturam furcâ expellas, tamen usque redibit*), lays claim to immediate certainty. But since it refers to something wholly distinct from us and, in fact, opposed to us, of which there is no evidence how it came into immediate consciousness, it must be regarded as nothing more than a prejudice—a natural and original one, to be sure, but nevertheless a prejudice.

The contradiction that a conclusion which in its nature cannot be immediately certain, is, nevertheless, blindly and without grounds, accepted as such, cannot be solved by transcendental philosophy, except on the assumption that this conclusion is implicitly, and without our being aware of it, not founded upon, but identical, and one and the same with an affirmation which is immediately certain. To demonstrate this identity will in reality be the task of transcendental philosophy.

2. Now, even for the ordinary use of reason, there exists nothing immediately certain except the affirmation *I am,* which, since it loses all significance outside of immediate consciousness, is the most individual of all truths, and the absolute prejudice, which must be assumed, if anything else is to be made certain. The affirmation *There are things outside of us,* will therefore be certain for the transcendental philosopher, solely because of its identity with the affirmation *I am;* and its certainty will also only be equal to the certainty of the affirmation from which it derives its own.

According to this view transcendental knowledge would be distinguished from common knowledge in two particulars.

First.—That for it the certainty of the existence of external things is a mere prejudice, which it transcends, in order to investigate the grounds of it. (It can never be the task for transcendental philosophy to prove the existence of things in themselves, but only to show that it is a natural and necessary prejudice to assume external objects as real.)

Second.—That it separates the two affirmations, *I am* and *There are things outside of me,* which run together in the ordinary consciousness, and places the one before the other, in order to prove their identity and that immediate connection which in the other is only felt. By this act of separation, when it is completed, one transports one's self in the transcendental act of contemplation, which is by no means a natural, but an artificial one.

3. If the subjective alone has reality for the transcendental philosopher he will also make only the subjective directly his object. The objective will be for him only indirectly an object, and, whereas, in ordinary knowledge, knowledge itself—the act of knowing—disappears in the object, in transcendental knowledge, on the contrary, the object as such disappears in the act of knowing. Transcendental knowledge is therefore a knowledge of knowing, in so far as it is purely subjective.

Thus, for example, in intuition it is the objective only that reaches the ordinary consciousness; the act of intuition is itself lost in the object; whereas on the contrary the transcendental mode of observation gets only a glimpse of the object of intuition by the act of intuition. Thus the ordinary thinking is a mechanism, in which ideas prevail, without, however, being distinguished as ideas; whereas the transcendental act of thought interrupts this mechanism, and in becoming conscious of the idea as an act, rises to the idea of the idea. In ordinary action, the acting is itself forgotten in the object of the action; philosophizing is also an action, but not an action only. It is likewise a continued self-intuition in this action.

The nature of the transcendental mode of thought must consist, therefore, in general in this: that, in it, that which in all other thinking, knowing, or acting escapes the consciousness, and is absolutely non-objective, is brought into consciousness, and becomes objective. In brief, it consists in a continuous act of becoming an object to itself on the part of the subjective.

The transcendental art will therefore consist in the ability to maintain one's self constantly in this duplicity of acting and thinking.

SECTION III: PRELIMINARY DIVISION OF TRANSCENDENTAL PHILOSOPHY

This division is preliminary, because the principles of the division can be derived only from the science itself.

We return to the idea of science.

Transcendental philosophy has to explain how knowledge is possible at all, assuming that the subjective in it is accepted as the ruling or first element.

It is therefore, not a single part, nor a special object of knowledge, but knowledge itself, and knowledge in general, that it takes for its object.

Now all knowledge can be reduced to certain original convictions or original prejudices. These different convictions transcendental philosophy must trace to one original conviction. This ultimate conviction from which all others are derived, is expressed in the first principle of this philosophy, and the task of finding such is none other than to find the absolutely certain by which all other certainty is attained.

The division of transcendental philosophy is determined through those original convictions, whose validity it affirms. These convictions must, in the first place, be sought in the common understanding. If, therefore, we go back to the standpoint of the ordinary view, we find the following convictions deeply engraven in the human understanding:—

A. That not only does there exist a world of things independent of us, but also that our representations agree with them in such a manner that there is nothing else in the things beyond what we represent by them. The necessity in our objective representations is explained by the belief that the things are unalterably determined, and that by this determination of things our representations appear to be mediately determined. By this first and most original conviction, the first problem of philosophy is determined, *viz.:* to explain how representations can absolutely agree with objects which exist entirely independent of them. Since it is upon the assumption that things are exactly as we represent them, and that we therefore certainly know things as they are in themselves, that the possibility of all experience rests (for what would experience be, and where would physics, for example, stray to, without that presupposition of the absolute identity of being and seeming?), the solution of this problem is identical with theoretical philosophy, which has to investigate the possibility of experience.

B. The second equally original conviction is, that representations which originate in us freely and without necessity can pass over from the world of thought into the real world, and attain objective reality.

This conviction is opposed to the first. According to the first, it is assumed that objects are unalterably determined, and our representations by them; according to the other, that objects are changeable, and that, too, by the causality of representations in us. According to the first conviction, a transition takes place within us from the real world into the world of representations, or a determining of the representations by the objective, according to the second, a transition takes place from the world of representations into the world of reality, or a determining of the objective by a (freely conceived) representation in us.

By this second conviction, a second problem is determined, *viz.* how, by something merely thought, an objective is changeable, so as entirely to correspond with that something thought.

Since the possibility of all free action rests upon that assumption, the solution of this problem is practical philosophy.

C. But with these two problems we find ourselves involved in a contradiction. According to B, the supremacy of thought (the ideal) over the world of sense is demanded. But how is such supremacy conceivable, if (according to A) the idea in its origin is already only the slave of the objective? On the other hand, if the real world is something wholly independent of us, and is something with which our ideas must conform as their pattern (by A), then it becomes inconceivable how, on the other hand, the real world can conform to the ideas in us (by B). In brief, in the theoretical certainty we lose the practical; in the practical we lose the theoretical. It is impossible that at the same time there should be truth in our knowledge and reality in our volition.

This contradiction must be solved, if there is to be a philosophy at all. The solution of this problem, or the answering of the question: How can ideas be conceived as conforming to objects, and at the same time objects as conforming to ideas?—is not the first, but is the chief task of transcendental philosophy.

It is easy to see that this problem cannot be solved either in theoretical or practical philosophy, but in a higher one, which is the connecting link of both, and is neither theoretical nor practical, but both at the same time.

How at the same time the objective world conforms to representations in us, and representations in us conform to the objective world, cannot be conceived, unless there exists a preestablished harmony between the two worlds of the ideal and the real. But this preestablished harmony is itself not conceivable unless the activity by which the objective world is produced, is originally identical with that which displays itself in volition, and *vice versa*.

Now it is certainly a *productive* activity which manifests itself in volition. All free action is productive, but productive only with consciousness. If, then, since the two activities are only one in principle, we suppose that the same activity which is productive *with* consciousness in free action, is productive *without* consciousness in the production of the world, this preestablished harmony is a reality, and the contradiction is solved. If we suppose that all this is actually the case, then that original identity of the activity which is engaged in the production of the world, with that which exhibits itself in volition, must manifest itself in the productions of the former, and these must necessarily appear as the productions of an activity at once conscious and unconscious.

Nature, as a whole, no less than in its different productions, will of necessity appear as a work produced with consciousness and yet at the same time as the production of the blindest mechanism. It is the result of purpose without being explainable as such. The philosophy of the aims of Nature, or teleology, is therefore the required point of union of theoretical and practical philosophy.

D. Heretofore, we have posited only in general terms the identity of the unconscious activity which has produced Nature and the conscious activity which manifests itself in volition, without having decided where the principle of this activity lies, whether in Nature or in us.

But now the system of knowledge can be regarded as complete only when it reverts to its principle. Transcendental philosophy would therefore be completed only when it also could demonstrate that identity—the highest solution of its entire problem—in its principle (the *Ego*).

It is therefore postulated, that activity, at once conscious and unconscious, can be shown in the subjective, that is in consciousness itself.

Such an activity can be no other than the *aesthetic,* and every work of art can only be conceived as the product of such. The ideal work of art and the real world of objects are therefore products of one and the same activity. The meeting of the two (of the conscious and the unconscious) gives *without* consciousness the real, *with* consciousness the aesthetic world.

The objective world is only the original still unconscious poetry of the soul. The universal organum of philosophy—the keystone of its entire arch—is the philosophy of art.

SECTION IV: ORGAN OF TRANSCENDENTAL PHILOSOPHY

1. The only immediate object of transcendental consideration is the subjective (§ 2). The sole organ of this method of philosophizing is therefore the *inner sense,* and its object is of such a nature that, unlike that of mathematics, it can never become the object of external intuition. The object of mathematics, to be sure, exists as little outside of knowledge, as that of philosophy. The entire existence of mathematics depends upon the intuition. It exists, therefore, only in the intuition; but this intuition itself is an external one. In addition to this the mathematician has never to do immediately with the intuition—the construction itself—but only with the thing constructed, which can certainly be presented outwardly. The philosopher, however, regards only the act of construction itself, which is purely an internal one.

2. Moreover, the objects of the transcendental philosopher have no existence, except in so far as they are freely produced. One cannot be compelled to this production any more than one can be compelled by the external drawing of a mathematical figure to regard it internally. Just as the existence of a mathematical figure depends upon external sense, so the entire reality of a philosophical concept depends upon the inner sense. The whole object of this philosophy is no other than the action of the intelligence according to fixed laws. This action can be conceived only through a peculiar, direct, inner intuition, and this again is possible only by production. But this is not enough. In philosophizing, one is not only the object, but is always at the same time the subject of the reflection. Two conditions are consequently demanded for the understanding of philosophy. First, the philosopher must be engaged in a continued inner activity, in a continuous production of those original actions

of intelligence; second, he must be engaged in continuous reflection upon this productive action; in a word, he must at the same time always be the contemplated (producing) and the contemplating.

3. By this continuous duplicity of production and of intuition, that must become an object which is otherwise reflected by nothing. It cannot be proved here, but will be proved later, that this becoming-reflected on the part of the absolutely unconscious and non-objective, is possible only by an aesthetic act of the imagination. Nevertheless, it is certain from what has already been proved that all philosophy is productive. Philosophy, therefore, as well as art, rests upon the productive faculty, and the difference between the two consists merely in the different direction of the productive power. For whereas production in art is directed outward, in order to reflect the unconscious by products; philosophical production is directed immediately inward, in order to reflect it in intellectual intuition. The special sense by which this kind of philosophy must be grasped is therefore the aesthetic sense, and hence it is that the philosophy of art is the true organum of philosophy (§ 3).

From the vulgar reality there exist only two outlets: poetry, which transports us into the ideal world, and philosophy, which causes the real world wholly to vanish before us. It is not clear why the sense for philosophy should be more widely diffused than that for poetry, especially among the classes of men who have not wholly lost the aesthetic organ either by memory work (nothing destroys more directly the productive power) or by dead speculation, which is ruinous to all imaginative power.

4. It is unnecessary to occupy more time with the commonplaces about the sense of truth, or about entire disregard for results, although it might be asked, what other conviction can be sacred to one who questions the most certain of all—that there are things outside of us. We may rather take a glance at the so-called claims of the common understanding.

The common understanding in matters of philosophy has no claims whatsoever, except those which all objects of investigations have, *viz.,* to be perfectly explained.

It is not, therefore, our business to prove that what is held for true, is true, but only to disclose the unavoidableness of its illusions. This implies that the objective world belongs only to the necessary limitations which render self-consciousness (the *I am*) possible; it is enough for the common understanding, if from this view the necessity of its own view is derived.

For this purpose it is necessary, not only that the inner machinery of our mental activity be disclosed, and the mechanism of necessary ideas revealed, but also that it should be shown by what peculiarity of our nature it is necessary that what has reality only in our intuition, is reflected to us as something existing outside of us.

As natural science produces idealism out of realism, when it intellectualizes the laws of nature into laws of intelligence, or superinduces the formal upon the material (§ 1), so transcendental philosophy produces realism out of idealism when it materializes the laws of intelligence into laws of nature, or introduces the material into the formal.

FIRST DIVISION: THE PRINCIPLE
OF TRANSCENDENTAL IDEALISM
Explanations

a. If now we revert to the fundamental principle of identity $A = A$, we discover that we can derive our principle directly from it. In every identical proposition it was affirmed that the thought is compared with itself; this undoubtedly takes place by means of an act of thought. The proposition A = A therefore presupposes a thought that becomes immediately an object to itself; but an act of thought which becomes its own object exists only in self-consciousness. It is certainly incomprehensible how one can seriously derive from a mere proposition of logic something real; but it is truly comprehensible how one can find in it by reflection upon the act of thought something real, *e.g.* the categories from the logical function of judgment, and similarly the act of self-consciousness from every identical proposition.

b. That the subject and object of thought are one in self-consciousness can become clear to every one solely by the act of self-consciousness itself. It is necessary for this purpose that one at the same time perform this act, and in so doing reflect again upon one's self. Self-consciousness is the act whereby the thinking itself immediately becomes the object, and conversely. This act and none other is self-consciousness. Such act is an absolutely free action, to which one can indeed be guided but cannot be compelled. The readiness to perceive one's self in this act, to discriminate one's self both as thought and as thinking, and again to recognize one's self as identical in such discrimination, is constantly presupposed in what follows.

c. Self-consciousness is an act, but by every act something is accomplished for us. Every thought is an act, and every definite thought is a definite act. By means of every such act there also arises in us a definite conception. The conception is nothing but the act of thinking itself, and abstracted from this act it is nothing. By the act of self-consciousness there must likewise originate a conception for us; and this is no other than the conception of the Ego. While I regard myself as the object by means of self-consciousness there originates in me the conception of the Ego; and conversely the conception of the Ego is only the conception of self becoming its own object.

d. The conception of the Ego is accomplished by the act of self-consciousness. Without the act, therefore, the Ego is nothing; its entire reality depends solely upon this act. The Ego can thus be conceived only as act, and it is otherwise nothing.

Whether the external object is nothing different from its conception, whether also here conception and object are one, is a question which is still to be decided. But that the conception of the Ego, that is, the act whereby thought becomes its own object, and the Ego itself (the object) are absolutely one, needs no proof, since the Ego is clearly nothing apart from the act, and in general exists only in this act.

Here, therefore, is that original identity of thought and of object, of appearance and of being, which we sought, and which is nowhere else met with. The Ego does not exist at all before that act whereby the thought becomes its own object. It is therefore nothing other than the thought becoming itself the object, and consequently absolutely nothing apart from the thought. The reason why so many fail to see, in case of the Ego, that its being conceived is identical with its being originated has its explanation solely in the fact, that they neither can perform the act of self-consciousness with freedom, nor are able to reflect upon what originates in this very act. As regards the first, it is to be remarked, that we make a clear distinction between self-consciousness as act, and mere empirical consciousness. What we commonly term consciousness is merely something which goes along with the representations of objects, something which maintains identity amid the change of representations. It is thus purely of an empirical character, for indeed I am thereby conscious of myself, but only as of one having representations. The act here spoken of is one, however, by which I am conscious of myself, not as having this or that determination, but originally, and this consciousness, in contrast with the other, is called pure consciousness, or self-consciousness.

The genesis of these two kinds of consciousness may be made clearer in the following way. Let one abandon himself wholly to the involuntary succession of representations, then, no matter how manifold or different these may be, they will nevertheless appear as belonging to one identical subject. But if I reflect upon this identity of the subject in the representations, there originates for me the proposition *I think.* It is this *I think* that accompanies all representations and maintains in them the continuity of consciousness. If however one frees one's self from every act of representation in order to become conscious of one's original self, there arises not the proposition *I think,* but the proposition *I am,* which is undoubtedly a higher one. In the proposition *I think* there exists already the expression of a determination or affection of the Ego; the proposition *I am,* on the contrary, is an infinite proposition, because it is one which has no real predicate, but which, for that very reason, may have an infinity of possible predicates.

e. The Ego is nothing distinct from the thought of it; the thought of the Ego and the Ego itself are absolutely one. The Ego, therefore, is absolutely nothing apart from the thought; it is therefore also no thing, no affair, but endlessly the non-objective. This is to be understood in the following way. The Ego is indeed object, but only for itself, and is thus not originally in the world of objects. It becomes an object only by the very fact that it makes itself its own object. It becomes the object not of something external, but always only of itself.

Everything that is not Ego is originally object, and for this very reason is an object not to itself, but to something perceiving outside of it. The original objective is always something known, never a knower. The Ego is known only through its own self-knowledge. Matter is called self-less for the very reason that it has nothing innermost, and exists only as something perceived in a foreign perception.

f. If the Ego is no thing, no affair, then one cannot ask concerning any predicate of the Ego. It has none except this, that it is no thing. The character of the Ego consists in having no other predicate except that of self-consciousness.

The same result can also be reached in other ways.

That which is the highest principle of knowledge cannot have its ground of knowledge in something higher. Its *principium essendi* and *cognoscendi,* must therefore be one, and coincide in one.

For this very reason the unconditioned can never be sought in any one thing; for what is object, is originally also object of knowledge; whereas what is a principle of all knowledge cannot become at all an object of knowledge, either originally or in itself, except only through a special act of freedom.

The unconditioned can therefore never be sought in the world of objects. (Therefore the purely objective, or matter, is for natural science nothing original, but is for it even as much appearance as it is for transcendental philosophy.)

Unconditioned is termed that which can by no means become a thing, or an affair. The first task of philosophy can therefore be thus expressed: to find something which absolutely cannot be thought as thing. But of this character is only the Ego, and conversely, the Ego is that which is in itself non-objective.

g. If now the Ego is absolutely no object, no thing, it appears difficult to explain how in general a knowledge of it is possible, or what kind of knowledge we have of it.

The Ego is pure act, pure doing, and, because it is the principle of all knowledge, must be absolutely non-objective in knowledge. If it is, therefore, to become an act of knowledge, it can become known only in a way entirely different from common knowledge.

This knowledge must be:

(*a*) Absolutely free, because all other knowledge is not free. It must, therefore, be a knowledge to which the way is not by proofs, conclusions, and the mediation of concepts. It is therefore in general an intuition.

(*b*) It must also be a knowledge whose object is not independent of it, and is therefore a knowledge which is at the same time productive of its object. It is an intuition which is altogether freely productive, and in which the producing is one and the same with the produced.

Such an intuition is termed *intellectual intuition,* in contrast with the sensible intuition, which never appears as productive of its object, and in which therefore the perceiving-itself is distinct from the perceived.

Such an intuition is the Ego, because through the knowledge the Ego has of itself, the Ego itself (the object) first originates. Since the Ego (as object) is none other than this very knowledge of itself, the Ego originates solely by the fact that it knows itself. The Ego itself is, therefore, a knowledge which at the same time creates itself (as object).

The intellectual intuition is the organ of all transcendental thinking. For the whole aim of transcendental thought is freely to transform into its own object something which is otherwise no object. It presupposes a faculty to produce and at the same time to perceive certain functions of the soul, so that the producing of the object and the perceiving are absolutely one. This faculty, however, is precisely the faculty of intellectual intuition.

Transcendental philosophizing must therefore be constantly accompanied by intellectual intuition. All pretence that this philosophizing cannot be understood has its cause not in the unintelligibility of it, but in the defect of the organ whereby it must be comprehended. Apart from this intuition, philosophizing has itself no substratum that might cause and support thought. This very intuition supplies the place of the objective world in the transcendental thought, and, as it were, carries the flight of speculation. The Ego itself is an object that exists by virtue of the fact that it has knowledge of itself, that is, it is a constant intellectual intuition. Since the sole object of transcendental philosophy is this self-producing activity, the intellectual intuition is for it precisely what space is for geometry. Just as without intuition of space, geometry would be absolutely incomprehensible, because all its constructions are only different methods and ways of qualifying that intuition, so without the intellectual intuition, all philosophy would be incomprehensible, because all its conceptions are only different qualifications of that production which has itself for an object, that is, of the intellectual intuition (cf. Fichte's "Einleitung in die Wissenschaftslehre" in the "Philosophisches Journal").

No reason need be given why people have perceived something mysterious in this intuition, some special sense feigned by a few, except that some persons are really without it. This, however, is no more strange than that they still entirely lack many another sense whose reality is as little involved in doubt.

h. The Ego is nothing other than a producing which becomes its own object, *i.e.* it is an intellectual intuition. But this intellectual intuition is itself an absolutely free act. It can therefore not be demonstrated, but only demanded. The Ego itself is solely this intuition; the Ego therefore as principle of philosophy is itself only something that is postulated.

Since the time that Reinhold made the scientific founding of philosophy his aim, there has been much talk of a first fundamental proposition from which philosophy would have to proceed. By this one generally understood a theorem in which the entire philosophy should be involved. But it is easily perceived that transcendental philosophy can proceed from no theorem, because it proceeds from the subjective, that is, from that which can become objective only by a distinct act of freedom. A theorem is a proposition which depends upon being. Transcendental philosophy, however, proceeds from no being, but from a free act; and this can only be postulated. Every science that is not empirical must by its first principle already exclude all empiricism, that is, must presuppose its object as not already existing but must create it. In this way, for example, geometry proceeds, since it starts not from theorems but from postulates. It is because the most primal construction in it is postulated, and is left to the pupil to create, that he is at the very outset sent back to self-construction. It is just the same with transcendental philosophy. Unless one bring to it the transcendental method of thought, one must find it incomprehensible. It is, therefore, necessary that one place one's self at the outset through freedom in that method of thought; and this takes place by means of the free act whereby the principle originates. If it be a fact that transcendental philosophy does not presuppose its objects, it certainly cannot presuppose its first object, the principle; it can postulate it only as one freely to be constructed. As the principle is of its own construction, so are also all its remaining concepts; and the entire science has to do with its own free constructions.

If the principle of philosophy is a postulate, then the object of this postulate must be the most primal construct for the inner sense, *i.e.* must be the Ego, not in so far as it is determined in this or that particular way, but the Ego in general, as production of itself. Through and in this primal construct, it is true, something definite is effected, just as always happens by every definite act of the soul. But the product is surely nothing without the construction; in fact it exists only in that it is constructed; abstracted from the construction it exists as little as the line of the geometer. The geometrical line also is nothing existing, for the line on the board is, as we know, not the line itself, but is recognized only as such because it is taken in connection with the original intuition of the line itself.

What the Ego is, is for this reason just as little demonstrable as what the line is: one can only describe the action by which it originates. If the line could be demonstrated it would not need to be postulated. It is just the same with that transcendental line of the production which must be originally intuited in transcendental philosophy, and from which all other constructions of the science first proceed (cf. "Allgemeine Uebersicht der philosophischen Literatur" in New Philos. Journal, 10. Hft).

i. What comes to us by the original act of intellectual intuition can be expressed in a fundamental principle which one can term the first fundamental principle of philosophy. Now the Ego originates through the intellectual intuition in so far as it is its own product, that is, is at the same time producing and produced. This identity between the Ego in so far as it is the producing and the Ego as produced is expressed in the proposition the $I = I$. This proposition, since it places opposites as equal, is by no means an identical, but a synthetic proposition.

By means of the proposition $I = I$, the proposition $A = A$ is therefore transformed into a synthetical proposition, and we have found the point where the identical knowledge springs immediately from the synthetical, and the synthetical knowledge from the identical. But at this point also is found (Chap. I) the principle of all knowledge. In the proposition $I = I$, therefore, the principle of all knowledge must be expressed, because this proposition is indeed the only possible one, that is at the same time identical and synthetic.

The mere reflection upon the proposition $A = A$ could have led us to the same conclusion. The proposition A = A appears, to be sure, identical; it could, however, very well also have synthetical significance, that is, if the one A were opposed to the other. One would therefore have to substitute in the place of A, a conception which expresses the original duplicity of identity, and *vice versa*.

Such a conception is that of an object which is at the same time opposed to and on an equality with itself. But of such character is only an object which in itself is both cause and effect, producing and produced, subject and object. The conception of an original identity in duplicity, and conversely, is therefore solely the conception of a subject-object, and this occurs originally only in self-consciousness.

Natural science sets out from nature as at once arbitrarily the producing and the produced, in order to derive the individual from that conception. The unmediated object of knowledge is such an identity only in the unmediated self-consciousness, in the highest potency of becoming its own object, in which the transcendental philosopher at the outset places himself, not arbitrarily, but with freedom. The original duplicity in nature is itself ultimately explained only by assuming nature to be intelligible.

k. The proposition I = I meets at the same time the second demand which is made of the principle of knowledge, that it establish at once both the form and the content of knowledge. For the highest formal fundamental proposition A = A, is of course only possible by the act which is expressed by the proposition I = I, that is, by the act of thinking which becomes its own object, and is identical with itself. The proposition I = I is therefore so far from being conditioned by the fundamental proposition of identity, that on the contrary this latter is conditioned by the former. For if I were not I, then A could also not be A, because the equality which is posited in that proposition expresses after all only an equality between the subject which judges and that in which A is posited as object, that is, an equality between the Ego as subject and object.

General Comments

1. The contradiction which has been solved by the foregoing deduction is the following: the science of knowledge can proceed from nothing objective, since it begins precisely with the universal doubt in the reality of the objective. The unconditioned-certain, therefore, exists for it only in the absolute non-objective which also proves the non-objectivity of the identical propositions as the solely unconditioned-certain. But how the objective could arise from this original non-objective would not be conceivable, unless that non-objective were an Ego, that is, a principle that becomes its own object. Only what is not originally object, can make itself the object, and thereby become an object. From this original duplicity in itself, every objective for the Ego is evolved that comes into consciousness; and it is that original identity in duplicity which alone brings union and coherence into all synthetic knowledge.

2. Some remarks may still be necessary on the use of language in this philosophy.

Kant in his anthropology finds it remarkable that a new world appears to spring up to the child as soon as it begins to speak of itself as I. This is in fact very natural: it is the intellectual world which reveals itself to him, since whatever can say I to itself lifts itself thereby above the objective world, and enters from a foreign intuition into its own. Philosophy must undoubtedly proceed from that conception in which the entire intellectuality is contained, and from which it is developed.

From this very fact one must see that in the conception of the Ego there exists something higher than the mere expression of individuality. It is the very act of self-consciousness in-deed, with which the consciousness of individuality makes its simultaneous appearance, but which itself contains nothing individual. Heretofore the discussion has been only of the Ego as the mere act of self-consciousness; and from it all individuality must yet be derived.

Under the Ego as principle, the individual I is thought of just as little as is the empiri-cal I,—the I which appears in empirical consciousness. The pure consciousness determined and restricted in a different way yields the empirical consciousness. The two, therefore, are separated merely by their restrictions. Remove the restrictions of the empirical and you have the absolute Ego, which is here treated. The pure self-consciousness is an act which lies out-side of all time and itself constitutes all time; the empirical consciousness is only one creat-ing itself in time, and in the succession of representations.

The question whether the Ego is a thing in itself, or a phenomenon, is of itself contra-dictory. It is in general no thing, neither thing in itself, nor phenomenon.

The dilemma which one may here bring forward in reply: Everything must either be something or nothing, etc., rests upon the ambiguity of the concept something. If the some-thing in general is intended to designate something real in contrast with the merely imag-ined, then the Ego must indeed be something real, since it is the principle of all reality. And just as clearly is it true that because the Ego is principle of all reality, it cannot then be real in the same sense as that to which belongs merely derived reality. The reality which such objector regards as the true one, namely that of things, is merely derived, and is only the reflection of that higher reality. The dilemma strictly viewed is thus equivalent to saying: Everything is either a *thing* or nothing. This is manifestly false, since there certainly exists a higher conception than that of the thing, namely, that of the deed, or of the activity.

This conception must indeed be higher than that of the thing, since the things them-selves are to be conceived only as modifications of an activity limited in different ways. The being of the thing does not indeed consist in mere rest or inactivity. For even all space-filling is only a degree of activity, and every thing is only a determined degree of activity with which space is filled.

Since none of the predicates which attach to things belong to the Ego, the paradox is thereby explained, that one cannot say of the Ego, that it is. One is unable to predicate being of the Ego, just because the Ego is being itself. The eternal act of self-consciousness conceived as in no time, which we term Ego, is what gives existence to all things, and which therefore needs no other existence by which to be supported; but appears self-carrying and self-supporting, objectively as the eternal becoming, subjectively as the infinite producing.

3. Before we proceed to the setting up of the system itself, it may be well to show how the principle can establish at the same time both theoretical and practical philosophy. That it does this is a necessary character of the principle, and is thus obvious.

That the principle should be at the same time the principle of theoretical and practical philosophy, is impossible, unless it be both theoretical and practical. Since now a theoretical principle is a theorem, but a practical principle is a command, something must be inter-mediate between the two. This is the postulate. It borders on the practical philosophy be-cause it is a pure demand, and on the theoretical because it requires a purely theoretical construction. What the postulate derives its compulsory power from is explained by the fact that it is allied to the practical demands. The intellectual intuition is something that one can demand and expect. Whoever has not such faculty at least ought to have it.

4. What every one who has attentively followed us thus far perceives for himself is that the beginning and the end of this philosophy is freedom, the absolutely indemonstrable,

that which proves itself by itself. What in all other systems threatens the destruction of freedom is in this system derived from itself. Being, in this system, is only suspended freedom. In a system which makes being the first and highest, not only must knowledge be a mere copy of an original being, but all freedom must also be only a necessary deception, because one is ignorant of the principle whose movements constitute the apparent manifestations of freedom.

. . . .

SCHOPENHAUER

1788–1860

Born in the Free City of Danzig, Arthur Schopenhauer was sent to boarding school in Hamburg. After his father, a successful merchant, committed suicide, young Schopenhauer went to live in Weimar with his mother, a novelist. In 1809 he enrolled at the University of Göttingen but then moved to the University of Berlin to study with Fichte. He completed his doctorate in philosophy at the University of Jena.

Schopenhauer's highly original philosophy developed from the idealism of Kant and Fichte. It is a rich blend of Kantian and Platonic theories, and owes much to Indian mysticism. His main philosophical influences were Goethe, Fichte, Schelling, Locke, and Hume. In his thirties Schopenhauer published his most important work, *The World as Will and Idea* (sometimes translated as *The World as Will and Representation*), convinced that it would cause a great stir. It was almost universally ignored for over three decades. The book did, however, help him to get a teaching position in philosophy at the University of Berlin at the same time as Hegel, whose ideas had already begun to dominate German philosophy. Schopenhauer was vehemently opposed to Hegel's use of the concept of reason as the basic force of the world, arguing that what is most fundamental to the world is not reason but *will.*

Schopenhauer tried, unsuccessfully, to compete with Hegel, even by scheduling his lectures at the same time as Hegel, but never managed to achieve any sort of following. Meanwhile, Hegel's influence spread like wildfire throughout Europe. Bitter and jealous, Schopenhauer left Berlin and had this to say about his colleague:

> Hegel, installed from above by the powers that be as the certified Great Philosopher, was a flat-headed, insipid, nauseating, illiterate charlatan, who reached the pinnacle of audacity in scribbling together and dishing up the craziest mystifying nonsense.

Nevertheless, Schopenhauer continued writing. In 1844 he issued a second edition of *The World as Will and Idea,* with fifty additional chapters. Unlike the first edition, this new version finally brought fame to the author, who was now in his sixties. Soon Schopenhauer found himself famous throughout Europe. He has continued to exert enormous influence on philosophers, psychologists, and writers, including Friedrich Nietzsche, Richard Wagner, Leo Tolstoy, Joseph Conrad, Marcel Proust, Thomas Mann, and Sigmund Freud.

Our selection from *The World as Will and Idea* begins with Schopenhauer explaining how everything in your present experience *is you yourself.* The world of your experience and everything in it is, literally, your dream, expressed in the proposition "The world is my idea." This sounds like a very positive and enlightening philosophy: your life is a dream, the world is a dream, and so on. But actually it is a very negative, dark philosophy. For then one must ask, if the world is but my own idea, why then is there so much suffering and evil in it? Here is Schopenhauer's unflattering answer: "The world is my will." The reason the world is so full of violence, pain, and suffering is that you willed it to be so.

To understand Schopenhauer's reasoning, we must go back to Kant's distinction between phenomena, the world of appearances, and noumena, things in themselves. For Schopenhauer applies this distinction to us, to our own experience of ourselves. Kant had claimed that the noumenal world is forever beyond reach of the phenomena and even of reason, because the noumena transcend the categories of the mind. But Schopenhauer argues that the noumenal world is much involved in each aspect of experience, because he equates the noumenal world of things in themselves with the *will.*

Schopenhauer's concept of will provides the missing bridge between phenomena and noumena. What is ultimately real for Schopenhauer is not any sort of rational world-*mind,* as Hegel had thought. Rather, the driving force of the world is a nonrational and blind force, the world-*will.* It is the dark momentum of existence that with an insatiable craving creates all and destroys all. The will that drives the world is not some benevolent God, not even is it rational. Hiding behind the veil of appearance, the will is invulnerable to the prying glances of its own creations. It creates in its creatures insatiable cravings that are the will objectified: sex, violence, greed, war, and domination. Behind all of these cravings is the eternal, dark, metaphysical world-will.

Schopenhauer claims that human beings can escape the tyranny of the will only through art. Because the will is not rational and yet it controls everything, the world cannot be understood through rational means. Therefore, true understanding can be attained only through aesthetic experience. Art exists, according to Schopenhauer, in the transcendental realm of "will-less" perception. Thus, as with Schelling, what Plato considered to be the worst aspect of art turns out to be the very solution to the problem of existence. That is, because art is not subservient to science and rational thinking, art provides the highest form of understanding and gives just enough elbow room for the possibility of freedom.

THE WORLD AS WILL AND IDEA

BOOK I: THE WORLD AS IDEA

§ 1. "The world is my idea:"—this is a truth which holds good for everything that lives and knows, though man alone can bring it into reflective and abstract consciousness. If he

From A. Schopenhauer, *The World as Will and Idea,* trans. R. B. Haldane and J. Kemp (London: Trübner, 1883), vol. i. With emendations by Daniel Kolak.

really does this, he has attained to philosophical wisdom. It then becomes clear and certain to him that what he knows is not a sun and an earth, but only an eye that sees a sun, a hand that feels an earth; that the world which surrounds him is there only as idea, *i.e.,* only in relation to something else, the consciousness, which is himself. If any truth can be asserted *a priori,* it is this: for it is the expression of the most general form of all possible and think-able experience: a form which is more general than time, or space, or causality, for they all presuppose it; and each of these, which we have seen to be just so many modes of the prin-ciple of sufficient reason, is valid only for a particular class of ideas; whereas the antithesis of object and subject is the common form of all these classes, is that form under which alone any idea of whatever kind it may be, abstract or intuitive, pure or empirical, is possible and thinkable. No truth therefore is more certain, more independent of all others, and less in need of proof than this, that all that exists for knowledge, and therefore this whole world, is only object in relation to subject, perception of a perceiver, in a word, idea. This is ob-viously true of the past and the future, as well as of the present, of what is farthest off, as of what is near; for it is true of time and space themselves, in which alone these distinctions arise. All that in any way belongs or can belong to the world is inevitably thus conditioned through the subject, and exists only for the subject. The world is idea.

This truth is by no means new. It was implicitly involved in the sceptical reflections from which Descartes started. Berkeley, however, was the first who distinctly enunciated it, and by this he has rendered a permanent service to philosophy, even though the rest of his teach-ing should not endure. Kant's primary mistake was the neglect of this principle. . . . How early again this truth was recognised by the wise men of India, appearing indeed as the fun-damental tenet of the Vedânta philosophy ascribed by Vyasa, is pointed out by Sir William Jones in the last of his essays: "On the Philosophy of the Asiatics" (*Asiatic Researches,* vol. iv, p. 164), where he says, "The fundamental tenet of the Vedanta school consisted not in de-nying the existence of matter, that is, of solidity, impenetrability, and extended figure (to deny which would be lunacy), but in correcting the popular notion of it, and in contending that it has no essence independent of mental perception; that existence and perceptibility are convertible terms." These words adequately express the compatibility of empirical reality and transcendental ideality.

In this first book, then, we consider the world only from this side, only so far as it is idea. The inward reluctance with which any one accepts the world as merely his idea, warns him that this view of it, however true it may be, is nevertheless one-sided, adopted in con-sequence of some arbitrary abstraction. And yet it is a conception from which he can never free himself. The defectiveness of this view will be corrected in the next book by means of a truth which is not so immediately certain as that from which we start here; a truth at which we can arrive only by deeper research and more severe abstraction, by the separation of what is different and the union of what is identical. This truth, which must be very se-rious and impressive if not awful to every one, is that a man can also say and must say, "The world is my will."

In this book, however, we must consider separately that aspect of the world from which we start, its aspect as knowable, and therefore, in the meantime, we must, without reserve, regard all presented objects, even our own bodies (as we shall presently show more fully), merely as ideas, and call them merely ideas. By so doing we always abstract from will (as we hope to make clear to every one further on), which by itself constitutes the other aspect of the world. For as the world is in one aspect entirely *idea,* so in another it is entirely *will.* A reality which is neither of these two, but an object in itself (into which the thing in itself has unfortunately dwindled in the hands of Kant), is the phantom of a dream, and its acceptance is an *ignis fatuus* in philosophy.

§ 2. That which knows all things and is known by none is the subject. Thus it is the supporter of the world, that condition of all phenomena, of all objects which is always presupposed throughout experience; for all that exists, exists only for the subject. Every one finds himself to be subject, yet only in so far as he knows, not in so far as he is an object of knowledge. But his body is object, and therefore from this point of view we call it idea. For the body is an object among objects and is conditioned by the laws of objects, although it is an immediate object. Like all objects of perception, it lies within the universal forms of knowledge, time and space, which are the conditions of multiplicity. The subject, on the contrary, which is always the knower, never the known, does not come under these forms, but is presupposed by them; it has therefore neither multiplicity nor its opposite unity. We never know it, but it is always the knower wherever there is knowledge.

So then the world as idea, the only aspect in which we consider it at present, has two fundamental, necessary, and inseparable halves. The one half is the object, the forms of which are space and time, and through these multiplicity. The other half is the subject, which is not in space and time, for it is present, entire and undivided, in every percipient being. So that any one percipient being, with the object, constitutes the whole world as idea just as fully as the existing millions could do; but if this one were to disappear, then the whole world as idea would cease to be. These halves are therefore inseparable even for thought, for each of the two has meaning and existence only through and for the other, each appears with the other and vanishes with it. They limit each other immediately; where the object begins the subject ends. The universality of this limitation is shown by the fact that the essential and hence universal forms of all objects, space, time, and causality, may, without knowledge of the object, be discovered and fully known from a consideration of the subject, *i.e.*, in Kantian language, they lie *a priori* in our consciousness. That he discovered this is one of Kant's principal merits, and it is a great one. I however go beyond this, and maintain that the principle of sufficient reason is the general expression for all these forms of the object of which we are *a priori* conscious; and that therefore all that we know purely *a priori*, is merely the content of that principle and what follows from it; in it all our certain *a priori* knowledge is expressed. In my essay on the principle of sufficient reason I have shown in detail how every possible object comes under it; that is, stands in a necessary relation to other objects, on the one side as determined, on the other side as determining: this is of such wide application, that the whole existence of all objects, so far as they are objects, ideas and nothing more, may be entirely traced to this their necessary relation to each other, rests only in it, is in fact merely relative; but of this more presently. I have further shown, that the necessary relation which the principle of sufficient reason expresses generally, appears in other forms corresponding to the classes into which objects are divided, according to their possibility; and again that by these forms the proper division of the classes is tested. I take it for granted that what I said in this earlier essay is known and present to the reader, for if it had not been already said it would necessarily find its place here.

§ 5. It is needful to guard against the grave error of supposing that because perception arises through the knowledge of causality, the relation of subject and object is that of cause and effect. For this relation subsists only between the immediate object and objects known indirectly, thus always between objects alone. It is this false supposition that has given rise to the foolish controversy about the reality of the outer world; a controversy in which dogmatism and scepticism oppose each other, and the former appears, now as realism, now as idealism. Realism treats the object as cause, and the subject as its effect. The idealism of Fichte reduces the object to the effect of the subject. Since however, and this cannot be too much emphasised, there is absolutely no relation according to the principle of sufficient reason between subject and object, neither of these views could be proved, and therefore scepticism attacked them both with success. Now, just as the law of causality precedes perception and experience as their condition, and therefore cannot (as Hume thought) be derived from them, so object and subject precede all knowledge, and hence the principle of sufficient reason in general, as its first condition; for this principle is merely the form of all objects, the whole nature and possibility of their existence as phenomena: but the object always presupposes the subject; and therefore between these two there can be no relation of reason and consequent. My essay on the principle of sufficient reason accomplishes just this: it explains the content of that principle as the essential form of every object—that is to say, as the universal nature of all objective existence, as something which pertains to the object as such; but the object as such always presupposes the subject as its necessary correlative; and therefore the subject remains always outside the province in which the principle of sufficient reason is valid. The controversy as to the reality of the outer world rests upon this false extension of the validity of the principle of sufficient reason to the subject also, and starting with this mistake it can never understand itself. On the one side realistic dogmatism, looking upon the idea as the effect of the object, desires to separate these two, idea and object, which are really one, and to assume a cause quite different from the idea, an object in itself, independent of the subject, a thing which is quite inconceivable; for even as object it presupposes subject, and so remains its ideas. Opposed to this doctrine is scepticism, which makes the same false presupposition that in the idea we have only the effect, never the cause, therefore never real being; that we always know merely the action of the object. But this object, it supposes, may perhaps have no resemblance whatever to its effect, may indeed have been quite erroneously received as the cause, for the law of causality is first to be gathered from experience, and the reality of experience is then made to rest upon it. Thus both of these views are open to the correction, firstly, that object and idea are the same; secondly, that the true being of the object of perception is its action, that the reality of the thing consists in this, and the demand for an existence of the object outside the idea of the subject, and also for an essence of the actual thing different from its action, has absolutely no meaning, and is contradiction: and that the knowledge of the nature of the effect of any perceived object, exhausts such an object itself, so far as it is object, *i.e.,* idea, for beyond this there is nothing more to be known. So far then, the perceived world in space and time, which makes itself known as causation alone, is entirely real, and is throughout simply what it appears to be, and it appears wholly and without reserve as idea, bound together according to the law of causality. This is its empirical reality. On the other hand, all causality is in the understanding alone, and for the understanding. The whole actual, that is, active world is determined as such through the understanding, and apart from it is nothing. This, however, is not the only reason for altogether denying such a reality of the outer world as is taught by the dogmatist, who explains its reality as its independence of the subject. We also deny it, because no object apart from a subject can be conceived without contradiction. The whole world of objects is and remains idea, and therefore wholly and for ever determined by the subject; that is to say, it has transcendental ideality. But it is not therefore illusion or mere appearance; it presents itself as that which it is, idea, and indeed as a series of ideas of which the common bond is the principle of sufficient reason. It is according to its inmost meaning quite comprehensible to the healthy understanding, and speaks a language quite intelligible to it. To dispute about its reality can only occur to a mind perverted by over-subtilty, and such discussion always arises from a false application of the principle of sufficient reason, which binds all ideas together of whatever kind they may be, but by no means connects them with the subject, nor yet with a something which is neither subject nor object, but only the ground of the object; an absurdity, for only objects can be and always are the ground of objects. If we examine more closely the source of this question as to the reality of the outer world, we find that besides the false application of the principle of sufficient reason generally to what lies beyond its province, a special confusion of its forms is also involved; for that form which it has only in reference to concepts or abstract ideas, is applied to perceived ideas, real objects; and a ground of knowing is demanded of objects, whereas they can have nothing but a ground of being. Among the abstract ideas, the concepts united in the judgment, the principle of sufficient reason appears in such a way that each of these has its worth, its validity, and its whole existence, here called *truth,* simply and solely through the relation of the judgment to something outside of it, its ground of knowledge, to which there must consequently always be a return. Among real objects, ideas of perception, on the other hand, the principle of sufficient reason appears not as the principle of the ground of *knowing,* but of *being,* as the law of causality: every real object has paid its debt to it, inasmuch as it has come to be, *i.e.,* has appeared as the effect of a cause. The demand for a ground of knowing has therefore here no application and no meaning, but belongs to quite another class of things. Thus the world of perception raises in the observer no question or doubt so long as he remains in contact with it: there is here neither error nor truth, for these are confined to the province of the abstract—the province of reflection. But here the world lies open for sense and understanding; presents itself with naïve truth as that which it really is—ideas of perception which develop themselves according to the law of causality.

So far as we have considered the question of the reality of the outer world, it arises from a confusion which amounts even to a misunderstanding of reason itself, and therefore thus far, the question could be answered only by explaining its meaning. After examination of the whole nature of the principle of sufficient reason, of the relation of subject and object, and the special conditions of sense perception, the question itself disappeared because it had no longer any meaning. There is, however, one other possible origin of this question, quite different from the purely speculative one which we have considered, a specially empirical origin, though the question is always raised from a speculative point of view, and in this form it has a much more comprehensible meaning than it had in the first. We have dreams; may not our whole life be a dream? or more exactly: is there a sure criterion of the distinction between dreams and reality? between phantasms and real objects? The assertion that what is dreamed is less vivid and distinct than what we actually perceive is not to the point, because no one has ever been able to make a fair comparison of the two; for we can only compare the recollection of a dream with the present reality. Kant answers the question thus: "The connection of ideas among themselves, according to the law of causality, constitutes the difference between real life and dreams." But in dreams, as well as in real life, everything is connected individually at any rate, in accordance with the principle of sufficient reason in all its forms, and this connection is broken only between life and dreams, or between one dream and another. Kant's answer therefore could only run thus:—the *long* dream (life) has throughout complete connection according to the principle of sufficient reason; it has not this connection, however, with *short* dreams, although each of these has in itself the same connection: the bridge is therefore broken between the former and the latter and on this account we distinguish them.

But to institute an enquiry according to this criterion, as to whether something was dreamed or seen, would always be difficult and often impossible. For we are by no means in a position to trace link by link the causal connection between any experienced event and the present moment, but we do not on that account explain it as dreamed. Therefore in real life we do not commonly employ that method of distinguishing between dreams and reality. The only sure criterion by which to distinguish them is in fact the entirely empirical one of awaking, through which at any rate the causal connection between dreamed events and those of waking life, is distinctly and sensibly broken off. This is strongly supported by the remark of Hobbes in the second chapter of Leviathan, that we easily mistake dreams for reality if we have unintentionally fallen asleep without taking off our clothes, and much more so when it also happens that some undertaking or design fills all our thoughts, and occupies our dreams as well as our waking moments. We then observe the awaking just as little as the falling asleep, dream and reality run together and becomes confounded. In such a case there is nothing for it but the application of Kant's criterion; but if, as often happens, we fail to establish by means of this criterion, either the existence of causal connection with the present, or the absence of such connection, then it must for ever remain uncertain whether an event was dreamed or really happened. Here, in fact, the intimate relationship between life and dreams is brought out very clearly, and we need not be ashamed to confess it, as it has been recognised and spoken of by many great men. The Vedas and Puranas have no better simile than a dream for the whole knowledge of the actual world, which they call the web of Mâyâ, and they use none more frequently. Plato often says that men live only in a dream; the philosopher alone strives to awake himself. . . . Beside which most worthily stands Shakespeare:—

> We are such stuff
> As dreams are made on, and our little life
> Is rounded with a sleep.—*Tempest,* Act IV. Sc. i.

Lastly, Calderon was so deeply impressed with this view of life that he sought to embody it in a kind of metaphysical drama—"Life a Dream."

After these numerous quotations from the poets, perhaps I also may be allowed to express myself by a metaphor. Life and dreams are leaves of the same book. The systematic reading of this book is real life, but when the reading hours (that is, the day) are over, we often continue idly to turn over the leaves, and read a page here and there without method or connection: often one we have read before, sometimes one that is new to us, but always in the same book. Such an isolated page is indeed out of connection with the systematic study of the book, but it does not seem so very different when we remember that the whole continuous perusal begins and ends just as abruptly, and may therefore be regarded as merely a larger single page.

Thus although individual dreams are distinguished from real life by the fact that they do not fit into that continuity which runs through the whole of experience, and the act of awaking brings this into consciousness, yet that very continuity of experience belongs to real life as its form, and the dream on its part can point to a similar continuity in itself. If, therefore, we consider the question from a point of view external to both, there is no distinct difference in their nature, and we are forced to concede to the poets that life is a long dream.

Let us turn back now from this quite independent empirical origin of the question of the reality of the outer world, to its speculative origin. We found that this consisted, first, in the false application of the principle of sufficient reason to the relation of subject and object; and secondly, in the confusion of its forms, inasmuch as the principle of sufficient reason of knowing was extended to a province in which the principle of sufficient reason of being is valid. But the question could hardly have occupied philosophers so constantly if it were entirely devoid of all real content, and if some true thought and meaning did not lie at its heart as its real source. Accordingly, we must assume that when the element of truth that lies at the bottom of the question first came into reflection and sought its expression, it became involved in these confused and meaningless forms and problems. This at least is my opinion, and I think that the true expression of that inmost meaning of the question, which it failed to find, is this:—What is this world of perception besides being my idea? Is that of which I am conscious only as idea, exactly like my own body, of which I am doubly conscious, in one aspect as *idea,* in another aspect as *will?* The fuller explanation of this question and its answer in the affirmative, will form the content of the second book, and its consequences will occupy the remaining portion of this work.

§ 6. For the present, however, in this first book we consider every thing merely as idea, as object for the subject. And our own body, which is the starting point for each of us in our perception of the world, we consider, like all other real objects, from the side of its knowableness, and in this regard it is simply an idea. Now the consciousness of every one is in general opposed to the explanation of objects as mere ideas, and more especially to the explanation of our bodies as such; for the thing in itself is known to each of us immediately in so far as it appears as our own body; but in so far as it objectifies itself in the other objects of perception, it is known only indirectly. But this abstraction, this one-sided treatment, this forcible separation of what is essentially and necessarily united, is only adopted to meet the demands of our argument; and therefore the disinclination to it must, in the meantime, be suppressed and silenced by the expectation that the subsequent treatment will correct the one-sidedness of the present one, and complete our knowledge of the nature of the world.

At present therefore the body is for us immediate object; that is to say, that idea which forms the starting point of the subject's knowledge; because the body, with its immediately known changes, precedes the application of the law of causality, and thus supplies it with its first data. The whole nature of matter consists, as we have seen, in its causal action. But cause and effect exist only for the understanding, which is nothing but their subjective correlative. The understanding, however, could never come into operation if there were not something else from which it starts. This is simple sensation—the immediate consciousness of the changes of the body, by virtue of which it is immediate object. Thus the possibility of knowing the world of perception depends upon two conditions; the first, *objectively expressed,* is the power of material things to act upon each other, to produce changes in each other, without which common quality of all bodies no perception would be possible, even by means of the sensibility of the animal body. And if we wish to express this condition *subjectively* we say: The understanding first makes perception possible; for the law of causality, the possibility of effect and cause, springs only from the understanding, and is valid only for it, and therefore the world of perception exists only through and for it. The second condition is the sensibility of animal bodies, or the quality of being immediate objects of the subject which certain bodies possess. The mere modification which the organs of sense sustain from without through their specific affections, may here be called ideas, so far as these affections produce neither pain nor pleasure, that is, have no immediate significance for the will, and are yet perceived, exist therefore only for *knowledge.* Thus far, then, I say that the body is immediately *known,* is *immediate object.* But the conception of object is not to be taken here in its fullest sense, for through this immediate knowledge of the body, which precedes the operation of the understanding, and is mere sensation, our own body does not exist specifically as *object,* but first the material things which affect it: for all knowledge of an object proper, of an idea perceived in space, exists only through and for the understanding; therefore not before, but only subsequently to its operation. Therefore the body as object proper, that is, an idea perceived in space, is first known indirectly, like all other objects, through the application of the law of causality to the action of one of its parts upon another, as, for example, when the eye sees the body or the hand touches it. Consequently the form of our body does not become known to us through mere feeling, but only through knowledge, only in idea; that is to say, only in the brain does our own body first come to appear as extended, articulate, organic. A man born blind receives this idea only little by little from the data afforded by touch. A blind man without hands could never come to know his own form; or at the most could infer and construct it little by little from the effects of other bodies upon him. If, then, we call the body an immediate object, we are to be understood with these reservations. . . .

§ 12. *Rational knowledge* is then all abstract knowledge—that is, the knowledge which is peculiar to the reason as distinguished from the understanding. Now, as reason only reproduces, for knowledge, what has been received in another way, it does not actually extend our knowledge, but only gives it another form. It enables us to know in the abstract and generally, what first became known in sense-perception, in the concrete. But this is much more important than it appears at first sight when so expressed. For it depends entirely upon the fact that knowledge has become rational or abstract knowledge, that it can be safely preserved, that it is communicable and susceptible of certain and wide-reaching application to practice. Knowledge in the form of sense-perception is valid only of the particular case, extends only to what is nearest, and ends with it, for sensibility and understanding can only comprehend one object at a time. Every enduring, arranged, and planned activity must therefore proceed from principles (that is, from abstract knowledge) and it must be conducted in accordance with them. Thus, for example, the knowledge of the relation of cause and effect arrived at by the understanding, is in itself far completer, deeper and more exhaustive than anything that can be thought about it in the abstract; the understanding alone knows in perception directly and completely the nature of the effect of a lever, of a pulley, or a cog-wheel, the stability of an arch, and so forth. But on account of the peculiarity of the knowledge of perception just referred to, that it only extends to what is immediately present, the mere understanding can never enable us to construct machines and buildings. Here reason must come in; it must substitute abstract concepts for ideas of perception, and take them as the guide of action; and if they are right, the anticipated result will happen. In the same way we have perfect knowledge in pure perception of the nature and constitution of the parabola, hyperbola, and spiral; but if we are to make trustworthy application of this knowledge to the real, it must first become abstract knowledge, and by this it certainty loses its character of intuition or perception, but on the other hand it gains the certainty and preciseness of abstract knowledge. The differential calculus does not really extend our knowledge of the curve, it contains nothing that was not already in the mere pure perception of the curve; but it alters the kind of knowledge, it changes the intuitive into an abstract knowledge, which is so valuable for application. . . .

The greatest value of rational or abstract knowledge is that it can be communicated and permanently retained. It is principally on this account that it is so inestimably important for practice. Anyone may have a direct perceptive knowledge through the understanding alone, of the causal connection, of the changes and motions of natural bodies, and he may find entire satisfaction in it; but he cannot communicate this knowledge to others until it has been made permanent for thought in concepts. Knowledge of the first kind is even sufficient for practice, if a man puts his knowledge into practice himself, in an action which can be accomplished while the perception is still vivid; but it is not sufficient if the help of others is required, or even if the action is his own but must be carried out at different times, and therefore requires a preconceived plan. Thus, for example, a practiced billiard player may have a perfect knowledge of the laws of the impact of elastic bodies upon each other, merely in the understanding, merely for direct perception; and for him it is quite sufficient; but on the other hand it is only the man who has studied the science of mechanics who has, properly speaking, a rational knowledge of these laws, that is, a knowledge of them in the abstract. . . . It is, however, remarkable that in the first kind of activity—in which we have supposed that one man alone, in an uninterrupted course of action, accomplishes something—abstract knowledge, the application of reason or reflection, may often be a hindrance to him; for example in the case of billiard playing, of fighting, of tuning an instrument, or in the case of singing. Here perceptive knowledge must directly guide action; its passage through reflection makes it uncertain, for it divides the attention and confuses the man. . . . In the same way it is of no use to me to know in the abstract the exact angle in degrees and minutes at which I must apply a razor if I do not know it intuitively, that is, if I have not got it in my touch. The knowledge of physiognomy, also, is interfered with by the application of reason. This knowledge must be gained directly through the understanding. We say that the expression, the meaning of the features, can only be *felt,* that is, it cannot be put into abstract concepts. Every man has his direct intuitive method of physiognomy and pathognomy, yet one man understands more clearly than another these *signatura rerum.* But an abstract science of physiognomy to be taught and learned is not possible; for the distinctions of difference are here so fine that concepts cannot reach them; therefore abstract knowledge is related to them as a mosaic is to a painting by a Van der Werft or a Denner. In mosaics, however fine they may be, the limits of the stones are always there, and therefore no continuous passage from one color to another is possible, and this is also the case with regard to concepts, with their rigidity and sharp delineation; however finely we may divide them by exact definition they are still incapable of reaching the finer modifications of the perceptible, and this is just what happens in the example we have taken, knowledge of physiognomy.

This quality of concepts by which they resemble the stones of a mosaic, and on account of which perception always remains their asymptote, is the reason why nothing good is produced in art by their means. If the singer or the virtuoso attempts to guide his execution by reflection he remains silent. And this is equally true of the composer, the painter, and the poet. The concept always remains unfruitful in art; it can only direct the technical part of it, its sphere is science. . . .

Lastly, virtue and holiness do not proceed from reflection, but from the inner depths of the will, and its relation to knowledge. The exposition of this belongs to another part of our work; this, however, I may remark here, that the dogmas relating to ethics may be the same in the reason of whole nations, but the action of every individual different; and the converse also holds good; action, we say, is guided by *feelings*—that is, simply not by concepts, but as a matter of fact by the ethical character. Dogmas occupy the idle reason; but action in the end pursues its own course independently of them, generally not according to abstract rules, but according to unspoken maxims, the expression of which is the whole man himself. Therefore, however different the religious dogmas of nations may be, yet in the case of all of them, a good action is accompanied by unspeakable satisfaction, and a bad action by endless remorse. No mockery can shake the former; no priest's absolution can deliver from the latter. Notwithstanding this, we must allow that for the pursuit of a virtuous life, the application of reason is needful; only it is not its source, but has the subordinate function of preserving resolutions which have been made, of providing maxims to withstand the weakness of the moment, and give consistency to action. It plays the same part ultimately in art also, where it has just as little to do with the essential matter, but assists in carrying it out, for genius is not always at call, and yet the work must be completed in all its parts and rounded off to a whole.

As regards the *content* of the sciences generally, it is, in fact, always the relation of the phenomena of the world to each other, according to the principle of sufficient reason, under the guidance of the *why,* which has validity and meaning only through this principle. *Explanation* is the establishment of this relation. Therefore explanation can never go further than to show two ideas standing to each other in the relation peculiar to that form of the principle of sufficient reason which reigns in the class to which they belong. If this is done we cannot further be asked the question, *why:* for the relation proved is that one which absolutely cannot be imagined as other than it is, *i.e.,* it is the form of all knowledge. Therefore we do not ask why $2 + 2 = 4$; or why the quality of the angles of a triangle determines the equality of the sides; or why its effect follows any given cause; or why the truth of the conclusion is evident from the truth of the premises. Every explanation which does not ultimately lead to a relation of which no "why" can further be demanded, stops at an accepted *qualitas occulta;* but this is the character of every original force of nature. Every explanation in natural science must ultimately end with such a *qualitas occulta,* and thus with complete obscurity. It must leave the inner nature of a stone just as much unexplained as that of a human being; it can give as little account of the weight, the cohesion, the chemical qualities, etc., of the former, as of the knowing and acting of the latter. . . . Philosophy is the most general rational knowledge, the first principles of which cannot therefore be derived from another principle still more general. The principle of contradiction establishes merely the agreement of concepts, but does not itself produce concepts. The principle of sufficient reason explains the connections of phenomena, but not the phenomena themselves; therefore philosophy cannot proceed upon these principles to seek a *causa efficiens* or a *causa finalis* of the whole world. My philosophy, at least, does not by any means seek to know *whence* or *wherefore* the world exists, but merely *what* the world is. But the *why* is here subordinated to the *what,* for it already belongs to the world, as it arises and has meaning and validity only through the form of its phenomena, the principle of sufficient reason. We might indeed say that every one knows what the world is without help, for he is himself that subject of knowledge of which the world is the idea; and so far this would be true. But that knowledge is empirical, is in the concrete; the task of philosophy is to reproduce this in the abstract, to raise to permanent rational knowledge the successive changing perceptions, and in general, all that is contained under the wide concept of feeling and merely negatively defined as not abstract, distinct, rational knowledge. It must therefore consist of a statement in the abstract, of the nature of the whole world, of the whole and of all the parts. . . .

BOOK II: THE WORLD AS WILL

FIRST ASPECT. THE OBJECTIFICATION OF THE WILL

§ 17. . . . What now impels us to inquiry is, that we are not satisfied with knowing that we have ideas, that they are such and such, and that they are connected according to certain laws, the general expression of which is the principle of sufficient reason. We wish to know the significance of these ideas; we ask whether this world is merely idea; in which case it would pass by us like an empty dream or a baseless vision, not worth our notice; or whether it is also something else, something more than idea, and if so, what. Thus much is certain, that this something we seek for must be completely and in its whole nature different from the idea; that the forms and laws of the idea must therefore be completely foreign to it; further, that we cannot arrive at it from the idea under the guidance of the laws which merely combine objects, ideas, among themselves, and which are the forms of the principle of sufficient reason.

Thus we see already that we can never arrive at the real nature of things from without. However much we investigate, we can never reach anything but images and names. We are like a man who goes round a castle seeking in vain for an entrance, and sometimes sketching the façades. And yet this is the method that has been followed by all philosophers before me.

§ 18. In fact, the meaning for which we seek of that world which is present to us only as our idea, or the transition from the world as mere idea of the knowing subject to whatever it may be besides this, would never be found if the investigator himself were nothing more than the pure knowing subject (a winged cherub without a body). But he is himself rooted in that world; he finds himself in it as an *individual,* that is to say, his knowledge, which is the necessary supporter of the whole world as idea, is yet always given through the medium of a body, whose affections are, as we have shown, the starting-point for the understanding in the perception of that world. His body is, for the pure knowing subject, an idea like every other idea, an object among objects. Its movements and actions are so far known to him in precisely the same way as the changes of all other perceived objects, and would be just as strange and incomprehensible to him if their meaning were not explained for him in an entirely different way. Otherwise he would see his actions follow upon given motives with the constancy of a law of nature just as the changes of other objects follow upon causes, stimuli, or motives. But he would not understand the influence of the motives any more than the connection between every other effect which he sees and its cause. He would then call the inner nature of these manifestations and actions of his body which he did not understand a force, a quality, or a character, as he pleased, but he would have no further insight into it. But all this is not the case; indeed the answer to the riddle is given to the subject of knowledge who appears as an individual, and the answer is *will.* This and this alone gives him the key to his own existence, reveals to him the significance, shows him the inner mechanism of his being, of his action, of his movements. The body is given in two entirely different ways to the subject of knowledge, who becomes an individual only through his identity with it. It is given as an idea in intelligent perception, as an object among objects and subject to the laws of objects. And it is also given in quite a different way as that which is immediately known to every one, and is signified by the word *will.* Every true act of his will is also at once and without exception a movement of his body. The act of will and the movement of the body are not two different things objectively known, which the bond of causality unites; they do not stand in the relation of cause and effect; they are one and the same, but they are given in entirely different ways,—immediately, and again in perception for the understanding. The action of the body is nothing but the act of the will objectified, *i.e.,* passed into perception. It will appear later that this is true of every movement of the body, not merely those which follow upon motives, but also involuntary movements which follow upon mere stimuli, and, indeed, that the whole body is nothing but objectified will, *i.e.,* will become idea. All this will be proved and made quite clear in the course of this work. In one respect, therefore, I shall call the body the *objectivity of will;* as in the previous book, and in this essay on the principle of sufficient reason, in accordance with the one-sided point of view intentionally adopted there (that of the idea), I called it *the immediate object.* Thus in a certain sense we may also say that will is the knowledge *a priori* of the body, and the body is the knowledge *a posteriori* of the will. Resolutions of the will which relate to the future are merely deliberations of the reason about what we shall will at a particular time, not real acts of will. Only the carrying out of the resolve stamps it as will, for till then it is never more than an intention that may be changed, and that exists only in the reason *in abstracto*. It is only in reflection that to will and to act are different; in reality they are one. Every true, genuine, immediate act of will is also, at once and immediately, a visible act of the body. And, corresponding to this, every impression upon the body is also, on the other hand, at once and immediately an impression upon the will. As such it is called pain when it is opposed to the will; gratification or pleasure when it is in accordance with it. The degrees of both are widely different. It is quite wrong, however, to call pain and pleasure ideas, for they are by no means ideas, but immediate affections of the will in its manifestation, the body; compulsory, instantaneous willing or not-willing of the impression which the body sustains. There are only a few impressions of the body which do not touch the will, and it is through these alone that the body is an immediate object of knowledge, for, as perceived by the understanding, it is already an indirect object like all others. These impressions are, therefore, to be treated directly as mere ideas, and excepted from what has been said. The impressions we refer to are the affections of the purely objective senses of sight, hearing, and touch, though only so far as these organs are affected in the way which is specially peculiar to their specific nature. This affection of them is so excessively weak an excitement of the heightened and specifically modified sensibility of these parts that it does not affect the will, but only furnishes the understanding with the data out of which the perception arises, undisturbed by any excitement of the will. But every stronger or different kind of affection of these organs of sense is painful, that is to say, against the will, and thus they also belong to its objectivity. Weakness of the nerves shows itself in this, that the impressions which have only such a degree of strength as would usually be sufficient to make them data for the understanding reach the higher degree at which they influence the will, that is to say, give pain or pleasure, though more often pain, which is, however, to some extent deadened and inarticulate, so that not only particular tones and strong light are painful to us, but there ensues a generally unhealthy and hypochondriacal disposition which is not distinctly understood. The identity of the body and the will shows itself further, among other ways, in the circumstance that every vehement and excessive movement of the will, *i.e.*, every emotion, agitates the body and its inner constitution directly, and disturbs the course of its vital functions. This is shown in detail in "Will in Nature," p. 27 of the second edition and p. 28 of the third.

Lastly, the knowledge which I have of my will, though it is immediate, cannot be separated from that which I have of my body. I know my will, not as a whole, not as a unity, not completely, according to its nature, but I know it only in its particular acts, and therefore in time, which is the form of the phenomenal aspect of my body, as of every object. Therefore the body is a condition of the knowledge of my will. Thus, I cannot really imagine this will apart from my body. In the essay on the principle of sufficient reason, the will, or rather the subject of willing, is treated as a special class of ideas or objects. But even there we saw this object become one with the subject; that is, we saw it cease to be an object. We there called this union the miracle, and the whole of the present work is to a certain extent an explanation of this. So far as I know my will specially as object, I know it as body. But then I am again at the first class of ideas laid down in that essay, *i.e.*, real objects. As we proceed we shall see always more clearly that these ideas of the first class obtain their explanation and solution from those of the fourth class given in the essay, which could no longer be properly opposed to the subject as object, and that, therefore, we must learn to understand the inner nature of the law of causality which is valid in the first class, and of all that happens in accordance with it from the law of motivation which governs the fourth class.

The identity of the will and the body, of which we have now given a cursory explanation, can only be proved in the manner we have adopted here. We have proved this identity for the first time, and shall do so more and more fully in the course of this work. By "proved" we mean raised from the immediate consciousness, from knowledge in the concrete to abstract knowledge of the reason, or carried over into abstract knowledge. On the other hand, from its very nature it can never be demonstrated, that is, deduced as indirect knowledge from some other more direct knowledge, just because it is itself the most direct knowledge; and if we do not apprehend it and stick to it as such, we shall expect in vain to receive it again in some indirect way as derivative knowledge. It is knowledge of quite a special kind, whose truth cannot therefore properly be brought under any of the four rubrics under which I have classified all truth in the essay on the principle of sufficient reason, § 29, the logical, the empirical, the metaphysical, and the metalogical, for it is not, like all these, the relation of an abstract idea to another idea, or to the necessary form of perceptive or of abstract ideation, but it is the relation of a judgment to the connection which an idea of perception, the body, has to that which is not an idea at all, but something *toto genere* different, will. I should like therefore to distinguish this from all other truth, and call it *philosophical truth.* We can turn the expression of this truth in different ways and say: My body and my will are one;—or, What as an idea of perception I call my body, I call my will, so far as I am conscious of it in an entirely different way which cannot be compared to any other;—or, My body is the *objectivity* of my will;—or, My body considered apart from the fact that it is my idea is still my will, and so forth.

§ 19. In the first book we were reluctantly driven to explain the human body as merely idea of the subject which knows it, like all the other objects of this world of perception. But it has now become clear that what enables us consciously to distinguish our own body from all other objects which in other respects are precisely the same, is that our body appears in consciousness in quite another way *toto genere* different from idea, and this we denote by the word *will;* and that it is just this double knowledge which we have our own body that affords us information about it, about its action and movement following on motives and also about what it experiences by means of external impressions; in a word, about what is it, not as idea, but as more than idea; that is to say, what it is *in itself.* None of this information have we got directly with regard to the nature, action, and experience of other real objects.

It is just because of this special relation to one body that the knowing subject is an individual. For regarded apart from this relation, his body is for him, only an idea like all other ideas. But the relation through which the knowing subject is an *individual,* is just on that account a relation which subsists only between him and one particular idea of all those which he has. Therefore he is conscious of this one idea, not merely as an idea, but in quite a different way as a will. If, however, he abstracts from that special relation, from that twofold and completely heterogeneous knowledge of what is one and the same, then that *one,* the body, is an idea like all other ideas. Therefore, in order to understand the matter, the individual who knows must either assume that what distinguishes that one idea from others is merely the fact that his knowledge stands in this double relation to it alone; that insight in two ways at the same time is open to him only in the case of this one object of perception, and that this is to be explained not by the difference of this object from all others, but only by the difference between the relation of his knowledge to this one object, and its relation to all other objects. Or else he must assume that this object is essentially different from all others; that it alone of all objects is at once both will and idea, while the rest are only ideas, *i.e.,* only phantoms. Thus he must assume that his body is the only real individual in the world, *i.e.,* the only phenomenon of will and the only immediate object of the subject. That other objects, considered merely as *ideas,* are like his body, that is, like it, fill space (which itself can only be present as idea), and also, like it, are causally active in space, is indeed demonstrably certain from the law of causality which is *a priori* valid for ideas, and which admits of no effect without a cause; but apart from the fact that we can only reason from an effect to a cause generally, and not to a similar cause, we are still in the sphere of mere ideas, in which alone the law of causality is valid, and beyond which it can never take us. But whether the objects known to the individual only as ideas are yet, like his own body, manifestations of a will, is, as was said in Book I the proper meaning of the question as to the reality of the external world. To deny this is *theoretical egoism,* which on that account regards all phenomena that are outside its own will as phantoms, just as in a practical reference exactly the same thing is done by practical egoism. For in it a man regards and treats himself alone as a person, and all other persons as mere phantoms. Theoretical egoism can never be demonstrably refuted, yet in philosophy it has never been used otherwise than as a sceptical sophism, *i.e.,* a pretence. As a serious conviction, on the other hand, it could only be found in a madhouse, and as such it stands in need of a cure rather than a refutation. We do not therefore combat it any further in this regard, but treat it as merely the last stronghold of scepticism, which is always polemical. Thus our knowledge, which is always bound to individuality and is limited by this circumstance, brings with it the necessity that each of us can only *be one,* while, on the other hand, each of us can *know all;* and it is this limitation that creates the need for philosophy. We therefore who, for this very reason, are striving to extend the limits of our knowledge through philosophy, will treat this sceptical argument of theoretical egoism which meets us, as an army would treat a small frontier fortress. The fortress cannot indeed be taken, but the garrison can never sally forth from it, and therefore we pass it by without danger, and are not afraid to have it in our rear.

The double knowledge which each of us has of the nature and activity of his own body, and which is given in two completely different ways, has now been clearly brought out. We shall accordingly make further use of it as a key to the nature of every phenomenon in nature, and shall judge of all objects which are not our own bodies, and are consequently not given to our consciousness in a double way but only as ideas, according to the analogy of our own bodies, and shall therefore assume that as in one respect they are idea, just like our bodies, and in this respect are analogous to them, so in another aspect, what remains of objects when we set aside their existence as idea of the subject, must in its inner nature be the same as that in us which we call *will.* For what other kind of existence or reality should we attribute to the rest of the material world? Whence should we take the elements out of which we construct such a world? Besides will and idea nothing is known to us or thinkable. If we wish to attribute the greatest known reality to the material world which exists immediately only in our idea, we give it the reality which our own body has for each of us; for that is the most real thing for every one. But if we now analyse the reality of this body and its actions, beyond the fact that it is idea, we find nothing in it except the will; with this its reality is exhausted. Therefore we can nowhere find another kind of reality which we can attribute to the material world. Thus if we hold that the material world is something more than merely our idea, we must say that besides being idea, that is, in itself and according to its inmost nature, it is that which we find immediately in ourselves as *will.* I say according to its inmost nature; but we must first come to know more accurately this real nature of the will, in order that we may be able to distinguish from it what does not belong to itself, but to its manifestation, which has many grades. . . .

§ 20. As we have said, the will proclaims itself primarily in the voluntary movements of our own body, as the inmost nature of this body, as that which it is besides being object of perception, idea. For these voluntary movements are nothing else but the visible aspect of the individual acts of will, with which they are directly coincident and identical, and only distinguished through the form of knowledge into which they have passed, and in which alone they can be known, the form of idea.

But these acts of will have always a ground or reason outside themselves in motives. Yet these motives never determine more than what I will at *this* time, in *this* place, and under *these* circumstances, not *that* I will in general, or *what* I will in general, that is, the maxims which characterize my volition generally. Therefore the inner nature of my volition cannot be explained from these motives; but they merely determine its manifestation at a given point of time: they are merely the occasion of my will showing itself; but the will itself lies outside the province of the law of motivation, which determines nothing but its appearance at each point of time. It is only under the presupposition of my empirical character that the motive is a sufficient ground of explanation of my action. But if I abstract from my character, and then ask why, in general, I will this and not that, no answer is possible, because it is only the manifestation of the will that is subject to the principle of sufficient reason, and not the will itself, which in this respect is to be called *groundless*. . . .

Thus, although every particular action, under the presupposition of the definite character, necessarily follows from the given motive, and although growth, the process of nourishment, and all the changes of the animal body take place according to necessarily acting causes (stimuli), yet the whole series of actions, and consequently every individual act, and also its condition, the whole body itself which accomplishes it, and therefore also the process through which and in which it exists, are nothing but the manifestation of the will, the becoming visible, *the objectification of the will*. Upon this rests the perfect suitableness of the human and animal body to the human and animal will in general, resembling, though far surpassing, the correspondence between an instrument made for a purpose and the will of the maker, and on this account appearing as design, *i.e.,* the teleological explanation of the body. The parts of the body must, therefore, completely correspond to the principal desires through which the will manifests itself; they must be the visible expression of these desires. Teeth, throat, and bowels are objectified hunger; the organs of generation are objectified sexual desire; the grasping hand, the hurrying feet, correspond to the more indirect desires of the will which they express. As the human form generally corresponds to the human will generally, so the individual bodily structure corresponds to the individually modified will, the character of the individual, and therefore it is throughout and in all parts characteristic and full of expression. . . .

§ 21. Whoever has now gained from all these expositions a knowledge *in abstracto,* and therefore clear and certain, of what every one knows directly *in concreto, i.e.,* as feeling, a knowledge that his will is the real inner nature of his phenomenal being, which manifests itself to him as idea, both in his actions and in their permanent substratum, his body, and that his will is that which is most immediate in his consciousness, though it has not as such completely passed into the form of idea in which object and subject stand over against each other, but makes itself known to him in a direct manner, in which he does not quite clearly distinguish subject and object, yet is not known as a whole to the individual himself, but only in its particular acts,—whoever, I say, has with me gained this conviction will find that of itself it affords him the key to the knowledge of the inmost being of the whole of nature; for he now transfers it to all those phenomena which are not given to him, like his own phenomenal existence, both in direct and indirect knowledge, but only in the latter, thus merely onesidedly as *idea* alone. He will recognise this will of which we are speaking not only in those phenomenal existences which exactly resemble his own, in men and animals as their inmost nature, but the course of reflection will lead him to recognise the force which germinates and vegetates in the plant, and indeed the force through which the crystal is formed, that by which the magnet turns to the North Pole, the force whose shock he experiences from the contact of two different kinds of metals, the force which appears in the elective affinities of matter as repulsion and attraction, decomposition and combination, and, lastly, even gravitation, which acts so powerfully throughout matter, draws the stone to the earth and the earth to the sun,—all these, I say, he will recognise as different only in their phenomenal existence, but in their inner nature as identical, as that which is directly known to him so intimately and so much better than anything else, and which in its most distinct manifestation is called *will*. It is this application of reflection alone that prevents us from remaining any longer at the phenomenon, and leads us to the *thing in itself*. Phenomenal existence is idea and nothing more. All idea, of whatever kind it may be, all *object*, is *phenomenal* existence, but the *will* alone is a *thing in itself*. As such, it is throughout not idea, but *toto genere* different from it; it is that of which all idea, all object, is the phenomenal appearance, the visibility, the objectification. It is the inmost nature, the kernel, of every particular thing, and also of the whole. It appears in every blind force of nature and also in the preconsidered action of man; and the great difference between these two is merely in the degree of the manifestation, not in the nature of what manifests itself.

§ 25. We know that *multiplicity* in general is necessarily conditioned by space and time, and is only thinkable in them. In this respect they are called the *principium individuationis*. But we have found that space and time are forms of the principle of sufficient reason. In this principle all our knowledge a priori is expressed, but, as we showed above, this a priori knowledge, as such, only applies to the knowableness of things, not to the things themselves, *i.e.*, it is only our form of knowledge, it is not a property of the thing-in-itself. The thing-in-itself is, as such, free from all forms of knowledge, even the most universal, that of being an object for the subject. In other words, the thing-in-itself is something altogether different from the idea. If, now, this thing-in-itself is *the will*, as I believe I have fully and convincingly proved it to be; then, regarded as such and apart from its manifestation, it lies outside time and space, and therefore knows no multiplicity, and is consequently *one*. Yet, as I have said, it is not one in the sense in which an individual or a concept is one, but as something to which the condition of the possibility of multiplicity, the *principium individuationis*, is foreign. The multiplicity of things in space and time, which collectively constitute the objectification of will, does not affect the will itself, which remains indivisible notwithstanding it. It is not the case that, in some way or other, a smaller part of will is in the stone and a larger part in the man, for the relation of part and whole belongs exclusively to space, and has no longer any meaning when we go beyond this form of intuition or perception. The more and the less have application only to the phenomenon of will, that is, its visibility, its objectification. Of this there is a higher grade in the plant than in the stone; in the animal a higher grade than in the plant: indeed, the passage of will into visibility, its objectification, has grades as innumerable as exist between the dimmest twilight and the brightest sunshine, the loudest sound and the faintest echo. We shall return later to the consideration of these grades of visibility which belong to the objectification of the will, to the reflection of its nature. But as the grades of its objectification do not directly concern the will itself, still less is it concerned by the multiplicity of the phenomena of these different grades, *i.e.,* the multitude of individuals of each form, or the particular manifestations of each force. For this multiplicity is directly conditioned by time and space, into which the will itself never enters. The will reveals itself as completely and as much in *one* oak as in millions. Their number and multiplication in space and time has no meaning with regard to it, but only with regard to the multiplicity of individuals who know in space and time, and who are themselves multiplied and dispersed in these. The multiplicity of these individuals itself belongs not to the will, but only to its manifestation. We may therefore say that if, *per impossibile,* a single real existence, even the most insignificant, were to be entirely annihilated, the whole world would necessarily perish with it. The great mystic Angelus Silesius feels this when he says:—

> I know God cannot live an instant without me,
> He must give up the ghost if I should cease to be.

Men have tried in various ways to bring the immeasurable greatness of the material universe nearer to the comprehension of us all, and then they have seized the opportunity to make edifying remarks. They have referred perhaps to the relative smallness of the earth, and indeed of man; or, on the contrary, they have pointed out the greatness of the mind of this man who is so insignificant—the mind that can solve, comprehend, and even measure the greatness of the universe, and so forth. Now, all this is very well, but to me, when I consider the vastness of the world, the most important point is this, that the thing-in-itself, whose manifestation is the world—whatever else it may be—cannot have its true self spread out and dispersed after this fashion in boundless space, but that this endless extension belongs only to its manifestation. The thing-in-itself, on the contrary, is present entire and undivided in every object of nature and in every living being. Therefore we lose nothing by standing still beside any single individual thing, and true wisdom is not to be gained by measuring out the boundless world, or, what would be more to the purpose, by actually traversing endless space. It is rather to be attained by the thorough investigation of any individual thing, for thus we seek to arrive at a full knowledge and understanding of its true and peculiar nature.

The subject which will therefore be fully considered in the next book, and which has, doubtless, already presented itself to the mind of every student of Plato, is, that these different grades of the objectification of will which are manifested in innumerable individuals, and exist as their unattained types or as the eternal forms of things, not entering themselves into time and space, which are the medium of individual things, but remaining fixed, subject to no change, always being, never becoming, while the particular things arise and pass away, always become and never are,—that these *grades of the objectification of will* are, I say, simply *Plato's Ideas.* I make this passing reference to the matter here in order that I may be able in future to use the word *Idea* in this sense. In my writings, therefore, the word is always to be understood in its true and original meaning given to it by Plato, and has absolutely no reference to those abstract productions of dogmatising scholastic reason, which Kant has inaptly and illegitimately used this word to denote, though Plato had already appropriated and used it most fitly. By Idea, then, I understand every definite and fixed grade of the objectification of will, so far as it is thing-in-itself, and therefore has no multiplicity. These grades are related to individual things as their eternal forms or prototypes. . . .

§ 26. The lowest grades of the objectification of will are to be found in those most universal forces of nature which partly appear in all matter without exception, as gravity and impenetrability, and partly have shared the given matter among them, so that certain of them reign in one species of matter and others in another species, constituting its specific difference, as rigidity, fluidity, elasticity, electricity, magnetism, chemical properties and qualities of every kind. They are in themselves immediate manifestations of will, just as much as human action; and as such they are groundless, like human character. Only their particular manifestations are subordinated to the principle of sufficient reason, like the particular actions of men. They themselves, on the other hand, can never be called either effect or cause, but are the prior and presupposed conditions of all causes and effects through which their real nature unfolds and reveals itself. It is therefore senseless to demand a cause of gravity or electricity, for they are original forces. . . . It is therefore a mistake to say "gravity is the cause of a stone falling"; for the cause in this case is rather the nearness of the earth, because it attracts the stone. Take the earth away and the stone will not fall, although gravity remains. The force itself lies quite outside the chain of causes and effects, which presupposes time, because it only has meaning in relation to it; but the force lies outside time. . . .

In the higher grades of the objectivity of will we see individuality occupy a prominent position, especially in the case of man, where it appears as the great difference of individual characters, *i.e.,* as complete personality, outwardly expressed in strongly marked individual physiognomy, which influences the whole bodily form. None of the brutes have this individuality in anything like so high a degree, though the higher species of them have a trace of it; but the character of the species completely predominates over it, and therefore they have little individual physiognomy. . . .

Thus every universal, original force of nature is nothing but a low grade of the objectification of will, and we call every such grade an eternal *Idea* in Plato's sense. But a *Law of Nature* is the relation of the Idea to the form of its manifestation. This form is time, space, and causality, which are necessarily and inseparably connected and related to each other. Through time and space the Idea multiplies itself in innumerable phenomena, but the order according to which it enters these forms of multiplicity is definitely determined by the law of causality; this law is as it were the norm of the limit of these phenomena of different Ideas, in accordance with which time, space, and matter are assigned to them. This norm is therefore necessarily related to the identity of the aggregate of existing matter, which is the common substratum of all those different phenomena. If all these were not directed to that common matter in the possession of which they must be divided, there would be no need for such a law to decide their claims. They might all at once and together fill a boundless space throughout an endless time. Therefore, because all these phenomena of the eternal Ideas are directed to one and the same matter, must there be a rule for their appearance and disappearance; for if there were not, they would not make way for each other. Thus the law of causality is essentially bound up with that of the permanence of substance; they reciprocally derive significance from each other. Time and space, again, are related to them in the same way. For time is merely the possibility of conflicting states of the same matter, and space is merely the possibility of the permanence of the same matter under all sorts of conflicting states. . . .

§ 27. . . . It follows from all that has been said that it is certainly an error on the part of natural science to seek to refer the higher grades of the objectification of will to the lower; for the failure to recognise, or the denial of, original and self-existing forces of nature is just as wrong as the groundless assumption of special forces when what occurs is merely a peculiar kind of manifestation of what is already known. Thus Kant rightly says that it would be absurd to hope for a blade of grass from a Newton, that is, from one who reduced the blade of grass to the manifestations of physical and chemical forces, of which it was the chance product, and therefore a mere freak of nature, in which no special Idea appeared, *i.e.,* the will did not directly reveal itself in it in a higher and specific grade, but just as in the phenomena of unorganised nature and by chance in this form. On the other hand, it is not to be overlooked that in all Ideas, that is, in all forces of unorganised, and all forms of organised nature, it is *one and the same* will that reveals itself, that is to say, which enters the form of the idea and passes into *objectivity*. Its unity must therefore be also recognisable through an inner relationship between all its phenomena. Now this reveals itself in the higher grades of the objectification of will, where the whole phenomenon is more distinct, thus in the vegetable and animal kingdoms, through the universally prevailing analogy of all forms, the fundamental type which recurs in all phenomena. . . . To discover this fundamental type has been the chief concern, or at any rate the praiseworthy endeavor, of the natural philosophers of the school of Schelling, who have in this respect considerable merit, although in many cases their hunt after analogies in nature degenerated into mere conceits. They have, however, rightly shown that that general relationship and family likeness exists also in the ideas of unorganised nature; for example, between electricity and magnetism, the identity of which was afterwards established; between chemical attraction and gravitation, and so forth. They specially called attention to the fact that *polarity,* that is, the sundering of a force into two qualitatively different and opposed activities striving after reunion, which also shows itself for the most part in space as a dispersion in opposite directions, is a fundamental type of almost all the phenomena of nature, from the magnet and the crystal to man himself. Yet this knowledge has been current in China from the earliest times, in the doctrine of opposition of Yin and Yang. . . .

According to the view I have expressed, the traces of chemical and physical modes of operation will indeed be found in the organism, but it can never be explained from them; because it is by no means a phenomenon even accidentally brought about through the united actions of such forces, but a higher Idea which has overcome these lower Ideas by *subduing assimilation;* for the *one* will which objectifies itself in all Ideas always seeks the highest possible objectification, and has therefore in this case given up the lower grades of its manifestation after a conflict, in order to appear in a higher grade, and one so much the more powerful. No victory without conflict: since the higher Idea or objectification of will can only appear through the conquest of the lower, it endures the opposition of these lower Ideas, which, although brought into subjection, still constantly strive to obtain an independent and complete expression of their being. The magnet that has attracted a piece of iron carries on a perpetual conflict with gravitation, which, as the lower objectification of will, has a prior right to the matter of the iron; and in this constant battle the magnet indeed grows stronger, for the opposition excites it, as it were, to greater effort. In the same way every manifestation of the will, including that which expresses itself in the human organism, wages a constant war against the many physical and chemical forces which, as lower Ideas, have a prior right to that matter. Thus the arm falls which for a while, overcoming gravity, we have held stretched out; thus the pleasing sensation of health, which proclaims the victory of the Idea of the self-conscious organism over the physical and chemical laws, which originally governed the humors of the body, is so often interrupted, and is indeed always accompanied by greater or less discomfort, which arises from the resistance of these forces, and on account of which the vegetative part of our life is constantly attended by slight pain. Thus also digestion weakens all the animal functions, because it requires the whole vital force to overcome the chemical forces of nature by assimilation. Hence also in general the burden of physical life, the necessity of sleep, and, finally, of death; for at last these subdued forces of nature, assisted by circumstances, win back from the organism, wearied even by the constant victory, the matter it took from them, and attain to an unimpeded expression of their being. We may therefore say that every organism expresses the Idea of which it is the image, only after we have subtracted the part of its force which is expended in subduing the lower Ideas that strive with it for matter. This seems to have been running in the mind of Jacob Böhme when he says somewhere that all the bodies of men and animals, and even all plants, are really half dead. According as the subjection in the organism of these forces of nature, which express the lower grades of the objectification of will, is more or less successful, the more or the less completely does it attain to the expression of its Idea; that is to say, the nearer it is to the *ideal* or the further from it—the *ideal* of beauty in its species.

Thus everywhere in nature we see strife, conflict, and alternation of victory, and in it we shall come to recognise more distinctly that variance with itself which is essential to the will. . . . Thus the will to live everywhere preys upon itself, and in different forms is its own nourishment, till finally the human race, because it subdues all the others, regards nature as a manufactory for its use. Yet even the human race, as we shall see in Book IV, reveals in itself with most terrible distinctness this conflict, this variance with itself of the will, and we find *homo homini lupus*. Meanwhile we can recognise this strife, this subjugation, just as well in the lower grades of the objectification of will. Many insects (especially ichneumon-flies) lay their eggs on the skin, and even in the body of the larvae of other insects, whose slow destruction is the first work of the newly hatched brood. . . . But the bulldog-ant of Australia affords us the most extraordinary example of this kind; for if it is cut in two, a battle begins between the head and the tail. The head seizes the tail with its teeth and the tail defends itself bravely by stinging the head: the battle may last for half an hour, until they die or are dragged away by other ants. This contest takes place every time the experiment is tried. On the banks of the Missouri one sometimes sees a mighty oak the stem and branches of which are so encircled, fettered, and interlaced by a gigantic wild vine, that it withers as if choked. . . .

Thus knowledge generally, rational as well as merely sensuous, proceeds originally from the will itself, belongs to the inner being of the higher grades of its objectification as a mere means of supporting the individual and the species, just like any organ of the body. Originally destined for the service of the will for the accomplishment of its aims, it remains almost throughout entirely subjected to its service: it is so in all brutes and in almost all men. . . .

BOOK III: THE WORLD AS IDEA

SECOND ASPECT. THE IDEA INDEPENDENT OF THE PRINCIPLE OF SUFFICIENT REASON: THE PLATONIC IDEA: THE OBJECT OF ART

§ 32. It follows from our consideration of the subject, that, for us, Idea and thing-in-itself are not entirely one and the same, in spite of the inner agreement between Kant and Plato, and the identity of the aim they had before them or the conception of the world which roused them and led them to philosophise. The Idea is for us rather the direct, and therefore adequate, objectivity of the thing-in-itself, which is, however, itself the *will*—the will as not yet objectified, not yet become idea. For the thing-in-itself must, even according to Kant, be free from all the forms connected with knowing as such; and it is merely an error on his part that he did not count among these forms, before all others, that of being object for a subject, for it is the first and most universal form of all phenomena, *i.e.,* of all idea; he should therefore have distinctly denied objective existence to this thing-in-itself, which would have saved him from a great inconsistency that was soon discovered. The Platonic

Idea, on the other hand, is necessarily object, something known, an idea, and in that respect is different from the thing-in-itself, but in that respect only. It has merely laid aside the subordinate forms of the phenomenon, all of which we include in the principle of sufficient reason, or rather it has not yet assumed them; but it has retained the first and most universal form, that of the idea in general, the form of being object for a subject. It is the forms which are subordinate to this (whose general expression is the principle of sufficient reason) that multiply the Idea in particular transitory individuals, whose number is a matter of complete indifference to the Idea. The principle of sufficient reason is thus again the form into which the Idea centers when it appears in the knowledge of the subject as individual. The particular thing that manifests itself in accordance with the principle of sufficient reason is thus only an indirect objectification of the thing-in-itself (which is the will), for between it and the thing-in-itself stands the Idea as the only direct objectivity of the will, because it has assumed none of the special forms of knowledge as such, except that of the idea in general, *i.e.,* the form of being object for a subject. Therefore it alone is the most *adequate objectivity* of the will or thing-in-itself which is possible; indeed it is the whole thing-in-itself, only under the form of the idea; and here lies the ground of the great agreement between Plato and Kant, although, in strict accuracy, that of which they speak is not the same. But the particular things are no really adequate objectivity of the will, for in them it is obscured by those forms whose general expression is the principle of sufficient reason, but which are conditions of the knowledge which belongs to the individual as such. If it is allowable to draw conclusions from an impossible presupposition, we would, in fact, no longer know particular things, not events, nor change, nor multiplicity, but would comprehend only Ideas,—only the grades of the objectification of that one will, of the thing-in-itself, in pure unclouded knowledge. Consequently our world would be a *nunc stans,* if it were not that, as knowing subjects, we are also individuals, *i.e.,* our perceptions come to us through the medium of a body, from the affections of which they proceed, and which is itself only concrete willing, objectivity of the will, and thus is an object among objects, and as such comes into the knowing consciousness in the only way in which an object can, through the forms of the principle of sufficient reason, and consequently already presupposes, and therefore brings in, time, and all other forms which that principle expresses. Time is only the broken and piecemeal view which the individual being has of the Ideas, which are outside time, and consequently *eternal.* Therefore Plato says time is the moving picture of eternity.

§ 33. Since now, as individuals, we have no other knowledge than that which is subject to the principle of sufficient reason, and this form of knowledge excludes the Ideas, it is certain that if it is possible for us to raise ourselves from the knowledge of particular things to that of the Ideas, this can only happen by an alteration taking place in the subject which is analogous and corresponds to the great change of the whole nature of the object, and by virtue of which the subject, so far as it knows an Idea, is no more individual.

It will be remembered from the preceding book that knowledge in general belongs to the objectification of will at its higher grades, and sensibility, nerves, and brain, just like the other parts of the organised being, are the expression of the will at this stage of its objectivity, and therefore the idea which appears through them is also in the same way bound to the service of will as a means for the attainment of its now complicated aims for sustaining a being of manifold requirements. Thus originally, and according to its nature, knowledge is completely subject to the will, and, like the immediate object which, by means of the application of the law of causality, is its starting-point, all knowledge which proceeds in accordance with the principle of sufficient reason remains in a closer or more distant relation to the will. For the individual finds his body as an object among objects, to all of which it is related and connected according to the principle of sufficient reason. Thus all investigations of these relations and connections lead back to his body, and consequently to his will. Since it is the principle of sufficient reason which places the objects in this relation to the body, and, through it, to the will, the one endeavor of the knowledge which is subject to this principle will be to find out the relations in which objects are placed to each other through this principle, and thus to trace their innumerable connections in space, time, and causality. For only through these is the object *interesting* to the individual, *i.e.,* related to the will. Therefore the knowledge which is subject to the will knows nothing further of objects than their relations, knows the objects only so far as they exist at this time, in this place, under these circumstances, from these causes, and with these effects—in a word, as particular things; and if all these relations were to be taken away, the objects would also have disappeared for it, because it knew nothing more about them. We must not disguise the fact that what the sciences consider in things is also in reality nothing more than this; their relations, the connections of time and space, the causes of natural changes, the resemblance of forms, the motives of actions—thus merely relations. What distinguishes science from ordinary knowledge is merely its systematic form, the facilitating of knowledge by the comprehension of all particulars in the universal, by means of the subordination of concepts, and completeness of knowledge which is thereby attained. . . .

Knowledge now, as a rule, remains always subordinate to the service of the will, as indeed it originated for this service, and grew, so to speak, to the will, as the head to the body. In the case of the brutes this subjection of knowledge to the will can never be abolished. In the case of men it can be abolished only in exceptional cases, which we shall presently consider more closely. This distinction between man and brute is outwardly expressed by the difference of the relation of the head to the body. In the case of the lower brutes both are deformed: in all brutes the head is directed towards the earth, where the objects of its will lie: even in the higher species the head and the body are still far more one than in the case of man, whose head seems freely set upon his body, as if only carried by and not serving it. . . .

§ 34. The transition which we have referred to as possible, but yet to be regarded as only exceptional, from the common knowledge of particular things to the knowledge of the Idea, takes place suddenly; for knowledge breaks free from the service of the will, by the subject ceasing to be merely individual, and thus becoming the pure will-less subject of knowledge, which no longer traces relations in accordance with the principle of sufficient reason, but rests in fixed contemplation of the object presented to it, out of its connection with all others, and rises into it. . . .

If, raised by the power of the mind, a man relinquishes the common way of looking at things, gives up tracing, under the guidance of the forms of the principle of sufficient reason, their relations to each other, the final goal of which is always a relation to his own will; if he thus ceases to consider the where, the when, the why, and the whither of things, and looks simply and solely at the *what;* if, further, he does not allow abstract thought, the concepts of the reason, to take possession of his consciousness, but, instead of all this, gives the whole power of his mind to perception, sinks himself entirely in this, and lets his whole consciousness be filled with the quiet contemplation of the natural object actually present, whether a landscape, a tree, a mountain, a building, or whatever it may be; inasmuch as he *loses* himself in this object (to use a pregnant German idiom), *i.e.,* forgets even his individuality, his will, and only continues to exist as the pure subject, the clear mirror of the object, so that it is as if the object alone were there, without any one to perceive it, and he can no longer separate the perceiver from the perception, but both have become one, because the whole consciousness is filled and occupied with one single sensuous picture; if thus the object has to such an extent passed out all relation to something outside it, and the subject out of all relation to the will, then that which is so known is no longer the particular thing as such; but it is the *Idea,* the eternal form, the immediate objectivity of the will at this grade; and, therefore, he who is sunk in this perception is no longer individual, for in such perception the individual has lost himself; but he is *pure,* will-less, painless, timeless *subject of knowledge.*

§ 35. In order to gain a deeper insight into the nature of the world, it is absolutely necessary that we should learn to distinguish the will as thing-in-itself from its adequate objectivity, and also the different grades in which this appears more and more distinctly and fully, *i.e.,* the Ideas themselves, from the merely phenomenal existence of these Ideas in the forms of the principle of sufficient reason, the restricted method of knowledge of the individual. We shall then agree with Plato when he attributes actual being only to the Ideas, and allows only an illusive, dream-like existence to things in space and time, the real world for the individual. Then we shall understand how one and the same Idea reveals itself in so many phenomena, and presents its nature only bit by bit to the individual, one side after another. Then we shall also distinguish the Idea itself from the way in which its manifestation appears in the observation of the individual, and recognise the former as essential and the latter as unessential. Let us consider this with the help of examples taken from the most insignificant things, and also from the greatest. When the clouds move, the figures which they form are not essential, but indifferent to them; but that as elastic vapour they are pressed together, drifted along, spread out, or torn asunder by the force of the wind: this is their nature, the essence of the forces which objectify themselves in them, the Idea; their actual forms are only for the individual observer. To the brook that flows over stones, the eddies, the waves, the foam-flakes which it forms are indifferent and unessential; but that it follows the attraction of gravity, and behaves as inelastic, perfectly mobile, formless, transparent fluid: this is its nature; this, *if known through perception,* is its Idea; these accidental forms are only for us so long as we know as individuals. The ice on the window-pane forms itself into crystals according to the laws of crystallisation, which reveal the essence of the force of nature that appears here, exhibit the Idea; but the trees and flowers which it traces on the pane are unessential, and are only there for us. What appears in the clouds, the brook, and the crystal is the weakest echo of that will which appears more fully in the plant, more fully still in the beast, and most fully in man. But only the essential in all these grades of its objectification constitutes the Idea; on the other hand, its unfolding or development, because broken up in the forms of the principle of sufficient reason into a multiplicity of many-sided phenomena, is unessential to the Idea, lies merely in the kind of knowledge that belongs to the individual and has reality only for this. The same thing necessarily holds good of the unfolding of that Idea which is the completest objectivity of will. Therefore, the history of the human race, the throng of events, the change of times, the multifarious forms of human life in different lands and countries, all this is only the accidental form of the manifestation of the Idea, does not belong to the Idea itself, in which alone lies the adequate objectivity of the will, but only to the phenomenon which appears in the knowledge of the individual, and is just as foreign, unessential, and indifferent to the Idea itself as the figures which they assume are to the clouds, the form of its eddies and foam-flakes to the brook, or its trees and flowers to the ice.

To him who has thoroughly grasped this, and can distinguish between the will and the Idea, and between the Idea and its manifestation, the events of the world will have significance only so far as they are the letters out of which we may read the Idea of man, but not in and for themselves. He will not believe with the vulgar that time may produce something actually new and significant; that through it, or in it, something absolutely real may attain to existence, or indeed that it itself as a whole has beginning and end, plan and development, and in some way has for its final aim the highest perfection (according to their conception) of the last generation of man, whose life is a brief thirty years. Therefore he will just as little, with Homer, people a whole Olympus with gods to guide the events of time, as, with Ossian, he will take the forms of the clouds for individual beings; for, as we have said, both have just as much meaning as regards the Idea which appears in them. In the manifold forms of human life and in the unceasing change of events, he will regard the Idea only as the abiding and essential, in which the will to live has its fullest objectivity, and which shows its different sides in the capacities, the passions, the errors and the excellences of the human race; in self-interest, hatred, love, fear, boldness, frivolity, stupidity, slyness, wit, genius, and so forth, all of which crowding together and combining in thousands of forms (individuals), continually create the history of the great and the little world, in which it is all the same whether they are set in motion by nuts or by crowns. Finally, he will find that in the world it is the same as in the dramas of Dozzi, in all of which the same persons appear, with like intention, and with a like fate; the motives and incidents are certainly different in each piece, but the spirit of the incidents is the same; the actors in one piece know nothing of the incidents of another, although they performed in it themselves; therefore, after all experience of former pieces, Pantaloon has become no more agile or generous, Tartaglia no more conscientious, Brighella no more courageous, and Columbine no more modest.

Suppose we were allowed for once a clearer glance into the kingdom of the possible, and over the whole chain of causes and effects; if the earth-spirit appeared and showed us in a picture all the greatest men, enlighteners of the world, and heroes, that chance destroyed before they were ripe for their work; then the great events that would have changed the history of the world and brought in periods of the highest culture and enlightenment, but which the blindest chance, the most insignificant accident, hindered at the outset; lastly, the splendid powers of great men, that would have enriched whole ages of the world, but which, either misled by error or passion, or compelled by necessity, they squandered uselessly on unworthy or unfruitful objects, or even wasted in play. If we saw all this, we would shudder and lament at the thought of the lost treasures of whole periods of the world. But the earth-spirit would smile and say, "The source from which the individuals and their powers proceed is inexhaustible and unending as time and space; for, like these forms of all phenomena, they also are only phenomena, visibility of the will. No finite measure can exhaust that infinite source; therefore an undiminished eternity is always open for the return of any event or work that was nipped in the bud. In this world of phenomena true loss is just as little possible as true gain. The will alone is; it is the thing-in-itself, and the source of all these phenomena. Its self-knowledge and its assertion or denial, which is then decided upon, is the only event in-itself."

§ 36. History follows the thread of events; it is pragmatic so far as it deduces them in accordance with the law of motivation, a law that determines the self-manifesting will wherever it is enlightened by knowledge. At the lowest grades of its objectivity, where it still acts without knowledge, natural science, in the form of etiology, treats of the laws of the changes of its phenomena, and, in the form of morphology, of what is permanent in them. This almost endless task is lightened by the aid of concepts, which comprehend what is general in order that we may deduce what is particular from it. Lastly, mathematics treats of the mere forms, time and space, in which the Ideas, broken up into multiplicity, appear for the knowledge of the subject as individual. All these, of which the common name is science, proceed according to the principle of sufficient reason in its different forms, and their theme is always the phenomenon, its laws, connections, and the relations which result from them. But what kind of knowledge is concerned with that which is outside and independent of all relations, that which alone is really essential to the world, the true content of its phenomena, that which is subject to no change, and therefore is known with equal truth for all time, in a word, the *Ideas,* which are the direct and adequate objectivity of the thing-in-itself, the will? We answer, *Art,* the work of genius. It repeats or reproduces the eternal Ideas grasped through pure contemplation, the essential and abiding in all the phenomena of the world; and according to what the material is in which it reproduces, it is sculpture or painting, poetry or music. Its one source is the knowledge of Ideas; its one aim the communication of this knowledge. While science, following the unresting and inconstant stream of the four-fold forms of reason and consequent, with each end attained sees further, and can never reach a final goal nor attain full satisfaction, any more than by running we can reach the place where the clouds touch the horizon; art, on the contrary, is everywhere at its goal. For it plucks the object of its contemplation out of the stream of the world's course, and has it isolated before it. And this particular thing, which in that stream was a small perishing part, becomes to art the representative of the whole, an equivalent of the endless multitude in space and time. It therefore pauses at this particular thing; the course of time stops; the relations vanish for it; only the essential, the Idea, is its object. We may, therefore, accurately define it as the *way of viewing things independent of the principle of sufficient reason,* in opposition to the way of viewing them which proceeds in accordance with that principle, and which is the method of experience and of science. This last method of considering things may be compared to a line infinitely extended in a horizontal direction, and the former to a vertical line which cuts it at any point. The method of viewing things which proceeds in accordance with the principle of sufficient reason is the rational method, and it alone is valid and of use in practical life and in science. The method which looks away from the content of this principle is the method of genius, which is only valid and of use in art. The first is the method of Aristotle; the second is, on the whole, that of Plato. The first is like the mighty storm, that rushes along without beginning and without aim, bending, agitating, and carrying away everything before it; the second is like the silent sunbeam, that pierces through the storm quite unaffected by it. The first is like the innumerable showering drops of the waterfall, which, constantly changing, never rest for an instant; the second is like the rainbow, quietly resting on this raging torrent. Only through the pure contemplation described above, which ends entirely in the object, can Ideas be comprehended; and the nature of *genius* consists in pre-eminent capacity for such contemplation. Now, as this requires that a man should entirely forget himself and the relations in which he stands, *genius* is simply the completest *objectivity, i.e.,* the objective tendency of the mind, as opposed to the subjective, which is directed to one's own self—in other words, to the will. Thus genius is the faculty of continuing the state of pure perception, of losing oneself in perception, and of enlisting in this service the knowledge which originally existed only for the service of the will; that is to say, genius is the power of leaving one's own interests, wishes, and aims entirely out of sight, thus of entirely renouncing one's own personality for a time, so as to remain *pure knowing subject,* clear vision of the world; and this not merely at moments, but for a sufficient length of time, and with sufficient consciousness, to enable one to reproduce by deliberate art what has thus been apprehended, and "to fix in lasting thoughts the wavering images that float before the mind." It is as if, when genius appears in an individual, a far larger measure of the power of knowledge falls to his lot than is necessary for the service of an individual will; and this superfluity of knowledge, being free, now becomes subject purified from will, a clear mirror of the inner nature of the world. This explains the activity, amounting even to disquietude, of men of genius, for the present can seldom satisfy them, because it does not fill their consciousness. This gives them that restless aspiration, that unceasing desire for new things, and for the contemplation of lofty things, and also that longing that is hardly ever satisfied, for men of similar nature and of like stature, to whom they might communicate themselves; while the common mortal, entirely filled and satisfied by the common present, ends in it, and finding everywhere his like, enjoys that peculiar satisfaction in daily life that is denied to genius.

. . . .

BOOK IV: THE WORLD AS WILL

SECOND ASPECT. THE ASSERTION AND DENIAL OF THE WILL TO LIVE, WHEN SELF-CONSCIOUSNESS HAS BEEN ATTAINED

§ 54. . . . The will, which, considered purely in itself, is without knowledge, and is merely a blind incessant impulse, as we see it appear in unorganized and vegetable nature and their laws, and also in the vegetative part of our own life, receives through the addition of the world as idea, which is developed in subjection to it, the knowledge of its own willing and of what it is that it wills. And this is nothing else but the world as idea, life, precisely as it exists. Therefore we called the phenomenal world the mirror of the will, its objectivity. And since what the will wills is always life, just because life is nothing but the representation of that willing for the idea, it is all one and a mere pleonasm if, instead of simply saying "the will," we say "the will to live." . . .

Above all things, we must distinctly recognise that the form of the phenomenon of will, the form of life or reality, is really only the *present,* not the future nor the past. The latter are only in the conception, exist only in the connection of knowledge, so far as it follows the principle of sufficient reason. No man has ever lived in the past, and none will live in the future; the *present* alone is the form of all life, and is its sure possession which can never be taken from it. . . . The present is the form essential to the objectification of the will. It cuts time, which extends infinitely in both directions, as a mathematical point, and stands immovably fixed, like an everlasting mid-day with no cool evening, as the actual sun burns without intermission, while it only seems to sink into the bosom of night. Therefore, if a man fears death as his annihilation, it is just as if he were to think that the sun cries out at evening, "Woe is me! for I go down into eternal night." And conversely, whoever is oppressed with the burdens of life, whoever desires life and affirms it, but abhors its torments, and especially can no longer endure the hard lot that has fallen to himself, such a man has no deliverance to hope for from death, and cannot right himself by suicide. The cool shades of Orcus allure him only with the false appearance of a haven of rest. The earth rolls from day into night, the individual dies, but the sun itself shines without intermission, an eternal noon. Life is assured to the will to live; the form of life is an endless present, no matter how the individuals, the phenomena of the Idea, arise and pass away in time, like fleeting dreams. . . .

But this that we have brought to clearest consciousness, that although the particular phenomenon of the will has a temporal beginning and end, the will itself as thing-in-itself is not affected by it, nor yet the correlative of all object, the knowing but never known subject, and that life is always assured to the will to live—this is not to be numbered with the doctrines of immortality. For permanence has no more to do with the will or with the pure subject of knowing, the eternal eye of the world, than transitoriness, for both are predicates that are only valid in time, and the will and the pure subject of knowing lie outside time. Therefore the egoism of the individual (this particular phenomenon of will enlightened by the subject of knowing) can extract as little nourishment and consolation for his wish to endure through endless time from the view we have expressed, as he could from the knowledge that after his death the rest of the eternal world would continue to exist, which is just the expression of the same view considered objectively, and therefore temporally. For every individual is transitory only as phenomenon, but as thing-in-itself is timeless, and therefore endless. But it is also only as phenomenon that an individual is distinguished from the other things of the world; as thing-in-itself he is the will which appears in all, and death destroys the illusion which separates his consciousness from that of the rest: this is immortality. . . . What we fear in death is the end of the individual which it openly professes itself to be, and since the individual is a particular objectification of the will to live itself, its whole nature struggles against death. Now when feeling thus exposes us helpless, reason can yet step in and for the most part overcome its adverse influence, for it places us upon a higher standpoint, from which we no longer contemplate the particular but the whole. Therefore a philosophical knowledge of the nature of the world, which extended to the point we have now reached in this work but went no farther, could even at this point of view overcome the terror of death in the measure in which reflection had power over direct feeling in the given individual. A man who had thoroughly assimilated the truths we have already advanced, but had not come to know, either from his own experience or from a deeper insight, that constant suffering is essential to life, who found satisfaction and all that he wished in life, and could calmly and deliberately desire that his life, as he had hitherto known it, should endure for ever or repeat itself ever anew, and whose love of life was so great that he willingly and gladly accepted all the hardships and miseries to which it is exposed for the sake of its pleasures—such a man would stand "with firm-knit bones on the well-rounded, enduring earth," and would have nothing to fear. Armed with the knowledge we have given him, he would await with indifference the death that hastens towards him on the wings of time. He would regard it as a false illusion, an impotent spectre, which frightens the weak but has no power over him who knows that he is himself the will of which the whole world is the objectification or copy, and that therefore he is always certain of life, and also of the present, the peculiar and only form of the phenomenon of the will. He could not be terrified by an endless past or future in which he would not be, for this he would regard as the empty delusion of the web of Mâyâ. Thus he would no more fear death than the sun fears the night. In the *Bhagavad-Gita*, Krishna thus raises the mind of his young pupil Arjuna, when, seized with compunction at the sight of the arrayed hosts (somewhat as Xerxes was), he loses heart and desires to give up the battle in order to avert the death of so many thousands. Krishna leads him to this point of view, and the death of those thousands can no longer restrain him; he gives the sign for battle. . . .

§ 57. At every grade that is enlightened by knowledge, the will appears as an individual. The human individual finds himself as finite in infinite space and time, and consequently as a vanishing quantity compared with them. He is projected into them, and, on account of their unlimited nature, he has always a merely relative, never absolute *when* and *where* of his existence; for his place and duration are finite parts of what is infinite and boundless. His real existence is only in the present, whose unchecked flight into the past is a constant transition into death a constant dying. For his past life, apart from its possible consequences for the present, and the testimony regarding the will that is expressed in it, is now entirely done with, dead, and no longer anything; and, therefore, it must be, as a matter of reason, indifferent to him whether the content of that past was pain or pleasure. But the present is always passing through his hands into the past; the future is quite uncertain and always short. Thus his existence, even when we consider only its formal side, is a constant hurrying of the present into the dead past, a constant dying. But if we look at it from the physical side, it is clear that, as our walking is admittedly merely a constantly prevented falling, the life of our body is only a constantly prevented dying, an ever-postponed death: finally, in the same way, the activity of our mind is a constantly deferred ennui. Every breath we draw wards off the death that is constantly intruding upon us. In this way we fight with it every moment, and again, at longer intervals, through every meal we eat, every sleep we take, every time we warm ourselves, etc. In the end, death must conquer, for we became subject to him through birth, and he only plays for a little while with his prey before he swallows it up. We pursue our life, however, with great interest and much solicitude as long as possible, as we blow out a soap-bubble as long and as large as possible, although we know perfectly well that it will burst.

We saw that the inner being of unconscious nature is a constant striving without end and without rest. And this appears to us much more distinctly when we consider the nature of brutes and man. Willing and striving is its whole being, which may be very well compared to an unquenchable thirst. But the basis of all willing is need, deficiency, and thus pain. Consequently, the nature of brutes and man is subject to pain originally and through its very being. If, on the other hand, it lacks objects of desire, because it is at once deprived of them by a too easy satisfaction, a terrible void and ennui comes over it, *i.e.,* its being and existence itself becomes an unbearable burden to it. Thus its life swings like a pendulum backwards and forwards between pain and ennui. This has also had to express itself very oddly in this way; after man had transferred all pain and torments to hell, there then remained nothing over for heaven but ennui.

But the constant striving which constitutes the inner nature of every manifestation of will obtains its primary and most general foundation at the higher grades of objectification, from the fact that here the will manifests itself as a living body, with the iron command to nourish it; and what gives strength to this command is just that this body is nothing but the objectified will to live itself. Man, as the most complete objectification of that will, is in like measure also the most necessitous of all beings: he is through and through concrete willing and needing; he is a concretion of a thousand necessities. With these he stands upon the earth, left to himself, uncertain about everything except his own need and misery. Consequently the care for the maintenance of that existence under exacting demands, which are renewed every day, occupies, as a rule, the whole of human life. To this is directly related the second claim, that of the propagation of the species. At the same time he is threatened from all sides by the most different kinds of dangers, from which it requires constant watchfulness to escape. With cautious steps and casting anxious glances round him he pursues his path, for a thousand accidents and a thousand enemies lie in wait for him. Thus he went while yet a savage, thus he goes in civilised life; there is no security for him. . . .

The life of the great majority is only a constant struggle for this existence itself, with the certainty of losing it at last. But what enables them to endure this wearisome battle is not so much the love of life as the fear of death, which yet stands in the background as inevitable, and may come upon them at any moment. Life itself is a sea, full of rocks and whirlpools, which man avoids with the greatest care and solicitude, although he knows that even if he succeeds in getting through with all his efforts and skill, he yet by doing so comes nearer at every step to the greatest, the total, inevitable, and irremediable shipwreck, death;

nay, even steers right upon it: this is the final goal of the laborious voyage, and worse for him than all the rocks from which he has escaped.

Now it is well worth observing that, on the one hand, the suffering and misery of life may easily increase to such an extent that death itself, in the flight from which the whole of life consists, becomes desirable, and we hasten towards it voluntarily; and again, on the other hand, that as soon as want and suffering permit rest to a man, ennui is at once so near that he necessarily requires diversion. The striving after existence is what occupies all living things and maintains them in motion. But when existence is assured, then they know not what to do with it; thus the second thing that sets them in motion is the effort to get free from the burden of existence, to make it cease to be felt, "to kill time," *i.e.,* to escape from ennui. Accordingly we see that almost all men who are secure from want and care, now that at last they have thrown off all other burdens, become a burden to themselves, and regard as a gain every hour they succeed in getting through, and thus every diminution of the very life which, till then, they have employed all their powers to maintain as long as possible. Ennui is by no means an evil to be lightly esteemed; in the end it depicts on the countenance real despair. It makes beings who love each other so little as men do, seek each other eagerly, and thus becomes the source of social intercourse. Moreover, even from motives of policy, public precautions are everywhere taken against it, as against other universal calamities. For this evil may drive men to the greatest excesses, just as much as its opposite extreme, famine: the people require *panem et circenses.* The strict penitentiary system of Philadelphia makes use of ennui alone as a means of punishment, through solitary confinement and idleness, and it is found so terrible that it has even led prisoners to commit suicide. As want is the constant scourge of the people, so ennui is that of the fashionable world. In middle-class life ennui is represented by the Sunday, and want by the six week-days.

Thus between desiring and attaining all human life flows on throughout. The wish is, in its nature, pain; the attainment soon begets satiety: the end was only apparent; possession takes away the charm; the wish, the need, presents itself under a new form; when it does not, then follows desolateness, emptiness, ennui, against which the conflict is just as painful as against want. That wish and satisfaction should follow each other neither too quickly nor too slowly reduces the suffering which both occasion to the smallest amount, and constitutes the happiest life. For that which we might otherwise call the most beautiful part of life, its purest joy, if it were only because it lifts us out of real existence and transforms us into disinterested spectators of it—that is, pure knowledge, which is foreign to all willing, the pleasure of the beautiful, the true delight in art—this is granted only to a very few, because it demands rare talents, and to these few only as a passing dream. And then, even these few, on account of their higher intellectual power, are made susceptible of far greater suffering than duller minds can ever feel, and are also placed in lonely isolation by a nature which is obviously different from that of others; thus here also accounts are squared. But to the great majority of men purely intellectual pleasures are not accessible. They are almost quite incapable of the joys which lie in pure knowledge. They are entirely given up to willing. If, therefore, anything is to win their sympathy, to be *interesting* to them, it must (as is implied in the meaning of the word) in some way excite their *will,* even if it is only through a distant and merely problematical relation to it; the will must not be left altogether out of the question, for their existence lies far more in willing than in knowing,—action and reaction is their one element. We may find in trifles and everyday occurrences that naïve expressions of this quality. Thus, for example, at any place worth seeing they may visit, they write their names, in order thus to react, to affect the place since it does not affect them.

Again, when they see a strange, rare animal, they cannot easily confine themselves to merely observing it; they must rouse it, tease it, play with it, merely to experience action and re-action; but this need for excitement of the will manifests itself very specially in the discovery and support of card-playing, which is quite peculiarly the expression of the miserable side of humanity.

But whatever nature and fortune may have done, whoever a man be and whatever he may possess, the pain which is essential to life cannot be thrown off. . . . The ceaseless efforts to banish suffering accomplish no more than to make it change its form. It is essentially deficiency, want, care for the maintenance of life. If we succeed, which is very difficult, in removing pain in this form, it immediately assumes a thousand others, varying according to age and circumstances, such as lust, passionate love, jealousy, envy, hatred, anxiety, am-bition, covetousness, sickness, etc., etc. If at last it can find entrance in no other form, it comes in the sad, grey garments of tediousness and ennui, against which we then strive in various ways. If finally we succeed in driving this away, we shall hardly do so without letting pain enter in one of its earlier forms, and the dance begin again from the beginning; for all human life is tossed backwards and forwards between pain and ennui.

. . . .

§ 58. All satisfaction, or what is commonly called happiness, is always really and essen-tially only *negative,* and never positive. It is not an original gratification coming to us of itself, but must always be the satisfaction of a wish. The wish, *i.e.,* some want, is the con-dition which precedes every pleasure. But with the satisfaction the wish and therefore the pleasure cease. Thus the satisfaction or the pleasing can never be more than the deliverance from a pain, from a want; for such is not only every actual, open sorrow, but every desire, the importunity of which disturbs our peace, and, indeed, the deadening ennui also that makes life a burden to us. It is, however, so hard to attain or achieve anything; difficulties and troubles without end are opposed to every purpose, and at every step hindrances accu-mulate. But when finally everything is overcome and attained, nothing can ever be gained but deliverance from some sorrow or desire, so that we find ourselves just in the same po-sition as we occupied before this sorrow or desire appeared. All that is even directly given us is merely the want, *i.e.,* the pain. The satisfaction and the pleasure we can only know indirectly through the remembrance of the preceding suffering and want, which ceases with its appearance. Hence it arises that we are not properly conscious of the blessings and ad-vantages we actually possess, nor do we prize them, but think of them merely as a matter of course, for they gratify us only negatively by restraining suffering. Only when we have lost them do we become sensible of their value; for the want, the privation, the sorrow, is the positive, communicating itself directly to us. Thus also we are pleased by the remembrances of past need, sickness, want, and such like, because this is the only means of enjoying the present blessings. And, further, it cannot be denied that in this respect, and from this stand-point of egoism, which is the form of the will to live, the sight or the description of the sufferings of others affords us satisfaction and pleasure. . . . Yet we shall see farther on that this kind of pleasure, through knowledge of our own well-being obtained in this way, lies very near the source of real, positive wickedness.

That all happiness is only of a negative not a positive nature, that just on this account it cannot be lasting satisfaction and gratification, but merely delivers us from some pain or want which must be followed either by a new pain, or by languor, empty longing, and ennui; this finds support in art, that true mirror of the world and life, and especially in poetry. Every epic and dramatic poem can only represent a struggle, an effort, and fight for happiness, never enduring and complete happiness itself. It conducts its heroes through a thousand difficulties and dangers to the goal; as soon as this is reached, it hastens to let the curtain fall; for now there would remain nothing for it to do but to show that the glittering goal in which the hero expected to find happiness had only disappointed him, and that after its attainment he was no better off than before. Because a genuine enduring happiness is not possible, it cannot be the subject of art. Certainly the aim of the idyll is the description of such a happiness, but one also sees that the idyll as such cannot continue. The poet always finds that it either becomes epical in his hands, and in this case it is a very insignificant epic, made up of trifling sorrows, trifling delights, and trifling efforts—this is the commonest case—or else it becomes a merely descriptive poem, describing the beauty of nature, *i.e.,* pure knowing free from will, which certainly, as a matter of fact, is the only pure happiness, which is neither preceded by suffering or want, nor necessarily followed by repentance, sorrow, emptiness, or satiety; but this happiness cannot fill the whole life, but is only possible at moments. What we see in poetry we find again in music; in the melodies of which we have recognised the universal expression of the inmost history of the self-conscious will, the most secret life, longing, suffering, and delight; the ebb and flow of the human heart. Melody is always a deviation from the keynote through a thousand capricious wanderings, even to the most painful discord, and then a final return to the keynote which expresses the satisfaction and appeasing of the will, but with which nothing more can then be done, and the continuance of which any longer would only be a wearisome and unmeaning monotony corresponding to ennui.

All that we intend to bring out clearly through these investigations, the impossibility of attaining lasting satisfaction and the negative nature of all happiness, finds its explanation in what is shown at the conclusion of Book II: that the will, of which human life, like every phenomenon, is the objectification, is a striving without aim or end. We find the stamp of this endlessness imprinted upon all the parts of its whole manifestation, from its most universal form, endless time and space, up to the most perfect of all phenomena, the life and efforts of man. We may theoretically assume three extremes of human life, and treat them as elements of actual human life. First, the powerful will, the strong passions (Radscha-Guna). It appears in great historical characters; it is described in the epic and the drama. But it can also show itself in the little world, for the size of the objects is measured here by the degree in which they influence the will, not according to their external relations. Secondly, pure knowing, the comprehension of the Ideas, conditioned by the freeing of knowledge from the service of will: the life of genius (Satwa-Guna). Thirdly and lastly, the greatest lethargy of the will, and also of the knowledge attaching to it, empty longing, life-benumbing languor (Tama-Guna). The life of the individual, far from becoming permanently fixed in one of these extremes, seldom touches any of them, and is for the most part only a weak and wavering approach to one or the other side, a needy desiring of trifling objects, constantly recurring, and so escaping ennui. It is really incredible how meaningless and void of significance when looked at from without, how dull and unenlightened by intellect when felt from within, is the course of the life of the great majority of men. It is a weary longing and complaining, a dream-like staggering through the four ages of life to death, accompanied by a series of trivial thoughts. Such men are like clockwork, which is wound up, and goes it knows not why; and every time a man is begotten and born, the clock of human life is wound up anew, to repeat the same old piece it has played innumerable times before, passage after passage, measure after measure, with insignificant variations. Every individual, every human being and his course of life, is but another short dream of the endless spirit of nature, of the persistent will to live; is only another fleeting form, which it carelessly sketches on its infinite page, space and time; allows to remain for a time so short that it vanishes into nothing in comparison with these, and then obliterates to make new room. And yet, and here lies the serious side of life, every one of these fleeting forms, these empty fancies, must be paid for by the whole will to live, in all its activity, with many and deep sufferings, and finally with a bitter death, long feared and coming at last. This is why the sight of a corpse makes us suddenly so serious.

The life of every individual, if we survey it as a whole and in general, and only lay stress upon its most significant features, is really always a tragedy, but gone through in detail, it has the character of a comedy. For the deeds and vexations of the day, the restless irritation of the moment, the desires and fears of the week, the mishaps of every hour, are all through chance, which is ever bent upon some jest, scenes of a comedy. But the never-satisfied wishes, the frustrated efforts, the hopes unmercifully crushed by fate, the unfortunate errors of the whole life, with increasing suffering and death at the end, are always a tragedy. Thus, as if fate would add derision to the misery of our existence, our life must contain all the woes of tragedy, and yet we cannot even assert the dignity of tragic characters, but in the broad detail of life must inevitably be the foolish characters of a comedy.

But however much great and small trials may fill human life, they are not able to conceal its insufficiency to satisfy the spirit; they cannot hide the emptiness and superficiality of existence, nor exclude ennui, which is always ready to fill up every pause that care may allow. Hence it arises that the human mind, not content with the cares, anxieties, and occupations which the actual world lays upon it, creates for itself an imaginary world also in the form of a thousand different superstitions, then finds all manner of employment with this, and wastes time and strength upon it, as soon as the real world is willing to grant it the rest which it is quite incapable of enjoying. This is accordingly most markedly the case with nations for which life is made easy by the congenial nature of the climate and the soil, most of all with the Hindus, then with the Greeks, the Romans, and later with the Italians, the Spaniards, etc. Demons, gods, and saints man creates in his own image; and to them he must then unceasingly bring offerings, prayers, temple decorations, vows and their fulfilment, pilgrimages, salutations, ornaments for their images, etc. Their service mingles everywhere with the real, and, indeed, obscures it. Every event of life is regarded as the work of these beings; the intercourse with them occupies half the time of life, constantly sustains hope, and by the charm of illusion often becomes more interesting than intercourse with real beings. It is the expression and symptom of the actual need of mankind, partly for help and support, partly for occupation and diversion; and if it often works in direct opposition to the first need, because when accidents and dangers arise valuable time and strength, instead of being directed to warding them off, are uselessly wasted on prayers and offerings; it serves the second end all the better by this imaginary converse with a visionary spirit world; and this is the by no means contemptible gain of all superstitions.

§ 68. All suffering, since it is a mortification and a call to resignation, has potentially a sanctifying power. This is the explanation of the fact that every great misfortune or deep pain inspires a certain awe. But the sufferer only really becomes an object of reverence when, surveying the course of his life as a chain of sorrows, or mourning some great and incurable misfortune, he does not really look at the special combination of circumstances which has plunged his own life into suffering, nor stops at the single great misfortune that has befallen him; for in so doing his knowledge still follows the principle of sufficient reason, and clings to the particular phenomenon; he still wills life, only not under the conditions which have happened to him; but only then, I say, is he truly worthy of reverence when he raises his glance from the particular to the universal, when he regards his suffering as merely an example of the whole, and for him, since in a moral regard he partakes of genius, one case stands for a thousand, so that the whole of life conceived as essentially suffering brings him to resignation. Therefore it inspires reverence when in Goethe's "Torquato Tasso" the princess speaks of how her own life and that of her relations has always been sad and joyless, and yet regards the matter from an entirely universal point of view.

A very noble character we always imagine with a certain trace of quiet sadness, which is anything but a constant fretfulness at daily annoyances (this would be an ignoble trait, and lead us to fear a bad disposition), but is a consciousness derived from knowledge of the vanity of all possessions, of the suffering of all life, not merely of his own. But such knowledge may primarily be awakened by the personal experience of suffering, especially some one great sorrow, as a single unfulfilled wish brought Petrarch to that state of resigned sadness concerning the whole of life which appeals to us so pathetically in his works; for the Daphne he pursued had to flee from his hands in order to leave him, instead of herself, the immortal laurel. When through some such great and irrevocable denial of fate the will is to some extent broken, almost nothing else is desired, and the character shows itself mild, just, noble, and resigned. When, finally, grief has no definite object, but extends itself over the whole of life, then it is to a certain extent a going into itself, a withdrawal, a gradual disappearance of the will, whose visible manifestation, the body, it imperceptibly but surely undermines, so that a man feels a certain loosening of his bonds, a mild foretaste of that death which promises to be the abolition at once of the body and of the will. Therefore a secret pleasure accompanies this grief, and it is this, as I believe, which the most melancholy of all nations has called "the joy of grief." But here also lies the danger of *sentimentality,* both in life itself and in the representation of it in poetry; when a man is always mourning and lamenting without courageously rising to resignation. In this way we lose both earth and heaven, and retain merely a watery sentimentality. Only if suffering assumes the form of pure knowledge, and this, acting as a *quieter of the will,* brings about resignation, is it worthy of reverence. In this regard, however, we feel a certain respect at the sight of every great sufferer which is akin to the feeling excited by virtue and nobility of character, and also seems like a reproach of our own happy condition. We cannot help regarding every sorrow, both our own and those of others, as at least a potential advance towards virtue and holiness, and, on the contrary, pleasures and worldly satisfactions as a retrogression from them. This goes so far, that every man who endures a great bodily or mental suffering, indeed every one who merely performs some physical labour which demands the greatest exertion, in the sweat of his brow and with evident exhaustion, yet with patience and without murmuring, every such man, I say, if we consider him with close attention, appears to us like a sick man who tries a painful cure, and who willingly, and even with satisfaction, endures the suffering it causes him, because he knows that the more he suffers the more the cause of his disease is affected, and that therefore the present suffering is the measure of his cure.

According to what has been said, the denial of the will to live, which is just what is called absolute, entire resignation, or holiness, always proceeds from that quieter of the will which the knowledge of its inner conflict and essential vanity, expressing themselves in the suffering of all living things, becomes. The difference, which we have represented as two paths, consists in whether that knowledge is called up by suffering which is merely and purely *known,* and is freely appropriated by means of the penetration of the *principium individuationis,* or by suffering which is directly *felt* by a man himself. True salvation, deliverance from life and suffering, cannot even be imagined without complete denial of the will. Till then, every one is simply this will itself, whose manifestation is an ephemeral existence, a constantly vain and empty striving, and the world full of suffering we have represented, to which all irrevocably and in like manner belong. For we found above that life is always assured to the will to live, and its one real form is the present, from which they can never escape, since birth and death reign in the phenomenal world. The Indian mythus expresses this by saying "they are born again." The great ethical difference of character means this, that the bad man is infinitely far from the attainment of the knowledge from which the denial of the will proceeds, and therefore he is in truth *actually* exposed to all the miseries which appear in life as *possible;* for even the present fortunate condition of his personality is merely a phenomenon produced by the *principium individuationis,* and a delusion of Mâyâ, the happy dream of a beggar. The sufferings which in the vehemence and ardour of his will he inflicts upon others are the measure of the suffering, the experience of which in his own person cannot break his will, and plainly lead it to the denial of itself. All true and pure love, on the other hand, and even all free justice, proceed from the penetration of the *principium individuationis,* which, if it appears with its full power, results in perfect sanctification and salvation, the phenomenon of which is the state of resignation described above, the unbroken peace which accompanies it, and the greatest delight in death.

COMTE

1798–1857

Auguste Comte was born in Montpellier, France. He attended the École Polytechnique at Paris for two years, then took part in the student rebellion that closed the school. He supported himself as a private tutor in mathematics. When the École Polytechnique reopened in 1833, Comte got a job there as an entrance examiner. When the administration discovered that he had been one of the revolutionaries, they fired him. But by then Comte had already been noticed by many leading figures of the time, including John Stuart Mill in England. Mill came to his defense, calling Comte an "original and bold new thinker."

Comte's writings became a major inspiration for the nineteenth-century shift from metaphysical to "scientific" philosophy, which meant, at the time, that knowledge was sanctified by some sort of social verification. Indeed, the knowledge-seeking enterprise known as science has since then become a social, not an individual, activity. This is a complete reversal of the Cartesian notion of "I think, therefore I am," in which certainty is grounded through the individual's own internal relation to the truth. Truth in the new, "scientific" sense meant truth publicly verified.

Our selection is from Comte's main philosophical work, *Cours de philosophie positive* (*The Positive Philosophy,* in six volumes, published from 1842 to 1854). Here Compte presented his law of the three "theoretical conditions" of intellectual development. In the first, primitive "theological or fictitious" stage, human beings rely on the power of supernatural beings existing beyond the seen world so that explanations are given ultimately in supernatural terms. In the second, "metaphysical" stage, explanation is ultimately theological, where supernatural entities are replaced with abstract notions. In the third and final, "positive" stage, the mind is freed by reason and observation from its vain egotistical search for "absolute notions."

Comte argues against the "vain" search for causes. He rejects causes as agents or forces. Further, in turning away from introspective philosophy, in which the appreciation of one's own psychological states is taken as an epistemological yardstick, and moving toward the public, "sociological" realm of cross-verification and "social facts," Comte provided the first systematic account of social science, which he called "sociology." His thinking along these lines helped inspire the early logical positivists and paved the way for the social, political, and moral philosophy of John Stuart Mill.

Like Nietzsche and Marx, Comte makes a radical break with religion. He argues that the positive philosophy has no room for traditional theological thinking. He calls for the eradication of religion on grounds that it obfuscates the truth and only stands in the way of humanity's progress. In place of traditional religion, humanity would establish a new "religion of humanity." The new priesthood would consist of scientists, businessmen, politicians, and a "calendar of saints." These figures would be placed as icons in the new educational institutions that would replace in society the traditional educational institutions run by the church, and the priesthood would include people like Adam Smith, Dante, Shakespeare, and the great philosophers, economists, and scientists of the future.

Comte's positive philosophy was a bold attempt to end the "error" that the mind can know anything more than phenomena and their relations. Just as we do not know the essence of the phenomena, we do not know their first causes nor their ultimate ends. All we know, by means of *controlling the phenomena* through experiment and observation, are the constant relations between phenomena, the relations of succession and of similarity, and the uniformities which we call their laws. Knowledge is therefore relative. There is no absolute knowledge because the "things in themselves" and the essence of facts are unreachable by the mind. All we know is that phenomenon *a* is connected with phenomenon *b*, because *b* always follows *a* as far as our observations go.

At the same time, although the positive philosophy rejects metaphysics, it does not lead either to idealism or to empiricism. Isolated, empirical observations are useless and unknowable as such; a phenomenon becomes useful and a part of knowledge only when it is defined and explained by a theory, or combined with other observations into a law of nature.

THE POSITIVE PHILOSOPHY

INTRODUCTION

CHAPTER I: VIEW OF THE NATURE AND IMPORTANCE OF THE POSITIVE PHILOSOPHY

. . . From the study of the development of the human mind, in all directions, and through all times, the discovery arises of a great fundamental law, to which it is necessarily subject, and which has a solid foundation of proof, both in the facts of our organization and in our historical experience. The law is this:—that each of our leading conceptions,—each branch of our knowledge,—passes successively through three different theoretical conditions: the theological, or fictitious; the metaphysical, or abstract; and the scientific, or positive. In other words, the human mind, by its nature, employs in its progress three methods of philosophizing, the character of which is essentially different, and even radically opposed: viz., the theological method, the metaphysical, and the positive. Hence arise three philosophies,

From the *Cours de Philosophie positive,* Paris, 1830–1842. Translated by Harriet Martineau. Reprinted from A. Comte's *The Positive Philosophy* (London, 1853). With emendations by Daniel Kolak.

or general systems of conceptions on the aggregate of phenomena, each of which excludes the others. The first is the necessary point of departure of the human understanding; and the third is its fixed and definitive state. The second is merely a state of transition.

In the theological state, the human mind, seeking the essential nature of beings, the first and final causes (the origin and purpose) of all effects,—in short, absolute knowledge,—supposes all phenomena to be produced by the immediate action of supernatural beings.

In the metaphysical state, which is only a modification of the first, the mind supposes, instead of supernatural beings, abstract forces, veritable entities (that is, personified abstractions) inherent in all beings, and capable of producing all phenomena. What is called the explanation of phenomena is, in this stage, a mere reference of each to its proper entity.

In the final, the positive state, the mind has given over the vain search after absolute notions, the origin and destination of the universe, and the causes of phenomena, and applies itself to the study of their laws,—that is, their invariable relations of succession and resemblance. Reasoning and observation, duly combined, are the means of this knowledge. What is now understood when we speak of an explanation of facts is simply the establishment of a connection between single phenomena and some general facts, the number of which continually diminishes with the progress of science.

The theological system arrived at the highest perfection of which it is capable when it substituted the providential action of a single Being for the varied operations of the numerous divinities which had been before imagined. In the same way, in the last stage of the metaphysical system, men substitute one great entity (nature) as the cause of all phenomena, instead of the multitude of entities at first supposed. In the same way, again, the ultimate perfection of the positive system would be (if such perfection could be hoped for) to represent all phenomena as particular aspects of a single general fact;—such as gravitation, for instance.

The importance of the working of this general law will be established hereafter. At present, it must suffice to point out some of the grounds of it.

There is no science which, having attained the positive stage, does not bear marks of having passed through the others. Some time since it was (whatever it might be) composed, as we can now perceive, of metaphysical abstractions; and, further back in the course of time, it took its form from theological conceptions. We shall have only too much occasion to see, as we proceed, that our most advanced sciences still bear very evident marks of the two earlier periods through which they have passed.

The progress of the individual mind is not only an illustration, but an indirect evidence of that of the general mind. The point of departure of the individual and of the race being the same, the phases of the mind of a man correspond to the epochs of the mind of the race. Now, each of us is aware, if he looks back upon his own history, that he was a theologian in his childhood, a metaphysician in his youth, and a natural philosopher in his manhood. All men who are up to their age can verify this for themselves.

Besides the observation of facts, we have theoretical reasons in support of this law.

The most important of these reasons arises from the necessity that always exists for some theory to which to refer our facts, combined with the clear impossibility that, at the outset of human knowledge, men could have formed theories out of the observation of facts. All good intellects have repeated, since Bacon's time, that there can be no real knowledge but that which is based on observed facts. This is incontestable, in our present advanced stage; but, if we look back to the primitive stage of human knowledge, we shall see that it must have been otherwise then. If it is true that every theory must be based upon observed facts, it is equally true that facts cannot be observed without the guidance of some theory. Without such guidance, our facts would be desultory and fruitless; we could not retain them: for the most part we could not even perceive them.

Thus, between the necessity of observing facts in order to form a theory, and having a theory in order to observe facts, the human mind would have been entangled in a vicious circle, but for the natural opening afforded by theological conceptions. This is the fundamental reason for the theological character of the primitive philosophy. This necessity is confirmed by the perfect suitability of the theological philosophy to the earliest researches of the human mind. It is remarkable that the most inaccessible questions,—those of the nature of beings, and the origin and purpose of phenomena,—should be the first to occur in a primitive state, while those which are really within our reach are regarded as almost unworthy of serious study. The reason is evident enough:—that experience alone can teach us the measure of our powers; and if men had not begun by an exaggerated estimate of what they can do, they would never have done all that they are capable of. Our organization requires this. At such a period there could have been no reception of a positive philosophy, whose function is to discover the laws of phenomena, and whose leading characteristic it is to regard as interdicted to human reason those sublime mysteries which theology explains, even to their minutest details, with the most attractive facility. It is just so under a practical view of the nature of the researches with which men first occupied themselves. Such inquiries offered the powerful charm of unlimited empire over the external world,—a world destined wholly for our use, and involved in every way with our existence. The theological philosophy, presenting this view, administered exactly the stimulus necessary to incite the human mind to the irksome labour without which it could make no progress. We can now scarcely conceive of such a state of things, our reason having become sufficiently mature to enter upon laborious scientific researches, without needing any such stimulus as wrought upon the imaginations of astrologers and alchemists. We have motive enough in the hope of discovering the laws of phenomena, with a view to the confirmation or rejection of a theory. But it could not be so in the earliest days; and it is to the chimeras of astrology and alchemy that we owe the long series of observations and experiments on which our positive science is based. Kepler felt this on behalf of astronomy, and Berthollet on behalf of chemistry. Thus was a spontaneous philosophy, the theological, the only possible beginning, method, and provisional system, out of which the positive philosophy could grow. It is easy, after this, to perceive how metaphysical methods and doctrines must have afforded the means of transition from the one to the other.

The human understanding, slow in its advance, could not step at once from the theological into the positive philosophy. The two are so radically opposed, that an intermediate system of conceptions has been necessary to render the transition possible. It is only in doing this, that metaphysical conceptions have any utility whatever. In contemplating phenomena, men substitute for supernatural direction a corresponding entity. This entity may have been supposed to be derived from the supernatural action: but it is more easily lost sight of, leaving attention free for the facts themselves, till, at length, metaphysical agents have ceased to be anything more than the abstract names of phenomena. It is not easy to say by what other process than this our minds could have passed from supernatural considerations to natural; from the theological system to the positive.

The law of human development being thus established, let us consider what is the proper nature of the positive philosophy.

As we have seen, the first characteristic of the positive philosophy is that it regards all phenomena as subjected to invariable natural *laws*. Our business is,—seeing how vain is any research into what are called *causes,* whether first or final,—to pursue an accurate discovery of these laws, with a view to reducing them to the smallest possible number. By speculating upon causes, we could solve no difficulty about origin and purpose. Our real business is to analyse accurately the circumstances of phenomena, and to connect them by the natural relations of succession and resemblance. The best illustration of this is in the case of the doctrine of gravitation. We say that the general phenomena of the universe are *explained* by it, because it connects under one head the whole immense variety of astronomical facts; exhibiting the constant tendency of atoms towards each other in direct proportion to their masses, and in inverse proportion to the squares of their distances; while the general fact itself is a mere extension of one which is perfectly familiar to us, and which we therefore say that we know;—the weight of bodies on the surface of the earth. As to what weight and attraction are, we have nothing to do with that, for it is not a matter of knowledge at all. Theologians and metaphysicians may imagine and refine about such questions; but positive philosophy rejects them. When any attempt has been made to explain them, it has ended only in saying that attraction is universal weight, and that weight is terrestrial attraction: that is, that the two orders of phenomena are identical; which is the point from which the question set out. Again, M. Fourier, in his fine series of researches on Heat, has given us all the most important and precise laws of the phenomena of heat, and many large and new truths, without once inquiring into its nature, as his predecessors had done when they disputed about calorific matter and the action of an universal ether. In treating his subject in the positive method, he finds inexhaustible material for all his activity of research, without betaking himself to insoluble questions.

Before ascertaining the stage which the positive philosophy has reached, we must bear in mind that the different kinds of our knowledge have passed through the three stages of progress at different rates, and have not therefore arrived at the same time. The rate of advance depends on the nature of the knowledge in question, so distinctly that, as we shall see hereafter, this consideration constitutes an accessory to the fundamental law of progress. Any kind of knowledge reaches the positive stage early in proportion to its generality, simplicity, and independence of other departments. Astronomical science, which is above all made up of facts that are general, simple, and independent of other sciences, arrived first; then terrestrial physics; then chemistry; and, at length, physiology.

It is difficult to assign any precise date to this revolution in science. It may be said, like everything else, to have been always going on; and especially since the labours of Aristotle and the school of Alexandria; and then from the introduction of natural science into the West of Europe by the Arabs. But, if we must fix upon some marked period, to serve as a rallying point, it must be that,—about two centuries ago,—when the human mind was astir under the precepts of Bacon, the conceptions of Descartes, and the discoveries of Galileo. Then it was that the spirit of the positive philosophy rose up in opposition to that of the superstitious and scholastic systems which had hitherto obscured the true character of all science. Since that date, the progress of the positive philosophy, and the decline of the other two, have been so marked that no rational mind now doubts that the revolution is destined to go on to its completion,—every branch of knowledge being, sooner or later, brought within the operation of positive philosophy. This is not yet the case. Some are still lying outside: and not till they are brought in will the positive philosophy possess that character of universality which is necessary to its definitive constitution.

In mentioning just now the four principal categories of phenomena,—astronomical, physical, chemical, and physiological,—there was an omission which will have been noticed. Nothing was said of social phenomena. Though involved with the physiological, social phenomena demand a distinct classification, both on account of their importance and of their difficulty. They are the most individual, the most complicated, the most dependent on all others; and therefore they must be the latest,—even if they had no special obstacle to encounter. This branch of science has not hitherto entered into the domain of positive philosophy. Theological and metaphysical methods, exploded in other departments, are as yet exclusively applied, both in the way of inquiry and discussion, in all treatment of social subjects, though the best minds are heartily weary of eternal disputes about divine right and the sovereignty of the people. This is the great, while it is evidently the only gap which has to be filled, to constitute, solid and entire, the positive philosophy. Now that the human mind has grasped celestial and terrestrial physics,—mechanical and chemical; organic physics, both vegetable and animal,—there remains one science, to fill up the series of sciences of observation,—Social physics. This is what men have now most need of: and this it is the principal aim of the present work to establish.

It would be absurd to pretend to offer this new science at once in a complete state. Others, less new, are in very unequal conditions of forwardness. But the same character of positivity which is impressed on all the others will be shown to belong to this. This once done, the philosophical system of the moderns will be in fact complete, as there will then be no phenomenon which does not naturally enter into some one of the five great categories. All our fundamental conceptions having become homogeneous, the positive state will be fully established. It can never again change its character, though it will be for ever in course of development by additions of new knowledge. Having acquired the character of universality which has hitherto been the only advantage resting with the two preceding systems, it will supersede them by its natural superiority, and leave to them only an historical existence.

We have stated the special aim of this work. Its secondary and general aim is this:—to review what has been effected in the sciences, in order to show that they are not radically separate, but all branches from the same trunk. If we had confined ourselves to the first and special object of the work, we should have produced merely a study of social physics: whereas, in introducing the second and general we offer a study of positive philosophy, passing in review all the positive sciences already formed.

The purpose of this work is not to give an account of the natural sciences. Besides that it would be endless, and that it would require a scientific preparation such as no one man possesses, it would be apart from our object, which is to go through a course of not positive science, but positive philosophy. We have only to consider each fundamental science in its relation to the whole positive system, and to the spirit which characterizes it; that is, with regard to its methods and its chief results.

The two aims, though distinct, are inseparable; for, on the one hand, there can be no positive philosophy without a basis of social science, without which it could not be all-comprehensive; and, on the other hand, we could not pursue social science without having been prepared by the study of phenomena less complicated than those of society, and furnished with a knowledge of laws and anterior facts which have a bearing upon social science. Though the fundamental sciences are not all equally interesting to ordinary minds, there is no one of them that can be neglected in an inquiry like the present; and, in the eye of philosophy, all are of equal value to human welfare. Even those which appear the least interesting have their own value, either on account of the perfection of their methods, or as being the necessary basis of all the others.

Lest it should be supposed that our course will lead us into a wilderness of such special studies as are at present the bane of a true positive philosophy, we will briefly advert to the existing prevalence of such special pursuit. In the primitive state of human knowledge there is no regular division of intellectual labour. Every student cultivates all the sciences. As knowledge accrues, the sciences part off; and students devote themselves each to some one branch. It is owing to this division of employment, and concentration of whole minds upon a single department, that science has made so prodigious an advance in modern times; and the perfection of this division is one of the most important characteristics of the positive philosophy. But, while admitting all the merits of this change, we cannot be blind to the eminent disadvantages which arise from the limitation of minds to a particular study. It is inevitable that each should be possessed with exclusive notions, and be therefore incapable of the general superiority of ancient students, who actually owed that general superiority to the inferiority of their knowledge. We must consider whether the evil can be avoided without losing the good of the modern arrangement; for the evil is becoming urgent. We all acknowledge that the divisions established for the convenience of scientific pursuit are radically artificial; and yet there are very few who can embrace in idea the whole of any one science; each science moreover being itself only a part of a great whole. Almost every one is busy about his own particular section, without much thought about its relation to the general system of positive knowledge. We must not be blind to the evil, nor slow in seeking a remedy. We must not forget that this is the weak side of the positive philosophy, by which it may yet be attacked, with some hope of success, by the adherents of the theological and metaphysical systems. As to the remedy, it certainly does not lie in a return to the ancient confusion of pursuits, which would be mere retrogression, if it were possible, which it is not. It lies in perfecting the division of employments itself,—in carrying it one degree higher,— in constituting one more specialty from the study of scientific generalities. Let us have a new class of students, suitably prepared, whose business it shall be to take the respective sciences as they are, determine the spirit of each, ascertain their relations and mutual connection, and reduce their respective principles to the smallest number of general principles, in conformity with the fundamental rules of the positive method. At the same time, let other students be prepared for their special pursuit by an education which recognizes the whole scope of positive science, so as to profit by the labours of the students of generalities, and so as to correct reciprocally, under that guidance, the results obtained by each. We see some approach already to this arrangement. Once established, there would be nothing to apprehend from many extent of division of employments. When we once have a class of learned men, at the disposal of all others, whose business it shall be to connect each new discovery with the general system, we may dismiss all fear of the great whole being lost sight of in the pursuit of the details of knowledge. The organization of scientific research will then be complete; and it will henceforth have occasion only to extend its development, and not to change its character. After all, the formation of such a new class as is proposed would be merely an extension of the principle which has created all the classes we have. While science was narrow, there was only one class: as it expanded, more were instituted. With a further advance a fresh need arises, and this new class will be the result.

The general spirit of a course of positive philosophy having been thus set forth, we must now glance at the chief advantages which may be derived, on behalf of human progression, from the study of it. . . .

The study of the positive philosophy affords the only rational means of exhibiting the logical laws of the human mind, which have hitherto been sought by unfit methods. To explain what is meant by this, we may refer to a saying of M. de Blainville, in his work on comparative anatomy, that every active, and especially every living being, may be regarded under two relations—the statical and the dynamical; that is, under conditions or in action.

It is clear that all considerations range themselves under the one or the other of these heads. Let us apply this classification to the intellectual functions.

If we regard these functions under their statical aspect—that is, if we consider the conditions under which they exist—we must determine the organic circumstances of the case, which inquiry involves it with anatomy and physiology. If we look at the dynamic aspect, we have to study simply the exercise and results of the intellectual powers of the human race, which is neither more nor less than the general object of the positive philosophy. In short, looking at all scientific theories as so many great logical facts, it is only by the thorough observation of these facts that we can arrive at the knowledge of logical laws. These being the only means of knowledge of intellectual phenomena, the illusory psychology, which is the last phase of theology, is excluded. It pretends to accomplish the discovery of the laws of the human mind by contemplating it in itself; . . .

The present exclusive specialty of our pursuits, and the consequent isolation of the sciences, spoil our teaching. If any student desires to form an idea of natural philosophy as a whole, he is compelled to go through each department as it is now taught, as if he were to be only an astronomer, or only a chemist; so that, be his intellect what it may, his training must remain very imperfect. And yet his object requires that he should obtain general positive conceptions of all the classes of natural phenomena. It is such an aggregate of conceptions, whether on a great or on a small scale, which must henceforth be the permanent basis of all human combinations. It will constitute the mind of future generations. In order to this regeneration of our intellectual system, it is necessary that the sciences, considered as branches from one trunk, should yield us, as a whole, their chief methods and their most important results. The specialities of science can be pursued by those whose vocation lies in that direction. They are indispensable; and they are not likely to be neglected; but they can never of themselves renovate our system of education; and, to be of their full use, they must rest upon the basis of that general instruction which is a direct result of the positive philosophy.

The same special study of scientific generalities must also aid the progress of the respective positive sciences: and this constitutes our third head of advantages.

The divisions which we establish between the sciences are, though not arbitrary, essentially artificial. The subject of our researches is one: we divide it for our convenience, in order to deal the more easily with its difficulties. But it sometimes happens—and especially with the most important doctrines of each science—that we need what we cannot obtain under the present isolation of the sciences,—a combination of several special points of view; and for want of this, very important problems wait for their solution much longer than they otherwise need do. To go back into the past for an example: Descartes' grand conception with regard to analytical geometry is a discovery which has changed the whole aspect of mathematical science, and yielded the germ of all future progress; and it issued from the union of two sciences which had always before been separately regarded and pursued. The case of pending questions is yet more impressive; as, for instance, in chemistry, the doctrine of definite proportions. Without entering upon the discussion of the fundamental principle of this theory, we may say with assurance that, in order to determine it—in order to determine whether it is a law of nature that atoms should necessarily combine in fixed numbers,—it will be indispensable that the chemical point of view should be united with the physiological. The failure of the theory with regard to organic bodies indicates that the cause of this immense exception must be investigated; and such an inquiry belongs as much to physiology as to chemistry. Again, it is as yet undecided whether azote is a simple or a compound body. It was concluded by almost all chemists that azote is a simple body; the illustrious Berzelius hesitated, on purely chemical considerations; but he was also influenced by the physiological observation that animals which receive no azote in their food have as much of it in their tissues as carnivorous animals. From this we see how physiology must unite with chemistry to inform us whether azote is simply or compound, and to institute a new series of researches upon the relation between the composition of living bodies and their mode of alimentation.

Such is the advantage which, in the third place, we shall owe to positive philosophy—the elucidation of the respective sciences by their combination. In the fourth place:

IV. The positive philosophy offers the only solid basis for that social reorganization which must succeed the critical condition in which the most civilized nations are now living.

It cannot be necessary to prove to anybody who reads this work that ideas govern the world, or throw it into chaos; in other words, that all social mechanism rests upon opinions. The great political and moral crisis that societies are now undergoing is shown by a rigid analysis to arise out of intellectual anarchy. While stability in fundamental maxims is the first condition of genuine social order, we are suffering under an utter disagreement which may be called universal. Till a certain number of general ideas can be acknowledged as a rallying-point of social doctrine, the nations will remain in a revolutionary state, whatever palliatives may be devised; and their institutions can be only provisional. But whenever the necessary agreement on first principles can be obtained, appropriate institutions will issue from them, without shock or resistance; for the causes of disorder will have been arrested by the mere fact of the agreement. It is in this direction that those must look who desire a natural and regular, a normal state of society.

Now, the existing order is abundantly accounted for by the existence, all at once, of three incompatible philosophies,—the theological, the metaphysical, and the positive. Any one of these might alone secure some sort of social order; but while the three co-exist, it is impossible for us to understand one another upon any essential point whatever. If this is true, we have only to ascertain which of the philosophies must, in the nature of things, prevail; and, this ascertained, every man, whatever may have been his former views, cannot but concur in its triumph. The problem once recognized cannot remain long unsolved; for all considerations whatever point to the positive philosophy as the one destined to prevail. It alone has been advancing during a course of centuries, throughout which the others have been declining. The fact is incontestable. Some may deplore it, but none can destroy it, nor therefore neglect it but under penalty of being betrayed by illusory speculations. This general revolution of the human mind is nearly accomplished. We have only to complete the positive philosophy by bringing social phenomena within its comprehension, and afterwards consolidating the whole into one body of homogeneous doctrine. The marked preference which almost all minds, from the highest to the commonest, accord to positive knowledge over vague and mystical conceptions, is a pledge of what the reception of this philosophy will be when it has acquired the only quality that it now wants—a character of due generality. When it has become complete, its supremacy will take place spontaneously, and will re-establish order throughout society. There is, at present, no conflict but between the theological and the metaphysical philosophies. They are contending for the task of reorganizing society; but it is a work too mighty for either of them. The positive philosophy has hitherto intervened only to examine both, and both are abundantly discredited by the process. It is time now to be doing something more effective, without wasting our forces in needless controversy. It is time to complete the vast intellectual operation begun by Bacon, Descartes, and Galileo, by constructing the system of general ideas which must henceforth prevail among the human race. This is the way to put an end to the revolutionary crisis which is tormenting the civilized nations of the world.

Leaving these four points of advantage, we must attend to one precautionary reflection.

Because it is proposed to consolidate the whole of our acquired knowledge into one body of homogeneous doctrine, it must not be supposed that we are going to study this vast variety as proceeding from a single principle, and as subjected to a single law. There is something so chimerical in attempts at universal explanation by a single law, that it may be as well to secure this work at once from any imputation of the kind, though its development will show how undeserved such an imputation would be. Our intellectual resources are too narrow, and the universe is too complex, to leave any hope that it will ever be within our power to carry scientific perfection to its last degree of simplicity. Moreover, it appears as if the value of such an attainment, supposing it possible, were greatly overrated. The only way, for instance, in which we could achieve the business, would be by connecting all natural phenomena with the most general law we know,—which is that of gravitation, by which astronomical phenomena are already connected with a portion of terrestrial physics. Laplace has indicated that chemical phenomena may be regarded as simple atomic effects of the Newtonian attraction, modified by the form and mutual position of the atoms. But supposing this view proveable (which it cannot be while we are without data about the constitution of bodies), the difficulty of its application would doubtless be found so great that we must still maintain the existing division between astronomy and chemistry, with the difference that we now regard as natural that division which we should then call artificial. Laplace himself presented his idea only as a philosophic device, incapable of exercising any useful influence over the progress of chemical science. Moreover, supposing this insuperable difficulty overcome, we should be no nearer to scientific unity, since we then should still have to connect the whole of physiological phenomena with the same law, which certainly would not be the least difficult part of the enterprise. Yet, all things considered, the hypothesis we have glanced at would be the most favourable to the desired unity.

MILL

1806–1873

Born and educated in London by his father, a prominent philosopher, historian, and economist, John Stuart Mill began studying Greek at the age of three. He had read all the works of Plato in the original by the time he was eight. By twelve he had learned Latin, Euclidean geometry, and algebra and had studied Aristotle's logical treatises. At fourteen he had a college-level understanding of logic, mathematics, and world history. In many ways he became Comte's philosophical successor, carrying on both his phenomenalist and presentationalist philosophy into the social arena of politics and ethics.

By twenty-five, Mill was emotionally burned out. He later wrote that "the habit of analysis has a tendency to wear away the feelings. . . . I was thus, as I said to myself, left stranded at the commencement of my voyage, with a well equipped ship and a rudder, but no sail." He says his life was turned around by Mrs. Harriet Taylor, with whom he fell in love and married after her husband died. She inspired Mill and helped him write many of his most important works, including *A System of Logic* (1843), *The Principles of Political Economy* (1848), and *On Liberty* (1859).

Mill had been raised by his father on the utilitarian doctrines of Jeremy Bentham (1748–1832) and the "philosophical radicals." Bentham defined his principle of utility as

> that property in any object whereby it tends to produce pleasure, good or happiness, or to prevent the happening of mischief, pain, evil or unhappiness to the party whose interest is considered.

According to Bentham, this principle takes account of the two main motives for all human action—pain and pleasure. Governments, social, political, and legal institutions, as well as individual citizens, should follow the *greatest happiness principle:* choose that course of action which leads to the greatest happiness for the greatest number of people. His utilitarianism, designed to free people from oppressive laws and to make governing bodies moral, provided a foundation for many democratic societies. Since leaders as well as individuals are thus morally bound to follow the same universal principle and one that is readily accessible to everyone—we all know what pain and pleasure are—there can be no manipulation, through rhetoric, of the weak by the powerful. In Bentham's system we are each our own best judge as to how to live and attain happiness. His utilitarianism is designed to break this repressive structure of laws imposed, under the guise of morality, on people by corrupt and exploiting leaders. Bentham openly called for the rejection of all monarchies and established churches, claiming that "all government is in itself one vast evil." The only justification for putting such evil into place would be to prevent some greater evil; governments should therefore never stray from the principle of utility—the greatest happiness for the greatest number.

Mill revolutionized utilitarian ideas in his most widely influential book, *Utilitarianism* (1863), from which our first selection is taken. His major modification of Bentham's ethical theory is that whereas Bentham had defined his utility principle in terms of avoiding pain and securing pleasure, Mill argues that such self-interest is an inadequate criterion of moral goodness. The main problem with Bentham's moral calculus, as Mill saw it, was that it lacked any qualitative distinction between various pleasures. Bentham had defined pains and pleasures using the seven categories of intensity, duration, certainty, proximity, fecundity, purity, and extent. Moral judgments were then to be calculated as follows. Suppose, for instance, that law X would produce an intense pleasure very briefly for only a few individuals, while causing many others a lot of pain for a long time. Then X was a bad law.

The problem, as Mill saw it, was that Bentham failed to distinguish between types of pleasure and pain sensations: "quantity of pleasure being equal, pushpin is as good as poetry." Mill therefore adds quality to the list, saying "better to be Socrates dissatisfied than a fool satisfied." The problem is that this addition makes Bentham's moral calculus no longer a straightforward objective question, since qualitative judgments are subjective. Mill tried to solve the problem by basing his moral theory on his political theory, stating that such moral judgments having to do with qualities would have to be decided *democratically,* through majority rule, since unlike quantitative judgments they were not objective but subjective.

The second selection is from Mill's *On Liberty* (1859), in which he argues that the fundamental utilitarian principle—the greatest amount of happiness for the greatest number of people—can be achieved only if all individuals are given as much freedom of thought and action as possible. The only constraint was a prohibition against causing harm to others. *On Liberty* was both popular in Europe and highly influential to the development of nineteenth- and early-twentieth-century democracy in the United States.

Plato had argued that democracy is the worst form of government. Having seen Socrates sentenced to death by the democratic state majority, he urged that there be rule by enlightened philosopher-kings. Mill comes to just the opposite conclusion. He reasons that the correct lesson from the past is that no one should have a monopoly on what people regard to be the truth. All our best philosophies keep evolving, as does science, and all human knowledge can attain is partial truths. The philosophical and political well-being of a society should therefore be dependent on *growth* and *change,* or else we end up at a dead end like the Byzantine and Roman Empires. Finally, and perhaps most important, if we let the wisest among us become the rulers in charge of everything, including our education, what will happen to the rest of the people? They will look up to the leaders. This may be good for a generation or two of leadership, but it will lead, Mill argues, in the long run to stagnation and decline. After a while the official "truths" will simply be passed down, generation to generation, and no one will achieve anything new.

To avoid the rise and inevitable fall of every precious empire, the wise society should therefore encourage not obedience to authority but the development of individuality, even rebellion. It must help spawn individuals through whom new ideas are born. Eccentricity, not conformity, should be the ideal. The majority must be tolerant and helpful to the minorities, the learned should be tolerant of the unlearned, and so on. This system will, in Mill's view, produce not just a healthy, vibrant society but a moral one that evolves over time to achieve the greatest happiness for the greatest number.

Although Mill never held an official academic post, he applied his theories to many causes. In *The Subjection of Women* (1869), he argued for the then-radical position that women should have careers and be allowed to vote. He fought discrimination against women, founded the first women's suffrage society, and was an early advocate of openly available birth control.

Mill made his living working for the East India Company. He had started at age seventeen as a clerk and had been quickly promoted to the highest post in his department. He retired in 1865 to run for Parliament and won. During his term in office he achieved many sweeping reforms for the British working class. He argued on behalf of exploited Jamaicans and for fair redistribution of land in Ireland.

UTILITARIANISM

The creed which accepts as the foundation of morals "utility" or the "greatest happiness principle" holds that actions are right in proportion as they tend to promote happiness, wrong as they tend to produce the reverse of happiness. By happiness is intended pleasure, and the absence of pain; by unhappiness, pain, and the privation of pleasure. To give a clear view of the moral standard set up by the theory, much more requires to be said; in particular, what things it includes in the ideas of pain and pleasure; and to what extent this is left an open question. But these supplementary explanations do not affect the theory of life on which this theory of morality is grounded—namely, that pleasure and freedom from pain are the only things desirable as ends; and that all desirable things (which are as numerous in the utilitarian as in any other scheme) are desirable either for the pleasure inherent in themselves, or as means to the promotion of pleasure and the prevention of pain.

Now such a theory of life excites in many minds, and among them in some of the most estimable in feeling and purpose, inveterate dislike. To suppose that life has (as they express it) no higher end than pleasure—no better and nobler object of desire and pursuit—they designate as utterly mean and groveling; as a doctrine worthy only of swine, to whom the followers of Epicurus were, at a very early period, contemptuously likened; and modern holders of the doctrine are occasionally made the subject of equally polite comparisons by its German, French, and English assailants.

When thus attacked, the Epicureans have always answered that it is not they, but their accusers, who represent human nature in a degrading light, since the accusation supposes human beings to be capable of no pleasures except those of which swine are capable. If this supposition were true, the charge could not be gainsaid, but would then be no longer an imputation; for if the sources of pleasure were precisely the same to human beings and to swine, the rule of life which is good enough for the one would be good enough for the other. The comparison of the Epicurean life to that of beasts is felt as degrading, precisely because a beast's pleasures do not satisfy a human being's conceptions of happiness. Human

From J. S. Mill, *Utilitarianism,* 1863.

beings have faculties more elevated than the animal appetites and, when once made conscious of them, do not regard anything as happiness which does not include their gratification. I do not, indeed, consider the Epicureans to have been by any means faultless in drawing out their scheme of consequences from the utilitarian principle. To do this in any sufficient manner, many Stoic, as well as Christian, elements require to be included. But there is no known Epicurean theory of life which does not assign to the pleasures of the intellect, of the feelings and imagination, and of the moral sentiments, a much higher value as pleasures than to those of mere sensation. It must be admitted, however, that utilitarian writers in general have placed the superiority of mental over bodily pleasures chiefly in the greater permanency, safety, uncostliness, etc., of the former—that is, in their circumstantial advantages rather than in their intrinsic nature. And on all these points utilitarians have fully proved their case; but they might have taken the other and, as it may be called, higher ground with entire consistency. It is quite compatible with the principle of utility to recognize the fact that some kinds of pleasure are more desirable and more valuable than others. It would be absurd that, while, in estimating all other things, quality is considered as well as quantity, the estimation of pleasures should be supposed to depend on quantity alone.

If I am asked what I mean by difference of quality in pleasures, or what makes one pleasure more valuable than another, merely as a pleasure, except its being greater in amount, there is but one possible answer. Of two pleasures, if there be one to which all or almost all who have experience of both give a decided preference, irrespective of any feeling of moral obligation to prefer it, that is the more desirable pleasure. If one of the two is, by those who are competently acquainted with both, placed so far above the other that they prefer it, even though knowing it to be attended with a greater amount of discontent, and would not resign it for any quantity of the other pleasure which their nature is capable of, we are justified in ascribing to the preferred enjoyment a superiority in quality so far outweighing quantity as to render it, in comparison, of small account.

Now it is an unquestionable fact that those who are equally acquainted with and equally capable of appreciating and enjoying both, do give a most marked preference to the manner of existence which employs their higher faculties. Few human creatures would consent to be changed into any of the lower animals for a promise of the fullest allowance of a beast's pleasures; no intelligent human being would consent to be a fool, no instructed person would be an ignoramus, no person of feeling and conscience would be selfish and base, even though they should be persuaded that the fool, the dunce, or the rascal is better satisfied with his lot than they are with theirs. They would not resign what they possess more than he for the most complete satisfaction of all the desires which they have in common with him. If they ever fancy they would, it is only in cases of unhappiness so extreme that to escape from it they would exchange their lot for almost any other, however undesirable in their own eyes. A being of higher faculties requires more to make him happy, is capable probably of more acute suffering, and certainly accessible to it at more points, than one of an inferior type; but in spite of these liabilities, he can never really wish to sink into what he feels to be a lower grade of existence. We may give what explanation we please of this unwillingness; we may attribute it to pride, a name which is given indiscriminately to some of the most and to some of the least estimable feelings of which mankind are capable: we may refer it to the love of liberty and personal independence, an appeal to which was with the Stoics one of the most effective means for the inculcation of it; to the love of power or to the love of excitement, both of which do really enter into and contribute to it; but its most appropriate appellation is a sense of dignity, which all human beings possess in one form or other, and in some, though by no means in exact, proportion to their higher faculties, and which is so essential a part of the happiness of those in whom it is strong that nothing which conflicts with it could be otherwise than momentarily an object of desire to them. Whoever supposes that this preference takes place at a sacrifice of happiness—that the superior being, in anything like equal circumstances, is not happier than the inferior—confounds the two very different ideas of happiness and content. It is undisputable that the being whose capacities of enjoyment are low has the greatest chance of having them fully satisfied; and a highly endowed being will always feel that any happiness which he can look for, as the world is constituted, is imperfect. But he can learn to bear its imperfections, if they are at all bearable; and they will not make him envy the being who is indeed unconscious of the imperfections, but only because he feels not at all the good which those imperfections qualify. It is better to be a human being dissatisfied than a pig satisfied; better to be Socrates dissatisfied than a fool satisfied. And if the fool, or the pig, are of a different opinion, it is because they only know their own side of the question. The other party to the comparison knows both sides.

It may be objected that many who are capable of the higher pleasures occasionally, under the influence of temptation, postpone them to the lower. But this is quite compatible with a full appreciation of the intrinsic superiority of the higher. Men often, from infirmity of character, make their election for the nearer good, though they know it to be the less valuable; and this no less when the choice is between two bodily pleasures than when it is between bodily and mental. They pursue sensual indulgences to the injury of health, though perfectly aware that health is the greater good. It may be further objected that many who begin with youthful enthusiasm for everything noble, as they advance in years, sink into indolence and selfishness. But I do not believe that those who undergo this very common change voluntarily choose the lower description of pleasures in preference to the higher. I believe that, before they devote themselves exclusively to the one, they have already become incapable of the other. Capacity for the nobler feelings is in most natures a very tender plant, easily killed, not only by hostile influences, but by mere want of sustenance; and in the majority of young persons it speedily dies away if the occupations to which their position in life has devoted them, and the society into which it has thrown them, are not favorable to keeping that higher capacity in exercise. Men lose their high aspirations as they lose their intellectual tastes, because they have not time or opportunity for indulging them; and they addict themselves to inferior pleasures, not because they deliberately prefer them, but because they are either the only ones to which they have access, or the only ones which they are any longer capable of enjoying. It may be questioned whether any one who has remained equally susceptible to both classes of pleasures, ever knowingly and calmly preferred the lower, though many, in all ages, have broken down in an ineffectual attempt to combine both.

From this verdict of the only competent judges, I apprehend there can be no appeal. On a question which is the best worth having of two pleasures, or which of two modes of existence is the most grateful to the feelings, apart from its moral attributes and from its consequences, the judgment of those who are qualified by knowledge of both, or, if they differ, that of the majority of them, must be admitted as final. And there needs to be less hesitation to accept this judgment respecting the quality of pleasures, since there is no other tribunal to be referred to even on the question of quantity. What means are there of determining which is the acutest of two pains, or the intensest of two pleasurable sensations, except the general suffrage of those who are familiar with both? Neither pains nor pleasures are homogeneous, and pain is always heterogeneous with pleasure. What is there to decide whether a particular pleasure is worth purchasing at the cost of a particular pain, except the feelings and judgment of the experienced? When, therefore, those feelings and judgment declare the pleasures derived from the higher faculties to be preferable *in kind,* apart from the question of intensity, to those of which the animal nature, disjoined from the higher faculties, is susceptible, they are entitled on this subject to the same regard.

I have dwelt on this point, as being a necessary part of a perfectly just conception of utility or happiness considered as the directive rule of human conduct. But it is by no means an indispensable condition to the acceptance of the utilitarian standard; for that standard is not the agent's own greatest happiness, but the greatest amount of happiness altogether; and if it may possibly be doubted whether a noble character is always the happier for its nobleness, there can be no doubt that it makes other people happier, and that the world in general is immensely a gainer by it. Utilitarianism, therefore, could only attain its end by the general cultivation of nobleness of character, even if each individual were only benefited by the nobleness of others, and his own, so far as happiness is concerned, were a sheer deduction from the benefit. But the bare enunciation of such an absurdity as this last renders refutation superfluous.

According to the greatest happiness principle, as above explained, the ultimate end, with reference to and for the sake of which all other things are desirable—whether we are considering our own good or that of other people—is an existence exempt as far as possible from pain, and as rich as possible in enjoyments, both in point of quantity and quality; the test of quality and the rule for measuring it against quantity being the preference felt by those who, in their opportunities of experience, to which must be added their habits of self-consciousness and self-observation, are best furnished with the means of comparison. This, being, according to the utilitarian opinion, the end of human action, is necessarily also the standard of morality, which may accordingly be defined "the rules and precepts for human conduct," by the observance of which an existence such as has been described might be, to the greatest extent possible, secured to all mankind; and not to them only, but, so far as the nature of things admits, to the whole sentient creation. . . .

The happiness which forms the utilitarian standard of what is right in conduct is not the agent's own happiness but that of all concerned. As between his own happiness and that of others, utilitarianism requires him to be as strictly impartial as a disinterested and benevolent spectator. In the golden rule of Jesus of Nazareth, we read the complete spirit of the ethics of utility. "To do as you would be done by," and "to love your neighbor as yourself," constitute the ideal perfection of utilitarian morality. As the means of making the nearest approach to this ideal, utility would enjoin, first, that laws and social arrangements should place the happiness or (as, speaking practically, it may be called) the interest of every individual as nearly as possible in harmony with the interest of the whole; and, secondly, that education and opinion, which have so vast a power over human character, should so use that power as to establish in the mind of every individual an indissoluble association between his own happiness and the good of the whole, especially between his own happiness and the practice of such modes of conduct, negative and positive, as regard for the universal happiness prescribes; so that not only he may be unable to conceive the possibility of happiness to himself, consistently with conduct opposed to the general good, but also that a direct impulse to promote the general good may be in every individual one of the habitual motives of action, and the sentiments connected therewith may fill a large and prominent place in every human being's sentient existence. If the impugners of the utilitarian morality represented it to their own minds in this its true character, I know not what recommendation possessed by any other morality they could possibly affirm to be wanting to it; what more beautiful or more exalted developments of human nature any other ethical system can be supposed to foster, or what springs of action, not accessible to the utilitarian, such systems rely on for giving effect to their mandates.

. . . The corollaries from the principle of utility, like the precepts of every practical art, admit of indefinite improvement, and, in a progressive state of the human mind, their improvement is perpetually going on. But to consider the rules of morality as improvable is one thing; to pass over the intermediate generalization entirely and endeavor to test each individual action directly by the first principle is another. It is a strange notion that the acknowledgment of a first principle is inconsistent with the admission of secondary ones. To inform a traveler respecting the place of his ultimate destination is not to forbid the use of landmarks and direction-posts on the way. The proposition that happiness is the end and aim of morality does not mean that no road ought to be laid down to that goal, or that persons going thither should not be advised to take one direction rather than another. Men really ought to leave off talking a kind of nonsense on this subject, which they would neither talk nor listen to on other matters of practical concernment. Nobody argues that the art of navigation is not founded on astronomy because sailors cannot wait to calculate the nautical almanac. Being rational creatures, they go to sea with it ready calculated; and all rational creatures go out upon the sea of life with their minds made up on the common questions of right and wrong, as well as on many of the far more difficult questions of wise and foolish. And this, as long as foresight is a human quality, it is to be presumed they will continue to do. Whatever we adopt as the fundamental principle of morality, we require subordinate principles to apply it by; the impossibility of doing without them, being common to all systems, can afford no argument against any one in particular; but gravely to argue as if no such secondary principles could be had, and as if mankind had remained till now, and always must remain, without drawing any general conclusions from the experience of human life, is as high a pitch, I think, as absurdity has ever reached in philosophical controversy. . . .

OF WHAT SORT OF PROOF THE PRINCIPLE OF UTILITY IS SUSCEPTIBLE

. . . Questions of ultimate ends do not admit of proof, in the ordinary acceptation of the term. To be incapable of proof by reasoning is common to all first principles, to the first premises of our knowledge, as well as to those of our conduct. But the former, being matters of fact, may be the subject of a direct appeal to the faculties which judge of fact—namely, our senses and our internal consciousness. Can an appeal be made to the same faculties on questions of practical ends? Or by what other faculty is cognizance taken of them?

Questions about ends are, in other words, questions what things are desirable. The utilitarian doctrine is that happiness is desirable, and the only thing desirable, as an end; all other things being only desirable as means to that end. What ought to be required of this doctrine, what conditions is it requisite that the doctrine should fulfill—to make good its claim to be believed?

The only proof capable of being given that an object is visible is that people actually see it. The only proof that a sound is audible is that people hear it; and so of the other sources of our experience. In like manner, I apprehend, the sole evidence it is possible to produce that anything is desirable is that people do actually desire it. If the end which the utilitarian doctrine proposes to itself were not, in theory and in practice, acknowledged to be an end, nothing could ever convince any person that it was so. No reason can be given why the general happiness is desirable, except that each person, so far as he believes it to be attainable, desires his own happiness. This, however, being a fact, we have not only all the proof which the case admits of, but all which it is possible to require, that happiness is a good; that each person's happiness is a good to that person, and the general happiness, therefore, a good to the aggregate of all persons. Happiness has made out its title as *one* of the ends of conduct, and consequently one of the criteria of morality.

But it has not, by this alone, proved itself to be the sole criterion. To do that, it would seem, by the same rule, necessary to show, not only that people desire happiness, but that they never desire anything else. Now it is palpable that they do desire things which, in common language, are decidedly distinguished from happiness. They desire, for example, virtue and the absence of vice, no less really than pleasure and the absence of pain. The desire of virtue is not as universal, but it is as authentic a fact as the desire of happiness. And hence the opponents of the utilitarian standard deem that they have a right to infer that there are other ends of human action besides happiness, and that happiness is not the standard of approbation and disapprobation.

But does the utilitarian doctrine deny that people desire virtue, or maintain that virtue is not a thing to be desired? The very reverse. It maintains not only that virtue is to be desired, but that it is to be desired disinterestedly, for itself. Whatever may be the opinion of utilitarian moralists as to the original conditions by which virtue is made virtue, however they may believe (as they do) that actions and dispositions are only virtuous because they promote another end than virtue, yet this being granted, and it having been decided, from considerations of this description, what *is* virtuous, they not only place virtue at the very head of the things which are good as means to the ultimate end, but they also recognize as a psychological fact the possibility of its being, to the individual, a good in itself, without looking to any end beyond it; and hold that the mind is not in a right state, not in a state conformable to utility, not in the state most conducive to the general happiness, unless it does love virtue in this manner—as a thing desirable in itself, even although, in the individual instance, it should not produce those other desirable consequences which it tends to produce, and on account of which it is held to be virtue. This opinion is not, in the smallest degree, a departure from the happiness principle. The ingredients of happiness are very various, and each of them is desirable in itself, and not merely when considered as swelling an aggregate. The principle of utility does not mean that any given pleasure, as music, for instance, or any given exemption from pain, as for example health, is to be looked upon as means to a collective something termed happiness, and to be desired on that account. They are desired and desirable in and for themselves; besides being means, they are a part of the end. Virtue, according to the utilitarian doctrine, is not naturally and originally part of the end, but it is capable of becoming so; and in those who love it disinterestedly it has become so, and is desired and cherished, not as a means to happiness, but as a part of their happiness.

To illustrate this further, we may remember that virtue is not the only thing originally a means, and which if it were not a means to anything else would be and remain indifferent, but which by association with what it is a means to comes to be desired for itself, and that too with the utmost intensity. What, for example, shall we say of the love of money? There is nothing originally more desirable about money than about any heap of glittering pebbles. Its worth is solely that of the things which it will buy; the desires for other things than itself, which it is a means of gratifying. Yet the love of money is not only one of the strongest moving forces of human life, but money is, in many cases, desired in and for itself; the desire to possess it is often stronger than the desire to use it, and goes on increasing when all the desires which point to ends beyond it, to be compassed by it, are falling off. It may, then, be said truly that money is desired not for the sake of an end, but as part of the end. From being a means to happiness, it has come to be itself a principal ingredient of the individual's conception of happiness. The same may be said of the majority of the great objects of human life: power, for example, or fame, except that to each of these there is a certain amount of immediate pleasure annexed, which has at least the semblance of being naturally inherent in them—a thing which cannot be said of money. Still, however, the strongest natural attraction, both of power and of fame, is the immense aid they give to the attainment of our other wishes; and it is the strong association thus generated between them and all our objects of desire which gives to the direct desire of them the intensity if often assumes, so as in some characters to surpass in strength all other desires. In these cases the means have become a part of the end, and a more important part of it than any of the things which they are means to. What was once desired as an instrument for the attainment of happiness has come to be desired for its own sake. In being desired for its own sake it is, however, desired as *part* of happiness. The person is made, or thinks he would be made, happy by its mere possession; and is made unhappy by failure to obtain it. The desire of it is not a different thing from the desire of happiness any more than the love of music or the desire of health. They are included in happiness. They are some of the elements of which the desire of happiness is made up. Happiness is not an abstract idea but a concrete whole; and these are some of its parts. And the utilitarian standard sanctions and approves their being so. Life would be a poor thing, very ill provided with sources of happiness, if there were not this provision of nature by which things originally indifferent, but conducive to, or otherwise associated with, the satisfaction of our primitive desires, become in themselves sources of pleasure more valuable than the primitive pleasures, both in permanency, in the space of human existence that they are capable of covering, and even in intensity.

Virtue, according to the utilitarian conception, is a good of this description. There was no original desire of it, or motive to it, save its conduciveness to pleasure, and especially to protection from pain. But through the association thus formed it may be felt a good in itself, and desired as such with as great intensity as any other good; and with this difference between it and the love of money, of power, or of fame, that all of these may, and often do, render the individual noxious to the other members of the society to which he belongs, whereas there is nothing which makes him so much a blessing to them as the cultivation of the disinterested love of virtue. And consequently, the utilitarian standard, while it tolerates and approves those other acquired desires, up to the point beyond which they would be more injurious to the general happiness than promotive of it, enjoins and requires the cultivation of the love of virtue up to the greatest strength possible, as being above all things important to the general happiness.

It results from the preceding considerations that there is in reality nothing desired except happiness. Whatever is desired otherwise than as a means to some end beyond itself, and ultimately to happiness, is desired as itself a part of happiness, and is not desired for itself until it has become so. Those who desire virtue for its own sake desire it either because the consciousness of it is a pleasure, or because the consciousness of being without it is a pain, or for both reasons united; as in truth the pleasure and pain seldom exist separately, but almost always together—the same person feeling pleasure in the degree of virtue attained, and pain in not having attained more. If one of these gave him no pleasure, and the other no pain, he would not love or desire virtue, or would desire it only for the other benefits which it might produce to himself or to persons whom he cared for.

We have now, then, an answer to the question, of what sort of proof the principle of utility is susceptible. If the opinion which I have now stated is psychologically true—if human nature is so constituted as to desire nothing which is not either a part of happiness or a means of happiness, we can have no other proof, and we require no other, that these are the only things desirable. If so, happiness is the sole end of human action, and the promotion of it the test by which to judge of all human conduct; from whence it necessarily follows that it must be the criterion of morality, since a part is included in the whole.

And now to decide whether this is really so, whether mankind do desire nothing for itself but that which is a pleasure to them, or of which the absence is a pain, we have evidently arrived at a question of fact and experience, dependent, like all similar questions, upon evidence. It can only be determined by practised self-consciousness and self-observation, assisted by observation of others. I believe that these sources of evidence, impartially consulted, will declare that desiring a thing and finding it pleasant, aversion to it and thinking of it as painful, are phenomena entirely inseparable or rather two parts of the same phenomenon; in strictness of language, two different modes of naming the same psychological fact; that to think of an object as desirable (unless for the sake of its consequences) and to think of it as pleasant are one and the same thing; and that to desire anything except in proportion as the idea of it is pleasant, is a physical and metaphysical impossibility.

So obvious does this appear to me that I expect it will hardly be disputed; and the objection made will be, not that desire can possibly be directed to anything ultimately except pleasure and exemption from pain, but that the will is a different thing from desire; that a person of confirmed virtue or any other person whose purposes are fixed carries out his purposes without any thought of the pleasure he has in contemplating them or expects to derive from their fulfilment, and persists in acting on them, even though these pleasures are much diminished by changes in his character or decay of his passive sensibilities, or are outweighed by the pains which the pursuit of the purposes may bring upon him. All this I fully admit and have stated it elsewhere as positively and emphatically as anyone. Will, the active phenomenon, is a different thing from desire, the state of passive sensibility, and, though originally an offshoot from it, may in time take root and detach itself from the parent stock, so much so that in the case of an habitual purpose, instead of willing the thing because we desire it, we often desire it only because we will it. This, however, is but an instance of that familiar fact, the power of habit, and is nowise confined to the case of virtuous actions. Many indifferent things which men originally did from a motive of some sort, they continue to do from habit. Sometimes this is done unconsciously; the consciousness coming only after the action; at other times with conscious volition, but volition which has become habitual and is put in operation by the force of habit, in opposition perhaps to the deliberate preference, as often happens with those who have contracted habits of vicious or hurtful indulgence. Third and last comes the case in which the habitual act of will in the individual instance is not in contradiction to the general intention prevailing at other times, but in fulfilment of it; as in the case of the person of confirmed virtue and of all who pursue deliberately and consistently any determinate end. The distinction between will and desire thus understood is an authentic and highly important psychological fact; but the fact consists solely in this—that will, like all other parts of our constitution, is amenable to habit, and that we may will from habit what we no longer desire for itself, or desire only because we will it. It is not the less true that will, in the beginning, is entirely produced by desire; including in that term the repelling influence of pain as well as the attractive one of pleasure. Let us take into consideration no longer the person who has a confirmed will to do right, but him in whom that virtuous will is still feeble, conquerable by temptation, and not to be fully relied on; by what means can it be strengthened? How can the will to be virtuous, where it does not exist in sufficient force, be implanted or awakened? Only by making the person *desire* virtue—by making him think of it in a pleasurable light, or of its absence in a painful one. It is by associating the doing right with pleasure, or the doing wrong with pain, or by eliciting and impressing and bringing home to the person's experience the pleasure naturally involved in the one or the pain in the other, that it is possible to call forth that will to be virtuous which, when confirmed, acts without any thought of either pleasure or pain. Will is the child of desire, and passes out of the dominion of its parent only to come under that of habit. That which is the result of habit affords no presumption of being intrinsically good; and there would be no reason for wishing that the purpose of virtue should become independent of pleasure and pain were it not that the influence of the pleasurable and painful associations which prompt to virtue is not sufficiently to be depended on for unerring constancy of action until it has acquired the support of habit. Both in feeling and in conduct, habit is the only thing which imparts certainty; and it is because of the importance to others of being able to rely absolutely on one's feelings and conduct, and to oneself of being able to rely on one's own, that the will to do right ought to be cultivated into this habitual independence. In other words, this state of the will is a means to good, not intrinsically a good; and does not contradict the doctrine that nothing is a good to human beings but in so far as it is either itself pleasurable or a means of attaining pleasure or averting pain.

But if this doctrine be true, the principle of utility is proved. Whether it is so or not, must now be left to the consideration of the thoughtful reader.

ON LIBERTY

CHAPTER I
Introductory

. . . The object of this essay is to assert one very simple principle, as entitled to govern absolutely the dealings of society with the individual in the way of compulsion and control, whether the means used be physical force in the form of legal penalties, or the moral coercion of public opinion. That principle is, that the sole end for which mankind are warranted, individually or collectively, in interfering with the liberty of action of any of their number, is self-protection. That the only purpose for which power can be rightfully exercised over any member of a civilized community, against his will, is to prevent harm to others. His own good, either physical or moral, is not a sufficient warrant. He cannot rightfully be compelled to do or forbear because it will be better for him to do so, because it will make him happier, because, in the opinions of others, to do so would be wise, or even right. These are good reasons for remonstrating with him, or reasoning with him, or persuading him, or entreating him, but not for compelling him, or visiting him with any evil in case

From J. S. Mill, *On Liberty*, first published in London in 1859.

he do otherwise. To justify that, the conduct from which it is desired to deter him must be calculated to produce evil to some one else. The only part of the conduct of anyone, for which he is amenable to society, is that which concerns others. In the part which merely concerns himself, his independence is, of right, absolute. Over himself, over his own body and mind, the individual is sovereign.

It is perhaps hardly necessary to say that this doctrine is meant to apply only to human beings in the maturity of their faculties. We are not speaking of children, or of young persons below the age which the law may fix as that of manhood or womanhood. Those who are still in a state to require being taken care of by others, must be protected against their own actions as well as against external injury. . . .

It is proper to state that I forego any advantage which could be derived to my argument from the idea of abstract right, as a thing independent of utility. I regard utility as the ultimate appeal on all ethical questions; but it must be utility in the largest sense, grounded on the permanent interests of a man as a progressive being. Those interests, I contend, authorized the subjection of individual spontaneity to external control, only in respect to those actions of each which concern the interest of other people. If anyone does an act hurtful to others, there is a *prima facie* case for punishing him, by law, or, where legal penalties are not safely applicable, by general disapprobation. There are also many positive acts for the benefit of others, which he may rightfully be compelled to perform: such as to give evidence in a court of justice; to bear his fair share in the common defense, or in any other joint work necessary to the interest of the society of which he enjoys the protection; and to perform certain acts of individual beneficence, such as saving a fellow-creature's life, or interposing to protect the defenseless against ill-usage, things which wherever it is obviously a man's duty to do, he may rightfully be made responsible to society for not doing. A person may cause evil to others not only by his actions but by his inaction, and in either case he is justly accountable to them for the injury. The latter case, it is true, requires a much more cautious exercise of compulsion than the former. To make anyone answerable for doing evil to others is the rule; to make him answerable for not preventing evil is, comparatively speaking, the exception. Yet there are many cases clear enough and grave enough to justify that exception. In all things which regard the external relations of the individual, he is *de jure* amenable to those whose interests are concerned, and, if need be, to society as their protector. There are often good reasons for not holding him to the responsibility; but these reasons must arise from the special expediencies of the case: either because it is a kind of case in which he is on the whole likely to act better, when left to his own discretion, than when controlled in any way in which society have it in their power to control him; or because the attempt to exercise control would produce other evils, greater than those which it would prevent. When such reasons as these preclude the enforcement of responsibility, the conscience of the agent himself should step into the vacant judgment seat, and protect those interests of others which have no external protection; judging himself all the more rigidly, because the case does not admit of his being made accountable to the judgment of his fellow-creatures.

But there is a sphere of action in which society, as distinguished from the individual, has, if any, only an indirect interest; comprehending all that portion of a person's life and conduct which affects only himself, or if it also affects others, only with their free, voluntary, and undeceived consent and participation. When I say only himself, I mean directly, and in the first instance; for whatever affects himself, may affect others through himself; and the objection which may be grounded on this contingency, will receive consideration in the sequel. This, then, is the appropriate region of human liberty. It comprises, *first,* the inward domain of consciousness; demanding liberty of conscience in the most comprehensive sense; liberty of thought and feeling; absolute freedom of opinion and sentiment on all sub-jects, practical or speculative, scientific, moral or theological. The liberty of expressing and publishing opinions may seem to fall under a different principle, since it belongs to that part of the conduct of an individual which concerns other people; but, being almost of as much importance as the liberty of thought itself, and resting in great part on the same rea-sons, is practically inseparable from it. *Secondly,* the principle requires liberty of tastes and pursuits; of framing the plan of our life to suit our own character; of doing as we like, subject to such consequences as may follow: without impediment from our fellow-creatures, so long as what we do does not harm them, even though they should think our conduct foolish, perverse, or wrong. *Thirdly,* from this liberty of each individual, follows the liberty, within the same limits, of combination among individuals; freedom to unite, for any pur-pose not involving harm to others: the persons combining being supposed to be of full age, and not forced or deceived.

No society in which these liberties are not, on the whole, respected, is free, whatever may be its form of government; and none is completely free in which they do not exist absolute and unqualified. The only freedom which deserves the name, is that of pursuing our own good in our own way, so long as we do not attempt to deprive others of theirs, or impede their efforts to obtain it. Each is the proper guardian of his own health, whether bodily, or mental and spiritual. Mankind are greater gainers by suffering each other to live as seems good to themselves, than by compelling each to live as seems good to the rest.

Though this doctrine is anything but new, and, to some persons, may have the air of a truism, there is no doctrine which stands more directly opposed to the general tendency of existing opinion and practice. . . . There is . . . an inclination to stretch unduly the powers of society over the individual, both by the force of opinion and even by that of legislation; and as the tendency of all the changes taking place in the world is to strengthen society, and diminish the power of the individual, this encroachment is not one of the evils which tend spontaneously to disappear, but, on the contrary, to grow more and more formidable. The disposition of mankind, whether as rulers or as fellow-citizens, to impose their own opin-ions and inclinations as a rule of conduct on others, is so energetically supported by some of the best and by some of the worst feelings incident to human nature, that it is hardly ever kept under restraint by anything but want of power; and as the power is not declining, but growing, unless a strong barrier of moral conviction can be raised against the mischief, we must expect, in the present circumstances of the world, to see it increase. . . .

CHAPTER II
Of the Liberty of Thought and Discussion

The time, it is to be hoped, is gone by, when any defence would be necessary of the "liberty of the press" as one of the securities against corrupt or tyrannical government. . . . Speak-ing generally, it is not, in constitutional countries, to be apprehended that the government, whether completely responsible to the people or not, will often attempt to control the ex-pression of opinion, except when in doing so it makes itself the organ of the general intol-erance of the public. Let us suppose, therefore, that the government is entirely at one with the people, and never thinks of exerting any power of coercion unless in agreement with what it conceives to be their voice. But I deny the right of the people to exercise such co-ercion, either by themselves or by their government. The power itself is illegitimate. The best government has no more title to it than the worst. It is as noxious, or more noxious, when exerted in accordance with public opinion, than when in opposition to it. If all mankind minus one were of one opinion, and only one person were of the contrary opinion, mankind would be no more justified in silencing that one person, than he, if he had the power, would be justified in silencing mankind. Were an opinion a personal possession of no value except to the owner; if to be obstructed in the enjoyment of it were simply a private injury, it would make some difference whether the injury was inflicted only on a few persons or on many. But the peculiar evil of silencing the expression of an opinion is, that it is robbing the human race: posterity as well as the existing generation; those who dissent from the opinion, still more than those who hold it. If the opinion is right, they are deprived of the opportunity of exchanging error for truth; if wrong, they lose, what is almost as great a benefit, the clearer perception and livelier impression of truth, produced by its collision with error.

It is necessary to consider separately these two hypotheses, each of which has a distinct branch of the argument corresponding to it. We can never be sure that the opinion we are endeavoring to stifle is a false opinion; and if we were sure, stifling it would be an evil still.

First: the opinion which it is attempted to suppress by authority may possibly be true. Those who desire to suppress it, of course deny its truth; but they are not infallible. They have no authority to decide the question for all mankind, and exclude every other person from the means of judging. To refuse a hearing to an opinion, because they are sure that it is false, is to assume that *their* certainty is the same thing as *absolute* certainty. All silencing of discussion is an assumption of infallibility. Its condemnation may be allowed to rest on this common argument, not the worse for being common.

Unfortunately for the good sense of mankind, the fact of their fallibility is far from carrying the weight in their practical judgment which is always allowed to it in theory; for while everyone well knows himself to be fallible, few think it necessary to take any precautions against their own fallibility, or admit the supposition that any opinion of which they feel very certain, may be one of the examples of the error to which they acknowledge themselves to be liable. Absolute princes, or others who are accustomed to unlimited deference, usually feel this complete confidence in their own opinions on nearly all subjects. People more happily situated, who sometimes hear their opinions disputed, and are not wholly unused to be set right when they are wrong, place the same unbounded reliance only on such of their opinions as are shared by all who surround them, or to whom they habitually defer; for in proportion to a man's want of confidence in his own solitary judgment, does he usually repose, with implicit trust, on the infallibility of "the world" in general. And the world, to each individual, means the part of it with which he comes in contact—his party, his sect, his church, his class of society; the man may be called, by comparison, almost liberal and large-minded to whom it means anything so comprehensive as his own country or his own age. Nor is his faith in this collective authority at all shaken by his being aware that other ages, countries, sects, churches, classes, and parties have thought, and even now think, the exact reverse. He devolves upon his own world the responsibility of being in the right against the dissentient worlds of other people; and it never troubles him that mere accident has decided which of these numerous worlds is the object of his reliance, and that the same causes which make him a Churchman in London, would have made him a Buddhist or a Confucian in Peking. Yet it is as evident in itself as any amount of argument can make it, that ages are no more infallible than individuals; every age having held many opinions which subsequent ages have deemed not only false but absurd; and it is as certain that many opinions now general will be rejected by future ages, as it is that many, once general, are rejected by the present.

The objection likely to be made to this argument would probably take some such form as the following. There is no greater assumption of infallibility in forbidding the propagation of error, than in any other thing which is done by public authority on its own judgment and responsibility. Judgment is given to men that they may use it. Because it may be used erroneously, are men to be told that they ought not to use it at all? To prohibit what they think pernicious, is not claiming exemption from error, but fulfilling the duty incumbent on them, although fallible, of acting on their conscientious conviction. If we were never to act on our opinions, because those opinions may be wrong, we should leave all our interests uncared for, and all our duties unperformed. An objection which applies to all conduct can be no valid objection to any conduct in particular. It is the duty of governments, and of individuals, to form the truest opinions they can; to form them carefully, and never impose them upon others unless they are quite sure of being right. But when they are sure (such reasoners may say), it is not conscientiousness but cowardice to shrink from acting on their opinions, and allow doctrines which they honestly think dangerous to the welfare of mankind, either in this life or in another, to be scattered abroad without restraint, because other people, in less enlightened times, have persecuted opinions now believed to be true. Let us take care, it may be said, not to make the same mistake; but governments and nations have made mistakes in other things, which are not denied to be fit subjects for the exercise of authority: they have laid on bad taxes, made unjust wars. Ought we therefore to lay on no taxes, and, under whatever provocation, make no wars? Men, and governments, must act to the best of their ability. There is no such thing as absolute certainty, but there is assurance sufficient for the purposes of human life. We may, and must, assume our opinion to be true for the guidance of our own conduct: and it is assuming no more when we forbid bad men to pervert society by the propagation of opinions which we regard as false and pernicious.

I answer that it is assuming very much more. There is the greatest difference between presuming an opinion to be true because, with every opportunity for contesting it, it has not been refuted, and assuming its truth for the purpose of not permitting its refutation. Complete liberty of contradicting and disproving our opinion is the very condition which justifies us in assuming its truth for purposes of action; and on no other terms can a being with human faculties have any rational assurance of being right.

When we consider either the history of opinion, or the ordinary conduct of human life, to what is it to be ascribed that the one and the other are no worse than they are? Not certainly to the inherent force of the human understanding; for, on any matter not self-evident, there are ninety-nine persons totally incapable of judging of it for one who is capable; and the capacity of the hundredth person is only comparative: for the majority of the eminent men of every past generation held many opinions now known to be erroneous, and did or approved numerous things which no one will now justify. Why is it, then, that there is on the whole a preponderance among mankind of rational opinions and rational conduct? If there really is this preponderance—which there must be unless human affairs are, and have always been, in an almost desperate state—it is owing to a quality of the human mind, the source of everything respectable in man either as an intellectual or as a moral being, namely, that his errors are corrigible. He is capable of rectifying his mistakes, by discussion and experience. Not by experience alone. There must be discussion, to show how experience is to be interpreted. Wrong opinions and practices gradually yield to fact and argument; but facts and arguments, to produce any effect on the mind, must be brought before it. Very few facts are able to tell their own story, without comments to bring out their meaning. The whole strength and value, then, of human judgment, depending on the one property, that it can be set right when it is wrong, reliance can be placed on it only when the means of setting it right are kept constantly at hand. In the case of any person whose judgment is really deserving of confidence, how has it become so? Because he has kept his mind open to criticism of his opinions and conduct. Because it has been his practice to listen to all that could be said against him; to profit by as much of it as was just, and expound to himself, and upon occasion to others, the fallacy of what was fallacious. Because he has felt that the only way in which a human being can make some approach to knowing the whole of a subject, is by hearing what can be said about it by persons of every variety of opinion, and studying all modes in which it can be looked at by every character of mind. No wise man ever acquired his wisdom in any mode but this; nor is it in the nature of human intellect to become wise in any other manner. The steady habit of correcting and completing his own opinion by collating it with those of others, so far from causing doubt and hesitation in carrying it into practice, is the only stable foundation for a just reliance on it: for, being cognizant of all that can, at least obviously, be said against him, and having taken up his position against all gainsayers—knowing that he has sought for objections and difficulties, instead of avoiding them, and has shut out no light which can be thrown upon the subject from any quarter—he has a right to think his judgment better than that of any person, or any multitude, who have not gone through a similar process.

It is not too much to require that what the wisest of mankind, those who are best entitled to trust their own judgment, find necessary to warrant their relying on it, should be submitted to by that miscellaneous collection of a few wise and many foolish individuals, called the public. The most intolerant of churches, the Roman Catholic Church, even at the canonization of a saint, admits, and listens patiently to, a "devil's advocate." The holiest of men, it appears, cannot be admitted to posthumous honors, until all that the devil could say against him is known and weighed. If even the Newtonian philosophy were not permitted to be questioned, mankind could not feel as complete assurance of its truth as they now do. The beliefs which we have most warrant for, have no safeguard to rest on but a standing invitation to the whole world to prove them unfounded. If the challenge is not accepted, or is accepted and the attempt fails, we are far enough from certainty still; but we have done the best that the existing state of human reason admits of; we have neglected nothing that could give the truth a chance of reaching us: if the lists are kept open, we may hope that if there be a better truth, it will be found when the human mind is capable of receiving it; and in the meantime we may rely on having attained such approach to truth as is possible in our own day. This is the amount of certainty attainable by a fallible being, and this the sole way of attaining it.

Strange it is that men should admit the validity of the arguments for free discussion, but object to their being "pushed to an extreme"; not seeing that unless the reasons are good for an extreme case, they are not good for any case. Strange that they should imagine that they are not assuming infallibility, when they acknowledge that there should be free discussion on all subjects which can possibly be *doubtful,* but think that some particular principle or doctrine should be forbidden to be questioned because it is so *certain,* that is, because *they are certain* that it is certain. To call any proposition certain while there is anyone who would deny its certainty if permitted, but who is not permitted, is to assume that we ourselves, and those who agree with us, are the judges of certainty, and judges without hearing the other side.

In the present age—which has been described as "destitute of faith, but terrified at scepticism"—in which people feel sure, not so much that their opinions are true, as that they should not know what to do without them—the claims of an opinion to be protected from public attack are rested not so much on its truth, as on its importance to society. There are, it is alleged, certain beliefs so useful, not to say indispensable, to well-being that it is as much the duty of governments to uphold those beliefs, as to protect any other of the interests of society. In a case of such necessity, and so directly in the line of their duty, something less than infallibility may, it is maintained, warrant, and even bind, governments to act on their own opinion, confirmed by the general opinion of mankind. It is also often argued, and still oftener thought, that none but bad men would desire to weaken these salutary beliefs; and there can be nothing wrong, it is thought, in restraining bad men, and prohibiting what only such men would wish to practice. This mode of thinking makes the justification of restraints on discussion not a question of the truth of doctrines, but of their usefulness; and flatters itself by that means to escape the responsibility of claiming to be an infallible judge of opinions. But those who thus satisfy themselves, do not perceive that the assumption of infallibility is merely shifted from one point to another. The usefulness of an opinion is itself matter of opinion: as disputable, as open to discussion, and requiring discussion as much as the opinion itself. There is the same need of an infallible judge of opinions to decide an opinion to be noxious, as to decide it to be false, unless the opinion condemned has full opportunity of defending itself. And it will not do to say that the heretic may be allowed to maintain the utility or harmlessness of his opinion, though forbidden to maintain its truth. The truth of an opinion is part of its utility. If we would know whether or not it is desirable that a proposition should be believed, is it possible to exclude the consideration of whether or not it is true? In the opinion, not of bad men, but of the best men, no belief which is contrary to truth can be really useful; and can you prevent such men from urging that plea, when they are charged with culpability for denying some doctrine which they are told is useful, but which they believe to be false? Those who are on the side of received opinions never fail to take all possible advantages of this plea: you do not find *them* handling the question of utility as if it could be completely abstracted from that of truth; on the contrary, it is, above all, because their doctrine is "the truth," that the knowledge or the belief of it is held to be so indispensable. There can be no fair discussion of the question of usefulness when an argument so vital may be employed on one side, but not on the other. And in point of fact, when law or public feeling do not permit the truth of an opinion to be disputed, they are just as little tolerant of a denial of its usefulness. The utmost they allow is an extenuation of its absolute necessity, or of the positive guilt of rejecting it.

In order more fully to illustrate the mischief of denying a hearing to opinions because we, in our own judgment, have condemned them, it will be desirable to fix down the discussion to a concrete case; and I choose, by preference, the cases which are least favorable to me—in which the argument against freedom of opinion, both on the score of truth and on that of utility, is considered the strongest. Let the opinions impugned be the belief in a God and in a future state, or any of the commonly received doctrines of morality. To fight the battle on such ground gives a great advantage to an unfair antagonist; since he will be sure to say (and many who have no desire to be unfair will say it internally), "Are these the doctrines which you do not deem sufficiently certain to be taken under the protection of laws? Is the belief in a God one of the opinions to feel sure of which you hold to be assuming infallibility?" But I must be permitted to observe that it is not the feeling sure of a doctrine (be it what it may) which I call an assumption of infallibility. It is the undertaking to decide that question *for others,* without allowing them to hear what can be said on the contrary side. And I denounce and reprobate this pretension not the less if put forth on the side of my most solemn convictions. However positive anyone's persuasion may be, not only of the falsity but of the pernicious consequences—not only of the pernicious consequences, but (to adopt expressions which I altogether condemn) the immorality and impiety of an opinion; yet if, in pursuance of that private judgment, though backed by the public judgment of his country or his contemporaries, he prevents the opinion from being heard in its defense, he assumes infallibility. And so far from the assumption being less objectionable or less dangerous because the opinion is called immoral or impious, this is the case of all others in which it is most fatal. These are exactly the occasions on which the men of one generation commit those dreadful mistakes which excite the astonishment and horror of posterity. It is among such that we find the instances memorable in history, when the arm of the law has been employed to root out the best men and the noblest doctrines; with deplorable success as to the men, though some of the doctrines have survived to be (as if in mockery) invoked in defense of similar conduct toward those who dissent from *them,* or from their received interpretation.

Mankind can hardly be too often reminded, that there was once a man named Socrates, between whom and the legal authorities and public opinion of his time there took place a memorable collision. Born in an age and country abounding in individual greatness, this man has been handed down to us by those who best knew both him and the age, as the most virtuous man in it; while *we* know him as the head and prototype of all subsequent teachers of virtue, the source equally of the lofty inspiration of Plato and the judicious utilitarianism of Aristotle, . . . the two head-springs of ethical as of all other philosophy. This acknowledged master of all the eminent thinkers who have since lived—whose fame, still growing after more than two thousand years, all but outweighs the whole remainder of the names which make his native city illustrious—was put to death by his countrymen, after a judicial conviction, for impiety and immorality. Impiety, in denying the gods recognized by the State; indeed his accuser asserted (see the *Apology*) that he believed in no gods at all. Immorality, in being, by his doctrines and instructions, a "corruptor of youth." Of these charges the tribunal, there is every ground for believing, honestly found him guilty, and condemned the man who probably of all then born had deserved best of mankind to be put to death as a criminal.

To pass from this to the only other instance of judicial iniquity, the mention of which, after the condemnation of Socrates, would not be an anticlimax: the event which took place on Calvary rather more than eighteen hundred years ago. The man who left on the memory of those who witnessed his life and conversation such an impression of his moral grandeur that eighteen subsequent centuries have done homage to him as the Almighty in person, was ignominiously put to death, as what? As a blasphemer. Men did not merely mistake their benefactor; they mistook him for the exact contrary of what he was, and treated him as that prodigy of impiety which they themselves are now held to be for their treatment of him. The feelings with which mankind now regard these lamentable transactions, especially the later of the two, render them extremely unjust in their judgment of the unhappy actors. These were, to all appearance, not bad men—not worse than men commonly are, but rather the contrary; men who possessed in a full, or somewhat more than a full measure, the religious, moral, and patriotic feelings of their time and people: the very kind of men who, in all times, our own included, have every chance of passing through life blameless and respected. The high-priest who rent his garments when the words were pronounced which, according to all the ideas of his country, constituted the blackest guilt, was in all probability quite as sincere in his horror and indignation as the generality of respectable and pious men now are in the religious and moral sentiments they profess; and most of those who now shudder at his conduct, if they had lived in his time, and been born Jews, would have acted precisely as he did. Orthodox Christians who are tempted to think that those who stoned to death the first martyrs must have been worse men than they themselves are, ought to remember that one of those persecutors was Saint Paul. . . .

Let us now pass to the second division of the argument, and dismissing the supposition that any of the received opinions may be false, let us assume them to be true, and examine into the worth of the manner in which they are likely to be held, when their truth is not freely and openly canvassed. However unwilling a person who has a strong opinion may admit the possibility that his opinion may be false, he ought to be moved by the consideration that, however true it may be, if it is not fully, frequently, and fearlessly discussed, it will be held as a dead dogma, not a living truth.

There is a class of persons (happily not quite so numerous as formerly) who think it enough if a person assents undoubtingly to what they think true, though he has no knowledge whatever of the grounds of the opinion, and could not make a tenable defense of it against the most superficial objections. Such persons, if they can once get their creed taught from authority, naturally think that no good, and some harm, comes of its being allowed to be questioned. Where their influence prevails, they make it nearly impossible for the received opinion to be rejected wisely and considerately, though it may still be rejected rashly and ignorantly; for to shut out discussion entirely is seldom possible, and when it once gets in, beliefs not grounded on conviction are apt to give way before the slightest semblance of an argument. Waiving, however, this possibility—assuming that the true opinion abides in the mind, but abides as a prejudice, a belief independent of, and proof against, argument—this is not the way in which truth ought to be held by a rational being. This is not knowing the truth. Truth, thus held, is but one superstition the more, accidentally clinging to the words which enunciate a truth.

If the intellect and judgment of mankind ought to be cultivated, a thing which Protestants at least do not deny, on what can these faculties be more appropriately exercised by anyone, than on the things which concern him so much that it is considered necessary for him to hold opinions on them? If the cultivation of the understanding consists in one thing more than in another, it is surely in learning the grounds of one's own opinions. Whatever people believe, on subjects on which it is of the first importance to believe rightly, they ought to be able to defend against at least the common objections. But, some one may say, "Let them be *taught* the grounds of their opinions. It does not follow that opinions must be merely parroted because they are never heard controverted. Persons who learn geometry do not simply commit the theorems to memory, but understand and learn likewise the demonstrations; and it would be absurd to say that they remain ignorant of the grounds of geometrical truths, because they never hear any one deny, and attempt to disprove them." Undoubtedly: and such teaching suffices on a subject like mathematics, where there is nothing at all to be said on the wrong side of the question. The peculiarity of the evidence of mathematical truths is that all the argument is on one side. There are no objections, and no answers to objections. But on every subject on which difference of opinion is possible, the truth depends on a balance to be struck between two sets of conflicting reasons. Even in natural philosophy, there is always some other explanation possible of the same facts—some geocentric theory instead of heliocentric, some phlogiston instead of oxygen—and it has to be shown why that other theory cannot be the true one; and until this is shown, and until we know how it is shown, we do not understand the grounds of our opinion. But when we turn to subjects infinitely more complicated, to morals, religion, politics, social relations, and the business of life, three-fourths of the arguments for every disputed opinion consist in dispelling the appearances which favor some opinion different from it. The greatest orator, save one, of antiquity, has left it on record that he always studied his adversary's case with as great, if not still greater, intensity than even his own. What Cicero practiced as the means of forensic success requires to be imitated by all who study any subject in order to arrive at the truth. He who knows only his own side of the case, knows little of that. His reasons may be good, and no one may have been able to refute them. But if he is equally unable to refute the reasons on the opposite side; if he does not so much as know what they are, he has no ground for preferring either opinion. The rational position for him would be suspension of judgment, and unless he contents himself with that, he is either led by authority, or adopts, like the generality of the world, the side to which he feels most inclination. Nor is it enough that he should hear the arguments of adversaries from his own teachers, presented as they state them, and accompanied by what they offer as refutations. That is not the way to do justice to the arguments, or bring them into real contact with his own mind. He must be able to hear them from persons who actually believe them; who defend them in earnest, and do their very utmost for them. He must know them in their more plausible and persuasive form; he must feel the whole force of the difficulty which the true view of the subject has to encounter and dispose of; else he will never really possess himself of the portion of truth which meets and removes that difficulty. Ninety-nine in a hundred of what are called educated men are in this condition; even of those who can argue fluently for their opinions. Their conclusion may be true, but it might be false for anything they know: they have never thrown themselves into the mental position of those who think differently from them, and considered what such persons may have to say; and consequently they do not, in any proper sense of the word, know the doctrine which they themselves profess. They do not know those parts of it which explain and justify the remainder; the considerations which show that a fact which seemingly conflicts with another is reconcilable with it, or that, of two apparently strong reasons, one and not the other ought to be preferred. All that part of the truth which turns the scale, and decides the judgment of a completely informed mind, they are strangers to; nor is it ever really known but to those who have attended equally and impartially to both sides, and endeavored to see the reasons of both in the strongest light. So essential is this discipline to a real understanding of moral and human subjects, that if opponents of all important truths do not exist, it is indispensable to imagine them, and supply them with the strongest arguments which the most skilful devil's advocate can conjure up. . . .

If, however, the mischievous operation of the absence of free discussion, when the received opinions are true, were confined to leaving men ignorant of the grounds of those opinions, it might be thought that this, if an intellectual, is no moral evil, and does not affect the worth of the opinions, regarded in their influence on the character. The fact, however, is that not only the grounds of the opinion are forgotten in the absence of discussion, but too often the meaning of the opinion itself. The words which convey it cease to suggest ideas, or suggest only a small portion of those they were originally employed to communicate. Instead of a vivid conception and a living belief, there remain only a few phrases retained by rote; or, if any part, the shell and husk only of the meaning is retained, the finer essence being lost. The great chapter in human history which this fact occupies and fills, cannot be too earnestly studied and meditated on. . . .

The same thing holds true, generally speaking, of all traditional doctrines—those of prudence and knowledge of life, as well as of morals or religion. All languages and literatures are full of general observations on life, both as to what it is, and how to conduct oneself in it; observations which everybody knows, which everybody repeats, or hears with acquiescence, which are received as truisms, yet of which most people first truly learn the meaning when experience, generally of a painful kind, has made it a reality to them. How often, when smarting under some unforeseen misfortune or disappointment, does a person call to mind some proverb or common saying, familiar to him all his life, the meaning of which, if he had ever before felt it as he does now, would have saved him from the calamity. There are indeed reasons for this, other than the absence of discussion; there are many truths of which the full meaning *cannot* be realized until personal experience has brought it home. But much more of the meaning even of these would have been understood, and what was understood would have been far more deeply impressed on the mind, if the man had been accustomed to hear it argued *pro* and *con* by people who did understand it. The fatal tendency of mankind to leave off thinking about a thing when it is no longer doubtful, is the cause of half their errors. A contemporary author has well spoken of "the deep slumber of a decided opinion."

But what! (it may be asked) Is the absence of unanimity an indispensable condition of true knowledge? Is it necessary that some part of mankind should persist in error to enable any to realize the truth? Does a belief cease to be real and vital as soon as it is generally received; and is a proposition never thoroughly understood and felt unless some doubt of it remains? As soon as mankind have unanimously accepted a truth, does the truth perish within them? The highest aim and best result of improved intelligence, it has hitherto been thought, is to unite mankind more and more in the acknowledgment of all important truths; and does the intelligence only last as long as it has not achieved its object? Do the fruits of conquest perish by the very completeness of the victory?

I affirm no such thing. As mankind improve, the number of doctrines which are no longer disputed or doubted will be constantly on the increase: and the well-being of mankind may almost be measured by the number and gravity of the truths which have reached the point of being uncontested. The cessation, on one question after another, of serious controversy, is one of the necessary incidents of the consolidation of opinion; a consolidation as salutary in the case of true opinions, as it is dangerous and noxious when the opinions are erroneous. But though this gradual narrowing of the bounds of diversity of opinion is necessary in both senses of the term, being at once inevitable and indispensable, we are not therefore obliged to conclude that all its consequences must be beneficial. The loss of so important an aid to the intelligent and living apprehension of a truth, as is afforded by the necessity of explaining it to, or defending it against, opponents, though not sufficient to outweigh, is no trifling drawback from, the benefit of its universal recognition. Where this advantage can no longer be had, I confess I should like to see the teachers of mankind endeavoring to provide a substitute for it; some contrivance for making the difficulties of the question as present to the learner's consciousness, as if they were pressed upon him by a dissentient champion, eager for his conversion. . . .

It is the fashion of the present time to disparage negative logic—that which points out weaknesses in theory or errors in practice, without establishing positive truths. Such negative criticism would indeed be poor enough as an ultimate result; but as a means to attaining any positive knowledge or conviction worthy the name, it cannot be valued too highly; and until people are again systematically trained to it, there will be few greater thinkers, and a low general average of intellect, in any but the mathematical and physical departments of speculation. On any other subject no one's opinions deserve the name of knowledge, except so far as he has either had forced upon him by others, or gone through of himself, the same mental process which would have been required of him in carrying on an active controversy with opponents. That, therefore, which when absent, it is so indispensable, but so difficult, to create, how worse than absurd it is to forego, when spontaneously offering itself! If there are any persons who contest a received opinion, or who will do so if law or opinion will let them, let us thank them for it, open our minds to listen to them, and rejoice that there is some one to do for us what we otherwise ought, if we have any regard for either the certainty or the vitality of our convictions, to do with much greater labor for ourselves.

It still remains to speak of one of the principal causes which make diversity of opinion advantageous, and will continue to do so until mankind shall have entered a stage of intellectual advancement which at present seems at an incalculable distance. We have hitherto considered only two possibilities: that the received opinion may be false, and some other opinion consequently true; or that, the received opinion being true, a conflict with the opposite error is essential to a clear apprehension and deep feeling of its truth. But there is a commoner case than either of these: when the conflicting doctrines, instead of being one true and the other false, share the truth between them; and the nonconforming opinion is needed to supply the remainder of the truth, of which the received doctrine embodies only a part. Popular opinions, on subjects not palpable to sense, are often true, but seldom or never the whole truth. They are a part of the truth; sometimes a greater, sometimes a smaller part, but exaggerated, distorted, and disjointed from the truths by which they ought to be accompanied and limited. Heretical opinions, on the other hand, are generally some of these suppressed and neglected truths, bursting the bonds which kept them down, and neither seeking reconciliation with the truth contained in the common opinion, or fronting it as enemies, and setting themselves up, with similar exclusiveness, as the whole truth. The latter case is hitherto the most frequent, as, in the human mind, one-sidedness has always been the rule, and many-sidedness the exception. Hence, even in revolutions of opinion, one part of the truth usually sets while another rises. Even progress, which ought to superadd, for the most part only substitutes, one partial and incomplete truth for another; improvement consisting chiefly in this, that the new fragment of truth is more wanted, more adapted to the needs of the time, than that which it displaces. Such being the partial character of prevailing opinions, even when resting on a true foundation, every opinion which embodies somewhat of the portion of truth which the common opinion omits, ought to be considered precious, with whatever amount of error and confusion that truth may be blended. No sober judge of human affairs will feel bound to be indignant because those who force on our notice truths which we should otherwise have overlooked, overlook some of those which we see. Rather, he will think that so long as popular truth is one-sided, it is more desirable than otherwise that unpopular truth should have one-sided assertors too; such being usually the most energetic, and the most likely to compel reluctant attention to the fragment of wisdom which they proclaim as if it were the whole.

Thus, in the eighteenth century, when nearly all the instructed, and all those of the uninstructed who were led by them, were lost in admiration of what is called civilization, and of the marvels of modern science, literature, and philosophy, and while greatly overrating the amount of unlikeness between the men of modern and those of ancient times, indulged the belief that the whole of the difference was in their own favor; with what a salutary shock did the paradoxes of Rousseau explode like bombshells in the midst, dislocating the compact mass of one-sided opinion, and forcing its elements to recombine in a better form and with additional ingredients. Not that the current opinions were on the whole farther from the truth than Rousseau's were: on the contrary, they were nearer to it: they contained more of positive truth, and very much less of error. Nevertheless there lay in Rousseau's doctrine, and has floated down the stream of opinion along with it, a considerable amount of exactly those truths which the popular opinion wanted; and these are the deposit which was left behind when the flood subsided. The superior worth of simplicity of life, the enervating and demoralizing effect of the trammels and hypocrisies of artificial society, are ideas which have never been entirely absent from cultivated minds since Rousseau wrote; and they will in time produce their due effect, though at present needing to be asserted as much as ever, and to be asserted by deeds, for words, on their subject, have nearly exhausted their power.

In politics, again, it is almost a commonplace, that a party of order or stability, and a party of progress or reform, are both necessary elements of a healthy state of political life; until the one or the other shall have so enlarged its mental grasp as to be a party equally of order and of progress, knowing and distinguishing what is fit to be preserved from what ought to be swept away. Each of these modes of thinking derives its utility from the deficiencies of the other; but it is in a great measure the opposition of the other that keeps each within the limits of reason and sanity. Unless opinions favorable to democracy and to aristocracy, to property and to equality, to cooperation and to competition, to luxury and to abstinence, to sociality and individuality, to liberty and discipline, and all the other standing antagonisms of practical life, are expressed with equal freedom, and enforced and defended with equal talent and energy, there is no chance of both elements obtaining their due: one scale is sure to go up, and the other down. Truth, in the great practical concerns of life, is so much a question of the reconciling and combining of opposites, that very few have minds sufficiently capacious and impartial to make the adjustment with an approach to correctness, and it has to be made by the rough process of a struggle between combatants fighting under hostile banners. On any of the great open questions just enumerated, if either of the two opinions has a better claim than the other, not merely to be tolerated, but to be encouraged and countenanced, it is the one which happens at the particular time and place to be in a minority. That is the opinion which, for the time being, represents the neglected interests, the side of human well-being which is in danger of obtaining less than its share. I am aware that there is not, in this country, any intolerance of differences of opinion on most of these topics. They are adduced to show, by admitted and multiplied examples, the universality of the fact that only through diversity of opinion is there, in the existing state of human intellect, a chance of fair play to all sides of the truth. When there are persons to be found who form an exception to the apparent unanimity of the world on any subject, even if the world is in the right, it is always probable that dissentients have something worth hearing to say for themselves, and that truth would lose something by their silence. . . .

We have now recognized the necessity to the mental well-being of mankind (on which all their other well-being depends) of freedom of opinion, and freedom of the expression of opinion, on four distinct grounds; which we will now briefly recapitulate.

First, if any opinion is compelled to silence, that opinion may, for aught we can certainly know, be true. To deny this is to assume our own infallibility.

Secondly, though the silenced opinion be an error, it may, and very commonly does, contain a portion of truth; and since the general or prevailing opinion on any subject is rarely or never the whole truth; it is only by the collision of adverse opinions that the remainder of the truth has any chance of being supplied.

Thirdly, even if the received opinion be not only true, but the whole truth; unless it is suffered to be, and actually is, vigorously and earnestly contested, it will, by most of those who receive it, be held in the manner of a prejudice, with little comprehension or feeling of its rational grounds. And not only this, but, fourthly, the meaning of the doctrine itself will be in danger of being lost, or enfeebled, and deprived of its vital effect on the character and conduct: the dogma becoming a mere formal procession, inefficacious for good, but cumbering the ground, and preventing the growth of any real and heartfelt conviction, from reason or personal experience. . . .

CHAPTER III
Of Individuality, As One of the Elements of Well-being

Such being the reasons which make it imperative that human beings should be free to form opinions, and to express their opinions without reserve; and such the baneful consequences to the intellectual, and through that to the moral nature of man, unless this liberty is either conceded, or asserted in spite of prohibition; let us next examine whether the same reasons do not require that men should be free to act upon their opinions—to carry these out in their lives, without hindrance, either physical or moral, from their fellow-men, so long as it is at their own risk and peril. This last proviso is of course indispensable. No one pretends that actions should be as free as opinions. On the contrary, even opinions lose their immunity when the circumstances in which they are expressed are such as to constitute their expression a positive instigation to some mischievous act. An opinion that corn-dealers are starvers of the poor, or that private property is robbery, ought to be unmolested when simply circulated through the press, but many justly incur punishment when delivered orally to an excited mob assembled before the house of a corn-dealer, or when handed about among the same mob in the form of a placard. Acts, of whatever kind, which without justifiable cause do harm to others, may be, and in the more important cases absolutely require to be, controlled by the unfavorable sentiments, and, when needful, by the active interference of mankind. The liberty of the individual must be thus far limited; he must not make himself a nuisance to other people. But if he refrains from molesting others in what concerns them, and merely acts according to his own inclination and judgment in things which concern himself, the same reasons which show that opinion should be free, without molestation, to carry his opinions into practice at his own cost. That mankind are not infallible; that their truths, for the most part, are only half-truths; that unity of opinion, unless resulting from the fullest and freest comparison of opposite opinions, is not desirable, and diversity not an evil, but a good, until mankind are much more capable than at present of recognizing all sides of the truth, are principles applicable to men's modes of action, not less than to their opinions. As it is useful that while mankind are imperfect there should be different opinions, so it is that there should be different experiments of living; that free scope should be given to varieties of character, short of injury to others; and that the worth of different modes of life should be proved practically, when any one thinks fit to try them. It is desirable, in short, that in things which do not primarily concern others, individuality should assert itself. Where not the person's own character, but the traditions or customs of other people are the rule of conduct, there is wanting one of the principal ingredients of human happiness, and quite the chief ingredient of individual and social progress.

In maintaining this principle, the greatest difficulty to be encountered does not lie in the appreciation of means toward an acknowledged end, but in the indifference of persons in general to the end in itself. If it were felt that the free development of individuality is one of the leading essentials of well-being; that it is not only a coordinate element with all that is designated by the terms civilization, instruction, education, culture, but is itself a necessary part and condition of all those things; there would be no danger that liberty should be undervalued, and the adjustment of the boundaries between it and social control would present no extraordinary difficulty. But the evil is, that individual spontaneity is hardly recognized by the common modes of thinking as having any intrinsic worth, or deserving any regard on its own account. The majority, being satisfied with the ways of mankind as they now are (for it is they who make them what they are), cannot comprehend why those ways should not be good enough for everybody; and what is more, spontaneity forms no part of the ideal of the majority of moral and social reformers, but is rather looked on with jealousy, as a troublesome and perhaps rebellious obstruction to the general acceptance of what these reformers, in their own judgment, think would be best for mankind.

. . . No one's idea of excellence in conduct is that people should do absolutely nothing but copy one another. No one would assert that people ought not to put into their mode of life, and into the conduct of their concerns, any impress whatever of their own judgment, or of their own individual character. On the other hand, it would be absurd to pretend that people ought to live as if nothing whatever had been known in the world before they came into it; as if experience had as yet done nothing toward showing that one mode of existence, or of conduct, is preferable to another. Nobody denies that people should be so taught and trained in youth as to know and benefit by the ascertained results of human experience. But it is the privilege and proper condition of a human being, arrived at the maturity of his faculties, to use and interpret experience in his own way. It is for him to find out what part of recorded experience is properly applicable to his own circumstances and character. The traditions and customs of other people are to a certain extent, evidence of what their experience has taught *them:* presumptive evidence, and as such, have a claim to his deference. But in the first place, their experience may be too narrow, or they may not have interpreted it rightly. Secondly, their interpretation of experience may be correct, but unsuitable to him. Customs are made for customary circumstances and customary characters, and his circumstances or his character may be uncustomary. Thirdly, though the customs be both good as customs, and suitable to him, yet to conform to custom, merely *as* custom, does not educate or develop in him any of the qualities which are the distinctive endowment of a human being. The human faculties of perception, judgment, discriminative feeling, mental activity, and even moral preference, are exercised only in making a choice. He who does anything because it is the custom makes no choice. He gains no practice either in discerning or in desiring what is best. The mental and moral, like the muscular powers, are improved only by being used. The faculties are called into no exercise by doing a thing merely because others do it, no more than by believing a thing only because others believe it. If the grounds of an opinion are not conclusive to the person's own reason, his reason cannot be strengthened, but is likely to be weakened, by his adopting it; and if the inducements to an act are not such as are consentaneous to his own feelings and character (where affection, or the rights of others, are not concerned) it is so much done toward rendering his feelings and character inert and torpid, instead of active and energetic.

He who lets the world, or his own portion of it, choose his plan of life for him, has no need of any other faculty than the ape-like one of imitation. He who chooses his plan for himself, employs all his faculties. He must use observation to see, reasoning and judgment to foresee, activity to gather materials for decision, discrimination to decide, and when he has decided, firmness and self-control to hold to his deliberate decision. And these qualities he requires and exercises exactly in proportion as the part of his conduct which he determines according to his own judgment and feelings is a large one. It is possible that he might be guided in some good path, and kept out of harm's way, without any of these things. But what will be his comparative worth as a human being? It really is of importance, not only what men do, but also what manner of men they are that do it. Among the works of man which human life is rightly employed in perfecting and beautifying, the first in importance surely is man himself. Supposing it were possible to get houses built, corn grown, battles fought, causes tried, and even churches erected and prayers said, by machinery—by automatons in human form—it would be a considerable loss to exchange for these automatons even the men and women who at present inhabit the more civilized parts of the world, and who assuredly are but starved specimens of what nature can and will produce. Human nature is not a machine to be built after a model, and set to do exactly the work prescribed for it, but a tree, which requires to grow and develop itself on all sides, according to the tendency of the inward forces which make it a living thing.

It will probably be conceded that it is desirable people shall exercise their understandings, and that an intelligent following of custom, or even occasionally an intelligent deviation from custom, is better than a blind and simply mechanical adhesion to it. To a certain extent it is admitted that our understanding should be our own: but there is not the same willingness to admit that our desires and impulses should be our own likewise; or that to possess impulses of our own, and of any strength, is anything but a peril and a snare. Yet desires and impulses are as much a part of a perfect human being as beliefs and restraints; and strong impulses are only perilous when not properly balanced—when one set of aims and inclinations is developed into strength, while others, which ought to coexist with them, remain weak and inactive. It is not because men's desires are strong that they act ill; it is because their consciences are weak. There is no natural connection between strong impulses and a weak conscience. The natural connection is the other way. To say that one person's desires and feelings are stronger and more various than those of another, is merely to say that he has more of the raw material of human nature, and is therefore capable, perhaps of more evil, but certainly of more good. Strong impulses are but another name for energy. Energy may be turned to bad uses; but more good may always be made of an energetic nature than of an indolent and impassive one. Those who have most natural feeling are always those whose cultivated feelings may be made the strongest. The same strong susceptibilities which make the personal impulses vivid and powerful, are also the source from whence are generated the most passionate love of virtue, and the sternest self-control. It is through the cultivation of these that society both does its duty and protects its interests; not by rejecting the stuff of which heroes are made because it knows not how to make them. A person whose desires and impulses are his own—are the expression of his own nature, as it has been developed and modified by his own culture—is said to have a character. One whose desires and impulses are not his own, has no character, no more than a steam-engine has a character. If, in addition to being his own, his impulses are strong, and are under the government of a strong will, he has an energetic character. Whoever thinks that individuality of desires and impulses should not be encouraged to unfold itself, must maintain that society has no need of strong natures—is not the better for containing many persons who have much character—and that a high general average of energy is not desirable. . . .

It is not by wearing down into uniformity all that is individual in themselves, but by cultivating it, and calling it forth, within the limits imposed by the rights and interests of others, that human beings become a noble and beautiful object of contemplation; and as the works partake the character of those who do them, by the same process human life also becomes rich, diversified, and animating, furnishing more abundant aliment to high thoughts and elevating feelings, and strengthening the tie which binds every individual to the race, by making the race infinitely better worth belong to. In proportion to the development of his individuality, each person becomes more valuable to himself, and is therefore capable of being more valuable to others. There is a greater fullness of life about his own existence, and when there is more life in the units there is more in the mass which is composed of them. As much compression as is necessary to prevent the stronger specimens of human nature from encroaching on the rights of others cannot be dispensed with; but for this there is ample compensation even in the point of view of human development. The means of development which the individual loses by being prevented from gratifying his inclinations to the injury of others, are chiefly obtained at the expense of the development of other people. And even to himself there is a full equivalent in the better development of the social part of his nature, rendered possible by the restraint put upon the selfish part. To be held to rigid rules of justice for the sake of others, develops the feelings and capacities which have the good of others for their object. But to be restrained in things not affecting their good, by their mere displeasure, develops nothing valuable, except such force of character as may unfold itself in resisting the restraint. If acquiesced in, it dulls and blunts the whole nature. To give any fair play to the nature of each, it is essential that different persons should be allowed to lead different lives. In proportion as this latitude has been exercised in any age, has that age been noteworthy to posterity. Even despotism does not produce its worst effects, so long as individuality exists under it; and whatever crushes individuality is despotism, by whatever name it may be called, and whether it professes to be enforcing the will of God or the injunctions of men.

Having said that the individuality is the same thing with development, and that it is only the cultivation of individuality which produces, or can produce, well-developed human beings, I might here close the argument: for what more or better can be said of any condition of human affairs than that it brings human beings themselves nearer to the best thing they can be? or what worse can be said of any obstruction to good than that it prevents this? Doubtless, however, these considerations will not suffice to convince those who most need convincing; and it is necessary further to show that these developed human beings are of some use to the undeveloped—to point out to those who do not desire liberty, and would not avail themselves of it, that they may be in some intelligible manner rewarded for allowing other people to make use of it without hindrance.

In the first place, then, I would suggest that they might possibly learn something from them. It will not be denied by anybody that originality is a valuable element in human affairs. There is always need of persons not only to discover new truths, and point out when what were once truths are true no longer, but also to commence new practices, and set the example of more enlightened conduct, and better taste and sense in human life. This cannot well be gainsaid by anybody who does not believe that the world has already attained perfection in all its ways and practices. It is true that this benefit is not capable of being rendered by everybody alike: there are but few persons, in comparison with the whole of mankind, whose experiments, if adopted by others, would be likely to be any improvement on established practice. But these few are the salt of the earth; without them, human life would become a stagnant pool. Not only is it they who introduce good things which did not before exist; it is they who keep the life in those which already exist. If there were nothing new to be done, would human intellect cease to be necessary? Would it be a reason why those who do the old things should forget why they are done, and do them like cattle, not like human beings? There is only too great a tendency in the best beliefs and practices to degenerate into the mechanical; and unless there were a succession of persons whose over-recurring originality prevents the grounds of those beliefs and practices from becoming merely traditional, such dead matter would not resist the smallest shock from anything really alive, and there would be no reason why civilization should not die out, as in the Byzantine Empire. Persons of genius, it is true, are, and are always likely to be, a small minority; but in order to have them, it is necessary to preserve the soil in which they grow. Genius can only breathe freely in an *atmosphere* of freedom. Persons of genius are, *ex vi termini* [by the force of the phraseology], more individual than any other people—less capable, consequently, of fitting themselves, without hurtful compression, into any of the small number of molds which society provides in order to save its members the trouble of forming their own character. If from timidity they consent to be forced into one of these molds, and to let all that part of themselves which cannot expand under the pressure remain unexpanded, society will be little the better for their genius. If they are of a strong character, and break their fetters, they become a mark for the society which has not succeeded in reducing them to commonplace, to point out with solemn warning as "wild," "erratic," and the like; much as if one should complain of the Niagara river for not flowing smoothly between its banks like a Dutch canal.

I insist thus emphatically on the importance of genius, and the necessity of allowing it to unfold itself freely both in thought and in practice, being well aware that no one will deny the position in theory, but knowing also that almost everyone, in reality, is totally indifferent to it. People think genius a fine thing if it enables a man to write an exciting poem, or paint a picture. But in its true sense, that of originality in thought and action, though no one says that it is not a thing to be admired, nearly all, at heart, think that they can do very well without it. Unhappily this is too natural to be wondered at. Originality is the one thing which unoriginal minds cannot feel the use of. They cannot see what it is to do for them: how should they? If they could see what it would do for them, it would not be originality. The first service which originality has to render them, is that of opening their eyes: which being once fully done, they would have a chance of being themselves original. Meanwhile, recollecting that nothing was ever yet done which someone was not the first to do, and that all good things which exist are the fruits of originality, let them be modest enough to believe that there is something still left for it to accomplish, and assure themselves that they are more in need of originality, the less they are conscious of the want.

In sober truth, whatever homage may be professed, or even paid, to real or supposed mental superiority, the general tendency of things throughout the world is to render mediocrity the ascendant power among mankind. In ancient history, in the Middle Ages, and in a diminishing degree through the long transition from feudality to the present time, the individual was a power in himself; and if he had either great talents or a high social position, he was a considerable power. At present individuals are lost in the crowd. In politics it is almost a triviality to say that public opinion now rules the world. The only power deserving the name is that of masses, and of governments while they make themselves the organ of the tendencies and instincts of masses. This is as true in the moral and social relations of private life as in public transactions. Those whose opinions go by the name of public opinion are not always the same sort of public: in America they are the whole white population; in England, chiefly the middle class. But they are always a mass, that is to say, collective mediocrity. And what is a still greater novelty, the mass do not now take their opinions from dignitaries in Church or State, from ostensible leaders, or from books. Their thinking is done for them by men much like themselves, addressing them or speaking in their name, on the spur of the moment, through the newspapers. I am not complaining of all this. I do not assert that anything better is compatible, as a general rule, with the present low state of the human mind. But that does not hinder the government of mediocrity from being mediocre government. No government by a democracy or a numerous aristocracy, either in its political acts or in the opinions, qualities, and tone of mind which it fosters, ever did or could rise above mediocrity, except in so far as the sovereign Many have let themselves be guided (which in their best times they always have done) by the counsels and influence of a more highly gifted and instructed One or Few. The initiation of all wise or noble things comes and must come from individuals; generally at first from some one individual. The honor and glory of the average man is that he is capable of following that initiative; that he can respond internally to wise and noble things, and be led to them with his eyes open. I am not countenancing the sort of "hero-worship" which applauds the strong man of genius for forcibly seizing on the government of the world and making it do his bidding in spite of itself. All he can claim is, freedom to point out the way. The power of compelling others into it is not only inconsistent with the freedom and development of all the rest, but corrupting to the strong man himself. It does seem, however, that when the opinions of masses of merely average men are everywhere become or becoming the dominant power, the counterpoise and corrective to that tendency would be the more and more pronounced individuality of those who stand on the higher eminences of thought. It is in these circumstances most especially, that exceptional individuals, instead of being deterred, should be encouraged in acting differently from the mass. In other times there was no advantage in their doing so, unless they acted not only differently but better. In this age, the mere example of nonconformity, the mere refusal to bend the knee to custom, is itself a service. Precisely because the tyranny of opinion is such as to make eccentricity a reproach, it is desirable, in order to break through that tyranny, that people should be eccentric. Eccentricity has always abounded when and where strength of character has abounded; and the amount of eccentricity in a society has generally been proportional to the amount of genius, mental vigor, and moral courage it contained. That so few now dare to be eccentric marks the chief danger of the time.

I have said that it is important to give the freest scope possible to uncustomary things, in order that it may in time appear which of these are fit to be converted into customs. But independence of action, and disregard of custom, are not solely deserving of encouragement for the chance they afford that better modes of action, and customs more worthy of general adoption, may be struck out; nor is it only persons of decided mental superiority who have a just claim to carry on their lives in their own way. There is no reason that all human existence should be constructed on some one or some small number of patterns. If a person possesses any tolerable amount of common sense and experience, his own mode of laying out his existence is the best, not because it is the best in itself, but because it is his own mode. Human beings are not like sheep; and even sheep are not undistinguishably alike. A man cannot get a coat or a pair of boots to fit him unless they are either made to his measure, or he has a whole warehouseful to choose from: and is it easier to fit him with a life than with a coat, or are human beings more like one another in their whole physical and spiritual conformation than in the shape of their feet? If it were only that people have diversities of taste, that is reason enough for not attempting to shape them all after one model. But different persons also require different conditions for their spiritual development; and can no more exist healthily in the same moral, than all the variety of plants can in the same physical, atmosphere and climate. The same things which are helps to one person towards the cultivation of his higher nature are hindrances to another. The same mode of life is a healthy excitement to one, keeping all his faculties of action and enjoyment in their best order, while to another it is a distracting burden, which suspends or crushes all internal life. Such are the differences among human beings in their sources of pleasure, their susceptibilities of pain, and the operation on them of different physical and moral agencies, that unless there is a corresponding diversity in their modes of life, they neither obtain their fair share of happiness, nor grow up to the mental, moral, and aesthetic stature of which their nature is capable. . . .

There is one characteristic of the present direction of public opinion peculiarly calculated to make it intolerant of any marked demonstration of individuality. The general average of mankind are not only moderate in intellect, but also moderate in inclinations: they have no tastes or wishes strong enough to incline them to do anything unusual, and they consequently do not understand those who have, and class all such with the wild and intemperate whom they are accustomed to look down upon. Now, in addition to this fact which is general, we have only to suppose that a strong movement has set in towards the improvement of morals, and it is evident what we have to expect. In these days such a movement has set in; much has actually been effected in the way of increased regularity of conduct and discouragement of excesses; and there is a philanthropic spirit abroad, for the exercise of which there is no more inviting field than the moral and prudential improvement of our fellow-creatures. These tendencies of the times cause the public to be more disposed than at most former periods to prescribe general rules of conduct, and endeavor to make every one conform to the approved standard. And that standard, express or tacit, is to desire nothing strongly. Its ideal of character is to be without any marked character; to maim by compression, like a Chinese lady's foot, every part of human nature which stands out prominently, and tends to make the person markedly dissimilar in outline to commonplace humanity.

As is usually the case with ideals which exclude one-half of what is desirable, the present standard of approbation produces only an inferior imitation of the other half. Instead of great energies guided by vigorous reason, and strong feelings strongly controlled by a conscientious will, its result is weak feelings, and weak energies, which therefore can be kept in outward conformity to rule without any strength either of will or of reason. Already energetic characters on any large scale are becoming merely traditional. There is now scarcely any outlet for energy in this country except business. The energy expended in this may still be regarded as considerable. What little is left from that employment is expended on some hobby; which may be a useful, even a philanthropic hobby, but is always some one thing, and generally a thing of small dimensions. The greatness of England is now all collective; individually small, we only appear capable of anything great by our habit of combining; and with this our moral and religious philanthropists are perfectly contented. But it was men of another stamp than this that made England what it has been; and men of another stamp will be needed to prevent its decline.

The despotism of custom is everywhere the standing hindrance to human advancement, being in unceasing antagonism to that disposition to aim at something better than customary, which is called, according to circumstances, the spirit of liberty, or that of progress or improvement. The spirit of improvement is not always a spirit of liberty, for it may aim at forcing improvements on an unwilling people; and the spirit of liberty, in so far as it resists such attempts, may ally itself locally and temporarily with the opponents of improvement; but the only unfailing and permanent source of improvement is liberty, since by it there are as many possible independent centers of improvement as there are individuals. The progressive principle, however, in either shape, whether as the love of liberty or of improvement, is antagonistic to the sway of custom, involving at least emancipation from that yoke; and the contest between the two constitutes the chief interest of the history of mankind. . . .

What has made the European family of nations an improving, instead of a stationary portion of mankind? Not any superior excellence in them, which, when it exists, exists as the effect not as the cause; but their remarkable diversity of character and culture. Individuals, classes, nations, have been extremely unlike one another; they have struck out a great variety of paths, each leading to something valuable; and although at every period those who traveled in different paths have been intolerant of one another, and each would have thought it an excellent thing if all the rest could have been compelled to travel his road, their attempts to thwart each other's development have rarely had any permanent success, and each has in time endured to receive the good which the others have offered. Europe is, in my judgment, wholly indebted to this plurality of paths for its progressive and many-sided development. But it already begins to possess this benefit in a considerably less degree. . . .

Formerly, different ranks, different neighborhoods, different trades and professions, lived in what might be called different worlds; at present to a great degree in the same. Comparatively speaking, they now read the same things, listen to the same things, see the same things, go to the same places, have their hopes and fears directed to the same objects, have the same rights and liberties, and the same means of asserting them. Great as are the differences of position which remain, they are nothing to those which have ceased. And the assimilation is still proceeding. All the political changes of the age promote it, since they all tend to raise the low and to lower the high. Every extension of education promotes it, because education brings people under common influences, and gives them access to the general stock of facts and sentiments. Improvement in the means of communication promotes it, by bringing the inhabitants of distant places into personal contact, and keeping up a rapid flow of changes of residence between one place and another. The increase of commerce and manufactures promotes it, by diffusing more widely the advantages of easy circumstances, and opening all objects of ambition, even the highest, to general competition, whereby the desire of rising becomes no longer the character of a particular class, but of all classes. A more powerful agency than even all these, in bringing about a general similarity among mankind, is the complete establishment, in this and other free countries, of the ascendancy of public opinion in the State. As the various social eminences which enabled persons entrenched on them to disregard the opinion of the multitude gradually become leveled; as the very idea of resisting the will of the public, when it is positively known that they have a will, disappears more and more from the minds of practical politicians: there ceases to be any social support for nonconformity—any substantive power in society which, itself opposed to the ascendancy of numbers, is interested in taking under its protection opinions and tendencies at variance with those of the public.

The combination of all these causes forms so great a mass of influences hostile to individuality, that it is not easy to see how it can stand its ground. It will do so with increasing difficulty, unless the intelligent part of the public can be made to feel its value—to see that it is good there should be differences, even though not for the better, even though, as it may appear to them, some should be for the worse. If the claims of individuality are ever to be asserted, the time is now, while much is still wanting to complete the enforced assimilation. It is only in the earlier stages that any stand can be successfully made against the encroachment. The demand that all other people shall resemble ourselves grows by what it feeds on. If resistance waits till life is reduced *nearly* to one uniform type, all deviations from that type will come to be considered impious, immoral, even monstrous and contrary to nature. Mankind speedily become unable to conceive diversity, when they have been for some time unaccustomed to see it.

CHAPTER

39

MARX

1818–1883

Karl Marx was born in Trèves (Trier), Germany, what was then Prussia. He went to the Universities of Berlin and Bonn and received his Ph.D. in philosophy from the University of Jena. His doctoral dissertation was on the Greek atomism of Democritus and Epicurus. At the time, the most influential philosophy in Germany and much of the rest of Europe was Hegel's. The Hegelian right consisted of older, more conservative philosophers steeped in an orthodox reading of Hegel's theories of religion and morality. The Hegelian left consisted of young radical philosophers such as Marx. Calling themselves "the Young Hegelians," they considered Hegel's social and political views false and saw in them deep, hidden truths implying the very opposite of what Hegel taught. Marx eventually claimed that his own system, which he called dialectic materialism, was a right-side-up version of Hegel's dialectic idealism.

Unable to find a teaching position, Marx found a job with the Cologne *Rheinische Zeitung* and was even the London correspondent for the *New York Tribune.* The pay was minimal, and he spent most of his life unemployed. Several of his children died of malnutrition.

Marx got some support from his friend and coauthor of the *Communist Manifesto* (1888), Frederick Engels, but remained extremely poor. Yet he was prolific. His deeply influential works have made him one of the most recognized names in history and an important socialist philosopher.

Marx's greatest influence came from Ludwig Feuerbach's *Essence of Christianity,* a work that inspired the Young Hegelian Leftists. Feuerbach had argued that ever since Plato, the greatest corrupter of human values has been the ideal images of universal values. In reality, Feuerbach claimed, there are no universal values and so all such Platonic goals are unattainable, the stuff of Christian religion. He argued that the human mind, by craving its own idealizations, alienates from itself. In this way the mind transfers its own desires onto an imaginary ideal being, God. By doing so, the human mind prevents its own ascension to the ideal. Religion is its greatest prison.

Marx continued Feuerbach's argument that religious imagery must be abolished. Only then can true peace, happiness, and self-illumination come to society. But Marx went further; in his *Theses on Feuerbach* (published posthumously in 1886), he criticizes Feuerbach on grounds that no such change in thinking could ever be attained by human beings so long as the argument remains philosophical. Philosophy itself merely manipulates ideas and images. He calls Feuerbach's "speculative" materialism in comparison to his own "practical materialism" and calls for a change in the actual material and economic relationships among human beings: "The philosophers have only *interpreted* the world in various ways, the point however is to *change* it."

The *Communist Manifesto,* from which our first selection is taken, became the rallying cry for world revolution involving a class struggle between the "bourgeoisie"—the capitalist employers of wage labor who owned the means of production—and the "proletariat"— wage laborers who had no means of production and are thus forced to sell their labor in order to live. Marx's criticism of capitalism and of all social, political, economic, and religious structures owes much to Hegelian dialectic. He claims that various capitalist theses lead to their opposites. Competition, for instance, leads to monopoly and the lack of competition. How does capitalism solve unemployment? By creating more money, which leads to inflation, which capitalism fixes by increasing unemployment. And so on.

The purpose of Communist revolution, which Marx advocated, was to bring about the collapse of capitalism. He wanted to replace capitalism with a temporary "dictatorship of the proletariat." This would be a worker's state in which the workers themselves would ultimately abolish the class-structured society. The false, capitalist democracy would thus be replaced by a true, Communist democrary. In the end, the revolutionary leaders would themselves be forced to resign. When this happened, history, which Marx defined in terms of class struggle, would itself come to an end.

In our second selection, *Alienation,* he argues how we subtly but permanently become imprisoned by capitalism. The key to understanding Marx's thought here is that human consciousness is itself not the cause of social processes. Rather, individual human consciousness is an effect. Human consciousness can thus become enlightened and evolve to a higher state only if the competition of capitalism is removed. The true individual can then emerge from the cocoon of society, and the world becomes an ideal state, a utopia. But what prevents this? The chief problem as Marx sees it is that through alienated labor our natural needs have become perverted. He explains why in the final selection, an insightful meditation on "The Power of Money."

COMMUNIST MANIFESTO

BOURGEOIS AND PROLETARIANS

The history of all hitherto existing society is the history of class struggles.

Free man and slave, patrician and plebeian, lord and serf, guild master and journeyman, in a word, oppressor and oppressed, stood in constant opposition to one another, carried on an uninterrupted, now hidden, now open fight, a fight that each time ended either in

From Karl Marx and Frederick Engels, *Communist Manifesto,* trans. Samuel Moore, 1888.

a revolutionary reconstitution of society at large or in the common ruin of the contending classes.

In the earlier epochs of history we find almost everywhere a complicated arrangement of society into various orders, a manifold gradation of social rank. In ancient Rome we have patricians, knights, plebeians, slaves; in the Middle Ages, feudal lords, vassals, guild masters, journeymen, apprentices, serfs; in almost all of these classes, again, subordinate gradations.

The modern bourgeois society that has sprouted from the ruins of feudal society has not done away with class antagonisms. It has but established new classes, new conditions of oppression, new forms of struggle in place of the old ones.

Our epoch, the epoch of the bourgeoisie, possesses, however, this distinctive feature: it has simplified the class antagonisms. Society as a whole is more and more splitting up into two great hostile camps, into two great classes directly facing each other: bourgeoisie and proletariat.

From the serfs of the Middle Ages sprang the chartered burghers of the earliest towns. From these burgesses the first elements of the bourgeoisie were developed.

The discovery of America, the rounding of the Cape, opened up fresh ground for the rising bourgeoisie. The East Indian and Chinese markets, the colonization of America, trade with the colonies, the increase in the means of exchange and in commodities generally, gave to commerce, to navigation, to industry an impulse never before known, and thereby, to the revolutionary element in the tottering feudal society, a rapid development.

The feudal system of industry, under which industrial production was monopolized by closed guilds, now no longer sufficed for the growing wants of the new markets. The manufacturing system took its place. The guild masters were pushed on one side by the manufacturing middle class; division of labor between the different corporate guilds vanished in the face of division of labor in each single workshop.

Meantime the markets kept ever growing, the demand ever rising. Even manufacture no longer sufficed. Thereupon steam and machinery revolutionized industrial production. The place of manufacture was taken by the giant, modern industry, the place of the industrial middle class by industrial millionaires, the leaders of whole industrial armies, the modern bourgeois.

Modern industry has established the world market, for which the discovery of America paved the way. This market has given an immense development to commerce, to navigation, to communication by land. This development has, in its turn, reacted on the extension of industry; and in proportion as industry, commerce, navigation, railways extended, in the same proportion the bourgeoisie developed, increased its capital, and pushed into the background every class handed down from the Middle Ages.

We see, therefore, how the modern bourgeoisie is itself the product of a long course of development, of a series of revolutions in the modes of production and of exchange.

Each step in the development of the bourgeoisie was accompanied by a corresponding political advance of that class. An oppressed class under the sway of the feudal nobility, an armed and self-governing association in the medieval commune; here independent urban republic (as in Italy and Germany), there taxable "third estate" of the monarchy (as in France), afterward, in the period of manufacture proper, serving either the semi-feudal or the absolute monarchy as a counterpoise against the nobility, and, in fact, cornerstone of the great monarchies in general, the bourgeoisie has at last, since the establishment of Modern Industry and of the world market, conquered for itself, in the modern representative

State, exclusive political sway. The executive of the modern State is but a committee for managing the common affairs of the whole bourgeoisie.

The bourgeoisie, historically, has played a most revolutionary part.

The bourgeoisie, wherever it has got the upper hand, has put an end to all feudal, patriarchal, idyllic relations. It has pitilessly torn asunder the motley feudal ties that bound man to his "natural superiors," and has left remaining no other nexus between man and man than naked self-interest, than callous "cash payment." It has drowned the most heavenly ecstasies of religious fervor, of chivalrous enthusiasm, of philistine sentimentalism, in the icy water of egotistical calculation. It has resolved personal worth into exchange value, and in place of the numberless indefeasible chartered freedoms has set up that single, unconscionable freedom—Free Trade. In one word, for exploitation, veiled by religious and political illusions, it has substituted naked, shameless, direct, brutal exploitation.

The bourgeoisie has stripped of its halo every occupation hitherto honored and looked up to with reverent awe. It has converted the physician, the lawyer, the priest, the poet, the man of science, into its paid wage-laborers.

The bourgeoisie has torn away from the family its sentimental veil, and has reduced the family relation to a mere money relation.

The bourgeoisie has disclosed how it came to pass that the brutal display of vigor in the Middle Ages, which Reactionists so much admire, found its fitting complement in the most slothful indolence. It has been the first to show what man's activity can bring about. It has accomplished wonders far surpassing Egyptian pyramids, Roman aqueducts and Gothic cathedrals; it has conducted expeditions that put in the shade all former Exoduses of nations and crusades.

The bourgeoisie cannot exist without constantly revolutionizing the instruments of production, and thereby the relations of production, and with them the whole relations of society. Conservation of the old modes of production in unaltered form was, on the contrary, the first condition of existence for all earlier industrial classes. Constant revolutionizing of production, uninterrupted disturbance of all social conditions, everlasting uncertainty and agitation distinguish the bourgeois epoch from all earlier ones. All fixed, fast-frozen relations, with their train of ancient and venerable prejudices and opinions, are swept away, all new-formed ones become antiquated before they can ossify. All that is solid melts into air, all that is holy is profaned, and man is at last compelled to face with sober senses his real conditions of life and his relations with his kind.

The need of a constantly expanding market for its products chases the bourgeoisie over the whole surface of the globe. It must nestle everywhere, settle everywhere, establish connections everywhere.

The bourgeoisie has through its exploitation of the world market given a cosmopolitan character to production and consumption in every country. To the great chagrin of Reactionists, it has drawn from under the feet of industry the national ground on which it stood. All old-established national industries have been destroyed or are daily being destroyed. They are dislodged by new industries, whose introduction becomes a life and death question for all civilized nations, by industries that no longer work up indigenous raw material but raw material drawn from the remotest zones; industries whose products are consumed, not only at home, but in every quarter of the globe. In place of the old wants, satisfied by the production of the country, we find new wants, requiring for their satisfaction the products of distant lands and climes. In place of the old local and national seclusion and self-sufficiency, we have intercourse in every direction, universal interdependence of nations. And as in material, so also in intellectual production. The intellectual creations of individual nations become common property. National one-sidedness and narrow-mindedness become more and more impossible, and from the numerous national and local literatures there arises a world literature.

The bourgeoisie, by the rapid improvement of all instruments of production, by the immensely facilitated means of communication, draws all, even the most barbarian, nations into civilization. The cheap prices of its commodities are the heavy artillery with which it batters down all Chinese walls, with which it forces the barbarians' intensely obstinate hatred of foreigners to capitulate. It compels all nations, on pain of extinction, to adopt the bourgeois mode of production; it compels them to introduce what it calls civilization into their midst, i.e., to become bourgeois themselves. In a word, it creates a world after its own image.

The bourgeoisie has subjected the country to the rule of the towns. It has created enormous cities, has greatly increased the urban population as compared with the rural, and has thus rescued a considerable part of the population from the idiocy of rural life. Just as it has made the country dependent on the towns, so it has made barbarian and semi-barbarian countries dependent on the civilized ones, nations of peasants on nations of bourgeois, the East on the West.

The bourgeoisie keeps doing away more and more with the scattered state of the population, of the means of production, and of property. It has agglomerated population, centralized means of production, and has concentrated property in a few hands. The necessary consequence of this was political centralization. Independent or but loosely connected provinces with separate interests, laws, governments and systems of taxation became lumped together into one nation, with one government, one code of laws, one national class interest, one frontier and one customs tariff.

The bourgeoisie during its rule of scarce one hundred years has created more massive and more colossal productive forces than have all preceding generations together. Subjection of nature's forces to man, machinery, application of chemistry to industry and agriculture, steam navigation, railways, electric telegraphs, clearing of whole continents for cultivation, canalization of rivers, whole populations conjured out of the ground—what earlier century had even a presentiment that such productive forces slumbered in the lap of social labor?

We see then: the means of production and of exchange, on the foundation of which the bourgeoisie built itself up, were generated in feudal society. At a certain stage in the development of these means of production and of exchange, the conditions under which feudal society produced and exchanged, the feudal organization of agriculture and manufacturing industry, in a word, the feudal relations of property became no longer compatible with the already developed productive forces; they became so many fetters. They had to be burst asunder; they were burst asunder.

Into their place stepped free competition, accompanied by a social and political constitution adapted to it and by the economic and political sway of the bourgeois class.

A similar movement is going on before our own eyes. Modern bourgeois society with its relations of production, of exchange and of property, a society that has conjured up such gigantic means of production and of exchange, is like the sorcerer who is no longer able to control the powers of the nether world whom he has called up by his spells. For many a decade past the history of industry and commerce is but the history of the revolt of modern productive forces against modern conditions of production, against the property relations that are the conditions for the existence of the bourgeoisie and of its rule. It is enough to mention the commercial crises that by their periodical return put on trial, each time more threateningly, the existence of the entire bourgeois society. In these crises a great part not only of the existing products, but also of the previously created productive forces, are periodically destroyed. In these crises there breaks out an epidemic that in all earlier epochs would have seemed an absurdity—the epidemic of over-production. Society suddenly finds itself put back into a state of momentary barbarism; it appears as if a famine, a universal war of devastation had cut off the supply of every means of subsistence; industry and commerce seem to be destroyed; and why? Because there is too much civilization, too much means of subsistence, too much industry, too much commerce. The productive forces at the disposal of society no longer tend to further the development of the conditions of bourgeois property; on the contrary, they have become too powerful for these conditions, by which they are fettered, and as soon as they overcome these fetters, they bring disorder into the whole of bourgeois society, endanger the existence of bourgeois property. The conditions of bourgeois society are too narrow to comprise the wealth created by them. And how does the bourgeoisie get over these crises? On the one hand by enforced destruction of a mass of productive forces, on the other, by the conquest of new markets and by the more thorough exploitation of the old ones. That is to say, by paving the way for more extensive and more destructive crises and by diminishing the means whereby crises are prevented.

The weapons with which the bourgeoisie felled feudalism to the ground are now turned against the bourgeoisie itself.

But not only has the bourgeoisie forged the weapons that bring death to itself; it has also called into existence the men who are to wield those weapons—the modern working class, the proletarians.

In proportion as the bourgeoisie, i.e., capital, is developed, in the same proportion is the proletariat, the modern working class, developed—a class of laborers who live only as long as they find work, and who find work only as long as their labor increases capital. These laborers, who must sell themselves piecemeal, are a commodity like every other article of commerce, and are consequently exposed to all the vicissitudes of competition, to all the fluctuations of the market.

Owing to the extensive use of machinery and to division of labor, the work of the proletarians has lost all individual character and, consequently, all charm for the workman. He becomes an appendage of the machine, and it is only the most simple, most monotonous, and most easily acquired knack that is required of him. Hence, the cost of production of a workman is restricted almost entirely to the means of subsistence that he requires for his maintenance and for the propagation of his race. But the price of a commodity, and therefore also of labor, is equal to its cost of production. In proportion, therefore, as the repulsiveness of the work increases, the wage decreases. Nay more, in proportion as the use of machinery and division of labor increase, in the same proportion the burden of toil also increases, whether by prolongation of the working hours, by increase of the work exacted in a given time or by increased speed of the machinery, etc.

Modern industry has converted the little workshop of the patriarchal master into the great factory of the industrial capitalist. Masses of laborers, crowded into the factory, are organized like soldiers. As privates of the industrial army they are placed under the command of a perfect hierarchy of officers and sergeants. Not only are they slaves of the bourgeois class and of the bourgeois State; they are daily and hourly enslaved by the machine, by the overseer and, above all, by the individual bourgeois manufacturer himself. The more openly this despotism proclaims gain to be its end and aim, the more petty, the more hateful and the more embittering it is.

The less the skill and exertion of stremgth implied in manual labor, in other words, the more modern industry becomes developed, the more is the labor of men superseded by that of women. Differences of age and sex no longer have any distinctive social validity for the working class. All are instruments of labor, more or less expensive to use, according to their age and sex.

No sooner is the exploitation of the laborer by the manufacturer so far at an end that he receives his wages in cash, than he is set upon by the other portions of the bourgeoisie, the landlord, the shopkeeper, the pawnbroker, etc.

The lower strata of the middle class—the small tradespeople, shopkeepers and retired tradesmen generally, the handicraftsmen and peasants—all these sink gradually into the proletariat, partly because their diminutive capital does not suffice for the scale on which Modern Industry is carried on and is swamped in the competition with the large capitalists, partly because their specialized skill is rendered worthless by new methods of production. Thus the proletariat is recruited from all classes of the population.

The proletariat goes through various stages of development. With its birth begins its struggle with the bourgeoisie. At first the contest is carried on by individual laborers, then by the work people of the factory, then by the operatives of one trade in one locality against the individual bourgeois who directly exploits them. They direct their attacks not against the bourgeois conditions of production, but against the instruments of production them- selves; they destroy imported wares that compete with their labor, they smash machinery to pieces, they set factories ablaze, they seek to restore by force the vanished status of the workman of the Middle Ages.

At this stage the laborers still form an incoherent mass scattered over the whole country and broken up by their mutual competition. If anywhere they unite to form more compact bodies, this is not yet the consequence of their own active union but of the union of the bourgeoisie, which class, in order to attain its own political ends, is compelled to set the whole proletariat in motion and, moreover is, for a time, yet able to do so. At this stage, therefore, the proletarians do not fight their enemies, but the enemies of their enemies, the remnants of absolute monarchy, the landowners, the non-industrial bourgeois, the petty bourgeoisie. Thus the whole historical movement is concentrated in the hands of the bour- geoisie; every victory so obtained is a victory for the bourgeoisie.

But with the development of industry the proletariat not only increases in number; it becomes concentrated in greater masses, its strength grows, and it feels that strength more. The various interests and conditions of life within the ranks of the proletariat are more and more equalized in proportion as machinery obliterates all distinctions of labor and nearly everywhere reduces wages to the same low level. The growing competition among the bour- geois, and the resulting commercial crises, make the wages of the workers ever more fluc- tuating. The unceasing improvement of machinery, ever more rapidly developing, makes their livelihood more and more precarious; the collisions between individual workmen and individual bourgeois take more and more the character of collisions between two classes. Thereupon the workers begin to form combinations (Trades' Unions) against the bour- geois; they club together in order to keep up the rate of wages; they found permanent associations in order to make provision beforehand for these occasional revolts. Here and there the contest breaks out into riots.

Now and then the workers are victorious, but only for a time. The real fruit of their battles lies, not in the immediate result, but in the ever expanding union of the workers. This union is helped on by the improved means of communication that are created by modern industry and that place the workers of different localities in contact with one another. It was just this contact that was needed to centralize the numerous local struggles, all of the same character, into one national struggle between classes. But every class struggle is a political struggle. And that union, to attain which the burghers of the Middle Ages with their miserable highways required centuries, the modern proletarians, thanks to railways, achieve in a few years.

This organization of the proletarians into a class and consequently into a political party is continually being upset again by the competition between the workers themselves. But it ever rises up again, stronger, firmer, mightier. It compels legislative recognition of particular interests of the workers, by taking advantage of the divisions among the bourgeoisie itself. Thus the ten-hours' bill in England was carried.

Altogether, collisions between the classes of the old society in many ways further the course of development of the proletariat. The bourgeoisie finds itself involved in a constant battle. At first with the aristocracy; later on, with those portions of the bourgeoisie itself whose interests have become antagonistic to the progress of industry; at all times with the bourgeoisie of foreign countries. In all these battles it sees itself compelled to appeal to the proletariat, to ask for its help, and thus to drag it into the political arena. The bourgeoisie itself, therefore, supplies the proletariat with its own elements of political and general education; in other words, it furnishes the proletariat with weapons for fighting the bourgeoisie.

Further, as we have already seen, entire sections of the ruling classes are precipitated into the proletariat by the advance of industry, or are at least threatened in their conditions of existence. These also supply the proletariat with fresh elements of enlightenment and progress.

Finally, in times when the class struggle nears the decisive hour, the process of dissolution going on within the ruling class, in fact within the whole range of old society, assumes such a violent, glaring character that a small section of the ruling class cuts itself adrift and joins the revolutionary class, the class that holds the future in its hands. Therefore, just as, at an earlier period a section of the nobility went over to the bourgeoisie, so now a portion of the bourgeoisie goes over to the proletariat, and in particular a portion of the bourgeois ideologists who have raised themselves to the level of comprehending theoretically the historical movement as a whole.

Of all the classes that stand face to face with the bourgeoisie today, the proletariat alone is a really revolutionary class. The other classes decay and finally disappear in the face of modern industry; the proletariat is its special and essential product.

The lower middle class, the small manufacturer, the shopkeeper, the artisan, the peasant, all these fight against the bourgeoisie to save from extinction their existence as fractions of the middle class. They are therefore not revolutionary, but conservative. Nay more, they are reactionary, for they try to roll back the wheel of history. If by chance they are revolutionary, they are so only in view of their impending transfer into the proletariat; they thus defend not their present, but their future interests; they desert their own standpoint to place themselves at that of the proletariat.

The "dangerous class," the social scum, that passively rotting mass thrown off by the lowest layers of the old society may here and there be swept into the movement by a proletariat revolution; its conditions of life, however, prepare it far more for the part of a bribed tool of reactionary intrigue.

In the conditions of the proletariat, those of the old society at large are already virtually swamped. The proletarian is without property; his relation to his wife and children has no longer anything in common with the bourgeois family relations; modern industrial labor, modern subjection to capital, the same in England as in France, in America as in Germany, has stripped him of every trace of national character. Law, morality, religion are to him so many bourgeois prejudices behind which lurk in ambush just as many bourgeois interests.

All the preceding classes that got the upper hand sought to fortify their already acquired status by subjecting society at large to their conditions of appropriation. The proletarians cannot become masters of the productive forces of society except by abolishing their own previous mode of appropriation, and thereby also every other previous mode of appropriation. They have nothing of their own to secure and to fortify; their mission is to destroy all previous securities for, and insurances of, individual property.

All previous historical movements were movements of minorities or in the interest of minorities. The proletarian movement is the self-conscious, independent movement of the immense majority in the interest of the immense majority. The proletariat, the lowest stratum of our present society, cannot stir, cannot raise itself up, without the whole superincumbent strata of official society being sprung into the air.

Though not in substance, yet in form, the struggle of the proletariat with the bourgeoisie is at first a national struggle. The proletariat of each country must, of course, first of all settle matters with its own bourgeoisie.

In depicting the most general phases of the development of the proletariat, we traced the more or less veiled civil war raging within existing society up to the point where that war breaks out into open revolution, and where the violent overthrow of the bourgeoisie lays the foundation for the sway of the proletariat.

Hitherto, every form of society has been based, as we have already seen, on the antagonism of oppressing and oppressed classes. But in order to oppress a class certain conditions must be assured to it under which it can, at least, continue its slavish existence. The serf, in the period of serfdom, raised himself to membership in the commune, just as the petty bourgeois, under the yoke of feudal absolutism, managed to develop into a bourgeois. The modern laborer, on the contrary, instead of rising with the progress of industry sinks deeper and deeper below the conditions of existence of his own class. He becomes a pauper, and pauperism develops more rapidly than population and wealth. And here it becomes evident that the bourgeoisie is unfit any longer to be the ruling class in society and to impose its conditions of existence upon society as an over-riding law. It is unfit to rule because it is incompetent to assure an existence to its slave within his slavery, because it cannot help letting him sink into such a state that it has to feed him instead of being fed by him. Society can no longer live under this bourgeoisie, in other words, its existence is no longer compatible with society.

The essential condition for the existence and for the sway of the bourgeois class is the formation and augmentation of capital; the condition for capital is wage labor. Wage labor rests exclusively on competition between the laborers. The advance of industry, whose involuntary promoter is the bourgeoisie, replaces the isolation of the laborers, due to competition, by their revolutionary combination due to association. The development of

Modern Industry therefore cuts from under its feet the very foundation on which the bourgeois produces and appropriates products. What the bourgeoisie therefore produces, above all, are its own grave-diggers. Its fall and the victory of the proletariat are equally inevitable.

PROLETARIANS AND COMMUNISTS

In what relation do the communists stand to the proletarians as a whole?

The communists do not form a separate party opposed to other working-class parties.

They have no interests separate and apart from those of the proletariat as a whole.

They do not set up any sectarian principles of their own, by which to shape and mold the proletarian movement.

The communists are distinguished from the other working-class parties by this only: (1) In the national struggles of the proletarians of the different countries they point out and bring to the front the common interests of the entire proletariat, independent of all nationality. (2) In the various stages of development which the struggle of the working class against the bourgeoisie has to pass through, they always and everywhere represent the interests of the movement as a whole.

The communists, therefore, are on the one hand, practically, the most advanced and resolute section of the working-class parties of every country, that section which pushes forward all others; on the other hand, theoretically, they have over the great mass of the proletariat the advantage of clearly understanding the line of march, the conditions, and the ultimate general results of the proletarian movement.

The immediate aim of the communists is the same as that of all the other proletarian parties: formation of the proletariat into a class, overthrow of the bourgeois supremacy, conquest of political power by the proletariat.

The theoretical conclusions of the communists are in no way based on ideas or principles that have been invented, or discovered, by this or that would-be universal reformer.

They merely express, in general terms, actual relations springing from an existing class struggle, from a historical movement going on under our very eyes. The abolition of existing property relations is not at all a distinctive feature of communism.

All property relations in the past have continually been subject to historical change consequent upon the change in historical conditions.

The French Revolution, for example, abolished feudal property in favor of bourgeois property.

The distinguishing feature of communism is not the abolition of property generally, but the abolition of bourgeois property. But modern bourgeois private property is the final and most complete expression of the system of producing and appropriating products that is based on class antagonisms, on the exploitation of the many by the few.

In this sense the theory of the communists may be summed up in the single sentence: Abolition of private property.

We communists have been reproached with the desire of abolishing the right of personally acquiring property as the fruit of a man's own labor, which property is alleged to be the groundwork of all personal freedom, activity, and independence.

Hard-won, self-acquired, self-earned property! Do you mean the property of the petty artisan and of the small peasant, a form of property that preceded the bourgeois form? There is no need to abolish that; the development of industry has to a great extent already destroyed it, and is still destroying it daily.

Or do you mean modern bourgeois private property?

But does wage labor create any property for the laborer? Not a bit. It creates capital, i.e., that kind of property which exploits wage labor, and which cannot increase except upon condition of begetting a new supply of wage labor for fresh exploitation. Property, in its present form, is based on the antagonism of capital and wage labor. Let us examine both sides of this antagonism.

To be a capitalist is to have not only a purely personal but a social *status* in production. Capital is a collective product, and only by the united action of many members, nay, in the last resort only by the united action of all members of society, can it be set in motion.

Capital is, therefore, not a personal, it is a social power.

When, therefore, capital is converted into common property, into the property of all members of society, personal property is not thereby transformed into social property. It is only the social character of the property that is changed. It loses its class character.

Let us now take wage labor.

The average price of wage labor is the minimum wage, i.e., that quantum of the means of subsistence which is absolutely requisite to keep the laborer in bare existence as a laborer. What, therefore, the wage laborer appropriates by means of his labor merely suffices to prolong and reproduce a bare existence. We by no means intend to abolish this personal appropriation of the products of labor, an appropriation that is made for the maintenance and reproduction of human life, and that leaves no surplus wherewith to command the labor of others. All that we want to do away with is the miserable character of this appropriation, under which the laborer lives merely to increase capital, and is allowed to live only insofar as the interest of the ruling class requires it.

In bourgeois society living labor is but a means to increase accumulated labor. In communist society accumulated labor is but a means to widen, to enrich, to promote the existence of the laborer.

In bourgeois society, therefore, the past dominates the present; in communist society the present dominates the past. In bourgeois society capital is independent and has individuality, while the living person is dependent and has no individuality.

And the abolition of this state of things is called by the bourgeois abolition of individuality and freedom! And rightly so. The abolition of bourgeois individuality, bourgeois independence, and bourgeois freedom is undoubtedly aimed at.

By freedom is meant, under the present bourgeois conditions of production, free trade, free selling and buying.

But if selling and buying disappear, free selling and buying disappear also. This talk about free selling and buying, and all the other "brave words" of our bourgeoisie about freedom in general, have a meaning, if any, only in contrast with restricted selling and buying, with the fettered traders of the Middle Ages, but have no meaning when opposed to the communistic abolition of buying and selling, of the bourgeois conditions of production, and of the bourgeoisie itself.

You are horrified at our intending to do away with private property. But in your existing society private property is already done away with for nine tenths of the population; its existence for the few is solely due to its non-existence in the hands of those nine tenths. You reproach us, therefore, with intending to do away with a form of property the necessary condition for whose existence is the non-existence of any property for the immense majority of society.

In one word, you reproach us with intending to do away with your property. Precisely so; that is just what we intend.

From the moment when labor can no longer be converted into capital, money, or rent, into a social power capable of being monopolized, i.e., from the moment when individual property can no longer be transformed into bourgeois property, into capital, from that moment, you say, individuality vanishes.

You must, therefore, confess that by "individual" you mean no other person than the bourgeois, than the middle-class owner of property. This person must, indeed, be swept out of the way and made impossible.

Communism deprives no man of the power to appropriate the products of society; all that it does is to deprive him of the power to subjugate the labor of others by means of such appropriation.

It has been objected that upon the abolition of private property all work will cease and universal laziness will overtake us.

According to this, bourgeois society ought long ago have gone to the dogs through sheer idleness, for those of its members who work acquire nothing and those who acquire anything do not work. The whole of this objection is but another expression of the tautology that there can no longer be any wage labor when there is no longer any capital.

All objections urged against the communistic mode of producing and appropriating material products have, in the same way, been urged against the communistic modes of producing and appropriating intellectual products. Just as, to the bourgeois, the disappearance of class property is the disappearance of production itself, so the disappearance of class culture is to him identical with the disappearance of all culture.

That culture, the loss of which he laments, is, for the enormous majority, a mere training to act as a machine.

But don't wrangle with us so long as you apply, to our intended abolition of bourgeois property, the standard of your bourgeois notions of freedom, culture, law, etc. Your very ideas are but the outgrowth of the conditions of your bourgeois production and bourgeois property, just as your jurisprudence is but the will of your class made into a law for all, a will whose essential character and direction are determined by the economic conditions of existence of your class.

The selfish misconception that induces you to transform into eternal laws of nature and of reason the social forms springing from your present mode of production and form of property—historical relations that rise and disappear in the progress of production—this misconception you share with every ruling class that has preceded you. What you see clearly in the case of ancient property, what you admit in the case of feudal property you are of course forbidden to admit in the case of your own bourgeois form of property.

Abolition of the family! Even the most radical flare up at this infamous proposal of the communists.

On what foundation is the present family, the bourgeois family, based? On capital, on private gain. In its completely developed form this family exists only among the bourgeoisie. But this state of things finds its complement in the practical absence of the family among the proletarians, and in public prostitution.

The bourgeois family will vanish as a matter of course when its complement vanishes, and both will vanish with the vanishing of capital.

Do you charge us with wanting to stop the exploitation of children by their parents? To this crime we plead guilty.

But, you will say, we destroy the most hallowed of relations when we replace home education by social.

And your education! Is not that also social, and determined by the social conditions under which you educate, by the intervention, direct or indirect, of society, by means of schools, etc.? The communists have not invented the intervention of society in education; they do but seek to alter the character of that intervention, and to rescue education from the influence of the ruling class.

The bourgeois claptrap about the family and education, about the hallowed co-relation of parent and child, becomes all the more disgusting, the more, by the action of modern industry, all family ties among the proletarians are torn asunder and their children transformed into simple articles of commerce and instruments of labor.

"But you communists would introduce community of women," screams the whole bourgeoisie in chorus.

The bourgeois sees in his wife a mere instrument of production. He hears that the instruments of production are to be exploited in common and, naturally, can come to no other conclusion than that the lot of being common to all will likewise fall to the women.

He has not even a suspicion that the real point aimed at is to do away with the status of women as mere instruments of production.

For the rest, nothing is more ridiculous than the virtuous indignation of our bourgeois at the community of women which, they pretend, is to be openly and officially established by the communists. The communists have no need to introduce community of women; it has existed almost from time immemorial.

Our bourgeois, not content with having the wives and daughters of their proletarians at their disposal, not to speak of common prostitutes, take the greatest pleasure in seducing each other's wives.

Bourgeois marriage is in reality a system of wives in common and thus, at the most, what the communists might possibly be reproached with is that they desire to introduce, in substitution for a hypocritically concealed, an openly legalized community of women. For the rest, it is self-evident that the abolition of the present system of production must bring with it the abolition of the community of women springing from that system, i.e., of prostitution, both public and private.

The communists are further reproached with desiring to abolish countries and nationality.

The workingmen have no country. We cannot take from them what they have not got. Since the proletariat must first of all acquire political supremacy, must rise to be the leading class of the nation, must constitute itself *the* nation, it is, so far, itself national, though not in the bourgeois sense of the word.

National differences and antagonisms between peoples are daily more and more vanishing, owing to the development of the bourgeoisie, to freedom of commerce, to the world market, to uniformity in the mode of production and in the conditions of life corresponding thereto.

The supremacy of the proletariat will cause them to vanish still faster. United action, of the leading civilized countries at least, is one of the first conditions for the emancipation of the proletariat.

In proportion as the exploitation of one individual by another is put to an end, the exploitation of one nation by another will also be put to an end. In proportion as the antagonism between classes within the nation vanishes, the hostility of one nation to another will come to an end.

The charges against communism made from a religious, a philosophical, and, generally, from an ideological standpoint are not deserving of serious examination.

Does it require deep intuition to comprehend that man's ideas, views, and conceptions, in one word, man's consciousness, change with every change in the conditions of his material existence, in his social relations, and in his social life?

What else does the history of ideas prove than that the intellectual production changes its character in proportion as material production is changed? The ruling ideas of each age have ever been the ideas of its ruling class.

When people speak of ideas that revolutionize society they do but express the fact that within the old society the elements of a new one have been created, and that the dissolution of the old ideas keeps even pace with the dissolution of the old conditions of existence.

When the ancient world was in its last throes, the ancient religions were overcome by Christianity. When Christian ideas succumbed in the eighteenth century to nationalist ideas, feudal society fought its death battle with the then revolutionary bourgeoisie. The ideas of religious liberty and freedom of conscience merely gave expression to the sway of free competition within the domain of knowledge.

"Undoubtedly," it will be said, "religious, moral, philosophical, and juridical ideas have been modified in the course of historical development. But religion, morality, philosophy, political science, and law constantly survived this change.

"There are, besides, eternal truths, such as freedom, justice, etc., that are common to all states of society. But communism abolishes eternal truths, it abolishes all religion, and all morality, instead of constituting them on a new basis; it therefore acts in contradiction to all past historical experience."

What does this accusation reduce itself to? The history of all past society has consisted in the development of class antagonisms, antagonisms that assumed different forms at different epochs.

But whatever form they may have taken, one fact is common to all past ages, viz., the exploitation of one part of society by the other. No wonder then that the social consciousness of past ages, despite all the multiplicity and variety it displays, moves within certain common forms, or general ideas, which cannot completely vanish except with the total disappearance of class antagonisms.

The communist revolution is the most radical rupture with traditional property relations; no wonder that its development involves the most radical rupture with traditional ideas.

But let us have done with the bourgeois objections to communism.

We have seen above that the first step in the revolution by the working class is to raise the proletariat to the position of ruling class, to win the battle of democracy.

The proletariat will use its political supremacy to wrest, by degrees, all capital from the bourgeoisie, to centralize all instruments of production in the hands of the state, i.e., of the proletariat organized as the ruling class, and to increase the total of productive forces as rapidly as possible.

Of course, in the beginning this cannot be effected except by means of despotic inroads on the rights of property and on the conditions of bourgeois production; by means of measures, therefore, which appear economically insufficient and untenable, but which, in the course of the movement, outstrip themselves, necessitate further inroads upon the old social order, and are unavoidable as a means of entirely revolutionizing the mode of production.

These measures will of course be different in different countries.

Nevertheless, in the most advanced countries the following will be pretty generally applicable:

1. Abolition of property in land and application of all rents of land to public purposes.

2. A heavy progressive or graduated income tax.

3. Abolition of all right of inheritance.

4. Confiscation of the property of all emigrants and rebels.

5. Centralization of credit in the hands of the state, by means of a national bank with state capital and an exclusive monopoly.

6. Centralization of the means of communication and transport in the hands of the state.

7. Extension of factories and instruments of production owned by the state; the bringing into cultivation of wastelands, and the improvement of the soil generally in accordance with a common plan.

8. Equal liability of all to labor. Establishment of industrial armies, especially for agriculture.

9. Combination of agriculture with manufacturing industries; gradual abolition of the distinction between town and country, by a more equable distribution of the population over the country.

10. Free education for all children in public schools. Abolition of children's factory labor in its present form. Combination of education with industrial production, etc.

When, in the course of development, class distinctions have disappeared and all production has been concentrated in the hands of a vast association of the whole nation, the public power will lose its political character. Political power, properly so called, is merely the organized power of one class for oppressing another. If the proletariat during its contest with the bourgeoisie is compelled, by the force of circumstances, to organize itself as a class, if, by means of a revolution, it makes itself the ruling class and, as such, sweeps away by force the old conditions of production, then it will, along with these conditions, have swept away the conditions for the existence of class antagonisms and of classes generally, and will thereby have abolished its own supremacy as a class.

In place of the old bourgeois society, with its classes and class antagonisms, we shall have an association in which the free development of each is the condition for the free development of all. . . .

In short, the communists everywhere support every revolutionary movement against the existing social and political order of things.

In all these movements they bring to the front, as the leading question in each, the property question, no matter what its degree of development at the time.

Finally, they labor everywhere for the union and agreement of the democratic parties of all countries.

The communists disdain to conceal their views and aims. They openly declare that their ends can be attained only by the forcible overthrow of all existing social conditions. Let the ruling classes tremble at a communistic revolution. The proletarians have nothing to lose but their chains. They have a world to win.

WORKINGMEN OF ALL COUNTRIES, UNITE!

ALIENATION

We have proceeded from the premises of political economy. We have accepted its language and its laws. We presupposed private property, the separation of labor, capital and land, and of wages, profit of capital and rent of land—likewise division of labor, competition, the concept of exchange-value, etc. On the basis of political economy itself, in its own words, we have shown that the worker sinks to the level of a commodity and becomes indeed the most wretched of commodities; that the wretchedness of the worker is in inverse proportion to the power and magnitude of his production; that the necessary result of competition is the accumulation of capital in a few hands, and thus the restoration of monopoly in a more terrible form; that finally the distinction between capitalist and land-rentier, like that between the tiller of the soil and the factory-worker, disappears and that the whole of society must fall apart into the two classes—the property-*owners* and the propertyless *workers*.

Political economy proceeds from the fact of private property, but it does not explain it to us. It expresses in general, abstract formulae the *material* process through which private property actually passes, and these formulae it then takes for *laws*. It does not *comprehend* these laws—i.e., it does not demonstrate how they arise from the very nature of private property. Political economy does not disclose the source of the division between labor and capital, and between capital and land. When, for example, it defines the relationship of wages to profit, it takes the interest of the capitalists to be the ultimate cause; i.e., it takes for granted what it is supposed to evolve. Similarly, competition comes in everywhere. It is explained from external circumstances. As to how far these external and apparently fortuitous circumstances are but the expression of a necessary course of development, political economy teaches us nothing. We have seen how, to it, exchange itself appears to be a fortuitous fact. The only wheels which political economy sets in motion are *avarice* and the *war among the avaricious—competition*.

Precisely because political economy does not grasp the connections within the movement, it was possible to counterpose, for instance, the doctrine of competition to the doctrine of monopoly, the doctrine of craft-liberty to the doctrine of the corporation, the doctrine of the division of landed property to the doctrine of the big estate—for competition, craft-liberty and the division of landed property were explained and comprehended only as fortuitous, premeditated and violent consequences of monopoly, the corporation, and feudal property, not as their necessary, inevitable and natural consequences.

Now, therefore, we have to grasp the essential connection between private property, avarice, and the separation of labor, capital and landed property; between exchange and competition, value and the devaluation of men, monopoly and competition, etc.; the connection between this whole estrangement and the *money*-system.

Do not let us go back to a fictitious primordial condition as the political economist does, when he tries to explain. Such a primordial condition explains nothing. He merely pushes the question away into a gray nebulous distance. He assumes in the form of fact, of an event, what he is supposed to deduce—namely, the necessary relationship between two

From Karl Marx, *Economic and Philosophic Manuscripts of 1844*, trans. Martin Milligan.

things—between, for example, division of labor and exchange. Theology in the same way explains the origin of evil by the fall of man; that is, it assumes as a fact, in historical form, what has to be explained.

We proceed from an *actual* economic fact.

The worker becomes all the poorer the more wealth he produces, the more his production increases in power and range. The worker becomes an ever cheaper commodity the more commodities he creates. With the *increasing value* of the world of things proceeds in direct proportion the *devaluation* of the world of men. Labor produces not only commodities: it produces itself and the worker as a *commodity*—and does so in the proportion in which it produces commodities generally.

This fact expresses merely the object which labor produces—labor's product—confronts it as *something alien,* as a *power independent* of the producer. The product of labor is labor which has been congealed in an object, which has become material: it is the *objectification* of labor. Labor's realization is its objectification. In the conditions dealt with by political economy this realization of labor appears as *loss of reality* for the workers; objectification as *loss of the object* and *object-bondage;* appropriation as *estrangement,* as *alienation.*

So much does labor's realization appear as loss of reality that the worker loses reality to the point of starving to death. So much does objectification appear as loss of the object that the worker is robbed of the objects most necessary not only for his life but for his work. Indeed, labor itself becomes an object which he can get hold of only with the greatest effort and with the most irregular interruptions. So much does the appropriation of the object appear as estrangement that the more objects the worker produces the fewer can he possess and the more he falls under the dominion of his product, capital.

All these consequences are contained in the definition that the worker is related to the *product of his labor* as to an *alien* object. For on this premise it is clear that the more the worker spends himself, the more powerful the alien objective world becomes which he creates over-against himself, the poorer he himself—his inner world—becomes, the less belongs to him as his own. It is the same in religion. The more man puts into God, the less he retains in himself. The worker puts his life into the object; but now his life no longer belongs to him but to the object. Hence, the greater this activity, the greater is the worker's lack of objects. Whatever the product of his labor is, he is not. Therefore the greater this product, the less is he himself. The *alienation* of the worker in his product means not only that his labor becomes an object, an *external* existence, but that it exists *outside him,* independently, as something alien to him, and that it becomes a power on its own confronting him; it means that the life which he has conferred on the object confronts him as something hostile and alien.

Let us now look more closely at the *objectification,* at the production of the worker; and therein at the *estrangement,* the *loss* of the object, his product.

The worker can create nothing without *nature,* without the *sensuous external world.* It is the material on which his labor is manifested, in which it is active, from which and by means of which it produces.

But just as nature provides labor with the *means of life* in the sense that labor cannot *live* without objects on which to operate, on the other hand, it also provides the *means of life* in the more restricted sense—i.e., the means for the physical subsistence of the *worker* himself.

Thus the more the worker by his labor *appropriates* the external world, sensuous nature, the more he deprives himself of *means of life* in the double respect: first, that the sensuous external world more and more ceases to be an object belonging to his labor—to be his labor's *means of life;* and secondly, that it more and more ceases to be *means of life* in the immediate sense, means for the physical subsistence of the worker.

Thus in this double respect the worker becomes a slave of his object, first, in that he receives an *object of labor,* i.e., in that he receives *work;* and secondly, in that he receives *means of subsistence.* Therefore, it enables him to exist, first, as a *worker;* and, second, as a *physical subject.* The extremity of this bondage is that it is only as a *worker* that he continues to maintain himself as a *physical subject,* and that it is only as a *physical subject* that he is a *worker.*

(The laws of political economy express the estrangement of the worker in his object thus: the more the worker produces, the less he has to consume; the more values he creates, the more valueless, the more unworthy he becomes; the better formed his product, the more deformed becomes the worker; the more civilized his object, the more barbarous becomes the worker; the mightier labor becomes, the more powerless becomes the worker; the more ingenious labor becomes, the duller becomes the worker and the more he becomes nature's bondsman.)

Political economy conceals the estrangement inherent in the nature of labor by not considering the direct relationship between the worker (labor) *and production.* It is true that labor produces for the rich wonderful things—but for the worker it produces privation. It produces palaces—but for the worker, hovels. It produces beauty—but for the worker, deformity. It replaces labor by machines—but some of the workers it throws back to a barbarous type of labor, and the other workers it turns into machines. It produces intelligence—but for the worker idiocy, cretinism.

The direct relationship of labor to its produce is the relationship of the worker to the objects of his production. The relationship of the man of means to the objects of production and to production itself is only a *consequence* of the first relationship—and confirms it. We shall consider this other aspect later.

When we ask, then, what is the essential relationship of labor we are asking about the relationship of the *worker* to production.

Till now we have been considering the estrangement, the alienation of the worker only in one of its aspects, i.e., the worker's *relationship to the products of his labor.* But the estrangement is manifested not only in the result but in the *act of production*—within the *producing activity* itself. How would the worker come to face the product of his activity as a stranger, were it not that in the very act of production he was estranging himself from himself? The product is after all but the summary of the activity, of production. If then the product of labor is alienation, production itself must be active alienation, the alienation of activity, the activity of alienation. In the estrangement of the object of labor is merely summarized the estrangement, the alienation, in the activity of labor itself.

What, then, constitutes the alienation of labor?

First, the fact that labor is *external* to the worker, i.e., it does not belong to his essential being; that in his work, therefore, he does not affirm himself but denies himself, does not feel content but unhappy, does not develop freely his physical and mental energy but mortifies his body and ruins his mind. The worker therefore only feels himself outside his work, and in his work feels outside himself. He is at home when he is not working, and when he is working he is not at home. His labor is therefore not voluntary, but coerced; it is *forced labor.* It is therefore not the satisfaction of a need; it is merely a *means* to satisfy needs external to it. Its alien character emerges clearly in the fact that as soon as no physical or other compulsion exists, labor is shunned like the plague. External labor, labor in which man alienates himself, is a labor of self-sacrifice, of mortification. Lastly, the external character of labor for the worker appears in the fact that it is not his own, but someone else's, that it does not belong to him, that in it he belongs, not to himself, but to another. Just as in religion the spontaneous activity of the human imagination, of the human brain and the human heart, operates independently of the individual—that is, operates on him as an alien, divine or diabolical activity—in the same way the worker's activity is not his spontaneous activity. It belongs to another; it is the loss of his self.

As a result, therefore, man (the worker) no longer feels himself to be freely active in any but his animal functions—eating, drinking, procreating, or at most in his dwelling and in dressing-up, etc.; and in his human functions he no longer feels himself to be anything but an animal. What is animal becomes human and what is human becomes animal.

Certainly drinking, eating, procreating, etc., are also genuinely human functions. But in the abstraction which separates them from the sphere of all other human activity and turns them into sole and ultimate ends, they are animal.

We have considered the act of estranging practical human activity, labor, in two of its aspects. (1) The relation of the worker to the *product of labor* as an alien object exercising power over him. This relation is at the same time the relation to the sensuous external world, to the objects of nature as an alien world antagonistically opposed to him. (2) The relation of labor to the *act of production* within the *labor* process. This relation is the relation of the worker to his own activity as an alien activity not belonging to him; it is activity as suffering, strength as weakness, begetting as emasculating, the worker's *own* physical and mental energy, his personal life or what is life other than activity—as an activity which is turned against him, neither depends on nor belongs to him. Here we have *self-estrangement,* as we had previously the estrangement of the *thing*.

We have yet a third aspect of *estranged labor* to deduce from the two already considered.

Man is a species being, not only because in practice and in theory he adopts the species as his object (his own as well as those of other things), but—and this is only another way of expressing it—but also because he treats himself as the actual, living species; because he treats himself as a *universal* and therefore a free being.

The life of the species, both in man and in animals, consists physically in the fact that man (like the animal) lives on inorganic nature; and the more universal man is compared with an animal, the more universal is the sphere of inorganic nature on which he lives. Just as plants, animals, stones, the air, light, etc., constitute a part of human consciousness in the realm of theory, partly as objects of natural science, partly as objects of art—his spiritual inorganic nature, spiritual nourishment which he must first prepare to make it palatable and digestable—so too in the realm of practice they constitute a part of human life and human activity. Physically man lives only on these products of nature, whether they appear in the form of food, heating, clothes, a dwelling, or whatever it may be. The universality of man is in practice manifested precisely in the universality which makes all nature his *inorganic* body—both inasmuch as nature is (1) his direct means of life, and (2) the material, the object, and the instrument of his life-activity. Nature is man's *inorganic body*—nature, that is, insofar as it is not itself the human body. Man *lives* on nature—means that nature is his *body,* with which he must remain in continuous intercourse if he is not to die. That man's physical and spiritual life is linked to nature means simply that nature is linked to itself, for man is a part of nature.

In estranging from man (1) nature, and (2) himself, his own active functions, his life-activity, estranged labor estranges the *species* from man. It turns for him the *life of the species* into a means of individual life. First it estranges the life of the species and individual life, and secondly it makes individual life in its abstract form the purpose of the life of the species, likewise in its abstract and estranged form.

For in the first place labor, *life-activity, productive life* itself, appears to man merely as a *means* of satisfying a need—the need to maintain the physical existence. Yet the productive life is the life of the species. It is life-engendering life. The whole character of a species—its species character—is contained in the character of its life-activity; and free, conscious activity is man's species character. Life itself appears only as a *means to life*.

The animal is immediately identical with its life-activity. It does not distinguish itself from it. It is *its life-activity*. Man makes his life-activity itself the object of his will and of his consciousness. He has conscious life-activity. It is not a determination with which he directly merges. Conscious life-activity directly distinguishes man from animal life-activity. It is just because of this that he is a species being. Or it is only because he is a species being that he is a Conscious Being, i.e., that his own life is an object for him. Only because of that is his activity free activity. Estranged labor reverses this relationship, so that it is just because man is a conscious being that he makes his life-activity, his *essential* being, a mere means to his *existence*.

In creating an *objective world* by his practical activity, in *working-up* inorganic nature, man proves himself a conscious species being, i.e., as a being that treats the species as its own essential being, or that treats itself as a species being. Admittedly animals also produce. They build themselves nests, dwellings, like the bees, beavers, ants, etc. But an animal only produces what it immediately needs for itself or its young. It produces one-sidedly, while man produces universally. It produces only under the dominion of immediate physical need, while man produces even when he is free from physical need and only truly produces in freedom therefrom. An animal produces only itself, while man reproduces the whole of nature. An animal's product belongs immediately to its physical body, while man freely confronts his proudct. An animal forms things in accordance with the standard and the need of the species to which it belongs, while man knows how to produce in accordance with the standard of every species, and knows how to apply everywhere the inherent standard to the object. Man therefore also forms things in accordance with the laws of beauty.

It is just in the working-up of the objective world, therefore, that man first really proves himself to be a *species being*. This production is his active species life. Through and because of this production, nature appears as *his* work and his reality. The object of labor is, therefore, the *objectification of man's species life:* for he duplicates himself not only, as in consciousness, intellectually, but also actively, in reality, and therefore he contemplates himself in a world that he has created. In tearing away from man the object of his production, therefore, estranged labor tears from him his *species life,* his real species objectivity, and transforms his advantage over animals into the disadvantage that his inorganic body, nature, is taken from him.

Similarly, in degrading spontaneous activity, free activity, to a means, estranged labor makes man's species life a means to his physical existence.

The consciousness which man has of his species is thus transformed by estrangement in such a way that the species life becomes for him a means.

Estranged labor turns thus: (3) *Man's species being,* both nature and his spiritual species property, into a being *alien* to him, into a *means* to his *individual existence*. It estranges man's own body from him, as it does external nature and his spiritual essence, his *human* being. (4) An immediate consequence of the fact that man is estranged from the product of his labor, from his life-activity, from his species being is the *estrangement of man* from *man.* If a man is confronted by himself, he is confronted by the *other* man. What applies to a man's relation to his work, to the product of his labor and to himself, also holds of a man's relation to the other man, and to the other man's labor and object of labor.

In fact, the proposition that man's species nature is estranged from him means that one man is estranged from the other, as each of them is from man's essential nature.

The estrangement of man, and in fact every relationship in which man stands to himself, is first realized and expressed in the relationship in which a man stands to other men.

Hence within the relationship of estranged labor each man views the other in accordance with the standard and the position in which he finds himself as a worker.

We took our departure from a fact of political economy—the estrangement of the worker and his production. We have formulated the concept of this fact—*estranged, alienated* labor. We have analyzed this concept—hence analyzing merely a fact of political economy.

Let us now see, further, how in real life the concept of estranged, alienated labor must express and present itself.

If the product of labor is alien to me, if it confronts me as an alien power, to whom, then, does it belong?

To a being *other* than me.

Who is this being?

The *gods?* To be sure, in the earliest times the principal production (for example, the building of temples, etc., in Egypt, India and Mexico) appears to be in the service of the gods, and the product belongs to the gods. However, the gods on their own were never the lords of labor. No more was *nature.* And what a contradiction it would be if, the more man subjugated nature by his labor and the more the miracles of the gods were rendered superfluous by the miracles of industry, the more man were to renounce the joy of production and the enjoyment of the produce in favor of these powers.

The *alien* being, to whom labor and the produce of labor belongs, in whose service labor is done and for whose benefit the produce of labor is provided, can only be *man* himself.

If the product of labor does not belong to the worker, if it confronts him as an alien power, this can only be because it belongs to some *other man than the worker.* If the worker's activity is a torment to him, to another it must be *delight* and his life's joy. Not the gods, not nature, but only man himself can be this alien power over man.

We must bear in mind the above-stated proposition that man's relation to himself only becomes *objective* and *real* for him through his relation to the other man. Thus, if the product of his labor, his labor *objectified,* is for him an *alien,* hostile, powerful object independent of him, then his position towards it is such that someone else is master of this object, someone who is alien, hostile, powerful, and independent of him. If his own activity is to him an unfree activity, then he is treating it as activity performed in the service, under the dominion, the coercion and the yoke of another man.

Every self-estrangement of man from himself and from nature appears in the relation in which he places himself and nature to men other than and differentiated from himself. For this reason religious self-estrangement necessarily appears in the relationship of the layman to the priest, or again to a mediator, etc., since we are here dealing with the intellectual world. In the real practical world self-estrangement can only become manifest through the real practical relationship to other men. The medium through which estrangement takes place is itself *practical*. Thus through estranged labor man not only engenders his relationship to the object and to the act of production as to powers that are alien and hostile to him; he also engenders the relationship in which other men stand to his production and to his product, and the relationship in which he stands to these other men. Just as he begets his own production as the loss of his reality, as his punishment; just as he begets his own product as a loss, as a product not belonging to him; so he begets the dominion of the one who does not produce over production and over the product. Just as he estranges from himself his own activity, so he confers to the stranger activity which is not his own.

Till now we have only considered this relationship from the standpoint of the worker and later we shall be considering it also from the standpoint of the non-worker.

Through *estranged, alienated labor,* then, the worker produces the relationship to this labor of a man alien to labor and standing outside it. The relationship of the worker to labor engenders the relation to it of the capitalist, or whatever one chooses to call the master of labor. *Private property* is thus the product, the result, the necessary consequence, of *alienated labor,* of the external relation of the worker to nature and to himself.

Private property thus results by analysis from the concept of *alienated labor*—i.e., of *alienated man,* of estranged labor, of estranged life, of *estranged* man.

True, it is as a result of the *movement of private property* that we have obtained the concept of *alienated labor (of alienated life)* from political economy. But on analysis of this concept it becomes clear that though private property appears to be the source, the cause of alienated labor, it is really its consequence, just as the gods *in the beginning* are not the cause but the effect of man's intellectual confusion. Later this relationship becomes reciprocal.

Only at the very culmination of the development of private property does this, its secret, re-emerge, namely, that on the one hand it is the *product* of alienated labor, and that secondly it is the *means* by which labor alienates itself, the *realization of this alienation.*

This exposition immediately sheds light on various hitherto unsolved conflicts.

1. Political economy starts from labor as the real soul of production; yet to labor it gives nothing, and to private property everything. From this contradiction Proudhon has concluded in favor of labor and against private property. We understand, however, that this apparent contradiction is the contradiction of *estranged labor* with itself, and that political economy has merely formulated the laws of estranged labor.

We also understand, therefore, that *wages* and *private property* are identical: where the product, the object of labor pays for labor itself, the wage is but a necessary consequence of labor's estrangement, for after all in the wage of labor, labor does not appear as an end in itself but as the servant of the wage. We shall develop this point later, and meanwhile will only deduce some conclusions.

A *forcing-up of wages* (disregarding all other difficulties, including the fact that it would only be by force, too, that the higher wages, being an anomaly, could be maintained) would therefore be nothing but *better payment for the slave,* and would not conquer either for the worker or for labor their human status and dignity.

Indeed, even the *equality of wages* demanded by Proudhon only transforms the relationship of the present-day worker to his labor into the relationship of all men to labor. Society is then conceived as an abstract capitalist.

Wages are a direct consequence of estranged labor, and estranged labor is the direct cause of private property. The downfall of the one aspect must therefore mean the downfall of the other.

2. From the relationship of estranged labor to private property it further follows that the emancipation of society from private property, etc., from servitude, is expressed in the *political* form of the *emancipation of the workers;* not that *their* emancipation alone was at stake but because the emancipation of the workers contains universal human emancipation—and it contains this, because the whole of human servitude is involved in the relation of the worker to production, and every relation of servitude is but a modification and consequence of this relation.

Just as we have found the concept of *private property* from the concept of *estranged, alienated labor* by analysis, in the same way every *category* of political economy can be evolved with the help of these two factors; and we shall find again in each category, e.g., trade, competition, capital, money, only a *definite* and *developed expression* of the first foundations.

Before considering this configuration, however, let us try to solve two problems.

1. To define the general *nature of private property,* as it has arisen as a result of estranged labor, in its relation to *truly human, social property.*

2. We have accepted the *estrangement of labor,* its *alienation,* as a fact, and we have analyzed this fact. How, we now ask, does *man* come to *alienate,* to estrange, *his labor?* How is this estrangement rooted in the nature of human development? We have already gone a long way to the solution of this problem by *transforming* the question as to the *origin of private property* into the question as to the relation of *alienated labor* to the course of humanity's development. For when one speaks of *private property,* one thinks of being concerned with something external to man. When one speaks of labor, one is directly concerned with man himself. This new formulation of the question already contains its solution.

As to (1): The general nature of private property and its relation to truly human property.
Alienated labor has resolved itself for us into two elements which mutually condition one another, or which are but different expressions of one and the same relationship. *Appropriation* appears as *estrangement,* as *alienation;* and *alienation* appears as *appropriation, estrangement* as true *enfranchisement.*

We have considered the one side—*alienated* labor in relation to the *worker* himself, i.e., the *relation of alienated labor to itself.* The *property-relation of the non-worker to the worker and to labor* we have found as the product, the necessary outcome of this relation of alienated labor. *Private property,* as the material, summary expression of alienated labor, embraces both relations—the *relation of the worker to work, to the product of his labor and to the non-worker,* and the relation of the *non-worker to the worker and to the product of his labor.*

Having seen that in relation to the worker who *appropriates* nature by means of his labor, this appropriation appears as estrangement, his own spontaneous activity as activity for another and as an activity of another, vitality as a sacrifice of life, production of the object as loss of the object to an alien power, to an *alien* person—we shall now consider the relation to the worker, to labor and its object of this person who is *alien* to labor and the worker.

First it has to be noted, that everything which appears in the worker as an *activity of alienation, of estrangement,* appears in the non-worker as a *state of alienation, of estrangement.*

Secondly, that the worker's *real, practical attitude* in production and to the product (as a state of mind) appears in the non-worker confronting him as a *theoretical* attitude.

Thirdly, the non-worker does everything against the worker which the worker does against himself; but he does not do against himself what he does against the worker.

Let us look more closely at these three relations.

THE POWER OF MONEY

If man's *feelings,* passions, etc., are not merely anthropological phenomena in the [narrower] sense, but truly *ontological* affirmations of essential being (of nature), and if they are only really affirmed because their *object* exists for them as an object of *sense,* then it is clear:

1. That they have by no means merely one mode of affirmation, but rather that the distinctive character of their existence, of their life, is constituted by the distinctive mode of their affirmation. In what manner the object exists for them, is the characteristic mode of their *gratification.*

2. Wherever the sensuous affirmation is the direct annulment of the object in its independent form (as in eating, drinking, working up of the object, etc.), this is the affirmation of the object.

3. Insofar as man, and hence also his feeling, etc., are *human,* the affirmation of the object by another is likewise his own enjoyment.

4. Only through developed industry—i.e., through the medium of private property—does the ontological essence of human passion come to be both in its totality and in its humanity; the science of man is therefore itself a product of man's establishment of himself by practical activity.

5. The meaning of private property—liberated from its estrangement—is the *existence of essential objects* for man, both as objects of enjoyment and as objects of activity.

By possessing the *property* of buying everything, by possessing the property of appropriating all objects, *money* is thus the *object* of eminent possession. The universality of its *property* is the omnipotence of its being. It therefore functions as the almighty being. Money is the *pimp* between man's need and the object, between his life and his means of life. But *that which* mediates *my* life for me, also *mediates* the existence of other people *for me.* For me it is the *other* person.

> What, man! confound it, hands and feet
> And head and backside, are all yours!

From Karl Marx, *Economic and Philosophic Manuscripts of 1844,* trans. Martin Milligan.

And what we take while life is sweet,
Is that to be declared not ours?
Six stallions, say, I can afford,
Is not their strength my property?
I tear along, a sporting lord,
As if their legs belonged to me.
      (GOETHE: *Faust*—Mephistopheles)

Shakespeare in *Timon of Athens:*

Gold? Yellow, glittering, precious gold? No, Gods,
I am no idle votarist! . . . Thus much of this will
    make black white, foul fair,
Wrong, right, base noble, old young, coward valiant.
. . . Why, this
Will lug your priests and servants from your sides,
Pluck stout men's pillows from below their heads:
This yellow *slave*
Will knit and break religions, bless the accursed;
Make the hoar leprosy adored, place thieves
And give them title, knee and approbation
With senators on the bench: This is it
That makes the wappen'd widow wed again;
She, whom the spital-house and ulcerous sores
Would cast the gorge at, this embalms and spices
To the April day again. . . . Damned earth,
Thou common whore of mankind, that putt'st odds
Among the rout of nations.

And also later:

O thou sweet king-killer, and dear divorce
Twixt natural son and sire! thou bright defiler
of Hymen's purest bed! thou valiant Mars!
Thou ever young, fresh, loved and delicate wooer,
Whose blush doth thaw the consecrated snow
That lies on Dian's lap! Thou *visible God!*
That solder'st close *impossibilities,*
And maest them kiss! That speak'st with every tongue,
To every purpose! O thou touch of hearts!
Think, thy slave man rebels, and by thy virtue
Set them into confounding odds, that beasts
May have the world in empire!

Shakespeare excellently depicts the real nature of *money*. To understand him, let us begin, first of all, by expounding the passage from Goethe.

That which is for me through the medium of *money*—that for which I can pay (i.e., which money can buy)—that am *I,* the possessor of the money. The extent of the power of money is the extent of my power. Money's properties are my properties and essential powers—the properties and powers of its possessor. Thus, what I *am* and *am capable* of is by no means determined by my individuality. I am ugly, but I can buy for myself the most *beautiful* of women. Therefore I am not *ugly,* for the effect of *ugliness*—its deterrent power—is nullified by money. I, in my character as an individual, am *lame,* but money furnishes me with twenty-four feet. Therefore I am not lame. I am bad, dishonest, unscrupulous, stupid; but money is honored, and therefore so is its possessor. Money is the supreme good, therefore its possessor is good. Money, besides, saves me the trouble of being dishonest: I am therefore presumed honest. I am *stupid,* but money is the *real mind* of all things and how then should its possessor be stupid? Besides, he can buy talented people for himself, and is he who has power over the talented not more talented than the talented? Do not I, who thanks to money am capable of *all* that the human heart longs for, possess all human capacities? Does not my money therefore transform all my incapacities into their contrary?

If *money* is the bond binding me to *human* life, binding society to me, binding me and nature and man, is not money the bond of all *bonds?* Can it not dissolve and bind all ties? Is it not, therefore, the universal *agent of divorce?* It is the true *agent of divorce* as well as the true *binding agent*—the [universal] *galvano-chemical* power of Society.

Shakespeare stresses especially two properties of money: (1) It is the visible divinity—the transformation of all human and natural properties into their contraries, the universal confounding and overturning of things: it makes brothers of impossibilities. (2) It is the common whore, the common pimp of people and nations.

The overturning and confounding of all human and natural qualities, the fraternization of impossibilities—the *divine* power of money—lies in its *character* as men's estranged, alienating and self-disposing *species-nature.* Money is the alienated *ability of mankind.*

That which I am unable to do as a *man,* and of which therefore all my individual essential powers are incapable, I am able to do by means of *money.* Money thus turns each of these powers into something which in itself it is not—turns it, that is, into its *contrary.*

If I long for a particular dish or want to take the mail-coach because I am not strong enough to go by foot, money fetches me the dish and the mail-coach: that is, it converts my wishes from something in the realm of imagination, translates them from their meditated, imagined or willed existence into their *sensuous, actual* existence—from imagination to life, from imagined being into real being. In effecting this mediation, money is the *truly creative* power.

No doubt *demand* also exists for him who has no money, but his demand is a mere thing of the imagination without effect or existence for me, for a third party, for the others, and which therefore remains for me *unreal* and *objectless.* The difference between effective demand based on money and ineffective demand based on my need, my passion, my wish, etc., is the difference between *being* and *thinking,* between the imagined which *exists* merely within me and the imagined as it is for me outside me as a *real object.*

If I have no money for travel, I have no *need*—that is, no real and self-realizing need—to travel. If I have the *vocation* for study but no money for it, I have *no* vocation for study—that is, no *effective,* no *true* vocation. On the other hand, if I have really *no* vocation for study but have the will *and* the money for it, I have an *effective* vocation for it. Being the external, common *medium* and *faculty* for turning an *image* into *reality* and *reality* into a mere *image* (a faculty not springing from man as man or from human society as society), *money* transforms the *real essential powers of man and nature* into what are merely abstract conceits and therefore *imperfections*—into tormenting chimeras—just as it transforms *real imperfections and chimeras*—essential powers which are really impotent, which exist only in the imagination of the individual—into *real powers* and *faculties.*

In the light of this characteristic alone, money is thus the general overturning of *individualities* which turns them into their contrary and adds contradictory attributes to their attributes.

Money, then, appears as this *overturning* power both against the individual and against the bonds of society, etc., which claim to be *essences* in themselves. It transforms fidelity into infidelity, love into hate, hate into love, virtue into vice, vice into virtue, servant into master, master into servant, idiocy into intelligence and intelligence into idiocy.

Since money, as the existing and active concept of value, confounds and exchanges all things, it is the general *confounding* and *compounding* of all things—the world upside-down—the confounding and compounding of all natural and human qualities.

He who can buy bravery is brave, though a coward. As money is not exchanged for any one specific quality, for any one specific thing, or for any particular human essential power, but for the entire objective world of man and nature, from the standpoint of its possessor it therefore serves to exchange every property for every other, even contradictory, property and object: it is the fraternization of impossibilities. It makes contradictions embrace.

Assume *man* to be *man* and his relationship to the world to be a human one: then you can exchange love only for love, trust for trust, etc. If you want to enjoy art, you must be an artistically cultivated person; if you want to exercise influence over other people, you must be a person with a stimulating and encouraging effect on other people. Every one of your relations to man and to nature must be a *specific expression,* corresponding to the object of your will, of your *real individual* life. If you love without evoking love in return—that is, if your loving as loving does not produce reciprocal love; if through a *living expression* of yourself as a loving person you do not make yourself a *loved person,* then your love is impotent—a misfortune.

CHAPTER

40

MACH

1838–1916

Ernst Mach was born at Turas in Moravia, a province in what is now the Czech Republic and educated in Vienna. He was professor of physics, first at Graz from 1864 to 1867 and then at Prague from 1867 to 1895, and then returned to Vienna as a professor of philosophy. His work both as a physicist and as a philosopher has had a tremendous influence on twentieth-century thought and on both fields. Mach is generally regarded as the founder of the philosophical movement known as *logical positivism,* especially of the variety espoused by the Vienna Circle. His name is also widely recognized in the "Mach number" relating an airplane's air speed with the local speed of sound.

As a radical empiricist, Mach formalized the view now shared by most scientists that only empirically verifiable statements are meaningful. He was also one of the clearest advocates of *phenomenalism,* the view that physical object propositions are analyzable into statements about sensations in terms of either actual or possible perceptual experience. Although his views are reminiscent of Berkeley and Kant, they have often been presented in purely Berkeleian or Kantian terms; whereas in Berkeley's view the elements of the mind are conditioned by an unknown external cause that Berkeley identified as God, and Kant relied on the "thing-in-itself," Mach argued that the elements of the mind depend only on each other and require no other substance or cause for a complete explanation. He influenced not only the leading members of the Vienna Circle but also John Stuart Mill and the young A. J. Ayer. So thoroughly rigorous were Mach's criteria of verifiability that he managed in his early work to criticize Newton's empirical system as inadequate, paving the way for Einstein's theory of relativity. In his *Analysis of Sensations* (1886), from which the following selection is taken, Mach describes his foray into philosophy, marked by a lifelong indebtedness to Kant's *Prolegomena.*

THE ANALYSIS OF SENSATIONS
AND THE RELATION OF THE PHYSICAL
TO THE PSYCHICAL

INTRODUCTORY REMARKS: ANTIMETAPHYSICAL

The great results achieved by physical science in modern times—results not restricted to its own sphere but embracing that of other sciences which employ its help—have brought it about that physical ways of thinking and physical modes of procedure enjoy on all hands unwonted prominence, and that the greatest expectations are associated with their application. In keeping with this drift of modern inquiry, the physiology of the senses, gradually abandoning the method of investigating sensations in themselves followed by men like Goethe, Schopenhauer, and others, but with greatest success by Johannes Müller, has also assumed an almost exclusively physical character. This tendency must appear to us as not altogether appropriate, when we reflect that physics, despite its considerable development, nevertheless constitutes but a portion of a *larger* collective body of knowledge, and that it is unable, with its limited intellectual implements, created for limited and special purposes, to exhaust all the subject-matter in question. Without renouncing the support of physics, it is possible for the physiology of the senses, not only to pursue its own course of development, but also to afford to physical science itself powerful assistance. The following simple considerations will serve to illustrate this relation between the two.

Colors, sounds, temperatures, pressures, spaces, times, and so forth, are connected with one another in manifold ways; and with them are associated dispositions of mind, feelings, and volitions. Out of this fabric, that which is relatively more fixed and permanent stands prominently forth, engraves itself on the memory, and expresses itself in language. Relatively greater permanency is exhibited, first, by certain complexes of colors, sounds, pressures, and so forth, functionally connected in time and space, which therefore receive special names, and are called bodies. Absolutely permanent such complexes are not.

My table is now brightly, now dimly lighted. Its temperature varies. It may receive an ink stain. One of its legs may be broken. It may be repaired, polished, and replaced part by part. But, for me, it remains the table at which I daily write.

My friend may put on a different coat. His countenance may assume a serious or a cheerful expression. His complexion, under the effects of light or emotion, may change. His shape may be altered by motion, or be definitely changed. Yet the number of the permanent features presented, compared with the number of the gradual alterations, is always so great, that the latter may be overlooked. It is the same friend with whom I take my daily walk.

My coat may receive a stain, a tear. My very manner of expressing this shows that we are concerned here with a sum-total of permanency, to which the new element is added and from which that which is lacking is subsequently taken away.

Our greater intimacy with this sum-total of permanency, and the preponderance of its importance for me as contrasted with the changeable element, impel us to the partly instinc-

From Ernst Mach, *The Analysis of Sensations,* trans. C. M. Williams, 1906, revised by S. Waterlow, 1914.

tive, partly voluntary and conscious economy of mental presentation and designation, as expressed in ordinary thought and speech. That which is presented in a single image receives a single designation, a single name.

Further, that complex of memories, moods, and feelings, joined to a particular body (the human body), which is called the "I" or "Ego," manifests itself as relatively permanent. I may be engaged upon this or that subject, I may be quiet and cheerful, excited and ill-humored. Yet, pathological cases apart, enough durable features remain to identify the ego. Of course, the ego also is only of relative permanency.

The apparent permanency of the ego consists chiefly in the single fact of its continuity, in the slowness of its changes. The many thoughts and plans of yesterday that are continued to-day, and of which our environment in waking hours incessantly reminds us (whence in dreams the ego can be very indistinct, doubled, or entirely wanting), and the little habits that are unconsciously and involuntarily kept up for long periods of time, constitute the groundwork of the ego. There can hardly be greater differences in the egos of different people, than occur in the course of years in one person. When I recall to-day my early youth, I should take the boy that I then was, with the exception of a few individual features, for a different person, were it not for the existence of the chain of memories. Many an article that I myself penned twenty years ago impresses me now as something quite foreign to myself. The very gradual character of the changes of the body also contributes to the stability of the ego, but in a much less degree than people imagine. Such things are much less analyzed and noticed than the intellectual and the moral ego. Personally, people know themselves very poorly. When I wrote these lines in 1886, Ribot's admirable little book, *The Diseases of Personality,* was unknown to me. Ribot ascribes the principal role in preserving the continuity of the ego to the general sensibility. Generally, I am in perfect accord with his views.

The ego is as little absolutely permanent as are bodies. That which we so much dread in death, the annihilation of our permanency, actually occurs in life in abundant measure. That which is most valued by us, remains preserved in countless copies, or, in cases of exceptional excellence, is even preserved of itself. In the best human being, however, there are individual traits, the loss of which neither he himself nor others need regret. Indeed, at times, death, viewed as a liberation from individuality, may even become a pleasant thought. Such reflections of course do not make physiological death any the easier to bear.

After a first survey has been obtained, by the formation of the substance-concepts "body" and "ego" (matter and soul), the will is impelled to a more exact examination of the changes that take place in these relatively permanent existences. The element of change in bodies and the ego, is in fact, exactly what moves the will to this examination. Here the component parts of the complex are first exhibited as its properties. A fruit is sweet; but it can also be bitter. Also, other fruits may be sweet. The red color we are seeking is found in many bodies. The neighborhood of some bodies is pleasant; that of others, unpleasant. Thus, gradually, different complexes are found to be made up of common elements. The visible, the audible, the tangible, are separated from bodies. The visible is analyzed into colors and into form. In the manifoldness of the colors, again, though here fewer in number, other component parts are discerned—such as the primary colors, and so forth. The complexes are disintegrated into elements, that is to say, into their ultimate component parts, which hitherto we have been unable to subdivide any further. The nature of these elements need not be discussed at present; it is possible that future investigations may throw light on it. We need not here be disturbed by the fact that it is easier for the scientist to study relations of relations of these elements than the direct relations between them.

The useful habit of designating such relatively permanent compounds by single names, and of apprehending them by single thoughts, without going to the trouble each time of an analysis of their component parts, is apt to come into strange conflict with the tendency to isolate the component parts. The vague image which we have of a given permanent complex, being an image which does not perceptibly change when one or another of the component parts is taken away, seems to be something which exists in itself. Inasmuch as it is possible to take away singly every constituent part without destroying the capacity of the image to stand for the totality and to be recognized again, it is imagined that it is possible to subtract all the parts and to have something still remaining. Thus naturally arises the philosophical notion, at first impressive, but subsequently recognized as monstrous, of a "thing-in-itself," different from its "appearance," and unknowable.

Thing, body, matter, are nothing apart from the combinations of the elements—the colors, sounds, and so forth—nothing apart from their so-called attributes. That protean pseudo-philosophical problem of the single thing with its many attributes, arises wholly from a misinterpretation of the fact that summary comprehension and precise analysis, although both are provisionally justifiable and for many purposes profitable, cannot be carried on simultaneously. A body is one and unchangeable only so long as it is unnecessary to consider its details. Thus both the earth and a billiard-ball are spheres, if we are willing to neglect all deviations from the spherical form, and if greater precision is not necessary. But when we are obliged to carry on investigations in orography or microscopy, both bodies cease to be spheres.

Man is pre-eminently endowed with the power of voluntarily and consciously determining his own point of view. He can at one time disregard the most salient features of an object, and immediately thereafter give attention to its smallest details; now consider a stationary current, without a thought of its contents (whether heat, electricity, or fluidity), and then measure the width of a Fraunhofer line in the spectrum; he can rise at will to the most general abstractions or bury himself in the minutest particulars. Animals possess this capacity in a far less degree. They do not assume a point of view, but are usually forced to it by their sense-impressions. The baby that does not know its father with his hat on, the dog that is perplexed at the new coat of its master, have both succumbed in this conflict of points of view. Who has not been worsted in similar plights? Even the man of philosophy at times succumbs, as the grotesque problem, above referred to, shows.

In this last case, the circumstances appear to furnish a real ground of justification. Colors, sounds, and the odors of bodies are evanescent. But their tangibility, as a sort of constant nucleus, not readily susceptible of annihilation, remains behind, appearing as the vehicle of the more fugitive properties attached to it. Habit thus keeps our thought firmly attached to this central nucleus, even when we have begun to recognize that seeing, hearing, smelling, and touching are intimately akin in character. A further consideration is that, owing to the singularly extensive development of mechanical physics, a kind of higher reality is ascribed to the spatial and to the temporal than to colors, sounds, and odors; agreeably to which, the temporal and spatial links of colors, sounds, and odors appear to be more real than the colors, sounds, and odors themselves. The physiology of the senses, however, demonstrates that spaces and times may just as appropriately be called sensations as colors and sounds. But of this later.

Not only the relation of bodies to the ego, but the ego itself also, gives rise to similar pseudo-problems, the character of which may be briefly indicated as follows:

Let us denote the above-mentioned elements by the letters $A\ B\ C \ldots, K\ L\ M \ldots,$ $\alpha\ \beta\ \gamma \ldots.$ Let those complexes of colors, sounds, and so forth, commonly called bodies, be denoted, for the sake of clearness, by $A\,B\,C\ldots$; the complex, known as our own body, which is a part of the former complexes distinguished by certain peculiarities, may be called $K\,L\,M\ldots$; the complex composed of volitions, memory-images, and the rest, we shall represent by $\alpha\,\beta\,\gamma\ldots$. Usually, now, the complex $\alpha\,\beta\,\gamma\ldots K\,L\,M\ldots$, as making up the ego, is opposed to the complex $A\,B\,C\ldots$, as making up the world of physical objects; sometimes also, $\alpha\,\beta\,\gamma\ldots$ is viewed as ego, and $K\,L\,M\ldots A\,B\,C\ldots$ as world of physical objects. Now, at first blush, $A\,B\,C\ldots$ appears independent of the ego, and opposed to it as a separate existence. But this independence is only relative, and gives way upon closer inspection. Much, it is true, *may* change in the complex $\alpha\,\beta\,\gamma\ldots$ without much perceptible change being induced in $A\,B\,C\ldots$; and vice versa. But many changes in $\alpha\,\beta\,\gamma\ldots$ do pass, by way of changes in $K\,L\,M\ldots$, to $A\,B\,C\ldots$; and vice versa. (As, for example, when powerful ideas burst forth into acts, or when our environment induces noticeable changes in our body.) At the same time the group $K\,L\,M\ldots$ appears to be more intimately connected with $\alpha\,\beta\,\gamma\ldots$ and with $A\,B\,C\ldots$, than the latter with one another; and their relations find their expression in common thought and speech.

Precisely viewed, however, it appears that the group $A\,B\,C\ldots$ is always codetermined by $K\,L\,M\ldots$. A cube when seen close at hand, looks large; when seen at a distance, small; its appearance to the right eye differs from its appearance to the left; sometimes it appears double; with closed eyes it is invisible. The properties of one and the same body, therefore, appear modified by our own body; they appear conditioned by it. But where, now, is that *same* body, which appears so *different?* All that can be said is, that with different $K\,L\,M\ldots$ different $A\,B\,C\ldots$ are associated.

A common and popular way of thinking and speaking is to contrast "appearance" with "reality." A pencil held in front of us in the air is seen by us as straight; dip it into the water, and we see it crooked. In the latter case we say that the pencil *appears* crooked, but is in *reality* straight. But what justifies us in declaring one fact rather than another to be the reality, and degrading the other to the level of appearance? In both cases we have to do with facts which present us with different combinations of the elements, combinations which in the two cases are differently conditioned. Precisely because of its environment, the pencil dipped in water is optically crooked; but it is tactually and metrically straight. An image in a concave or flat mirror is *only* visible, whereas under other and ordinary circumstances a tangible body as well corresponds to the visible image. A bright surface is brighter beside a dark surface than beside one brighter than itself. To be sure, our expectation is deceived when, not paying sufficient attention to the conditions, and substituting for one another different cases of the combination, we fall into the natural error of expecting what we are accustomed to, although the case may be an unusual one. The facts are not to blame for that. In these cases, to speak of "appearance" may have a practical meaning, but cannot have a scientific meaning. Similarly, the question which is often asked, whether the world is real or whether we merely dream it, is devoid of all scientific meaning. Even the wildest dream is a fact as much as any other. If our dreams were more regular, more connected, more stable, they would also have more practical importance for us. In our waking hours the relations of the elements to one another are immensely amplified in comparison with what they were in our dreams. We recognize the dream for what it is. When the process is reversed, the field of psychic vision is narrowed; the contrast is almost entirely lacking. Where there is no contrast, the distinction between dream and waking, between appearance and reality, is quite otiose and worthless.

The popular notion of an antithesis between appearance and reality has exercised a very powerful influence on scientific and philosophical thought. We see this, for example, in

Plato's pregnant and poetical fiction of the Cave, in which, with our backs turned towards the fire, we observe merely the shadows of what passes (*Republic,* Book VII). But this conception was not thought out to its final consequences, with the result that it has had an unfortunate influence on our ideas about the universe. The universe, of which nevertheless we are a part, became completely separated from us, and was removed an infinite distance away. Similarly, many a young man, hearing for the first time of the refraction of stellar light, has thought that doubt was cast on the whole of astronomy, whereas nothing is required but an easily effected and unimportant correction to put everything right again.

We see an object having a point S. If we touch S, that is, bring it into connection with our body, we receive a prick. We can see S, without feeling the prick. But as soon as we feel the prick we find S on the skin. The visible point, therefore, is a permanent nucleus, to which the prick is annexed, according to circumstances, as something accidental. From the frequency of analogous occurrences we ultimately accustom ourselves to regard all properties of bodies as "effects" proceeding from permanent nuclei and conveyed to the ego through the medium of the body; which effects we call sensations. By this operation, however, these nuclei are deprived of their entire sensory content, and converted into mere mental symbols. The assertion, then, is correct that the world consists only of our sensations. In which case we have knowledge *only* of sensations, and the assumption of the nuclei referred to, or of a reciprocal action between them, from which sensations proceed, turns out to be quite idle and superfluous. Such a view can only suit with a half-hearted realism or a half-hearted philosophical criticism.

Ordinarily the complex $\alpha\,\beta\,\gamma \ldots K\,L\,M \ldots$ is contrasted as ego with the complex $A\,B\,C \ldots$. At first only those elements of $A\,B\,C \ldots$ that more strongly alter $\alpha\,\beta\,\gamma \ldots$, as a prick, a pain, are wont to be thought of as comprised in the ego. Afterwards, however, through observations of the kind just referred to, it appears that the right to annex $A\,B\,C \ldots$ to the ego nowhere ceases. In conformity with this view, the ego can be so extended as ultimately to embrace the entire world. The ego is not sharply marked off, its limits are very indefinite and arbitrarily displaceable. Only by failing to observe this fact, and by unconsciously narrowing those limits, while at the same time we enlarge them, arise, in the conflict of points of view, the metaphysical difficulties met with in this connection.

As soon as we have perceived that the supposed unities "body" and "ego" are only makeshifts, designed for provisional orientation and for definite practical ends (so that we may take hold of bodies, protect ourselves against pain, and so forth), we find ourselves obliged, in many more advanced scientific investigations, to abandon them as insufficient and inappropriate. The antithesis between ego and world, between sensation (appearance) and thing, then vanishes, and we have simply to deal with the connection of the elements $\alpha\,\beta\,\gamma \ldots$ $A\,B\,C \ldots K\,L\,M \ldots$, of which this antithesis was only a partially appropriate and imperfect expression. This connection is nothing more or less than the combination of the above-mentioned elements with other similar elements (time and space). Science has simply to accept this connection, and to get its bearings in it, without at once wanting to explain its existence.

On a superficial examination the complex $\alpha\,\beta\,\gamma \ldots$ appears to be made up of much more evanescent elements than $A\,B\,C \ldots$ and $K\,L\,M \ldots$, in which last the elements seem to be connected with greater stability and in a more permanent manner (being joined to solid nuclei as it were). Although on closer inspection the elements of all complexes prove to be homogeneous, yet even when this has been recognized, the earlier notion of an antithesis of body and spirit easily slips in again. The philosophical spiritualist is often sensible of the difficulty of imparting the needed solidity to his mind-created world of bodies; the materialist is at a loss when required to endow the world of matter with sensation. The monistic point of view, which reflection has evolved, is easily clouded by our older and more powerful instinctive notions.

The difficulty referred to is particularly felt when we consider the following case. In the complex $A\,B\,C\ldots$, which we have called the world of matter, we find as parts, not only our own body $K\,L\,M\ldots$, but also the bodies of other persons (or animals) $K'\,L'\,M'\ldots$, $K''\,L''\,M''\ldots$, to which, by analogy, we imagine other $\alpha'\,\beta'\,\gamma'\ldots$, $\alpha''\,\beta''\,\gamma''\ldots$, annexed, similar to $\alpha\,\beta\,\gamma\ldots$. So long as we deal with $K'\,L'\,M'\ldots$, we find ourselves in a thoroughly familiar province which is at every point accessible to our senses. When, however, we inquire after the sensations or feelings belonging to the body $K'\,L'\,M'\ldots$, we no longer find these in the province of sense: we add them in thought. Not only is the domain which we now enter far less familiar to us, but the transition into it is also relatively unsafe. We have the feeling as if we were plunging into an abyss. Persons who adopt this way of thinking only, will never thoroughly rid themselves of that sense of insecurity, which is a very fertile source of illusory problems.

But we are not restricted to this course. Let us consider, first, the reciprocal relations of the elements of the complex $A\,B\,C\ldots$, without regarding $K\,L\,M\ldots$ (our body). All physical investigations are of this sort. A white ball falls upon a bell; a sound is heard. The ball turns yellow before a sodium lamp, red before a lithium lamp. Here the elements $(A\,B\,C\ldots)$ appear to be connected only with one another and to be independent of our body $(K\,L\,M\ldots)$. But if we take santonine, the ball again turns yellow. If we press one eye to the side, we see two balls. If we close our eyes entirely, there is no ball there at all. If we sever the auditory nerve, no sound is heard. The elements $A\,B\,C\ldots$, therefore, are not only connected with one another, but also with $K\,L\,M\ldots$. To this extent, and to this extent only, do we call $A\,B\,C\ldots$ *sensations,* and regard $A\,B\,C\ldots$ as belonging to the ego. In what follows, wherever the reader finds the terms "sensation," "sensation-complex," used alongside of or instead of the expressions "element," "complex of elements," it must be borne in mind that it is *only* in the connection and relation in question, *only* in their functional dependence, that the elements are sensations. In another functional relation they are at the same time physical objects. We only use the additional term "sensations" to describe the elements, because most people are much more familiar with the elements in question *as* sensations (colors, sounds, pressures, spaces, times, etc.), while according to the popular conception it is particles of mass that are considered as physical elements, to which the elements, in the sense here used, are attached as "properties" or "effects."

In this way, accordingly, we do not find the gap between bodies and sensations above described, between what is without and what is within, between the material world and the spiritual world. All elements $A\,B\,C\ldots$, $K\,L\,M\ldots$, constitute a *single* coherent mass only, in which, when any one element is disturbed, *all* is put in motion; except that a disturbance in $K\,L\,M\ldots$ has a more extensive and profound action than one in $A\,B\,C\ldots$. A magnet in our neighborhood disturbs the particles of iron near it; a falling boulder shakes the earth; but the severing of a nerve sets in motion the *whole* system of elements. Quite involuntarily does this relation of things suggest the picture of a viscous mass, at certain places (as in the ego) more firmly coherent than in others. I have often made use of this image in lectures.

Thus the great gulf between physical and psychological research persists only when we acquiesce in our habitual stereotyped conceptions. A color is a physical object as soon as we consider its dependence, for instance, upon its luminous source, upon other colors, upon temperatures, upon spaces, and so forth. When we consider, however, its dependence upon the retina (the elements $K L M \ldots$), it is a psychological object, a sensation. Not the subject-matter, but the direction of our investigation, is different in the two domains.

Both in reasoning from the observation of the bodies of other men or animals, to the sensations which they possess, as well as in investigating the influence of our own body upon our own sensations, we have to complete observed facts by analogy. This is accomplished with much greater ease and certainty, when it relates, say, only to nervous processes, which cannot be fully observed in our own bodies—that is, when it is carried out in the more familiar physical domain—than when it is extended to the psychical domain, to the sensations and thoughts of other people. Otherwise there is no essential difference.

The considerations just advanced, expressed as they have been in an abstract form, will gain in strength and vividness if we consider the concrete facts from which they flow. Thus, I lie upon my sofa. If I close my right eye, the picture represented in the accompanying cut is presented to my left eye. In a frame formed by the ridge of my eyebrow, by my nose, and by my moustache, appears a part of my body, so far as visible, with its environment. My body differs from other human bodies—beyond the fact that every intense motor idea is immediately expressed by a movement of it, and that, if it is touched, more striking changes are determined than if other bodies are touched—by the circumstance that it is only seen piecemeal, and, especially, is seen without a head. If I observe an element A within my field of vision, and investigate its connection with another element B within the same field, I step out of the domain of physics into that of physiology or psychology, provided B, to use the apposite expression of a friend of mine made upon seeing this drawing, passes through my skin. Reflections like that for the field of vision may be made with regard to the province of touch and the perceptual domains of the other senses.

Reference has already been made to the different character of the groups of elements denoted by $A B C \ldots$ and $\alpha \beta \gamma \ldots$. As a matter of fact, when we see a green tree before us, or remember a green tree, that is, represent a green tree to ourselves, we are perfectly aware of the difference of the two cases. The represented tree has a much less determinate, a much more changeable form; its green is much paler and more evanescent; and, what is of especial note, it plainly appears in a different domain. A movement that we will execute is never more than a represented movement, and appears in a different domain from that of the executed movement, which always takes place when the image is vivid enough. Now the statement that the elements A and α appear in different domains, means, if we go to the bottom of it, simply this, that these elements are united with different other elements. Thus far, therefore, the fundamental constituents of $A B C \ldots, \alpha \beta \gamma \ldots$ would seem to be *the same* (colors, sounds, spaces, times, motor sensations . . .), and only the character of their connection different.

Ordinarily pleasure and pain are regarded as different from sensations. Yet not only tactual sensations, but all other kinds of sensations, may pass gradually into pleasure and pain. Pleasure and pain also may be justly termed sensations. Only they are not so well analyzed or so familiar, nor, perhaps, limited to so few organs as the common sensations. In fact, sensations of pleasure and pain, however faint they may be, really constitute an essential part of the content of all so-called emotions. Any additional element that emerges into consciousness when we are under the influence of emotions may be described as more or less diffused and not sharply localized sensations. William James, and after him Théodule Ribot, have investigated the physiological mechanism of the emotions: they hold that what is essential is purposive tendencies of the body to action—tendencies which correspond to circumstances and are expressed in the organism. Only a part of these emerges into consciousness. We are sad because we shed tears, and not vice versa, says James. And Ribot justly observes that a cause of the backward state of our knowledge of the emotions is that we have always confined our observation to so much of these physiological processes as emerges into consciousness. At the same time, he goes too far when he maintains that everything psychical is merely "*surajouté*" to the physical, and that it is only the physical that produces effects. For us this distinction is non-existent.

Thus, perceptions, presentations, volitions, and emotions, in short the whole inner and outer world, are put together, in combinations of varying evanescence and permanence, out of a small number of homogeneous elements. Usually, these elements are called sensations. But as vestiges of a one-sided theory inhere in that term, we prefer to speak simply of elements, as we have already done. The aim of all research is to ascertain the mode of connection of these elements. If it proves impossible to solve the problem by assuming *one* set of such elements, then more than one will have to be assumed. But for the questions under discussion it would be improper to begin by making complicated assumptions in advance.

That in this complex of elements, which fundamentally is only one, the boundaries of bodies and of the ego do not admit of being established in a manner definite and sufficient for all cases, has already been remarked. To bring together elements that are most intimately connected with pleasure and pain into one ideal mental-economical unity, the ego; this is a task of the highest importance for the intellect working in the service of the pain-avoiding, pleasure-seeking will. The delimitation of the ego, therefore, is instinctively effected, is rendered familiar, and possibly becomes fixed through heredity. Owing to their high practical importance, not only for the individual, but for the entire species, the composites "ego" and "body" instinctively make good their claims, and assert themselves with elementary force. In special cases, however, in which practical ends are not concerned, but where knowledge is an end in itself, the delimitation in question may prove to be insufficient, obstructive, and untenable.

The primary fact is not the ego, but the elements (sensations). What was said just above as to the term "sensation" must be borne in mind. The elements constitute the I. "*I* have the sensation green," signifies that the element green occurs in a given complex of other elements (sensations, memories). When *I* cease to have the sensation green, when *I* die, then the elements no longer occur in the ordinary, familiar association. That is all. Only an ideal mental-economical unity, not a real unity, has ceased to exist. The ego is not a definite, unalterable, sharply bounded unity. None of these attributes are important, for all vary even within the sphere of individual life; in fact their alteration is even sought after by the individual. *Continuity* alone is important. This view accords admirably with the position which Weismann has reached by biological investigations. But continuity is only a means of preparing and conserving what is contained in the ego. This content, and not the ego, is the principal thing. This content, however, is not confined to the individual. With the exception of some insignificant and valueless personal memories, it remains preserved in others even after the death of the individual. The elements that make up the consciousness of a given individual are firmly connected with one another, but with those of another individual they are only feebly connected, and the connection is only casually apparent. Contents of consciousness, however, that are of universal significance, break through these limits of the individual, and, attached of course to individuals again, can enjoy a continued existence of an impersonal, superpersonal kind, independently of the personality by means of which they were developed. To contribute to this is the greatest happiness of the artist, the scientist, the inventor, the social reformer, etc.

The ego must be given up. It is partly the perception of this fact, partly the fear of it, that has given rise to the many extravagances of pessimism and optimism, and to numerous religious, ascetic, and philosophical absurdities. In the long run we shall not be able to close our eyes to this simple truth, which is the immediate outcome of psychological analysis. We shall then no longer place so high a value upon the ego, which even during the individual life greatly changes, and which, in sleep or during absorption in some idea, just in our very happiest moments, may be partially or wholly absent. We shall then be willing to renounce individual immortality, and not place more value upon the subsidiary elements than upon the principal ones. In this way, we shall arrive at a freer and more enlightened view of life, which will preclude the disregard of other egos and the overestimation of our own. The ethical ideal founded on this view of life will be equally far removed from the ideal of the ascetic, which is not biologically tenable for whoever practises it, and vanishes at once with his disappearance, and from the ideal of an overweening Nietzschean "superman," who cannot, and I hope will not be tolerated by his fellow-men.

If a knowledge of the connection of the elements (sensations) does not suffice us, and we ask, "*Who* possesses this connection of sensations, *Who* experiences it?" then we have succumbed to the old habit of subsuming every element (every sensation) under some unanalyzed complex, and we are falling back imperceptibly upon an older, lower, and more limited point of view. It is often pointed out, that a psychical experience which is not the experience of a determinate subject is unthinkable, and it is held that in this way the essential part played by the unity of consciousness has been demonstrated. But the Ego-consciousness can be of many different degrees and composed of a multiplicity of chance memories. One might just as well say that a physical process which does not take place in some environment or other, or at least somewhere in the universe, is unthinkable. In both cases, in order to make a beginning with our investigation, we must be allowed to abstract from the environment, which, as regards its influence, may be very different in different cases, and in special cases may shrink to a minimum. Consider the sensations of the lower animals, to which a subject with definite features can hardly be ascribed. It is out of sensations that the subject is built up, and, once built up, no doubt the subject reacts in turn on the sensations.

The habit of treating the unanalyzed ego-complex as an indiscerptible unity frequently assumes in science remarkable forms. First, the nervous system is separated from the body as the seat of the sensations. In the nervous system again, the brain is selected as the organ best fitted for this end, and finally, to save the supposed psychical unity, a *point* is sought in the brain as the seat of the soul. But such crude conceptions are hardly fit even to foreshadow the roughest outlines of what future research will do for the connection of the physical and the psychical. The fact that the different organs and parts of the nervous system are physically connected with, and can be readily excited by, one another, is probably at the bottom of the notion of "psychical unity."

I once heard the question seriously discussed, how the perception of a large tree could find room in the little head of a man. Now, although this "problem" is no problem, yet it renders us vividly sensible of the absurdity that can be committed by thinking sensations spatially into the brain. When I speak of the sensations of another person, those sensations are, of course, not exhibited in any optical or physical space; they are mentally added, and I conceive them causally, not spatially, attached to the brain observed, or rather, functionally presented. When I speak of my own sensations, these sensations do not exist spatially in my head, but rather my "head" shares with them the same spatial field, as was explained above.

The unity of consciousness is not an argument in point. Since the apparent antithesis between the real world and the world given through the senses lies entirely in our mode of view, and no actual gulf exists between them, a complicated and variously interconnected content of consciousness is no more difficult to understand than is the complicated interconnection of the world.

If we regard the ego as a real unity, we become involved in the following dilemma: either we must set over against the ego a world of unknowable entities (which would be quite idle and purposeless), or we must regard the whole world, the egos of other people included, as comprised in our own ego (a proposition to which it is difficult to yield serious assent).

But if we take the ego simply as a practical unity, put together for purposes of provisional survey, or as a more strongly cohering group of elements, less strongly connected with other groups of this kind, questions like those above discussed will not arise, and research will have an unobstructed future.

In his philosophical notes Lichtenberg says: "We become conscious of certain presentations that are not dependent upon us; of others that we at least think are dependent upon us. Where is the border-line? We know only the existence of our sensations, presentations, and thoughts. We should say, '*It thinks*,' just as we say, '*It lightens*.' It is going too far to say *Cogito*, if we translate *Cogito* by '*I think*.' The assumption, or postulation, of the ego is a mere practical necessity." Though the method by which Lichtenberg arrived at this result is somewhat different from ours, we must nevertheless give our full assent to his conclusion.

Bodies do not produce sensations, but complexes of elements (complexes of sensations) make up bodies. If, to the physicist, bodies appear the real, abiding existences, while the "elements" are regarded merely as their evanescent, transitory appearance, the physicist forgets, in the assumption of such a view, that all bodies are but thought-symbols for complexes of elements (complexes of sensations). Here, too, the elements in question form the real, immediate, and ultimate foundation, which it is the task of physiologico-physical research to investigate. By the recognition of this fact, many points of physiology and physics assume more distinct and more economical forms, and many spurious problems are disposed of.

For us, therefore, the world does not consist of mysterious entities, which by their interaction with another, equally mysterious entity, the ego, produce sensations, which alone are accessible. For us, colors, sounds, spaces, times, . . . are provisionally the ultimate elements, whose given connection it is our business to investigate. It is precisely in this that the exploration of reality consists. In this investigation we must not allow ourselves to be impeded by such abridgments and delimitations as body, ego, matter, spirit, etc., which have been formed for special, practical purposes and with wholly provisional and limited ends in view. On the contrary, the fittest forms of thought must be created in and by that research itself, just as is done in every special science. In place of the traditional, instinctive ways of thought, a freer, fresher view, conforming to developed experience, and reaching out beyond the requirements of practical life, must be substituted throughout.

Science always has its origin in the adaptation of thought to some definite field of experience. The results of the adaptation are thought-elements, which are able to represent the whole field. The outcome, of course, is different, according to the character and extent of the field. If the field of experience is enlarged, or if several fields heretofore disconnected are united, the traditional, familiar thought-elements no longer suffice for the extended field. In the struggle of acquired habit with the effort after adaptation, problems arise, which disappear when the adaptation is perfected, to make room for others which have arisen meanwhile.

To the physicist, *qua* physicist, the idea of "body" is productive of a real facilitation of view, and is not the cause of disturbance. So, also, the person with purely practical aims is materially supported by the idea of the *I* or ego. For, unquestionably, every form of thought that has been designedly or undesignedly constructed for a given purpose, possesses for that purpose a *permanent* value. When, however, physics and psychology meet, the ideas held in the one domain prove to be untenable in the other. From the attempt at mutual adaptation arise the various atomic and monadistic theories—which, however, never attain their end. If we regard sensations, in the sense above defined, as the elements of the world, the problems referred to appear to be disposed of in all essentials, and the first and most important adaptation to be consequently effected. This fundamental view (without any pretension to being a philosophy for all eternity) can at present be adhered to in all fields of experience; it is consequently the one that accommodates itself with the least expenditure of energy, that is, more economically than any other, to the present temporary collective state of knowledge. Furthermore, in the consciousness of its purely economical function, this fundamental view is eminently tolerant. It does not obtrude itself into fields in which the current conceptions are still adequate. It is also ever ready, upon subsequent extensions of the field of experience, to give way before a better conception.

The presentations and conceptions of the average man of the world are formed and dominated, not by the full and pure desire for knowledge as an end in itself, but by the struggle to adapt himself favorably to the conditions of life. Consequently they are less exact, but at the same time also they are preserved from the monstrosities which easily result from a one-sided and impassioned pursuit of a scientific or philosophical point of view. The unprejudiced man of normal psychological development takes the elements which we have called $A\,B\,C\ldots$ to be spatially contiguous and external to the elements $K\,L\,M\ldots$, and he holds this view *immediately,* and not by any process of psychological projection or logical inference or construction; even were such a process to exist, he would certainly not be conscious of it. He sees, then, an "external world" $A\,B\,C\ldots$ different from his body $K\,L\,M\ldots$ and existing outside it. As he does not observe at first the dependence of the $A\,B\,C$'s $\ldots$ on the $K\,L\,M$'s $\ldots$ (which are always repeating themselves in the same way and consequently receive little attention), but is always dwelling upon the fixed connection of the $A\,B\,C$'s $\ldots$ with one another, there appears to him a world of things independent of his Ego. This Ego is formed by the observation of the special properties of the particular thing $K\,L\,M\ldots$ with which pain, pleasure, feeling, will, etc., are intimately connected. Further, he notices things $K'\,L'\,M'\ldots$, $K''\,L''\,M''\ldots$, which behave in a manner perfectly analogous to $K\,L\,M\ldots$, and whose behavior he thoroughly understands as soon as he has thought of analogous feelings, sensations, etc., as attached to them in the same way as he observed these feelings, sensations, etc., to be attached to himself. The analogy impelling him to this result is the same as determines him, when he has observed that a wire possesses *all* the properties of a conductor charged with an electric current, except *one* which has not yet been directly demonstrated, to conclude that the wire possesses this one property as well. Thus, since he does not perceive the sensations of his fellow-men or of animals but only supplies them by analogy, while he infers from the behavior of his fellow-men that they are in the same position over against himself, he is led to ascribe to the sensations, memories, etc., a particular $A\,B\,C\ldots K\,L\,M\ldots$ of a different nature, always differently conceived according to the degree of civilization he has reached; but this process, as was shown above, is unnecessary, and in science leads into a maze of error, although the falsification is of small significance for practical life.

These factors, determining as they do the intellectual outlook of the plain man, make their appearance alternately in him according to the requirements of practical life for the time being, and persist in a state of nearly stable equilibrium. The scientific conception of the world, however, puts the emphasis now upon one, now upon the other factor, makes sometimes one and sometimes the other its starting-point, and, in its struggle for greater precision, unity, and consistency, tries, so far as seems possible, to thrust into the background all but the most indispensable conceptions. In this way dualistic and monistic systems arise.

The plain man is familiar with blindness and deafness, and knows from his everyday experience that the look of things is influenced by his senses; but it never occurs to him to regard the whole world as the creation of his senses. He would find an idealistic system, or such a monstrosity as solipsism, intolerable in practice.

It may easily become a disturbing element in unprejudiced scientific theorizing when a conception which is adapted to a particular and strictly limited purpose is promoted in advance to be the foundation of *all* investigation. This happens, for example, when all experiences are regarded as "effects" of an external world extending into consciousness. This conception gives us a tangle of metaphysical difficulties which it seems impossible to unravel. But the specter vanishes at once when we look at the matter as it were in a mathematical light, and make it clear to ourselves that all that is valuable to us is the discovery of *functional relations,* and that what we want to know is merely the dependence of experiences on one another. It then becomes obvious that the reference to unknown fundamental variables which are not given (things-in-themselves) is purely fictitious and superfluous. But even when we allow this fiction, uneconomical though it be, to stand at first, we can still easily distinguish different classes of the mutual dependence of the elements of "the facts of consciousness"; and this alone is important for us.

$$
\begin{array}{ll}
\left.\begin{array}{l}
A\,B\,C\ldots K\,L\,M\ldots \\
K'\,L'\,M'\ldots \\
K''\,L''\,M''\ldots
\end{array}\right| &
\left.\begin{array}{l}
\alpha\,\beta\,\gamma\ldots \\
\alpha'\,\beta'\,\gamma'\ldots \\
\alpha''\,\beta''\,\gamma''\ldots
\end{array}\right\|
\end{array}
$$

The system of the elements is indicated in the above scheme. Within the space surrounded by a single line lie the elements which belong to the sensible world—the elements whose regular connection and peculiar dependence on one another represent both physical (lifeless) bodies and the bodies of men, animals, and plants. All these elements, again, stand in a relation of quite peculiar dependence to certain of the elements $K\,L\,M\ldots$—the nerves of our body, namely—by which the facts of sense-physiology are expressed. The space surrounded by a double line contains the elements belonging to the higher psychic life, memory-images and presentations, including those which we form of the psychic life of our fellow-men. These may be distinguished by accents. These presentations, again, are connected with one another in a different way (association, fancy) from the sensational elements $A\,B\,C\ldots K\,L\,M\ldots$, but it cannot be doubted that they are very closely allied to the latter, and that in the last resort their behavior is determined by $A\,B\,C\ldots K\,L\,M\ldots$ (the totality of the physical world), and especially by our body and nervous system. The presentations $\alpha'\,\beta'\,\gamma'\ldots$ of the contents of the consciousness of our fellow-men play for us the part of *intermediate substitutions,* by means of which the behavior of our fellow-men—the functional relation of $K'\,L'\,M'\ldots$ to $A\,B\,C\ldots$—becomes intelligible, in so far as in and for itself (physically) it would remain unexplained.

It is therefore important for us to recognize that in all questions in this connection that can be asked intelligibly and that can interest us, everything turns on taking into consideration different *ultimate variables* and different *relations of dependence.* That is the main point.

Nothing will be changed in the actual facts or in the functional relations, whether we regard all the data as contents of consciousness, or as partially so, or as completely physical.

The biological task of science is to provide the fully developed human individual with as perfect a means of orientating himself as possible. No other scientific ideal can be realized, and any other must be meaningless.

The philosophical point of view of the average man—if that term may be applied to his naïve realism—has a claim to the highest consideration. It has arisen in the process of immeasurable time without the intentional assistance of man. It is a product of nature, and is preserved by nature. Everything that philosophy has accomplished—though we may admit the biological justification of every advance, nay, of every error—is, as compared with it, but an insignificant and ephemeral product of art. The fact is, every thinker, every philosopher, the moment he is forced to abandon his one-sided intellectual occupation by practical necessity, immediately returns to the general point of view of mankind. Professor X., who theoretically believes himself to be a solipsist, is certainly not one in practice when he has to thank a Minister of State for a decoration conferred upon him, or when he lectures to an audience. The Pyrrhonist who is cudgeled in Molière's *Le Mariage Forcé* does not go on saying "It seems to me that you are hitting me," but takes his beating as really received.

41

PEIRCE

1839–1914

Charles Sanders Peirce was born in Cambridge, Massachusetts. He was educated mainly by his father, a Harvard mathematician, though he graduated from Harvard University at the bottom of his class. As a result, the only job he could find was with the U.S. Coast and Geodetic Survey. He never secured a permanent teaching position, but taught logic as an adjunct at the Johns Hopkins University from 1879 to 1884. Subsequently, he went back to work for the U.S. Coast and Geodetic Survey. He was, however, a member of the "metaphysical club" in Cambridge, which included William James and Oliver Wendell Holmes. His own view of metaphysics owes much to Kant and Hegel, and was highly influenced by the then-recent evolutionary theory of Charles Darwin (1809–1882).

Peirce initiated the movement in American philosophy known as *pragmatism,* which he developed from Kant. As a new theory of truth, pragmatism relies on one's own personal experience tempered with the practical significance of propositions. The pragmatist as espoused by Peirce involves the "clarification of thought" according to what Peirce called "the pragmatic principle": "Consider what effects, that conceivably might have practical bearings, we conceive the object of our conception to have. Then our conception of these effects is the whole of our conception of the object." Beliefs according to Peirce are psychological habits predisposing us to respond in specific ways to specific situations. Any situation in our experience causes either physical movement of the body or psychological expectation in the mind. In our first selection, "The Fixation of Belief," his most famous article, Peirce claims there are four basic ways for our habits, customs, traditions, and folkways to become "fixed" in our minds. These apply to everything from personal convictions to metaphysical philosophical systems, and are used for both settling opinions and resolving doubt: tenacity, authority, the a priori method, and the method of science.

The method of *tenacity* exists through the impoverished domain of common sense. The method of *authority* arises through military, governmental, and church organizations conditioning individuals against disobedience. The *a priori* method, which has been practiced by great philosophers from Plato to Descartes, is only slightly better than the first two. But ultimately it amounts to an elaborate form of rationalization. These three methods have their social and institutional functions. But the only reliable method is the "self-corrective" way of Peirce's version of the *scientific method.*

The key to the fourth method is, first, to not know in advance where you are going or what you are looking for. It requires for its initial stimulus the experience, not of a feeling of certainty, but of *doubt*. The end result is the settlement of opinion by a *method,* which is science. In other words, all inquiry must proceed experientially, as a felt problem. It is not formal or mechanical. If you don't feel the problem, or are not puzzled, or are not in a psychological state of doubt, then you are not engaged in real inquiry.

The second selection, "How to Make Our Ideas Clear," is a follow-up to his "Fixation of Belief." He begins with a criticism of Descartes's notion of clear and distinct ideas, which he claims is *itself* not clear and distinct. Peirce's complaint about Descartes's notion is that it relies solely on the a priori method, which he rejects on grounds that it appeals, ultimately, to nonverifiable self-evidence. This is but the first level of clarity, not itself sufficient. Similarly, he rejects Leibniz's method of abstract definition on the grounds that "nothing new can ever be learned by analyzing definitions." This is but the second level of clarity, also not sufficient. Peirce thus calls for a third grade of clearness, itself predicated upon and identical with his pragmatic maxim, which renders as meaningless any terms or concepts that go beyond the possible effects on observable objects: beliefs must be judged solely by the habits they produce, the practical rules of action they govern. His system thus comes full circle and completes itself.

THE FIXATION OF BELIEF

Few persons care to study logic, because everybody conceives himself to be proficient enough in the art of reasoning already. But I observe that this satisfaction is limited to one's own ratiocination, and does not extend to that of other men.

We come to the full possession of our power of drawing inferences, the last of all our faculties, for it is not so much a natural gift as a long and difficult art. The history of its practice would make a grand subject for a book.

We are, doubtless, in the main logical animals, but we are not perfectly so. Most of us, for example, are naturally more sanguine and hopeful than logic would justify. We seem to be so constituted that, in the absence of any facts to go upon, we are happy and self-satisfied; so that the effect of experience is continually to counteract our hopes and aspirations. Yet a lifetime of the application of this corrective does not usually eradicate our sanguine disposition. Where hope is unchecked by any experience, it is likely that our optimism is extravagant. Logicality in regard to practical matters is the most useful quality an animal can possess, and might, therefore, result from the action of natural selection; but outside of these, it is probably of more advantage to the animal to have his mind filled with pleasing and encouraging visions, independently of their truth; and thus, upon unpractical subjects, natural selection might occasion a fallacious tendency of thought.

From Charles Sanders Peirce, "The Fixation of Belief," *Popular Science Monthly,* 1877.

That which determines us, from given premises, to draw one inference rather than another, is some habit of mind, whether it be constitutional or acquired. The habit is good or otherwise, according as it produces true conclusions from true premises or not; and an inference is regarded as valid or not, without reference to the truth or falsity of its conclusion specially, but according as the habit which determines it is such as to produce true conclusions in general or not. The particular habit of mind which governs this or that inference may be formulated in a proposition whose truth depends on the validity of the inferences which the habit determines; and such a formula is called a *guiding principle* of inference. . . .

We generally know when we wish to ask a question and when we wish to pronounce a judgment, for there is a dissimilarity between the sensation of doubting and that of believing.

But this is not all which distinguishes doubt from belief. There is a practical difference. Our beliefs guide our desires and shape our actions. The Assassins, or followers of the Old Man of the Mountain, used to rush into death at his least command, because they believed that obedience to him would insure everlasting felicity. Had they doubted this, they would not have acted as they did. So it is with every belief, according to its degree. The feeling of believing is a more or less sure indication of there being established in our nature some habit which will determine our actions. Doubt never has such an effect.

Nor must we overlook a third point of difference. Doubt is an uneasy and dissatisfied state from which we struggle to free ourselves and pass into the state of belief; while the latter is a calm and satisfactory state which we do not wish to avoid, or to change to a belief in anything else. On the contrary, we cling tenaciously, not merely to believing, but to believing just what we do believe.

Thus, both doubt and belief have positive effects upon us, though very different ones. Belief does not make us act at once, but puts us into such a condition that we shall behave in a certain way, when the occasion arises. Doubt has not the least effect of this sort, but stimulates us to action until it is destroyed. This reminds us of the irritation of a nerve and the reflex action produced thereby; while for the analogue of belief, in the nervous system, we must look to what are called nervous associations—for example, to that habit of the nerves in consequence of which the smell of a peach will make the mouth water.

The irritation of doubt causes a struggle to attain a state of belief. I shall term this struggle *inquiry,* though it must be admitted that this is sometimes not a very apt designation.

The irritation of doubt is the only immediate motive for the struggle to attain belief. It is certainly best for us that our beliefs should be such as may truly guide our actions so as to satisfy our desires; and this reflection will make us reject any belief which does not seem to have been so formed as to insure this result. But it will only do so by creating doubt in the place of that belief. With the doubt, therefore, the struggle begins, and with the cessation of doubt it ends. Hence, the sole object of inquiry is the settlement of opinion. We may fancy that this is not enough for us, and that we seek, not merely an opinion, but a true opinion. But put this fancy to the test, and it proves groundless; for as soon as a firm belief is reached we are entirely satisfied, whether the belief be false or true. And it is clear that nothing out of the sphere of our knowledge can be our object, for nothing which does not affect the mind can be a motive for mental effort. The most that can be maintained is that we seek for a belief that we shall *think* to be true. But we think each one of our beliefs to be true, and, indeed, it is mere tautology to say so.

That the settlement of opinion is the sole end of inquiry is a very important proposition. It sweeps away, at once, various vague and erroneous conceptions of proof. A few of these may be noticed here.

1. Some philosophers have imagined that to start an inquiry it was only necessary to utter a question or set it down on paper, and have even recommended us to begin our studies with questioning everything! But the mere putting of a proposition into the interrogative form does not stimulate the mind to any struggle after belief. There must be a real and living doubt, and without this all discussion is idle.

2. It is a very common idea that a demonstration must rest on some ultimate and absolutely undubitable propositions. These, according to one school, are first principles of a general nature; according to another, are first sensations. But, in point of fact, an inquiry, to have that completely satisfactory result called demonstration, has only to start with propositions perfectly free from all actual doubt. If the premises are not in fact doubted at all, they cannot be more satisfactory than they are.

3. Some people seem to love to argue a point after all the world is fully convinced of it. But no further advance can be made. When doubt ceases, mental action on the subject comes to an end; and, if it did go on, it would be without a purpose.

If the settlement of opinion is the sole object of inquiry, and if belief is of the nature of a habit, why should we not maintain the desired end by taking any answer to a question, which we may fancy, and constantly reiterating it to ourselves, dwelling on all which may conduce to that belief, and learning to turn with contempt and hatred from anything which might disturb it? This simple and direct method is really pursued by many men. I remember once being entreated not to read a certain newspaper lest it might change my opinion upon free trade. "Lest I might be entrapped by its fallacies and misstatements," was the form of expression. "You are not," my friend said, "a special student of political economy. You might, therefore, easily be deceived by fallacious arguments upon the subject. You might, then, if you read this paper, be led to believe in protection. But you admit that free trade is the true doctrine; and you do not wish to believe what is not true." I have often known this system to be deliberately adopted. Still oftener, the instinctive dislike of an undecided state of mind, exaggerated into a vague dread of doubt, makes men cling spasmodically to the views they already take. The man feels that, if he only holds to his belief without wavering, it will be entirely satisfactory. Nor can it be denied that a steady and immovable faith yields great peace of mind. It may, indeed, give rise to inconveniences, as if a man should resolutely continue to believe that fire would not burn him, or that he would be eternally damned if he received his *ingesta* otherwise than through a stomach-pump. But then the man who adopts this method will not allow that its inconveniences are greater than its advantages. He will say, "I hold steadfastly to the truth and the truth is always wholesome." And in many cases it may very well be that the pleasure he derives from his calm faith overbalances any inconveniences resulting from its deceptive character. Thus, if it be true that death is annihilation, then the man who believes that he will certainly go straight to heaven when he dies, provided he has fulfilled certain simple observances in this life, has a cheap pleasure which will not be followed by the least disappointment. A similar consideration seems to have weight with many persons in religious topics, for we frequently hear it said, "Oh, I could not believe so-and-so, because I should be wretched if I did." When an ostrich buries its head in the sand as danger approaches, it very likely takes the happiest course. It hides the danger, and then calmly says there is no danger; and, if it feels perfectly sure there is none, why should it raise its head to see? A man may go through life systematically keeping out of view all that might cause a change in his opinions, and if he only succeeds—basing his method, as he does, on two fundamental psychological laws—I do not see what can be said against his doing so. It would be an egotistical impertinence to object that his procedure is irrational, for that only amounts to saying that his method of settling belief is not ours. He does not propose to himself to be rational, and, indeed, will often talk with scorn of man's weak and illusive reason. So let him think as he pleases.

But this method of fixing belief, which may be called the method of tenacity, will be unable to hold its ground in practice. The social impulse is against it. The man who adopts it will find that other men think differently from him, and it will be apt to occur to him in some saner moment that their opinions are quite as good as his own, and this will shake his confidence in his belief. This conception, that another man's thought or sentiment may be equivalent to one's own, is a distinctly new step, and a highly important one. It arises from an impulse too strong in man to be suppressed without danger of destroying the human species. Unless we make ourselves hermits, we shall necessarily influence each other's opinions, so that the problem becomes how to fix belief, not in the individual merely, but in the community.

Let the will of the state act, then, instead of that of the individual. Let an institution be created which shall have for its object to keep correct doctrines before the attention of the people, to reiterate them perpetually, and to teach them to the young; having at the same time power to prevent contrary doctrines from being taught, advocated, or expressed. Let all possible causes of a change of mind be removed from men's apprehensions. Let them be kept ignorant, lest they should learn of some reason to think otherwise than they do. Let their passions be enlisted, so that they may regard private and unusual opinions with hatred and horror. Then, let all men who reject the established belief be terrified into silence. Let the people turn out and tar-and-feather such men, or let inquisitions be made into the manner of thinking of suspected persons, and, when they are found guilty of forbidden beliefs, let them be subjected to some signal punishment. When complete agreement could not otherwise be reached, a general massacre of all who have not thought in a certain way has proved a very effective means of settling opinion in a country. If the power to do this be wanting, let a list of opinions be drawn up, to which no man of the least independence of thought can assent, and let the faithful be required to accept all these propositions, in order to segregate them as radically as possible from the influence of the rest of the world.

This method has, from the earliest times, been one of the chief means of upholding correct theological and political doctrines, and of preserving their universal or catholic character. In Rome, especially, it has been practiced from the days of Numa Pompilius to those of Pius Nonus. This is the most perfect example in history; but wherever there is a priesthood—and no religion has been without one—this method has been more or less made use of. Wherever there is an aristocracy, or a guild, or any association of a class of men whose interests depend, or are supposed to depend, on certain propositions, there will be inevitably found some traces of this natural product of social feeling. Cruelties always accompany this system; and when it is consistently carried out, they become atrocities of the most horrible kind in the eyes of any rational man. Nor should this occasion surprise, for the officer of a society does not feel justified in surrendering the interests of that society for the sake of mercy, as he might his own private interests. It is natural, therefore, that sympathy and fellowship should thus produce a most ruthless power.

In judging this method of fixing belief, which may be called the method of authority, we must, in the first place, allow its immeasurable mental and moral superiority to the method of tenacity. Its success is proportionately greater; and, in fact, it has over and over again worked the most majestic results. The mere structures of stone which it has caused to be put together—in Siam, for example, in Egypt, and in Europe—have many of them a sublimity hardly more than rivalled by the greatest works of Nature. And, except the geological epochs, there are no periods of time so vast as those which are measured by some of these organized faiths. If we scrutinize the matter closely, we shall find that there has not been one of their creeds which has remained always the same; yet the change is so slow as to be imperceptible during one person's life, so that individual belief remains sensibly fixed. For the mass of mankind, then, there is perhaps no better method than this. If it is their highest impulse to be intellectual slaves, then slaves they ought to remain.

But no institution can undertake to regulate opinions upon every subject. Only the most important ones can be attended to, and on the rest men's minds must be left to the action of natural causes. This imperfection will be no source of weakness so long as men are in such a state of culture that one opinion does not influence another—that is, so long as they cannot put two and two together. But in the most priest-ridden states some individuals will be found who are raised above that condition. These men possess a wider sort of social feeling; they see that men in other countries and in other ages have held to very different doctrines from those which they themselves have been brought up to believe; and they cannot help seeing that it is the mere accident of their having been taught as they have, and of their having been surrounded with the manners and associations they have, that has caused them to believe as they do and not far differently. Nor can their candor resist the reflection that there is no reason to rate their own views at a higher value than those of other nations and other centuries; thus giving rise to doubts in their minds.

They will further perceive that such doubts as these must exist in their minds with reference to every belief which seems to be determined by the caprice either of themselves or of those who originated the popular opinions. The willful adherence to a belief, and the arbitrary forcing of it upon others, must, therefore, both be given up. A different new method of settling opinions must be adopted, that shall not only produce an impulse to believe, but shall also decide what proposition it is which is to be believed. Let the action of natural preferences be unimpeded, then, and under their influence let men, conversing together and regarding matters in different lights, gradually develop beliefs in harmony with natural causes. This method resembles that by which conceptions of art have been brought to maturity. The most perfect example of it is to be found in the history of metaphysical philosophy. Systems of this sort have not usually rested upon any observed facts, at least not in any great degree. They have been chiefly adopted because their fundamental propositions seemed "agreeable to reason." This is an apt expression; it does not mean that which agrees with experience, but that which we find ourselves inclined to believe. Plato, for example, finds it agreeable to reason that the distances of the celestial spheres from one another should be proportional to the different lengths of strings which produce harmonious chords. Many philosophers have been led to their main conclusions by considerations like this; but this is the lowest and least developed from which the method takes, for it is clear that another man might find Kepler's theory, that the celestial spheres are proportional to the inscribed and circumscribed spheres of the different regular solids, more agreeable to *his* reason. But the shock of opinions will soon lead men to rest on preferences of a far more universal nature. Take, for example, the doctrine that man only acts selfishly—that is, from the consideration that acting in one way will afford him more pleasure than acting in another. This rests on no fact in the world, but it has had a wide acceptance as being the only reasonable theory.

This method is far more intellectual and respectable from the point of view of reason than either of the others which we have noticed. But its failure has been the most manifest. It makes of inquiry something similar to the development of taste; but taste, unfortunately, is always more or less a matter of fashion, and accordingly metaphysicians have never come to any fixed agreement, but the pendulum has swung backward and forward between a more material and a more spiritual philosophy, from the earliest times to the latest. And so from this, which has been called the *a priori* method, we are driven, in Lord Bacon's phrase, to a true induction. We have examined this *a priori* method as something which promised to deliver our opinions from their accidental and capricious element. But development, while it is a process which eliminates the effect of some casual circumstances, only magnifies that of others. This method, therefore, does not differ in a very essential way from that of authority. The government may not have lifted its finger to influence my convictions; I may have been left outwardly quite free to choose, we will say, between monogamy and polygamy, and appealing to my conscience only, I may have concluded that the latter practice is in itself licentious. But when I come to see that the chief obstacle to the spread of Christianity among a people of as high culture as the Hindus has been a conviction of the immorality of our way of treating women, I cannot help seeing that, though governments do not interfere, sentiments in their development will be very greatly determined by accidental causes. Now, there are some people, among whom I must suppose that my reader is to be found, who, when they see that any belief of theirs is determined by any circumstance extraneous to the facts, will from that moment not merely admit in words that that belief is doubtful, but will experience a real doubt of it, so that it ceases in some degree to be a belief.

To satisfy our doubts, therefore, it is necessary that a method should be found by which our beliefs may be caused by nothing human, but by some external permanency—by something upon which our thinking has no effect. Some mystics imagine that they have such a method in a private inspiration from on high. But that is only a form of the method of tenacity, in which the conception of truth as something public is not yet developed. Our external permanency would not be external, in our sense, if it was restricted in its influence to one individual. It must be something which affects, or might affect, every man. And, though these affections are necessarily as various as are individual conditions, yet the method must be such that the ultimate conclusion of every man shall be the same. Such is the method of science. Its fundamental hypothesis, restated in more familiar language, is this: There are Real things, whose characters are entirely independent of our opinions about them; those realities affect our senses according to regular laws, and, though our sensations are as different as are our relations to the objects, yet, by taking advantage of the laws of perception, we can ascertain by reasoning how things really are; and any man, if we have sufficient experience and he reason enough about it, will be led to the one True conclusion. The new conception here involved is that of Reality. It may be asked how I know that there are any realities. If this hypothesis is the sole support of my method of inquiry, my method of inquiry must not be used to support my hypothesis. The reply is this: (1) If investigation cannot be regarded as proving that there are Real things, it at least does not lead to a contrary conclusion; but the method and the conception on which it is based remain ever in harmony. No doubts of the method, therefore, necessarily arise from its practice, as is the case with all the others. (2) The feeling which gives rise to any method of fixing belief is a dissatisfaction at two repugnant propositions. But here already is a vague concession that there is some *one* thing to which a proposition should conform. Nobody, therefore, can really doubt that there are realities, for, if he did, doubt would not be a source of dissatisfaction. The hypothesis, therefore, is one which every mind admits. So that the social impulse does not cause men to doubt it. (3) Everybody uses the scientific method about a great many things, and only ceases to use it when he does not know how to apply it. (4) Experience of the method has not led us to doubt it, but, on the contrary, scientific investigation has had the most wonderful triumphs in the way of settling opinion. These afford the explanation of my not doubting the method or the hypothesis which it supposes; and not having any doubt, nor believing that anybody else whom I could influence has, it would be the merest babble for me to say more about it. If there be anybody with a living doubt upon the subject, let him consider it. . . .

This is the only one of the four methods which presents any distinction of a right and a wrong way. If I adopt the method of tenacity, and shut myself out from all influences, whatever I think necessary to doing this, is necessary according to that method. So with the method of authority: the state may try to put down heresy by means which, from a scientific point of view, seem very ill-calculated to accomplish its purposes; but the only test *on that method* is what the state thinks; so that it cannot pursue the method wrongly. So with the *a priori* method. The very essence of it is to think as one is inclined to think. All metaphysicians will be sure to do that, however they may be inclined to judge each other to be perversely wrong. Hegel's system of Nature represents tolerably the science of that day; and one may be sure that whatever scientific investigation has put out of doubt will presently receive *a priori* demonstration on the part of the metaphysicians. But with the scientific method the case is different. I may start with known and observed facts to proceed to the unknown; and yet the rules which I follow in doing so may not be such as investigation would approve. The test of whether I am truly following the method is not an immediate appeal to my feelings and purposes, but, on the contrary, itself involves the application of the method. Hence it is that bad reasoning as well as good reasoning is possible; and this fact is the foundation of the practical side of logic.

It is not to be supposed that the first three methods of settling opinion present no advantage whatever over the scientific method. On the contrary, each has some peculiar convenience of its own. The *a priori* method is distinguished for its comfortable conclusions. It is the nature of the process to adopt whatever belief we are inclined to, and there are certain flatteries to the vanity of man which we all believe by nature, until we are awakened from our pleasing dream by rough facts. The method of authority will always govern the mass of mankind; and those who wield the various forms of organized force in the state will never be convinced that dangerous reasoning ought not to be suppressed in some way. If liberty of speech is to be untrammelled from the grosser forms of constraint, then uniformity of opinion will be secured by a moral terrorism to which the respectability of society will give its thorough approval. Following the method of authority is the path of peace. Certain non-conformities are permitted; certain others (considered unsafe) are forbidden. These are different in different countries and in different ages; but, wherever you are, let it be known that you seriously hold a tabooed belief, and you may be perfectly sure of being treated with a cruelty less brutal but more refined than hunting you like a wolf. Thus, the greatest intellectual benefactors of mankind have never dared, and dare not now, to utter the whole of their thought; and thus a shade of *prima facie* doubt is cast upon every proposition which is considered essential to the security of society. Singularly enough, the persecution does not all come from without; but a man torments himself and is oftentimes more distressed at finding himself believing propositions which he has been brought up to regard with aversion. The peaceful and sympathetic man will, therefore, find it hard to resist the temptation to submit his opinions to authority. But most of all I admire the method of tenacity for its strength, simplicity, and directness. Men who pursue it are distinguished for their decision of character, which becomes very easy with such a mental rule. They do not waste time in trying to make up their minds what they want, but, fastening like lightning upon whatever alternative comes first, they hold it to the end, whatever happens, without an instant's irresolution. This is one of the splendid qualities which generally accompany brilliant, unlasting success. It is impossible not to envy the man who can dismiss reason, although we know how it must turn out at last.

Such are the advantages which the other methods of settling opinion have over scientific investigation. A man should consider well of them; and then he should consider that, after all, he wishes his opinions to coincide with the fact and that there is no reason why the result of those three methods should do so. To bring about this effect is the prerogative of the method of science. Upon such considerations he has to make his choice—a choice which is far more than the adoption of any intellectual opinion, which is one of the ruling decisions of his life, to which, when once made, he is bound to adhere. The force of habit will sometimes cause a man to hold on to old beliefs, after he is in a condition to see that they have no sound basis. But reflection upon the state of the case will overcome these habits, and he ought to allow reflection its full weight. People sometimes shrink from doing this, having an idea that beliefs are wholesome which they cannot help feeling rest on nothing. But let such persons suppose an analogous though different case from their own. Let them ask themselves what they would say to a reformed Mussulman who should hesitate to give up his old notions in regard to the relations of the sexes; or to a reformed Catholic who should still shrink from reading the Bible. Would they not say that these persons ought to consider the matter fully, and clearly understand the new doctrine, and then ought to embrace it, in its entirety? But, above all, let it be considered that what is more wholesome than any particular belief is integrity of belief, and that to avoid looking into the support of any belief from a fear that it may turn out rotten is quite as immoral as it is disadvantageous. The person who confesses that there is such a thing as truth, which is distinguished from falsehood simply by this, that if acted on it will carry us to the point we aim at and not astray, and then, though convinced of this, dares not know the truth and seeks to avoid it, is in a sorry state of mind indeed.

Yes, the other methods do have their merits: a clear logical conscience does cast something—just as any virtue, just as all that we cherish, costs us dear. But we should not desire it to be otherwise. The genius of a man's logical method should be loved and reverenced as his bride, whom he has chosen from all the world. He need not condemn the others; on the contrary, he may honor them deeply, and in doing so he only honors her the more. But she is the one that he has chosen, and he knows that he was right in making that choice. And having made it, he will work and fight for her, and will not complain that there are blows to take, hoping that there may be as many and as hard to give, and will strive to be the worthy knight and champion of her from the blaze of whose splendors he draws his inspiration and his courage.

HOW TO MAKE OUR IDEAS CLEAR

When Descartes set about the reconstruction of philosophy, his first step was to (theoretically) permit scepticism and to discard the practice of the schoolmen of looking to authority as the ultimate source of truth. That done, he sought a more natural fountain of true principles, and professed to find it in the human mind; thus passing, in the directest way, from the method of authority to that of a priority, as described in my first paper. Self-consciousness was to furnish us with our fundamental truths, and to decide what was agreeable to reason. But since, evidently, not all ideas are true, he was led to note, as the first condition of infallibility, that they must be clear. The distinction between an idea *seeming* clear and really being so, never occurred to him. Trusting to introspection, as he did, even for a knowledge of external things, why should he question its testimony in respect to the contents of our own minds? But then, I suppose, seeing men, who seemed to be quite clear and positive, holding opinions upon fundamental principles, he was further led to say that clearness of ideas is not sufficient, but that they need also to be distinct, *i.e.,* to have nothing unclear about them. What he probably meant by this (for he did not explain himself with precision) was, that they must sustain the test of dialectical examination; that they must not only seem clear at the outset, but that discussion must never be able to bring to light points of obscurity connected with them.

Such was the distinction of Descartes, and one sees that it was precisely on the level of his philosophy. It was somewhat developed by Leibniz. This great and singular genius was as remarkable for what he failed to see as for what he saw. That a piece of mechanism could not do work perpetually without being fed with power in some form, was a thing perfectly apparent to him; yet he did not understand that the machinery of the mind can only transform knowledge, but never originate it, unless it be fed with facts of observation. He thus missed the most essential point of the Cartesian philosophy, which is, that to accept propositions which seem perfectly evident to us is a thing which, whether it be logical or illogical, we cannot help doing. Instead of regarding the matter in this way, he sought to reduce the first principles of science to formulas which cannot be denied without self-contradiction, and was apparently unaware of the great difference between his position and that of Descartes. So he reverted to the old formalities of logic, and, above all, abstract definitions played a great part in his philosophy. It was quite natural, therefore, that on observing that the method of Descartes labored under the difficulty that we may seem to ourselves to have clear apprehensions of ideas which in truth are very hazy, no better remedy occurred to him than to require an abstract definition of every important term. Accordingly, in adopting the distinction of *clear* and *distinct* notions, he described the latter quality as the clear apprehension of everything contained in the definition; and the books have ever since copied his words. There is no danger that his chimerical scheme will ever again be overvalued. Nothing new can ever be learned by analyzing definitions. Nevertheless, our existing beliefs can be

From Charles S. Peirce, "How to Make Our Ideas Clear," *Popular Science Monthly,* 1878.

set in order by this process, and order is an essential element of intellectual economy, as of every other. It may be acknowledged, therefore, that the books are right in making familiarity with a notion the first step toward clearness of apprehension, and the defining of it the second. But in omitting all mention of any higher perspicuity of thought, they simply mirror a philosophy which was exploded a hundred years ago. That much-admired "ornament of logic"—the doctrine of clearness and distinctness—may be pretty enough, but it is high time to relegate to our cabinet of curiosities the antique *bijou* and to wear about us something better adapted to modern uses.

The very first lesson that we have a right to demand that logic shall teach us is, how to make our ideas clear; and a most important one it is, depreciated only by minds who stand in need of it. To know what we think, to be masters of our own meaning, will make a solid foundation for great and weighty thought. It is most easily learned by those whose ideas are meager and restricted; and far happier they than such as wallow helplessly in a rich mud of conceptions. A nation, it is true, may, in the course of generations, overcome the disadvantage of an excessive wealth of language and its natural concomitant, a vast, unfathomable deep of ideas. We may see it in history, slowly perfecting its literary forms, sloughing at length its metaphysics, and, by virtue of the untirable patience which is often a compensation, attaining great excellence in every branch of mental acquirement.

. . . the action of thought is excited by the irritation of doubt, and ceases when belief is attained; so that the production of belief is the sole function of thought. All these words, however, are too strong for my purpose. It is as if I had described the phenomena as they appear under a mental microscope. Doubt and Belief, as the words are commonly employed, relate to religious or other grave discussions. But here I use them to designate the starting of any question, no matter how small or how great, and the resolution of it. If, for instance, in a horse-car, I pull out my purse and find a five-cent nickel and five coppers, I decide, while my hand is going to the purse, in which way I will pay my fare. To call such a question Doubt, and my decision Belief, is certainly to use words very disproportionate to the occasion. To speak of such a doubt as causing an irritation which needs to be appeased, suggests a temper which is uncomfortable to the verge of insanity. Yet, looking at the matter minutely, it must be admitted that, if there is the least hesitation as to whether I shall pay the five coppers or the nickel (as there will be sure to be, unless I act from some previously contracted habit in the matter), though irritation is too strong a word, yet I am excited to such small mental activity as may be necessary to deciding how I shall act. Most frequently doubts arise from some indecision, however momentary, in our action. Sometimes it is not so. I have, for example, to wait in a railway-station, and to pass the time I read the advertisements on the walls, I compare the advantages of different trains and different routes which I never expect to take, merely fancying myself to be in a state of hesitancy, because I am bored with having nothing to trouble me. Feigned hesitancy, whether feigned for mere amusement or with a lofty purpose, plays a great part in the production of scientific inquiry. However the doubt may originate, it stimulates the mind to an activity which may be slight or energetic, calm or turbulent. Images pass rapidly through consciousness, one incessantly melting into another, until at last, when all is over—it may be in a fraction of a second, in an hour, or after long years—we find ourselves decided as to how we should act under such circumstances as those which occasioned our hesitation. In other words, we have attained belief. . . .

And what, then, is belief? It is the demicadence which closes a musical phrase in the symphony of our intellectual life. We have seen that it has just three properties: First, it is something that we are aware of; second, it appeases the irritation of doubt; and, third, it involves the establishment in our nature of a rule of action, or, say, for short, a *habit*. As it appeases the irritation of doubt, which is the motives for thinking, thought relaxes, and comes to rest for a moment when belief is reached. But, since belief is a rule for action, the application of which involves further doubt and further thought, at the same time that it is a stopping-place, it is also a new starting-place for thought. That is why I have permitted myself to call it thought at rest, although thought is essentially an action. The *final* upshot of thinking is the exercise of volition; and of this thought no longer forms a part; but belief is only a stadium of mental action, an effect upon our nature due to thought, which will influence future thinking.

The essence of belief is the establishment of a habit, and different beliefs are distinguished by the different modes of action to which they give rise. If beliefs do not differ in this respect, if they appease the same doubt by producing the same rule of action, then no mere differences in the manner of consciousness of them can make them different beliefs, any more than playing a tune in different keys is playing different tunes. Imaginary distinctions are often drawn between beliefs which differ only in their mode of expression;—the wrangling which ensues is real enough, however. To believe that any objects are arranged as in Figure 1, and to believe that they are arranged [as] in Figure 2, are one and the same belief; yet it is conceivable that a man should assert one proposition and deny the other. Such false distinctions do as much harm as the confusion of beliefs really different, and are among the pitfalls of which we ought constantly to beware, especially when we are upon metaphysical ground. One singular deception of this sort, which often occurs, is to mistake the sensation produced by our own unclearness of thought for a character of the object we are thinking. Instead of perceiving that the obscurity is purely subjective, we fancy that we contemplate a quality of the object which is essentially mysterious; and if our conception be afterward presented to us in a clear form we do not recognize it as the same, owing to the absence of the feeling of unintelligibility. So long as this deception lasts, it obviously puts an impassable barrier in the way of perspicuous thinking; so that it equally interests the opponent of rational thought to perpetuate it, and its adherents to guard against it.

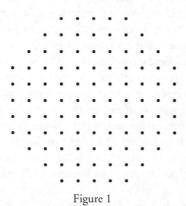

Figure 1

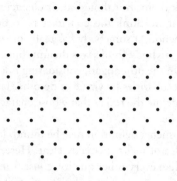

Figure 2

Another such deception is to mistake a mere difference in the grammatical construction of two words for a distinction between the ideas they express. In this pedantic age, when the general mob of writers attend so much more to words than to things, this error is common enough. When I just said that thought is an *action,* and that it consists in a relation, although a person performs an action, but not a relation, which can only be the result of an action, yet there was no inconsistency in what I said, but only a grammatical vagueness.

From all these sophisms we shall be perfectly safe so long as we reflect that the whole function of thought is to produce habits of action; and that whatever there is connected with a thought, but irrelevant to its purpose, is an accretion to it, but no part of it. If there be a unity among our sensations which has no reference to how we shall act on a given occasion, as when we listen to a piece of music, why, we do not call that thinking. To develop its meaning, we have, therefore, simply to determine what habits it produces, for what a thing means is simply what habits it involves. Now, the identity of a habit depends on how it might lead us to act, not merely under such circumstances as are likely to arise, but under such as might possibly occur, no matter how improbable they may be. What the habit is depends on *when* and *how* it causes us to act. As for the when, every stimulus to action is derived from perception; as for the how, every purpose of action is to produce some sensible result. Thus, we come down to what is tangible and conceivably practical, as the root of every real distinction of thought, no matter how subtle it may be; and there is no distinction of meaning so fine as to consist in anything but a possible difference of practice.

Let us now approach the subject of logic, and consider a conception which particularly concerns it, that of *reality.* Taking clearness in the sense of familiarity, no idea could be clearer than this. Every child uses it with perfect confidence, never dreaming that he does not understand it. As for clearness in its second grade, however, it would probably puzzle most men, even among those of a reflective turn of mind, to give an abstract definition of the real. Yet such a definition may perhaps be reached by considering the points of difference between reality and its opposite, fiction. A figment is a product of somebody's imagination; it has such characters as his thought impresses upon it. That whose characters are independent of how you or I think is an external reality. There are, however, phenomena within our own minds, dependent upon our thought, which are at the same time real in the sense that we really think them. But though their characters depend on how we think, they do not depend on what we think those characters to be. Thus, a dream has a real existence as a menu phenomenon, if somebody has really dreamt it; that he dreamt so and so does not depend on what anybody thinks was dreamt, but is completely independent of all opinion on the subject. On the other hand, considering not the fact of dreaming but the thing dreamt, it retains its peculiarities by virtue of no other fact than that it was dreamt to possess them. Thus we may define the real as that whose characters are independent of what anybody may think them to be.

But, however satisfactory such a definition may be found, it would be a great mistake to suppose that it makes the idea of reality perfectly clear. Here, then, let us apply our rules. According to them, reality, like every other quality, consists in the peculiar sensible effects which things partaking of it produce. The only effect which real things have is to cause belief, for all the sensations which they excite emerge into consciousness in the form of beliefs. The question therefore is, how is true belief (or belief in the real) distinguished from false belief (or belief in fiction).

. . . Now, as we have seen in the former paper, the ideas of truth and falsehood, in their full development, appertain exclusively to the scientific method of settling opinion. A person who arbitrarily chooses the propositions which he will adopt can use the word truth only to emphasize the expression of his determination to hold on to his choice. Of course, the method of tenacity never prevailed exclusively; reason is too natural to men for that. But in the literature of the dark ages we find some fine examples of it. When Scotus Erigena is commenting upon a poetical passage in which Hellebore is spoken of as having caused the death of Socrates, he does not hesitate to inform the inquiring reader that Helleborus and Socrates were two eminent Greek philosophers, and that the latter having been overcome in argument by the former took the matter to heart and died of it! . . .

The real spirit of Socrates, who I hope would have been delighted to have been "overcome in argument," because he would have learned something by it, is in curious contrast with the naive idea of the glossist, for whom discussion would seem to have been simply a struggle. When philosophy began to awake from its long slumber, and before theology completely dominated it, the practice seems to have been for each professor to seize upon any philosophical position he found unoccupied and which seemed a strong one, to intrench himself in it, and to sally forth from time to time to give battle to the others.

. . . Since the time of Descartes, the defect in the conception of truth has been less apparent. Still, it will sometimes strike a scientific man that the philosophers have been less intent on finding out what the facts are, than on inquiring what belief is most in harmony with their system. It is hard to convince a follower of the *a priori* method by adducing facts; but show him that an opinion he is defending is inconsistent with what he has laid down elsewhere, and he will be very apt to retract it. These minds do not seem to believe that disputation is ever to cease; they seem to think that the opinion which is natural for one man is not so for another, and that belief will, consequently, never be settled. In contenting themselves with fixing their own opinions by a method which would lead another man to a different result, they betray their feeble hold of the conception of what truth is. . . .

They may at first obtain different results, but, as each perfects his method and his processes, the results will move steadily together toward a destined center. So with all scientific research. Different minds may set out with the most antagonistic views, but the progress of investigation carries them by a force outside of themselves to one and the same conclusion. This activity of thought by which we are carried, not where we wish, but to a foreordained goal, is like the operation of destiny. No modification of the point of view taken, no selection of other facts for study, no natural bent of mind even, can enable a man to escape the predestinate opinion. This great law is embodied in the conception of truth and reality. The opinion which is fated to be ultimately agreed to by all who investigate, is what we mean by the truth, and the object represented in this opinion is the real. That is the way I would explain reality . . . though the object of the final opinion depends on what that opinion is, yet what that opinion is does not depend on what you or I or any man thinks. Our perversity and that of others may indefinitely postpone the settlement of opinion; it might even conceivably cause an arbitrary proposition to be universally accepted as long as the human race should last. Yet even that would not change the nature of the belief, which alone could be the result of investigation carried sufficiently far; and if, after the extinction of our race, another should arise with faculties and disposition for investigation, that true opinion must be the one which they would ultimately come to. "Truth crushed to earth shall rise again," and the opinion which would finally result from investigation does not depend on how anybody may actually think. But the reality of that which is real does depend on the real fact that investigation is destined to lead, at last, if continued long enough, to a belief in it.

JAMES

1842–1910

William James was born in New York City. After studying science and medicine at the Lawrence Scientific School, he went to Harvard Medical School. James's lifelong search for philosophical meaning and understanding took him across a variety of disciplines. After his initial work in medical physiology, he made profound and important contributions to psychology and several areas of philosophy, including epistemology, the philosophy of mind, and the philosophy of religion. His interest in philosophy began when he had a mystical experience that he says changed his life:

> I went one evening into a dressing-room in the twilight to procure some article that was there; when suddenly there fell upon me without any warning, just as if it came out of the darkness, a horrible fear of my own existence. . . . It was as if something hitherto solid within my breast gave way entirely, and I became a mass of quivering fear. After this the universe was changed for me altogether. I awoke morning after morning with a horrible dread at the pit of my stomach, and with a sense of the insecurity of life that I never knew before, and that I have never felt since. It was like a revelation. . . . For months I was unable to go out into the dark alone. In general I dreaded to be left alone. I remember wondering how other people could live, how I myself had ever lived, so unconscious of that pit of insecurity beneath the surface of life.

After graduating with an M.D. in 1869, James became an instructor in comparative physiology at Harvard, then taught physiology and psychology at Johns Hopkins University. He returned to Harvard in 1880 to join an illustrious philosophy department that included Josiah Royce and graduate student George Santayana (1863–1952).

Ten years later, James published his famous *Principles of Psychology,* which helped lay the philosophical foundation for the newly developing science of psychology. James founded the American Psychological Association and served as its first president.

Our first selection is a famous lecture that James delivered to a combined meeting of the philosophy clubs of Yale and Brown Universities. Titled "The Will to Believe," it is an apology for religious belief. James claims that it can be rational to believe in God even in the absence of adequate evidence. The thesis has been criticized as an example of how badly a philosopher can go awry if he or she gives up the notion of objective truth. For instance, Bertrand Russell (Chapter 49), a devout atheist, criticizes James's principle that "if the hypothesis of God works satisfactorily in the widest sense of the word, it is true," on the grounds that "this simply omits as unimportant the question whether God really is in His heaven; if He is a useful hypothesis, that is enough." But even the pope, a devout believer, condemned James's pragmatic defense of religion. In the essay, James tries to develop a pragmatic theory of truth, inspired by Peirce and Dewey; as a result, both Peirce and Dewey dissociated themselves from James's version of pragmatism. The reason was that Peirce and Dewey modeled their pragmatism on scientific thinking and the scientific method, whereas James's analysis relies primarily on religious and moral considerations: "An idea is 'true' so long as to believe it is profitable to our lives."

In saying that truth is but something that "happens to an idea," James was reacting against modern representationalist views of truth according to which an idea "represents" reality and is true insofar as it is a good copy in the mind of what exists "out there" in the "objective world." Bertrand Russell, who otherwise greatly admired James, especially for his work in psychology and the philosophy of mind, labeled James's theory of truth "subjectivist madness."

James ignored his many critics and continued working on his *Varieties of Religious Experience* (1902). A blend of philosophical psychology, philosophy of religion, and philosophy of mysticism, it tries to put mysticism in a positive light. The work is widely regarded today as a definitive study of mystical experience. After its publication, James decided to respond to his earlier critics with an effort to provide a solid philosophical basis for his pragmatic theory of truth.

In 1907 James succeeded to a certain degree with *Pragmatism: A New Name for Some Old Ways of Thinking,* from which the second selection is taken. Here, James presents the roots of his version of pragmatism in the context of John Stuart Mill, to whom the book is dedicated. In his attempt to make pragmatism philosophically respectable, James developed a bold new theory of mind, based on a careful analysis of percepts and concepts. Now known as radical empiricism, it turned out to be James's main philosophical achievement. In many ways a psychological version of logical positivism, the idea grew out of an attempt to wed the basic tenets of his earlier version of pragmatism with a new emphasis on experience along the lines espoused by the increasingly influential logical positivist movement, itself derived from the earlier positivism of Auguste Comte (Chapter 37).

James argues that a proposition is true or false depending *not* on "what difference it makes to you and me," as he had claimed in his earlier version of pragmatism, but on whether it *succeeds or fails to predict new sense experience.* Propositions that do not successfully make any such predictions one way or the other are meaningless because the world itself consists entirely of experience. This idea led James to his alternative to both traditional forms of idealism and materialism, what he called "neutral monism," according to which neither matter nor consciousness exists. Influenced by the philosophical views of physicist Ernst Mach, James's theory is both phenomenalistic and yet reminiscent of naive realism. The basic but radical innovation, though in many ways extremely subtle, is this: ideas are the only existent *given* but that does not necessarily mean they are *mental.* James thus accepts as true certain basic aspects of absolute idealism while rejecting as false the existence of an intrinsically subjective consciousness.

The third selection, "Does 'Consciousness' Exist?" gives a detailed account of James's radical empiricist position of neutral monism through a detailed analysis of consciousness, leading up to the conclusion that what, ordinarily, we call consciousness, *does not exist.* What exists is "pure experience." The mind according to James is not just a passive observer of reality but has an active role in the structuring of reality. Like many nineteenth-century idealists, James gives up Kant's notion of the "thing-in-itself" and the noumenal world existing independently of the mind. Some two decades after James's article appeared, Bertrand Russell wrote:

> Twenty-three years have elapsed since William James startled the world with his article entitled, "Does 'Consciousness' Exist?" In this article . . . he set out the view that "there is only one primal stuff or material in the world," and that the word "consciousness" stands for a function, not an entity. He holds that there are "thoughts," which perform the function of "knowing," but that thoughts are not made of any different "stuff" from that of which material objects are made. He thus laid the foundations for what is called "neutral monism," a view advocated by most American realists.

Russell too will argue that the mind-body problem as originally posed by Descartes can be resolved with some type of neutral monism according to which the mind and physical matter are but different constructions out of the same basic stuff that is neither mental nor physical.

In many ways, neutral monism was an attempt to transcend the entire subjective-objective distinction. It gave rise to the Darwin-inspired theory known as *naturalism*, highly influential in the twentieth century up to the present day, according to which not just the mind but the human being and the world entire are conceived as interactions among *natural* processes, a view that gave rise to the corresponding theory of knowledge known as *naturalized epistemology.*

THE WILL TO BELIEVE

I

Let us give the name of *hypothesis* to anything that may be proposed to our belief; and just as the electricians speak of live and dead wires, let us speak of any hypothesis as either *live* or *dead.* A live hypothesis is one which appeals as a real possibility to him to whom it is proposed. If I ask you to believe in the Mahdi, the notion makes no electric connection with your nature—it refuses to scintillate with any credibility at all. As an hypothesis it is completely dead. To an Arab, however (even if he be not one of the Mahdi's followers), the hypothesis is among the mind's possibilities: it is alive. This shows that deadness and liveness in an hypothesis are not intrinsic properties, but relations to the individual thinker. They are measured by his willingness to act. The maximum of liveness in an hypothesis means willingness to act irrevocably. Practically, that means belief; but there is some believing tendency wherever there is willingness to act at all.

Next, let us call the decision between two hypotheses an *option.* Options may be of several kinds. They may be—first, *living* or *dead;* secondly, *forced* or *avoidable;* thirdly,

An Address to the Philosophical Clubs of Yale and Brown Universities. Published in the *New World,* June 1896.

momentous or *trivial;* and for our purposes we may call an option a genuine option when it is of the forced, living, and momentous kind.

1. A living option is one in which both hypotheses are live ones. If I say to you: "Be a theosophist or be a Mohammedan," it is probably a dead option, because for you neither hypothesis is likely to be alive. But if I say: "Be an agnostic or be a Christian," it is otherwise: trained as you are, each hypothesis makes some appeal, however small, to your belief.

2. Next, if I say to you: "Choose between going out with your umbrella or without it," I do not offer you a genuine option, for it is not forced. You can easily avoid it by not going out at all. Similarly, if I say, "Either love me or hate me," "Either call my theory true or call it false," your option is avoidable. You may remain indifferent to me, neither loving nor hating, and you may decline to offer any judgment as to my theory. But if I say, "Either accept this truth or go without it," I put on you a forced option, for there is no standing place outside of the alternative. Every dilemma based on a complete logical disjunction, with no possibility of not choosing, is an option of this forced kind.

3. Finally, if I were Dr. Nansen and proposed to you to join my North Pole expedition, your option would be momentous; for this would probably be your only similar opportunity, and your choice now would either exclude you from the North Pole sort of immortality altogether or put at least the chance of it into your hands. He who refuses to embrace a unique opportunity loses the prize as surely as if he tried and failed. *Per contra,* the option is trivial when the opportunity is not unique, when the stake is insignificant, or when the decision is reversible if it later prove unwise. Such trivial options abound in the scientific life. A chemist finds an hypothesis live enough to spend a year in its verification: he believes in it to that extent. But if his experiments prove inconclusive either way, he is quit for his loss of time, no vital harm being done.

It will facilitate our discussion if we keep all these distinctions well in mind.

II

The next matter to consider is the actual psychology of human opinion. When we look at certain facts, it seems as if our passional and volitional nature lay at the root of all our convictions. When we look at others, it seems as if they could do nothing when the intellect had once said its say. Let us take the latter facts up first.

Does it not seem preposterous on the very face of it to talk of our opinions being modifiable at will? Can our will either help or hinder our intellect in its perceptions of truth? Can we, by just willing it, believe that Abraham Lincoln's existence is a myth, and that the portraits of him in *McClure's Magazine* are all of some one else? Can we, by any effort of our will, or by any strength of wish that it were true, believe ourselves well and about when we are roaring with rheumatism in bed, or feel certain that the sum of the two one-dollar bills in our pocket must be a hundred dollars? We can *say* any of these things, but we are absolutely impotent to believe them; and of just such things is the whole fabric of the truths that we do believe in made up—matters of fact, immediate or remote, as Hume said, and relations between ideas, which are either there or not there for us if we see them so, and which if not there cannot be put there by any action of our own.

In Pascal's *Thoughts* there is a celebrated passage known in literature as Pascal's wager. In it he tries to force us into Christianity by reasoning as if our concern with truth resembled our concern with the stakes in a game of chance. Translated freely his words are these: You must either believe or not believe that God is—which will you do? Your human reason cannot say. A game is going on between you and the nature of things which at the day of judgment will bring out either heads or tails. Weigh what your gains and your losses would be if you should stake all you have on heads, or God's existence: if you win in such case, you gain eternal beatitude; if you lose, you lose nothing at all. If there were an infinity of chances, and only one for God in this wager, still you ought to stake your all on God; for though you surely risk a finite loss by this procedure, any finite loss is reasonable, even a certain one is reasonable, if there is but the possibility of infinite gain. Go, then, and take holy water, and have masses said; belief will come and stupefy your scruples—*Cela vous fera croire et vous abêtira.* Why should you not? At bottom, what have you to lose?

You probably feel that when religious faith expresses itself thus, in the language of the gaming-table, it is put to its last trumps. Surely Pascal's own personal belief in masses and holy water had far other springs; and this celebrated page of his is but an argument for others, a last desperate snatch at a weapon against the hardness of the unbelieving heart. We feel that a faith in masses and holy water adopted wilfully after such a mechanical calculation would lack the inner soul of faith's reality; and if we were ourselves in the place of the Deity, we should probably take particular pleasure in cutting off believers of this pattern from their infinite reward. It is evident that unless there be some pre-existing tendency to believe in masses and holy water, the option offered to the will by Pascal is not a living option. Certainly no Turk ever took to masses and holy water on its account; and even to us Protestants these means of salvation seem such foregone impossibilities that Pascal's logic, invoked for them specifically, leaves us unmoved. As well might the Mahdi write to us, saying, "I am the Expected One whom God has created in his effulgence. You shall be infinitely happy if you confess me; otherwise you shall be cut off from the light of the sun. Weigh, then, your infinite gain if I am genuine against your finite sacrifice if I am not!" His logic would be that of Pascal; but he would vainly use it on us, for the hypothesis he offers us is dead. No tendency to act on it exists in us to any degree.

The talk of believing by our volition seems, then, from one point of view, simply silly. From another point of view it is worse than silly, it is vile. When one turns to the magnificent edifice of the physical sciences, and sees how it was reared; what thousands of disinterested moral lives of men lie buried in its mere foundations; what patience and postponement, what choking down of preference, what submission to the icy laws of outer fact are wrought into its very stones and mortar; how absolutely impersonal it stands in its vast augustness—then how besotted and contemptible seems every little sentimentalist who comes blowing his voluntary smoke-wreaths, and pretending to decide things from out of his private dream! Can we wonder if those bred in the rugged and manly school of science should feel like spewing such subjectivism out of their mouths? The whole system of loyalties which grow up in the schools of science go dead against its toleration; so that it is only natural that those who have caught the scientific fever should pass over to the opposite extreme, and write sometimes as if the incorruptibly truthful intellect ought positively to prefer bitterness and unacceptableness to the heart in its cup.

> It fortifies my soul to know
> That though I perish, Truth is so—

sings Clough, while Huxley exclaims: "My only consolation lies in the reflection that, however bad our posterity may become, so far as they hold by the plain rule of not pretending to believe what they have no reason to believe, because it may be to their advantage so to pretend [the word 'pretend' is surely here redundant], they will not have reached the lowest depth of immorality." And that delicious *enfant terrible* Clifford writes: "Belief is desecrated when given to unproved and unquestioned statements for the solace and private pleasure of the believer. . . . Whoso would deserve well of his fellows in this matter will guard the purity of his belief with a very fanaticism of jealous care, lest at any time it should rest on an unworthy object, and catch a stain which can never be wiped away. . . . If [a] belief has been accepted on insufficient evidence [even though the belief be true, as Clifford on the same page explains] the pleasure is a stolen one. . . . It is sinful because it is stolen in defiance of our duty to mankind. That duty is to guard ourselves from such beliefs as from a pestilence which may shortly master our own body and then spread to the rest of the town. . . . It is wrong always, everywhere, and for every one, to believe anything upon insufficient evidence."

III

All this strikes one as healthy, even when expressed, as by Clifford, with somewhat too much of robustious pathos in the voice. Free will and simple wishing do seem, in the matter of our credences, to be only fifth wheels to the coach. Yet if any one should thereupon assume that intellectual insight is what remains after wish and will and sentimental preference have taken wing, or that pure reason is what then settles our opinions, he would fly quite as directly in the teeth of the facts.

It is only our already dead hypotheses that our willing nature is unable to bring to life again. But what has made them dead for us is for the most part a previous action of our willing nature of an antagonistic kind. When I say "willing nature," I do not mean only such deliberate volitions as may have set up habits of belief that we cannot now escape from—I mean all such factors of belief as fear and hope, prejudice and passion, imitation and partisanship, the circumpressure of our caste and set. As a matter of fact we find ourselves believing, we hardly know how or why. Mr. Balfour gives the name of "authority" to all those influences, born of the intellectual climate, that make hypotheses possible or impossible for us, alive or dead. Here in this room, we all of us believe in molecules and the conservation of energy, in democracy and necessary progress, in Protestant Christianity and the duty of fighting for "the doctrine of the immortal Monroe," all for no reasons worthy of the name. We see into these matters with no more inner clearness, and probably with much less, than any disbeliever in them might possess. His unconventionality would probably have some grounds to show for its conclusions; but for us, not insight, but the *prestige* of the opinions, is what makes the spark shoot from them and light up our sleeping magazines of faith. Our reason is quite satisfied, in nine hundred and ninety-nine cases out of every thousand of us, if it can find a few arguments that will do to recite in case our credulity is criticized by some one else. Our faith is faith in some one else's faith, and in the greatest matters this is most the case. Our belief in truth itself, for instance, that there is a truth, and that our minds and it are made for each other—what is it but a passionate affirmation of desire, in which our social system backs us up? We want to have a truth; we want to believe that our experiments and studies and discussions must put us in a continually better and better position towards it; and on this line we agree to fight out our thinking lives. But if a Pyrrhonistic sceptic asks us *how we know* all this, can our logic find a reply? No! certainly it cannot. It is just one volition against another—we willing to go in for life upon a trust or assumption which he, for his part, does not care to make.

As a rule we disbelieve all facts and theories for which we have no use. Clifford's cosmic emotions find no use for Christian feelings. Huxley belabors the bishops because there is no use for sacerdotalism in his scheme of life. Newman, on the contrary, goes over to Romanism, and finds all sorts of reasons good for staying there, because a priestly system is for him an organic need and delight. Why do so few "scientists" even look at the evidence for telepathy, so called? Because they think, as a leading biologist, now dead, once said to me, that even if such a thing were true, scientists ought to band together to keep it suppressed and concealed. It would undo the uniformity of Nature and all sorts of other things without which scientists cannot carry on their pursuits. But if this very man had been shown something which as a scientist he might *do* with telepathy, he might not only have examined the evidence, but even have found it good enough. This very law which the logicians would impose upon us—if I may give the name of logicians to those who would rule out our willing nature here—is based on nothing but their own natural wish to exclude all elements for which they, in their professional quality of logicians, can find no use.

Evidently, then, our non-intellectual nature does influence our convictions. There are passional tendencies and volitions which run before and others which come after belief, and it is only the latter that are too late for the fair; and they are not too late when the previous passional work has been already in their own direction. Pascal's argument, instead of being powerless, then seems a regular clincher, and is the last stroke needed to make our faith in masses and holy water complete. The state of things is evidently far from simple; and pure insight and logic, whatever they might do ideally, are not the only things that really do produce our creeds.

IV

Our next duty, having recognized this mixed-up state of affairs, is to ask whether it be simply reprehensible and pathological, or whether, on the contrary, we must treat it as a normal element in making up our minds. The thesis I defend is, briefly stated, this: *Our passional nature not only lawfully may, but must, decide an option between propositions, whenever it is a genuine option that cannot by its nature be decided on intellectual grounds; for to say, under such circumstances, "Do not decide, but leave the question open," is itself a passional decision—just like deciding yes or no—and is attended with the same risk of losing the truth.* The thesis thus abstractly expressed will, I trust, soon become quite clear. But I must first indulge in a bit more of preliminary work.

V

It will be observed that for the purposes of this discussion we are on "dogmatic" ground— ground, I mean, which leaves systematic philosophical scepticism altogether out of account. The postulate that there is truth, and that it is the destiny of our minds to attain it, we are deliberately resolving to make, though the sceptic will not make it. We part company with him, therefore, absolutely, at this point. But the faith that truth exists, and that our minds can find it, may be held in two ways. We may talk of the *empiricist* way and of the *absolutist* way of believing in truth. The absolutists in this matter say that we not only can attain to knowing truth, but we can *know when* we have attained to knowing it; while the empiricists think that although we may attain it, we cannot infallibly know when. To *know* is one thing, and to know for certain *that* we know is another. One may hold to the first being possible without the second; hence the empiricists and the absolutists, although neither of them is a sceptic in the usual philosophic sense of the term, show very different degrees of dogmatism in their lives.

If we look at the history of opinions, we see that the empiricist tendency has largely prevailed in science, while in philosophy the absolutist tendency has had everything its own way. The characteristic sort of happiness, indeed, which philosophies yield has mainly consisted in the conviction felt by each successive school or system that by it bottom-certitude had been attained. "Other philosophies are collections of opinions, mostly false; *my* philosophy gives standing-ground forever"—who does not recognize in this the key-note of every system worthy of the name? A system, to be a system at all, must come as a *closed* system, reversible in this or that detail, perchance, but in its essential features never!

Scholastic orthodoxy, to which one must always go when one wishes to find perfectly clear statement, has beautifully elaborated this absolutist conviction in a doctrine which it calls that of "objective evidence." If, for example, I am unable to doubt that I now exist before you, that two is less than three, or that if all men are mortal then I am mortal too, it is because these things illumine my intellect irresistibly. The final ground of this objective evidence possessed by certain propositions is the *adaequatio intellectûs nostri cum rê*. The certitude it brings involves an *aptitudinem ad extorquendum certum assensum* on the part of the truth envisaged, and on the side of the subject a *quietem in cognitione*, when once the object is mentally received, that leaves no possibility of doubt behind; and in the whole transaction nothing operates but the *entitas ipsa* of the object and the *entitas ipsa* of the mind. We slouchy modern thinkers dislike to talk in Latin,—indeed, we dislike to talk in set terms at all; but at bottom our own state of mind is very much like this whenever we uncritically abandon ourselves: You believe in objective evidence, and I do. Of some things we feel that we are certain: we know, and we know that we do know. There is something that gives a click inside of us, a bell that strikes twelve, when the hands of our mental clock have swept the dial and meet over the meridian hour. The greatest empiricists among us are only empiricists on reflection: when left to their instincts, they dogmatize like infallible popes. When the Cliffords tell us how sinful it is to be Christians on such "insufficient evidence," insufficiency is really the last thing they have in mind. For them the evidence is absolutely sufficient, only it makes the other way. They believe so completely in an anti-Christian order of the universe that there is no living option: Christianity is a dead hypothesis from the start.

VI

But now, since we are all such absolutists by instinct, what in our quality of students of philosophy ought we to do about the fact? Shall we espouse and endorse it? Or shall we treat it as a weakness of our nature from which we must free ourselves, if we can?

I sincerely believe that the latter course is the only one we can follow as reflective men. Objective evidence and certitude are doubtless very fine ideals to play with, but where on this moonlit and dream-visited planet are they found? I am, therefore, myself a complete empiricist so far as my theory of human knowledge goes. I live, to be sure, by the practical faith that we must go on experiencing and thinking over our experience, for only thus can our opinions grow more true; but to hold any one of them—I absolutely do not care which—as if it never could be reinterpretable or corrigible, I believe to be a tremendously mistaken attitude, and I think that the whole history of philosophy will bear me out. There is but one indefectibly certain truth, and that is the truth that Pyrrhonistic scepticism itself leaves standing—the truth that the present phenomenon of consciousness exists. That, however, is the bare starting-point of knowledge, the mere admission of a stuff to be philosophized about. The various philosophies are but so many attempts at expressing what this stuff really is. And if we repair to our libraries what disagreement do we discover! Where is a certainly true answer found? Apart from abstract propositions of comparison (such as two and two are the same as four), propositions which tell us nothing by themselves about concrete reality, we find no proposition ever regarded by any one as evidently certain that has not either been called a falsehood, or at least had its truth sincerely questioned by some one else. The transcending of the axioms of geometry, not in play but in earnest, by certain of our contemporaries (as Zöllner and Charles H. Hinton), and the rejection of the whole Aristotelian logic by the Hegelians, are striking instances in point.

No concrete test of what is really true has ever been agreed upon. Some make the criterion external to the moment of perception, putting it either in revelation, the *consensus gentium,* the instincts of the heart, or the systematized experience of the race. Others make the perceptive moment its own test—Descartes, for instance, with his clear and distinct ideas guaranteed by the veracity of God; Reid with his "common-sense"; and Kant with his forms of synthetic judgment *a priori.* The inconceivability of the opposite; the capacity to be verified by sense; the possession of complete organic unity or self-relation, realized when a thing is its own other—are standards which, in turn, have been used. The much lauded objective evidence is never triumphantly there; it is a mere aspiration or *Grenzbegriff,* marking the infinitely remote ideal of our thinking life. To claim that certain truths now possess it, is simply to say that when you think them true and they *are* true, then their evidence is objective, otherwise it is not. But practically one's conviction that the evidence one goes by is of the real objective brand, is only one more subjective opinion added to the lot. For what a contradictory array of opinions have objective evidence and absolute certitude been claimed! The world is rational through and through—its existence is an ultimate brute fact; there is a personal God—a personal God is inconceivable; there is an extra-mental physical world immediately known—the mind can only know its own ideas; a moral imperative exists—obligation is only the resultant of desires; a permanent spiritual principle is in every one—there are only shifting states of mind; there is an endless chain of causes—there is an absolute first cause; an eternal necessity—a freedom; a purpose—no purpose; a primal One—a primal Many; a universal continuity—an essential discontinuity in things; an infinity—no infinity. There is this—there is that; there is indeed nothing which some one has not thought absolutely true, while his neighbor deemed it absolutely false; and not an absolutist among them seems ever to have considered that the trouble may all the time be essential, and that the intellect, even with truth directly in its grasp, may have no infallible signal for knowing whether it be truth or no. When, indeed, one remembers that the most striking practical application to life of the doctrine of objective certitude has been the conscientious labors of the Holy Office of the Inquisition, one feels less tempted than ever to lend the doctrine a respectful ear.

But please observe, now, that when as empiricists we give up the doctrine of objective certitude, we do not thereby give up the quest or hope of truth itself. We still pin our faith on its existence, and still believe that we gain an ever better position towards it by systematically continuing to roll up experiences and think. Our great difference from the scholastic lies in the way we face. The strength of his system lies in the principles, the origin, the *terminus a quo* of his thought; for us the strength is in the outcome, the upshot, the *terminus ad quem.* Not where it comes from but what it leads to is to decide. It matters not to an empiricist from what quarter an hypothesis may come to him: he may have acquired it by fair means or by foul; passion may have whispered or accident suggested it; but if the total drift of thinking continues to confirm it, that is what he means by its being true.

VII

One more point, small but important, and our preliminaries are done. There are two ways of looking at our duty in the matter of opinion—ways entirely different, and yet ways about whose difference the theory of knowledge seems hitherto to have shown very little concern. *We must know the truth;* and *we must avoid error*—these are our first and great commandments as would-be knowers; but they are not two ways of stating an identical commandment, they are two separable laws. Although it may indeed happen that when we believe the truth *A,* we escape as an incidental consequence from believing the falsehood *B,* it hardly ever happens that by merely disbelieving *B* we necessarily believe *A.* We may in escaping *B* fall into believing other falsehoods, *C* or *D,* just as bad as *B;* or we may escape *B* by not believing anything at all, not even *A.*

Believe truth! Shun error!—these, we see, are two materially different laws; and by choosing between them we may end by coloring differently our whole intellectual life. We may regard the chase for truth as paramount, and the avoidance of error as secondary; or we may, on the other hand, treat the avoidance of error as more imperative, and let truth take its chance. Clifford, in the instructive passage which I have quoted, exhorts us to the latter course. Believe nothing, he tells us, keep your mind in suspense forever, rather than by closing it on insufficient evidence incur the awful risk of believing lies. You, on the other hand, may think that the risk of being in error is a very small matter when compared with the blessings of real knowledge, and be ready to be duped many times in your investigation rather than postpone indefinitely the chance of guessing true. I myself find it impossible to go with Clifford. We must remember that these feelings of our duty about either truth or error are in any case only expressions of our passional life. Biologically considered, our minds are as ready to grind out falsehood as veracity, and he who says, "Better go without belief forever than believe a lie!" merely shows his own preponderant private horror of becoming a dupe. He may be critical of many of his desires and fears, but this fear he slavishly obeys. He cannot imagine any one questioning its binding force. For my own part, I have also a horror of being duped; but I can believe that worse things than being duped may happen to a man in this world: so Clifford's exhortation has to my ears a thoroughly fantastic sound. It is like a general informing his soldiers that it is better to keep out of battle forever than to risk a single wound. Not so are victories either over enemies or over nature gained. Our errors are surely not such awfully solemn things. In a world where we are so certain to incur them in spite of all our caution, a certain lightness of heart seems healthier than this excessive nervousness on their behalf. At any rate, it seems the fittest thing for the empiricist philosopher.

VIII

And now, after all this introduction, let us go straight at our question. I have said, and now repeat it, that not only as a matter of fact do we find our passional nature influencing us in our opinions, but that there are some options between opinions in which this influence must be regarded both as an inevitable and as a lawful determinant of our choice.

I fear here that some of you my hearers will begin to scent danger, and lend an inhospitable ear. Two first steps of passion you have indeed had to admit as necessary—we must think so as to avoid dupery, and we must think so as to gain truth; but the surest path to those ideal consummations, you will probably consider, is from now onwards to take no further passional step.

Well, of course, I agree as far as the facts will allow. Wherever the option between losing truth and gaining it is not momentous, we can throw the chance of *gaining truth* away, and at any rate save ourselves from any chance of *believing falsehood,* by not making up our minds at all till objective evidence has come. In scientific questions, this is almost always the case; and even in human affairs in general, the need of acting is seldom so urgent that a false belief to act on is better than no belief at all. Law courts, indeed, have to decide on the best evidence attainable for the moment, because a judge's duty is to make law as well as to ascertain it, and (as a learned judge once said to me) few cases are worth spending much time over: the great thing is to have them decided on *any* acceptable principle, and got out of the way. But in our dealings with objective nature we obviously are recorders, not makers, of the truth; and decisions for the mere sake of deciding promptly and getting on to the next business would be wholly out of place. Throughout the breadth of physical nature facts are what they are quite independently of us, and seldom is there any such hurry about them that the risks of being duped by believing a premature theory need be faced. The questions here are always trivial options, the hypotheses are hardly living (at any rate not living for us spectators), the choice between believing truth or falsehood is seldom forced. The attitude of sceptical balance is therefore the absolutely wise one if we would escape mistakes. What difference, indeed, does it make to most of us whether we have or have not a theory of the Röntgen rays, whether we believe or not in mind-stuff, or have a conviction about the causality of conscious states? It makes no difference. Such options are not forced on us. On every account it is better not to make them, but still keep weighing reasons *pro et contra* with an indifferent hand.

I speak, of course, here of the purely judging mind. For purposes of discovery such indifference is to be less highly recommended, and science would be far less advanced than she is if the passionate desires of individuals to get their own faiths confirmed had been kept out of the game. See for example the sagacity which Spencer and Weismann now display. On the other hand, if you want an absolute duffer in an investigation, you must, after all, take the man who has no interest whatever in its results: he is the warranted incapable, the positive fool. The most useful investigator, because the most sensitive observer, is always he whose eager interest in one side of the question is balanced by an equally keen nervousness lest he become deceived. Science has organized this nervousness into a regular *technique,* her so-called method of verification; and she has fallen so deeply in love with the method that one may even say she has ceased to care for truth by itself at all. It is only truth as technically verified that interests her. The truth of truths might come in merely affirmative form, and she would decline to touch it. Such truth as that, she might repeat with Clifford, would be stolen in defiance of her duty to mankind. Human passions, however, are stronger than technical rules. "*Le cœur a ses raisons,*" as Pascal says, "*que la raison ne connaît pas*" ("The heart has its reasons which reason does not know."); and however indifferent to all but the bare rules of the game the umpire, the abstract intellect, may be, the concrete players who furnish him the materials to judge of are usually, each one of them, in love with some pet "live hypothesis" of his own. Let us agree, however, that wherever there is no forced option, the dispassionately judicial intellect with no pet hypothesis, saving us, as it does, from dupery at any rate, ought to be our ideal.

The question next arises: Are there not somewhere forced options in our speculative questions, and can we (as men who may be interested at least as much in positively gaining truth as in merely escaping dupery) always wait with impunity till the coercive evidence shall have arrived? It seems *a priori* improbable that the truth should be so nicely adjusted to our needs and powers as that. In the great boarding-house of nature, the cakes and the butter and the syrup seldom come out so even and leave the plates so clean. Indeed, we should view them with scientific suspicion if they did.

IX

Moral questions immediately present themselves as questions whose solution cannot wait for sensible proof. A moral question is a question not of what sensibly exists, but of what is good, or would be good if it did exist. Science can tell us what exists; but to compare the *worths,* both of what exists and of what does not exist, we must consult not science, but what Pascal calls our heart. Science herself consults her heart when she lays it down that the infinite ascertainment of fact and correction of false belief are the supreme goods for man. Challenge the statement, and science can only repeat it oracularly, or else prove it by show-ing that such ascertainment and correction bring man all sorts of other goods which man's heart in turn declares. The question of having moral beliefs at all or not having them is decided by our will. Are our moral preferences true or false, or are they only odd biological phenomena, making things good or bad for *us,* but in themselves indifferent? How can your pure intellect decide? If your heart does not *want* a world of moral reality, your head will assuredly never make you believe in one. Mephistophelian scepticism, indeed, will satisfy the head's play-instincts much better than any rigorous idealism can. Some men (even at the student age) are so naturally cool-hearted that the moralistic hypothesis never has for them any pungent life, and in their supercilious presence the hot young moralist always feels strangely ill at ease. The appearance of knowingness is on their side, of *naïveté* and gullibility on his. Yet, in the inarticulate heart of him, he clings to it that he is not a dupe, and that there is a realm in which (as Emerson says) all their wit and intellectual superiority is no better than the cunning of a fox. Moral scepticism can no more be refuted or proved by logic than intellectual scepticism can. When we stick to it that there *is* truth (be it of either kind), we do so with our whole nature, and resolve to stand or fall by the results. The sceptic with his whole nature adopts the doubting attitude; but which of us is the wiser, Omniscience only knows.

Turn now from these wide questions of good to a certain class of questions of fact, questions concerning personal relations, states of mind between one man and another. *Do you like me or not?*—for example. Whether you do or not depends, in countless instances, on whether I meet you half-way, am willing to assume that you must like me, and show you trust and expectation. The previous faith on my part in your liking's existence is in such cases what makes your liking come. But if I stand aloof, and refuse to budge an inch until I have objective evidence, until you shall have done something apt, as the absolutists say, *ad extorquendum assensum meum,* ten to one your liking never comes. How many women's hearts are vanquished by the mere sanguine insistence of some man that they *must* love him! he will not consent to the hypothesis that they cannot. The desire for a certain kind of truth here brings about that special truth's existence; and so it is in innumerable cases of other sorts. Who gains promotions, boons, appointments, but the man in whose life they are seen to play the part of live hypotheses, who discounts them, sacrifices other things for their sake before they have come, and takes risks for them in advance? His faith acts on the powers above him as a claim, and creates its own verification.

A social organism of any sort whatever, large or small, is what it is because each member proceeds to his own duty with a trust that the other members will simultaneously do theirs. Wherever a desired result is achieved by the co-operation of many independent persons, its existence as a fact is a pure consequence of the precursive faith in one another of those immediately concerned. A government, an army, a commercial system, a ship, a college, an athletic team, all exist on this condition, without which not only is nothing achieved, but nothing is even attempted. A whole train of passengers (individually brave enough) will be looted by a few highwaymen, simply because the latter can count on one another, while each passenger fears that if he makes a movement of resistance, he will be shot before any one else backs him up. If we believed that the whole car-full would rise at once with us, we should each severally rise, and train-robbing would never even be attempted. There are, then, cases where a fact cannot come at all unless a preliminary faith exists in its coming. *And where faith in a fact can help create the fact,* that would be an insane logic which should say that faith running ahead of scientific evidence is the "lowest kind of immorality" into which a thinking being can fall. Yet such is the logic by which our scientific absolutists pretend to regulate our lives!

X

In truths dependent on our personal action, then, faith based on desire is certainly a lawful and possibly an indispensable thing.

But now, it will be said, these are all childish human cases, and have nothing to do with great cosmical matters, like the question of religious faith. Let us then pass on to that. Religions differ so much in their accidents that in discussing the religious question we must make it very generic and broad. What then do we now mean by the religious hypothesis? Science says things are; morality says some things are better than other things; and religion says essentially two things.

First, she says that the best things are the more eternal things, the overlapping things, the things in the universe that throw the last stone, so to speak, and say the final word. "Perfection is eternal"—this phrase of Charles Secrétan seems a good way of putting this first affirmation of religion, an affirmation which obviously cannot yet be verified scientifically at all.

The second affirmation of religion is that we are better off even now if we believe her first affirmation to be true.

Now, let us consider what the logical elements of this situation are *in case the religious hypothesis in both its branches be really true.* (Of course, we must admit that possibility at the outset. If we are to discuss the question at all, it must involve a living option. If for any of you religion be a hypothesis that cannot, by any living possibility, be true, then you need go no farther. I speak to the "saving remnant" alone.) So proceeding, we see, first, that religion offers itself as a *momentous* option. We are supposed to gain, even now, by our belief, and to lose by our non-belief, a certain vital good. Secondly, religion is a *forced* option, so far as that good goes. We cannot escape the issue by remaining sceptical and waiting for more light, because, although we do avoid error in that way *if religion be untrue,* we lose the good, *if it be true,* just as certainly as if we positively chose to disbelieve. It is as if a man should hesitate indefinitely to ask a certain woman to marry him because he was not perfectly sure that she would prove an angel after he brought her home. Would he not cut himself off from that particular angel-possibility as decisively as if he went and married some one else? Scepticism, then, is not avoidance of option; it is option of a certain particular kind of risk. *Better risk loss of truth than chance of error*—that is your faith-vetoer's exact position. He is actively playing his stake as much as the believer is; he is backing the field against the religious hypothesis, just as the believer is backing the religious hypothesis against the field. To preach scepticism to us as a duty until "sufficient evidence" for religion be found, is tantamount therefore to telling us, when in presence of the religious hypothesis, that to yield to our fear of its being error is wiser and better than to yield to our hope that it may be true. It is not intellect against all passions, then; it is only intellect with one passion laying down its law. And by what, forsooth, is the supreme wisdom of this passion warranted? Dupery for dupery, what proof is there that dupery through hope is so much worse than dupery through fear? I, for one, can see no proof; and I simply refuse obedience to the scientist's command to imitate his kind of option, in a case where my own stake is important enough to give me the right to choose my own form of risk. If religion be true and the evidence for it be still insufficient, I do not wish, by putting your extinguisher upon my nature (which feels to me as if it had after all some business in this matter), to forfeit my sole chance in life of getting upon the winning side—that chance depending, of course, on my willingness to run the risk of acting as if my passional need of taking the world religiously might be prophetic and right.

All this is on the supposition that it really may be prophetic and right, and that, even to us who are discussing the matter, religion is a live hypothesis which may be true. Now, to most of us religion comes in a still further way that makes a veto on our active faith even more illogical. The more perfect and more eternal aspect of the universe is represented in our religions as having personal form. The universe is no longer a mere *It* to us, but a *Thou*, if we are religious; and any relation that may be possible from person to person might be possible here. For instance, although in one sense we are passive portions of the universe, in another we show a curious autonomy, as if we were small active centres on our own account. We feel, too, as if the appeal of religion to us were made to our own active good-will, as if evidence might be forever withheld from us unless we met the hypothesis half-way. To take a trivial illustration: just as a man who in a company of gentlemen made no advances, asked a warrant for every concession, and believed no one's word without proof, would cut himself off by such churlishness from all the social rewards that a more trusting spirit would earn—so here, one who should shut himself up in snarling logicality and try to make the gods extort his recognition willy-nilly, or not get it at all, might cut himself off forever from his only opportunity of making the gods' acquaintance. This feeling, forced on us we know not whence, that by obstinately believing that there are gods (although not to do so would be so easy both for our logic and our life) we are doing the universe the deepest service we can, seems part of the living essence of the religious hypothesis. If the hypothesis *were* true in all its parts, including this one, then pure intellectualism, with its veto on our making willing advances, would be an absurdity; and some participation of our sympathetic nature would be logically required. I, therefore, for one, cannot see my way to accepting the agnostic rules for truth-seeking, or wilfully agree to keep my willing nature out of the game. I cannot do so for this plain reason, that *a rule of thinking which would absolutely prevent me from acknowledging certain kinds of truth if those kinds of truth were really there, would be an irrational rule.* That for me is the long and short of the formal logic of the situation, no matter what the kinds of truth might materially be.

I confess I do not see how this logic can be escaped. But sad experience makes me fear that some of you may still shrink from radically saying with me, *in abstracto,* that we have the right to believe at our own risk any hypothesis that is live enough to tempt our will. I suspect, however, that if this is so, it is because you have got away from the abstract logical point of view altogether, and are thinking (perhaps without realizing it) of some particular religious hypothesis which for you is dead. The freedom to "believe what we will" you apply to the case of some patent superstition; and the faith you think of is the faith defined by the schoolboy when he said, "Faith is when you believe something that you know ain't true." I can only repeat that this is misapprehension. *In concreto,* the freedom to believe can only cover living options which the intellect of the individual cannot by itself resolve; and living options never seem absurdities to him who has them to consider. When I look at the religious question as it really puts itself to concrete men, and when I think of all the possibilities which both practically and theoretically it involves, then this command that we shall put a stopper on our heart, instincts, and courage, and *wait*—acting of course meanwhile more or less as if religion were *not* true—till doomsday, or till such time as our intellect and senses working together may have raked in evidence enough—this command, I say, seems to me the queerest idol ever manufactured in the philosophic cave. Were we scholastic absolutists, there might be more excuse. If we had an infallible intellect with its objective certitudes, we might feel ourselves disloyal to such a perfect organ of knowledge in not trusting to it exclusively, in not waiting for its releasing word. But if we are empiricists, if we believe that no bell in us tolls to let us know for certain when truth is in our grasp, then it seems a piece of idle fantasticality to preach so solemnly our duty of waiting for the bell. Indeed we *may* wait if we will—I hope you do not think that I am denying that—but if we do so, we do so at our peril as much as if we believed. In either case we *act,* taking our life in our hands. No one of us ought to issue vetoes to the other, nor should we bandy words of abuse. We ought, on the contrary, delicately and profoundly to respect one another's mental freedom: then only shall we bring about the intellectual republic; then only shall we have that spirit of inner tolerance without which all our outer tolerance is soulless, and which is empiricism's glory; then only shall we live and let live, in speculative as well as in practical things.

I began by a reference to Fitz-James Stephen; let me end by a quotation from him. "What do you think of yourself? What do you think of the world? . . . These are questions with which all must deal as it seems good to them. They are riddles of the Sphinx, and in some way or other we must deal with them. . . . In all important transactions of life we have to take a leap in the dark. . . . If we decide to leave the riddles unanswered, that is a choice; if we waver in our answer, that, too, is a choice: but whatever choice we make, we make it at our peril. If a man chooses to turn his back altogether on God and the future, no one can prevent him; no one can show beyond reasonable doubt that he is mistaken. If a man thinks otherwise and acts as he thinks, I do not see that any one can prove that *he* is mistaken. Each must act as he thinks best; and if he is wrong, so much the worse for him. We stand on a mountain pass in the midst of whirling snow and blinding mist, through which we get glimpses now and then of paths which may be deceptive. If we stand still we shall be frozen to death. If we take the wrong road we shall be dashed to pieces. We do not certainly know whether there is any right one. What must we do? 'Be strong and of a good courage.' Act for the best, hope for the best, and take what comes. . . . If death ends all, we cannot meet death better."

PRAGMATISM

A New Name for Some Old Ways of Thinking

WHAT PRAGMATISM MEANS

Some years ago, being with a camping party in the mountains, I returned from a solitary ramble to find every one engaged in a ferocious metaphysical dispute. The *corpus* of the dispute was a squirrel—a live squirrel supposed to be clinging to one side of a tree-trunk; while over against the tree's opposite side a human being was imagined to stand. This human witness tries to get sight of the squirrel by moving rapidly round the tree, but no matter how fast he goes, the squirrel moves as fast in the opposite direction, and always keeps the tree between himself and the man, so that never a glimpse of him is caught. The resultant metaphysical problem now is this: *Does the man go round the squirrel or not?* He goes round the tree, sure enough, and the squirrel is on the tree; but does he go round the squirrel? In the unlimited leisure of the wilderness, discussion had been worn threadbare. Every one had taken sides, and was obstinate; and the numbers on both sides were even. Each side, when I appeared, therefore appealed to me to make it a majority. Mindful of the scholastic adage that whenever you meet a contradiction you must make a distinction, I immediately sought and found one, as follows: "Which party is right," I said, "depends on what you *practically mean* by 'going round' the squirrel. If you mean passing from the north of him to the east, then to the south, then to the west, and then to the north of him again, obviously the man does go round him, for he occupies these successive positions. But if on the contrary you mean being first in front of him, then on the right of him, then behind him, then on his left, and finally in front again, it is quite as obvious that the man fails to go round him, for by the compensating movements the squirrel makes, he keeps his belly turned towards the man all the time, and his back turned away. Make the distinction, and there is no occasion for any further dispute. You are both right and both wrong according as you conceive the verb 'to go round' in one practical fashion or the other."

Although one or two of the hotter disputants called my speech a shuffling evasion, saying they wanted no quibbling or scholastic hair-splitting, but meant just plain honest English "round," the majority seemed to think that the distinction had assuaged the dispute.

I tell this trivial anecdote because it is a peculiarly simple example of what I wish now to speak of as *the pragmatic method.* The pragmatic method is primarily a method of settling metaphysical disputes that otherwise might be interminable. Is the world one or many?— fated or free?—material or spiritual?—here are notions either of which may or may not hold good of the world; and disputes over such notions are unending. The pragmatic method in such cases is to try to interpret each notion by tracing its respective practical consequences. What difference would it practically make to any one if this notion rather than that notion were true? If no practical difference whatever can be traced, then the alternatives mean practically the same thing, and all dispute is idle. Whenever a dispute is

From William James, *Pragmatism: A New Name for Some Old Ways of Thinking,* 1907.

serious, we ought to be able to show some practical difference that must follow from one side or the other's being right.

A glance at the history of the idea will show you still better what pragmatism means. The term is derived from the same Greek word πράγμα, meaning action, from which our words "practice" and "practical" come. It was first introduced into philosophy by Mr. Charles Peirce in 1878. In an article entitled "How to Make Our Ideas Clear," in the *Popular Science Monthly* for January of that year Mr. Peirce, after pointing out that our beliefs are really rules for action, said that, to develop a thought's meaning, we need only determine what conduct it is fitted to produce: that conduct is for us its sole significance. And the tangible fact at the root of all our thought-distinctions, however subtle, is that there is no one of them so fine as to consist in anything but a possible difference of practice. To attain perfect clearness in our thoughts of an object, then, we need only consider what conceivable effects of a practical kind the object may involve—what sensations we are to expect from it, and what reactions we must prepare. Our conception of these effects, whether immediate or remote, is then for us the whole of our conception of the object, so far as that conception has positive significance at all. . . .

PRAGMATISM'S CONCEPTION OF TRUTH

When Clerk-Maxwell was a child it is written that he had a mania for having everything explained to him, and that when people put him off with vague verbal accounts of any phenomenon he would interrupt them impatiently by saying. "Yes; but I want you to tell me the *particular go* of it!" Had his question been about truth, only a pragmatist could have told him the particular go of it. I believe that our contemporary pragmatists, especially Messrs. Schiller and Dewey, have given the only tenable account of this subject. It is a very ticklish subject, sending subtle rootlets into all kinds of crannies, and hard to treat in the sketchy way that alone befits a public lecture. But the Schiller-Dewey view of truth has been so ferociously attacked by rationalistic philosophers, and so abominably misunderstood, that here, if anywhere, is the point where a clear and simple statement should be made.

I fully expect to see the pragmatist view of truth run through the classic stages of a theory's career. First, you know, a new theory is attacked as absurd; then it is admitted to be true, but obvious and insignificant; finally it is seen to be so important that its adversaries claim that they themselves discovered it. Our doctrine of truth is at present in the first of these three stages, with symptoms of the second stage having begun in certain quarters. I wish that this lecture might help it beyond the first stage in the eyes of many of you.

Truth, as any dictionary will tell you, is a property of certain of our ideas. It means their "agreement," as falsity means their disagreement, with "reality." Pragmatists and intellectualists both accept this definition as a matter of course. They begin to quarrel only after the question is raised as to what may precisely be meant by the term "agreement," and what by the term "reality," when reality is taken as something for our ideas to agree with.

In answering these questions the pragmatists are more analytic and painstaking, the intellectualists more offhand and irreflective. The popular notion is that a true idea must copy its reality. Like other popular views, this one follows the analogy of the most usual experience. Our true ideas of sensible things do indeed copy them. Shut your eyes and think of yonder clock on the wall, and you get just such a true picture or copy of its dial. But your idea of its "works" (unless you are a clockmaker) is much less of a copy, yet it passes muster, for it in no way clashes with the reality. Even though it should shrink to the mere word "works," that word still serves you truly; and when you speak of the "time-keeping function" of the clock, or of its spring's "elasticity," it is hard to see exactly what your ideas can copy.

You perceive that there is a problem here. Where our ideas cannot copy definitely their object, what does agreement with that object mean? Some idealists seem to say that they are true whenever they are what God means that we ought to think about that object. Others hold the copy-view all through, and speak as if our ideas possessed truth just in proportion as they approach to being copies of the absolute's eternal way of thinking.

These views, you see, invite pragmatistic discussion. But the great assumption of the intellectualists is that truth means essentially an inert static relation. When you've got your true idea of anything, there's an end of the matter. You're in possession; you *know;* you have fulfilled your thinking destiny. You are where you ought to be mentally; you have obeyed your categorical imperative; and nothing more need follow on that climax of your rational destiny. Epistemologically you are in stable equilibrium.

Pragmatism, on the other hand, asks its usual question. "Grant an idea or belief to be true," it says, "what concrete difference will its being true make in any one's actual life? How will the truth be realized? What experiences will be different from those which would obtain if the belief were false? What, in short, is the truth's cash-value in experiential terms?"

The moment pragmatism asks this question, it sees the answer: *True ideas are those that we can assimilate, validate, corroborate and verify. False ideas are those that we can not.* That is the practical difference it makes to us to have true ideas; that, therefore, is the meaning of truth, for it is all that truth is known-as.

This thesis is what I have to defend. The truth of an idea is not a stagnant property inherent in it. Truth *happens* to an idea. It *becomes* true, is *made* true by events. Its verity *is* in fact an event, a process: the process namely of its verifying itself, its veri-*fication.* Its validity is the process of its valid-*ation.*

But what do the words verification and validation themselves pragmatically mean? They again signify certain practical consequences of the verified and validated idea. It is hard to find any one phrase that characterizes these consequences better than the ordinary agreement-formula—just such consequences being what we have in mind whenever we say that our ideas "agree" with reality. They lead us, namely, through the acts and other ideas which they instigate, into or up to, or towards, other parts of experience with which we feel all the while—such feeling being among our potentialities—that the original ideas remain in agreement. The connections and transitions come to us from point to point as being progressive, harmonious, satisfactory. This function of agreeable leading is what we mean by an idea's verification. . . .

The possession of true thoughts means everywhere the possession of invaluable instruments of action; and that our duty to gain truth, so far from being a blank command from out of the blue, or a "stunt" self-imposed by our intellect, can account for itself by excellent practical reasons.

The importance to human life of having true beliefs about matters of fact is a thing too notorious. We live in a world of realities that can be infinitely useful or infinitely harmful. Ideas that tell us which of them to expect count as the true ideas in all this primary sphere of verification, and the pursuit of such ideas is a primary human duty. The possession of truth, so far from being here an end in itself, is only a preliminary means towards other vital satisfactions. If I am lost in the woods and starved, and find what looks like a cow-path, it is of the utmost importance that I should think of a human habitation at the end of it, for if I do so and follow it, I save myself. The true thought is useful here because the house which is its object is useful. The practical value of true ideas is thus primarily derived from the practical importance of their objects to us. Their objects are, indeed, not important at all times. I may on another occasion have no use for the house; and then my idea of it, however verifiable, will be practically irrelevant, and had better remain latent. Yet since almost any object may some day become temporarily important, the advantage of having a general stock of *extra* truths, of ideas that shall be true of merely possible situations, is obvious. We store such extra truths away in our memories, and with the overflow we fill our books of reference. Whenever such an extra truth becomes practically relevant to one of our emergencies, it passes from cold-storage to do work in the world and our belief in it grows active. You can say of it then either that "it is useful because it is true" or that "it is true because it is useful." Both these phrases mean exactly the same thing, namely that here is an idea that gets fulfilled and can be verified. True is the name for whatever idea starts the verification-process, useful is the name for its completed function in experience. True ideas would never have been singled out as such, would never have acquired a class-name, least of all a name suggesting value, unless they had been useful from the outset in this way.

From this simple cue pragmatism gets her general notion of truth as something essentially bound up with the way in which one moment in our experience may lead us towards other moments which it will be worth while to have been led to. Primarily, and on the commonsense level, the truth of a state of mind means this function of *a leading that is worth while.* When a moment in our experience, of any kind whatever, inspires us with a thought that is true, that means that sooner or later we dip by that thought's guidance into the particulars of experience again and make advantageous connection with them. This is a vague enough statement, but I beg you to retain it, for it is essential.

Our experience meanwhile is all shot through with regularities. One bit of it can warn us to get ready for another bit, can "intend" or be "significant of" that remoter object. The object's advent is the significance's verification. Truth, in these cases, meaning nothing but eventual verification, is manifestly incompatible with waywardness on our part. Woe to him whose beliefs play fast and loose with the order which realities follow in his experience; they will lead him nowhere or else make false connections.

By "realities" or "objects" here, we mean either things of common sense, sensibly present, or else common-sense relations, such as dates, places, distances, kinds, activities. Following our mental image of a house along the cow-path, we actually come to see the house; we get the image's full verification. *Such simply and fully verified leadings are certainly the originals and prototypes of the truth-process.* Experience offers indeed other forms of truth-process, but they are all conceivable as being primary verifications arrested, multiplied or substituted one for another.

Take, for instance, yonder object on the wall. You and I consider it to be a "clock," although no one of us has seen the hidden works that make it one. We let our notion pass for true without attempting to verify. If truths mean verification-process essentially, ought we then to call such unverified truths as this abortive? No, for they form the overwhelmingly large number of the truths we live by. Indirect as well as direct verifications pass muster. Where circumstantial evidence is sufficient, we can go without eye-witnessing. Just as we here assume Japan to exist without ever having been there, because it *works* to do so, everything we know conspiring with the belief, and nothing interfering, so we assume that thing to be a clock. We *use* it as a clock, regulating the length of our lecture by it. The verification of the assumption here means its leading to no frustration or contradiction. Verifi*ability* of wheels and weights and pendulum is as good as verification. For one truth-process completed there are a million in our lives that function in this state of nascency. They turn us *towards* direct verification; lead us into the *surroundings* of the objects they envisage; and then, if everything runs on harmoniously, we are so sure that verification is possible that we omit it, and are usually justified by all that happens.

Truth lives, in fact, for the most part on a credit system. Our thoughts and beliefs "pass," so long as nothing challenges them, just as bank-notes pass so long as nobody refuses them. But this all points to direct face-to-face verifications somewhere, without which the fabric of truth collapses like a financial system with no cash-basis whatever. You accept my verification of one thing, I yours of another. We trade on each other's truth. But beliefs verified concretely by *somebody* are the posts of the whole superstructure.

Another great reason—beside economy of time—for waiving complete verification in the usual business of life is that all things exist in kinds and not singly. Our world is found once for all to have that peculiarity. So that when we have once directly verified our ideas about one specimen of a kind, we consider ourselves free to apply them to other specimens without verification. A mind that habitually discerns the kind of thing before it, and acts by the law of the kind immediately, without pausing to verify, will be a "true" mind in ninety-nine out of a hundred emergencies, proved so by its conduct fitting everything it meets, and getting no refutation.

Indirectly or only potentially verifying processes may thus be true as well as full verification-processes. They work as true processes would work, give us the same advantages, and claim our recognition for the same reasons. All this on the common-sense level of matters of fact, which we are alone considering.

But matters of fact are not our only stock in trade. *Relations among purely mental ideas* form another sphere where true and false beliefs obtain, and here the beliefs are absolute, or unconditional. When they are true they bear the name either of definitions or of principles. It is either a principle or a definition that 1 and 1 make 2, that 2 and 1 make 3, and so on; that white differs less from gray than it does from black; that when the cause begins to act the effect also commences. Such propositions hold of all possible "ones," of all conceivable "whites" and "grays" and "causes." The objects here are mental objects. Their relations are perceptually obvious at a glance, and no sense-verification is necessary. Moreover, once true, always true, of those same mental objects. Truth here has an "eternal" character. If you can find a concrete thing anywhere that is "one" or "white" or "gray" or an "effect," then your principles will everlastingly apply to it. It is but a case of ascertaining the kind, and then applying the law of its kind to the particular object. You are sure to get truth if you can but name the kind rightly, for your mental relations hold good of everything of that kind without exception. If you, then, nevertheless, failed to get truth concretely, you would say that you had classed your real objects wrongly.

In this realm of mental relations, truth again is an affair of leading. We relate one abstract idea with another, framing in the end great systems of logical and mathematical truth, under the respective terms of which the sensible facts of experience eventually arrange themselves, so that our eternal truths hold good of realities also. The marriage of fact and theory is endlessly fertile. What we say is here already true in advance of special verification, *if we have subsumed our objects rightly.* Our ready-made ideal framework for all sorts of possible objects follows from the very structure of our thinking. We can no more play fast and loose with these abstract relations than we can do with our sense-experiences. They coerce us; we must treat them consistently, whether or not we like the results. The rules of addition apply to our debts as rigorously as to our assets. The hundredth decimal of π, the ratio of the circumference to its diameter, is predetermined ideally now, though no one may have computed it. If we should ever need the figure in our dealings with an actual circle we should need to have it given rightly, calculated by the usual rules; for it is the same kind of truth that those rules elsewhere calculate.

Between the coercions of the sensible order and those of the ideal order, our mind is thus wedged tightly. Our ideas must agree with realities, be such realities concrete or abstract; be they facts or be they principles, under penalty of endless inconsistency and frustration.

So far, intellectualists can raise no protest. They can only say that we have barely touched the skin of the matter.

Realities mean, then, either concrete facts, or abstract kinds of thing and relations perceived intuitively between them. They furthermore and thirdly mean, as things that new ideas of ours must no less take account of, the whole body of other truths already in our possession. But what now does "agreement" with such threefold realities mean?—to use again the definition that is current.

Here it is that pragmatism and intellectualism began to part company. Primarily, no doubt, to agree means to copy, but we saw that the mere word "clock" would do instead of a mental picture of its works, and that of many realities our ideas can only be symbols and not copies. "Past time," "power," "spontaneity,"—how can our mind copy such realities?

To "agree" in the widest sense with a reality *can only mean to be guided either straight up to it or into its surroundings, or to be put into such working touch with it as to handle either it or something connected with it better than if we disagreed.* Better either intellectually or practically! And often agreement will only mean that nothing contradictory from the quarter of that reality comes to interfere with the way in which our ideas guide us elsewhere. To copy a reality is, indeed, one very important way of agreeing with it, but it is far from being essential. The essential thing is the process of being guided. Any idea that helps us to *deal,* whether practically or intellectually, with either the reality or its belongings, that doesn't entangle our progress in frustrations, that *fits,* in fact, and adapts our life to the reality's whole setting, will agree sufficiently to meet the requirement. It will hold true of that reality.

Thus, *names* are just as "true" or "false" as definite mental pictures are. They set up similar verification-processes, and lead to fully equivalent practical results.

All human thinking gets discursified; we exchange ideas; we lend and borrow verifications, get them from one another by means of social intercourse. All truth thus gets verbally built out, stored up, and made available for every one. Hence, we must *talk* consistently just as we must *think* consistently: for both in talk and thought we deal with kinds. Names are arbitrary, but once understood they must be kept to. We mustn't now call Abel "Cain" or Cain "Abel." If we do, we ungear ourselves from the whole book of Genesis, and from all its connections with the universe of speech and fact down to the present time. We throw ourselves out of whatever truth that entire system of speech and fact may embody.

The overwhelming majority of our true ideas admit of no direct or face-to-face verification—those of past history, for example, as of Cain and Abel. The stream of time can be remounted only verbally, or verified indirectly by the present prolongations or effects of what the past harbored. Yet if they agree with these verbalities and effects, we can know that our *ideas of the past* are true. *As true as past time itself was,* so true was Julius Caesar, so true were antediluvian monsters, all in their proper dates and settings. That past time itself was, is guaranteed by its coherence with everything that's present. True as the present *is,* the past *was* also.

Agreement thus turns out to be essentially an affair of leading—leading that is useful because it is into quarters that contain objects that are important. True ideas lead us into useful verbal and conceptual quarters as well as directly up to useful sensible termini. They lead to consistency, stability and flowing human intercourse. They lead away from eccentricity and isolation, from foiled and barren thinking. The untrammelled flowing of the leading-process, its general freedom from clash and contradiction, passes for its indirect verification; but all roads lead to Rome, and in the end and eventually, all true processes must lead to the face of directly verifying sensible experiences *somewhere,* which somebody's ideas have copied.

Such is the large loose way in which the pragmatist interprets the word agreement. He treats it altogether practically. He lets it cover any process of conduction from a present idea to a future terminus, provided only it run prosperously. It is only thus that "scientific" ideas, flying as they do beyond common sense, can be said to agree with their realities. It is, as I have already said, *as if* reality were made of ether, atoms or electrons, but we mustn't think so literally. The term "energy" doesn't even pretend to stand for anything "objective." It is only a way of measuring the surface of phenomena so as to string their changes on a simple formula.

Yet in the choice of these man-made formulas we can not be capricious with impunity any more than we can be capricious on the common-sense practical level. We must find a theory that will *work;* and that means something extremely difficult; for our theory must mediate between all previous truths and certain new experiences. It must derange common sense and previous belief as little as possible, and it must lead to some sensible terminus or other that can be verified exactly. To "work" means both these things; and the squeeze is so tight that there is little loose play for any hypothesis. Our theories are wedged and controlled as nothing else is. Yet sometimes alternative theoretic formulas are equally compatible with all the truths we know, and then we choose between them for subjective reasons. We choose the kind of theory to which we are already partial; we follow "elegance" or "economy." Clerk-Maxwell somewhere says it would be "poor scientific taste" to choose the more complicated of two equally well-evidenced conceptions; and you will all agree with him. Truth in science is what gives us the maximum possible sum of satisfactions, taste included, but consistency both with previous truth and with novel fact is always the most imperious claimant.

I have led you through a very sandy desert. But now, if I may be allowed so vulgar an expression, we begin to taste the milk in the cocoanut. Our rationalist critics here discharge their batteries upon us, and to reply to them will take us out from all this dryness into full sight of a momentous philosophical alternative.

Our account of truth is an account of truths in the plural, of processes of leading, realized *in rebus* [in things], and having only this quality in common, that they *pay.* They pay by guiding us into or towards some part of a system that dips at numerous points into sense-percepts, which we may copy mentally or not, but with which at any rate we are now in the kind of commerce vaguely designated as verification. Truth for us is simply a collective name for verification-processes, just as health, wealth, strength, etc., are names for other processes connected with life, and also pursued because it pays to pursue them. Truth is *made,* just as health, wealth and strength are made, in the course of experience.

Here rationalism is instantaneously up in arms against us. I can imagine a rationalist to talk as follows:

"Truth is not made," he will say; "it absolutely obtains, being a unique relation that does not wait upon any process, but shoots straight over the head of experience, and hits its reality every time. Our belief that yon thing on the wall is a clock is true already, although no one in the whole history of the world should verify it. The bare quality of standing in that transcendent relation is what makes any thought true that possesses it, whether or not there be verification. You pragmatists put the cart before the horse in making truth's being reside in verification-processes. These are merely signs of its being, merely our lame ways of ascertaining after the fact, which of our ideas already has possessed the wondrous quality. The quality itself is timeless, like all essences and natures. Thoughts partake of it directly, as they partake of falsity or of irrelevancy. It can't be analyzed away into pragmatic consequences."

The whole plausibility of this rationalist tirade is due to the fact to which we have already paid so much attention. In our world, namely, abounding as it does in things of similar kinds and similarly associated, one verification serves for others of its kind, and one great use of knowing things is to be led not so much to them as to their associates, especially to human talk about them. The quality of truth, obtaining *ante rem* [before the thing], pragmatically means, then, the fact that in such a world innumerable ideas work better by their indirect or possible than by their direct and actual verification. Truth *ante rem* means only verifiability, then; or else it is a case of the stock rationalist trick of treating the *name* of a concrete phenomenal reality as an independent prior entity, and placing it behind the reality as its explanation. Professor Mach quotes somewhere an epigram of Lessing's:

> Said crafty Hans to Cousin Fritz,
> "Why is it, Cousin Fritz,
> That those ranked richest in the world,
> The most wealth do possess?"

Hans here treats the principle "wealth" as something distinct from the facts denoted by the man's being rich. It antedates them; the facts become only a sort of secondary coincidence with the rich man's essential nature.

In the case of "wealth" we all see the fallacy. We know that wealth is but a name for concrete processes that certain men's lives play a part in, and not a natural excellence found in Messrs. Rockefeller and Carnegie, but not in the rest of us.

Like wealth, health also lives *in rebus*. It is a name for processes, as digestion, circulation, sleep, etc., that go on happily, though in this instance we are more inclined to think of it as a principle and to say the man digests and sleeps so well *because* he is so healthy.

With "strength" we are, I think, more rationalistic still, and decidedly inclined to treat it as an excellence pre-existing in the man and explanatory of the herculean performances of his muscles.

With "truth" most people go over the border entirely, and treat the rationalistic account as self-evident. But really all these words in *th* are exactly similar. Truth exists *ante rem* just as much and as little as the other things do.

The scholastics, following Aristotle, made much of the distinction between habit and act. Health *in actu* means, among other things, good sleeping and digesting. But a healthy man need not always be sleeping, or always digesting, any more than a wealthy man need be always handling money, or a strong man always lifting weights. All such qualities sink to the status of "habits" between their times of exercise; and similarly truth becomes a habit of certain of our ideas and beliefs in their intervals of rest from their verifying activities. But those activities are the root of the whole matter, and the condition of their being any habit to exist in the intervals.

"The true," to put it very briefly, *is only the expedient in the way of our thinking, just as "the*

right" is only the expedient in the way of our behaving. Expedient in almost any fashion; and expedient in the long run and on the whole of course; for what meets expediently all the experience in sight won't necessarily meet all farther experiences equally satisfactorily. Experience, as we know, has ways of *boiling over,* and making us correct our present formulas.

The "absolutely" true, meaning what no farther experience will ever alter, is that ideal vanishing-point towards which we imagine that all our temporary truths will some day converge. It runs on all fours with the perfectly wise man, and with the absolutely complete experience; and, if these ideals are ever realized, they will all be realized together. Meanwhile we have to live to-day by what truth we can get to-day, and be ready to-morrow to call it falsehood. Ptolemaic astronomy, euclidean space, aristotelian logic, scholastic metaphysics, were expedient for centuries, but human experience has boiled over those limits, and we now call these things only relatively true, or true within those borders of experience. "Absolutely" they are false; for we know that those limits were casual, and might have been transcended by past theorists just as they are by present thinkers.

When new experiences lead to retrospective judgments, using the past tense, what these judgments utter *was* true, even though no past thinker had been led there. We live forwards, a Danish thinker has said, but we understand backwards. The present sheds a backward light on the world's previous processes. They may have been truth-processes for the actors in them. They are not so for one who knows the later revelations of the story.

This regulative notion of a potential better truth to be established later, possibly to be established some day absolutely, and having powers of retroactive legislation, turns its face, like all pragmatist notions, towards concreteness of fact, and towards the future. Like the half-truths, the absolute truth will have to be *made,* made as a relation incidental to the growth of a mass of verification-experience to which the half-true ideas are all along contributing their quota.

I have already insisted on the fact that truth is made largely out of previous truths. Men's beliefs at any time are so much experience *funded.* But the beliefs are themselves parts of the sum total of the world's experience, and become matter, therefore, for the next day's funding operations. So far as reality means experienceable reality, both it and the truths men gain about it are everlastingly in process of mutation—mutation towards a definite goal, it may be—but still mutation.

Mathematicians can solve problems with two variables. On the Newtonian theory, for instance, acceleration varies with distance, but distance also varies with acceleration. In the realm of truth-processes facts come independently and determine our beliefs provisionally. But these beliefs make us act, and as fast as they do so, they bring into sight or into existence new facts which re-determine the beliefs accordingly. So the whole coil and ball of truth, as it rolls up, is the product of a double influence. Truths emerge from facts; but they dip forward into facts again and add to them; which facts again create or reveal new truth (the word is indifferent) and so on indefinitely. The "facts" themselves meanwhile are not *true.* They simply *are.* Truth is the function of the beliefs that start and terminate among them.

The case is like a snowball's growth, due as it is to the distribution of the snow on the one hand, and to the successive pushes of the boys on the other, with these factors co-determining each other incessantly.

The most fateful point of difference between being a rationalist and being a pragmatist is now fully in sight. Experience is in mutation, and our psychological ascertainments of truth are in mutation—so much rationalism will allow; but never that either reality itself or truth itself is mutable. Reality stands complete and ready-made from all eternity, rationalism insists, and the agreement of our ideas with it is that unique unanalyzable virtue in them of which she has already told us. As that intrinsic excellence, their truth has nothing to do with our experiences. It adds nothing to the content of experience. It makes no difference to reality itself; it is supervenient, inert, static, a reflection merely. It doesn't *exist,* it *holds* or *obtains,* it belongs to another dimension from that of either facts or fact-relations, belongs, in short, to the epistemological dimension—and with that big word rationalism closes the discussion.

Thus, just as pragmatism faces forward to the future, so does rationalism here again face backward to a past eternity. True to her inveterate habit, rationalism reverts to "principles," and thinks that when an abstraction once is named, we own an oracular solution.

The tremendous pregnancy in the way of consequences for life of this radical difference of outlook will only become apparent in my later lectures. I wish meanwhile to close this lecture by showing that rationalism's sublimity does not save it from inanity.

When, namely, you ask rationalists, instead of accusing pragmatism of desecrating the notion of truth, to define it themselves by saying exactly what *they* understand by it, the only positive attempts I can think of are these two:

1. "Truth is the system of propositions which have an unconditional claim to be recognized as valid."

2. Truth is a name for all those judgments which we find ourselves under obligation to make by a kind of imperative duty.

The first thing that strikes one in such definitions is their unutterable triviality. They are absolutely true, of course, but absolutely insignificant until you handle them pragmatically. What do you mean by "claim" here, and what do you mean by "duty"? As summary names for the concrete reasons why thinking in true ways is overwhelmingly expedient and good for mortal men, it is all right to talk of claims on reality's part to be agreed with, and of obligations on our part to agree. We feel both the claims and the obligations, and we feel them for just those reasons.

But the rationalists who talk of claim and obligation *expressly say that they have nothing to do with our practical interests or personal reasons.* Our reasons for agreeing are psychological facts, they say, relative to each thinker, and to the accidents of his life. They are his evidence merely, they are no part of the life of truth itself. That life transacts itself in a purely logical or epistemological, as distinguished from a psychological, dimension, and its claims antedate and exceed all personal motivations whatsoever. Though neither man nor God should ever ascertain truth, the word would still have to be defined as that which *ought* to be ascertained and recognized.

There never was a more exquisite example of an idea abstracted from the concretes of experience and then used to oppose and negate what it was abstracted from.

Philosophy and common life abound in similar instances. The "sentimentalist fallacy" is to shed tears over abstract justice and generosity, beauty, etc., and never to know these qualities when you meet them in the street, because the circumstances make them vulgar. Thus I read in the privately printed biography of an eminently rationalistic mind: "It was strange that with such admiration for beauty in the abstract, my brother had no enthusiasm for fine architecture, for beautiful painting, or for flowers." And in almost the last philosophic work I have read, I find such passages as the following: "Justice is ideal, solely ideal. Reason conceives that it ought to exist, but experience shows that it can not. . . . Truth, which ought to be, can not be. . . . Reason is deformed by experience. As soon as reason enters experience it becomes contrary to reason."

The rationalist's fallacy here is exactly like the sentimentalist's. Both extract a quality from the muddy particulars of experience, and find it so pure when extracted that they contrast it with each and all its muddy instances as an opposite and higher nature. All the while it is *their* nature. It is the nature of truths to be validated, verified. It pays for our ideas to be validated. Our obligation to seek truth is part of our general obligation to do what pays. The payments true ideas bring are the sole why of our duty to follow them. Identical whys exist in the case of wealth and health.

Truth makes no other kind of claim and imposes no other kind of ought than health and wealth do. All these claims are conditional; the concrete benefits we gain are what we mean by calling the pursuit a duty. In the case of truth, untrue beliefs work as perniciously in the long run as true beliefs work beneficially. Talking abstractly, the quality "true" may thus be said to grow absolutely precious and the quality "untrue" absolutely damnable: the one may be called good, the other bad, unconditionally. We ought to think the true, we ought to shun the false, imperatively.

But if we treat all this abstraction literally and oppose it to its mother soil in experience, see what a preposterous position we work ourselves into.

We can not then take a step forward in our actual thinking. When shall I acknowledge this truth and when that? Shall the acknowledgment be loud?—or silent? If sometimes loud, sometimes silent, which *now?* When may a truth go into cold-storage in the encyclopedia? and when shall it come out for battle? Must I constantly be repeating the truth "twice two are four" because of its eternal claim on recognition? or is it sometimes irrelevant? Must my thoughts dwell night and day on my personal sins and blemishes, because I truly have them?—or may I sink and ignore them in order to be a decent social unit, and not a mass of morbid melancholy and apology?

It is quite evident that our obligation to acknowledge truth, so far from being unconditional, is tremendously conditioned. Truth with a big T, and in the singular, claims abstractly to be recognized, of course; but concrete truths in the plural need be recognized only when their recognition is expedient. A truth must always be preferred to a falsehood when both relate to the situation; but when neither does, truth is as little of a duty as falsehood. If you ask me what o'clock it is and I tell you that I live at 95 Irving Street, my answer may indeed be true, but you don't see why it is my duty to give it. A false address would be as much to the purpose.

With this admission that there are conditions that limit the application of the abstract imperative, *the pragmatistic treatment of truth sweeps back upon us in its fullness.* Our duty to agree with reality is seen to be grounded in a perfect jungle of concrete expediencies.

When Berkeley had explained what people meant by matter, people thought that he denied matter's existence. When Messrs. Schiller and Dewey now explain what people mean by truth, they are accused of denying *its* existence. These pragmatists destroy all objective standards, critics say, and put foolishness and wisdom on one level. A favorite formula for describing Mr. Schiller's doctrines and mine is that we are persons who think that by saying whatever you find it pleasant to say and calling it truth you fulfil every pragmatistic requirement.

I leave it to you to judge whether this be not an impudent slander. Pent in, as the pragmatist more than any one else sees himself to be, between the whole body of funded truths squeezed from the past and the coercions of the world of sense about him, who so well as he feels the immense pressure of objective control under which our minds perform their operations? If any one imagines that this law is lax, let him keep its commandment one day, says Emerson. We have heard much of late of the uses of the imagination in science.

It is high time to urge the use of a little imagination in philosophy. The unwillingness of some of our critics to read any but the silliest of possible meanings into our statements is as discreditable to their imaginations as anything I know in recent philosophic history. Schiller says the true is that which "works." Thereupon he is treated as one who limits verification to the lowest material utilities. Dewey says truth is what gives "satisfaction." He is treated as one who believes in calling everything true which, if it were true, would be pleasant.

Our critics certainly need more imagination of realities. I have honestly tried to stretch my own imagination and to read the best possible meaning into the rationalist conception, but I have to confess that it still completely baffles me. The notion of a reality calling on us to "agree" with it, and that for no reasons, but simply because its claim is "unconditional" or "transcendent," is one that I can make neither head nor tail of. I try to imagine myself as the sole reality in the world, and then to imagine what more I would "claim" if I were allowed to. If you suggest the possibility of my claiming that a mind should come into being from out of the void inane and stand and *copy* me, I can indeed imagine what the copying might mean, but I can conjure up no motive. What good it would do me to be copied, or what good it would do that mind to copy me, if further consequences are expressly and in principle ruled out as motives for the claim (as they are by our rationalist authorities) I can not fathom. When the Irishman's admirers ran him along to the place of banquet in a sedan chair with no bottom, he said, "Faith, if it wasn't for the honor of the thing, I might as well have come on foot." So here: but for the honor of the thing, I might as well have remained uncopied. Copying is one genuine mode of knowing (which for some strange reason our contemporary transcendentalists seem to be tumbling over each other to repudiate); but when we get beyond copying, and fall back on unnamed forms of agreeing that are expressly denied to be either copyings or leadings or fittings, or any other processes pragmatically definable, the *what* of the "agreement" claimed becomes as unintelligible as the why of it. Neither content nor motive can be imagined for it. It is an absolutely meaningless abstraction.

Surely in this field of truth it is the pragmatists and not the rationalists who are the more genuine defenders of the universe's rationality. . . .

I am well aware how odd it must seem to some of you to hear me say that an idea is "true" so long as to believe it is profitable to our lives. That it is *good,* for as much as it profits, you will gladly admit. If what we do by its aid is good, you will allow the idea itself to be good in so far forth, for we are the better for possessing it. But is it not a strange misuse of the word "truth," you will say, to call ideas also "true" for this reason? . . .

. . . Let me now say only this, that truth is *one species of good,* and not, as is usually supposed, a category distinct from good, and co-ordinate with it. *The true is the name of whatever proves itself to be good in the way of belief, and good, too, for definite, assignable reasons.* Surely you must admit this, that if there were *no* good for life in true ideas, or if the knowledge of them were positively disadvantageous and false ideas the only useful ones, then the current notion that truth is divine and precious, and its pursuit a duty, could never have grown up or become a dogma. In a world like that, our duty would be to *shun* truth, rather. But in this world, just as certain foods are not only agreeable to our taste, but good for our teeth, our stomach, and our tissues; so certain ideas are not only agreeable to think about, or agreeable as supporting other ideas that we are fond of, but they are also helpful in life's practical struggles. If there be any life that it is really better we should lead, and if there be any idea which, if believed in, would help us to lead that life, then it would be really *better for us* to believe in that idea, *unless, indeed, belief in it incidentally clashed with other greater vital benefits.*

"What would be better for us to believe!" This sounds very like a definition of truth. It comes very near to saying "what we *ought* to believe"; and in *that* definition none of you would find any oddity. Ought we ever not to believe what it is *better for us* to believe? And can we then keep the notion of what is better for us, and what is true for us, permanently apart?

Pragmatism says no, and I fully agree with her. Probably you also agree, so far as the abstract statement goes, but with a suspicion that if we practically did believe everything that made for good in our own personal lives, we should be found indulging all kinds of fancies about this world's affairs, and all kinds of sentimental superstitions about a world hereafter. Your suspicion here is undoubtedly well founded, and it is evident that something happens when you pass from the abstract to the concrete that complicates the situation.

I said just now that what is better for us to believe is true *unless the belief incidentally clashes with some other vital benefit.* Now in real life what vital benefits is any particular belief of ours most liable to clash with? What indeed except the vital benefits yielded by *other beliefs* when these prove incompatible with the first ones? In other words, the greatest enemy of any one of our truths may be the rest of our truths. Truths have once for all this desperate instinct of self-preservation and of desire to extinguish whatever contradicts them.

DOES "CONSCIOUSNESS" EXIST?

"Thoughts" and "things" are names for two sorts of object, which common sense will always find contrasted and will always practically oppose to each other. Philosophy, reflecting on the contrast, has varied in the past in her explanations of it, and may be expected to vary in the future. At first, "spirit and matter," "soul and body," stood for a pair of equipollent substances quite on a par in weight and interest. But one day Kant undermined the soul and brought in the transcendental ego, and ever since then the bipolar relation has been very much off its balance. The transcendental ego seems nowadays in rationalist quarters to stand for everything, in empiricist quarters for almost nothing. . . .

[T]he spiritual principle attenuates itself to a thoroughly ghostly condition, being only a name for the fact that the "content" of experience *is known.* It loses personal form and activity—these passing over to the content—and becomes a bare *Bewusstheit* [consciousness] or *Bewusstsein überhaupt* [consciousness in general], of which in its own right absolutely nothing can be said.

I believe that "consciousness," when once it has evaporated to this estate of pure diaphaneity, is on the point of disappearing altogether. It is the name of a nonentity, and has no right to a place among first principles. Those who still cling to it are clinging to a mere echo, the faint rumor left behind by the disappearing "soul" upon the air of philosophy. . . . For twenty years past I have mistrusted "consciousness" as an entity; for seven or

From the *Journal of Philosophy, Psychology and Scientific Methods*, Vol. I, No. 18, September, 1904.

eight years past I have suggested its non-existence to my students, and tried to give them its pragmatic equivalent in realities of experience. It seems to me that the hour is ripe for it to be openly and universally discarded.

To deny plumply that "consciousness" exists seems so absurd on the face of it—for undeniably "thoughts" do exist—that I fear some readers will follow me no farther. Let me then immediately explain that I mean only to deny that the word stands for an entity, but to insist most emphatically that it does stand for a function. There is, I mean, no aboriginal stuff or quality of being, contrasted with that of which material objects are made, out of which our thoughts of them are made; but there is a function in experience which thoughts perform, and for the performance of which this quality of being is invoked. That function is *knowing*. "Consciousness" of supposed necessary to explain the fact that things not only are, but get reported, are known. Whoever blots out the notion of consciousness from his list of first principles must still provide in some way for that function's being carried on.

1

My thesis is that if we start with the supposition that there is only one primal stuff or material in the world, a stuff of which everything is composed, and if we call that stuff "pure experience," then knowing can easily be explained as a particular sort of relation towards one another into which portions of pure experience may enter. The relation itself is a part of pure experience; one of its "terms" becomes the subject or bearer of the knowledge, the knower, the other becomes the object known. This will need much explanation before it can be understood. The best way to get it understood is to contrast it with the alternative view; and for that we may take the recentest alternative, that in which the evaporation of the definite soul-substance has proceeded as far as it can go without being yet complete. If neo-Kantism has expelled earlier forms of dualism, we shall have expelled all forms if we are able to expel neo-Kantism in its turn.

For the thinkers I call neo-Kantian, the word consciousness to-day does no more than signalize the fact that experience is indefeasibly dualistic in structure. It means that not subject, not object, but object-plus-subject is the minimum that can actually be. The subject-object distinction meanwhile is entirely different from that between mind and matter, from that between body and soul. Souls were detachable, had separate destinies; things could happen to them. To consciousness as such nothing can happen, for, timeless itself, it is only a witness of happenings in time, in which it plays no part. It is, in a word, but the logical correlative of "content" in an Experience of which the peculiarity is *that fact comes to light* in it, that *awareness of content* takes place. Consciousness as such is entirely impersonal—"self" and its activities belong to the content. To say that I am self-conscious, or conscious of putting forth volition, means only that certain contents, for which "self" and "effort of will" are the names, are not without witness as they occur.

Thus, for these belated drinkers at the Kantian springs, we should have to admit consciousness as an "epistemological" necessity, even if we had no direct evidence of its being there.

But in addition to this, we are supposed by almost every one to have an immediate consciousness of consciousness itself. When the world of outer facts ceases to be materially present, and we merely recall it in memory, or fancy it, the consciousness is believed to stand out and to be felt as a kind of impalpable inner flowing, which, once known in this sort of experience, may equally be detected in presentations of the outer world. . . .

This supposes that the consciousness is one element, moment, factor—call it what you like—of an experience of essentially dualistic inner constitution, from which, if you abstract the content, the consciousness will remain revealed to its own eye. Experience, at this rate, would be much like a paint of which the world pictures were made. Paint has a dual constitution, involving, as it does, a menstruum (oil, size or what not) and a mass of content in the form of pigment suspended therein. We can get the pure menstruum by letting the pigment settle, and the pure pigment by pouring off the size or oil. We operate here by physical subtraction; and the usual view is, that by mental subtraction we can separate the two factors of experience in an analogous way—not isolating them entirely, but distinguishing them enough to know that they are two.

2

Now my contention is exactly the reverse of this. *Experience, I believe, has no such inner duplicity; and the separation of it into consciousness and content comes, not by way of subtraction, but by way of addition*—the addition, to a given concrete piece of it, of other sets of experiences, in connection with which severally its use or function may be of two different kinds.

The paint will also serve here as an illustration. In a pot in a paint-shop, along with other paints, it serves in its entirety as so much saleable matter. Spread on a canvas, with other paints around it, it represents, on the contrary, a feature in a picture and performs a spiritual function. Just so, I maintain, does a given undivided portion of experience, taken in one context of associates, play the part of a knower, of a state of mind, of "consciousness"; while in a different context the same undivided bit of experience plays the part of a thing known, of an objective "content." In a word, in one group it figures as a thought, in another group as a thing. And, since it can figure in both groups simultaneously we have every right to speak of it as subjective and objective both at once. The dualism connoted by such double-barrelled terms as "experience," "phenomenon," "datum," "*Vorfindung*"—terms which, in philosophy at any rate, tend more and more to replace the single-barrelled terms of "thought" and "thing"—that dualism, I say, is still preserved in this account, but reinterpreted, so that, instead of being mysterious and elusive, it becomes verifiable and concrete. It is an affair of relations, it falls outside, not inside, the single experience considered, and can always be particularized and defined.

The entering wedge for this more concrete way of understanding the dualism was fashioned by Locke when he made the word "idea" stand indifferently for thing and thought, and by Berkeley when he said that what common sense means by realities is exactly what the philosopher means by ideas. Neither Locke nor Berkeley thought his truth out into perfect clearness, but it seems to me that the conception I am defending does little more than consistently carry out the "pragmatic" method which they were the first to use.

If the reader will take his own experiences, he will see what I mean. Let him begin with a perceptual experience, the "presentation," so called, of a physical object, his actual field of vision, the room he sits in, with the book he is reading as its centre; and let him for the present treat this complex object in the commonsense way as being "really" what it seems to be, namely, a collection of physical things cut out from an environing world of other physical things with which these physical things have actual or potential relations. Now at the same time it is just *those self-same things* which his mind, as we say, perceives; and the whole philosophy of perception from Democritus's time downwards has been just one long wrangle over the paradox that what is evidently one reality should be in two places at once, both in outer space and in a person's mind. "Representative" theories of perception avoid the logical paradox, but on the other hand they violate the reader's sense of life, which knows no intervening mental image but seems to see the room and the book immediately just as they physically exist.

The puzzle of how the one identical room can be in two places is at bottom just the puzzle of how one identical point can be on two lines. It can, if it be situated at their intersection; and similarly, if the "pure experience" of the room were a place of intersection of two processes, which connected it with different groups of associates, respectively, it could be counted twice over, as belonging to either group, and spoken of loosely as existing in two places, although it would remain all the time a numerically single thing.

Well, the experience is a member of diverse processes that can be followed away from it along entirely different lines. The one self-identical thing has so many relations to the rest of experience that you can take it in disparate systems of association, and treat it as belonging with opposite contexts. In one of these contexts it is your "field of consciousness"; in another it is "the room in which you sit," and it enters both contexts in its wholeness, giving no pretext for being said to attach itself to consciousness by one of its parts or aspects, and to outer reality by another. What are the two processes, now, into which the room-experience simultaneously enters in this way?

One of them is the reader's personal biography, the other is the history of the house of which the room is part. The presentation, the experience, the *that* in short (for until we have decided *what* it is it must be a mere *that*) is the last term of a train of sensations, emotions, decisions, movements, classifications, expectations, etc., ending in the present, and the first term of a series of similar 'inner' operations extending into the future, on the reader's part. On the other hand, the very same *that* is the *terminus ad quem* of a lot of previous physical operations, carpentering, papering, furnishing, warming, etc., and the *terminus a quo* of a lot of future ones, in which it will be concerned when undergoing the destiny of a physical room. The physical and the mental operations form curiously incompatible groups. As a room, the experience has occupied that spot and had that environment for thirty years. As your field of consciousness it may never have existed until now. As a room, attention will go on to discover endless new details in it. As your mental state merely, few new ones will emerge under attention's eye. As a room, it will take an earthquake, or a gang of men, and in any case a certain amount of time, to destroy it. As your subjective state, the closing of your eyes, or any instantaneous play of your fancy will suffice. In the real world, fire will consume it. In your mind, you can let fire play over it without effect. As an outer object you must pay so much a month to inhabit it. As an inner content, you may occupy it for any length of time rent-free. If, in short, you follow it in the mental direction, taking it along with events of personal biography solely, all sorts of things are true of it which are false, and false of it which are true if you treat it as a real thing experienced, follow it in the physical direction, and relate it to associates in the outer world.

3

So far, all seems plain sailing, but my thesis will probably grow less plausible to the reader when I pass from percepts to concepts, or from the case of things presented to that of things remote. I believe, nevertheless, that here also the same law holds good. If we take conceptual manifolds, or memories, or fancies, they also are in their first intention mere bits of pure experience, and, as such, are single *thats* which act in one context as objects, and in another context figure as mental states. By taking them in their first intention, I mean ignoring their relation to possible perceptual experiences with which they may be connected, which they may lead to and terminate in, and which then they may be supposed to "represent." Taking them in this way first, we confine the problem to a world merely "thought-of" and not directly felt or seen. This world, just like the world of percepts, comes to us at first as a chaos of experiences, but lines of order soon get traced. We find that any bit of it which we may cut out as an example is connected with distinct groups of associates, just as our perceptual experiences are, that these associates link themselves with it by different relations, and that one forms the inner history of a person, while the other acts as an impersonal "objective" world, either spatial and temporal, or else merely logical or mathematical, or otherwise "ideal."

The first obstacle on the part of the reader to seeing that these non-perceptual experiences have objectivity as well as subjectivity will probably be due to the intrusion into his mind of *percepts,* that third group of associates with which the non-perceptual experiences have relations, and which, as a whole, they "represent," standing to them as thoughts to things. This important function of the non-perceptual experiences complicates the question and confuses it; for, so used are we to treat percepts as the sole genuine realities that, unless we keep them out of the discussion, we tend altogether to overlook the objectivity that lies in non-perceptual experiences by themselves. We treat them, "knowing" percepts as they do, as through and through subjective, and say that they are wholly constituted of the stuff called consciousness, using this term now for a kind of entity, after the fashion which I am seeking to refute.

Abstracting, then, from percepts altogether, what I maintain is, that any single non-perceptual experience tends to get counted twice over, just as a perceptual experience does, figuring in one context as an object or field of objects, in another as a state of mind: and all this without the least internal self-diremption on its own part into consciousness and content. It is all consciousness in one taking; and, in the other, all content. . . .

And yet, just as the seen room (to go back to our late example) is *also* a field of consciousness, so the conceived or recollected room is *also* a state of mind; and the doubling-up of the experience has in both cases similar grounds.

The room thought-of, namely, has many thought-of couplings with many thought-of things. Some of couplings are inconstant, others are stable. In the reader's personal history the room occupies a single date—he saw it only once perhaps, a year ago. Of the house's history, on the other hand, it forms a permanent ingredient. Some couplings have the curious stubbornness, to borrow Royce's term of fact; others show the fluidity of fancy—we let them come and go as we please. Grouped with the rest of its house, with the name of its town, of its owner, builder, value, decorative plan, the room maintains a definite foothold, to which, if we try to loosen it, it tends to return, and to reassert itself with force. With these associates, in a word, it coheres, while to other houses, other towns, other owners, etc., it shows no tendency to cohere at all. The two collections, first of its cohesive, and, second, of its loose associates, inevitably come to be contrasted. We call the first collection the system of external realities, in the midst of which the room, as "real," exists; the other we call the stream of our internal thinking, in which, as a "mental image," it for a moment floats. The room thus again gets counted twice over. It plays two different roles, being thought-of-an-object, and the object-thought-of, both in one; and all this without paradox or mystery, just as the same material thing may be both low and high, or small and great, or bad and good, because of its relations to opposite parts of an environing world.

As "subjective" we say that the experience represents; as "objective" it is represented. What represents and what is represented is here numerically the same; but we must remember that no dualism of being represented and representing resides in the experience *per se.*

In its pure state, or when isolated, there is no self-splitting of it into consciousness and what the consciousness is "of." Its subjectivity and objectivity are functional attributes solely, realized only when the experience is "taken," *i.e.,* talked-of, twice, considered along with its two differing contexts respectively, by a new retrospective experience, of which that whole past complication now forms the fresh content.

The instant field of the present is at all times what I call the "pure" experience. It is only virtually or potentially either object or subject as yet. For the time being, it is plain, un-qualified actuality, or existence, a simple *that.* In this *naïf* immediacy it is of course *valid;* it is *there,* we *act* upon it; and the doubling of it in retrospection into a state of mind and a reality intended thereby, is just one of the acts. The "state of mind," first treated explicitly as such in retrospection, will stand corrected or confirmed, and the retrospective experience in its turn will get a similar treatment; but the immediate experience in its passing is always "truth," practical truth, *something to act on,* at its own movement. If the world were then and there to go out like a candle, it would remain truth absolute and objective, for it would be "the last word," would have no critic, and no one would ever oppose the thought in it to the reality intended.

I think I may now claim to have made my thesis clear. Consciousness connotes a kind of external relation, and does not denote a special stuff or way of being. *The peculiarity of our experiences, that they not only are, but are known, which their 'conscious' quality is invoked to explain, is better explained by their relations—these relations themselves being experiences—to one another.*

43

NIETZSCHE

1844–1900

Friedrich Nietzsche was born in Röcken, Germany. His father and both grandfathers were Lutheran ministers. When he was four his father died, leaving him and his sister to be raised by his mother and grandmother. As a young man at the famous *Schulpforta,* he excelled in the study of ancient languages, religion, literature, and philosophy, especially the ancient Greeks—his favorite was Plato. He entered the University of Bonn but found the students and professors so "shallow" and "unphilosophical" that he transferred to Leipzig. Inspired by Schopenhauer's philosophy and Richard Wagner's music, Nietzsche began writing and publishing important papers. He became such a brilliant student that the University of Basel in Switzerland offered him professorship before he even completed his doctorate at Leipzig. He accepted and a year later, while only twenty-four, was awarded the doctorate without an examination.

At Basel, Nietzsche became friends with Richard Wagner. He taught there for ten years and then resigned so that he could work full time on his various books. He produced fourteen highly original and provocative works. Among his most influential are *Thus Spake Zarathustra* (1883, 1884, and 1885, published in three installments), *Beyond Good and Evil* (1886), *The Genealogy of Morals* (1887), *The Anarchist* (1888), and *The Will to Power* (published posthumously in 1901).

In *Beyond Good and Evil,* our first selection, Nietzsche argues that concepts like "good," "bad," and "evil" come about through the weak trying to corrupt the strong, what he calls the "transvaluation of classical values." Religion is part of the process, especially the "philosophically blind" Jewish and Christian priests who "transvalue" human biological and psychological nature. Philosophy, too, is guilty, and Nietzsche mounts an equally searing attack on philosophers, suggesting that philosophers are as blinded by the "chimera" of "objective knowledge" as much as the Christians are blinded from the truth by their concept of God. The only remedy is truth, itself subjective and perspectival, which is created not by the weak but by the strong, through the will to power.

Nietzsche wanted to literally revolutionize philosophy by taking it back to its pre-Socratic, Sophist roots. According to him, the only true morality is that of the powerful imposing their will upon the weak, much in the way as espoused by the authoritarian nihilist Thrasymachus in the fifth century B.C.E. To "know" for Nietzsche means to *invent,* and to invent *authentically* for human beings means to lie. Traditional lying is inauthentic lying in which one lies using the terms and methods of religious, political, and educational institutions; this is but an elaborate form of *self*-deception.

To lie authentically according to Nietzsche is the very essence of authentic creativity because it subjugates others to one's will to power. One thereby forces reality into a shape to which others must then bend. According to Nietzsche, only a few individuals are brave enough to retain their authentic power after passing through the self-destructive gauntlet of social "normalization." Most people get absorbed by the previous lies imposed upon them through institutions that are themselves the decaying remnants of others' will to power. To use language is to lie, for language works by lying. Words deny what is real—the perpetual flux of ephemeral things—by imposing fictitious similarities between appearances through the power of repetition.

While many other philosophers of the time, most notably Kierkegaard (1813–1855), argued for individual identity Nietzsche claims that there is no true individual identity, no authentic personal self. The concept of a self is but a clever lie and self-deception. The only *authentic* action left to the conscious mind is the willful construction of *masks* with which to further exert unto the otherwise insubstantial world its own will to power. Language is such a mask, imposed upon us "as a condition of life," which because of the fact that it *must* by its very nature lie becomes the source of new creative possibilities.

Language in Nietzsche's view is a "mobile army of metaphors." Because language in its origin was metaphoric, language had the same origin and function as poetry. The division between the "literal" "scientific," and "logical," nature of language, on the one hand, and its "metaphoric," "figurative," or "poetic" nature on the other, Nietzsche views as wholly artificial. He says this division is the leading cause of error in philosophy. In his voluminous writings he attempts to return language to its original, primordial function as poetry. Indeed, Nietzsche refers to his philosophical works as elaborate "poems." They do not provide philosophical insights into being itself, some *"true reality,"* but are merely *poetical* interpretations of being.

But not all interpretations are created equal. The powerful poetic lies that "affirm life"— what following Thrasymachus he calls the *noble* lies—he regards as *true*. Common lies, such as found in both Platonism and Christianity, Nietzsche condemns as bad poetry consisting of ignoble lies. For both Platonism and Christianity deny reality for what it really is, a chaotic flux to be molded in the image of each will. They set up a false and unfulfillable longing for another world through the theory of formal ideas, heaven, and so on. Nietzsche claims that what these other-worldly philosophical and religious congregations truly long for are *nothingness* and *death*. Religions are not life-affirming but life-denying. This, in Nietzsche's view, makes them utterly decrepit and false.

Nietzsche attacks all traditional forms of authority, including, and most of all, morality. In stating that "slave-morality is essentially the morality of utility," he means to attack the utilitarian systems of the time, in particular that of John Stuart Mill (Chapter 38). Again, in his view, nowhere is this more evident than in religion, which is the social machinery for "turning values upside down," and the religion that is the most culpable is Christianity. In *The Will to Power,* from which the second selection is taken, he calls Christianity the most "fatal and seductive lie that has ever yet existed" for the suppression of humanity, urging everyone to declare "open war with it." Along with a call to arms against Christianity, Nietzsche here presents his perspectival analysis of truth and an instrumentalist theory of knowledge.

BEYOND GOOD AND EVIL

PREFACE

Supposing that Truth is a woman—what then? Is there not ground for suspecting that all philosophers, in so far as they have been dogmatists, have failed to understand women— that the terrible seriousness and clumsy importunity with which they have usually paid their addresses to Truth, have been unskilled and unseemly methods for winning a woman? Certainly she has never allowed herself to be won; and at present every kind of dogma stands with sad and discouraged mien—*if,* indeed, it stands at all! For there are scoffers who maintain that it has fallen, that all dogma lies on the ground—nay more, that it is at its last gasp. But to speak seriously, there are good grounds for hoping that all dogmatising in philosophy, whatever solemn, whatever conclusive and decided airs it has assumed, may have been only a noble puerilism and tyronism; and probably the time is at hand when it will be once and again understood *what* has actually sufficed for the basis of such imposing and absolute philosophical edifices as the dogmatists have hitherto reared: perhaps some popular superstition of immemorial time (such as the soul-superstition, which, in the form of subject- and ego-superstition, has not yet ceased doing mischief): perhaps some play upon words, a deception on the part of grammar, or an audacious generalisation of very restricted, very personal, very human—all-too-human facts. The philosophy of the dogmatists, it is to be hoped, was only a promise for thousands of years afterwards, as was astrology in still earlier times, in the service of which probably more labour, gold, acuteness, and patience have been spent than on any actual science hitherto: we owe to it, and to its "super-terrestrial" pretensions in Asia and Egypt, the grand style of architecture. It seems that in order to inscribe themselves upon the heart of humanity with everlasting claims, all great things have first to wander about the earth as enormous and awe-inspiring caricatures: dogmatic philosophy has been a caricature of this kind—for instance, the Vedanta doctrine in Asia, and Platonism in Europe. Let us not be ungrateful to it, although it must certainly be confessed that the worst, the most tiresome, and the most dangerous of errors hitherto has been a dogmatist error—namely, Plato's invention of Pure Spirit and the Good in Itself. But now when it has been surmounted, when Europe, rid of this nightmare, can again draw breath freely and at least enjoy a healthier—sleep, we, *whose duty is wakefulness itself,* are the heirs of all the strength which the struggle against this error has fostered. It amounted to the very inversion of truth, and the denial of the *perspective*—the fundamental condition— of life, to speak of Spirit and the Good as Plato spoke of them; indeed one might ask, as a physician: "How did such a malady attack that finest product of antiquity, Plato? Had the wicked Socrates really corrupted him? Was Socrates after all a corrupter of youths, and deserved his hemlock?" But the struggle against Plato, or—to speak plainer, and for the "people"—the struggle against the ecclesiastical oppression of millenniums of Christianity (for Christianity is Platonism for the "people"), produced in Europe a magnificent tension

From Friedrich Nietzsche, *Beyond Good and Evil,* trans. Helen Zimmern.

of soul, such as had not existed anywhere previously; with such a tensely strained bow one can now aim at the furthest goals. As a matter of fact, the European feels this tension as a state of distress, and twice attempts have been made in grand style to unbend the bow: once by means of Jesuitism, and the second time by means of democratic enlightenment— which, with the aid of liberty of the press and newspaper-reading, might, in fact, bring it about that the spirit would not so easily find itself in "distress"! (The Germans invented gunpowder—all credit to them! But they again made things square—they invented print- ing.) But we, who are neither Jesuits, nor democrats, nor even sufficiently Germans, we *good Europeans,* and free, *very* free spirits—we have it still, all the distress of spirit and all the tension of its bow! And perhaps also the arrow, the duty, and, who knows? *the goal to aim at.* . . .

SILS-MARIA, UPPER ENGADINE,
June 1885

PREJUDICES OF PHILOSOPHERS

The Will to Truth, which is to tempt us to many a hazardous enterprise, the famous Truth- fulness of which all philosophers have hitherto spoken with respect, what questions has this Will to Truth not laid before us! What strange, perplexing, questionable questions! It is already a long story; yet it seems as if it were hardly commenced. Is it any wonder if we at last grow distrustful, lose patience, and turn impatiently away? That this Sphinx teaches us at last to ask questions ourselves? *Who* is it really that puts questions to us here? *What* really is this "Will to Truth" in us? In fact we made a long halt at the question as to the origin of this Will—until at last we came to an absolute standstill before a yet more fundamental question. We inquired about the *value* of this Will. Granted that we want the truth: *why not rather* untruth? And uncertainty? Even ignorance? The problem of the value of truth presented itself before us—or was it we who presented ourselves before the problem? Which of us is the Oedipus here? Which the Sphinx? It would seem to be a rendezvous of questions and notes of interrogation. And could it be believed that it at last seems to us as if the problem had never been propounded before, as if we were the first to discern it, get a sight of it, and *risk raising* it. For there is risk in raising it, perhaps there is no greater risk.

"*How could* anything originate out of its opposite? For example, truth out of error? or the Will to Truth out of the will to deception? or the generous deed out of selfishness? or the pure sun-bright vision of the wise man out of covetousness? Such genesis is impossible; whoever dreams of it is a fool, nay, worse than a fool; things of the highest value must have a different origin, an origin of *their own*—in this transitory, seductive, illusory, paltry world, in this turmoil of delusion and cupidity, they cannot have their source. But rather in the lap of Being, in the intransitory, in the concealed God, in the 'Thing-in-itself'—*there* must be their source, and nowhere else!"—This mode of reasoning discloses the typical prejudice by which metaphysicians of all times can be recognised, this mode of valuation is at the back of all their logical procedure; through this "belief" of theirs, they exert themselves for their "knowledge," for something that is in the end solemnly christened "the Truth." The fundamental belief of metaphysicians is *the belief in antitheses of values.* It never occurred even to the wariest of them to doubt here on the very threshold (where doubt, however, was most necessary); though they had made a solemn vow, "*de omnibus dubitandum.*" For it may be doubted, firstly, whether antitheses exist at all; and secondly, whether the popular valuations and antitheses of value upon which metaphysicians have set their seal, are not perhaps merely superficial estimates, merely provisional perspectives, besides being probably made from some corner, perhaps from below—"frog perspectives," as it were, to borrow an expression current among painters. In spite of all the value which may belong to the true, the positive, and the unselfish, it might be possible that a higher and more fundamental value for life generally should be assigned to pretence, to the will to delusion, to selfishness, and cupidity. It might even be possible that *what* constitutes the value of those good and respected things, consists precisely in their being insidiously related, knotted, and crocheted to these evil and apparently opposed things—perhaps even in being essentially identical with them. Perhaps! But who wishes to concern himself with such dangerous "Perhapses"! For that investigation one must await the advent of a new order of philosophers, such as will have other tastes and inclinations, the reverse of those hitherto prevalent—philosophers of the dangerous "Perhaps" in every sense of the term. And to speak in all seriousness, I see such new philosophers beginning to appear.

Having kept a sharp eye on philosophers, and having read between their lines long enough, I now say to myself that the greater part of conscious thinking must be counted amongst the instinctive functions, and it is so even in the case of philosophical thinking; one has here to learn anew, as one learned anew about heredity and "innateness." As little as the act of birth comes into consideration in the whole process and procedure of heredity, just as little is "being-conscious" *opposed* to the instinctive in any decisive sense; the greater part of the conscious thinking of a philosopher is secretly influenced by his instincts, and forced into definite channels. And behind all logic and its seeming sovereignty of movement, there are valuations, or to speak more plainly, physiological demands, for the maintenance of a definite mode of life. For example, that the certain is worth more than the uncertain, that illusion is less valuable than "truth": such valuations, in spite of their regulative importance for *us,* might notwithstanding be only superficial valuations, special kinds of *niaiserie,* such as may be necessary for the maintenance of beings such as ourselves. Supposing, in effect, that man is not just the "measure of things." . . .

The falseness of an opinion is not for us any objection to it: it is here, perhaps, that our new language sounds most strangely. The question is, how far an opinion is life-furthering, life-preserving, species-preserving, perhaps species-rearing; and we are fundamentally inclined to maintain that the falsest opinions (to which the synthetic judgments *a priori* belong), are the most indispensable to us; that without a recognition of logical fictions, without a comparison of reality with the purely *imagined* world of the absolute and immutable, without a constant counterfeiting of the world by means of numbers, man could not live—that the renunciation of false opinions would be a renunciation of life, a negation of life. *To recognise untruth as a condition of life:* that is certainly to impugn the traditional ideas of value in a dangerous manner, and a philosophy which ventures to do so, has thereby alone placed itself beyond good and evil.

That which causes philosophers to be regarded half-distrustfully and half-mockingly, is not the oft-repeated discovery how innocent they are—how often and easily they make mistakes and lose their way, in short, how childish and childlike they are,—but that there is not enough honest dealing with them, whereas they all raise a loud and virtuous outcry when the problem of truthfulness is even hinted at in the remotest manner. They all pose as though their real opinions had been discovered and attained through the self-evolving of a cold, pure, divinely indifferent dialectic (in contrast to all sorts of mystics, who, fairer and foolisher, talk of "inspiration"); whereas, in fact, a prejudiced proposition, idea, or "suggestion," which is generally their heart's desire abstracted and refined, is defended by them with arguments sought out after the event. They are all advocates who do not wish to be regarded as such, generally astute defenders, also, of their prejudices, which they dub "truths"—and *very* far from having the conscience which bravely admits this to itself; very far from having the good taste of the courage which goes so far as to let this be understood, perhaps to warn friend or foe, or in cheerful confidence and self-ridicule. The spectacle of the Tartuffery of old Kant, equally stiff and decent, with which he entices us into the dialectic by-ways that lead (more correctly mislead) to his "categorical imperative"—makes us fastidious ones smile, we who find no small amusement in spying out the subtle tricks of old moralists and ethical preachers. Or, still more so, the hocus-pocus in mathematical form, by means of which Spinoza has as it were clad his philosophy in mail and mask—in fact, the "love of *his* wisdom," to translate the term fairly and squarely—in order thereby to strike terror at once into the heart of the assailant who should dare to cast a glance on that invincible maiden, that Pallas Athene:—how much of personal timidity and vulnerability does this masquerade of a sickly recluse betray!

It has gradually become clear to me what every great philosophy up till now has consisted of—namely, the confession of its originator, and a species of involuntary and unconscious auto-biography; and moreover that the moral (or immoral) purpose in every philosophy has constituted the true vital germ out of which the entire plant has always grown. Indeed, to understand how the abstrusest metaphysical assertions of a philosopher have been arrived at, it is always well (and wise) to first ask oneself: "What morality do they (or does he) aim at?" Accordingly, I do not believe that an "impulse to knowledge" is the father of philosophy; but that another impulse, here as elsewhere, has only made use of knowledge (and mistaken knowledge!) as an instrument. But whoever considers the fundamental impulses of man with a view to determining how far they may have here acted as *inspiring* genii (or as demons and cobolds), will find that they have all practised philosophy at one time or another, and that each one of them would have been only too glad to look upon itself as the ultimate end of existence and the legitimate *lord* over all the other impulses. For every impulse is imperious, and as *such*, attempts to philosophise. To be sure, in the case of scholars, in the case of really scientific men, it may be otherwise—"better," if you will; there may really be such a thing as an "impulse to knowledge," some kind of small, independent clockwork, which, when well wound up, works away industriously to that end, *without* the rest of the scholarly impulses taking any material part therein. The actual "interests" of the scholar, therefore, are generally in quite another direction—in the family, perhaps, or in money-making, or in politics; it is, in fact, almost indifferent at what point of research his little machine is placed, and whether the hopeful young worker becomes a good philologist, a mushroom specialist, or a chemist; he is not *characterised* by becoming this or that. In the philosopher, on the contrary, there is absolutely nothing impersonal; and above all, his morality furnishes a decided and decisive testimony as to *who he is,*—that is to say, in what order the deepest impulses of his nature stand to each other.

You desire to *live* "according to Nature"? Oh, you noble Stoics, what fraud of words! Imagine to yourselves a being like Nature, boundlessly extravagant, boundlessly indifferent, without purpose or consideration, without pity or justice, at once fruitful and barren and uncertain: imagine to yourselves *indifference* as a power—how *could* you live in accordance with such indifference? To live—is not that just endeavouring to be otherwise than this Nature? Is not living valuing, preferring, being unjust, being limited, endeavouring to be different? And granted that your imperative, "living according to Nature," means actually the same as "living according to life"—how could you do *differently*? Why should you make a principle out of what you yourselves are, and must be? In reality, however, it is quite otherwise with you: while you pretend to read with rapture the canon of your law in Nature, you want something quite the contrary, you extraordinary stage-players and self-deluders! In your pride you wish to dictate your morals and ideals to Nature, to Nature herself, and to incorporate them therein; you insist that it shall be Nature "according to the Stoa," and would like everything to be made after your own image, as a vast, eternal glorification and generalisation of Stoicism! With all your love for truth, you have forced yourselves so long, so persistently, and with such hypnotic rigidity to see Nature *falsely,* that is to say, Stoically, that you are no longer able to see it otherwise—and to crown all, some unfathomable superciliousness gives you the Bedlamite hope that *because* you are able to tyrannise over yourselves—Stoicism is self-tyranny—Nature will also allow herself to be tyrannised over: is not the Stoic a *part* of Nature? . . . But this is an old and everlasting story: what happened in old times with the Stoics still happens to-day, as soon as ever a philosophy begins to believe in itself. It always creates the world in its own image; it cannot do otherwise; philosophy is this tyrannical impulse itself, the most spiritual Will to Power, the will to "creation of the world," the will to the *causa prima.*

The eagerness and subtlety, I should even say craftiness, with which the problem of "the real and the apparent world" is dealt with at present throughout Europe, furnishes food for thought and attention; and he who hears only a "Will to Truth" in the background, and nothing else, cannot certainly boast of the sharpest ears. In rare and isolated cases, it may really have happened that such a Will to Truth—a certain extravagant and adventurous pluck, a metaphysician's ambition of the forlorn hope—has participated therein: that which in the end always prefers a handful of "certainty" to a whole cartload of beautiful possibilities; there may even be puritanical fanatics of conscience, who prefer to put their last trust in a sure nothing, rather than in an uncertain something. But that is Nihilism, and the sign of a despairing, mortally wearied soul, notwithstanding the courageous bearing such a virtue may display. It seems, however, to be otherwise with stronger and livelier thinkers who are still eager for life. In that they side *against* appearance, and speak superciliously of "perspective," in that they rank the credibility of their own bodies about as low as the credibility of the ocular evidence that "the earth stands still," and thus, apparently, allowing with complacency their securest possession to escape (for what does one at present believe in more firmly than in one's body?),—who knows if they are not really trying to win back something which was formerly an even *securer* possession, something of the old domain of the faith of former times, perhaps the "immortal soul," perhaps "the old God," in short, ideas by which they could live better, that is to say, more vigorously and more joyously, than by "modern ideas"? There is *distrust* of these modern ideas in this mode of looking at things, a disbelief in all that has been constructed yesterday and to-day; there is perhaps some slight admixture of satiety and scorn, which can no longer endure the *bric-à-brac* of ideas of the most varied origin, such as so-called Positivism at present throws on the market; a disgust of the more refined taste at the village-fair motleyness and patchiness of all these reality-philosophasters, in whom there is nothing either new or true, except this motleyness. Therein it seems to me that we should agree with those sceptical anti-realists and knowledge-microscopists of the present day; their instinct, which repels them from *modern* reality, is unrefuted . . . what do their retrograde by-paths concern us! The main thing about them is *not* that they wish to go "back," but that they wish to get *away* therefrom. A little *more* strength, swing, courage, and artistic power, and they would be *off*—and not back!

It seems to me that there is everywhere an attempt at present to divert attention from the actual influence which Kant exercised on German philosophy, and especially to ignore prudently the value which he set upon himself. Kant was first and foremost proud of his Table of Categories; with it in his hand he said: "This is the most difficult thing that could ever be undertaken on behalf of metaphysics." Let us only understand this "could be"! He was proud of having *discovered* a new faculty in man, the faculty of synthetic judgment *a priori*. Granting that he deceived himself in this matter; the development and rapid flourishing of German philosophy depended nevertheless on his pride, and on the eager rivalry of the younger generation to discover if possible something—at all events "new faculties"— of which to be still prouder!—But let us reflect for a moment—it is high time to do so. "How are synthetic judgments *a priori possible?*" Kant asks himself—and what is really his answer? "*By means of a means* (faculty)"—but unfortunately not in five words, but so circumstantially, imposingly, and with such display of German profundity and verbal flourishes, that one altogether loses sight of the comical *niaiserie allemande* involved in such an answer. People were beside themselves with delight over this new faculty, and the jubilation reached its climax when Kant further discovered a moral faculty in man—for at that time Germans were still moral, not yet dabbling in the "Politics of hard fact." Then came the honeymoon of German philosophy. All the young theologians of the Tübingen institution went immediately into the groves—all seeking for "faculties." And what did they not find—in that innocent, rich, and still youthful period of the German spirit, to which Romanticism, the malicious fairy, piped and sang, when one could not yet distinguish between "finding" and "inventing"! Above all a faculty for the "transcendental"; Schelling christened it, intellectual intuition, and thereby gratified the most earnest longings of the naturally pious-inclined Germans. One can do no greater wrong to the whole of this exuberant and eccentric movement (which was really youthfulness, notwithstanding that it disguised itself so boldly in hoary and senile conceptions), than to take it seriously, or even treat it with moral indignation. Enough, however—the world grew older, and the dream vanished. A time came when people rubbed their foreheads, and they still rub them to-day. People had been dreaming, and first and foremost—old Kant. "By means of a means (faculty)"— he had said, or at least meant to say. But, is that—an answer? An explanation? Or is it not rather merely a repetition of the question? How does opium induce sleep? "By means of a means (faculty)," namely the *virtus dormitiva*, replies the doctor in Molière,

> *Quia est in eo virtus dormitiva,*
> *Cujus est natura sensus assoupire.*

But such replies belong to the realm of comedy, and it is high time to replace the Kantian question, "How are synthetic judgments *a priori* possible?" by another question, "Why is belief in such judgments *necessary?*"—in effect, it is high time that we should understand that such judgments must be *believed* to be true, for the sake of the preservation of creatures like ourselves; though they still might naturally be *false* judgments! Or, more plainly spoken, and roughly and readily—synthetic judgments *a priori* should not "be possible" at all; we have no right to them; in our mouths they are nothing but false judgments. Only, of course, the belief in their truth is necessary, as plausible belief and ocular evidence belonging to the perspective view of life. And finally, to call to mind the enormous influence which "German philosophy"—I hope you understand its right to inverted commas (goosefeet)?—has exercised throughout the whole of Europe, there is no doubt that a certain *virtus dormitiva* had a share in it; thanks to German philosophy, it was a delight to the noble idlers, the virtuous, the mystics, the artists, the three-fourths Christians, and the political obscurantists of all nations, to find an antidote to the still overwhelming sensualism which overflowed from the last century into this, in short—"*sensus assoupire.*" . . .

As regards materialistic atomism, it is one of the best refuted theories that have been advanced, and in Europe there is now perhaps no one in the learned world so unscholarly as to attach serious signification to it, except for convenient everyday use (as an abbreviation of the means of expression)—thanks chiefly to the Pole Boscovich: he and the Pole Copernicus have hitherto been the greatest and most successful opponents of ocular evidence. For while Copernicus has persuaded us to believe, contrary to all the senses, that the earth does *not* stand fast, Boscovich has taught us to abjure the belief in the last thing that "stood fast" of the earth—the belief in "substance," in "matter," in the earth-residuum, and particle-atom: it is the greatest triumph over the senses that has hitherto been gained on earth. One must, however, go still further, and also declare war, relentless war to the knife, against the "atomistic requirements" which still lead a dangerous after-life in places where no one suspects them, like the more celebrated "metaphysical requirements": one must also above all give the finishing stroke to that other and more portentous atomism which Christianity has taught best and longest, the *soul-atomism.* Let it be permitted to designate by this expression the belief which regards the soul as something indestructible, eternal, indivisible, as a monad, as an *atomon: this* belief ought to be expelled from science! Between ourselves, it is not at all necessary to get rid of "the soul" thereby, and thus renounce one of the oldest and most venerated hypotheses—as happens frequently to the clumsiness of naturalists, who can hardly touch on the soul without immediately losing it. But the way is open for new acceptations and refinements of the soul-hypothesis; and such conceptions as "mortal soul," and "soul as subjective multiplicity," and "soul as social structure of the instinct and passions," want henceforth to have legitimate rights in science. In that the *new* psychologist is about to put an end to the superstitions which have hitherto flourished with almost tropical luxuriance around the idea of the soul, he is really, as it were, thrusting himself into a new desert and a new distrust—it is possible that the older psychologists had a merrier and more comfortable time of it; eventually, however, he finds that precisely thereby he is also condemned to *invent*—and, who knows? perhaps to *discover* the new.

Psychologists should bethink themselves before putting down the instinct of self-preservation as the cardinal instinct of an organic being. A living thing seeks above all to *discharge* its strength—life itself is *Will to Power;* self-preservation is only one of the indirect and most frequent *results* thereof. In short, here, as everywhere else, let us beware of *superfluous* teleological principles!—one of which is the instinct of self-preservation (we owe it to Spinoza's inconsistency). It is thus, in effect, that method ordains, which must be essentially economy of principles.

It is perhaps just dawning on five or six minds that natural philosophy is only a world-exposition and world-arrangement (according to us, if I may say so!) and *not* a world-explanation; but in so far as it is based on belief in the senses, it is regarded as more, and for a long time to come must be regarded as more—namely, as an explanation. It has eyes and fingers of its own, it has ocular evidence and palpableness of its own: this operates fascinatingly, persuasively, and *convincingly* upon an age with fundamentally plebeian tastes—in fact, it follows instinctively the canon of truth of eternal popular sensualism. What is clear, what is "explained"? Only that which can be seen and felt—one must pursue every problem thus far. Obversely, however, the charm of the Platonic mode of thought, which was an *aristocratic* mode, consisted precisely in *resistance to* obvious sense-evidence—perhaps among men who enjoyed even stronger and more fastidious senses than our contemporaries, but who knew how to find a higher triumph in remaining masters of them: and this by means of pale, cold, grey conceptional networks which they threw over the motley whirl of the senses—the mob of the senses, as Plato said. In this overcoming of the world, and interpreting of the world in the manner of Plato, there was an *enjoyment* different from that which the physicists of to-day offer us—and likewise the Darwinists and antiteleologists among the physiological workers, with their principles of the "smallest possible effort," and the greatest possible blunder. "Where there is nothing more to see or to grasp, there is also nothing more for men to do"—that is certainly an imperative different from the Platonic one, but it may notwithstanding be the right imperative for a hardy, labourious race of machinists and bridge-builders of the future, who have nothing but *rough* work to perform.

To study physiology with a clear conscience, one must insist on the fact that the sense-organs are *not* phenomena in the sense of the idealistic philosophy; as such they certainly could not be causes! Sensualism, therefore, at least as regulative hypothesis, if not as heuristic principle. What? And others say even that the external world is the work of our organs? But then our body, as a part of this external world, would be the work of our organs! But then our organs themselves would be the work of our organs! It seems to me that this is a complete *reductio ad absurdum,* if the conception *causa sui* is something fundamentally absurd. Consequently, the external world is *not* the work of our organs—?

There are still harmless self-observers who believe that there are "immediate certainties"; for instance, "I think," or as the superstition of Schopenhauer puts it, "I will"; as though cognition here got hold of its object purely and simply as "the thing in itself," without any falsification taking place either on the part of the subject or the object. I would repeat it, however, a hundred times, that "immediate certainty," as well as "absolute knowledge" and the "thing in itself," involve a *contradictio in adjecto;* we really ought to free ourselves from the misleading significance of words! The people on their part may think that cognition is knowing all about things, but the philosopher must say to himself: "When I analyse the process that is expressed in the sentence, 'I think,' I find a whole series of daring assertions, the argumentative proof of which would be difficult, perhaps impossible: for instance, that it is *I* who think, that there must necessarily be something that thinks, that thinking is an activity and operation on the part of a being who is thought of as a cause, that there is an "ego," and finally, that it is already determined what is to be designated by thinking—that I *know* what thinking is. For if I had not already decided within myself what it is, by what standard could I determine whether that which is just happening is not perhaps 'willing' or 'feeling'? In short, the assertion 'I think,' assumes that I *compare* my state at the present moment with other states of myself which I know, in order to determine what it is; on account of this retrospective connection with further 'knowledge,' it has at any rate no immediate certainty for me."—In place of the "immediate certainty" in which the people may believe in the special case, the philosopher thus finds a series of metaphysical questions presented to him, veritable conscience questions of the intellect, to wit: "From whence did I get the notion of 'thinking'? Why do I believe in cause and effect? What gives me the right to speak of an 'ego,' and even of an 'ego' as cause, and finally of an 'ego' as cause of thought?" He who ventures to answer these metaphysical questions at once by an appeal to a sort of *intuitive* perception, like the person who says, "I think, and know that this, at least, is true, actual, and certain"—will encounter a smile and two notes of interrogation in a philosopher nowadays. "Sir," the philosopher will perhaps give him to understand, "it is improbable that you are not mistaken, but why should it be the truth?"

With regard to the superstitions of logicians, I shall never tire of emphasising a small, terse fact, which is unwillingly recognised by these credulous minds—namely, that a thought comes when "it" wishes, and not when "I" wish; so that it is a *perversion* of the facts of the case to say that the subject "I" is the condition of the predicate "think." *One* thinks; but that this "one" is precisely the famous old "ego," is, to put it mildly, only a supposition, an assertion, and assuredly not an "immediate certainty." After all, one has even gone too far with this "one thinks"—even the "one" contains an *interpretation* of the process, and does not belong to the process itself. One infers here according to the usual grammatical formula—"To think is an activity; every activity requires an agency that is active; consequently" . . . It was pretty much on the same lines that the older atomism sought, besides the operating "power," the material particle wherein it resides and out of which it operates—the atom. More rigorous minds, however, learned at last to get along without this "earth-residuum," and perhaps some day we shall accustom ourselves, even from the logician's point of view, to get along without the little "one" (to which the worthy old "ego" has refined itself).

It is certainly not the least charm of a theory that it is refutable; it is precisely thereby that it attracts the more subtle minds. It seems that the hundred-times-refuted theory of the "free will" owes its persistence to this charm alone; some one is always appearing who feels himself strong enough to refute it.

Philosophers are accustomed to speak of the will as though it were the best-known thing in the world; indeed, Schopenhauer has given us to understand that the will alone is really known to us, absolutely and completely known, without deduction or addition. But it again and again seems to me that in this case Schopenhauer also only did what philosophers are in the habit of doing—he seems to have adopted a *popular prejudice* and exaggerated it. Willing—seems to me to be above all something *complicated,* something that is a unity only in name—and it is precisely in a name that popular prejudice lurks, which has got the mastery over the inadequate precautions of philosophers in all ages. So let us for once be more cautious, let us be "unphilosophical": let us say that in all willing there is firstly a plurality of sensations, namely, the sensation of the condition "*away from which* we go," the sensation of the condition "*towards which* we go," the sensation of this "*from*" and "*towards*" itself, and then besides, an accompanying muscular sensation, which, even without our putting in motion "arms and legs," commences its action by force of habit, directly we "will" anything. Therefore, just as sensations (and indeed many kinds of sensations) are to be recognised as ingredients of the will, so, in the second place, thinking is also to be recognised; in every act of the will there is a ruling thought;—and let us not imagine it possible to sever this thought from the "willing," as if the will would then remain over! In the third place, the will is not only a complex of sensation and thinking, but it is above all an *emotion,* and in fact the emotion of the command. That which is termed "freedom of the will" is essentially the emotion of supremacy in respect to him who must obey: "I am free, 'he' must obey"—this consciousness is inherent in every will; and equally so the straining of the attention, the straight look which fixes itself exclusively on one thing, the unconditional judgment that "this and nothing else is necessary now," the inward certainty that obedience will be rendered—and whatever else pertains to the position of the commander. A man who *wills* commands something within himself which renders obedience, or which he believes renders obedience. But now let us notice what is the strangest thing about the will,— this affair so extremely complex, for which the people have only one name. Inasmuch as in the given circumstances we are at the same time the commanding *and* the obeying parties, and as the obeying party we know the sensations of constraint, impulsion, pressure, resistance, and motion, which usually commence immediately after the act of will; inasmuch as, on the other hand, we are accustomed to disregard this duality, and to deceive ourselves about it by means of the synthetic term "I": a whole series of erroneous conclusions, and consequently of false judgments about the will itself, has become attached to the act of willing—to such a degree that he who wills believes firmly that willing *suffices* for action. Since in the majority of cases there has only been exercise of will when the effect of the command—consequently obedience, and therefore action—was to be *expected,* the *appear-*

ance has translated itself into the sentiment, as if there were there a *necessity of effect;* in a word, he who wills believes with a fair amount of certainty that will and action are somehow one; he ascribes the success, the carrying out of the willing, to the will itself, and thereby enjoys an increase of the sensation of power which accompanies all success. "Freedom of Will"—that is the expression for the complex state of delight of the person exercising volition, who commands and at the same time identifies himself with the executor of the order—who, as such, enjoys also the triumph over obstacles, but thinks within himself that it was really his own will that overcame them. In this way the person exercising volition adds the feelings of delight of his successful executive instruments, the useful "underwills" or under-souls—indeed, our body is but a social structure composed of many souls—to his feelings of delight as commander. *L'effet c'est moi:* what happens here is what happens in every well-constructed and happy commonwealth, namely, that the governing class identifies itself with the successes of the commonwealth. In all willing it is absolutely a question of commanding and obeying, on the basis, as already said, of a social structure composed of many "souls"; on which account a philosopher should claim the right to include willing-as-such within the sphere of morals—regarded as the doctrine of the relations of supremacy under which the phenomenon of "life" manifests itself.

That the separate philosophical ideas are not anything optional or autonomously evolving, but grow up in connection and relationship with each other; that, however suddenly and arbitrarily they seem to appear in the history of thought, they nevertheless belong just as much to a system as the collective members of the fauna of a Continent—is betrayed in the end by the circumstance: how unfailingly the most diverse philosophers always fill in again a definite fundamental scheme of *possible* philosophies. Under an invisible spell, they always revolve once more in the same orbit; however independent of each other they may feel themselves with their critical or systematic wills, something within them leads them, something impels them in definite order the one after the other—to wit, the innate methodology and relationship of their ideas. Their thinking is in fact far less a discovery than a re-recognising, a remembering, a return and a homecoming to a far-off, ancient common-household of the soul, out of which those ideas formerly grew: philosophising is so far a kind of atavism of the highest order. The wonderful family resemblance of all Indian, Greek, and German philosophising is easily enough explained. In fact, where there is affinity of language, owing to the common philosophy of grammar—I mean owing to the unconscious domination and guidance of similar grammatical functions—it cannot but be that everything is prepared at the outset for a similar development and succession of philosophical systems; just as the way seems barred against certain other possibilities of world-interpretation. It is highly probable that philosophers within the domain of the Ural-Altaic languages (where the conception of the subject is least developed) look otherwise "into the world," and will be found on paths of thought different from those of the Indo-Germans and Mussulmans, the spell of certain grammatical functions is ultimately also the spell of *physiological* valuations and racial conditions.—So much by way of rejecting Locke's superficiality with regard to the origin of ideas.

The *causa sui* is the best self-contradiction that has yet been conceived, it is a sort of logical violation and unnaturalness; but the extravagant pride of man has managed to entangle itself profoundly and frightfully with this very folly. The desire for "freedom of will" in the superlative, metaphysical sense, such as still holds sway, unfortunately, in the minds of the half-educated, the desire to bear the entire and ultimate responsibility for one's actions oneself, and to absolve God, the world, ancestors, chance, and society therefrom, involves nothing less than to be precisely this *causa sui,* and, with more than Munchausen daring, to pull oneself up into existence by the hair, out of the slough of nothingness. If any one should find out in this manner the crass stupidity of the celebrated conception of "free will" and put it out of his head altogether, I beg of him to carry his "enlightenment" a step further, and also put out of his head the contrary of this monstrous conception of "free will": I mean "non-free will," which is tantamount to a misuse of cause and effect. One should not wrongly *materialise* "cause" and "effect," as the natural philosophers do (and whoever like them naturalise in thinking at present), according to the prevailing mechanical doltishness which makes the cause press and push until it "effects" its end; one should use "cause" and "effect" only as pure *conceptions,* that is to say, as conventional fictions for the purpose of designation and mutual understanding,—*not* for explanation. In "being-in-itself" there is nothing of "causal-connection," of "necessity," or of "psychological non-freedom;" there the effect does *not* follow the cause, there "law" does not obtain. It is *we* alone who have devised cause, sequence, reciprocity, relativity, constraint, number, law, freedom, motive, and purpose; and when we interpret and intermix this symbol-world, as "being in itself," with things, we act once more as we have always acted—*mythologically.* The "non-free will" is mythology; in real life it is only a question of *strong* and *weak* wills.— It is almost always a symptom of what is lacking in himself, when a thinker, in every "causal-connection" and "psychological necessity," manifests something of compulsion, indigence, obsequiousness, oppression, and non-freedom; it is suspicious to have such feelings—the person betrays himself. And in general, if I have observed correctly, the "non-freedom of the will" is regarded as a problem from two entirely opposite standpoints, but always in a profoundly *personal* manner: some will not give up their "responsibility," their belief in *themselves,* the personal right to *their* merits, at any price (the vain races belong to this class); others on the contrary, do not wish to be answerable for anything, or blamed for anything, and owing to an inward self-contempt, seek *to get out of the business,* no matter how. The latter, when they write books, are in the habit at present of taking the side of criminals; a sort of socialistic sympathy is their favourite disguise. And as a matter of fact, the fatalism of the weak-willed embellishes itself surprisingly when it can pose as "*la religion de la souffrance humaine*"; that is *its* "good taste."

Let me be pardoned, as an old philologist who cannot desist from the mischief of putting his finger on bad modes of interpretation, but "Nature's conformity to law," of which you physicists talk so proudly, as though—why, it exists only owing to your interpretation and bad "philology." It is no matter of fact, no "text," but rather just a naïvely humanitarian adjustment and perversion of meaning, with which you make abundant concessions to the democratic instincts of the modern soul! "Everywhere equality before the law—Nature is not different in that respect, nor better than we": a fine instance of secret motive, in which the vulgar antagonism to everything privileged and autocratic—likewise a second and more refined atheism—is once more disguised. "*Ni dieu, ni maître*"—that, also, is what you want; and therefore "Cheers for natural law!"—is it not so? But, as has been said, that is interpretation, not text; and somebody might come along, who, with opposite intentions and modes of interpretation, could read out of the same "Nature," and with regard to the same phenomena, just the tyrannically inconsiderate and relentless enforcement of the claims of power—an interpreter who should so place the unexceptionalness and unconditionalness of all "Will to Power" before your eyes, that almost every word, and the word "tyranny" itself, would eventually seem unsuitable, or like a weakening and softening, metaphor—as being too human; and who should, nevertheless, end by asserting the same about this world as you do, namely, that it has a "necessary" and "calculable" course, *not,* however, because laws obtain in it, but because they are absolutely *lacking,* and every power effects its ultimate consequences every moment. Granted that this also is only interpretation—and you will be eager enough to make this objection?—well, so much the better.

All psychology hitherto has run aground on moral prejudices and timidities, it has not dared to launch out into the depths. In so far as it is allowable to recognise in that which has hitherto been written, evidence of that which has hitherto been kept silent, it seems as if nobody had yet harboured the notion of psychology as the Morphology and *Development-doctrine of the Will to Power*, as I conceive of it. The power of moral prejudices has penetrated deeply into the most intellectual world, the world apparently most indifferent and unprejudiced, and has obviously operated in an injurious, obstructive, blinding, and distorting manner. A proper physio-psychology has to contend with unconscious antagonism in the heart of the investigator, it has "the heart" against it: even a doctrine of the reciprocal conditionalness of the "good" and the "bad" impulses, causes (as refined immorality) distress and aversion in a still strong and manly conscience—still more so, a doctrine of the derivation of all good impulses from bad ones. If, however, a person should regard even the emotions of hatred, envy, covetousness, and imperiousness as life-conditioning emotions, as factors which must be present, fundamentally and essentially, in the general economy of life (which must, therefore, be further developed if life is to be further developed), he will suffer from such a view of things as from sea-sickness. And yet this hypothesis is far from being the strangest and most painful in this immense and almost new domain of dangerous knowledge; and there are in fact a hundred good reasons why every one should keep away from it who *can* do so! On the other hand, if one has once drifted hither with one's bark, well! very good! now let us set our teeth firmly! let us open our eyes and keep our hand fast on the helm! We sail away right *over* morality, we crush out, we destroy perhaps the remains of our own morality by daring to make our voyage thither—but what do *we* matter! Never yet did a *profounder* world of insight reveal itself to daring travellers and adventurers, and the psychologist who thus "makes a sacrifice"—it is *not* the *sacrifizio dell' intelletto,* on the contrary!—will at least be entitled to demand in return that psychology shall once more be recognised as the queen of the sciences, for whose service and equipment the other sciences exist. For psychology is once more the path to the fundamental problems.

THE FREE SPIRIT

It is the business of the very few to be independent; it is a privilege of the strong. And whoever attempts it, even with the best right, but without being *obliged* to do so, proves that he is probably not only strong, but also daring beyond measure. He enters into a labyrinth, he multiplies a thousandfold the dangers which life in itself already brings with it; not the least of which is that no one can see how and where he loses his way, becomes isolated, and is torn piecemeal by some minotaur of conscience. Supposing such a one comes to grief, it is so far from the comprehension of men that they neither feel it, nor sympathise with it. And he cannot any longer go back! He cannot even go back again to the sympathy of men!

Our deepest insights must—and should—appear as follies, and under certain circumstances as crimes, when they come unauthorisedly to the ears of those who are not disposed and predestined for them. The exoteric and the esoteric, as they were formerly distinguished by philosophers—among the Indians, as among the Greeks, Persians, and Mussulmans, in short, wherever people believed in gradations of rank and *not* in equality and equal rights—are not so much in contradistinction to one another in respect to the exoteric class, standing without, and viewing, estimating, measuring, and judging from the outside, and not from the inside; the more essential distinction is that the class in question views things from below upwards—while the esoteric class views things *from above downwards*. There are heights of the soul from which tragedy itself no longer appears to operate tragically; and if all the woe in the world were taken together, who would dare to decide whether the sight of it would *necessarily* seduce and constrain to sympathy, and thus to a doubling of the woe? . . . That which serves the higher class of men for nourishment or refreshment, must be almost poison to an entirely different and lower order of human beings. The virtues of the common man would perhaps mean vice and weaknesses in a philosopher; it might be possible for a highly developed man, supposing him to degenerate and go to ruin, to acquire qualities thereby alone, for the sake of which he would have to be honoured as a saint in the lower world into which he had sunk. There are books which have an inverse value for the soul and the health according as the inferior soul and the lower vitality, or the higher and more powerful, makes use of them. In the former case they are dangerous, disturbing, unsettling books, in the latter case they are herald-calls which summon the bravest to *their* bravery. Books for the general reader are always ill-smelling books, the odour of paltry people clings to them. Where the populace eat and drink, and even where they reverence, it is accustomed to stink. One should not go into churches if one wishes to breathe *pure* air. . . .

It cannot be helped: the sentiment of surrender, of sacrifice for one's neighbour, and all self-renunciation-morality, must be mercilessly called to account, and brought to judgment; just as the aesthetics of "disinterested contemplation," under which the emasculation of art nowadays seeks insidiously enough to create itself a good conscience. There is far too much witchery and sugar in the sentiments "for others" and "*not* for myself," for one not needing to be doubly distrustful here, and for one asking promptly: "Are they not perhaps—*deceptions?*"—That they *please*—him who has them, and him who enjoys their fruit, and also the mere spectator—that is still no argument in their *favour,* but just calls for caution. Let us therefore be cautious!

At whatever standpoint of philosophy one may place oneself nowadays, seen from every position, the *erroneousness* of the world in which we think we live is the surest and most certain thing our eyes can light upon: we find proof after proof thereof, which would fain allure us into surmises concerning a deceptive principle in the "nature of things." He, however, who makes thinking itself, and consequently "the spirit," responsible for the falseness of the world—an honourable exit, which every conscious or unconscious *advocatus dei* avails himself of—he who regards this world, including space, time, form, and movement, as falsely *deduced,* would have at least good reason in the end to become distrustful also of all thinking; has it not hitherto been playing upon us the worst of scurvy tricks? and what guarantee would it give that it would not continue to do what it has always been doing? In all seriousness, the innocence of thinkers has something touching and respect-inspiring in it, which even nowadays permits them to wait upon consciousness with the request that it will give them *honest* answers: for example, whether it be "real" or not, and why it keeps the outer world so resolutely at a distance, and other questions of the same description. The belief in "immediate certainties" is a *moral naïveté* which does honour to us philosophers; but—we have now to cease being "*merely* moral" men! Apart from morality, such belief is a folly which does little honour to us! If in middle-class life an ever-ready distrust is regarded as the sign of a "bad character," and consequently as an imprudence, here amongst us, beyond the middle-class world and its Yeas and Nays, what should prevent us being imprudent and saying: the philosopher has at length a *right* to "bad character," as the being who has hitherto been most befooled on earth—he is now under *obligation* to distrustfulness, to the wickedest squinting out of every abyss of suspicion.—Forgive me the joke of this gloomy grimace and turn of expression; for I myself have long ago learned to think and estimate differently with regard to deceiving and being deceived, and I keep at least a couple of pokes in the ribs ready for the blind rage with which philosophers struggle against being deceived. Why *not*? It is nothing more than a moral prejudice that truth is worth more than semblance; it is, in fact, the worst proved supposition in the world. *So* much must be conceded: there could have been no life at all except upon the basis of perspective estimates and semblances; and if, with the virtuous enthusiasm and stupidity of many philosophers, one wished to do away altogether with the "seeming world"—well, granted that *you* could do that,—at least nothing of your "truth" would thereby remain! Indeed, what is it that forces us in general to the supposition that there is an essential opposition of "true" and "false"? Is it not enough to suppose degrees of seemingness, and as it were lighter and darker shades and tones of semblance—different *valeurs,* as the painters say? Why might not the world *which concerns us*—be a fiction? And to any one who suggested: "But to a fiction belongs an originator?"—might it not be bluntly replied: *Why?* May not this "belong" also belong to the fiction? Is it not at length permitted to be a little ironical towards the subject, just as towards the predicate and object? Might not the philosopher elevate himself above faith in grammar? All respect to governesses, but is it not time that philosophy should renounce governess-faith?

O Voltaire! O humanity! O idiocy! There is something ticklish in "the truth," and in the *search* for the truth; and if man goes about it too humanely—"*il ne cherche le vrai que pour faire le bien*"—I wager he finds nothing!

Supposing that nothing else is "given" as real but our world of desires and passions, that we cannot sink or rise to any other "reality" but just that of our impulses—for thinking is only a relation of these impulses to one another:—are we not permitted to make the attempt and to ask the question whether this which is "given" does not *suffice,* by means of our counterparts, for the understanding even of the so-called mechanical (or "material") world? I do not mean as an illusion, a "semblance," a "representation" (in the Berkeleyan and Schopenhauerian sense), but as possessing the same degree of reality as our emotions themselves—as a more primitive form of the world of emotions, in which everything still lies locked in a mighty unity, which afterwards branches off and develops itself in organic processes (naturally also, refines and debilitates)—as a kind of instinctive life in which all organic functions, including self-regulation, assimilation, nutrition, secretion, and change of matter, are still synthetically united with one another—as a *primary form* of life?—In the end, it is not only permitted to make this attempt, it is commanded by the conscience of *logical method.* Not to assume several kinds of causality, so long as the attempt to get along with a single one has not been pushed to its furthest extent (to absurdity; if I may be allowed to say so): that is a morality of method which one may not repudiate nowadays—it follows "from its definition," as mathematicians say. The question is ultimately whether we really recognise the will as *operating,* whether we believe in the causality of the will; if we do so—and fundamentally our belief *in this* is just our belief in causality itself—we *must* make the attempt to posit hypothetically the causality of the will as the only causality. "Will" can naturally only operate on "will"—and not on "matter" (not on "nerves," for instance): in short, the hypothesis must be hazarded, whether will does not operate on will wherever "effects" are recognised—and whether all mechanical action, inasmuch as a power operates therein, is not just the power of will, the effect of will. Granted, finally, that we succeeded in explaining our entire instinctive life as the development and ramification of one fundamental form of will—namely, the Will to Power, as *my* thesis puts it; granted that all organic functions could be traced back to this Will to Power, and that the solution of the problem of generation and nutrition—it is one problem—could also be found therein: one would thus have acquired the right to define *all* active force unequivocally as *Will to Power*. The world seen from within, the world defined and designated according to its "intelligible character"—it would simply be "Will to Power," and nothing else.

"What? Does not that mean in popular language: God is disproved, but not the devil?"—On the contrary! On the contrary, my friends! And who the devil also compels you to speak popularly! a mind might be measured by the amount of "truth" it could endure—or to speak more plainly, by the extent to which it *required* truth attenuated, veiled, sweetened, damped, and falsified. But there is no doubt that for the discovery of certain *portions* of truth the wicked and unfortunate are more favourably situated and have a greater likelihood of success; not to speak of the wicked who are happy—a species about whom moralists are silent. Perhaps severity and craft are more favourable conditions for the development of strong, independent spirits and philosophers than the gentle, refined, yielding good-nature, and habit of taking things easily, which are prized, and rightly prized in a learned man. Presupposing always, to begin with, that the term "philosopher" be not confined to the philosopher who writes books, or even introduces *his* philosophy into books!—Stendhal furnishes a last feature of the portrait of the free-spirited philosopher, which for the sake of German taste I will not omit to underline—for it is *opposed* to German taste. "*Pour être bon philosophe*," says this last great psychologist, "*il faut être sec, clair, sans illusion. Un banquier, qui a fait fortune, a une partie du caractère requis pour faire des découvertes en philosophie, c'est-à-dire pour voir clair dans ce qui est.*"

Everything that is profound loves the mask; the profoundest things have a hatred even of figure and likeness. Should not the *contrary* only be the right disguise for the shame of a God to go about in? A question worth asking!—it would be strange if some mystic has not already ventured on the same kind of thing. There are proceedings of such a delicate nature that it is well to overwhelm them with coarseness and make them unrecognisable; there are actions of love and of an extravagant magnanimity after which nothing can be wiser than to take a stick and thrash the witness soundly: one thereby obscures his recollection. Many a one is able to obscure and abuse his own memory, in order at least to have vengeance on this sole party in the secret: shame is inventive. They are not the worst things of which one is most ashamed: there is not only deceit behind a mask—there is so much goodness in craft. I could imagine that a man with something costly and fragile to conceal, would roll through life clumsily and rotundly like an old, green, heavily hooped wine-cask: the refinement of his shame requiring it to be so. A man who has depths in his shame meets his destiny and his delicate decisions upon paths which few ever reach, and with regard to the existence of which his nearest and most intimate friends may be ignorant; his mortal danger conceals itself from their eyes, and equally so his regained security. Such a hidden nature, which instinctively employs speech for silence and concealment, and is inexhaustible in evasion of communication, *desires* and insists that a mask of himself shall occupy his place in the hearts and heads of his friends; and supposing he does not desire it, his eyes will some day be opened to the fact that there is nevertheless a mask of him there—and that it is well to be so. Every profound spirit needs a mask; nay, more, around every profound spirit there continually grows a mask, owing to the constantly false, that is to say, *superficial* interpretation of every word he utters, every step he takes, every sign of life he manifests.

One must subject oneself to one's own tests that one is destined for independence and command, and do so at the right time. One must not avoid one's tests, although they constitute perhaps the most dangerous game one can play, and are in the end tests made only before ourselves and before no other judge. Not to cleave to any person, be it even the dearest—every person is a prison and also a recess. Not to cleave to a fatherland, be it even the most suffering and necessitous—it is even less difficult to detach one's heart from a victorious fatherland. Not to cleave to a sympathy, be it even for higher men, into whose peculiar torture and helplessness chance has given us an insight. Not to cleave to a science, though it tempt one with the most valuable discoveries, apparently specially reserved for *us*. Not to cleave to one's own liberation, to the voluptuous distance and remoteness of the bird, which always flies further aloft in order always to see more under it—the danger of the flier. Not to cleave to our own virtues, nor become as a whole a victim to any of our specialities, to our "hospitality" for instance, which is the danger of dangers for highly developed and wealthy souls, who deal prodigally, almost indifferently with themselves, and push the virtue of liberality so far that it becomes a vice. One must know how *to conserve oneself*—the best test of independence.

A new order of philosophers is appearing; I shall venture to baptize them by a name not without danger. As far as I understand them, as far as they allow themselves to be understood—for it is their nature to *wish* to remain something of a puzzle—these philosophers of the future might rightly, perhaps also wrongly, claim to be designated as *"tempters."* This name itself is after all only an attempt, or, if it be preferred, a temptation.

Will they be new friends of "truth," these coming philosophers? Very probably, for all philosophers hitherto have loved their truths. But assuredly they will not be dogmatists. It must be contrary to their pride, and also contrary to their taste, that their truth should still be truth for every one—that which has hitherto been the secret wish and ultimate purpose of all dogmatic efforts. "My opinion is *my* opinion: another person has not easily a right to it"—such a philosopher of the future will say, perhaps. One must renounce the bad taste of wishing to agree with many people. "Good" is no longer good when one's neighbour takes it into his mouth. And how could there be a "common good"! The expression contradicts itself; that which can be common is always of small value. In the end things must be as they are and have always been—the great things remain for the great, the abysses for the profound, the delicacies and thrills for the refined, and, to sum up shortly, everything rare for the rare.

Need I say expressly after all this that they will be free, *very* free spirits, these philosophers of the future—as certainly also they will not be merely free spirits, but something more, higher, greater, and fundamentally different, which does not wish to be misunderstood and mistaken? But while I say this, I feel under *obligation* almost as much to them as to ourselves (we free spirits who are their heralds and forerunners), to sweep away from ourselves altogether a stupid old prejudice and misunderstanding, which, like a fog, has too long made the conception of "free spirit" obscure. In every country of Europe, and the same in America, there is at present something which makes an abuse of this name: a very narrow, prepossessed, enchained class of spirits, who desire almost the opposite of what our intentions and instincts prompt—not to mention that in respect to the *new* philosophers who are appearing, they must still more be closed windows and bolted doors. Briefly and regrettably, they belong to the *levellers,* these wrongly named "free spirits"—as glib-tongued and scribe-fingered slaves of the democratic taste and its "modern ideas": all of them men without solitude, without personal solitude, blunt honest fellows to whom neither courage nor honourable conduct ought to be denied; only, they are not free, and are ludicrously superficial, especially in their innate partiality for seeing the cause of almost *all* human misery and failure in the old forms in which society has hitherto existed—a notion which happily inverts the truth entirely! What they would fain attain with all their strength, is the universal, green-meadow happiness of the herd, together with security, safety, comfort, and alleviation of life for every one; their two most frequently chanted songs and doctrines are called "Equality of Rights" and "Sympathy with all Sufferers"—and suffering itself is looked upon by them as something which must be *done away with*. We opposite ones, however, who have opened our eye and conscience to the question how and where the plant "man" has hitherto grown most vigorously, believe that this has always taken place under the opposite conditions, that for this end the dangerousness of his situation had to be increased enormously, his inventive faculty and dissembling power (his "spirit") had to develop into subtlety and daring under long oppression and compulsion, and his Will to Life had to be increased to the unconditioned Will to Power:—we believe that severity, violence, slavery, danger in the street and in the heart, secrecy, stoicism, tempter's art and devilry of every kind,—that everything wicked, terrible, tyrannical, predatory, and serpentine in man, serves as well for the elevation of the human species as its opposite:—we do not even say enough when we only say *this much;* and in any case we find ourselves here, both with our speech and our silence, at the *other* extreme of all modern ideology and gregarious desirability, as their antipodes perhaps? What wonder that we "free spirits" are not exactly the most communicative spirits? that we do not wish to betray in every respect *what* a spirit can free itself from, and *where* perhaps it will then be driven? And as to the import of the dangerous formula, "Beyond Good and Evil," with which we at least avoid confusion, we *are* something else than *"libres-penseurs," "liberi pensatori,"* "free-thinkers," and whatever these honest advocates of "modern ideas" like to call themselves. Having been at home, or at least guests, in many realms of the spirit; having escaped again and again from the gloomy, agreeable nooks in which preferences and prejudices, youth, origin, the accident of men and books, or even the weariness of travel seemed to confine us; full of malice against the seductions of dependency which lie concealed in honours, money, positions, or exaltation of the senses; grateful even for distress and the vicissitudes of illness, because they always free us from some rule, and its "prejudice," grateful to the God, devil, sheep, and worm in us; inquisitive to a fault, investigators to the point of cruelty, with unhesitating fingers for the intangible, with teeth and stomachs for the most indigestible, ready for any business that requires sagacity and acute senses, ready for every adventure, owing to an excess of "free will"; with anterior and posterior souls, into the ultimate intentions of which it is difficult to pry, with foregrounds and backgrounds to the end of which no foot may run; hidden ones under the mantles of light, appropriators, although we resemble heirs and spendthrifts, arrangers and collectors from morning till night, misers of our wealth and our full-crammed drawers, economical in learning and forgetting, inventive in scheming; sometimes proud of tables of categories, sometimes pendants, sometimes night-owls of work even in full day; yea, if necessary, even scarecrows—and it is necessary nowadays, that is to say, inasmuch as we are the born, sworn, jealous friends of *solitude,* of our own profoundest midnight and midday solitude:—such kind of men are we, we free spirits! And perhaps *ye* are also something of the same kind, ye coming ones? ye *new* philosophers?

WHAT IS NOBLE?

Every elevation of the type "man," has hitherto been the work of an aristocratic society—and so will it always be—a society believing in a long scale of gradations of rank and differences of worth among human beings, and requiring slavery in some form or other. Without the *pathos of distance,* such as grows out of the incarnated difference of classes, out of the constant outlooking and downlooking of the ruling caste on subordinates and instruments, and out of their equally constant practice of obeying and commanding, of keeping down and keeping at a distance—that other more mysterious pathos could never have arisen, the longing for an ever new widening of distance within the soul itself, the formation of ever higher, rarer, further, more extended, more comprehensive states, in short, just the elevation of the type "man," the continued "self-surmounting of man," to use a moral formula in a supermoral sense. To be sure, one must not resign oneself to any humanitarian illusions about the history of the origin of an aristocratic society (that is to say, of the preliminary condition for the elevation of the type "man"): the truth is hard. Let us acknowledge unprejudicedly how every higher civilisation hitherto has *originated!* Men with a still natural nature, barbarians in every terrible sense of the word, men of prey, still in possession of unbroken strength of will and desire for power, threw themselves upon weaker, more moral, more peaceful races (perhaps trading or cattle-rearing communities), or upon old mellow civilisations in which the final vital force was flickering out in brilliant fireworks of wit and depravity. At the commencement, the noble caste was always the barbarian caste: their superiority did not consist first of all in their physical, but in their psychical power—they were more *complete* men (which at every point also implies the same as "more complete beasts").

Corruption—as the indication that anarchy threatens to break out among the instincts, and that the foundation of the emotions, called "life," is convulsed—is something radically different according to the organisation in which it manifests itself. When, for instance, an aristocracy like that of France at the beginning of the Revolution, flung away its privileges with sublime disgust and sacrificed itself to an excess of its moral sentiments, it was corruption:—it was really only the closing act of the corruption which had existed for centuries, by virtue of which that aristocracy had abdicated step by step its lordly prerogatives and lowered itself to a *function* of royalty (in the end even to its decoration and parade-dress). The essential thing, however, is a good and healthy aristocracy is that it should *not* regard itself as a function either of the kingship or the commonwealth, but as the *significance* and highest justification thereof—that it should therefore accept with a good conscience the sacrifice of a legion of individuals, who, *for its sake,* must be suppressed and reduced to imperfect men, to slaves and instruments. Its fundamental belief must be precisely that society is *not* allowed to exist for its own sake, but only as a foundation and scaffolding, by means of which a select class of beings may be able to elevate themselves to their higher duties, and in general to a higher *existence:* like those sun-seeking climbing plants in Java—they are called *Sipo Matador,*—which encircle an oak so long and so often with their arms, until at last, high above it, but supported by it, they can unfold their tops in the open light, and exhibit their happiness.

To refrain mutually from injury, from violence, from exploitation, and put one's will on a par with that of others: this may result in a certain rough sense in good conduct among individuals when the necessary conditions are given (namely, the actual similarity of the individuals in amount of force and degree of worth, and their co-relation within one organisation). As soon, however, as one wished to take this principle more generally, and if possible even as *the fundamental principle of society,* it would immediately disclose what it really is—namely, a Will to the *denial* of life, a principle of dissolution and decay. Here one must think profoundly to the very basis and resist all sentimental weakness: life itself is *essentially* appropriation, injury, conquest of the strange and weak, suppression, severity, obtrusion of peculiar forms, incorporation, and at the least, putting it mildest, exploitation;—but why should one for ever use precisely these words on which for ages a disparaging purpose has been stamped? Even the organisation within which, as was previously supposed, the individuals treat each other as equal—it takes place in every healthy aristocracy—must itself, if it be a living and not a dying organisation, do all that towards other bodies, which the individuals within it refrain from doing to each other: it will have to be the incarnated Will to Power, it will endeavour to grow, to gain ground, attract to itself and acquire ascendency—not owing to any morality or immorality, but because it *lives,* and because life *is* precisely Will to Power. On no point, however, is the ordinary consciousness of Europeans more unwilling to be corrected than on this matter; people now rave everywhere, even under the guise of science, about coming conditions of society in which "the exploiting character" is to be absent:—that sounds to my ears as if they promised to invent a mode of life which should refrain from all organic functions. "Exploitation" does not belong to a depraved, or imperfect and primitive society: it belongs to the *nature* of the living being as a primary organic function; it is a consequence of the intrinsic Will to Power, which is precisely the Will to Life.—Granting that as a theory this is a novelty—as a reality it is the *fundamental fact* of all history: let us be so far honest towards ourselves!

In a tour through the many finer and coarser moralities which have hitherto prevailed or still prevail on the earth, I found certain traits recurring regularly together, and connected with one another, until finally two primary types revealed themselves to me, and a radical distinction was brought to light. There is *master-morality* and *slave-morality;*—I would at once add, however, that in all higher and mixed civilisations, there are also attempts at the reconciliation of the two moralities; but one finds still oftener the confusion and mutual misunderstanding of them, indeed, sometimes their close juxtaposition—even in the same man, within one soul. The distinctions of moral values have either originated in a ruling caste, pleasantly conscious of being different from the ruled—or among the ruled class, the slaves and dependents of all sorts. In the first case, when it is the rulers who determine the conception "good," it is the exalted, proud disposition which is regarded as the distinguishing feature, and that which determines the order of rank. The noble type of man separates from himself the beings in whom the opposite of this exalted, proud disposition displays itself: he despises them. Let it at once be noted that in this first kind of morality the antithesis "good" and "bad" means practically the same as "noble" and "despicable";—the antithesis "good" and "*evil*" is of a different origin. The cowardly, the timid, the insignificant, and those thinking merely of narrow utility are despised; moreover, also, the distrustful, with their constrained glances, the self-abasing, the dog-like kind of men who let themselves be abused, the mendicant flatterers, and above all the liars:—it is a fundamental belief of all aristocrats that the common people are untruthful. "We truthful ones"—the nobility in ancient Greece called themselves. It is obvious that everywhere the designations of moral value were at first applied to *men,* and were only derivatively and at a later period applied to *actions;* it is a gross mistake, therefore, when historians of morals start with questions like, "Why have sympathetic actions been praised?" The noble type of man regards *himself* as a determiner of values; he does not require to be approved of; he passes the judgment: "What is injurious to me is injurious to itself"; he knows that it is he himself only who confers honour on things; he is a *creator of values.* He honours whatever he recognises in himself: such morality is self-glorification. In the foreground there is the feeling of plenitude, of power, which seeks to overflow, the happiness of high tension, the consciousness of a wealth which would fain give and bestow:—the noble man also helps the unfortunate, but not—or scarcely—out of pity, but rather from an impulse generated by the superabundance of power. The noble man honours in himself the powerful one, him also who has power over himself, who knows how to speak and how to keep silence, who takes pleasure in subjecting himself to severity and hardness, and has reverence for all that is severe and hard. "Wotan placed a hard heart in my breast," says an old Scandinavian Saga: it is thus rightly expressed from the soul of a proud Viking. Such a type of man is even proud of *not* being made for sympathy; the hero of the Saga therefore adds warningly: "He who has not a hard heart when young, will never have one." The noble and brave who think thus are the furthest removed from the morality which sees precisely in sympathy, or in acting for the good of others, or in *désintéressement,* the characteristic of the moral; faith in oneself, pride in oneself, a radical enmity and irony towards "selflessness," belong as definitely to noble morality, as do a careless scorn and precaution in presence of sympathy and the "warm heart."—It is the powerful who *know* how to honour, it is their art, their domain for invention. The profound reverence for age and for tradition—all law rests on this double reverence,—the belief and prejudice in favour of ancestors and unfavourable to newcomers, is typical in the morality of the powerful; and if, reversely, men of "modern ideas" believe almost instinctively in "progress" and the "future," and are more and more lacking in respect for old age, the ignoble origin of these "ideas" has complacently betrayed itself thereby. A morality of the ruling class, however, is more especially foreign and irritating to present-day taste in the sternness of its principle that one has duties only to one's equals; that one may act towards beings of a lower rank, towards all that is foreign, just as seems good to one, or "as the heart desires," and in any case "beyond good and evil": it is here that sympathy and similar sentiments can have a place. The ability and obligation to exercise prolonged gratitude and prolonged revenge—both only within the circle of equals,—artfulness in retaliation, *raffinement* of the idea in friendship, a certain necessity to have enemies (as outlets for the emotions of envy, quarrelsomeness, arrogance—in fact, in order to be a good *friend*): all these are typical characteristics of the noble morality, which, as has been pointed out, is not the morality of "modern ideas," and is therefore at present difficult to realise, and also to unearth and disclose.—It is otherwise with the second type of morality, *slave-morality.* Supposing that the abused, the oppressed, the suffering, the unemancipated, the weary, and those uncertain of themselves, should moralise, what will be the common element in their moral estimates? Probably a pessimistic suspicion with regard to the entire situation of man will find expression, perhaps a condemnation of man, together with his situation. The slave has an unfavourable eye for the virtues of the powerful; he has a scepticism and distrust, a *refinement* of distrust of everything "good" that is there honoured—he would fain persuade himself that the very happiness there is not genuine. On the other hand, *those* qualities which serve to alleviate the existence of sufferers are brought into prominence and flooded with light; it is here that sympathy, the kind, helping hand, the warm heart, patience, diligence, humility, and friendliness attain to honour; for here these are the most useful qualities, and almost the only means of supporting the burden of existence. Slave-morality is essentially the morality of utility. Here is the seat of the origin of the famous antithesis "good" and "*evil*":—power and dangerousness are assumed to reside in the evil, a certain dreadfulness, subtlety, and strength, which do not admit of being despised. According to slave-morality, therefore, the "evil" man arouses fear; according to master-morality, it is precisely the "good" man who arouses fear and seeks to arouse it, while the bad man is regarded as the despicable being. The contrast attains its maximum when, in accordance with the logical consequences of slave-morality, a shade of depreciation—it may be slight and well-intentioned—at last attaches itself even to the "good" man of this morality; because, according to the servile mode of thought, the good man must in any case be the *safe* man: he is good-natured, easily deceived, perhaps a little stupid, *un bonhomme.* Everywhere that slave-morality gains the ascendency, language shows a ten-

dency to approximate the significations of the words "good" and "stupid."—A last fundamental difference: the desire for *freedom,* the instinct for happiness and the refinements of
the feeling of liberty belong as necessarily to slave-morals and morality, as artifice and enthusiasm in reverence and devotion are the regular symptoms of an aristocratic mode of
thinking and estimating.—Hence we can understand without further detail why love *as
a passion*—it is our European speciality—must absolutely be of noble origin; as is well
known, its invention is due to the Provençal poet-cavaliers, those brilliant ingenious men
of the *"gai saber,"* to whom Europe owes so much, and almost owes itself.

Vanity is one of the things which are perhaps most difficult for a noble man to understand: he will be tempted to deny it, where another kind of man thinks he sees it self-
evidently. The problem for him is to represent to his mind beings who seek to arouse a
good opinion of themselves which they themselves do not possess—and consequently also
do not "deserve,"—and who yet *believe* in this good opinion afterwards. This seems to him
on the one hand such bad taste and so self-disrespectful, and on the other hand so gro-
tesquely unreasonable, that he would like to consider vanity an exception, and is doubtful
about it in most cases when it is spoken of. He will say, for instance: "I may be mistaken
about my value, and on the other hand may nevertheless demand that my value should be
acknowledged by others precisely as I rate it:—that, however, is not vanity (but self-conceit,
or, in most cases, that which is called 'humility,' and also 'modesty')." Or he will even say:
"For many reasons I can delight in the good opinion of others, perhaps because I love and
honour them, and rejoice in all their joys, perhaps also because their good opinion endorses
and strengthens my belief in my own good opinion, perhaps because the good opinion
of others, even in cases where I do not share it, is useful to me, or gives promise of usefulness:—all this, however, is not vanity." The man of noble character must first bring it home
forcibly to his mind, especially with the aid of history, that, from time immemorial, in all
social strata in any way dependent, the ordinary man *was* only that which he *passed for:*—
not being at all accustomed to fix values, he did not assign even to himself any other value
than that which his master assigned to him (it is the peculiar *right of masters* to create values).
It may be looked upon as the result of an extraordinary atavism, that the ordinary man,
even at present, is still always *waiting* for an opinion about himself, and then instinctively
submitting himself to it; yet by no means only to a "good" opinion, but also to a bad
and unjust one (think, for instance, of the greater part of the self-appreciations and self-
depreciations which believing women learn from their confessors, and which in general the
believing Christian learns from his Church). In fact, conformably to the slow rise of the
democratic social order (and its cause, the blending of the blood of masters and slaves), the
originally noble and rare impulse of the masters to assign a value to themselves and to "think
well" of themselves, will now be more and more encouraged and extended; but it has at all
times an older, ampler, and more radically ingrained propensity opposed to it—and in the
phenomenon of "vanity" this older propensity overmasters the younger. The vain person
rejoices over *every* good opinion which he hears about himself (quite apart from the point
of view of its usefulness, and equally regardless of its truth or falsehood), just as he suffers
from every bad opinion: for he subjects himself to both, he *feels* himself subjected to both,
by that oldest instinct of subjection which breaks forth in him.—It is "the slave" in the
vain man's blood, the remains of the slave's craftiness—and how much of the "slave" is still
left in woman, for instance!—which seeks to *seduce* to good opinions of itself; it is the slave,
too, who immediately afterwards falls prostrate himself before these opinions, as though he
had not called them forth.—And to repeat it again: vanity is an atavism. . . .

At the risk of displeasing innocent ears, I submit that egoism belongs to the essence of a noble soul, I mean the unalterable belief that to a belief such as "we," other beings must naturally be in subjection, and have to sacrifice themselves. The noble soul accepts the fact of his egoism without question, and also without consciousness of harshness, constraint, or arbitrariness therein, but rather as something that may have its basis in the primary law of things:—if he sought a designation for it he would say: "It is justice itself." He acknowledges under certain circumstances, which made him hesitate at first, that there are other equally privileged ones; as soon as he has settled this question of rank, he moves among those equals and equally privileged ones with the same assurance, as regards modesty and delicate respect, which he enjoys in intercourse with himself—in accordance with an innate heavenly mechanism which all the stars understand. It is an *additional* instance of his egoism, this artfulness and self-limitation in intercourse with his equals—every star is a similar egoist; he honours *himself* in them, and in the rights which he concedes to them, he has no doubt that the exchange of honours and rights, as the *essence* of all intercourse, belongs also to the natural condition of things. The noble soul gives as he takes, prompted by the passionate and sensitive instinct of requital, which is at the root of his nature. The notion of "favour" has, *inter pares,* neither significance nor good repute; there may be a sublime way of letting gifts as it were light upon one from above, and of drinking them thirstily like dew-drops; but for those arts and displays the noble soul has no aptitude. His egoism hinders him here: in general, he looks "aloft" unwillingly—he looks either *forward,* horizontally and deliberately, or downwards—*he knows that he is on a height. . . .*

—What is noble? What does the word "noble" still mean for us nowadays? How does the noble man betray himself, how is he recognised under this heavy overcast sky of the commencing plebeianism, by which everything is rendered opaque and leaden?—It is not his actions which establish his claim—actions are always ambiguous, always inscrutable; neither is it his "works." One finds nowadays among artists and scholars plenty of those who betray by their works that a profound longing for nobleness impels them; but this very *need of* nobleness is radically different from the needs of the noble soul itself, and is in fact the eloquent and dangerous sign of the lack thereof. It is not the works, but the *belief* which is here decisive and determines the order of rank—to employ once more an old religious formula with a new and deeper meaning,—it is some fundamental certainty which a noble soul has about itself, something which is not to be sought, is not to be found, and perhaps, also, is not to be lost.—*The noble soul has reverence for itself.*— . . .

. . . Every philosophy also *conceals* a philosophy; every opinion is also a *lurking-place,* every word is also a *mask.*

Every deep thinker is more afraid of being understood than of being misunderstood. The latter perhaps wounds his vanity; but the former wounds his heart, his sympathy, which always says: "Ah, why would *you* also have as hard a time of it as I have?"

Man, a *complex,* mendacious, artful, and inscrutable animal, uncanny to the other animals by his artifice and sagacity, rather than by his strength, has invented the good conscience in order finally to enjoy his soul as something *simple;* and the whole of morality is a long, audacious falsification, by virtue of which generally enjoyment at the sight of the soul becomes possible. From this point of view there is perhaps much more in the conception of "art" than is generally believed.

A philosopher: that is a man who constantly experiences, sees, hears, suspects, hopes, and dreams extraordinary things; who is struck by his own thoughts as if they came from the outside, from above and below, as a species of events and lightning-flashes *peculiar to him;* who is perhaps himself a storm pregnant with new lightnings; a portentous man, around whom there is always rumbling and mumbling and gaping and something uncanny going on. A philosopher: alas, a being who often runs away from himself, is often afraid of himself—but whose curiosity always makes him "come to himself" again.

A man who says: "I like that, I take it for my own, and mean to guard and protect it from every one"; a man who can conduct a case, carry out a resolution, remain true to an opinion, keep hold of a woman, punish and overthrow insolence; a man who has his indignation and his sword, and to whom the weak, the suffering, the oppressed, and even the animals willingly submit and naturally belong; in short, a man who is a *master* by nature—when such a man has sympathy, well! *that* sympathy has value! But of what account is the sympathy of those who suffer! Or of those even who preach sympathy! There is nowadays, throughout almost the whole of Europe, a sickly irritability and sensitiveness towards pain, and also a repulsive irrestrainableness in complaining, an effeminising, which, with the aid of religion and philosophical nonsense, seeks to deck itself out as something superior—there is a regular cult of suffering. The *unmanliness* of that which is called "sympathy" by such groups of visionaries, is always, I believe, the first thing that strikes the eye.—One must resolutely and radically taboo this latest form of bad taste; and finally, I wish people to put the good amulet, *"gai saber"* ("gay science," in ordinary language), on heart and neck, as a protection against it.

The Olympian Vice.—Despite the philosopher who, as a genuine Englishman, tried to bring laughter into bad repute in all thinking minds—"Laughing is a bad infirmity of human nature, which every thinking mind will strive to overcome" (Hobbes),—I would even allow myself to rank philosophers according to the quality of their laughing—up to those who are capable of *golden* laughter. And supposing that Gods also philosophise, which I am strongly inclined to believe, owing to many reasons—I have no doubt that they also know how to laugh thereby in an overman-like and new fashion—and at the expense of all serious things! Gods are fond of ridicule: it seems that they cannot refrain from laughter even in holy matters.

The genius of the heart, as that great mysterious one possesses it, the tempter-god and born rat-catcher of consciences, whose voice can descend into the nether-world of every soul, who neither speaks a word nor casts a glance in which there may not be some motive or touch of allurement, to whose perfection it pertains that he knows how to appear,—not as he is, but in a guise which acts as an *additional* constraint on his followers to press ever closer to him, to follow him more cordially and thoroughly;—the genius of the heart, which imposes silence and attention on everything loud and self-conceited, which smooths rough souls and makes them taste a new longing—to lie placid as a mirror, that the deep heavens may be reflected in them;—the genius of the heart, which teaches the clumsy and too hasty hand to hesitate, and to grasp more delicately; which scents the hidden and forgotten treasure, the drop of goodness and sweet spirituality under thick dark ice, and is a divining-rod for every grain of gold, long buried and imprisoned in mud and sand; the genius of the heart, from contact with which every one goes away richer; not favoured or surprised, not as though gratified and oppressed by the good things of others; but richer in himself, newer than before, broken up, blown upon, and sounded by a thawing wind; more uncertain perhaps, more delicate, more fragile, more bruised, but full of hopes which as yet lack names, full of a new will and current, full of a new ill-will and counter-current . . . but what am I doing, my friends? Of whom am I talking to you? Have I forgotten myself so far that I have not even told you his name? Unless it be that you have already divined of your own accord who this questionable God and spirit is, that wishes to be *praised* in such a manner? For, as it happens to every one who from childhood onward has always been on his legs, and in foreign lands, I have also encountered on my path many strange and dangerous spirits; above all, however, and again and again, the one of whom I have just spoken: in fact, no less a personage than the God *Dionysus,* the great equivocator and tempter, to whom, as you know, I once offered in all secrecy and reverence my first-fruits—the last, as it seems to me, who has offered a *sacrifice* to him, for I have found no one who could understand what I was then doing. In the meantime, however, I have learned much, far too much, about the philosophy of this God, and, as I said, from mouth to mouth—I, the last disciple and initiate of the God Dionysus: and perhaps I might at last begin to give you, my friends, as far as I am allowed, a little taste of this philosophy? In a hushed voice, as is but seemly: for it has to do with much that is secret, new, strange, wonderful, and uncanny. The very fact that Dionysus is a philosopher, and that therefore Gods also philosophise, seems to me a novelty which is not unensnaring, and might perhaps arouse suspicion precisely amongst philosophers;—amongst you, my friends, there is less to be said against it, except that it comes too late and not at the right time; for, as it has been disclosed to me, you are loth nowadays to believe in God and gods. It may happen, too, that in the frankness of my story I must go further than is agreeable to the strict usages of your ears? Certainly the God in question went further, very much further, in such dialogues, and was always many paces ahead of me. . . . Indeed, if it were allowed, I should have to give him, according to human usage, fine ceremonious titles of lustre and merit, I should have to extol his courage as investigator and discoverer, his fearless honesty, truthfulness, and love of wisdom. But such a God does not know what to do with all that respectable trumpery and pomp. "Keep that," he would say, "for thyself and those like thee, and whoever else require it! I—have no reason to cover my nakedness!" One suspects that this kind of divinity and philosopher perhaps lacks shame?—He once said: "Under certain circumstances I love mankind"—and referred thereby to Ariadne, who was present; "in my opinion man is an agreeable, brave, inventive animal, that has not his equal upon earth, he makes his way even through all labyrinths. I like man, and often think how I can still further advance him, and make him stronger, more evil, and more profound."—"Stronger, more evil, and more profound?" I asked in horror. "Yes," he said again, "stronger, more evil, and more profound; also more beautiful"—and thereby the tempter-god smiled with his halcyon smile, as though he had just paid some charming compliment. One here sees at once that it is not only shame that this divinity lacks;—and in general there are good grounds for supposing that in some things the Gods could all of them come to us men for instruction. We men are—more human.—

Alas! what are you, after all, my written and painted thoughts! Not long ago you were so variegated, young, and malicious, so full of thorns and secret spices, that you made me sneeze and laugh—and now? You have already doffed your novelty, and some of you, I fear, are ready to become truths, so immortal do they look, so pathetically honest, so tedious! And was it ever otherwise? What then do we write and paint, we mandarins with Chinese brush, we immortalisers of things which *lend* themselves to writing, what are we alone capable of painting? Alas, only that which is just about to fade and begins to lose its odour! Alas, only exhausted and departing storms and belated yellow sentiments! Alas, only birds strayed and fatigued by flight, which now let themselves be captured with the hand—with *our* hand! We immortalise what cannot live and fly much longer, things only which are exhausted and mellow! And it is only for your *afternoon,* you, my written and painted thoughts, for which alone I have colours, many colours perhaps, many variegated softenings, and fifty yellows and browns and greens and reds;—but nobody will divine thereby how ye looked in your morning, you sudden sparks and marvels of my solitude, you, my old, beloved—*evil* thoughts!

THE WILL TO POWER

I regard Christianity as the most fatal and seductive lie that has ever yet existed—as the greatest and most *impious* lie: I can discern the last sprouts and branches of its ideal beneath every form of disguise, I decline to enter into any compromise or false position in reference to it—I urge people to declare open war with it.

The morality of paltry people as the measure of all things: this is the most repugnant kind of degeneracy that civilisation has ever yet brought into existence. And this *kind of ideal* is hanging still, under the name of "God," over men's heads!!

However modest one's demands may be concerning intellectual cleanliness, when one touches the New Testament one cannot help experiencing a sort of inexpressible feeling of discomfort; for the unbounded cheek with which the least qualified people will have their say in its pages, in regard to the greatest problems of existence, and claim to sit in judgment on such matters, exceeds all limits. The impudent levity with which the most unwieldy problems are spoken of here (life, the world, God, the purpose of life), as if they were not problems at all, but the most simple things which these little bigots *know all about!!!*

This was the most fatal form of insanity that has ever yet existed on earth:—when these little lying abortions of bigotry begin laying claim to the words "God," "last judgment," "truth," "love," "wisdom," "Holy Spirit," and thereby distinguishing themselves from the rest of the world; when such men begin to transvalue values to suit themselves, as though they were the sense, the salt, the standard, and the measure of all things; then all that one should do is this: build lunatic asylums for their incarceration. To *persecute* them was an egregious act of antique folly: this was taking them too seriously; it was making them serious.

The whole fatality was made possible by the fact that a similar form of megalomania was already *in existence,* the *Jewish* form (once the gulf separating the Jews from the Christian-Jews was bridged, the Christian-Jews *were compelled* to employ those self-preservative measures afresh which were discovered by the Jewish instinct, for their own self-preservation, after having accentuated them); and again through the fact that Greek moral philosophy had done everything that could be done to prepare the way for moral-fanaticism, even among Greeks and Romans, and to render it palatable. . . . Plato, the great importer of corruption, who was the first who refused to see Nature in morality, and who had already deprived the Greek gods of all their worth by his notion "*good,*" was already tainted with *Jewish bigotry* (in Egypt?). . . .

The *law,* which is the fundamentally realistic formula of certain self-preservative measures of a community, forbids certain actions that have a definite tendency to jeopardise the welfare of that community: it does *not* forbid the attitude of mind which gives rise to these actions—for in the pursuit of other ends the community requires these forbidden actions, namely, when it is a matter of opposing its *enemies.* The moral idealist now steps forward and says: "God sees into men's hearts: the action itself counts for nothing; the reprehensible attitude of mind from which it proceeds must be extirpated. . . ." In normal conditions

From Friedrich Nietzsche, *The Will to Power,* trans. A. M. Ludovici.

men laugh at such things; it is only in exceptional cases, when a community lives *quite* beyond the need of waging war in order to maintain itself, that an ear is lent to such things. Any attitude of mind is abandoned, the utility of which cannot be conceived.

This was the case, for example, when Buddha appeared among a people that was both peaceable and afflicted with great intellectual weariness.

This was also the case in regard to the first Christian community (as also the Jewish), the primary condition of which was the absolutely *unpolitical* Jewish society. Christianity could grow only upon the soil of Judaism—that is to say, among a people that had already renounced the political life, and which led a sort of parasitic existence within the Roman sphere of government. Christianity goes a step *farther:* it allows men to "emasculate" themselves even more; the circumstances actually favour their doing so.—*Nature* is *expelled* from morality when it is said, "Love ye your enemies": for *Nature's* injunction, "Ye shall *love* your neighbour and *hate* your enemy," has now become senseless in the law (in instinct); now, even *the love a man feels for his neighbour* must first be based upon something (*a sort of love of God*). *God* is introduced everywhere, and *utility* is withdrawn; the natural *origin* of morality is denied everywhere: the *veneration of Nature,* which lies in *acknowledging a natural morality,* is *destroyed* to the roots. . . .

Whence comes the *seductive charm* of this emasculate ideal of man? Why are we not *disgusted* by it, just as we are disgusted at the thought of a eunuch? . . . The answer is obvious: it is not the voice of the eunuch that revolts us, despite the cruel mutilation of which it is the result; for, as a matter of fact, it has grown sweeter. . . . And owing to the very fact that the "male organ" has been amputated from virtue, its voice now has a feminine ring, which, formerly, was not to be discerned.

On the other hand, we have only to think of the terrible hardness, dangers, and accidents to which a life of manly virtues leads—the life of a Corsican, even at the present day, or that of a heathen Arab (which resembles the Corsican's life even to the smallest detail: the Arab's songs might have been written by Corsicans)—in order to perceive how the most robust type of man was fascinated and moved by the voluptuous ring of this "goodness" and "purity." . . . A pastoral melody . . . an idyll . . . the "good man": such things have most effect in ages when tragedy is abroad.

The *Astuteness of moral castration.*—How is war waged against the virile passions and valuations? No violent physical means are available; the war must therefore be one of ruses, spells, and lies—in short, a "spiritual war."

First recipe: One appropriates virtue in general, and makes it the main feature of one's ideal; the older ideal is denied and declared to be *the reverse of all ideals.* Slander has to be carried to a fine art for this purpose.

Second recipe: One's own type is set up as a general *standard;* and this is projected into all things, behind all things, and behind the destiny of all things—as God.

Third recipe: The opponents of one's ideal are declared to be the opponents of God; one arrogates to oneself a *right* to great pathos, to power, and a right to curse and to bless.

Fourth recipe: All suffering, all gruesome, terrible, and fatal things are declared to be the results of opposition to *one's* ideal—all suffering is *punishment* even in the case of one's adherents (except it be a trial, etc.).

Fifth recipe: One goes so far as to regard Nature as the reverse of one's ideal, and the lengthy sojourn amid natural conditions is considered a great trial of patience—a sort of martyrdom; one studies contempt, both in one's attitudes and one's looks towards all "natural things."

Sixth recipe: The triumph of anti-naturalism and ideal castration, the triumph of the world of the pure, good, sinless, and blessed, is projected into the future as the consummation, the finale, the great hope, and the "Coming of the Kingdom of God."

I hope that one may still be allowed to laugh at this artificial hoisting up of a small species of man to the position of an absolute standard of all things?

To what extent psychologists have been corrupted by the moral idiosyncrasy!—Not one of the ancient philosophers had the courage to advance the theory of the non-free will (that is to say, the theory that denies morality);—not one had the courage to identify the typical feature of happiness, of every kind of happiness ("pleasure"), with the will to power: for the pleasure of power was considered immoral;—not one had the courage to regard virtue as a *result of immorality* (as a result of a will to power) in the service of a species (or of a race, or of a *polis*); for the will to power was considered immoral.

In the whole of moral evolution, there is no sign of truth: all the conceptual elements which come into play are fictions; all the psychological tenets are false; all the forms of logic employed in this department of prevarication are sophisms. The chief feature of all moral philosophers is their total lack of intellectual cleanliness and self-control: they regard "fine feelings" as arguments: their heaving breasts seem to them the bellows of godliness. . . . Moral philosophy is the most suspicious period in the history of the human intellect.

The first great example: in the name of morality and under its patronage, a great wrong was committed, which as a matter of fact was in every respect an act of decadence. Sufficient stress cannot be laid upon this fact, that the great Greek philosophers not only represented the decadence of *every kind of Greek ability,* but also made it *contagious.* . . . This "virtue" made wholly abstract was the highest form of seduction; to make oneself abstract means to *turn one's back on the world.*

The moment is a very remarkable one: the Sophists are within sight of the first *criticism* of morality, the first *knowledge* of morality:—they classify the majority of moral valuations (in view of their dependence upon local conditions) together;—they lead one to understand that every form of morality is capable of being upheld dialectically: that is to say, they guessed that all the fundamental principles of a morality must be *sophistical*—a proposition which was afterwards proved in the grandest possible style by the ancient philosophers from Plato onwards (up to Kant);—they postulate the primary truth that there is no such thing as a "moral *per se,*" a "good *per se,*" and that it is madness to talk of "truth" in this respect.

Wherever was *intellectual uprightness* to be found in those days?

The Greek culture of the Sophists had grown out of all the Greek instincts; it belongs to the culture of the age of Pericles as necessarily as Plato does not: it has its predecessors in Heraclitus, Democritus, and in the scientific types of the old philosophy; it finds expression in the elevated culture of Thucydides, for instance. And—it has ultimately shown itself to be right: every step in the science of epistemology and morality has *confirmed the attitude* of the Sophists. . . . Our modern attitude of mind is, to a great extent, Heraclitean, Democritean, and Protagorean . . . to say that it is *Protagorean* is even sufficient: because Protagoras was in himself a synthesis of the two men Heraclitus and Democritus.

(*Plato: a great Cagliostro,*—let us think of how Epicurus judged him; how Timon, Pyrrho's friend, judged him—Is Plato's integrity by any chance beyond question? . . . But we at least know what he wished to have *taught* as absolute truth—namely, things which were to him not even relative truths: the separate and immortal life of "souls.") . . .

Of all the interpretations of the world attempted heretofore, the *mechanical* one seems to-day to be most prominent. Apparently it has a clean conscience on its side; for no science believes inwardly in progress and success unless it be with the help of mechanical procedures. Everyone knows these procedures: "reason" and "purpose" are kept out of consideration as far as possible; it is shown that, provided a sufficient amount of time be allowed to elapse, everything can evolve out of everything else, and no one attempts to suppress his malicious satisfaction, when the "apparent design in the fate" of a plant or of the yolk of an egg, may be traced to stress and thrust—in short, people are heartily glad to pay respect to this principle of profoundest stupidity, if I may be allowed to pass a playful remark concerning these serious matters. Meanwhile, among the most select intellects to be found in this movement, some presentiment of evil, some anxiety is noticeable, as if the theory had a rent in it that sooner or later might be its last: I mean the sort of rent that denotes the end of all balloons inflated with such theories.

Stress and thrust themselves cannot be "explained," one cannot get rid of the *actio in distans*. The belief even in the ability to explain is now lost, and people peevishly admit that one can only describe, not explain, that the dynamic interpretation of the world, with its denial of "empty space" and its little agglomerations of atoms, will soon get the better of physicists: although in this way *Dynamis* is certainly granted an inner quality.

The triumphant concept *energy*, with which our physicists created God and the world, needs yet to be completed: it must be given an inner will which I characterize as the "*Will to Power*"—that is to say, as an insatiable desire to manifest power; or the application and exercise of power as a creative instinct, etc. Physicists cannot get rid of the "*actio in distans*" in their principles; any more than they can a repelling force (or an attracting one). There is no help for it, all movements, all "appearances," all "laws" must be understood as *symptoms* of an *inner* phenomenon, and the analogy of man must be used for this purpose. It is possible to trace all the instincts of an animal to the will to power; as also all the functions of organic life to this one source.

Is the "Will to Power" a kind of will, or is it identical with the concept will? Is it equivalent to desiring or commanding; is it the Will that Schopenhauer says is the essence of things?

My proposition is that the will of psychologists hitherto has been an unjustifiable generalization, and there is no such thing as this sort of will, that instead of the development of one will into several forms being taken as a fact, the character of will has been cancelled owing to the fact that its content, its "whither," was subtracted from it. In Schopenhauer this is so in the highest degree; what he calls "Will" is merely an empty word. There is even less plausibility in the Will to Live, for life is simply one of the manifestations of the Will to Power; it is quite arbitrary and ridiculous to suggest that everything is striving to enter into this particular form of the Will to Power.

How is it that the fundamental article of faith in all psychologies is a piece of most outrageous contortion and fabrication? "Man strives after happiness," for instance—how much of this is true? In order to understand what life is, and what kind of striving and tenseness life contains, the formula should hold good not only of trees and plants, but of animals also. "What does the plant strive after?"—But here we have already invented a false entity that does not exist—concealing and denying the fact of an infinitely variegated growth, with individual and semi-individual starting-points—when we give it the clumsy title "plant" as if it were a unit. It is very obvious that the ultimate and smallest "individuals" cannot be understood in the sense of metaphysical individuals or atoms; their sphere of power is continually shifting its ground: but with all these changes, can it be said that any of them strives after happiness?—All this expanding, this incorporation and growth, is a search for resistance; movement is essentially related to states of pain: the driving power here must represent some other desire if it leads to such continual willing and seeking of pain.—To what end do the trees of a virgin forest contend with each other? "For happiness"?—For power! . . .

Man is now master of the forces of nature, and master too of his own wild and unbridled feelings (the passions have followed suit, and have learned to become useful)—in comparison with primeval man, the man of to-day represents an enormous quantum of power, but not an increase in happiness! How can one maintain, then, that he has striven after happiness? . . .

The new concept of the universe. The universe exists; it is nothing that grows into existence and that passes out of existence. Or, better still, it develops, it passes away, but it never began to develop, and has never ceased from passing away; it *maintains* itself in both states. . . . It lives on itself, its excrements are its nourishment.

We need not concern ourselves for one instant with the hypothesis of a *created* world. The concept "create" is today utterly indefinable and unrealizable; it is but a word that hails from superstitious ages; nothing can be explained with a word. The last attempt to conceive of a world that *began* was recently made in diverse ways, with the help of logical reasoning chiefly, as you will guess, with an ulterior theological motive.

Several attempts have been made lately to show that the concept that "the universe has an infinite past" (*regressus in infinitum*) is contradictory: in fact, it was even demonstrated, at the price of confounding the head with the tail. Nothing can prevent me from calculating backward from this moment of time, and of saying: "I shall never reach the end"; just as I can calculate without end in a forward direction, from the same moment. It is only when I wish to commit the error—I shall be careful to avoid it—of reconciling this correct concept of a *regressus in infinitum* with the absolutely unrealizable concept of an infinite *progressus* up to the present; only when I consider the direction (forward or backward) as logically indifferent, that I take hold of the head—this very moment—and think I hold the tail: this pleasure I leave to you. . . .

I have come across this thought in other thinkers before me, and every time I found that it was determined by other ulterior motives (chiefly theological, in favor of a *creator spiritus*). If the universe were in any way able to congeal, to dry up, to perish; or if it were capable of attaining to a state of equilibrium; or if it had any kind of goal at all which a long lapse of time, immutability, and finality reserved for it (in short, to speak metaphysically, if becoming could resolve itself into being or into nonentity), this state ought already to have been reached. But it has not been reached: it therefore follows. . . . This is the only certainty we can grasp, which can serve as a corrective to a host of cosmic hypotheses possible in themselves. If, for instance, materialism cannot consistently escape the conclusion of a final state, . . . then materialism is thereby refuted.

If the universe may be conceived as a definite quantity of energy, as a definite number of centres of energy—and every other concept remains indefinite and therefore useless—it follows that the universe must go through a calculable number of combinations in the great game of chance that constitutes its existence. In infinity at some moment or other, every possible combination must have been realized; not only this, but it must have been realised an infinite number of times. And inasmuch as between every one of these combinations and its next recurrence every other possible combination would necessarily have been undergone, and since every one of these combinations would determine the whole series in the same order, a circular movement of absolutely identical series is thus demonstrated: the universe is shown to be a circular movement that has already repeated itself an infinite number of times, and that plays its game for all eternity.—This conception is not simply materialistic; for if it were this, it would not involve an infinite recurrence of identical cases, but a final state. Owing to the fact that the universe has not reached this final state, materialism shows itself to be but an imperfect and provisional hypothesis.

And do you know what "the universe" is to my mind? Shall I show it to you in my mirror? This universe is a monster of energy, without beginning or end; a fixed and brazen quantity of energy that grows neither bigger nor smaller, does not consume itself, but only alters its face; as a whole its bulk is immutable, it is a household without either losses or gains, but likewise without increase and without sources of revenue, surrounded by nonentity as by a frontier. It is nothing vague or wasteful, it does not stretch into infinity; but is a definite quantum of energy located in limited space, and not in space that would be anywhere empty. It is rather energy everywhere, the play of forces and force-waves, at the same time one and many, agglomerating here and diminishing there, a sea of forces storming and raging in itself, forever changing, forever rolling back over incalculable ages to recurrence, with an ebb and flow of its forms, producing the most complicated things out of the most simple structures; producing the most ardent, most savage, and most contradictory things out of the quietest, most rigid, and most frozen material, and then returning from multifariousness to uniformity, from the play of contradictions back into the delight of consonance, saying Yea unto itself, even in this homogeneity of its courses and ages; forever blessing itself as something which recurs for all eternity—a becoming that knows not satiety, or disgust, or weariness—this, my Dionysian world of eternal self-creation, of eternal self-destruction, this mysterious world of twofold voluptuousness; this, my "Beyond Good and Evil," without aim, unless there is an aim in the bliss of the circle, without will, unless a ring must by nature keep good will to itself—would you have a name for my world? A *solution* of all your riddles? Do you also want a light, you most concealed, strongest and most undaunted men of the blackest midnight?—*This world is the Will to Power—and nothing else!* And even you yourselves are this Will to Power—and nothing else!

. . . He, however, who has reflected deeply concerning the question, how and where the plant man has hitherto grown most vigorously, is forced to believe that this has always taken place under the opposite conditions; that to this end the danger of the situation has to increase enormously, his inventive faculty and dissembling powers have to fight their way up under long oppression and compulsion, and his Will to Life has to be increased to the unconditioned Will to Power, to *over-power:* he believes that danger, severity, violence, peril in the street and in the heart, inequality of rights, secrecy, stoicism, seductive art, and devilry of every kind—in short, the opposite of all gregarious desiderata—are necessary for the elevation of man. Such a morality with opposite designs, which would rear man upwards instead of to comfort and mediocrity; such a morality, with the intention of producing a ruling caste—the future lords of the earth—must, in order to be taught at all, introduce itself as if it were in some way correlated to the prevailing moral law, and must come forward under the cover of the latter's words and forms. But seeing that, to this end, a host of transitionary and deceptive measures must be discovered, and that the life of a single individual stands for almost nothing compared to the accomplishment of such lengthy tasks and aims, the first thing that must be done is to rear *a new kind* of man in whom the duration of the necessary will and the necessary instincts is guaranteed for many generations. This must be a new kind of ruling species and caste—this ought to be quite as clear as the somewhat lengthy and not easily expressed consequences of this thought. The aim should be to prepare a *transvaluation of values* for a particularly strong kind of man, most highly gifted in intellect and will, and, to this end, slowly and cautiously to liberate in him a whole host of slandered instincts hitherto held in check: whoever meditates about this problem belongs to us, the free spirits. . . .

From now henceforward there will be such favourable first conditions for greater ruling powers as have never yet been found on earth. And this is by no means the most important point. The establishment has been made possible of international race unions which will set themselves the task of rearing a ruling race, the future "lords of the earth"—a new, vast aristocracy based upon the most severe self-discipline, in which the will of philosophical men of power and artist-tyrants will be stamped upon thousands of years: a higher species of men who, thanks to their preponderance of will, knowledge, riches, and influence, will avail themselves of democratic Europe as the most suitable and supple instrument they can have for taking the fate of the earth into their own hands, and working as artists upon man himself. Enough! The time is coming for us to transform all our views on politics.

I fancy I have divined some of the things that lie hidden in the soul of the highest man; perhaps every man who has divined so much must go to ruin. But he who has seen the highest man must do all he can to make him *possible*.

Fundamental thought: we must make the future the standard of all our valuations—and not seek the laws for our conduct behind us.

Not "mankind," but *Superman,* is the goal. . . .

BRADLEY

1846–1924

Francis Herbert Bradley was born in Clapham, Surrey (now London), one of twenty-two children fathered by an evangelical preacher. After graduating from University College, Oxford, he was elected to a fellowship at Merton College. His unique brand of absolute idealism grew out of opposition to both the past British empiricists (Locke, Berkeley, and Hume) and the then-current empiricism of J. S. Mill. Like most post-Kantian idealist metaphysicians, Bradley conceives the totality of what really exists in terms of "the Absolute," an essentially whole world-mind similar to Hegel's and Schelling's conceptions except Bradley's more atheistic system does not involve any type of God.

The Absolute as conceived by Bradley requires us to transcend all the fundamental categories of human thought: quality and relation, substance and cause, subject and object, time and space, and so on, are but mere appearance. Neither one nor many, the Absolute is a "unity in diversity." Individuals, which are not collections of attributable properties, get their unity and character from the relations of their properties. This means that in Bradley's view there are no external relations: all relations are *internal.*

Suppose an individual named Socrates has a property—say, that of being a teacher—in virtue of which he has a relation *R* to some other individual or individuals; in that case, *R* is an *internal relation* of Socrates. Socrates is a teacher; the relation of being someone's teacher is one of Socrates's internal relations. An external relation is one in which there is no property in virtue of which an individual is *necessarily R*-related to anyone else. For instance, if Socrates is taller than Plato, this is an external relation. Now, since according to Bradley and other British absolute idealists (most notably T. H. Green and B. Bosanquet), all relations are internal, this means that any individual has relations to absolutely all other individuals; to assert any truth about Socrates is thus to assert a truth about the Absolute (the whole world of actually existing things). In other words, to say anything at all about any individual part of the universe is really to say something about the whole universe.

In the following selection, taken from his most famous work, *Appearance and Reality,* Bradley presents his unique brand of absolute idealism devoid of religious metaphysics and grounded in a logic distinct from both psychology and physics: the Absolute must be understood not as a system of appearances but as the container of that system such that each appearance is itself an essential constituent of reality. Bertrand Russell was greatly influenced by Bradley's views, first by agreement and then through opposition, and so was G. E. Moore; even while rejecting Bradley's positive theses, both Moore and Russell remained under the influence of Bradley's sharply critical dialectic as well as the approach to logic he developed in *The Principles of Logic* (1883; 2nd ed., 1922, corrected 1928). Three months before his death, Bradley became the first philosopher to be appointed to the Order of Merit.

APPEARANCE AND REALITY

BOOK II: REALITY

CHAPTER XXVI: THE ABSOLUTE AND ITS APPEARANCES

. . . All is appearance, and no appearance, or any combination of these, is the same as Reality. This is half the truth, and by itself it is a dangerous error. We must turn at once to correct it by adding its counterpart and supplement. The Absolute *is* its appearances, it really is all and every one of them. That is the other half-truth which we have already insisted on, and which we must urge once more here. And we may remind ourselves at this point of a fatal mistake. If you take appearances, singly or all together, and assert barely that the Absolute is either one of them or all—the position is hopeless. Having first set these down as appearance, you now proclaim them as the very opposite; for that which is identified with the Absolute is no appearance but is utter reality. But we have seen the solution of this puzzle, and we know the sense and meaning in which these half-truths come together into one. The Absolute is each appearance, and is all, but it is not any one as such. And it is not all equally, but one appearance is more real than another. In short the doctrine of degrees in reality and truth is the fundamental answer to our problem. Everything is essential, and yet one thing is worthless in comparison with others. Nothing is perfect, as such, and yet everything in some degree contains a vital function of Perfection. Every attitude of experience, every sphere or level of the world, is a necessary factor in the Absolute. Each in its own way satisfies, until compared with that which is more than itself. Hence appearance is error, if you will, but not every error is illusion. At each stage is involved the principle of that which is higher, and every stage (it is therefore true) is already inconsistent. But on the other hand, taken for itself and measured by its own ideas, every level has truth. It meets, we may say, its own claims, and it proves false only when tried by that which is already beyond it. And thus the Absolute is immanent alike through every region of appearances. There are degrees and ranks, but, one and all, they are alike indispensable.

We can find no province of the world so low but the Absolute inhabits it. Nowhere is there even a single fact so fragmentary and so poor that to the universe it does not matter.

From F. H. Bradley, *Appearance and Reality: A Metaphysical Essay* (London: George Allen & Unwin Ltd.; New York: Macmillan, 1893; 2nd ed., 1897).

There is truth in every idea however false, there is reality in every existence however slight; and, where we can point to reality or truth, there is the one undivided life of the Absolute. Appearance without reality would be impossible, for what then could appear? And reality without appearance would be nothing, for there certainly is nothing outside appearances. But on the other hand Reality (we must repeat this) is not the sum of things. It is the unity in which all things, coming together, are transmuted, in which they are changed all alike, though not changed equally. And, as we have perceived, in this unity relations of isolation and hostility are affirmed and absorbed. These also are harmonious in the Whole, though not of course harmonious as such, and while severally confined to their natures as separate. Hence it would show blindness to urge, as an objection against our view, the opposition found in ugliness and in conscious evil. The extreme of hostility implies an intenser relation, and this relation falls within the Whole and enriches its unity. The apparent discordance and distraction is overruled into harmony, and it is but the condition of fuller and more individual development. But we can hardly speak of the Absolute itself as either ugly or evil. The Absolute is indeed evil in a sense and it is ugly and false, but the sense, in which these predicates can be applied, is too forced and unnatural. Used of the Whole each predicate would be the result of an indefensible division, and each would be a fragment isolated and by itself without consistent meaning. Ugliness, evil, and error, in their several spheres, are subordinate aspects. They imply distinctions falling, in each case, within one subject province of the Absolute's kingdom; and they involve a relation, in each case. of some struggling element to its superior, though limited, whole. Within these minor wholes the opposition draws its life from, and is overpowered by the system which supports it. The predicates evil, ugly, and false must therefore stamp, whatever they qualify, as a mere subordinate aspect, an aspect belonging to the province of beauty or goodness or truth. And to assign such a position to the sovereign Absolute would be plainly absurd. You may affirm that the Absolute *has* ugliness and error and evil, since it owns the provinces in which these features are partial elements. But to assert that it *is* one of its own fragmentary and dependent details would be inadmissible.

It is only by a licence that the subject-systems, even when we regard them as wholes, can be made qualities of Reality. It is always under correction and on sufferance that we term the universe either beautiful or moral or true. And to venture further would be both useless and dangerous at once.

If you view the Absolute morally at all, then the Absolute is good. It cannot be one factor contained within and overpowered by goodness. In the same way, viewed logically or aesthetically, the Absolute can only be true or beautiful. It is merely when you have so termed it, and while you still continue to insist on these preponderant characters, that you can introduce at all the ideas of falsehood and ugliness. And, so introduced, their direct application to the Absolute is impossible. Thus to identify the supreme universe with a partial system may, for some end, be admissible. But to take it as a single character within this system, and as a feature which is already overruled, and which as such is suppressed there, would, we have seen, be quite unwarranted. Ugliness, error, and evil, all are owned by, and all essentially contribute to the wealth of the Absolute. The Absolute, we may say in general, has no assets beyond appearances; and again, with appearances alone to its credit, the Absolute would be bankrupt. All of these are worthless alike apart from transmutation. But, on the other hand once more, since the amount of change is different in each case, appearances differ widely in their degrees of truth and reality. There are predicates which, in comparison with others, are false and unreal.

To survey the field of appearances, to measure each by the idea of perfect individuality, and to arrange them in an order and in a system of reality and merit—would be the task of metaphysics. This task (I may repeat) is not attempted in these pages. I have however endeavoured here, as above, to explain and to insist on the fundamental principle. And, passing from that, I will now proceed to remark on some points of interest. There are certain questions which at this stage we may hope to dispose of.

Let us turn our attention once more to Nature or the physical world. Are we to affirm that ideas are forces, and that ends operate and move there? And, again, is Nature beautiful and an object of possible worship? On this latter point, which I will consider first, I find serious confusion. Nature, as we have seen, can be taken in various senses. We may understand by it the whole universe, or again merely the world in space, or again we may restrict it to a very much narrower meaning. We may first remove everything which in our opinion is only psychical, and the abstract residue—the primary qualities—we may then identify with Nature. These will be the essence, while all the rest is accessory adjective, and, in the fullest sense, is immaterial. Now we have found that Nature, so understood, has but little reality. It is an ideal construction required by science, and it is a necessary working fiction. And we may add that reduction to a result, and to a particular instance, of this fiction, is what is meant by a strictly physical explanation. But in this way there grows up a great confusion. For the object of natural science is the full world in all its sensible glory, while the essence of Nature lies in this poor fiction of primary qualities, a fiction believed not to be idea but solid fact. Nature then, while unexplained, is still left in its sensuous splendor, while Nature, if explained, would be reduced to this paltry abstraction. On one side is set up the essence—the final reality—in the shape of a bare skeleton of primary qualities; on the other side remains the boundless profusion of life which everywhere opens endlessly before our view. And these extremes then are confused, or are conjoined, by sheer obscurity or else by blind mental oscillation. If explanation reduces facts to be adjectives of something which they do not qualify at all, the whole connection seems irrational, and the process robs us of the facts. But if the primary essence after all *is* qualified, then its character is transformed. The explanation, in reducing the concrete, will now also have enriched and have individualized the abstract, and we shall have started on our way towards philosophy and truth. But of this latter result in the present case there can be no question. And therefore we must end in oscillation with no attempt at an intelligent unity of view. Nature is, on the one hand, that show whose reality lies barely in primary qualities. It is, on the other hand, that endless world of sensible life, which appeals to our sympathy and extorts our wonder. It is the object loved and lived in by the poet and by the observing naturalist. And, when we speak of Nature, we have often no idea which of these extremes, or indeed what at all, is to be understood. We in fact pass, as suits the occasion, from one extreme unconsciously to the other.

I will briefly apply this result to the question before us. Whether Nature is beautiful and adorable will depend entirely on the sense in which Nature is taken. If the genuine reality of Nature is bare primary qualities, then I cannot think that such a question needs serious discussion. In a word Nature will be dead. It could possess at the most a kind of symmetry; and again by its extent, or by its practical relation to our weaknesses or needs, it might excite in us feelings of a certain kind. But these feelings, in the first place, would fall absolutely within ourselves. They could not rationally be applied to, nor in the very least could they qualify Nature. And, in the second place, these feelings would in our minds hardly take the form of worship. Hence when Nature, as the object of natural science, is either asserted to be beautiful, or is set up before us as divine, we may make our answer at once.

If the reality of the object is to be restricted to primary qualities, then surely no one would advocate the claims we have mentioned. If again the whole perceptible world and the glory of it is to be genuinely real, and if this splendor and this life are of the very essence of Nature, then a difficulty will arise in two directions. In the first place this claim has to get itself admitted by physical science. The psychical has to be adopted as at least co-equal in reality with matter. The relation to the organism and to the soul has to be included in the vital being of a physical object. And the first difficulty will consist in advancing to this point. Then the second difficulty will appear at once when this point has been reached. For, having gone so far, we have to justify our refusal to go further. For why is Nature to be confined to the perceptible world? If the psychical and the "subjective" is in any degree to make part of its reality, then upon what principle can you shut out the highest and most spiritual experience? Why is Nature viewed and created by the painter, the poet, and the seer, not essentially real? But in this way Nature will tend to become the total universe of both spirit and matter. And our main conclusion so far must be this. It is evidently useless to raise such questions about the object of natural science, when you have not settled in your mind what that object is, and when you supply no principle on which we can decide in what its reality consists.

But turning from this confusion, and once more approaching the question from, I trust, a more rational ground, I will try to make a brief answer. Into the special features and limits of the beautiful in Nature I cannot enter. And I cannot discuss how far, and in what sense, the physical world is included in the true object of religion. These are special enquiries which fall within the scope of my volume. But whether Nature is beautiful or adorable at all, and whether it possesses such attributes really and in truth,—to the question, asked thus in general, we may answer, Yes. We have seen that Nature, regarded as bare matter, is a mere convenient abstraction. The addition of secondary qualities, the included relation to a body and to a soul, in making Nature more concrete makes it thereby more real. The sensible life, the warmth and color, the odor and the tones, without these Nature is a mere intellectual fiction. The primary qualities are a construction demanded by science, but, while divorced from the secondary, they have no life as facts. Science has a Hades from which it returns to interpret the world, but the inhabitants of its Hades are merely shades. And, when the secondary qualities are added, Nature, though more real, is still incomplete. The joys and sorrows of her children, their affections and their thoughts—how are we to say that these have no part in the reality of Nature? Unless to a mind restricted by a principle the limitation would be absurd, and our main principle on the other hand insists that Nature, when more full, is more real. And this same principle will carry us on to a further conclusion. The emotions, excited by Nature in the considering soul, must at least in part be referred to, and must be taken as attributes of Nature. If there is no beauty there, and if the sense of that is to fall somewhere outside, why in the end should there be any qualities in Nature at all? And, if no emotional tone is to qualify Nature, how and on what principle are we to attribute to it anything else whatever? Everything there without exception is "subjective," if we are to regard the matter so; and an emotional tone cannot, solely on this account, be excluded from Nature. And, otherwise, why should it not have reality there as a genuine quality? For myself I must follow the same principle and can accept the fresh consequence. The Nature that we have lived in, and that we love, is really Nature. Its beauty and its terror and its majesty are no illusion, but qualify it essentially. And hence that, in which at our best moments we all are forced to believe, is the literal truth.

This result, however, needs some qualification from another side. It is certain that everything is determined by the relations in which it stands. It is certain that, with increase of determinateness, a thing becomes more and more real. On the other hand anything, fully determined, would be the Absolute itself. There is a point where increase of reality implies passage beyond self. A thing by enlargement becomes a mere factor in the whole next above it; and, in the end, all provinces and all relative wholes cease to keep their separate characters. We must not forget this while considering the reality of Nature. By gradual increase of that reality you reach a stage at which Nature, as such, is absorbed. Or, as you reflect on Nature, your object identifies itself gradually with the universe or Absolute. And the question arises at what point, when we begin to add psychical life or to attribute spiritual attributes to Nature, we have ceased to deal with Nature in any proper sense of that term. Where do we pass from Nature, as an outlying province in the kingdom of things, to Nature as a suppressed element in a higher unity? These enquiries are demanded by philosophy, and their result would lead to clearer conclusions about the qualities of Nature. I can do no more than allude to them here, and the conclusion, on which I insist, can in the main be urged independently. Nothing is lost to the Absolute, and all appearances have reality. The Nature, studied by the observer and by the poet and painter, is in all its sensible and emotional fulness a very real Nature. It is in most respects more real than the strict object of physical science. For Nature, as the world whose real essence lies in primary qualities, has not a high degree of reality and truth. It is a mere abstraction made and required for a certain purpose. And the object of natural science may either mean this skeleton, or it may mean the skeleton made real by blood and flesh of secondary qualities. Hence, before we dwell on the feelings Nature calls for from us, it would be better to know in what sense we are using the term. But the boundary of Nature can hardly be drawn even at secondary qualities. Or, if we draw it there, we must draw it arbitrarily, and to suit our convenience. Only on this ground can psychical life be excluded from Nature, while, regarded otherwise, the exclusion would not be tenable. And to deny aesthetic qualities in Nature, or to refuse it those which inspire us with fear or devotion, would once more surely be arbitrary. It would be a division introduced for a mere working theoretical purpose. Our principle, that the abstract is the unreal, moves us steadily upward. It forces us first to rejection of bare primary qualities, and it compels us in the end to credit Nature with our higher emotions. That process can cease only where Nature is quite absorbed into spirit, and at every stage of the process we find increase in reality.

And this higher interpretation, and this eventual transcendence of Nature lead us to the discussion of another point which we mentioned above. Except in finite souls and except in volition may we suppose that ends operate in Nature, and is ideality, in any other sense, a working force there? How far such a point of view may be permitted in aesthetics or in the philosophy of religion, I shall not enquire. But considering the physical world as a mere system of appearances in space, are we on metaphysical grounds to urge the insufficiency of the mechanical view? In what form (if in any) are we to advocate a philosophy of Nature? On this difficult subject I will very briefly remark in passing.

The mechanical view plainly is absurd as a full statement of truth. Nature so regarded has not ceased at all (we may say) to be ideal, but its ideality throughout falls somewhere outside itself. And that even for working purposes this view can everywhere be rigidly maintained, I am unable to assert. But upon one subject I have no doubts. Every special science must be left at liberty to follow its own methods, and, if the natural sciences reject every way of explanation which is not mechanical, that is not the affair of metaphysics. For myself, in other ways ignorant, I venture to assume that these sciences understand their own business. But where, quite beyond the scope of any special science, assertions are made, the metaphysician may protest. He may insist that abstractions are not realities, and that working fictions are never more than useful fragments of truth. And on another point also he may claim a hearing. To adopt one sole principle of valid explanation, and to urge that, if phenomena are to be explicable, they must be explained by one method—this is of course competent to any science. But it is another thing to proclaim phenomena as already explained, or as explicable, where in certain aspects or in certain provinces they clearly are not explained, and where, perhaps, not even the first beginning of an explanation has been made. In these lapses or excursions beyond its own limits natural science has no rights. But within its boundaries I think every wise man will consider it sacred. And this question of the operation of Ends in Nature is one which, in my judgment, metaphysics should leave untouched.

Is there then no positive task which is left to metaphysics, the accomplishment of which might be called a philosophy of Nature? I will briefly point out the field which seems to call for occupation. All appearances for metaphysics have degrees of reality. We have an idea of perfection or of individuality; and, as we find that any form of existence more completely realizes this idea, we assign to it its position in the scale of being. And in this scale (as we have seen) the lower, as its defects are made good, passes beyond itself into the higher. The end, or the absolute individuality, is also the principle. Present from the first it supplies the test of its inferior stages, and, as these are included in fuller wholes, the principle grows in reality. Metaphysics in short can assign a meaning to perfection and progress. And hence, if it were to accept from the sciences the various kinds of natural phenomena, if it were to set out these kinds in an order of merit and rank, if it could point out how within each higher grade the defects of the lower are made good, and how the principle of the lower grade is carried out in the higher—metaphysics surely would have contributed to the interpretation of Nature. And, while myself totally incapable of even assisting in such work, I cannot see how or on what ground it should be considered unscientific. It is doubtless absurd to wear the airs of systematic omniscience. It is worse than absurd to pour scorn on the detail and on the narrowness of devoted specialism. But to try to give system from time to time to the results of the sciences, and to attempt to arrange these on what seems a true principle of worth, can be hardly irrational.

Such a philosophy of Nature, if at least it were true to itself, could not intrude on the province of physical science. For it would, in short, abstain wholly and in every form from speculation on genesis. How the various stages of progress come to happen in time, in what order or orders they follow, and in each case from what causes, these enquiries would, as such, be no concern of philosophy. Its idea of evolution and progress in a word should not be temporal. And hence a conflict with the sciences upon any question of development or of order could not properly arise. "Higher" and "lower," terms which imply always a standard and end, would in philosophy be applied solely to designate rank. Natural science would still be free, as now, to use, or even to abuse, such terms at its pleasure, and to allow them any degree of meaning which is found convenient. Progress for philosophy would never have any temporal sense, and it could matter nothing if the word elsewhere seemed to bear little or no other. With these brief remarks I must leave a subject which deserves serious attention.

In a complete philosophy the whole world of appearance would be set out as a progress. It would show a development of principle though not a succession in time. Every sphere of experience would be measured by the absolute standard, and would be given a rank answering to its own relative merits and defects. On this scale pure Spirit would mark the extreme most removed from lifeless Nature. And, at each rising degree of this scale, we should find more of the first character with less of the second. The ideal of spirit, we may say, is directly opposite to mechanism. Spirit is a unity of the manifold in which the externality of the manifold has utterly ceased. The universal here is immanent in the parts, and its system does not lie somewhere outside and in the relations between them. It is above the relational form and has absorbed it in a higher unity, a whole in which there is no division between elements and laws. And, since this principle shows itself from the first in the inconsistencies of bare mechanism, we may say that Nature at once is realized and transmuted by spirit. But each of these extremes, we must add, has no existence as fact. The sphere of dead mechanism is set apart by an act of abstraction, and in that abstraction alone it essentially consists. And, on the other hand, pure spirit is not realized except in the Absolute. It can never appear as such and with its full character in the scale of existence. Perfection and individuality belong only to that Whole in which all degrees alike are at once present and absorbed. This one Reality of existence can, as such, nowhere exist among phenomena. And it enters into, but is itself incapable of, evolution and progress.

FREGE
1848–1925

Gottlob Frege was born at Wismar, Germany. He studied at the University of Jena and the University of Göttingen. He became a professor of mathematics at Jena, but his work had a deep and lasting influence on philosophy, especially mathematical logic, the philosophy of mathematics, and the philosophy of language. His ground-breaking *Grundgesetze der Arithmetik* (The basic laws of arithmetic, 1884) begins with a warning to unphilosophical mathematicians, telling them they should not bother reading his book: "Mathematicians reluctant to venture into the labyrinths of philosophy are requested to leave off reading. . . ."

Many philosophers, from Plato and Pythagoras to Descartes and Leibniz, made important contributions to mathematics and considered mathematics important for philosophy. Kant, for instance, took mathematical truths to be a paradigm of the synthetic a priori. As a mathematician, Frege was puzzled why philosophy itself had never developed a sufficiently technical language of its own, and why philosophers seemed to shun the formal language of mathematics and logic and preferred instead to state their philosophies in the sloppy constraints of *natural* language. Why, he wondered, did Descartes, the inventor of analytic geometry, and Leibniz, the inventor of calculus, write philosophy not in the language of mathematics but in French, Latin, German, and so on? Even the philosophers doing fundamental work in logic presented the subject matter of logic itself in natural language. Likewise, Spinoza, who modeled his system after the axiomatic system of Euclidean geometry, uses mathematics only as an example and states his system in natural language.

Frege inspired many philosophers, including Bertrand Russell, to try to achieve the technical rigor of mathematics within philosophy. In his *Basic Laws of Arithmetic* he puts forth the ground-breaking thesis that has since become known as *logicism,* the view that mathematics reduces to pure logic. This was further developed by Bertrand Russell and others, who claimed that perhaps all natural languages—English, German, French, etc.—are reducible to logic.

Frege argued that proofs in mathematics must be constructed using a completely perspicuous machinery, where every demonstration is clear and distinct, both mathematically and philosophically. Every step must be explicit so that nothing is left to intuition or psychology. In this way, the Cartesian notion of clearness and distinctness, an internal state of the mind expressed as a psychological sensation, is replaced by a purely formalized system of symbolic clarity.

According to Frege, the propositions of arithmetic and analysis are pure a priori expressions of logic. This is in marked contrast to Kant, who thought they were synthetic a priori, and John Stuart Mill, who thought they were empirical. In his *Begriffsschrift* (1879), Frege develops a new formal language whose vocabulary and modes of construction owe much to the *calculus philosophicus et ratiocinator* originally envisioned by Leibniz. It is Frege who invented the concepts of quantifiers and variables, symbolic constructions that allowed the giant first step to be taken toward the formalization of natural language. He even developed a revolutionary analysis of sense and meaning, giving primacy to reference (*Bedeutung*), which influenced philosophers as varied as Bertrand Russell, Edmund Husserl, and Martin Heidegger and continues to exert enormous influence still today.

In his *Basic Laws of Arithmetic,* Frege argues against both subjective idealism and psychologism (the view that psychology and introspection are primary methods of inquiry). He offers proof for the thesis that the mind has access to what is beyond itself. The proof is based on a distinction between the *meaning* of a term, its *Sinn* ("sense") and its *Bedeutung* ("reference"), and then demonstrating that two terms can have different meanings even when they have the same reference. Frege makes this clear in his famous "Über Sinn und Bedeutung" (On sense and reference), from which our selection is taken.

ON SENSE AND REFERENCE

The idea of identity challenges reflection and raises questions that are not easy to answer. Is identity a relation? A relation between objects or between names or signs of objects? I assumed the latter in my *Begriffsschrift*. The reasons that seem to favor this are the following: "a = a" and "a = b" are sentences of obviously different cognitive value: "a = a" is valid *a priori* and according to Kant is to be called analytic, while sentences of the form "a = b" often contain very valuable extensions of our knowledge and cannot always be justified *a priori*. The discovery that it is not a different and new sun which rises every morning, but always the very same, certainly was one of the most important discoveries in astronomy. Even today the re-cognition (identification) of a planet or a comet is not always a case of self-evidence. If we wanted to view identity as a relation between the objects designated by the names 'a' and 'b' then "a = b" and "a = a" would seem the same if "a = b" is true. This would express a relation of a thing to itself, and indeed one that holds between every thing and itself but never between one thing and another. What one wants to express with "a = b" seems to be that the signs or names 'a' and 'b' name the same thing; and in that case we would be dealing with those signs: a relation between them would be asserted. But this relation would hold only in so far as they name or designate something. The relation would be mediated through the connection of each sign with the same reference [designated object]. This connection, however, is arbitrary. You cannot forbid the use of an arbitrarily

From Gottlob Frege, "On Sense and Reference," (Veber Sinn und Bedeutung, 1892) trans. Daniel Kolak.

producible event or object as a sign for something else. In that case, the sentence "a = b" would no longer refer to the subject matter but only to its mode of designation; no genuine knowledge would be expressed by it. But this is exactly what we want to do in many cases. If the sign 'a' differs from the sign 'b' only as an object (here by its shape) but not as a sign, that is, not by the manner in which it designates something, then the cognitive value of "a = a" would be essentially the same as that of "a = b", if "a = b" is true. A difference can arise only if the difference of the signs corresponds to a difference in the way the designated objects are presented. Let a, b, c be straight lines connecting the corners of a triangle with the midpoints of the opposite sides. The point of intersection of a and b is then the same as that of b and c. Thus we have different designations for the same point and these names ('intersection of a and b', 'intersection of b and c') indicate also the way in which these points are presented. Therefore the sentence expresses genuine knowledge.

Now it is natural to connect with a sign (name, word combination, letter) not only the designated object, which may be called the reference of the sign, but also the sense (connotation, meaning) of the sign in which the mode of presentation is presented. Accordingly, in our example the reference of the expressions 'the point of intersection of a and b' and 'the point of intersection of b and c' would be the same, but not their senses. The reference of 'evening star' and 'morning star' is the same but not their senses.

In this context it is clear that I here understand by 'sign' or 'name' any expression which functions as a proper name, whose reference accordingly is a definite object (in the widest sense of this word), but not a concept or relation. These matters will be dealt with in another article. The designation of a single object can consist of several words or other signs. For brevity, every such designation will be called a proper name.

The sense of a proper name is grasped by everybody who knows the language or the totality of designations of which the proper name belongs; this, however, illuminates a single aspect of the reference, if there is any. Complete knowledge of the reference would require that we could tell immediately in the case of any given sense whether it belongs to the reference. We can never attain such knowledge.

The regular connection between a sign, its sense and its reference is such that there corresponds a definite sense to the sign and to this sense there corresponds in turn a definite reference; whereas any given reference (object) there does not belong only a single sign. In different languages, and even in one language, the same sense can have different expressions. It is true, there are exceptions to this rule. Certainly there should be a definite sense for every expression in a complete totality of signs, but the natural languages often do not satisfy this condition. We must be content if the same word, at least in the same context, has the same sense. It may perhaps be granted that every expression has a sense if it is formed in a grammatically correct manner and stands for a proper name. But that is not to say that there to the sense corresponds a reference. The words 'the heavenly body most distant from the earth' have a sense; but it is very doubtful if they also have a reference. The expression 'the least rapidly convergent series' has a sense; but it can be proved that it has no reference, since for any given convergent series, one can find another one that is less convergent. Therefore in grasping a sense one is not assured of a reference.

If words are used in the ordinary way what is talked about are their referents. But it may happen that one wishes to speak about the words themselves or about their senses. The first case happens when one quotes someone else's words in direct (ordinary) discourse. In this case one's own words immediately name (denote) the words of the other person and only the latter words have their usual reference. We then have signs of signs. In writing the words are in this case enclosed in quotation marks. A word in quotes must therefore not be taken as having its ordinary reference.

If we want to speak of the sense of an expression 'A' we can do this simply through the phrase 'the sense of the expression 'A''. In direct discourse we speak of the sense, e.g., someone else's words. From this it becomes clear that also in indirect discourse words do not have their customary reference but designate what customarily would be their sense. In order to formulate this succinctly we will say: words in indirect discourse are used *indirectly*, or have *indirect* referents. Thus we distinguish the *customary* from the *indirect* reference of a word; and similarly, its *customary* sense from its *indirect* sense. The indirect reference of a word is accordingly its customary sense. Such exceptions must be kept in mind if the mode of connection between signs, senses and referents in any given case is to be correctly understood.

The reference and the sense of a sign must be distinguished from the associated idea. If the reference of a sign is an object of sense perception, my idea of it is an internal image arising from memories of sense impressions and my activities, internal or external. (With the ideas we can align also the percepts in which the sense impressions and activities themselves take the place of those traces left in the mind. For our purposes this difference is unimportant, especially since besides sensations and activities recollections of such help in completing the mental presentation. 'Percept' may also be understood as the object, inasmuch as it is spatial or capable of sensory apprehension.) Frequently such an idea is saturated with feelings; the clarity of its various parts may vary and fluctuate. Even with the same person the same sense is not always accompanied by the same idea. The idea is subjective; one person's idea is not that of another. Hence, the various differences between the ideas associated with one and the same sense. A painter, a horseback rider, a zoologist probably connect different ideas with the name 'Bucephalus' [i.e., Alexander the Great's horse, a mettlesome riding horse, and a genus of flatworm, respectively—ED.]. The idea thereby differs essentially from the sense of a sign, which may be the common property of many and therefore is not a part or mode of the individual mind; for it cannot be denied that human beings possess a common store of thoughts which is transmitted from generation to generation.

Accordingly, one can speak without qualification of the sense in regard to ideas; however, we must, to be precise, add *whose* ideas they are and at what time they occur. One might say: just as words are associated with different images in different people, the same is true of different senses. Yet this difference would consist merely in the manner of association. It does not prevent both from grasping the same sense, but they cannot have the same idea. *Si duo idem faciunt, non est idem.* If two persons imagine the same thing, each still has his own idea. It is sometimes possible to detect differences in the images or even in the sensations of different persons. But an exact comparison is impossible because these ideas cannot be had together in the same consciousness.

The reference of a proper name is the object itself which is designated thereby; the idea which we may have along with it is quite subjective; the sense lies in between, not subjective as is the idea, but not the object either. The following analogy may help clarify these relationships. Someone observes the moon through a telescope. The moon I compare to the reference; it is the object of the observation mediated through the real image projected by the object lens into the interior of the telescope, and through the retinal image of the observer. The former I compare with the sense, the latter with the presentation (or idea in the psychological sense). The optical image inside the telescope, however, is relative; it depends upon the standpoint; yet, it is objective in that it can be used by several observers. Arrangements could be made so that several observers could use it. But each one would have his own retinal image. Because of the diverse shapes of the observers eyes not even geometrical congruence could be achieved; a real coincidence would be impossible. This analogy could be developed further by assuming that the retinal image of *A* could be visible to *B;* or *A* could see his own retinal image in a mirror. In this way one could possibly show how an idea can be made into an object; but even so, it would never be to the (outside) observer what it is to the one who possesses the idea. However, these thoughts lead us too far afield.

We can now recognize three levels of difference between words, expressions and complete sentences. The difference may concern at most the ideas, or else the sense but not the reference, or finally also the reference. Regarding the first level, we must note that, owing to the uncertain connection of ideas with words, a difference may exist for one person but not another. The difference of a translation and the original should properly not go beyond the first level. Among the differences possible here belong the shadings and colorings which poetry seeks to impart to the senses. Such shadings and colorings are not objective. Each hearer or reader has to add them according to the hints of the poet or speaker. Art would be impossible without some affinity among human ideas; but just how far the intentions of the poet are realized can never be known.

We shall in what follows no longer refer to the ideas and experiences; they were discussed only lest the idea evoked by a word be confused with its sense or its reference.

To facilitate concise and precise expression let us lay down the following formulations:

A proper name (word, sign, sign-combination, expression) expresses its sense, and designates its reference. We let a *sign express* its sense and *designate* its reference.

Perhaps the following objection from idealists or skeptics has been around for some time: "You talk without hesitation of the moon as an object; but how do you know that the name 'the moon' has any reference? How do you know that anything at all has a reference?" I reply that we do not intend to speak of the image of the moon, nor would we be satisfied with the sense when we say 'the moon'; instead, we presuppose a reference. We would completely misunderstand the sense if we assumed we referred to images in the sentence "the moon is smaller than the earth". Were that what we intended we would use say 'my image of the moon'. Of course, we may be mistaken about the presupposition, and such errors have occurred. However, the question whether we could possibly always be mistaken in this way need not be answered here; it will suffice to refer to our intention in speaking or thinking in order to justify mention of the reference of a sign; even if we have to add the reservation: if there is such a reference.

So far we have considered sense and reference only of such expressions, words or signs which we called proper names. We are now going to inquire into the sense and the reference of a whole declarative sentence. Such a sentence contains a thought. Is this thought to be regarded as the sense or the reference of the sentence? Let us for the time being assume that the sentence has a reference. If we now substitute a word in it by another word with the same reference but with a different sense, then this substitution cannot affect the reference of the sentence. But we realize that in such cases the thought changes; e.g., the thought in the sentence "the morning star is a body illuminated by the sun" is different from that of "the evening star is a body illuminated by the sun". Anybody who did not know that the evening star is the morning star could consider the one thought true and the other false. The thought can therefore not be the reference of the sentence; it will instead have to be considered its sense. But what about the reference? Can we even ask this question? Can a sentence as a whole have only sense and no reference? One may in any case expect that there are such sentences, just as there are parts of sentences which do have sense but no reference. Certainly, sentences containing proper names without referents must be of this kind. The sentence "Odysseus sound asleep was disembarked at Ithaca" obviously has a sense. But since it is doubtful as to whether the name 'Odysseus' occurring in this sentence has a reference, so it is also doubtful that the whole sentence has one. However, it is certain that whoever seriously regards the sentence either as true or as false also ascribes to the name 'Odysseus' a reference, not only a sense; for it is obviously the reference of this name to which the predicate is either affirmed or denied. If one does not acknowledge the reference, one cannot ascribe or deny a predicate to it. It might be claimed that the consideration of the reference of the name is superfluous; one could be satisfied with the sense, if one stayed with the thought. If all that mattered were only the sense of the sentence (i.e., the thought) then it would be unnecessary to bother with the referents of the sentence-components, for only the sense of the components can be relevant for the sense of the sentence. The thought remains the same, no matter whether or not the name 'Odysseus' has a reference. The fact that we are concerned about the reference of a sentence-component indicates that we generally recognize and expect a reference for the sentence itself. The thought loses value as soon as we recognize that one of its parts is lacks a reference. We are therefore justified to ask for the reference of a sentence, in addition to its sense. But why do we wish that every proper name have not only a sense but also a reference? Why is the thought alone not sufficient? Because what matters to us is the truth-value. This, however, is not always the case. In listening to an epic, for instance, we are fascinated by the euphony of the language and also by the sense of the sentences and by the images and feelings evoked. The question of truth causes us to disregard the artistic appreciation and pursue scientific investigation. Whether the name 'Odysseus' has a reference is therefore immaterial to us as long as we accept the poem as a work of art. (Expressions for signs which have sense only we could call 'icons'. Then the words of an actor on the stage would be icons; even the actor himself would be an icon.) Thus, it is the striving for truth that drives us to advance from the sense to the reference.

We have seen that we are to look for the reference of a sentence whenever the referents of the sentence-components are what matters; and that is the case when and only when we are inquiring of the truth-value.

Thus we find ourselves driven to accept the *truth-value* of a sentence as its reference. By the truth-value of a sentence I mean the circumstance of its being true or false. There are no other truth-values. For brevity's sake I shall call the one the True and the other the False. Every declarative sentence, in which what matters are the referents of the words, is therefore to be regarded as a proper name; and its reference, if there is any, is either the True or the False. These two objects are recognized, even if only implicitly, by everyone who makes judgments, holds anything as true, thus even by the skeptic. To designate truth-values as objects may thus far appear as an arbitrary idea or as a mere play on words, from which no profound conclusion should be drawn. What I call an object can be discussed only in connection with the nature of concepts and relations. That I will reserve for another essay. But this might be clear even here: in every judgment—no matter how trivial—a step is made from the level of thoughts to the level of the referents (the objective facts).

It may be tempting to regard the relation of a thought to the True not as that of sense to reference but as that of the subject to the predicate. One could indeed say: "the thought that 5 is a prime number is true". But on closer examination one notices that this does not say any more than is said in the simple sentence "5 is a prime number". This makes clear that the relation of a thought to the True may not be compared with the relation of subject and predicate. Subject and predicate (interpreted logically) are, after all, elements of a thought; they are on the same level as regards knowledge. By joining subject and predicate we always arrive only at a thought; in this way we never move from a sense to a reference or from a thought to its truth-value. One remains on the same level and never advances to the next one. Just as the sun cannot be part of a thought, so the truth-value, because it is not the sense, but an object, cannot be part of a thought.

If our supposition (that the reference of a sentence is its truth-value) is correct, then the truth-value must remain unchanged if a sentence-component is replaced by an expression with the same reference but with a different sense. Indeed, Leibnitz declares: "*Eadem sunt, quae sibi mutuo substitui possunt, salva veritate*". What else, but the truth-value, could be found, which generally belongs to every sentence and in regard to which the referents of the components are relevant and which remains unchanged by substitutions of the kind in question?

Now if the truth-value of a sentence is its reference, then all true sentences have the same reference, and so do all false ones. This implies that all detail is obliterated in the reference of a sentence. What interests us can therefore never be merely the reference; but the thought alone does not give knowledge; only the thought together with its reference, i.e., its truth-value, does. Judging may be viewed as a movement from a thought to its reference, i.e., its truth-value. Of course this is not intended as a definition. Judging is indeed something peculiar and unique. One might say that judging consists in the distinction of parts within the truth-value. Such distinction occurs by return to the thought. Every sense that belongs to a truth-value would correspond in its own manner to the analysis. I have here used the word 'part' in a particular manner: I have transferred the relation of whole and part from the sentence to its reference. This I did by viewing the reference of a word as part of the reference of a sentence, if the word itself is part of the sentence. True, this way of speaking is objectionable since, regarding the reference the whole and one part of it does not determine the other part; and also because the word 'part' in reference to bodies has a difference sense. A special term should be coined for what has been suggested above.

We shall now further test the supposition that the truth-value of a sentence is its reference. We have found that the truth-value of a sentence remains unchanged when an expression within the sentence is replaced by a synonymous one. But we have not yet considered the case in which the expression-to-be-replaced is itself a sentence. If our view is correct, then the truth-value of a sentence, which contains another sentence as a part, must remain unchanged when the part is replaced by another of the same truth-value. Exceptions are to be expected if the whole or the part are either direct or indirect quotations; for as we have seen, in such cases the referents of the words are not the usual ones. A sentence in direct quotation refers again to a sentence but in indirect quotation it refers to a thought.

Our attention is thus directed to subordinate sentences (i.e., dependent clauses). These occur of course as parts of a sentence-structure which from a logical point of view appears also as a sentence, and indeed as if it were a main clause. But here we face the question whether in the case of dependent clauses it also holds that their referents are truth-values. We know already that this is not the case with sentences in indirect quotation. The grammarians view clauses as representatives of sentence-parts and divide them accordingly into noun, adjective and adverbial clauses. This might suggest that the subordinate clause refers not to a truth-value but rather of the same kind as that of a noun or of an adjective or of an adverb; in short, it refers to a sentence-part whose sense is not a thought but only a part of a thought. Only a thorough investigation can provide clarity. We shall herein not follow strictly along grammatical lines, but rather group together what is logically of the same type. Let us first search for cases in which, as we just supposed, the sense of a clause is not an independent thought.

Among the abstract noun clauses beginning with 'that' there is also the indirect quotation, of which we have seen that in it the words have their indirect (oblique) referents which coincide with what are ordinarily their senses. In this case then the clause refers to a thought, not a truth-value; its sense is not a thought but it is the sense of the words 'the thought that . . .', which is only a part of the thought corresponding to the total sentence-structure. This happens with 'to say', 'to hear', 'to believe', 'to be convinced', 'to infer' and similar words. The situation is different, and rather complicated after words such as 'to recognize', 'to know', 'to believe', which we shall consider later.

One can see that in such cases the clause indeed refers to the thought, because whether that thought is true or false is immaterial for the truth of the whole sentence. Let us compare the following two sentences: "Copernicus believed that the planetary orbits are circles" and "Copernicus believed that the sun's apparent motion is produced by the real motion of the earth". Here the one clause can be substituted for the other without altering the truth. The sense of the main clause together with the subordinate clause is a single thought; and the truth of the whole implies neither the truth nor the falsity of the clause. In such cases it is not permissible to replace one expression in the clause by another of the same reference. Such replacement may be made only by expressions of the same indirect reference, i.e., of the same customary sense. If someone concluded that the reference of a sentence is not its truth-value ("because then a sentence could always be replaced by another with the same truth-value"), this would prove too much; one could just as well claim that the reference of the word 'morning star' is not Venus, for one cannot always substitute 'Venus' for 'morning star'. The only correct conclusion is that the reference of a sentence is *not always* its truth-value, and that 'morning star' does not always refer to the planet Venus; for this is indeed not the case when the word is used as an indirect reference. Such an exception occurs in the clauses just considered, whose reference is a thought. . . .

. . . In a logically perfect language (logical symbolism) every expression constructed as a proper name in a grammatically correct manner out of already introduced symbols, in fact designates an object; and no symbol can be introduced as a proper name unless we know it has a reference. It is customary in logic texts to warn against such ambiguity of expressions as a source of fallacies. I deem it equally important to issue a warning against apparent proper names that have no referents. The history of mathematics has many a tale to tell of exactly such errors. The demagogic misuse is close at hand, as in the case of ambiguous expressions. 'The will of the people' may serve as an example; for it is easy to show that there is no standard reference of that expression. Thus it is important to remove once and for all the source of these errors, at least in science. Then objections such as the one discussed above will become impossible, for then whether a proper name has a reference can never depend upon the truth of a thought.

Our considerations may be extended from these noun clauses to the logically related adjective and adverbial clauses. . . .

Places, dates and time-intervals are objects from a logical point of view; the linguistic symbol of a definite place, moment or span of time must therefore be considered a proper name. Adverbial clauses of space or time can then be used in the formation of such proper names in the same way as in the case of noun and adjective clauses. In the same way, expressions for concepts which comprise places, etc., can be formed. Here too, let us note, the sense of the subordinate clauses cannot be rendered in a principal clause, because the essential constituent—the determination of place and time—is missing and only hinted at by a relative pronoun or a conjunction. . . .

One cannot exhaust all possibilities that present themselves in language; but I hope essentially to have disclosed the reasons why, in view of the invariance of the truth of a whole sentence, a clause cannot always be replaced by another of the same truth-value. These reasons are:

1. the clause does not denote a truth-value but expresses only a part of a thought;
2. the clause, while it does denote a truth-value, is not restricted to this function in that its sense comprises, not just one thought but also a part of another.

The first case holds

a. with the indirect referents of the words;
b. if a clause indicates only indirectly without being a proper name.

In the second case the clause is to be interpreted in two ways; namely, once with its usual reference and once with its indirect reference; or else, the sense of a part of the clause may simultaneously be a constituent of another thought which, together with the sense expressed in the dependent clause, amounts to the total sense of the main and the dependent clause.

Thus it is reasonable that instances in which a clause is not replaceable by another of the same truth-value do not alter our view that the reference of a sentence is its truth-value and its sense a thought.

Let us return to our point of departure now.

When we discerned generally a difference in cognitive significance between "a = a" and "a = b" then this is now explained by the fact that for the cognitive significance of a sentence the sense (the thought expressed) is no less relevant than its reference (the truth-value). If a = b, then the reference of 'a' and of 'b' is indeed the same and therefore also the truth-value of "a = b" is the same as that of "a = a". Nevertheless, the sense of 'b' may differ from the sense of 'a'; and therefore the thought expressed by "a = b" may differ from the thought expressed by "a = a"; in that case the two sentences do not have the same cognitive significance. Thus if by 'judgment' we mean the transition from a thought to its truth-value, as we did above, then we can also say that the judgments differ from one another.

ROYCE

1855–1916

Josiah Royce was born in the California mining town of Grass Valley. He studied engineering at the University of California, then went to Germany to study philosophy at Leipzig and Göttingen. His greatest influence was Hegel. When he returned to the United States, he went to Johns Hopkins University and received his Ph.D at the age of twenty-three. He taught at the University of California and then at Harvard.

Royce attempted to construct a complete system of thought in the grand style of Hegel, and he founded a uniquely individualistic form of absolute idealism. For the British and German absolute idealists, the Absolute is beyond the categories of thought, hence inaccessible and incomprehensible to the individual mind. Royce argues that the individual mind can have complete knowledge of everything through an "absolute experience to which all facts are known and for which all facts are subject to universal law." He puts this view forth in his *Spirit of Modern Philosophy* (1892), from which our first selection is taken.

Royce identifies each aspect of the world in terms of the immediate presence of the world-soul. We ourselves are "such stuff as ideas are made of." Royce offers a brilliant and simple response to a traditional criticism of idealism. If, as the idealists argue, reality is not *material* but *mental* stuff, then why is so much of it fixed and impenetrable? If the world is my idea, why can't I just wish whatever I want into existence? Royce's response is that ideas themselves can be even more "stubborn" and "resilient" than the firmest concept of matter. That is, when you are literally in the grip of an idea, the fact is that you do not move *it* around with your wishes. It moves *you.* Ideas can be impenetrable to your prying into them, even though it is really their own prying into themselves. Royce's point is not that ideas cannot be altered in any way, merely that individual egos do not ordinarily have sufficient knowledge. Within the world-soul there exist *imperspicuous ideas* that correspond, within a materialistic framework, to impenetrable matter.

Royce distinguishes *epistemological* idealism—the claim that our knowledge of the world is ultimately subjective—from *metaphysical* idealism—the claim that the world itself is ultimately a mental, or spiritual entity. He argues, following Fichte, Schelling, and Hegel, against both materialist realism and empiricism, claiming that metaphysical idealism is the only system that makes genuine knowledge possible. Materialism and realism, in which the world is conceived in terms of some nonmental substance, such as physical atoms or material "things in themselves," ultimately make reality unknowable.

Royce's method requires us not to go beyond the ideas themselves as they are known in experience. But Royce is not content with putting forth an idealist view in opposition to nonidealist, materialistic views. He argues for idealism as the historical evolution of philosophy, similar to what Hegel did. The four stages of this evolution are described in his *The World and the Individual* (1899), from which the second selection is taken. These "four historical conceptions of Being" are realism, mysticism, critical rationalism, and Royce's own "teleological idealism." They can be summarized, respectively, as the view that *to be is to be independent,* that *to be is to be immediate,* and that *to be is to be valid.* Each involves a deep contradiction. The only consistent view, Royce argues, in his fourth conception, is summarized in the ancient mystic's chant, *"That art thou."*

THE SPIRIT OF MODERN PHILOSOPHY

REALITY AND IDEALISM: THE INNER WORLD AND ITS MEANING

I

I am very sorry that I cannot state my idealism in a simple and unproblematic form; but the nature of the doctrine forbids. I must first of all puzzle you with a paradox, by saying that my idealism has nothing in it which contradicts the principal propositions of what is nowadays called scientific Agnosticism, in so far, namely, as this agnosticism relates to that world of facts of experience which man sees and feels and which science studies. Of such agnosticism we learned something in our last lecture. But I must go on to say that the fault of our modern so-called scientific agnosticism is only that it has failed to see how the world in space and time, the world of causes and effects, the world of matter and of finite mind, whereof we know so little and long to know so much, is a very subordinate part of reality. It will be my effort to explain how we do know something very deep and vital about what reality is in its innermost essence. My explanation will indeed be very poor and fragmentary, but the outcome of it will be the very highly paradoxical assertion that while the whole finite world is full of dark problems for us, there is absolutely nothing, not even the immediate facts of our sense at this moment, so clear, so certain, as the existence and the unity of that infinite conscious Self of whom we have now heard so much. About the finite world, as I shall assert, we know in general only what experience teaches us and science records. There is nothing in the universe absolutely sure except the Infinite. That will be the curious sort of agnosticism that I shall try in a measure to expound. Of the infinite we know that it is one and conscious. Of the finite things, that is, of the particular fashions of behavior in terms of which the infinite Consciousness gives himself form and plays the world-game, we

From Josiah Royce, *The Spirit of Modern Philosophy,* 1892.

know only what we experience. Yet doubtless it will at once seem to you that in *one* important respect my announced doctrine is in obvious conflict with a wise agnosticism. For is it not confessedly anthropomorphic in its character? And is not anthropomorphism precisely the defect that modern thinkers have especially taught us to avoid?

Anthropomorphism was the savage view, which led primitive man to interpret extraordinary natural events as expressions of the will of beings like himself. However he came by his fancy, whether by first believing in the survival of the ghosts of his ancestors, and then conceiving them as the agents who produced lightning, and who moved the sun, or by a simple and irreducible instinct of his childish soul, leading him to see himself in nature, and to regard it all as animate; in any case he made the bad induction, created the gods in his own image, and then constituted them as the causes of all natural events. His ignorant self-multiplication we must avoid. Shall our limited inner experience be the only test of what sorts of causation may exist in the world? What we know is that events happen to us, and happen in a certain fixed order. We do not know the ultimate causes of these events. If we lived on some other planet, doubtless causes of a very novel sort would become manifest to us, and our whole view of nature would change. It is self-contradictory, it is absurd, to make our knowledge the measure of all that is! The real world that causes our experience is a great *x*, wholly unknown to us except in a few select phenomena, which happen to fall within our ken. How wild to guess about the mysteries of the infinite!

But now *this* agnosticism, too, as I assure you, I ardently and frankly agree with, so far as it concerns itself with precisely *that* world in which it pretends to move, and to which it undertakes to apply itself. I have no desire to refute it. Touching all the world in space and time beyond experience, in the scientific sense of the term experience, I repeat that I know nothing positive. I know, for instance, nothing about the stratification of Saturn, or the height of the mountains on the other side of the moon. For the same reason, also, I know nothing of any anthropomorphic daemons or gods here or there in nature, acting as causes of noteworthy events. Of these I know nothing, because science has at present no need for such hypotheses. There may be such beings; there doubtless are in nature many curious phenomena; but what curiosities further experience might show us, we must wait for experience to point out ere we shall know. I repeat, in its own world, agnosticism is in all these respects in the right. For reasons that you will later see, I object indeed to the unhappy word *unknowable*. In the world of experience, as in the world of abstracter problems, there are infinitely numerous things unknown to us. But there is no rational question that could not somehow be answered by a sufficiently wise person. There are things relatively unknowable for us, not things absolutely so. There are numberless experiences that I shall never have, in my individual capacity; and there are numberless problems that I shall never solve. But the only absolute insoluble mysteries, as I shall hereafter point out to you, would be the questions that it is essentially absurd to ask. Still, not to quarrel over words, what many agnostics mean by unknowable is simply the stubbornly unknown, and, in that sense, I fully agree and indeed insist that human knowledge is an island in the vast ocean of mystery, and that numberless questions, which it deeply concerns humanity to answer, will never be answered so long as we are in our present limited state, bound to one planet, and left for our experience to our senses, our emotions, and our moral activities.

But, if I thus accept this agnostic view of the world of experience, what chance is left, you will say, for anything like an absolute system of philosophy? In what sense can I pretend to talk of idealism, as giving any final view of the whole nature of things? In what sense, above all, can I pretend to be a theist, and to speak of the absolute Self as the very essence and life of the whole world? For is this not mere anthropomorphism? Isn't it making our private human experience the measure of all reality? Isn't it making hypotheses in terms of our experience, about things beyond our experience? Isn't it making our petty notions of causation a basis for judging of the nature of the unknown first cause? Isn't it another case of what the savage did when he saw his gods in the thunder-clouds, because he conceived that causes just like his own angry moods must be here at work? Surely, at best, this is sentiment, faith, mystical dreaming. It can't be philosophy.

I answer, just to change our whole view of the deeper reality of things, just to turn away our attention from any illusive search for first causes in the world of experience, just to get rid of fanciful faith about the gods in outer nature, and just to complete the spiritual task of agnosticism by sending us elsewhere than to phenomena for the true and inner nature of things,—for just this end was the whole agony of modern philosophy endured by those who have wrestled with its problems. Is any one agnostic about the finite world? Then I more. I know nothing of any first cause in the world of appearances yonder. I see no gods in the thunder-clouds, no Keplerian angels carrying the planets in conic sections around the sun; I imagine no world-maker far back in the ages, beginning the course of evolution. Following Laplace, I need, once more, no such hypothesis. I await the verdict of science about all facts and events in physical nature. And yet that is just *why* I am an idealist. It is my agnosticism about the causes of my experience that makes me search elsewhere than amongst causes for the meaning of experience. The outer world which the agnostic sees and despairs of knowing is not the region where I look for light. The living God, whom idealism knows, is not the first cause in any physical sense, at all. No possible experience could find him as a thing amongst things or show any outer facts that would prove his existence. He isn't anywhere in space or in time. He makes from without no worlds. He is no hypothesis of empirical science. But he is all the more real for that, and his existence is all the surer. For causes are, after all, very petty and subordinate truths in the world, and facts, phenomena, as such, could never demonstrate any important spiritual truth. The absolute Self simply doesn't *cause* the world. The very idea of causation belongs to things of finite experience, and is only a mythological term when applied to the real truth of things. Not because I interpret the causes of my experience in terms of my limited ideas of causation is the universe of God a live thing to me, but for a far deeper reason; for a reason which deprives this world of agnosticism of all substantiality and converts it once for all into mere show. I am ignorant of this world just because it is a show-world.

And this deeper reason of the idealist I may as well first suggest in a form which may perhaps seem just now even more mysterious than the problem which I solve by means of it. My reason for believing that there is one absolute World-Self, who embraces and is all reality, whose consciousness includes and infinitely transcends our own, in whose unity all the laws of nature and all the mysteries of experience must have their solution and their very being,—is simply that the profoundest agnosticism which you can possibly state in any coherent fashion, the deepest doubt which you can any way formulate about the world or the things that are therein, already presupposes, implies, demands, asserts, the existence of such a World-Self. The agnostic, I say, already asserts this existence—unconsciously, of course, as a rule, but none the less inevitably. For, as we shall find, there is no escape from the infinite Self except by self-contradiction. Ignorant as I am about first causes, I am at least clear, therefore, about the Self. If you deny him, you already in denying affirm him. You reckon ill when you leave him out. "Him when you fly, he is the wings." He is the doubter and the doubt. You in vain flee from his presence. The wings of the morning will not aid you. Nor do I mean all this now as any longer a sort of mysticism. This truth is, I assure you, simply a product of dry logic. When I try to tell you about it in detail, I shall weary you by my wholly unmystical analysis of commonplaces. Here is, in fact, as we shall soon find, the very presupposition of presuppositions. You cannot stir, nay, you cannot even stand still in thought without it. Nor is it an unfamiliar idea. On the contrary, philosophy finds trouble in bringing it to your consciousness merely *because* it is so familiar. When they told us in childhood that we could not see God just *because* he was everywhere, just because his omnipresence gave us no chance to discern him and to fix our eyes upon him, they told us a deep truth in allegorical fashion. The infinite Self, as we shall learn, is actually asserted by you in every proposition you utter, is there at the heart, so to speak, of the very multi-plication table. The Self is so little a thing merely guessed at as the unknowable source of experience, that already, *in* the very least of daily experiences you unconsciously know him as something present. This, as we shall find, is the deepest tragedy of our finitude, that continually he comes to his own, and his own receive him not, that he becomes flesh in every least incident of our lives; while we, gazing with wonder upon his world, search here and there for first causes, look for miracles, and beg him to show us the Father, since that alone will suffice us. No wonder that thus we have to remain agnostics. "Hast thou been so long time with me, and yet hast thou not *known* me?" Such is the eternal answer of the Logos to every doubting question. Seek him not as an outer hypothesis to explain experi-ence. Seek him not anywhere yonder in the clouds. He is no "thing in itself." But for all that, experience contains him. He is the reality, the soul of it. "Did not our heart burn within us while he talked with us by the way?" And, as we shall see, he does not talk merely to our hearts. He reveals himself to our coolest scrutiny.

II

But enough of speculative boasting. Coming to closer quarters with my topic, I must re-mind you that idealism has two aspects. It is, for the first, a kind of analysis of the world, an analysis which so far has no absolute character about it, but which undertakes, in a fashion that might be acceptable to any skeptic, to examine what you mean by all the things, whatever they are, that you believe in or experience. This idealistic analysis consists merely in a pointing out, by various devices, that the world of your knowledge, whatever it con-tains, is through and through such stuff as ideas are made of, that you never in your life believed in anything definable *but* ideas, that, as Berkeley put it, "this whole choir of heaven and furniture of earth" is nothing for any of us but a system of ideas which govern our belief and our conduct. Such idealism has numerous statements, interpretations, embodi-ments: forms part of the most various systems and experiences, is consistent with Berkeley's theism, with Fichte's ethical absolutism, with Professor Huxley's agnostic empiricism, with Clifford's mind-stuff theory, with countless other theories that have used such idealism as a part of their scheme. In this aspect idealism is already a little puzzling to our natural con-sciousness, but it becomes quickly familiar, in fact almost commonplace, and seems after all to alter our practical faith or to solve our deeper problems very little.

The other aspect of idealism is the one which gives us our notion of the absolute Self. To it the first is only preparatory. This second aspect is the one which from Kant, until the present time, has formed the deeper problem of thought. Whenever the world has become more conscious of its significance, the work of human philosophy will be, not nearly ended (Heaven forbid an end), but for the first time fairly begun. For then, in critically estimating our passions, we shall have some truer sense of whose passions they are.

I begin with the first and the less significant aspect of idealism. Our world, I say, whatever it may contain, is such stuff as ideas are made of. This preparatory sort of idealism is the one that, as I just suggested, Berkeley made prominent, and after a fashion familiar. I must state it in my own way, although one in vain seeks to attain novelty in illustrating so frequently described a view.

Here, then, is our so real world of the senses, full of light and warmth and sound. If anything could be solid and external, surely, one at first will say, it is this world. Hard facts, not mere ideas, meet us on every hand. Ideas any one can mould as he wishes. Not so facts. In idea socialists can dream out Utopias, disappointed lovers can imagine themselves successful, beggars can ride horses, wanderers can enjoy the fireside at home. In the realm of facts, society organizes itself as it must, rejected lovers stand for the time defeated, beggars are alone with their wishes, oceans roll drearily between home and the wanderer. Yet this world of fact is, after all, not entirely stubborn, not merely hard. The strenuous will can mould facts. We can form our world, in part, according to our ideas. Statesmen influence the social order, lovers woo afresh, wanderers find the way home. But thus to alter the world we must work, and just because the laborer is worthy of his hire, it is well that the real world should thus have such fixity of things as enables us to anticipate what facts will prove lasting, and to see of the travail of our souls when it is once done. This, then, is the presupposition of life, that we work in a real world, where house-walls do not melt away as in dreams, but stand firm against the winds of many winters, and can be felt as real. We do not wish to find facts wholly plastic; we want them to be stubborn, if only the stubbornness be not altogether unmerciful. Our will makes constantly a sort of agreement with the world, whereby, if the world will continually show some respect to the will, the will shall consent to be strenuous in its industry. Interfere with the reality of my world, and you therefore take the very life and heart out of my will.

The reality of the world, however, when thus defined in terms of its stubbornness, its firmness as against the will that has not conformed to its laws, its kindly rigidity in preserving for us the fruits of our labors,—such reality, I say, is still something wholly unanalyzed. In what does this stubbornness consist? Surely, many different sorts of reality, as it would seem, may be stubborn. Matter is stubborn when it stands in hard walls against us, or rises in vast mountain ranges before the path-finding explorer. But minds can be stubborn also. The lonely wanderer, who watches by the seashore the waves that roll between him and his home, talks of cruel facts, material barriers that, just because they *are* material, and not ideal, shall be the irresistible foes of his longing heart. "In wish," he says, "I am with my dear ones, but alas, wishes cannot cross oceans! Oceans are material facts, in the cold outer world. Would that the world of the heart were all!" But alas! to the rejected lover the world of the heart *is* all, and that is just his woe. Were the barrier between him and his beloved only made of those stubborn material facts, only of walls or of oceans how lightly might his will erelong transcend them all! Matter stubborn! Outer nature cruelly the foe of ideas! Nay, it is just an idea that now opposes him,—just an idea, and that, too, in the mind of the maiden he loves. But in vain does he call this stubborn bit of disdain a merely ideal fact. No flint was ever more definite in preserving its identity and its edge than this disdain may be. Place me for a moment, then, in an external world that shall consist wholly of ideas,— the ideas, namely, of other people about me, a world of maidens who shall scorn me, of old friends who shall have learned to hate me, of angels who shall condemn me, of God who shall judge me. In what piercing north winds, amidst what fields of ice, in the labyrinths of what tangled forests, in the depths of what thick-walled dungeons, on the edges of what tremendous precipices, should I be more genuinely in the presence of stubborn and unyielding facts than in that conceived world of ideas! So, as one sees, I by no means deprive my world of stubborn reality, if I merely call it a world of ideas. On the contrary, as every teacher knows, the ideas of the people are often the most difficult of facts to influence. We were wrong, then, when we said that while matter was stubborn, ideas could be moulded at pleasure. Ideas are often the most implacable of facts. Even my own ideas, the facts of my own inner life, may cruelly decline to be plastic to my wish. The wicked will that refuses to be destroyed,—what rock has often more consistency for our senses than this will has for our inner consciousness! . . .

No, here are barriers worse than any material chains. The world of ideas has its own horrible dungeons and chasms. Let those who have refuted Bishop Berkeley's idealism by the wonder why he did not walk over every precipice or into every fire if these things existed only in his idea, let such, I say, first try some of the fires and the precipices of the inner life, ere they decide that dangers cease to be dangers as soon as they are called ideal, or even subjectively ideal in me.

Many sorts of reality, then, may be existent at the heart of any world of facts. But this bright and beautiful sense-world of ours,—what, amongst these many possible sorts of reality, does that embody? Are the stars and the oceans, the walls and the pictures, real as the maiden's heart is real,—embodying the ideas of somebody, but none the less stubbornly real for that? Or can we make something else of their reality? For, of course, that the stars and the oceans, the walls and the pictures have *some* sort of stubborn reality, just as the minds of our fellows have, our analysis so far does not for an instant think of denying. Our present question is, what sort of reality? Consider, then, in detail, certain aspects of the reality that seems to be exemplified in our sense-world. The sublimity of the sky, the life and majesty of the ocean, the interest of a picture,—to what sort of real facts do these belong? Evidently here we shall have no question. So far as the sense-world is beautiful, is majestic, is sublime, this beauty and dignity exist only for the appreciative observer. If they exist beyond him, they exist only for some other mind, or as the thought and embodied purpose of some universal soul of nature. A man who sees the same world, but who has no eye for the fairness of it, will find all the visible facts, but will catch nothing of their value. At once, then, the sublimity and beauty of the world are thus truths that one who pretends to insight ought to see, and they are truths which have no meaning except for such a beholder's mind, or except as embodying the thought of the mind of the world. So here, at least, is so much of the outer world that is ideal, just as the coin or the jewel or the bank-note or the bond has its value not alone in its physical presence, but in the idea that it symbolizes to a beholder's mind, or to the relatively universal thought of the commercial world. But let us look a little deeper. Surely, if the objects yonder are unideal and outer, odors and tastes and temperatures do not exist in these objects in just the way in which they exist in us. Part of the being of these properties, at least, if not all of it, is ideal and exists for us, or at best is once more the embodiment of the thought or purpose of some world-mind. About tastes you cannot dispute, because they are not only ideal but personal. For the benumbed tongue and palate of diseased bodily conditions, all things are tasteless. As for temperatures, a well-known experiment will show how the same water may seem cold to one hand and warm to the other. But even so, colors and sounds are at least in part ideal. Their causes may have some other sort of reality; but colors themselves are not in the things, since they change with the light that falls on the things, vanish in the dark (while the things remained unchanged), and differ for different eyes. And as for sounds, both the pitch and the quality of tones depend for us upon certain interesting peculiarities of our hearing organs, and exist in nature only as voiceless sound-waves trembling through the air. All such sense qualities, then, are ideal. The world yonder may—yes, must—have attributes that give reasons why these qualities are thus felt by us; for so we assume. The world yonder may even be a mind that thus expresses its will to us. But these qualities need not, nay, cannot resemble the ideas that are produced in us, unless, indeed, that is because these qualities have place as ideas in some world-mind. Sound-waves in the air are not like our musical sensations; nor is the symphony as we hear it and feel it any physical property of the strings and the wind instruments; nor are the ether-vibrations that the sun sends us like our ideas when we see the sun; nor yet is the flashing of moonlight on the water as we watch the waves a direct expression of the actual truths of fluid motion as the water embodies them.

Unless, then, the real physical world yonder is itself the embodiment of some world-spirit's ideas, which he conveys to us, unless it is real only as the maiden's heart is real, namely, as itself a conscious thought, then we have so far but one result: that real world (to repeat one of the commonplaces of modern popular science) is in itself, apart from some-body's eyes and tongue and ears and touch, neither colored nor tasteful, neither cool nor warm, neither light nor dark, neither musical nor silent. All these qualities belong to our ideas, being indeed none the less genuine facts for that, but being in so far ideal facts. We must see colors when we look, we must hear music when there is playing in our presence; but this *must* is a must that consists in a certain irresistible presence of an idea in us under certain conditions. *That* this idea must come is, indeed, a truth as unalterable, once more, as the king's settled remorse in Hamlet. But like this remorse, again, it exists as an ideal truth, objective, but through and through objective *for* somebody, and not *apart from* any-body. What this truth implies we have yet to see. So far it is only an ideal truth for the beholder, with just the bare possibility that behind it all there is the thought of a world-spirit. And, in fact, *so* far we must all go together if we reflect.

But now, at this point, the Berkeleyan idealist goes one step further. The real outside world that is still left unexplained and unanalyzed after its beauty, its warmth, its odors, its tastes, its colors, and its tones, have been relegated to the realm of ideal truths, what do you now *mean* by calling it real? No doubt it *is* known as somehow real, but *what* is this reality *known* as being? If you know that this world is still there and outer, as by hypothesis you know, you are bound to say *what* this outer character implies for your thought. And here you have trouble. Is the outer world, as it exists outside of your ideas, or of anybody's ideas, something having shape, filling space, possessing solidity, full of moving things? That would in the first place seem evident. The sound isn't outside of me, but the sound-waves, you say, are. The colors are ideal facts; but the ether-waves don't need a mind to know them. Warmth is ideal, but the physical fact called heat, this playing to and fro of molecules, is real, and is there apart from any mind. But once more, *is* this so evident? What do I *mean* by the shape of anything, or by the size of anything? Don't I mean just the idea of shape or of size that I am obliged to get under certain circumstances? What is the meaning of any property that I give to the real outer world? How can I express that property except in case I think it in terms of my ideas? As for the sound-waves and the ether-waves, what are they but things ideally conceived to explain the facts of nature? The conceptions have doubtless their truth, but it is an ideal truth. What I mean by saying that the things yonder have shape and size and trembling molecules, and that there is air with sound-waves, and ether with light-waves in it,—what I *mean* by all this is that experience forces upon me, directly or indirectly, a vast system of ideas, which may indeed be founded in truth beyond me, which in fact *must* be founded in such truth if my experience has any sense, but which, like my ideas of color and of warmth, are simply expressions of how the world's order must appear to me, and to anybody constituted like me. Above all, is this plain about space. The real things, I say, outside of me, fill space, and move about in it. But what do I mean by space?

Only a vast system of ideas which experience and my own mind force upon me. Doubtless these ideas have a validity. They have *this* validity, that I, at all events, when I look upon the world, am bound to see it in space, as much bound as the king in Hamlet was, when he looked within, to see himself as guilty and unrepentant. But just as his guilt was an idea,— a crushing, an irresistible, an overwhelming idea,—but still just an idea, so, too, the space in which I place my world is one great formal idea of mine. That is just why I can describe it to other people. "It has three dimensions," I say, "length, breadth, depth." I describe each. I form, I convey, I construct, an idea of it through them. I know space, as an idea, very well. I can compute all sorts of unseen truths about the relations of its parts. I am sure that you, too, share this idea. But, then, for all of us alike it is just an idea; and when we put our world into space, and call it real there, we simply think one idea into another idea, not voluntarily, to be sure, but inevitably, and yet without leaving the realm of ideas.

Thus, all the reality that *we* attribute to our world, in so far as *we* know and can tell what we mean thereby, becomes ideal. There is, in fact, a certain system of ideas, forced upon us by experience, which we have to use as the guide of our conduct. This system of ideas we can't change by our wish; it is for us as overwhelming a fact as guilt, or as the bearing of our fellows towards us, but we know it only *as* such a system of ideas. And we call it the world of matter. John Stuart Mill very well expressed the puzzle of the whole thing, as we have now reached the statement of this puzzle, when he called matter a mass of "permanent possibilities of experience" for each of us. Mill's definition has its faults, but it is a very fair beginning. You know matter as something that either now gives you this idea or experience, or that would give you some other idea or experience under other circumstances. A fire, while it burns, is for you a permanent possibility of either getting the idea of an agreeable warmth, or of getting the idea of a bad burn, and you treat it accordingly. A precipice amongst mountains is a permanent possibility of your experiencing a fall, or of your getting a feeling of the exciting or of the sublime in mountain scenery. You have no experience just now of the tropics or of the poles, but both tropical and polar climates exist in your world as permanent possibilities of experience. When you call the sun 92,000,000 miles away, you mean that between you and the sun (that is, between your present experience and the possible experience of the sun's surface) there would inevitably lie the actually inaccessible, but still numerically conceivable series of experiences of distance expressed by the number of miles in question. In short, your whole attitude towards the real world may be summed up by saying: "I have experiences now which I seem bound to have, experiences of color, sound, and all the rest of my present ideas; and I am also bound by experience to believe that in case I did certain things (for instance, touched the wall, traveled to the tropics, visited Europe, studied physics), I then should get, in a determinate order, dependent wholly upon *what* I had done, certain other experiences (for instance, experiences of the wall's solidity, or of a tropical climate, or of the scenes of an European tour, or of the facts of physics)." And this acceptance of actual experience, this belief in possible experience, constitutes all that you mean by your faith in the outer world.

But, you say, Is not, then, all this faith of ours after all well founded? Isn't there really something yonder that corresponds in fact to this series of experiences in us? Yes, indeed, there no doubt is. But what if this, which so shall correspond without us to the ideas within us, what if this hard and fast reality should itself be a system of ideas, outside of our minds but not outside of every mind? As the maiden's disdain is outside the rejected lover's mind, unchangeable so far for him, but not on that account the less ideal, not the less a fact in a mind, as, to take afresh a former fashion of illustration, the price of a security or the ob-jective existence of this lecture is an ideal fact, but real and external for the individual person,—even so why might not this world beyond us, this "permanent possibility of experience," be in essence itself a system of ideal experiences of some standard thought of which ours is only the copy? Nay, must it not be such a system in case it has any reality at all? For, after all, isn't this precisely what our analysis brings us to? Nothing whatever can I say about my world yonder that I do not express in terms of mind. *What* things are, extended, moving, colored, tuneful, majestic, beautiful, holy, *what* they are in any aspect of their nature, mathematical, logical, physical, sensuously pleasing, spiritually valuable, all this must mean for me only something that I have to express in the fashion of ideas. The more I am to know my world, the more of a mind I must have for the purpose. The closer I come to the truth about the things, the more ideas I get. Isn't it plain, then, that *if* my world yonder is anything knowable at all, it must be in and for itself essentially a mental world? Are my ideas to *resemble* in any way the world? Is the truth of my thought to consist in its *agreement* with reality? And am I thus capable, as common sense supposes, of *conforming* my ideas to things? Then reflect. What can, after all, so well agree with an idea as another idea? To what can things that go on in my mind conform unless it be to another mind? If the more my mind grows in mental clearness, the nearer it gets to the nature of reality, then surely the reality that my mind thus resembles must be in itself mental.

After all, then, would it deprive the world here about me of reality, nay, would it not rather save and assure the reality and the knowableness of my world of experience, if I said that this world, as it exists outside of my mind, and of any other human minds, exists in and for a standard, a universal mind, whose system of ideas simply constitutes the world? Even if I fail to prove that there is such a mind, do I not at least thus make plausible that, as I said, our world of common sense has no fact in it which we cannot interpret in terms of ideas, so that this world is throughout such stuff as ideas are made of? To say this, as you see, in no way deprives our world of its due share of reality. If the standard mind knows now that its ideal fire has the quality of burning those who touch it, and if I in my finitude are bound to conform in my experiences to the thoughts of this standard mind, then in case I touch that fire I shall surely get the idea of a burn. The standard mind will be at least as hard and fast and real in its ideal consistency as is the maiden in her disdain for the rejected lover; and I, in presence of the ideal stars and the oceans, will see the genuine realities of fate as certainly as the lover hears his fate in the voice that expresses her will.

I need not now proceed further with an analysis that will be more or less familiar to many of you, especially after our foregoing historical lectures. What I have desired thus far is merely to give each of you, as it were, the sensation of being an idealist in this first and purely analytical sense of the word idealism. The sum and substance of it all is, you see, this: you know your world in fact as a system of ideas about things, such that from moment to moment you find this system forced upon you by experience. Even matter you know just as a mass of coherent ideas that you cannot help having. Space and time, as you think them, are surely ideas of yours. Now, what more natural than to say that *if* this be so, the real world beyond you must in itself be a system of somebody's ideas? If it is, then you can comprehend what its existence means. If it isn't, then since all you can know of it is ideal, the real world must be utterly unknowable, a bare *x*. Minds I can understand, because I myself am a mind. An existence that has no mental attribute is wholly opaque to me. So far, however, from such a world of ideas, existent beyond me in another mind, seeming to coherent thought essentially *un*real, ideas and minds and their ways, are, on the contrary, the hardest and stubbornest facts that we can name. *If* the external world is in itself mental, then, be this reality a standard and universal thought, or a mass of little atomic minds constituting the various particles of matter, in any case one can comprehend what it is, and will have at the same time to submit to its stubborn authority as the lover accepts the reality of the maiden's moods. If the world *isn't* such an ideal thing, then indeed all our science, which is through and through concerned with our mental interpretations of things, can neither have objective validity, nor make satisfactory progress towards truth. For as science is concerned with ideas, the world beyond all ideas is a bare *x*.

III

But with this bare *x,* you will say, this analytical idealism after all leaves me, as with something that, spite of all my analyses and interpretations, may after all be there beyond me as the real world, which my ideas are vainly striving to reach, but which eternally flees before me. So far, you will say, what idealism teaches is that the real world can only be interpreted by treating it as if it were somebody's thought. So regarded, the idealism of Berkeley and of other such thinkers is very suggestive; yet it doesn't tell us what the true world is, but only that *so much* of the true world as we ever get into our comprehension has to be conceived in ideal terms. Perhaps, however, while neither beauty, nor majesty, nor odor, nor warmth, nor tone, nor color, nor form, nor motion, nor space, nor time (all these being but ideas of ours), can be said to belong to the extra-mental world,—perhaps, after all, there does exist there yonder an extra-mental world, which has nothing to do, except by accident, with *any* mind, and which is through and through just extra-mental, something unknowable, inscrutable, the basis of experience, the source of ideas, but itself never experienced as it is in itself, never adequately represented by any idea in us. Perhaps it is there. Yes, you will say, *must* it not be there? Must not one accept our limitations once for all, and say, "What reality is, we can never hope to make clear to ourselves. That which has been made clear becomes an idea in us. But always there is the beyond, the mystery, the inscrutable, the real, the *x.* To be sure, perhaps we can't even know so much as that this *x* after all does exist. But then we feel bound to regard it as existent; or even if we doubt or deny it, may it not be there all the same?" In such doubt and darkness, then, this first form of idealism closes. If that were all there were to say, I should indeed have led you a long road in vain. Analyzing what the known world is for you, in case there is haply any world known to you at all,—this surely isn't proving that there is any real world, or that the real world can be known. Are we not just where we started?

No; there lies now just ahead of us the goal of a synthetic idealistic conception, which will not be content with this mere analysis of the colors and forms of things, and with the mere discovery that all these are for us nothing but ideas. In this second aspect, idealism grows bolder, and fears not the profoundest doubt that may have entered your mind as to whether there is any world at all, or as to whether it is in any fashion knowable. State in full the deepest problem, the hardest question about the world that your thought ever conceived. In this new form idealism offers you a suggestion that indeed will not wholly answer nor do away with every such problem, but that certainly will set the meaning of it in a new light. What this new light is, I must in conclusion seek to illustrate.

Note the point we have reached. *Either,* as you see, your real world yonder is through and through a world of ideas, an outer mind that you are more or less comprehending through your experience, *or else,* in so far as it is real and outer it is unknowable, an inscrutable *x,* an absolute mystery. The dilemma is perfect. There is no third alternative. Either a mind yonder, or else the unknowable; that is your choice. Philosophy loves such dilemmas, wherein all the mightiest interests of the spirit, all the deepest longings of human passion, are at stake, waiting as for the fall of a die. Philosophy loves such situations, I say, and loves, too, to keep its scrutiny as cool in the midst of them as if it were watching a game of chess, instead of the great world-game. Well, try the darker choice that the dilemma gives you. The world yonder shall be an *x,* an unknowable something, outer, problematic, foreign, opaque. And you,—you shall look upon it and believe in it. Yes, you shall for argument's sake first put on an air of resigned confidence, and say, "I do not only fancy it to be an extra-mental and unknowable something there, an impenetrable *x,* but I know it to be such. I can't help it. I didn't make it unknowable. I regret the fact. But there it is. I have to admit its existence. But I know that I shall never solve the problem of its nature." Ah, its nature is a *problem,* then. But what do you mean by this *"problem"*? Problems are, after a fashion, rather familiar things,—that is, in the world of ideas. There are problems soluble and problems insoluble in that world of ideas. It is a soluble problem if one asks what whole number is the square root of 64. The answer is 8. It is an insoluble problem if one asks me to find what whole number is the square root of 65. There is, namely, no such whole number. If one asks me to name the length of a straight line that shall be equal to the circumference of a circle of a known radius, that again, in the world of ideas, is an insoluble problem, because, as can be proved, the circumference of a circle is a length that cannot possibly be exactly expressed in terms of any statable number when the radius is of a stated length. So in the world of ideas, problems are definite questions which can be asked in knowable terms. Fair questions of this sort either may be fairly answered in our present state of knowledge, or else they could be answered if we knew a little or a good deal more, or finally they could not possibly be answered. But in the latter case, if they could not possibly be answered, they always must resemble the problem how to square the circle. They then always turn out, namely, to be absurdly stated questions and it is their absurdity that makes these problems absolutely insoluble. Any fair question could be answered by one who knew enough. No fair question has an unknowable answer. But now, *if* your unknowable world out there is a thing of wholly, of absolutely problematic and inscrutable nature, is it so because you don't *yet* know enough about it, or because in its very nature and essence it is an absurd thing, an *x* that *would* answer a question, which actually it is nonsense to ask? Surely one must choose the former alternative. The real world may be unknown; it can't be essentially unknowable.

This subtlety is wearisome enough, I know, just here, but I shall not dwell long upon it. Plainly *if* the unknowable world out there is through and through in its nature a really inscrutable problem, this must mean that in nature it resembles such problems as, What is the whole number that is the square root of 65? Or, What two adjacent hills are there that have no valley between them? For in the world of thought such are the *only* insoluble problems. All others either may now be solved, or would be solved if we knew more than we now do. But, once more, *if* this unknowable is only just the real world as now unknown to us, but capable some time of becoming known, then remember that, as we have just seen, only a mind can ever become an object known to a mind. If I know you as external to me, it is only because you are minds. If I can come to know *any* truth, it is only in so far as this truth is essentially mental, is an idea, is a thought, that I can ever come to know it. Hence, if that so-called unknowable, that unknown outer world there, ever could, by any device, come within our ken, then it is already an ideal world. For just that is what our whole idealistic analysis has been proving. Only ideas are knowable. And nothing absolutely unknowable can exist. For the absolutely unknowable, the *x* pure and simple, the Kantian thing in itself, simply cannot be admitted. The notion of it is nonsense. The assertion of it is a contradiction. Round-squares, and sugar salt-lumps, and Snarks, and Boojums, and Jabberwocks, and Abracadabras; such, I insist, are the only unknowables there are. The unknown, that which our human and finite selfhood hasn't grasped, exists spread out before us in a boundless world of truth; but the unknowable is essentially, confessedly, *ipso facto* a fiction.

The nerve of our whole argument in the foregoing is now pretty fairly exposed. We have seen that the outer truth must be, if anything, a "possibility of experience." But we may now see that a *bare* "possibility" as such, is, like the unknowable, something meaningless. That which, whenever I come to know it, turns out to be through and through an idea, an experience, must be in itself, before I know it, either somebody's idea, somebody's experience, or it must be nothing. What is a "possibility" of experience that is outside of me, and that is still nothing *for* any one else than myself? Isn't it a bare *x*, a nonsense phrase? Isn't it like an unseen color, an untasted taste, an unfelt feeling? In proving that the world is one of "possible" experience, we have proved that in so far as it is real it is one of actual experience.

Once more, then, to sum up here, *if*, however vast the world of the unknown, only the essentially knowable can exist, and *if* everything knowable is an idea, a mental somewhat, the content of some mind, then once for all we are the world of ideas. Your deepest doubt proves this. Only the nonsense of that inscrutable *x*, of that Abracadabra, of that Snark, the Unknowable of whose essence you make your real world, prevents you from seeing this.

To return, however, to our dilemma. *Either* idealism, we said, *or* the unknowable. What we have now said is that the absolutely unknowable is essentially an absurdity, a nonexistent. For any fair and stable problem admits of an answer. *If* the world exists yonder, its essence is then already capable of being known by some mind. If capable of being known by a mind, this essence is then already essentially ideal and mental. A mind that knew the real world would, for instance, find it a something possessing qualities. But qualities are ideal existences, just as much as are the particular qualities called odors or tones or colors. A mind knowing the real world would again find in it relations, such as equality and inequality, attraction and repulsion, likeness and unlikeness. But such relations have no meaning except as objects of a mind. In brief, then, the world as known would be found to be a world that had all the while been ideal and mental, even before it became known to the particular mind that we are to conceive as coming into connection with it. Thus, then, we are driven to the second alternative. The real world must be a mind, or else a group of minds.

IV

But with this result we come in presence of a final problem. All this, you say, depends upon my assurance that there is after all a real and therefore an essentially knowable and rational world yonder. Such a world would have to be in essence a mind, or a world of minds. But after all, how does one ever escape from the prison of the inner life? Am I not in all this merely wandering amidst the realm of my own ideas? *My* world, of course, isn't and can't be a mere *x*, an essentially unknowable thing, just because it *is my* world, and I have an idea of it. But then does not this mean that *my* world is, after all, forever just *my* world, so that I never get to any truth beyond myself? Isn't this result very disheartening? My world is thus a world of ideas, but alas! how do I then ever reach those ideas of the minds beyond me?

The answer is a simple, but in one sense a very problematic one. You, in one sense, namely, never *do* or can get beyond your own ideas, nor ought you to wish to do so, because in truth all those other minds that constitute your outer and real world are in essence one with your own self. This whole world of ideas is essentially *one* world, and so it is essentially the world of one self and *That art Thou.*

The truth and meaning of this deepest proposition of all idealism is now not at all remote from us. The considerations, however, upon which it depends are of the dryest possible sort, as commonplace as they are deep.

Whatever objects you may think about, whether they are objects directly known to you, or objects infinitely far removed, objects in the distant stars, or objects remote in time, or objects near and present,—such objects, then, as a number with fifty places of digits in it, or the mountains on the other side of the moon, or the day of your death, or the character of Cromwell, or the law of gravitation, or a name that you are just now trying to think of and have forgotten, or the meaning of some mood or feeling or idea now in your mind,— all such objects, I insist, stand in a certain constant and curious relation to your mind whenever you are thinking about them,—a relation that we often miss because it is so familiar. What is this relation? Such an object, while you think about it, needn't be, as popular thought often supposes it to be, the *cause* of your thoughts concerning it. Thus, when you think about Cromwell's character, Cromwell's character isn't just now *causing* any ideas in you,—isn't, so to speak, doing anything to you. Cromwell is dead, and after life's fitful fever his character is a very inactive thing. Not as the *cause,* but as the *object* of your thought is Cromwell present to you. Even so, if you choose now to think of the moment of your death, that moment is somewhere off there in the future, and you can make it your object, but it isn't now an active cause of your ideas. The moment of your death has no present physical existence at all, and just now causes nothing. So, too, with the mountains on the other side of the moon. When you make them the object of your thought, they remain indifferent to you. They do not affect you. You never saw them. But all the same you can think about them.

Yet this thinking *about* things is, after all, a very curious relation in which to stand to things. In order to think *about* a thing, it is *not* enough that I should have an idea in me that merely resembles that thing. This last is a very important observation. I repeat, it is *not* enough that I should merely have an idea in me that resembles the thing whereof I think. I have, for instance, in me the idea of a pain. Another man has a pain just like mine. Say we both have toothache; or have both burned our finger-tips in the same way. Now my idea of pain is just like the pain in him, but I am not on that account necessarily thinking about *his* pain, merely because what I am thinking about, namely my own pain, resembles his pain. No; to think about an object you must not merely have an idea that resembles the object, but you must *mean* to have your idea resemble that object. Stated in other form, to think of an object you must consciously aim at that object, you must pick out that object, you must already in some measure possess that object enough, namely, to identify it as what you mean. But how can you *mean,* how can you *aim at,* how can you *possess,* how can you *pick out,* how can you *identify* what is not already present in essence to your own hidden self? Here is surely a deep question. When you aim at yonder object, be it the mountains in the moon or the day of your death, you really say, "I, as my real self, as my larger self, as my complete consciousness, already in deepest truth possess that object, have it, own it, identify it. And that, and that alone, makes it possible for me in my transient, my individual, my momentary personality, to mean yonder object, to inquire about it, to be partly aware of it and partly ignorant of it." You can't mean what is utterly foreign to you. You mean an object, you assert about it, you talk about it, yes, you doubt or wonder about it, you admit your private and individual ignorance about it, only in so far as your larger self, your deeper personality, your total of normal consciousness already *has* that object. Your momentary and private wonder, ignorance, inquiry, or assertion, about the object, implies, asserts, presupposes, that your total self is in full and immediate possession of the object. This, in fact, is the very nature of that curious relation of a thought to an object which we are now considering. The self that is doubting or asserting, or that is even feeling its private ignorance about an object, and that still, even in consequence of all this, is *meaning*, is *aiming at* such object, is in essence identical with the self for which this object exists in its complete and consciously known truth.

So paradoxical seems this final assertion of idealism that I cannot hope in one moment to make it very plain to you. . . . But what I intend by thus saying that the self which thinks about an object, which really, even in the midst of the blindest ignorance and doubt concerning its object still means the object,—that this self is identical with the deeper self which possesses and truly knows the object,—what I intend hereby I can best illustrate by simple cases taken from your own experience. You are in doubt, say, about a name that you have forgotten, or about a thought that you just had, but that has now escaped you. As you hunt for the name or the lost idea, you are all the while sure that you mean just one particular name or idea and no other. But you don't yet know what name or idea this is. You try, and reject name after name. You query, "Was this what I was thinking of, or this?" But after searching you erelong find the name or the idea, and now at once you *recognize* it. "Oh, that," you say, "was what I meant all along, only—I didn't know what I meant." Did you know? Yes, in one sense you knew all the while,—that is, your deeper self, your true consciousness knew. It was your momentary self that did not know. But when you found the long-sought name, recalled the lost idea, you recognized it at once, because it was all the while your own, because you, the true and larger self, who owned the name or the idea and were aware of what it was, now were seen to include the smaller and momentary self that sought the name or tried to recall the thought. Your deeper consciousness of the lost idea was all the while there. In fact, did you not presuppose this when you sought the lost idea? How can I mean a name, or an idea, unless I in truth am the self who knows the name, who possesses the idea? In hunting for the name or the lost idea, I am hunting for my own thought. Well, just so I know nothing about the far-off stars in detail, but in so far as I mean the far-off stars at all, as I speak of them, I am identical with that remote and deep thought of my own that already knows the stars. When I study the stars, I am trying to find out what I really mean by them. To be sure, only experience can tell me, but that is because only experience can bring me into relation with my larger self. The escape from the prison of the inner self is simply the fact that the inner self is through and through an appeal to a larger self. The self that inquires, either inquires without meaning, or if it has a meaning, this meaning exists in and for the larger self that knows.

Here is a suggestion of what I mean by Synthetic Idealism. No truth, I repeat, is more familiar. That I am always meaning to inquire into objects beyond me, what clearer fact could be mentioned? That only in case it is already I who, in deeper truth, in my real and hidden thought, *know* the lost object yonder, the object whose nature I seek to comprehend, that only in this case I can truly *mean* the thing yonder,—this, as we must assert, is involved in the very idea of *meaning*. That is the logical analysis of it. You can mean what your deeper self knows; you cannot mean what your deeper self doesn't know. To be sure, the complete illustration of this most critical insight of idealism belongs elsewhere. Few see the familiar. Nothing is more common than for people to think that they mean objects that have nothing to do with themselves. Kant it was, who, despite his things in themselves, first showed us that nobody really means an object, really knows it, or doubts it, or aims at it, unless he does so by aiming at a truth that is present to his own larger self. Except for the unity of my true self, taught Kant, I have no objects. And so it makes no difference whether I know a thing or am in doubt about it. So long as I really *mean* it, that is enough. The self that *means* the object is identical with the larger self that possesses the object, just as when you seek the lost idea you are already in essence with the self that possesses the lost idea.

In this way I suggest to you the proof which a rigid analysis of the logic of our most commonplace thought would give for the doctrine that in the world there is but *one* Self, and that it is *his* world which we all alike are truly meaning, whether we talk of one another or of Cromwell's character or of the fixed stars or of the far-off eons of the future. The relation of my thought to its object has, I insist, this curious character, that *unless* the thought and its object are parts of one larger thought I can't even be *meaning* that object yonder, can't even be in error about it, can't even doubt its existence. You, for instance, are part of one larger self with me, or else I can't even be meaning to address you as outer beings. You are part of one larger self along with the most mysterious or most remote fact of nature, along with the moon, and all the hosts of heaven, along with all truth and all beauty. Else could you not even intend to speak of such objects beyond you. For whatever you speak of you will find that your world is meant by you as just your world. Talk of the unknowable, and it forthwith becomes your unknowable, your problem, whose solution, unless the problem be a mere nonsense question, your larger self must own and be aware of. The deepest problem of life is, "What is this deeper self?" And the only answer is, *It is the self that knows in unity all truth.* This, I insist, is no hypothesis. It is actually the presupposition of your deepest doubt. And that is why I say: Everything finite is more or less obscure, dark, doubtful. Only the Infinite Self, the problem-solver, the complete thinker, the one who knows what we mean even when we are most confused and ignorant, the one who includes us, who has the world present to himself in unity, before whom all past and future truth, all distant and dark truth is clear in one eternal moment, to whom far and forgot is near, who thinks the whole of nature, and in whom are all things, the Logos, the world-possessor,—only his existence, I say, is perfectly sure.

V

Yet I must not state the outcome thus confidently without a little more analysis and exemplification. Let me put the whole matter in a slightly different way. When a man believes that he knows any truth about a fact beyond his present and momentary thought, what is the position, with reference to that fact, which he gives himself? We must first answer, He believes that one who really knew his, the thinker's, thought, and compared it with the fact yonder, would perceive the agreement between the two. Is this *all*, however, that the believer holds to be true of his own thought? No, not so, for he holds not only that his thought, as it is, agrees with *some* fact outside his present self (as my thought, for instance, of my toothache may agree with the fact yonder called my neighbor's toothache), but also that his thought agrees with the fact with which it *meant* to agree. To *mean* to agree, however, with a specific fact beyond my present self, involves such a relation to that fact that if I could somehow come directly into the presence of the fact itself, could somehow absorb it into my present consciousness, I should become immediately aware of it as the fact that I all along had meant. Our previous examples have been intended to bring clearly before us this curious and in fact unique character of the relation called *meaning* an object of our thought. To return, then, to our supposed believer: he believes that he *knows* some fact beyond his present consciousness. This involves, as we have now seen, the assertion that he believes himself to stand in such an actual relation to the fact yonder that were it in, instead of out of his present consciousness, he would recognize it both as the object *meant* by his present thought, and also as in agreement therewith; and it is all this which, as he believes, an immediate observer of his own thought and of the object—that is, an observer who should include our believer's present self, and the fact yonder, and who should reflect on their relations—would find as the real relation. Observe, however, that only by *reflection* would this higher observer find out that real relation. Nothing but Reflective Self-consciousness could discover it. To believe that you know anything beyond your present and momentary self, is, therefore, to believe that you do stand in such a relation to truth as only a larger and reflectively observant self, that included you and your object, could render intelligible. Or once more, so to believe is essentially to appeal confidently to a possible larger self for approval. But now to say, I know a truth, and yet to say, This larger self to whom I appeal is appealed to only as to a possible self, that needn't be real,—all this involves just the absurdity against which our whole idealistic analysis has been directed in case of all the sorts of fact and truth in the world. To believe, is to say, I stand in a *real* relation to truth, a relation which transcends wholly my present momentary self; and this real relation is of such a curious nature that only a larger inclusive self which consciously reflected upon my meaning and consciously possessed the object that I mean, could know or grasp the reality of the relation. If, however, this *relation* is a real one, it must, like the colors, the sounds, and all the other things of which we spoke before be real *for* somebody. Bare possibilities are nothing. Really possible things are already in some sense real. If, then, my relation to the truth, this complex relation of meaning an object and conforming to it, when the object, although at this moment meant by me, is not now present to my momentary thought,—if this relation is genuine, and yet is such as only a possible larger self could render intelligible, then my possible larger self must be real in order that my momentary self should in fact possess the truth in question. Or, in briefest form, The relation of conforming one's thought to an outer object meant by this thought is a relation which only a Reflective Larger Self could grasp or find real. If the relation is real, the larger self is real, too.

So much, then, for the case when one *believes* that one has grasped a truth beyond the moment. But now for the case when one is actually in *error* about some object of his momentary and finite thought. Error is the actual failure to agree, not with any fact taken at random, but with just the fact that one had meant to agree with. Under what circumstances, then, is error possible? Only in case one's real thought, by virtue of its meaning, does transcend his own momentary and in so far ignorant self. As the true believer, meaning the truth that he believes, must be in real relation thereto, even so the blunderer, really meaning, as he does, the fact yonder, in order that he should be able even to blunder about it, must be, in so far, in the same real relation to truth as the true believer. His error lies in missing that conformity with the meant object at which he aimed. None the less, however, did he really mean and really aim; and, therefore, is he in error, because his real and larger self finds him to be so. True thinking and false thinking alike involve, then, the same fundamental conditions, in so far as both are carried on in moments; and in so far as, in both cases, the false moment and the true are such by virtue of being organic parts of a larger, critical, reflective, and so conscious self.

To sum up so far: Of no object do I speak either falsely or truly, unless I mean that object. Never do I mean an object, unless I stand in such relation thereto that were the object in this conscious moment, and immediately present to me, I should myself recognize it as completing and fulfilling my present and momentary meaning. The relation of meaning an object is thus one that only conscious Reflection can define, or observe, or constitute. No merely *foreign* observer, no external test, could decide upon what is meant at any moment. Therefore, when what is meant is outside of the moment which means, only a Self inclusive of the moment and its object could complete, and so confirm or refute, the opinion that the moment contains. Really to mean an object, then, whether in case of true opinion or in case of false opinion, involves the real possibility of such a reflective test of one's meaning from the point of view of a larger self. But to say, My relation to the object is such that a reflective larger self, and *only* such a reflective and inclusive self, could see that I meant the object, is to assert a fact, a relation, an existent truth in the world, that either is a truth for nobody, or is a truth for an actual reflective self, inclusive of the moment, and critical of its meaning. Our whole idealistic analysis, however, from the beginning of this discussion, has been to the effect that facts must be facts for somebody, and can't be facts for nobody, and that *bare* possibilities are really impossible. Hence whoever believes, whether truly or falsely, about objects beyond the moment of his belief, is an organic part of a reflective and conscious larger self that has those objects immediately present to itself, and has them in organic relation with the erring or truthful momentary self that believes.

Belief, true and false, having been examined, the case of doubt follows at once. To doubt about objects beyond my momentary self is to admit the "possibility of error" as to such objects. Error would involve my inclusion in a larger self that has directly present to it the object meant by me as I doubt. Truth would involve the same inclusion. The inclusion itself, then, is, so far, no object of rational doubt. To doubt the inclusion would be merely to doubt whether I meant anything at all beyond the moment, and not to doubt as to my particular knowledge about the *nature* of some object beyond, when once the object had been supposed to be meant. Doubt presupposes then, whenever it is a definite doubt, the real possibility, and so, in the last analysis, the reality of the normal self-consciousness that possesses the object concerning which one doubts.

But if, passing to the extreme of skepticism, and stating one's most despairing and most uncompromising doubt, one so far confines himself to the prison of the inner life as to doubt whether one ever does mean any object beyond the moment at all, there comes the final consideration that in doubting one's power to transcend the moment, one has already transcended the moment, just as we found in following Hegel's analysis. To say, It is impossible to mean any object beyond this moment of my thought, and the moment is for itself "the measure of all things," is at all events to give a meaning to the words *this moment.* And *this moment* means something only in opposition to *other* moments. Yes, even in saying *this moment,* I have already left this moment, and am meaning and speaking of a past moment. Moreover, to deny that one can mean an object "beyond the moment" is already to give a meaning to the phrase *beyond the moment,* and then to deny that anything is meant to fall within the scope of this meaning. In every case, then, one must transcend by one's meaning the moment to which one is confined by one's finitude.

Flee where we will, then, the net of the larger Self ensnares us. We are lost and imprisoned in the thickets of its tangled labyrinth. The moments are not at all in themselves, for as moments they have no meaning; they exist only in relation to the beyond. The larger Self alone is, and they are by reason of it, organic parts of it. They perish, but it remains; they have truth or error only in its overshadowing presence.

And now, as to the unity of this Self. Can there be many such organic selves, mutually separate unities of moments and of the objects that these moments mean? Nay, were there *many* such, would not their manifoldness be a truth? Their relations, would not these be real? Their distinct places in the world-order, would not these things be objects of possible true or false thoughts? If so, must not there be once more the inclusive real Self for whom these truths were true, these separate selves interrelated, and their variety absorbed in the organism of its rational meaning?

There is, then, at last, but one Self, organically, reflectively, consciously inclusive of all the selves, and so of all truth. I have called this self, Logos, problem-solver, all-knower. Consider, then, last of all, his relation to problems. In the previous lecture we doubted many things; we questioned the whole seeming world of the outer order; we wondered as to space and time, as to nature and evolution, as to the beginning and the end of things. Now he who wonders is like him who doubts. Has his wonder any rationality about it? Does he *mean* anything by his doubt? Then the truth that he means, and about which he wonders, has its real constitution. As wonderer, he in the moment possesses not this solving truth; he appeals to the self who can solve. That self must possess the solution just as surely as the problem has a meaning. The real nature of space and time, the real beginning of things, where matter was at any point of time in the past, what is to become of the world's energy: these are matters of truth, and truth is necessarily present to the Self as in one all-comprehending self-completed moment, beyond which is naught, within which is the world.

The world, then, is such stuff as ideas are made of. Thought possesses all things. But the world isn't unreal. It extends infinitely beyond our private consciousness, because it is the world of a universal mind. What facts it is to contain only experience can inform us. There is no magic that can anticipate the work of science. Absolutely the *only* thing sure from the first about this world, however, is that it is intelligent, rational, orderly, essentially comprehensible, so that all its problems are somewhere solved, all its darkest mysteries are known to the supreme Self. This Self infinitely and reflectively transcends our consciousness, and therefore, since it includes us, it is at the very least a person, and more definitely conscious than we are; for what it possesses is self-reflecting knowledge, and what is knowledge aware of itself, but consciousness? Beyond the seeming wreck and chaos of our finite problems, its eternal insight dwells, therefore, in absolute and supreme majesty. Yet it is not far from every one of us. There is no least or most transient thought that flits through a child's mind, or that troubles with the faintest line of care a maiden's face, and that still does not contain and embody something of this divine Logos.

THE WORLD AND THE INDIVIDUAL

There is an ancient doctrine that whatever is, is ultimately something Individual. Realism early came to that view; and only Critical Rationalism has ever explicitly maintained that the ultimate realities are universals, namely, valid possibilities of experience, or mere truths as such. Now at the close of the last lecture, after analyzing the whole basis of Critical Rationalism, the entire conception of the Real as merely valid, we reinstated the Individual as the only ultimate form of Being. In so far we returned to a view that, in the history of thought, Realism already asserted. But we gave a new reason of our own for this view. Our reason was that the very defect of our finite ideas which sends us seeking for Being lies in the fact that whether we long for practical satisfaction, or think of purely theoretical prob-

From Josiah Royce, *The World and the Individual* (New York: Macmillan, 1899).

lems, we, as we now are, are always seeking another object than what is yet present to our ideas. Now any ultimate reality, for us while as finite thinkers we seek it, is always such another fact. Yet this other object is always an object for our thought only in so far as our thought already means it, defines it, and wills it to be our object. But what is for us this other? In its essence it is already defined even before we undertake to know it. For this other is precisely the fulfilment of our purpose, the satisfaction of the will now imperfectly embodied in our ideas, the completion of what we already partially possess in our finite insight. This completion is for us another, solely because our ideas, in their present momentary forms, come to us as general ideas,—ideas of what is now merely a kind of relative fulfilment and not an entire fulfilment. Other fulfilment of the same general kind is needed before we can face the whole Being that we seek. This kind of fulfilment we want to bring, however, to some integral expression, to its own finality, to its completeness as a whole fact. And this want of ours, so I asserted, not only sets us looking for Being, but gives us our only ground and means for defining Being.

Being itself we should directly face in our own experience only in case we experienced finality, *i.e.* full expression of what our finite ideas both mean and seek. Such expression, however, would be given to us in the form of a life that neither sought nor permitted another to take its own place as the expression of its own purpose. Where no other was yet to be sought, there alone would our ideas define no other, no Being, of the type in question, lying yet beyond themselves, in the direction of their own type of fulfilment. The other would be found, and so would be present. And there alone should we consequently stand in the presence of what is real. Conversely, whoever grasps only the nature of a general concept, whoever merely thinks of light or colors, or gravitation, or of man, whoever lacks, longs, or in any way seeks another, has not in his experience the full expression of his own meaning. Hence it is that he has to seek his object elsewhere. And so he has not yet faced any ultimate Being. He has upon his hands mere fragments, mere aspects of Being. Thus an entire instance of Being must be precisely that which permits your ideas to seek no other than what is present. Such a being is an Individual. Only, for our present conception of Being, an individual being is not a fact independent of any experience, nor yet a merely valid truth, nor yet a merely immediate datum that quenches ideas. For all these alternatives we have already faced and rejected. On the contrary an individual being is a Life of Experience fulfilling Ideas, in an absolutely final form. And this we said is the essential nature of Being. The essence of the Real is to be Individual, or to permit no other of its own kind, and this character it possesses only as the unique fulfilment of purpose.

Or, once more, as Mysticism asserted, so we too assert of your world, *That art thou.* Only the Self which is your world is your completely integrated Self, the totality of the life that at this instant you fragmentarily grasp. Your present defect is a matter of the mere form of your consciousness at this instant. Were your eyes at this instant open to your own meaning, your life as a whole would be spread before you as a single and unique life, for which no other could be substituted without a less determinate expression of just your individual will. Now this complete life of yours, is. Only such completion can be. Being can possess no other nature than this. And this, in outline, is our Fourth Conception of Being. . . .

But with this result we come in presence of a final problem. All this, you say, depends upon my assurance that there is after all a real and therefore an essentially knowable and rational world yonder. Such a world would have to be in essence a mind, or a world of minds. But after all, how does one ever escape from the prison of the inner life? Am I not in all this merely wandering amidst the realm of my own ideas? *My* world, of course, isn't and can't be a mere *x*, an essentially unknowable thing, just because it *is my* world, and I have an idea of it. But then does not this mean that *my* world is, after all, forever just *my* world, so that I never get to any truth beyond myself? Isn't this result very disheartening? My world is thus a world of ideas, but alas! how do I then ever reach those ideas of the minds beyond me?

The answer is a simple, but in one sense a very problematic one. You, in one sense, namely, never *do* or can get beyond your own ideas, nor ought you to wish to do so, because in truth all these other minds that constitute your outer and real world are in essence one with your own self. This whole world of ideas is essentially *one* world, and so it is essentially the world of one self and *That art Thou.*

The truth and meaning of this deepest proposition of all idealism is now not at all remote from us. The considerations, however, upon which it depends are of the dryest possible sort, as commonplace as they are deep.

Whatever objects you may think about, whether they are objects directly known to you, or objects infinitely far removed, objects in the distant stars, or objects remote in time, or objects near and present—such objects, then, as a number with fifty places of digits in it, or the mountains on the other side of the moon, or the day of your death, or the character of Cromwell, or the law of gravitation, or a name that you are just now trying to think of and have forgotten, or the meaning of some mood or feeling or idea now in your mind,— all such objects, I insist, stand in a certain constant and curious relation to your mind whenever you are thinking about them,—a relation that we often miss because it is so familiar. What is this relation? Such an object, while you think about it, needn't be, as popular thought often supposes it to be, the *cause* of your thoughts concerning it. Thus, when you think about Cromwell's character, Cromwell's character isn't just now *causing* any ideas in you,—isn't, so to speak, doing anything to you. Cromwell is dead, and after life's fitful fever his character is a very inactive thing. Not as the *cause*, but as the *object* of your thought is Cromwell present to you. Even so, if you choose now to think of the moment of your death, that moment is somewhere off there in the future, and you can make it your object, but it isn't now an active cause of your ideas. The moment of your death has no present physical existence at all, and just now causes nothing. So, too, with the mountains on the other side of the moon. When you make them the object of your thought, they remain indifferent to you. They do not affect you. You never saw them. But all the same you can think about them.

Yet this thinking *about* things is, after all, a very curious relation in which to stand to things. In order to think *about* a thing, it is *not* enough that I should have an idea in me that merely resembles that thing. This last is a very important observation. I repeat, it is *not* enough that I should merely have an idea in me that resembles the thing whereof I think. I have, for instance, in me the idea of a pain. Another man has a pain just like mine. Say we both have toothache; or have both burned our finger-tips in the same way. Now my idea of pain is just like the pain in him, but I am not on that account necessarily thinking about *his* pain, merely because what I am thinking about, namely my own pain, resembles his pain. No; to think about an object you must not merely have an idea that resembles the object, but you must *mean* to have your idea resemble that object. Stated in other form, to think of an object you must consciously aim at that object, you must pick out that object, you must already in some measure possess that object enough, namely, to identify it as what you mean. But how can you *mean*, how can you *aim at*, how can you *possess*, how can you *pick out*, how can you *identify* what is not already present in essence to your own hidden self? Here is surely a deep question. When you aim at yonder object, be it the mountains in the moon or the day of your death, you really say, "I, as my real self, as my larger self, as my complete consciousness, already in deepest truth possess that object, have it, own it, identify it. And that, and that alone, makes it possible for me in my transient, my individual, my momentary personality, to mean yonder object, to inquire about it, to be partly aware of it and partly ignorant of it." You can't mean what is utterly foreign to you. You mean an object, you assert about it, you talk about it, yes, you doubt or wonder about it, you admit your private and individual ignorance about it, only in so far as your larger self, your deeper personality, your total of normal consciousness already *has* that object. Your momentary and private wonder, ignorance, inquiry, or assertion, about the object, implies, asserts, presupposes, that your total self is in full and immediate possession of the object. This, in fact, is the very nature of that curious relation of a thought to an object which we are now considering. The self that is doubting or asserting, or that is even feeling, its private ignorance about an object, and that still, even in consequence of all this, is *meaning*, is *aiming at* such object, is in essence identical with the self for which this object exists in its complete and consciously known truth.

So paradoxical seems this final assertion of idealism that I cannot hope in one moment to make it very plain to you. . . . But what I intend by thus saying that the self which thinks about an object, which really, even in the midst of the blindest ignorance and doubt concerning its object still means the object,—that this self is identical with the deeper self which possesses and truly knows the object,—what I intend hereby I can best illustrate by simple cases taken from your own experience. You are in doubt, say, about a name that you have forgotten, or about a thought that you just had, but that has now escaped you. As you hunt for the name or the lost idea, you are all the while sure that you mean just one particular name or idea and no other. But you don't yet know what name or idea this is. You try, and reject name after name. You query, "Was this what I was thinking of, or this?" But after searching you erelong find the name or the idea, and now at once you *recognize* it. "Oh, that," you say, "was what I meant all along, only—I didn't know what I meant." Did you know? Yes, in one sense you knew all the while,—that is, your deeper self, your true consciousness knew. It was your momentary self that did not know. But when you found the long-sought name, recalled the lost idea, you recognized it at once, because it was all the while your own, because you, the true and larger self, who owned the name or the idea and were aware of what it was, now were seen to include the smaller and momentary self that sought the name or tried to recall the thought. Your deeper consciousness of the lost idea was all the while there. In fact, did you not presuppose this when you sought the lost idea? How can I mean a name, or an idea, unless I in truth am the self who knows the name, who possesses the idea? In hunting for the name or the lost idea, I am hunting for my own thought. Well, just so I know nothing about the far-off stars in detail, but in so far as I mean the far-off stars at all, as I speak of them, I am identical with that remote and deep thought of my own that already knows the stars. When I study the stars, I am trying to find out what I really mean by them. To be sure, only experience can tell me, but that is because only experience can bring me into relation with my larger self. The escape from the prison of the inner self is simply the fact that the inner self is through and through an appeal to a larger self. The self that inquires, either inquires without meaning, or if it has a meaning, this meaning exists in and for the larger self that knows.

Here is a suggestion of what I mean by Synthetic Idealism. No truth, I repeat, is more familiar. That I am always meaning to inquire into objects beyond me, what clearer fact could be mentioned? That only in case it is already I who, in deeper truth, in my real and hidden thought, *know* the lost object yonder, the object whose nature I seek to comprehend, that only in this case I can truly *mean* the thing yonder,—this, as we must assert, is involved in the very idea of *meaning*. That is the logical analysis of it. You can mean what your deeper self knows; you cannot mean what your deeper self doesn't know. To be sure, the complete illustration of this most critical insight of idealism belongs elsewhere. Few see the familiar. Nothing is more common than for people to think that they mean objects that have nothing to do with themselves. Kant it was, who, despite his things in themselves, first showed us that nobody really means an object, really knows it, or doubts it, or aims at it, unless he does so by aiming at a truth that is present to his own larger self. Except for the unity of my true self, taught Kant, I have no objects. And so it makes no difference whether I know a thing or am in doubt about it. So long as I really *mean* it, that is enough. The self that *means* the object is identical with the larger self that possesses the object, just as when you seek the lost idea you are already in essence with the self that possesses the lost idea.

In this way I suggest to you the proof which a rigid analysis of the logic of our most commonplace thought would give for the doctrine that in the world there is but *one* Self, and that it is *his* world which we all alike are truly meaning, whether we talk of one another or of Cromwell's character or of the fixed stars or of the far-off eons of the future. The relation of my thought to its object has, I insist, this curious character, that *unless* the thought and its object are parts of one larger thought I can't even be *meaning* that object yonder, can't even be in error about it, can't even doubt its existence. You, for instance, are part of one larger self with me, or else I can't even be meaning to address you as outer beings. You are part of one larger self along with the most mysterious or most remote fact of nature, along with the moon, and all the hosts of heaven, along with all truth and beauty. Else could you not even intend to speak of such objects beyond you. For whatever you speak of you will find that your world is meant by you as just your world. Talk of the unknowable, and it forthwith becomes your unknowable, your problem, whose solution, unless the problem be a mere nonsense question, your larger self must own and be aware of. The deepest problem of life is, "What is this deeper self?" And the only answer is, *It is the self that knows in unity all truth.* This, I insist, is no hypothesis. It is actually the presupposition of your deepest doubt. And that is why I say: Everything finite is more or less obscure, dark, doubtful. Only the Infinite Self, the problem-solver, the complete thinker, the one who knows what we mean even when we are most confused and ignorant, the one who includes us, who has the world present to himself in unity, before whom all past and future truth, all distant and dark truth is clear in one eternal moment, to whom far and forgot is near, who thinks the whole of nature, and in whom are all things, the Logos, the world-possessor,—only his existence, I say, is perfectly sure.

CHAPTER

47

BERGSON

1859–1941

Henri Bergson was born in Paris to Jewish immigrants; his father was from Poland, his mother from England. At the prestigious École Normale Supérieure, his studies turned from mathematics, in which he had shown early prodigal abilities, to science, and then finally philosophy. By the time he became philosophy professor at the Collège de France in 1900, after having taught at a variety of places, he had already become famous in philosophical circles for his doctoral dissertation, published in 1889 as *Essai sur les données immédiates de la conscience* (Essay on the immediate data of consciousness). He argued in his *Essay* that experience will forever be beyond the reach of the intellect because experience is an indivisible continuum (in the mathematical sense) and therefore cannot ever be adequately represented as a succession of demarcated conscious states (as required by the intellect). Like Edmund Husserl, Bergson drew a sharp distinction between the concept of time and the experience of time; *real* time is not the static (abstract) time of being but the dynamic time of becoming as given in experience. Experiential time is apprehended solely by intuition as duration, which ultimately is inaccessible to the conceptual objectifications of the intellect. From this initial work Bergson came to reject all mechanistic and scientific reductionisms of the human mind to any sort of mechanistic explanation. By the turn of the century, his philosophy of "dynamism" extended beyond philosophical and scientific circles and attracted a wide public following through his lectures on human freedom and spirituality against the growing scientific determinism. His method and unique style is presented most clearly in his *Introduction to Metaphysics* (1903), from which our selection is taken.

With the publication in 1907 of *Creative Evolution*, excerpted in our selection, Bergson became world renowned. William James called the work "a pure classic in point of form." In it, Bergson argues that the inner creative urge, a vital principle, or *élan vital*, is the teleological force behind evolution, rather than the (blind) natural selection envisioned by Charles Darwin. He presents reality as an integrated whole and yet undetermined in a way that allows individual minds to play an active role. The ultimate goal of human existence, according to Bergson, is to enter into a mystical union with the ultimate, a state beyond all rationality. This enlightened experience is the culmination of the *élan vital*, the key ingredient in Bergson's dynamic universe of becoming: at its pinnacle, the human mind joins mystic intuition with scientific experiment, thereby taking an active and central role in "the essential function of the universe, which is a machine for the making of gods."

Bergson was elected to the Council of the Legion of Honor, the French Academy, and the Academy of Sciences, and served as president of the League of Nations Committee for Intellectual Cooperation. In 1928 he won the Nobel Prize for literature.

AN INTRODUCTION TO METAPHYSICS

A comparison of the definitions of metaphysics and the various conceptions of the absolute leads to the discovery that philosophers, in spite of their apparent divergencies, agree in distinguishing two profoundly different ways of knowing a thing. The first implies that we move round the object; the second that we enter into it. The first depends on the point of view at which we are placed and on the symbols by which we express ourselves. The second neither depends on a point of view nor relies on any symbol. The first kind of knowledge may be said to stop at the *relative;* the second, in those cases where it is possible, to attain the *absolute.*

Consider, for example, the movement of an object in space. My perception of the motion will vary with the point of view, moving or stationary, from which I observe it. My expression of it will vary with the systems of axes, or the points of reference, to which I relate it: that is, with the symbols by which I translate it. For this double reason I call such motion *relative:* in the one case, as in the other, I am placed outside the object itself. But when I speak of an *absolute* movement, I am attributing to the moving object an interior and, so to speak, states of mind; I also imply that I am in sympathy with those states, and that I insert myself in them by an effort of imagination. Then, according as the object is moving or stationary, according as it adopts one movement or another, what I experience will vary. And what I experience will depend neither on the point of view I may take up in regard to the object, since I am inside the object itself, nor on the symbols by which I may translate the motion, since I have rejected all translations in order to possess the original. In short, I shall no longer grasp the movement from without, remaining where I am, but from where it is, from within, as it is in itself. I shall possess an absolute.

Consider, again, a character whose adventures are related to me in a novel. The author may multiply the traits of his hero's character, may make him speak and act as much as he pleases, but all this can never be equivalent to the simple and indivisible feeling which I should experience if I were able for an instant to identify myself with the person of the hero himself. Out of that indivisible feeling, as from a spring, all the words, gestures, and actions of the man would appear to me to flow naturally. They would no longer be accidents which, added to the idea I had already formed of the character, continually enriched that idea,

From Henri Bergson, *An Introduction to Metaphysics,* trans. T. E. Hulme (New York: Putnam, 1912).

without ever completing it. The character would be given to me all at once, in its entirety, and the thousand incidents which manifest it, instead of adding themselves to the idea and so enriching it, would seem to me, on the contrary, to detach themselves from it, without, however, exhausting it or impoverishing its essence. All the things I am told about the man provide me with so many points of view from which I can observe him. All the traits which describe him, and which can make him known to me only by so many comparisons with persons or things I know already, are signs by which he is expressed more or less symbolically. Symbols and points of view, therefore, place me outside him; they give me only what he has in common with others, and not what belongs to him and to him alone. But that which is properly himself, that which constitutes his essence, cannot be perceived from without, being internal by definition, nor be expressed by symbols, being incommensurable with everything else. Description, history, and analysis leave me here in the relative. Coincidence with the person himself would alone give me the absolute.

It is in this sense, and in this sense only, that *absolute* is synonymous with *perfection.* Were all the photographs of a town, taken from all possible points of view, to go on indefinitely completing one another, they would never be equivalent to the solid town in which we walk about. Were all the translations of a poem into all possible languages to add together their various shades of meaning and, correcting each other by a kind of mutual retouching, to give a more and more faithful image of the poem they translate, they would yet never succeed in rendering the inner meaning of the original. A representation taken from a certain point of view, a translation made with certain symbols, will always remain imperfect in comparison with the object of which a view has been taken, or which the symbols seek to express. But the absolute, which is the object and not its representation, the original and not its translation, is perfect, by being perfectly what it is.

It is doubtless for this reason that the *absolute* has often been identified with the *infinite.* Suppose that I wished to communicate to someone who did not know Greek the extraordinarily simple impression that a passage in Homer makes upon me; I should first give a translation of the lines, I should then comment on my translation, and then develop the commentary; in this way, by piling up explanation on explanation, I might approach nearer and nearer to what I wanted to express; but I should never quite reach it. When you raise your arm, you accomplish a movement of which you have, from within, a simple perception; but for me, watching it from the outside, your arm passes through one point, then through another, and between these two there will be still other points; so that, if I began to count, the operation would go on for ever. Viewed from the inside, then, an absolute is a simple thing; but looked at from the outside, that is to say, relatively to other things, it becomes, in relation to these signs which express it, the gold coin for which we never seem able to finish giving small change. Now, that which lends itself at the same time both to an indivisible apprehension and to an inexhaustible enumeration, is, by the very definition of the word, an infinite.

It follows from this that an absolute could only be given in an *intuition,* while everything else falls within the province of *analysis.* By intuition is meant the kind of *intellectual sympathy* by which one places oneself within an object in order to coincide with what is unique in it and consequently inexpressible. Analysis, on the contrary, is the operation which reduces the object to elements already known, that is, to elements common both to it and other objects. To analyze, therefore, is to express a thing as a function of something other than itself. All analysis is thus a translation, a development into symbols, a representation taken from successive points of view from which we note as many resemblances as possible between the new object which we are studying and others which we believe we know already. In its eternally unsatisfied desire to embrace the object around which it is compelled to turn, analysis multiplies without end the number of its points of view in order to complete its always incomplete representation, and ceaselessly varies its symbols that it may perfect the always imperfect translation. It goes on, therefore, to infinity. But intuition, if intuition is possible, is a simple act.

Now it is easy to see that the ordinary function of positive science is analysis. Positive science works, then, above all, with symbols. Even the most concrete of the natural sciences, those concerned with life, confine themselves to the visible form of living beings, their organs and anatomical elements. They make comparisons between these forms, they reduce the more complex to the more simple; in short, they study the workings of life in what is, so to speak, only its visual symbol. If there exists any means of possessing a reality absolutely instead of knowing it relatively, of placing oneself within it instead of looking at it from outside points of view, of having the intuition instead of making the analysis: in short, of seizing it without any expression, translation, or symbolic representation—metaphysics is that means. *Metaphysics, then, is the science which claims to dispense with symbols.*

There is one reality, at least, which we all seize from within, by intuition and not by simple analysis. It is our own personality in its flowing through time—our self which endures. We may sympathize intellectually with nothing else, but we certainly sympathize with our own selves.

When I direct my attention inward to contemplate my own self (supposed for the moment to be inactive), I perceive at first, as a crust solidified on the surface, all the perceptions which come to it from the material world. These perceptions are clear, distinct, juxtaposed, or juxtaposable one with another; they tend to group themselves into objects. Next, I notice the memories which more or less adhere to these perceptions and which serve to interpret them. These memories have been detached, as it were, from the depth of my personality, drawn to the surface by the perceptions which resemble them; they rest on the surface of my mind without being absolutely myself. Lastly, I feel the stir of tendencies and motor habits—a crowd of virtual actions, more or less firmly bound to these perceptions and memories. All these clearly defined elements appear more distinct from me, the more distinct they are from each other. Radiating, as they do, from within outwards, they form, collectively, the surface of a sphere which tends to grow larger and lose itself in the exterior world. But if I draw myself in from the periphery toward the center, if I search in the depth of my being that which is most uniformly, most constantly, and most enduringly myself, I find an altogether different thing.

There is, beneath these sharply cut crystals and this frozen surface, a continuous flux which is not comparable to any flux I have ever seen. There is a succession of states, each of which announces that which follows and contains that which precedes it. They can, properly speaking, only be said to form multiple states when I have already passed them and turn back to observe their track. While I was experiencing them they were so solidly organized, so profoundly animated with a common life, that I could not have said where any one of them finished or where another commenced. In reality no one of them begins or ends, but all extend into each other.

This inner life may be compared to the unrolling of a coil, for there is no living being who does not feel himself coming gradually to the end of his role; and to live is to grow old. But it may just as well be compared to a continual rolling up, like that of a thread on a ball, for our past follows us, it swells incessantly with the present that it picks up on its way; and consciousness means memory.

But actually it is neither an unrolling nor a rolling up, for these two similes evoke the idea of lines and surfaces whose parts are homogeneous and superposable on one another. Now, there are no two identical moments in the life of the same conscious being. Take the simplest sensation, suppose it constant, absorb in it the entire personality: the consciousness which will accompany this sensation cannot remain identical with itself for two consecutive moments, because the second moment always contains, over and above the first, the memory that the first has bequeathed to it. A consciousness which could experience two identical moments would be a consciousness without memory. It would die and be born again continually. In what other way could one represent unconsciousness?

It would be better, then, to use as a comparison the myriad-tinted spectrum, with its insensible gradations leading from one shade to another. A current of feeling which passed along the spectrum, assuming in turn the tint of each of its shades, would experience a series of gradual changes, each of which would announce the one to follow and would sum up those which preceded it. Yet even here the successive shades of the spectrum always remain external one to another. They are juxtaposed; they occupy space. But pure duration, on the contrary, excludes all idea of juxtaposition, reciprocal externality, and extension.

Let us, then, rather, imagine an infinitely small elastic body, contracted, if it were possible, to a mathematical point. Let this be drawn out gradually in such a manner that from the point comes a constant lengthening line. Let us fix our attention not on the line as a line, but on the action by which it is traced. Let us bear in mind that this action, in spite of its duration, is indivisible if accomplished without stopping, that if a stopping point is inserted, we have two actions instead of one, that each of these separate actions is then the indivisible operation of which we speak, and that it is not the moving action itself which is divisible, but, rather, the stationary line it leaves behind it as its track in space. Finally, let us free ourselves from the space which underlies the movement in order to consider only the movement itself, the act of tension or extension; in short, pure mobility. We shall have this time a more faithful image of the development of our self in duration.

However, even this image is incomplete, and, indeed, every comparison will be insufficient, because the unrolling of our duration resembles in some of its aspects the unity of an advancing movement and in others the multiplicity of expanding states; and, clearly, no metaphor can express one of these two aspects without sacrificing the other. If I use the comparison of the spectrum with its thousand shades, I have before me a thing already made, while duration is continually in the making. If I think of an elastic which is being stretched, or of a spring which is extended or relaxed, I forget the richness of color, characteristic of duration that is lived, to see only the simple movement by which consciousness passes from one shade to another. The inner life is all this at once: variety of qualities, continuity of progress, and unity of direction. It cannot be represented by images.

But it is even less possible to represent it by *concepts,* that is, by abstract, general, or simple ideas. It is true that no image can reproduce exactly the original feeling I have of the flow of my own conscious life. But it is not even necessary that I should attempt to render it. If a man is incapable of getting for himself the intuition of the constitutive duration of his own being, nothing will ever give it to him, concepts no more than images. Here the single aim of the philosopher should be to promote a certain effort, which in most men is usually fettered by habits of mind more useful to life. Now the image has at least this advantage, that it keeps us in the concrete. No image can replace the intuition of duration, but many diverse images, borrowed from very different orders of things, may, by the convergence of their action, direct consciousness to the precise point where there is a certain intuition to be seized. By choosing images as dissimilar as possible, we shall prevent any one of them from usurping the place of the intuition it is intended to call up, since it would then be driven away at once by its rivals. By providing that, in spite of their differences of aspect, they all require from the mind the same kind of attention, and in some sort the same degree of tension, we shall gradually accustom consciousness to a particular and clearly defined disposition—that precisely which it must adopt in order to appear to itself as it really is, without any veil. But, then, consciousness must at least consent to make the effort. For it will have been shown nothing: it will simply have been placed in the attitude it must take up in order to make the desired effort, and so come by itself to the intuition. Concepts on the contrary—especially if they are simple—have the disadvantage of being in reality symbols substituted for the object they symbolize, and demand no effort on our part. Examined closely, each of them, it would be seen, retains only that part of the object which is common to it and to others, and expresses, still more than the image does, a *comparison* between the object and others which resemble it. But as the comparison has made manifest a resemblance, as the resemblance is a property of the object, and as a property has every appearance of being a *part* of the object which possesses it, we easily persuade ourselves that by setting concept beside concept we are reconstructing the whole of the object with its parts, thus obtaining, so to speak, its intellectual equivalent. In this way we believe that we can form a faithful representation of duration by setting in line the concepts of unity, multiplicity, continuity, finite or infinite divisibility, etc. There precisely is the illusion. There also is the danger. Just insofar as abstract ideas can render service to analysis, that is, to the scientific study of the object in its relations to other objects, so far are they incapable of replacing intuition, that is, the metaphysical investigation of what is essential and unique in the object. For on the one hand these concepts, laid side by side, never actually give us more than an artificial reconstruction of the object, of which they can only symbolize certain general, and, in a way, impersonal aspects; it is, therefore, useless to believe that with them we can seize a reality of which they present to us the shadow alone. And, on the other hand, besides the illusion there is also a very serious danger. For the concept generalizes at the same time as it abstracts. The concept can only symbolize a particular property by making it common to an infinity of things. It therefore always more or less deforms the property by the extension it gives to it. Replaced in the metaphysical object to which it belongs, a property coincides with the object, or at least moulds itself on it, and adopts the same outline. Extracted from the metaphysical object, and presented in a concept, it grows indefinitely larger, and goes beyond the object itself, since henceforth it has to contain it, along with a number of other objects. Thus the different concepts that we form of the properties of a thing inscribe round it so many circles, each much too large and none of them fitting it exactly. And yet, in the thing itself the properties coincided with the thing, and coincided consequently with one another. So that, if we are bent on reconstructing the object with concepts, some artifice must be sought whereby this coincidence of the object and its properties can be brought about. For example, we may choose one of the concepts and try, starting from it, to get round to the others. But we shall then soon discover that, according as we start from one concept or another, the meeting and combination of the concepts will take place in an altogether different way. According as we start, for example, from unity or from multiplicity, we shall have to conceive differently the multiple unity of duration. Everything will depend on the weight we attribute to this or that concept, and this weight will always be arbitrary, since the concept extracted from the object has no weight, being only the shadow of a body. In this way, as many different *systems* will spring up as there are external points of view from which the reality can be examined, or larger circles in which it can be enclosed. Simple concepts have, then, not only the inconvenience of dividing the concrete unity of the object into so many symbolical expressions; they also divide philosophy into distinct schools, each of which takes its seat, chooses its counters, and carries on with the others a game that will never end. Either metaphysics is only this play of ideas, or else, if it is a serious occupation of the mind, if it is a science and not simply an exercise, it must transcend concepts in order to reach intuition. Certainly, concepts are necessary to it, for all the other sciences work as a rule with concepts, and metaphysics cannot dispense with the other sciences. But it is only truly itself when it goes beyond the concept, or at least when it frees itself from rigid and ready-made concepts in order to create a kind very different from those which we habitually use; I mean supple, mobile, and almost fluid representations, always ready to mould themselves on the fleeting forms of intuition. We shall return later to this important point. Let it suffice us for the moment to have shown that our duration can be presented to us directly in an intuition, that it can be suggested to us indirectly by images, but that it can never—if we confine the word concept to its proper meaning—be enclosed in a conceptual representation.

Let us try for an instance to consider our duration as a multiplicity. It will then be necessary to add that the terms of this multiplicity, instead of being distinct, as they are in any other multiplicity, encroach on one another; and that, while we can no doubt, by an effort of imagination, solidify duration once it has elapsed, divide it into juxtaposed portions and count all these portions, yet this operation is accomplished on the frozen memory of the duration, on the stationary trace which the mobility of duration leaves behind it, and not on the duration itself. We must admit, therefore, that if there is a multiplicity here, it bears no resemblance to any other multiplicity we know. Shall we say, then, that duration has unity? Doubtless, a continuity of elements which prolong themselves into one another participates in unity as much as in multiplicity; but this moving, changing, colored, living unity has hardly anything in common with the abstract, motionless, and empty unity which the concept of pure unity circumscribes. Shall we conclude from this that duration must be defined as unity and multiplicity at the same time? But singularly enough, however much I manipulate the two concepts, portion them out, combine them differently, practice on them the most subtle operations of mental chemistry, I never obtain anything which resembles the simple intuition that I have of duration; while, on the contrary, when I replace myself in duration by an effort of intuition, I immediately perceive how it is unity, multiplicity, and many other things besides. These different concepts, then, were only so many standpoints from which we could consider duration. Neither separated nor reunited have they made us penetrate into it.

We do penetrate into it, however, and that can only be by an effort of intuition. In this sense, an inner, absolute knowledge of the duration of the self by the self is possible. But if metaphysics here demands and can obtain an intuition, science has none the less need of an analysis. Now it is a confusion between the function of analysis and that of intuition which gives birth to the discussions between the schools and the conflicts between systems.

Psychology, in fact, proceeds like all the other sciences by analysis. It resolves the self, which has been given to it at first in a simple intuition into sensations, feelings, ideas, etc., which it studies separately. It substitutes, then, for the self a series of elements which form the facts of psychology. But are these *elements* really *parts?* That is the whole question, and it is because it has been evaded that the problem of human personality has so often been stated in insoluble terms.

It is incontestable that every psychical state, simply because it belongs to a person, reflects the whole of a personality. Every feeling, however simple it may be, contains virtually within it the whole past and present of the being experiencing it, and, consequently, can only be separated and constituted into a "state" by an effort of abstraction or of analysis. But it is no less incontestable that without this effort of abstraction or analysis there would be no possible development of the science of psychology. What, then, exactly, is the operation by which a psychologist detaches a mental state in order to erect it into a more or less independent entity? He begins by neglecting that special coloring of the personality which cannot be expressed in known and common terms. Then he endeavors to isolate, in the person already thus simplified, some aspect which lends itself to an interesting inquiry. If he is considering inclination, for example, he will neglect the inexpressible shade which colors it, and which makes the inclination mine and not yours; he will fix his attention on the movement by which our personality *leans towards* a certain object: he will isolate this attitude, and it is this special aspect of the personality, this snapshot of the mobility of the inner life, this "diagram" of concrete inclination, that he will erect into an independent fact. There is in this something very like what an artist passing through Paris does when he makes, for example, a sketch of a tower of Notre Dame. The tower is inseparably united to the building, which is itself no less inseparably united to the ground, to its surroundings, to the whole of Paris, and so on. It is first necessary to detach it from all these; only one aspect of the whole is noted, that formed by the tower of Notre Dame. Moreover, the special form of this tower is due to the grouping of the stones of which it is composed; but the artist does not concern himself with these stones, he notes only the silhouette of the tower. For the real and internal organization of the thing he substitutes, then, an external and schematic representation. So that, on the whole, his sketch corresponds to an observation of the object from a certain point of view and to the choice of a certain means of representation. But exactly the same thing holds true of the operation by which the psychologist extracts a single mental state from the whole personality. This isolated psychical state is hardly anything but a sketch, the commencement of an artificial reconstruction; it is the whole considered under a certain elementary aspect in which we are specially interested and which we have carefully noted. It is not a part, but an element. It has not been obtained by a natural dismemberment, but by analysis.

Now beneath all the sketches he has made at Paris the visitor will probably, by way of memento, write the word "Paris." And as he has really seen Paris, he will be able, with the help of the original intuition he had of the whole, to place his sketches therein, and so join them up together. But there is no way of performing the inverse operation; it is impossible, even with an infinite number of accurate sketches, and even with the word "Paris" which indicates that they must be combined together, to get back to an intuition that one has never had, and to give oneself an impression of what Paris is like if one has never seen it. This is because we are not dealing here with real *parts*, but with mere *notes* of the total impression. To take a still more striking example, where the notation is more completely symbolic, suppose that I am shown, mixed together at random, the letters which make up a poem I am ignorant of. If the letters were *parts* of the poem, I could attempt to reconstitute the poem with them by trying the different possible arrangements, as a child does with the pieces of a Chinese puzzle. But I should never for a moment think of attempting such a thing in this case, because the letters are not *component parts,* but only *partial expressions,* which is quite a different thing. That is why, if I know the poem, I at once put each of the letters in its proper place and join them up without difficulty by a continuous connection, while the inverse operation is impossible. Even when I believe I am actually attempting this inverse operation, even when I put the letters end to end, I begin by thinking of some plausible meaning. I thereby give myself an intuition, and from this intuition I attempt to redescend to the elementary symbols which would reconstitute its expression. The very idea of reconstituting a thing by operations practiced on symbolic elements alone implies such an absurdity that it would never occur to anyone if [he] recollected that [he was] not dealing with fragments of the thing, but only, as it were, with fragments of its symbol.

Such is, however, the undertaking of the philosophers who try to reconstruct personality with psychical states, whether they confine themselves to those states alone, or whether they add a kind of thread for the purpose of joining the states together. Both empiricists and rationalists are victims of the same fallacy. Both of them mistake *partial notations* for *real parts,* thus confusing the point of view of analysis and of intuition, of science and of metaphysics.

DEWEY

1859–1952

John Dewey was born in Burlington, Vermont, the son of a local grocer. At the University of Vermont he expressed little interest in academics until his senior year when he discovered philosophy. He was most influenced by Hume and Kant and their respective followers, and says that at first he could not make up his mind between "Scottish empirical realism" and "German rational idealism." He taught high school for two years, then decided to pursue graduate studies at the Johns Hopkins University. He received his doctorate in only two years for his dissertation, *The Psychology of Kant*. A few years later he published a work on Leibniz, *Leibniz's New Essays Concerning Human Understanding: A Critical Exposition* (1888).

Dewey taught at the University of Michigan for ten years before he became chairman of the department of philosophy, psychology, and education at the University of Chicago, where he designed and ran his "Laboratory School." This was an experimental learning environment where he tried out his unorthodox methods of teaching children from ages four to fifteen. In 1905 he moved to New York to join the philosophy department at Columbia University and remained there for the rest of his life, exerting a tremendous influence on subsequent American philosophers.

Dewey, like many philosophers of the time, started out as a Hegelian. He believed that individuals do not exist in isolation from history, culture, and environment. This remained a central aspect of Dewey's later philosophy of education, even after he modified his idealism into a version of Kant-inspired pragmatism: Hegel, he writes, "left a permanent deposit in my thinking." Dewey's philosophy was also influenced by William James's *Principles of Psychology* (1890). Dewey credits James's *Principles* with awakening him to the idea of pragmatism and the development of his theory of experience.

Dewey conceives not just the mind but the human being and the world entire as interactions among *natural* processes. Breaking down the boundary between knowers and what is known within his strictly positivistic outlook leads to a completely *naturalized epistemology*. In Dewey's view, we ourselves as knowers are not mere spectators of reality. As Kant, Hegel, and the German idealists, especially Fichte, had argued, the relation between knowers and the known is itself an *act*. Reality involves a participatory existence between the knower and the known.

According to Dewey, the quest for certainty from Aristotle to the present has wrongly emphasized the theoretical and ideal rather than the practical and useful. The intellectual alienation away from practical experience leads philosophers to overestimate the power of pure reason and to underestimate the cognitive significance of ordinary experience. Dewey thus tries to unite reflective and concrete experience in a way that makes philosophy more "relevant" to the world as it is conceived out of experience rather than as something transcendent to, or the cause of, experience. In *Democracy and Education* (1916), he applies this theory to education, arguing for the central importance of practical experience to any type of thinking: "An experience, a very humble experience, is capable of generating and carrying any amount of theory (or intellectual content), but a theory apart from an experience cannot be definitely grasped even as a theory." He argues that there can be no Kantian transcendental deduction. It is impossible to go beyond experience in either the transcendental or transcendent direction—we cannot deduce anything about things in themselves nor about the categories of thought. He then returns to where he began early on, with a distinctly Humean account of the primacy of the empirical.

The purpose of philosophy according to Dewey is not to make *distinctions* but to make *connections* among our actions and their consequences. Thinking itself is not an activity of the intellect but a type of reflective experience.

THOUGHT AND EXPERIENCE

1. *The Nature of Experience.* The nature of experience can be understood only by noting that it includes an active and a passive element peculiarly combined. On the active hand, experience is *trying*—a meaning which is made explicit in the connected term experiment. On the passive, it is *undergoing*. When we experience something we act upon it, we do something with it; then we suffer or undergo the consequences. We do something to the thing and then it does something to us in return: such is the peculiar combination. The connection of these two phases of experience measures the fruitfulness or value of the experience. Mere activity does not constitute experience. It is dispersive, centrifugal, dissipating. Experience as trying involves change, but change is meaningless transition unless it is consciously connected with the return wave of consequences which flow from it. When an activity is continued *into* the undergoing of consequences, when the change made by action is reflected back into a change made in us, the mere flux is loaded with significance. We learn something. It is not experience when a child merely sticks his finger into a flame; it is experience when the movement is connected with the pain which he undergoes in consequence. Henceforth the sticking of the finger into flame *means* a burn. Being burned is a mere physical change, like the burning of a stick of wood, if it is not perceived as a consequence of some other action.

Blind and capricious impulses hurry us on heedlessly from one thing to another. So far as this happens, everything is writ in water. There is none of that cumulative growth which

From John Dewey, *Democracy and Education*, 1911.

makes an experience in any vital sense of that term. On the other hand, many things happen to us in the way of pleasure and pain which we do not connect with any prior activity of our own. They are mere accidents so far as we are concerned. There is no before or after to such experience; no retrospect nor outlook, and consequently no meaning. We get nothing which may be carried over to foresee what is likely to happen next, and no gain in ability to adjust ourselves to what is coming—no added control. Only by courtesy can such an experience be called experience. To "learn from experience" is to make a backward and forward connection between what we do to things and what we enjoy or suffer from things in consequence. Under such conditions, doing becomes a trying; an experiment with the world to find out what it is like; the undergoing becomes instruction—discovery of the connection of things.

Two conclusions important for education follow. (1) Experience is primarily an active-passive affair; it is not primarily cognitive. But (2) the *measure of the value* of an experience lies in the perception of relationships or continuities to which it leads up. It includes cognition in the degree in which it is cumulative or amounts to something, or has meaning. In schools, those under instruction are too customarily looked upon as acquiring knowledge as theoretical spectators, minds which appropriate knowledge by direct energy of intellect. The very word pupil has almost come to mean one who is engaged not in having fruitful experiences but in absorbing knowledge directly. Something which is called mind or consciousness is severed from the physical organs of activity. The former is then thought to be purely intellectual and cognitive; the latter to be an irrelevant and intruding physical factor. The intimate union of activity and undergoing its consequences which leads to recognition of meaning is broken; instead we have two fragments: mere bodily action on one side, and meaning directly grasped by "spiritual" activity on the other.

It would be impossible to state adequately the evil results which have flowed from this dualism of mind and body, much less to exaggerate them. Some of the more striking effects, may, however, be enumerated. (*a*) In part bodily activity becomes an intruder. Having nothing, so it is thought, to do with mental activity, it becomes a distraction, an evil to be contended with. For the pupil has a body, and brings it to school along with his mind. And the body is, of necessity, a wellspring of energy; it has to do something. But its activities, not being utilized in occupation with things which yield significant results, have to be frowned upon. They lead the pupil away from the lesson with which his "mind" ought to be occupied; they are sources of mischief. The chief source of the "problem of discipline" in schools is that the teacher has often to spend the larger part of the time in suppressing the bodily activities which take the mind away from its material. A premium is put on physical quietude; on silence, on rigid uniformity of posture and movement; upon a machine-like simulation of the attitudes of intelligent interest. The teachers' business is to hold the pupils up to these requirements and to punish the inevitable deviations which occur.

The nervous strain and fatigue which result with both teacher and pupil are a necessary consequence of the abnormality of the situation in which bodily activity is divorced from the perception of meaning. Callous indifference and explosions from strain alternate. The neglected body, having no organized fruitful channels of activity, breaks forth, without knowing why or how, into meaningless boisterousness, or settles into equally meaningless fooling—both very different from the normal play of children. Physically active children become restless and unruly; the more quiescent, so-called conscientious ones spend what energy they have in the negative task of keeping their instincts and active tendencies suppressed, instead of in a positive one of constructive planning and execution; they are thus educated not into responsibility for the significant and graceful use of bodily powers, but into an enforced duty not to give them free play. It may be seriously asserted that a chief cause for the remarkable achievements of Greek education was that it was never misled by false notions into an attempted separation of mind and body.

(*b*) Even, however, with respect to the lessons which have to be learned by the application of "mind," some bodily activities have to be used. The senses—especially the eye and ear—have to be employed to take in what the book, the map, the blackboard, and the teacher say. The lips and vocal organs, and the hands, have to be used to reproduce in speech and writing what has been stowed away. The senses are then regarded as a kind of mysterious conduit through which information is conducted from the external world into the mind; they are spoken of as gateways and avenues of knowledge. To keep the eyes on the book and the ears open to the teacher's words is a mysterious source of intellectual grace. Moreover, reading, writing, and figuring—important school arts—demand muscular or motor training. The muscles of eye, hand, and vocal organs accordingly have to be trained to act as pipes for carrying knowledge back out of the mind into external action. For it happens that using the muscles repeatedly in the same way fixes in them an automatic tendency to repeat.

The obvious result is a mechanical use of the bodily activities which (in spite of the generally obtrusive and interfering character of the body in mental action) have to be employed more or less. For the senses and muscles are used not as organic participants in having an instructive experience, but as external inlets and outlets of mind. Before the child goes to school, he learns with his hand, eye, and ear, because they are organs of the process of doing something from which meaning results. The boy flying a kite has to keep his eye on the kite, and has to note the various pressures of the string on his hand. His senses are avenues of knowledge not because external facts are somehow "conveyed" to the brain, but because they are *used* in doing something with a purpose. The qualities of seen and touched things have a bearing on what is done, and are alertly perceived; they have a meaning. But when pupils are expected to use their eyes to note the form of words, irrespective of their meaning, in order to reproduce them in spelling or reading, the resulting training is simply of isolated sense organs and muscles. It is such isolation of an act from a purpose which makes it mechanical. It is customary for teachers to urge children to read with expression, so as to bring out the meaning. But if they originally learned the sensory-motor technique of reading—the ability to identify forms and to reproduce the sounds they stand for—by methods which did not call for attention to meaning, a mechanical habit was established which makes it difficult to read subsequently with intelligence. The vocal organs have been trained to go their own way automatically in isolation; and meaning cannot be tied on at will. Drawing, singing, and writing may be taught in the same mechanical way; for, we repeat, any way *is* mechanical which narrows down the bodily activity so that a separation of body from mind—that is, from recognition of meaning—is set up. Mathematics, even in its higher branches, when undue emphasis is put upon the technique of calculation, and science, when laboratory exercises are given for their own sake, suffer from the same evil.

(*c*) On the intellectual side, the separation of "mind" from direct occupation with things throws emphasis on *things* at the expense of *relations* or connections. It is altogether too common to separate perceptions and even ideas from judgments. The latter are thought to come after the former in order to compare them. It is alleged that the mind perceives things apart from relations; that it forms ideas of them in isolation from their connections—with what goes before and comes after. Then judgment or thought is called upon to combine the separated items of "knowledge" so that their resemblance or causal connection shall be brought out. As matter of fact, every perception and every idea is a sense of the bearings, use, and cause, of a thing. We do not really know a chair or have an idea of it by inventorying and enumerating its various isolated qualities, but only by bringing these qualities into connection with something else—the purpose which makes it a chair and not a table; or its difference from the kind of chair we are accustomed to, or the "period" which it represents, and so on. A wagon is not perceived when all its parts are summed up; it is the characteristic connection of the parts which makes it a wagon. And these connections are not those of mere physical juxtaposition; they involve connection with the animals that draw it, the things that are carried on it, and so on. Judgment is employed in the perception; otherwise the perception is mere sensory excitation or else a recognition of the result of a prior judgment, as in the case of familiar objects.

Words, the counters for ideals, are, however, easily taken for ideas. And in just the degree in which mental activity is separated from active concern with the world, from doing something and connecting the doing with what is undergone, words, symbols, come to take the place of ideas. The substitution is the more subtle because *some* meaning is recognized. But we are very easily trained to be content with a minimum of meaning, and to fail to note how restricted is our perception of the relations which confer significance. We get so thoroughly used to a kind of pseudo-idea, a half perception, that we are not aware how half-dead our mental action is, and how much keener and more extensive our observations and ideas would be if we formed them under conditions of a vital experience which required us to use judgment: to hunt for the connections of the thing dealt with.

There is no difference of opinion as to the theory of the matter. All authorities agree that that discernment of relationships is the genuinely intellectual matter; hence, the educative matter. The failure arises in supposing that relationships can become perceptible without *experience*—without that conjoint trying and undergoing of which we have spoken. It is assumed that "mind" can grasp them if it will only give attention, and that this attention may be given at will irrespective of the situation. Hence the deluge of half-observations, of verbal ideas, and unassimilated "knowledge" which afflicts the world. An ounce of experience is better than a ton of theory simply because it is only in experience that any theory has vital and verifiable significance. An experience, a very humble experience, is capable of generating and carrying any amount of theory (or intellectual content), but a theory apart from an experience cannot be definitely grasped even as theory. It tends to become a mere verbal formula, a set of catchwords used to render thinking, or genuine theorizing, unnecessary and impossible. Because of our education we use words, thinking they are ideas, to dispose of questions, the disposal being in reality simply such an obscuring of perception as prevents us from seeing any longer the difficulty.

2. *Reflection in Experience.* Thought or reflection, as we have already seen virtually if not explicitly, is the discernment of the relation between what we try to do and what happens in consequence. No experience having a meaning is possible without some element of thought. But we may contrast two types of experience according to the proportion of reflection found in them. All our experiences have a phase of "cut and try" in them—what psychologists call the method of trial and error. We simply do something, and when it fails, we do something else, and keep on trying till we hit upon something which works, and then we adopt that method as a rule of thumb measure in subsequent procedure. Some experiences have very little else in them than this hit and miss or succeed process. We see *that* a certain way of acting and a certain consequence are connected, but we do not see *how* they are. We do not see the details of the connection; the links are missing. Our discernment is very gross. In other cases we push our observation farther. We analyze to see just what lies between so as to bind together cause and effect, activity and consequence. This exten-

sion of our insight makes foresight more accurate and comprehensive. The action which rests simply upon the trial and error method is at the mercy of circumstances; they may change so that the act performed does not operate in the way it was expected to. But if we know in detail upon what the result depends, we can look to see whether the required conditions are there. The method extends our practical control. For if some of the conditions are missing, we may, if we know what the needed antecedents for an effect are, set to work to supply them; or, if they are such as to produce undesirable effects as well, we may eliminate some of the superfluous causes and economize effort.

In discovery of the detailed connections of our activities and what happens in consequence, the thought implied in cut and dry experience is made explicit. Its quantity increases so that its proportionate value is very different. Hence the quality of the experience changes; the change is so significant that we may call this type of experience reflective— that is, reflective *par excellence*. The deliberate cultivation of this phase of thought constitutes thinking as a distinctive experience. Thinking, in other words, is the intentional endeavor to discover specific connections between something which we do and the consequences which result, so that the two become continuous. Their isolation, and consequently their purely arbitrary going together, is cancelled; a unified developing situation takes its place. The occurrence is now understood; it is explained; it is reasonable, as we say, that the thing should happen as it does.

Thinking is thus equivalent to an explicit rendering of the intelligent element in our experience. It makes it possible to act with an end in view. It is the condition of our having aims. As soon as an infant begins to *expect* he begins to use something which is now going on as a sign of something to follow; he is, in however simple a fashion, judging. For he takes one thing as *evidence* of something else, and so recognizes a relationship. Any future development, however elaborate it may be, is only an extending and a refining of this simple act of inference. All that the wisest man can do is to observe what is going on more widely and more minutely and then select more carefully from what is noted just those factors which point to something to happen. The opposites, once more, to thoughtful action are routine and capricious behavior. The former accepts what has been customary as a full measure of possibility and omits to take into account the connections of the particular things done. The latter makes the momentary act a measure of value, and ignores the connections of our personal action with the energies of the environment. It says, virtually, "things are to be just as I happen to like them at this instant," as routine says in effect "let things continue just as I have found them in the past." Both refuse to acknowledge responsibility for the future consequences which flow from present action. Reflection is the acceptance of such responsibility.

The starting point of any process of thinking is something going on, something which just as it stands is incomplete or unfulfilled. Its point, its meaning lies literally in what it is going to be, in how it is going to turn out. As this is written, the world is filled with the clang of contending armies. For an active participant in the war, it is clear that the momentous thing is the issue, the future consequences, of this and that happening. He is identified, for the time at least, with the issue; *his* fate hangs upon the course things are taking. But even for an onlooker in a neutral country, the significance of every move made, of every advance here and retreat there, lies in what it portends. To *think* upon the news as it comes to us is to attempt to see what is indicated as probable or possible regarding an outcome. To fill our heads, like a scrapbook, with this and that item as a finished and done-for thing, is not to think. It is to turn ourselves into a piece of registering apparatus. To consider the *bearing* of the occurrence upon what may be, but is not yet, is to think. Nor will the reflective experience be different in kind if we substitute distance in time for separation in space. Imagine the war done with, and a future historian giving an account of it. The episode is, by assumption, past. But he cannot give a thoughtful account of the war save as he preserves the time sequence; the meaning of each occurrence, as he deals with it, lies in what was future for *it,* though not for the historian. To take it by itself as a complete existence is to take it unreflectively.

Reflection also implies concern with the issue—a certain sympathetic identification of our own destiny, if only dramatic, with the outcome of the course of events. For the general in the war, or a common soldier, or a citizen of one of the contending nations, the stimulus to thinking is direct and urgent. For neutrals, it is indirect and dependent upon imagination. But the flagrant partisanship of human nature is evidence of the intensity of the tendency to identify ourselves with one possible course of events, and to reject the other as foreign. If we cannot take sides in overt action, and throw in our little weight to help determine the final balance, we take sides emotionally and imaginatively. We desire this or that outcome. One wholly indifferent to the outcome does not follow or think about what is happening at all. From this dependence of the act of thinking upon a sense of sharing in the consequences of what goes on, flows one of the chief paradoxes of thought. Born in partiality, in order to accomplish its tasks it must achieve a certain detached impartiality. The general who allows his hopes and desires to affect his observations and interpretations of the existing situation will surely make a mistake in calculation. While hopes and fears may be the chief motive for a thoughtful following of the war on the part of an onlooker in a neutral country, he too will think ineffectively in the degree in which his preferences modify the stuff of his observations and reasonings. There is, however, no incompatibility between the fact that the occasion of reflection lies in a personal sharing in what is going on and the fact that the value of the reflection lies upon keeping one's self out of the data. The almost insurmountable difficulty of achieving this detachment is evidence that thinking originates in situations where the course of thinking is an actual part of the course of events and is designed to influence the result. Only gradually and with a widening of the area of vision through a growth of social sympathies does thinking develop to include what lies beyond our *direct* interests: a fact of great significance for education.

To say that thinking occurs with reference to situations which are still going on, and incomplete, is to say that thinking occurs when things are uncertain or doubtful or problematic. Only what is finished, completed, is wholly assured. Where there is reflection there is suspense. The object of thinking is to help *reach* a conclusion, to project a possible termination on the basis of what is already given. Certain other facts about thinking accompany this feature. Since the situation in which thinking occurs is a doubtful one, thinking is a process of inquiry, of looking into things, of investigating. *Acquiring is always secondary, and instrumental to the act of in*quiring. It is seeking, a quest, for something that is not at hand. We sometimes talk as if "original research" were a peculiar prerogative of scientists or at least of advanced students. But all thinking is research, and all research is native, original, with him who carries it on, even if everybody else in the world already is sure of what he is still looking for.

It also follows that all thinking involves a risk. Certainty cannot be guaranteed in advance. The invasion of the unknown is of the nature of an adventure; we cannot be sure in advance. The conclusions of thinking, till confirmed by the event, are, accordingly, more or less tentative or hypothetical. Their dogmatic assertion as final is unwarranted, short of the issue, in fact. The Greeks acutely raised the question: How can we learn? For either we know already what we are after, or else we do not know. In neither case is learning possible;

on the first alternative because we know already; on the second, because we do not know what to look for, nor if, by chance, we find it can we tell that it is what we were after. The dilemma makes no provision for *coming* to know, for learning; it assumes either complete knowledge or complete ignorance. Nevertheless the twilight zone of inquiry, of thinking, exists. The possibility of *hypothetical* conclusions, of *tentative* results, is the fact which the Greek dilemma overlooked. The perplexities of the situation suggest certain ways out. We try these ways, and either push our way out, in which case we know we have found what we were looking for, or the situation gets darker and more confused—in which case, we know we are still ignorant. Tentative means trying out, feeling one's way along provisionally. Taken by itself, the Greek argument is a nice piece of formal logic. But it is also true that as long as men kept a sharp disjunction between knowledge and ignorance, science made only slow and accidental advance. Systematic advance in invention and discovery began when men recognized that they could utilize doubt for purposes of inquiry by forming conjectures to guide action in tentative explorations, whose development would confirm, refute, or modify the guiding conjecture. While the Greeks made knowledge more than learning, modern science makes conserved knowledge only a means to learning, to discovery.

To recur to our illustration. A commanding general cannot base his actions upon either absolute certainty or absolute ignorance. He has a certain amount of information at hand which is, we will assume, reasonably trustworthy. He then *infers* certain prospective movements, thus assigning meaning to the bare facts of the given situation. His inference is more or less dubious and hypothetical. But he acts upon it. He develops a plan of procedure, a method of dealing with the situation. The consequences which directly follow from his acting this way rather than that test and reveal the worth of his reflections. What he already knows functions and has value in what he learns. But will this account apply in the case of the one in a neutral country who is thoughtfully following as best he can the progress of events? In form, yes, though not of course in content. It is self-evident that his guesses about the future indicated by present facts, guesses by which he attempts to supply meaning to a multitude of disconnected data, cannot be the basis of a method which shall take effect in the campaign. *That* is not *his* problem. But in the degree in which he is actively thinking, and not merely passively following the course of events, his tentative inferences will take effect in *a* method of procedure appropriate to *his* situation. He will anticipate certain future moves, and will be on the alert to see whether they happen or not. In the degree in which he is intellectually concerned, or thoughtful, he will be *actively* on the lookout; he will take steps which although they do not affect the campaign, modify in some degree *his* subsequent actions. Otherwise his later "I told you so" has no intellectual quality at all; it does not mark any testing or verification of prior thinking, but only a coincidence that yields emotional satisfaction—and includes a large factor of self-deception.

The case is comparable to that of an astronomer who from given data has been led to foresee (infer) a future eclipse. No matter how great the mathematical probability, the inference is hypothetical—a matter of probability. The hypothesis as to the date and position of the anticipated eclipse becomes the material of forming a method of future conduct. Apparatus is arranged; possibly an expedition is made to some far part of the globe. In any case, some active steps are taken which actually change *some* physical conditions. And apart from such steps and the consequent modification of the situation, there is no completion of the act of thinking. It remains suspended. Knowledge, already attained knowledge, controls thinking and makes it fruitful.

So much for the general features of a reflective experience. They are (*i*) perplexity, confusion, doubt, due to the fact that one is implicated in an incomplete situation whose full character is not yet determined; (*ii*) a conjectural anticipation—a tentative interpretation of the given elements, attributing to them a tendency to effect certain consequences; (*iii*) a careful survey (examination, inspection, exploration, analysis) of all attainable consideration which will define and clarify the problem in hand; (*iv*) a consequent elaboration of the tentative hypothesis to make it more precise and more consistent, because squaring with a wider range of facts; (*v*) taking one stand upon the projected hypothesis as a plan of action which is applied to the existing state of affairs: doing something overtly to bring about the anticipated result, and thereby testing the hypothesis. It is the extent and accuracy of steps three and four which mark off a distinctive reflective experience from one on the trial and error plane. They make *thinking* itself into an experience. Nevertheless, we never get wholly beyond the trial and error situation. Our most elaborate and rationally consistent thought has to be tried in the world and thereby tried out. And since it can never take into account all the connections, it can never cover with perfect accuracy all the consequences. Yet a thoughtful survey of conditions is so careful, and the guessing at results so controlled, that we have a right to mark off the reflective experience from the grosser trial and error forms of action.

Summary. In determining the place of thinking in experience we first noted that experience involves a connection of doing or trying with something which is undergone in consequence. A separation of the active doing phase from the passive undergoing phase destroys the vital meaning of an experience. Thinking is the accurate and deliberate instituting of connections between what is done and its consequences. It notes not only that they are connected, but the details of the connection. It makes connecting links explicit in the form of relationships. The stimulus to thinking is found when we wish to determine the significance of some act, performed or to be performed. Then we anticipate consequences. This implies that the situation as it stands is, either in fact or to us, incomplete and hence indeterminate. The projection of consequences means a proposed or tentative solution. To perfect this hypothesis, existing conditions have to be carefully scrutinized and the implications of the hypothesis developed—an operation called reasoning. Then the suggested solution—the idea or theory—has to be tested by acting upon it. If it brings about certain consequences, certain determinate changes, in the world, it is accepted as valid. Otherwise it is modified, and another trial made. Thinking includes all of these steps,—the sense of a problem, the observation of conditions, the formation and rational elaboration of a suggested conclusion, and the active experimental testing. While all thinking results in knowledge, ultimately the value of knowledge is subordinate to its use in thinking. For we live not in a settled and finished world, but in one which is going on, and where our main task is prospective, and where retrospect—and all knowledge as distinct from thought is retrospect—is of value in the solidity, security, and fertility it affords our dealings with the future.

CHAPTER

49

∞

RUSSELL

1872–1970

Bertrand Russell was born to a noble family in Monmouthshire, England. His parents died while he was still a child and he was raised by his grandfather, Lord John Russell. He studied mathematics and philosophy at Cambridge University, where under the influence of Bradley (Chapter 44) he became a Hegelian idealist. Inspired by fellow pupil G. E. Moore (Chapter 50), Russell gave up Hegelianism in favor of commonsense philosophy, which in the end he rejected even more vehemently in favor of scientific and logical realism.

In his first major work, the ground-breaking *Principles of Mathematics* (1903), Russell was inspired by Frege to equate meaning and reference. He argues that any meaningful terms must have real entities as references, even mathematical terms (numbers, points, lines, etc.). He and mathematician Alfred North Whitehead (1861–1947) collaborated on *Principia Mathematica* (in three volumes, 1910–1913). The idea was to start with logically primitive, irreducible concepts stated as axioms and then to derive the whole of mathematics. Each step would be perspicuous, with nothing left to intuition, as Frege had called for, to prove that mathematics reduces to pure logic.

Russell developed a theory of logical constructions showing how the foundations of mathematics could be established using "contextual definitions" in which mathematical concepts are translated into their logical equivalents. His axiom of infinity, the set theoretical paradox that now bears his name (Russell's paradox), and the theory of types revolutionized the way both philosophy and mathematics are done. He also inspired and was mentor to another one of the greatest philosophers of the twentieth century, Ludwig Wittgenstein, who in turn came to have a lasting influence on Russell's views on logic and the philosophy of language.

Russell was a lifelong critic not just of religion but of traditional morality and education, and an outspoken pacifist, which got him fired from his teaching post in England during World War I. He was jailed many times in his life; at the age of eighty-nine he was arrested for protesting against nuclear arms. In 1940 he was prevented from accepting a teaching position at the College of the City of New York because of his liberal views on sex.

A prolific writer, Russell published over seventy books and hundreds of articles and essays on virtually every topic. He was awarded the Order of Merit in 1949, and in 1950 he won the Nobel Prize for literature.

In *Our Knowledge of the External World* (1914), Russell argued for his Frege-inspired view that logic is the essence of philosophy. But he questions the adequacy of traditional subject-predicate logic in favor of his theory of the twofold nature of logic, which is his logical atomism. Whereas the "old logic" in his words put "thought in fetters," his "new logic gives it wings." According to Russell, the only real entities in the world are *logical atoms* analogous to Leibniz's monads. Just about all the objects we ordinarily take to be real turn out to be nothing more than elaborate fictions, much in the way that David Hume had supposed. In a unique blend of cosmic mysticism and technical logic, Russell offers an explicit proof of the logical impossibility of the existence of the world—the universe entire—conceived as a whole.

In his *Mysticism and Logic,* Russell explains why logic is the essence not just of philosophy but of the world as well; thus, in *Our Knowledge of the External World,* from which our first selection is taken, he makes clear how his logical atoms differ from the concept of physical atoms by presenting a devastating problem for any naive realist conception of physical reality based on physical science. In *Mysticism and Logic,* from which the second selection is taken, he gives up mind-body dualism in favor of a version of the thesis that the ultimate elements of the world are neither physical nor mental "things" but, rather, logical particulars—the logical atoms—and their external relations. He extends his logical-analytic method to the question of the relation between sense perception and physical objects. By combining his theory of descriptions in which meaning and reference are equated with his logical construction principle (the substitution, wherever possible, of constructions out of known entities for inference to unknown ones), he shows how even the symbols of physics—points in space, moments in time (instants), physical particles, and so on—can be analyzed (translated) into their sentential contexts, that is, into logical statements about empirical entities.

Like the early William James (Chapter 42), Russell became an advocate of a type of "neutral monism," resolving the mind-body problem raised by Descartes through an analysis in which mind and physical matter are viewed as different constructions out of the same, basic *logical* elements. Russell didn't merely offer a metaphysical claim about how the world must therefore be understood as neither mental nor physical, but showed it was logical. *logical.* The key concept is his notion of *sense-data.* Just as the mind's cognitive function—thought, mathematics, and logic—consists in logical atoms, so its perceptual function—seeing, feeling, smelling, emoting, etc.—consists in their atomic form as individual sense-data. And, as Russell clearly states, "I regard sense-data as not mental." Ultimately the mind's cognitive and perceptual functions consist in external relations. In taking such a functional approach to both mind and matter, Russell helped pave the way toward a purely logico-mathematical model of mind and reality. The key passage appears in his *Principles of Mathematics:*

> Philosophy asks of Mathematics: What does it mean? Mathematics in the past was unable to answer, and Philosophy answered by introducing the totally irrelevant notion of mind. But now Mathematics is able to answer, so far at least as to reduce the whole of its propositions to certain fundamental notions of logic. At this point, the discussion must be resumed by Philosophy.

In our final selection, "The Value of Philosophy," Russell gives his philosophy of philosophy—what philosophy is for, what it is about, and how it ought to be done. He argues that in other disciplines, such as physics, medicine, architecture, and engineering, the value of the discipline can be known and appreciated without knowing the discipline itself. For instance, one can experience the benefits of engineering technology without knowing anything about engineering. But because philosophy has no direct utility outside the lives of those who partake in it, it must be known and understood by the individual before it can provide its highest value: the attainment of "union with the universe."

OUR KNOWLEDGE OF THE EXTERNAL WORLD
Logic as the Essence of Philosophy

The topics we discussed in our first lecture, and the topics we shall discuss later, all reduce themselves, in so far as they are genuinely philosophical, to problems of logic. This is not due to any accident, but to the fact that every philosophical problem, when it is subjected to the necessary analysis and purification, is found either to be not really philosophical at all, or else to be, in the sense in which we are using the word, logical. But as the word "logic" is never used in the same sense by two different philosophers, some explanation of what I mean by the word is indispensable at the outset.

Logic, in the Middle Ages, and down to the present day in teaching, meant no more than a scholastic collection of technical terms and rules of syllogistic inference. Aristotle had spoken, and it was the part of humbler men merely to repeat the lesson after him. The trivial nonsense embodied in this tradition is still set in examinations, and defended by eminent authorities as an excellent "propaedeutic," *i.e.* a training in those habits of solemn humbug which are so great a help in later life. But it is not this that I mean to praise in saying that all philosophy is logic. Ever since the beginning of the seventeenth century, all vigorous minds that have concerned themselves with inference have abandoned the mediaeval tradition, and in one way or other have widened the scope of logic.

The first extension was the introduction of the inductive method by Bacon and Galileo—by the former in a theoretical and largely mistaken form, by the latter in actual use in establishing the foundations of modern physics and astronomy. This is probably the only extension of the old logic which has become familiar to the general educated public. But induction, important as it is when regarded as a method of investigation, does not seem to remain when its work is done: in the final form of a perfected science, it would seem that everything ought to be deductive. If induction remains at all, which is a difficult question, it will remain merely as one of the principles according to which deductions are effected. Thus the ultimate result of the introduction of the inductive method seems not the creation of a new kind of non-deductive reasoning, but rather the widening of the scope of deduction by pointing out a way of deducing which is certainly not syllogistic, and does not fit into the mediaeval scheme.

The question of the scope and validity of induction is of great difficulty, and of great importance to our knowledge. Take such a question as, "Will the sun rise tomorrow?" Our

From Bertrand Russell, *Our Knowledge of the External World* (London: George Allen & Unwin, Ltd., 1914).

first instinctive feeling is that we have abundant reason for saying that it will, because it has risen on so many previous mornings. Now, I do not myself know whether this does afford a ground or not, but I am willing to suppose that it does. The question which then arises is: What is the principle of inference by which we pass from past sunrises to future ones? The answer given by Mill is that the inference depends upon the law of causation. Let us suppose this to be true; then what is the reason for believing in the law of causation? There are broadly three possible answers: (1) that it is itself known *a priori*; (2) that it is a postulate; (3) that it is an empirical generalisation from past instances in which it has been found to hold. The theory that causation is known *a priori* cannot be definitely refuted, but it can be rendered very unplausible by the mere process of formulating the law exactly, and thereby showing that it is immensely more complicated and less obvious than is generally supposed. The theory that causation is a postulate, *i.e.* that it is something which we choose to assert although we know that it is very likely false, is also incapable of refutation; but it is plainly also incapable of justifying any use of the law in inference. We are thus brought to the theory that the law is an empirical generalisation, which is the view held by Mill.

But if so, how are empirical generalisations to be justified? The evidence in their favour cannot be empirical, since we wish to argue from what has been observed to what has not been observed, which can only be done by means of some known relation of the observed and the unobserved; but the unobserved, by definition, is not known empirically, and therefore its relation to the observed, if known at all, must be known independently of empirical evidence. Let us see what Mill says on this subject.

According to Mill, the law of causation is proved by an admittedly fallible process called "induction by simple enumeration." This process, he says, "consists in ascribing the nature of general truths to all propositions which are true in every instance that we happen to know of." As regards its fallibility, he asserts that "the precariousness of the method of simple enumeration is in an inverse ratio to the largeness of the generalisation. The process is delusive and insufficient, exactly in proportion as the subject-matter of the observation is special and limited in extent. As the sphere widens, this unscientific method becomes less and less liable to mislead; and the most universal class of truths, the laws of causation for instance, and the principles of number and of geometry, are duly and satisfactorily proved by that method alone, nor are they susceptible of any other proof."

In the above statement, there are two obvious lacunae: (1) How is the method of simple enumeration itself justified? (2) What logical principle, if any, covers the same ground as this method, without being liable to its failures? Let us take the second question first.

A method of proof which, when used as directed, gives sometimes truth and sometimes falsehood—as the method of simple enumeration does—is obviously not a valid method, for validity demands invariable truth. Thus, if simple enumeration is to be rendered valid, it must not be stated as Mill states it. We shall have to say, at most, that the data render the result *probable*. Causation holds, we shall say, in every instance we have been able to test; therefore it *probably* holds in untested instances. There are terrible difficulties in the notion of probability, but we may ignore them at present. We thus have what at least *may* be a logical principle, since it is without exception. If a proposition is true in every instance that we happen to know of, and if the instances are very numerous, then, we shall say, it becomes very probable, on the data, that it will be true in any further instance. This is not refuted by the fact that what we declare to be probable does not always happen, for an event may be probable on the data and yet not occur. It is, however, obviously capable of further analysis, and of more exact statement. We shall have to say something like this: that every instance of a proposition being true increases the probability of its being true in a fresh instance, and that a sufficient number of favourable instances will, in the absence of instances to the contrary, make the probability of the truth of a fresh instance approach indefinitely near to certainty. Some such principle as this is required if the method of simple enumeration is to be valid.

But this brings us to our other question, namely, how is our principle known to be true? Obviously, since it is required to justify induction, it cannot be proved by induction; since it goes beyond the empirical data, it cannot be proved by them alone; since it is required to justify all inferences from empirical data to what goes beyond them, it cannot itself be even rendered in any degree probable by such data. Hence, *if* it is known, it is not known by experience, but independently of experience. I do not say that any such principle is known: I only say that it is required to justify the inferences from experience which empiricists allow, and that it cannot itself be justified empirically.

A similar conclusion can be proved by similar arguments concerning any other logical principle. Thus logical knowledge is not derivable from experience alone, and the empiricist's philosophy can therefore not be accepted in its entirety, in spite of its excellence in many matters which lie outside logic.

Hegel and his followers widened the scope of logic in quite a different way—a way which I believe to be fallacious, but which requires discussion if only to show how their conception of logic differs from the conception which I wish to advocate. In their writings, logic is practically identical with metaphysics. In broad outline, the way this came about is as follows. Hegel believed that, by means of *a priori* reasoning, it could be shown that the world *must* have various important and interesting characteristics, since any world without these characteristics would be impossible and self-contradictory. Thus what he calls "logic" is an investigation of the nature of the universe, in so far as this can be inferred merely from the principle that the universe must be logically self-consistent. I do not myself believe that from this principle alone anything of importance can be inferred as regards the existing universe. But, however that may be, I should not regard Hegel's reasoning, even if it were valid, as properly belonging to logic: it would rather be an application of logic to the actual world. Logic itself would be concerned rather with such questions as what self-consistency is, which Hegel, so far as I know, does not discuss. And though he criticises the traditional logic, and professes to replace it by an improved logic of his own, there is some sense in which the traditional logic, with all its faults, is uncritically and unconsciously assumed throughout his reasoning. It is not in the direction advocated by him, it seems to me, that the reform of logic is to be sought, but by a more fundamental, more patient, and less ambitious investigation into the presuppositions which his system shares with those of most other philosophers.

The way in which, as it seems to me, Hegel's system assumes the ordinary logic which it subsequently criticises, is exemplified by the general conception of "categories" with which he operates throughout. This conception is, I think, essentially a product of logical confusion, but it seems in some way to stand for the conception of "qualities of Reality as a whole." Mr. Bradley has worked out a theory according to which, in all judgment, we are ascribing a predicate to Reality as a whole; and this theory is derived from Hegel. Now the traditional logic holds that every proposition ascribes a predicate to a subject, and from this it easily follows that there can be only one subject, the Absolute, for if there were two, the proposition that there were two would not ascribe a predicate to either. Thus Hegel's doctrine, that philosophical propositions must be of the form, "the Absolute is such-and-such," depends upon the traditional belief in the universality of the subject-predicate form. This belief, being traditional, scarcely self-conscious, and not supposed to be important, operates underground, and is assumed in arguments which, like the refutation of relations, appear at first sight such as to establish its truth. This is the most important respect in which Hegel uncritically assumes the traditional logic. Other less important respects—though important enough to be the source of such essentially Hegelian conceptions as the "concrete universal" and the "union of identity in difference"—will be found where he explicitly deals with formal logic. Hegel's argument in this portion of his "Logic" depends throughout upon confusing the "is" of predication, as in "Socrates is mortal" with the "is" of identity, as in "Socrates is the philosopher who drank the hemlock." Owing to this confusion, he thinks that "Socrates" and "mortal" must be identical. Seeing that they are different, he does not infer, as others would, that there is a mistake somewhere, but that they exhibit "identity in difference." Again, Socrates is particular, "mortal" is universal. Therefore, he says, since Socrates is mortal, it follows that the particular is the universal—taking the "is" to be throughout expressive of identity. But to say "the particular is the universal" is self-contradictory. Again Hegel does not suspect a mistake, but proceeds to synthesise particular and universal in the individual, or concrete universal. This is an example of how, for want of care at the start, vast and imposing systems of philosophy are built upon stupid and trivial confusions, which, but for the almost incredible fact that they are unintentional, one would be tempted to characterise as puns.

There is quite another direction in which a large technical development of logic has taken place: I mean the direction of what is called logistic or mathematical logic. This kind of logic is mathematical in two different senses: it is itself a branch of mathematics, and it is the logic which is specially applicable to other more traditional branches of mathematics. Historically, it began as *merely* a branch of mathematics: its special applicability to other branches is a more recent development. In both respects, it is the fulfilment of a hope which Leibniz cherished throughout his life, and pursued with all the ardour of his amazing intellectual energy. Much of his work on this subject has been published recently, after his discoveries had been remade by others; but none was published by him, because his results persisted in contradicting certain points in the traditional doctrine of the syllogism. We now know that on these points the traditional doctrine is wrong, but respect for Aristotle prevented Leibniz from realising that this was possible.

The modern development of mathematical logic dates from Boole's *Laws of Thought* (1854). But in him and his successors, before Peano and Frege, the only thing really achieved, apart from certain details, was the invention of a mathematical symbolism for deducing consequences from the premisses which the newer methods shared with those of Aristotle. This subject has considerable interest as an independent branch of mathematics, but it has very little to do with real logic. The first serious advance in real logic since the time of the Greeks was made independently by Peano and Frege—both mathematicians. They both arrived at their logical results by an analysis of mathematics. Traditional logic regarded the two propositions, "Socrates is mortal" and "All men are mortal," as being of the same form; Peano and Frege showed that they are utterly different in form. The philosophical importance of logic may be illustrated by the fact that this confusion—which is still committed by most writers—obscured not only the whole study of the forms of judgment and inference, but also the relations of things to their qualities, of concrete existence to abstract concepts, and of the world of sense to the world of Platonic ideas. Peano and Frege, who pointed out the error, did so for technical reasons, and applied their logic mainly to technical developments; but the philosophical importance of the advance which they made is impossible to exaggerate.

Mathematical logic, even in its most modern form, is not *directly* of philosophical importance except in its beginnings. After the beginnings, it belongs rather to mathematics than to philosophy. Of its beginnings, which are the only part of it that can properly be called *philosophical* logic, I shall speak shortly. But even the later developments, though not directly philosophical, will be found of great indirect use in philosophising. They enable us to deal easily with more abstract conceptions than merely verbal reasoning can enumerate; they suggest fruitful hypotheses which otherwise could hardly be thought of; and they enable us to see quickly what is the smallest store of materials with which a given logical or scientific edifice can be constructed. Not only Frege's theory of number, which we shall deal with in Lecture VII., but the whole theory of physical concepts which will be outlined in our next two lectures, is inspired by mathematical logic, and could never have been imagined without it.

In both these cases, and in many others, we shall appeal to a certain principle called "the principle of abstraction." This principle, which might equally well be called "the principle which dispenses with abstraction," and is one which clears away incredible accumulations of metaphysical lumber, was directly suggested by mathematical logic, and could hardly have been proved or practically used without its help. The principle will be explained in our fourth lecture, but its use may be briefly indicated in advance. When a group of objects have that kind of similarity which we are inclined to attribute to possession of a common quality, the principle in question shows that membership of the group will serve all the purposes of the supposed common quality, and that therefore, unless some common quality is actually known, the group or class of similar objects may be used to replace the common quality, which need not be assumed to exist. In this and other ways, the indirect uses of even the later parts of mathematical logic are very great; but it is now time to turn our attention to its philosophical foundations.

In every proposition and in every inference there is, besides the particular subject-matter concerned, a certain *form,* a way in which the constituents of the proposition or inference are put together. If I say, "Socrates is mortal," "Jones is angry," "The sun is hot," there is something in common in these three cases, something indicated by the word "is." What is in common is the *form* of the proposition, not an actual constituent. If I say a number of things about Socrates—that he was an Athenian, that he married Xantippe, that he drank the hemlock—there is a common constituent, namely Socrates, in all the propositions I enunciate, but they have diverse forms. If, on the other hand, I take any one of these propositions and replace its constituents, one at a time, by other constituents, the form remains constant, but no constituent remains. Take (say) the series of propositions, "Socrates drank the hemlock," "Coleridge drank the hemlock," "Coleridge drank opium," "Coleridge ate opium." The form remains unchanged throughout this series, but all the constituents are altered. Thus form is not another constituent, but is the way the constituents are put together. It is forms, in this sense, that are the proper object of philosophical logic.

It is obvious that the knowledge of logical forms is something quite different from knowledge of existing things. The forms of "Socrates drank the hemlock" is not an existing thing like Socrates or the hemlock, nor does it even have that close relation to existing things that drinking has. It is something altogether more abstract and remote. We might understand all the separate words of a sentence without understanding the sentence: if a sentence is long and complicated, this is apt to happen. In such a case we have knowledge of the constituents, but not of the form. We may also have knowledge of the form without having knowledge of the constituents. If I say, "Rorarius drank the hemlock," those among you who have never heard of Rorarius (supposing there are any) will understand the form, without having knowledge of all the constituents. In order to understand a sentence, it is necessary to have knowledge both of the constituents and of the particular instance of the form. It is in this way that a sentence conveys information, since it tells us that certain known objects are related according to a certain known form. Thus some kind of knowledge of logical forms, though with most people it is not explicit, is involved in all understanding of discourse. It is the business of philosophical logic to extract this knowledge from its concrete integuments, and to render it explicit and pure.

In all inference, form alone is essential: the particular subject-matter is irrelevant except as securing the truth of the premises. This is one reason for the great importance of logical form. When I say, "Socrates was a man, all men are mortal, therefore Socrates was mortal," the connection of premises and conclusion does not in any way depend upon its being Socrates and man and mortality that I am mentioning. The general form of the inference may be expressed in some such words as, "If a thing has a certain property, and whatever has this property has a certain other property, then the thing in question also has that other property." Here no particular things or properties are mentioned: the proposition is absolutely general. All inferences, when stated fully, are instances of propositions having this kind of generality. If they seem to depend upon the subject-matter otherwise than as regards the truth of the premises, that is because the premises have not been all explicitly stated. In logic, it is a waste of time to deal with inferences concerning particular cases: we deal throughout with completely general and purely formal implications, leaving it to other sciences to discover when the hypotheses are verified and when they are not.

But the forms of propositions giving rise to inferences are not the simplest forms: they are always hypothetical, stating that if one proposition is true, then so is another. Before considering inference, therefore, logic must consider those simpler forms which inference presupposes. Here the traditional logic failed completely: it believed that there was only one form of simple proposition (*i.e.* of proposition not stating a relation between two or more other propositions), namely, the form which ascribes a predicate to a subject. This is the appropriate form in assigning the qualities of a given thing—we may say "This thing is round, and red, and so on." Grammar favours this form, but philosophically it is so far from universal that it is not even very common. If we say "this thing is bigger than that," we are not assigning a mere quality of "this," but a relation of "this" and "that." We might express the same fact by saying "that thing is smaller than this," where grammatically the subject is changed. Thus propositions stating that two things have a certain relation have a different form from subject-predicate propositions, and the failure to perceive this difference or to allow for it has been the source of many errors in traditional metaphysics.

The belief or unconscious conviction that all propositions are of the subject-predicate form—in other words, that every fact consists in some thing having some quality—has rendered most philosophers incapable of giving any account of the world of science and daily life. If they had been honestly anxious to give such an account, they would probably have discovered their error very quickly; but most of them were less anxious to understand the world of science and daily life, than to convict it of unreality in the interests of a super-sensible "real" world. Belief in the unreality of the world of sense arises with irresistible force in certain moods—moods which, I imagine, have some simple physiological basis, but are none the less powerfully persuasive. The conviction born of these moods is the source of most mysticism and of most metaphysics. When the emotional intensity of such a mood subsides, a man who is in the habit of reasoning will search for logical reasons in favour of the belief which he finds in himself. But since the belief already exists, he will be very hospitable to any reason that suggests itself. The paradoxes apparently proved by his logic are really the paradoxes of mysticism, and are the goal which he feels his logic must reach if it is to be in accordance with insight. It is in this way that logic has been pursued by those of the great philosophers who were mystics—notably Plato, Spinoza, and Hegel. But since they usually took for granted the supposed insight of the mystic emotion, their logical doctrines were presented with a certain dryness, and were believed by their disciples to be quite independent of the sudden illumination from which they sprang. Nevertheless their origin clung to them, and they remained—to borrow a useful word from Mr. Santayana—"malicious" in regard to the world of science and common sense. It is only so that we can account for the complacency with which philosophers have accepted the inconsistency of their doctrines with all the common and scientific facts which seem best established and most worthy of belief.

The logic of mysticism shows, as is natural, the defects which are inherent in anything malicious. While the mystic mood is dominant, the need of logic is not felt; as the mood fades, the impulse to logic reasserts itself, but with a desire to retain the vanishing insight, or at least to prove that it *was* insight, and that what seems to contradict it is illusion. The logic which thus arises is not quite disinterested or candid, and is inspired by a certain hatred of the daily world to which it is to be applied. Such an attitude naturally does not tend to the best results. Everyone knows that to read an author's books simply in order to refute him is not the way to understand him; and to read the book of Nature with a conviction that it is all illusion is just as unlikely to lead to understanding. If our logic is to find the common world intelligible, it must not be hostile, but must be inspired by a genuine acceptance such as is not usually to be found among metaphysicians.

Traditional logic, since it holds that all propositions have the subject-predicate form, is unable to admit the reality of relations: all relations, it maintains, must be reduced to properties of the apparently related terms. There are many ways of refuting this opinion; one of the easiest is derived from the consideration of what are called "asymmetrical" relations. In order to explain this, I will first explain two independent ways of classifying relations.

Some relations, when they hold between A and B, also hold between B and A. Such, for example, is the relation "brother or sister." If A is a brother or sister of B, then B is a brother or sister of A. Such again is any kind of similarity, say similarity of colour. Any kind of dissimilarity is also of this kind: if the colour of A is unlike the colour of B, then the colour of B is unlike the colour of A. Relations of this sort are called *symmetrical.* Thus a relation is symmetrical if, whenever it holds between A and B, it also holds between B and A.

All relations that are not symmetrical are called *non-symmetrical.* Thus "brother" is non-symmetrical, because if A is a brother of B, it may happen that B is a *sister* of A.

A relation is called *asymmetrical* when, if it holds between A and B, it *never* holds between B and A. Thus husband, father, grandfather, etc., are asymmetrical relations. So are *before, after, greater, above, to the right of,* etc. All the relations that give rise to series are of this kind.

Classification into symmetrical, asymmetrical, and merely non-symmetrical relations is the first of the two classifications we had to consider. The second is into transitive, intransitive, and merely non-transitive relations, which are defined as follows.

A relation is said to be *transitive,* if, whenever it holds between A and B and also between B and C, it holds between A and C. Thus *before, after, greater, above* are transitive. All relations giving rise to series are transitive, but so are many others. The transitive relations just mentioned were asymmetrical, but many transitive relations are symmetrical—for instance, equality in any respect, exact identity of colour, being equally numerous (as applied to collections), and so on.

A relation is said to be *non-transitive* whenever it is not transitive. Thus "brother" is non-transitive, because a brother of one's brother may be oneself. All kinds of dissimilarity are non-transitive.

A relation is said to be *intransitive* when, if A has the relation to B, and B to C, A never has it to C. Thus "father" is intransitive. So is such a relation as "one inch taller" or "one year later."

Let us now, in the light of this classification, return to the question whether all relations can be reduced to predications.

In the case of symmetrical relations—*i.e.* relations which, if they hold between A and B, also hold between B and A—some kind of plausibility can be given to this doctrine. A symmetrical relation which is transitive, such as equality, can be regarded as expressing possession of some common property, while one which is not transitive, such as inequality, can be regarded as expressing possession of different properties. But when we come to asymmetrical relations, such as before and after, greater and less, etc., the attempt to reduce them to properties becomes obviously impossible. When for example, two things are merely known to be unequal, without our knowing which is greater, we may say that the inequality results from their having different magnitudes, because inequality is a symmetrical relation; but to say that when one thing is *greater* than another, and not merely unequal to it, that means that they have different magnitudes, is formally incapable of explaining the facts. For if the other thing had been greater than the one, the magnitudes would also have been different, though the fact to be explained would not have been the same. Thus mere *difference* of magnitude is not *all* that is involved, since, if it were, there would be no difference between one thing being greater than other, and the other being greater than the one. We shall have to say that the one magnitude is *greater* than the other, and thus we shall have failed to get rid of the relation "greater." In short, both possession of the same property and possession of different properties are *symmetrical* relations, and therefore cannot account for the existence of *asymmetrical* relations.

Asymmetrical relations are involved in all series—in space and time, greater and less, whole and part, and many others of the most important characteristics of the actual world. All these aspects, therefore, the logic which reduces everything to subjects and predicates is compelled to condemn as error and mere appearance. To those whose logic is not malicious, such a wholesale condemnation appears impossible. And in fact there is no reason except prejudice, so far as I can discover, for denying the reality of relations. When once their reality is admitted, all *logical* grounds for supposing the world of sense to be illusory disappear. If this is to be supposed, it must be frankly and simply on the ground of mystic insight unsupported by argument. It is impossible to argue against what professes to be insight, so long as it does not argue in its own favour. As logicians, therefore, we may admit the possibility of the mystic's world, while yet, so long as we do not have his insight, we must continue to study the everyday world with which we are familiar. But when he contends that our world is impossible, then our logic is ready to repel his attack. And the first step in creating the logic which is to perform this service is the recognition of the reality of relations.

Relations which have two terms are only one kind of relations. A relation may have three terms, or four, or any number. Relations of two terms, being the simplest, have received more attention than the others, and have generally been alone considered by philosophers, both those who accepted and those who denied the reality of relations. But other relations have their importance, and are indispensable in the solution of certain problems. Jealousy, for example, is a relation between three people. Professor Royce mentions the relation "giving": when A gives B to C, that is a relation of three terms. When a man says to his wife: "My dear, I wish you could induce Angelina to accept Edwin," his wish constitutes a relation between four people, himself, his wife, Angelina, and Edwin. Thus such relations are by no means recondite or rare. But in order to explain exactly how they differ from relations of two terms, we must embark upon a classification of the logical forms of facts, which is the first business of logic, and the business in which the traditional logic has been most deficient.

The existing world consists of many things with many qualities and relations. A complete description of the existing world would require not only a catalogue of the things, but also a mention of all their qualities and relations. We should have to know not only this, that, and the other thing, but also which was red, which yellow, which was earlier than which, which was between which two others, and so on. When I speak of a "fact," I do not mean one of the simple things in the world; I mean that a certain thing has a certain quality, or that certain things have a certain relation. Thus, for example, I should not call Napoleon a fact, but I should call it a fact that he was ambitious, or that he married Josephine. Now a fact, in this sense, is never simple, but always has two or more constituents. When it simply assigns a quality to a thing, it has only two constituents, the thing and the quality. When it consists of a relation between two things, it has three constituents, the things and the relation. When it consists of a relation between three things, it has four constituents, and so on. The constituents of facts, in the sense in which we are using the word "fact," are not other facts, but are things and qualities or relations. When we say that there are relations of more than two terms, we mean that there are single facts consisting of a single relation and more than two things. I do not mean that one relation of two terms may hold between A and B, and also between A and C, as, for example, a man is the son of his father and also the son of his mother. This constitutes two distinct facts: if we choose to treat it as one fact, it is a fact which has facts for its constituents. But the facts I am speaking of have no facts among their constituents, but only things and relations. For example, when A is jealous of B on account of C, there is only one fact, involving three people; there are not two instances of jealousy, but only one. It is in such cases that I speak of a relation of three terms, where the simplest possible fact in which the relation occurs is one involving three things in addition to the relation. And the same applies to relations of four terms or five or any other number. All such relations must be admitted in our inventory of the logical forms of facts: two facts involving the same number of things have the same form, and two which involve different numbers of things have different forms.

Given any fact, there is an assertion which expresses the fact. The fact itself is objective, and independent of our thought or opinion about it; but the assertion is something which involves thought, and may be either true or false. An assertion may be positive or negative: we may assert that Charles I was executed, or that he did *not* die in his bed. A negative assertion may be said to be a *denial*. Given a form of words which must be either true or false, such as "Charles I died in his bed," we may either assert or deny this form of words: in the one case we have a positive assertion, in the other a negative one. A form of words which must be either true or false I shall call a *proposition*. Thus a proposition is the same as what may be significantly asserted or denied. A proposition which expresses what we have called a fact, *i.e.* which, when asserted, asserts that a certain thing has a certain quality, or that certain things have a certain relation, will be called an atomic proposition, because, as we shall see immediately, there are other propositions into which atomic propositions enter in a way analogous to that in which atoms enter into molecules. Atomic propositions, although, like facts, they may have any one of an infinite number of forms, are only one kind of propositions. All other kinds are more complicated. In order to preserve the parallelism in language as regards facts and propositions, we shall give the name "atomic facts" to the facts we have hitherto been considering. Thus atomic facts are what determine whether atomic propositions are to be asserted or denied.

Whether an atomic proposition, such as "this is red," or "this is before that," is to be asserted or denied can only be known empirically. Perhaps one atomic fact may sometimes be capable of being inferred from another, though I do not believe this to be the case; but in any case it cannot be inferred from premises no one of which is an atomic fact. It follows that, if atomic facts are to be known at all, some at least must be known without inference. The atomic facts which we come to know in this way are the facts of sense-perception; at any rate, the facts of sense-perception are those which we most obviously and certainly come to know in this way. If we knew all atomic facts, and also knew that there were none except those we knew, we should, theoretically, be able to infer all truths of whatever form. Thus logic would then supply us with the whole of the apparatus required. But in the first acquisition of knowledge concerning atomic facts, logic is useless. In pure logic, no atomic fact is ever mentioned: we confine ourselves wholly to forms, without asking ourselves what objects can fill the forms. Thus pure logic is independent of atomic facts; but conversely, they are, in a sense, independent of logic. Pure logic and atomic facts are the two poles, the wholly *a priori* and the wholly empirical. But between the two lies a vast intermediate region, which we must now briefly explore.

"Molecular" propositions are such as contain conjunctions—*if, or, and, unless,* etc.— and such words are the marks of a molecular proposition. Consider such an assertion as, "If it rains, I shall bring my umbrella." This assertion is just as capable of truth or falsehood as the assertion of an atomic proposition, but it is obvious that either the corresponding fact, or the nature of the correspondence with fact, must be quite different from what it is in the case of an atomic proposition. Whether it rains, and whether I bring my umbrella, are each severally matters of atomic fact, ascertainable by observation. But the connection of the two involved in saying that *if* the one happens, *then* the other will happen, is something radically different from either of the two separately. It does not require for its truth that it should actually rain, or that I should actually bring my umbrella; even if the weather is cloudless, it may still be true that I should have brought my umbrella if the weather had been different. Thus we have here a connection of two propositions, which does not depend upon whether they are to be asserted or denied, but only upon the second being inferable from the first. Such propositions, therefore, have a form which is different from that of any atomic proposition.

Such propositions are important to logic, because all inference depends upon them. If I have told you that if it rains I shall bring my umbrella, and if you see that there is a steady downpour, you can infer that I shall bring my umbrella. There can be no inference except where propositions are connected in some way, so that from the truth or falsehood of the one something follows as to the truth or falsehood of the other. It seems to be the case we can sometimes know molecular propositions, as in the above instance of the umbrella, when we do not know whether the component atomic propositions are true or false. The *practical* utility of inference rests upon this fact.

The next kind of propositions we have to consider are *general* propositions, such as "all men are mortal," "all equilateral triangles are equiangular." And with these belong propositions in which the word "some" occurs, such as "some men are philosophers" or "some philosophers are not wise." These are the denials of general propositions, namely (in the above instances), of "all men are non-philosophers" and "all philosophers are wise." We will call propositions containing the word "some" *negative* general propositions, and those containing the word "all" *positive* general propositions. These propositions, it will be seen, begin to have the appearance of the propositions in logical text-books. But their peculiarity and complexity are not known to the text-books, and the problems which they raise are only discussed in the most superficial manner.

When we were discussing atomic facts, we saw that we should be able, theoretically, to infer all other truths by logic if we knew all atomic facts and also knew that there were no other atomic facts besides those we knew. The knowledge that there are no other atomic facts is positive general knowledge; it is the knowledge that "all atomic facts are known to me," or at least "all atomic facts are in this collection"—however the collection may be given. It is easy to see that general propositions, such as "all men are mortal," cannot be known by inference from atomic facts alone. If we could know each individual man, and know that he was mortal, that would not enable us to know that all men are mortal, unless we *knew* that those were all the men there are, which is a general proposition. If we knew every other existing thing throughout the universe, and knew that each separate thing was not an immortal man, that would not give us our result unless we *knew* that we had explored the whole universe, *i.e.* unless we knew "all things belong to this collection of things I have examined." Thus general truths cannot be inferred from particular truths alone, but must, if they are to be known, be either self-evident, or inferred from premises of which at least one is a general truth. But all *empirical* evidence is of *particular* truths. Hence, if there is any knowledge of general truths at all, there must be *some* knowledge of general truths which is independent of empirical evidence, *i.e.* does not depend upon the data of sense.

The above conclusion, of which we had an instance in the case of the inductive principle, is important, since it affords a refutation of the older empiricists. They believed that all our knowledge is derived from the senses and dependent upon them. We see that, if this view is to be maintained, we must refuse to admit that we know any general propositions. It is perfectly possible logically that this should be the case, but it does not appear to be so in fact, and indeed no one would dream of maintaining such a view except a theorist at the last extremity. We must therefore admit that there is general knowledge not derived from sense, and that some of this knowledge is not obtained by inference but is primitive.

Such general knowledge is to be found in logic. Whether there is any such knowledge not derived from logic, I do not know; but in logic, at any rate, we have such knowledge. It will be remembered that we excluded from pure logic such propositions as, "Socrates is a man, all men are mortal, therefore Socrates is mortal," because *Socrates* and *man* and *mortal* are empirical terms, only to be understood through particular experience. The corresponding proposition in pure logic is: "If anything has a certain property, and whatever has this property has a certain other property, then the thing in question has the other property." This proposition is absolutely general: it applies to all things and all properties. And it is quite self-evident. Thus in such propositions of pure logic we have the self-evident general propositions of which we were in search.

A proposition such as "If Socrates is a man, and all men are mortal, then Socrates is mortal," is true in virtue of its *form* alone. Its truth, in this hypothetical form, does not depend upon whether Socrates actually is a man, nor upon whether in fact all men are mortal; thus it is equally true when we substitute other terms for *Socrates* and *man* and *mortal.* The general truth of which it is an instance is purely formal, and belongs to logic. Since it does not mention any particular thing, or even any particular quality or relation, it is wholly independent of the accidental facts of the existent world, and can be known, theoretically, without any experience of particular things or their qualities and relations.

Logic, we may say, consists of two parts. The first part investigates what propositions are and what forms they may have; this part enumerates the different kinds of atomic propositions, of molecular propositions, of general propositions, and so on. The second part consists of certain supremely general propositions, which assert the truth of all propositions of certain forms. This second part merges into pure mathematics, whose propositions all turn out, on analysis, to be such general formal truths. The first part, which merely enumerates forms, is the more difficult, and philosophically the more important; and it is the recent progress in this first part, more than anything else, that has rendered a truly scientific discussion of many philosophical problems possible.

The problem of the nature of judgment or belief may be taken as an example of a problem whose solution depends upon an adequate inventory of logical forms. We have already seen how the supposed universality of the subject-predicate form made it impossible to give a right analysis of serial order, and therefore made space and time unintelligible. But in this case it was only necessary to admit relations of two terms. The case of judgment demands the admission of more complicated forms. If all judgments were true, we might suppose that a judgment consisted in apprehension of a *fact,* and that the apprehension was a relation of a mind to the fact. From poverty in the logical inventory, this view has often been held. But it leads to absolutely insoluble difficulties in the case of error. Suppose I believe that Charles I died in his bed. There is no objective fact "Charles I's death in his bed" to which I can have a relation of apprehension. Charles I and death and his bed are objective, but they are not, except in my thought, put together as my false belief supposes. It is therefore necessary, in analysing a belief, to look for some other logical form than a two-term relation. Failure to realise this necessity has, in my opinion, vitiated almost everything that has hitherto been written on the theory of knowledge, making the problem of error insoluble and the difference between belief and perception inexplicable.

Modern logic, as I hope is now evident, has the effect of enlarging our abstract imagination, and providing an infinite number of possible hypotheses to be applied in the analysis of any complex fact. In this respect it is the exact opposite of the logic practised by the classical tradition. In that logic, hypotheses which seem *prima facie* possible are professedly proved impossible, and it is decreed in advance that reality must have a certain special character. In modern logic, on the contrary, while the *prima facie* hypotheses as a rule remain admissible, others, which only logic would have suggested, are added to our stock, and are very often found to be indispensable if a right analysis of the facts is to be obtained. The old logic put thought in fetters, while the new logic gives it wings. It has, in my opinion, introduced the same kind of advance into philosophy as Galileo introduced into physics, making it possible at last to see what kinds of problems may be capable of solution, and what kinds must be abandoned as beyond human powers. And where a solution appears possible, the new logic provides a method which enables us to obtain results that do not merely embody personal idiosyncrasies, but must command the assent of all who are competent to form an opinion.

MYSTICISM AND LOGIC

I. THE RELATION OF SENSE-DATA TO PHYSICS

Physics is said to be an empirical science, based upon observation and experiment.

It is supposed to be verifiable, i.e. capable of calculating beforehand results subsequently confirmed by observation and experiment.

What can we learn by observation and experiment?

Nothing, so far as physics is concerned, except immediate data of sense: certain patches of colour, sounds, tastes, smells, etc., with certain spatio-temporal relations.

The supposed contents of the physical world are *prima facie* very different from these: molecules have no colour, atoms make no noise, electrons have no taste, and corpuscles do not even smell.

If such objects are to be verified, it must be solely through their relation to sense-data: they must have some kind of correlation with sense-data, and must be verifiable through their correlation *alone*.

But how is the correlation itself ascertained? A correlation can only be ascertained empirically by the correlated objects being constantly *found* together. But in our case, only one term of the correlation, namely, the sensible term, is ever *found:* the other term seems essentially incapable of being found. Therefore, it would seem, the correlation with objects of sense, by which physics was to be verified, is itself utterly and for ever unverifiable.

There are two ways of avoiding this result.

1. We may say that we know some principle *a priori,* without the need of empirical verification, e.g. that our sense-data have *causes* other than themselves, and that something can be known about these causes by inference from their effects. This way has been often adopted by philosophers. It may be necessary to adopt this way to some extent, but in so far as it is adopted physics ceases to be empirical or based upon experiment and observation alone. Therefore this way is to be avoided as much as possible.

2. We may succeed in actually defining the objects of physics as functions of sense-data. Just in so far as physics leads to expectations, this *must* be possible, since we can only *expect* what can be experienced. And in so far as the physical state of affairs is inferred from sense-data, it must be capable of expression as a function of sense-data. The problem of accomplishing this expression leads to much interesting logico-mathematical work.

In physics as commonly set forth, sense-data appear as functions of physical objects: when such-and-such waves impinge upon the eye, we see such-and-such colours, and so on. But the waves are in fact inferred from the colours, not vice versa. Physics cannot be regarded as validly based upon empirical data until the waves have been expressed as functions of the colours and other sense-data.

Thus if physics is to be verifiable we are faced with the following problem: Physics

From Bertrand Russell, *Mysticism and Logic* (London: Longmans, Green Co., 1918).

exhibits sense-data as functions of physical objects, but verification is only possible if physical objects can be exhibited as functions of sense-data. We have therefore to solve the equations giving sense-data in terms of physical objects, so as to make them instead give physical objects in terms of sense-data.

II. CHARACTERISTICS OF SENSE-DATA

When I speak of a "sense-datum," I do not mean the whole of what is given in sense at one time. I mean rather such a part of the whole as might be singled out by attention: particular patches of colour, particular noises, and so on. There is some difficulty in deciding what is to be considered *one* sense-datum: often attention causes divisions to appear where, so far as can be discovered, there were no divisions before. An observed complex fact, such as that this patch of red is to the left of that patch of blue, is also to be regarded as a datum from our present point of view: epistemologically, it does not differ greatly from a simple sense-datum as regards its function in giving knowledge. Its *logical* structure is very different, however, from that of sense: *sense* gives acquaintance with particulars, and is thus a two-term relation in which the object can be *named* but not asserted, and is inherently incapable of truth or falsehood, whereas the observation of a complex fact, which may be suitably called perception, is not a two-term relation, but involves the propositional form on the object-side, and gives knowledge of a truth, not mere acquaintance with a particular. This logical difference, important as it is, is not very relevant to our present problem; and it will be convenient to regard data of perception as included among sense-data for the purposes of this paper. It is to be observed that the particulars which are constituents of a datum of perception are always sense-data in the strict sense.

Concerning sense-data, we know that they are there while they are data, and this is the epistemological basis of all our knowledge of external particulars. (The meaning of the word "external" of course raises problems which will concern us later.) We do not know, except by means of more or less precarious inferences, whether the objects which are at one time sense-data continue to exist at times when they are not data. Sense-data at the times when they are data are all that we directly and primitively know of the external world; hence in epistemology the fact that they are *data* is all-important. But the fact that they are all that we directly know gives, of course, no presumption that they are all that there is. If we could construct an impersonal metaphysic, independent of the accidents of our knowledge and ignorance, the privileged position of the actual data would probably disappear, and they would probably appear as a rather haphazard selection from a mass of objects more or less like them. In saying this, I assume only that it is probable that there are particulars with which we are not acquainted. Thus the special importance of sense-data is in relation to epistemology, not to metaphysics. In this respect, physics is to be reckoned as metaphysics: it is impersonal, and nominally pays no special attention to sense-data. It is only when we ask how physics can be *known* that the importance of sense-data re-emerges.

III. SENSIBILIA

I shall give the name *sensibilia* to those objects which have the same metaphysical and physical status as sense-data, without necessarily being data to any mind. Thus the relation of a *sensibile* to a sense-datum is like that of a man to a husband: a man becomes a husband by entering into the relation of marriage, and similarly a *sensibile* becomes a sense-datum by entering into the relation of acquaintance. It is important to have both terms; for we wish to discuss whether an object which is at one time a sense-datum can still exist at a time when it is not a sense-datum. We cannot ask "Can sense-data exist without being given?" for that is like asking "Can husbands exist without being married?" We must ask "Can *sensibilia* exist without being given?" and also "Can a particular *sensibile* be at one time a sense-datum, and at another not?" Unless we have the word *sensibile* as well as the word "sense-datum," such questions are apt to entangle us in trivial logical puzzles.

It will be seen that all sense-data are *sensibilia*. It is a metaphysical question whether all *sensibilia* are sense-data, and an epistemological question whether there exist means of inferring *sensibilia* which are not data from those that are.

A few preliminary remarks, to be amplified as we proceed, will serve to elucidate the use which I propose to make of *sensibilia*.

I regard sense-data as not mental, and as being, in fact, part of the actual subject-matter of physics. There are arguments, shortly to be examined, for their subjectivity, but these arguments seem to me only to prove *physiological* subjectivity, i.e. causal dependence on the sense-organs, nerves, and brain. The appearance which a thing presents to us is causally dependent upon these, in exactly the same way as it is dependent upon intervening fog or smoke or coloured glass. Both dependences are contained in the statement that the appearance which a piece of matter presents when viewed from a given place is a function not only of the piece of matter, but also of the intervening medium. (The terms used in this statement—"matter," "view from a given place," "appearance," "intervening medium"—will all be defined in the course of the present paper.) We have not the means of ascertaining how things appear from places not surrounded by brain and nerves and sense-organs, because we cannot leave the body; but continuity makes it not unreasonable to suppose that they present *some* appearance at such places. Any such appearance would be included among *sensibilia*. If—*per impossibile*—there were a complete human body with no mind inside it, all those *sensibilia* would exist, in relation to that body, which would be sense-data if there were a mind in the body. What the mind adds to *sensibilia*, in fact, is *merely* awareness: everything else is physical or physiological.

IV. SENSE-DATA ARE PHYSICAL

Before discussing this question it will be well to define the sense in which the terms "mental" and "physical" are to be used. The word "physical," in all preliminary discussions, is to be understood as meaning "what is dealt with by physics." Physics, it is plain, tells us something about some of the constituents of the actual world; what these constituents are may be doubtful, but it is they that are to be called physical, whatever their nature may prove to be.

The definition of the term "mental" is more difficult, and can only be satisfactorily given after many difficult controversies have been discussed and decided. For present purposes therefore I must content myself with assuming a dogmatic answer to these controversies. I shall call a particular "mental" when it is aware of something, and I shall call a fact "mental" when it contains a mental particular as a constituent.

It will be seen that the mental and the physical are not necessarily mutually exclusive, although I know of no reason to suppose that they overlap.

The doubt as to the correctness of our definition of the "mental" is of little importance in our present discussion. For what I am concerned to maintain is that sense-data are physical, and this being granted it is a matter of indifference in our present inquiry whether or not they are also mental. Although I do not hold, with Mach and James and the "new realists," that the difference between the mental and the physical is *merely* one of arrangement, yet what I have to say in the present paper is compatible with their doctrine and might have been reached from their standpoint.

In discussions on sense-data, two questions are commonly confused, namely: (1) Do sensible objects persist when we are not sensible of them? in other words, do *sensibilia* which are data at a certain time sometimes continue to exist at times when they are not data? And (2) are sense-data mental or physical?

I propose to assert that sense-data are physical, while yet maintaining that they probably never persist unchanged after ceasing to be data. The view that they do not persist is often thought, quite erroneously in my opinion, to imply that they are mental; and this has, I believe, been a potent source of confusion in regard to our present problem. If there were, as some have held, a *logical impossibility* in sense-data persisting after ceasing to be data, that certainly would tend to show that they were mental; but if, as I contend, their non-persistence is merely a probable inference from empirically ascertained causal laws, then it carries no such implication with it, and we are quite free to treat them as part of the subject-matter of physics.

Logically a sense-datum is an object, a particular of which the subject is aware. It does not contain the subject as a part, as for example beliefs and volitions do. The existence of the sense-datum is therefore not logically dependent upon that of the subject; for the only way, so far as I know, in which the existence of *A* can be *logically* dependent upon the existence of *B* is when *B* is part of *A*. There is therefore no *a priori* reason why a particular which is a sense-datum should not persist after it has ceased to be a datum, nor why other similar particulars should not exist without ever being data. The view that sense-data are mental is derived, no doubt, in part from their physiological subjectivity, but in part also from a failure to distinguish between sense-data and "sensations." By a sensation I mean the fact consisting in the subject's awareness of the sense-datum. Thus a sensation is a complex of which the subject is a constituent and which therefore is mental. The sense-datum, on the other hand, stands over against the subject as that external object of which in sensation the subject is aware. It is true that the sense-datum is in many cases in the subject's body, but the subject's body is as distinct from the subject as tables and chairs are, and is in fact merely a part of the material world. So soon, therefore, as sense-data are clearly distinguished from sensations, and as their subjectivity is recognised to be physiological not psychical, the chief obstacles in the way of regarding them as physical are removed.

V. "SENSIBILIA" AND "THINGS"

But if "sensibilia" are to be recognised as the ultimate constituents of the physical world, a long and difficult journey is to be performed before we can arrive either at the "thing" of common sense or at the "matter" of physics. The supposed impossibility of combining the different sense-data which are regarded as appearances of the same "thing" to different people has made it seem as though these "sensibilia" must be regarded as mere subjective phantasms. A given table will present to one man a rectangular appearance, while to another it appears to have two acute angles and two obtuse angles; to one man it appears brown, while to another, towards whom it reflects the light, it appears white and shiny. It is said, not wholly without plausibility, that these different shapes and different colours cannot co-exist simultaneously in the same place, and cannot therefore both be constituents of the physical world. This argument I must confess appeared to me until recently to be irrefutable. . . . The supposed impossibility derives its apparent force from the phrase: "*in the same place*," and it is precisely in this phrase that its weakness lies. The conception of space is too often treated in philosophy—even by those who on reflection would not defend such treatment—as though it were as given, simple, and unambiguous as Kant, in his psychological innocence, supposed. It is the unperceived ambiguity of the word "place" which, as we shall shortly see, has caused the difficulties to realists and given an undeserved advantage to their opponents. Two "places" of different kinds are involved in every sense-datum, namely the place *at* which it appears and the place *from* which it appears. These belong to different spaces, although, as we shall see, it is possible, with certain limitations, to establish a correlation between them. What we call the different appearances of the same thing to different observers are each in a space private to the observer concerned. No place in the private world of one observer is identical with a place in the private world of another observer. There is therefore no question of combining the different appearances in the one place; and the fact that they cannot all exist in one place affords accordingly no ground whatever for questioning their physical reality. The "thing" of common sense may in fact be identified with the whole class of its appearances—where, however, we must include among appearances not only those which are actual sense-data, but also those "sensibilia," if any, which, on grounds of continuity of resemblance, are to be regarded as belonging to the same system of appearances, although there happen to be no observers to whom they are data.

An example may make this clearer. Suppose there are a number of people in a room, all seeing, as they say, the same tables and chairs, walls and pictures. No two of these people have exactly the same sense-data, yet there is sufficient similarity among their data to enable them to group together certain of these data as appearances of one "thing" to the several spectators, and others as appearances of another "thing." Besides the appearances which a given thing in the room presents to the actual spectators, there are, we may suppose, other appearances which it would present to other possible spectators. If a man were to sit down between two others, the appearance which the room would present to him would be intermediate between the appearances which it presents to the two others: and although this appearance would not exist as it is without the sense-organs, nerves and brain, of the newly arrived spectator, still it is not unnatural to suppose that, from the position which he now occupies, *some* appearance of the room existed before his arrival. This supposition, however, need merely be noticed and not insisted upon.

Since the "thing" cannot, without indefensible partiality, be identified with any single one of its appearances, it came to be thought of as something distinct from all of them and underlying them. But by the principle of Occam's razor, if the class of appearances will fulfill the purposes for the sake of which the thing was invented by the prehistoric metaphysicians to whom common sense is due, economy demands that we should identify the thing with the class of its appearances. It is not necessary to *deny* a substance or substratum underlying these appearances; it is merely expedient to abstain from asserting this unnecessary entity. Our procedure here is precisely analogous to that which has swept away from the philosophy of mathematics the useless menagerie of metaphysical monsters with which it used to be infested.

VI. CONSTRUCTIONS VERSUS INFERENCES

Before proceeding to analyse and explain the ambiguities of the word "place," a few general remarks on method are desirable. The supreme maxim in scientific philosophising is this: *Wherever possible, logical constructions are to be substituted for inferred entities.*

Some examples of the substitution of construction for inference in the realm of mathematical philosophy may serve to elucidate the uses of this maxim. Take first the case of irrationals. In old days, irrationals were inferred as the supposed limits of series of rationals which had no rational limit; but the objection to this procedure was that it left the existence of irrationals merely optative, and for this reason the stricter methods of the present day no longer tolerate such a definition. We now define an irrational number as a certain class of ratios, thus constructing it logically by means of ratios, instead of arriving at it by a doubtful inference from them. Take again the case of cardinal numbers. Two equally numerous collections appear to have something in common: this something is supposed to be their cardinal number. But so long as the cardinal number is inferred from the collections, not constructed in terms of them, its existence must remain in doubt, unless in virtue of a metaphysical postulate *ad hoc.* By defining the cardinal number of a given collection as the class of all equally numerous collections, we avoid the necessity of this metaphysical postulate, and thereby remove a needless element of doubt from the philosophy of arithmetic. A similar method, as I have shown elsewhere, can be applied to classes themselves, which need not be supposed to have any metaphysical reality, but can be regarded as symbolically constructed fictions.

The method by which the construction proceeds is closely analogous in these and all similar cases. Given a set of propositions nominally dealing with the supposed inferred entities, we observe the properties which are required of the supposed entities in order to make these propositions true. By dint of a little logical ingenuity, we then construct some logical function of less hypothetical entities which has the requisite properties. This constructed function we substitute for the supposed inferred entities, and thereby obtain a new and less doubtful interpretation of the body of propositions in question. This method, so fruitful in the philosophy of mathematics, will be found equally applicable in the philosophy of physics, where, I do not doubt, it would have been applied long ago but for the fact that all who have studied this subject hitherto have been completely ignorant of mathematical logic. I myself cannot claim originality in the application of this method to physics, since I owe the suggestion and the stimulus for its application entirely to my friend and collaborator Dr. Whitehead, who is engaged in applying it to the more mathematical portions of the region intermediate between sense-data and the points, instants and particles of physics.

A complete application of the method which substitutes constructions for inferences would exhibit matter wholly in terms of sense-data, and even, we may add, of the sense-data of a single person, since the sense-data of others cannot be known without some element of inference. This, however, must remain for the present an ideal, to be approached as nearly as possible, but to be reached, if at all, only after a long preliminary labour of which as yet we can only see the very beginning. The inferences which are unavoidable can, however, be subjected to certain guiding principles. In the first place they should always be made perfectly explicit, and should be formulated in the most general manner possible. In the second place the inferred entities should, whenever this can be done, be similar to those whose existence is given, rather than, like the Kantian *Ding an sich,* something wholly remote from the data which nominally support the inference. The inferred entities which I shall allow myself are of two kinds: (*a*) the sense-data of other people, in favour of which there is the evidence of testimony, resting ultimately upon the analogical argument in favour of minds other than my own; (*b*) the "sensibilia" which would appear from places where there happen to be no minds, and which I suppose to be real although they are no one's data. Of these two classes of inferred entities, the first will probably be allowed to pass unchallenged. It would give me the greatest satisfaction to be able to dispense with it, and thus establish physics upon a solipsistic basis; but those—and I fear they are the majority— in whom the human affections are stronger than the desire for logical economy, will, no doubt, not share my desire to render solipsism scientifically satisfactory. The second class of inferred entities raises much more serious questions. It may be thought monstrous to maintain that a thing can present any appearance at all in a place where no sense-organs and nervous structure exist through which it could appear. I do not myself feel the monstrosity; nevertheless I should regard these supposed appearances only in the light of a hypothetical scaffolding, to be used while the edifice of physics is being raised, though possibly capable of being removed as soon as the edifice is completed. These "sensibilia" which are not data to anyone are therefore to be taken rather as an illustrative hypothesis and as an aid in preliminary statement than as a dogmatic part of the philosophy of physics in its final form.

VII. PRIVATE SPACE AND THE SPACE OF PERSPECTIVES

We have now to explain the ambiguity in the word "place," and how it comes that two places of different sorts are associated with every sense-datum, namely the place *at* which it is and the place *from* which it is perceived. The theory to be advocated is closely analogous to Leibniz's monadology, from which it differs chiefly in being less smooth and tidy.

The first fact to notice is that, so far as can be discovered, no sensibile is ever a datum to two people at once. The things seen by two different people are often closely similar, so similar that the same *words* can be used to denote them, without which communication with others concerning sensible objects would be impossible. But, in spite of this similarity, it would seem that some difference always arises from difference in the point of view. Thus each person, so far as his sense-data are concerned, lives in a private world. This private world contains its own space, or rather spaces, for it would seem that only experience teaches us to correlate the space of sight with the space of touch and with the various other spaces of other senses. This multiplicity of private spaces, however, though interesting to the psychologist, is of no great importance in regard to our present problem, since a merely solipsistic experience enables us to correlate them into the one private space which embraces all our own sense-data. The place *at* which a sense-datum is, is a place in private space. This place therefore is different from any place in the private space of another percipient. For if we assume, as logical economy demands, that all position is relative, a place is only definable by the things in or around it, and therefore the same place cannot occur in two private worlds which have no common constituent. The question, therefore, of combining what we call different appearances of the same thing in the same place does not arise, and the fact that a given object appears to different spectators to have different shapes and colours affords no argument against the physical reality of all these shapes and colours.

In addition to the private spaces belonging to the private worlds of different percipients, there is, however, another space, in which one whole private world counts as a point, or at least as a spatial unit. This might be described as the space of points of view, since each private world may be regarded as the appearance which the universe presents from a certain point of view. I prefer, however, to speak of it as the space of *perspectives,* in order to obviate the suggestion that a private world is only real when someone views it. And for the same reason, when I wish to speak of a private world without assuming a percipient, I shall call it a "perspective."

We have now to explain how the different perspectives are ordered in one space. This is effected by means of the correlated "sensibilia" which are regarded as the appearances, in different perspectives, of one and the same thing. By moving, and by testimony, we discover that two different perspectives, though they cannot both contain the same "sensibilia," may nevertheless contain very similar ones; and the spatial order of a certain group of "sensibilia" in private space of one perspective is found to be identical with, or very similar to, the spatial order of the correlated "sensibilia" in the private space of another perspective. In this way one "sensibile" in one perspective is correlated with one "sensibile" in another. Such correlated "sensibilia" will be called "appearances of one thing." In Leibniz's monadology, since each monad mirrored the whole universe, there was in each perspective a "sensibile" which was an appearance of each thing. In our system of perspectives, we make no such assumption of completeness. A given thing will have appearances in some perspectives, but presumably not in certain others. The "thing" being defined as the class of its appearances, if κ is the class of perspectives in which a certain thing θ appears, then θ is a member of the multiplicative class of κ, κ being a class of mutually exclusive classes of "sensibilia." And similarly a perspective is a member of the multiplicative class of the things which appear in it.

The arrangement of perspectives in a space is effected by means of the differences between the appearances of a given thing in the various perspectives. Suppose, say, that a certain penny appears in a number of different perspectives; in some it looks larger and in some smaller, in some it looks circular, in others it presents the appearance of an ellipse of varying eccentricity. We may collect together all those perspectives in which the appearance of the penny is circular. These we will place on one straight line, ordering them in a series by the variations in the apparent size of the penny. Those perspectives in which the penny appears as a straight line of a certain thickness will similarly be placed upon a plane (though in this case there will be many different perspectives in which the penny is of the same size; when one arrangement is completed these will form a circle concentric with the penny), and ordered as before by the apparent size of the penny. By such means, all those perspectives in which the penny presents a visual appearance can be arranged in a three-dimensional spatial order. Experience shows that the same spatial order of perspectives would have resulted if, instead of the penny, we had chosen any other thing which appeared in all the perspectives in question, or any other method of utilising the differences between the appearances of the same things in different perspectives. It is this empirical fact which has made it possible to construct the one all-embracing space of physics.

The space whose construction has just been explained, and whose elements are whole perspectives, will be called "perspective-space."

VIII. THE PLACING OF "THINGS" AND "SENSIBILIA" IN PERSPECTIVE SPACE

The world which we have so far constructed is a world of six dimensions, since it is a three-dimensional series of perspectives, each of which is itself three-dimensional. We have now to explain the correlation between the perspective space and the various private spaces contained within the various perspectives severally. It is by means of this correlation that the one three-dimensional space of physics is constructed; and it is because of the unconscious performance of this correlation that the distinction between perspective space and the percipient's private space has been blurred, with disastrous results for the philosophy of physics. Let us revert to our penny: the perspectives in which the penny appears larger are regarded as being nearer to the penny than those in which it appears smaller, but as far as experience goes the apparent size of the penny will not grow beyond a certain limit, namely, that where (as we say) the penny is so near the eye that if it were any nearer it could not be seen. By touch we may prolong the series until the penny touches the eye, but no further. If we have been travelling along a line of perspectives in the previously defined sense, we may, however, by imagining the penny removed, prolong the line of perspectives by means, say, of another penny; and the same may be done with any other line of perspectives defined by means of the penny. All these lines meet in a certain place, that is, in a certain perspective. This perspective will be defined as "the place where the penny is."

It is now evident in what sense two places in constructed physical space are associated with a given "sensibile." There is first the place which is the perspective of which the "sensibile" is a member. This is the place *from* which the "sensibile" appears. Secondly there is the place where the thing is of which the "sensibile" is a member, in other words an appearance; this is the place *at* which the "sensibile" appears. The "sensibile" which is a member of one perspective is correlated with another perspective, namely, that which is the place where the thing is of which the "sensibile" is an appearance. To the psychologist the "place from which" is the more interesting, and the "sensibile" accordingly appears to him subjective and where the percipient is. To the physicist the "place at which" is the more interesting, and the "sensibile" accordingly appears to him physical and external. The causes, limits and partial justification of each of these two apparently incompatible views are evident from the above duplicity of places associated with a given "sensibile."

We have seen that we can assign to a physical thing a place in the perspective space. In this way different parts of our body acquire positions in perspective space, and therefore there is a meaning (whether true or false need not much concern us) in saying that the perspective to which our sense-data belong is inside our head. Since our mind is correlated with the perspective to which our sense-data belong, we may regard this perspective as being the position of our mind in perspective space. If, therefore, this perspective is, in the above defined sense, inside our head, there is a good meaning for the statement that the mind is in the head. We can now say of the various appearances of a given thing that some of them are nearer to the thing than others; those are nearer which belong to perspectives that are nearer to "the place where the thing is." We can thus find a meaning, true or false, for the statement that more is to be learned about a thing by examining it close to than by viewing it from a distance. We can also find a meaning for the phrase "the things which intervene between the subject and a thing of which an appearance is a datum to him." One reason often alleged for the subjectivity of sense-data is that the appearance of a thing may change when we find it hard to suppose that the thing itself has changed—for example, when the change is due to our shutting our eyes, or to our screwing them up so as to make the thing look double. If the thing is defined as the class of its appearances (which is the definition adopted above), there is of course necessarily *some* change in the thing whenever any one of its appearances changes. Nevertheless there is a very important distinction between two different ways in which the appearances may change. If after looking at a thing I shut my eyes, the appearance of my eyes changes in every perspective in which there is such an appearance, whereas most of the appearances of the thing will remain unchanged. We may say, as a matter of definition, that a thing changes when, however near to the thing an appearance of it may be, there are changes in appearances as near as, or still nearer to, the thing. On the other hand we shall say that the change is in some other thing if all appearances of the thing which are at not more than a certain distance from the thing remain unchanged, while only comparatively distant appearances of the thing are altered. From this consideration we are naturally led to the consideration of *matter,* which must be our next topic.

IX. THE DEFINITION OF MATTER

We defined the "physical thing" as the class of its appearances, but this can hardly be taken as a definition of matter. We want to be able to express the fact that the appearance of a thing in a given perspective is causally affected by the matter between the thing and the perspective. We have found a meaning for "between a thing and a perspective." But we want matter to be something other than the whole class of appearances of a thing, in order to state the influence of matter on appearances.

We commonly assume that the information we get about a thing is more accurate when the thing is nearer. Far off, we see it is a man, then we see it is Jones; then we see he is smiling. Complete accuracy would only be attainable as a limit: if the appearances of Jones as we approach him tend towards a limit, that limit may be taken to be what Jones really is. It is obvious that from the point of view of physics the appearances of a thing close to "count" more than the appearances far off. We may therefore set up the following tentative definition:

The *matter* of a given thing is the limit of its appearances as their distance from the thing diminishes.

It seems probable that there is something in this definition, but it is not quite satisfactory, because empirically there is no such limit to be obtained from sense-data. The definition will have to be eked out by constructions and definitions. But probably it suggests the right direction in which to look.

We are now in a position to understand in outline the reverse journey from matter to sense-data which is performed by physics. The appearance of a thing in a given perspective is a function of the matter composing the thing and of the intervening matter. The appearance of a thing is altered by intervening smoke or mist, by blue spectacles or by alterations in the sense-organs or nerves of the percipient (which also must be reckoned as part of the intervening medium). The nearer we approach to the thing, the less its appearance is affected by the intervening matter. As we travel further and further from the thing, its appearances diverge more and more from their initial character; and the causal laws of their divergence are to be stated in terms of the matter which lies between them and the thing. Since the appearances at very small distances are less affected by causes other than the thing itself, we come to think that the limit towards which these appearances tend as the distance diminishes is what the thing "really is," as opposed to what it merely seems to be. This, together with its necessity for the statement of causal laws, seems to be the source of the entirely erroneous feeling that matter is more "real" than sense-data.

Consider for example the infinite divisibility of matter. In looking at a given thing and approaching it, one sense-datum will become several, and each of these will again divide. Thus *one* appearance may represent *many* things, and to this process there seems no end. Hence in the limit, when we approach indefinitely near to the thing, there will be an indefinite number of units of matter corresponding to what, at a finite distance, is only one appearance. This is how infinite divisibility arises.

The whole causal efficacy of a thing resides in its matter. This is in some sense an empirical fact, but it would be hard to state it precisely, because "causal efficacy" is difficult to define.

What can be known empirically about the matter of a thing is only approximate, because we cannot get to know the appearances of the thing from very small distances, and cannot accurately infer the limit of these appearances. But it *is* inferred *approximately* by means of the appearances we can observe. It then turns out that these appearances can be exhibited by physics as a function of the matter in our immediate neighbourhood; e.g. the visual appearance of a distant object is a function of the light-waves that reach the eyes. This leads to confusions of thought, but offers no real difficulty.

One appearance, of a visible object for example, is not sufficient to determine its other simultaneous appearances, although it goes a certain distance towards determining them. The determination of the hidden structure of a thing, so far as it is possible at all, can only be effected by means of elaborate dynamical inferences.

X. TIME

It seems that the one all-embracing time is a construction, like the one all-embracing space. Physics itself has become conscious of this fact through the discussions connected with relativity.

Between two perspectives which both belong to one person's experience, there will be a direct time-relation of before and after. This suggests a way of dividing history in the same sort of way as it is divided by different experiences, but without introducing experience or any thing mental: we may define a "biography" as everything that is (directly) earlier or later than, or simultaneous with, a given "sensibile." This will give a series of perspectives, which *might* all form parts of one person's experience, though it is not necessary that all or any of them should actually do so. By this means, the history of the world is divided into a number of mutually exclusive biographies.

We have now to correlate the times in the different biographies. The natural thing would be to say that the appearances of a given (momentary) thing in two different perspectives belonging to different biographies are to be taken as simultaneous; but this is not convenient. Suppose *A* shouts to *B,* and *B* replies as soon as he hears *A*'s shout. Then between *A*'s hearing of his own shout and his hearing of *B*'s there is an interval; thus if we made *A*'s and *B*'s hearing of the same shout exactly simultaneous with each other, we should have events exactly simultaneous with a given event but not with each other. To obviate this, we assume a "velocity of sound." That is, we assume that the time when *B* hears *A*'s shout is half-way between the time when *A* hears his own shout and the time when he hears *B*'s. In this way the correlation is effected.

What has been said about sound applies of course equally to light. The general principle is that the appearances, in different perspectives, which are to be grouped together as constituting what a certain thing is at a certain moment, are not to be all regarded as being at that moment. On the contrary they spread outward from the thing with various velocities according to the nature of the appearances. Since no *direct* means exist of correlating the time in one biography with the time in another, this temporal grouping of the appearances belonging to a given thing at a given moment is in part conventional. Its motive is partly to secure the verification of such maxims as that events which are exactly simultaneous with the same event are exactly simultaneous with one another, partly to secure convenience in the formulation of causal laws.

XI. THE PERSISTENCE OF THINGS AND MATTER

Apart from any of the fluctuating hypotheses of physics, three main problems arise in connecting the world of physics with the world of sense, namely:

1. the construction of a single space;
2. the construction of a single time;
3. the construction of permanent things or matter.

We have already considered the first and second of these problems; it remains to consider the third.

We have seen how correlated appearances in different perspectives are combined to form one "thing" at one moment in the all-embracing time of physics. We have now to consider how appearances at different times are combined as belonging to one "thing," and how we arrive at the persistent "matter" of physics. The assumption of permanent substance, which technically underlies the procedure of physics, cannot of course be regarded as metaphysically legitimate: just as the one thing simultaneously seen by many people is a construction, so the one thing seen at different times by the same or different people must be a construction, being in fact nothing but a certain grouping of certain "sensibilia."

We have seen that the momentary state of a "thing" is an assemblage of "sensibilia," in different perspectives, not all simultaneous in the one constructed time, but spreading out from "the place where the thing is" with velocities depending upon the nature of the "sensibilia." The time *at* which the "thing" is in this state is the lower limit of the times at which these appearances occur. We have now to consider what leads us to speak of another set of appearances as belonging to the same "thing" at a different time.

For this purpose, we may, at least to begin with, confine ourselves within a single biography. If we can always say when two "sensibilia" in a given biography are appearances of one thing, then, since we have seen how to connect "sensibilia" in different biographies as appearances of the same momentary state of a thing, we shall have all that is necessary for the complete construction of the history of a thing.

It is to be observed, to begin with, that the identity of a thing for common sense is not always correlated with the identity of matter for physics. A human body is one persisting thing for common sense, but for physics its matter is constantly changing. We may say, broadly, that the common-sense conception is based upon continuity in appearances at the ordinary distances of sense-data, while the physical conception is based upon the continuity of appearances at very small distances from the thing. It is probable that the common-sense conception is not capable of complete precision. Let us therefore concentrate our attention upon the conception of the persistence of matter in physics.

The first characteristic of two appearances of the same piece of matter at different times is *continuity*. The two appearances must be connected by a series of intermediaries, which, if time and space form compact series, must themselves form a compact series. The colour of the leaves is different in autumn from what it is in summer; but we believe that the change occurs gradually, and that, if the colours are different at two given times, there are intermediate times at which the colours are intermediate between those at the given times.

But there are two considerations that are important as regards continuity.

First, it is largely hypothetical. We do not observe any one thing continuously, and it is merely a hypothesis to assume that, while we are not observing it, it passes through conditions intermediate between those in which it is perceived. During uninterrupted observation, it is true, continuity is nearly verified, but even here, when motions are very rapid, as in the case of explosions, the continuity is not actually capable of direct verification. Thus we can only say that the sense-data are found to *permit* a hypothetical complement of "sensibilia" such as will preserve continuity, and that therefore there *may* be such a complement. Since, however, we have already made such use of hypothetical "sensibilia," we will let this point pass, and admit such "sensibilia," as are required to preserve continuity.

Secondly, continuity is not a sufficient criterion of material identity. It is true that in many cases, such as rocks, mountains, tables, chairs, etc., where the appearances change slowly, continuity is sufficient, but in other cases, such as the parts of an approximately homogeneous fluid, it fails us utterly. We can travel by sensibly continuous gradations from any one drop of the sea at any one time to any other drop at any other time. We infer the motions of sea-water from the effects of the current, but they cannot be inferred from direct sensible observation together with the assumption of continuity.

The characteristic required in addition to continuity is conformity with the laws of dynamics. Starting from what common sense regards as persistent things, and making only such modifications as from time to time seem reasonable, we arrive at assemblages of "sensibilia" which are found to obey certain simple laws, namely those of dynamics. By regarding "sensibilia" at different times as belonging to the same piece of matter, we are able to define *motion,* which presupposes the assumption or construction of something persisting throughout the time of the motion. The motions which are regarded as occurring, during a period in which all the "sensibilia" and the times of their appearance are given, will be different according to the manner in which we combine "sensibilia" at different times as belonging to the same piece of matter. Thus even when the whole history of the world is given in every particular, the question what motions take place is still to a certain extent arbitrary even after the assumption of continuity. Experience shows that it is possible to determine motions in such a way as to satisfy the laws of dynamics, and that this determination, roughly and on the whole, is fairly in agreement with the common-sense opinions about persistent things. This determination, therefore, is adopted, and leads to a criterion by which we can determine, sometimes practically, sometimes only theoretically, whether two appearances at different times are to be regarded as belonging to the same piece of matter. The persistence of all matter throughout all time can, I imagine, be secured by definition.

To recommend this conclusion, we must consider what it is that is proved by the empirical success of physics. What is proved is that its hypotheses, though unverifiable where they go beyond sense-data, are at no point in contradiction with sense-data, but, on the contrary, are ideally such as to render all sense-data calculable when a sufficient collection of "sensibilia" is given. Now physics has found it empirically possible to collect sense-data into series, each series being regarded as belonging to one "thing" and behaving, with regard to the laws of physics, in a way in which series not belonging to one thing would in general not behave. If it is to be unambiguous whether two appearances belong to the same thing or not, there must be only one way of grouping appearances so that the resulting things obey the laws of physics. It would be very difficult to prove that this is the case, but for our present purposes we may let this point pass, and assume that there is only one way. Thus we may lay down the following definition: *Physical things are those series of appearances whose matter obeys the laws of physics.* That such series exist is an empirical fact, which constitutes the verifiability of physics.

XII. ILLUSIONS, HALLUCINATIONS, AND DREAMS

It remains to ask how, in our system, we are to find a place for sense-data which apparently fail to have the usual connection with the world of physics. Such sense-data are of various kinds, requiring somewhat different treatment. But all are of the sort that would be called "unreal," and therefore, before embarking upon the discussion, certain logical remarks must be made upon the conceptions of reality and unreality. . . .

1. The belief that dream-objects are not given comes, I think, from failure to distinguish, as regards waking life, between the sense-datum and the corresponding "thing." In dreams, there is no such corresponding "thing" as the dreamer supposes; if, therefore, the "thing" were given in waking life, as *e.g.* Meinong maintains, then there would be a difference in respect of givenness between dreams and waking life. But if, as we have maintained, what is given is never the thing, but merely one of the "sensibilia" which compose the thing, then what we apprehend in a dream is just as much given as what we apprehend in waking life.

Exactly the same argument applies as to the dream-objects being "there." They have their position in the private space of the perspective of the dreamer; where they fail is in their correlation with other private spaces and therefore with perspective space. But in the only sense in which "there" can be a datum, they are "there" just as truly as any of the sense-data of waking life.

2. The conception of "illusion" or "unreality," and the correlative conception of "reality," are generally used in a way which embodies profound logical confusions. Words that go in pairs, such as "real" and "unreal," "existent" and "non-existent," "valid" and "invalid," etc., are all derived from the one fundamental pair, "true" and "false." Now "true" and "false" are applicable only—except in derivative significations—to *propositions.* Thus wherever the above pairs can be significantly applied, we must be dealing either with propositions or with such incomplete phrases as only acquire meaning when put into a context which, with them, forms a proposition. Thus such pairs of words can be applied to *descriptions,* but not to proper names: in other words, they have no application whatever to data, but only to entities or non-entities described in terms of data.

Let us illustrate by the terms "existence" and "non-existence." Given any datum *x,* it is meaningless either to assert or to deny that *x* "exists." We might be tempted to say: "Of course *x* exists, for otherwise it could not be a datum." But such a statement is really meaningless, although it is significant and true to say "My present sense-datum exists," and it may also be true that "*x* is my present sense-datum." The inference from these two propositions to "*x* exists" is one which seems irresistible to people unaccustomed to logic; yet the apparent proposition inferred is not merely false, but strictly meaningless. To say "My present sense-datum exists" is to say (roughly): "There is an object of which 'my present sense-datum' is a description." But we cannot say: "There is an object of which '*x*' is a description," because '*x*' is (in the case we are supposing) a name, not a description. Dr. Whitehead and I have explained this point fully elsewhere with the help of symbols, without which it is hard to understand; I shall not therefore here repeat the demonstration of the above propositions, but shall proceed with their application to our present problem.

The fact that "existence" is only applicable to descriptions is concealed by the use of what are grammatically proper names in a way which really transforms them into descriptions. It is, for example, a legitimate question whether Homer existed; but here "Homer" means "the author of the Homeric poems," and is a description. Similarly we may ask whether God exists; but then "God" means "the Supreme Being" or "the *ens realissimum*" or whatever other description we may prefer. If "God" were a proper name, God would have to be a datum; and then no question could arise as to His existence. The distinction between existence and other predicates, which Kant obscurely felt, is brought to light by the theory of descriptions, and is seen to remove "existence" altogether from the fundamental notions of metaphysics.

What has been said about "existence" applies equally to "reality," which may, in fact, be taken as synonymous with "existence." Concerning the immediate objects in illusions, hallucinations, and dreams, it is meaningless to ask whether they "exist" or are "real." There they are, and that ends the matter. But we may legitimately inquire as to the existence or reality of "things" or other "sensibilia" inferred from such objects. It is the unreality of these "things" and other "sensibilia," together with a failure to notice that they are not data, which has led to the view that the objects of dreams are unreal.

We may now apply these considerations in detail to the stock arguments against realism, though what is to be said will be mainly a repetition of what others have said before.

1. We have first the variety of normal appearances, supposed to be incompatible. This is the case of the different shapes and colours which a given thing presents to different spectators. Locke's water which seems both hot and cold belongs to this class of cases. Our system of different perspectives fully accounts for these cases, and shows that they afford no argument against realism.

2. We have cases where the correlation between different senses is unusual. The bent stick in water belongs here. People say it looks bent but is straight: this only means that it is straight to the touch, though bent to sight. There is no "illusion," but only a false inference, if we think that the stick would feel bent to the touch. The stick would look just as bent in a photograph, and, . . . "the photograph cannot lie." The case of seeing double also belongs here, though in this case the cause of the unusual correlation is physiological, and would therefore not operate in a photograph. It is a mistake to ask whether the "thing" is duplicated when we see it double. The "thing" is a whole system of "sensibilia," and it is only those visual "sensibilia" which are data to the percipient that are duplicated. The phenomenon has a purely physiological explanation; indeed, in view of our having two eyes, it is in less need of explanation than the single visual sense-datum which we normally obtain from the things on which we focus.

3. We come now to cases like dreams, which may, at the moment of dreaming, contain nothing to arouse suspicion, but are condemned on the ground of their supposed incompatibility with earlier and later data. Of course it often happens that dream-objects fail to behave in the accustomed manner: heavy objects fly, solid objects melt, babies turn into pigs or undergo even greater changes. But none of these unusual occurrences *need* happen

in a dream, and it is not on account of such occurrences that dream-objects are called "unreal." It is their lack of continuity with the dreamer's past and future that makes him, when he wakes, condemn them; and it is their lack of correlation with other private worlds that makes others condemn them. Omitting the latter ground, our reason for condemning them is that the "things" which we infer from them cannot be combined according to the laws of physics with the "things" inferred from waking sense-data. This might be used to condemn the "things" inferred from the data of dreams. Dream-data are no doubt appearances of "things," but not of such "things" as the dreamer supposes. I have no wish to combat psychological theories of dreams, such as those of the psycho-analysts. But there certainly are cases where (whatever psychological causes may contribute) the presence of physical causes also is very evident. For instance, a door banging may produce a dream of a naval engagement, with images of battleships and sea and smoke. The whole dream will be an appearance of the door banging, but owing to the peculiar condition of the body (especially the brain) during sleep, this appearance is not that expected to be produced by a door banging, and thus the dreamer is led to entertain false beliefs. But his sense-data are still physical, and are such as a completed physics would include and calculate.

4. The last class of illusions are those which cannot be discovered within one person's experience, except through the discovery of discrepancies with the experiences of others. Dreams might conceivably belong to this class, if they were jointed sufficiently neatly into waking life; but the chief instances are recurrent sensory hallucinations of the kind that lead to insanity. What makes the patient, in such cases, become what others call insane is the fact that, within his own experience, there is nothing to show that the hallucinatory sense-data do not have the usual kind of connection with "sensibilia" in other perspectives. Of course he may learn this through testimony, but he probably finds it simpler to suppose that the testimony is untrue and that he is being wilfully deceived. There is, so far as I can see, no theoretical criterion by which the patient can decide, in such a case, between the two equally satisfactory hypotheses of his madness and of his friends' mendacity.

From the above instances it would appear that abnormal sense-data, of the kind which we regard as deceptive, have intrinsically just the same status as any others, but differ as regards their correlations or causal connections with other "sensibilia" and with "things." Since the usual correlations and connections become part of our unreflective expectations, and even seem, except to the psychologist, to form part of our data, it comes to be thought, mistakenly, that in such cases the data are unreal, whereas they are merely the causes of false inferences. The fact that correlations and connections of unusual kinds occur adds to the difficulty of inferring things from sense and of expressing physics in terms of sense-data. But the unusualness would seem to be always physically or physiologically explicable, and therefore raises only a complication, not a philosophical objection.

I conclude, therefore, that no valid objection exists to the view which regards sense-data as part of the actual substance of the physical world, and that, on the other hand, this view is the only one which accounts for the empirical verifiability of physics. In the present paper, I have given only a rough preliminary sketch. In particular, the part played by *time* in the construction of the physical world is, I think, more fundamental than would appear from the above account. I should hope that, with further elaboration, the part played by unperceived "sensibilia" could be indefinitely diminished, probably by invoking the history of a "thing" to eke out the inferences derivable from its momentary appearance.

THE VALUE OF PHILOSOPHY

Having now come to the end of our brief and very incomplete review of the problems of philosophy, it will be well to consider, in conclusion, what is the value of philosophy and why it ought to be studied. It is the more necessary to consider this question, in view of the fact that many men, under the influence of science or of practical affairs, are inclined to doubt whether philosophy is anything better than innocent but useless trifling, hair-splitting distinctions, and controversies on matters concerning which knowledge is impossible.

This view of philosophy appears to result, partly from a wrong conception of the ends of life, partly from a wrong conception of the kind of goods which philosophy strives to achieve. Physical science, through the medium of inventions, is useful to innumerable people who are wholly ignorant of it; thus the study of physical science is to be recommended, not only, or primarily, because of the effect on the student, but rather because of the effect on mankind in general. Thus utility does not belong to philosophy. If the study of philosophy has any value at all for others than students of philosophy, it must be only indirectly, through its effects upon the lives of those who study it. It is in these effects, therefore, if anywhere, that the value of philosophy must be primarily sought.

But further, if we are not to fail in our endeavour to determine the value of philosophy, we must first free our minds from the prejudices of what are wrongly called "practical" men. The "practical" man, as this word is often used, is one who recognizes only material needs, who realizes that men must have food for the body, but is oblivious of the necessity of providing food for the mind. If all men were well off, if poverty and disease had been reduced to their lowest possible point, there would still remain much to be done to produce a valuable society; and even in the existing world the goods of the mind are at least as important as the goods of the body. It is exclusively among the goods of the mind that the value of philosophy is to be found; and only those who are not indifferent to these goods can be persuaded that the study of philosophy is not a waste of time.

Philosophy, like all other studies, aims primarily at knowledge. The knowledge it aims at is the kind of knowledge which gives unity and system to the body of the sciences, and the kind which results from a critical examination on the grounds of our convictions, prejudices, and beliefs. But it cannot be maintained that philosophy has had any very great measure of success in its attempts to provide definite answers to its questions. If you ask a mathematician, a mineralogist, a historian, or any other man of learning, what definite body of truths has been ascertained by his science, his answer will last as long as you are willing to listen. But if you put the same question to a philosopher, he will, if he is candid, have to confess that his study has not achieved positive results such as have been achieved by other sciences. It is true that this is partly accounted for by the fact that, as soon as definite knowledge concerning any subject becomes possible, this subject ceases to be called phi-

From Bertrand Russell, *The Problems of Philosophy,* 1912.

losophy, and becomes a separate science. The whole study of the heavens, which now belongs to astronomy, was once included in philosophy; Newton's great work was called "the mathematical principles of natural philosophy." Similarly, the study of the human mind, which was a part of philosophy, has now been separated from philosophy and has become the science of psychology. Thus, to a great extent, the uncertainty of philosophy is more apparent than real: those questions which are already capable of definite answers are placed in the sciences, while those only to which, at present, no definite answer can be given, remain to form the residue which is called philosophy.

This is, however, only a part of the truth concerning the uncertainty of philosophy. There are many questions—and among them those that are of the profoundest interest to our spiritual life—which, so far as we can see, must remain insoluble to the human intellect unless its powers become of quite a different order from what they are now. Has the universe any unity of plan or purpose, or is it a fortuitous concourse of atoms? Is consciousness a permanent part of the universe, giving hope of indefinite growth in wisdom, or is it a transitory accident on a small planet on which life must ultimately become impossible? Are good and evil of importance to the universe or only to man? Such questions are asked by philosophy, and variously answered by various philosophers. But it would seem that, whether answers be otherwise discoverable or not, the answers suggested by philosophy are none of them demonstrably true. Yet, however slight may be the hope of discovering an answer, it is part of the business of philosophy to continue the consideration of such questions, to make us aware of their importance, to examine all the approaches to them, and to keep alive that speculative interest in the universe which is apt to be killed by confining ourselves to definitely ascertainable knowledge.

Many philosophers, it is true, have held that philosophy could establish the truth of certain answers to such fundamental questions. They have supposed that what is of most importance in religious beliefs could be proved by strict demonstration to be true. In order to judge of such attempts, it is necessary to take a survey of human knowledge, and to form an opinion as to its methods and its limitations. On such a subject it would be unwise to pronounce dogmatically; but if the investigations of our previous chapters have not led us astray, we shall be compelled to renounce the hope of finding philosophical proofs of religious beliefs. We cannot, therefore, include as part of the value of philosophy any definite set of answers to such questions. Hence, once more, the value of philosophy must not depend upon any supposed body of definitely ascertainable knowledge to be acquired by those who study it.

The value of philosophy is, in fact, to be sought largely in its very uncertainty. The man who has no tincture of philosophy goes through life imprisoned in the prejudices derived from common sense, from the habitual beliefs of his age or his nation, and from convictions which have grown up in his mind without the co-operation or consent of his deliberate reason. To such a man the world tends to become definite, finite, obvious; common objects rouse no questions, and unfamiliar possibilities are contemptuously rejected. As soon as we begin to philosophize, on the contrary, we find, as we saw in our opening chapters, that even the most everyday things lead to problems to which only very incomplete answers can be given. Philosophy, though unable to tell us with certainty what is the true answer to the doubts which it raises, is able to suggest many possibilities which enlarge our thoughts and free them from the tyranny of custom. Thus, while diminishing our feeling of certainty as to what things are, it greatly increases our knowledge as to what they may be; it removes the somewhat arrogant dogmatism of those who have never travelled into the region of liberating doubt, and it keeps alive our sense of wonder by showing familiar things in an unfamiliar aspect.

Apart from its utility in showing unsuspected possibilities, philosophy has a value—perhaps its chief value—through the greatness of the objects which it contemplates, and the freedom from narrow and personal aims resulting from this contemplation. The life of the instinctive man is shut up within the circle of his private interests: family and friends may be included, but the outer world is not regarded except as it may help or hinder what comes within the circle of instinctive wishes. In such a life there is something feverish and confined, in comparison with which the philosophic life is calm and free. The private world of instinctive interests is a small one, set in the midst of a great and powerful world which must, sooner or later, lay our private world in ruins. Unless we can so enlarge our interests as to include the whole outer world, we remain like a garrison in a beleaguered fortress, knowing that the enemy prevents escape and that ultimate surrender is inevitable. In such a life there is no peace, but a constant strife between the insistence of desire and the powerlessness of will. In one way or another, if our life is to be great and free, we must escape this prison and this strife.

One way of escape is by philosophic contemplation. Philosophic contemplation does not, in its widest survey, divide the universe into two hostile camps—friends and foes, helpful and hostile, good and bad—it views the whole impartially. Philosophic contemplation, when it is unalloyed, does not aim at proving that the rest of the universe is akin to man. All acquisition of knowledge is an enlargement of the Self, but this enlargement is best attained when it is not directly sought. It is obtained when the desire for knowledge is alone operative, by a study which does not wish in advance that its objects should have this or that character, but adapts the Self to the characters which it finds in its objects. This enlargement of Self is not obtained when, taking the Self as it is, we try to show that the world is so similar to this Self that knowledge of it is possible without any admission of what seems alien. The desire to prove this is a form of self-assertion and, like all self-assertion, it is an obstacle to the growth of Self which it desires, and of which the Self knows that it is capable. Self-assertion, in philosophic speculation as elsewhere, views the world as a means to its own ends; thus it makes the world of less account than Self, and the Self sets bounds to the greatness of its goods. In contemplation, on the contrary, we start from the non-Self, and through its greatness the boundaries of Self are enlarged; through the infinity of the universe the mind which contemplates it achieves some share in infinity.

For this reason greatness of soul is not fostered by those philosophies which assimilate the universe to Man. Knowledge is a form of union of Self and not-Self; like all union, it is impaired by dominion, and therefore by any attempt to force the universe into conformity with what we find in ourselves. There is a widespread philosophical tendency towards the view which tells us that Man is the measure of all things, that truth is man-made, that space and time and the world of universals are properties of the mind, and that, if there be anything not created by the mind, it is unknowable and of no account for us. This view, if our previous discussions were correct, is untrue; but in addition to being untrue, it has the effect of robbing philosophic contemplation of all that gives it value, since it fetters contemplation to Self. What it calls knowledge is not a union with the not-Self, but a set of prejudices, habits, and desires, making an impenetrable veil between us and the world beyond. The man who finds pleasure in such a theory of knowledge is like the man who never leaves the domestic circle for fear his word might not be law.

The true philosophic contemplation, on the contrary, finds its satisfaction in every enlargement of the not-Self, in everything that magnifies the objects contemplated, and thereby the subject contemplating. Everything, in contemplation, that is personal or private, everything that depends upon habit, self-interest, or desire, distorts the object, and hence impairs the union which the intellect seeks. By thus making a barrier between subject and object, such personal and private things become a prison to the intellect. The free intellect will see as God might see, without a *here* and *now,* without hopes and fears, without the trammels of customary beliefs and traditional prejudices, calmly, dispassionately, in the sole and exclusive desire of knowledge—knowledge as impersonal, as purely contemplative, as it is possible for man to attain. Hence also the free intellect will value more the abstract and universal knowledge into which the accidents of private history do not enter, than the knowledge brought by the senses, and dependent, as such knowledge must be, upon an exclusive and personal point of view and a body whose sense-organs distort as much as they reveal.

The mind which has become accustomed to the freedom and impartiality of philosophic contemplation will preserve something of the same freedom and impartiality in the world of action and emotion. It will view its purposes and desires as parts of the whole, with the absence of insistence that results from seeing them as infinitesimal fragments in a world of which all the rest is unaffected by any one man's deeds. The impartiality which, in contemplation, is the unalloyed desire for truth, is the very same quality of mind which, in action, is justice, and in emotion is that universal love which can be given to all, and not only to those who are judged useful or admirable. Thus contemplation enlarges not only the objects of our thoughts, but also the objects of our actions and our affections: it makes us citizens of the universe, not only of one walled city at war with all the rest. In this citizenship of the universe consists man's true freedom, and his liberation from the thraldom of narrow hopes and fears.

Thus, to sum up our discussion of the value of philosophy: Philosophy is to be studied, not for the sake of any definite answers to its questions, since no definite answers can, as a rule, be known to be true, but rather for the sake of the questions themselves; because these questions enlarge our conception of what is possible, enrich our intellectual imagination and diminish the dogmatic assurance which closes the mind against speculation; but above all because, through the greatness of the universe which philosophy contemplates, the mind also is rendered great, and becomes capable of that union with the universe which constitutes its highest good.

50

MOORE

1873–1958

Born and raised in London, the son of a doctor, George Edward Moore was educated first at Dulwich College and then at Trinity College, Cambridge, where in 1898 he was elected to a prize fellowship. His early work had an enormous influence on early-twentieth-century philosophy in Britain where he became an instrumental figure in the shift away from the Hegelianism and Kantianism dominant at the time. In 1951, one year before Russell, he was awarded the Order of Merit.

Moore and Russell met in the fall semester of 1892, in Cambridge. Their meeting has been called a "landmark" in the development of philosophy. Russell decided that Moore was a genius (as he would later decide about Wittgenstein) when he heard Moore read a paper in class that began "In the beginning was matter, and matter begat the devil, and the devil begat God. . . ." Russell wrote, "I was quickly attracted by the clarity and passion of his thinking, and by a kind of flame-like sincerity which roused in me deep admiration." Likewise, Moore claimed that Russell was the greatest philosopher he had ever known and had exerted the greatest influence on him.

Our selection, "The Refutation of Idealism" (1903), played a leading part in undermining Hegel's and Kant's influence on subsequent 20th century British philosophy. Moore argues for epistemological realism about the objects of empirical knowledge. For instance, introspection reveals that the color red is logically distinct from the awareness of red and, therefore, that the *being* of the color does not depend on the perception of it. Berkeley's famous dictum *"Esse* is *percipi"* is thus, according to Moore, nullified. Like Russell, Moore goes on to argue that sense-data—the objects of sensation—are fundamentally real, non-mental entities. But whereas Russell was adamantly against commonsense views of the world, calling them "religious myths" and "metaphysics of the Stone Age," the far more conservative Moore took the preservation of common sense to be the goal of his philosophy and eventually gave up metaphysics altogether.

THE REFUTATION OF IDEALISM

Modern Idealism, if it asserts any general conclusion about the universe at all, asserts that it is *spiritual*. There are two points about this assertion to which I wish to call attention. These points are that, whatever be its exact meaning, it is certainly meant to assert (1) that the universe is very different indeed from what it seems, and (2) that it has quite a large number of properties which it does not seem to have. Chairs and tables and mountains *seem* to be very different from us; but, when the whole universe is declared to be spiritual, it is certainly meant to assert that they are far more like us than we think. The idealist means to assert that they are *in some sense* neither lifeless nor unconscious, as they certainly seem to be; and I do not think his language is so grossly deceptive, but that we may assume him to believe that they really are very different indeed from what they seem. And secondly when he declares that they are *spiritual,* he means to include in that term quite a large number of different properties. When the whole universe is declared to be spiritual, it is meant not only that it is in some sense *conscious,* but that it has what we recognise in ourselves as the *higher* forms of consciousness. That it is intelligent; that it is purposeful; that it is not mechanical; all these different things are commonly asserted of it. In general, it may be said, this phrase 'reality is spiritual' excites and expresses the belief that the *whole* universe possesses *all the qualities* the possession of which is held to make us so superior to things which seem to be inanimate: at least, if it does not possess exactly those which we possess, it possesses not one only, but several others, which, by the same ethical standard, would be judged equal to or better than our own. When we say it is *spiritual* we mean to say that it has quite a number of excellent qualities, different from any which we commonly attribute either to stars or planets or to cups and saucers.

Now why I mention these two points is that when engaged in the intricacies of philosophic discussion, we are apt to overlook the vastness of the difference between this idealistic view and the ordinary view of the world, and to overlook the number of *different* propositions which the idealist must prove. It is, I think, owing to the vastness of this difference and owing to the number of different excellences which Idealists attribute to the universe, that it seems such an interesting and important question whether Idealism be true or not. But, when we begin to argue about it, I think we are apt to forget what a vast number of arguments this interesting question must involve: we are apt to assume, that if one or two points be made on either side, the whole case is won. I say this lest it should be thought that any of the arguments which will be advanced in this paper would be sufficient to disprove, or any refutation of them sufficient to prove, the truly interesting and important proposition that reality is spiritual. For my own part I wish it to be clearly understood that I do not suppose that anything I shall say has the smallest tendency to prove that reality is not spiritual: I do not believe it possible to refute a single one of the many important propositions contained in the assertion that it is so. Reality may be spiritual, for all I know;

From G. E. Moore, "The Refutation of Idealism," 1903.

and I devoutly hope it is. But I take "Idealism" to be a wide term and to include not only this interesting conclusion but a number of arguments which are supposed to be, if not sufficient, at least *necessary,* to prove it. Indeed I take it that modern Idealists are chiefly distinguished by certain arguments which they have in common. That reality is spiritual has, I believe, been the tenet of many theologians; and yet, for believing that alone, they should hardly be called Idealists. There are besides, I believe, many persons, not improperly called Idealists, who hold certain characteristic propositions, without venturing to think them quite sufficient to prove so grand a conclusion. It is, therefore, only with Idealistic *arguments* that I am concerned; and if any Idealist holds that *no* argument is necessary to prove that reality is spiritual, I shall certainly not have refuted him. I shall, however, attack at least one argument, which, to the best of my belief, is considered necessary to their position by *all* Idealists. And I wish to point out a certain advantage which this procedure gives me—an advantage which justifies the assertion that, if my arguments are sound, they will have refuted Idealism. If I can refute a single proposition which is a necessary and essential step in all Idealistic arguments, then, no matter how good the rest of these arguments may be, I shall have proved that Idealists have *no reason whatever* for their conclusion.

Suppose we have a chain of argument which takes the form: Since A is B, and B is C, and C is D, it follows A is D. In such an argument though "B is C" and "C is D" may both be perfectly true, yet if "A is B" be false, we have no more reason for asserting A is D than if all three were false. It does not, indeed, follow that A is D is false; nor does it follow that no other arguments would prove it to be true. But it does follow that, so far as this argument goes, it is the barest supposition, without the least bit of evidence. I propose to attack a proposition which seems to me to stand in this relation to the conclusion "Reality is spiritual." I do not propose to dispute that "Reality is spiritual"; I do not deny that there may be reasons for thinking that it is: but I do propose to show that one reason upon which, to the best of my judgment, all other arguments ever used by Idealists depend is *false.* These other arguments may, for all I shall say, be eminently ingenious and true; they are very many and various, and different Idealists use the most different arguments to prove the same most important conclusions. Some of these *may* be sufficient to prove that B is C and C is D; but if, as I shall try to show, their "A is B" is false the conclusion A is D remains a pleasant supposition. I do not deny that to suggest pleasant and plausible suppositions may be the proper function of philosophy: but I am assuming that the name Idealism can only be properly applied where there is a certain amount of argument, intended to be cogent.

The subject of this paper is, therefore, quite uninteresting. Even if I prove my point, I shall have proved nothing about the Universe in general. Upon the important question whether Reality is or is not spiritual my argument will not have the remotest bearing. I shall only attempt to arrive at the truth about a matter, which is in itself quite trivial and insignificant, and from which, so far as I can see and certainly so far as I shall say, no conclusions can be drawn about any of the subjects about which we most want to know. The only importance I can claim for the subject I shall investigate is that it seems to me to be a matter upon which not Idealists only, but all philosophers and psychologists also, have been in error, and from their erroneous view of which they have inferred (validly or invalidly) their most striking and interesting conclusions. And that it has even this importance I cannot hope to prove. If it has this importance, it will indeed follow that all the most striking results of philosophy—Sensationalism, Agnosticism and Idealism alike—have, for all that has hitherto been urged in their favour, no more foundation than the supposition that a chimera lives in the moon. It will follow that, unless new reasons never urged hitherto can be found, all the most important philosophic doctrines have as little claim to assent as the most superstitious beliefs of the lowest savages. Upon the question what we have *reason* to believe in the most interesting matters, I do therefore think that my results will have an important bearing; but I cannot too clearly insist that upon the question whether these beliefs are true they will have none whatever.

The trivial proposition which I propose to dispute is this: that *esse* is *percipi*. This is a very ambiguous proposition, but, in some sense or other, it has been very widely held. That it is, in some sense, essential to Idealism, I must for the present merely assume. What I propose to show is that, in all the senses ever given to it, it is false.

But, first of all, it may be useful to point out briefly in what relation I conceive it to stand to Idealistic arguments. That wherever you can truly predicate *esse* you can truly predicate *percipi*, in some sense or other, is, I take it, a necessary step in all arguments, properly to be called Idealistic, and, what is more, in all arguments hitherto offered for the Idealistic conclusion. If *esse* is *percipi*, this is at once equivalent to saying that whatever is, is experienced; and this, again, is equivalent, in a sense, to saying that whatever is, is something mental. But this is not the sense in which the Idealist *conclusion* must maintain that Reality is *mental*. The Idealist *conclusion* is that *esse* is *percipere;* and hence, whether *esse* be *percipi* or not, a further and different discussion is needed to show whether or not it is also *percipere*. And again, even if *esse* be *percipere,* we need a vast quantity of further argument to show that what has *esse* has also those higher mental qualities which are denoted by spiritual. This is why I said that *the* question I should discuss, namely, whether or not *esse* is *percipi*, must be utterly insufficient either to prove or to disprove that reality is spiritual. But, on the other hand, I believe that every argument ever used to show that reality is spiritual has inferred this (validly or invalidly) from "*esse* is *percipere*" as one of its premises; and that this again has never been pretended to be proved except by use of the premiss that *esse* is *percipi*. The type of argument used for the latter purpose is familiar enough. It is said that since whatever is, is experienced, and since some things are which are not experienced by the individual, these must at least form part of some experience. Or again that, since an object necessarily implies a subject, and since the whole world must be an object, we must conceive it to belong to some subject or subjects, in the same sense in which whatever is the object of our experience belongs to us. Or again, that, since thought enters into the essence of all reality, we must conceive behind it, in it, or as its essence, a spirit akin to ours, who think: that "spirit greets spirit" in its object. Into the validity of these inferences I do not propose to enter: they obviously require a great deal of discussion. I only desire to point out that, however correct they may be, yet if *esse* is not *percipi*, they leave us as far from a proof that reality is spiritual, as if they were all false too.

But now: Is *esse percipi?* There are three very ambiguous terms in this proposition, and I must begin by distinguishing the different things that may be meant by some of them.

And first with regard to *percipi*. This term need not trouble us long at present. It was, perhaps, originally used to mean "sensation" only; but I am not going to be so unfair to modern Idealists—the only Idealists to whom the term should now be applied without qualification—as to hold that, if they say *esse* is *percipi*, they mean by *percipi* sensation only. On the contrary I quite agree with them that, if *esse* be *percipi* at all, *percipi* must be understood to include not sensation only, but that other type of mental fact, which is called "thought"; and, whether *esse* be *percipi* or not, I consider it to be the main service of the philosophic school, to which modern Idealists belong, that they have insisted on distinguishing "sensation" and "thought" and on emphasising the importance of the latter. Against Sensationalism and Empiricism they have maintained the true view. But the distinction between sensation and thought need not detain us here. For, in whatever respects they differ, they have at least this in common, that they are both forms of consciousness or, to use a term that seems to be more in fashion just now, they are both ways of experiencing. Accordingly, whatever *esse* is *percipi* may mean, it does *at least* assert that whatever it is, is *experienced.* And since what I wish to maintain is, that even this is untrue, the question whether it be experienced by way of sensation or thought or both is for my purpose quite irrelevant. If it be not experienced at all, it cannot be either an object of thought or an object of sense. It is only if being involves "experience" that the question, whether it involves sensation or thought or both, becomes important. I beg, therefore, that *percipi* may be understood, in what follows, to refer merely to what is *common* to sensation and thought. A very recent article states the meaning of *esse* is *percipi* with all desirable clearness in so far as *percipi* is concerned. "I will undertake to show," says Mr. Taylor, "that what makes [any piece of fact] real can be nothing but its presence as an inseparable aspect of *a sentient experience.*" I am glad to think that Mr. Taylor has been in time to supply me with so definite a statement that this is the ultimate premiss of Idealism. My paper will at least refute Mr. Taylor's Idealism, if it refutes anything at all: for I *shall* undertake to show that what makes a thing real cannot possibly be its presence as an inseparable aspect of a sentient experience.

But Mr. Taylor's statement though clear, I think, with regard to the meaning of *percipi* is highly ambiguous in other respects. I will leave it for the present to consider the next ambiguity in the statement: *Esse* is *percipi.* What does the copula mean? What can be meant by saying that Esse *is* percipi? There are just three meanings, one or other of which such a statement *must* have, if it is to be true; and of these there is only one which it can have, if it is to be important. (1) The statement may be meant to assert that the word "esse" is used to signify nothing either more or less than the word "percipi": that the two words are precise synonyms: that they are merely different names for one and the same thing: that what is meant by *esse* is absolutely identical with what is meant by *percipi.* I think I need not prove that the principle *esse* is *percipi* is *not* thus intended merely to define a word; nor yet that, if it were, it would be extremely bad definition. But if it does *not* mean this, only two alternatives remain. The second is (2) that what is meant by *esse,* though not absolutely identical with what is meant by *percipi,* yet *includes* the latter as a *part* of its meaning. If this were the meaning of "esse is percipi," then to say that a thing was real would not be the same thing as to say that it was experienced. That it was *real* would mean that it was experienced and *something else besides:* "being experienced" would be *analytically essential* to reality, but would not be the whole meaning of the term. From the fact that a thing was real we should be able to infer, by the law of contradiction, that it was experienced; since the latter would be *part* of what is meant by the former. But, on the other hand, from the fact a thing was experienced we should *not* be able to infer that it was real; since it would not follow from the fact that it had one of the attributes essential to reality, that it *also* had the other or others. Now, if we understand *esse* is *percipi* in this second sense, we must distinguish *three* different things which it asserts. First of all, it gives a definition of the word "reality," asserting that word stands for a complex whole, of which what is meant by "percipi" forms a part. And secondly it asserts that "being experienced" forms a part of a certain whole. Both these propositions may be true, and at all events I do not wish to dispute them. I do not, indeed, think that the word "reality" is commonly used to include "percipi": but I do not wish to argue about the meaning of words. and that many things which are experienced are also something else—that to be experienced forms part of certain wholes, is, of course, indisputable. But what I wish to point out is, that neither of these propositions is of any importance, unless we add to them a *third.* That "real" is a convenient name for a union of attributes which *sometimes* occurs, it could not be worth any one's while to assert: no inferences of any importance could be drawn from such an assertion. Our principle could only mean that when a thing happens to have *percipi* as well as the other qualities included under *esse,* it has *percipi:* and we should never be able to *infer* that it was experienced, except from a proposition which already asserted that it was both experienced and something else. Accordingly, if the assertion that *percipi* forms part of the whole meant by reality is to have any importance, it must mean that the whole is organic, at least in this sense, that the other constituent or constituents of it *cannot* occur without percipi, even if percipi can occur without them. Let us call these other constituents *x.* The proposition that *esse* includes *percipi,* and that therefore from *esse percipi* can be inferred, can only be important if it is meant to assert that *percipi* can be inferred from *x.* The only importance of the question whether the whole *esse* includes the part *percipi* rests therefore on the question whether the part *x* is necessarily connected with the part *percipi.* And this is (3) the third possible meaning of the assertion *esse* is *percipi:* and, as we now see, the only important one. *Esse* is *percipi* asserts that wherever you have *x* you also have *percipi* that whatever has the property *x* also has the property that is *experienced.* And this being so, it will be convenient if, for the future, I may be allowed to use the term *"esse"* to denote *x alone.* I do not wish thereby to beg the question whether what we commonly mean by the word "real" does or does not include *percipi* as well as *x.* I am quite content that my definition of *"esse"* to denote *x,* should be regarded merely as an arbitrary verbal definition. Whether it is so or not, the only question of interest is whether from *x percipi* can be inferred, and I should prefer to be able to express this in the form: can *percipi* be inferred from *esse?* Only let it be understood that when I say *esse,* that term will not for the future *include percipi:* it denotes only that *x,* which Idealists, perhaps rightly include *along with percipi* under *their* term *esse.* That there is such an *x* they must admit on pain of making the proposition an *absolute* tautology; and that from this *x percipi* can be inferred they must admit, on pain of making it a perfectly barren analytic proposition. Whether *x* alone should or should not be called *esse* is not worth a dispute: what is worth dispute is whether *percipi* is necessarily connected with *x.*

We have therefore discovered the ambiguity of the copula in *esse* is *percipi,* so far as to see that this principle asserts two distinct terms to be so related, that whatever has the *one,* which I call *esse,* has *also* the property that it is experienced. It asserts a necessary connection between *esse* on the one hand and *percipi* on the other; these two words denoting each a distinct term, and *esse* denoting a term in which that denoted by *percipi* is not included. We have, then in *esse* is *percipi,* a *necessary synthetic* proposition which I have undertaken to refute. And I may say at once that, understood as such, it cannot be refuted. If the Idealist chooses to assert that it is merely a self-evident truth, I have only to say that it does not appear to me to be so. But I believe that no Idealist ever has maintained it to be so. Although this—that two distinct terms are necessary related—is the only sense which "esse is percipi" can have if it is to be true and important, it *can* have another sense, if it is to be an important falsehood. I believe that Idealists all hold this important falsehood. They do not perceive that *Esse* is *percipi* must, if true, be *merely* a self-evident synthetic truth; they either identify with it or give as a reason for it another proposition which must be false because it is self-contradictory. Unless they did so, they would have to admit that it was a perfectly unfounded assumption; and if they recognised that it was *unfounded,* I do not think they would maintain its truth to be evident. *Esse* is *percipi,* in the sense I have found for it, *may* indeed be true; I cannot refute it: but if this sense were clearly apprehended, no one, I think, would *believe* that it was true.

Idealists, we have seen, must assert that whatever is experienced, is *necessarily* so. And this doctrine they commonly express by saying that "the object of experience is inconceivable apart from the subject." I have hitherto been concerned with pointing out what meaning this assertion must have, if it is to be an important truth. I now propose to show that it may have an important meaning, which must be false, because it is self-contradictory.

It is a well-known fact in the history of philosophy that *necessary* truths in general, but especially those of which it is said that the opposite is inconceivable, have been commonly supposed to be *analytic,* in the sense that the proposition denying them was self-contradictory. It was in this way, commonly supposed, before Kant, that many truths could be proved by the law of contradiction alone. This is, therefore, a mistake which it is plainly easy for the best philosophers to make. Even since Kant many have continued to assert it; but I am aware that among those Idealists, who most properly deserve the name, it has become more fashionable to assert that truths are *both* analytic and synthetic. Now with many of their reasons for asserting this I am not concerned; it is possible that in some connections the assertion may bear a useful and true sense. But if we understand "analytic" in the sense just defined, namely, what is proved by the law of contradiction *alone,* it is plain that, if "synthetic" means what is *not* proved by this alone, no truth can be both analytic and synthetic. Now it seems to me that those who do maintain truths to be both, do nevertheless maintain that they are so in this as well as in other senses. It is, indeed, extremely unlikely that so essential a part of the historical meaning of "analytic" and "synthetic" should have been entirely discarded, especially since we find no express recognition that it is discarded. In that case it is fair to suppose that modern Idealists have been influenced by the view that certain truths can be proved by the law of contradiction alone. I admit they also expressly declare that they can *not:* but this is by no means sufficient to prove that they do not also think they are; since it is very easy to hold two mutually contradictory opinions. What I suggest then is that Idealists hold the particular doctrine in question, concerning the relation of subject and object in experience, because they think it is an analytic truth in this restricted sense that it is proved by the law of contradiction alone.

I am suggesting that the Idealist maintains that object and subject are necessarily connected, mainly because he fails to see that they are *distinct,* that they are *two,* at all. When he thinks of "yellow" and when he thinks of the "sensation of yellow," he fails to see that there is anything whatever in the latter which is not in the former. This being so, to deny that yellow can ever *be* apart from the sensation of yellow is merely to deny that yellow can ever be other than it is; since yellow and sensation of yellow are absolutely identical. To assert that yellow is necessarily an object of experience is to assert that yellow is necessarily yellow—a purely identical proposition, and therefore proved by the law of contradiction alone. Of course, the proposition also implies that experience is, after all, something distinct from yellow—else there would be no reason for insisting that yellow is a sensation: and that the argument thus both affirms and denies that yellow and sensation of yellow are distinct, is what sufficiently refutes it. But this contradiction can easily be overlooked, because though we are convinced, in other connections, that "experience" does mean something and something most important, yet we are never distinctly aware *what* it means, and thus in every particular case we do not notice its presence. The facts present themselves as a kind of antinomy: (1) Experience *is* something unique and different from anything else; (2) Experience of green is entirely indistinguishable from green; two propositions which cannot both be true. Idealists, holding both, can only take refuge in arguing from the one in some connections and from the other in others.

But I am well aware that there are many idealists who would repel it as an utterly unfounded charge that they fail to distinguish between a sensation or idea and what I will call its object. And there are, I admit, many who not only imply, as we all do, that green is distinct from the sensation of green, but expressly insist upon the distinction as an important part of their system. They would perhaps only assert that the two form an inseparable unity. But I wish to point out that many, who use this phrase, and who do admit the distinction, are not thereby absolved from the charge that they deny it. For there is a certain doctrine, very prevalent among philosophers nowadays, which by a very simple reduction may be seen to assert that two distinct things both are and are not distinct. A distinction is asserted; but it is *also* asserted that the things distinguished form an "organic unity." But, forming such a unity, it is held, each would not be what it is *apart from its relation to the other*. Hence to consider either by itself is to make an *illegitimate abstraction*. The recognition that there are "organic unities" and "illegitimate abstractions" in this sense is regarded as one of the chief conquests of modern philosophy. But what is the sense attached to these terms? An abstraction is illegitimate, when and only when we attempt to assert of *a part*— of something abstracted—that which is true only of the *whole* to which it belongs: and it may perhaps be useful to point out that this should not be done. But the application actually made of this principle, and what perhaps would be expressly acknowledged as its meaning, is something much the reverse of useful. The principle is used to assert that certain abstractions are *in all cases* illegitimate; that whenever you try to assert *anything whatever* of that which is *part* of an organic whole, what you assert can only be true of the whole. And this principle, so far from being a useful truth, is necessarily false. For if the whole can, nay *must*, be substituted for the part in all propositions and for all purposes, this can only be because the whole is absolutely identical with the part. When, therefore, we are told that green and the sensation of green are certainly distinct but yet are not separable, or that it is an illegitimate abstraction to consider the one apart from the other, what these provisos are used to assert is, that though the two things are distinct yet you not only can but must treat them as if they were not. Many philosophers, therefore, when they admit a distinction, yet (following the lead of Hegel) boldly assert their right, in a slightly more obscure form of words, *also* to deny it. The principle of organic unities, like that of combined analysis and synthesis, is mainly used to defend the practice of holding *both* of two contradictory propositions, wherever this may seem convenient. In this, as in other matters, Hegel's main service to philosophy has consisted in giving a name to and erecting into a principle, a type of fallacy to which experience had shown philosophers, along with the rest of mankind, to be addicted. No wonder that he has followers and admirers.

I have shown then, so far, that when the Idealist asserts the important principle "*Esse* is *percipi*" he must, if it is to be true, mean by this that: Whatever is experienced also *must* be experienced. And I have also shown that he *may* identify with, or give as a reason for, this proposition, one which must be false, because it is self-contradictory. But at this point I propose to make a complete break in my argument. "*Esse* is *percipi*," we have seen, asserts of two terms, as distinct from one another as "green" and "sweet," that whatever has the one has also the other: it asserts that "being" and "being experienced" are necessarily connected: that whatever *is* is *also* experienced. And this, I admit cannot be directly refuted. But I believe it to be false; and I have asserted that anybody who saw that "*esse* and *percipi*" *were* as distinct as "green" and "sweet" would be no more ready to believe that whatever *is* is *also* experienced, than to believe that whatever is green is also sweet. I have asserted that no one would believe that "*esse* is *percipi*" if they saw how different *esse* is from *percipi*: but *this* I shall not try to prove. I have asserted that all who do believe that "*esse* is *percipi*" identify with it or take as a reason for it a self-contradictory proposition: but this I shall not try to prove. I shall only try to show that certain propositions which I assert to be believed, are false. That they are believed, and that without this belief "*esse* is *percipi*" would not be believed either, I must leave without a proof.

I pass, then, from the uninteresting question Is "*esse percipi?*" to the still more uninteresting and apparently irrelevant question "What is a sensation or idea?"

We all know that the sensation of blue differs from that of green. But it is plain that if both are *sensations* they also have some point in common. What is it that they have in common? And how is this common element related to the points in which they differ?

I will call the common element "consciousness" without yet attempting to say what the thing I so call *is*. We have then in every sensation two distinct terms, (1) "consciousness," in respect of which all sensations are alike; and (2) something else, in respect of which one sensation differs from another. It will be convenient if I may be allowed to call this second term the "object" of a sensation: this also without yet attempting to say what I mean by the word.

We have then in every sensation two distinct elements, one which I call consciousness, and another which I call the object of consciousness. This must be so if the sensation of blue and the sensation of green, though different in one respect, are alike in another: blue is one object of sensation and green is another, and consciousness, which both sensations have in common, is different from either.

But, further, sometimes the sensation of blue exists in my mind and sometimes it does not; and knowing, as we now do, that the sensation of blue includes two different elements, namely consciousness and blue, the question arises whether, when the sensation of blue exists, it is the consciousness which exists, or the blue which exists, or both. And one point at least is plain: namely that these three alternatives are all different from one another. So that, if any one tells us that to say "Blue exists" is the *same* thing as to say that "Both blue and consciousness exists," he makes a mistake and a self-contradictory mistake.

But another point is also plain, namely, that when the sensation exists, the consciousness, at least, certainly does exist; for when I say that the sensations of blue and of green both exist, I certainly mean that what is common to both and in virtue of which both are called sensations, exists in each case. The only alternative left, then, is that *either* both exist or the consciousness exists alone. If, therefore, any one tells us that the existence of blue is the same thing as the existence of the sensation of blue he makes a mistake and a self-contradictory mistake, for he asserts *either* that blue is the same thing as blue together with consciousness, *or* that it is the same thing as consciousness alone.

Accordingly to identify either "blue" or any other of what I have called "*objects*" of sensation, with the corresponding sensation is in every case, a self-contradictory error. It is to identify a part either with the whole of which it is a part or else with the other part of the same whole. If we are told that the assertion "Blue exists" is *meaningless* unless we mean by it that "The sensation of blue exists," we are told what is certainly false and self-contradictory. If we are told that the existence of blue is inconceivable apart from the existence of the sensation, the speaker *probably* means to convey to us, by this ambiguous expression, what is a self-contradictory error. For we can and must conceive the existence of blue as something quite distinct from the existence of the sensation. We can and must conceive that blue might exist and yet the sensation of blue not exist. For my own part I not only conceive this, but conceive it to be true. Either therefore this terrific assertion of inconceivability means what is false and self-contradictory or else it means only that *as a matter of fact* blue never can exist unless the sensation of it exists also.

And at this point I need not conceal my opinion that no philosopher has ever yet succeeded in avoiding this self-contradictory error: that the most striking results both of Idealism and of Agnosticism are only obtained by identifying blue with the sensation of blue: that *esse* is held to be *percipi,* solely because *what is experienced* is held to be identical with *the experience of it.* That Berkeley and Mill committed this error will, perhaps, be granted: that modern Idealists make it will, I hope, appear more probable later. But that my opinion is plausible, I will now offer two pieces of evidence. The first is that language offers us no means of referring to such objects as "blue" and "green" and "sweet," except by calling them sensations: it is an obvious violation of language to call them "things" or "objects" or "terms." And similarly we have no natural means of referring to such objects as "causality" or "likeness" or "identity," except by calling them "ideas" or "notions" or "conceptions." But it is hardly likely that if philosophers had clearly distinguished in the past between a sensation or idea and what I have called its object, there should have been no separate name for the latter. They have always used the same name for these two different "things" (if I may call them so): and hence there is some probability that they have supposed these "things" *not* to be two and different, but one and the same. And, secondly, there is a very good reason why they should have supposed so, in the fact that when we refer to introspection and try to discover what the sensation of blue is, it is very easy to suppose that we have before us only a single term. The term "blue" is easy enough to distinguish, but the other element which I have called "consciousness"—that which sensation of blue has in common with sensation of green—is extremely difficult to fix. That many people fail to distinguish it at all is sufficiently shown by the fact that there are materialists. And, in general, that which makes the sensation of blue a mental fact seems to escape us: it seems, if I may use a metaphor, to be transparent—we look through it and see nothing but the blue; we may be convinced that there *is something* but *what* it is no philosopher, I think, has yet clearly recognised.

But this was a digression. The point I had established so far was that in every sensation or idea we must distinguish two elements, (1) the "object," or that in which one differs from another; and (2) "consciousness," or that which all have in common—that which makes them sensations or mental facts. This being so, it followed that when a sensation or idea exists, we have to choose between the alternatives that either object alone, or consciousness alone, or both, exist; and I showed that of these alternatives one, namely that the object only exists, is excluded by the fact that what we mean to assert is certainly the existence of a mental fact. There remains the question: Do both exist? Or does the consciousness alone? And to this question one answer has hitherto been given universally: That both exist.

This answer follows from the analysis hitherto accepted of the relation of what I have called "object" to "consciousness" in any sensation or idea. It is held that what I call the object is merely the "content" of a sensation or idea. It is held that in each case we can distinguish two elements and two only, (1) the fact that there is feeling or experience, and (2) *what* is felt or experienced; the sensation or idea, it is said, forms a whole, in which we must distinguish two "inseparable aspects," "content" and "existence." I shall try to show that this analysis is false; and for that purpose I must ask what may seem an extraordinary question: namely what is meant by saying that one thing is "content" of another? It is not usual to ask this question; the term is used as if everybody must understand it. But since I am going to maintain that "blue" is *not* the content of the sensation of blue, and what is more important, that, even if it were this analysis would leave out the most important element in the sensation of blue, it is necessary that I should try to explain precisely what it is that I shall deny.

What then is meant by saying that one thing is the "content" of another? First of all I wish to point out that "blue" is rightly and properly said to be part of the content of a blue flower. If, therefore, we also assert that it is part of the content of the sensation of blue, we assert that it has to the other parts (if any) of this whole the same relation which it has to the other parts of a blue flower—and we assert only this: we cannot mean to assert that it has to the sensation of blue any relation which it does not have to the blue flower. And we have seen that the sensation of blue contains at least one other element beside blue—namely, what I call "consciousness," which makes it a sensation. So far then as we assert that blue is the content of the sensation, we assert that it has to this "consciousness" the same relation which it has to the other parts of a blue flower: we do assert this, and we assert no more than this. Into the question what exactly the relation is between blue and a blue flower in virtue of which we call the former part of its "content" I do not propose to enter. It is sufficient for my purpose to point out that it is the general relation most commonly meant when we talk of a thing and its qualities; and that this relation is such that to say the thing exists implies that the qualities also exist. The *content* of the thing is *what* we assert to exist, when we assert *that* the thing exists.

When, therefore, blue is said to be part of the content of the "sensation of blue," the latter is treated as if it were a whole constituted in exactly the same way as any other "thing." The "sensation of blue," on this view, differs from a blue bead or a blue beard, in exactly the same way in which the two latter differ from one another: the blue bead differs from the blue beard, in that while the former contains glass, the latter contains hair; and the "sensation of blue" differs from both in that, instead of glass or hair, it contains consciousness. The relation of the blue to the consciousness is conceived to be exactly the same as that of the blue to the glass or hair: it is in all three cases the *quality* of a *thing*.

But I said just now that the sensation of blue was analysed into "content" and "existence," and that blue was said to be *the* content of the idea of blue. There is an ambiguity in this and a possible error, which I must note in passing. The term "content" may be used in two senses. If we use "content" as equivalent to what Mr. Bradley calls the "*what*"—if we mean by it the *whole* of what is said to exist, when the thing is said to exist, then blue is certainly not *the* content of the sensation of blue: part of the *content* of the sensation is, in this sense of the term, that other element which I have called consciousness. The analysis of this sensation into the "content" "blue," on the one hand, and mere existence on the other, is therefore certainly false; in it we have again the self-contradictory identification of "Blue exists" with "The sensation of blue exists." But there is another sense in which "blue" might properly be said to be *the* content of the sensation—namely, the sense in which "content," like $\varepsilon\iota\delta o\varsigma$, is opposed to "substance" or "matter." For the element "consciousness," being common to all sensations, may be and certainly is regarded as in some sense their "substance," and by the "content" of each is only meant that in respect of which one differs from another. In this sense then "blue" might be said to be *the* content of the sensation; but, in that case, the analysis into "content" and "existence" is, at least, misleading, since under "existence" must be included "*what* exists" in the sensation other than blue.

We have it, then, as a universally received opinion that blue is related to the sensation or idea of blue, as its *content,* and that this view, if it is to be true, must mean that blue is part of *what* is said to exist when we say that the sensation exists. To say that the sensation exists is to say both that blue exists and that "consciousness," whether we call it the substance of which blue is *the* content or call it another part of the content, exists too. Any sensation or idea is a "*thing*," and what I have called its object is the quality of this thing. Such a "thing" is what we think of when we think of a *mental image*. A mental image is conceived as if it were related to that of which it is the image (if there be any such thing) in exactly the same way as the image in a looking-glass is related to that of which it is the reflection; in both cases there is identity of content, and the image in the looking-glass differs from that in the mind solely in respect of the fact that in the one case the other constituent of the image is "glass" and in the other case it is consciousness. If the image is of blue, it is not conceived that this "content" has any relation to the consciousness but what it has to the glass: it is conceived *merely* to be its *content*. And owing to the fact that sensations and ideas are all considered to be *wholes* of this description—things in the mind—the question: What do we know? is considered to be identical with the question: What reason have we for supposing that there are things outside the mind *corresponding* to these that are inside it?

What I wish to point out is (1) that we have no reason for supposing that there are such things as mental images at all—for supposing that blue *is* part of the content of the sensation of blue, and (2) that even if there are mental images, no mental image and no sensation or idea is *merely* a thing of this kind: that "blue," even if it is part of the content of the image or sensation or idea of blue, is always *also* related to it in quite another way, and that this other relation, omitted in the traditional analysis, is the *only* one which makes the sensation of blue a mental fact at all.

The true analysis of a sensation or idea is as follows. The element that is common to them all, and which I have called "consciousness," really *is* consciousness. A sensation is, in reality, a case of "knowing" or "being aware of" or "experiencing" something. When we know that the sensation of blue exists, the fact we know is that there exists an awareness of blue. And this awareness is not merely, as we have hitherto seen it must be, itself something distinct and unique, utterly different from blue: it also has a perfectly distinct and unique relation to blue, a relation which is *not* that of thing or substance to content, nor of one part of content to another part of content. This relation is just that which we mean in every case by "knowing." To have in your mind "knowledge" of blue, is *not* to have in your mind a "thing" or "image" of which blue is the content. To be aware of the sensation of blue is *not* to be aware of a mental image—of a "thing," of which "blue" and some other element are constituent parts in the same sense in which blue and glass are constituents of a blue bead. It is to be aware of an awareness of blue; awareness being used, in both cases, in exactly the same sense. This element, we have seen, is certainly neglected by the "content" theory: that theory entirely fails to express the fact that there is, in the sensation of blue, this unique relation between blue and the other constituent. And what I contend is that this omission is *not* mere negligence of expression, but is due to the fact that though philosophers have recognised that *something* distinct is meant by consciousness, they have never yet had a clear conception of *what* that something is. They have not been able to hold *it* and *blue* before their minds and to compare them, in the same way in which they can compare *blue* and *green*. And this for the reason I gave above: namely that the moment we try to fix our attention upon consciousness and to see *what*, distinctly, it is, it seems to vanish: it seems as if we had before us a mere emptiness. When we try to introspect the sensation of blue, all we can see is the blue: the other element is as if it were diaphanous. Yet it *can* be distinguished if we look attentively enough, and if we know that there is something to look for. My main object in this paragraph has been to try to make the reader *see* it; but I fear I shall have succeeded very ill.

It being the case, then, that the sensation of blue includes in its analysis, beside blue, *both* a unique element "awareness" *and* a unique relation of this element to blue, I can make plain what I meant by asserting, as two distinct propositions, (1) that blue is probably not part of the content of the sensation at all, and (2) that, even if it were, the sensation would nevertheless not be the sensation *of* blue, if blue had only this relation to it. The first hypothesis may now be expressed by saying that, if it were true, then, when the sensation of blue exists, there exists a *blue awareness:* offence may be taken at the expression, but yet it expresses just what should be and is meant by saying that blue is, in this case, a *content* of consciousness or experience. Whether or not, when I have the sensation of blue, my consciousness of awareness is thus blue, my introspection does not enable me to decide with certainty: I only see no reason for thinking that it is. But whether it is or not, the point is unimportant, for introspection *does* enable me to decide that something else is also true: namely that I am aware *of* blue, and by this I mean, that my awareness has to blue a quite different and distinct relation. It is possible, I admit, that my awareness is blue *as well* as being *of* blue: but what I am quite sure of is that it is *of* blue; that it has to blue the simple and unique relation of a thing from this thing known, indeed in distinguishing mind from matter. And this result I may express by saying that what is called the *content* of a sensation is in very truth what I originally called it—the sensation's *object.*

But, if all this be true, what follows?

Idealists admit that some things really exist of which they are not aware: there are some things, they hold, which are not inseparable aspects of *their* experience, even if they be inseparable aspects of some experience. They further hold that some of the things of which they are sometimes aware do really exist, even when they are not aware of them: they hold for instance that they are sometimes aware of other minds, which continue to exist even when they are not aware of them. They are, therefore, sometimes aware of something which is *not* an inseparable aspect of their own experience. They do *know some* things which are *not* a mere part or content of their experience. And what my analysis of sensation has been designed to show is, that whenever I have a mere sensation or idea, the fact is that I am then aware of something which is equally and in the same sense *not* an inseparable aspect of my experience. The awareness which I have maintained to be included in sensation is the very same unique fact which constitutes every kind of knowledge: "blue" is as much an object, and as little a mere content, of my experience, when I experience it, as the most exalted and independent real thing of which I am ever aware. There is, therefore, no question of how we are to "get outside the circle of our own ideas and sensations." Merely to have a sensation is already to *be* outside that circle. It is to know something which is as truly and really *not* a part of my experience, as anything which I can ever know.

Now I think I am not mistaken in asserting that the reason why Idealists suppose that everything which *is* must be an inseparable aspect of some experience, is that they suppose some things, at least, to be inseparable aspects of *their* experience. And there is certainly nothing which they are so firmly convinced to be an inseparable aspect of their experience as what they call the *content* of their ideas and sensations. If, therefore, *this* turns out in every case, whether it be also the content or not, to be at least *not* an inseparable aspect of the experience of it, it will be readily admitted that nothing else which *we* experience ever is such an inseparable aspect. But if we never experience anything but what is *not* an inseparable aspect of *that* experience, how can we infer that anything whatever, let alone *everything,* is an inseparable aspect of *any* experience? How utterly unfounded is the assumption that "*esse* is *percipi*" appears in the clearest light.

But further I think it may be seen that if the object of an Idealist's sensation were, as he supposes, *not* the object but merely the content of that sensation, if, that is to say, it really were an inseparable aspect of his experience, each Idealist could never be aware either of himself or of any other real thing. For the relation of a sensation to its object is certainly the same as that of any other instance of experience to its object; and this, I think, is generally admitted even by Idealists: they state as readily that *what is* judged or thought or perceived is the *content* of that judgment or thought or perception, as that blue is the content of the sensation of blue. But, if so, then when any Idealist thinks he is *aware* of himself or of any one else, this cannot really be the case. The fact is, on his own theory, that himself and that other person are in reality mere *contents* of an awareness, which is aware *of* nothing whatever. All that can be said is that there is an awareness in him, *with* a certain content: it can never be true that there is in him a consciousness *of* anything. And similarly he is never aware either of the fact that he exists or that reality is spiritual. The real fact, which he describes in those terms, is that his existence and the spirituality of reality are *contents* of an awareness, which is aware of nothing—certainly not, then, of its own content.

And further if everything, of which he thinks he is aware, is in reality merely a content of his own experience he has certainly no *reason* for holding that anything does not exist except himself: it will, of course, be possible that other persons do exist; solipsism will not be necessarily true; but he cannot possibly infer from anything he holds that is not true. That he himself exists will of course follow from his premiss that many things are contents of *his* experience. But since everything, of which he thinks himself aware, is in reality merely an inseparable aspect of that awareness; this premiss allows no inference that any of these contents far less any other consciousness, exists at all except as an inseparable aspect of his awareness, that is, as part of himself.

Such, and not those which he takes to follow from it, are the consequences which *do* follow from the Idealist's supposition that the object of an experience is in reality merely a content or inseparable aspect of that experience. If, on the other hand, we clearly recognise the nature of that peculiar relation which I have called "awareness of anything"; if we see that *this* is involved equally in the analysis of *every* experience—from the merest sensation to the most developed perception or reflection, and that *this* is in fact the only essential element in an experience—the only thing that is both common and peculiar to all experiences—the only thing which gives us reason to call any fact mental; if, further, we recognise that this awareness is and must be in all cases of such a nature that its object, when we are aware of it, is precisely what it would be, if we were not aware: then it becomes plain that the existence of a table in space is related to my experience of *it* in precisely the same way as the existence of my own experience is related to my experience of *that*. Of both we are merely aware: if we are aware that the one exists, we are aware in precisely the same sense that the other exists; and if it is true that my experience can exist, even when I do not happen to be aware of its existence, we have exactly the same reason for supposing that the table can do so also. When, therefore, Berkeley, supposed that the only thing of which I am directly aware is my own sensations and ideas, he supposed what was false; and when Kant supposed that the objectivity of things in space *consisted* in the fact that they were "Vorstellungen" having to one another different relations from those which the same "Vorstellungen" have to one another in subjective experience, he supposed what was equally false. I am as directly aware of the existence of material things in space as of my own sensations; and *what* I am aware of with regard to each is exactly the same—namely that in one case the material thing, and in the other case my sensation does really exist. The question requiring to be asked about material things is thus not: What reason have we for supposing that anything exists *corresponding* to our sensations? but: What reason have we for supposing that material things do *not* exist, since *their* existence has precisely the same evidence as that of our sensations? That either exist *may* be false; but if it is a reason for doubling the existence of matter, that it is an inseparable aspect of our experience, the same reasoning will prove conclusively that our experience does not exist either, since that must also be an inseparable aspect of our experience of *it*. The only *reasonable* alternative to the admission that matter exists *as well* as spirit, is absolute Scepticism—that, as likely as not *nothing* exists at all. All other suppositions—the Agnostic's, that something, at all events, does exist, as much as the Idealist's, that spirit does—are, if we have no reason for believing in matter, as baseless as the grossest superstitions.

51

WITTGENSTEIN

1889–1951

Ludwig Wittgenstein was born in Vienna to a prominent Jewish family that had converted to Roman Catholicism. Owners of the largest steel company in Austria, they used their money to support many Viennese artists, musicians, and writers. Wittgenstein was educated at home by the best tutors until the age of fourteen, when he entered the *Realschule* in Linz, where he studied mathematics and physics. After receiving a degree in engineering in Berlin, he moved to England with the idea of going to the University of Manchester to study aeronautical engineering. But a growing interest in the foundations of mathematics prevailed, and instead he went to Cambridge University.

In his autobiography, Bertrand Russell describes his meeting Wittgenstein, who apparently had become deeply puzzled, studying his engineering mathematics, about what made mathematics possible. Russell says:

> He was perhaps the most perfect example I have ever known of genius as traditionally conceived, passionate, profound, intense, and dominating. . . . His life was turbulent and troubled, and his personal force was extraordinary. . . . He used to come to see me every evening at midnight, and pace up and down my room like a wild beast for three hours in agitated silence. Once I said to him: "Are you thinking about logic or about your sins?" "Both," he replied, and continued his pacing. I did not like to suggest that it was time for bed, as it seemed probable both to him and me that on leaving me he would commit suicide. At the end of his first term at Trinity, he came to me and said: "Do you think I am an absolute idiot?" I said: "Why do you want to know?" He replied: "Because if I am I shall become an aeronaut, but if I am not I shall become a philosopher." I said to him: "My dear fellow, I don't know whether you are an absolute idiot or not, but if you will write me an essay during the vacation upon any philosophical topic that interests you, I will read it and tell you." He did so, and brought it to me at the beginning of the next term. As soon as I read the first sentence, I became persuaded that he was a man of genius. . . .

Russell once asked his colleague G. E. Moore what he thought of Wittgenstein. Moore replied that he thought Wittgenstein was brilliant, "Because at my lectures he looks puzzled, and nobody else ever looks puzzled."

World War I interrupted Wittgenstein's studies, and he left England to serve as an officer in the Austrian army. In the trenches he began writing what would become his doctoral dissertation, which he completed in an Italian prison camp: *Tractatus Logico-Philosophicus* (German ed. 1921, English ed. 1922), from which our selection is taken. It created a revolution in philosophy. In it, Wittgenstein tries to make clear the relationship between language and thought by delineating the limit of language as the expression of thought and showing how the mind uses language to picture reality; language itself is the medium of representation as to how things are in the world. Just as Kant tried to show the necessary conditions that would make experience-as-representation possible, Wittgenstein tries to show the necessary conditions that would make language-as-representation possible by claiming that the world consists ultimately not of things but of "elementary facts" made in part accessible by the sentential logic as developed by Russell. Elementary sentences are the linguistic counterparts of elementary facts, to which they are related as pictures are to the things they depict, in virtue of what Wittgenstein calls their "logical form."

The *Tractatus* gave much impetus to the antimetaphysical views of the logical positivists. And yet, ironically, it is also a call to a unique type of mysticism: in trying to say what can only properly be "shown," Wittgenstein claims he is trying to stand outside language. According to his own view, however—since sense exists only within the limits of language—everything he is saying in the *Tractatus* is therefore, strictly speaking, "nonsense." Acknowledging this, he claims his book is a very special type of illuminating nonsense.

The initial reception of the *Tractatus* was mixed. In his introduction to the book, Russell called it an "important event in the philosophical world." But another important twentieth-century philosopher, C. I. Lewis, who also did foundational work in logic, wrote in a letter to the editor of the prestigious *Journal of Philosophy*:

> Have you looked at Wittgenstein's new book yet? I am much discouraged by Russell's foolishness in writing the introduction to such nonsense. I fear it will be looked upon as what symbolic logic leads to. If so, it will be the death of the subject.[1]

Lewis apparently changed his mind a decade later when he claimed that "the nature of logical truth itself has become more definitely understood, largely through the discussions of Wittgenstein."[2]

The *Tractatus* contains seven sentences, numbered 1–7, along with secondary sentences that are commentaries on the first, 1.1, 2.1, and so on, each of which is followed by tertiary sentences that are commentaries on the commentaries, 1.11, 2.11, and so forth. Wittgenstein's picture theory of language and his austere tone of logical rigor sever what can be said—sense—from what cannot be said—the mystical—with explicit statements to the affect that philosophy must remain completely silent about that which is beyond language. This led the logical positivists, who viewed the traditional philosophical domain of metaphysics as bankrupt, to praise the *Tractatus*. Wittgenstein himself regarded the positivist's interpretation of his work as too narrow and as having missed the essential point of the mystical allusions. Overall, however, Wittgenstein was fully satisfied with his work; he felt

---

1. See Lewis's cover letter to his "A Pragmatic Conception of the A Priori," in *Journal of Philosophy* 20 (1923): 169–77; quoted in Burton Dreben and Juliet Floyd, "Tautology: How Not to Use a Word," *Synthese* 87 (1991): 23–49.

2. Quoted in Dreben and Floyd, "Tautology," p. 23.

certain that he had successfully answered all of philosophy's main questions and thus abandoned the profession in favor of teaching elementary school in the Austrian Alps. Shunning what he considered the trappings of wealth, Wittgenstein had by then given away his share of the family fortune, and so when he grew disillusioned with teaching elementary school he worked as a gardener in a nearby monastery, taking time off to design a house for one of his sisters.

Seven years later, in 1929, Russell arranged that Wittgenstein would be awarded a doctorate in philosophy on the basis of the *Tractatus.* Wittgenstein thus returned to Cambridge University and remained there as lecturer. In 1937 he succeeded G. E. Moore in the chair of philosophy. He shunned academic life, however, and lectured mostly in his own rooms, spontaneously and without notes, in an effort to always create something new by his method of "philosophizing out loud." Although he wrote much and circulated some of his writings among his students, he did not allow any of them to be published during his lifetime. In 1947 he resigned from Cambridge and spent the rest of his life in seclusion, working on unfinished manuscripts and occasionally visiting his former students.

It has often been said that Wittgenstein is unique in the history of philosophy for having inspired two very different and in many ways antithetical philosophical movements. Just as the *Tractatus* inspired a generation of logical positivists, his *Philosophical Investigations,* published in 1953, two years after his death, was instrumental in advancing ordinary language philosophy. In the preface, Wittgenstein writes:

> The thoughts which I publish in what follows are the precipitate of philosophical investigations which have occupied me for the last sixteen years. They concern many subjects: the concepts of meaning, of understanding, of a proposition, of logic, the foundations of mathematics, states of consciousness, and other things. I have written down all these thoughts as *remarks,* short paragraphs, of which there is sometimes a fairly long chain about the same subject, while I sometimes make a sudden change, jumping from one topic to another.

The work begins with a criticism of his former picture theory of language and of the *Tractatus* as a whole, with an Augustine-like confession regarding his previous views: "I have been forced to recognize grave mistakes in what I wrote." He claims that the *Tractatus* had captured only one of the many uses of language. The other legitimate uses can be found in ordinary language through meanings derived from social, tribal, cultural, scientific, and psychological contexts. Thus, according to his new and improved theory, "the meaning of a word is its use in the language." In his *Investigations,* Wittgenstein puts forth his new game theory of language, according to which the rules of the game change from one game to another. For instance, he uses the example of pain to argue that mental concepts do not refer to inner private states; uncovering the "logical grammar of pain" reveals that our sensations, thoughts, and experiences cannot be understood using a private language. Language exists through usage defined by social constructions; correct language use cannot be stipulated by private rules of application.

Although Wittgenstein's *Investigations* exemplifies his philosophical shift, on the one hand, from a pictorial to a descriptive view of language and, on the other, from logical atomism to linguistic pluralism, the task of Wittgensteinian philosophy remains in many ways the same. Philosophy according to Wittgenstein is still the "battle against the bewitchment of our intelligence by means of language," whose ultimate purpose is to show "the fly the way out of the fly-bottle."

TRACTATUS LOGICO-PHILOSOPHICUS

1   The world is all that is the case.

1.1   The world is the totality of facts, not of things.[1]

1.11   The world is determined by the facts, and by these being all the facts.

1.12   For the totality of facts determines all that is the case and also all that is not the case.

1.13   The facts in logical space are the world.

1.2   The world can be broken down into facts.

1.21   Each one can be the case or not be the case while all else remains the same.[2]

2   What is the case—a fact—is the existence of particular[3] states of affairs.[4]

From *Wittgenstein's Tractatus,* trans. Daniel Kolak (Mayfield, 1998).

---

1. Compare this to Schopenhauer's assertion, "The world is my idea," which influenced Wittgenstein. The generic and fundamental point is that what the mind has direct access to is not things as they exist independently of the mind (as conceived in materialist metaphysics) but its own items: perceptions, thoughts, and language. For illuminating avatars to Wittgenstein's linguistic variation of the idealistic theme, see the introduction to Berkeley's *Treatise Concerning Human Understanding,* reprinted in this anthology and the related discussion in my *From the Presocratics to the Present: A Personal Odyssey* (Mayfield, 1998). However, we must be careful to note that Wittgenstein is here *not* (at least not straightforwardly) denying the existence of things! If he were, the statements he makes below in which he uses the word *thing* (*ding*) would be the sort of nonsense that Wittgenstein most definitely thinks he is *not* writing, namely, nonilluminating nonsense; for although there is a tension in many of his sentences that, as we shall see, play on contradiction to make their philosophical "showings" clear, it is supposed to be the sort of *illuminating* "nonsense" that sentences in logic express.

2. Many have thought that this is a mistake. If "one" refers to facts, how can a fact *not* be the case? Others have held that this is not just a mistake, that Wittgenstein is here reverting to an earlier formulation of *Tatsache* as a complex conjunction of elementary, or simple, facts. Thus "It is raining and it is warm" may or may not be the case, while "it is warm and it is dark" remain, in his words, "the same." But I think *this* puzzle is solved in the next sentence (2), where he explains what *he* means by fact: facts are not construed in some *standard* type of realism but as "states of affairs" (*Sachverhalten*), such that I think he really meant that any particular *Sachverhalt* may or may not be the case. Indeed, in that regard he talks in 2.06 about positive and negative facts, where a positive fact is the existence of a particular state of affairs and a negative fact is the nonexistence of a particular state of affairs. Thus, for instance, "The Eiffel Tower is taller than Mt. Everest" is a negative fact and "Mt. Everest is taller than the Eiffel Tower" is a positive fact. Finally, 1.21 neatly establishes the distinction between that which Wittgenstein thinks the world is made of—facts—from what common sense says it is made of—things. One major difference between things as ordinarily understood, especially by German-speaking philosophers, is that "if one thing changes its qualities, this can have an effect upon another thing. Things affect each other and resist each one another. . . . This description of things and their interdependence corresponds to what we call the 'natural conception of the world'" (Heidegger, *What Is a Thing* [South Bend, Ind.: Regnery/Gateway, 1967], p. 33). Notice that here Heidegger, who as much as Wittgenstein but in a different way is wildly antithetical to any natural conception of the world, nicely and no doubt unintentionally illustrates for us why Wittgenstein would have wanted to insist (and did) that the *world* did not consist of *such* items (things) but items that are most implicitly *not* linked into a cosmos as conceived in natural science.

3. *Sachverhalt* has been variously translated as "atomic state of affairs," "elementary fact," "atomic fact," and so on. "Particular" I think has the better connotation, since the word *atomic* is erroneously ambiguous in that it can mean both "something that does not have parts and cannot be further broken down" and "something that consists of [basic] elements." "Particular" would do just as well as "elementary" if we kept in mind the additional sense, "consists of particles," that is, of distinct elements.

4. In translating *Sachverhalt* as "particular states of affairs" and *Tatsache* as "fact," let us keep in mind what Wittgenstein meant regarding the all-important relation between the two. *Sachverhalt* corresponds to a simple

2.01   A particular state of affairs is a combination of objects (items, things).[5]

2.02   Objects are simple.

2.03   In a particular state of affairs the objects hang in one another like the links of a chain.[6]

2.04   The world is a totality of all existing states of affairs.

2.05   The totality of all existing particular states of affair determines which particular states of affair do not exist.

2.06   The existence and nonexistence of particular states of affair is reality.[7]

   (We also call the existence of particular states of affair a positive fact, and their nonexistence a negative fact.)

---

declarative sentence if it is true. *Tatsache* corresponds to the totality of all simple declarative sentences when this totality is true. Here is my understanding of this. "Kolak is in his study" is at this moment a true simple declarative sentence. It describes a particular state of affairs. Likewise, "Kolak is sitting in a chair" is also true. It describes a different particular state of affairs. "Kolak is writing" is also true and describes yet another particular state of affairs. These three states of affairs just described using the above three sentences are all related by virtue of a *fact*. It is difficult, perhaps impossible, to say exactly what this fact is, even to specify its boundaries or enumerate it (i.e., count it) in relation to other facts about the world. In an important sense, we don't know of how many facts the world consists because we cannot specify their borders, only the boundary of the world (something the whole *Tractatus* sets out to delineate). Facts are thus in that sense as elusive to the mind as Kant's things-in-themselves (*ding-an-sich*). However, unlike facts, sentences—which are their linguistic representatives—can be enumerated and there exists the totality of true statements within a language, and so on. So in speaking of particular states of affairs, Wittgenstein is alluding to the fact that, for instance, it can be observed or seen that Kolak is in his study, sitting in a chair, writing, and so on, particular states of affairs all of which can be, via the content of simple declarative sentences (I just did it), "information bundles" packaged either in linguistic terms (sentences describing observed situations) or in experiential terms (items in a visual field). Often, but not always, it may help the understanding to think of "states of affairs" as synonymous to what is available to the perceiving subject in a particular visual field, in terms of the relations of the objects present in that visual field. Indeed, it is in saying that we cannot talk about anything beyond what is present in such states of affairs that Wittgenstein made himself so useful to the logical positivists and members of the Vienna Circle. Likewise, it may also help to think of "states of affairs" as a synonym for visual "statement." For a discussion of this sense, in which both visual events and linguistic events can be seen as the mind's "statement to itself" (my terminology, not Wittgenstein's), see below.

5. The original says: "Der Sachverhalt ist eine Verbindung von Gegenständen (Sachen, Dingen).'' Wittgenstein here means to regard *Ding, Sache,* and *Gegenstand* as synonymous. Clearly, both in ordinary usage and in the classical metaphysical implicature they are not (i.e., the problematic nature of the relation between [phenomenal] objects and things [in themselves, in Kant's sense]). This is not, I think, carelessness on Wittgenstein's part but, rather, it merely emphasizes what he conceives the world to *be.* In speaking of x as a *thing,* a collection of *things* or *somethings,* and so on, Wittgenstein—like many philosophers from Kant to Heidegger—is trying to refer to x in the most neutral way possible. "Object" already is specific, it has a direction; the German *Gegenstand* means "against" (*gegen*) + "stand" (*stand*). That which it stands against is of course the subject, and there is a long philosophical tradition—not just in idealism but in a variety of radical empiricisms, phenomenalisms, and presentationalisms—which holds that in order to exist objects as such require a subject. *Thing,* on the other hand, implies therefore something that can stand on its own, independently of being directed at (or, in some views [Fichte's, Schelling's, Schopenhauer's] *from*) a subject. This minimizes one Wittgensteinian tension only to leave us with the problem of how we should then interpret 1.1. Here, however, I think we can help ourselves by helping Wittgenstein to avail himself of straightforward idealism; although Wittgenstein's view of what the world is—like Schopenhauer's—is that the world is, literally, *his* world and no one else's, the items of which it is composed and that stand independently of the ego are not things but facts. And this, again, is to move away from the kind of linkage presented in scientific theories to the unique type of linkage that Wittgenstein is here constructing for us.

   So much for the ordinary, pretheoretical sense of these words. Now we turn to the important way in which we shall use certain words in our English rendition of Wittgenstein's *thoughts,* which are often clear in the original German without our having to evoke (in this case rather artificial) technical usage. Here it is: the *world* (*Die Welt*) is the totality of *facts* (*Tatsachen*), which consist of particular states of affairs (*Sachverhalte*), which, in turn, consist of configurations of *objects* (*Gegenstande*).

6. Here Wittgenstein means that nothing connects the links: the links themselves connect with one another. That is—and this is a key point—there is nothing in addition to the links, such as glue or solder, that keeps them together; they keep each other together.

7. In other words, the world collectively organized into a coherent whole is reality.

2.063   The sum total of reality is the world.

2.1   We make pictures of facts to ourselves.

2.11   Such a picture represents a particular state of affairs in logical space, the existence and nonexistence of particular states of affairs.

2.12   Such a picture is a model of reality.

2.13   To the objects correspond,[8] in such a picture, the elements of the picture.

2.14   The picture consists in its elements being combined in a definite way.[9]

2.141   The picture is a fact.[10]

2.15   The definite way in which the picture elements combine represents how things are related.

　　　Let us call this combination of elements[11] the *structure* of the picture, and let us call the possibility[12] of this structure the *form of representation* of the picture.

2.151   The form of representation is the possibility that things[13] combine in the same way as do the pictorial elements.

2.1511   In this way the picture makes contact with, or reaches up to, reality.

2.16   To be a picture, a fact[14] must have something in common with what it depicts.

2.17   What a picture must have in common with reality to be capable of depicting it the way it does—rightly or wrongly—is its form of representation.

2.18   What any such picture, of any form, must have in common with reality to be capable of representing it the way it does—rightly or wrongly—is logical form, that is, the form of reality.

2.19   Logical pictures are depictions of the world.

2.2   A picture must have the logical form of representation in common with what it depicts.

2.21   Such a picture agrees with reality or not; it is right or wrong, true or false.

2.22   Such a picture represents what it represents independently of its truth or falsity, via its representational form.[15]

2.221   What this picture represents is its sense.

2.222   Its truth or falsity consists in the agreement or disagreement of its sense with reality.

---

8. The German word here, "*entsprechen*," translated in line with its usual usage as "correspond," has an extremely revealing etymology that accords with Wittgenstein's overall theory: it means "to speak for." The world speaks. Experiences are its sayings. That's what Wittgenstein has in mind while building his bridge between sentences and facts.

9. A technical note against what has become a commonplace misinterpretation due to the Pears-McGuinness translation: the German *sich zu einander verhalten* means "being combined," and so the Pears-McGuinness translation of 2.14 as "What constitutes a picture is that its elements are related *to one another* in a determinate way" is a paradigm example of how that translation continues to be erroneous and deeply misleading.

10. That is, an *interpreted* fact. And keep in mind that Wittgenstein is not trying to make a point in esthetics about the nature of pictures but, rather, that he is talking about those pictures we make to ourselves when we picture facts. In other words, he's not informing you about the nature of objects hanging in a gallery but, rather, about the nature of objects hanging inside you, and he is using the analogy of pictures of the sort that hang in galleries to make his point.

11. That is, the structure of the fact.

12. That is, the form of the fact.

13. Meaning both the objects depicted and the picture elements that represent them.

14. Keep in mind that what Wittgenstein means by "fact" is a conglomerate of particular states of affairs.

15. In other words, a picture means something independently of whether it is true or false.

3.0   A thought is a logical picture of a fact.[16]

3.01   The totality of all true thoughts is a picture of the world.

3.02   A thought contains the possibility of the facts that it thinks. What is thinkable is also possible.

3.03   Thought cannot be of anything illogical, else we would have to think illogically.[17]

3.1   In a sentence the thought expresses itself perceptibly.[18]

3.11   We use a sentence (spoken or written, etc.) as a projection of a possible fact.[19]

        The method of projection is our thinking the sense of the sentence.

3.12   The sign with which a thought expresses itself, I will call a *sentential sign.* A sentence is a sentential sign conceived in its projective relation to the world.

3.13   The sentence has everything that the projection has, except what is projected.

        Therefore, the possibility of what is projected is in the sentence, but not the projection itself.

        And so the sentence does not yet contain its sense; what it does contain is the possibility of expressing that sense.

        ("The content of the sentence" means the content of a sentence that makes sense.)

        The sentence contains the [empty, logical] form[20] of its sense, without any content.

3.14   What constitutes a sentence is that its elements, the words, stand in a determinate relation to one another.

        A sentential sign is a fact.

3.2   In sentences, thoughts can be expressed such that the objects of the thoughts correspond[21] to the elements of the sentential signs.

3.21   The configuration of simple signs[22] in the sentential sign corresponds to the configuration of objects in the fact.

3.22   In a sentence a name signifies an object.

3.3   Only sentences make sense; only in the context of a sentence does a name signify anything.

3.31   Any part of a sentence that characterizes the sense of the sentence I call an *expression* (a symbol).[23]

        (A sentence is itself an expression.)

        Expressions are everything essential for the sense of the sentence that sentences can have in common with each other.

        An expression characterizes the form and content.

---

16. According to Wittgenstein, to think is to form mental pictures.

17. In other words, what is not possible is not thinkable.

18. In Wittgenstein's view, (meaningful) sentences are thoughts expressed in a communicable way.

19. It helps here to think of a projection in geometry, where say a 3-D cube is projected onto a 2-D coordinate system. I think this is an eminently illuminating image that takes us all the way back to Plato's ideal forms, where the relation of an elementary sentence to a particular state of affairs is like a projective shadow of an ideal form.

20. That is, the form of the possible state of affairs presented.

21. Here I think my earlier point about "speak for" being an illuminating etymological substitute for "correspond" is especially useful.

22. That is, symbols.

23. Wittgenstein means that an expression is itself a symbol.

3.32   A sign is the perceptible aspect of a symbol.

3.33   The meaning of a sign should never play a role in logical syntax. It must be possible to formulate logical syntax without mentioning the *meaning* of a sign; the meaning ought *only* to presuppose the description of the expressions.

3.34   A sentence has essential and accidental features.

        The accidental features arise in the way the sentence is produced; the essential features are the ones without which the sense of the sentence would be lost.

3.4   A sentence determines a place in logical space. The existence of this logical place is guaranteed by the existence of the expressions of which the sentence is composed— by the existence of the meaningful sentence.

3.41   The sentential sign with logical coordinates: that is the logical place.

3.42   Although a sentence may determine only one place in logical space, the whole logical space must already be given by it.

3.5   A sentential sign, applied and thought, is a thought.

4.0   A sentence that makes sense is a thought.[24]

4.01   A sentence is a picture of reality.

        A sentence is a model of reality as we think it is.

4.02   This we see from the fact that we understand the sense of a sentence without having had it explained to us.

4.021   A sentence is a picture of reality, for if I understand the sentence I know the fact represented by it. And I understand the sentence without its sense having been explained to me.

4.03   A sentence must communicate a new sense with old words.

        A sentence communicates a fact to us; therefore it must be *essentially* connected with the fact.

        And the connection is that a sentence is its logical picture.

        A sentence asserts something only insofar as it is a picture.

4.04   In a sentence there must be exactly as many things distinguishable as there are in the fact that it represents.

4.05   The reality is compared with the sentence.

4.06   Sentences can be true or false only by being pictures of the reality.

4.1   A sentence presents the existence and nonexistence of particular states of affairs.

4.2   The sense of a sentence is in its agreement and disagreement with the possibilities of the existence and nonexistence of particular states of affairs.

4.3   Truth-possibilities of elementary sentences signify the possibilities of the existence and nonexistence of particular states of affairs.[25]

4.4   A sentence is an expression of agreement and disagreement with the truth-possibilities of elementary sentences.[26]

---

24. Now this, of course, can be taken in two different ways, one which I call the conservative, *linguistic* sense and the other which I call the radical, *semiotic* sense: I take 4.0 in the radical, semiotic sense to mean that, yes, a sentence that makes sense *is* what a thought is; in other words, minds or consciousness as conceived in some superlinguistic (i.e., supernatural) terms are absolutely not required. In my view, the early Wittgenstein, like the early Russell and Charles Peirce before them both, is intuiting a computational approach to the problem of consciousness, where the computations are logical processes and the items processed are linguistic objects.

25. If we here interpret Wittgenstein to be talking about possible worlds, we thereby counterinvert the state of the *Tractatus* from within Wittgenstein's own world (regarded in its complete form) from the false (as the "later" Wittgenstein would "view" it) into the profound.

26. This is the famous *principle of extensionality,* as it would later come to be called.

4.5   We are in a position now to state the most general form of a sentence—that is, to describe the sentence of any symbolic language whatsoever such that every sense can be expressed by a symbol satisfying the description and that every symbol satisfying the description can express a sense, provided that the signification of each name is well chosen.

   Clearly, only what is essential to the most general form of a sentence may be included in its description—otherwise, it would not be the most general form.

   The existence of a general form of a sentence is proved in that no sentence can be given whose form could not have been foreseen (i.e., constructed). The general form of a sentence is: so and so[27] is the case.

5.0   A sentence is a truth-function of elementary sentences.[28]

   (An elementary sentance is a truth-function of itself.)

5.1   The truth-functions can be ordered in a series.

   This is the foundation for the theory of probability.

5.2   The structures of sentences stand to one another in internal relations.

5.3   All sentences are the result of truth-operations on the elementary sentences.

5.4   It is here that the nonexistence of "logical objects" or "logical constants" (in the sense of Frege and Russell) shows itself.

5.5   Each truth-function is a result of successive applications of the operation "(-----T) (ξ,....)."

   This operation negates all the sentences in the right-hand brackets and so I call it the negation of those sentences.

5.6   *The boundary of my language* is the boundary of my world.

5.61   Logic fills the world: the boundary of logic is also the boundary of the world.

   So in logic we cannot say, "The world has this in it and this, but not that."

   For this apparently presupposes that some possibilities were thereby being excluded, which cannot possibly be the case, since this would require that logic should extend beyond the boundary of the world; for only then could it have a view from the other side of the boundary.

   What we cannot think, that we cannot think: we cannot therefore *say* what we cannot think.

5.62   This thought itself shows how much truth there is in solipsism.

   What the solipsist intends to say is absolutely correct. The problem is that the truth cannot speak but only shows itself.

   That the world is *my* world reveals itself in the fact that the boundary of language (the language that I alone understand) is the boundary of *my* world.

5.621   The world and life are one.[29]

5.63   I am my world (the microcosm).

5.631   The thinking, perceiving subject does not exist.

   If I were to write a book, *The World as I Found It,* I would also have to include an account of my body in it, and report which parts are subject to my will and which not, etc. This then would be a method of isolating the subject, or rather of

---

27. I borrow this happy term from Nelson Goodman.

28. Another statement of the famous thesis of extensionality.

29. But let us quickly note that in his *Notebooks* Wittgenstein follows up this sentence immediately with "Physiological life is of course not 'Life.' And neither is psychological life. Life is the world" (77 [6]).

showing that in an important sense there is no subject; that is to say: of it alone in this book mention could *not* be made.

5.632   The subject does not belong to the world but is the boundary of the world.

5.633   Where *in* the world could a metaphysical subject be?

You say this is just like the case with the eye and the visual field. But you do *not* really see the eye.

And there is nothing *in the visual field* to let you infer that it is being seen through an eye.

5.64   Here we can see that solipsism[30] thoroughly thought out coincides with pure realism. The *I* in solipsism shrinks to an extensionless point and there remains the reality coordinated with it.

5.641   Thus there really is a sense in which philosophy can speak about the self in a non-psychological way.

The *I* occurs in philosophy through the fact that "the world is my world."

The philosophical *I* is not the human being, not the human body, not the human soul with which psychology deals. The philosophical self is the metaphysical subject, the boundary—nowhere in the world.

6   The general form of a truth-function is $[p,\xi,N(\xi)]$.

This is the general form of a sentence.

6.1   The sentences of logic are tautologies.

6.11   The sentences of logic therefore say nothing. (They are analytic sentences.)

6.12   The fact that the sentences of logic are tautologies shows the formal—logical—properties of language, of the world.

6.13   Logic is not a theory about the world but a reflection of it, its mirror image.

Logic is transcendent.[31]

6.2   Mathematics is a logical method.

Mathematical sentences are equations and, therefore, pseudostatements.[32]

6.21   Mathematical sentences express no thoughts.

6.3   The investigation of logic means the investigation of *all* conformity to *laws*. And outside logic all is accident.

6.4   All sentences are of equal value.

6.41   The meaning of the world must lie outside the world. In the world everything is as

---

30. I agree half-heartedly with Hintikka's contention that what Wittgenstein means by *solipsism* is not *merely* what philosophers usually meant, namely, that there are no other minds besides one's own. (See Hintikka's "On Wittgenstein's 'Solipsism,'" *Mind*, n.s. LXVII, 1958.) That there are no other minds besides my own I take to be a truth not in the limiting sense but in the cosmic sense as perhaps implied by Averroes and others, that all minds are numerically identical beings. (This is a complicated but illuminating notion. See my *I Am You: A Philosophical Explanation of the Possibility That We Are All the Same Person* [Ann Arbor: UMI, 1986] and my *In Search of Self: Life, Death, and Personal Identity* [Belmont, Calif.: Wadsworth, 1998].) Stenius too agrees with Hintikka, "at least in so far as Wittgenstein ought to have used the word 'idealism' rather than 'solipsism,' because what he calls 'solipsism' is exactly his linguistic turn of Kantian idealism" (Erik Stenius, *Wittgenstein's Tractatus: A Critical Exposition of Its Main Lines of Thought* [Ithaca, N.Y.: Cornell University Press, 1964]). I say "half-heartedly" not because I do not fully agree with Hintikka (I would not dare) but because I *more* than agree with him: I think Wittgenstein (whether he consciously realized it or not) meant both the (linguistic turn of) Kantian (transcendental, or critical) idealism and the cosmic truth "there are no other minds but mine".

31. Wittgenstein says "transcendental," but I think this is a mistake; he means "transcendent." See my comment regarding the ethical, in note 33.

32. Once again, this is not meant pejoratively.

it is, everything happens as it does happen; there is no value *in* it—if there were any, the value would be worthless.

For a value to be worth something, it must lie outside all happening and outside being this way or that. For all happening and being this way or that is accidental.

The nonaccidental cannot be found in the world, for otherwise this too would then be accidental.

The value of the world lies outside it.

6.42 Likewise, there can be no sentences in ethics. Sentences cannot express anything higher.

6.421 Clearly, ethics cannot be put into words.

Ethics is transcendent.[33]

(Ethics and esthetics are one.)

6.422 As soon as we set up an ethical law having the form "thou shalt . . . ," our first thought is: So then what if I don't do it? But clearly ethics has nothing to do with punishment and reward in the ordinary sense. The question about the consequences of my action must therefore be irrelevant. At least these consequences will not be events. For there must be something right in that formulation of the question. There must be some sort of ethical reward and ethical punishment, but this must lie in the action itself.

6.423 We cannot speak of the will as if it were the ethical subject.

And the will as a phenomenon is only of interest to psychology.[34]

6.43 If good or bad willing changes the world, it changes only the boundaries of the world, not the facts—not the things that can be expressed in language.

6.431 In death, too, the world does not change but only ceases.

6.4311 Death is not an event in life. Death is not lived through.

If by *eternity* we mean not endless temporal duration but timelessness, then to live eternally is to live in the present.

In the same way as our visual field is without boundary, our life is endless.

6.4312 The temporal immortality of the human soul—its eternal survival after death—is not only without guarantee, this assumption could never have the desired effect. Is a riddle solved by the fact that I survive forever? Is eternal life not as enigmatic as our present life? The solution to the riddle of life in space and time lies *outside* of space and time.

(Certainly the solution to this riddle does not involve solutions to any of the problems of natural science.)

6.432 *How* the world is, is completely indifferent to what is higher. God does not reveal himself *in* the world.

---

33. Wittgenstein says "transcendental," but this is a mistake; he means "transcendent." By my lights, "transcendental" is used by both Kant and Wittgenstein (but by neither always consistently) to mean the limits of theoretical knowledge as known by reaching beyond experience not outside the mind but into the inner workings of the mind, via the categories and forms of perception and thought; "transcendent" refers to what exists beyond that limit, not on the inside but outside, beyond the categories of thought, "outside the mind" (such as Kant's things-in-themselves). For further clarifications on this fundamental point, see the sections on Kant and Wittgenstein in my *From the Presocratics to the Present* (Mayfield, 1998), my *Lovers of Wisdom* (Wadsworth, 1997), and my *In Search of Kant* (Wadsworth, 1998).

34. That is, that it seems people's intentions obviously affect the course of events is merely an appearance, a phenomenon, of superficial psychological interest, without any philosophical significance.

6.4321   The facts all belong to the setting up of the problem,[35] not to its solution.

6.44   It's not *how* the world is that is mystical but *that* it is.

6.45   To view the world *sub specie aeternitatis* is the view of it as a bounded whole.

The feeling of the world as a bounded whole is the mystical feeling.

6.5   If the answer cannot be put into words, the question, too, cannot be put into words.

The riddle does not exist.

If a question can be put at all, then it *can* also be answered.

6.51   Skepticism is *not* irrefutable, only nonsensical, insofar as it tries to raise doubts about what cannot be asked.

For doubt can exist only if there is a question; a question can exist only if there is an answer, and this can be the case only if something *can* be *said.*

6.52   We feel that even if *all possible* scientific questions were answered, the problems of life would still not have been touched at all. To be sure, there would then be no question left, and just this is the answer.

6.521   The vanishing of this problem is the solution to the problem of life.

(Is this not the very reason people to whom after long bouts of doubt the meaning of life became clear, could not then say what this meaning is?)

6.522   The inexpressible indeed exists. It *shows* itself. It is the mystical.

6.53   The right method in philosophy would be to say nothing except what can be said using sentences such as those of natural science—which of course has nothing to do with philosophy—and then, to show those wishing to say something metaphysical that they failed to give any meaning to certain signs in their sentences. Although they would not be satisfied—they would feel you weren't teaching them any philosophy—*this* would be the only right method.

6.54   My sentences are illuminating in the following way: to understand me you must recognize my sentences—once you have climbed out through them, on them, over them—as senseless. (You must, so to speak, throw away the ladder, after you have climbed up on it.)

You must climb out through my sentences; then you will see the world correctly.

7   Of what we cannot speak we must be silent.

---

35. In German, *Aufgabe* refers to trivial elementary school exercises, such as spelling, multiplication tables, and so on—an expression of which Wittgenstein was extremely fond.

CHAPTER

52

QUINE

1908–

Willard Van Orman Quine was born in Akron, Ohio. He says that while still in high school he saw the falseness of religion and tried to enlighten friends away from "their Episcopalian faith to atheism." It was not the rejection of religion that inspired him to philosophy, but rather a poem—Edgar Allan Poe's *Eureka,* which "for all its outrageousness fostered the real thing: the desire to understand the universe. So did the antireligious motive." At Oberlin College Quine concentrated on the study of mathematics and mathematical philosophy, including the works of Russell, Whitehead, and the mathematician Peano. He went to graduate school at Harvard and received his doctorate in philosophy after only two years. His dissertation, "The Logic of Sequences: A Generalization of 'Principia Mathematica,'" was subsequently published as his first book, *A System of Logic.*

The work of course owes much to Russell and Whitehead's *Principia Mathematica.* But Quine develops an original view of logic that he says is in "kinship with the most general and systematic aspects of natural science, farthest from observation. Mathematics and logic are supported by observation only in the indirect way that those aspects of natural science are supported by observation; namely, as participating in an organized whole which, way up at its empirical edges, squares with observation."

Quine held a series of positions in Vienna, Prague, and Warsaw. In Europe, Quine studied with the logical positivist Moritz Schlick, who founded the Vienna Circle, the brilliant philosopher of science Hans Reichenbach, the logical positivist Rudolf Carnap, and the great mathematician and logician Adolph Tarski. In 1936 Quine returned to the United States and became an instructor at Harvard. He published *Mathematical Logic* (1940) and *Elementary Logic* (1941) during a time in which "Germans massacred Jews, Germans swarmed over France, Japanese bombed Hawaii. Logic seemed off the point." He joined the navy and ended up working for radio intelligence in Washington.

After the war Quine returned to Harvard, where he became a full professor in 1948. At a lecture delivered at Yale and published a few years later in *From a Logical Point of View,* Quine addresses the age-old problem of "ontological commitment"—the fundamental question of how to decide philosophical disputes over *what there is.* Is the universe a mental object? A material object? Does consciousness exist? Influenced by pragmatism, by Russell, by Occam's razor, Quine tries to solve disputes over the "old Platonic riddle of non-being" in an ingenious way, by arguing for relativity: different, even opposing, philosophical stances, such as phenomenalism and physicalism, should best be viewed as essentially different but equally fundamental points of view, whose preference must be determined depending on one's practical purposes.

Ultimately, according to Quine, "the ontological controversy should tend into controversy over language." In other words, the issue of what exists resolves itself into the question of what some statement or doctrine *says* exists. Such "ontological relativity" would later be even further developed by Quine in his *Ontological Relativity.*

In 1951 Quine delivered a lecture to the American Philosophical Association that became an instant classic: "Two Dogmas of Empiricism." Subsequently published as the second chapter of *From a Logical Point of View,* it presents a challenge to the fundamental, age-old distinction between analytic and synthetic truth by claiming that "a boundary between analytic and synthetic statements simply has not been drawn": That such a distinction can be drawn in the first place is the first dogma of empiricism. It is, Quine argues, a metaphysical article of faith.

The second dogma of empiricism is reductionism. According to reductionism, every meaningful statement can be translated into a statement about immediate experience. But Quine shows that any conceptual scheme we bring to it "is a man-made fabric which impinges on experience only along the edges." According to Quine there are no analytic truths; that is, there are no propositions that can be known to be true a priori just in virtue of their meaning. He therefore concludes that "no statement is immune to revision."

In *Ontological Relativity* (1969), Quine develops two of his most important philosophical theses about meaning—the indeterminacy of translation and the inscrutability of reference—into a view that one cannot say what a language is about. This view holds not just for natural language but even for scientific and formal languages. In other words, theories of meaning are like scientific theories in that they are underdetermined by the available data. Vastly and often incommensurate competing theories can all account for the same data.

According to Quine, whether theory A or theory B is better—whether it explains more or is more correct in its ontological claims—is relative. Whether one theory is better than another competing theory ultimately depends on the purposes of the theory. In other words, we cannot even tell what really exists—what the actual objects of the world are—independently of the conceptual schemes of the theory and the terms of the language in which the theory is stated. Quine argues that there will always be equally competing alternative theories, each of which is encased in a number of conflicting conceptual schemes. Therefore, we must always make room for the possibility of new theories, better views improved according to established scientific principles.

Quine would agree with Wittgenstein that it is not possible to have a private language. It is communication through language that gives us access to each other's conceptual schemes, making possible what Quine calls "semantic ascent." But this always involves developing a more inclusive conceptual scheme in which the speakers of the language must make intelligent "ontic decisions" about what they are talking about. This must be done by the speakers of the language despite the fact that, if they are philosophers, they know that the translation of meanings must forever remain indeterminate. In this way, the indeterminacy of the world and the incompleteness of our theories are mirrored within ourselves.

TWO DOGMAS OF EMPIRICISM

Modern empiricism has been conditioned in large part by two dogmas. One is a belief in some fundamental cleavage between truths which are *analytic,* or grounded in meanings independently of matters of fact, and truths which are *synthetic,* or grounded in fact. The other dogma is *reductionism:* the belief that each meaningful statement is equivalent to some logical construct upon terms which refer to immediate experience. Both dogmas, I shall argue, are ill-founded. One affect of abandoning them is, as we shall see, a blurring of the supposed boundary between speculative metaphysics and natural science. Another effect is a shift toward pragmatism.

1. BACKGROUND FOR ANALYTICITY

Kant's cleavage between analytic and synthetic truths was foreshadowed in Hume's distinction between relations of ideas and matters of fact, and in Leibniz's distinction between truths of reason and truths of fact. Leibniz spoke of the truths of reason as true in all possible worlds. Picturesqueness aside, this is to say that the truths of reason are those which could not possibly be false. In the same vein we hear analytic statements defined as statements whose denials are self-contradictory. But this definition has small explanatory value; for the notion of self-contradictoriness, in the quite broad sense needed for this definition of analyticity, stands in exactly the same need of clarification as does the notion of analyticity itself. The two notions are the two sides of a single dubious coin.

Kant conceived of an analytic statement as one that attributes to its subject no more than is already conceptually contained in the subject. This formulation has two shortcomings: it limits itself to statements of subject-predicate form, and it appeals to a notion of containment which is left at a metaphorical level. But Kant's intent, evident more from the use he makes of the notion of analyticity than from his definition of it, can be restated thus: a statement is analytic when it is true by virtue of meanings and independently of fact. Pursuing this line, let us examine the concept of *meaning* which is presupposed.

Meaning, let us remember, is not to be identified with naming. Frege's example of 'Evening Star' and 'Morning Star', and Russell's of 'Scott' and 'the author of *Waverley*', illustrate that terms can name the same thing but differ in meaning. The distinction between meaning and naming is no less important at the level of abstract terms. The terms '9' and 'the number of the planets' name one and the same abstract entity but presumably must be regarded as unlike in meaning; for astronomical observation was needed, and not mere reflection on meanings, to determine the sameness of the entity in question.

The above examples consist of singular terms, concrete and abstract. With general terms, or predicates, the situation is somewhat different but parallel. Whereas a singular term purports to name an entity, abstract or concrete, a general term does not; but a general term

From *Philosophical Review*, 1951.

is *true of* an entity, or of each of many, or of none. The class of all entities of which a general term is true is called the *extension* of the term. Now paralleling the contrast between the meaning of a singular term and the entity named, we must distinguish equally between the meaning of a general term and its extension. The general terms 'creature with a heart' and 'creature with kidneys', for example, are perhaps alike in extension but unlike in meaning.

Confusion of meaning with extension, in the case of general terms, is less common than confusion of meaning with naming in the case of singular terms. It is indeed a commonplace in philosophy to oppose intension (or meaning) to extension, or, in a variant vocabulary, connotation to denotation.

The Aristotelian notion of essence was the forerunner, no doubt, of the modern notion of intension or meaning. For Aristotle it was essential in men to be rational, accidental to be two-legged. But there is an important difference between this attitude and the doctrine of meaning. From the latter point of view it may indeed be conceded (if only for the sake of argument) that rationality is involved in the meaning of the word 'man' while two-leggedness is not; but two-leggedness may at the same time be viewed as involved in the meaning of 'biped' while rationality is not. Thus from the point of view of the doctrine of meaning it makes no sense to say of the actual individual, who is at once a man and a biped, that his rationality is essential and his two-leggedness accidental or vice versa. Things had essences, for Aristotle, but only linguistic forms have meanings. Meaning is what essence becomes when it is divorced from the object of reference and wedded to the word.

For the theory of meaning a conspicuous question is the nature of its objects: what sort of things are meanings? A felt need for meant entities may derive from an earlier failure to appreciate that meaning and reference are distinct. Once the theory of meaning is sharply separated from the theory of reference, it is a short step to recognizing as the primary business of the theory of meaning simply the synonymy of linguistic forms and the analyticity of statements; meanings themselves, as obscure intermediary entities, may well be abandoned.

The problem of analyticity then confronts us anew. Statements which are analytic by general philosophical acclaim are not, indeed, far to seek. They fall into two classes. Those of the first class, which may be called *logically true,* are typified by:

(1) No unmarried man is married.

The relevant feature of this example is that it not merely is true as it stands, but remains true under any and all reinterpretations of 'man' and 'married'. If we suppose a prior inventory of *logical* particles, comprising 'no', 'un-', 'not', 'if', 'then', 'and', etc., then in general a logical truth is a statement which is true and remains true under all reinterpretations of its components other than the logical particles.

But there is also a second class of analytic statements, typified by:

(2) No bachelor is married.

The characteristic of such a statement is that it can be turned into a logical truth by putting synonyms for synonyms; thus (2) can be turned into (1) by putting 'unmarried man' for its synonym 'bachelor'. We still lack a proper characterization of this second class of analytic statements, and therewith of analyticity generally, inasmuch as we have had in the above description to lean on a notion of "synonymy" which is no less in need of clarification than analyticity itself.

In recent years Carnap has tended to explain analyticity by appeal to what he calls state-descriptions. A state-description is any exhaustive assignment of truth values to the atomic, or noncompound, statements of the language. All other statements of the language are, Carnap assumes, built up of their component clauses by means of the familiar logical devices, in such a way that the truth value of any complex statement is fixed for each state-description by specifiable logical laws. A statement is then explained as analytic when it comes out true under every state-description. This account is an adaptation of Leibniz's "true in all possible worlds." But note that this version of analyticity serves its purpose only if the atomic statements of the language are, unlike 'John is a bachelor' and 'John is married', mutually independent. Otherwise there would be a state-description which assigned truth to 'John is a bachelor' and to 'John is married', and consequently 'No bachelors are married' would turn out synthetic rather than analytic under the proposed criterion. Thus the criterion of analyticity in terms of state-descriptions serves only for languages devoid of extralogical synonym-pairs, such as 'bachelor' and 'unmarried man'—synonym-pairs of the type which give rise to the "second class" of analytic statements. The criterion in terms of state-descriptions is a reconstruction at best of logical truth, not of analyticity.

I do not mean to suggest that Carnap is under any illusions on this point. His simplified model language with its state-descriptions is aimed primarily not at the general problem of analyticity but at another purpose, the clarification of probability and induction. Our problem, however, is analyticity; and here the major difficulty lies not in the first class of analytic statements, the logical truths, but rather in the second class, which depends on the notion of synonymy.

2. DEFINITION

There are those who find it soothing to say that the analytic statements of the second class reduce to those of the first class, the logical truths, by *definition;* 'bachelor', for example, is *defined* as 'unmarried man'. But how do we find that 'bachelor' is defined as 'unmarried man'? Who defined it thus, and when? Are we to appeal to the nearest dictionary, and accept the lexicographer's formulation as law? Clearly this would be to put the cart before the horse. The lexicographer is an empirical scientist, whose business is the recording of antecedent facts; and if he glosses 'bachelor' as 'unmarried man' it is because of his belief that there is a relation of synonymy between those forms, implicit in general or preferred usage prior to his own work. The notion of synonymy presupposed here has still to be clarified, presumably in terms relating to linguistic behavior. Certainly the "definition" which is the lexicographer's report of an observed synonymy cannot be taken as the ground of the synonymy.

Definition is not, indeed, an activity exclusively of philologists. Philosophers and scientists frequently have occasion to "define" a recondite term by paraphrasing it into terms of a more familiar vocabulary. But ordinarily such a definition, like the philologist's, is pure lexicography, affirming a relation of synonymy antecedent to the exposition in hand.

Just what it means to affirm synonymy, just what the interconnections may be which are necessary and sufficient in order that two linguistic forms be properly describable as synonymous, is far from clear; but, whatever these interconnections may be, ordinarily they are grounded in usage. Definitions reporting selected instances of synonymy come then as reports upon usage.

There is also, however, a variant type of definitional activity which does not limit itself to the reporting of preexisting synonymies. I have in mind what Carnap calls *explication*—an activity to which philosophers are given, and scientists also in their more philosophical moments. In explication the purpose is not merely to paraphrase the definiendum into an outright synonym, but actually to improve upon the definiendum by refining or supplementing its meaning. But even explication, though not merely reporting a preexisting synonymy between definiendum and definiens, does rest nevertheless on *other* preexisting synonymies. The matter may be viewed as follows. Any word worth explicating has some contexts which, as wholes, are clear and precise enough to be useful; and the purpose of explication is to preserve the usage of these favored contexts while sharpening the usage of other contexts. In order that a given definition be suitable for purposes of explication, therefore, what is required is not that the definiendum in its antecedent usage be synonymous with the definiens, but just that each of these favored contexts of the definiendum, taken as a whole in its antecedent usage, be synonymous with the corresponding context of the definiens.

Two alternative definientia may be equally appropriate for the purposes of a given task of explication and yet not be synonymous with each other; for they may serve interchangeably within the favored contexts but diverge elsewhere. By cleaving to one of these definientia rather than the other, a definition of explicative kind generates, by fiat, a relation of synonymy between definiendum and definiens which did not hold before. But such a definition still owes its explicative function, as seen, to preexisting synonymies.

There does, however, remain still an extreme sort of definition which does not hark back to prior synonymies at all: namely, the explicitly conventional introduction of novel notations for purposes of sheer abbreviation. Here the definiendum becomes synonymous with the definiens simply because it has been created expressly for the purpose of being synonymous with the definiens. Here we have a really transparent case of synonymy created by definition; would that all species of synonymy were as intelligible. For the rest, definition rests on synonymy rather than explaining it.

The word 'definition' has come to have a dangerously reassuring sound, owing no doubt to its frequent occurrence in logical and mathematical writings. We shall do well to digress now into a brief appraisal of the role of definition in formal work.

In logical and mathematical systems either of two mutually antagonistic types of economy may be striven for, and each has its peculiar practical utility. On the one hand we may seek economy of practical expression—ease and brevity in the statement of multifarious relations. This sort of economy calls usually for distinctive concise notations for a wealth of concepts. Second, however, and oppositely, we may seek economy in grammar and vocabulary; we may try to find a minimum of basic concepts such that, once a distinctive notation has been appropriated to each of them, it becomes possible to express any desired further concept by mere combination and iteration of our basic notations. This second sort of economy is impractical in one way, since a poverty in basic idioms tends to a necessary lengthening of discourse. But it is practical in another way: it greatly simplifies theoretical discourse *about* the language, through minimizing the terms and the forms of construction wherein the language consists.

Both sorts of economy, though prima facie incompatible, are valuable in their separate ways. The custom has consequently arisen of combining both sorts of economy by forging in effect two languages, the one a part of the other. The inclusive language, though redundant in grammar and vocabulary, is economical in message lengths, while the part, called

primitive notation, is economical in grammar and vocabulary. Whole and part are correlated by rules of transition whereby each idiom not in primitive notation is equated to some
complex built up of primitive notation. These rules of translation are the so-called *definitions* which appear in formalized systems. They are best viewed not as adjuncts to one
language but as correlations between two languages, the one a part of the other.

But these correlations are not arbitrary. They are supposed to show how the primitive
notations can accomplish all purposes, save brevity and convenience, of the redundant language. Hence the definiendum and its definiens may be expected, in each case, to be related
in one or another of the three ways lately noted. The definiens may be a faithful paraphrase
of the definiendum into the narrower notation, preserving a direct synonymy as of antecedent usage; or the definiens may, in the spirit of explication, improve upon the antecedent
usage of the definiendum; or finally, the definiendum may be a newly created notation,
newly endowed with meaning here and now.

In formal and informal work alike, thus, we find that definition—except in the extreme
case of the explicitly conventional introduction of new notations—hinges on prior relations
of synonymy. Recognizing then that the notion of definition does not hold the key to
synonymy and analyticity, let us look further into synonymy and say no more of definition.

3. INTERCHANGEABILITY

A natural suggestion, deserving close examination, is that the synonymy of two linguistic
forms consists simply in their interchangeability in all contexts without change of truth
value—interchangeability, in Leibniz's phrase, *salva veritate*. Note that synonyms so conceived need not even be free from vagueness, as long as the vaguenesses match.

But it is not quite true that the synonyms 'bachelor' and 'unmarried man' are everywhere
interchangeable *salva veritate*. Truths which become false under substitution of 'unmarried
man' for 'bachelor' are easily constructed with the help of 'bachelor of arts' or 'bachelor's
buttons'; also with the help of quotation, thus:

'Bachelor' has less than ten letters.

Such counterinstances can, however, perhaps be set aside by treating the phrases 'bachelor
of arts' and 'bachelor's buttons' and the quotation ''bachelor'' each as a single indivisible
word and then stipulating that the interchangeability *salva veritate* which is to be the touch-
stone of synonymy is not supposed to apply to fragmentary occurrences inside of a word.
This account of synonymy, supposing it acceptable on other counts, has indeed the drawback of appealing to a prior conception of "word" which can be counted on to present
difficulties of formulation in its turn. Nevertheless some progress might be claimed in having reduced the problem of synonymy to a problem of wordhood. Let us pursue this line a
bit, taking "word" for granted.

The question remains whether interchangeability *salva veritate* (apart from occurrences
within words) is a strong enough condition for synonymy, or whether, on the contrary,
some heteronymous expressions might be thus interchangeable. Now let us be clear that we
are not concerned here with synonymy in the sense of complete identity in psychological
associations or poetic quality; indeed no two expressions are synonymous in such a sense.
We are concerned only with what may be called *cognitive* synonymy. Just what this is cannot
be said without successfully finishing the present study; but we know something about it

from the need which arose for it in connection with analyticity in §1. The sort of synonymy needed there was merely such that any analytic statement could be turned into a logical truth by putting synonyms for synonyms. Turning the tables and assuming analyticity, indeed, we could explain cognitive synonymy of terms as follows (keeping to the familiar example): to say that 'bachelor' and 'unmarried man' are cognitively synonymous is to say no more nor less than that the statement:

(3) All and only bachelors are unmarried men

is analytic.

What we need is an account of cognitive synonymy not presupposing analyticity—if we are to explain analyticity conversely with help of cognitive synonymy as undertaken in §1. And indeed such an independent account of cognitive synonymy is at present up for consideration, namely, interchangeability *salva veritate* everywhere except within words. The question before us, to resume the thread at last, is whether such interchangeability is a sufficient condition for cognitive synonymy. We can quickly assure ourselves that it is, by examples of the following sort. The statement:

(4) Necessarily all and only bachelors are bachelors

is evidently true, even supposing 'necessarily' so narrowly construed as to be truly applicable only to analytic statements. Then, if 'bachelor' and 'unmarried man' are interchangeable *salva veritate,* the result:

(5) Necessarily all and only bachelors are unmarried men

of putting 'unmarried man' for an occurrence of 'bachelor' in (4) must, like (4), be true. But to say that (5) is true is to say that (3) is analytic, and hence that 'bachelor' and 'unmarried man' are cognitively synonymous.

Let us see what there is about the above argument that gives it its air of hocus-pocus. The condition of interchangeability *salva veritate* varies in its force with variations in the richness of the language at hand. The above argument supposes we are working with a language rich enough to contain the adverb 'necessarily', this adverb being so constructed as to yield truth when and only when applied to an analytic statement. But can we condone a language which contains such an adverb? Does the adverb really make sense? To suppose that it does is to suppose that we have already made satisfactory sense of 'analytic'. Then what are we so hard at work on right now?

Our argument is not flatly circular, but something like it. It has the form, figuratively speaking, of a closed curve in space.

Interchangeability *salva veritate* is meaningless until relativized to a language whose extent is specified in relevant respects. Suppose now we consider a language containing just the following materials. There is an indefinitely large stock of one-place predicates (for example, 'F' where 'Fx' means that x is a man) and many-place predicates (for example, 'G' where 'Gxy' means that x loves y), mostly having to do with extralogical subject matter. The rest of the language is logical. The atomic sentences consist each of a predicate followed by one or more variables 'x', 'y', etc.; and the complex sentences are built up of the atomic ones by truth functions ('not', 'and', 'or', etc.) and quantification. In effect such a language enjoys the benefits also of descriptions and indeed singular terms generally, these being contextually definable in known ways. Even abstract singular terms naming classes, classes of classes, etc., are contextually definable in case the assumed stock of predicates includes the two-place predicate of class membership. Such a language can be adequate to classical mathematics and indeed to scientific discourse generally, except in so far as the latter involves debatable devices such as contrary-to-fact conditionals or modal adverbs like 'necessarily'. Now a language of this type is extensional, in this sense: any two predicates which agree extensionally (that is, are true of the same objects) are interchangeable *salva veritate*.

In an extensional language, therefore, interchangeability *salva veritate* is no assurance of cognitive synonymy of the desired type. That 'bachelor' and 'unmarried man' are interchangeable *salva veritate* in an extensional language assures us of no more than that (3) is true. There is no assurance here that the extensional agreement of 'bachelor' and 'unmarried man' rests on meaning rather than merely on accidental matters of fact, as does the extensional agreement of 'creature with a heart' and 'creature with kidneys'.

For most purposes extensional agreement is the nearest approximation to synonymy we need care about. But the fact remains that extensional agreement falls far short of cognitive synonymy of the type required for explaining analyticity in the manner of §1. The type of cognitive synonymy required there is such as to equate the synonymy of 'bachelor' and 'unmarried man' with the analyticity of (3), not merely with the truth of (3).

So we must recognize that interchangeability *salva veritate,* if constructed in relation to an extensional language, is not a sufficient condition of cognitive synonymy in the sense needed for deriving analyticity in the manner of §1. If a language contains an intensional adverb 'necessarily' in the sense lately noted, or other particles to the same effect, then interchangeability *salva veritate* in such a language does afford a sufficient condition of cognitive synonymy; but such a language is intelligible only in so far as the notion of analyticity is already understood in advance.

The effort to explain cognitive synonymy first, for the sake of deriving analyticity from it afterward as in §1, is perhaps the wrong approach. Instead we might try explaining analyticity somehow without appeal to cognitive synonymy. Afterward we could doubtless derive cognitive synonymy from analyticity satisfactorily enough if desired. We have seen that cognitive synonymy of 'bachelor' and 'unmarried man' can be explained as analyticity of (3). The same explanation works for any pair of one-place predicates, of course, and it can be extended in obvious fashion to many-place predicates. Other syntactical categories can also be accommodated in fairly parallel fashion. Singular terms may be said to be cognitively synonymous when the statement of identity formed by putting '=' between them is analytic. Statements may be said simply to be cognitively synonymous when their biconditional (the result of joining them by 'if and only if') is analytic. If we care to lump all categories into a single formulation, at the expense of assuming again the notion of "word" which was appealed to early in this section, we can describe any two linguistic forms as cognitively synonymous when the two forms are interchangeable (apart from occurrences within "words") *salva* (no longer *veritate* but) *analyticitate.* Certain technical questions arise, indeed, over cases of ambiguity or homonymy; let us not pause for them, however, for we are already digressing. Let us rather turn our backs on the problem of synonymy and address ourselves anew to that of analyticity.

4. SEMANTICAL RULES

Analyticity at first seemed most naturally definable by appeal to a realm of meanings. On refinement, the appeal to meanings gave way to an appeal to synonymy or definition. But definition turned out to be a will-o'-the-wisp, and synonymy turned out to be best understood only by dint of a prior appeal to analyticity itself. So we are back at the problem of analyticity.

I do not know whether the statement 'Everything green is extended' is analytic. Now does my indecision over this example really betray an incomplete understanding, an incomplete grasp of the "meanings", of 'green' and 'extended'? I think not. The trouble is not with 'green' or 'extended', but with 'analytic'.

It is often hinted that the difficulty in separating analytic statements from synthetic ones in ordinary language is due to the vagueness of ordinary language and that the distinction is clear when we have a precise artificial language with explicit "semantical rules." This, however, as I shall now attempt to show, is a confusion.

The notion of analyticity about which we are worrying is a purported relation between statements and languages: a statement S is said to be *analytic for* a language L, and the problem is to make sense of this relation generally, that is, for variable 'S' and 'L'. The gravity of this problem is not perceptibly less for artificial languages than for natural ones. The problem of making sense of the idiom 'S is analytic for L', with variable 'S' and 'L', retains its stubbornness even if we limit the range of the variable 'L' to artificial languages. Let me now try to make this point evident.

For artificial languages and semantical rules we look naturally to the writings of Carnap. His semantical rules take various forms, and to make my point I shall have to distinguish certain of the forms. Let us suppose, to begin with, an artificial language L_0 whose semantical rules have the form explicitly of a specification, by recursion or otherwise, of all the analytic statements of L_0. The rules tell us that such and such statements, and only those, are the analytic statements of L_0. Now here the difficulty is simply that the rules contain the word 'analytic', which we do not understand! We understand what expressions the rules attribute analyticity to, but we do not understand what the rules attribute to those expressions. In short, before we can understand a rule which begins 'A statement S is analytic for language L_0 if and only if . . .', we must understand the general relative term 'analytic for'; we must understand 'S is analytic for L' where 'S' and 'L' are variables.

Alternatively we may, indeed, view the so-called rule as a conventional definition of a new simple symbol 'analytic-for-L_0', which might better be written untendentiously as 'K' so as not to seem to throw light on the interesting word 'analytic'. Obviously any number of classes K, M, N, etc. of statements of L_0 can be specified for various purposes or for no purpose; what does it mean to say that K, as against M, N, etc., is the class of the "analytic" statements of L_0?

By saying what statements are analytic for L_0 we explain 'analytic-for-L_0' but not 'analytic', not 'analytic for'. We do not begin to explain the idiom 'S is analytic for L' with variable 'S' and 'L', even if we are content to limit the range of 'L' to the realm of artificial languages.

Actually we do know enough about the intended significance of 'analytic' to know that analytic statements are supposed to be true. Let us then turn to a second form of semantical rule, which says not that such and such statements are analytic but simply that such and such statements are included among the truths. Such a rule is not subject to the criticism of containing the un-understood word 'analytic'; and we may grant for the sake of argument that there is no difficulty over the broader term 'true'. A semantical rule of this second type, a rule of truth, is not supposed to specify all the truths of the language; it merely stipulates, recursively or otherwise, a certain multitude of statements which, along with others unspecified, are to count as true. Such a rule may be conceded to be quite clear. Derivatively, afterward, analyticity can be demarcated thus: a statement is analytic if it is (not merely true but) true according to the semantical rule.

Still there is really no progress. Instead of appealing to an unexplained word 'analytic', we are now appealing to an unexplained phrase 'semantical rule'. Not every true statement which says that the statements of some class are true can count as a semantical rule— otherwise *all* truths would be "analytic" in the sense of being true according to semantical rules. Semantical rules are distinguishable, apparently, only by the fact of appearing on a page under the heading 'Semantical Rules'; and this heading is itself then meaningless.

We can say indeed that a statement is *analytic-for-L_0* if and only if it is true according to such and such specifically appended "semantical rules," but then we find ourselves back at essentially the same case which was originally discussed: '*S* is analytic-for L_0 if and only if. . . .' Once we seek to explain '*S* is analytic for *L*' generally for variable '*L*' (even allowing limitation of '*L*' to artificial languages), the explanation 'true according to the semantical rules of *L*' is unavailing; for the relative term 'semantical rule of' is as much in need of clarification, at least, as 'analytic for'.

It may be instructive to compare the notion of semantical rule with that of postulate. Relative to a given set of postulates, it is easy to say what a postulate is: it is a member of the set. Relative to a given set of semantical rules, it is equally easy to say what a semantical rule is. But given simply a notation, mathematical or otherwise, and indeed as thoroughly understood a notation as you please in point of the translations or truth conditions of its statements, who can say which of its true statements rank as postulates? Obviously the question is meaningless—as meaningless as asking which points in Ohio are starting points. Any finite (or effectively specifiable infinite) selection of statements (preferably true ones, perhaps) is as much *a* set of postulates as any other. The word 'postulate' is significant only relative to an act of inquiry; we apply the word to a set of statements just in so far as we happen, for the year or the moment, to be thinking of those statements in relation to the statements which can be reached from them by some set of transformations to which we have seen fit to direct our attention. Now the notion of semantical rule is as sensible and meaningful as that of postulate, if conceived in a similarly relative spirit—relative, this time, to one or another particular enterprise of schooling unconversant persons in sufficient conditions for truth of statements of some natural or artificial language *L*. But from this point of view no one signalization of a subclass of the truths of *L* is intrinsically more a semantical rule than another; and, if 'analytic' means 'true by semantical rules', no one truth of *L* is analytic to the exclusion of another.

It might conceivably be protested that an artificial language *L* (unlike a natural one) is a language in the ordinary sense *plus* a set of explicit semantical rules—the whole constituting, let us say, an ordered pair; and that the semantical rules of *L* then are specifiable simply as the second component of the pair *L*. But, by the same token and more simply, we might construe an artificial language *L* outright as an ordered pair whose second component is the class of its analytic statements; and then the analytic statements of *L* become specifiable simply as the statements in the second component of *L*. Or better still, we might just stop tugging at our bootstraps altogether.

Not all the explanations of analyticity known to Carnap and his readers have been covered explicitly in the above considerations, but the extension to other forms is not hard to see. Just one additional factor should be mentioned which sometimes enters: sometimes the semantical rules are in effect rules of translation into ordinary language, in which case the analytic statements of the artificial language are in effect recognized as such from the analyticity of their specified translations in ordinary language. Here certainly there can be no thought of an illumination of the problem of analyticity from the side of the artificial language.

From the point of view of the problem of analyticity the notion of an artificial language with semantical rules is a *feu follet par excellence.* Semantical rules determining the analytic statements of an artificial language are of interest only in so far as we already understand the notion of analyticity; they are of no help in gaining this understanding.

Appeal to hypothetical languages of an artificially simple kind could conceivably be useful in clarifying analyticity, if the mental or behavioral or cultural factors relevant to analyticity—whatever they may be—were somehow sketched into the simplified model. But a model which takes analyticity merely as an irreducible character is unlikely to throw light on the problem of explicating analyticity.

It is obvious that truth in general depends on both language and extralinguistic fact. The statement 'Brutus killed Caesar' would be false if the world had been different in certain ways, but it would also be false if the word 'killed' happened rather to have the sense of 'begat'. Thus one is tempted to suppose in general that the truth of a statement is somehow analyzable into a linguistic component and a factual component. Given this supposition, it next seems reasonable that in some statements the factual component should be null; and these are the analytic statements. But, for all its a priori reasonableness, a boundary between analytic and synthetic statements simply has not been drawn. That there is such a distinction to be drawn at all is an unempirical dogma of empiricists, a metaphysical article of faith.

5. THE VERIFICATION THEORY AND REDUCTIONISM

In the course of these somber reflections we have taken a dim view first of the notion of meaning, then of the notion of cognitive synonymy, and finally of the notion of analyticity. But what, it may be asked, of the verification theory of meaning? This phrase has established itself so firmly as a catchword of empiricism that we should be very unscientific indeed not to look beneath it for a possible key to the problem of meaning and the associated problems.

The verification theory of meaning, which has been conspicuous in the literature from Peirce onward, is that the meaning of a statement is the method of empirically confirming or infirming it. An analytic statement is that limiting case which is confirmed no matter what.

As urged in §1, we can as well pass over the question of meanings as entities and move straight to sameness of meaning, or synonymy. Then what the verification theory says is that statements are synonymous if and only if they are alike in point of method of empirical confirmation or information.

This is an account of cognitive synonymy not of linguistic forms generally, but of statements. However, from the concept of synonymy of statements we could derive the concept of synonymy for other linguistic forms, by considerations somewhat similar to those at the end of §3. Assuming the notion of "word," indeed, we could explain any two forms as synonymous when the putting of the one form for an occurrence of the other in any statement (apart from occurrences within "words") yields a synonymous statement. Finally, given the concept of synonymy thus for linguistic forms generally, we could define analyticity in terms of synonymy and logical truth as in §1. For that matter, we could define analyticity more simply in terms of just synonymy of statements together with logical truth; it is not necessary to appeal to synonymy of linguistic forms other than statements. For a statement may be described as analytic simply when it is synonymous with a logically true statement.

So, if the verification theory can be accepted as an adequate account of statement synonymy, the notion of analyticity is saved after all. However, let us reflect. Statement synonymy is said to be likeness of method of empirical confirmation or information. Just what are these methods which are to be compared for likeness? What, in other words, is the nature of the relation between a statement and the experiences which contribute to or detract from its confirmation?

The most naive view of the relation is that it is one of direct report. This is *radical reductionism*. Every meaningful statement is held to be translatable into a statement (true or false) about immediate experience. Radical reductionism, in one form or another, well antedates the verification theory of meaning explicitly so called. Thus Locke and Hume held that every idea must either originate directly in sense experience or else be compounded of ideas thus originating; and taking a hint from Tooke we might rephrase this doctrine in semantical jargon by saying that a term, to be significant at all, must be either a name of a sense datum or a compound of such names or an abbreviation of such a compound. So stated, the doctrine remains ambiguous as between sense data as sensory events and sense data as sensory qualities; and it remains vague as to the admissible ways of compounding. Moreover, the doctrine is unnecessarily and intolerably restrictive in the term-by-term critique which it imposes. More reasonably, and without yet exceeding the limits of what I have called radical reductionism, we may take full statements as our significant units—thus demanding that our statements as wholes be translatable into sense-datum language, but not that they be translatable term by term.

This emendation would unquestionably have been welcome to Locke and Hume and Tooke, but historically it had to await an important reorientation in semantics—the reorientation whereby the primary vehicle of meaning came to be seen no longer in the term but in the statement. This reorientation, seen in Bentham and Frege, underlies Russell's concept of incomplete symbols defined in use; also it is implicit in the verification theory of meaning, since the objects of verification are statements.

Radical reductionism, conceived now with statements as units, set itself the task of specifying a sense-datum language and showing how to translate the rest of significant discourse, statement by statement, into it. Carnap embarked on the project in the *Aufbau*.

The language which Carnap adopted as his starting point was not a sense-datum language in the narrowest conceivable sense, for it included also the notations of logic, up through higher set theory. In effect it included the whole language of pure mathematics. The ontology implicit in it (that is, the range of values of its variables) embraced not only sensory events but classes, classes of classes, and so on. Empiricists there are who would boggle at such prodigality. Carnap's starting point is very parsimonious, however, in its extralogical or sensory part. In a series of constructions in which he exploits the resources of modern logic with much ingenuity, Carnap succeeds in defining a wide array of important additional sensory concepts which, but for his constructions, one would not have dreamed were definable on so slender a basis. He was the first empiricist who, not content with asserting the reducibility of science to terms of immediate experience, took serious steps toward carrying out the reduction.

If Carnap's starting point is satisfactory, still his constructions were, as he himself stressed, only a fragment of the full program. The construction of even the simplest statements about the physical world was left in a sketchy state. Carnap's suggestions on this subject were, despite their sketchiness, very suggestive. He explained spatio-temporal point-instants as quadruples of real numbers and envisaged assignment of sense qualities to point-instants according to certain canons. Roughly summarized, the plan was that qualities should be assigned to point-instants in such a way as to achieve the laziest world compatible with our experience. The principle of least action was to be our guide in constructing a world from experience.

Carnap did not seem to recognize, however, that his treatment of physical objects fell short of reduction not merely through sketchiness, but in principle. Statements of the form 'Quality q is at point-instant $x; y; z; t$' were, according to his canons, to be apportioned truth values in such a way as to maximize and minimize certain over-all features, and with growth of experience the truth values were to be progressively revised in the same spirit. I think this is a good schematization (deliberately oversimplified, to be sure) of what science really does; but it provides no indication, not even the sketchiest, of how a statement of the form 'Quality q is at $x; y; z; t$' could ever be translated into Carnap's initial language of sense data and logic. The connective 'is at' remains an added undefined connective; the canons counsel us in its use but not in its elimination.

Carnap seems to have appreciated this point afterward; for in his later writings he abandoned all notion of the translatability of statements about the physical world into statements about immediate experience. Reductionism in its radical form has long since ceased to figure in Carnap's philosophy.

But the dogma of reductionism has, in a subtler and more tenuous form, continued to influence the thought of empiricists. The notion lingers that to each statement, or each synthetic statement, there is associated a unique range of possible sensory events such that the occurrence of any of them would add to the likelihood of truth of the statement, and that there is associated also another unique range of possible sensory events whose occurrence would detract from that likelihood. This notion is of course implicit in the verification theory of meaning.

The dogma of reductionism survives in the supposition that each statement, taken in isolation from its fellows, can admit of confirmation or infirmation at all. My counter-suggestion, issuing essentially from Carnap's doctrine of the physical world in the *Aufbau,* is that our statements about the external world face the tribunal of sense experience not individually but only as a corporate body.

The dogma of reductionism, even in its attenuated form, is intimately connected with the other dogma—that there is a cleavage between the analytic and the synthetic. We have found ourselves led, indeed, from the latter problem to the former through the verification theory of meaning. More directly, the one dogma clearly supports the other in this way: as long as it is taken to be significant in general to speak of the confirmation and infirmation of a statement, it seems significant to speak also of a limiting kind of statement which is vacuously confirmed, *ipso facto,* come what may; and such a statement is analytic.

The two dogmas are, indeed, at root identical. We lately reflected that in general the truth of statements does obviously depend both upon language and upon extralinguistic fact; and we noted that this obvious circumstance carries in its train, not logically but all too naturally, a feeling that the truth of a statement is somehow analyzable into a linguistic component and a factual component. The factual component must, if we are empiricists, boil down to a range of confirmatory experiences. In the extreme case where the linguistic component is all that matters, a true statement is analytic. But I hope we are now impressed with how stubbornly the distinction between analytic and synthetic has resisted any straightforward drawing. I am impressed also, apart from prefabricated examples of black and white balls in an urn, with how baffling the problem has always been of arriving at any explicit theory of the empirical confirmation of a synthetic statement. My present suggestion is that it is nonsense, and the root of much nonsense, to speak of a linguistic component and a factual component in the truth of any individual statement. Taken collectively, science has its double dependence upon language and experience; but this duality is not significantly traceable into the statements of science taken one by one.

The idea of defining a symbol in use was, as remarked, an advance over the impossible term-by-term empiricism of Locke and Hume. The statement, rather than the term, came with Bentham to be recognized as the unit accountable to an empiricist critique. But what I am now urging is that even in taking the statement as unit we have drawn our grid too finely. The unit of empirical significance is the whole of science.

6. EMPIRICISM WITHOUT THE DOGMAS

The totality of our so-called knowledge or beliefs, from the most casual matters of geography and history to the profoundest laws of atomic physics or even of pure mathematics and logic, is a man-made fabric which impinges on experience only along the edges. Or, to change the figure, total science is like a field of force whose boundary conditions are experience. A conflict with experience at the periphery occasions readjustments in the interior of the field. Truth values have to be redistributed over some of our statements. Reevaluation of some statements entails reevaluation of others, because of their logical interconnections—the logical laws being in turn simply certain further statements of the system, certain further elements of the field. Having reevaluated one statement we must reevaluate some others, which may be statements logically connected with the first or may be the statements of logical connections themselves. But the total field is so underdetermined by its boundary conditions, experience, that there is much latitude of choice as to what statements to reevaluate in the light of any single contrary experience. No particular experiences are linked with any particular statements in the interior of the field, except indirectly through considerations of equilibrium affecting the field as a whole.

If this view is right, it is misleading to speak of the empirical content of an individual statement—especially if it is a statement at all remote from the experiential periphery of the field. Furthermore it becomes folly to seek a boundary between synthetic statements, which hold contingently on experience, and analytic statements, which hold come what may. Any statement can be held true come what may, if we make drastic enough adjustments elsewhere in the system. Even a statement very close to the periphery can be held true in the face of recalcitrant experience by pleading hallucination or by amending certain statements of the kind called logical laws. Conversely, by the same token, no statement is immune to revision. Revision even of the logical law of the excluded middle has been proposed as a means of simplifying quantum mechanics; and what difference is there in principle between such a shift and the shift whereby Kepler superseded Ptolemy, or Einstein Newton, or Darwin Aristotle?

For vividness I have been speaking in terms of varying distances from a sensory periphery. Let me try now to clarify this notion without metaphor. Certain statements, though *about* physical objects and not sense experience, seem peculiarly germane to sense experience—and in a selective way: some statements to some experiences, others to others. Such statements, especially germane to particular experiences, I picture as near the periphery. But in this relation of "germaneness" I envisage nothing more than a loose association reflecting the relative likelihood, in practice, of our choosing one statement rather than another for revision in the event of recalcitrant experience. For example, we can imagine recalcitrant experiences to which we would surely be inclined to accommodate our system by reevaluating just the statement that there are brick houses on Elm Street, together with related statements on the same topic. We can imagine other recalcitrant experiences to which we would be inclined to accommodate our system to reevaluating just the statement that there are not centaurs, along with kindred statements. A recalcitrant experience can, I have urged, be accommodated by any of various alternative reevaluations in various alternative quarters of the total system; but, in the cases which we are now imagining, our natural tendency to disturb the total system as little as possible would lead us to focus our revisions upon these specific statements concerning brick houses or centaurs. These statements are felt, therefore, to have a sharper empirical reference than highly theoretical statements of physics or logic or ontology. The latter statements may be thought of as relatively centrally located within the total network, meaning merely that little preferential connection with any particular sense data obtrudes itself.

As an empiricist I continue to think of the conceptual scheme of science as a tool, ultimately, for predicting future experience in the light of past experience. Physical objects are conceptually imported into the situation as convenient intermediaries—not by definition in terms of experience, but simply as irreducible posits comparable, epistemologically, to the gods of Homer. For my part I do, qua lay physicist, believe in physical objects and not in Homer's gods; and I consider it a scientific error to believe otherwise. But in point of epistemological footing the physical objects and the gods differ only in degree and not in kind. Both sorts of entities enter our conception only as cultural posits. The myth of physical objects is epistemologically superior to most in that it has proved more efficacious than other myths as a device for working a manageable structure into the flux of experience.

Positing does not stop with macroscopic physical objects. Objects at the atomic level are posited to make the laws of macroscopic objects, and ultimately the laws of experience, simpler and more manageable; and we need not expect or demand full definition of atomic and subatomic entities in terms of macroscopic ones, any more than definition of macroscopic things in terms of sense data. Science is a continuation of common sense, and it continues the common-sense expedient of swelling ontology to simplify theory.

Physical objects, small and large, are not the only posits. Forces are another example; and indeed we are told nowadays that the boundary between energy and matter is obsolete. Moreover, the abstract entities which are the substance of mathematics—ultimately classes and classes of classes and so on up—are another posit in the same spirit. Epistemologically these are myths on the same footing with physical objects and gods, neither better nor worse except for differences in the degree to which they expedite our dealings with sense experiences.

The over-all algebra of rational and irrational numbers is underdetermined by the algebra of rational numbers, but is smoother and more convenient; and it includes the algebra of rational numbers as a jagged or gerrymandered part. Total science, mathematical and natural and human, is similarly but more extremely underdetermined by experience. The edge of the system must be kept squared with experience; the rest, with all its elaborate myths or fictions, has as its objective the simplicity of laws.

Ontological questions, under this view, are on a par with questions of natural science. Consider the question whether to countenance classes as entities. This, as I have argued elsewhere, is the question whether to quantify with respect to variables which take classes as values. Now Carnap [6] has maintained that this is a question not of matters of fact but of choosing a convenient language form, a convenient conceptual scheme or framework for science. With this I agree, but only on the proviso that the same be conceded regarding scientific hypotheses generally. Carnap ([6], p. 32n) has recognized that he is able to preserve a double standard for ontological questions and scientific hypotheses only by assuming an absolute distinction between the analytic and the synthetic; and I need not say again that this is a distinction which I reject.

The issue over there being classes seems more a question of convenient conceptual scheme; the issue over there being centaurs, or brick houses on Elm Street, seems more a question of fact. But I have been urging that this difference is only one of degree, and that it turns upon our vaguely pragmatic inclination to adjust one strand of the fabric of science rather than another in accommodating some particular recalcitrant experience. Conservatism figures in such choices, and so does the quest for simplicity.

Carnap, Lewis, and others take a pragmatic stand on the question of choosing between language forms, scientific frameworks; but their pragmatism leaves off at the imagined boundary between the analytic and the synthetic. In repudiating such a boundary I espouse a more thorough pragmatism. Each man is given a scientific heritage plus a continuing barrage of sensory stimulation; and the considerations which guide him in warping his scientific heritage to fit his continuing sensory promptings are, where rational, pragmatic.